Ellen Percy: or, the Memoirs of an Actress.

George W. M. Reynolds

12620. *Reg* 58.

ELLEN PERCY; OR, THE MEMOIRS OF AN ACTRESS.

ELLEN PERCY:

OR, THE

MEMOIRS OF AN ACTRESS.

BY

GEORGE W. M. REYNOLDS,

AUTHOR OF THE FIRST AND SECOND SERIES OF "THE MYSTERIES OF LONDON," "THE MYSTERIES OF THE COURT OF LONDON," "MARY PRICE," "JOSEPH WILMOT," "ROSA LAMBERT," "THE SOLDIER'S WIFE," "THE NECROMANCER," "POPE JOAN," "THE PIXY," "ROBERT MACAIRE," "KENNETH," "THE DAYS OF HOGARTH," "WAGNER THE WEHR-WOLF," "THE RYE HOUSE PLOT," "THE BRONZE STATUE," "THE LOVES OF THE HAREM," "OMAR," "LEILA," "THE SEAM-STRESS," "THE CORAL ISLAND," "MARGARET; OR, THE DISCARDED QUEEN," "MAY MIDDLETON," "FAUST," "PICKWICK ABROAD," "THE YOUNG DUCHESS," ETC., ETC.

BEAUTIFULLY ILLUSTRATED,

BY F. GILBERT.

VOL. II.

LONDON:
PUBLISHED, FOR THE PROPRIETOR, BY JOHN DICKS,
No. 7, WELLINGTON STREET NORTH, STRAND.
1857.

INDEX TO ENGRAVINGS.

INDEX TO VOL. II.

ELLEN PERCY;

OR, THE MEMOIRS OF AN ACTRESS.

CHAPTER LXXI.

AN UNEXPECTED RETURN.

MY nerves were so agitated by the scenes which had just taken place—first with Juliet, and then with her husband—that I experienced the neces-

sity of seeking some means to allay my perturbation. I left the unhappy couple together, and walked forth from the house. It was the middle of April—the weather was beautiful—there was a flush of green upon the hedges, the trees, and the fields—and there was just a sufficiency of the saline breeze blowing from the sea to mitigate the sultriness of the sun's heat. The sky was cloudless; and the change of scene from the presence of the unhappy wife and distracted husband, imparted a certain degree of elasticity to my spirits. Still it was impossible that I could feel cheerful; for even if that unfortunate young couple had been almost complete strangers to me, I should have felt much affected by their position: therefore as Juliet was my dearest and most intimate friend, how could I possibly be otherwise than grieved and anguished on her account? How it would all end I could not foresee: but that there must be a speedy termination of a state of affairs so shocking and unnatural, was only to be too seriously expected.

I thought to myself that I was glad Mr. Norman still remained upon the Continent; for if he had been in England he might at this very moment be paying a visit to his daughter and son-in-law;—and would he as Juliet's father sit down tranquilly and ask no questions while her husband wore that sable fillet bound about his head, and obstinately refused to seek medical advice either for the alleged injury he had received upon his brow or for the hurt sustained by the recent fall from his horse? And in reference to this latter misfortune, I could not help thinking that Frederick must have experienced some internal injury: for as no bones were broken, and as it did not appear that he complained of any external bruises—yet as he evidently suffered much, and seemed at least to have been excessively shaken, the apprehension that he was hurt inwardly seemed to be borne out by facts; and the longer I reflected upon the idea, the more was I convinced of the necessity for the young nobleman to take medical advice.

I was walking along the road between River House and Dover, inhaling the freshness of the breeze—it being now nearly five o'clock in the afternoon—when at a little distance I beheld a gentleman approaching. He was dressed in deep black, had a cloak thrown over his arm, and wore a travelling cap. There was something in his gait which immediately struck me: I looked again—yes, I could not be mistaken!—it was Mr. Norman himself whom I beheld advancing!—and I who but a few minutes back had been congratulating myself on his supposed continuous sojourn on the Continent! Only three months and a half had elapsed since the death of his wife: his original intention had been to remain abroad for some time longer: and yet here he was again upon the English soil, and proceeding to a house where naught but a spectacle of distress and misery awaited him.

"Now," thought I to myself, with a sad and sudden tightening at the heart, "Mr. Norman's presence will assuredly bring matters to some species of termination!"

I sped forward to welcome him: he greeted me with all the parental kindness which he had ever been wont to display towards me,—exclaiming, "This is indeed an unexpected pleasure, dearest Ellen, to encounter you almost at the very first instant when setting foot upon my native soil. But how are they at River House?"

"I regret to say," I answered, scarcely knowing how to reply, "that Lord Frederick has experienced a little accident—indeed two accidents——"

"Accidents, Ellen?" ejaculated Mr. Norman, with terror upon his countenance. "What do you mean?—are they serious?"

"Nothing serious I hope——indeed I am almost certain, so far as Lord Frederick's life is concerned: but—but"—and I hesitated—"he has received a wound or injury of some sort which threatens to disfigure him——"

"Ah! then this is indeed most serious," said Mr. Norman. "But your looks are troubled, Ellen? I am afraid that you have not as yet told me everything.—You are preparing me for something worse? For God's sake leave me not in suspense!"

"In a word, my dear Mr. Norman," I said, now regaining my self-possession as I saw the absolute necessity of speaking in some sense to the point,—"in a word, Lord Frederick went up to London about three weeks ago, and there he sustained the injury which threatens to disfigure him, he fears, for life. Misfortunes never come alone; and thus three or four days back he was thrown from his horse—but no limbs were broken."

"All these tidings are sorrowful indeed, Ellen," said Mr. Norman, with agitated looks. "But that first injury to which you have alluded, and which threatens to disfigure him——"

"I will tell you the tale, my dear sir," I responded, "precisely as you will hear it at River House. It is to the effect that Lord Frederick on visiting London, was knocked down by some public vehicle—that his head came in contact with the kerbstone of the pavement—that he received a dreadful wound upon the forehead—and that he apprehends a ghastly scar will remain there for the rest of his life.

"This is indeed sad—very sad!" said Mr. Norman; "because young people value their personal beauty and their good looks!"

"Lord Frederick," I continued, "has bound his forehead with a black fillet, which he vows that he will wear for ever sooner than display the naked scar——"

"What! wear a black ribbon for ever?" exclaimed Mr. Norman. "This is outrageous and preposterous! A wound must heal; and however marked the scar, it must assuredly be less unsightly than a permanent bandage round the head. What says the medical man?"

"Lord Frederick consulted an eminent physician in London," I replied, "and has since followed, I believe, the advice which he thus obtained: but he has consulted no professional adviser since his return home; and as he is irritable—obstinate—prejudiced——"

"And self-willed perhaps?" added Mr. Norman. "I understand!—he will not send for the surgeon? This is often the case with invalids; and it is always a bad sign. But you say that the accident took place upwards of three weeks ago. Since then I have received a letter from Juliet; and she did not allude to the circumstance. I wonder why she should have thus maintained silence?"

"For the very best of motives, my dear sir," I hastily answered, "and which you can have no difficulty in comprehending. She did not choose to distress you with the communication of her own sorrows: she thought that it would be time enough on your return to England to hear of all these things——"

"Poor Juliet!" said Mr. Norman; "she is a good and affectionate daughter—she knew that I was already sufficiently afflicted by the loss which I had sustained——"

Here he stopped short, and wiped from his eyes the tears which had gathered there at the recollection of his late bereavement.

"You perhaps wonder, Ellen," he presently resumed, "that I have returned to England sooner than I originally intended: but a very few words will explain the cause—and after everything you have told me I am glad, for dear Juliet's sake, that I *have* come back. The truth is, the solitude which I sought on the Continent had become intolerable; and instead of diminishing my grief on account of my poor wife's death, it only appeared to increase it. I may have written somewhat differently in my letters to you and dear Juliet, because *I* also was unwilling to afflict either of you; and besides, I endeavoured to persuade myself that my mind was really and truly becoming tranquillized. At length I could endure no longer this separation from all whom I held dear in my native land; and my resolve was suddenly taken to return to England. Alas! I thought that my presence at River House would be welcomed with joy——"

"Oh, my dear sir!" I exclaimed, "you know that you will be welcomed! But still——"

"But still," added Mr. Norman, "I am prepared to find much unhappiness within those walls—an unhappiness to which it scarcely seems as if the presence of friends or relatives may be enabled to impart any solace! How long have you been there, my dear Ellen?"

"I only arrived this afternoon—I left London very early this morning. I came forth to breathe the fresh air for half-an-hour, little expecting to meet you——"

"And as little did I expect to meet you, my dear girl. But you are always at your post, Ellen: for where sorrow and sickness are, *there* are you to be found!"

We now reached River House: I would fain have invented some pretext to hasten forward and prepare both Juliet and Lord Frederick for Mr. Norman's presence—but I could not adopt this course: he had kept me with him in conversation, and I dared do nothing to excite his suspicion that matters were worse than I had represented, or that anything had been kept back from his knowledge. My soul was full of trouble, and apprehension, and evil presentiments; for I dreaded lest some painful, if not fatal crisis should be now at hand. For a moment—but only for a moment—the thought had flashed to me that I would tell Mr. Norman everything, so that he might rather aid in concealing Lord Frederick's fearful secret from Juliet's knowledge; but the idea was discarded as soon as formed. The secret was not my own—it was too terrible to violate—and besides I could not possibly tell how Mr. Norman himself might act if it came to his knowledge that the husband of his daughter had been branded like a felon.

We reached River House: the front door was opened—and just at that very moment Juliet was descending the staircase. With a cry of astonishment and joy she sprang forward and was received in her father's arms. I availed myself of the opportunity to glide up the staircase; and I sped into the drawing-room. There I found Lord Frederick lying upon the sofa: a book which he had taken, had fallen from his hand and was upon the carpet,—the circumstance being a painful indication of the fearfully uneasy state of the young nobleman's mind which could settle itself to no soothing avocation. On beholding me he started up to a sitting posture, exclaiming, "What new calamity has happened, Miss Percy?—for your looks are troubled!"

"My lord!" I hastily said, "you are more than ever in need of all your firmness and self-possession! Summon all your courage to your aid—for Mr. Norman has returned to England!"

"Mr. Norman?" ejaculated the unhappy young nobleman, with a start. "But he must not come hither—write to him at once—or hasten to him! Go!—speed, Miss Percy!"

"Hush!—for heaven's sake tranquillize yourself!" I said, in a tone of passionate and vehement entreaty. "Mr. Norman is here—beneath this roof! Juliet is now with him—in a few minutes he will be in your presence."

Lord Frederick sank back upon the sofa with a deep hollow groan; and in the incautiousness of his mental anguish he pressed his hands to his brow. Then it was almost a shriek or yell of agony which he sent forth from his lips: but I could not comprehend whether it was produced by physical pain arising from pressure on the branded part, or whether it arose from the mere fact of touching the sable ribbon which so vividly reminded him of his horrible condition.

"Now, my lord," I hastily went on to say, "if there were ever in your life a moment when you stood in need of all your fortitude, that moment is come—it is now present! I have prepared Mr. Norman—"

"Ellen!" ejaculated Lord Frederick, again starting up to a sitting posture—and his looks were full of the ghastliest horror: "have you dared violate——"

"No, my lord! Of this you know that I am incapable—or at least you ought to know it! If I have kept the secret from your wife, how much more should I seek to cover it with a veil in the presence of your father-in-law? So far as I am concerned, I have done all that human being can do to ward off a catastrophe:—the rest depends upon yourself!"

I now glided forth from the drawing-room, and hastened to my chamber, where I put off my walking apparel. As I glanced from the window, I beheld a carrier's van stopping at the gate: a couple of trunks were being brought into the house; and this circumstance made me reflect that Mr. Norman might possibly purpose to make a somewhat lengthy sojourn beneath that roof.

"And this," I said to myself, "is all the more probable; for he will linger here in the hope of seeing happiness restored to his daughter's mind. But every moment that this visit is prolonged, will increase the chances of a deplorable catastrophe! The interview must now be taking place in the drawing-room. Shall I remain here? No! my presence may perhaps prove useful towards the preservation of the secret: a timely word thrown in may in such circumstances avert the dreaded result! At all events I must watch the proceedings in all their stages, and act accordingly."

I hastened down to the drawing-room, the door of which I reached just as Mr. Norman and Juliet were passing into that apartment.

"Welcome, Mr. Norman, back to England!—welcome likewise to River House!" said Lord Frederick, rising from the sofa and extending his hand to his father-in-law with a certain degree of composure, the maintenance of which I knew must be costing the unhappy young nobleman the most painful efforts.

"I am truly sorry," replied Mr. Norman, grasping the hand of his son-in-law, "to find that you have sustained such injuries."

"The less said upon the subject the better, Mr. Norman," replied Frederick: then with a sickly smile he added, "We all have our little vanity, I presume: and it is a very painful thing to be—to be"——he gasped and seemed as if about to suffocate; but regaining his firmness, he went on to say, "to be so cruelly disfigured, and to be compelled to wear this cursed bandage!"

"Let us sit down and talk quietly upon the subject," said Mr. Norman.

"Surely it is the dinner-hour?" ejaculated Frederick, consulting his watch; "and you must be hungry, Mr. Norman?—you too, Miss Percy?"

"I have not the slightest appetite," interrupted Mr. Norman; "and I would much rather——"

"But I have a good appetite!" exclaimed Lord Frederick; "and it is close upon six o'clock. Dinner must be served up:"—and hastening across the room, he pulled the bell violently; for I could full well understand that he was a prey to a terrific under-current of excitement. "I have not felt in better spirits," he said, "for some days past. Your presence"—glancing towards Mr. Norman and myself—"has quite cheered me!"

He now affected to laugh: but the attempt was a ghastly and a sickly one; and I saw that Mr. Norman was not deceived by it—for he looked both grave and distressed.

"Let him have his own way, my dear father," whispered Juliet entreatingly. "He is indeed in better spirits — your return has enlivened him!"

At this moment the footman entered the apartment to announce that dinner was served up in the dining-room; and Lord Frederick, hastening to give me his arm, led the way down stairs. Mr. Norman and Juliet followed. Juliet was whispering something to her sire,—no doubt entreating him to humour her husband in all things, and to touch as little as possible upon the topic which so much excited him. As for Lord Frederick himself, he affected to be chatting gaily; but as I knew full well how hollow was this cheerfulness on his part, it sounded terribly unnatural to my ears,—just for all the world as if a corpse itself was giving utterance to tones of merriment!

"It is astonishing how well and happy I feel this afternoon," he exclaimed: "these visits have quite enlivened me! No bad compliment to Juliet! The dear girl has done all she could to cheer my spirits: but different voices and different circumstances are as effective as change of scene. I shall soon be well! I feel that I have a capital appetite; and that is an excellent sign. I suppose you came across by the steamer, Mr. Norman?"

The reply was in the affirmative: but it was given in a grave mournful tone, as if Mr. Norman

himself was not deceived by his son-in-law's assumed hilarity—and as if he could not bring himself to join in it.

"Well then, you likewise must have a good appetite; and we will sit down and enjoy ourselves," proceeded Lord Frederick, as we entered the dining-room.

"He is evidently much better," said Juliet in a hasty whisper to me, as she passed my chair to take her own seat at the head of the table. "Let us encourage him in this mood!"

The dinner progressed: Lord Frederick rattled away—Juliet was deceived by the apparent cheerfulness of his manner—but I saw that it was not so with her father, who continued to wear a grave and distressed look, as if he felt convinced that Lord Frederick was acting a part the necessity for which he could not altogether comprehend. I saw that the young nobleman was overdoing the thing, and taking the very course to excite sinister suspicions in his father-in-law's mind. But I could not check him; I dared not so much as make him a significant sign; for I sat precisely opposite to Mr. Norman—and every now and then his looks seemed painfully to interrogate me as to the meaning of the strange scene which was passing before him. At length the dessert was placed upon the table; and the footman withdrew. After a little while Juliet rose; and I prepared to accompany her to the drawing-room. Then Lord Frederick started up, exclaiming, "You need not leave us by ourselves! I have had enough wine—and I know that Mr. Norman does not linger over the bottle."

"I will nevertheless take another glass with you," said Mr. Norman, maintaining his seat.

For a moment Lord Frederick looked undecided and uneasy. I saw that he dreaded to be left alone with his father-in-law; and I came to his rescue by saying, "Well, Juliet, as this is no formal party nor ceremonial occasion, we also can remain."

We accordingly resumed our seats: but in a few minutes Mr. Norman, who really did not care about drinking wine, said, "Perhaps, after all, it would be more agreeable if we ascended to the drawing-room?"

Again Lord Frederick offered me his arm: this time Juliet and her father were in advance of us; and the young nobleman, lingering behind them, whispered to me in feverish haste, "You did well, Miss Percy, not to leave us together! For God's sake don't suffer me to be for a moment alone with Mr. Norman! I must manage to get rid of him as soon as possible—at least in a day or two: but heaven only knows how!"

I was about to advise Lord Frederick to abstain from overacting his part, when it struck me that in his unnatural and morbid state of mind the least check which he might experience would produce the strongest reaction, and would plunge him from the height of a cheerfulness which was assumed into the depths of a despondency which he would not be able to conceal. I therefore said nothing upon the subject. But here I must observe that whatsoever assistance I lent to the maintenance of this fearful secret, was for the sake of his wife and that of his father-in-law: for apart from these considerations I had too little esteem and respect for the young nobleman's character to condescend to the slightest shade of duplicity on his account alone.

We all took our seats in the drawing-room, and coffee was served up. But Lord Frederick now began to exhibit unmistakable signs of weariness and exhaustion beneath the exciting influence of the part which he had been playing.

"As an invalid," said Mr. Norman, "you must not sit up too late. It is now nine o'clock—and I should advise you to seek your couch."

It was with a sense of relief which to my perception was visible enough, and which methought did not escape the notice of Mr. Norman, that Lord Frederick availed himself of this hint. He rose—bade us good night—and exclaimed in a tone of assumed cheerfulness as before, "I already feel so much better! I know I shall be quite well tomorrow! The presence of friends is better than the advice of all the doctors in the world."

Juliet followed her husband from the apartment; and now I was left alone with Mr. Norman. This was a circumstance which I had alike foreseen and dreaded: it was another ordeal through which I had nerved myself to pass. For some few minutes after the door had closed behind his daughter and son-in-law, Mr. Norman remained silent; and I affected to be occupied by turning over a portfolio of prints which lay upon the table.

"Ellen," at length said Mr. Norman, speaking in a very grave voice and with corresponding looks, "what am I to understand by all this? It appears as if a scene, which I cannot comprehend, were passing around me. There is something forced and unnatural on the part of Ravenscliffe, as if he were striving far more than could possibly be necessary under ordinary circumstances to conceal the effects of indisposition. Juliet was deceived by his manner: but I was *not*—and I very much doubt whether *you* were."

"Is it not natural, my dear sir," I asked, "for Lord Frederick to seek as much as possible to cheer and enliven his wife?"

"Yes—if such had been his course all along," answered Mr. Norman; "but the case is different. Alike from your lips and from Juliet's I have heard how depressed and desponding he has been; and I am too well experienced in the world, Ellen, to imagine for a moment that my arrival can alone have thus tended to cheer him. Indeed, it is impossible, considering all past circumstances," proceeded Mr. Norman, his tone becoming more solemn and his looks more grave, "that he can entertain towards me so strong an affection ——"

"You know, my dear sir," I interjected, "that Lord Frederick's disposition has much altered since his marriage—that he has been kind and good to Juliet ——"

"Yes, it is his destiny which he has accepted—to which he has resigned himself—and which he has made as it were a habit and a custom for his mind to fall into. Now, Ellen, understand me well! I am not satisfied with appearances: there is something concealed—something in the background—something that has to be glossed over by this assumed air of cheerfulness. What this something is, I know not—nor can I form any conjecture. Lord Frederick evidently dreads to find himself alone with me. I meant to have spoken seriously to him after dinner; then he rose from his chair and expressed a desire to repair to the drawing-room. There is something mysterious, I repeat, in all this—something which I might even proclaim to be suspicious, only that I know not what to suspect!"

I listened in a species of subdued consternation: I made no comment and gave no answer. Mr. Norman continued.

"I have made up my mind, Ellen," he said, "to summon medical advice. It may be painful to oppose the will of an invalid: but there are certain considerations which render it necessary that I should fulfil the duty I owe my daughter. Lord Frederick's reason may be affected—his mind may be in a morbid condition; and if so, it will become a question whether it is safe to leave him beyond the pale of restraint—and if otherwise, of what nature such restraint must be. Nevertheless, Ellen," continued Mr. Norman, "I scarcely know how to believe this tale of the accident by concussion with the kerbstone. What wound could have left a scar so dreadful that it must needs be covered up? I again say that I know not what to think: but there are uneasy feelings in my mind—vague indefinite suspicions, for which I can scarcely account, and yet which I cannot conquer!"

Again Mr. Norman paused; and again I continued silent—but so composing my looks as to prevent him from catching at the idea that I knew more than I had chosen to tell.

"Now, the matter stands precisely thus, Ellen," he continued: "there are two alternatives. If the whole tale of the accident with the kerbstone be true, the violence of the concussion may have injured the brain, and Frederick may scarcely be held accountable for his actions. If this be so, medical advice should be speedily sought: for it is impossible to say to what extent the aberration of the intellect may reach when once the reason is unsettled. The individual may become dangerous—he may burst forth into a sudden paroxysm of fury—and the dreadful violence of a lunatic often falls upon the very being who in his rational moments is best loved. On the other hand, Ellen," continued Mr. Norman, "the whole tale of the accident with the kerbstone may be false—though God knows how the disfigurement of the young man's face is to be otherwise accounted for: because in this country wrongdoers are not branded on the brow, as they are in some parts of Germany."

"Mr. Norman!" I involuntarily ejaculated, as a sensation of horror smote me.

"The allusion may not have been a proper one, Ellen," observed Mr. Norman; "and perhaps I was wrong to make it: but it arose in my mind at the instant. Indeed, it had already struck me when you first mentioned that Lord Frederick persisted in wearing a black band; and again it struck me when I first entered this room and beheld him with a ribbon on his brow. However, we of course know that it is impossible such a thing could take place in this country; and therefore, again supposing the tale of the concussion with the kerbstone to be untrue, it is absolutely necessary to find out what the truth really *is*. For this purpose medical assistance must be procured, as in the former case which I have suggested. I think that the name of the surgeon who used to attend at River House ——"

"Mr. Singleton," I said,—"a worthy and talented man. He attended upon Juliet in her confinement, on me in my illness, and on poor Mrs. Oldcastle in the last moments of her existence."

"I will do nothing to-night, Ellen," said Mr. Norman: "it is too late. But to-morrow morning——"

"And you will do nothing, my dear sir," I said, "without consulting Juliet?"

"Here she is to answer for herself," ejaculated Mr. Norman, as Lady Frederick Ravenscliffe entered the room at the moment. "Come and sit down with us, my dear child," continued her sire: "we are speaking most seriously in reference to Frederick——"

"Oh! what would you advise, my dear father?" exclaimed Juliet, as she placed herself by his side. "I am dreadfully alarmed on poor Frederick's account! I was in hopes that his spirits were cheering up: but the instant he entered his chamber just now, his mind seemed suddenly to give way —he threw himself upon the bed and burst into a perfect agony of weeping!"

"To tell you the truth, Juliet," said Mr. Norman, "I apprehended some such reaction as this: for with an invalid extremes are always followed by extremes. Now compose yourself, Juliet—do not be alarmed—I am doing everything for the best—and therefore you must answer me a question or two."

"Speak, my dear father—speak!" said Juliet, full of nervous agitation. "I am glad you have come——But pray speak!"

"I think I understood you," said Mr. Norman, "in the course of the few hurried words which we exchanged when I first entered the house, that you have never seen the mark which the accident has left upon Frederick's forehead?"

"No, not once," responded Juliet.

"You have not so much as caught a glimpse of it?" proceeded her father inquiringly.

"Not once," again answered Juliet.

Mr. Norman proceeded to question his daughter; and he elicited from her lips some of the particulars which she had already given to me: namely, that Frederick returned from London with a black bandage bound about his head—that he had never removed it in her presence—that he would not listen to her entreaty that Mr. Singleton's advice should be asked—that the lamp was excluded from the bed-chamber at night—that Frederick suffered from horrible dreams, crying out in anguish—and that he had been altogether wretched and miserable until within the last few hours, when his spirits had apparently experienced so sudden and remarkable an elevation.

Mr. Norman listened with the deepest attention to everything that Juliet told him; and when she had finished speaking, he reflected profoundly for upwards of a minute. At length he said, addressing his daughter, "My dear girl, I deem it absolutely necessary—for a variety of reasons which I will not now explain to you—that medical advice should be called in on your husband's behalf."

"It is useless, father, to offer such a suggestion!" exclaimed Juliet: "for I know that he will refuse it. I know likewise that it will only afflict and anger him."

"Nevertheless, the course must be adopted," answered Mr. Norman. "We must not always consult the wishes of invalids. Your own poor mother Juliet, had an aversion to the doctor— whereas if she had oftener consulted him, she might be spared to us now. Say nothing to Frederick of my intention—it will be time enough to address him on the point when Mr. Singleton shall be in the house."

"I will follow your advice, my dear father, in all things," rejoined Juliet, in a mournful tone and with a look of deep sadness; "for I do indeed feel that something must be done—and I know that whatsoever you do will be for the best!"

We retired early to our respective chambers; but before I sought my couch, I sat down to reflect upon Mr. Norman's intention in respect to Mr. Singleton. Should I seek the earliest opportunity on the morrow to whisper to Lord Frederick a warning of Mr. Norman's resolve?—or should I now let matters take their own course, as a catastrophe seemed inevitable, and it was only aggravating suspense and anxiety in some quarters, and painful apprehensions in others, to endeavour to ward it off? Besides, I disliked the idea of doing anything in a direct and positive manner to frustrate Mr. Norman's designs or to baffle his views. I therefore came to the conclusion that I would suffer the affair in respect to the summoning of medical assistance to take its own course.

I retired to rest; and slumber was just stealing upon my eyes, when I was startled by a cry which almost resembled a yell of human agony; so that the blood stagnated in my veins and I felt as if my hair was standing on end. I sat up in bed and listened. Two or three other cries—but more subdued than the first—reached my ear: and then all was still. The chamber which I occupied was on the same floor as that where Lord and Lady Frederick Ravenscliffe slept: there was an untenanted room between the two—the walls were thick—and yet I had heard those sounds with a fearful plainness. Oh! how deeply I pitied poor Juliet, lying by the side of one who started up in the midst of his dreams and gave vent to such hideous yells!

"Yes," I said to myself, "all this must assuredly be brought to an end of some kind or another—and the sooner the better!"

It was long before I could compose myself to slumber; and even when sleep did visit my eyes, the appalling yells of mental anguish seemed still to be ringing in my brain. I rose in the morning with a headach, with a pale countenance, and with depressed spirits. My toilet was soon accomplished, and I descended to the breakfast-parlour. I found no one there: and yet I had heard Mr. Norman leave his own room at least three quarters of an hour previously. I looked out into the hall: his hat was not there on the peg where he had hung it; and I therefore felt convinced he had already gone forth to put his design into execution and to see Mr. Singleton.

In a few minutes Mr. Norman entered the house; and on joining me in the breakfast parlour, he said in a low voice, and with looks in which a subdued horror was expressed, "Ellen, did you hear those fearful cries last night? That wretched man has a guilty conscience—I am convinced he has! Some fearful mystery attaches itself to him; and I am resolved to fathom it. Not for worlds would I leave my beloved daughter in the society of such a husband without ascertaining the whole truth!"

"You have doubtless been to see Mr. Singleton?" I said inquiringly.

"I have seen Mr. Singleton," answered Mr. Norman; "and I have found him everything you represented. He is evidently a talented, a discreet, and a humane man. I have dealt candidly with him—I have told him everything I know in respect to this most unfortunate case."

"And he is coming?" I inquired, inwardly shuddering with apprehension.

Mr. Norman looked at his watch, and said, "It is now half-past nine o'clock: I allowed an hour for breakfast; and I have therefore requested Mr. Singleton to be here at half-past ten precisely. He has promised to be punctual. I am prepared, Ellen, to deal resolutely with this case; for some secret voice within me seems to whisper that the happiness of my beloved daughter is cruelly involved."

Here the conversation was interrupted by the entrance of Juliet, who was almost immediately followed by her husband. I need hardly say that Lord Frederick still wore the ominous black fillet around his head: but I may add that I noticed how Mr. Norman's eyes were shudderingly withdrawn from it, as if the presentiment were indeed strong in his mind that it concealed something dreadful. The young nobleman again affected to be cheerful and happy: he assured us that he was much better—and he talked of taking a ride in the afternoon. It was the Sabbath-day; but not a syllable was spoken by any one about proceeding to a place of worship:—the thoughts of those who would otherwise have gone thither, were now absorbed in more engrossing if not more important considerations.

CHAPTER LXXII.

THE CLERGYMAN'S NARRATIVE.

LORD FREDERICK RAVENSCLIFFE lingered over the breakfast,—sometimes rattling away in a manner which he deemed calculated to inspire the belief that he was gay and cheerful, and sometimes directing his attention to the London newspapers which had arrived by the post. By that assumed hilarity on his part, he endeavoured to cheat his wife and father-in-law into the belief that his mind was really becoming settled and cheerful: but as for myself, the wretched young nobleman knew only but too well that I was not to be thus deluded—for I was aware of the tremendous secret which had for ever rendered happiness a mere name to his experience!

Precisely at half-past ten o'clock Mr. Singleton was seen threading his way through the little enclosure in front of the house; and Lord Frederick Ravenscliffe, dropping a newspaper from his hand, started up from his seat, exclaiming in a voice of terror, "There is the surgeon!"

"I know it, my dear Lord Frederick," said Mr. Norman: "it is I who have requested his attendance here."

"You, sir!" ejaculated Ravenscliffe fiercely; for

he momentarily lost his temper under the influence of the harrowed feelings which seized upon him.

"Yes—I, my lord!" responded Mr. Norman, with a grave and firm composure. "If you do not perform the duty which you owe to yourself and to your wife, it is incumbent on your friends to perform that duty on your behalf. Be reasonable, my lord——"

"But why should I see a doctor?" demanded Ravenscliffe. "I tell you that I am now quite well——"

"Forgive me, my lord, for observing," said Mr. Norman, "that it is impossible one who has recently suffered such injuries as you have sustained, can be altogether well. Indeed, I fear that the fall from your horse may have hurt you internally; and it is on this point chiefly that I am desirous Mr. Singleton should be consulted."

"My dear Frederick," said Juliet, throwing her arms about her husband's neck, "do pray listen to my father! I beseech you to be reasonable!—he is doing everything for the best!"

"Well, well, Juliet—I yield—I consent!" ejaculated Frederick. "Pardon me, my dear sir," he immediately added, advancing to Mr. Norman and proffering his hand, "if for a moment I spoke abruptly and perhaps ungratefully—but I appreciate your kindness!"

"Enough, Frederick—enough!" exclaimed Mr. Norman: "say not another word upon the subject. And now go and see Mr. Singleton: for I gave instructions that he was to be shown up into the drawing-room."

I saw that Lord Frederick darted a look upon me as if to ascertain whether I were privy to that proceeding on Mr. Norman's part: but I maintained so complete a control over my looks that it was utterly impossible for him to judge anything thereby—unless it were that I had most sacredly respected his secret. He issued from the room; and as the door closed behind him, Juliet clasped her hands together, murmuring with an expression of anguished terror upon her countenance, "Heaven grant that the result of all this may not be to irritate or excite poor Frederick's mind even still more than it has yet been disturbed!"

"Tranquillize yourself, Juliet," said Mr. Norman; "be composed, my dear child!—for the step which I have taken was an indispensable one; and whatever may be the result, I cannot reproach myself."

Mr. Norman now quitted the breakfast-parlour for a few minutes—in order, as he afterwards informed me, that he might leave his daughter to the soothing influence of my friendly consolations. But it was not his purpose to ascend to the drawing-room, nor be present at the interview between his son-in-law and Mr. Singleton.

"Dearest Ellen," said Juliet, the instant we were alone together, "what did my father mean by saying last night that in the step that he was thus taking, he was swayed by circumstances which he would not then explain to me?"

"Mr. Norman," I replied, "is naturally apprehensive on your husband's account——"

"Tell me, dearest Ellen," asked Juliet, quickly, and with a sad woe-begone expression of countenance,—"tell me, did you last night hear—did my father hear——"

"It were useless to deceive you, Juliet," I rejoined, with a sickening sensation at the heart. "I *did* hear those dreadful cries—and your father also heard them in his own chamber!"

"Oh! it was a dreadful, dreadful thing!" cried Juliet, joining her hands together in anguish,— "all in the deep darkness of our chamber—the lamp extinguished—the curtains closely drawn over the windows, so that not the faintest glimmering of the beautiful clear moonlight could penetrate!—and I to be suddenly startled up from my slumber! But God knows I do not say this to complain—I would do anything for poor Frederick——"

"My sweet friend," I said, unable to restrain my tears, "it is indeed a trying time for you; and deeply, deeply do I sympathise with you!"

Juliet threw herself into my arms; and she clung to me, weeping and sobbing, for some minutes. At length, slowly disengaging herself from my embrace, she said in a low deep voice, and with a look which proved that she dreaded to put the question, "What did my father think, Ellen, of those dreadful cries?"

"He said but very little on the subject," I answered: "but the observation which he *did* make was to the effect that he was more than ever convinced of the propriety of consulting Mr. Singleton."

Mr. Norman now returned to the breakfast-parlour: Juliet quickly composed her looks; and her father began to converse on different topics, evidently with the considerate design of soothing the painfulness of his daughter's suspense during the interview that was taking place in the apartment overhead. This interview lasted altogether for upwards of half-an-hour; and then we heard the drawing-room bell ring as a signal that the surgeon was taking his leave of his patient. Mr. Norman issued from the parlour, met Mr. Singleton in the hall, and led him into the dining-room opposite. Almost immediately afterwards Lord Frederick descended the stairs, and joined Juliet and myself in the breakfast-parlour. I can scarcely describe the look that he wore. He was smiling with an air of cheerfulness: but it seemed as if this gaiety were only a gloss or varnish over a haggard anguished expression which the recent trial of his feelings had left behind.

"Well," he said, in a light tone, "I knew it was all useless, and that it would end in comparatively nothing!"

"Then there is naught serious?" exclaimed Juliet joyously, as she took her husband's hand and pressed it between both her own.

"Serious?—no, my dear girl!" answered Frederick. "I have been shaken by the fall from the horse—Singleton recommends repose and rest —and he is going to send me some medicine— opiates, sedatives, or something of that kind. Then as for my restlessness at night," continued Ravenscliffe, his countenance suddenly changing as he thus alluded to the topic—and he glanced with uneasy furtiveness at Juliet, then at me,— "it is only a repetition in my dreams of the dreadful accident——but you know what I mean, and there is enough upon the subject! I am now going to lie down on the sofa in the drawing-room. Get me some books, Juliet."

"I will come and sit by you, Frederick," she responded: "I will get you the books and join you immediately."

With these words she issued from the room: and Lord Frederick, hastily accosting me, whispered in a low rapid tone, "My secret is still safe! A thousand, thousand thanks, Miss Percy! I see that you have not let fall a syllable that might betray it! Singleton suspects nothing. He was keen—searching—minute in all his questions; and, Oh, my God! it seemed as if he were probing a wound that was already hideously painful! Nevertheless, I satisfied him; and he will satisfy Mr. Norman likewise. Heaven only knows how it must all end at last!—but for the present I am as happy as the doomed criminal who has obtained a respite."

Lord Frederick quitted the breakfast parlour, and ascended to the drawing room,—whither he was immediately followed by Juliet, who had been to procure some books from the library. In a few minutes the door of the dining-room opened, and I went out into the hall to speak to Mr. Singleton.

"How do you do, Miss Percy?" he exclaimed, taking my hand. "Once more at River House? I am delighted to see you!"

We exchanged a few observations on indifferent topics; and just as Mr. Singleton was taking his leave, he hastily whispered, "Try and favour me with a call in the course of the day. Come between one and two if possible: I wish to speak to you."

He significantly placed his finger upon his lips, and hastened away. Mr. Norman had re-entered the breakfast-parlour, where I now joined him. His countenance wore a somewhat lighter expression than before his interview with the surgeon; and I therefore thought that Lord Frederick was correct in his idea that Mr. Singleton would satisfy the mind of Juliet's father.

"You are anxious to know, Ellen, what has taken place," said Mr. Norman; "and I will tell you exactly. Mr. Singleton represented to Lord Frederick that he ought to deal candidly with him, and not trifle with his health on account of any silly punctilio or prejudice which he might entertain. Lord Frederick mentioned certain symptoms which he felt; and Mr. Singleton heard enough to convince him that Frederick had been very much shaken by the fall from the horse. But relative to the accident which occurred in London, Frederick positively refused to suffer Mr. Singleton to see the wound. He said that it was almost completely healed, but that the scar was horrible, and nothing should induce him to remove the bandage. He mentioned circumstances which convinced Mr. Singleton that when in London he had positively obtained advice from an eminent physician: indeed he displayed the prescription for certain soothing medicines which he had received from that medical practitioner. And now I come, Ellen," continued Mr. Norman, "to Mr. Singleton's own opinion upon the case. He says that there can be no doubt Lord Frederick must have sustained when in London some accident which produced a very great shock to the whole nervous system, and that this influence has since been aggravated by the fall from the horse. It is by no means unnatural nor strange that Frederick should have horrible dreams, or that he should start up in the midst of them and give vent to wild and mournful cries; for these results are consistent with the nervous

febrile symptoms previously spoken of. Mr. Singleton thinks that I ought not to attach much importance to what I may look upon as Lord Frederick's obstinate perseverance in keeping the black ribbon upon his brow. A high degree of sensitiveness belongs to certain dispositions; and it becomes enhanced into a positive excruciation when the whole nervous system has received a very severe shock. This sensitiveness is naturally greater with young persons who have reason to be proud of their good looks, and who have any special vanity and conceit on that point. Mr. Singleton has known many patients who have recoiled from the idea of having their disfiguring wounds or scars revealed even to the eye of their medical attendant. Indeed so singular is sometimes the conduct of invalids when the nervous system is unsettled, that if they be afraid of death, for instance, they will study their utmost to persuade themselves there is no real danger, and in

this morbid mood they will even endeavour to conceal from their medical attendant what they experience and make him believe that they never felt better in their lives. In the same way a patient will recoil from the idea of suffering a medical man to see with his own eyes the extent to which he is disfigured by an accident or a disease; and thus, Ellen, according to all these theories and reasonings, I ought not perhaps to be surprised that my son-in-law has doomed himself to wear the black fillet around his head, and that he will not so much as remove it before the eyes of his wife nor for surgical inspection."

"Then you are now satisfied, Mr. Norman?" I asked.

He did not immediately reply to my question: he meditated—the cloud again came over his features; and at length he said, "Perhaps I ought to be satisfied, Ellen: but still I cannot consistently with strict truth affirm that I am. I know not how it is:—perhaps the excessive love which I bear my daughter renders me painfully apprehensive on her account—perhaps my own nerves are by recent circumstances more or less unstrung—perhaps likewise the knowledge of Lord Frederick's antecedents have had their influence in rendering me suspicious; for you know very well, Ellen, that after all his conduct towards Juliet previous to their marriage, it is impossible for me to entertain a very exalted opinion of his character. However, as I was saying, it may perhaps be all these circumstances to which I have alluded, that are acting upon my mind, and which leave certain vague and indefinite misgivings floating there despite everything I have heard from Mr. Singleton's lips. But we will now say no more upon the subject. I have done all that a father can do when he fancies that the happiness of his daughter is compromised; and I can do no more. You return to town the day after to-morrow—and I will accompany you. In two or three weeks I shall come back to River House and see how Frederick is getting on. Till then I must endeavour to remain satisfied, and if possible, to set these vague misgivings of mine at rest."

Mr. Norman and I then temporarily separated,—he going out to take a walk, and I retiring to my own chamber. The evil appeared to be staved off: Lord Frederick's secret seemed to be safe for the present. But Mr. Singleton desired to have a private interview with me. For what purpose could this be? Did he suspect something? had he with a kind discretion forborne from mentioning such suspicion, whatsoever it were, to Mr. Norman? and was he anxious to consult me on the position of affairs? I could not conjecture; but I was resolved to call and see the surgeon between the hours which he had indicated. Accordingly, at about one o'clock, I left the house and proceeded to the little village of River, which was close by, and where Mr. Singleton resided. On reaching his dwelling, I was at once shown by a neatly-dressed maid-servant into a parlour where Mr. Singleton was seated with another gentleman and lady. The gentleman—whom I judged by his dress to be a clergyman, and who was a benevolent-looking man of middle age—was introduced to me as Mr. Singleton's brother. The lady was the surgeon's wife; and she received me with a friendly welcome. It was evident that the clergyman was already aware of my expected presence, and that he had been informed who I was; for he expressed his gratification at thus meeting me, and he was a liberal-minded man who had no prejudice against the stage, its influences, or its votaries. Indeed he presently gave me to understand that he had seen me in two or three of my favourite characters; for it appeared that he lived in London. I may here add that he had come to pass a few days with his brother, and he had only arrived at River at a late hour on the preceding evening.

"You may continue that tale which you were telling us," said Mr. Singleton the surgeon, thus addressing himself to his brother, after I had taken the seat which was placed for my accommodation. "Miss Percy is doubtless in no hurry for a few minutes; and as it is perhaps no secret ——"

"Not precisely a secret," answered the clergyman, "though as a matter of course, from its very nature, it is not a narrative to which full publicity ought to be given. I was telling my brother and sister at the moment you were announced, Miss Percy," continued the clergyman, "of a very painful scene at which I was present the day before yesterday, and which indeed, contrary to my original intention, delayed my departure from London until yesterday. I had scarcely commenced my narrative when you knocked at the door; and therefore I will again begin it. You will see, Miss Percy, that wild and thrilling romance is not limited only to novels or to the stage, but that in the range of real life it often assumes more vivid forms and takes more wondrous embodiments."

I felt interested by this preface, and prepared to listen with attention,—although I was in suspense as to what Mr. Singleton the surgeon's object might be in seeking a private interview with me.

"It was, as I have said, the day before yesterday," continued Mr. Singleton the clergyman, "that just as I was completing my preparations to set off on this long-promised visit to River, I received a message requesting me to repair immediately to a neighbouring hotel and administer the last sacrament to a gentleman who was at the point of death. I should tell you, Miss Percy, that my incumbency is at the West End of London, and that the hotel to which I was thus summoned is situated in a fashionable quarter. Of course such a message was imperative: my preparations for departure from the metropolis were at once abandoned, and I hastened to the hotel. The name of the dying gentleman had been mentioned to me: but this, for reasons which will presently become obvious, I suppress. I was conducted up to an ante-chamber, where I found two physicians; and they gave me to understand that their patient in the adjoining room was engaged with a lawyer who had been sent for to receive and record the dying man's last testamentary instructions. One of the physicians proceeded to announce that I had arrived: he returned in a few moments with the intelligence that the will was drawn up, that it merely awaited signature, and that when the ceremony was over I should be free to enter into the dying man's presence. The two physicians passed into the death-chamber to attest the will; and in a few minutes they came forth, accompanied by the lawyer. I then entered the inner room. The dying gentleman was completely sensible: he was in full possession of his mental faculties. I found him to be an elderly man; and from the conversation which presently took place between us, I discovered that he was very rich, and that he had endured the saddest calamities: for, alas! the wealthy in this world are as liable to misfortune as the rest of human beings. It is the common lot of humanity."

The clergyman paused for a few moments, and then continued in the following strain:—

"I found the dying gentleman, as I have said, in the full possession of his mental faculties, and perfectly aware that his end was approaching. He was not perishing of any particular disease—but was literally and truly dying through grief and with a breaking heart. Under these influences he was sinking out of existence. It appeared that he had been calm and collected when giving his final instructions to the attorney; but he grew dreadfully agitated while unbosoming his feelings to me. He declared that throughout his life he had never until within the last few weeks committed a single deed of a nature calculated to trouble his mind as he lay stretched upon the bed of death. But within those few weeks it was different! He had done something in the perpetration of which he considered himself fully and completely justified at the time; but now that the hand of death was upon him, grave and serious doubts had arisen in his soul whether it were not a crime which he had thus committed. Indeed it was a terrible vengeance which he had wreaked; and I shuddered from head to foot, while my blood ran cold within me, as I listened to his explanations. It appeared that his daughter—his only child, whom he had loved with the fondest parental devotion—had been basely seduced by a young nobleman ——"

It was here with the greatest difficulty that I could prevent an ejaculation from escaping my lips. The tale which was being told, seemed suddenly to be fitting itself into the framework of circumstances already known to me. I however conquered my emotion; but it was with suspended breath and with the deepest suspense that I listened to the progress of the clergyman's narrative.

"Yes," continued the Reverend Mr. Singleton, "the unfortunate gentleman's beloved and only daughter had been rendered the victim of a most atrocious villany: she had perished, and her babe with her! Then this gentleman resolved to wreak a terrific vengeance upon the author of these calamities. The name of this guilty young nobleman was not mentioned to me: the gentleman had pledged himself, it appears, to respect the secret of the fearful chastisement which he inflicted on his daughter's seducer. And what think you was this chastisement? The vindictive father had enticed the young nobleman to the house which he occupied at the time; and there, in the same room where the dead daughter and the babe lay,—there, in that room, certain ruffians hired for the purpose seized upon the young nobleman, held him forcibly in a chair, and upon his brow impressed a red-hot iron!"

"Good God, Miss Percy! you are ill!" exclaimed Mr. Singleton the surgeon, springing up from his chair. "Come with me into the next room!—No! no!" he ejaculated, thus addressing himself to his wife and his brother; "do you both of you remain here!"—for they likewise had now sprung up from their seats, and were anxious to render whatsoever assistance lay in their power.

I had not swooned—I had not lost my consciousness: on the contrary, all my mental faculties were most keenly and vividly alive within me. But a deadly pallor had come over my countenance: I had started as if galvanized with sudden horror; and then I had sunk back in my chair. Mr. Singleton led me from the sitting-room, and conducted me into his surgery, where he gave me volatile essences to inhale; and I quickly recovered—or rather, I should say, regained my self-possession. And now, when I glanced up at his countenance, I saw in a moment that Lord Frederick Ravenscliffe's fatal secret was no longer in my keeping *alone!*

"Do not be excited, Miss Percy!—compose yourself!" he said, with a kind voice and look. "It is one of those extraordinary coincidences which some persons would call accidental, but which I cannot help looking upon as evidences of the inscrutable working out of providential designs!"

"It is useless, Mr. Singleton, for me to deny," I said, in a low voice, "that you have fathomed one of the most fearful mysteries which ever came within my knowledge!"

"Ah! then, it is so!" ejaculated the surgeon. "Good heavens! that wretched young nobleman! But his unfortunate wife—does *she* also know it? and is she striving to keep it secret from her father?"

"No—Oh, no!" I exclaimed; "heaven forbid that she should learn this hideous truth! But leave me here by myself for a few minutes," I continued; "return to your brother—ascertain from him whether that gentleman of whom he was speaking actually died——"

"I can answer this question, Miss Percy," responded Mr. Singleton, "without seeking my brother for further information; because when he began to tell my wife and me the tale before you knocked at the front door, he commenced by saying that he had the day before yesterday attended at the death-bed of a penitent who died in peace in his arms!"

"Then Mr. Gower is no more," I thought within myself: "the avenger is gone to his last account! And oh! was not his life cut short beneath the blighting influence of that wickedness which crushed his hapless daughter down into the grave? Frederick Ravenscliffe, you have indeed much to answer for!"

"You are reflecting sorrowfully and painfully, Miss Percy," said Mr. Singleton, gently breaking in upon my meditations. "This is a frightful secret which has been in your keeping!"

"And lest you should think it strange, Mr. Singleton," I responded, "that the hideous secret should be known to *me*, and not to the wife of the delinquent sufferer himself, I must give you some explanations."

I then told Mr. Singleton a sufficiency of past events to make him comprehend how it was that I had been a witness of the horrible ceremony of branding Lord Frederick Ravenscliffe: I informed the surgeon that it was merely through motives of the kindest consideration for Juliet that I had in any way aided her husband to keep his disgrace a secret; and I concluded by repeating the vehement, impassioned, and anguished language in which Lord Frederick had spoken to me on the preceding day when he alluded to suicide and the various means that had suggested themselves to his fevered imagination for accomplishing the work of self-destruction.

"And now tell me, Mr. Singleton," I said, "why did you ask me to come to your house on the present occasion? why did you seek a private interview with me?"

"I will tell you, Miss Percy. During my interview in the forenoon with Lord Frederick Ravenscliffe, the suspicion entered my mind that there was something kept in the background—some mystery enveloping him! Indeed, I shared the suspicion which Mr. Norman had previously confessed to me with frankness, that the tale of the accident with the kerbstone was more or less liable to doubt, and that there was something in the whole business which remained to be probed and fathomed. But I could not tell Lord Frederick what ideas were thus floating in my mind: neither could I obtain any information from his lips to confirm those ideas. His tale, though extraordinary, was consistent, and *might* be strictly true. Remember, I say it *might* be strictly true! Still there was a little incident which somewhat strengthened my misgiving——".

"And that incident?" I asked.

"Lord Frederick informed me that soon after the accident in London, he consulted an eminent physician. He showed me a prescription which that physician had given him; and I saw that it was for calming and soothing medicines. I inquired if the physician had not given an additional prescription—an ointment for instance, or any other application for the wounded forehead? For a moment Lord Frederick appeared to be thrown off his guard: but quickly recovering himself, he searched amongst certain papers in a writing-desk, and then told me that he had lost the other prescription. I repeat, Miss Percy, this little incident seemed suspicious; and yet it might on the other hand be strictly consistent with facts. Indeed, everything which emanated from Lord Frederick's lips *might* have been the actual truth to the very letter; and as a medical man I was bound to report accordingly to Mr. Norman. This report was given with strict reference to the knowledge which I actually *possessed*; and I carefully avoided suffering my report to be biassed by any misgivings, suspicions, or sinister ideas which might have been floating in my mind."

"You could not possibly have acted more conscientiously or honourably," I observed. "But you have now to tell me, Mr. Singleton, why you sought this interview with me?"

"A few words will suffice to give the requisite information," responded the surgeon. "I tell you that though bound by circumstances to make to Mr. Norman a report which to a certain degree was satisfactory, I was not satisfied in my own mind. I was like a juror who having to judge only by the circumstances actually presented to him, finds himself constrained to return a verdict favourable to the accused, though in his own mind there may be lingering suspicions and misgivings tending to suggest a very opposite decision. Such was my position as the medical juror in this case. But the matter was not to end there. I had undertaken to send medicine to the young nobleman: I was to treat him professionally: I therefore naturally wished to obtain as deep an insight as possible into the particulars of his case. I thought that if there were anything in the background—any secret, in short—his wife would be acquainted with it, and *you*, as her most intimate friend, would have been taken into her confidence. Therefore I considered that there would be no harm in my having a little private conversation with you, Miss Percy, upon the point—though when I asked you to come hither, I little foresaw it would be for you to hear a tale which was so much to affect you, and which was so singularly destined to elucidate the mystery concerning Lord Frederick Ravenscliffe."

"And now, Mr. Singleton," I said, "what course will you adopt? Will you suffer the wife of that unhappy young nobleman, as well as her father, to learn the tale of this deep branding infamy?"

"Heaven forbid, Miss Percy," exclaimed the kind-hearted surgeon, "that I should be the means of inflicting unnecessary pain!".

"I expected nothing less than such an assurance from your lips. But carefully though Lord Frederick has endeavoured to conceal from his neighbours the fact that he wears a bandage about his head, yet servants will whisper and gossip—perhaps Mrs. Singleton already suspects from your brother's narrative——"

"I can assure you she suspects nothing!" answered the surgeon; "for I looked at her countenance the very moment when the truth flashed to my knowledge. On my return from River House I mentioned nothing to her of what had there taken place: I never reveal professional secrets even to my wife. It is not as yet known in the neighbourhood that Lord Frederick wears the black fillet; for when he has been seen riding out, he wears his hat so low down upon his head as to conceal the ribbon. My brother departs the day after to-morrow; and he is little likely to catch any floating gossip, even if it were really current. At the same time, Miss Percy," added Mr. Singleton, speaking seriously, "I need not tell you as a young lady of sense, that it will be utterly impossible for the fact that Lord Frederick *does* wear that black band to be long concealed. It must ooze out sooner or later; my wife may hear of it—she may put two and two together, recollecting my brother's story——But this much I can promise, that she will maintain silence upon her lips!"

"More than all this, Mr. Singleton," I responded, "you can neither say nor do. But tell me, is it impossible—is it utterly, absolutely impossible that the mark of the brand can be removed from the brow of that wretched young nobleman?"

"Utterly, absolutely impossible!" answered Mr. Singleton: "there is no surgical operation by which it can be accomplished."

"At all events," I said, "you now know precisely the sad particulars of the case with which you have to deal. Perhaps though you cannot help the physical disfigurement, you may possibly be enabled to minister to the diseased mind?"

"Such shall be my study, Miss Percy," rejoined the surgeon.

I now rose to take my leave. I returned for a moment into the parlour to pay my farewell respects to Mrs. Singleton and the surgeon's brother; and I bent my way towards River House. On arriving there, I found that Mr. Norman had gone out again after luncheon; and ascending to the drawing-room, I perceived Lord Frederick sleeping on the sofa, Juliet being seated near him with her arms thrown about his form. I wondered how he could be so incautious as thus to suffer repose to steal over him in the broad daylight, when the finger of curiosity might lift the black fillet from his brow; and I marvelled all the more on remembering the numerous precautions which he took at night-time to prevent the revelation of the Cain-brand in case that black fillet should happen to come off in the midst of his slumbers. But Juliet whispered to me that sleep had now insensibly stolen over him, as on the previous day it had done.

Gently disengaging her arms from about his form, Lady Frederick Ravenscliffe motioned me to follow her from the room. We proceeded into another apartment; and there she at once exclaimed, with a singular expression of mingled joy and anguish upon her countenance, "Thank God that you came, Ellen! It was heaven which sent you at that moment!"

The shuddering conviction of what my unhappy friend meant, struck me; and I said earnestly and entreatingly, "I conjure you, Juliet, to rise superior to this temptation!"

"Oh! I pray to heaven to give me strength to do so!" she replied: "but there are moments when this dreadful curiosity becomes stronger than myself! Last night, Ellen, those hideous cries—they ring in my brain! they vibrate in my ears! I feel as if I were going mad! I am convinced too that my father entertains some ideas—some suspicions—though God knows what they are or can be: for how can the tale be by any possibility otherwise than Frederick has represented it? Of what other interpretation or construction are the incidents themselves susceptible? It is this that bewilders me! I think there *must* be something; and yet I know not what it *can* be. I seem to be catching at shadows—phantom forms, hideous and undefined, as they flit past in the gloomy obscurity of my soul! And that my father has his doubts and misgivings, I am convinced!—and these have only tended to aggravate mine! Oh, Ellen! it is dreadful—and you cannot wonder that a horrible resistless curiosity should sometimes seize upon me—especially when I am alone with him, when he is asleep, and I have naught to do but perform an act so slight, so brief, and so simple in itself as that of lifting the black fillet with my finger!"

"No, Juliet," I answered, "you must not do it—you must no more violate your husband's will in this respect than you might open a letter which he had forbidden you to read, or peer amongst the contents of a writing-desk which he had forbidden you to touch."

"I will endeavour, my sweet friend," answered Juliet, "to obey your recommendation! Oh, rest assured that I will strive my utmost to perform my duty in this respect! And now, that at the present moment, I feel myself strong—for your words, dear Ellen, inspire me with energy—I wonder at that weakness which almost betrayed me into error, and I am ashamed of myself! God grant that I shall not again experience such a failing of the moral courage, and that I shall not be compelled to make such painful and humiliating confessions to you, dear Ellen!"

I was much pleased to listen to these words which came from Juliet's lips, and all the more so because her countenance assumed a look which appeared to indicate that her soul was indeed recovering some of its lost fortitude; and as she pressed my hand, she said, "It is your friendship, dearest Ellen, that has nerved me in many a trial; and it shall still prove equally effective! I will return to him—I will sit by his side. Be not afraid, dearest Ellen!—the dark mood will not come over me again!"

Having thus spoken, Juliet sped back to the drawing-room, while I ascended to my own chamber for a little while. At the expiration of about half-an-hour I thought I would again seek Juliet; for as she assured me that my presence inspired her with courage, I deemed it better to leave her as little alone with her husband as possible. To the drawing-room I accordingly repaired: but at the very instant that I opened the door, a shriek smote my ears; and rushing in, I beheld Juliet with the black ribbon in her hand, and with a wild, horror-stricken countenance — while Lord Frederick, startled by that cry from his slumber, was thus suddenly wakened up to the consciousness that his terrible secret had at length become revealed to his wife!

CHAPTER LXXIII.

THE BRANDED ONE.

THE scene which now took place almost defies the power of language for its description. In my terror lest any of the servants should have happened to hear that wild shriek and should speed to the apartment, I closed and locked the door behind me: then I sprang forward—and snatching the black bandage from the hand of Juliet, I tossed it towards her miserable, guilty husband. Juliet was holding the ribbon with the firm grasp of convulsive tenacity,—that firmness which derived its energy from the strength of her anguish itself; so that it was with a certain degree of violence and with an abrupt jerk that I snatched the fillet from her. Then the unfortunate Juliet threw herself into my arms, and burst into a perfect agony of weeping. At the same time Lord Frederick was giving way to the bitterest lamentations as he sat upon the sofa with a wild horror depicted on his ghastly countenance. And now for the first time since that fatal night on which the mark of Cain was impressed upon his brow, did I catch a glimpse of the hideous braud. It was a long mark of vivid scarlet, stretching lengthways almost entirely across the forehead; and my blood ran cold within me as I quickly averted my eyes from the appalling spectacle.

"My God! my God! what have I done?" moaned the wretched Juliet, her voice broken with convulsive sobbings.

"Accursed being that I am!" exclaimed Lord Frederick: "how have I lived to meet this moment which was inevitable!"—and with a species of frenzy he thrust both his hands into his hair and tore it as if he sought to wrench it out by the roots.

"O Ellen! you will despise me—you will hate me!" continued Juliet, in a tone of the most woful lamentation: "but the dark mood came over me again—it was irresistible—and I did it! Frederick!" she suddenly exclaimed, bursting from my arms and rushing towards him, "I adjure you to tell me what means that dreadful mark!"

There was frenzy in the looks of the wretched wife as she stood before him: there was frenzy likewise in the looks of the perhaps still more wretched husband as he now gazed up at her with a wild bewilderment. Oh, it was a dreadful scene! Full well did I know that behind that branded brow there was a maddening brain, racked with the most horrible excruciation—and a scarcely less frenzied brain throbbing behind the pure white brow of the miserable man's wretched wife! Yes—it was a scene that to be looked upon only for a moment, would leave an ineffaceable impression on the mind of the beholder,—a scene which even as I am now writing, appears to rise up vividly before me with all its terrible incidents as strongly marked as they were at that moment.

"Frederick!" repeated Juliet, "I adjure you to answer me!"

She wept no longer: her eye-balls, unmoistened by tears, seemed to burn; her countenance was ghastly pale—the features were rigid: a terrible energy seemed to be inspiring her, as if she were resolved to know the worst at once. For a few instants longer did her husband continue to gaze up at her in that same horror-stricken manner; and then suddenly throwing himself upon his knees, he exclaimed in tones of the most rending anguish, "Have pity upon your miserable husband, Juliet! I am accursed!—the punishment of crime is upon the brow of the criminal!"

"My God!" moaned Juliet, all her energy giving way in an instant: and she sank senseless into my arms.

"I will leave you with her, Miss Percy," said Lord Frederick. "Tell her everything! let the whole truth be made known to her! The time for deception is past! Tell her everything, I say!—spare me not in the unfolding of your narrative! Let all my guilt be made known——aye, and my sufferings likewise! Tell her also that she is now the arbitress of my destinies! Whatever she may decide upon, I will do! It is now my wish to go abroad and hide myself for ever——But let it be," he ejaculated,—"yes, let it be all as she shall dictate!"

Lord Frederick had spoken with rapid and excited utterance; and having hastily tied the fillet round his head, he quitted the room. While he was still speaking, I had deposited Juliet upon the sofa: I now lost no time in applying a bottle of volatile essence to her nostrils; and she slowly began to recover. How I dreaded lest her father should return from his walk at the moment, and find his daughter in a state that must inevitably lead to explanations!—though, under any circumstances, I now scarcely saw how such explanations were to be avoided.

Juliet seemed to awaken as if from a wild and horrible dream: she looked up vacantly at me—then she glanced rapidly around, with the light of intelligence, painfully vivid, flashing in her eyes; and when she beheld not the branded being whom she had expected to behold, it seemed as if her mind suddenly experienced a feeling of relief. I took a chair and sat by her. I did not immediately speak: I knew not what to say, nor how to enter upon the explanations which I was charged to give. Deep sighs, having even the strength of sobs, were convulsing Juliet's bosom, as she gazed upon me with a look which seemed to indicate that she expected me to speak, but that she herself dared not ask me to do so, as she knew that they could be only dread revealings which must issue from my lips.

"My poor friend," I at length said, bending over her and speaking in a low tone, "this is indeed a wretched day for you! But yet, after all, it is perhaps better that you should know the worst——"

"Yes—it is better, Ellen," she answered: "it is a relief, though of a horrible kind! What did he say ere he left the room?—for doubtless he said something."

"He told me, Juliet, that I was to explain everything to you——"

"Ah! then you know everything, Ellen?" said Juliet.

"Yes—all along I have known everything: and if I have dissembled——"

"Oh! you need not tell me that it has been for the very best of motives!—for do I not know you well, Ellen? have I not received a thousand proofs of the excellence of your disposition? Tell me all!—tell me everything, whatever it may be! Did I hear aright"—and she shuddered visibly—"did I indeed hear that he has been branded as a criminal?"

"Not branded by the law," I rejoined: "for you know that this punishment exists not legally in England. It is a terrible tale, Juliet!—a tale of dark iniquity on the one hand and of fearful vengeance on the other!"

"Tell it me, Ellen: I am nerved to hear it! Let me know the worst; for it is indeed time that so unnatural a state of things should cease—and I see that there is a decision to be arrived at. But answer me at once:—am I to understand that the branding-iron of infamy——"

"The branding-iron of vengeance," I said, "has been imprinted upon the brow of the wretched Frederick Ravenscliffe! Listen, and I will tell you the tale; for his parting words were, as he left the room, that you are now to know everything—that you are to become the arbitress of his destinies—and that whatever you ordain, he will fulfil."

I then proceeded to describe to Juliet all those circumstances with which the reader has been made acquainted,—how Mr. Gower was the author of the vengeance which had left its ineffaceable sign upon Lord Frederick's brow—how Felicia had been seduced, had become a mother, and had perished with the babe—how I had been rendered the witness of the horrible chastisement—how Mr. Gower had died two days back—and how I had just before heard the tale of that death from the lips of Mr. Singleton's brother. But all these revealings were gradually broken by me with the most delicate care and consideration; for mine indeed was no pleasing task, to be compelled thus to speak to a wife of her husband! Juliet listened in profound silence: her face was as pale as death—her looks were fixed—her features were still rigid. It seemed as if she were indeed now thoroughly nerved to hear the very worst. When I had concluded my narrative, she remained a long time silent; she was reflecting deeply; but not the slightest change came over her countenance. I saw that she was taking some fixed resolve—that she was making up her mind how to act—and that she did not intend to consult me, nor her father, nor any one upon the point, but that she felt that she alone must decide in the midst of the circumstances wherein she found herself placed.

"Lord Frederick's guilt towards the unfortunate Felicia Gower," she at length said, "took place before he became my husband; and for this reason perhaps I ought to think the more mercifully of him—were it not that the whole tenour of the crime was so black, so infamous! Still I must remember that he was forced into that marriage with me, and that this very marriage perhaps prevented him from performing an act of justice towards Miss Gower. I must not therefore abandon him altogether: I have accepted the position of a wife, and to a certain extent must I perform its duties. Frederick has agreed to abide by my decision; and I am now enunciating it. We will continue to live beneath the same roof; we will endeavour to maintain certain appearances before the world: but in other respects we shall dwell apart. Never again will I incur the risk of being startled from my slumbers by the wild cries which in his horrible dreams he sends forth! As for his secret, for my sake as well as for his own must it be respected!—not for worlds would I have it come to the knowledge of my father! No! before *him* we must both dissemble! And now, Ellen, do me one more act of kindness—seek my husband, and tell him all that I have just said to you."

Juliet spoke with a mournful calmness, but with a firm decisiveness of tone. As I had expected, she dictated her decision and consulted me not upon it. I therefore offered not a syllable of comment: but I rose from my seat, with the simple intimation that I would do her bidding—and I left the room for the purpose. Deeply, deeply as I pitied her, yet I was almost glad, and I certainly experienced a relief, that the crisis should be brought about; for it put an end to a most unnatural state of things, or at least brought matters to a settled point.

Lord Frederick had doubtless expected that I should presently have something to communicate to him: he was waiting to hear the drawing-room door open; and he descended from the landing above. I led the way in silence to the library; and when we were there alone together, I explained to him Juliet's decision. He himself was now calm and nerved—though I could not help suspecting that there was something fearfully forced and unnatural in this composure. He listened in silence until I had finished speaking; and he then said, "It shall be as Juliet has ordained. Miss Percy, you have acted a noble part throughout these distressing transactions; and I can only say that I am deeply, deeply grateful."

He then quitted the library: and I returned to Juliet.

"I have still for a day or two a most difficult part to perform," she said; "for as long as my father is with us, I must dissemble—I must endeavour to wear a look that will betray nothing. But you know not, Ellen, how different I now feel!—for it is far better to ascertain the worst, than to live amidst the tortures of anxiety and suspense."

Mr. Norman soon afterwards returned; and then Lord Frederick joined us again in the drawing-room. He and his wife were courteous and polite to each other: but words and epithets of endearment were dropped. During the dinner-hour I did my best to sustain the conversation on a variety of topics, until I almost began to fear

that Mr. Norman would suspect I was straining to keep his attention diverted from particular subjects. The evening wore away; and I was glad when the moment came for us to retire to our respective chambers.

It was a long time before I could get to sleep: but at last slumber came upon my eyes. When I awoke in the morning, I felt rejoiced that I had not been disturbed by those cries which on the preceding night had penetrated so fearfully into my room; and I said to myself, "Heaven grant that all may now go on tranquilly, and that nothing may transpire to reveal the dread secret to Mr. Norman!"

When we were all assembled at the breakfast-table, Juliet and Lord Frederick still adopted towards each other an outward air of friendly politeness; and as I furtively watched Mr. Norman's countenance, I trembled as I fancied that his eye occasionally wandered suspiciously from his daughter to his son-in-law. After breakfast Mr. Singleton called: he remained alone with Lord Frederick for a few minutes, and then took his departure. I did not see him—neither did Juliet or Mr. Norman; nor did the last-mentioned seek an interview with the surgeon. It struck me that this circumstance was favourable, and that Mr. Norman was now resolved to suffer matters to take their own course. Juliet and I asked him to walk out with us—to which he readily assented, Lord Frederick having casually observed that he had some letters to write, and should shut himself in the library for a few hours.

Nothing of any consequence transpired during the day: we all assembled at the usual hour in the dining-room, and still Lord Frederick and his wife maintained towards each other that external demeanour which it seemed they had tacitly resolved to adopt. After the dessert I went out to roam in the garden; and I had not been many minutes there, when I was joined by Mr Norman. I at once perceived by his looks that he had something of importance to say to me; and I dreaded a recurrence to the one terrible subject.

"Ellen," he abruptly exclaimed, "I cannot understand all this! Circumstances seem to have taken a new phase: I feel as if I were in the midst of a scene which I am utterly at a loss to comprehend! At first Juliet and Frederick were all tenderness towards each other: but since yesterday afternoon it seems to me as if a change had come over them. Their demeanour is altogether different. I am not to be deceived: there is a coldness—a constraint which is not to be glossed over by a simple bearing of courtesy! They now show each other mere polite attentions, as if they were friends: but affection is visibly dead between them. And you too, Ellen, appear to be in a strange and unnatural element. You converse as if you were inwardly conscious of the painful necessity of keeping up a discourse which would otherwise droop and dwindle into silence. And there is another thing too, Ellen:—my daughter and her husband occupied different chambers last night; for I heard distinct doors closing, despite the caution that was used by Juliet in shutting her own door. Ah! circumstances have rendered me keenly alive to every fresh incident; for in the present strange and unnatural posture of affairs, everything is significant—nothing is trivial!"

I listened in silence; and I still held my peace when Mr. Norman had done speaking. I knew not how to answer him. I was sick of dissembling; and I was resolved not to give utterance to any direct untruths. Yet I was cruelly embarrassed.

"What am I to understand, Ellen?" asked Mr. Norman. "You do not reply to me. I know the subject must be a most painful one: but I fancied that you were in my daughter's confidence—and if you are not, who could be?"

"My dear sir," I ejaculated; "for heaven's sake distress not yourself any more in these matters! I thought you had resolved to let them take their course—that you would return in a few weeks——"

"Yes, yes," said Mr. Norman; "I see that this is indeed all I can do!"

We walked together for some minutes in silence; and it was in the little enclosure in front of the house that this scene took place. Presently we heard the gate opening; and looking in that direction, we beheld an elderly gentleman, dressed in black, entering the garden. He had grey hair; and he walked quickly with a certain bustling air which seemed professional in some sense or another. Accosting us, he said, "Could I speak to Miss Percy for a few moments?—or perhaps I have now the honour of addressing her?"

"I am Miss Percy," I said, wondering who the gentleman could be and what he wanted.

He immediately drew forth his card, which announced him to be Mr. Aspinall, a solicitor of Lincoln's Inn.

"You must prepare yourself, Miss Percy," he proceeded to say, "for a very startling and extraordinary communication."

"There is nothing wrong, I hope?" exclaimed Mr. Norman anxiously, just as my own lips were about to put a similar question.

"The tidings are in some sense agreeable," continued the lawyer, "but the pleasure they may impart, has its drawback. In plain terms, Miss Percy, you have the chance of inheriting a very considerable fortune—but if ultimately obtained, it will only be when you shall have passed through the ordeal of a lawsuit, which I am afraid will be both tedious and expensive."

The idea for a moment struck me that Mr. Aspinall must be alluding to the fortune which my grandfather had left, but of which I had been so infamously defrauded by Mrs. Parks and her son. Yet a second thought made me feel convinced that the present business could have nothing to do with the other: for the latter could scarcely be now brought to my cognisance in such a shape. As for Mr. Norman, he looked bewildered; and he said, "I really think, sir, you must be making some mistake. Perhaps this is not the Miss Percy whom the business concerns?"

"There can be no mistake, sir," answered Mr. Aspinall, with a courteous smile, "if I have the honour of speaking to Miss Percy the great tragedian?"

"Then pray explain yourself!" cried Mr. Norman, "for your announcement is startling enough."

"When I mention the name of Mr. Gower, Miss Percy——"

"Ah, Mr. Gower!" I ejaculated with a sudden excitement, as if I were all in a moment brought to the very threshold of some new calamitous phase in the subject which I so much yearned to avoid.

"That gentleman," continued the lawyer, "died on Friday last; and I was employed to receive and draw up his testamentary instructions. He has bequeathed, Miss Percy, the great bulk of his property to you. Immediately after his death, I communicated the fact, as in duty bound, to his nephew Major Gower; and I regret to add that this gentleman lost no time in instituting legal proceedings by taking out a *caveat* against the proving or administering of the will."

"Ellen," said Mr. Norman, bending upon me a very grave and serious look, "what is the meaning of this?"

"Nothing prejudicial to that high character which Miss Percy bears," the lawyer hastened to interpose. "Not only did I receive this solemn assurance from Mr. Gower's lips when he lay stretched upon his death-bed, but the fact itself is as solemnly recorded in the will. The bulk of Mr. Gower's property is bequeathed to Miss Percy as a token of gratitude for the sympathy which she displayed towards the late Felicia Gower, and likewise as a reparation for certain evil constructions which the testator, Mr. Gower, at one time put upon Miss Percy's conduct."

"My dear Ellen," exclaimed Mr. Norman, grasping my hand, "forgive me if for a moment I looked suspiciously upon this matter!—and I now hope to God it will prove a subject on which I may congratulate you——though I certainly like as little as possible the aspect of the threatened law-proceedings."

"I considered it my duty," said Mr. Aspinall, "to see you, Miss Percy, with the least possible delay, and I deemed it better to have a personal interview with you than to write on so important a topic. I called on Saturday afternoon at your house in Great Ormond-street. I learnt that you were temporarily staying here; and I therefore came down to Dover this afternoon. The fortune is very large; and the chance of obtaining it is worth a battle in the law courts. But of course you will see your own legal adviser with the least possible delay. I am now powerless to act in the face of the *caveat* which has been served upon me by Major Gower."

"It is my purpose to return to London to-morrow," I said; "and I will lose no time in making you aware of my intentions. I have friends to consult——"

"Naturally so, Miss Percy!" exclaimed the lawyer. "I have now performed my duty—and I may add that you have my best wishes for your success."

Mr. Norman invited Mr. Aspinall to enter the house and partake of some refreshment; but he declined, as he was anxious to get back into Dover to see one or two persons with whom he was acquainted in that town.

The reader must bear in mind that Mr. Norman was utterly ignorant of every circumstance that had borne any reference to Mr. Gower, beyond the simple fact that I had happened to become acquainted with such a gentleman a few months back. All that he had therefore heard from Mr. Aspinall's lips had naturally stricken him with the greatest astonishment; and it was really

ALINE MARCY

no wonder that he should have looked suspiciously on this bequest of a large fortune to myself on the part of one whom he fancied to be almost a perfect stranger to me.

"This, my dear Ellen," he said, as soon as Mr. Aspinall had taken his departure, "is a strange mixture of good and bad luck; for all in a moment you find yourself the heiress of a fortune and a lawsuit! However, we will proceed cautiously in this matter, and take the best possible advice. But how were you enabled to show any sympathy towards Felicia Gower?—and what evil construction

could her father at any time have put upon your motives?"

"It is all too long a tale to tell at present," I said : "but there were circumstances a little while back——"

"Ah, my dear Ellen," cried Mr. Norman, "you choose to do good in secret!—quietly and unostentatiously do you pour forth your sympathy where it is needed! Perhaps there is some little mystery in this case?—perhaps there were circumstances connected with the young lady which you would rather not reveal?—and if so, my dear girl, act according to your discretion, for you know that I have no undue curiosity."

"There were indeed circumstances connected with Felicia Gower," I gravely and solemnly answered, "which I would rather not explain—no, not even to *you*, my kind friend——though if to any one I revealed them——"

"Yes, Ellen, I know that it would be to myself. But you shall not speak another word upon the subject——"

"And in order that I may not be asked for explanations indoors," I said, thus alluding to Lord Frederick and Juliet, "let us for the present keep silence in respect to this visit of Mr. Aspinall:"—for, as the reader may suppose, the name of Gower was the very last which I could wish to be breathed in the presence of the two afflicted beings who had so much reason to recoil in horror from that name.

"It shall be as you say, Ellen," rejoined Mr. Norman: "you always have good motives for everything that you do!"

I was heartily glad that I had thus succeeded in avoiding the necessity of entering into any explanations with Mr. Norman in reference to the legacy bequeathed to me, and that I had also put the seal of silence upon his lips, so that the mention of Mr. Gower's name might be avoided in the presence of Lord and Lady Frederick Ravenscliffe. We re-entered the house: coffee was soon served up; and at ten o'clock we retired to our respective chambers—for both Mr. Norman and myself had to rise somewhat early in the morning to take our departure for London.

When I was alone in my own room, I reflected upon the communication which I had received from the London solicitor. I cannot say that I was particularly elated by the tidings; for it was evident that if, after consulting legal opinions, I advanced my claim to the property, I should have to enter upon the painful harassing ordeal of a lawsuit. That Mr. Gower had been stricken by remorse for his inhuman conduct towards me, was evident enough; and when he lay upon his death-bed he had doubtless reflected that his treatment of me was indeed most cruelly outrageous after having but a comparatively short time before thanked me with so much fervour for the sympathy I had displayed towards his daughter. But though upon his death-bed he conceived (as I had heard from the clergyman's lips) that he had usurped the attributes of the Divinity by wreaking so frightful a vengeance on Lord Frederick Ravenscliffe, yet his remorse on this score evidently had not reached to such an extent as to induce him to make atonement, or seek to make it, for *that* deed.

I fell asleep in the midst of my meditations: but all of a sudden I was startled up by the wild and fearful cries which denoted the mental agonies of the wretched young nobleman in his dreams. Then I heard a door open—then hasty footsteps passing on the landing—and then another door opening. What could it be? Was Mr. Norman seeking his son-in-law's room? A terrible presentiment of a new crisis seized upon me: I glided from my couch—thrust my feet into slippers—hastily threw on a wrapper—and looked forth from my chamber. The door of Lord Frederick's room stood half open; and there was a light burning within. The branded being was crying out in his slumber; for this was evident by what he was saying—and I caught the words plainly enough.

"No, no! you shall not do it! Stand back, miscreants! Good God! a hot iron? No, no! you shall not! Mr. Gower, are you a fiend——"

"Ah! that name! Gower!" ejaculated the voice of Mr. Norman. "By heaven the mystery shall be cleared up!"

The next instant there was a half-stifled cry of anguish, followed by a deep moan, these sounds being on the part of Ravenscliffe: while simultaneously therewith an exclamation of horror burst from the lips of Mr. Norman. Then the door of the wretched young nobleman's room was abruptly closed—no doubt by Mr. Norman's hand; and the next moment Juliet came forth from her own separate chamber, pale as a ghost, and half-wild with affright. Rushing towards me, she exclaimed, "Good heavens, Ellen! what is the matter?"

"I fear, Juliet," I said, hastily drawing her into my chamber and shutting the door,—"I fear—alas! I am only too certain that everything is at length discovered!"

For a moment I perceived, by the light burning in my chamber, that a ghastly pallor like that of death came over Juliet: but the next instant she exerted all her power of self-control—and she said, in a voice which was low but strangely, perhaps unnaturally composed, "It is better thus, Ellen!—better that everything should be known to my father than that we should all continue to exist in a hideous state of fear, uncertainty, and suspense!"

"Remain with me, my dear friend," I said,—"remain here for the rest of the night:"—for notwithstanding this calmness on her part, I thought that she might need consolation, and I was fearful lest she should experience a reaction and be plunged into wildest grief.

Scarcely had I spoken when there was a gentle tap at the door; and as I partially opened it, Mr. Norman inquired in a voice that was hoarse with the strong feelings which possessed him, "Where is Juliet?"

"I am here, father—I am here with Ellen," was her response.

"I am glad of it," he said: "remain with your friend! I know everything——but thank heaven, the servants have not been alarmed—the house is now quiet! Good night."

Mr. Norman at once retired to his own chamber; and when the door of my room was again closed, Juliet asked, "What, think you, will my father do?"

"It is useless for us to speculate, my dear friend," I replied: "but one thing is certain—that it is impossible for matters to be rendered worse than they have been: whatever now takes place must assuredly be for the better."

Juliet said nothing more; and as she lay by my side in the couch, I knew not whether she slept, or whether she were absorbed in deep painful thoughts: but I sincerely hoped for her own sake that her senses were steeped in slumber.

———

CHAPTER LXXI.

THE DECISION.

I AWOKE at a very early hour in the morning; and then I perceived that Juliet was sleeping. I noiselessly performed my toilet in the adjoining dressing-room: Juliet still slumbered;—and issuing from my chamber, I descended the stairs. I proceeded towards the breakfast-parlour: but on reaching the door, I caught the sounds of voices speaking inside the room; and I immediately retreated, for I now knew Mr. Norman and his son-in-law were in conference together. I went out into the garden to woo the refreshing breeze to my brows which were feverishly throbbing; and in a few minutes I was joined by Mr. Norman. His face was pale: the expression of his countenance was that of mingled resoluteness and grief. I felt assured that some decision had been arrived at; and with no small degree of suspense did I await the explanation.

"During the past night, Ellen," he said, "everything was at length most fearfully cleared up to my knowledge; and the lips of that wretched young nobleman have just revealed the fullest details of the horrible narrative. To you I find it was all along known: but to poor Juliet it was a mystery until the day before yesterday. I do not blame you, Ellen, for having kept the dreadful secret: you were only obeying the dictates of your humane and generous heart. Ah! and now too I comprehend wherefore the deceased Mr. Gower should have thought it right to make you an atonement for the pain and horror of the ordeal through which as a witness he dragged you. Ellen!" added Mr. Norman, stopping short in the midst of the gravel-walk of the garden, and gazing fixedly upon my countenance, "I scarcely believe that there is a wretch upon the face of the earth the sum of whose iniquities is greater than that of the man who has become my son-in-law! I thank God that he took my poor wife away from me before all these horrors transpired!"

There was a pause, during which we slowly continued our way along the path; and at length Mr. Norman again spoke.

"You will not be astonished to learn," he resumed; "that I have made up my mind to an immediate and eternal separation between Lord Frederick and Juliet. It is impossible that I can suffer my daughter to live for another day beneath the same roof with a man who bears the indelible mark of a felon upon his brow! It is true that the mark was not branded by the law itself: but it is impossible to blind one's eyes to the fact that there was a terrible justice in the retribution dealt by the hand of private vengeance. In a word, Ellen, Lord Frederick is about to take his departure for the Continent; and he has assured me he shall there bury himself in some seclusion for the remainder of his days. Have you anything to urge against the decision which has thus been arrived at?"

"It is not for me, my dear sir," I answered, "to offer an opinion in matters of such exceeding delicacy."

"Yes, Ellen—as a friend of the family may you speak: and it is in this light," added Mr. Norman, "that I appeal to you."

"But Juliet must be consulted," I said, endeavouring to evade the necessity of giving any direct reply; "and if she as well as her husband be agreeable——"

"Frederick is now with Juliet," answered Mr. Norman; "and it is scarcely possible to doubt what her decision will be. I have suggested certain precautions to prevent a scandal in the house or in the neighbourhood; and thus Lord Frederick will presently intimate to the servants that pressing business suddenly calls him upon the Continent. It is my intention to remain here: and nothing therefore need prevent you, my dear Ellen, from fulfilling your original intention of returning to London to-day."

After a little more conversation we re-entered the house; and I ascended the staircase to seek Juliet. On the first landing I met Lord Frederick: his face was exceedingly pale—he was dressed as if for a journey—he had on his hat, and it was drawn so far down over his forehead as to conceal the black band.

"Farewell, Miss Percy," he said, in a low, hurried, and excited tone: "you will never see me again."

He did not offer me his hand, nor did he stop for any answer that I might have made: but he sped down the stairs and soon afterwards quitted the house. I ascended to my chamber—but Juliet was not there: I proceeded to her own room, where I found her. She was enveloped in a morning wrapper—her long hair was floating all dishevelled over her shoulders and down her back: she was seated upon a chair, evidently absorbed in profound and painful reflections. But she was not weeping: there was not a tear upon her cheeks:—her's was not now the affliction which could find a vent by such means. She did not immediately perceive me as I entered the room; and her aspect was such that I felt a kind of solemn awe which prevented me from intruding with speech on her profound and painful reverie. At length she started slightly; and then taking my hand, she said in a low half-stifling voice, "It is all over now, Ellen—the last scene of the drama is played out! Frederick and I"—here she gasped, and she repeated the words, "Frederick and I have bidden each other an eternal farewell!"

In silence I embraced her; and there was a long pause ere she again spoke.

"I feel, Ellen," she at last said, "that I am in some sense righteously punished for the ambition which I entertained. My mirror told me that I was beautiful; and, as you well know, I longed to form a brilliant matrimonial alliance and obtain a high social position. Oh! I recollect that when you first came to live with us in Hunter Street, I told you that such was my ambition, and in my vanity I looked upon my face as my fortune. It is true that when Frederick first presented himself as my suitor, I loved him—and therefore I am spared the bitterness of the reflection of having thrown myself into his arms entirely through ambition and without the purer and more feminine impulse of attachment. Nevertheless, I feel that I am punished for whatsoever amount of ambition I did entertain——"

"Speak not thus, Juliet!" I said: "why reproach yourself at a time when you ought to seek all means of consolation? It is useless to repine for the past——"

"But this past leaves me so little hope for the future!" said Juliet, with a certain degree of bitterness in her accents. "I bear a patrician title —but it becomes a mockery, situated as I now find myself!"

"Yet you must admit, Juliet," I said, "that you have many elements of happiness still left? You possess a competency—you have a kind and affectionate father, who purposes to remain here with you, at least for the present——"

"And I have a kind friend in you, dearest Ellen!" answered Juliet, as she threw her arms about my neck. "I must accept my destiny!—whatever evils have overtaken me, were more or less prepared by my own hand——"

"No, Juliet," I said; "I cannot even allow you to reproach yourself to this extent! After everything which had originally occurred between yourself and Lord Frederick Ravenscliffe, it was alike natural and proper that you should avail yourself of the opportunity to become his lawfully wedded wife; and at the time you knew not of his deep criminality in respect to the unfortunate Felicia Gower. All the evils which have recently occurred, therefore, were directly and solely the fruit of his own wickedness; and you were as innocent as the unborn child of any complicity in the preparation of these sad destinies. Look up, my dear Juliet, from the depth of your affliction!—take courage—put your faith in heaven—be thankful for the bounties and blessings which still remain to you—and recollect, moreover, that you have a father whose heart will continue deeply wounded so long as he perceives that you abandon yourself to despair!"

In this strain I continued to address her for some little time longer, until she was cheered, encouraged, and consoled; and then, so soon as her toilet was completed, we descended to the breakfast-parlour. Lord Frederick had made a show of partaking of the morning meal previous to his departure, in order to diminish the chances of the domestics suspecting something wrong; and he had already left the house when Juliet and I joined Mr. Norman in that room. It soon became evident that Juliet, in obedience to my counsel, strove to summon all her fortitude to her aid: I nevertheless offered to remain a few days longer with her and send up some fitting excuse to Mr. Richards for my non-appearance at the theatre. But Juliet would not listen to the idea that I should thus violate my engagement and incur the risk of paying the heavy pecuniary penalties which the lessee might inflict upon me. Mr. Norman also urged me to depart; and finally with reluctance I yielded. I bade my friends adieu, and set out on my return to London. During the journey thither I thought to myself that no three days of my existence had on any previous occasion been so replete with wildly romantic and painful incidents as those three days that I had just passed at River House.

I reached Great Ormond Street between three and four o'clock in the afternoon; and Mary Glentworth, who knew the period of my probable return, was expecting me. Without entering into any of the painful particulars which are known to the reader, I briefly informed her that Mr. Norman had returned to England, and that Lord Frederick Ravenscliffe had gone abroad upon the Continent,—adding that it unfortunately proved that the marriage was not altogether a happy one, and that the separation might possibly be eternal. Mary Glentworth expressed much surprise and grief at this announcement: but as I have before remarked, she had no undue share of curiosity, and she did not question me minutely on the subject. Notwithstanding that I was depressed in spirits and unsettled in mind by all the events which had recently occurred at River House, I was compelled to appear upon the stage that evening; for the engagements with lessees and managers are rigidly binding and the public are sternly exacting in respect to the duties of persons of my profession. Thus, unless actual indisposition or deep domestic calamity intervene, the dramatic professional must ever be in readiness to appear at the hour and the moment—to put aside as it were all private feelings—and to assume the character, whether comic or tragic, gay or grave, announced for the particular occasion. Nevertheless, when the heart and soul are thoroughly absorbed in the avocation, and when the profession is pursued not merely as a means of gain but likewise with a veritable enthusiasm, it is surprising how readily one can adapt oneself to the exigencies of the position. And so it was with me; and thus on the particular night of which I am speaking, I made my appearance with as much eclat as ever.

On the following day I saw my father, to whom I of course in confidence revealed everything that had taken place; and I likewise told him of the particulars of the visit of Mr. Aspinall, the solicitor, to River House. My father spoke in much the same sense that Mr. Norman had adopted in reference to the matter, congratulating me on the prospect of obtaining a fortune, but sorrowing that there should be the expense, anxiety, and uncertainty of a lawsuit,—recommending likewise that the opinion of an honest, intelligent, and respectable attorney should at once be taken. I asked my father to go and see Mr. Aspinall in the first instance, and glean from him the minutest particulars, for fear lest I should have forgotten or misinterpreted anything that this gentleman might have said during the hurried interview that took place between us in the garden at River House. My father set off; and it was about one o'clock in the afternoon when he returned from Lincoln's Inn, where Mr. Aspinall's offices were situated. I had ordered my carriage for that hour; and it was waiting at the door.

"Come, Ellen," said my father; "I have learnt all particulars—the affair is precisely as you explained it to me, with this important addition that it is a property of no less than fifteen thousand a-year which is at stake. We have somewhere to go at once, to put the matter into a proper train; for if we decide on fighting the battle, it must be in the Chancery Court—or if on the other hand we negotiate a compromise with Major Gower, it must be through the medium of a solicitor."

I was ready apparelled to go out: my father and I accordingly took our seats in the carriage, he having given some instructions to the coachman, which did not however reach my ears.

"Mr. Aspinall," said my father, as we pursued our way in the carriage, "is an honest, straightforward, and intelligent man. It is a pity he should be so situated, as the solicitor who drew up the will, to render it inexpedient that he should conduct the business on your behalf. But he has given me a letter of introduction to a lawyer whom he recommends for the purpose; and it is to this gentleman's office we are now proceeding. Do not forget, Ellen, that I am appearing in the matter as Mr. Forsyth, your uncle."

The carriage soon drove through a gateway into a moderately-sized square; and it stopped at the door of one of the numerous houses all of which had the appearance of constituting lawyers' offices. We alighted; and on entering the passage, my father stopped for a moment to seek amidst the names painted on the wall for the particular one to which his letter of introduction was addressed.

"First floor—Mr. Wilkinson," he said, thus reading the indication which he sought.

"Mr. Wilkinson?" I ejaculated, instantaneously struck by the name. "Is this Furnival's Inn?"

"The same," replied my father. "But why do you ask? Do you happen to know Mr. Wilkinson?"

"Not personally—but I have heard of him before, in some little matter connected with Mary Glentworth."

While thus speaking, we had ascended the first flight; and my father now opened the door of the clerks' office. Mr. Wilkinson was in his own private room, and disengaged at the instant. The letter of introduction was taken to him by one of the clerks; and almost immediately afterwards the lawyer himself came forth to invite us into his own office. He was a gentlemanly-looking person, between fifty and sixty years of age; and the appearance of his offices, with the numerous clerks, and the quantities of legal documents scattered about, as well as with the arrays of japanned boxes bearing the names of titled clients, amongst which names my eye caught that of the Duke of Ardleigh,—all indicated a large, respectable, and prosperous business.

Mr. Wilkinson conducted us into his private room, and placing seats for our accommodation, he said, "I am delighted, Miss Percy, to have the honour of becoming personally acquainted with you. I have frequently been gratified by beholding you elsewhere; and I have also heard of your kindness in respect to a certain young lady——"

"And now, sir," I hastened to interject, for my father was unacquainted with the mysterious circumstances which regarded Mary Glentworth,—"we have called upon you on a most important business."

"So I perceive, by my friend Mr. Aspinall's letter," remarked Mr. Wilkinson. "We will at once enter upon the subject; and I thank you for the honour you have done me in confiding the business to my hands."

My father had obtained from Mr. Aspinall a copy of Mr. Gower's will; and Mr. Wilkinson carefully perused it. But he required a copy of the caveat which Major Gower, the nephew of the deceased, had entered against the proving or administering of the will; and my father volunteered

to hasten to Lincoln's Inn to procure it if I would wait at Mr. Wilkinson's chambers until his return. I agreed; and when he was gone, Mr. Wilkinson said, "I perceived that everything which relates to Mary Glentworth has been kept a secret from your uncle Mr. Forsyth; and I am sure that the Duke and Duchess of Ardleigh will fully appreciate the delicacy and generosity which have signalized your entire conduct."

"It is now upwards of six months," I said, "since the Duke and Duchess of Ardleigh went abroad: I was given to understand that having wintered upon the Continent they would return to England——"

"Their Graces are expected almost immediately," rejoined Mr. Wilkinson; "and then I have no doubt some decisive step will be taken in reference to Miss Glentworth. I presume that young lady is still staying beneath your hospitable roof?"

"Yes," I replied; "and as you are well aware, she is most anxious to see her supposed uncle. Indeed, of this anxiety you very recently had a proof; and Mary is very grateful for the kindness which you showed her."

Mr. Wilkinson looked, methought, somewhat astonished as if he did not precisely comprehend me; and he said, "I really had no opportunity of showing any kindness to Miss Glentworth: it was merely a professional visit which I paid her some six months back when she was living with you in Hunter Street."

It was now my turn to look astonished, as I said, "But you have seen her since then?"

"Never, to my knowledge," answered Mr. Wilkinson.

I was completely confounded: the lawyer perceived that there was some strange misunderstanding; and he said, "Perhaps it would have been more kind and courteous on my part to have called upon Miss Glentworth—but I have been so occupied—and moreover I thought it better to let the matter rest until the return of the Ardleigh family——"

"Then I must have been mistaken," I said: "I must have erroneously interpreted something that Mary Glentworth remarked to me. But my impression really was that about three weeks or a month back Miss Glentworth called upon you to inquire when there was a chance of her supposed uncle returning to England."

"She might have inquired of my clerks," said Mr. Wilkinson; "but I can assure you that I have never seen the young lady since I paid my respects to her in Hunter Street—and that was six months ago."

"Then it must have been my mistake," I observed, with an outwardly quiet air; but inwardly I was much distressed.

My father shortly afterwards returned, the distance between Furnival's Inn and Lincoln's Inn being very short, and he having had the use of my carriage. He brought the copy of the caveat, which he gave to Mr. Wilkinson. This gentleman read it, and said, "I will at once devote my best attention to the business. I will send notice to Major Gower's attorneys that I am engaged on your behalf; and as I happen to be privately acquainted with them, I will ascertain in a day or two whether there be any chance of effecting a compromise. What character does this Major Gower bear?"

My father answered the question, saying, "I learn from Mr. Aspinall that Major Gower is an honourable and upright young man—for though he bears a military rank comparatively high, he is not above five-and-twenty years of age. I am further informed that he quarrelled with his deceased uncle some twelve or eighteen months back; but with the reason of this dispute I am unacquainted. Certain however it is that the late Mr. Gower was very bitter against his nephew,—though from this circumstance it must be by no means assumed that the nephew was in the wrong, or that he gave the provocation in the first instance—for Mr. Gower was a peculiar character, passionate, impulsive, and vindictive."

"You have spoken very fairly, Mr. Forsyth," said Mr. Wilkinson; "and the impartial manner in which you deal with the case as far as Major Gower is concerned, commands my admiration."

"It were perhaps better," I said, "that at this stage of the proceedings I should explain my own sentiments. Mr. Gower had clearly a right to dispose of his property as he thought fit; and it can be proved to you, Mr. Wilkinson—not merely on the evidence of Mr. Aspinall—but likewise on that of two respectable physicians, as well as on the testimony of the Reverend Mr. Singleton, that his mind was perfectly lucid and sane in his last moments. If therefore he chose to bequeath his property to me, I do not consider that I am called upon to renounce my claim to it. But still, as he was a man of strong and violent prejudices, swayed by powerful and passionate impulses, doing things in haste and repenting at leisure, I should be sorry if his nephew Major Gower were made to suffer unjustly in consequence of the will which his uncle has left behind him. For this reason, therefore, I am perfectly willing to compromise the business at issue in an amicable manner. In short, Mr. Wilkinson, if you find the opposing party agreeable to make a compromise, I leave the settlement of the business entirely to your discretion."

We now took our leave of the solicitor; and shortly afterwards I and my father also separated. While returning to Great Ormond Street, I reflected painfully upon the unmistakable fact that Mary Glentworth had deceived me in reference to her pretended visits to Mr. Wilkinson. What could have been her motive? Was it to account for her absence from home on two occasions when that absence was prolonged to hours? I shuddered and trembled—but I strove to the utmost to prevent my mind from prejudging her whom I looked upon as a friend and loved almost as much as if she were a sister.

On reaching the house, I found Mary at work in the drawing-room; and I requested her to accompany me to my chamber. Whether it were that she had a guilty conscience, or that there was something in my look which made her suspect that all was not right, I knew not at the time: but certain it was that a flush transiently passed over her features as I thus addressed her. When we were together in my room, I said to her, "You will be surprised to learn that having some little law-business to transact, I was led by accident to call upon a gentleman who is known to you—— I mean Mr. Wilkinson of Furnival's Inn."

A deep blush immediately suffused Mary's countenance: but it quickly vanished, leaving her face very pale—and she burst into tears. Then she threw herself into my arms, exclaiming, "Forgive me, Ellen! I see that you have discovered that I deceived you!—and Oh! I am very unhappy that I should have done so!"

"Tell me, Mary," I said,—"tell me at once I conjure you—what was your motive?"

She sat down—wiped away her tears—reflected for a few moments—and at length said, "Pray do not question me, Ellen!—do not, I beseech you!"

I was now seriously alarmed; and I exclaimed, "Oh, Mary! is it possible that you can have any secrets from me? Do I not love you——"

"Yes, yes—I know it!" she murmured, again bursting into tears; and her bosom was now convulsed with sobs. "But still, Ellen——"

"There is something in all this, Mary, which fills me with apprehension on your account! Do, for heaven's sake, relieve my mind——"

"Oh!" she ejaculated, starting up from her seat, "if you think that I have done anything wrong, Ellen——I mean to say if you think that I am lost and no longer worthy of your love and friendship——you misjudge me—Oh! you misjudge me!"

"I believe you, Mary," I said: "I am confident that you are innocence itself! But you will see the necessity of explaining why you practised that little deception upon me. Remember, you told me that on one occasion you were for two or three hours at Mr. Wilkinson's office—then you said that you dined at his private house at Highbury, with his wife and daughters. Oh, Mary! now that I recall these tales, I see that there was something deliberate and circumstantial in them—and it must have been for an object of great importance that you condescended to such falsehoods!"

Mary Glentworth did not answer me; but with her countenance bent downward, she wept and she played nervously with her kerchief. She was all in a trepidation—her bosom rose and fell with powerful heavings—she was deeply agitated.

"Mary," I said, in the kindest, most affectionate, and yet most urgent tone, "I beseech you, let there be the fullest confidence between us! For some little time past it has struck me that you were unhappy. You have had fits of abstraction—you have been pensive—I have asked you whether there was anything upon your mind—then your countenance has brightened up—you have made an effort to be gay—and I candidly confess that there has been a vague uneasiness floating in my brain——"

"Ellen—dearest Ellen, do not distress yourself on my account!" exclaimed Mary Glentworth, once more flinging her arms about my neck: but as she embraced me, methought it was with a species of convulsive vehemence, as if she were still labouring under a strong nervous agitation.

"You surely will not deny your confidence," I said, "to one who loves you like a sister? I have no impertinent curiosity, Mary—I do not seek to pry into your affairs——"

"Oh! how you distress me by such assurances as these!" she said, in a voice of anguish, and it even struck me for a moment that she wrung her hands.

"Do be candid with me, Mary!" I entreatingly urged; "for your conduct frightens me. Recollect! it was only a couple of months back that you experienced an adventure which proved to me your innocence—your artlessness—your unsuspecting nature! You remember, Mary, when you were accosted by a woman in the Burlington Arcade—when the Marquis of Tynedale insulted you—and when a young gentleman rescued you from his importunities?"

The blushes were now burning upon Mary Glentworth's countenance; and I know not precisely how it was, but a suspicion made me instantaneously in my own mind associate those incidents with her subsequent peculiarities of conduct.

"Answer me," I said,—"answer me, I conjure you!—have you renewed those acquaintances?—have you since encountered any one of the persons to whom I have just referred?"

"Oh, Ellen!" she exclaimed, for the third time throwing herself into my arms, and weeping on my bosom; "is it a sin to be beloved? is it a sin to love in return? or is it a crime to endeavour to keep the secret after being emphatically assured that this secret is not my own?"

"Ah!" I ejaculated. "Now, Mary, you are telling me the truth—or at least you are approaching it. You love, my sweet friend? Come, place yourself by my side," I continued, making her sit next to me upon a sofa which was in my bedchamber; "and speak to me as if it were to a sister!"

Mary, whose countenance was still suffused with blushes, sat down by my side; and as I held her hand in my own, I gently entreated her to give me her confidence.

"I have already told you, Ellen," she said, in a low murmuring voice, and with diffidently averted looks, "that the secret is not altogether mine own——"

"What mean you, Mary? You have doubtless been enjoined by the object of this love of yours to maintain it as a secret for the present——"

"Oh! I spoke to him of my uncle Mr. Glentworth—I spoke to him likewise of you, Ellen—and he assured me that it were better that our love should remain a secret! He advanced a thousand reasons—I do not recollect them now—I am so bewildered and confused——but I yielded to his representations; and therefore did I remain silent. At first my conscience smote me, and I could scarcely endure to look you in the face, dear Ellen; for I felt that I was acting with duplicity towards you. Often and often have I been on the very point of throwing myself into your arms, or even at your feet—and confessing everything—but my feelings held me back; for in my soul there appeared to be two distinct currents of emotions—one prompting me to do my duty and act frankly towards you, Ellen, as my best and dearest friend—the other impelling me to make almost any sacrifice on behalf of that love which is so sweet to experience and to be reciprocated!"

There was an unmistakable artlessness, an unquestionable sincerity in Mary Glentworth's language, tone, and looks, as she thus spoke; and I

felt convinced that if she had been acting with imprudence she had not fallen into frailty or error. Thus my mind was infinitely relieved; and I could now proceed to question her with comparative calmness.

"But you have not told me, Mary," I said, "who is the object of this love of yours? Confident am I that notwithstanding all this secrecy he cannot be an unworthy one——"

"Oh! if you did but know him, Ellen," exclaimed Mary, with all the enthusiasm of her young and loving heart, "you would like him—you would not wonder that he should have made an impression upon me—his voice is so harmonious—his language is so tender—his looks are so full of affection——And then too," she added, with a deepening blush upon her cheeks, "he is so handsome—he possesses such a beautiful figure—his manners are so elegant——"

"But his name, Mary?" I said; "what is his name? and who is he?"

"His name is Clarence," replied Miss Glentworth: "is it not a pretty one? He is a young gentleman of fortune—having no profession—free to follow his own inclinations——"

"Clarence I presume is his Christian name," I said: "but what is his surname? and where does he live?"

"Clarence Beauchamp—that is his name," rejoined Mary, all these revealings being characterised by mingled artlessness and reluctance, by sincerity and hesitation, as if she felt that she was sacrificing to her friendship for me the pledges of secrecy which she had made to her lover. "He lives at an hotel at the West-End—he belongs to two or three clubs——"

"So far so good," I interjected, with an increased feeling of relief and satisfaction, for I was now convinced of the respectability of the object of Mary's affection. "But how came you to form his acquaintance? If I might hazard a conjecture, this is the same young gentleman who behaved so handsomely to you two months ago, when you were accosted by that bad designing woman, and when the Marquis of Tynedale so grossly insulted you?"

"Yes—he is the same," responded Mary. "A few days after that incident I met him again—it was of course quite by accident—and he accosted me. I could not do otherwise than speak to him: he kept me in conversation for a little while—but his manner was so respectful and yet so kind, that when we were about to separate and he asked if he might have the honour of paying his respects to me at my own residence, I was about to answer with all frankness in the affirmative, when it suddenly struck me that I had no right to give an invitation to any one to visit at your house without your permission being previously obtained."

"And what therefore did you say, Mary?" I inquired.

"I told him that I was not living with parents or relatives, but that I was residing with a very dear friend—and then I named you, speaking of you as Miss Trafford. The young gentleman was surprised at the announcement—but he immediately began to praise you in a manner which gave me infinite pleasure, because I always like to read or to hear the eulogies which are passed upon you! He however said that it assuredly would be improper for him to call at your house without your permission; and then we parted. It was my purpose to mention this incident to you, Ellen—but I scarcely know how it was—I feared that you might blame me for having stopped to speak to that young gentleman after the earnest advice you had given me to be ever on my guard in reference to strangers—I did not then know his name—I thought that of course you would ask me, and that I should feel myself foolish and embarrassed in being compelled to reply that I really did not know. So I remained silent: but—but—I must candidly confess, Ellen"—and here Mary Glentworth reposed her blushing countenance upon my shoulder—"that I thought of that young gentleman and that his image had made a certain impression upon my mind!"

"And doubtless you again met him shortly?" I inquiringly said, thus endeavouring piecemeal to elicit the facts of the whole proceeding.

"Yes—it was so," replied Mary. "Two or three days afterwards, while you were at rehearsal, I went out to make a few little purchases—and I met him in a neighbouring street. He immediately accosted me—he seemed delighted to see me—and in the course of conversation he told me his name—he gave me to understand that he was rich and his own master. Then—I can scarcely tell how—but I found myself listening to the assurances which he was giving me, but in language so gentlemanly and delicate, to the effect that he had never ceased to think of me from the moment we first met, and that he felt unhappy till he beheld me again. I was trembling all over—it seemed to me that I was doing wrong to listen to such language—or at least that I was in duty bound to communicate everything afterwards to you: but he besought me to grant him another meeting on the following day and to remain altogether silent upon the subject in the interval. I did not promise that I would—neither did I say that I would not. We parted—and—and——"

"On the following day you met him again?" I said.

"Yes, Ellen—I met him—he then spoke to me more plainly—he declared that he had never loved before—but that he felt he loved me deeply, and that he could not live without me. He besought me to tell him whether I could love him in return; and he vowed that the most delightful moment of his life would be that in which he should conduct me to the altar. Afterwards we met frequently, Ellen—for I am now confessing everything——"

"But what arguments did he use, my dear Mary," I inquired, "as a reason for not calling at the house and for keeping all these proceedings a secret?"

"I could not tell him that I loved him in return—I experienced some feeling, I scarcely know how to explain it—but it was a reluctance to admit that in so short a time he had made an impression upon my heart. Ah! perhaps it was that I feared he might think it was levity on my part, and I wished to merit his esteem—his love——"

"But did it not strike you, Mary," I gently inquired, "that you might suffer in his estimation by continuing to meet him thus stealthily?"

"Oh! he begged and implored me to meet him—he said that until I came to know him better

and could give him a positive decision, it were more prudent that he should abstain from calling at the house—and in a word that he would not visit me there until he could be introduced to you and to my uncle as my accepted suitor. And then too, Ellen, I must admit that there was such soft persuasion in his language — I felt myself as if under a spell when in his company——"

"But now tell me, Mary," I said, "on that particular evening when I returned from Petersfield, and you said you had been to dine with Mr. Wilkinson——"

"Ah! I will explain everything, my dear Ellen," she exclaimed. "The day before you returned from Petersfield I met Clarence Beauchamp, and he asked me to accompany him to the Gardens in the Regent's Park. We went: and as I was two or three hours absent from home—much longer than I had ever before been absent, when not using the carriage—I thought on my return that it would appear strange to the servants; and not knowing precisely what excuse to make, I suddenly recollected that it would seem natural enough if I had been engaged in some business with a solicitor. So the name of Mr. Wilkinson came uppermost; and as if quite casually, I dropped a hint to that effect. I had promised that I would meet Clarence again on the following evening, and that I would then give him my decision—for as yet I had not suffered him to elicit from my lips an avowal of reciprocal affection: but as I had by that time known him exactly one month, I thought that I need no longer conceal the true state of my feelings—and all the less so because he must have fully comprehended them from the fact of my consenting to meet him from time to time, and that I had listened to the language of love which he breathed in my ear. I had promised to meet him again in the Regent's Park; and foreseeing that my absence would once more be prolonged, I again used the name of Mr. Wilkinson as a pretext with the servants:—I said that I was going to dine with that gentleman. Now believe me, my dear Ellen, if you had been at home on these two occasions, I could not have brought myself to give utterance to those untruths deliberately to your face: but to servants one will casually throw out excuses which one would not breathe to one's friends or equals. Nevertheless, when on returning that evening at about nine o'clock, I found you had come back from Petersfield—unexpectedly indeed, for I thought that your business would most probably detain you a day or two longer there—I was seized as it were with a species of consternation, and I found myself compelled to repeat deliberately the pretext which I had lightly and casually thrown out in the presence of the lady's-maid. For you must understand, Ellen, I had promised Clarence that the secret of our love should be maintained until he himself considered that a proper time had elapsed when everything might be revealed to you and when my uncle should have returned——"

"But nearly a month has passed, Mary," I interjected, "since you suffered Mr. Beauchamp to elicit the avowal of love from your lips—you have now known him about two months altogether—and yet during all this time you have kept the secret——"

"Yes, Ellen," responded Mary, "because Clarence Beauchamp convinced me by arguments that it was necessary. He said that if I were to mention everything to you, you would insist that I should desist from seeing him until the return of my uncle to England; and as the date of his return is so uncertain—it may still be weeks, or it may be months — Clarence pleaded so hard that I would take no step which would put an end to these interviews and prevent us from seeing each other occasionally. So I yielded to this reasoning —and I pledged myself that I would say nothing to you until the return of my uncle. This is why I assured you when you ere now began to press me, that the secret was not my own. But I could no longer refuse my confidence; and now you know everything! Tell me, my dear Ellen—tell me—for there is indeed a sisterly affection between us — are you angry with me? and have I done very wrong?"

"It may seem strange, Mary," I answered seriously but with kindness, "that I, who am only of your own age, should take it on myself to speak as one having greater experience——"

"Oh! but you *do* possess greater experience in the world, Ellen!" exclaimed Mary; "for you have seen so much, whereas I lived for the greater part of my existence in country places——"

"Well, my dear Mary," I resumed, "if you admit this superior experience on my part, you will not be offended that I speak candidly. You ought not to have kept all these things a secret from me. Had you told me in the first instance that Mr. Beauchamp addressed you in the language of love—that he had made a certain impression on your heart—and that you had every reason to suppose him to be a highly honourable and respectable young gentleman, I should have said to you, 'Let him call at the house, Mary: let him pay his attentions openly; and at least let his courtship have the sanction and countenance of the friend with whom you live.'—But you have adopted another course; you have acted secretly, until this secresy has assumed the character of duplicity, and you have even been led into the utterance of untruths —of which however, heaven be thanked! I see that you are ashamed."

Mary Glentworth was now weeping: I began to fear that I had spoken too severely to her, and that in the fervor of my friendship I had exercised a greater authority and power than I ought properly to usurp. I therefore threw my arms about her neck, saying, "Do not weep, Mary— and do not think that I am reproaching you with harshness or unkindness! You know that I love you—and whatsoever I may say is only for your good!"

"What am I to do, then, Ellen?" asked Mary Glentworth, continuing to sob convulsively and weep plenteously. "I feel that I have been guilty of duplicity, and I have been led into the utterance of untruths to which I could never deliberately condescend, and from which my soul now recoils! But I will make every possible atonement. How shall I act? I will be altogether guided by your counsel and advice. Can I say more, Ellen?—can I do more?"

"Nothing, dear Mary!—and believe me when I assure you that your present conduct is a complete atonement in my estimation for the past. Have you promised to meet Mr. Beauchamp again? If so, when and where?"

"Yes—I have promised," she murmuringly replied. "The day after to-morrow—at the West End of the town——"

"Then you will suffer me to accompany you on the occasion," I said. "I will exculpate you from any wilful breach of faith towards Mr. Beauchamp in confessing everything to me. He is doubtless an honourable young gentleman, and he will be satisfied. I will invite him to the house— he shall henceforth visit you openly—and when your uncle returns to England, he will not object to your receiving the attentions of an eligible suitor. On the contrary, it will be a subject for congratulation——"

"Oh, how kind you are, Ellen!" exclaimed Mary, wiping away her tears, and an expression of joy animating her countenance. "Yes—you shall accompany me at my next meeting with Clarence——"

"And we will therefore now say no more upon the subject," I interrupted her. "I have a little treat in store for you this evening, if you like to avail yourself of it. There is to be a grand debate in the House of Commons—I have never as yet visited the legislative assemblies—and I purpose to be present there on this occasion. Do you feel inclined to accompany me?"

Mary expressed her readiness to accept my invitation; and we therefore partook of an early dinner that we might be at the House at five o'clock, the hour when the debate was expected to commence.

——

CHAPTER LXXII.

LUIGI.

THE reader will recollect that when I first resided with the Norman family, they were accustomed to see a great deal of company; and thus I had become acquainted with many noblemen, Members of the House of Commons, and other persons of distinction. After the unfortunate circumstances connected with Lord Frederick Ravenscliffe and Juliet—I allude to the mock-marriage and the events which ensued directly therefrom—the Normans gave up receiving company to the same extent as formerly: and the circle of their visiting friends became chiefly limited to their dramatic acquaintances. When I was compelled by Mrs. Norman's death to have an establishment of my own, I narrowed the limits of my visiting acquaintances to a very small circle: but still several of the noblemen, gentlemen, and other persons of distinction to whom I have above alluded, occasionally left their cards as a token of respect, as I believe, to my eminence as a tragedian. A County Member, having called some little time previous to the incidents which have occupied the last few chapters, happened to inquire of me whether I had ever been to the House of Commons?—and on my answering in the negative, he volunteered to send me admissions for myself and my friend Miss Glentworth on the very first occasion when there should happen to be a debate worth hearing. He had kept his word; and it was of these admissions that Mary and I now availed ourselves.

The compartment allotted for the accommodation of ladies in the old House of Commons, was a species of little wooden cage, or dungeon, situated at the back of the Speaker's Gallery, and capable only of containing about a dozen persons. When Mary and I arrived at our destination and were shown up into this wretched little place, we found that it was already nearly filled by elegantly dressed ladies,—most of them, as I presently learnt, being the wives or daughters of the leading Members who were to take a part in the debate. Amongst these ladies was Mrs. St. Clair; and immediately upon our entrance she came and sat by our side. Mary was already acquainted with her, for on two or three occasions she had called upon me in Great Ormond Street; and she now expressed her delight at meeting us both on the present occasion. She had been there before: she was therefore enabled to point out to us the different arrangements of the House—the Treasury benches where the Ministers sat, the Opposition benches, the Reporters' Gallery, and so forth. She likewise indicated, from personal knowledge, the leading members of all parties; and thus it was fortunate we had fallen in with her on the occasion. She did not mention her husband's name: but I beheld Edwin St. Clair seated on the front Treasury bench, amongst the leading Cabinet Ministers; and in a whisper I directed Mary Glentworth's attention to him. I should observe that Zarah looked exceedingly well. She was very handsomely dressed; and she was treated with marked distinction by most of the ladies who were present in the little cage-like compartment where we all sat, screened off from the male portion of the auditory in the Speaker's Gallery.

At first there was only some routine business of an uninteresting nature—the reading of private bills for docks, turnpike-roads, canals, railways, and so forth; and during the hour thus occupied Zarah and I had leisure for a little whispered discourse.

"Nearly a month has elapsed, my dear Zarah," I observed, "since you and I parted after our return from Petersfield; and you have not as yet suggested what course is to be adopted in reference to the forger and assassin Mr. Parks."

"I called at your house, Ellen, last Saturday," replied Zarah; "and I learnt that you had gone to Dover. I wished to discourse upon the matter with you; and I will therefore visit you to-morrow, if you should be disengaged, in the afternoon."

"I shall be disengaged, and I shall be delighted to see you," was my answer. "Indeed, the sooner something is now done in reference to Mr. Parks, the better. You know my resolution!—the man shall not escape punishment!"

"Nor is it my wish that he should continue in the enjoyment of impunity," replied Mrs. St. Clair,—"especially, my dear Ellen, as it would afford me infinite pleasure to behold you in possession of the fortune of which you were so cruelly plundered. I have not been unmindful of the subject—I have already revolved several plans in my imagination, and I have settled upon one which I think will be effective. But more of this to-morrow. By the bye, I experienced a little adventure the other day, which, if I had seen you on Saturday, it was my intention to communicate."

"No adventure of an unpleasant character, let me hope?" I said.

"It was by no means agreeable, I can assure you, Ellen," was the response. "But you know that I am tolerably strong-minded," she added, with a smile; "and therefore it produced upon me a more mitigated impression than it would have made upon most persons of our sex. But to the tale:—A few days ago," continued Mrs. St. Clair, "I went to call upon a lady residing in our neighbourhood; and as the distance was very short, I proceeded on foot. On my way thither I perceived a crowd gathered at the entrance of a diverging street; and I saw that it was assembled to behold the performances of a party of Italian mountebanks. They were about half-a-dozen in number: they were dressed in a quaint style—and they were performing various feats after the usual manners of itinerant *acrobats*. I was passing towards the other side of the way in order to avoid this crowd, when my attention was suddenly directed to one of the mountebanks, who came rushing forward with a saucer in his hand to solicit a donation. I quickly drew forth a coin from my purse: but just at that very instant these strange words hissed in my ears—'The day is yet to come when I will wreak a deadly vengeance upon you! Much as I once loved you, so bitterly do I now hate you!'"

"Good heavens, Zarah!" I whisperingly ejaculated: "could it possibly have been——"

"Yes, Ellen—I see that you already suspect who the man was! It was the wretch Luigi!"

"The murderer of his unfortunate master, the Count of Carboni!" I exclaimed, though still speaking in a low whispering tone: "or at least there is too much reason to suppose that he was the Count's assassin! I told you that dreadful tragedy at the time——"

"Yes—and most assuredly I had not forgotten it!" responded Zarah. "But listen to my narrative. When the mountebank first approached me, I paid no particular attention to him—I did not even glance at his countenance: I was in haste to bestow my donation and escape from the notice of the crowd. But when those words suddenly hissed upon my ear as if breathed from the mouth of a hideous reptile, I flung my eyes upon the countenance of the speaker; and then, through the mask of paint which bedaubed his face, I at once recognised Luigi. 'Wretched murderer! assassin!' I ejaculated: but scarcely had the words gone forth from my lips, when he darted away with the speed of lightning——not rejoining his companions, nor mingling amongst the crowd, but turning into another street and disappearing from the view as if it were a phantom melting into the thin air. A police-constable instantaneously accosted me and asked if I had been robbed?—'No,' I hastily responded; 'but that man who has just fled from my presence, is the supposed assassin of the Count of Carboni who about six months ago was murdered at Dover!'—'Ah, I recollect!' ejaculated the constable: and without saying another word he set off in pursuit."

"But he did not overtake him?" I exclaimed: "he did not capture him?—for I saw nothing of the incident in the papers!"

"And I heard nothing more of it," rejoined Zarah: "I therefore conclude that the wretch succeeded in effecting his escape. I must however add a few more words to my narrative. The incident which I have described took place, so to speak, in the twinkling of an eye; and as it was apart from the crowd, none of those bystanders overheard anything that was thus said—but there was of course a general sensation when the people beheld the occurrence. From certain ejaculations which burst forth, I perceived the impression to be that the mountebank had snatched my purse from my hand and had fled. Cries of 'Stop, thief!' therefore soon became general; and I, anxious to escape from the notice of the crowd, bent my hurried steps to the house whither I was proceeding at the time."

"Luigi thus discovered," I said, "that he is suspected as the murderer of his late master; and since he succeeded in evading the pursuit of the police on that occasion when his mountebank dress ought to have rendered him an object so easy to capture, there can be little doubt that by this time he has got safely out of the country. If this be so, I shall feel glad for one reason—that you, my dear Zarah, will remain in security against the execution of the villain's vindictive threats; though on the other hand, I should be sorry if justice were to be cheated of its due and that the murderer should escape the arm of the law."

Our conversation now ceased; for the order of the day initiating the grand debate was read. Then some leading member of the Opposition rose to bring forward an amendment, of which, as it appeared, he had given notice; and he spoke for about an hour and a half upon the subject. His oration was an eloquent one; and he sat down amongst the loud cheers of his party. Then, upon the Ministerial side rose Edwin St. Clair; and a profound silence prevailed. I glanced at Zarah, and I saw that through the duskiness of her gipsy-complexion the rich blood was mantling; for though she loved not her husband, and though there continued to reign a species of strong, stern, tacit warfare between them, yet was she proud of him,—proud of being the wife of the Right Hon. Edwin St. Clair who was now about to command the attention of the listening senate!

I must confess on my own part that much as I loathed and abhorred the character of this man— much as I had reason to deplore that an individual whose soul I knew to be blackened with crimes, should occupy a post of public authority— I was nevertheless inspired by curiosity to hear him; for I had learnt how brilliant was his style of oratory and what a commanding genius he as a statesman possessed. I will also acknowledge that as he proceeded with his oration, I was so led away by his eloquence as to forget for intervals that it was a man of such a character who was speaking,—until I was suddenly startled as it were by the recollection. He began in a voice that was comparatively low, and yet so clear in its mas-culine harmony that not a syllable was lost even in the remote screened-off nook where I was seated. Presently a cheer burst forth from the Ministerial side of the House: then, as he re-sumed, he raised his voice—he became animated— his tones swelled—they rolled through the build-ing in continuous waves of harmonious sound; and when he again paused, the cheering was perfectly enthusiastic. He proceeded, sometimes breaking forth with withering sarcasm against his political opponents—but chiefly pursuing a line of argument most logically and closely reasoned, de-molishing one by one the statements set forth by the proposer of the amendment. Then again he indulged in bitter taunts and overwhelming sar-casms,—the fluctuations of his voice being most skilfully modulated so as to suit the various styles of oratory which he thus successively in-troduced into his speech. Frequent cheers burst forth; and it soon became apparent that the effect he produced was immense. And now his eloquence became ornate with flowers and metaphors: and this portion of his speech was surpassingly beautiful. He never hesitated for a word, and he never used an inappropriate one: he had the most perfect command of language—and yet there was not the slightest shadow of a proof that he had previously studied his speech. It seemed entirely to be the spontaneous effusion of the mind, evoked by the circumstances of the moment. As he stood there, elegantly dressed— looking in every sense the polished gentleman— his countenance glowing with the fervour that carried him onward, and with anticipated triumph, —as he sometimes drew his tall slender form up to its full height, and by his gestures as well as his words hurled defiance at his antagonists on the opposite benches—or as he burst forth into pas-sages of thrilling eloquence, full of argument and beauty,—as he stood there indeed, with the *pres-tige* of having raised himself by his own talent to

be what he was, I could not help thinking during a pause in his speech — but a pause that was occupied by loud cheering—how lamentable and shocking a thing it was that a man so highly gifted should be so inwardly depraved, and that a being capable of deeds the noblest and the grandest, should have condescended to the perpetration of the vilest and the worst.

Ever and anon I glanced towards Zarah; and I perceived that her eyes were beaming and her cheeks were flushing with a triumph of her own. Full well could I understand what was passing in her mind. She was the wife of that man—she bore the name of him who was thus commanding the applause of the assembly of British represen-tatives! the glory which sat upon his brow was reflected on her own! The two hours that his speech lasted were two hours of pride and satisfaction for her; and when at length he sat down amidst bursts of loud cheering that was prolonged for several minutes, she hastily applied her kerchief to her eyes: the strong-minded Zarah was for a moment overpowered by the very luxury of her feelings, — feelings of pride, and satisfaction, and triumph!

The debate lasted until about half-past eleven o'clock: several Members took part in the discus-sion—but none spoke with the same effect as Edwin St. Clair. When the division ensued, the Government obtained an immense majority; and the Ministerial triumph was proclaimed in the newspapers of the following day to be entirely owing to the eloquent oration of the Right Honour-able Edwin St. Clair. For my own part, when I returned with Mary Glentworth on that evening from the House of Commons, it was with a certain depression of spirits: I felt shocked for humanity's sake that a person of St. Clair's genius should be the fiend-like, remorseless, unprincipled creature that I knew he was.

On the following day a note from Mr. Wilkin-son compelled my attendance at his office; and I was therefore under the necessity of leaving a billet for Zarah, apologizing for my absence from home, and requesting her to favour me with a call on the day but one next ensuing (for on the fol-lowing day I was to accompany Mary Glentworth in her interview with Clarence Beauchamp). On arriving at Mr. Wilkinson's offices, I found that he had not suffered the grass to grow under his feet; for he had already seen Major Gower's solicitors, and they had given him to understand that their client was willing to compromise the matter amicably. They had however suggested that I should renounce two-thirds of the property on Major Gower's behalf. To this arrangement Mr. Wilkinson by no means counselled me to agree; and he proposed that the whole property should be equally divided. I left the matter entirely to his discretion; and he promised that he would speedily communicate with Major Gower's at-torneys.

In the evening of that day I appeared at the theatre in some new character; but what it was I do not remember, for I accidentally omitted to re-cord it in the diary which I have been accus-tomed to keep, and which has formed the ground-work of the complete narrative which I am now giving to the public. The announcement, how-ever, of my appearance in this character for the first time, drew one of the most crowded houses to which I have ever played; and on sweeping my eyes around the closely-packed tiers, I caught sight of Edwin St. Clair and Zarah. Zarah frequently attended the theatre: but her husband seldom visited places of public entertainment since his appointment to the Ministerial office demanded so much of his time and attention. But on this occasion he *was* present; and until I entered upon the stage, he and his handsome wife were the objects of almost universal notice. At the conclusion of the drama I was greeted with the usual testimonies of applause; and on proceeding to my dressing-room, I was speedily joined by Mary Glentworth and Aline Marcy, who had occupied one of the stage-boxes. They enthusiastically congratulated me on my triumph; and I saw that Aline's beautiful blue eyes glistened with hopefulness on her own account when the day of her *debut* should come. Mary Glentworth likewise experienced an inspiration of a somewhat kindred character: for she whispered to me, "Oh, my dear Ellen! how happy should I be if I were the heroine of this evening's triumph, but without depriving you of the honour!"

I was about to make her some answer, when sounds indicative of agitation and confusion reached our ears,—several voices speaking hurriedly and in an excited manner, blended with ejaculations expressive of horror, as if something dreadful had occurred. Then there was the rush of many footsteps in the narrow corridor from which my dressing-room opened; and indeed everything indicated that some unusual and alarming event was transpiring. The apprehension of fire struck me; and as I was half undressed, I besought my maid to go and see what was the matter. She and Mary Glentworth hastened forth together: but Mary almost immediately returned with the assurance that there was no danger of the kind I had apprehended. The cause of the excitement was some outrage which had been perpetrated upon a lady at the entrance of the theatre—but what it was Mary Glentworth had not been enabled to glean from the person to whom she had addressed herself for information. My lady's-maid had however gone to prosecute the inquiry.

By the assistance of Aline and Mary I speedily finished my toilet; and scarcely was it completed, when the maid returned, with horror and consternation in her looks.

"Oh, Miss!" she cried, "what a dreadful occurrence!" and she sank all pale and trembling upon a seat.

"Good heavens! what is it?" I inquired, while my own terror and anxiety were shared by Mary and Aline.

"A villain," gasped the maid, "has just thrown a quantity of vitriol——"

"Vitriol!" I shudderingly ejaculated. "Upon whom?"

"Upon your friend, Miss,' was the response,— "upon Mrs. St. Clair!"

"O horror!" I ejaculated, instantaneously smitten with the conviction that this was the hideous work of the vindictive miscreant Luigi.

"But is she much injured?"

"We feared so, Miss! Her screams were dreadful—she was instantaneously placed in her carriage——"

"And the villain?" I anxiously asked: "was he captured?"

"No, Miss—he escaped in the midst of the confusion: but he will no doubt be speedily taken, for he wore a peculiar dress——"

"Oh! heaven's justice," I exclaimed, in anguish of mind on poor Zarah's account, "will not suffer him to evade the righteous vengeance of the law! But Mrs. St. Clair——"

"She was at once placed in her carriage, and her husband gave a hurried order for the coachman to drive to the nearest surgeon's."

"We will go and make inquiries!" I said: and I rushed from my dressing-room.

The utmost confusion prevailed in the theatre, both behind and before the curtain. The actors and actresses were conversing in detached groups: the theatre itself was half-emptied of an audience that but a few minutes back was overflowing; and Mr. Richards, the lessee, was now announcing that in consequence of the horrible impression made by the fiend-like deed, the after-piece would not be presented and the performances would at once close for the evening. Although my carriage was in attendance, I did not immediately seek it at the private door where it was drawn up: but I issued forth by a nearer avenue, for my mind was dreadfully excited, and I was anxious to learn to what extent my unfortunate friend Zarah had suffered. There was a great crowd collected in front of the theatre: but the moment I was recognised, a passage was cleared for me, followed closely as I was by Aline Marcy, Mary Glentworth, and my maid. I hurriedly inquired of a police-official in which direction Mrs. St. Clair's carriage had gone?—and I speedily ascertained that it was at no very great distance. Thither I hastened,—thus for the first time voluntarily seeking any place where I stood a chance of encountering Edwin St. Clair: but I thought not of him—all my ideas and feelings were most painfully absorbed in Zarah's calamity. The crowd extended all the way to the surgeon's residence, where the carriage had stopped; and just as I reached the spot, I beheld Zarah issuing forth, supporting herself on the arm of her husband. A large black veil (which, as it subsequently appeared, the surgeon's wife had furnished) completely wrapped her head; and the sickening conviction smote me that her countenance was disfigured. A dizziness seized upon my brain—a dimness came over my vision—my tongue was paralysed—I could not give utterance to a word; and it was only by a strong effort that I saved myself from falling. The carriage drove rapidly away; and Mary Glentworth, drawing my arm in her own, said, "You look very ill, Ellen! Let me entreat you to get out of this crowd?"

Though I did not faint, yet I had scarcely any subsequent recollection of how I got to my own carriage: but I presently found myself seated therein, with Mary, Aline, and my maid. I was determined that before I returned to Great Ormond Street, I would make personal inquiries concerning my friend Zarah; and the order was accordingly given to the coachman. I cannot describe the suspense, excruciating to a degree, which I endured while proceeding to the neighbourhood of the Regent's Park; and on our arriving at St. Clair's house, I was too ill to alight from my carriage. I begged Mary Glentworth to make the inquiries for me. She descended—knocked at the door—and remained for a few minutes in conversation with the footman who opened it. Then she returned to me, saying in a hurried manner, "Mrs. St. Clair is much injured—she is in a dangerous state—two or three physicians are with her —but the servant does not as yet know of what nature the injuries are, nor to what extent they have reached."

By this time several other carriages came driving up to the house; for many persons who were at the theatre at the time of the dreadful occurrence, were thus coming to make the same inquiries which had led me thither. I at once perceived that it would be indiscreet on my part to ask to see Zarah; and I accordingly, though with considerable reluctance, gave orders to return home. On reaching Great Ormond Street, I sent the carriage to convey Aline Marcy back to the theatre, where Lady Kelvedon's equipage was to be in attendance to fetch her to Eaton Square.

I passed a sad anxious night—sleeping but little, and then only feverishly; and as early as eight o'clock in the morning I sent off the coachman in a cab to the Regent's Park to make inquiries relative to Mrs. St. Clair. But before the domestic returned, I obtained, through the medium of the morning newspapers, a deeper insight than I already possessed into the hideous transaction. I read a paragraph which was couched in the following terms:—

"DIABOLICAL OUTRAGE.—We regret to be compelled to record a most diabolical outrage which was last night perpetrated against Mrs. St. Clair, wife of the Right Honourable Edwin St. Clair. It appears that the lady and her husband visited the Theatre Royal —— ——, to witness the performance of the accomplished Miss Trafford. When the drama was over, the Right Honourable gentleman and his lady were preparing to quit the theatre, when just at the very moment that the former was handing the latter into the carriage, a quantity of corrosive fluid was thrown from behind the equipage. Cries of pain burst from the lips of Mrs. St. Clair—ejaculations of horror from those of her husband and the bystanders. A rush was made to capture the miscreant who had perpetrated the fiend-like deed: but he darted away with incredible celerity, and succeeded in effecting his escape. This was all the more remarkable inasmuch as he was dressed in a strange mountebank garb which rendered him conspicuous. Mrs. St. Clair was immediately conveyed in the carriage to the residence of the nearest surgeon, by whom it was soon ascertained that she had suffered severely from the effects of the corrosive fluid. Indeed we regret to state that this lady's countenance, so remarkable for its beauty, is threatened with complete disfigurement. We have instituted inquiries until the latest moment before going to press, at which time the miscreant was not captured: but the police were actively engaged in his pursuit, and it is hoped that by the time this statement comes under the notice of our readers he will be in custody. There is reason to believe that this is not the only crime which may be brought against him; but that a deed of still darker iniquity will be laid to his charge. We allude to the murder of the Count of Carboni, an Italian nobleman, who some months ago was hurled from the cliffs at Dover. Only vague conjectures can be formed in reference to any probable reason which might have instigated the villain to make this atrocious attack upon Mrs. St. Clair; nor is it even certain that it was intended expressly for herself instead of her husband. Indeed, it is surmised that the latter may have been the real object of the wretch's vengeance; for it will not be forgotten that on a recent occasion the Right Honourable gentleman animadverted very strongly from his place in parliament on the secret machinations which were going on in this country on the part of certain Italian refugee desperadoes whose ideas and hopes are to excite the flame of revolution in Italy. It is not therefore improbable that political vengeance may have instigated a deed of which the Right Honourable gentleman's wife has become the victim instead of that gentleman himself. We need hardly add that Mrs. St. Clair is totally unaware of having ever given umbrage to the vile author of this crime; and therefore the hypothesis we have just set forth, and which ascribes the deed to a political vengeance directed against her husband, seems all the more probable."

Scarcely had I read this paragraph, when the coachman came back; and the tidings which he brought most painfully corroborated all the worst fears which I already entertained on poor Zarah's account. It appeared from the inquiries he had made, that Zarah was shockingly burnt upon the face, neck, and bosom—that the sight of one eye was entirely destroyed—and that the loss of the other was apprehended. In a word, her beauty was ruined, and her life was pronounced to be in danger. I was greatly distressed on receiving this intelligence; and my first impulse was to order the carriage that I might hasten to Zarah's abode and offer to bestow the most assiduous attentions upon my poor friend: but a second thought induced me to recall the mandate. I reflected that perhaps it might be imprudent to take a step which would at once show the world on what intimate terms Zarah and I had been together; and I also thought that if she required my presence, she would send for me. She could not fail to know that I had left my card on the preceding evening, and that I had sent again at an early hour in the morning to make inquiries concerning her; and her natural intelligence would enable her to understand the motives which prevented me from personally seeking her. I should add that Mary Glentworth—who, as I have already said, was acquainted with Zarah—experienced much generous sympathy on her behalf.

The day was passing, and as no message came I sent up in the evening to make fresh inquiries. My messenger returned with the intelligence that Mrs. St. Clair was much worse, and that her life was almost despaired of. I procured the evening paper; and I thereby learnt that Luigi was still at large, and that the endeavours of the police to discover him had as yet proved ineffectual. I was reflecting with a sad depression of spirits upon my unfortunate friend's calamity, when at about eight o'clock in the evening her own confidential maid arrived, with a request that I would immediately hasten to see her mistress, who, it was supposed could not survive the night. The lady's-maid had come in a cab: I did not therefore wait to order out my own carriage—but I at once accompanied her. I had not now the slightest fear of setting foot beneath the roof of Edwin St. Clair; for unprincipled though I knew him to be, I could not suppose that in existing circumstances he would attempt to do me a mischief. Besides, I knew that he maintained a large establishment of domestics of a different character from those who were the ready accomplices of his misdeeds at the time when I was a captive at that house; and I likewise reflected that the physicians would be sure to be present within the walls—so that in every sense I was safe.

During the drive to St. Clair's residence I learnt from the lady's-maid a full confirmation of the distressing report which my own servant had brought me in reference to the disfigurement of Zarah. I inquired how she bore up against her misfortune?—and I was assured that she supported it with an heroic fortitude. Of her own accord the maid added that her master seemed greatly distressed, and that he was assiduous in his attentions to his wife. On arriving at the house, I was in the first instance shown to the drawing-room, where I remained alone for a few minutes; and then the maid returned to me with a request that I would follow her. On ascending the staircase leading to Mrs. St. Clair's chamber, I met two elderly gentlemen coming down; and these I knew to be the physicians. The maid conducted me to the room, which I entered—and I was now left alone with Zarah.

CHAPTER LXXIII.

A LAST INTERVIEW WITH ZARAH.

A LAMP burnt upon the toilet-table; and Zarah, in a voice which had in it but little of the feebleness of indisposition, bade me approach the couch in which she lay. It was with a sad palpitation of the heart that I obeyed; and the first glance which I threw upon her, showed me how her countenance was almost completely concealed with the bandages which enveloped her head. I sank weeping upon a chair by the side of the couch, and taking her hand, I pressed it to my lips, murmuring, "Oh! Zarah, how wretched I am! It was in the aid of my designs that you made an enemy of Luigi——"

"Do not weep for me, my dearest friend!" said Zarah, pressing my hand warmly: "and do not reproach yourself! I am resigned to die—and a career which for a long while was a life of vagabondage, but which was of late elevated into a sphere of lofty ambition, is drawing fast towards its close!"

"No, Zarah," I said; "you will live!—your voice has lost little of its power——"

"Ellen," she suddenly interrupted me, "I tell you that this is my death-bed!—and inasmuch as I am about to render you a service, I demand one at your hands."

"Speak, my dearest friend!" I exclaimed, suffering the excruciations of the wildest grief; "and whatsoever you ask of me, I will accomplish!"

"You swear, Ellen," asked Zarah, with solemn impressiveness, "that you will fulfil this pledge, and that you will accord this boon which I am about to ask?"

So overcome was I by my anguished feelings and so immense was the compassion which I entertained for my unfortunate friend, that I should at the moment have promised almost anything which did not militate against my own honour as a woman or the safety of my immortal soul. I therefore replied, "Yes, Zarah—I swear to do your bidding! Oh, how could I refuse you anything in existing circumstances?"

"A thousand thanks, dear Ellen!" she said, again pressing my hand with fervour. "I knew full well that I could rely upon you! The boon I demand is simply this,—that when you hear or read of my death, which must shortly happen, you will remain altogether silent in respect to me—you will abstain from any comment which your knowledge of past circumstances might possibly suggest—and that if you speak of me at all, it will only be with the sympathy of a friend?"

"Dearest Zarah," I exclaimed, the tears streaming from my eyes, "could you for a moment suppose that I should act otherwise than in the very manner which your words have just pointed out? No, no! it were impossible! Think you, my dear friend, that I am so heartless as to be capable of breathing a syllable that might in any way taint your memory?"

"Rest assured, Ellen," she rejoined, "that not for a single instant did I suspect your friendship: but still it was a satisfaction and consolation to obtain this pledge from your lips. And do not forget it, my dear Ellen! Remember the terms in which you have couched it,—that when I shall be no more, you will not breathe a syllable in any way calculated to taint the memory of one who has loved you so sincerely and so well!"

I was still weeping bitterly, as in a broken voice I murmuringly repeated the assurance that the pledge should be most faithfully observed; and then I exclaimed, "But you will not die, Zarah——Oh, no! you will not die! You may be injured—disfigured—but there is a strong vitality yet inspiring you——"

"Enough upon that point, Ellen!" she interrupted me, in a grave and solemn tone: "you know not my feelings as I myself experience and comprehend them! The pledge you have given me will soothe my last moments; and let it be to you likewise a consolation that you have been enabled to impart this solace! And now we will speak on another subject. Our interview must be short—and therefore what I have to say will be restricted to as few words as possible. I had devised a project for dealing with Mr. Parks in such a manner as I hoped and believed would reduce him to the necessity of doing you an act of justice. I thought perhaps that if he were forced to disgorge the fortune of which he has plundered you, Ellen, you would be satisfied: for rest assured your vengeance would thereby be complete enough! I had not been idle on your behalf since we parted on our return from Petersfield: I have instituted inquiries—and I have obtained the positive certainty that if Mr. Parks were to restore you your fortune with all accumulations of interest, he would be utterly beggared—he, his wife, and his children. Yes, they would be reduced to destitution!—and surely this would prove sufficient chastisement for the crimes of which he has been guilty? Murderer though he may be, yet is there not a punishment equal to that of sending him to the gibbet?—or indeed I would ask whether the long agony of want, penury, and destitution, which for the remainder of his life he must endure, be not even a greater punishment than the shorter agony of trial, condemnation, and the preliminaries to death upon the scaffold? Dispossess him utterly of his ill-gotten gains, and you leave him to his own remorse—you leave him likewise to the excruciation of beholding his wife and children wanting the common necessaries of existence—and thus terrible must be the penalties that he will have to pay for his complicity in the death of your grandsire! But even in this very vengeance will you be exercising a mercy, Ellen! —for you will leave a husband to the wife and a father to the children—whereas if you gave him to the scaffold you would be striking a blow that would not fail to redound upon the heads of the innocent! And there is yet one other consideration which I have to offer. I have hitherto been reasoning as if you absolutely possessed the power of sending that man to the scaffold:—but I will now ask, 'What if you have *not* that power?' You may be morally certain of his guilt—but how would you establish it in a court of justice? Where is your witness? That wretched woman —my grandmother—who sold him the poison, is no longer in England. True, you and Beda might repeat the confession which you extorted from her lips at the cottage near Petersfield: but this would be regarded only as hearsay evidence. In a word, you would *not* be enabled to convict Mr. Parks; and therefore, for this reason *alone*, apart from all other considerations, I put it to you whether it were not better to inflict the other vengeance which I have suggested?—a vengeance which will be sure in its execution and equally certain in its effects,—I mean the process of compelling him to the restitution of your long usurped fortune, and leaving the man to misery and destitution, with his wife and his children?"

My feelings were so absorbed in the distress produced by Zarah's fearful calamity—and the idea that she was actually upon her death-bed, was, after all she had previously said, so paramount in my mind—that I had no faculty for deliberate reflection upon matters personally regarding myself, and which, indeed, under such circumstances involved only selfish considerations. And then too, any appeal, no matter of what nature, which was made to me by one who declared that she was hovering upon the very threshold of the grave, exercised an influence which at any other time and in different circumstances might have been far less potent. In a word, my mind was so attenuated by the shock it had received on her account, that I was prepared to give my assent to any appeal which she might make to my reason, as well as to any favour she might ask at my hands.

"Yes, my dear Zarah," I said, still weeping and sobbing, "I yield to your arguments! Give me your counsel, and with gratitude will I follow it!"

"Our interview must soon terminate," she said; "and I have therefore but a brief opportunity for speech. Look in the centre drawer of that toilet-table—and you will perceive, in the left hand inner corner, a scrap of paper containing a name and an address. Hesitate not to seek that man at his abode: he is already prepared to go through fire and water to serve you, because Zarah has so willed it! On this point I need say no more; for he is acquainted with the plan which I had conceived in reference to Mr. Parks—and he will carry it out."

I proceeded to the toilet-table—I opened the drawer, and possessed myself of the scrap of paper. I glanced at the words written upon it: but my eyes were dimmed with tears, and I could not decipher them. I therefore thrust the paper into my bosom, and returned to the side of Zarah's bed.

"Tell me, my dearest friend," I asked,—"tell me, I entreat you, is he——you know to whom I allude——"

"My husband?" she said in a firm tone.

"Yes! Is he indeed kind to you under existing circumstances?"

"Oh, Ellen!" ejaculated Zarah, "is it possible that you know so little of Edwin St. Clair as to suppose that he is capable of a real and genuine kindness towards one whom he has never ceased to hate as the wife that forced herself upon him? No, no!—it suits him to maintain an appearance before the world, as he has hitherto maintained it! Is he not a Minister? is he not one of the rulers of the people? and must he not study any point which may in any sense affect his reputation? Yes!—and this *is* his study!" added Zarah, with bitterness and scorn in her accents. "When he is in this room, and my maid or the physicians are present, he is full of endearment, and he manifests the deepest distress; while I on my part, with a corresponding dissimulation, seem to accept his language as the outpouring of a sincere and genuine grief. Yes!—because I would not have it known, nor even suspected by the world at large that instead of being the loved and cherished wife, I have been the hated and the loathed one!—instead of being the woman whom for her beauty he voluntarily espoused, I was the woman who forced myself upon him! The same feelings of vanity and ambition which inspired me when I sought the elevation which this marriage would give, extend beyond the grave: I am careful of what shall be said of me when I go hence and exist no longer in this world! Perhaps you may wonder at such feelings, such ideas, and such precautions?—but if you have studied my character aright, you will perceive that they are consistent therewith."

There was a brief pause, during which I reflected with mingled painfulness and perplexity on this last speech of Zarah's; and at length she proceeded in the following manner:—

"I have told you how St. Clair behaves towards me when others are present: I will now tell you how he acts when he is alone in this chamber with me. He does not condescend to what he would deem the pettiness, the paltriness, and the meanness of expressing his triumph in words: but his looks full well demonstrate that he is veritably triumphant at what may be termed my downfall! You know that at one period I thought I might possibly win back his love: but that for some time

past I have seen to be impossible! His hatred has endured; and therefore he gloats in silence over the fearful calamity which has overtaken me and which must speedily have its termination in the tomb. Faithful to his entire policy of seeming to brave the opinion of the world on my account, and of suffering it to be believed that he espoused me because he really loved me, he will give me a grand funeral—he will follow in deep mourning—he will gather his friends to do the last honours to my name—his hypocrisy and his dissimulation will endure throughout the obsequies themselves! But in his heart he is glad—he is rejoiced—he is triumphant——"

"For heaven's sake, speak not thus, Zarah!" I said, shocked and horrified at everything I now heard. "It is dreadful—it is terrible——"

"Then we will quit the subject, my dear friend," said Zarah. "Yet one thing I must mention. Do not for an instant suppose that Edwin St. Clair

No. 57.—ELLEN PERCY.

would seek to abridge the remnant of life that may still be left in me!—do not think that even if it were possible that I *could* live on, he would inflict death upon me to rid himself of one who has become a loathsome and disgusting object! No! Rest assured that it would please his hatred and his vengeance if I were to live yet awhile, excruciated with the sense of my ruined beauty—my hideously disfigured countenance! Therefore, Ellen, whatsoever you may hear or read in reference to my last moments, do not for a single instant imagine that St. Clair dealt foully with me! As surely as I behold you here, by my side,—so confident am I that in this sense I am completely safe at his hands. Therefore, dear Ellen, in a single word, let me conjure you to entertain not the slightest suspicion against my husband, no matter what circumstances may attend my last moments!"

I was so full of grief—I was weeping and sobbing so bitterly—that at the time I had but a very dim comprehension of what Zarah was saying,—though afterwards I was enabled fully to recall every syllable that had been thus spoken.

"And now farewell, my dear friend!" she said, her voice becoming tremulous with emotion for the first time throughout this interview : "we are about to part, never to meet again in this world! May heaven bless you, Ellen!—may God in his mercy shower his choicest gifts upon your head, for you deserve them all! Farewell, my sweet friend! Leave me quickly——or this parting will be more than I can endure!"

I carried her hand to my lips—I covered it with kisses and with tears. Fervidly did she press my hand in return; and then again she said, "Leave me, Ellen!—leave me, I conjure you!"

I staggered forth from the chamber, reeling like a tipsy person—my heart rent with the most torturing pangs—my soul a prey to the most passionate grief. How I found my way down the staircase, I scarcely remember : but on the landing below I met the maid who had been sent to fetch me—and she sustained me to the cab which was waiting to bear me home. I felt exceedingly ill : I had no power for deliberate reflection—my brain was a confused whirl of harrowing and distracting thoughts; and on reaching Great Ormond Street, I was at once compelled to seek my chamber. Mary Glentworth and Beda were so alarmed on my account, that they sent for a neighbouring physician, who prescribed some medicine calculated to soothe the excited nerves, and under the opiate influence of which I speedily fell into a profound slumber.

When I awoke in the morning, I was languid and depressed—all my energies seemed prostrated—and it was even some time before I could give utterance to a word : moreover in one sense I feared to breathe the inquiry which in another sense I longed to put. At length I asked if any tidings had been received in reference to Mrs. St. Clair, and if the morning newspapers had yet arrived? It appeared that no message of any kind had been delivered, and that the newspapers were late. I at once sent off a domestic to make inquiries relative to the invalid : but during the interval the journals were brought in, and a paragraph in two brief lines recorded the death of Mrs. St. Clair : a presentiment had prepared me for the intelligence : but still it came upon me with a shock which even for a few minutes prevented the tears from finding a vent; but at last they gushed forth, and I wept copiously to the memory of my perished friend. All the good offices I had ever received at her hands swept vividly in unto my memory : I thought likewise of the numerous excellent qualities which she had possessed, and I deplored her fate.

Before my own domestic returned from the Regent's Park, the late Mrs. St. Clair's lady's-maid arrived in Great Ormond Street; and she sought a private interview with me. This was the same confidential person who on the previous evening had fetched me to the death-bed of her mistress. I saw that she had been weeping—she was much affected—and some little interval elapsed, after we were alone together, before she could enter upon the explanations which she had come to give.

"And Mrs. St. Clair is gone?" I said. "I just now read her death in the newspaper——"

"Yes, Miss Percy," responded the maid; "she breathed her last precisely at the hour of midnight. And Oh, it was so sudden! I was scarcely five minutes absent from the room—it really seems as if death struck her as if with a lightning-stroke——"

"Indeed!" I said : "so suddenly as this?"

"Yes, Miss Percy. The death of my poor mistress was not only sudden, but it was attended with circumstances which I scarcely know whether to describe as more strange or more affecting——"

"Strange circumstances?" I asked—and I know not how it was, but some peculiar and bewildering suspicion arose in my mind : yet it was scarcely a suspicion—it was a species of vague bewildering uneasy thought that the singular character of Zarah had been destined to have something mysterious associated with it until the very last.

"I will tell you all, Miss Percy," resumed the lady's-maid; "for I know that my mistress loved you very much—and almost the last words she spoke were in reference to yourself."

"Proceed," I said, deeply affected, but also inspired with a solemn curiosity.

"Soon after you had left the house last night, Miss Percy," continued the maid, "my mistress said that she felt death to be approaching. The physicians begged her to entertain a hope that it would be otherwise—for that her constitution was strong and her health had throughout life been vigorous, so that there was every reason to anticipate that she might successfully battle against the effects of the injuries she had sustained. I was present in the room at the time : her husband was also there. In reply to the physicians she spoke with a serene firmness. She said that she herself could best tell what she felt—that she gave her medical attendants all possible credit for the professional knowledge which prompted their opinion and the kindness with which they had enunciated it, but that her own sensations, alike mental and physical, told her that she had received a shock from which she never could recover. Then I saw that the countenances of the physicians became grave and serious; and I felt convinced that they recognised only too fatally and despondingly the probable truth of the words just spoken by their patient. Mrs. St. Clair desired to be left alone with her husband, that she might take of him a last farewell; for she said that she already had the sensation as if life were ebbing away. The physicians and I accordingly retired; and she was left alone with her husband."

"And how long did this parting interview last?" I inquired.

"Probably half-an-hour," replied the lady's-maid. "At the end of that time Mr. St. Clair came forth with his kerchief to his eyes; and I saw that he was weeping bitterly."

"The hypocrite!" I thought within myself. "Oh, heavens! was it not monstrous that this dissimulation should be continued until the very last?"

"On thus coming forth from my mistress's chamber," continued the maid, "Captain St. Clair bade me not enter thither for the present, for that he was about to return for a few minutes. He proceeded to his own room, where he however stayed not more than a few seconds; and then he went back to the chamber of his wife. I think that he must have gone to fetch something which she wished to see before she died—and perhaps it was the very flower——"

"The flower?" I ejaculated, with something like a start.

"Ah! I was proceeding too rapidly with my narrative," rejoined the maid; "but my mind is still full of grief—and there are moments when I grow bewildered. But I will endeavour to speak calmly and collectedly."

"Proceed," I said, now experiencing a painful degree of curiosity. "Mr. St. Clair went to his own room—then he returned to that where his perishing wife lay——"

"Yes, Miss—it was thus that it happened," continued the maid. "But in a very few minutes he came forth again; and he said to me in a broken voice, 'The catastrophe is approaching; my poor wife has not long to live: I would remain with her until the last, but she will not permit me. Go to her: she requires your presence; hasten, delay not!'—It was thus that he spoke; but I inquired whether the physicians were not also to return into the sick room?—'No,' replied Mr. St. Clair; 'your mistress will see them no more, unless indeed she be very much mistaken in her sad presentiment, and this should be a mere passing crisis which will leave her better afterwards. But of this I fear there is no hope.'— Mr. St. Clair then hastened away, with his kerchief to his eyes; and as he repaired to his own room, I returned into the chamber where my poor dying mistress lay. I found her perfectly calm, resigned, and collected. She told me that the bitterness of death was now passed since she had taken the final leave of her husband. She proceeded to thank me for what she was pleased to term the kind attentions I had displayed towards her: she presented me with her watch and chain, several other little articles of jewellery, and a purse filled with gold, telling me that it was with Mr. St. Clair's perfect concurrence that she thus rewarded me for my services. I need scarcely tell you, Miss Percy, how affected I was while pouring forth the assurances of my gratitude."

Here the maid wept; and for some moments she was unable to pursue her narrative. At length she continued in the following manner:—

"My dying mistress then proceeded to speak of you, Miss Percy. She said how much she loved you—how highly she had ever esteemed your character—how consoled and comforted she was by the visit which you had paid her. She went on to say that as she knew her death to be approaching, and that she had not even an hour to live, she begged that I would see you in the morning and remind you of the generous promises you had made her, but to the nature of which she did not allude. She entreated that through my lips you should be enjoined to keep those promises——"

"Oh, it was not necessary!" I exclaimed: "I am incapable of violating them! Proceed—tell me the rest of this sad, sad narrative!"

"My mistress said that she knew it was unnecessary to remind you of your promises; and

yet she could not help doing so, because they involved matters of importance:—but she desired me to abstain from speaking to any other living soul besides yourself of what was then passing between us. When she had ceased giving me these instructions, she lay profoundly quiet for upwards of half-an-hour, as if absorbed in the deepest meditation—doubtless in prayer. I sat as motionless by her bedside as if I had been a statue: there was something awful in the silence which prevailed in that chamber—I can scarcely describe the sensations that possessed me. Then indeed I knew that death was close at hand: the presentiment that it was so sat like a nightmare upon my mind. At last my mistress spoke again. She bade me open a bureau, of which she gave me the key, and which key she took from beneath her pillow. I obeyed her; and she directed me to bring her a little rosewood box, about six inches square, which I should find on a particular shelf in that bureau. This also I did. She took the box in her hands, and desired me to raise her up somewhat in the couch by placing additional pillows behind her head. When I had fulfilled this mandate, she went on speaking in a low, plaintive, but clear and firm voice. As nearly as as I can recollect she spoke to the following effect :—'This box contains an artificial flower which was bequeathed to me by my mother, and which was almost superstitiously associated with her own fate. What the tale was I cannot tell you, for I feel that my life is rapidly ebbing away. But it is a strange wild tale : I firmly believe that it was prophetic of my own fate! I wish to pray alone; and my prayers will be influenced by the presence of this object, trifling as it may seem in your eyes, yet dear as it is to me because it was bequeathed by my deceased mother. Now leave me, and return in five minutes. You need not go far ! Remain just outside the door; and I repeat, in five minutes you can return. Ah!' she added; 'a thought strikes me! The very moment that I am no more, go and summon my husband: it is my wish, and I desire that it may be fulfilled.'—I had a presentiment that I should not again see my poor mistress alive : I knelt down and pressed her hand to my lips. The tears were flowing fast from my eyes as I issued from the room. I did not close the door : I merely left it ajar—for I thought that if my mistress wanted anything I ought to be readily accessible to the summoning of her voice, which had become low and feeble. I remained outside—and all continued still within the chamber. That very stillness seemed to me to be solemnly presentient of death ; and never in my life had I before experienced such feelings. At length, when I conceived that the prescribed interval of five minutes had elapsed, I slowly and tremblingly pushed the door open and crossed the threshold. I at once saw that all was over : my mistress lay dead upon the pillows ! One arm was by her side, the other hung down over the edge of the couch—and upon her bosom was an artificial flower resembling a faded white rose."

I moaned inwardly; for I had a horrible comprehension of it all ! But my lips gave expression to no sound ; and whatsoever feelings my features may have expressed, might well appear to the maid to be simply those of deep affliction for my friend Zarah's death.

"I stood upon the threshold for upwards of a minute," she continued, "contemplating that spectacle; and then suddenly recollecting the last injunction my mistress had given, I hastened to Mr. St. Clair's room to inform him that all was over. I cannot tell you, Miss Percy, with what a wild rapidity he flew to the chamber where his wife lay: he shut himself in there—for several minutes he remained alone with the corpse—and when he came forth, he had the little rosewood box in his hand. He was very, very pale; but he was not *then* weeping. He muttered some words to me in a broken voice; I could not exactly catch their sense—but methought he said something to the effect that the faded flower contained in that box should be cherished by him to the end of his life, as it was found upon the bosom of his beloved and lamented Zarah."

The maid ceased speaking—and I was plunged into the most painful meditations; for only too able was I to furnish a fearful clue to the mystery of that white rose. At length, after a long pause, I asked, "And what said the physicians relative to the death of your mistress?"

"They expressed some little surprise that it should have taken place so suddenly," answered the maid; "but they spoke of the shock which her nervous system had sustained—and what else they said I know not, for my mind was too much distressed to enable me to devote much attention to them. They soon took their departure; for, alas! Miss Percy, their patient was gone, and all their skill had been unavailing to arrest the approach of death! I believe there is to be a splendid funeral——"

"No doubt of it! no doubt of it!" I said, with some degree of bitterness, though the maid perceived it not—but at the same time I remembered the parting words which Zarah had addressed to me in reference to her husband.

The confidential maid of the late Mrs. St. Clair remained with me a little time longer in conversation; and then she went away.

When I was by myself, I reflected on all that had taken place and on everything that I had just heard. I must describe the nature of my meditations to my readers. I felt convinced that Zarah had perished by suicide—that she had poisoned herself by means of that white rose the deadly secret of which had been acquired in foreign parts by her criminal grandmother! But that the allusions she had thrown out in reference to a fatal association between that rose and her own mother's fate, were pure fictions in order to prevent her maid from suspecting anything strange, I was equally well convinced;—and the same degree of certitude did I entertain in reference to the complicity of St. Clair in his wife's self-destruction. The physicians were no doubt right when they had asserted that her naturally vigorous constitution would have enabled her to triumph over the shock which her nerves had sustained: but Zarah was not the being who could consent to live with ruined beauty—a disfigured, hideous, loathsome-looking creature! Thus she had all along, from the moment of the outrage, contemplated self-destruction. She knew that the white rose would prove most fatally efficient in enabling her to accomplish her deadly purpose, and that no suspicion of suicide would remain behind. She doubtless knew likewise that her husband had one of those fatal flowers in his possession, and that he would only too gladly place it at her disposal when finding that it was to rid him for ever of the wife whom he hated. That these conjectures on my part were borne out by facts, was sufficiently evident, inasmuch as portions of the tale which I had just heard from the lady's-maid confirmed everything in this respect. In the last hour of his wife's existence St. Clair had fetched something from his own room. What could this *something* be unless it was the rosewood box which the maid had subsequently taken from the bureau?—and how could the key of the bureau have been under Zarah's pillow unless her husband himself given it to her to place there? Besides, the injunctions which Zarah had given to me, and the observance of which she had enjoined almost with her last breath through the medium of her maid, proved that she contemplated suicide at the time. Her object was to prevent me from giving publicity to any facts which might prove that she had sought relief in self-destruction from the calamity which had overtaken her. She had enjoined me that when she should be no more, I would not breathe a syllable in any way calculated to taint her memory—that I would remain altogether silent in respect to her—that I would abstain from any comment which my knowledge of past circumstances might possibly suggest—and that if I spoke of her at all, it would only be with the sympathizing regretfulness of a friend. And then too, she had so earnestly enjoined me not to entertain any suspicion injurious to her husband, no matter what might be the circumstances attending her last moments; and she had so skilfully contrived everything that St. Clair should not even be in the room with her when she inhaled the fatal poison of the white rose. Yes—it was all a deliberate calculation on her part,—a tissue of proceedings woven with a horrible calmness by a woman whose strength of mind had endured until the very last! And so skilfully were these arrangements combined—with such a fearful clearness of intellect were they all conducted—that the very physicians themselves were cheated into the belief of a natural death, and the confidential maid utterly failed to suspect that there was aught sinister! She simply looked upon the closing scene as superstitiously strange and affecting; and as if dissimulation were most fully to crown the extraordinary drama, the grief of the widowed husband was so well assumed that it passed for genuine.

I was shocked and appalled at the whole tremendous tragedy. I, the constant actress in tragedies upon the stage, shrank with feelings of indescribable horror from this tragedy of real life! It looked like an awful dream—a tremendous vision impossible of realization: and yet it was all true! But after a little while I reflected even still more deeply upon the details of the occurrence, and upon the minutest springs of action which had influenced the perished Zarah. An immense ambition and a high degree of vanity had for a while past been the influences that ruled her. She found herself the envied wife of the Right Honourable Edwin St. Clair, a Cabinet Minister, and one of the most rising statesmen of the day. Life had charms only so long as her beauty embellished, so to speak, the position to which she was raised ; and when she became a loathsome object, she could exist no longer. But might she not in her last moments have wreaked upon her husband a horrible vengeance for all his conduct towards her ?—might she not have proclaimed the tale of his crimes and bequeathed him her vengeance as a legacy ? Yes : or she might have lived to inflict this vengeance, to mark its progress, and to gloat over its results. But no !— Zarah, whether living or dead, was resolved that her husband should continue great and honoured and renowned, so that *her* name and *her* memory might be illuminated by the reflecting halo. She had perished, carrying with her to the wilfully sought tomb the secret of her husband's enormities,—leaving the world to suppose that she was a beloved and cherished wife, so that the historian and the biographer when writing of the great statesman, might make favourable mention of the handsome gipsy who had become his bride !

But now, in reference to myself—what course was I to adopt ? Could I do otherwise than keep the pledges which I had so solemnly given to Zarah ?—could I falsify those promises by proclaiming all that I knew, or at least suspected, in reference to the closing scene of the tragedy ? No !—I could not. I had not the heart to destroy with a breath the false fabric of fame which Zarah had so laboriously piled up for herself : I could not stand before the world and pronounce it to have been all a hideous fiction ! Such a course would have been to heap dirt upon the memory of the dead—to deprive the unfortunate Zarah of the rites of Christian burial, and to brand her as a deliberate suicide. Fully evident was it that if St. Clair was an accomplice in that deed of self-destruction by supplying her with the means, he at all events had neither urged her to its accomplishment—nor had treacherously and murderously taken away her life. I therefore came to the conclusion that I must respect the fatal secret as Zarah's own, and leave her husband to whatsoever remorse his evil conscience might sooner or later inflict, or else to whatsoever punishment heaven might eventually send down upon his head.

CHAPTER LXXIV.

MARY'S LOVER.

THROUGHOUT that day I kept my own chamber—for I was a prey to all the influences of the painful thoughts and meditations which I have been describing ; and my self-seclusion seemed natural enough to Mary Glentworth and the servants, for they knew that I was a friend of the deceased Mrs. St. Clair and that I might well be expected to mourn for her loss. A medical certificate procured my exemption from appearing at the theatre in the evening ; and the public were neither surprised nor indignant when Mr. Richards announced that my absence on the occasion arose from the shock my nerves had sustained on account of the hideous outrage perpetrated on a lady with whom I was well acquainted, and which outrage had terminated in her death.

I will here observe that a few days afterwards a grand funeral took place ; and Zarah was buried with all the pomp and ceremony which in her last hour she had anticipated, and which did indeed seem most appropriate as the crowning incident of her ambitious career. But previous to her funeral events occurred which I must proceed to relate in due order ; and if I have now out of place alluded to these obsequies, it was merely that I might thus without interruption terminate the episode which so sadly and horribly concerned my gipsy friend.

The day after the diabolical outrage at the theatre, was the one on which I was to accompany Mary Glentworth to keep her appointment with Clarence Beauchamp : but on that day I was so dreadfully distressed in mind—so anxious and nervous on Zarah's account—that I could think of scarcely anything else ; and I asked Mary Glentworth if it were not possible for her to postpone her appointment with Clarence Beauchamp ? She at once replied that she could ; for though she did not remember the name (even if she had ever heard it) of the hotel at which, as he alleged, he resided, she nevertheless knew that he belonged to the Union Club in Trafalgar Square. Indeed, he had requested that if at any time circumstances should transpire to render correspondence necessary, she would communicate with him at that Club. I was pleased to behold the willingness with which in order to suit my own frame of mind as well as my convenience, she offered to postpone that appointment ; for it proved that she was now ready to be guided by my counsel in all things. I therefore requested her to write to Mr. Beauchamp and to intimate her inability to keep the appointment on the particular day for which it was given, but at the same time to promise that she would shortly see her lover. The day after the one on which Zarah's death was announced to me—and which, to be particular in dates, was the 30th of April, 1842—I reflected that the business which so intimately concerned Mary Glentworth, was not one which ought to be postponed ; and I therefore begged her to write and make an appointment with Clarence Beauchamp for the ensuing day. This she did : but she said nothing in the correspondence of the discovery that I had made of their love-affair, nor of my intention to accompany her at the interview which was thus arranged.

Mary Glentworth had written to Mr. Beauchamp to the effect that she would meet him at one o'clock precisely, near the church in Langham Place ; for I thought that we might thence walk together into the Regent's Park, where I could have some serious conversation with the young gentleman on her account. It was now the commencement of May—the weather was remarkably fine—we dispensed with the carriage for the occasion—and we proceeded on foot towards the place of appointment. I could judge from Mary's looks that her heart palpitated with a nervous anxiety ; but I assured her that I would address Clarence Beauchamp in such a manner as should prevent him from being in the slightest degree annoyed with herself on account of the interposing part I was taking in their affairs. As we were somewhat too early for the appointment—and as I had a little purchase to make at a jeweller's in Oxford Street, where I was accustomed to deal—

we proceeded in that direction. I was going to order a mourning ring to forward to Zarah's confidential maid, as an acknowledgment of the attention she had displayed towards myself in the recent unfortunate occurrences. Mary and I reached the jeweller's shop: but just as we entered it whom should I at the first glance recognise standing at the counter making purchases, but the Duke and Duchess of Ardleigh?

"My uncle! my dear uncle!" ejaculated Mary: and with a cry of joy she precipitated herself towards that titled nobleman whom she believed to be plain Mr. Glentworth.

The Duke caught her in his arms; for he was discomfited and bewildered—he was seized with confusion—he knew not how to act. At that very instant the assistant who was serving behind the counter, was addressing some observation to the Duke, whom he of course styled "My Lord" and "Your Grace;"—and not more bewildered with confusion was the nobleman himself, than Mary suddenly became with amazement on hearing her supposed uncle thus spoken to with those lofty sounding titles. At once perceiving the necessity of avoiding a scene in the shop, which might lead to unpleasant revelations and exposures before the assistants who were serving there, I caught Mary somewhat violently by the arm,—drew her hastily aside — and whispered, "For heaven's sake be composed! — say nothing! — I will tell you all presently!"

Mary gazed upon me for a moment with a species of consternation, as if utterly at a loss what to think:—then abruptly turning to an assistant who was serving on that side of the shop to which I had led her across, she demanded, "Who is that gentleman?"

There was something so positive if not absolutely imperious in her tone, that the assistant, taken by surprise—in fact at a loss to comprehend the entire scene or to think how he himself had better act—at once answered, "That, Miss—that is a great nobleman—the Duke of Ardleigh."

Mary Glentworth turned deadly pale, staggered back a pace or two—and was about to sink upon the floor when I caught her in my arms. Consciousness had abandoned her; and one of the assistants, rushing into the adjoining parlour, returned with some water, which I hastened to sprinkle upon the poor girl's face.

"Good heavens!" said the Duke, rushing about the shop like one demented, "what a scene! what a coincidence! Here's a pretty business! I wish Peaseblossom was present——"

"Silence, my lord!" said the voice of the Duchess, speaking in that habitual tone of command which at once operated like magic upon her husband. "We will retire to the carriage immediately. Miss Trafford, let me see you and Miss Glentworth at Ardleigh House in one hour from this time. You can tell her what you think fit in the meanwhile," she added, bending down towards me so as to whisper these last words in my ears.

The proprietor of the establishment and his wife now came hastening into the shop to render assistance or offer their services; and the Duchess hastily said, "Mrs. Brooks, have the kindness to let this young lady be borne into your sitting-room. Mr. Brooks, I reckon upon the discretion of yourself and your assistants in the observance of implicit silence with regard to this scene!"

The Duchess of Ardleigh, who was perfectly calm and collected, though her countenance indicated mingled anger and mortification, issued her various directions and injunctions with the completest self-possession. She then made an imperious sign for her husband to follow her, and they went forth from the establishment. The carriage—which had proceeded a little way along the street in order to turn the more conveniently, and which therefore was not at the door when Mary Glentworth and I reached the establishment—had drawn up while the scene was taking place in the shop. The Duke and Duchess entered the vehicle, and the equipage drove away. Mrs. Brooks, the jeweller's wife, assisted me to convey Mary Glentworth to a chamber up-stairs: but nearly a quarter of an hour elapsed before the poor girl could be brought back to complete consciousness. As she began to recover I requested Mrs. Brooks to leave us alone together; and she at once retired. Mary Glentworth threw herself into my arms and wept passionately on my bosom. For several minutes she was unable to give utterance to a word: she was convulsed with sobs; and I felt only too painfully convinced that the scene in the shop below had smitten her soul with some suspicion, if not with a full knowledge of the real truth.

"Ellen, dearest Ellen!" she at length murmuringly faltered; "I always knew there was some mystery——at least for a long time I have fancied it——I thought there was something with which you were acquainted, but which you were hiding from me——"

"Do not excite yourself, Mary!—compose your feelings!" I said; "and let us converse tranquilly."

"Ah! then you do not deny it?" she exclaimed with another passionate ebullition of grief; "and I—and I am compelled——But tell me, Ellen, I adjure you!" she abruptly demanded: "in what relation does the Duke of Ardleigh stand towards me?"

"Mary," I answered, much excited and affected, "I see that you already know it——or at least the suspicion has entered your mind——it is therefore useless to trifle with the matter. The Duke of Ardleigh is—is—your father!"

I saw that Mary Glentworth was shaken as if by a cold tremor suddenly passing through her entire frame; and for upwards of a minute she remained altogether silent. At first she gazed fixedly upon me with a strange vacant look: then her regards gradually sank—and as her eyes were bent downward, the tears started forth anew, the big drops rolling upon her pale cheeks. Yes!—for those cheeks which were wont to bloom with the carnation hues of health, were now of dead pallor.

"The Duke of Ardleigh my father!" she at length said in a musing tone and in a low voice: "the Duke of Ardleigh my father! Then what can I now think? Alas, alas! the reputation of that mother whose memory I sought to revere as that of one deserving all veneration——But oh! I cannot think of it! Alas, my poor mother! you must have been cruelly betrayed——and I am almost called upon to hate the author of my being for having so betrayed you!"

Mary Glentworth ceased; and again for upwards of a minute she bent her looks downward, while the tears trickled upon her cheeks. I took her hand and pressed it in my own: but I said nothing.

"The Duke of Ardleigh my father!" she at length repeated. "Oh, my dear Ellen! you must all along have known this from the commencement of our acquaintance!"

"It is true, Mary," I replied in a sorrowful voice, "that I *have* known the secret from a very early stage of our acquaintance; and if I have kept it, your own heart will tell you that it has been from the best and kindest of motives. But I always foresaw that the day must inevitably come when it would be revealed to you——"

"And that day has come at length!" said Mary. "And would to heaven," she added, passionately wringing her hands, "that I had ever remained ignorant of this secret! You know how I loved my mother, Ellen—you know how I revered her—how I looked upon her as the very personification of all virtues!—and it is hard—Oh! it is hard to have the idol of one's worship suddenly destroyed! It shakes one's faith in the existence of truth and purity and rectitude in the world!"

"But as you say, Mary," I interrupted her, while the tears were flowing down my own cheeks, —"as you say, my dear friend, your mother may have been betrayed, and therefore she was perhaps more to be pitied than blamed. At all events it is for you as her daughter to afford your sympathy to her memory, and not to look upon her with the bitterness of reproach!"

"Heaven forbid that I should now think lightly of her!" exclaimed Mary, clasping her hands with deprecating anguish.

"Besides, my dear friend," I hastened to interject, "remember that within the range of your own knowledge there was in your mother's conduct no reason for reproach. She dwelt in respectability and seclusion——"

"Yes—Oh, yes!" ejaculated Mary. "But even still more must I remember that her love for me partook of the character of devotedness—that she reared me with the tenderest care—that she was to me a moral teacher and a guide as well as a parent——"

"Then think of her in this sacred light!" I hastened to interpose; for I was glad to clutch at any recommendation which might serve as a source of solace to my afflicted friend. "It is not for us frail human creatures to judge each other harshly in the world, liable as we all are to error and to failing!—much less should a child judge harshly of a parent!"

Mary reflected for a few moments: she was evidently becoming calm and resigned; and she presently said, "Where is the Duke of Ardleigh now?—was that the Duchess who was with him?—and how am I to act?"

"The Duke and Duchess have taken their departure—and it is almost time that we ourselves should go hence," I continued, "in order to keep an appointment which the Duchess whispered to me, at Ardleigh House."

"An appointment?" ejaculated Mary. "And that other appointment——"

"The hour has long passed," I said, looking at my watch; "the appointment with Clarence Beau-champ was for one o'clock—and it is now a quarter to two. In a few minutes we must be at Ardleigh House: the appointment with Clarence Beauchamp must therefore be postponed until another occasion—because it is vitally important to your interests, my dear Mary, that you should learn to what extent you may reckon on your father's love and protection."

"I do not want to see my father!" she petulantly exclaimed. "I can only look upon him——"

"Have you not told me, Mary," I interrupted her, with a tone and look of remonstrance, "that he has ever treated you with kindness?—and so long as you believed him to be your uncle, have you not loved him?—and have you not for months past been hoping that he would soon return?"

"Perhaps he has never been absent," she interjected with renewed petulance: "perhaps it was only a subterfuge——"

"No—he has been absent," I said; "and he has only just come back to London. He and the Duchess have been upon the Continent—I saw them at Dover previous to their departure: her Grace knows that you are her husband's daughter—and she promised that on the return of the family to England something should be done for you."

"Now listen to me, Ellen," said Mary Glentworth, speaking with a calm firmness: "I will accept no favours from the Duke and Duchess of Ardleigh! The stigma of illegitimacy rests upon me—and there is no compensation which can mitigate or efface it. Whatever they might give me would be in charity; and perhaps I have already accepted too much from the Duke's hand! As for the Duchess, she cannot possibly regard me with favour—she can only look upon me as the living proof of her husband's infidelity towards herself. No!—I will accept nothing at their hands: and I will *not* go to Ardleigh House. I have now no consent to ask of him whom I believed to be my uncle, in reference to my marriage with Clarence Beauchamp. Circumstances are altered; Clarence will joyfully make me his bride with the least possible delay—and you, my sweet friend, will not interpose a syllable to dissuade me from obtaining a settled position, a name, and a home?"

"If Mr. Beauchamp be all that you suppose and represent, my dear Mary," I answered, "not for worlds would I say or do aught to delay your happiness for a single hour! You now seem to be fully able to discuss your affairs with calmness and firmness. Listen therefore, I entreat, to the counsel which I am about to give!"

"Oh, yes—I will listen!" exclaimed Mary. "Your advice, dearest Ellen, shall ever have its due weight with me!"

"You say that Mr. Beauchamp is rich," I continued: "but no young gentleman ever has any objection against his wife possessing a dower. You have nothing, Mary, beyond the few hundreds of pounds which are invested in your name in the Bank of England. The Duke of Ardleigh will most assuredly act handsomely by you—or at least I hope so; and you would be wrong to reject whatsoever he may propose to give. Besides, notwithstanding the circumstances of your birth, he has a certain claim, if he choose to assert it, upon your obedience. Remember, he is the author of your being; and this fact imposes its obligations. I now therefore entreat you to accompany me to Ard-leigh House. Indeed, it would be ungracious and improper to refuse: for the Duchess has given the invitation, and she has taken the matter in hand. She will behave liberally:—you owe it to yourself and to whomsoever may become your husband to accept the worldly gifts that are offered you from such sources."

Mary Glentworth suffered herself to be per-suaded by this reasoning; and she agreed to accom-pany me. We now descended from the chamber: we cordially thanked Mr. and Mrs. Brooks for their kindness—I hastily made the little purchase which I required—and issuing from the establish-ment, we took a cab to Ardleigh House. As the vehicle drew up in front of the palatial mansion, Mary heaved a profound sigh, saying, "Oh! if the circumstances of my birth were different, I might have been a dweller beneath that proud roof!"

We alighted—we ascended the steps—and we entered the hall. A half-shrieking querulous voice was at the moment resounding through that hall, and giving vent in an angry tone to these ejacu-lations:—"What! the Duchess not visible and the Duke engaged—and this too at lunch-time, when you know that I am always welcome! It is scandalous!—and if poor dear Lord Mangold were alive——"

"Really, my lady," said the hall-porter, to whom the irate expostulations were addressed, "it is not my fault—I only repeat the orders I re-ceived——"

"Stuff and nonsense!" ejaculated Lady Man-gold, with a disdainful toss of her head. "Am I not the aunt of her Grace of Ardleigh? and have I not a right of *entrée* at all times? I tell you that if poor dear Lord Mangold were alive——"

"I am sorry, my lady," said the hall-porter, "but my instructions——Be so kind as to walk that way, ladies!" he said, thus suddenly turning to address himself to Mary and me.

"What!" cried Lady Mangold, now positively furious; "the play-actress to be received—and I, the aunt to the Duchess, to be denied at the very threshold! If Lord Mangold were alive——But thank God he is dead! or it would break his heart, the good old soul——"

"That way, ladies!" repeated the hall-porter, looking very uneasy, as if he dreaded a compli-cation of the unpleasant scene. "Now, James, make haste and show these ladies——"

"This way, ladies!" said the footman who was about to escort us.

"I won't have it! I declare I won't have it!" shrieked forth Lady Mangold. "What! to be eclipsed by a play-actress, who refused to let me appear as Venus amidst clouds and attended by a host of little Cupids! It is preposterous!—and if poor dear Lord Mangold were alive——"

I waited to hear no more, but hurried onward with Mary Glentworth. The footman conducted us up the spacious staircase; and we were es-corted into an apartment, where we found the Duchess of Ardleigh alone, waiting for us. The Duke was not there. Her Grace looked coldly affable: hauteur and condescension were in her bearing. Methought that I could comprehend what was passing in her mind: she did not like to seem ungenerously repulsive towards Mary Glent-worth—she did not on the other hand choose to

appear too kind and friendly; and thus she had a difficult part to perform. Slightly rising for an instant from the sofa on which she was seated, she motioned with her hand for Mary and myself to take chairs; and she at once entered upon the business by saying, "I suppose, Miss Trafford, you have communicated everything to your friend Miss Glentworth?"

I answered in the affirmative; and the Duchess went on to observe, "It was an unpleasant scene which took place just now: but not for a single instant do I blame Miss Glentworth! She had been deceived and misled. Yet under all circum-stances, it ought to be a subject of rejoicing that the day of elucidation has arrived. You will both of you agree with me that it is better his Grace should not be present at this interview. Certain arrangements must be made—and I am prepared to make them. Perhaps you will inform me, Miss Trafford, what are your friend's views and aims in life?—or perhaps Miss Glentworth herself will explain them? In a word——"

"I have already advised Miss Glentworth to accept," I said, "that which his Grace of Ardleigh may deem consistent with his position towards her, to bestow."

"For myself," said Mary Glentworth, speaking with calmness and decision, "I will frankly con-fess that at one time I experienced a strong in-clination for the stage; and I should even now adopt it, were it not that circumstances have arisen——"

Here she blushed and suddenly became seized with confusion. I accordingly took up the thread of the discourse which she herself was too much embarrassed to pursue.

"As your Grace thinks fit on this occasion," I said, "to appear as the representative of the Duke of Ardleigh, the same statements must be made to your ladyship which, were the Duke present, would have been made to his lordship. The hand of Miss Glentworth has been sought in marriage by a young gentleman whom there is every reason to believe to be the occupant of an honourable position and possessed of some fortune——"

"His name?" inquired the Duchess.

"His name is Mr. Beauchamp," I replied.

"I have the fullest confidence in your pru-dence, Miss Trafford," said the Duchess of Ard-leigh; "and therefore if you assure me that this is an eligible alliance, I shall at once assent on the Duke's part; and indeed I shall congratulate Miss Glentworth on the prospect of so advanta-geously settling herself in life. She shall not go a dowerless bride to the altar: but the secret of her birth must be maintained inviolate——"

"I ought to inform your Grace," I here broke in, "that I am as yet totally unacquainted with Mr. Beauchamp: but this very day was he to have been introduced to me——"

"And you would have satisfied yourself," said the Duchess, "that he is in every sense an honourable character? I thought, Miss Traf-ford," she added, with an approving smile, "that I was not wrong when I declared that I could trust to your prudence and discretion. But Ah! I fancied that Miss Glentworth lived altogether with you; and if this be the case, how happens it that she should have formed so intimate an acquaintance who is entirely unknown to your-

self? You will bear in mind that I represent the Duke upon this occasion—that I am therefore asking these questions through no motive of impertinent curiosity—but, to speak plainly, because I will not suffer the Duke's purse to furnish a dower for Miss Glentworth with the chance of its being expended by some extravagant person."

"I will pledge my existence," exclaimed Mary Glentworth indignantly, "for the honourable character of Clarence Beauchamp! But I do not want the dower; and he will gladly espouse me without it. Come, Ellen!—let us depart! I had a presentiment that I should be insulted within these walls!"

"Miss Glentworth," said the Duchess, coldly and severely, "no one has insulted you; and your friend Miss Trafford will inform you that I am only adopting a reasonable and prudential course."

"Her Grace speaks truly, my dear Mary," I said; "and I beseech you to be calm."

"Prove to my satisfaction," continued the Duchess, addressing herself to me, "that this Mr. Beauchamp is an honourable and well principled young gentleman—as indeed I have little doubt, from what Miss Glentworth says, that he is—and I will present her with a dower of ten thousand pounds. But let it be well understood that this is on the condition of the secret of her birth being inviolably kept! I can assure Miss Glentworth that I had no intention of insulting her——"

"I thought that your Grace," said Mary, now speaking with the utmost civility, "endeavoured to throw a slur over Mr. Beauchamp's character, just because it happens that my friend Ellen is as yet unacquainted with him."

"I am incapable of prejudging persons in this light or reckless manner," responded the Duchess of Ardleigh: "but when I was informed that he was a total stranger to Miss Trafford, I thought that if there was not something strange, there was at least something which required explanation."

"And as we are not here to be catechised in this manner," said Mary Glentworth, "we will take our departure."

Thus speaking, she rose abruptly from her seat. Her mind had been chafed by the incidents preceding our arrival at Ardleigh House : she had looked upon her father as the betrayer of her mother rather than in any other light—and she now felt that she stood in the position of one who was about to receive charitable or eleemosynary assistance from the proud Duchess. Therefore that spirit which was usually latent under the mild amiability of her disposition and the ingenuous artlessness of her character, had flamed up. The Duchess of Ardleigh was by no means a lady formed to brook any display of temper of this kind ; and she said with haughty indignation, "I little thought to find so forward and perverse a disposition in the young person whose best interests I was endeavouring to serve. She may do as she pleases : but until I am convinced that her hand is sought by a respectable young man, not one single shilling of the Duke of Ardleigh's money shall be forthcoming with the chance of its being recklessly expended by an unprincipled adventurer !"

"Unprincipled adventurer?" ejaculated Mary Glentworth, her cheeks flushing with indignation —and I noticed that she quivered with rage.

"Hush, my dear Mary ! hush !" I hastened to interpose—for I saw that she was indeed damaging all her best interests, and even proving ungrateful towards the Duchess of Ardleigh who was disposed to treat her with liberality : "you are not behaving right towards her Grace——"

"Did she not call Clarence Beauchamp an unprincipled adventurer?" demanded Mary, with the glow still upon her cheeks ; "and have not I over and over again proclaimed that he is in every way worthy——But ah !" she ejaculated, in a tone of joy and amazement ; "here he is to speak for himself !"

They were likewise ejaculations of amazement —though heaven knows with nothing of joy in them—which almost simultaneously burst from the lips of the startled Duchess and myself as Mary Glentworth bounded towards the individual who entered the room at the moment : for he whom she believed to be Clarence Beauchamp, was none other than the Marquis of Dalrymple, the Duke and Duchess of Ardleigh's son !

CHAPTER LXXV.

THE HALF-BROTHER AND SISTER.

A HORRIBLE shudder swept through my entire frame at the thought of the fearful precipice on which not merely Mary Glentworth had been standing, but likewise that young nobleman himself. The half-brother and half-sister had formed a mutual passion ; and though for a variety of reasons I was in a moment struck by the conviction that on Herbert Dalrymple's part it was no genuine love, but merely the inclination of a libertine, yet for this very reason it was perhaps all

the more shocking that he should have breathed the language of a deceptive tenderness in the ears of one who by blood was related to him. That Mary was completely innocent—that she was pure and chaste — that she had escaped whatsoever seductive wiles the young Marquis had hitherto been with a systematic craftiness practising towards her, I had not the slightest doubt : but were it not for the combination of circumstances which had led to this explosion, as it may be termed, heaven only knows to what miserable catastrophe my too trusting and confiding friend might have been hurried onward !

The scene which was now occurring in that apartment presented what in theatrical language may be denominated a perfect *tableau*. It indicated several varieties of interest, sentiment, and feeling. For myself, I was, as I have already said, for an instant shocked and smitten with a shuddering tremor at the discovery : and then the next moment my heart leaped with satisfaction that this discovery should have been made ere it was too late : but in another instant my mind experienced an equally powerful revulsion, and I thought of the anguish that was now in store for poor Mary, who had learnt to love her own half-brother ! The Duchess of Ardleigh was smitten with amazement on finding that her son had been unconsciously wooing his half-sister, evidently with no honourable purpose, but with the seductive design of a profligate ; and as I glanced towards her Grace, I saw that the colour was coming and going in rapid transitions upon her haughtily handsome countenance. The Marquis of Dalrymple had entered that room in ignorance of whom he was to meet there : he was seized with a sudden confusion on beholding Mary Glentworth and myself ; and when the former bounded towards him, he mechanically sustained her in his arms—but it was with the embarrassed air of a guilty person whose criminal designs were on the point of receiving the fullest exposure. Yet be it understood he was still utterly unaware of the peculiar circumstances attaching themselves to Mary Glentworth : these startling facts he had yet to learn. As for Mary herself, she had at first flown towards him with all the confidence of her sincere and artless love, delighted that he should suddenly present himself to vindicate a character which she believed to have been unjustly aspersed, or at least suspected, by the Duchess of Ardleigh : — she dreamt not of aught sinister lurking in the background and being about to transpire ; and even when she perceived that her lover was stricken with confusion, she attributed it not to a guilty conscience, but to the embarrassment of a sudden meeting with me, in the presence too of the mistress of the mansion.

Yes, it was a veritable *tableau*, — lasting for nearly a minute — during which every lip was sealed by the sentiments that were respectively experienced. Mary Glentworth was the first to break that silence ; and looking up into her lover's countenance, she exclaimed, "Oh, I am so glad you have come, Clarence !"

"Unhappy girl !" cried the Duchess of Ardleigh, hastening forward ; "you know not what you say ! you know not what you do !"

"Mary, for God's sake pardon me !" exclaimed the young Marquis, in a voice of anguish—for he was not utterly depraved, and his conscience smote him severely:—"I have deceived you—I am not Clarence Beauchamp——"

A cry burst from the lips of Mary Glentworth as she started back from the arm to which she had been clinging; and she gazed with consternation and affright upon the countenance of that young nobleman.

"But I swear to you," he continued, with rapid and excited utterance, "that I will make you amends! My eyes are open to all your virtuous qualities—and I will lead you to the altar!"

It was with a cry of joy that Mary Glentworth bounded back into his arms: the poor girl's brain was in confusion—the shock which she had for an instant sustained by being told that she was deceived, had yielded to an equally sudden sense of delight on hearing that she should become the bride of him she loved. But rapid as the changes of the kaleidoscope, another phase in the hurried and excited drama was now to ensue. Literally wresting Mary from the arms of the young nobleman, the Duchess of Ardleigh exclaimed, almost with a shriek of mingled anguish and horror, "Wretched girl! unhappy boy! ye know not what ye are doing!"

"Madam, unhand me!" ejaculated Mary, her cheeks flushed with indignation.

"Mother," exclaimed Herbert, "I will not be domineered over by you!"

"Ah!" cried Mary, now smitten with a new cause of amazement and affright: "the Duchess of Ardleigh your mother?——O heavens! No, no! Say not *that!* But the Duke—the Duke——"

"Is my father!" cried the Marquis. "Yes, my beloved! I am not Clarence Beauchamp—and you shall become the Marchioness of Dalrymple!"

"Oh, my God! is this possible?"—and now it was a wild cry of horror and distress that thrilled from Mary's lips as she sank down on the carpet from the hold which the Duchess had laid upon her.

"Good God! how can I make known the truth?" exclaimed her Grace. "Be tranquil, Mary!—stand back, Herbert! It is your own half-sister whom you behold there!—the offspring of your father's infidelity towards myself!"

A groan of indescribable horror was but too fearfully indicative of the shock thus given to the wretched young nobleman: but for the moment I had no leisure to pay any attention to him nor to his mother the Duchess—for I was sustaining the half-fainting Mary Glentworth in my arms. I had flown to her the instant she sank down upon the carpet, crushed, overpowered, almost annihilated by the awful revelation which had just been made to her that it was her own half-brother the Marquis of Dalrymple whom she had loved! Complete consciousness did not however abandon her: she became fearfully agitated—her bosom heaved and sank with convulsive sobs—the most piteous lamentations came gaspingly from her ashy pale lips—and with a nervous violence did she keep pressing my hand as I retained her's in my clasp. I got her to a sofa—I entreated her to be calm—and I whispered to her in a tone of the most earnest prayer, "You displayed courage and fortitude ere now in your dealings with the Duchess: for heaven's sake lose not your presence of mind

at a moment when it is more than ever necessary to sustain you!"

I perceived that the unfortunate girl exerted a powerful effort over herself; and she said—though it was in a hollow voice that she spoke—"Ellen, the calamity is frightful; but I will be courageous—I will be calm!"

I now glanced towards the Duchess of Ardleigh and her son: they were whispering together in a corner of the apartment—the young nobleman leant against the wall—his countenance was as pale as death—his features had a look of unutterable anguish. I could not see his mother's face—her back was towards me; but it was evident that she was giving some hasty details explanatory in respect to Mary Glentworth. All of a sudden the young Marquis uttered an ejaculation as if his mind had thus abruptly taken some fixed resolve; and striding across the room, he said to Mary Glentworth, "Pardon me for the past!—on my knees do I entreat your pardon. There was all along something which made me treat you with a degree of respect—though to my shame and sorrow I confess that my intentions were vile to a degree! Forgive me—for God's sake forgive me! You are my sister—and whether so acknowledged or not by my family, yet in that light will I regard you—will I love you—will I cherish you—will I protect and defend you!"

No! that young man was *not* utterly depraved! All the natural generosity of his disposition—all the native magnanimity of his character, were now asserting themselves and rising dominant above other influences and feelings. He sank upon his knees: his countenance wore a look of ineffable anguish and entreaty as he made this appeal to Mary and took her hand. For an instant she abandoned that hand to him, and a violent struggle was evidently taking place within her. But it was only for an instant that she thus remained a prey to doubt and indecision: the next moment her resolve was taken. Abruptly withdrawing her hand, she started up from her seat; and with indignant looks, she exclaimed, "Rise, my lord!—kneel not to me!—ask not a pardon which never can be accorded!"

"Speak not thus, Mary my sister!" cried the young nobleman, quitting his suppliant posture, but now joining his hands in anguished entreaty. "You will drive me mad—you will plunge me into despair, if you refuse to accept whatsoever atonement I offer for the past!"

"I will receive no boon, no favour, no kindness from any member of the Ardleigh family!" and Mary's voice was sombre and gloomy, but stern and decisive; and Oh! it was terrible to think that one so young, not yet twenty years of age, should become acquainted with calamities and feelings which thus influenced her speech and her language. "The Duke of Ardleigh was the betrayer of my mother—and in this light only can I henceforth regard him! The Duchess of Ardleigh has insulted me with her insolently-proffered charities: but, Oh! infinitely worse, has been *your* conduct!"—and here she bent her eyes with the bitterest reproach upon the countenance of the young Marquis. "You sought to ruin me—you deceived me with a display of affection—you were gradually winding your meshes about me——your character must be infamous! I now hate you—I hate every one belonging to your family! The stigma that rests upon my birth is derived, proud Duchess, from your own husband!—unprincipled Marquis, from your own father! No—I seek not kindness here! Give me your hatred, as I give you mine."

It was with a frightful bitterness and a terribly passionate vehemence that Mary Glentworth thus spoke; the fury of the volcano was in her heart—the stormy ocean seemed to have lent its tumultuous heavings to her bosom. The Duchess looked appalled — Herbert was dreadfully distressed—and I myself was smitten with consternation.

"Come, Ellen, my only friend!" exclaimed Mary, suddenly turning towards me and taking my hand; "come—let us depart hence! You are the only being except my poor betrayed mother that ever loved me! Come, I say! let us leave this house where the very atmosphere itself is oppressive as if laden with the breath of crime!"

Thus speaking, she drew me with violence from the sofa; and now recovering my self-possession, I made a rapid sign to the Duchess to imply that it would be better for me to take the half distracted girl away.

"For heaven's sake depart not thus!" exclaimed the Marquis of Dalrymple, rushing forward to detain his half-sister.

"Back, back, my lord," she cried, with hysterical violence and with actual affright, as if it were a wild beast that was about to spring or a reptile to dart upon her. "Touch me not, I say! but let me go!"

She rushed to the door—I was with her—and the next instant it closed behind us.

"Now, Mary," I said, "for heaven's sake be calm—or the domestics will notice that there is something strange!"

"Fear not, Ellen," she replied; "I am perfectly calm:"—but it was in a forced unnatural tone that she spoke—a tone that was broken likewise by a short hysterical laugh which it did me harm to hear.

She was very pale; her features were now rigid —and I trembled for the consequences of the frightful things that had taken place. Within the comparatively brief interval of two hours she had learnt two startling facts: first, that she was the illegitimate daughter of the Duke of Ardleigh —second that the individual who under a feigned name had sought her love was that Duke's son, her own half-brother! It was sufficient to overwhelm her; and if she had given way to hours and hours of passionate weeping, I should have been more better on her account than I was now that I found her in this mood of forced composure and unnatural calmness.

We descended the staircase—we passed out of the mansion—we resumed our seats in the cab that had brought us thither. Mary Glentworth remained plunged in deep silence: her looks were fixed—her countenance continued very pale—no tears trickled from her eyes — her bosom had ceased to heave—it was completely still. She had the air of a person who was making up her mind to some desperate resolve. It was a silence which I dared not break, for I knew not what to say to her. My own reflections and apprehensions were painful enough. As I thought of past incidents I remembered amongst other things that conversation which about six weeks back I had overheard at the Polytechnic Institution between Mr. Ormond and Mr. Trevelyan, relative to the Marquis of Dalrymple having been seen walking in a street at the West End with a young and beautiful lady. I had now no doubt that this was Mary Glentworth; for it was the precise period when her acquaintance with him was in its infancy, and when she might well have appeared timid, diffident, and affrighted, as I remembered to have heard Mr. Ormond describe that she was. Oh! how deeply, deeply did I pity my poor friend!—and in respect to myself I felt that adventures and incidents of a painful character were coming upon me as if striking me blow upon blow, and without absolutely injuring me, yet with bitterness enlarging my experience of life.

At least ten minutes had elapsed since we left Ardleigh House before a word was spoken by either of us: and then Mary, slowly raising her head and looking towards me, said, "This is a day of trials, Ellen."

"And you, my dearest Mary," I replied, "must collect all your courage and fortitude——"

"I am fully nerved with both," she answered, in a cold, level, unnaturally monotonous voice. "Within the space of a few hours I have acquired the experiences of a lifetime. My heart seems dead within me——or at least it beats only with two feelings: an illimitable commiseration for the memory of my deceased mother, and the equally boundless affection of a sister towards yourself! The rest of the world I hate and hold almost in abhorrence."

I was about to tell her that it was wrong to speak in this latter strain—but I checked myself: I thought it better that she should have her own way, and that the present despairing mood should take its course and either wear itself out or else in reaction yield to some other state of mind.

"I am resolved how to act," she continued: "my future career is sketched forth so far as my own ideas can determine it. From all those thoughts and feelings which have recently agitated me I fall back upon my original inclination as a relief. Ellen," she added, after a brief pause, and speaking with even more firmness than she had before adopted, "I shall go upon the stage."

"You shall do as you like, Mary," I answered, in the kindest possible tone: "but for awhile—for a few months, or at least for a few weeks—you shall remain quiet and tranquil; you shall have leisure to compose yourself——"

"I require not the leisure of even a few days," she interrupted me; and it was still with firmness though with kindness that she spoke. "I am already composed—and the only means by which I can retain that composure is by following my inclinations. I shall adopt a profession which will absorb all my attention—all my thoughts and ideas—and which I hope will give me bread."

"This last consideration, Mary," I said, in a gentle tone of remonstrance, "need not enter into your thoughts; for you have told me that you love me as if you were my sister—and as I entertain a similar affection towards yourself, everything that I possess is at your disposal. Besides, you have money of your own——"

"Now, my dear Ellen, let us not argue the

point!" interrupted Mary. "A great change has taken place within me: and you shall see that it is so. Everything is now to give place in my mind to the execution of the resolve I have adopted;—and this is to go upon the stage. I shall become your pupil, my dearest friend, as Aline Marcy already is. You will instruct me—will you not? Yes—I know you will!—and oh! you shall soon see the smiles come back to my lips——"

Here she stopped short and averted her face for a moment. Hastily she lifted the kerchief to her eyes—then she looked at me again, and said in a lower, more tremulous tone, "I have gone through a great deal in a very short time; and I cannot all in a moment shake off the effects. But let us not speak of the past—let us think only of the present and the future; for from this instant I commence a new epoch of my existence!"

We now reached Great Ormond Street, and Aline Marcy was there to receive her usual lesson. Mary Glentworth insisted upon joining her: I remonstrated but feebly—for on seeing that she was resolute, I thought it was better to let her have her own way, and to succour her in any course which might tend to wean her mind from reflecting gloomily on recent occurrences. I was astonished at the cheerfulness with which she received her lesson: there was no abstraction—no wandering of the thoughts to other subjects. Her mind was a strong one, but peculiar in its strength; and I sincerely hoped that it would experience no relapse nor reaction.

On the following morning I received a note from Mr. Wilkinson, requesting me to call at his office at eleven o'clock in the forenoon. I did not tell Mary that I had received this communication; for I had a suspicion that it might probably relate to her own affairs rather than to those which I had recently entrusted to Mr. Wilkinson's guidance:—but I set out alone to keep the appointment.

"This is altogether a sad affair," said the attorney, the moment I had taken a seat in his private office; and though the observation was so abruptly made, yet I comprehended full well to what subject it related.

"Then you have doubtless received some communication from Ardleigh House?" I said inquiringly.

"Her Grace sent for me last evening," responded the attorney, "and she told me everything that had occurred. She likewise gave me certain instructions how to act. This is the reason I requested a visit from you, Miss Percy; for as yet I have nothing to communicate in respect to your own personal matters. Her Grace——for perhaps you know that she does everything and her husband is but a cipher——has directed that the sum of ten thousand pounds be offered to Miss Glentworth, on condition that an inviolable secrecy be maintained——"

"If the money be proffered as a bribe, Mr. Wilkinson," I interrupted him, "the proposal becomes a direct insult——"

"Come, come, Miss Percy," said the lawyer good-naturedly, "do not take things in this light! You and I can understand each other—though your friend Miss Glentworth may be smarting, as is natural enough, under the sense of recent

circumstances. The Duchess wishes to provide for the young lady——"

"I can give you the positive assurance, Mr. Wilkinson, that Mary Glentworth has not the slightest inclination to afford publicity to matters the painfulness of which has already induced her to express the positive desire that they cease to be a topic of conversation even between herself and me. She has decided upon going on the stage. In her present humour she will accept of nothing at the hands of the Ardleigh family——"

"But you will give her better advice, Miss Percy?" exclaimed the lawyer.

"I shall most assuredly counsel her to accept the fortune which her own father offers her," I replied. "It is no boon which he confers—no charity which he bestows: it is a mere duty which he fulfils. But I tell you candidly that I do not for a moment think Mary Glentworth will follow my advice on this point. I never saw such decision on the part of any human being!—her resolve is firmly taken to reject everything at the hands of the Ardleigh family."

"This mood of mind is forced and unnatural," said the solicitor, "and will not last."

"I thought so yesterday," I rejoined; "but I think differently to-day. Within the last few hours I have acquired a greater insight than ever I before possessed into the state of Mary Glentworth's mind. It is strong; and if once she adopt an idea—it may become a prejudice, a perverseness, an obstinacy, call it what you will—but nevertheless she will adhere to it! I shall of course communicate to her the proposal of the Duke of Ardleigh——"

"And if she reject it," exclaimed Mr. Wilkinson, "we must accomplish the matter secretly—we must invest the money in the funds in her name; and she need know nothing about it until the day shall come when in an altered state of mind she will gladly accept the little fortune thus provided for her."

I reflected for a few moments; and then I said, "Since you have the power to do this, it will be infinitely better to adopt such a course than that I should reopen the subject and enter into a fresh series of unavailing arguments. If you will act as trustee, the investment need not become known to Miss Glentworth until a more opportune moment shall arrive."

"Be it so," rejoined the lawyer. "And now to another point. The Marquis of Dalrymple, knowing of my intention to have this interview with you to-day, most earnestly and vehemently entreated that he might be allowed a few minutes' private conversation with you. I gave no promise: I simply informed him that he might call here at half-past twelve o'clock, when, if you decided upon seeing him——"

"Yes, I will see him," I said. "He may have something to communicate; and it would be wrong, considering all circumstances, that I should refuse to hear him."

"Then I will ascertain if he be arrived," said the attorney: and he passed out into the front office.

Almost immediately afterwards the door again opened, and the Marquis of Dalrymple made his appearance. His looks were haggard and careworn: his eyes were red and swollen as if he had passed a sleepless night: he had an abashed, a diffident, and guilty air as he entered into my presence. He closed the door behind him; and on perceiving how coldly severe my demeanour was, he seemed to be overwhelmed with distress. Averting his countenance, he covered his face with his hands and sobbed audibly. Then bursting forth with vehement and passionate utterance, he exclaimed, "Oh! how the vices of men may lead to the most fearful consequences and hurry them onward unconsciously to the brink of crime! My father's folly and his infidelity towards my mother gave birth to her who is my half-sister—accident threw me in her way—evil thoughts took possession of me—and but for the sudden discoveries of yesterday a hideous crime might have been perpetrated!"

"I hope, my lord," I said, "that all this will prove a salutary lesson for you——"

"Oh! it will, it will, I can assure you!" he exclaimed, with unquestionable sincerity. "It has rendered me an altered being. As God is my judge I am telling you the truth! Never, never again will I strive to seduce an innocent girl from the path of virtue! I am going abroad, Miss Percy—to-morrow I shall leave England. If henceforth you hear of me, it will only be in a manner creditable to myself; and if we ever meet again, you will not blush to know me. I do not ask you to forgive me for my past conduct——"

"Remember, my lord," I said, "that in no sense do I stand towards you in a position which necessitates you to ask my forgiveness, nor which entitles me to expect such a prayer from your lips."

"Yes, Miss Percy! as the bosom-friend—as the more than sister of poor Mary, you have a right to demand proofs of contrition from me; and you have the power to vouchsafe a promise of forgiveness if my future conduct shall render me deserving of it! And there is another reason," he continued, hesitatingly and diffidently; "for there was a time when—and Oh! at *that* time I was an honourable young man—pure and uncontaminated ——and then I dared love you and in all sincerity offer you my hand——"

"Enough, my lord!" I interrupted him: and I could not help adding, "The Marquis of Dalrymple of the present time is very different from the Marquis of Dalrymple of the other day. Look, my lord, at the whole tenour of your conduct towards the unfortunate Mary Glentworth; and for ever blush for it as the darkest chapter in your life's history! It was a tissue of the most complicated deceptions; and Ah, my lord! in one sense it furnishes the most potent reason why you ought to sink down with shame in alluding to whatsoever once took place between yourself and me. For what was your conduct to Mary Glentworth? Accident rendered you acquainted with her: you became smitten with her beauty—you threw yourself in her way—you dared to talk to her of an honourable love—and yet it was the basest design which you cherished. Yes!—for it was no headlong passion which hurried you on: it was from the outset a deliberately conceived, and I may almost say a cold-blooded plan to accomplish the poor girl's ruin. You adopted a feigned name; and in case of any circumstance arising to render correspondence necessary, you bribed some underling at your Club to receive whatsoever letter might come addressed to you under that fictitious name. Was not all this the proof of a deep-laid and studied scheme of villany? But you did more! When you learnt, no doubt to your great surprise, that Mary Glentworth lived with me, you put forward all kinds of pretexts to prevent her from revealing the secret to my ears; for you dared not come to my house under your false name to woo her—and you dreaded likewise that I should detect and expose your wickedness before it was entirely consummated. Ah, my lord! I have heard from Mary's lips all the sophistries which you called into requisition to blind and to bewilder her, and to leave clear the pathway of villany along which you were dragging her towards the precipice at the end! When you think of all this, my lord, you must indeed feel that you have played a part on which you never can look back otherwise than with shame, remorse, and regret. And not even that love with which you say that I myself had some time back inspired you—not even the brotherly friendship which at that period you proclaimed towards me when you found that I would not accept your hand,—and not even the respect which you might have borne for one whom but the other day you professed to love,—no, none of these considerations availed to arrest you in the path of wickedness when once your mind was bent on rendering poor Mary Glentworth your victim!"

I had not intended at the outset to make this long speech, nor even to condescend to enter into any details with the young Marquis apart from the business, whatsoever it were, on which he had sought an interview with me: but the subject grew upon me as I progressed—and thus was my discourse elaborated. Herbert Dalrymple was thoroughly abashed, cowed, crushed down: he was overwhelmed with shame and remorse. I continued to speak mercilessly, because when I perceived that he displayed a real contrition, I fancied that the castigation would prove beneficial to his future welfare.

"But heaven was resolved," I continued, "in its goodness and mercy to save you from the accomplishment of an aim which in the long run would have proved to be a crime of darker dye and greater magnitude than you could have at first conceived. Yes—heaven has been merciful to you, and has stretched out its helping hand to lift you from the precipice down which you were falling. Let all this be a lesson to you! I have spoken severely: there are deep wounds in your soul—and you may think that I have been probing them unmercifully. But I will confess that there is no need to despair of you for the future! All good principles and generous sentiments have not been crushed out of you. If, my lord, you avoid evil society for the future—the gaming-table—and the company of those who make evil actions the subject of their applause, and who consider it manly to lead a life of profligacy and debauchery,—if you avoid such society as this, I say, you will prosper—you will redeem yourself—and you will atone for the past. Now, my lord, if I at first spoke severely, I have at last spoken hopefully; and I will even go so far as to add that with a friendly interest shall I watch your future career."

"Generous Miss Percy!" exclaimed the young

nobleman, in a tone tremulous with emotions; "it required but an angel-voice such as yours to lift me completely up from the depths into which I have been plunging! Yours is the voice of sincerest friendship: you rebuke me for my misdeeds —but you tell me that there is hope for me in the future. My God! that I could ever have gone wrong! But by heaven! it was not altogether my fault. Not upon others would I unjustly throw the blame of my own delinquencies; but judge whether I speak not truly when I declare that my father's frivolities and my mother's imperiousness first drove me from home by rendering that home intolerable. Then what was I to do? I naturally associated with young men in my own sphere; and they led me astray. Most solemnly do I swear to you, Miss Percy, that I have gone forth from Ardleigh House of an evening when if my home had been comfortable I would infinitely rather have remained within its walls. I have sought the society of dissipated young men about town—not because I preferred it, but because it presented itself as the only resource. I have drunk deep of wine because others drank, although my heart sickened at it after the few first glasses. I have gambled and thrown my money about, because others around me did the same, and I felt that if I sought that society I was bound to follow its example. Oh! believe me therefore—since you have permitted me to make these confessions—since you have listened to them with patience—and I think— I hope, not altogether without sympathy,—believe me, I say, my reformation is an easier task than you may have supposed: but even if it were the most difficult ever undertaken by man, I swear that it should be accomplished!"

It was impossible to listen to this speech, so frank, so genuine, and so sincere in its depth of feeling, without being moved: it was likewise impossible for me to avoid expressing myself in a kind and encouraging manner after having at the outset expostulated with the young nobleman so severely and so mercilessly.

"My lord," I therefore said, "it is with a friendly sympathy that I have listened to you; for I know that when our acquaintance began some eighteen or twenty months ago, you possessed the loftiest sentiments and the most generous disposition. Neither have I forgotten certain kind services which you rendered towards myself. It is therefore with satisfaction I have heard all those confessions, avowals, and assurances from your lips; and I repeat I shall watch your future career with a friendly interest. But now, my lord, tell me—for what special purpose did you seek the present interview?"

"Oh, Miss Percy!" he exclaimed, "I had a thousand things to say to you! I wished to speak to you of her whom I sincerely love as if she were my legitimately-born sister! She is well-principled and virtuous. She believed that in Clarence Beauchamp she had an honourable suitor; and in her artless confidence she consented to meet me from time to time. But if ever I sought to bestow even the simplest token which a lover may offer to the object of his affections—a kiss or the pressure of a hand—her natural modesty recoiled; and she invariably by the very purity of her character kept me at a distance. I will now confess

that the very difficulties that I thus encountered in the prosecution of my villanous design, piqued me, urged me on, and made me feel as if it were almost a point of honour that I should persevere until I might achieve success. Thank God that Mary was thus right-principled, and that my wicked persistence was so timeously baffled as it was yesterday! All these assurances I have just given you for your satisfaction, that you may the better know how to appreciate the good qualities, the innate chastity, and the correct principles of your bosom friend Mary."

I was indeed delighted to learn these things from Dalrymple's lips; for favourably as I had before thought of Mary Glentworth's conduct, she now stood infinitely higher in my estimation. I could scarcely now accuse her of even a display of the slightest weakness: I could only think of her as one whose too confiding nature and unsuspecting artlessness had rendered her incautious.

"And now tell me, Miss Percy," continued Herbert, "how does poor Mary support the blows which have smitten her?"

"With courage and fortitude," I answered. "But I will not deceive you, my lord: she entertains bitter feelings against the entire house of Ardleigh!"

"And this sum which my mother proposes through Mr. Wilkinson's agency——"

"I am convinced that Mary will not in her present frame of mind accept it. But Mr. Wilkinson and I have agreed upon a plan, according to which the little fortune may be invested for her benefit so as to be available on any future occasion."

"Heaven be thanked!" exclaimed the young Marquis fervently. "But tell me, Miss Percy— may I not hope ere leaving England that she will see me — that we may meet as brother and sister——"

"Do not think of it, my lord!" I replied. "I have already told you that I will not deceive you— nor would I unnecessarily wound your feelings, for I see that they are already deeply lacerated. You cannot hope to have an interview with Mary: she is bitter against yourself as well as against your parents; and if I give you this assurance, it is only that you may not persevere in any idea that you may have formed to obtain a parting interview with her."

"No, no! I will not!" said the young Marquis: "I will do nothing against your advice. But you, Miss Percy, will continue to watch over her—you will continue to be her friend—and in whatsoever circumstances she may be placed——"

"Fear not, my lord," I interrupted him, "that I shall ever be otherwise to your half-sister than I now am. Circumstances as well as inclinations have riveted between us the bonds of sincerest affection. I was with her at the time when her mother died—I then obtained for her a home at the house of Mrs. Oldcastle, a relative of mine— and when this lady also died, Mary took up her abode altogether with me, first in Hunter Street, and subsequently where I now dwell."

"Yes—all these particulars has Mary at different times told me," responded the Marquis; "and she has ever spoken to me in sisterly terms of you. I know therefore that with you she will be happy——"

"It is my duty to inform you of one thing," I

said, "since you take so deep and generous an interest in your half-sister—she has resolved to embrace the stage as a profession——"

"Ah!" said Herbert; "that was one point on which I was likewise desirous to speak to you! From her conversation at times I have gleaned that she had an inclination for the stage——"

"And she will adopt it as a profession," I rejoined. "If you wish it I will endeavour to dissuade her——in fact it is an idea which I have never encouraged; for where one achieves success, there are so many failures——although I must candidly inform your lordship that Mary has the talent——"

"Act as you will, Miss Percy! do precisely as you think fit!" interjected the Marquis of Dalrymple. "And now I have detained you long enough: I renew the assurances of my gratitude for all the generous and kind things you have said to me—and believe me, Oh! believe me, the seed has not fallen upon barren ground!"

Thus speaking with much genuine feeling, the Marquis wrung my hand and hastened from the room. Shortly afterwards I likewise took my departure from the lawyer's office in Furnival's Inn; and I returned to Great Ormond Street. During the dinner time I touched delicately and gently upon the forbidden topic, in order to ascertain whether I might venture to proceed and explain to Mary Glentworth what had taken place: but she at once turned the conversation into another channel—not with rudeness nor unkindness, but still with a firmness which rendered it impossible for me to give utterance to another syllable on the point.

CHAPTER LXXVI.

GILDEROY HEMP.

IT was about nine o'clock in the evening, three or four days after the incidents which I have been just relating, that I and Beda found ourselves plunging into the midst of a maze of wretched, narrow, ill-paved, ill-lighted streets or rather lanes and alleys somewhere in the district of Clerkenwell. We were both dressed in our commonest costume, and had veils closely drawn over our countenances. Although it was in the month of May, yet the night was dark and stormy; and I had more than half selected it on account of its gloominess for the enterprise which I had in hand —because, as the reader may suppose, I was by no means anxious to stand the chance of being recognised in the low vile quarter into which I was now penetrating. To be brief, I was following a portion of the parting instructions which Zarah had given me,—that portion which so especially regarded my own personal concerns. In reference to the name which was written on the scrap of paper that I had taken from the table-drawer in her chamber, she had said to me, "Hesitate not to seek that man at his abode." Therefore, after much deliberation with myself as well as with Beda, I had determined upon following Zarah's instructions to the very letter— namely, by calling in person upon the man instead of sending for him to come to me at my

own house. Beda knew nothing of him—she had never before heard his name; and she was therefore unable to afford me the slightest idea of his character and disposition. But Zarah had assured me that he was prepared to go through fire and water to serve me; and I knew perfectly well that I might place the fullest reliance on the words she had thus spoken. I should add that in the forenoon of the day on which I had now resolved to visit the man, I had sent Beda into the neighbourhood to ascertain the precise whereabouts of his abode, so as to avoid the necessity of inquiring our way or standing the chance of losing it in the evening.

It was, therefore, as I have said, at about nine o'clock that Beda and I were bending our steps thither. The gaslights were few and far between; and they seemed to burn more dimly in this neighbourhood than anywhere else. Most of the shops were already closed; and even those that were still open, had merely a candle or two burning feebly inside, and which shed no light into the alleys and lanes themselves. There were not many persons abroad in those narrow thoroughfares: but from the public-houses, which were sprinkled pretty numerously about, issued the din of uncouth uproarious revelry, "making night hideous."

"Is it much farther, Beda?" I inquired in a low tone; for I feared lest my faithful guide must have lost herself amidst the maze of lanes and alleys into which we had already so deeply penetrated.

"It is here close at hand," replied Beda. "You are not afraid, Miss?" she asked.

"No—not afraid," I responded: "but the sooner we reach our destination, the better; for if I happen to meet any one who may recognise me, even through the folds of this thick black veil, it would not be very agreeable——"

Scarcely had I thus spoken, when the door of a public-house which we were passing at the instant was thrown suddenly open; and a man issued forth. I at once recognised him: it was Black Ned, the gipsy who had been our gaoler at the ruined farm-buildings near Petersfield, and whom Beda and I had overpowered and bound when we effected our escape from our prison-chamber. He hurried past us, proceeding in the same direction as ourselves; and he was quickly lost to our view in the obscurity which prevailed farther along the narrow street.

"Do you know who that was, Beda?" I inquired, stopping suddenly short and clutching her by the arm: "did you recognise him?"

"Yes, Miss," she responded: "it was Black Ned. But he did not perceive us—or at least I think not."

"Perhaps not," I said: "but yet he may probably be going to the same house which is our destination—and I should not like to fall in with him, I can assure you."

"And I have not the least apprehension in encountering him," rejoined Beda. "Rest assured that Zarah's promise may be thoroughly relied upon: Gilderoy will prove faithful—and he will protect you, Miss, from all harm."

"But remember, Beda," I resumed, still lingering in the street, "Black Ned can entertain no very favourable sentiments towards you and me; and perhaps he may be only too glad of an oppor-

tunity to avenge himself on us for his discomfiture at the ruined farm-buildings."

"I can only repeat, Miss, my conviction," replied Beda, "from the assurances which poor Zarah gave you, that the man Gilderoy Hemp will prove a safeguard against all enemies. He must be a person not merely of energy, but also wielding some authority with the tribe; or else Zarah would not have thought of making use of his services in the business that her death cut short, and which you are now taking up. Besides, it is by no means certain that Black Ned was going to his house at all: for this is a district much frequented by gipsy tramps when they come to London."

Still I hesitated, for I was afraid of incurring unnecessary risks; and I was almost inclined to postpone the enterprise to another evening, or else to alter my plan by sending and desiring Gilderoy Hemp to come to me at my own house, when Beda went on speaking.

No. 59.—ELLEN PERCY.

"If you do not like to proceed, Miss," she said, "let me go on. I will see Gilderoy—explain to him your fears—and ascertain whether he be able and willing to protect you against any enemies that may present themselves?"

"No, my faithful Beda," I at once answered; "not for worlds would I expose you to any danger which I myself am afraid to dare! Courageous girl, you are always equal to any emergency! We have been together in perils and difficulties before: we will remain together now. Let us proceed."

We continued our path accordingly; and in a few minutes we reached an archway leading into the court where dwelt the object of our visit to this vile neighbourhood. That archway appeared to be the entrance into a cavern of densest blackness: a dead silence prevailed in this particular spot—and instead of that silence, I should even rather have heard the uproarious sounds of revelry which had startled and disgusted me elsewhere.

"Give me your hand, Miss," said Beda; "and I will lead you along. The court is dark—but I know my way thoroughly; I studied it well in the morning."

I had really hesitated through fear: I was now ashamed to display it—particularly after the little colloquy which had taken place between Beda and myself a few minutes back in reference to Black Ned; so I gave her my hand, and she led me into the court. When once the archway was passed under, the gloomy black clouds could be seen over-head, as I looked upward from between two ranges of buildings which were separated by an interval of about four yards, this being the width of the court. And now a feeble glimmering might be discerned through the dingy panes of three or four windows, or through the gaping chinks of some half-dilapidated shutters. But the deep silence still prevailed, as if it were ominous of impending evil. Mischief seemed to be lying in ambush in that dark court, like a wild beast in its cave.

"It is here," said Beda, as she stopped at the door of one of the houses, which only appeared to be two storeys high above the ground floor. "Shall I knock, Miss?"

"Yes," I answered, now summoning all my fortitude to my aid.

Beda knocked accordingly: three or four minutes elapsed before the summons drew any response—then a light which had been previously glimmering through the shutter of the ground-floor window disappeared—and the next moment a thin thread of light was thrown through the keyhole of the door. That door opened: and for a moment I looked in surprise to see who had thus opened it, and by whom the candle was carried; for on a level with my own face I could distinguish no human being — naught but the passage which the light feebly revealed. Instinctively lowering my gaze, I became aware of the presence of a hideous old man of dwarfish proportions. He positively was not more than three feet in stature; and contrary to the general rule which prevails amongst the stunted race, he had a very small head which hung over all on one side—not being so carried habitually, but evidently fixed in that position either by disease or some injury sustained. He had thin grey hair —shaggy overhanging grey brows—and a mouth which was all awry in the same direction as that in which the head bent over. I presently noticed likewise that the arm on the same side was stiff and motionless; so that I concluded the unfortunate wretch had received a paralytic stroke which had thus afflicted him. He was very meanly dressed: his threadbare patched black coat was much too large for him, and the tails actually hung down to his heels. He had a sinister, penetrating, knowing look; and as I glanced down upon him in the manner already described, I encountered his eyes so suddenly, as they were staring up at me, that for an instant I was seized with affright. It was the effect sustained by meeting the gaze of a reptile.

"What do you want?" he inquired, in a quick harsh voice, as he held the candle to the height of the outstretched arm the use of which he possessed; and I saw that he was endeavouring to penetrate with his regards through the thick black veils which covered our countenances.

"Does a person named Gilderoy Hemp live here?" I inquired.

"And if so be he does," said the dwarf, "who may have sent you to ask for him?"

"The deceased Zarah," I answered, in altered and mournful accents.

"Ah! then perhaps you are Miss Percy?" at once exclaimed the old man, now raising himself on his tiptoes in his anxiety to peer up into my countenance.

"Yes—that is my name," I rejoined.

"And the other?" demanded the dwarf, flinging his looks with the rapidity of lightning upon my faithful attendant.

"This is my young friend and companion, Beda," was my response.

"All right!" said the dwarf, grinning with satisfied significancy; so that his distorted mouth seemed to have the most horrible expression that can possibly be imagined, as it revealed a set of large yellow teeth. "Walk this way, Miss Percy. And you, Beda," added the man with a significancy which I regarded as allusive to my faithful dependant's gipsy origin, "have even a better right than your mistress to enter within these walls."

We crossed the threshold: the dwarf closed the front door, and drew a somewhat heavy bolt into its socket. He then threw open a door leading from the passage, and desired us to pass into the room which was thus disclosed to our view. It was a back room: a light was burning upon the table. The place was furnished with some little regard to comfort, though in a humble style; but there was a certain air of cleanliness which I scarcely expected to behold in such a house and in such a neighbourhood. The dwarf, closing the door, left me and Beda alone together: we heard him ascend the staircase—and then all was silent.

"I fancy, Beda," I said in a whisper, "that this place must constitute some species of head-quarters of the Zingari tribes; for that dwarf evidently alluded with emphasis to your special right to enter hither."

"I know, dear Miss, that there are houses in London," interjected Beda, "which the gipsies use as their head-quarters for a variety of purposes. For instance, it is the business of some to assume various disguises, frequent the West End of the town, throw themselves in the way of the servants of wealthy families, and by the exercise of a little ingenuity extract from them whatsoever gossip or tittle-tattle they may have to relate in reference to their masters and mistresses. All the particulars thus elicited are duly chronicled in a book for use on future occasions. It is likewise a favourite practice with these gipsies who go about thus disguised, to throw themselves in the way of nurse-maids in the Parks; and from the lips of those girls much information is obtained in respect to the families in whose service they live."

"And how does this information serve the purposes of the gipsies?" I inquired. "Perhaps it is to enable them to tell fortunes——"

"Precisely so," responded Beda. "The morning newspapers are regularly watched when the London season is over—notes are taken of the aristocratic and wealthy families going out of town to their country-seats—and then, by a reference to the book of records, it is seen what information has been gleaned in respect to such-and-such families. This is communicated to the wandering gipsies in different parts of the country; and by them it is rendered available with their usual tact and ingenuity. Let us suppose, for instance, a nobleman, his wife, and his daughter, living at some grand mansion in Park Lane. From the little-tattle of the domestics it has been ascertained that the daughter favours the suit of some gentleman whose pretensions are not agreeable to her parents. Let us also suppose that he is an officer in the Guards—tall, handsome, and dark-haired—and about three-and-twenty years of age. That noble family goes to its country-seat. Well, some fine morning the young lady is rambling by herself through the park or the fields, when she meets a gipsy-woman who offers to tell her fortune. The young lady indignantly repels the proposal as an insult to her common sense. The gipsy-woman besets her with the usual mystical jargon, in the midst of which she dexterously throws out something which startles the young lady and rivets her attention. Of course it is an allusion to the handsome dark-haired military lover. In nine cases out of ten the result is that the young lady remains to listen: the gipsy-woman, availing herself of the information which she possesses, says everything that is flattering to the hopes and inclinations of the deluded fair one; and it would be strange indeed if the hand of the bewildered and delighted young lady did not cross with a piece of gold the palm of the seeming prophetess. This is one illustration of the manner in which the system works; and your own quick intelligence, Miss," added Beda, "will readily enable you to comprehend how these methods of proceeding may be ramified and diversified in all kinds of ways according to the amount and the nature of the information originally obtained in London."

"Yes—I understand this well enough, Beda," I remarked; "and I am well aware likewise that the world contains an immense number of credulous persons who are easily duped and deceived by such means as these."

We had thus been discoursing for a few minutes in low whispers: silence now supervened: a few more minutes passed—and I began to wonder that we should be left thus long alone. At length I whispered to Beda, "Do you think that the dwarf can be Gilderoy Hemp himself?"

"I should assuredly think not," replied Beda; "or else he would doubtless have at once announced that such was the fact. Besides, everything would lead us to suppose that he is only a menial in the house."

There was again an interval of silence, during which I glanced round the little room in which we were seated. There were several pictures suspended to the walls,—common prints, in cheap black frames, and having a somewhat dingy appearance. One of these pictures hung exactly in the middle of the wall which separated that room from the adjoining one; and under it there was a chest of drawers, with the sloping top contrived to form a writing-desk by letting down a lid upon two sliding pieces of wood that could be drawn out at pleasure. Indeed, it was an old-fashioned *escritoire*; and upon the top of it were several specimens of china ornaments. I was looking at these ornaments from the spot where I was seated, when methought that the picture suspended over the escritoire began to move. I was startled by the idea; and my eyes were now riveted upon that print in its common black-stained frame. Yes—it assuredly moved:—it was opening upward, as if it were a flap or panel with hinges on the upper part. In some degree of alarm I nudged Beda with my elbow: she glanced in the same direction: the picture was now raised completely with a sudden movement—and the countenance of Black Ned for a moment appeared in the aperture which was thus disclosed. The picture was instantaneously lowered again; and so great a consternation seized upon me that it was only this feeling of dismay which prevented a cry from pealing forth from my lips. Beda grasped my hand with violence, hastily whispering, "Be silent, dear Miss! Let us not show that we are afraid!"

"Whose face was it that you saw?" I inquired, also speaking in a low whisper; and I put the question in order to ascertain whether my own idea upon the point was the correct one.

"It was Black Ned," responded Beda: but her countenance was composed and settled—nor in her fine black eyes was there the slightest glittering of uneasiness.

"Let us leave the house, Beda!" I said: "I am sorry, my dear girl, that I should have brought you hither; for my mind is now filled with the direst misgivings!"

"I certainly wish such an incident as this had not occurred," whispered Beda: "for it looks suspicious. But on the other hand, it is no proof that harm is intended, as it is rather an indication of mere curiosity on Black Ned's part. As for leaving the house, rest assured, dear Miss, that this will be impossible if indeed it be the intention of the inmates to detain us here. After all, we cannot suppose that Zarah's friendship in her lifetime towards you and me would have terminated on her deathbed with an act of treachery."

Beda spoke calmly and with a perfect self-possession; but I must confess that I was haunted with vague and fearful misgivings. In a very few moments footsteps were heard descending the stairs—the door of the room was opened—and the dwarf reappeared.

"I am sorry you should be kept waiting," said the hideous monster; "but it was not immediately convenient to attend to your business. Be so kind as to follow me."

He had a candle in his hand. I flung an inquiring look upon Beda; and she at once made me a sign to accompany the dwarf. He opened a door at the end of the passage, and which door I thought would probably lead into some yard at the back of the house; so that I for a moment wondered with renewed apprehension whither he was about to conduct us. The door however disclosed a continuation of the passage: it was rather a long one—at the extremity there was another door—then we ascended a few steps—and it struck me that we had now entered another house. The dwarf, still leading the way, conducted us up a staircase: we reached a small landing, where he threw open a door, and standing aside, bade us pass on. We entered a respectably-furnished room, where we found a venerable-looking old man, whose age could not have been far off from ninety, seated at a table on which were a few books and papers. The door had closed behind us—the dwarf had not followed us into that room—we were alone with that old man ; and my courage at once revived, for I felt assured that I was at length in the presence of the individual whom I had come to seek. In reference to this person I should add that he had a white beard, which threw out the natural swarthiness of his complexion in strong relief, as the light of the candle streamed upon it: his forehead was one mass of wrinkles—his nose was large and of the aquiline form—his mouth had completely fallen in through the loss of all his teeth: but it was not difficult to perceive that his profile must have once been handsome. His thin spare form was enveloped in a somewhat shabby dressing-gown of cloth with blue and black stripes—or rather I should say a species of plaid : a black silk skull cap was upon the table, as well as a large pair of horn spectacles with great circular glasses. He was sitting in a large arm-chair, from which he did not move as we entered : but he bowed with an air of grave patronising solemnity as if he were a personage of authority.

"Be seated," he said; and his voice was clear and firm, neither mumbling through the loss of his teeth, nor tremulous with old age. "You are Miss Percy," he continued, fixing upon me the dark eyes which still retained much of the fire that must have been vivid in his earlier years, and which were still keen and penetrating. "And you are, Beda, who on more occasions than one rendered essential services to the deceased Zarah?"

"I am that same Beda," replied the girl. "I need not tell you that I am of the same Zingari race to which you belong; and therefore I am confident that beneath this roof my beloved mistress and myself are in perfect security."

"Why should you doubt it ?" inquired the old man, turning somewhat in his chair to fix a still more penetrating gaze upon Beda.

"I will answer you frankly," she responded. "There was a little circumstance which for a moment seemed calculated to engender suspicion. We were shown into a room where we beheld a picture lifted up—a countenance looked in upon us—and we recognised a man who has no very great reason to entertain a friendly feeling towards us."

"You mean Black Ned ?" said the white-bearded individual. "Yes—I knew that he was in the house : he is even now waiting to see me upon business. You have been alarmed by a display of impertinent curiosity on his part—that is all. Believe me——"

"I cannot admit," interrupted Beda, "that I was exactly alarmed ; for I had faith in the promises and assurances which poor Zarah upon her deathbed gave my mistress."

"And you were right to put faith in those assurances," rejoined the old man. "I know the cause of animosity which Black Ned has against you : but beneath this roof he is powerless to injure you ; and I will presently speak to him in a way which shall disarm him of all resentment for the future. Alas! woe was it to Zarah, that forsaking the habits, the manners, and the creed of her race, she should have aspired to become the fine lady! Had she been without this fatal ambi-

tion, she might now be in the enjoyment of life, blooming in her marvellous beauty—with hundreds of our faithful tribe ready to succour her in all legitimate undertakings, and to do her bidding. She might be free and happy : but now she is a cold corpse! Alas, poor Zarah! I knew her from her birth—I loved her as if she were my own child ; and even though she renounced her race and her creed, thereby violating the laws which govern us, yet was I ready and willing to use my power on her behalf or in obedience to her dictates. And in the same way, Miss Percy, that I had undertaken to perform a certain thing according to her desire, I am still prepared to carry it out ; for it is in reference to this that you have sought me ?"

"Then, you," I said, "must be Gilderoy Hemp ? and it is you that are to succour me in the recovery of my lost fortune ?"

The old man bowed an affirmative response to these questions. He then consulted a memorandum-book which lay upon the table before him; and he said, "I suppose I may take it for granted that the deceased Zarah explained to you the conditions on which I will act on your behalf. I will undertake to compel Mr. Parks to surrender up the fortune of which he plundered you; but I will not consent to become a party to the handing him over to the grasp of the law. On the contrary, I expressly stipulate that when once he shall have rendered you an act of justice in respect to the restoration of that fortune, it shall be considered that his punishment is sufficient and that an adequate atonement will have been made."

"I pledged myself to this effect to Zarah," I said; "and though I candidly confess that for many reasons I regret the promise which under the influence of my distress and affliction I made at the time, yet I consider the vow to be sacred, and by no subterfuge will I seek to evade it."

"You speak fairly, Miss Percy," replied Gilderoy; "and I repose the fullest faith in your assurances. On the present occasion I have nothing more to say to you : but within a few days all shall be accomplished. I know that your dramatic engagements occupy particular evenings in the week : be so good as to intimate those when your time is at your own disposal ?"

I mentioned the evenings : and Gilderoy, putting on his great pair of horn spectacles, entered the *memoranda* in his book.

"You must be prepared," he continued, "to obey the summons which you may receive on any of these evenings—and I promise you it shall be an early one—for your presence will be again required here. You have my pledge for your safety and that of your handmaiden : hesitate not therefore to obey the summons when you may receive it! I need scarcely add that inasmuch as I am working in your interest, the seal of inviolable secrecy must rest upon your lips in reference to anything that may pass within these walls."

"I should hold that I was performing a perfidious part," was my response, "if I were to act otherwise :"—then with some little degree of hesitation I took out my purse, saying, "There will doubtless be expenses connected with these proceedings on your part ; and you must permit me to defray them."

"No," rejoined Gilderoy: "I receive not gold nor silver from the hands of one whom the deceased Zarah loved."

He then rose from his seat: and I was astonished at the height of his stature. I had judged that he was tall; but as his form seemed somewhat bowed as he sat in the arm-chair, that posture had concealed his actual height. He now drew himself up to the fulness of his stature: he stood before me erect, at least six feet two inches high. He had a commanding and venerable appearance; and there was a certain grave dignity in his manner which well became a personage exercising power and authority, no matter how that influence had been obtained.

He rang a bell which stood upon a table: the door opened, and the dwarf made his appearance. Gilderoy merely waved his hand to the deformed being, who thereby understood that he was to escort us from the room. Gilderoy bowed with grave affability to me; but he shook Beda by the hand, saying in a kind tone, "I learn that you are faithfully serving a good mistress—continue faithful—but seek not to step beyond the bounds of the sphere in which you are placed; and above all things avoid the temptations of that ambition which proved so fatal to our friend Zarah!"

Having thus spoken, Gilderoy made a sign for us to depart; and we followed the dwarf down the staircase. Instead of conducting us forth by the way we had entered, he led us along the passage with which that staircase immediately communicated—he opened a door—we passed out into the street—and the instant the dwarf had clutched the sovereign which I placed in his hand, that door was closed behind us.

It was not into a dark gloomy court that we thus found egress: it was, as I have said, in a street; and my impression was realised that the establishment of Gilderoy Hemp consisted of two distinct houses communicating by means of the long passage which we had threaded.

"I told you there was no danger, dear Miss," said Beda, "and it was impossible Zarah could have deceived us! Do you not think that the strange old man whose presence we have just left, must really possess the power of accomplishing all he has undertaken?"

"Yes, my dear girl," I replied: "such is indeed the impression the interview has left upon my mind."

While conversing upon the particulars of that interview, Beda and I pursued our way: we speedily issued forth from that neighbourhood—and we reached Great Ormond Street in safety. I retired to rest, wondering by what means Gilderoy would accomplish the task he had undertaken.

But taking leave of this subject for the present, I must now speak more particularly than I have hitherto done of that beautiful French girl Aline Marcy, whom I had gratuitously undertaken to prepare for the stage. I have already said that she was about nineteen or twenty—that she possessed delicate features—and that the expression of her countenance was full of an amiable *naiveté* blended with intelligence. I may now proceed to give a few additional particulars in reference to her personal appearance. Her complexion was re-

markably fair, the purity of her skin being without a blemish; and a slight tint of the carnation rested upon her cheeks. She had a profusion of light brown hair, which she was accustomed to wear in the French fashion then prevalent—turned back from her forehead and clustering in heavy tresses behind her ears. But her eyes were a dark hazel, and the brows were two or three shades darker than the colour of her hair. Fine large eyes were those, shaded by long lashes, — the orbs being habitually full of softness, but sparkling with animation when engaged in the study of the particular dramatic parts in which I was instructing her. Her *nose was not perfectly straight*—it was in the slightest degree *retroussée;* yet it was beautifully formed. The configuration of the mouth was faultless, and it had the sweetest expression that it is possible to conceive. When she smiled, the rosy lips disclosed a set of white well-formed teeth. A little above the middle stature, her figure was symmetry itself,—softly rounded into proportions which promised to become of a more expansive luxuriance at the period of a riper womanhood. She had a very fine bust: but her waist was exceedingly slender —naturally so, without any artificial compressure. I have seldom seen more beautifully formed arms or more exquisitely shaped *feet* and ankles. In disposition she resembled Mary Glentworth, being artless, innocent, and confiding: but her manners had a more exquisite polish than those of Mary. The latter was perfectly lady-like; but it was easy to perceive that she had never experienced an acquaintance with the saloons of fashion—whereas Aline Marcy had that peculiar refinement which seems almost natural to French ladies. Nevertheless, as I have already said, she had been reared in England since her childhood; and though to some little extent she followed the fashions of her native land—such as in the arrangement of her hair— yet she might almost be called an English girl. As for the English language, she spoke it without the slightest foreign accent, and with as much fluency as a native of this country.

She had now been under my tuition for about five weeks; and I had conceived a great affection towards her. In her dramatic studies she progressed so satisfactorily that I now saw no reason why she should not soon think of making her *debut*—for which indeed I had already arranged with Mr. Richards. Mary Glentworth was now likewise studying arduously to prepare herself for the stage; and she took an opportunity of informing Mr. Richards that she also meant to appear under his auspices. Mr. Richards, having a keen eye to business, thought that it would be a grand stroke of theatrical policy if both the young ladies could make their *debut* on the same evening; and Mary Glentworth was delighted at the idea. Aline Marcy, who was good-nature itself, readily agreed to postpone her own appearance until Mary should be sufficiently prepared to present herself to a London audience on the same occasion; and I threw no obstacle in the way. Everything was therefore settled in accordance with this aim; and Aline Marcy herself gave Mary Glentworth lessons when I was otherwise engaged.

Three or four days after my interview with Gilderoy Hemp, I found myself alone with Aline Marcy one forenoon; and in the course of conversation I said to her, "Are you sure that when once you have taken so serious a step as that of appearing upon the stage, you will not regret it?"

"Why should I regret it, my dear Miss Percy?" asked Aline, contemplating me with some degree of surprise.

"I will tell you," I responded; "and I was determined to take an opportunity of speaking to you thus seriously upon the point before you shall have gone too far to retreat. I am not going to compliment you, Aline, when I say that you are a young lady in every sense of the term. You are accomplished—you are beautiful—your manners are refined: if you were the daughter of a duchess, you could not be in this sense superior to what you are. Now, remember that when once you set your foot upon the stage you are risking, if not indeed abdicating, this position; for there is no denying the fact that the social *status* of an actress is more or less held to be an equivocal one——"

"Tell me not so, my dear Miss Percy," interjected Aline, "when I see that you are universally respected and esteemed—everywhere spoken of with deference—courted far more than you wish to be courted—able if you thought fit to visit in the best society——"

"No, my dear Aline," I said; "there you are wrong. The haughty ladies of the English aristocracy might tolerate me—but nothing more. There are a few,—amongst whom is Lady Kelvedon, and likewise my friend Cecilia the Countess of Belgrave—who are on the most friendly terms with me: but as a general rule this is not the case. English ladies cannot forget *the actress*; and knowing such to be the fact, I have always sedulously avoided placing myself in a false position. What I am now saying is on your account. That by your conduct and character you will command the respect and merit the esteem of the world as I do, I have not the slightest doubt: but do not deceive yourself, Aline!—you will no longer remain *a lady* according to the general acceptance of the term! In a word, you will to a certain extent be abdicating your present position. It is this that I am desirous to impress upon you."

"If I possessed a fortune," replied Aline, "or had the chance of possessing one, it might be different. But, as you know, I am dependent either upon the bounty of friends or upon my own exertions. In the former state of dependence I cannot exist: I have my little pride, Miss Percy—but I am sure you will admit that it is only in a sense which is laudable——"

"Oh! nothing can be more laudable," I exclaimed, "than that pride which urges the individual to eat the bread of independence! It was this pride which made me what I am. You have the true dramatic genius, Aline—and your success is certain. Do not therefore for a moment think that I seek to throw a damp upon your spirits. No—Heaven forbid! But I deemed it my duty, as your friend and well-wisher, to speak to you thus seriously—to bring you to envisage as it were your true position, so that you may not now take any step of which you may hereafter repent."

There was a long pause, during which Aline Marcy seemed to be buried in profound reflection; and I surveyed her with a deep interest, not altogether unmingled with mournfulness—for I could not help feeling that it was a pity circumstances should compel that fair creature to descend as it were from the position which she might otherwise so brightly occupy. At length raising her large soft hazel eyes towards my countenance, she asked in a low gentle voice, "Are you sure, my dear Miss Percy, that you have not some reason as yet unexplained for speaking to me as you have been doing?"

I did not immediately answer: I meditated—and then I said, "Perhaps, dear Aline, there may have been something in my thoughts—something suggested by my own experiences of the past ——"

"Do tell me what you mean?" said Mademoiselle Marcy, as I again hesitated.

"I will be candid with you, Aline," I continued: "yes, I will speak openly! At the outset of my own professional career I concealed the secret of my having embraced it, from one who was dear to me—who is still very dear—and it engendered the most threatening complications. Prejudice had to be overcome — painful explanations to be given——"

I stopped short: for there was something in Aline Marcy's countenance which suddenly struck me with the idea that I had touched a chord which was vibrating painfully in her heart. From each hazel eye did a pearly tear-drop start forth: she hastily wiped them from her cheeks; and laying her hand upon mine, she looked up into my countenance with an expression of indescribable sweetness, saying in a low tremulous voice, "I understand you, Miss Percy! Your heart is bestowed upon some one who must be proud and happy in possessing your love? May heaven grant that in all things you shall be blessed and prosperous!"

The very tone in which she spoke, as well as the look that accompanied her words, seemed to indicate that with a species of sympathetic feeling she was wishing me a happiness to which she herself had once aspired but which she sadly felt was no longer within her reach. I pressed the hand that had been laid upon my own; and I said, "Now, perhaps, my dear Aline, you begin to comprehend wherefore I seized the present opportunity to address you in so serious a manner? I knew nothing of your secrets—I did not seek to penetrate them. But I thought within myself that it was scarcely possible that one so beautiful, so accomplished, and so fascinating as you are, could have failed to win the affection of some one whose honourable love you might reciprocate. And then methought, Aline, that if you happened to be taking this step either without his knowledge or contrary to his wish, there might be in store for you the same bitter experiences which at one time marked my own career! Believe me, therefore, that it was for the most friendly purpose I addressed you so seriously."

"Oh, I appreciate all your kindness, dearest Ellen!" exclaimed the grateful girl; "and as you have given me your confidence, I will give you mine in return!"

She paused for a few moments—bashfully hung down her head—and then, with her eyes still bent upon the carpet, she continued thus in a low voice:—

"Yes, Ellen—there has been some one who told me of his own love and who asked me for mine in return. And he did not ask in vain! I loved him——I love him still——but all is at an end between us!"

Again she paused: her countenance was averted —but I saw that her bosom heaved with a silent convulsing sob: and I warmly pressed the hand which I still retained in mine own.

"It was no fault of his," she presently continued, "that everything was broken off between us. His pecuniary means were limited; and though he had wealthy relatives, yet for certain reasons he had no expectations in that quarter. As for myself, I was penniless and dependent on the bounty of friends. In the fulness of his generous love—in the magnanimity of his disposition —he would have wedded me; for he declared that by dint of the strictest economy his means would be ample enough for us both. I knew the contrary; and I would not reward so much generous love on his part by selfishness on mine own. No! I would not make him feel the bitterness of poverty by espousing me! I explained my motives. Two months have elapsed since that last interview took place——we parted—with what feelings I leave you to imagine: but I felt that I had done my duty—and the approval of my own conscience has sustained me ever since."

"And did you tell him," I gently inquired, "that you purposed to seek the stage as a means of eating the bread of independence?"

"Yes—I dealt frankly with him on all points," replied Aline. "Oh! it was with the most passionate entreaties he conjured me to alter my decision and consent to become his wife; and it was with the bitterest anguish in my own heart that I implored him to consider everything to be at an end between us. I told him that I loved him too much to permit him to make such great sacrifices on my account: I conjured him likewise not to seek to alter my decision, nor to renew the pain of that interview by meeting me again. And since that time I have not seen him—I have not heard of him!"

I had listened with the deepest interest to this narrative, which afforded me a striking illustration of the generosity and self-sacrificing magnanimity of Aline Marcy's disposition. But as I reflected gravely upon the subject, I said, "Is not everything you have told me a reason, my dear Aline, why you should pause and hesitate ere you take the final step which may render your severance from him whom you love, complete and irrevocable? It is not wealth that constitutes happiness: he himself assured you that though his means were limited, yet they would suffice for both——"

"Do not endeavour to persuade me, my dear Ellen," interrupted Mademoiselle Marcy, "to reconsider my decision. Oh! it is such representations as these that weaken the purpose——and mine must not be weakened! He whom I loved is devoted to the profession to which he belongs; and this profession requires that he should maintain a certain appearance. Such an appearance he could not support with limited means:—shall I therefore become the cause of thus limiting them? No, no!—heaven forbid! Such conduct would not be a proof of love on my part, but an evidence of selfishness. To see his pride wounded by the necessity of making those shifts and contrivances to which one is reduced by a limited purse—to see him unable to join in the recreations of his companions—to know that he felt the cold

iron of poverty entering into his soul——Oh! this would be more than I could endure! On all these things I reflected; and thus was my decision taken. Besides," added Aline abruptly, "that decision has been proclaimed—but alas! it produced words of excitement and anger at parting; for he accused me of a want of love; and I—I, Ellen, preferred to rest under the weight of a charge which crushed my very soul with affliction, rather than abandon a decision which was formed conscientiously and adopted after the most serious self-communing!"

There was again a brief pause, and then Aline said in a low soft voice, "Therefore you perceive, Ellen, that even if I were not disposed to revoke that decision of mine, it is too late! The bonds are broken—and it was I who severed them! He has not again sought me—he has not communicated with me—and I have every reason to believe that he has made no endeavour to ascertain whither I went after I quitted the home that was so generously afforded me by Lady Kelvedon's parents, Mr. and Mrs. Wyvill. Therefore he may be angry—he may really believe that I loved him not to the extent which my assurances conveyed: or else, on the other hand, he may have listened to the dictates of reason, and he may have satisfied himself that what I did was for the best!"

"Your conduct, Aline, has been most noble and generous—most self-denying and admirable," I exclaimed. "May heaven grant that you never will have reason to repent of it!"

"I do not tell you, Ellen, that I am happy," replied the beautiful girl; "but my soul is resigned to its destiny—and in the consciousness of having performed one's duty there is a certain reward."

Here the conversation was terminated by the announcement that Lady Kelvedon's carriage had arrived to take Aline Marcy to Eaton Square.

In the evening of that same day, as I and Mary Glentworth were seated at the dinner-table, a note was brought in by the servant; and on opening it I read the following words, written in a bold round hand:—"To-night at nine o'clock your presence is required. Fail not!"

I knew full well from whom this missive came: it was a summons from the gipsy patriarch Gilderoy.

CHAPTER LXXVII.

THE ACCUSED.

PRECISELY at nine o'clock Beda and myself, dressed in our plainest apparel, and closely veiled as on the former occasion, turned into the dark court forming the approach to the establishment of Gilderoy Hemp. We had at first thought of seeking admittance by the door which had afforded us egress into the adjacent street; but inasmuch as on the occasion referred to, we had received no intimation to the effect that we might adopt this course, we concluded that it would be better to proceed by the route which we were now taking. This time it was without the slightest hesitation as well as without fear that I repaired to Gilderoy's abode,—although I was more or less in a nervous state of anxiety as to the means which might be adopted to compel Mr. Parks to disgorge the wealth of which he had plundered me.

Beda knocked at the door; and the summons was immediately answered by the hideous-looking dwarf, who carried a light in his hand, and who gave a significant grin on beholding us. We were conducted into the same back-room to which we had in the first instance been shown on the former occasion of our visit to that place. The dwarf left us; and we were again alone together.

In a few minutes the dwarf returned; and he requested us to follow him. He led us up the staircase belonging to that house in which we found ourselves; for the reader will remember that the premises tenanted by Gilderoy consisted of two houses, looking into different streets, but connected, as I have before described. On reaching the first-floor landing, the dwarf paused; and turning to me, he said, " You remember, Miss Percy, the vow of inviolable secrecy you made in respect to everything which you may behold within these walls? I now require your equally solemn pledge that you will interfere in nothing that may pass before your eyes—that you will remain altogether silent—and that you will so far conquer your feelings as to give way to no excitement during the progress of those things which are about to be done."

I hesitated—and I said, " Your words frighten me! If there be aught very terrible—if cruelty or torture be had recourse to——"

" If you hesitate, Miss Percy," interrupted the dwarf, " you can at once depart—and nothing more shall be done. But by such conduct you will be proving that you have no faith in the venerable Gilderoy; and you will be making a most ungrateful return for everything that he is doing in your behalf."

" All this is so vague that it terrifies me!" I said. " You have not promised that personal torture is not to be had recourse to in order to compel that wretched man to render up his usurped wealth; and vile though he be, yet I could not stand by and patiently behold the infliction of torture. No! I would sooner leave the house at once!"

" Do as you think fit, Miss Percy," said the dwarf. " I have no power to give you any further assurances."

" Suffer me to see the venerable Gilderoy?" I exclaimed.

" I will communicate your wish," rejoined the dwarf. " Have the goodness to accompany me down stairs again, to the room from which I have conducted you."

Beda and I accordingly descended the stairs; and in a few moments we again found ourselves alone together in the little room hung with the shabby-looking pictures.

" You do not blame me, Beda," I said, in a low whisper, " for my refusal to give the pledge so vaguely and so mysteriously required of me?"

" Oh, no!" she responded; " I admire you, Miss, for the generosity which prompted hesitation. But still I do not think that Gilderoy would have recourse to such dreadful means—or that if such were his purpose, he would have sent for you hither to witness the spectacle."

" Such also is my hope," I rejoined. " But you know your own people better than I——"

I stopped short, my gaze riveted with consternation and dismay upon a certain object. Beda's looks were immediately flung in the same direction; and an ejaculation of surprise burst from her lips. The picture above the *escritoire* was raised; and there was the countenance of the old harridan, Dame Betty, filling up the aperture like the hideous head of Medusa set in a frame! Indescribably malicious, wicked, and fiendlike seemed the haggard wrinkled countenance; and the reptile eyes were fixed with malignant keenness upon us. Then the picture suddenly fell; and the hideous apparition vanished from our view. I felt that I was as pale as death; for the thought struck me that the presence of that old wretch within those walls boded no good to Beda and myself; and once more did all the most horrible suspicions of impending treachery flame up in my mind, as vivid as when on the previous occasion I had seen the countenance of Black Ned looking down from the same aperture.

I had scarcely begun to recover from the fright thus caused me—and I was about to say something to Beda—when the door opened, and the dwarf again made his appearance.

" I am instructed by the venerable Gilderoy," he immediately said, " to assure you, Miss Percy —and you likewise, Beda—that he is incapable of inflicting torture upon the person of the lawyer Parks. He has no such design. You will now follow me."

" In the first place tell me," I said, " who is in the adjacent room?"

" I don't know," responded the dwarf doggedly.

" But I know," I rejoined; " and I will not remain in the house——"

" Do as you like, Miss Percy," interrupted the dwarf, with an air of the supremest indifference. " The door of the house shall be opened at your command; and if I was Gilderoy I should be only too glad to get rid of you—for you seem to want others to render you all sorts of services, but you give yourself all kinds of airs——"

" Cease this impertinence!" interrupted Beda, in a tone so imperious and dignified that the stunted being looked as if he were overawed in a moment, and he gazed with surprise and dismay upon the girl's beautiful countenance, which was flushed with indignation, while her luminous eyes appeared to be darting forth fires:—then turning to me, Beda said in a hasty whisper, " Trust to the patriarch Gilderoy! trust to him, dear Miss, I conjure you!"

Beda's advice always had its weight with me, more especially when it related to anything connected with the people of the race to which she belonged: and with only a moment's hesitation I said, " Be it so, my dear girl!"—then addressing myself to the dwarf, I added, " Lead the way: I am prepared to follow."

" And the pledge?" said the deformed being, who now spoke sullenly and doggedly,—" the pledge which I have demanded of you, and which the patriarch Gilderoy exacts?"

" Give it," hastily whispered Beda. " Take my word that everything will be for the best!"

" I pledge myself thus far," I said,—" that I

will remain altogether silent and abstain from every species of interference, so long as no cruel outrage of a physical nature—no infliction of torture or corporeal pain, in reference to the culprit Parks, shall be inflicted in my presence. Will that vow suffice?"

"I suppose it must," answered the dwarf sullenly. "And now follow me."

I glanced for an instant towards the picture over the *escritoire :* but it remained in its place—the hideous countenance of the old hag did not again make its appearance. The dwarf conducted Beda and me up the staircase ; and on reaching the landing, he opened a door which revealed a passage. I by this time comprehended enough of the geography of the premises to be aware that this passage was precisely over the one that had been threaded on a former occasion to conduct us into the other house. But I was now to learn more of the arrangements of those

premises ; and I may as well at once state that the two back yards of the two houses had been almost completely built over, leaving merely at each end of these intermediate buildings a sufficient interval for light to be admitted into whichsoever rooms had windows looking upon the open spaces thus left. These facts I presently comprehended from the position of such parts of the premises as I was about to make an acquaintance with.

Having proceeded some half-a-dozen paces along the passage, the dwarf opened a door, and stood aside for myself and Beda to enter. A feeble light was burning inside a spacious apartment, the aspect of which at the first glance made me recoil with a cold shudder. But Beda gently pushed me : I crossed the threshold—my faithful dependant was close behind—and the dwarf entering last, closed the door. He hurried us behind a black curtain which was at the extremity of the room close by that door. The curtain fell again into its place; and Beda and I sat down in the chairs which we found behind that sable screen. There were two round holes in the curtain, each about six inches in diameter; and through these we could command a view of the spectacle that was before us. This I shall now proceed to describe.

I have already said that it was a spacious apartment. The walls were hung with black; and at the extremity there was a species of raised platform, on which sat a figure in an arm-chair. This figure was clad in a sable robe, and had a high pointed black cap upon his head; indeed it was shaped like that which in pictures is assigned to astrologers. But by the white beard and the swarthy countenance it was by no means difficult to recognise the patriarch Gilderoy. At a table placed in front of the platform, at a little distance from it, and covered with black cloth, sat a person whose office was evidently that of clerk to this tribunal. On black-covered benches on either side were several gipsy men—perhaps two dozen in all —dressed in their usual apparel, and all maintaining a solemn silence. In the middle of the room was a species of dock, with a railing and an ascent of three steps. Two candles were burning on the clerk's table: and this was all the light which prevailed in the apartment. A small portion of the room had been screened off by the curtain, evidently to enable myself and Beda to witness the proceedings, without ourselves being observed. Behind us was a window; and a glance through it showed another window. This latter was one of the back ones of the house; and the two were at such a short distance that persons might shake hands from one to the other. It was thus that I comprehended how the back yards had been almost completely built over.

I must confess that the aspect of this tribunal produced a strange effect upon me; and I had strong scruples about remaining there. It was only too evident that the patriarch Gilderoy was arrogating to himself a power altogether beyond that of the regular law of the land; and I knew not whether it might not constitute an offence, or at least a great impropriety on my part, to become an accomplice in such proceedings, and to suffer Beda to remain in the same position.

"I do not think I shall stay," I whispered to her; "for either this must be a mockery of justice —or else if the proceedings take a serious turn——"

"Hush, Miss! hush!" said Beda. "Hear you those footsteps in the passage?"

I remained silent: for at the moment that Beda spoke, there was the tread of several persons in the adjoining passage. The door was almost immediately opened by the dwarf who had posted himself there; and four gipsy men entered, conducting Mr. Parks in their midst. Although the light was so feeble, yet it was sufficient to show that the lawyer's countenance was as pale as death, and that his features were literally smitten with an expression of wild affright, as on crossing the threshold he obtained a view of this tribunal. It was a downright agony of alarm—a mortal terror which seized upon the wretch; and his gipsy-guards were compelled to bear him into the dock, for his limbs were evidently sinking under him. On being released from their hold, he clutched the rail to sus-

tain himself; and then he faltered forth, "Why am I brought here? who has dared to do this?"

"It is vain for you, Thomas Parks," said Gilderoy, in a solemn voice, "to question the authority of those, who, as you perceive, have the power to enforce their will."

"But tell me what I have done? whom have I offended?" exclaimed the lawyer, now becoming somewhat the master of himself. "Inveigled here by an old woman under the pretext that she had important business to communicate, I find a snare set for me——"

"Silence!" interposed Gilderoy; "and listen! If your conscience tells you that you are sinless, you have no occasion for apprehension; for I emphatically proclaim that in all these proceedings you shall experience the same justice here as if you were in the presence of one of the legally constituted tribunals of the country."

"Perhaps it is all a jest," said Mr. Parks, clutching at the idea; "and you are making merry at my expense? If so——"

But he stopped short, evidently smitten with the conviction that it was very far from being a jest, and that there was a terrible earnestness in the sombre serious looks of the men whom he saw on his right and on his left, as well as in the grave stern countenance of the black-robed self-constituted judge.

"Listen to the accusation which is made against you!" resumed Gilderoy. "You, Thomas Parks, are charged with having been a direct accessory to the foul and mysterious murder of an old gentleman named Forsyth——"

The manner in which the wretched attorney started was plainly visible to Beda and myself behind the curtain. It seemed as if he were suddenly galvanized; and again he clung to the rail for support. We could not see his countenance, for his back was towards us: but that his form was thus shaken by the quick convulsive spasm shooting through it, there could be no doubt.

"And this foul murder," continued Gilderoy, "was perpetrated towards the close of the year 1834, in the town of Leeds. The indictment further charges you, Thomas Parks, with having aided and abetted your mother, the housekeeper of the deceased, to commit the crime in order that the fortune of the deceased, amounting to the sum of thirty thousand pounds, should fall into your hands, the additional crime of forgery being perpetrated to consummate the iniquity. These are the charges which are brought against you; and you are asked in the usual manner, whether you plead *Guilty* or *Not Guilty?*"

It seemed as if during this last speech from the lips of the venerable Gilderoy, Mr. Parks had time to collect himself again; and there is no doubt that a sense of his position made him wind up his courage to the utmost for the purpose of making one last desperate stand against the present proceedings.

"I refuse to plead!" he exclaimed: "I do not acknowledge your authority! You know as well as I that you are a lawless tribunal: and by the look of you, you are a still more lawless horde! Do you know what a series of offences you are committing against me, all constituting the most serious misdemeanours? You are accomplices in the fact of my being inveigled by false pretences to this place—you have detained me by force—you are keeping me here against my will — you are putting me in bodily fear—it is an assault and battery—conspiracy—violent abduction——"

"Be silent!" exclaimed Gilderoy. "If you have naught to advance but this tissue of declamatory verbiage, which produces not the slightest effect upon us, you had better hold your peace : we take upon ourselves the responsibility of what we are doing—even as you, Thomas Parks, have taken upon yourself still more frightful responsibilities, if the details of the indictment against you be correct. There is however this difference—that with *you* the day of reckoning is come, whereas *we* repose in the fullest confidence that no such day will ever come for us on account of these proceedings !"

"Be not too sure !" retorted Parks. "I instantaneously demand my liberty; and if it is refused, I will raise such a clamour—I will shout for assistance——"

"Enough of this child's play !" interrupted Gilderoy. "Shout if you please : the walls will beat back the sounds of your voice, even though it be raised to the loudest pitch—and you will benefit not yourself ! But inasmuch as for mercy's sake I am disposed to bear with you patiently yet a little while, seeing how awful is the position in which you stand——"

"Awful?" said Mr. Parks : and the word appeared to strike him with more or less consternation.

"Yes, awful !" repeated Gilderoy solemnly ; "for it is a matter of life or death with you—and if not death, at least the fullest atonement !"

"No, no—you dare not threaten my life !" cried the wretched man, whose courage was abandoning him, and who glanced around with terrified and haggard looks.

"Talk not of what we dare do, or what we dare not do," said Gilderoy sternly : "for perhaps, if you look into your own heart, you know to what an extent human daring can go for purposes of evil:—how far greater, then, may be its range for purposes of good ! And our purpose is a good one ! But I was ere now on the point of giving you a word of salutary counsel. Listen, therefore ! You threatened to cry and to shout with a hope of summoning hither the officers of justice. Do you know what would be the consequences if you succeeded ? Instead of remaining to be judged by this tribunal, which has the power to enter into terms with you if the result should render you a suppliant for mercy, you would be transferred into the presence of another tribunal, —a tribunal whose legality you would not dare challenge—whose authority you would not venture to question,—a tribunal which would have a stern and solemn duty to perform, and which if the result were against you, could negotiate no terms—could show no mercy ! Now, Thomas Parks, have I at length succeeded in awakening you to a due sense of your position ? and will you plead to the indictment which is brought against you ?"

There was a silence—an awful silence of nearly a minute, during which both Beda and myself continued narrowly to watch the prisoner through the holes perforated in the curtain. Though the light was so dim, yet were we enabled to discern sufficient evidences of the agitation under which he laboured. There were nervous spasmodic twitchings, so to speak, throughout his entire frame; his hands kept clutching at the rail ; he first rested the weight of his body on one leg, then upon the other ; and at last he said, "I am innocent ! I did nothing of all that is imputed to me ! I have deeds to prove that certain transactions have taken place betwixt myself and Miss Percy—she has acknowledged the validity of the will—you dare not say it is a forgery—and if it were valid, what interest had I in making away with the old man Forsyth ?"

"Be not too sure of all these matters, whereupon you seem to rely," said Gilderoy, in a tone of marked significancy. "When a man is placed in a certain position, the ground upon which his feet rest, and which he flatters himself is firm as a rock, becomes a quicksand to engulph him."

"What do you mean ?" asked the lawyer, his accents now proving that he was again labouring under a vague and fearful consternation. "Who are you, that you set yourself up for a judge ?"

"No matter who I am," rejoined Gilderoy ; "it is sufficient that I have the power to judge you—and that power I am exercising. Let there be no more waste of time : you have exhausted my patience; and as you have proclaimed yourself innocent, the declaration will be taken as tantamount to a plea of *Not Guilty*. The trial shall proceed."

There was again an awful silence ; and I should observe that I had now not the slightest inclination to leave my seat or to quit the apartment. Indeed, all the scruples that for an instant I had entertained, became absorbed in the sensation of profound interest with which I had listened to the opening proceedings on the introduction of Mr. Parks to the dock of the tribunal. So far as those proceedings as yet extended, Beda and I had watched them with suspended breath : we were both motionless as statues behind that sable curtain which concealed us from the view of all the rest. As the darkness was nearly complete behind that curtain, a feeble glimmering only penetrating through the window, the holes could not be perceived by any one in the body of the apartment; and thus, when Mr. Parks had in an agony of affright looked round the room, gazing behind him as well as on every side, his eyes were not attracted particularly towards the curtain.

"Is not this solemn and awful ?" whispered Beda to me during the last pause to which I have alluded.

"Little did I anticipate such a scene as this, Beda !" I answered, also speaking in the lowest tone possible. "The agony of mind which the wretched man is suffering, becomes already no mean chastisement for the odious crimes of which he has been guilty !"

"Call the first witness !" said the individual who performed the duties of Clerk of the Court.

The dwarf opened the door and looked out into the passage for a moment : almost immediately afterwards a young man entered. I immediately recognised him; and I whispered to Beda, "The affair does indeed become more and more serious. This is Mr. Moss, the lawyer's clerk."

We both narrowly watched Mr. Parks ; and we saw him start with affright as Moss thus made his appearance : but instantaneously becoming colected again, he exclaimed, "It is well that you are here, Mr. Moss, to become a witness of the violence to which I am subjected!"

Moss made no reply, and did not even look at his master; so that I felt convinced he had been by some means or another won over to mine own interests. The dwarf conducted him towards the clerk's table, placing him in such a position that his countenance might be seen by all present as he gave his testimony.

"Mr. Moss," said the Clerk of the Court, "do you remember any particular occurrences in reference to the prisoner Thomas Parks, and certain deeds in which a young lady of the name of Percy was interested?"

"I remember such occurrences," answered Moss: "they happened on the 5th of October of last year—consequently upwards of seven months back."

"And what were those occurrences?" inquired the Clerk.

"On that day," resumed Moss, "I witnessed a couple of deeds in the private office of Mr. Parks. Miss Percy and a gentleman were present. One of those documents was a conveyance from Mr. Parks to Miss Percy of a certain house at Leeds; and this was of course signed by Mr. Parks himself."

"To whom had that house belonged?" inquired the Clerk.

"To Miss Percy's deceased grandfather, Mr. Forsyth," was the response.

"Has Miss Percy taken possession of that house?"

"Yes—she has been to Leeds and taken formal possession of it. This I know for certain, as Mr. Parks received a letter to that effect from Mr. Jacobs, a house agent at Leeds, who had the letting of the premises."

"And what was the nature of the second document which you witnessed on the 5th of October?" inquired the Clerk of the Court.

"It was a deed which Miss Percy signed," answered Moss. "Its contents were to the effect that she recognised the validity of a will purporting to be that of Mr. Forsyth, and which had been administered to by Mrs. Parks, the mother of Thomas Parks who stands there. All the provisions of that will were duly set forth in the deed—and, in short, it was a kind of release given to Mr. Parks, he telling me at the time that it was an amicable arrangement to avoid a Chancery suit that would prove ruinous to both parties."

"And was there not a cheque given upon that occasion?" asked the Clerk of the Court.

"There was," responded Moss.

"And now," said the Clerk, "have you anything more to tell us in reference to these transactions?"

"Yes," replied Moss. "Something took place on the following day—namely, the 6th of October."

"And what was that?" inquired the Clerk, putting these questions from written *memoranda* which lay before him.

"I must here observe," said Mr. Moss, "that I had my suspicion that all was not quite right. When I was called up to witness those deeds on the 5th of October, there seemed something suspicious in my employer's manner—I can't

exactly describe what—but still I was not altogether satisfied. I feared that Miss Percy was being deceived; and I had a great respect for that young lady: I was uneasy on her account. Therefore, when she called at the office on the ensuing day, accompanied by the same gentleman as before, I listened at the door, and I learnt certain facts——"

"And what were those facts," inquired the Clerk of the Court.

"A cheque had been given to Miss Percy, as I have already said; but this cheque had proved to be a blank slip of paper. Some altercation took place—I was summoned and sent off into the City to get Mr. Parks's pass-book from the bankers—and on my return I again listened at the door, when from what ensued no doubt remained in my mind that some deed of villany had been perpetrated. Yet it was not for me to say a word upon the subject; for if Miss Percy could not adduce any evidence to prove the fraud, my bare proclamation of a suspicion would have still less availed her purpose, while it would only have lost me my situation."

"You therefore held your peace," said Gilderoy, now interposing in the examination; "and no one can blame you for doing so under the circumstances."

"Have you anything more to tell us, Mr. Moss?" inquired the Clerk of the Court, again referring to his notes.

"Yes," was the response. "In consequence of certain communications made to me within the last few days——"

"I will here at once admit," said the Clerk of the Court, addressing himself to the prisoner Parks, "that it was I who made these communications to Mr. Moss. Proceed, Sir," he added, turning towards the witness.

"I was about to observe," continued Moss, "that in consequence of the communications you made to me, I searched in Mr. Parks's office when he was absent: I discovered a bottle of ink, which was altogether different from the ink used in his establishment. I produce it. Here it is."

Thus speaking, he placed the ink-bottle upon the table.

"And what have you discovered in reference to this ink?" asked the Clerk.

"You yourself may test it, Sir," answered Moss. "I wrote you a note with that ink this morning, and sealed it with a particular seal."

"I received the note," said the Clerk: "I perused its contents—and I remember them. The writing was quite plain and legible—the ink in which it was penned was of the usual blackness. Here is the note:"—and he took a letter from beneath the papers on the table.

"Yes—that is it," said Mr. Moss; "I recognise it by the seal."

"But the writing on the envelope has disappeared," said the Clerk of the Court: and then opening the letter itself, he exclaimed, "The writing inside has likewise vanished! it is a blank piece of paper!"

There was a moment's sensation on the part of the gipsy auditory seated on the benches; and Beda whispered to me, "Look at the guilty Parks!—he trembles in every limb! his guilt is being thoroughly brought home to him!"

"Yes," I answered; "these proceedings are indeed calculated to strike terror into his soul! A thought has struck me, Beda! Perchance, after all, the presence of that old hag Dame Betty is portentous only to the cause of Mr. Parks, and implies no danger to us?"

"Look at all that is passing, dear Miss," rejoined Beda: "and then reflect whether the venerable Gilderoy would suffer the slightest injury to be done unto you?"

I had not time to make any reply; for the proceedings were being continued.

"Have you anything more to communicate, Mr. Moss?" inquired the Clerk of the Court.

"Yes," responded Moss: "I have one more fact to mention. From the communications made to me by you, Sir, I felt convinced that my original suspicion was correct, and that Miss Percy had been foully wronged. I saw that she had been duped into the signature of that deed of release—or rather, I should say, of amicable arrangement—which I witnessed. I therefore had no hesitation in searching amongst my employer's papers—I discovered that deed—I abstracted it—I brought it here. I produce it!"

Thus speaking, he laid the document upon the table, and both I and Beda again noticed that the prisoner Parks was seized with a violent agitation.

"I have nothing more to state," said Mr. Moss.

"Thomas Parks," exclaimed Gilderoy, "you are now at liberty to put any questions to this witness."

But the lawyer answered not a word: he maintained a dogged silence, as he leant over the rail, with his eyes bent downward.

Moss retired to a seat; and Gilderoy said in a loud voice, "Call the next witness!"

The dwarf again opened the door, and in a few moments Dame Betty made her appearance. That she was thoroughly prepared for the scene which she was to behold on entering, was sufficiently apparent from the nature of the glance of indifference which she flung around her. But then she looked more slowly and scrutinizingly about the apartment, perhaps expecting to find myself and Beda there. If so, in this she was disappointed: at least I am very certain that she had no suspicion of the fact of our concealment behind the curtain. She was much better dressed than ever I had before seen her; she supported herself with a stick; and her countenance indicated no degree of trouble. The dwarf conducted her to the same spot near the table where Moss had previously stood; and Gilderoy addressing her, said, "Woman, remember everything that has already been said to you, and tell the truth upon the present occasion!"

"And do you, Gilderoy," she answered, "solemnly renew in the presence of these witnesses the pledge which you gave me of my own safety——"

"That pledge is renewed," interrupted Gilderoy; "and now let the proceedings take their course."

"You know the man who stands there?" said the Clerk of the Court, indicating Thomas Parks.

"Yes—I know him well enough," replied Dame Betty. "There is no use in making a long tale of it—I know what I have to say—and I will say it at once. I met that man at York some eight or nine years ago: he spoke to me on a particular subject—we soon understood each other—and I sold him certain lozenges——"

"And those lozenges," said the Clerk,—"what did they contain?"

"Poison," rejoined the harridan.

"Do you believe," continued the Clerk, "that the deceased Mr. Forsyth was put to death by means of those poisoned lozenges?"

"I am sure of it," responded the Dame: "for immediately after his death I met Parks at Leeds: I said to him, 'So you have done the business:' he did not deny it—but he gave me an additional sum of money. That is all I have to state."

"Prisoner," said Gilderoy, "have you any questions to put to this witness?"

But Mr. Parks still maintained a dogged silence. There was a pause of nearly a minute; and then Gilderoy said, "Let the woman depart."

Dame Betty seemed only too glad to avail herself of this permission; she hobbled towards the door, which the dwarf opened; and he accompanied her from the room. Ten minutes elapsed before he returned.

"The case," said the Clerk of the Court, "is now complete against the prisoner Thomas Parks."

"I will make a few observations upon it," said Gilderoy: "and the prisoner may afterwards, if he think fit, give any explanation or say anything in his defence. The case, so far as it has gone, Thomas Parks, tells grievously against you. You purchased poison—the deceased Mr. Forsyth died under suspicious circumstances—and from the evidence of the last witness it would appear that his death was caused by that poison. You had a direct and most iniquitous interest in thus cutting off that old man. Years elapsed—and in your transactions with Miss Percy you were guilty of a tissue of frauds which are proved by your own clerk. There can be no doubt that the will to which your mother administered, and which is now at Doctors' Commons, was a forgery. Perhaps I need not remind you that if Miss Percy were here present, she might give additional evidence, proving that you had acknowledged that will to be a forgery: but it has suited my purpose to conduct the present proceedings without requiring the testimony of that young lady. The fortune of which your mother and yourself plundered her, amounted to thirty thousand pounds in sterling money; but with the accumulations of interest down to the date of the 5th of October, the total sum was estimated at thirty-six thousand three hundred pounds. It may be useful to mention these facts: but before I proceed any further, I await anything that you may have to urge in explanation or in your defence."

The lawyer still maintained a dogged silence; and I said in a low tone to Beda, "He evidently waits to see what is to follow. I myself am at a loss to comprehend how Gilderoy will now proceed: for if the wretched criminal refuse to make restoration of my fortune, how can he be compelled to do so? Gilderoy has pledged himself not to have recourse to torture—and I fear that the threat of handing Parks over to another tribunal will not have its weight with him."

"Let us see," said Beda. "Depend upon it that Gilderoy has not gone thus far without being fully conscious of the power to carry the matter to an issue as decisive as the proceedings have hitherto been solemnly and awfully regular."

There was this time a very long pause, during which Gilderoy waited to see if Parks would urge anything in his defence: but as the prisoner still maintained a dogged silence, the venerable old gipsy proceeded in the following strain:—

"It remains for you," addressing those who were seated upon the benches, "to decide whether the man who stands before you has received a fair trial this night. If you be of opinion that the trial is a fair one, you will decide whether he be guilty, or not guilty, of the various crimes laid to his charge?"

Gilderoy ceased; and all those men who were seated upon the benches, exclaimed as if with one accord, "He is guilty!"

At this point the interest which I felt in the proceedings was wound up to an almost painful degree of tension: for though I could not conceive what was now to follow, yet I had a presentiment that it would be something solemnly awful. Parks continued silent: but his whole attitude, as he leant over the rail of what may be termed the dock, indicated a fearful state of suspense. There was again a pause, after the verdict had been delivered; and then Gilderoy spoke with the deepest solemnity.

"Thomas Parks, you have been declared guilty of the foul crimes laid to your charge. Of this guilt no one present can possibly entertain the slightest doubt. By the vilest machinations you obtained the signature of Miss Percy to a certain document, by means of which you flattered yourself that with impunity you might retain possession of your ill-gotten riches, and that you might hold that young lady at defiance. The document lies upon the table: it was obtained by fraud—let it now be destroyed!"

The Clerk of the Court at once took up the document—tore it to pieces—and setting a light to the fragments, suffered them to burn upon the floor, stirring them with his foot so that they might be all the more quickly consumed. In a few moments the document to which my signature had been so fraudulently obtained, was reduced to blackened tinder, which the Clerk stamped upon with his foot, crushing out the last scintillating sparks.

"Now, prisoner," resumed Gilderoy, "you stand in the position of one who has not even the slightest legal ground to sustain the impunity hitherto enjoyed. But it remains for me to place before you the alternatives between which you have to choose; and that decision on your part must be quickly given. You have perpetrated crimes which render you deserving of death. *Death* therefore is one of those alternatives to which I have alluded. But on the other hand, this tribunal will be satisfied if you consent to make complete restitution of Miss Percy's fortune, and carry out the agreement according to the terms arranged on the 5th of October, 1841. If the latter alternative is your choice, you will be detained a prisoner within these walls until the sum of thirty-six thousand three hundred pounds be transferred by you to the name of Miss Ellen Percy in the books of the Bank of England—or until any other arrangement which may best suit your convenience be carried out, having the same effect. That you

possess sufficiency of resources to enable you to make this atonement, I have already acquired the certitude. Let that atonement be made, therefore—and the very instant that I find it to be irrevocably accomplished, you shall be set at freedom. In that case you best know, Mr. Parks, whether it will suit your interests to bury in oblivion all the proceedings of this night. But if you tell the tale to the world, remember that at the same time you will be publishing your own infamy: and the forged will still remains at Doctors' Commons as an evidence against you! That will must ever exist to be held in terror over you; and in order that you might not be absolved from the consequences of that forgery should your future conduct merit castigation, I ordained the destruction of the document which now lies a blackened piece of tinder upon the floor. But I have said enough! It is now for you to decide——Immediate death, or else the speediest atonement!"

Scarcely had Gilderoy thus ceased speaking, when a fearful spectacle began to develop itself. The low platform on which his chair was placed, had hitherto seemed to stand against a wall, covered, as the rest of the apartment was, with black drapery. But now that black drapery parted in the middle: the two portions into which that sable curtain was thus divided, were slowly drawn aside—and it became apparent that it had merely screened off a section of the apartment, which thus proved to be even more spacious than it at first appeared. There was a window at the further extremity; and in the space that was now being disclosed to view, a sinister object was gradually discovered. This was nothing else than a gibbet, with the halter pendant to the beam; and beneath that halter stood a man dressed in black, and wearing a sable mask upon his countenance. A cold shudder crept through me: I laid my hand upon Beda's arm—I was about to say that not for worlds would I suffer the awful sentence of death to be carried into execution in case Mr. Parks should refuse to make the required atonement—but I gasped for utterance—I could not articulate a syllable. No tragedy in which I had ever appeared upon the stage, was so awful, so fearful as this! Beda comprehended what was passing in my mind, and why I thus laid my hand upon her; for she hastily whispered, "For heaven's sake breathe not a word, dear Miss! that wretched man will prefer the milder alternative!"

There was a solemn silence throughout the apartment. Parks stood immoveable in the dock; and there, at the extremity of that dimly-lighted tribunal—making me shudderingly think of the Inquisition and Vehm-Gerichts of past ages,—there was that sinister object looming through the obscurity, the executioner standing beneath the pendant rope!

"Prisoner," said Gilderoy, at length breaking that solemn pause, "you have five minutes for your decision:"—and drawing forth a watch, the old man held it in his hand, fixing his eyes upon its dial.

There was again a deep silence—but this time it was of short duration; for the wretched Parks, evidently impressed with the terrible earnestness of the whole scene, suddenly gasped forth, "Spare my life! I will make the atonement—I will pay the money—but—but—when I have done it, you will give me my liberty?"

"Rest assured," replied Gilderoy, "no pledge which comes from my lips shall be violated! If your death were resolved upon, it would have been sufficient to hand you over to one of the regular tribunals of the country, in the presence of which all your guilt would have been made apparent the same as it is here this night; and not merely would Miss Percy have recovered her fortune, but you would be doomed to the scaffold! As it is, we are contented with the atonement—and your life is spared. Your clerk is present: he is provided with certain necessary papers for you to sign. I will myself to-morrow see that the negotiation is fully carried out; and the moment that Miss Percy's fortune irrevocably stands in her name in the Bank of England, or elsewhere, shall you be restored to liberty."

Mr. Parks advanced towards the table, which Mr. Moss likewise approached; and though neither myself nor Beda caught what was said, yet was it plainly apparent that the lawyer in his malignity gave vent to some reproach or insulting observation to Mr. Moss; for Gilderoy at once sternly interfering, exclaimed, "Silence, Sir! That young man is protected: he has given his assistance in a righteous cause—and he must not be made the object of your malevolence!"

There was now silence for a few minutes, during which Mr. Moss produced some papers, which Mr. Parks proceeded to fill up. At the same time the sable curtains behind Gilderoy's chair were gradually closed; and the sinister *paraphernalia* of death were concealed from the view. It appeared as if I could breathe more freely when this was done; and Beda whispered to me as she warmly pressed my hand, "Everything has ended well, dear Miss Percy! Accept my fervid congratulations!".

"Thanks, dear Beda," I replied: "but we will not be too sure. I have already experienced so many disappointments, that not until the money shall be actually in my possession dare I flatter myself with the enjoyment of such good fortune. I know that so far as it depends upon that sagacious and friendly old man, as well as those by whom he is so ably succoured in these proceedings, all will be done to ensure a successful issue. But you know the old proverb—which though vulgar, is a true one—'There is many a slip between the cup and the lip;' and my past experiences prevent me from being sanguine."

"And yet," said Beda, "I scarcely now see how there can be any possibility of failure. Depend upon it, Gilderoy knows full well what he is about—and there is Mr. Moss, who is not only faithful to your interests, but he is a thorough man of business——"

"Well, my dear Beda, we shall see," I interrupted her. "I confess that there appear to be ninety-nine chances to one that I shall recover the fortune of which I have so long been despoiled: but still there is that one chance which the chapter of accidents may turn up; and therefore if my star should still prove unlucky in this respect, Beda, you will see with what fortitude and calm resignation I shall endure the misfortune."

Here our softly whispered discourse was cut short by a movement at the table; for the business was evidently ended. Gilderoy took possession of the papers which had been signed: the gipsy-guards went forward to conduct Mr. Parks from the room. When the prisoner was led away, the men who had formed alike the auditory and the jury, rose from their seats and also quitted the apartment, followed by the individual who had officiated as Clerk. Gilderoy, Mr. Moss, and the dwarf alone remained, in addition to Beda and myself.

The hideous hunchback approached the curtain which concealed us—raised it—and invited us to come forth. I placed a couple of sovereigns in the dwarf's hand; and any angry feeling which he might have cherished towards me on account of my conduct prior to the proceedings which had just terminated, vanished in a smile which distorted his countenance into a still more dreadful hideousness, if possible, and which displayed his large yellow teeth. I now approached Gilderoy, who was conversing with Mr. Moss; and to both of them did I express my sincerest gratitude for the good offices they had rendered with a view to procure me my rights.

"You have of course lost your situation with your late employer," I said to Moss; "or at all events you would not resume it after everything which has occurred. You must permit me to make you such recompense as both my duty and my gratitude suggest——"

"Let all this stand over until to-morrow," said Gilderoy: "it will be time enough, Miss Percy, when you are put in possession of your fortune. Mr. Moss, in obedience to my directions, brought hither with him to-night the requisite printed forms for Mr. Parks to fill up, to effect the transfer of the money in the Bank of England. To-morrow Mr. Moss and I will attend to that business. Do you therefore at once return to your own abode, Miss Percy; for you must doubtless be wearied with the excitement arising from these proceedings."

"Permit me to ask one question, my venerable friend," I said. "What has become of Dame Betty, the deceased Zarah's grandmother?"

"She was on the Continent," replied Gilderoy, "when the intelligence reached her of her granddaughter's death. She came back to England—I scarcely know whether it was to remain here altogether—or whether it was to ascertain upon the spot all the particulars connected with that death. I learnt that she was in London; and this being the case, I was resolved to make her services available to-night; for I must tell you that in this respect I departed from the plan as it was originally sketched out by the deceased Zarah. Being fully aware of everything that concerns that vile old woman, I had her completely in my power: I threatened her—I made use of her as the means of inveigling Parks to this place—I forced her to give her testimony, as you heard it ere now. I had pledged myself for her safety; but on the express condition that she should depart immediately on her return to France: for this purpose she was led away from the room the moment her testimony was given; and I hope and trust that she will never again set foot in London. But with such a wretch nothing is certain; and moreover she seems to have got hold of some idea that her granddaughter Zarah experienced foul play at the hands of her husband——"

"Indeed ?" I ejaculated.

"Yes—such seems to be her belief," responded Gilderoy, not observing anything peculiar in the emotion I had displayed: "but I have no doubt it is a mere idle fantasy on her part—for according to all accounts St. Clair was devotedly attached to the unfortunate Zarah."

I said not a word: the dwarf came forward to conduct me and Beda from the house; we took leave of Gilderoy and Mr. Moss—and we followed the hunchback. He afforded us egress by the same avenue through which we had quitted the premises on the preceding night; and the nearest church clock was striking the hour of twelve as we emerged into the street.

———

CHAPTER LXXVIII.

THE FIRE.

WE hastened to the nearest point where a hackney-vehicle could be obtained, in order that the servants might not think it strange if we returned on foot. On reaching the house, I found Mary Glentworth anxiously awaiting my arrival; for she was acquainted with the purpose for which I had set out, and the affectionate girl dreaded lest I and Beda should have experienced some perfidious treatment. She was therefore rejoiced on beholding our safe return; and instead of immediately returning to rest, I sat with her in the drawing-room, describing all that had occurred. Mary—as Beda had previously done—proffered the warmest congratulations: but I answered in a similar strain, to the effect that I was not sanguine and that I should not believe in my good fortune until it was placed beyond the possibility of doubt.

It was close upon one o'clock when Mary and I separated to retire to our respective chambers. Beda was in readiness to attend upon me, as usual, and assist me in my night-toilet : but I besought her to seek her own couch without delay, for I thought she must be thoroughly weary. She however insisted upon remaining with me; and she expatiated in glowing terms upon the sagacity which the patriarch Gilderoy had displayed in all the arrangements for the memorable scene of that night. I assured Beda that on the morrow I should behave most liberally to Mr. Moss, and that I should insist upon Gilderoy's acceptance of a very handsome reward, whether I recovered my fortune or not.

My night-toilet was nearly completed, when Beda and I were startled by the rapid crashing rush of a fire-engine tearing along the street. To a dweller in the metropolis, where the fires average pretty nearly five hundred in the course of the year, the din of the speeding engine has always something ominous and alarming. I started up from the chair in which I was seated while Beda was combing out my hair; and we both instinctively rushed to the window. But thence we could discern no evidence of a conflagration. My chamber was in the front of the house, looking towards the south. We hastened into Mary Glentworth's room, which was immediately behind my own. She was just getting into bed : but we told her what we had heard—and she joined us at

the window of her apartment. Thence we could command a view of the northern sky, as well as a portion of the eastern; and now in this latter direction—namely, the eastern one—we discerned that strong luminous halo which is thrown up by a conflagration. We opened the windows—we looked out—the intervening mazes of buildings prevented us from distinguishing precisely where the fire was: but the overhanging glare grew brighter and brighter—and we therefore were only too painfully convinced that the fire must be an extensive and a serious one. While sympathizing with the unfortunate creatures who might be made sufferers thereby, we nevertheless congratulated ourselves on the certainty that it was much too remote to cause any apprehension to the dwellers in Great Ormond Street. We therefore at length bade each other "good night" and retired to rest.

It was not until a late hour in the morning that I awoke; and, as usual, I rang for Beda. Another maid-servant answered the summons, saying that Beda had gone out for some purpose which she had not mentioned, and that she was not yet returned. It was now nearly ten o'clock, for I had considerably overslept myself through having been up so late; and Beda had already been an hour and a half absent. I could not understand it; but at the same time I experienced no uneasiness—for I knew the girl well enough to be assured that she would have a satisfactory explanation to give on her return.

"I think you must have seen the fire last night, Miss?" said the maid who was taking Beda's place: "for I heard you go into Miss Glentworth's room and open the windows soon after the fire-engine dashed past."

"Yes—I saw the glare," I answered. "But have you heard any particulars——"

"The milkman told me and Beda," replied the maid, "that the fire took place somewhere in Clerkenwell, in one of the very worst neighbourhoods in the quarter of Saffron Hill. Several houses were totally consumed, and others were much injured."

"In Clerkenwell ?" I said, musingly repeating the name; and then a sudden idea occurred to me : Beda's absence seemed now to be explained —I felt convinced that she must have been startled by the intelligence received from the milkman, and that she had set off to see whether Gilderoy's establishment had suffered.

Scarcely had this thought occurred to me, when Beda herself entered the room; and the other maid immediately withdrew.

"Oh, my dear Miss!" exclaimed the faithful girl, her countenance now exhibiting the distress which she no longer strove to conceal; "you will be so afflicted——"

"Beda!" I said, "is it possible that the very place where we were last night——"

"Yes, Miss—it was there that the fire broke out——It is all a shapeless heap of ruins——But that is not the worst ! The poor old man——"

"O Beda !" I cried, clasping my hands, "do not tell me that the venerable Gilderoy——Ah ! it is so !"—and the deepest affliction seized upon me, as Beda's countenance denoted the sad truth.

"Yes, dear Miss—that poor old man perished

in the conflagration! It is known likewise that at least two or three others—perhaps even more —must have likewise met their death——"

"Oh, this is terrible, Beda!" I said, shocked and horrified by the intelligence of the frightful calamity. "But are you sure that the patriarch Gilderoy——is there no hope——"

"Alas, Miss! there is none!" replied Beda mournfully. "The poor old man was seen struggling amidst the burning rafters—battling as it were for his life against the rage of the devouring element—his garments on fire——Oh! even in imagination the picture is horrible: what must the reality have been?"

The tears were now running down my cheeks: I thought not of the probability of my own hopes in respect to the recovery of my fortune being utterly wrecked: I thought only of that good old man who had so befriended me, perishing so horribly.

"Yes," continued Beda, with a shudder, "he was seen battling for his life amidst the blazing pile! — then all suddenly gave way — and — and——"

But here she stopped, for her own feelings choked her utterance.

"And you say there were others, Beda?" I tremulously murmured,—"other victims? Did you learn anything——"

"Few were the details that I could pick up," responded Beda; and though I put many questions, without appearing pointedly to do so, yet I could ascertain nothing which gave me any certainty in respect to Mr. Parks. There is however no doubt that there were at least three or four victims—perhaps more: but the flames spread with such terrific rapidity that long before the engines arrived the whole place was in a blaze. From what I can learn," continued Beda, with an ominous expression of countenance, "the fire must have broken out in that very apartment where we were last night. Thence it spread to both houses—and thence to the adjacent ones. I saw the ruins—no one could now suspect that there had been a place there which had served for so solemn and fearful a scene as that whereof we were the witnesses! As for Mr. Parks, it is next to certain that he must have been one of the victims; for you remember that he was to be detained a captive——"

"And there was Mr. Moss!" I suddenly exclaimed, with a renewed apprehension. "You remember that we left him there——And yet let us hope," I hurriedly continued, "that he stayed not with the poor old man!"

"If he be safe," responded Beda, "he will be certain to call very soon and make you aware of the extent to which you may be a sufferer: for Oh! I fear that when you last night told me that you were not sanguine, and that out of a hundred chances there was at least one against you—I fear lest there must have been in your mind a mysterious presentiment of evil, though you comprehended it not at the time!"

Mary Glentworth now entered my chamber; and I told her everything which Beda had been relating. She was much shocked and horrified; and we were still conversing on the subject, when a double knock resounded through the house. I then recollected that I had written to my father to call upon me at ten o'clock on the morning of which I am speaking.

I had hitherto told my sire nothing of all my proceedings in respect to Gilderoy; and in observing this secrecy I had more reasons than one. In the first place I feared lest his apprehensions of treachery might prompt him to insist that I should not again launch into such enterprises as the one that so seriously menaced me with danger at Petersfield; or at all events I knew that he would insist upon accompanying me;—and having a vivid recollection of the painful scene which had taken place on the occasion we were together in the presence of Mr. Parks, I had ever since determined to avoid bringing my father into contact with that man. But when everything should be over in respect to Gilderoy's proceedings, it was my intention to reveal all those particulars to my parent. For this reason, therefore, I had written to him on the preceding day, desiring him to come to me at about ten in the morning of the ensuing one. He had now arrived in obedience to that appointment.

In a few minutes he and I were alone together in the drawing-room; and I told him everything that had occurred. He did not blame me for any rashness on my part in having again plunged into an enterprise where gipseys were concerned; because up to a certain point all had progressed satisfactorily; and if there were now a failure it must be attributed wholly and solely to the conflagration. That such a failure would indeed ensue, there was only too much reason to apprehend; but my father set out with the least possible delay to institute certain inquiries.

About three hours passed—and I remained in a state of considerable agitation until my father returned. This was between one and two o'clock in the afternoon; and the intelligence which he brought was alike mysterious and distressing. It was distressing, because Beda's information was confirmed in respect to old Gilderoy, who had beyond all doubt perished in the conflagration. It was also distressing because Mr. Moss had not since been heard of. In respect to the mysteriousness of certain incidents, a few words of explanation will be sufficient on this head. Mr. Parks had disappeared—but whether he had perished in the fire, or having survived, had fled, was left entirely to conjecture. His wife and children had also disappeared: they had left their house at about nine o'clock on that same morning, Mrs. Parks taking all her plate and valuables with her. But this was not all. The sum of thirty-eight thousand pounds which stood in Mr. Parks's name at the Bank of England, had been disposed of soon after the doors of that establishment opened: the business was transacted on behalf of some gentleman, whom the stockbroker described to my father, but with whose personal appearance my sire was altogether unacquainted. He had given his name as Jenkinson; and only one thing was certain, which was that it was not Mr. Parks himself.

Thus stood the matter. My father was disposed to think that Parks had survived the fire, but that finding I was resolute in recovering my rights, either by direct or indirect means, he had deemed it prudent to flee the country. Not for an instant did my father suspect that Mr. Moss had played a treacherous game, and getting possession of the Bank papers from Gilderoy, had used them for his own purpose. For in the first place the individual that gave the name of Jenkinson to the stockbroker who transacted the business, answered not to the description of Mr. Moss. In the second place the transfer-papers were filled up to the full amount which Mr. Parks possessed in the Bank, and not for the sum of thirty-six thousand three hundred pounds which on the previous night had been assigned to me. In the third place the papers themselves were antedated three or four days. And in the fourth place there was the sudden disappearance of Mrs. Parks and the children, with all the valuables which in their hurried flight they could possibly carry away with them. These circumstances, taken together, formed strong corroborative evidence to acquit Moss of treachery, and to prove that Parks had by some unaccountable means survived the conflagration. Still there was a degree of mystery enveloping the affair, and which merely giving scope for conjecture, prevented the mind from arriving at any certainty upon the point. The only thing that seemed but too positive was that my evil star had continued in the ascendant in reference to my rightful heritage, and that I was not merely deprived of it for the present, but that I must at length look upon it as utterly gone for ever. My father was deeply afflicted,—as were likewise Mary Glentworth and Beda, when these things were communicated to them; but I reminded them that I had all along assured them I was not too sanguine, and that if I failed to recover my just rights I should sit down with calm resignation under the misfortune, instead of uselessly repining at it.

The evening newspapers, in giving a description of the fire, made not the slightest allusion to the fact that there had been anything peculiar connected with Gilderoy Hemp's establishment. They merely spoke of the houses which were destroyed, as having been occupied by "gipseys, tramps, and other persons belonging to the very refuse of society." There was however a painfully vivid picture given of the death scene of poor Gilderoy —to which Beda had so forcibly alluded, according to the information which she had gathered from the bystanders on the spot at the time she visited the ruins.

A week now passed; and one morning I received a note from Mr. Wilkinson requesting me to favour him with a call at Furnival's Inn in the course of the day. Thither I accordingly repaired at about two in the afternoon, having previously sent a message to the effect that I would be there at that hour. I was at once introduced into Mr. Wilkinson's private office; and he said to me, "You will be pleased to hear, Miss Percy, that I have at length succeeded in arranging this business according to your desire. It seems that Major Gower himself has all along been reasonable enough—and indeed, from everything which I have learnt, he is a young man of estimable character. It was only by the advice of his attorneys that he held out—or rather, perhaps, I should say, they insisted on holding out for him, by the preposterous demand of two-thirds of the entire property bequeathed by the late Mr. Gower,—and which bequest was legally made unto yourself."

"Now, therefore, I am to understand," I said, "that Major Gower is willing to share the property with me?"

"He is not only willing," responded Mr. Wilkinson, "but he most gratefully accepts your proposal. He considers that you have acted most nobly and generously. In a word, Miss Percy, he called upon me this morning—he was here when your message came specifying the hour when you would be with me—and he entreated my permission to return at this hour, in order that he might personally express all the gratitude he feels towards you. I gave my assent. Have I done wrong?"

"Assuredly not," I replied; "and I am excessively glad that the business is thus amicably settled without the further perplexities of the law. And to you, Mr. Wilkinson, my gratitude is due, for having conducted the affair to such an inexpensive issue."

"Not another syllable upon that point," ejaculated the lawyer. "And now while we have a little leisure before Major Gower arrives, tell me about your friend Mary Glentworth."

"She is still in the same mood with reference to the Ardleigh family: she is bent upon going upon the stage—and in another fortnight she makes her *debut*, simultaneously with a young lady of great promise——"

Here one of the clerks entered to announce Major Gower. I rose from my seat, and beheld before me a tall handsome man, about five-and-twenty years of age, with a faultless Grecian profile, and with an expression of countenance which indicated a generous frankness of disposition. He had dark hair—very fine eyes—and good teeth: he wore a moustache;—his form was slender and perfectly symmetrical. He was dressed in plain clothes; and altogether his appearance was what may be termed most prepossessing. Mr. Wilkinson introduced him to me; and he at once said, with all the frankness which his looks denoted,

"Permit me to shake you by the hand, Miss Percy; for instead of regarding you as a hostile litigant, it is as a benefactress—a real benefactress," he added, emphatically, "that I greet you!"

There was so much enthusiasm—so much natural fervour in the strain in which Major Gower thus addressed me, that it was impossible to doubt the generosity of his own disposition while he was eulogizing mine. I was therefore doubly glad that the matter was amicably settled: but I said, "I really cannot receive the credit for so much magnanimity as you seem, Major Gower, inclined to attribute to me."

"Oh! if you knew all, Miss Percy," he ejaculated, "you would not wonder that I feel my heart so light—my spirits so buoyant——"

"At all events," I said, with a smile, "it is better that this business should be arranged in a friendly manner, than that we should assume the attitude of enemies and waste in law the property relative to which a temporary dispute arose."

"And yet, Miss Percy," rejoined Major Gower, "there are few—very few indeed who would argue in a manner at once so rational and so generous. There is no doubt your claim to the entire property is excellent, and that my pretensions were but vague and shadowy in the presence of my deceased uncle's will. I am aware of the motives which have been mainly influential in prompting you to this settlement. While maintaining the strict justice of your own claim, you nevertheless hesitated to enrich yourself to the prejudice of one who was most unjustly disinherited by his deceased relative. Oh, yes! I have learnt from Mr. Wilkinson all the kindness, the delicacy, and the forbearance with which you have acted; and it is for this that I thank you! I know likewise that when you were informed that I was no undeserving nor unprincipled character — no extravagant spendthrift nor depraved libertine—you expressed your sorrow that I should have been so completely deprived of that fortune which I had more or less right to regard as my legitimate heritage. In a word, Miss Percy, your conduct has been most admirable—you have laid me under a lasting obligation—and I experience the utmost gratitude towards you!"

"I certainly did not think, Major Gower," I said, "from all that I have learnt relative to your character and disposition, that you could have given your deceased uncle such dire offence as to deserve such retribution."

"No, Miss Percy," ejaculated the officer; "and on this point I am bound to give you every explanation."

"I do not desire it, Major Gower," I interjected, "if family secrets be involved——"

"Alas! those of whom I have to speak are both gone, and there can be no violation of any secrecy in the few words I am about to utter. My uncle Mr. Gower was a man of most peculiar disposition and character. Those who knew him superficially, believed him to be a frank-hearted, generous-minded, unsophisticated country gentleman——"

"Such was the impression he made upon me," I observed, "the first time I ever saw him."

"But perhaps there was never a man," continued Major Gower, "more inveterate in his prejudices—more doggedly persistent in his obstinacy—or more unrelenting in any aversions that he might conceive. He could be a stanch friend: but heaven help the individual who provoked his hatred and fell into his power! I know not, Miss Percy, to what extent you may have been acquainted with my uncle's true character——"

"I knew sufficient of it to be convinced, as I now listen to you, that in no sense is your description exaggerated:"—and I shuddered as I thought of the horrible vengeance that was wreaked upon the wretched Lord Frederick Ravenscliffe.

"I should inform you, Miss Percy," continued Major Gower, "that at an early age I was left an orphan, and totally dependent upon my uncle. He behaved towards me as if I were his own son: he spared no expense to give me a good education at a military college—and on the very day that I completed my sixteenth year, I was gazetted to a commission in the army. My uncle purchased my promotions step by step as rapidly as gold could achieve these objects. I thought I had every reason to bless him: but at that time I was obedient to all his wishes and mandates, and nothing therefore transpired between us to develop his character in its true light to my comprehension. I am now about to speak of an incident which occurred some fourteen or fifteen months ago. At that time I had just fallen in with a young lady who had made a certain impression upon my heart. One day my uncle summoned me to his country-seat, with the intimation that he had a matter of some importance on which he was desirous of speaking to me;—and thither I accordingly repaired. I could not conceive what this important business might possibly be: but on finding myself alone with my uncle, it was very soon explained. In a letter to my cousin Felicia — alas, poor Felicia!—I had mentioned the fact of having been impressed with the beauty of the young lady to whom I have just alluded. I had no secrets from Felicia: I had known her from her infancy—I looked upon her as a sister—and I knew that she regarded me as a brother. She entertained for me no sentiment of a more tender nature; and thus I had not the slightest hesitation in making her the confidante of the little secret to which I have referred. She in her unsuspecting artlessness showed the letter to her father; and hence the summons that was sent off to command my immediate presence at the country-seat. Mr. Gower questioned me concerning the young lady of whom I had spoken in that letter. I told him frankly that I had only been very recently introduced to her, and that no serious step had as yet been taken—no avowal of love as yet made. Indeed, with that habit of deference with which all my conduct towards my uncle was characterized, I should not have thought of entering into any engagement without having previously communicated my desire to him and received his sanction to my proceedings. All these assurances I gave him at the interview of which I am speaking. He appeared much pleased; and then for the first time I to my astonishment learnt that he entertained certain views which he went on to describe. He intended me to become the husband of his daughter! I was not merely surprised—I was even shocked: for though Felicia and myself were in reality only cousins, yet as we had been brought up together from childhood, I looked upon her as a sister. I frankly explained

my feelings to Mr. Gower; and I assured him that if he questioned Felicia, he would find that hers were of a kindred nature. But he would not listen patiently to my representations: he said that his mind was made up how to act. He had pushed me on rapidly in life with the idea that I was to become his heir, and that this heritage would not be to the prejudice of his daughter inasmuch as by means of marriage we should become the joint possessors of his wealth. I remonstrated —I entreated—I implored: but all to no effect! I prayed that he would consult his daughter: his only answer was that he knew Felicia was ready and willing to obey him in all things. At length matters came to that point which compelled me to assure my uncle that much as I loved Felicia in one sense—that is to say, as a cousin or as a sister —I could not possibly love her in the sense which would justify me in conducting her to the altar. Besides, my heart was already impressed with the image of another; and I felt that this *other* could alone constitute my happiness. Then it was that my uncle's true disposition developed itself: he suddenly revealed his character to me as that of the stern, self-willed, obstinate tyrant. He bade me yield to his wishes or else consider myself for evermore cast off from his favour. I fell upon my knees at his feet—I besought him not to treat me thus—I adjured him by all his former kindness towards me to maintain the same generous treatment. He was inexorable. 'Assent to what I have proposed,' he said, 'or depart hence and see my face no more.'—Then it was that my own spirit rebelled: I could not bring myself to be trampled upon by the foot of a domestic tyrant—high words ensued between us—and he banished me from his presence. Yet even *then* I could scarcely think that he would maintain his stern decision, until in the course of a few days I received a letter full of the bitterest reproaches, taxing me with the blackest ingratitude, and withdrawing the allowance which I had hitherto enjoyed. Now I indeed saw that everything was at an end between my uncle and myself! I have detained you a long time, Miss Percy—longer than I had at first anticipated, with this narrative of explanations: but it is finished, and you perceive that I was really guilty towards my uncle of no offence which deserved so great a punishment as that of complete disinheritance."

"Far from it, Major Gower," I said: "it would be most unreasonable to blame you! But as you have treated me with so much frankness, may I venture to hope that in respect to the young lady to whom you have alluded, all has progressed smoothly and in a manner calculated to ensure your happiness?"

"Ah, Miss Percy!" exclaimed the officer, "you can now perhaps understand wherefore my joy was so enthusiastic, and why I was even prepared to worship you as a benefactress, when I learnt that you were disposed to settle everything in an amicable manner. Yes!—no doubt my happiness may now be insured! Ah, believe me, Miss Percy"— and here a deep mournfulness suddenly overspread the Major's countenance,—"believe me when I declare that I was greatly distressed on hearing of poor Felicia's death! And perhaps you will not deem me a hypocrite or a dissembler if I add that I was shocked likewise at the death of my uncle following so soon upon the bereavement he had experienced in respect to his daughter! I fear that there were some mysterious circumstances connected with the latter days of poor Felicia,—those circumstances which afforded you an opportunity of displaying that kind sympathy to which such special allusion was made in my uncle's last will and testament."

"There were painful circumstances, Major Gower," I said: "but we will not further allude to them."

"There was a time," said the officer,—"it may have been some nine or ten months back—when I happened to hear it rumoured that Felicia was to be conducted to the altar by Lord Frederick Ravenscliffe; and then to my astonishment I one day read in the newspaper that this young nobleman had suddenly espoused the beautiful Miss Norman: so that I feared lest poor Felicia should have been unhandsomely treated by Lord Frederick. I dared not call upon my cousin, nor present myself at her father's house: I was stationed with my regiment at a country-town at the time —and I had no means of ascertaining any particulars in reference to those subjects to which I have just been alluding."

"And those subjects are indeed painful, Major Gower," I said: "but perhaps I ought to inform you that your surmise was only too correct. Your unfortunate cousin Felicia loved Lord Frederick—he espoused another—his conduct was most unhandsome——and Felicia died of a broken heart!"

There was a pause, during which Major Gower meditated sadly and mournfully. Whether he suspected that I had left anything untold, I cannot say: but he put no further questions and said not another syllable upon the painful topic. He took his leave of me, reiterating the assurances of his most fervid gratitude and declaring that he regarded me as a benefactress.

When he had departed from the office, I had a consultation with Mr. Wilkinson; and this gentleman entered into minute explanations relative to the property left by the deceased Mr. Gower. It appeared that from the rents of the estate and from money in the funds there was an income of fifteen thousand pounds. In addition to this there was the country-seat with the domain attached, and it was worth about sixty thousand pounds. It was the desire of Major Gower to obtain possession of the landed estates, and to leave me my fair commensurate portion in the shape of funded property. In short, after entering minutely into figures and calculations, it was shown that if I accepted this arrangement I should enjoy a clear income of about twelve thousand a year, as well as being absolute mistress of the capital producing this amount. Without a moment's hesitation I consented; and Mr. Wilkinson informed me that as both parties were now agreed as to the mode of settling the affairs, they could be brought to a termination in the course of a very few weeks. I therefore took my departure from the lawyer's office, with a heart elate at the brilliant prospects that were open before me. On my return to Great Ormond Street I lost no time in communicating the pleasing intelligence to my father; and I likewise wrote to the same effect to Mr. Norman. But I said nothing upon the subject to Mary Glentworth, Aline Marcy, or any other friends; for my experiences of life had already most severely taught me to boast of no hopes until they were completely realized.

CHAPTER LXXIX.

THE TWOFOLD DEBUT.

THE reader may perhaps be surprised that throughout so many chapters I should have scarcely mentioned the name of Henry Wakefield. Nearly ten months had now elapsed since I separated from him at Paisley, and since his departure from England on his return to the United States. But because I have been thus comparatively silent with regard to him, it must not for an instant be supposed that my love had diminished. On the contrary, my heart remained faithfully devoted to my cousin, and my affection had, if possible, become more tender and more deeply rooted. We corresponded frequently; and all the letters which I received from him, contained not merely the assurances of his own unalterable love, but likewise the gratifying intelligence that the affairs in which he was concerned on behalf of Mr. Macdonald of Paisley were still progressing in a most favourable manner. In about six weeks, or two months at the outside, Henry expected to be enabled to set foot again upon the British soil; and I looked forward with the most joyous feelings to the prospect of our meeting.

In my own letters to Henry Wakefield I had said nothing of my hopes which were at different times excited (and then most cruelly disappointed) of obtaining from Mr. Parks the fortune bequeathed to me by my deceased grandfather. I thought that if those hopes should be realized, it would prove time enough to transmit the happy information to my cousin. I now entertained the same view in reference to the far more brilliant prospects which appeared to spread themselves out before me in reference to my share of the late Mr. Gower's wealth. Thus, in again writing to Henry, I said nothing upon this subject. But Oh! I thought to myself—what happiness, what delight would be mine if on Henry's return to Great Britain I could say to him, "There is henceforth no necessity for me to remain upon the stage, nor for you to wade through the anxieties and perplexities of mercantile pursuits: for we are rich—we have immense wealth — we possess twelve thousand a year!"

I must candidly confess that when writing to Henry Wakefield, I could scarcely restrain myself from committing to paper the intelligence which I knew would afford him so much delight: but still I thought that if by any possible accident—if by any circumstance at present unforeseen and undreamt of—there should be a disappointment, the affliction of Henry would on my account be all the greater because of the very hopes which had been indulged. Therefore, all things considered, I deemed it more prudent to remain silent on that topic for the present—and I did so.

A fortnight passed from the date of my interview with Major Gower; and on calling two or three times at Mr. Wilkinson's office, I learnt that everything was progressing satisfactorily. The day was now close at hand when Aline Marcy and Mary Glentworth were to make their *debut* at the theatre. I felt tolerably confident that they would both achieve a signal success; and I sincerely hoped that such would be the case—not only for their own sake—but for that of Mr. Richards. The lessee had treated me with generosity, as well as with the strictest punctuality and integrity in his dealings; and I thought to myself that if I should shortly leave the stage, it would be a source of gratification for me to know that the services of my two pupils would still prove lucrative to the manager's treasury.

The evening fixed for the *debut* arrived; and both my pupils were full of courage and confidence. We were all three to appear in a new piece, which had been expressly written for the purpose of introducing us in three distinguished parts upon the stage. I conceived that the drama had by its own intrinsic merits every possible chance of success: the author had proved most willing to listen to certain suggestions that I had offered; and thus I was resolved to exert all my energies to ensure the triumph of his production. I felt confident that in this endeavour I should be ably supported by Aline and Mary; and from other circumstances every encouragement was to be derived. The announcement of the twofold *debut*, in connexion with my own appearance in the same piece, had excited the utmost sensation in the theatre-going world: every box was engaged beforehand—and the instant the doors were thrown open, there was a tremendous rush on the part of the assembled crowd, not more than one-third of whom could possibly hope to succeed in obtaining admittance. The vast theatre was quickly filled to suffocation; while hundreds and hundreds went away in disappointment from the portals.

In the meantime Aline Marcy, Mary Glentworth, and myself were assembled in my dressing-room,—where, assisted by Beda, we were performing our respective toilets. If I suffer the reader to peep into that dressing-room for a few moments, he may discern a *tableau* which is not perhaps altogether uninteresting. Let me sketch it at a moment when, my own toilet being finished, I was resting myself upon a species of *chaise longue*, or ottoman with a back to it. My costume was characterized rather by an elegant simplicity than by richness. A wreath of flowers was the only ornament which I wore for my hair: my arms were bare to the shoulders,—each embellished with a simple bracelet. At the dressing-table Mary Glentworth, whose toilet was not as yet quite achieved, was waiting while Beda brought the muslin dress which alone remained to be put on. She looked exceedingly handsome; and a crescent gleaming above her forehead, was the sole ornament for her luxuriant light brown hair. The costume in which she was to appear, was admirably calculated to set off her fine shape to the fullest advantage; and I knew that the beauty of her person could not fail to make its impression upon the spectators. I entertained the same idea in reference to the lovely Aline Marcy. Her toilet was already finished: it was somewhat a fanciful one—for she was to represent a lady of the Court of Louis the Fifteenth of France. The bodice of her dress was elaborately embroidered and worked: her light hair was turned back from her forehead,

in precisely the same style which she usually adopted, and which so much became her. A little velvet cap, with a single feather, gave her a most *piquante* appearance. Her arms were bare,—those arms which, as I have already stated on a former occasion, were so beautifully modelled! In a word, her costume, as well as that of Mary Glentworth, was most exquisitely suited for the display of all the graces and elegancies of the person.

"You are full of confidence, Mary?" I said, thus addressing Miss Glentworth as I rested myself on the ottoman; "and you recollect every line—every word of your part?"

"Every line—every word," she answered, turning towards me from the toilet-table, where she had just been arranging a stray tress before the mirror. "As for confidence, my dear Ellen, I feel sure that the moment the first sense of bewilderment shall have passed when the curtain draws up and reveals to me the gaze of the immense audience, I shall be as calm and collected as when rehearsing my part this morning to empty benches."

"And you, Aline," I said, turning towards Mademoiselle Marcy, who having finished her own toilet, was at the instant studying an attitude in front of the full-length looking-glass, or *psyche*, which stood in the middle of the dressing-room,—"you, I have no doubt, can give an equally favourable account?"

"Yes, my dear friend," replied the beautiful French girl. "I am full of confidence and courage: but do not think that I am possessed by an overweening vanity or conceit——"

"No, no!" I exclaimed: "there is a wide difference between the confidence which one reposes in oneself, and that conceit to which you allude. By the bye, Aline, I presume Lord and Lady Kelvedon are to be here this evening?"

"Oh, yes!" responded Mademoiselle Marcy: "her ladyship assured me this afternoon that they should make a point of attending. They have engaged a box, and will be accompanied by several friends."

I glanced at Mary Glentworth, to ascertain, if possible, by her looks, whether she were thinking of the Ardleigh family, and wondering whether they also would be present. Our eyes met: Mary's countenance was perfectly composed: she evidently fathomed what was passing in my mind —for bending down, she whispered to me, "Let them be there! Their presence assuredly will not ruffle me! On the contrary, if I succeed, my triumph will be the more complete by being enabled to prove to them that I shall henceforth eat the bread earned by myself, and that therefore I am more than ever independent of their eleemosynary charity."

Beda now proceeded to assist in the completion of Mary Glentworth's toilet; and rising from my seat on the ottoman, I glanced in the *psyche* to assure myself that nothing was wanting in respect to my own costume. At that moment Aline Marcy drew me aside; and she said in a low hurried whisper, "There is only one point on which I experience the least uneasiness! I should not like that *he* of whom I have once spoken to you, Ellen, should by any chance be present on this occasion!"

I should here inform the reader that Aline Marcy had adopted a feigned name in the announcement of her intended *debut*: but Mary Glentworth had retained that which she usually bore. Thus I understood full well the meaning of Aline Marcy's observation. The individual whom she loved might possibly be in London—he might be present at the theatre, little suspecting that in one of the young ladies who were that night to make their *debut*, he would behold Aline Marcy! I saw that the poor girl trembled at the idea of the effect which so sudden a surprise would produce upon the young gentleman to whom she alluded, if he *should* happen to be present; and I dreaded lest this apprehension should impair the courage and confidence which in all other respects she experienced. I therefore hastened to say a few encouraging words; and Aline, pressing my hand fervently, whispered, "Fear not, my dear friend, on my account! I have foreseen the possibility of such an occurrence—I have nerved myself—and therefore I am prepared if it should arise."

Mary Glentworth's toilet was now finished; and Beda stood at a little distance, surveying us all three as we were grouped together in the middle of the room. The eyes of the faithful girl were filled with admiration: I saw that something wavered upon her lips,—something which she wished to say, but to which she feared to give utterance: and then, unable to restrain herself, she suddenly burst forth.

"It would be impossible for all England to produce three more perfect specimens of beauty," she cried with enthusiasm, "than I now behold before me!"

We smiled at this artless and genuine expression of Beda's admiration; and Mary Glentworth said, "If there be the least truth in your remark, my dear girl, any other observer standing by might increase the number to four, by including yourself amongst them."

This assertion was indeed so far correct, that if so high an eulogium were merited by whatsoever good looks Aline, Mary, and myself might possess, Beda was equally worthy of such a compliment. For as I have already assured the reader, a more beautiful fairy-like gipsy than my young attendant could not possibly exist on the face of the earth; and more than ever lovely did she now seem with her superb eyes fixed in luminous enthusiasm upon us, and her cheeks mantling with the blush which Mary's flattering observation had conjured up.

But the important business of the evening was now about to commence. The overture was finished: we knew that the curtain had just drawn up on the first scene of the new drama. It was arranged, according to the plan of the author and the cast of the characters, that Mary Glentworth was to appear in the second scene—Aline Marcy in the third—and I was to appear at the commencement of the Second Act—and that at the close of the Second Act we should all three find ourselves upon the boards at the same time.

We issued from the dressing-room; Mr. Richards was anxiously awaiting our presence: and I saw by the expression of his countenance, as he flung a hasty look at my two pupils, that he

was inspired by the liveliest hope. A manager can tell at a glance whether a new aspirant to dramatic fame be endowed with firmness and self-possession on the eve of a first appearance; and in the present instance his survey was completely satisfactory. Those actors and actresses who were not engaged in the opening scene, came crowding about us; and I caught several whispers floating around.

"The young French lady is exquisitely beautiful!" said one.

"Miss Glentworth is remarkably handsome!" said another.

"What beautiful arms! and what a lovely complexion!" whispered a third, alluding to Aline Marcy.

"And what a fine grown girl is Miss Glentworth!" observed a fourth.

"After all," added a fifth, "our own Miss Trafford remains unrivalled in beauty, as I am confident she will continue unsurpassed in the profession!"

It is through no sentiment of vanity that I have recorded this last speech—but simply, as a truthful autobiographer, for the purpose of displaying the sentiments of the brother and sister professionals whose remarks caught my ear on the present occasion. But now the second scene was on the point of commencing; and in another minute Mary Glentworth was to appear for the first time on the boards of a theatre. At that instant all my feelings and sensations when exactly two years back I made my own *debut*, came rushing into my mind. I recollect how when I suddenly emerged into the full glare of light and became the focus for three thousand pair of eyes, my heart sank within me and I felt my courage rapidly evaporating. I glanced anxiously at Mary Glentworth's countenance: it was composed—its look was firm: I was astonished at the fortitude which she displayed. All my anxiety on her account vanished in a moment: I pressed her hand—and the next instant she was upon the stage. Then arose a tremendous shout of welcome; and Mary acknowledged it in the most graceful manner. I saw that her self-possession continued to be complete. She entered upon the part in a manner which gave every promise of success; she evidently bore in mind all the tutorings and instructions she had received; and yet she impersonated the character with an air as natural as if she were absolutely identified with it. When she came off the stage the entire audience testified its approbation in the most enthusiastic style.

"I do not think the Ardleighs are here," she took an opportunity of whispering to me after having received the congratulations of those who pressed around her—and the reader may be assured that Aline's and mine were not amongst the coldest.

"Ah! had you self-possession sufficient," I said "to scan the occupants of the boxes? I am astonished, Mary!" I added, with the most delighted feelings. "You have displayed more firmness and fortitude than I did on the night of my own *debut* which took place exactly two years ago!"

"If it had not been for those circumstances, dear Ellen," replied Mary Glentworth, "which finally settled my mind upon the stage, and which

made me resolve within myself that I would succeed, I do verily believe that I should have
failed!"

She however sighed as she spoke, and turned
away.

It was soon Aline Marcy's turn to make her appearance. She likewise was inspired with calmness and courage: the welcome she experienced
was quite as flattering as that which had so recently greeted Mary Glentworth; and she acquitted herself with the same degree of success.
Nothing could exceed the joy which I experienced
on being enabled to repeat to her the congratulations I had already proffered to her fellow-pupil:
I saw that both would that night achieve a splendid triumph; and I was delighted not merely for
their own sakes, but likewise because they did
such credit to the tuition I had afforded them.

When I appeared upon the stage at the commencement of the Second Act, I was greeted in
the most flattering manner: the vast building
rang with the applause which my presence elicited;
—and I felt that this enthusiastic demonstration
was not merely the usual testimonial given to my
repute as an actress, but that it was likewise an
acknowledgment of the efficiency with which I
had proved the preceptress of the two beauteous
debutantes. I saw Lord and Lady Kelvedon,
with their friends, in one box: I recognised the
Earl and Countess of Belgrave, with the Marquis
and Marchioness of Campanella, and Beatrice Di
Carboni, in another box. Many other friends and
acquaintances did I likewise discern amidst the
galaxy of rank and fashion; and in a less distinguished part of the theatre I caught a glimpse of
the countenance of my father. When I rejoined
Mary and Aline, the latter whispered to me, "You
see that Lord and Lady Kelvedon are here: but
I caught not a glimpse of *him* whom I confess I
dreaded to behold!"

I pressed Aline's hand in silent congratulation
at this circumstance; and now the moment arrived when we were all three to appear upon the
stage in the same scene. Nothing could exceed
the enthusiasm of the applause with which we
were greeted: and if it were flattering to myself,
accustomed as I was to such receptions, what a
rapturous thrill of delight must it have carried to
the hearts of Aline and Mary! I felt proud of
them as my pupils: and as they stood there—the
former on one side of me, the latter on the other
side—there, amidst the blaze of light, I thought
that Mary had never looked so eminently handsome nor Aline so bewitchingly beautiful, and
that if personal loveliness had aught to do with
the success of a *debutante*, they had indeed everything in their favour,—talent, lady-like manners,
graceful demeanours, clear pure voices, and all
the attractions of beauty. The scene in which we
thus appeared closed amidst another tremendous
burst of applause on the part of the audience.

The Second Act concluded; and then, according to the plot of the drama, Mary Glentworth
had to sustain the chief interest in the Third Act,
neither Aline nor myself appearing on the boards
during that interval. In the Fourth Act it was
my part to sustain the chief interest, neither of
my pupils having any concern with that portion
of the drama's progress. Then for the Fifth Act
Aline Marcy had to take her own share, until the

closing scene brought us all three again together
upon the stage for a grand *donouement*. Mary
continued to enact her own part with the most
perfect success throughout the Third Act; and
precisely the same observation applies to Aline
Marcy in the Fifth Act. And now came the final
closing scene, in which we all three appeared upon
the stage together. Nothing could exceed the
sensation which was thus created: never on any
former occasion had I felt my own energies so
completely commensurate with the task which I
had to perform—never was I so ably supported in
any drama as I then was by Mary and Aline!
The piece terminated—the curtain fell—and the
triumph of the two *debutantes* was complete.

Then from the entire audience came cries invoking us forward;—and giving to my two pupils
each a hand, I led them upon the stage while the
curtain was again drawn up. A perfect *furor* of
applause awaited us: bouquets were thrown from
all parts; but in the midst of this inspiring scene,
I felt Aline's hand suddenly tighten convulsively
as it clasped my own—a faint shriek escaped her
lips—and she fainted. Mary and myself instantaneously bore her back, while the curtain fell;
and as if to express sympathy with the occurrence, the shouts of applause gave place all in a
moment to a dead silence on the part of the audience. We bore Aline to the dressing-room: and
by the way I hastily whispered to Mr. Richards,
" Go and say that it is nothing but a swoon produced by excess of emotion!"

A very few instants after the dressing-room was
reached, and while assisted by Mary and Beda I
was administering restoratives, the shouts which
again burst forth from the audience reached our ears,
—thus proving that Mr. Richards had made some
successful speech, and that there was no suspicion
of any other motive than the one which he had
assigned at my bidding. Indeed, who could suspect any other motive, unless it were myself who
was acquainted with Aline's secret, and the object of her love whom she had doubtless espied in
the theatre? For that such was the cause of her
sudden swoon, I felt all but convinced: for up to
the instant when her hand tightened its grasp
upon my own, she had appeared as collected and
self-possessed as either Mary or I.

" The excitement has overcome her," said Miss
Glentworth, as we administered restoratives: " but
she will soon recover."

" Yes—it is nothing," I said. " Unloosen her
dress, Beda. Quick, my dear girl!"

This however proved unnecessary; for Aline
now opened her eyes—and for a few moments
gazed vacantly around her. Then all in an instant
I beheld the fire of intelligence light up in those
beautiful eyes: I comprehended that her recollections had suddenly returned; and bending down
as if to embrace her, while she lay stretched upon
the ottoman, I whispered, " Do not betray yourself, dearest Aline!"

There was now a knock at the door: one of the
actresses had come on the part of the rest to inquire how the young French lady found herself.
I bade Beda give a satisfactory answer: at the
same moment I desired Mary Glentworth to bring
a tumbler of water: and as they were both thus
temporarily engaged with their backs towards us,
I received a significant look from Aline.

"No one suspects anything," I hastily whispered: "it is attributed to a very natural excitement! Do not betray yourself!"

Aline Marcy wrung my hand; and then rising from the ottoman, she displayed a perfect self-possession. Mary Glentworth presented the tumbler of water: Aline imbibed some of its contents; and she was about to commence the task of disapparelling herself, when I begged her to rest a little while longer.

"No," she said, with a sweet expression of countenance, on which however there was a shade of sadness: "I now feel perfectly restored."

"Your triumph is complete!—and your's also, dear Mary!" I exclaimed, embracing them one after the other. "The results have far transcended all the most sanguine hopes that I dared entertain!"

Beda likewise proffered her congratulations: but I saw that Aline had received a shock—though

NO. 62.—ELLEN PERCY.

neither Mary nor Beda suspected it. We now began to change our toilets, putting off our dramatic costumes and resuming our own apparel. When the task was ended, I said to Aline, "Will you not come and pass the night at my house? I can send round a message to Lady Kelvedon's box to the effect that you will not return to Eaton Square until to-morrow."

"It was my intention," replied Aline, "to ask this favour of you:"—then drawing me a little aside, she added, "The step is now taken—and I am an actress! I have not forgotten all that you told me a short time ago; and I had resolved that the day of my *debut* should be the last of my sojourn at Eaton Square. A great gulf has suddenly opened between Lady Kelvedon and myself; and though her kindness and delicacy would induce her to grant me an asylum so long as she remains in London, yet not for worlds would I place her by my presence in a false position. I accept your kind offer, my dear Ellen; and perhaps I may intrude upon you for a few days until I provide myself with a suitable lodging."

"If you thus leave Lady Kelvedon," I said, "it shall be to remain with me altogether: for where can you find yourself more happy than with your fellow-pupil Mary, and with myself who am your preceptress?"

Aline pressed my hand; her heart was too full of emotions, arising from various sources, to allow her to give utterance to a word; and I said, "I will now go and send a message to Lady Kelvedon."

"I had already written her this note," said Aline, producing one; "and confident beforehand that you would afford me an asylum, I have informed her ladyship whither I am going."

I took the billet; and issuing forth, gave it to some underling to take round to Lady Kelvedon's box. My carriage was in readiness; and we all prepared to quit the theatre. On our way to the equipage, we found Mr. Richards waiting for us; and having expressed his congratulations to Aline and Mary, he said, "Ladies, I beg to offer you an engagement on whatever terms Miss Trafford may suggest. For my part I leave the settlement of those terms entirely to Miss Trafford; and I am confident that you, ladies, will be equally willing that she should thus kindly decide between us."

Both my friends expressed in a suitable manner their acknowledgments of this generous conduct on the lessee's part: he escorted us to the carriage—and we repaired to Great Ormond Street. When we sat down to supper, Mary Glentworth was in tolerably good spirits: but Aline was only enabled to affect a gaiety, beneath which I could discern the under-current of sadness. Miss Glentworth however, having no reason for suspicion, took that assumed cheerfulness to be genuine.

When the hour for retiring came, I conducted Aline to the chamber which she was to occupy; and she begged me to remain with her for a few minutes. We sat down together; and she now gave vent to the tears which she had hitherto kept back, and the restraining of which must have proved so painful.

"Was it not hard, dear Ellen," she said, in a broken voice, "that at the very moment of my success, something should have transpired to plunge a dagger in my heart? Yet, alas! it was so! Throughout those five Acts—or at least whenever I was upon the stage—I looked in every direction with the dread of meeting the eyes of one whom I wished not to behold there! Suddenly, just as the curtain was about to fall upon us three, as we stood hand in hand behind the footlights—the bouquets showering around us, and the shouts of applause resounding through the vast building—I saw the door of a box open —some one entered——it was he! As plainly, Ellen, as I behold you at this moment—for the box was only the second on the left-hand side of the stage,—as plainly, I say, as I now behold your countenance, did I catch the expression of wonderment and consternation which seized upon his features. Then, as if suddenly stricken a death-blow, I lost all consciousness!"

"But you thought yourself prepared, Aline—you fancied yourself nerved," I said, in the kindest

and gentlest tone, "for such an eventuality?—but it was more, my poor friend, than you could endure! My only wonder is, that labouring under that apprehension, you could have acquitted yourself as brilliantly as you did! Indeed, your performance was admirable—your triumph was immense! Oh, I hope that you do not fear lest on future occasions——But perhaps—who knows?— he whom you still love, Aline, may seek you out——"

Here I suddenly checked myself; for I felt that I was wrong to encourage a hope which peradventure never could be realized.

"I know what you would have said, Ellen," she answered; "and I can comprehend likewise what has suddenly flashed to your mind. No! I dare not entertain such a hope. As I have before told you, everything is irrevocably at an end betwixt him and me. It was a momentary weakness on my part this evening——it was a paroxysm that under certain circumstances was almost inevitable: but it cannot occur again! Do you not understand what ideas swept through my mind? It was that the step had been taken which opened the impassable abyss betwixt him and me!—it was the conviction that the death-knell had rung for any faint lingering hope that might possibly have hovered in my mind! But now, Ellen, all is over! —that one last feeling has found its vent—and henceforth you shall see that my calmness and fortitude will be fully equal to those of our friend Mary!"

I remained a little longer in Aline's chamber until I was convinced that she was in a perfectly settled frame of mind; and then I bade her good night. On returning to my own room, I was saddened by the reflection,—which indeed I had often made before,—that there is no happiness in this world without its alloy—no moment of triumph without its inevitably associated feeling of bitterness! On the night of my own brilliant *debut* two years back, I had felt that I was taking a step unknown to my aunt and cousin: now, on this night, when I had so much reason to rejoice in the success of my two beautiful pupils, I was compelled to mourn that complete bliss was not in *their* hearts. For Aline had been suddenly afflicted in the manner described; and I knew enough of Mary Glentworth to be certain that she still retained a sense of the cruel blow which had been stricken her a short time back.

I awoke in the morning at an earlier hour than usual; and on descending to the breakfast-parlour, I found that neither Mary nor Aline had as yet made their appearance. The newspapers had just arrived: I hastened to open them, and I was rejoiced at the flattering notices that were given of the performance of the two fair *debutantes* on the preceding evening. The morning journals were unanimous in their verdict of approval: they spoke highly of the talents and the personal beauty of Mary and Aline; and they enthusiastically complimented me for having introduced two such promising young ladies to the public. I sped upstairs to their chambers, and in a very short time communicated to each the nature of the reviews that were given of their performance. Mary Glentworth, desisting from her toilet, sat down greedily to devour the *critiques* in the journals which I left with her; but I found that Aline was far less enthusiastic upon the point. There was an expression of sweet sadness on her lovely countenance; and I feared that she had miscalculated her own strength of mind when on the preceding night she had assured me that her feelings having once found a vent, would leave her endowed with the utmost fortitude. I however thought it better not to speak to her on the point; and hearing a double knock at the door, I made it an excuse for hastily quitting her.

I wondered who could be calling at that hour in the morning—for it was only a little past nine o'clock; yet I thought it might possibly be my father—for though I had seen him at a distance on the preceding evening, and therefore knew he was at the theatre, we had not met. I reached the hall just as the servant was opening the front door; and to my surprise, I beheld Major Gower.

"A thousand apologies, Miss Percy," he said, "for intruding upon you at this unseemly hour:—but may I enter?"

"Pray walk in," I said; and I was immediately smitten with a misgiving that something was wrong in respect to the fortune which we had been hoping to share between us.

He followed me into the breakfast-parlour; and I saw that his look was swept around the room as he crossed the threshold. My apprehension was almost confirmed, as I said to myself, "He wishes to be alone with me! Yes, alas! he has assuredly some evil tidings to communicate."

"Miss Percy," he said in an agitated manner, "where—where is Aline?"

"Aline!"—and all in a moment a light flashed in unto my comprehension: the lover of Aline—that lover whose name she had never mentioned—could be none other than the gentleman who stood before me!

"What!" he exclaimed, "is it possible that you do not know everything by this time?—has she not made a confidante of you?"

"I understand it all, Major Gower," I said, my heart thrilling with delight on Aline's account; "but it is only this instant that I have understood it!"

"Oh! where is Aline?" he said, trembling with impatience. "Let me see her, I beseech you!—let me throw myself at her feet—prove to her how much I love her—tell her that I am now rich—and offer her my hand! Oh, let me do all this, Miss Percy!—and I beseech you to delay not!"

"Major Gower," I said, mechanically giving him my hand, while the tears of joy trickled down my cheeks, "your conduct is admirable!—you possess the noblest of hearts!—and Oh! bitterly, bitterly should I have repented any harshness on my part or any selfishness in respect to your uncle's fortune!"

"Miss Percy," he said, "it will be the happiest moment of my life if Aline will now consent to become mine!"

"She will! she will!" I said; "for she loves you! At this moment she is sad and mournful in her chamber——"

"Poor Aline!" murmured Major Gower; "could she think that I had proved faithless, or that I had abandoned her? My God! the bare idea is bitterness! But go to her, Miss Percy—go to her, I beseech you!—and tell her——Oh! I have so much to explain! I know not where to begin — I am bewildered with suspense and joy!"

I hastened from the apartment; I flew up to Aline's room—and it was only at the instant that my fingers touched the handle of the door that I recollected the necessity of breaking the intelligence with some degree of caution; for joy produces its evil effects as well as grief, if it strikes with the suddenness of a blow. Therefore composing my countenance somewhat, I entered; and I found that Aline was just completing her toilet—while the newspapers which I had brought up about a quarter of an hour back, lay on the table in precisely the same position as I had there left them: so that at a glance it was clear that Aline had not the heart to read the history of her own brilliant success.

"My dear friend," I said, "you are still mournful and sad: but as sorrows sometimes come in troops, so do joys! Last night you achieved a magnificent triumph: this morning——".

"Believe me, dear Ellen," she said, "I shall be perfectly calm and happy presently! But sometimes one miscalculates one's mental powers——"

"Aline," I said, taking her hand, "you are too good and gentle and beautiful to be deserted by heaven. No! heaven would not leave you long in affliction! Cheer up, Aline!—there is some one waiting to see you——"

"Some one?" and she started: then she trembled violently from head to foot, while the colour went and came in rapid transitions upon her cheeks.

Not for another instant could I keep that lovely and interesting girl in suspense: but throwing my arms about her neck, I exclaimed, "Your heart has already told you, Aline, what it is that I mean!—you know who is here! It is one who loves you—who is now rich, and who is come to lay his fortune at your feet!"

It seemed as if a faintness came over the young lady: she reeled—she appeared as if about to fall—but I sustained her; and I continued to pour in her ears those assurances which I was warranted to give from everything that had so recently emanated from the lips of Major Gower.

"But, Oh! is this possible?" she murmured; "is it not too late? is not the fatal step taken? I have appeared upon the stage! You remember all that you yourself told me, Ellen——"

"Come with me, and see whether I am deceiving you, Aline! Come—and you will be clasped in the arms of one who possesses the noblest of hearts, and who thinks only of his beloved and beautiful Aline! Not for an instant can you hesitate how to act or what to say to him! By his present conduct he is giving you every possible proof of the most devoted love!"

But still it seemed as if all this were too much happiness for Aline to place reliance upon; and I was compelled to reiterate the assurances over again. Then, as if suddenly convinced that it was really no dream — no hallucination of her own thoughts—it was literally a cry of wild joy to which she gave vent, as she said, "Oh, Ellen, it is destined that you are to prove an angel of goodness unto me! I will go with you."

I conducted her from the apartment: we hastened down the stairs—we entered the breakfast-parlour,—and with ejaculations of delight the lovers were clasped in each other's arms. I left them together, for I knew that they must have much to say and many things to explain after their separation. I ascended to Mary Glentworth's chamber; for it was now needless to keep from her any longer the secret of Aline Marcy's love—and indeed it was absolutely necessary to acquaint her therewith, as I had no doubt that the beautiful French girl would cease to be Mary's companion upon the stage. Miss Glentworth listened with a deep interest to all that I told her: I saw that she once or twice exerted a powerful effort to repress a sigh; and when I had finished speaking she said, "I am rejoiced that such happiness should have overtaken the amiable and kind-hearted Aline. Ah, my dear Ellen!" she added, "it must be sweet indeed to find that the channel of the heart's love at length flows smoothly, and that all the bright hopes which have once been entertained are at length to receive their realization!"

Perceiving that Mary's thoughts were settling upon a topic which engendered painful reminiscences for herself, I hastened to change the discourse by renewing my congratulations on the flattering *critiques* which had appeared in reference to her *debut*. Then her countenance grew animated—her eyes sparkled—and she exclaimed, as if bringing her previous reflections to a sudden climax, "Yes—henceforth my only love must be the profession which I have embraced!"

We now descended together, and repaired to the breakfast parlour. There we found the lovers seated hand in hand.—Aline's countenance radiant with happiness. Starting up from her seat, she flew towards me, exclaiming, "Oh, Ellen! to think that it should be after all entirely owing to yourself that I am indebted for so much happiness! To think that you should have known Alfred"—thus alluding to Major Gower—"and that by your generosity in surrendering up half of the fortune bequeathed to you, you should have proved so great a benefactress to us both!"

Aline embraced me fervently: I introduced Major Gower to Miss Glentworth: and we all sat down to breakfast. When the repast was over, Major Gower took his leave, saying significantly to Aline, "I shall see you this afternoon in Eaton Square."

When he had departed, Aline proceeded to give Mary Glentworth and myself some few explanations in reference to her lover. She was staying at the residence of Mr. and Mrs. Wyvill, Lady Kelvedon's parents, at a distant country-town, when nearly three months back she bade adieu to Alfred Gower—as she thought for ever! The Major was infinitely distressed at Aline's decision, especially as at the same time she had informed him of her intention to seek the stage as a means of eating the bread of independence. He had prayed, implored, and entreated that she would abandon these resolves and become his wife—but all in vain! From everything that passed between them, he felt assured that her determination was irrevocably taken; and he prepared to resign himself to a destiny which it seemed impossible to avert. Obtaining leave of absence from his regiment, he came to London; and at the expiration of a few weeks he received the intelligence that his uncle had died and bequeathed all his property to Miss Ellen Percy, *alias* Trafford,

the eminent tragedian. Any lingering hope which he might have entertained of the possibility of his uncle's heart relenting towards him, was now utterly destroyed; and it was therefore natural enough that he should catch at the suggestion thrown out by his solicitors to dispute his deceased relative's will. Little however did he expect that so speedy and so amicable a settlement would be arrived at; and the reader has already seen how enthusiastic was his joy and how boundless his gratitude when he met me at Mr. Wilkinson's office.

But wherefore had he not immediately sought for Aline Marcy and communicated to her his good fortune? He fancied that she must be still staying with Mr. and Mrs. Wyvill. He did not know that Lord and Lady Kelvedon were in London; nor had he any idea that Aline, having left the hospitable dwelling of her ladyship's parents, had subsequently found an asylum with the kind-hearted Hermione herself. Thus, Alfred Gower imagined that at any moment he should be enabled to find his beloved Aline; and he was resolved to prepare a surprise for her. He remained in London to hasten on the settlement of the pending affairs as much as possible; and he looked forward with a joyous anticipation to the moment when, all being satisfactorily finished, he should be enabled to speed off into the country to seek his Aline at the Wyvills' house, to announce the happy intelligence that he was now rich, and to recompense her for that generous self-sacrifice which she had made of her own love in regard to his worldly interests. Such delightful visions and anticipations was Major Gower indulging in, little dreaming that his Aline was in London all the time, and that she was studying for the dramatic profession. It happened that on the evening of her *debut*, Major Gower was invited to dine with some friends who had taken a box at the theatre for the purpose of witnessing the appearance of the two young lady-aspirants to histrionic honours. Alfred Gower dined with his friends; but he had no inclination to accompany them to the theatre:—he had conceived a dislike for everything that regarded the drama since the day that Aline had revealed to him her intention of embracing the stage as a profession. He did not therefore go with his friends to the theatre: but as they informed him that they should leave immediately after the first piece, he thought that it would only be an act of becoming courtesy for him to be in readiness to escort them home. Hence his appearance in the box just at the moment when the two *debutantes* and myself were receiving the plaudits of the audience at the conclusion of the drama. Aline Marcy had full well comprehended the nature of the feelings which at the moment were expressed by her lover's countenance: he was almost overwhelmed with surprise and consternation. His eyes had met the looks of Aline: she fainted—and he fathomed the cause. A painful incertitude smote him as to the course which he ought now to pursue,—whether he should at once attempt to obtain an interview with Aline, or whether he should await a more suitable opportunity. He espied Lady Kelvedon in another box; and he hastened thither. Her ladyship had just received Aline's note stating that she purposed to find an asylum beneath the roof of my dwelling. Up to that moment Lady Kelvedon was utterly ignorant of the love which had subsisted between Aline Marcy and Major Gower: she knew that they were acquainted, but suspected nothing more. Her astonishment may therefore be conceived when the Major, entering her ladyship's box, whispered to her a few half-distracted words which at once revealed his secret. There was so much excitement prevailing in the house in consequence of Aline's swoon and Mr. Richards' speech, as well as so much discussion going on in reference to the brilliant success achieved by the *debutantes*, that Major Gower's agitation passed unnoticed by any one except Lady Kelvedon herself. In consequence of the few words that he spoke to her, she showed him the note which she had just received from Aline: she earnestly counselled him not to make any attempt to obtain an interview with her at the theatre, nor to send her any billet, as such a proceeding might only tend to compromise her reputation; and she advised him to wait until the morning before he called at my house in Great Ormond Street, lest a visit at such an hour of the night might prove offensive to myself. All this excellent advice did Alfred Gower follow: but when the morning came he sped as early as he thought he might possibly venture to do, to my abode. The rest is known to the reader.

Aline Marcy was now completely happy. Every barrier to a union with the man whom she loved was completely removed. He had become rich; and he would have to make no sacrifices in respect to his own comforts or requirements in espousing a dowerless bride. Not for an instant had her appearance upon the stage excited any prejudice in his breast: on the contrary, he admired her all the more for the determined spirit which had impelled her to embrace a profession that would have enabled her to eat the bread of independence. But if the happy Alfred Gower was now to win a bride, and if the equally happy Aline Marcy was to win a husband, the public were destined to lose an actress of brilliant promise. My readers have no doubt heard of "stars" upon the stage: but this was a meteor that appeared there for a moment, dazzled all eyes with its brilliant but evanescent light, and then darted away into another sphere.

To resume however the immediate thread of my narrative, I must state that Aline Marcy was about to return to Kelvedon House in Eaton Square; her friend Hermione had sent to beg that she would remain with her until the celebration of the nuptials. Most affectionate was the leave-taking on Aline's part towards myself and Mary Glentworth; and with tears in her eyes, but with smiles upon her lips, she assured us of her imperishable friendship.

CHAPTER LXXX.

THE TESTIMONIAL.

In another fortnight the complete settlement of the late Mr. Gower's affairs was accomplished; and one morning I attended at Mr. Wilkinson's office to sign certain releases and discharges and to be put into possession of my share of the fortune. Although for the last month and upwards I had seen all the details of the business steadily progressing towards a prosperous issue, yet when the moment came at which this end was reached, I could scarcely believe it was otherwise than a dream. An amount of capital calculated to produce an income of twelve thousand pounds a year, was now transferred to my name in the Bank of England! Major Gower was present, with his own solicitor, at that final settlement: it was a busy day, for we had to go to Doctors' Commons —thence to the Bank of England—and back again to Furnival's Inn, all for the purpose of adjusting the different details of the amicable settlement that was taking place. At length the business was concluded: this time there had been no impediment to the fulfilment of my hopes—no sudden disappointment—no slip between the cup and the lip, as was more than once the case in the affairs connected with Mr. Parks. All progressed in a straightforward manner until the end; and about three o'clock in the afternoon of the 16th of June, 1842, I received the congratulations of those who were present on becoming the possessor of twelve thousand a-year!

In the evening of that same day the nuptials of Major Gower and Aline Marcy were privately solemnized, by special license, at Kelvedon House in Eaton Square: and by the express wish of the happy couple, as well as of Lady Kelvedon herself, both Mary Glentworth and I were present on the occasion. Old Lord Kelvedon was exceedingly polite and affable to us both. Mr. and Mrs. Wyvill and a few other friends were present, by all of whom I found myself treated with the most marked distinction. It was one of the happiest dates to which my memory now looks back; for I felt that to a certain extent I had been the means of accomplishing the happiness of an amiable girl and a generous-hearted man.

On the day when I gave certain explanations to Mary Glentworth in reference to the loves of those whose union I have just recorded, I was necessarily compelled to unfold to her the fact that I was in some way interested in the will of the deceased Mr. Gower: but still I did not on that occasion enter into minute details nor specify the amount of fortune which might possibly become my own. To my faithful Beda I revealed precisely as much as I unfolded to Mary Glentworth; and thus they neither suspected the magnitude of the affairs which so interested me. But now, when everything was accomplished—when the entire business was brought to a conclusion—and when all danger of disappointment, mishap, or delay was past, I revealed to my friend Mary and my faithful Beda the extent of riches which I had inherited, they were stupified with amazement. For awhile they could not speak: but at length their congratulations were poured forth with an enthusiasm which was almost wild in its fervour.

I now resolved to retire from the stage; and accordingly, on the day after the settlement of the business which gave me so handsome a fortune, I sent a note to Mr. Richards, requesting him to call upon me. It happened that my engagement for the past season had just closed, for the usual period of the vacation had arrived. So closely had the secret been kept in reference to Mr. Gower's will, that the lessee remained altogether unsuspicious of the good fortune which had overtaken me : therefore, on presenting himself in Great Ormond Street according to my summons, he was very far from entertaining the slightest apprehension that he was about to lose my services. I received him alone in the drawing-room ; and after the exchange of a few observations on general topics, I said, "Mr. Richards, it would be unhandsome on my part to keep you any longer in the dark in reference to my future intentions. Therefore I must at once inform you of my determination to withdraw from the stage."

He literally bounded upon his chair : for a few moments he surveyed me with a look of silent consternation ; and then he exclaimed, "No, Miss Trafford ! it is impossible ! Let me hope that you cannot be serious——"

"It is my purpose, Mr. Richards," I said, "to deal with you frankly. I have accepted no engagement from any rival house—I am not seeking by means of a subterfuge for an increase of emoluments from your treasury : I am incapable of behaving in an underhand manner towards you——"

"I know it, Miss Trafford—I know it !" said the lessee, who was much affected : "but the loss of your services comes upon me with the violence of a blow ! Is there no inducement I can hold out ? I hopefully anticipated a renewal of your engagement, under which circumstances it was my intention to offer of my own accord a considerable increase of salary——"

"I was about to inform you," I said, "that the sudden accession of some little amount of fortune, totally unexpected by me a few weeks back, has led me to the resolve which I am now communicating to you. To be frank, I find myself independent of the stage ; and to be still more completely candid with you, Mr. Richards——indeed, that there may not be the slightest mistake as to my position——I may add that in a short time I shall perhaps be altogether settled in life."

"I assuredly wish you all happiness, Miss Trafford ! But the intelligence of your withdrawal from the stage is, I repeat, a sad blow for me. First of all I lost that young French lady whose *debut* was so brilliant—now I am to lose you——"

"But Miss Glentworth remains," I interjected : "her success is already immense—she is devoted to the profession which she has embraced—and there is no chance of your losing her services for the present."

"This is at least a consolation," said Mr. Richards : then after a few moments' reflection, he added, "You do not purpose, I hope, to leave London immediately ?"

"By no means," I rejoined.

"Might I request," proceeded the lessee, "that you will favour me with your presence at the theatre for a single hour the day after to-morrow ? —let us say at noon precisely. In a word, Miss Trafford, I am sure that you will afford the ladies and gentlemen of my company that opportunity of expressing their friendship towards you, their regret at the severance of your professional alliance with them, and their sincere wishes for your prosperity and welfare."

"Not for an instant, Mr. Richards," I answered, "can I hesitate to accept an invitation which is every way so flattering to myself ! I will meet you, and the ladies and gentlemen of your company, at noon precisely the day after to-morrow."

"There is one more topic on which I ought to touch," said Mr. Richards. "During the two years which your professional career has lasted, you have always refused to avail yourself of the privilege of a Benefit. Would it be indiscreet on my part to offer you such an opportunity of bidding farewell to the public ?"

"While thanking you for the generosity of your proposal," I answered, "permit me to decline it. I am possessed of pecuniary resources ample enough to render such a proceeding unnecessary ; and though I will candidly admit that I have had my pride and my ambition in pursuing my professional career, yet I do not wish to quit the stage with the *eclat* of a formal announcement. I would rather disappear from it privately, so to speak : my withdrawal need not be at once generally made known—it will be time enough for it to transpire at the opening of the next season, when you put forward your usual announcements."

Mr. Richards took his leave of me, deeply regretting the loss of my services. I had already spoken seriously to Mary Glentworth in respect to her own interests : I had assured her that if she would leave the stage and continue to live with me as my friend and sister—the welcome partaker of my riches—I should be only too much delighted by such a decision on her part ; and at the same time I gave her to understand that if she preferred to remain upon the stage, such a resolve need not make the slightest difference in any other respect ; for that she must live with me as heretofore—and indeed it would grieve me infinitely if through my own altered circumstances she were to dream of a separation. Her decision was quickly made known ; she was determined to pursue the dramatic career on which she had so hopefully entered ; but she would never separate from me so long as I chose that we should dwell together as bosom-friends or sisters.

Although now possessed of a large fortune, and thus enabled to live in a style far superior to that which I had hitherto maintained, I nevertheless determined to make no alteration in this respect. The time was close at hand when my cousin Henry would return to his native shores ; and I knew, or at least hoped that nothing need prevent the consummation of our happiness by the solemnization of our nuptials. It would *then* be time sufficient to decide upon our future course of life—the quarter of the metropolis in which we might choose to fix our residence—and the degree of style which we should keep up. Therefore I determined for the present to make no change in my establishment, nor for any such purpose to avail myself of the riches that had come into my possession.

Precisely at the hour of noon on the appointed day I proceeded with Mary Glentworth to the theatre. Having received a hint to the effect that a collation was to be served in Mr. Richards' private apartment, we first of all repaired to the dressing-room which for two years had been mine, but which was now my friend Mary's only. Here we took off our bonnets and scarfs ; and thence we proceeded to the lessee's room. An elegant luncheon was prepared ; and when the repast was concluded, Mr. Richards requested that I would step to the Green Room as the most appropriate place for a little ceremony that was about to ensue. Thither I accordingly led the way; and in a few minutes the lessee, at the head of his company, entered that apartment. He bore a superb piece of plate of most exquisite workmanship; and he addressed me in the following terms:—

"Miss Trafford, I have on the present occasion to perform a duty which is alike fraught with pain and pleasure. It is associated with painful feelings, inasmuch as we are now assembled to mark your retirement from a stage which you have embellished and adorned. But on the other hand my duty is a pleasing one, inasmuch as it includes the presentation of this testimonial of the kind feelings, the sincere regard, and the genuine friendship entertained towards you by those whose sentiments I am now speaking. Miss Trafford, I should inform you that during the last few weeks a subscription has been privately made by the ladies and gentlemen present, and to which I have had the honour to contribute, for the purpose of presenting you at the close of the season some slight testimonial of our admiration for your brilliant talents and our appreciation of your moral worth. Little did we foresee that the testimonial which was in preparation would be presented on your retirement from the stage, and that an inscription to this effect would have to be substituted for another already drawn up to express the hope that for many a long year to come you might continue to be the leading star of your profession. But while, Miss Trafford, we regret that you should be about to withdraw yourself from us,—yet on the other hand we offer you our sincerest congratulations that circumstances enable you to take this step. The public in general will be inspired by the same feelings as those which we now experience; and when the time comes for your retirement to be made known, there will be thousands and thousands ready almost to blame that fortune which in its kindness towards *yourself* proved unkind to *them*, by withdrawing from the theatrical sphere a star on which they so much loved to gaze. I will now say no more, Miss Trafford—unless it be to reiterate the earnest wishes and prayers of all now present for your health and happiness; and ever hereafter, amongst our reminiscences, one of the most agreeable periods of our lives must appear to have been that in which we had the honour to be associated with a lady who in every sense has commanded our esteem, our respect, and our admiration."

There was no dramatic pomposity in the delivery of this speech—no attempt at theatrical display: it was spoken with a gentlemanly ease, and with much sincere and genuine feeling. I was greatly affected; but I composed my sensations sufficiently to make a suitable reply; and when the ceremony was finished, I shook hands with all who were assembled there, one after another. The superb piece of plate which had been presented to me, was conveyed to my carriage, in which Mary Glentworth and I took our seats; and we returned home.

That testimonial had been given to me on my retirement from the stage; and as the reader may have gleaned from the tenour of the speech delivered by Mr. Richards, there was an appropriate inscription. Possessed as I was of a large fortune, could I conceive it possible that I should ever

again return to that stage from which I had withdrawn?—could I, on that day, while contemplating the testimonial, have possibly foreseen that circumstances would sooner or later take such a course——But I am anticipating!—and I must resume the thread of my narrative.

Two or three days after the scene at the theatre, I received a letter from my cousin Henry Wakefield, to inform me that he had arrived at Liverpool, that Mr. Macdonald was there to meet him, and that within twenty-four hours after the receipt of this letter I might positively expect to see him in London. What joy and happiness now filled my soul!—with what delight did I hasten to inform Beda of the safe arrival of my cousin in his native land!—and with what flutterings of the heart did I seek Mary Glentworth in order to reveal to her a secret which she had yet to learn! I now told her of my engagement to my cousin: she asked me a thousand questions concerning him; and when I had informed her that he was about two years older than myself—tall, slender, and handsome, with dark hair, and large earnest brown eyes,—she exclaimed, "Oh, Ellen! how happy you ought to be, to know that you are beloved by such an Adonis as you are describing!"

This little incident, as well as a variety of others which I had at different times observed since the terrific exposure took place at Ardleigh House, proved to me that though Mary Glentworth might have ceased to love the Marquis of Dalrymple, yet that her thoughts were frequently concentrated on that lost sentiment, and that she assuredly had a yearning to love and be beloved in return. Even at those times when she would assure me that the power of love was now dead within her, I felt certain that it was otherwise, and that it was merely in the bitterness of her feelings that she thus spoke—and not because she had the deliberate conviction that her youthful affections had all been blighted by the one cruel blow she had received.

The hours passed away—evening came—and I thought it still probable that Henry might yet make his appearance that day. My heart kept fluttering with suspense at every sound that might seem to herald the approach of the fondly expected one: but at length the hour for retiring came, and my cousin did not make his appearance.

"Within four-and-twenty hours after the receipt of his letter," I said to myself. "Oh, assuredly he will keep his word—and to-morrow by breakfast-time he will be here!"

It was a long while before I could get to sleep that night. Fondly and devotedly did I love my cousin: there seemed to be now no barrier to our union; and thus in a few weeks, or in a few months, so soon as all the arrangements should be made, our happiness might be complete. As I lay reflecting in this strain, I found myself wondering whether Henry would be much altered—whether the lapse of a year could have effected any considerable change in his personal appearance? Then I blamed myself for being so foolish as to give way to such ideas; for his age was but twenty-two—and if there were any alteration in him at all it could only be for the better, and tending to give him a more manly appearance. His forehead, I thought to myself, would still be the same high, smooth, shining throne of intelligence—his dark hair would still curl in rich natural clusters about his well-shaped head — his classic features could have lost none of their delicate outlines—and there would still be a world of intelligence and thought in the handsome dark brown eyes. As for his heart, I knew that it was the same towards me, unchanged and unchangeable—for all the letters that I had received from him breathed tenderness, love, and affection.

In the midst of my meditations sleep stole over me; but I awoke at an early hour in the morning. I at once rose and commenced my toilet. And now I will confess that I looked at myself earnestly in the mirror, to ascertain whether the lapse of a year had effected any alteration in my own appearance,—whether late hours, the exertions of my profession, and a heated atmosphere on those nights when I had performed at the theatre, had left their traces upon my countenance? But no!—there was not the faintest sign or evidence of any of those marring influences! I was determined not to deceive myself: I was prepared to acknowledge the truth of any tale which ·my mirror should tell. But I was only twenty years of age; and was it indeed likely that my beauty had been in any way marred or impaired? No!—and it was with a feeling of ineffable joy that I could conscientiously say within myself that never had I looked better. My complexion was as pure and clear as it was before I ever set foot upon the stage: my eyes shone with as great a brilliancy; and the vermilion of my lips was as bright as in my girlhood. A little less of the Sylph and a little more of the Hebe in my figure,—this was the only perceptible change that might be associated with the lapse of the one year since Henry and I parted at Paisley. The reader must not think me vain and conceited that I thus consulted my mirror. What young woman of twenty, when being about to meet the object of her love after a twelvemonth's separation, does not seek to assure herself that in person as well as in feelings she is as worthy of his love as ever?—and who does not feel flattered by the admiration of that being whose approving smile is more precious than all the wealth of the East? If such sentiments as these constitute weakness, then assuredly was I weak on that morning when I thus stood before my mirror to ascertain whether there was the same luxuriance of the raven hair—the same lustre in the large dark eyes—the same vermilion of the lips—the same pearly whiteness of the teeth! Yes—all were the same!—and I confess that my heart swelled with emotions at the thought that if my cousin had ever admired me for my personal beauty, he would be more than ever certain to admire me now.

When I descended to the breakfast-parlour shortly after eight o'clock, I said to Beda, who had followed me thither, "Tell Anna"—thus alluding to the parlour-maid—"to lay places for three; and tell the cook to send up everything nice that the larder will afford."

"For three, dear Miss?" said Beda. "There are only you and Miss Glentworth——for I do not suppose that Mr. Wakefield will come at this hour?"

"Depend upon it, Beda, he will come!" I emphatically interjected. "Within four-and-twenty hours after the receipt of the letter I was to expect him. The letter came yesterday morning at nine o'clock; by nine this morning he will be here!"

Beda's beautiful countenance became animated with joy when she found me so confident; and she hastened to superintend the arrangements of the breakfast-table according to my mandates. Scarcely had she finished when a cab drove up to the door: I rushed to the window——Oh joy! it was Henry who alighted—Beda sped to the front door—in a few moments I was clasped in my cousin's arms!

The heart of the reader must comprehend those rapturous feelings which no language has power to describe,—the feelings attendant upon a meeting such as this. Term it a luxury of the mind—the phrase falls far short of the real meaning which it is intended to convey! Term it an ecstacy of the soul—and still the power of a complete description is wanting! As the Garden of Eden must have been infinitely superior in delights, and beauties, and captivations, to any other earthly garden which has ever since existed,—so were the feelings to which I am now alluding transcendent beyond all other emotions which the human heart can know. When the lips meet in the chastest kisses—when heart beats against heart with the purest though most thrilling sensations—when arms are thrown about each other's necks, or hands are fondly clasped—when the lips being withdrawn, the deep earnest gaze is fixed upon one another, the breath fanning each other's cheeks, and then the lips meeting again and again, and the bosom of one palpitating against the breast of the other,—when the tongue has no utterance for aught but broken words or fervid ejaculations—and when a holy ecstacy seems to enwrap the soul, as if there were a sense of worship mutually offered up betwixt each other,—then is indeed a happiness felt which no language can adequately describe!—then does the heart experience a veritable paradise of feelings! And Oh, for how many sorrows and fears, anxieties and afflictions—for how many perils passed through and mental tortures undergone—does such a period as this prove a recompense! It seems as if heaven itself often plunged human beings into the vortex of suffering, or dragged them through the fiery furnace of excruciating afflictions, in order that they might all the more rapturously appreciate the happiness of such a scene as was mine that morning!

Yes—Henry had returned! And all that my imagination had been depicting was realized; for the lapse of a year had improved his appearance and had constituted the last transition from a lingering boyishness to a complete manliness of look. On the other hand my own hope was likewise realized, when the superb dark brown eyes of my cousin were fixed upon me with tenderest admiration, and he exclaimed, "Ellen, my beloved Ellen! you are more beautiful than ever!"

Mary Glentworth presently made her appearance; and I introduced Henry Wakefield to her—for this was the first time they had ever met. We then sat down to breakfast: but Mary seized an opportunity of whispering in my ear, "He is even handsomer, Ellen, than you represented him!"

During the repast but little was said in the

shape of any of those explanations which Henry and I might mutually have to give; for we knew that we should shortly be again alone together—and it is sweet for lovers to impart their mutual confidences without restraint of any kind. It is an opportunity for which they always watch. Henry therefore conversed with us upon general topics. He had already perused in a newspaper the account of Mary Glentworth's success as a *debutante;* and he offered his congratulations. I was pleased to see that he had not the faintest scintillation of a lingering prejudice against the stage. He described to us many interesting particulars of his recent voyage across the Atlantic; and he gave us sketches of American life and manners. Thus more than an hour passed; and Mary Glentworth then left me and my cousin again alone together.

I first of all suffered him to give me whatever

NO. 63.—ELLEN PERCY.

explanations he might have to afford; and accordingly he lost no time in commencing.

"Dearest Ellen," he said, "you will be pleased to receive from my lips the confirmation of all I have previously told you by letter in reference to the success of the speculations which I have conducted at New York on behalf of Mr. Macdonald. Believe me, dear Ellen, that the very moment when I set foot on shore at Liverpool I should have commenced the journey which was to bring me to London to fold you in my arms; but if I tarried for four-and-twenty hours——"

"It was very natural and proper you should do so, my dear Henry," I said: "for inasmuch as Mr. Macdonald went from Paisley to Liverpool expressly to meet you on your landing, it was because he felt that business-matters must take precedence of every other consideration——"

"No, dearest Ellen," interrupted Henry: "Mr.

Macdonald was not so anxious as may appear, to enter into the accounts with me. He already knew, by the letters I had written him, the remittance of money I had made, and the invoices of goods I had sent, that the enterprises with which he had entrusted me had turned out most advantageous. Indeed, within a single twelvemonth I have not merely enabled him to realize enormous profits—but I have founded connexions, established agencies, and opened channels in the United States, which cannot fail to render the firm of *Macdonald and Company*—and here my cousin smiled significantly—"one of the richest and most prosperous in the world."

"Macdonald and *Company ?*" I said, half starting with the idea that somewhat unpleasantly struck me. "I did not know Mr. Macdonald had any partners ?"

"Dearest Ellen," exclaimed Henry, seizing my hand and pressing it with rapture, "I have glorious intelligence for you! I am Mr. Macdonald's partner !"

"Ah, my dear Henry," I said, "most sincerely should I congratulate you, were it not that——"

"What, my dear Ellen ?" he said, starting with surprise; "is there any drawback to your joy at the announcement I have made? No, no! there cannot be? Do you not remember when you were at Paisley, and when you were introduced to the Macdonalds, the worthy old gentleman made more than a half-promise that if I were successful in the speculations then contemplated, he would make me his partner? And I *have* been successful,—far more successful than even his most sanguine hopes could have led him to anticipate; so that with the zeal of a truthful man and the readiness of a generous one, he hastened to meet me at Liverpool that his promise might be accomplished. It was for this that I tarried, Ellen—it was that the necessary papers and agreements might be signed: for Oh! thought I to myself how proud should I be to announce, and how delighted would you be to hear, that I have thus attained an established position; and at the age of twenty-two have become the partner in one of the greatest mercantile houses of the North !"

"Oh! no reward is too great, my dear Henry," I exclaimed, "for your honest industry—no recompense is too large, for the exertions you have made and the successes you have achieved on behalf of your patron! Receive, then, my warmest congratulations !"

"Ah! now, dearest Ellen," cried Henry joyously, "you are speaking as I expected and hoped that you would speak : for, Oh! believe me, darling girl, that it was for your sake I have been enabled to do so much—for your sake likewise that I was so glad to receive the reward! And now, Ellen, there is naught to impede the accomplishment of our happiness; for I shall enjoy an income that will maintain us handsomely—and you shall leave the stage, dear Ellen——"

"I have already left it, Henry," I answered, with a smile.

"You have left it ?" he ejaculated, with a look of mingled astonishment and joy. "But when, dear Ellen? for in the file of papers which I saw at Liverpool your name was mentioned at only a recent date——"

"Look !" I said; and leading him towards the sideboard, I showed him the testimonial with the inscription upon it.

"Oh! then you have really left the stage !" he cried; "and I rejoice! For though you have been an honour and an ornament to the stage, and have thereon won a glorious renown—and though, dearest Ellen, I have not the slightest lingering prejudice against it,—yet now that I have by mine own industry obtained a good position, and ensured a competent income, I would not have you toil and waste your best years at a theatre——"

"And this, my dear Henry," I interrupted him, "is the very reason why I also would not have you toil and waste your own best years in a counting-house !—and this also is why I perhaps for a moment just now seemed vexed at the idea that you should have accepted Mr. Macdonald's offer to take you into partnership !"

"Good heavens, my dear Ellen !" exclaimed Henry, "do you not comprehend that there is an immense difference betwixt being a partner and a mere clerk or agent ?"

"You need not be either, Henry," I said, taking his hand and pressing it in my own; "and therefore you may undo as soon as possible whatsoever you have done with Mr. Macdonald in respect to the partnership. I will not keep you any longer in suspense, Henry! Read these papers—I will return to you in a quarter of an hour."

Thus speaking, I handed my cousin a packet of papers; and I then hurried from the room. Those papers consisted of a copy of Mr. Gower's will—the several letters which I had received from Mr. Wilkinson during the progress of the business—and other letters from Major Gower to Mr. Wilkinson, and which I had requested the solicitor to give me. All these papers tended to show that there was nothing in the slightest degree suspicious against my own character in the bequest made by the late Mr. Gower. If, in connexion with Henry I knew of any fault, it was that he had shown himself on one occasion too apt to judge by outward appearances and first impressions: and I feared that there might now possibly be a recurrence of the same jealous suspicion. For this reason, therefore I left him alone with all those documents, that he might obtain a full insight into the matter. I passed into another room; and there I beheld a scene which for an instant filled me with surprise. Beda was seated on the sofa; and a young man was kneeling at her feet. But the next instant I recognised her sailor-lover, William Lardner, who had rendered me such special services in the affair of the yacht at Ramsgate, and who had subsequently proved so useful when Zarah was consigned by the treacheries of Edwin St. Clair to a mad-house.

William Lardner did not immediately perceive me—for indeed his back was towards me as he knelt before Beda. But Beda herself gave a sudden start—the rich blood mantled upon her countenance—and then William sprang up to his feet. Beda bounded towards me; and taking my hand she looked up into my face in so deprecating a manner, as if afraid that I should be very angry with her, that I could not help smiling as I thought to myself, "It is a strange coincidence that Beda's lover should return at the same moment as mine: but it would be even still more remarkable if she had not the same right to receive a visit from

William Lardner as I have from Henry Wakefield!"

Caressingly smoothing down Beda's jetty dark hair with my hand, I said; "You have nothing to be afraid of, my dear girl! And as for William, he is most welcome here!"

The youth now came forward, and bowed with the profoundest respect. I have said on a former occasion that he was remarkably handsome—of the gipsy tribe—and swarthy. He was now about nineteen, and he had grown more manly in appearance since last I saw him. He was dressed with the utmost neatness; and I was not surprised when on turning round towards Beda, I perceived that she was surveying him with a species of bashful admiration. I inquired whether William had made a prosperous voyage and had done any good for himself?—and these questions elicited some particulars which were not as yet known to Beda, as it appeared that William Lardner had not been many minutes in the room when I made my appearance. He had originally hired himself on board an East Indiaman: but on touching at the Cape of Good Hope, he and two or three other sailors were attacked with such a violent fever that it was deemed expedient to land them at Cape Town. William Lardner recovered; and when his strength was sufficiently restored, he obtained a passage back to England in another ship belonging to the same owner as the first. On board this latter ship he had attracted the notice of a military man of high rank in the East India service; and this personage had offered to provide for him. But William Lardner had given no decisive answer; he wished to consult Beda on the subject—and, as he diffidently added, "he thought likewise that I should not refuse to give him my own advice." I cheerfully promised to pay the utmost attention to his interests, and assured him that in the course of a day or two I would hear all he had to say on the point; for it did not appear that there was any necessity for him to give a hasty decision to the personage who offered to become his patron.

Leaving William and Beda again alone together I returned to the room where I had left Henry: and the moment I opened the door, he bounded forward and caught me in his arms, exclaiming, "Oh, Ellen! you feared that I was not cured of that mad readiness of mine to judge hastily and by first appearances! Ah, if you knew how often and often I have since blamed myself for my almost unpardonable conduct towards you at River House——".

"Not another syllable on that point, my dear Henry!" I interrupted him: "I am glad that incident should have occurred, since I see that you profit so well by the experience it gave you. You have read those papers?"

"Ellen, it all looks like a dream!" he cried. "But, Oh! how rejoiced I am on your account! And you indeed possess——"

"Twelve thousand a-year, Henry! And now tell me," I continued, "what necessity is there for you to toil and slave behind the desk of a counting-house——".

"Oh! this is most generous on your part, dearest Ellen!" exclaimed Henry; "for I know what you mean!"

"Yes, dearest cousin," I replied: "in the same way that if you had suddenly become rich, you would rejoice to lay your fortune at my feet—so do I now bless the moment which enables me to do the same towards you!"

"Oh! but if I possessed something of my own, Ellen," cried Henry—"if through mine own industry I had obtained but the smallest competency, no matter how small, would you not think better of me?"

"Henry, how can you speak thus?" I exclaimed. "What matters it from which side the riches come, so long as we possess them? There is my fortune, Henry—take it—consider it to be your own——"

"Ellen, dearest Ellen!" he said, pressing my hand to his lips; "not another syllable of argument dare I use! You are the arbitress of my destiny——and Oh! happy indeed am I to possess the love of such a goddess of generosity, and beauty, and goodness as you are!"

"I honour you, Henry," I said, "for that inclination which you have shown to pursue an active employment and to earn riches by your own industry. But under existing circumstances it were the height of folly for you to render yourself the slave of commercial avocations. It is not because you retire from the mercantile world and I retire from the stage, that we need both lead a life of idleness, rendering us worthless members of society. Those who possess riches ought to seek every opportunity of doing good. Such a pursuit will furnish occupation; and thus, you see, there are useful, substantial, and pleasurable avocations apart from those of business. Then, too, there is leisure for the improvement of the mind—for the study of useful and valuable literature—and for the cultivation of the arts and sciences. Idleness need not be the inevitable associate of wealth: on the contrary, wealth itself may be rendered the fertile source of employments and avocations calculated to benefit not merely ourselves, but many of our fellow-creatures likewise."

Henry listened to me with the deepest attention,—his looks expressing the tenderest approval of all that thus flowed from my lips. After some little further conversation, it was agreed that he should write that very day to Mr. Macdonald at Paisley, to represent that his prospects enabled him to retire from the commercial world, and that he requested therefore the deeds of partnership might be cancelled. He promised to set off for Paisley in a couple of days that he might finally wind up his accounts with Mr. Macdonald, and take leave of that gentleman and his family.

I sent for my father in the course of the day, that he might be introduced to Henry Wakefield; for they had not as yet met. Henry's deceased mother had been my father's sister; and thus Henry was my father's nephew. He knew that my father had been unfortunate and criminal; for these revelations I made to Henry when we met at Paisley a year back. But the demeanour of my lover towards my father was of the kindest and the most magnanimous description. As for my father himself, he was proud of possessing such a nephew for the present, and of the prospect of shortly having him as a son-in-law.

Having remained two days in London, Henry set off for the North, in order that he might get his business finished with Mr. Macdonald as soon as possible. He calculated that he should be altogether a week absent; and we both felt at parting that brief though the interval of separation was to be, we wished that it was over, and that we were reunited, to part no more!

CHAPTER LXXXI.

THE POOR AUTHOR.

IT was on the day after Henry Wakefield's departure—and I was seated alone in the drawing-room, at about mid-day, Mary Glentworth having gone out on a shopping excursion,—when a domestic entered with the intimation that a person who gave the name of Jingleton desired to see me.

"Jingleton!" I said. "Are you sure it is Jingleton? I know a·gentleman named Singleton——"

"But this, Miss, is a Mr. Jingleton."

"Jingleton?" I repeated. "No! I do not remember such a name. Who is this person?"

"He looks, Miss, like some decayed tradesman —or else a very poor gentleman; and he was so uncommonly polite to me, bowing and scraping, and speaking so earnestly, as if he really thought that it depended on myself whether he could obtain access to you!"

"Poor man!" I said; for I began to suspect that he must either be an actor or else a dramatic author who had fallen upon evil days—for I frequently received visits from unfortunate persons belonging to those fraternities.

I at once desired that Mr. Jingleton might be shown up; and accordingly, in a few minutes, a very strange-looking person made his appearance. He was about five-and-forty years of age—very tall and lanky—and very shabbily dressed. He wore a kind of shooting jacket; his pantaloons hung loose upon his thin legs; and the toes of his worn unshapely boots turned upward. His person was not of the most scrupulous cleanliness; and in respect to his linen, truth compels me to declare that his shirt seemed to indicate a suspicion of credit on the part of his laundress for at least a fortnight back. His hat was much worn, and had that sort of battered, broken appearance which implied that he was frequently in the habit of knocking the crown against the tops of doorways that were too low for him to pass under without stooping, and that he always forgot to stoop. It was quite clear that his garments were not very often treated to a contact with the brush; for though it was now most beautiful weather, towards the close of the month of June, and there had not been any rain for the last ten days, yet were the lower parts of the pantaloons spattered with mud which had dried on in spots. As for the expression of this individual's countenance, it was that of the most servile humility blended with a certain under-current of conceit and self-importance, as if Mr. Jingleton felt that in reality he was one of the cleverest persons in the world, but that adverse circumstances had reduced him to the adoption of a meek, humble, grovelling demeanour towards those of whom he sought assistance or succour.

On being introduced into the drawing-room,

Mr. Jingleton made a very low bow: then he advanced a few paces, and bowed again: then he drew a little nearer still, but halted to make another salaam; and then he continued to shamble forward in a nervous hesitating way, which was so painful for me to behold that I endeavoured to put the poor man at once at his ease by saying, "Pray be seated, Mr. Jingleton."

"Thank you, Miss Trafford," he replied, with the most cringing manner and the humblest bow that could possibly be conceived; and then in his awkwardness and confusion he missed the chair on which he was about to seat himself, and sprawled backward upon the carpet.

I could scarcely help laughing: but compassion for the unfortunate man enabled me to exercise sufficient control over myself to restrain even a smile that might have been calculated to wound his feelings; and it was in the midst of the most painful confusion, and agitation, and nervous embarrassment that the poor wretch scrambled up.

"Dear me, Miss Trafford," he faltered out, "to think that I should be so awkward!"

"Oh! it was an accident which might happen to anybody," I said. "Pray be seated, Mr. Jingleton! Take your time—tell me your business; and if——"

"Ah! if, Miss Trafford!" interjected my strange visitor, theatrically extending his right arm, while his countenance lost somewhat of its expression of cringing humility: "that is the very point! That little preposition if, though brief to spell and curtly facile to pronounce, nevertheless often constitutes the most stupendous of barriers! Why, Miss Trafford, everything from the beginning of time seems to have depended upon an if! If Eve had not plucked the fruit in the Garden of Eden——"

"I presume, sir, you are a literary gentleman?" I interrupted him, with the hope of thus escaping from an essay or lecture which commencing at so remote a date, threatened to take a range which would prove interminable.

"If Shakspere had never written," responded Mr. Jingleton, with a most affected air of mingled humility and conceit, "I should style myself a dramatist. But who, Miss Trafford, in the face of the unapproachable Shakspere—who in the presence of the bard who stands on so sublime an eminence,—who, I ask, Miss Trafford, would dare——"

"Certainly not," I hastened to exclaim; for my strange visitor was now gesticulating so fiercely that I feared lest he should be working himself up into a sort of poetic rage, for his eye was assuredly "in a fine frenzy rolling."

"No, certainly not!" he vociferated. "And therefore, Miss Trafford, I call myself a dramatic author, and not a dramatist. Mark the distinction!" and here he raised his forefinger, which he kept obliquely pointing at a distance of about a foot from his own nose and three or four feet from mine. "You cannot say it is a distinction without a difference; for in less than one hour would I undertake to prove to the satisfaction of the whole world——"

"No doubt of it!" I hastened to interject. "And now, Mr. Jingleton, would you be kind enough to inform me of the purpose for which I am honoured with this visit?"

"Oh, Miss Trafford! it is I who am honoured!"—and now he was all cringing humility again. "I, the poor and comparatively obscure dramatic writer, seek you, the great tragedian—to ask not coin, Miss Trafford——Perish the vile thought! No mean and grovelling selfishness is here!"—and he hit his left breast a tremendous thump with his clenched fist, at the same time suddenly assuming a look of fierce defiance against the whole world to gainsay the truth of his assertion.

"No, my dear sir," I said, beginning to be fearful that I had to do with a lunatic who might possibly prove a dangerous one, "I am sure no one could impute selfishness to a literary gentleman such as you. But might I ask what is it you seek?"

"Your countenance and favour," replied Mr. Jingleton: and again his right arm was theatrically extended. "Now are my aim and object both revealed!"

"Yet still I do not quite understand," I said, "in what manner you require my assistance."

Mr. Jingleton slowly thrust his right hand into the pocket of his short coat of shooting-jacket appearance; and thence he drew forth a packet enveloped in brown paper, very greasy, and smelling of stale tobacco-smoke. This packet he proceeded to open with a most mysterious air: but I already more than half-suspected that it contained a manuscript—and such indeed proved to be the fact.

"Here," said Mr. Jingleton, with the manuscript upon his knees—and as he slowly turned over the leaves, I saw that they were very dirty, very much thumbed, and soiled at the edges, as if the unfortunate work had been through the hands of all the managers and lessees in London without experiencing success,—"here is a drama, Miss Trafford, in five acts—a legitimate drama, I may venture to call it—a drama in which the unities are preserved—a drama over which I spent days and nights of anxious toil,—a toil that hitherto has unrewarded been! But now, unless I mock myself with hopes vain and illusive as night's airy dreams, the moment of my triumph's near at hand: for you, Miss Trafford, will delight to shed the glory of your own bright genius on the fair creation of my heroine!"

"Am I to understand, Mr. Jingleton," I asked, smiling as I perceived that he endeavoured to speak in blank verse,—"am I to understand that you are desirous for me to recommend your drama for representation and take the character of the heroine?"

"Such is my wish, my hope, my aspiration!" answered Mr. Jingleton, whose diffidence was every moment losing itself in theatrical gestures and dramatic effects.

"I am really afraid," I said, "that I must at once disappoint you in this hope; for my engagement with Mr. Richards has ceased—I have no interest with that gentleman to enable me to forward your views——"

"Is this the truth? or a mere pretext made to let me down, with courteous ease and lightness, from the high culmination of my hopes into the abysm of a dark despair?"—and Mr. Jingleton sent forth the syllable -pair with a fierce sardonic prolongation and rolling accentuation, which rendered both his appearance and his conduct so exceedingly ludicrous that it was with the greatest difficulty I could keep myself from laughing.

"I am truly sorry," I said, "to be compelled——"

"At least give me a kindly written word," interjected Mr. Jingleton, "to the great Thespian manager Ricardo, vulgarly y-clept Richards! Perhaps you'll say that you must see the drama? Well, 'tis here!"

"It is indeed useless, Mr. Jingleton," I said, "to read any of your production. I have little doubt of its merit: but I am unable to forward your views in the manner you have suggested. Permit me, however, without giving offence, to state that if a little pecuniary aid would be acceptable——"

"Ah, Miss Trafford!" said the poor author, now dropping the rant and gesticulation, and relapsing into the cringing servility as at first; "report did not deceive me when it whispered in my ear that you were kind and generous. I have long been connected with the stage—I have seen and admired you from a distance——"

"You mean, I presume, that you have been connected with the stage as an author?"

"Well, Miss Trafford, to speak the truth, I have sometimes taken a character in one of my own plays. You see, it enabled me to eke out. I used to write for the Tom and Jerry Saloon: the price was half-a-guinea a play—so that five shillings extra on the Saturday night for taking a part——"

"Good heavens!" I ejaculated, "you have written plays for ten shillings and sixpence?"

"Alas, I have, Miss Trafford!" was Mr. Jingleton's response, delivered with a lugubrious solemnity which had something singularly ludicrous in it. "But on the other hand I have received remuneration as fair as any other writer. For instance, there was my crack piece which came out at the Adelphi and ran for a hundred and fifty nights. I'll tell you how it was, Miss. One day I was sitting in my room at my lodgings, busily engaged in meditating on the vanities of the world and the deceitfulness of riches—for I had nothing to do at the moment but thus to give way to my reflections—when there was a knock at the door. I called out, 'Come in:' but a hoarse voice on the other side exclaimed, 'It's deuced easy to talk about coming in, but I can't reach the latch.' I was nearly flying into a rage, for it was the gruff voice of a man that spoke, and so I naturally thought that it was ridiculous for him to pretend he could not reach the latch when any child of only five or six years old could easily lift it. However, I thought I wouldn't say anything rude; so I went to the door—I opened it—and in walked a little fellow only two feet high;—that is to say, one foot for the length of his head, and the other foot for the length of his body——and that's all, for he had no legs whatsoever!"

"And yet," I said with a smile, "you just now stated that he walked into the room?"

"So he did, Miss Trafford—I can assure you!" exclaimed Mr. Jingleton: "but he positively had no legs, and only little bits of feet fastened on to his body, just like the fins of a seal; and he flapped away too in just the same style that the seal moves itself along. He was handsomely dressed, with a gold chain which nearly touched the floor as he entered the room. He asked if I were that celebrated dramatic writer who bore the name of Jingleton? I answered that I was. He then asked what I could do for him? I said he must first tell me what he wanted. It then came out that he was going to perform at the Adelphi, but that he must have a particular style of piece to introduce him; for his abilities consisted only in leaping and flitting about, or gliding along with those fin-like feet and long monkey-arms of his, at a most astonishing pace. In fact, he gave me a specimen of his powers; and I then knew what I could do for him. Miss Trafford," added Mr. Jingleton, with the utmost solemnity, "you are now acquainted with the origin of that piece which took the whole town by storm——I mean *The Musical Musk-Rat.*"

"Oh, indeed!" I said, affecting to be greatly interested, so as not to wound the poor man's feelings. "And you were the author——"

"Yes, Miss Trafford—I was the author of that wonderful piece which ran a hundred and fifty nights! I need not inform a young lady of your brilliant intelligence, that my little friend the dwarf played the part of the musk-rat."

"I thought so. But did he sing?" I inquired.

"Oh, no!" exclaimed the dramatic author: "he could not sing a note. But when he appeared, the orchestra played low strains. There was the musk-rat—there also was the music: imagination ascribed the melody to the animal—and thus you had the Musical Musk-Rat!"

"Very ingenious," I said: and at the same time taking out my purse, I proceeded to observe, "And now, Mr. Jingleton——"

"Ingenious indeed!" he exclaimed: "it was the plot, Miss Trafford, that was ingenious! I will give you the outline."

"Really, my dear sir," I said, shrinking with horror from the idea of such an infliction, "I could not think of troubling you——"

"Oh, no trouble whatsoever!" ejaculated Mr. Jingleton; "and I am convinced that you will experience a rare pleasure in listening to the outline of this plot. The curtain, on rising, displays the gorgeous scenery of an uninhabited island, where the King surrounded by his courtiers and in the presence of crowds of his people——"

"How then," I gently asked, "could the island be an uninhabited one?"

"Uninhabited? Did I say uninhabited?" cried Mr. Jingleton, catching at the word as if to retrieve the error. "I meant to say *an unknown island!*"

"Well, pray proceed," I said; "though I am at a loss to comprehend how you could be supposed to discover what was going on in an *unknown* island?"

"Oh, Miss Trafford! you who have so perfect an experience of the stage, not to admit how much is left in that sphere to the imagination! When once the fancy can bring itself to believe that a stage of wooden boards constitutes a spot of earth, and that there is any reality in the wooden trees at the sides, the wooden waterfall at the end, and the wooden clouds overhead—surely Miss Trafford, I say, if an audience can sit patiently and comfortably, and delude itself thus far, it may also fancy that an island is unknown to all the rest of the world?"

"True, Mr. Jingleton," I said, beginning to get

wearied of his tediousness. "And now will you do me the favour to accept of this bank-note——"

"Miss Trafford, a thousand, thousand thanks!" exclaimed the delighted author, as he received the note for five pounds which I placed in his hand. "You know not half the service you have done me! My baker's bill shall now be liquidated—my butcher's also: from the cobbler's hands the boots I sent to sole shall be released: comfort shall likewise be infused into my washerwoman's soul; and from the spout my Sunday raiment soon shall be redeemed!"

Thus did Mr. Jingleton address me with theatrical declamation and outstretched arm. Again it was with the greatest difficulty I could prevent myself from smiling: but I succeeded in keeping my countenance; and when I beheld him carefully consign the bank-note to a greasy old pocket-book containing playbills and *memoranda* written on dirty paper, I was in hopes that he was about to take his departure. But nothing of the kind!—for on abruptly turning towards me, he exclaimed, "Now, Miss Trafford, for the plot of my celebrated piece!"

"Pray, Mr. Jingleton," I said, "do not give yourself the trouble. And then too," I added, looking at my watch, "my own time is precious——"

"Everybody's time is precious, Miss Trafford!" exclaimed the visitor. "But I could not possibly think of taking my departure before I had fulfilled my promise of giving you the outline of that remarkable and extraordinary drama."

I thought it best to resign myself to my fate, as it was evident that Mr. Jingleton was inexorably bent upon this cruel infliction. So I sat and listened.

"The first scene," resumed Mr. Jingleton, "discloses the King of the Unknown Island, attended by his courtiers and by an immense crowd of his loyal subjects. By the bye, the Adelphi management was liberal in respect to the crowd: it consisted of three men and a boy, and produced a startling effect. Well, the King—who of course is very splendidly dressed, in robes of purple, orange, red, and green, all spangled, with a crown on his head and a sceptre in his hand—begins by telling his courtiers and his people that he is ninety years of age, that he has reigned over them for exactly sixty years, that he had the misfortune to lose his Queen (here he weeps) fifty years ago——"

"His grief, then," I could not help observing, "had lasted exactly half a century?"

"It shows how faithful the good old King was to the memory of his beloved Queen," responded Mr. Jingleton. "But I was about to describe how the King went on to inform his courtiers and his people that the only living scion of his race was his beautiful granddaughter, the Princess Mimosetta, exactly sixteen years of age and a perfect miracle of loveliness."

"Of course," I interjected, "this good King of yours was telling his courtiers and his subjects all this for the same reason that Puff gives in the *Critic?*"

"Precisely so, Miss Trafford. The courtiers and the subjects must have known very well beforehand everything the King was telling them: but the audience at the Adelphi knew nothing about it. Well, his gracious Majesty proceeds to inform his assembled lieges that his most delicious experiences of life had been derived from the extreme sensitiveness of two tastes which he possessed. One was a passion for the odour of flowers, sweet essences, and everything fragrant: the other was a devoted love of melody in all its forms, whether vocal or instrumental, the singing of birds, the humming of insects, or the rippling of streams. The King went on to say that he could not help thinking that the natural mercifulness of his disposition arose from the soft influences of these qualities or tastes, whichever you may choose to call them; and he appealed to his courtiers and the assembled myriads of his subjects to pronounce whether his reign had been a mild one or not? Then of course the courtiers and the people are most loyal in their devotion, love, and admiration towards their aged monarch—all shout enthusiastically, clap their hands, and begin dancing for joy around that venerable king; so that he is greatly affected and begins to dance likewise."

"What! dance at ninety?" I inquired.

"Oh, yes! to be sure!" answered Mr. Jingleton: "one may do anything on the stage, you know, and also in an unknown island."

"No doubt. Pray proceed."

"I will, Miss Trafford. Well, the dance being over, and the King having wiped away his tears, his Majesty proceeds to inform his courtiers and his people that he is about to choose a husband for his charming granddaughter, the Princess Mimosetta. He announces that he has made up his mind to put all ideas of rank out of the question, and to judge of the qualities of a bridegroom according to those very tastes which he himself possessed to such a degree, and which have had the effect of rendering his own disposition so mild and merciful. This great King therefore orders proclamation to be made that whosoever can prove the possession of the most exquisite taste in respect to music, and likewise the most delicate sensitiveness in respect to sweet odours and fragrances, shall be honoured with the hand of the Princess Mimosetta, and shall be recognised as heir to the crown of the Unknown Island. The heralds make proclamation to this effect; and the first scene closes with a tableau of courtiers kneeling to their good old King, who stretches out his sceptre over them to bless them. Grand effect there, Miss Trafford, I can assure you!"

"It must have been, Mr. Jingleton. But do you not think that if you were to favour me with a call on some future occasion——"

"You might be out—you might be engaged—or a thousand things—and you would miss the remainder of the plot! I beseech you therefore to let me finish my description now. The second scene commences; and the stage represents a grand hall in the royal palace. The King is seated on his throne; the Princess Mimosetta occupies another throne; and there is a vacant one to be filled by the bridegroom, for this is the day of competition. The Princess is beautifully apparelled in a lavender-coloured satin dress, and with a tiara upon her head. In addition to the royal personages, there are courtiers, heralds, populace, and guards assembled. The proclamation is again made; several aspirants come forward—but they fail to convince the King of the excellence of their

tastes in respect to music and fragrances. At last the trumpets sound, and a beautiful young Prince makes his appearance."

"Where is the Prince supposed to come from?" I asked; "because the old King had no relations except his granddaughter—and no other land is known to this unknown island."

"True, Miss Trafford," said Mr. Jingleton, with a somewhat puzzled air; "I did not think of explaining where the Prince came from. But it did not much matter, you know—as the audience would not ask the question! Besides, on the stage as well as in fairy tales, a Prince is always forthcoming when wanted; and we have this advantage over the occurrences of real life,—that it is not necessary to explain who our Princes are. They announce their names, and that is sufficient. Well, this beautiful young Prince who suddenly appears in the palace-hall, makes an excellent speech, declaring his name to be Melodoriferous——"

"Rather a singular name for a royal personage —was it not?" I asked.

"Pray, Miss Trafford," exclaimed Mr. Jingleton, "pause for a moment to analyze the name —pronounce it in soft accents, so as to estimate its euphony—and study its combination of meanings, so as to judge of its appropriate expressiveness. Melodoriferous! Does it not convey the joint ideas of melody and odours—music and fragrance? It is a name alike harmonious and sweet-scented. So thought the King of the Unknown Island; and so thought the Princess Mimosetta. Conceive therefore the delight of King, Princess, courtiers, heralds, guards, and people, when they begin to perceive that the atmosphere is filled with the most delicious odours—eau-de-cologne, lavender-water, bergamot, otto of roses, millefleurs——"

"The millefleurs would alone be sufficient, I should conceive, for the purpose of appropriately and satisfactorily introducing the Prince?"

"Well, Miss Trafford, there was no harm in having all the other scents. The King was rejoiced—the Princess was enchanted; for that young Prince was a veritable embodiment of perfume—a substantial concentration of fragrance—a peripatetic nosegay. Then he raised his voice, and sang in the most ravishing manner. In a word, all present were thrown into ecstacies: for the beautiful Prince showed how well he merited his name of Melodoriferous. He is welcomed as a worthy bridegroom for the Princess and as the future King of the Unknown Island. All is happiness—when suddenly a clap of thunder startles everybody; the earth opens——that is to say a trap in the stage does—and up comes a horrible old hag, the Fairy Pestiferosa. This vile creature has always cherished a deadly enmity towards the beautiful young Prince, and by certain untoward circumstances she has now an opportunity of wreaking her vengeance——"

"And these untoward circumstances," I said.

"Well, Miss Trafford," responded Mr. Jingleton, "they were fully explained in my original manuscript of the play: they were embodied indeed in a dialogue which I represented as taking place between Prince Melodoriferous and the Fairy Pestiferosa—very thrilling and very startling, I can assure you!—but the manager cut it all out, to my infinite horror and disgust. Alas! there was no diverting him from his ruthless purpose! So the 'untoward circumstances' were all left to the imagination."

"Perhaps it was best," I said: and I had no doubt the audience must have thought so likewise.

"Well, Miss Trafford, if you say so, it must have been," rejoined Mr. Jingleton meekly. "Then came a terrible scene—the Fairy Pestiferosa stretched out her wand, touched the Prince therewith, and bade him quit the form of a man and take that of a rat. The courtiers, the guards, the heralds, and the people crowded around in horror and consternation: the Prince went down the trap—and up it in his place came my little friend the legless dwarf, for whom the piece was written. There he was, dressed as a rat!—so that when the guards, heralds, courtiers, and people fell back at the moment when the malignant fairy had done her dreadful work, the audience beheld the rat in the place where the young Prince had previously stood! Grand tableau—horror, consternation, petrifaction—Princess senseless in the arms of her maid—good old King speechless and transfixed on his throne. End of the second scene."

"It must have been very effective, Mr. Jingleton," I said. "But now, if you will permit me to order you up some luncheon——"

"Not for the world, until I have finished this description!" he exclaimed, thus reminding me of the persevering tediousness of the Barber of Bagdad in the Arabian Nights Entertainments.

"I am sure you must be wearied, Mr. Jingleton," I said.

"Wearied?" he cried. "Not an atom! I could talk another hour without ceasing!"

I almost groaned in despair; for I thought that he was fully capable of this terrible infliction.

"The third scene," he resumed, "opens with a dialogue between First and Second Citizen. First Citizen tells Second Citizen that it is now exactly seven years since the terrible event which deprived Princess Mimosetta of a handsome bridegroom and transformed Prince Melodoriferous into a rat. Second Citizen clasps his hands in sympathizing sorrow, and speaks of the affliction of the old King——"

"What! is the old King still alive?" I asked.

"Oh, yes!" exclaimed Mr. Jingleton. "It would not do to kill him before he had seen everything put right and happiness restored. Well, as I was saying, Second Citizen deplores the good old King's sorrow and draws an affecting picture of how the Princess Mimosetta sits in her bower, the picture of despair—always silent—never smiling—refusing all sustenance——"

"What! for seven long years?" I exclaimed

"Well, truly, it does seem rather odd," observed Mr. Jingleton: "but I positively make it so in the play: Second Citizen says it with all suitable gravity and distress—and the audience never once failed to be affected by it throughout a hundred and fifty nights!"

"Well, my dear sir," I said, "if so many audiences were satisfied, I have no right to complain. Pray proceed. The Princess had taken no sustenance for seven long years——"

"Yes—that was where I left off," said Mr. Jingleton. "In short, First and Second Citizen drew a most deplorable picture of the condition of their island ever since the catastrophe. But it appeared from this dialogue that though the wicked Fairy Pestiferosa had transmogrified Prince Melodoriferous into a rat, she could not crush out of him, so to speak, those very exquisite qualities which were the source and origin of all the umbrage she had spitefully taken against him. The consequence was that the power of melody still clung to him; and the fragrance with which his princely garments had been perfumed, survived in his rat-skin. It is true that the qualities of harmony and odour were modified and influenced by the change of form, though they could not be annihilated thereby. Thus the enchanted Prince had become a Musical Musk Rat! Pray, Miss Trafford, might I ask whether you think this was an ingenious method of introducing the little dwarf?"

"Nothing could be more ingenious," I replied. "You deserve infinite credit, Mr. Jingleton, for your tact and cleverness in this particular."

The wrinkled half-starved countenance of the poor author became animated with delight as I bestowed this praise upon him; and he was so elated and inspired by it that when I again suggested something relative to luncheon, he would not listen to it, but insisted on proceeding with the description of his piece.

"Well, Miss Trafford, presently First Citizen cries, 'Hush! here comes the King!'—and Second Citizen answers, 'We'll stand aside and watch the good old man!' The King enters, with his crown upon his head, his sceptre in his hand, and in his gorgeous robes of purple, orange, red, and green, all covered with spangles——"

"Just as he was seven years ago?" I observed.

"Precisely, Miss Trafford. His beard was as white as silver at first; so it could not be any whiter, you know——"

"And doubtless, as his granddaughter had taken no sustenance for seven long years, the King had not changed his garments during the same period?" I remarked.

"Most likely not," said Mr. Jingleton, taking quite seriously that which I meant in jest. "The King soliloquises; and from this soliloquy the audience learn that his majesty has had a dream during the past night. In this dream a good fairy appeared to him, and told him that if the musical rat can only be enticed to enter a trap, the spell will be broken and he will instantaneously recover his proper shape. So the King has come out to meditate upon this——"

"Don't you think that it would have been more natural," I asked, "if the King instead of wasting time in soliloquising, had at once set to work to bait a trap and entice the rat into it?"

"Well, perhaps it would," said Mr. Jingleton, slowly and thoughtfully: "but then such a course would have interfered with the arrangements and requirements of my plot."

"Oh, that is different!" I exclaimed. "Of course everything must be sacrificed to that! Pray proceed."

"I will, Miss Trafford. The King at the end of his soliloquy speaks in a broken voice relative to his granddaughter; and then he suddenly exclaims, 'Hush! she comes!'"

"Why does he say hush," I asked, "when no one is speaking but himself, and he can of course hold his tongue in a moment if he chooses?"

"Oh, Miss Trafford! What! with all your experience on the stage ——"

"Well, well," I exclaimed, laughing, "excuse a little piece of good-natured irony. I suppose there must always be some formal manner of announcing the approach of the principal characters upon the stage."

"If it wer'n't for 'Hush! he comes!' or 'Hush! she comes!'" rejoined Mr. Jingleton, "I really don't know how matters would ever get on satisfactorily upon the stage at all. However, to return to my own piece. The King saw his granddaughter coming; and she appears accordingly."

"Then she has left the bower at last, after having sat in it disconsolate for seven years?" I said.

"At last! Poor Mimosetta! Still beautiful—still with the same loveliness of countenance and the same rounded symmetry of form——"

"Well, that is extraordinary," I interjected,

No. 64.—ELLEN PERCY.

"seeing that she had not eaten anything for so long a period. One would have thought that she must at least have fallen away a little."

"Not an atom, Miss Trafford! and that is the peculiarity of heroines in plays and in novels when in affliction : they spend all their time in weeping, never think of eating, and yet do not find themselves physically the worse for it—so that when their lovers come back at the end, they always find their lady-loves more beautiful than ever. Mimosetta was no exception to the general rule. There she was, beautiful as ever !—with the tiara upon her brow, the symmetry of her shape set off by the lavender-coloured dress——"

"What!" I ejaculated, "then she wore just the same clothes as she did when we first saw her seven years back?"

"Well, it would appear so," said Mr. Jingleton, dubiously and thoughtfully. "Yet when we come to reflect upon it, it would appear more natural if we supposed that she had made some little change in her raiment during that period. However, so it was—in this manner did the Princess appear—and she also began to soliloquise for some little while——"

"Without seeing her royal grandfather, of course?" I said.

"Oh, of course!" ejaculated Mr. Jingleton; "because she was not to see him until she reached a particular part, when the King interjected something; and then with a cry of joy on beholding him, she threw herself into his arms. This always proved an effective point—particularly with the Gallery. It gave the old King a fine opportunity of displaying silent emotion; while the Princess Mimosetta found an equally good opportunity for a passionate appeal to her grandsire to restore her bridegroom to her arms."

"But the King had not taken the Prince away from her," I remarked.

"No, Miss Trafford: but yet I think it was a natural hit on my part—I mean in respect to what I thus made Princess Mimosetta do: for when people are in affliction they always appeal to their friends or relatives to extricate them, just for all the world as if the persons thus appealed to could perform impossibilities!"

"Yes—and so it was in this case," I said; "for even if the old King had taken away the Prince from his granddaughter, he could not very easily restore him to her arms so long as he maintained the form of a rat. But I beg you to proceed. What happened next?"

"The King waited till his granddaughter had finished that long and passionate appeal; and then he acquainted the Princess with his dream. She was rejoiced——"

"But why did he not at once tell her of the vision," I inquired, "and put as speedy an end as possible to the agony of her grief?"

"And then what would have become of the pathetic speech which I had taken so much pains to compose for the Princess Mimosetta? It would have been rendered useless; and my feelings as an author would have been sacrificed for the mere purpose of making the incidents of the piece seem a trifle more natural!"

"Ah! under those circumstances," I said, scarcely able to maintain my gravity, "it was better to make the piece so progress that nature should be outraged instead of your feelings."

"To be sure, Miss Trafford!" rejoined Mr. Jingleton: "that is precisely the way in which authors, whether dramatists or novelists, always reason. But to resume the thread of my description. I was stating that the King informed his granddaughter of his vision, and she was delighted. She insisted upon having a golden trap made, as one of that precious metal was alone worthy for so great a purpose. The King accordingly sent for a goldsmith, who undertook to make such a trap in three hours——"

"Three days you mean?" I interjected.

"No—three hours. We must suppose, Miss Trafford, that science and art can accomplish miracles in that Unknown Island. Besides, his Majesty threatened to cut off the goldsmith's head if he did not use the utmost despatch——"

"I admit that such an argument must have been persuasive enough with the goldsmith. But it would seem, Mr. Jingleton, that the good old King had become a bit of a tyrant?"

"Well, Miss Trafford, you must make some little allowance for afflictions and sorrows, which are terribly souring to the temper—particularly of Kings!"

"No doubt. So the golden cage was to be made in three hours——"

"Yes. And now the courtiers, the guards, the heralds, and the populace all came crowding around their Monarch and the Princess to offer their congratulations on account of the hope which has presented itself—and the third scene closes with a tableau alike affecting and effective. The fourth scene," continued Mr Singleton, rushing on with scarcely a break, for he was doubtless afraid that I should seize the opportunity to cut his description short,—"the fourth scene opens with the representation of a beautiful garden. In short, it is the palace-garden; and it is filled with trees covered with the most delicious fruits. There the Musical Musk-Rat is discovered at his sports; for this is the scene specially intended for the display of the dwarf's qualities. With surprising nimbleness he darted up the trees—swung himself from branch to branch—then rushed along the stage—bounded over the footlights and sprang into the pit. From the pit he darted up into the boxes—ascended to the gallery—swung himself by wires across the ceiling—lowered himself to the stage again—and recommenced his antics amidst the trees, First and Second Citizen enter. First Citizen tells Second Citizen that ever since his dreadful transformation the unfortunate Prince has lived in that garden. Then commences that splendid speech where Second Citizen says, ' Full well I know it all : the city too doth know the same as you yourself do know !' "

"Then why did the First Citizen tell the Second Citizen a thing that was so well known?" I asked, though of course I could easily anticipate what the answer would be.

"The audience did not know it," answered Mr. Jingleton, "But that splendid speech——"

"You must really spare the speech," I said, again looking at my watch; "and get on with the description. The rat, you say, was disporting in the gardens——"

"Yes—and a most delicious odour of musk was diffused around. There was seldom a night that some old lady did not faint and have to be carried out into the lobby, where very few of them ever recovered until hot brandy-and-water had been poured down their throats——"

"The odour of the musk must have been very powerful," I remarked.

"Very, Miss Trafford. At the same time the orchestra sent out low strains of a delicious music; and this was done so effectively that it really seemed as if the rat itself were the source of the melody. So, altogether, the effect was admirable, and the hero seemed well to deserve the appellation of the Musical Musk-Rat."

"And a happy ending soon came, I suppose?" I said.

"Not quite yet, Miss Trafford," answered the dramatic author. "The golden cage was brought into the garden : the King and Princess followed, attended by the whole Court; and Mimosetta with her own beautiful hand plucked an orange from one of the trees and therewith baited the trap. But the Musical Musk-Rat only played heedlessly about, as before—and did not even take the slightest notice of the Princess. Then she plucked a pomegranate, and substituted it for the orange. Still without avail! In short, she tried all the fruits of the garden successively—but still without effect; so that reduced to despair, she flung herself weeping into her grandsire's arms."

"But if the rat had the run of the garden," I said, "and could freely devour the fruits as he thought fit, it was scarcely to be supposed that he would be attracted by those self-same fruits when placed in a golden cage?"

"Well, the rat certainly was *not* attracted to the cage, Miss Trafford," answered Mr. Jingleton; "and everybody was reduced to despair. One Lord of the Council suggested that the trap should be baited with jelly or blancmange—another proposed trifle—a grave bishop thought that tipsy-cake would have the desired effect—the Lord Mayor of the capital insisted upon the efficacy of turtle—an alderman spoke of venison—a fat school-boy proposed mince pies. All these things were tried in succession. Hour after hour the trap was filled with a varying succession of delicacies: but the rat took not the slightest notice thereof. The King was almost worn out with grief: the Princess was reduced to despair: the courtiers, the heralds, the guards, and the people stood transfixed as statues in mute ineffable woe. Tableau accordingly. End of the fourth scene."

"I do not wonder," I said, "that the Princess Mimosetta was reduced to despair—for I assure you that I very nearly am!"

"Ah, no doubt, Miss Trafford!" observed the dramatic author: "all your tenderest sympathies are enlisted—you can feel for that poor Princess——"

"I hope her woes are ended?" I said.

"You shall hear," resumed Mr. Jingleton. "Scene fifth and last. A sumptuous room in the palace. Door in the centre, opening on the garden, where the rat is seen playing. The golden trap is on the threshold of that open door. It is baited with gooseberry tart and custards: but the rat takes no more notice of these luxuries than he did of any of the former delicacies. The King the Princess, with their whole Court, are assembled in the apartment, together with heralds, guards, and people."

"The people always seem to hang about their King in that island," I said.

"Naturally so: they deeply sympathize with him. He is telling his counsellors that seven days have elapsed since the golden trap first began to be baited, and the fulfilment of the vision which instigated the proceeding seems to be further off than ever. As for the poor Princess, she does nothing but weep and lament, exclaiming passionately, 'Oh, Rat! Rat! wherefore art thou Rat?' It is very piteous; and at this point the audience is always deeply affected: there is snivelling in the pit, whimpering in the boxes, and downright crying in the gallery. All of a sudden a domestic enters the royal apartment, and announces to the King that Professor Wiseacre, in obedience to the King's mandate, has just arrived at the palace. It then appears from what his gracious Majesty says, that Professor Wiseacre is the greatest philosopher in the world—a sage of such wonderful erudition that all the Universities put together could not form an aggregate of knowledge equal to that which was enclosed within his brain. No wonder, then, if the arrival of so profound a sage produced an immense excitement in the royal dwelling! The orchestra played a slow and solemn strain as the Professor entered upon the stage——"

"What was that for?" I asked.

"To give the greater effect to the appearance of so famous a scholar. He was clad in a long black gown covered with hieroglyphics and mystic symbols; and he had a high-pointed black cap upon his head, decorated with the signs of the Zodiac. His long white beard reached below his waist; and he carried a huge black-letter volume under his arm."

"Rather a strange figure," I said, "to be seen walking about in the streets of a city."

"Oh, but he was a philosopher!" exclaimed Mr. Jingleton.

"Ah, true! I forgot! Of course, a philosopher cannot be dressed like any other rational person. But pray proceed: I am now all anxiety to arrive at the *dénouement*."

"Ah! I knew you would be," exclaimed the author, quite rejoiced at the degree of interest which he flattered himself had been excited within me. "The *dénouement* is grand, I can assure you! Indeed, the whole of this last scene is so arranged as to conduct the drama with solemn and stately march to the happy conclusion. You shall see. Professor Wiseacre enters the royal apartment, and is conducted by the King to a seat of honour. Then his Majesty tells this great philosopher the whole story from first to last; and the sage listens with that erudite and profoundly learned expression of countenance which shows that an appeal to his wisdom will not be made in vain. At length the King winds up his doleful narrative by explaining how the golden trap has been vainly baited with jelly, blancmange, cream, trifle, tipsy-cake, turtle, venison, plum-pudding, mince pies, gooseberry tart and custards—in short, how every imaginable dainty has been fruitlessly placed within that golden trap. More erudite, if possible, grows the philosopher's look—more sage the expression of his eyes, as seen through the circular glasses of his great horn spectacles. The suspense which prevails is awe-felt to a degree! 'The case is a difficult one,' says the learned man, speaking in the most solemn tone: 'but the difficulty is not insuperable. The question is how to bait the trap? Now I should not have tried in the first instance all the luxuries, the dainties, and delicacies which have been used. For my part I should have been inclined at the outset to try'—— 'What? what?' asked the venerable old King, in terrific suspense.—'Speak, O sage! for heaven's sake speak!' shrieked forth Mimosetta, tremendously excited: 'what would you have tried as a means wherewith to bait the golden trap?'—Nothing could exceed the look of profound wisdom with which Professor Wiseacre gives his answer. 'What would I have tried?' he says: 'what would I *now* try? Why, a little bit of cheese!'—Immense was the excitement: away ran the Lord Chancellor himself to the pantry to fetch the cheese: it is brought—a morsel of the rind is put into the trap in place of the gooseberry tart and custards—and the whole assemblage stand by to witness the effect. Not long do they wait. The Musical Musk-Rat begins to hover about the trap—the odour of the musk grows stronger—the orchestra sends forth a delicious harmony; and Oh! at length the rat fairly glides into the trap. Then the transformation instantaneously ensues——"

"But is the Prince himself now an inmate of the trap?" I inquired.

"Not an atom of it!" replied Mr. Jingleton. "The young Prince comes forward in his own natural shape—of course the Princess flies into his arms—the old King blesses them both—they kneel in gratitude at the feet of the sagest of all philosophers whose unapproachable wisdom brought about this happy *denôuement;* and the curtain falls, while the King is giving orders to ring the marriage bells at once and prepare the most magnificent banquet ever seen within those walls."

"I sincerely congratulate you, Mr. Jingleton," I said, "on having brought all your characters to so agreeable a *denôuement.* And now——"

"Just hear the prologue of my new drama! Pray in mercy do, Miss Trafford!" he ejaculated. "I could not for worlds go without your opinion upon it!"

Before I could give utterance to another syllable of remonstrance he caught up a music-stand —placed it in the middle of the room—settled his manuscript-book upon it—and then as I was on the point of assuring him that I could not give him another minute of my time, he launched forth into the midst of his prologue. Now he ranted and raved and declaimed at so furious a rate that nothing more ludicrous than his appearance could be well conceived. Indeed it was with more difficulty than ever that I prevented myself from laughing outright. He did not notice the effect he thus produced: but on he went, ranting and declaiming and gesticulating, so that at last I was actually afraid lest the servants should become alarmed and wish to know if anything had happened. Nothing could stop him: I was compelled to allow him to get to the end of his prologue; and then he offered to read the epilogue. But this was more than human nature could endure; and I was therefore compelled to speak in a tone more peremptory than I had hitherto adopted. His manner became all meekness and humility, as it was when first he entered into my presence: the poor gentleman looked quite abashed and confused; and it now seemed to occur to him for the first time that he had been intruding. I however said a few kind words to set him at his ease on the point; and with many expressions of gratitude for the bounty I had bestowed upon him, he took his departure.

CHAPTER LXXXII.

WILLOWBRIDGE MANOR.

It was about five o'clock in the evening of that same day, and I was seated in the drawing-room conversing with Mary Glentworth during the half-hour prior to the announcement that dinner was served up,—when a loud double knock at the front door warned us of the presence of visitors. In a few moments Mr. Norman and Juliet made their appearance; and I need hardly say that they experienced a most cordial reception. This visit was not altogether unexpected on my part; for Juliet had written some days previously to say that if I did not go down to see her at Dover, she would come up to see me in London: but I was not aware of the precise time when she and her father would be likely to make their appearance in the metropolis.

Mr. Norman looked pale, ill, and careworn: Juliet's mien likewise denoted mental despondency; for though two months had now elapsed since the terrific exposures at River House, yet the impression naturally remained strong upon the minds of the father and daughter. They congratulated me upon my extraordinary good fortune: they likewise congratulated Mary Glentworth in respect to the success which she had achieved upon the stage. When alone with Juliet I inquired if she had seen or heard anything of her wretched husband Lord Frederick Ravenscliffe since the day when he went forth an exile and a wanderer from his home?

"No," answered Juliet; "we have heard nothing more of him. My father believes that he must have gone upon the Continent to bury himself in some strict seclusion: but this is only conjecture. Perhaps never more may we hear of him! —perhaps under some fictitious name, and in some far-distant land, he may pass out of existence, and the fact may continue unknown to me! Ah, mine is a wretched fate, dearest Ellen! But I have not come hither to render you unhappy, to inflict my sorrows upon you——"

"You are aware, Juliet," I said, "that you have my sincerest sympathies; and if it be any consolation for you to speak to me of your sorrows, heaven knows that I will listen with patience, and that now as heretofore I will do all I can to console you. But I had hoped that by this time your mind would have regained its fortitude and composure——"

"I shall never be happy," interrupted Juliet— "I shall never experience mental calmness and tranquillity, so long as I remain in ignorance of what has become of my unfortunate husband! To think that at any moment he might come forward to claim me as his wife——"

"Rest assured, Juliet, he will never do it!" I exclaimed. "What! after everything that has taken place at River House—after he must have known that your love had received so dreadful a shock—and with the burning sense of utter humiliation and infamy——"

"True, Ellen! it is scarcely probable that he will ever seek me again! But still there is that possibility; and there are times when the idea haunts me like a spectre. My father knows that this is the case——"

"And do you not see, Juliet," I said, "that your father is suffering on your account? Oh! you ought to exercise all your mental powers——"

"Believe me I will do so!" rejoined Lady Frederick Ravenscliffe. "Now that I am once more with you, my best and dearest friend, I shall derive salutary influences from such sweet companionship."

"I am glad you have come therefore, Juliet," I

exclaimed. "You evidently required change of scene—you ought not to have remained so long in that gloomy house where such frightful things took place!"

"Let us talk no more upon the subject," said Juliet. "I mean to stay a few weeks with you, and to be very happy the whole time. So do not be afraid," she added, smiling, "that I am come to throw a damp upon your own spirits!"

For the remainder of the evening Juliet was comparatively cheerful; and as I watched her attentively, though without appearing to do so, I could perceive that this improvement in her spirits was really natural and was not the result of continuous effort. Mr. Norman's countenance grew brighter as he contemplated his daughter; and when the hour for retiring came, he significantly whispered in my ear, "Your society, Ellen, has already produced a good effect upon Juliet!"

On the following morning Mr. Norman and I met in the breakfast parlour before Mary or Juliet had descended; and I was glad to find myself thus alone with my excellent friend, for I had something of importance to say to him.

"I am sure, my dear Mr. Norman," I said, "you will excuse one who entertains towards you a filial regard, and who never can forget that you gave her a home when she found herself surrounded by perplexities, a stranger in this great metropolis,—you will excuse me, I say, for speaking to you in reference to your affairs. You know that I am now rich. The instant that I received my fortune, I thought of taking some step that should place at your disposal whatsoever amount you might be enabled to render available for any purpose beneficial to yourself. But I was afraid of offending—I knew that I should shortly see you—I thought that I would then speak to you upon the subject——"

"Noble-minded girl that you are!" exclaimed Mr. Norman; "ever the same!—warm-hearted, generous, and full of gratitude! My poor afflicted Juliet had not been an hour beneath this roof before she experienced the genial influence of your kind disposition. I also have been cheered and comforted by finding myself again with you! But in reference to myself, Ellen, I require nothing. You know that Mrs. Oldcastle left me a thousand pounds; and then there was the produce of the sale of all the effects in Hunter Street. During the six months which have now elapsed since my poor wife breathed her last, I have expended but little; and therefore I have ample funds at my command. Besides, Juliet is well off; and I shall doubtless make my home with her for the future—unless indeed some happier change shall take place in her lot."

"A change, Mr. Norman?" I said, not precisely catching his meaning.

"Ah! perhaps you may think me worldly-minded, coldly calculating, and selfish," he responded: "but remember that I am a father, full of solicitude for the welfare of his daughter! Suppose therefore that anything was to happen to that wretched being whom I am forced to call my son-in-law—suppose that he should die soon, either by a broken heart, or by his own hand in a moment of madness,—then Lady Frederick Ravenscliffe, with an aristocratic title, endowed with personal beauty, and possessing an independence of nearly a thousand a year, need not long remain a widow, but might form some distinguished alliance. It was to the possibility of such a change as this in Juliet's lot that I was alluding. And now, Ellen, with these ideas in my mind you may conceive how painful it is for me to be left in suspense relative to the proceedings of that wretched young man. I know not where he is: all I do know is that he embarked at Dover for the Continent:—but who can tell whether he may not have returned to England?"

"Juliet told me last evening," I said, "that you believe him to be still upon the Continent?"

"Yes—but still there is no certainty upon the point. However, it is now my purpose to institute inquiries. Juliet will remain here with you for a few weeks, while I repair to the Continent; and I shall endeavour to lay some train to serve as a clue towards obtaining information at any time of the wretched Frederick Ravenscliffe. With the police-regulations which exist on the Continent, this is by no means so difficult as it might at first appear to you, especially as the passport-system furnishes the authorities with a personal description of all foreigners residing or travelling in the Continental States. In a word, Ellen, it is my intention to discover, if possible, some traces of the wretched young nobleman, and to adopt some measures whereby I may at any time learn if aught occurs to him."

Here our conversation was interrupted by the entrance of Mary Glentworth, who was shortly followed by Juliet. We sat down to breakfast. The morning newspapers lay upon the table; and I turned to a particular portion of the advertisement pages of the *Times*, there being something that I was now in search of. My attention was soon riveted upon an advertisement, which, if its announcements could be relied upon, seemed to promise the realization of the very requirement which I entertained. I had already acquainted Mr. Norman and Juliet of my engagement to my cousin Harry Wakefield; and I now therefore had no hesitation in directing their attention to the advertisement to which I am alluding. It announced for sale a country mansion, with about a hundred acres of land attached: the size and conveniences of the house itself were fully explained: in short every usual detail was given, and the little estate was situated at a distance of about twenty miles from London. I should here observe that my cousin Harry and I had spoken together of our future plans. I saw that his taste lay in favour of a country residence, with a little land of our own; and I had promised that during his absence in the North, I would look out for anything that I thought might suit us. The advertisement of which I have been speaking, afforded every reason to believe and hope that Willowbridge Manor, as the place was called, would suit our views, our purposes, and our means. Accordingly, after breakfast, Juliet and I went to the estate-agent who had the sale of Willowbridge. He showed us the drawings of the mansion and plans of the estate; and all the information received from his lips was entirely satisfactory. I therefore determined upon visiting Willowbridge on the morrow: for it was also on the morrow that Mr. Norman was to take his departure for the Continent—I thought that Juliet might feel dull and depressed at parting from her father—and I therefore arranged this expedition for that day in order to divert her mind as much as possible.

After breakfast on the ensuing morning Mr. Norman bade us farewell; and at about ten o'clock a postchaise drove up to the door to take Juliet and myself to Willowbridge; for Mary Glentworth expressed no desire to accompany us, and of late I had never pressed her to do anything which did not seem entirely to suit her inclination. Juliet and I therefore set off together. The estate was situated in Hertfordshire; and it was consequently in a northerly direction that we proceeded.

"If the house correspond with the drawings and the plans," said Juliet, "it must be a handsome as well as a commodious one. My only fear, Ellen, is that you will find it considerably out of repair; for you remember the estate-agent informed you that the mansion had not been tenanted for the last seven or eight years, though the land had been kept in good order."

"Yes—I am prepared to find that it is necessary to expend some money upon the repairs of the house: but the estate-agent assured us, if you recollect, that all this is taken into consideration in the price that is asked for the property. If we like the appearance of the mansion and the grounds, it will be easy to take farther advice upon the subject,—which of course I should do before completing the purchase. Henry himself must see it. I shall get my father to come and give his opinion—then a competent surveyor would be employed—and, in short, there are plenty of business details to be accomplished before a bargain of this kind can be concluded."

"And now tell me, Ellen," said Juliet; "if after your marriage you live away from London, what will Mary Glentworth do?"

"She has already assured me," I answered, "that on no consideration will she continue to live with me after my marriage. But understand me well, Juliet! She has not in this sense spoken unkindly nor ungratefully: on the contrary, it was with the utmost delicacy of feeling that Mary announced to me her intention on the subject. She said that young married persons ought not to be subjected to the restraint of visitors or friends residing with them: in short, Juliet, Mary's reasoning is most considerate—and though I argued against it, she nevertheless remained firm to her purpose. It will grieve me to separate from her: but what am I to do? She must have a home of her own: I will make her a present of all my furniture in Great Ormond Street—she seems to like the house—and she may therefore continue to live there."

By means of conversation the time was whiled away; and we drew near to the end of our journey. The mansion took its name from a picturesque little village near which it stood, at an interval of only about a mile and a half. As we had been informed there was an old couple in charge of the premises, and as there was consequently no necessity to halt in the village in the first instance, we might have driven straight up to the door of the mansion; but as the weather was deliciously fine, and we were also desirous of obtaining a full view of the landscape, we decided upon walking for that short distance. We accordingly alighted at the village-inn, where we ordered the postchaise to be put up; and we then set off on our ramble towards the mansion.

We pursued the main road for nearly a mile; and then we stopped at a gate opening into the grounds belonging to the house. There was a porter's lodge: but this was shut up, and the gate was left unlocked. We entered. A gradually ascending carriage-drive, intersecting fields thinly planted with trees, and what might by some little stretch of the imagination be looked upon as " a park," led up towards the edifice itself. This, even at a distance, had a dilapidated and tumble-down look: but the nearer we drew the less satisfactory or inviting became its appearance. Its condition was evidently far worse than the estate-agent had given me to understand: but the site was picturesque—we obtained a view of spacious gardens attached to the mansion—and all the surrounding scenery was of the most attractive description. Nevertheless, I saw that Juliet had conceived a strong repugnance for Willowbridge Manor; and I myself began to fear that in consequence of the dilapidated state of the house it was not calculated to prove a bargain which I should be justified in concluding.

"Shall you go over the premises?" inquired Juliet, as we halted at a little distance from the portico.

"You mean, my dear friend," I said, "that you have already seen sufficient to disgust you with Willowbridge?—you think we have lost sufficient time, and the best thing we can do is to return at once to London?"

"To speak candidly, Ellen," replied Lady Frederick Ravenscliffe, "I do not think the place will suit you. It is prettily situated: but it is lonely. Look!—between this spot and the village, a distance of a mile and a half, there are actually only two houses—the little wayside inn yonder, and the turnpike through which we passed on emerging from the hamlet. If you glance around, there is scarcely another habitation to be seen——"

"But country-residences are generally lonely in a certain sense," I observed. "River House, my dear Juliet, is not surrounded by habitations——"

"No!—but it is within a few hundred yards of several, and altogether is far less lonely than this. Then bear in mind likewise that it will cost you a mint of money to put this house in repair! Look at the Venetian shutters, all falling away from their fastenings and hinges—many of the window-frames broken out—great cracks in the brick-work—the whole structure wearing an aspect of dilapidation——But for heaven's sake, my dear Ellen, do not suffer me to set you against the place, if you really fancy it!"

"I confess that I have been deceived," I said, "by the terms of the advertisement and the representations of the agent. But still, as we have come thus far, we will peep into the interior."

"By all means," said Juliet, "if you wish it!"

We accordingly approached the front door, which was all rotting upon its hinges, large pieces of the wood-work having been broken off, and thus exposing the decaying condition of the remainder; while a glance upward at the portico itself showed a huge gaping crack all across the masonry overhead, — producing the disagreeable impression that it was about to tumble down that very moment. There was no knocker: but I rang a bell—and for several minutes the summons remained unanswered; so that we began to think there was nobody on the premises. I rang again; and then an old woman, emerging from a side-gate, made her appearance. She was a good-natured-looking dame, with a red, wrinkled, weather-beaten face; and bustling forward, she curtsied with the profoundest respect, apologizing for not having come at first, but excusing herself, on the ground "that she had gone out into the garden to fetch some taturs which her old man was digging up." She then asked what our business might be.

"We have come to look over the premises," I said; "and here is the card of the estate agent in London."

"Oh! it's all right, ladies, for the matter of that!" exclaimed the old woman: "but if I looked a bit flabbergasted, it was only because one so seldom sees anybody up here at the Manor."

"Then you have very few applications on the part of persons thinking to buy the estate?" I said inquiringly.

"Lor, no, Miss! very few!" answered the dame. "Sometimes, when my old man goes down to smoke his pipe yonder and take his pint at the *Leather Bottle*—that's the public-house down the road there—he hears of persons now and then having come as far as the willage; but when once they have axed a few questions, away they goes, and never wastes no more time in coming to wisit the premises!"

"Ah, is it so?" I exclaimed. "But what do persons hear in the village which thus sets them against the Manor so that they take their departure without even so much as inspecting the premises?"

"Why, Miss, use your own eyes, and see how much the place is out of repair. And then too it's so lonely—there's no society in the neighbourhood—and it would take a power of money to put the old house to rights. So when people hears all this——"

"They do as we should have done," said Juliet, smiling, "if *we* had paused in the village to make any inquiries."

I was on the point of saying to the old woman that we would not trouble her any further, and that we would take our departure,—when the thought occurred to me that it would be after all a pity to judge of matters so hastily and to depart without casting even so much as a look inside the building after having come all that way for the express purpose. So I said to Juliet, "I begin to think with you that it is not likely anything will come of our visit to Willowbridge: but still, as we are not pressed for time, and we are indeed so completely the mistresses of our own leisure, we may as well linger for a brief half-hour to look into the interior of the place."

"By all means!" said Juliet. "And after all," she added, "who can tell but that if you really take a fancy to the place you might obtain such a diminution of the price demanded, as will be amply commensurate for an extra outlay in the repairs of the edifice?"

When I told the old woman that I thought I should like to look over the premises, it struck me that for an instant she seemed somewhat confused,

—though if so, she immediately recovered herself, and said, "Oh, certainly, Miss, if you choose! But the place is in a sad dirty condition—the ceilings have fell in in some parts and kivered the floors with the white muck and dust——"

"Never mind," I said. "We see that the house is in a dilapidated condition, and we do not therefore expect to find ourselves walking on drawing-room carpets."

The dame had emerged from a side-gate in the boundary-wall enclosing the kitchen offices; and we followed her into that part of the premises. She now shrieked out at the top of her voice, "Jan! Jan! here be two ladies, a-come to look over the Manor 'ouse!"

Mr. Janson—for such, as we subsequently learnt, was the name of this couple, familiarly abbreviated into *Jan* when the wife specially adjured her husband—now presented himself to our view; and a very singular presence it was. He was thin almost to emaciation, with peaked features, a sinister expression of countenance, and a shuffling shambling walk as if his shoes were too large for him and he was compelled to manœuvre to keep them on his feet. The thinness of his legs was most painfully shown by the costume which he wore upon his limbs—namely, knee-breeches and stockings: he stooped in his gait, and seemed altogether very infirm, for his age could be scarcely less than seventy. Touching the brim of his old battered hat, he looked as much surprised as his wife had done on beholding Juliet and myself; and shuffling towards us, he said, "You don't think, ladies, of purchasing this here property—do 'ee?"

"It depends upon what we now see of it," I answered. "Your wife is about to conduct us over the house——"

"It's of no use, Miss," said Janson; "you'll never buy it! Why, it's all to pieces; so that when the wind blows high, me and my old 'ooman here is always afeard lest the ceiling should come tumbling about our ears. Don't bother about the house; but if so be you'll come and take a walk in the garden and eat some of my strawberries——"

"Thank you," I said; "we will look over the house, if you please:"—and I spoke rather decisively, for it struck me that the old people had some motive or another for not wishing to show the premises.

"Oh, to be sure! to be sure!" mumbled the old man: "to be sure, ladies! Here, Mrs. Janson——"

"Hold your tongue, Jan!—go back and 'tend to your taturs, and I'll show the ladies over the 'ouse."

The old man shuffled off into the garden again; while Mrs. Janson slowly conducted Juliet and myself into the house. We passed from room to room, and found that the place was indeed in a most terribly dilapidated condition. The Jansons lived in the kitchen, which accordingly had a few little articles of furniture for their accommodation; but all the other rooms which we entered were empty. These apartments were certainly spacious and lofty: indeed there were all the evidences of a handsome mansion before it was suffered to fall into decay. We visited all the rooms on the ground floor: we then began ascending the staircase,—the old woman continuously expressing her fears "that our bootiful dresses would get kivered with dust;" so that I was more and more convinced that she had some reason for wishing to get speedily rid of us. I whispered something to this effect to Juliet,—who said in reply, "Perhaps the old couple fear that if the property be sold, they will cease to live rent free and have the run of the garden; so that they endeavour to set persons against it to the utmost of their ability."

"Yes—this must be the solution of the mystery," I said, also in a low tone.

We now reached the drawing-room floor: we entered apartment after apartment—dilapidation was everywhere fast merging into utter ruin.

"We will go up to the next floor," I said; for though I had by this time fully determined upon ceasing to think of Willowbridge as an estate to be purchased, yet I could not help feeling a certain satisfaction in annoying the old woman whom I looked upon as being so selfishly anxious to get rid of us.

I saw that she looked excessively annoyed: Juliet likewise remarked the circumstance; and she smiled significantly at me. We ascended to the next floor: room after room did we enter, until only one apartment on that floor was left unvisited. As we drew near it, methought that a strange odour came stealing upon my nose,—a strong pungent sickly smell, as if of some chemical material. I saw that Juliet also observed it; and as we glanced at the old woman, we perceived that she was now excessively troubled. The odour evidently came from the interior of the apartment which we had not entered, and into which she did not offer to introduce us.

"Well, ladies, d'ye think you have seen enough? You'd better come down stairs and walk in the garden to eat some of Jan's nice strawberries," said the hag.

"But why have you not opened this door?" I asked; and I put my fingers upon the handle.

"It's locked," said the old woman curtly: "you can't get in there. It's only a store-room where Jan keeps things—and he's got the key."

"A very strange odour emanates from your husband's stores," I said. "But it is of no consequence! We of course will not intrude where our entrance would prove inconvenient or disagreeable."

We prepared to descend the stairs; and the dame's countenance brightened up. On reaching the garden, Juliet and I readily accepted the invitation to partake of some of the fruit—for we were wearied and thirsty, and the noxious odour upstairs had left a most unpleasant taste in our throats. We saw old Jan exchange a rapid glance of intelligence with his wife: but it would seem that the look she threw on him was completely reassuring—for his countenance brightened up somewhat, and he became particularly civil as he conducted us through the garden. We remained there about half-an-hour: we then took our leave of the old couple, having liberally remunerated them for whatsoever trouble we had given and for the fruit which we had eaten.

"I have renounced all thoughts of purchasing this little estate," I said to Juliet, as we wended our way towards the gate leading into the main road.

"You are right, Ellen," answered Lady Frederick Ravenscliffe. "But I wonder why that apartment was shut up, and what that strange odour could have been? I am almost inclined to think that the old couple must have had some deeper and more serious motive than the mere apprehension of losing their situation——"

"Yes, I think so likewise," I observed: "for the old woman was evidently most anxious to prevent us from ascending to the higher storeys; and her look was very peculiar when we stood at the door of that apartment."

"It is some little mystery," said Juliet, "which will doubtless never be cleared up to our knowledge. But Ah! there is some one following us!"

She had happened to look back towards the Manor, and she caught sight of the object which evoked this ejaculation from her lips. I now glanced behind; and I beheld some gentleman coming along the carriage-drive, but still at so great a distance behind us as to render it impossible for us to discern his features.

"It may be some one," I said, "who is thus taking what may be a short cut across the Willowbridge estate, from one point to another."

"Yes—it must be something of that sort," said Juliet; "for there are assuredly no accommodations at the Manor for a well-dressed gentleman as this appears to be——unless indeed," she added with a smile, "it be the mysterious apartment into which, like the heroine in the Blue Beard story, we were forbidden to enter."

We reached the gate leading into the road; and as we closed it behind us, we perceived, while glancing back, that the gentleman was now cutting diagonally across the field, in a manner which must bring him into the main road at a point considerably lower down, and therefore nearer to the village, than that where we were thus entering that road.

"One would almost be inclined to think," said Juliet, "that having failed to overtake us down the pathway, he is now trying to intercept us on our way to the village."

"For what earthly purpose could he do this," I asked, "unless to speak to us in an insulting manner? And that is barely probable—for at this distance he has not seen our faces."

"No," said Juliet: "and yet does it not really seem as if he had a motive in some way connected with ourselves?"

"Don't be foolish, my dear friend," I interjected. "Come—let us make the best of our way into the village, where we will take some luncheon at the little inn and then return to London."

We accordingly continued our way along the road, which was slightly circuitous. As we turned a winding which had a larger sweep than any other, we suddenly came upon a stile at the very spot to which the diagonal path that the gentleman had last pursued, led down. There was here a group of trees; and just as we were passing the stile, Juliet hastily whispered, "There he is!"

I glanced partially round; and there, in the shade of the trees, I caught a glimpse of the figure of the individual to whom she had alluded. The next instant he was coming towards us. His hat was pulled so low down over his face that we could not immediately obtain the slightest view of his features: but now, as he emerged from the shade of

the trees, his figure—his walk—his gait—all were familiar! He looked up——yes! the face too! Juliet screamed—for it was her husband Lord Frederick Ravenscliffe!

CHAPTER LXXXIII.

THE APPOINTMENT AT FOUR O'CLOCK.

It was a cry of amazement mingled also with terror which thus rang from Juliet's lips; for there was something mysteriously ominous in the stealthy way in which the wretched young nobleman had thus stolen as it were upon us. At the same time an ejaculation of surprise had fallen from my tongue; and a cold shudder swept over me at the thought that I stood once more in the

presence of that branded being. Yes!—and that glacial sensation was succeeded by one of horror and affright, lest the appearance of Juliet's miserable husband should prove the signal of fresh woes, calamities, or afflictions for herself. As for Lord Frederick, his face—or rather, I should say, as much as we could see of it, for his hat was pulled down to his very eyes — his face was ghastly pale, the lips themselves were ashy, and they were quivering nervously as he accosted us.

Juliet now clung to me for support: she was fearfully agitated: indeed the apparition itself was so sudden that it was a wonder it did not send her off into a fit. I sustained her; and addressing her husband, I said, "My lord, what brings you hither?"

"Ah!" he ejaculated: "then it is not intentional! But rest assured, Miss Percy," he continued, "I have not come into this part of the world to seek you, nor my poor afflicted Juliet.

On the contrary, I fancied that ye two must have come to seek me——"

"What do you mean?" I asked. "Is it possible that you are living in this neighbourhood!"

"Yes—I am living here," he replied, his voice continuing to be profoundly mournful. "I saw you just now—but only at the moment when you were leaving——"

"Are you living at the Manor?" I inquired, as the thought of the shut-up apartment flashed to my mind.

He seemed to hesitate how he should reply to the question; and then he somewhat abruptly said, "Yes—I am living there!"

"And you thought," I continued, "that we had come——"

"What other idea could I form?" he interrupted me. "And even now I can scarcely bring myself to believe that it was otherwise: for would not the coincidence be most marvellous—most extraordinary——"

"You mean the coincidence of our coming into the same neighbourhood where you are? Yes—it is extraordinary!"

"Extraordinary!" repeated Ravenscliffe, in a moody, thoughtful manner. "Ah! and the incident has its fearful significancy likewise——"

"What, what," gasped Juliet, "does he mean?"

"Ah, poor tortured girl!" said Ravenscliffe, with mournful bitterness; "do I hear your voice again? But no matter what I meant by those words which fell from my lips! Do you too, Juliet, tell me that it was accident——"

"Look at this card," I said; "it contains the address of the house-agent who is entrusted with the sale of Willowbridge Manor. I thought of buying Willowbridge—hence our visit. But do not for a single moment imagine, unhappy being that you are——"

"No, no!" exclaimed Ravenscliffe bitterly: "there is no hope with which I ought to buoy myself up! Yet for an instant I thought it possible that by some means or another you had become acquainted with the place of my seclusion,—and that you had therefore come hither to seek me. But yet, the instant I emerged from beneath the trees, I saw by the looks of both that I was mistaken; for my appearance filled you with amazement and affright! Well then, it is destiny —it is heaven itself, which has thrown us thus again together! Juliet, does it not seem so to you?"

"My brain is in confusion—my thoughts are all in a whirl," said poor Juliet, who still leaning upon my arm, was trembling violently. "Oh, what would you say to me, Frederick? Is it possible that you could have desired this meeting? did you have a presentiment of it?"

"No, no! I thought that here I would bury myself," he exclaimed, "for a long period——at least until——But ah! no matter what I thought! Of what avail is it thus to explain our thoughts— our feelings? You are now saw enough, Juliet, to convince you that even when I fancied you had come to seek me, I nevertheless approached with fear and trembling—I crept like a guilty thing towards you——"

"Lord Frederick," I said, "pray let this scene cease. You perceive how cruelly poor Juliet is afflicted——"

"It shall cease!" he ejaculated, with a strange suddenness. "When do you propose to return to London, or to whichsoever place whence you came?"

"We purpose to set off in less than an hour," I responded,—"indeed as soon as we have partaken of some little refreshment."

"It is now two o'clock," said the young nobleman, looking at his watch: "you must delay your departure somewhat! Yes—it is important—believe me that it is important! At four o'clock precisely must you return to yonder Manor——"

"Return thither?" I asked in astonishment, while I felt that poor Juliet was trembling more and more violently as she clung to my arm.

"Yes—at four o'clock," repeated Ravenscliffe vehemently: "at that hour must you both be punctual! The old couple will have a message for you! Be assured that this message will prove of the first importance! I conjure you therefore —I entreat—command—implore—whatsoever you will—that this appointment be kept!"

Having thus spoken, Lord Frederick Ravenscliffe dashed abruptly away from the spot, leaving myself and Juliet under the influence of feelings which it may perhaps be more easy for my reader to imagine than for me to describe. It must however of course be understood that Juliet was more likely to experience a greater impression than I myself was; for it was her own husband whom she had thus met—whereas to me the meeting was one of comparative indifference, beyond the sympathy which I felt for my afflicted friend. I had therefore maintained a greater degree of self-possession than she could possibly command; and I recovered a complete fortitude before she was even enabled to shake off the first effects of the encounter. Her handsome face was very pale—her entire form was quivering nervously—and she still clung to me for support for some moments after he had disappeared from our view.

"Good heavens, Ellen!" she murmured, "what can all this mean?—and does it not appear to you to be something as wild in its reality as if it were an episode which we were reading in the page of a romance?"

"Come, Juliet," I said, "let us hasten away from the spot!—let us return to the village! Surely it was some strange fatality which brought us hither!"

We walked on in silence, respectively absorbed in our reflections,—Juliet leaning on my arm, and seeming as if she had sustained some shock from which she could not very readily recover. I was meditating the while whether I should presently advise her to keep the appointment which her husband had given, or whether I should counsel her to quit the neighbourhood with the least possible delay, and return to London, where I might consult with my father and get him to come down to Willowbridge and ascertain what communication the wretched young nobleman might be desirous to make to his wife. For a moment I thought of offering to keep the appointment alone on Juliet's behalf: but this idea I almost immediately rejected, as the execution of it might prove perilous to my reputation—for it might be supposed that I had purposely come into those parts to seek an interview with a particular person under circumstances of secrecy and stealth.

"What shall I do, Ellen?" Juliet at length inquired, now speaking in a somewhat firmer tone. "I have strange misgivings—I know not what they are—I cannot comprehend them——"

"You must act entirely according to your own judgment, Juliet," I said: "it is a subject almost too delicate for me to advise you upon; for I feel that it is the sacred intervention of a third party between husband and wife."

Lady Frederick Ravenscliffe reflected for a few moments; and then she said, in a voice of increasing firmness, "Yes, Ellen—I will keep this appointment——at least if you will accompany me, my dearest friend!—for I should be courageous in your society—but without you, I should be a coward. What will you do?"

"Since such is your resolve, I will go with you, Julie," I said. "It is a duty which I owe you not only as your friend, but likewise as being cognizant of all the fatal, fatal circumstances connected with your married life, and with the crimes as well as afflictions of that unhappy young nobleman! But let us anticipate nothing—let us not torture ourselves with vain conjectures. One thing is very certain:—he cannot mean you any harm."

"No, no! I am convinced that he does not!" exclaimed Juliet with fervour; "for in reference to myself he can only have the remembrance of much love shown in contradistinction to much wrong sustained at his hands. Oh, wretched, wretched Frederick!" she ejaculated with a burst of passion: "what a state of mind must be your's, that you have sought such a seclusion as this wherein to bury yourself!"

"Tranquillize your feelings, my dear Julie," I said, pressing her hand in my own; "and let us await the issue of this next interview which is to take place; for he would not have demanded—he would not have particularized the hour in such a manner, if he had not intended the issue should be one of importance."

Thus conversing, we drew near to the village; and again I begged Juliet to compose her feelings as much as possible. We reached the little inn, and obtained a private sitting room. I ordered refreshments to be served up—not because we required them, but for the good of the house, and because I did not wish the inmates to suspect that there was anything peculiar in the circumstances which now attended our presence in that neighbourhood. I presently bethought myself of making a few private inquiries on certain points; and I therefore quitted the room, bidding Juliet await my return. I was descending the stairs in order to seek the landlady, when I fortunately encountered her as she was coming up; and I told her that I wished to speak to her in private. She conducted me to another apartment. She was an elderly person, with a look and manner of matronly kindness—exceedingly civil and good-tempered.

"Perhaps you may have already suspected," I began, "the object which has brought me and my friend into this neighbourhood?"

"I should say, Miss," she replied, "that you came to look at the Manor with a view of buying it?"

"Such was my aim," I answered. "And now, will you be good enough to give me a little infor-mation concerning it? I learnt from the old persons who have charge of the premises, that there are frequent inquiries made in the village—but that very few visitors who come originally with the same intention as myself, choose to give themselves the trouble to inspect the house and little estate after having once made those inquiries."

"Well, Miss," rejoined the landlady, "I always tell the truth when I am questioned—though it would no doubt be to my interest to have some good family residing there. It would create business, you know, for my house in more ways than one: visitors coming to call at the Manor would put up their horses here—and the servants would be sure more or less to patronise my little bar-parlour."

"Then you *do* know something against Willow-bridge Manor?" I said; "and being truthfully disposed, you are compelled to give such information as deters persons from becoming purchasers? Is it so?" I asked.

"Why, Miss, pretty nearly all I know is that the place has been much neglected, and that the advertisements which I from time to time see inserted in the London papers are calculated to mislead; because it will require a power of money to do up the house in a style to render it habitable. That is all I know—that is what I always say when questioned on the subject."

"And that much I know already," I answered; "because I have just been over the house. Has it been utterly uninhabited during the last few years, except by the old people who are in charge of it?"

"Well, not exactly, Miss," replied the landlady. "There was a strange character who had a room or two at the Manor for some three or four years: he was a foreigner——let me see, what was his name again? Oh! Professor Steinbach they called him, I think!"

"And he resided there?" I said. "What? as the tenant of the entire estate?"

"Oh, no, Miss!—he was just allowed to live there till the place should be sold or let. It used to be in the hands of one Humphreys—a house-agent in the village; and as the owner never came near the place, Humphreys thought he might just as well turn a pound or two for his own benefit by letting Professor Steinbach occupy a room in the premises. But the Professor died about a year ago: Humphreys did something wrong, and was compelled to leave the neighbourhood, and has not since been heard of. So then no other agent was appointed here; and old Janson and his wife have had it all their own way."

"And who was this Professor Steinbach?" I inquired.

"Well, Miss," responded the landlady, "no one seemed rightly to have any knowledge on the subject. He was a queer old man, with an unpleasant look—and during the whole period he lived at Willowbridge he did not come half-a-dozen times into the village; and as for ever so much as crossing my threshold to take a social glass, he never did such a thing! Not that I am prejudiced against him on that account: but he certainly was not a person that one would like by his looks."

"And what did he do with himself in such a seclusion?" I asked. "Had he any family?"

"None, Miss," was the reply. "As for what he did with himself, nobody exactly could tell—unless it was old Janson and his wife, who kept everything very close to themselves; for they *are* close people, Miss!"

"I suppose, then, that this foreigner possessed independent means, and had a fancy for the retirement in which he dwelt?"

"Well, Miss, there was certainly something mysterious about him; and people in a little village like this *will* talk, you know. Some one said that he was a great chemist—but that having meddled in the politics of his native country, he was turned away from the College or University at which he was a professor—and that he was a writer of books on chemistry. How true all this might be, I can't tell: but if he didn't go on practising his chemistry up at the Manor, he did something else—and it was this that made people talk."

"What, then, did they think that he did?" I asked, perceiving by the landlady's look that she had some mysterious communication to make—though I more than half fancied there was a great deal of idle gossip and tittle-tattle in all she was telling me.

"Why, Miss," she replied, "I am not one of those who like to repeat unpleasant things; and heaven forbid that I should say a word to take away a person's character, particularly when he's dead and gone, and has had to give an account elsewhere for his actions. So you must bear in mind I am only going to tell what I heard other people whisper amongst themselves."

"I give you credit, my good woman, for the most charitable motives," I said, wearied by her verbiage; "and therefore you can tell me without further preface what it was that people whispered about this Professor Steinbach?"

"Well, Miss," answered the landlady, with an air of mysterious confidence, "I know it was some people's opinion that he was a coiner. You know what I mean?—a person who manufactures base money."

"But that was a very serious accusation," I observed; "and whether true or false, there was doubtless some cause for it."

"Oh, to be sure, there was some cause!" rejoined the landlady; "and I must tell you for my own sake, for fear you should think I am capable of inventing anything about this foreigner. No sooner had he, with Mr. Humphreys' consent, taken up his abode at the Manor, than a bricklayer was sent for to make something in the room which he occupied. And what do you think it was, Miss? Why, a sort of furnace."

"And probable enough!" I interjected, "if the gentleman were really a professor of chemistry, and desired to pursue his studies and experiments in the retirement which he thus sought. The incident you have just mentioned seems to corroborate the idea that he was really what he represented himself—or what the more charitably disposed portion of your little community thought fit to represent him."

"Well, Miss, so I used to say," rejoined the landlady: "but somehow or another the folks who visited my bar-parlour seemed to have got it into their heads that all was not right with the German professor, and that if he wasn't a chemist, he must be a coiner; for every now and then the carrier brought from the neighbouring town a package of strange-looking instruments——"

"How did you happen to see them?" I inquired.

"Oh! you musn't think, Miss," exclaimed the landlady, "that I myself was given to curiosity and opened the packages: but some of my customers *did*—I couldn't very well prevent them, you know, for they were good customers of mine; and they were very anxious to find out whatever they could in respect to the queer-looking old German."

"And what, then, did you see in these packages," I asked.

"Strange instruments," rejoined the landlady—"some of glass and some of iron."

"Rest assured," I exclaimed, "that the poor German was nothing more nor less than what he represented himself to be, and that all the things to which you allude were implements and materials for his chemical experiments."

"Well, Miss, I daresay it was so," answered the landlady: "and I hope it was for his sake."

At this moment a recollection flashed to my mind. I remembered that strange odour which had emanated from the shut-up room at the Manor; and I could not help associating it with the idea that a laboratory had probably been fitted up there—though I was still at a loss to conceive how Lord Frederick Ravenscliffe could be in any way following in the wake of Professor Steinbach; for I had never heard that the young nobleman had the slightest taste for chemical experiments, or that he indeed possessed any knowledge of them.

"Do you believe," I inquired, "that the Jansons are now altogether alone at the Manor? or does any one else reside there?"

"Well, Miss," answered the landlady, "I have heard it said within the last few weeks, that a gentleman was seen walking two or three times through the grounds: but I really do not know how true it may be——and that was the reason I said nothing to you on the subject, and should not even have hinted at it unless you had mentioned it yourself; for I want to be as cautious as possible in saying anything in respect to the Manor. But as you have just been over the premises, perhaps you know best——"

"My good woman," I interrupted her, "it certainly did strike me that there was some one——"

"And if you have been through all the rooms, Miss," exclaimed the landlady, "you must have seen whether there is one with a little furnace in it—unless indeed the Jansons had it pulled down again, after the Professor died."

"I saw no furnace," I answered, thus telling the actual truth, though somewhat evasively perhaps; for I said nothing about the room that was shut up.

"Then no doubt old Janson pulled it down," rejoined the landlady; "for I know that there *was* a furnace there—because the bricklayer who made it to the Professor's own directions, has said so twenty times in my hearing. However, nothing of all this can be considered as having any concern with the property itself, whether or not it is eligible as a purchase; and the only thing I can possibly have to say against it is the ruined condition of the premises. But on the other hand there is plenty to be said in favour of the estate; for the land is very good and very productive—and Farmer Jenkins who holds the best part of it for the time-being, would tell you so, Miss, if you were to call upon him."

I pretended to reflect for a few moments, and then I said, "I shall return presently and look over the house again."

"By all means do, Miss?" exclaimed the woman eagerly; "for if you did buy it I'm sure it would be a good thing for the village; and you would not forget that I told you all the truth as far as I knew it, when you questioned me?"

"Rest assured," I replied, with a kind manner, "I shall not forget the sincerity and frankness with which you have spoken."

We then separated; and I returned to the apartment where I had left Juliet. I thought it better to tell her all that I had gleaned from the lips of the landlady, because I knew not to what extent any of those details might presently be found to associate themselves with Lord Frederick Ravenscliffe—though I could not see how any such connexion might possibly transpire. Juliet listened with attention, and with a sort of suspenseful interest; though she was quite as much at a loss as myself to comprehend why her husband should be practising chemical experiments—unless it were as a relaxation for his afflicted mind; for it was scarcely possible to suppose that he entertained the hope of discovering a means to efface the fearful Cain-brand from his brow!

It still wanted a full hour to the appointed time, when Juliet proposed that we should set off on our return to Willowbridge Manor. I represented to her that we had ample leisure before us, as the distance was but a mile and a half, and that therefore less than half-an-hour would suffice for the purpose of reaching the place. But Juliet—like all persons who are suffering suspense—was anxious to anticipate, if possible, the strictly appointed moment; and as I saw that she was getting uneasy and restless at the inn, I agreed to set out with her. We walked slowly; and ever and anon Juliet kept expressing her wonder what would be the result of the interview, and why her husband had seemed to attach so much importance to it? She spoke as if she had some vague and shadowy presentiment in her mind; while on my own part I experienced a certain uneasiness, which was however indefinite, and pointed to no particular evil as the probable issue of the present adventure.

As we again drew near the building, I thought for a moment of singling out the window which belonged to the room that was shut up: but as I mentally studied the geography of the interior of the Manor, I recollected that this apartment must be at the back. I should observe that it was scarcely to be wondered at that I should be in any doubt or uncertainty for awhile upon this point, inasmuch as there were several passages in the house, which somewhat confused a memory that was as yet but very slightly acquainted with the arrangements of the place.

We reached the Manor House; and instead of ringing at the front door, we passed on to that side-gate whence we had first seen Mrs. Janson emerge. The old woman quickly made her appear-

ance; and it was now with the most profound respect, mingled with timidity and diffidence, that she curtsied to us both. The friendly familiarity which had characterized her manner towards us at our first visit, had given place to a visible constraint, as if she had learnt something which rendered our presence completely overawing.

"I'm sure, my lady," she faltered out, thus addressing herself to Juliet, "I didn't know—I wasn't aweer—leastways I hadn't the slightest hidear that it was a ladyship as I was a speaking to just now—a real lord's wife!—or else I should have been on my very best behaviour, and should have hastened off to put on my best gownd——"

"You behaved yourself very civilly, my good woman," answered Juliet; "and we have not the slightest fault to find with you."

While the old woman had been speaking, Juliet and I both noticed that there was some little improvement in her appearance—that she was more cleanly in person—and that she had on a better dress. Her husband now emerged from the kitchen premises to our view: he also was apparelled in his Sunday's best; and he made the lowest bows as he approached towards us hat in hand. Having thus paid his respects, he was about to resume his hat, when his wife screamed out, "Don't think of such a thing, Jan! don't think of such a thing! Keep your hat in your hand, man! You know in whose presence you stand!"—and she again bobbed and curtsied to Juliet.

"Let your husband put on his hat, my good woman," said Juliet.

"There, Jan! do you hear? you are to put on your hat," cried the dame; "and you ought to go down upon your knees and thank her ladyship for such gracious condescension. Beg pardon, my lady—but here is the letter I was ordered to deliver into your ladyship's own hand; and as for the little festival, it will be ready presently——"

"A letter?" exclaimed Juliet, snatching at the one which was now presented to her: and then she impatiently demanded, "Why did you not give it me at first?"

The two old people shrank back in dismay at the sort of rebuke thus conveyed: but I hastened to reassure them with a glance, while Juliet tore open the letter which had been placed in her hand. For some moments she went on reading with a look which expressed a species of bewildered amazement, as if all her ideas had been thrown into a dismayed confusion and were so maintained.

"I can make nothing of this, Ellen," she murmured, as she handed me the letter. "I think that I must be dreaming, or that my senses are abandoning me!"

"Come with me," I said: "let us be alone together:"—and I led her into the adjacent garden.

There we sat down in an arbour; and I read the letter audibly—slowly and deliberately likewise—so that Juliet might be enabled to follow me with earnest attention as she listened. The contents of that document ran as follow:—

"Willowbridge Manor. June 29, 1842.
"3 o'clock in the afternoon.
"My dearest Juliet,
"Words have no power to convey the gratitude

which I experience towards you, for having sought me out in my solitude to assure me of your forgiveness for the past, and to propose that it shall all be buried in oblivion, so that we may be reunited at our home near Dover. Yes, dearest Juliet! you have performed the part of a kind, affectionate and loving wife; and henceforth shall you find me a tender and loving husband! I know, Juliet, that I do not deserve so much goodness at your hands; for my conduct previous to our separation was most unkind towards you. However, you have shown yourself as an affectionate wife and a forgiving Christian; and such an example cannot fail to have a beneficial effect upon my own heart and disposition. And while I am expressing my deep gratitude to yourself, my dearest wife, for having thus come to assure me of your pardon, and to declare that all the past shall be buried in oblivion,—let me not forget to record my thankfulness likewise to your amiable and generous-hearted friend Miss Percy, who I have no doubt countenanced and strengthened you in the step which you are just taking, and has demonstrated her approval thereof by accompanying you to this seclusion where I have buried myself.

"You may think it strange, my dearest Juliet, that I should pen this letter to be placed in your hands when in so short a time we are to meet again to part no more. But my motive can be speedily explained, and will doubtless be as readily understood. You have suggested that a complete veil should be thrown over the past, and that it should be no more alluded to—that enough was said upon the point when we are now met in the road—and that when we presently meet again, it will be to celebrate a new era in our existence. All this was most delicate, generous, kind, and considerate on your part, dearest Juliet; but I feel that some little explanation is due unto you. Two months and upwards have elapsed since, after that quarrel in which I was so completely in the wrong, I withdrew from River House,—vowing, like a wretch as I was, that everything was at an end between us, and that you should never hear of me any more! But what have I been doing during these two months and upwards? It is this that you have a right to know. First I went upon the Continent; and at Boulogne accident threw me in the way of an Englishman named Humphreys, who was involved in some distresses which I was fortunately enabled to relieve. In consequence of information which I obtained from his lips in the course of conversation, I resolved to return to England: for I had thus learnt that there was a spot which would serve as the solitude and retirement that I sought. It was in this manner that I fixed my abode at Willowbridge. You know, my dearest Juliet, that for some time past I had been fond of experimentalizing in the chemical art; and here was an opportunity for me to give ampler range for the scientific taste that I had acquired. For I should tell you that the celebrated German Professor Steinbach—the author of several standard works on chemical analysis, and who was expelled on account of his political opinions from the chair of chemistry at the University of Gottingen—was for some while a resident within these same walls. Yes—and for the last six weeks I have been the successor of that philosophic recluse; I have

worked at the same furnace—practised with the same alembics and retorts—profited by the suggestions of the same books—and travelled as a novice in the footsteps of the accomplished man of science who was here before me. These have been my pursuits, Juliet. I have remained almost completely shut up in my laboratory since my arrival here, and have had little or no taste for recreation or exercise in the garden and pleasure-grounds. Those worthy old people, the Jansons, have behaved most kindly to me from the moment that I came to Willowbridge and presented to them the letter of introduction which Mr. Humphreys gave me at Boulogne.

"For the last few days I have been making experiments on a very grand scale, but with a material that is somewhat dangerous to use,—though I can assure you that I have been very careful. I was in the midst of these experiments when you, my dearest Juliet, and your excellent friend, Miss Percy, arrived at the Manor. Yes—and I was thinking of you at the instant, Juliet! I thought that all the love you had borne for me had been but badly requited by my conduct. A nobler-hearted or more virtuous woman than yourself, Juliet, does not breathe! As there is a heaven above me, it was this very thought that was passing in my mind at the moment when you and your friend Miss Percy were passing through the Manor House. Was not this a strange coincidence, that I should be thus thinking of you at the very moment when you were beneath the roof?—that I was deploring my own past conduct at the instant when you arrived to proclaim its forgiveness? Oh, yes, Juliet! I hesitate not now to confess that I have behaved most vilely towards you, and that your conduct towards me has been of the noblest, the kindest, and the most affectionate description! I do not pen these words lightly, nor in a moment of enthusiasm because you have come to tell me that I am forgiven and that we shall live together again: but it is a deliberate opinion that I gravely and solemnly record—and if death were at the moment staring me in the face, I should avow precisely the same sentiments!

"Now that I have penned these lines, my dear Juliet, my heart feels relieved of a load. You will read the letter before we meet—you will comprehend what my sentiments are—you will give me credit for all the remorse which I feel on account of my past conduct—and you will believe me when I assure you of my firm resolve to prove all that I ought to be towards you for the future. And thus, Juliet, as I have written all this, there will be no necessity to revive the subject by word of mouth; —and hence the relief that I experience in having committed my sentiments to paper. In another hour we shall meet, according to our arrangement; we shall meet, as if unavoidable circumstances only had separated us, and not the wilfulness of my own perverse headstrong disposition! We shall meet as man and wife who throw themselves into each other's arms after an interval of separation! Yes—for us, my beloved Juliet, it must be the era of a new existence! Therefore we will celebrate it. I have asked the Jansons to make all the preparations in their power for a little banquet: we will meet at the board—you, I, and Miss Percy—as if to celebrate some joyous occasion!—as if we were to be married over again and this were our wedding feast! And afterwards, my dear Juliet, I shall be ready to accompany you to London; and thence we will repair with the least possible delay to River House—that home which hitherto has not been a happy one, but which henceforth shall prove the scene of smiles, and contentment, and domestic bliss!

"And now, Juliet, in bringing this long letter to a conclusion, I must repeat that the process of penning it has afforded a vent for my feelings, and has yielded an unspeakable relief to my mind. All that I could say to you from the lips, has now been said through the medium of this letter. Keep it, my dear Juliet; and if on any future occasion I should speak or look unkindly towards you—or if I should act harshly—produce the letter—hold it before my eyes—and a glance thereat will be sufficient to remind me of my solemn pledges and of my duty as a husband! Yes—keep this letter, Juliet!—for though I do not believe that you will ever find it necessary to produce it for the purpose that I have just specified, yet I must not forget that human nature is frail—that we are all weak and liable to error; and therefore it were as well that in the shape of this epistle you should posess a talisman the mere sight of which will at any moment recall me into the right path if I display the slightest inclination to deviate from it!

"I lay down my pen, Juliet, after having renewed and completed the assurance that I am henceforth your faithful, devoted, and affectionate husband,

"FREDERICK RAVENSCLIFFE."

It was no wonder that when Juliet commenced the perusal of this singular epistle her mind should have been amazed and confused, and that this bewilderment should have speedily assumed the character of downright dismay. Was it the letter of a madman? or was it the letter of a fiend, who under the pretence of affection was mocking her with the most cruel and caustic irony? She might have asked herself these questions; and even I was at first in a vague and dreamy uncertainty as to what construction was to be put upon the tenour of such an epistle:—but I had not read very deeply into it before the conviction began stealing into my mind to the effect that the letter was written with a studied and settled purpose of serving some ulterior object of grave and serious importance. It occurred to me that it was a letter penned entirely with a view of being published to the world, so as to give a particular colour to certain incidents that had already happened, or to others that *might* happen; and the nearer I drew towards the close of the document, the more did I feel convinced that it was the forerunner of something that would presently startle or appal!

Juliet listened with a half vague, half affrighted bewilderment, as I continued the reading of the letter; and when I had brought it to a termination, she looked up at me with a sort of silent stupefaction, as if waiting for me to afford some clue to the mystery.

"Juliet," I said, "it is now close upon four o'clock: let us hasten to the appointment!"

"But that letter, dear Ellen?" she wildly exclaimed: "what in the name of heaven can it mean? It does not seem as if written to myself!

—it appears as if it were addressed to the world at large, and that I must prepare myself to corroborate its statements! It misrepresents many things—it is not truthful: but its deviations from fact all appear to have a fixed purpose, and to be conceived in the idea that I, if appealed to, shall fall into the same views or tell the same tale! Does it not thus seem to you, dearest Ellen?"

"Yes, Juliet—and I should be wrong to assert the contrary. This letter is not the offspring of a madman's brain: there is all the reality of a terrible method in it! Neither is it meant to mock or insult you, Juliet. No!—on the contrary, it has the air of being the last atonement which a guilty husband has it in his power to make!"

"The *last* atonement, Ellen?" ejaculated Juliet. "Ah! there is something foreboding in your words! — they seem to associate themselves with the ominous character of the letter itself! Ah! you have formed some conjecture, Ellen?—there is something in your mind? Let us hasten—Oh! let us hasten and see what it all means; for I suddenly feel as if I were standing on the threshold of some hideous catastrophe!"

"Come then, Juliet—come!" I said, unable to add anything that was hopeful or reassuring; for I myself experienced the conviction that something of a terrific character would occur ere the day was done.

We issued from the garden; and as we entered the kitchen-premises, the old couple came forward to receive us—the husband hat in hand, the wife bobbing and curtseying as if she felt it was impossible to testify too much respect.

"If you please, ladies," said the old man, "we have done our best to make the dining-room look as neat as possible—we have moved our own little table there——"

"Hold your tongue, Jan—and let me speak!" cried the dame. "Beg your pardon, my lady—but my husband has no more hidear how to address himself to genteel folks——"

"You know, my good woman," I interrupted her, "who is the writer of this letter——"

"And we who never knowed that it was a lord until just now, when he come in, all of a flurry, and told us, says he, 'There's my dear blessed wife, an angel of goodness, which has some how or another heard that I was here; but not being quite sure upon the pint, she and her friend Miss Percy comes down under pretence of wanting to buy the Manor——"

"And we," exclaimed old Janson, "who thought we mustn't say a word about anybody else living on the premises, for fear when you went back to London you should tell the house-agent——"

"Hold your tongue, Jan—and let me speak!" interrupted his wife. "Well, ladies, so the young gentleman tells us right out that his name was no more Mr. Thompson than mine was—but that it was Lord Frederick Ravenscliffe—and that the stoutest young lady of the two was his own blessed wife whom he had cruelly and shamefully deserted a couple of months ago, and who was come to be reconciled to him; and that he was now as happy as the day was long! So he ordered us to prepare a nice little dinner—and Jan hobbles off to the *Leather Bottle* to get some wine——"

"We have no doubt," I said, "that all your preparations will be most admirably conducted.

But have the kindness to inform Lord Frederick Ravenscliffe that we are here;—or suffer us to proceed to his apartment—which perhaps will be the better plan."

"I'm sure you can do as you like, ladies," replied Mrs. Janson. "Use the house just for all the world as if it was your own!"

"We will proceed alone together to Lord Frederick's apartment," I said: "you need not attend upon us my worthy dame: but you may continue your preparations for the little festival."

I said these last words because I had a settled conviction of the necessity—or at least the prudence and propriety of maintaining those appearances which Lord Frederick had for his own ulterior purpose (whatever it were) already conjured up, and to which he had given a particular gloss. At the same time there was a sense—an almost awful sense of foreboding within me that there would be no dinner, nor festival, nor banquet there that day!

Juliet and I left the old couple together; and we entered into the dilapidated edifice. We ascended the staircase—we reached the drawing-room floor—and as we began the ascent towards the next storey, that same sickly odour which had before assailed our nostrils, was experienced with additional strength and pungency. I felt myself shuddering: horrible recollections began creeping in unto my mind—recollections of mad threats and wild menaces which the young nobleman in his frenzy had proclaimed in my hearing at River House upwards of two months back; so that it was no wonder if my heart palpitated, my frame quivered, or that my brain had confusion and hurry in it. I glanced at Juliet: I saw that she likewise was considerably agitated—though her ideas (as I afterwards learnt) were very far from pointing to any such conclusion as that towards which my own thoughts were now fearfully trooping.

We reached the second storey landing: we passed along the corridor leading to the *one* apartment which on the former occasion on that same day had remained unvisited by us; and as we drew nearer and nearer towards the door, more pungent and more sickly became the odour which assailed our nostrils. It came upon the nerves with an almost overwhelming power; and the effect was all the greater on account of the other influences which were already acting upon the nervous system of each of us.

I knocked at the door: there was no answer. That silence struck me as still more ominous than even the tenour of my thoughts had hitherto been. Juliet gasped, and looked up at me with an expression of the most anxious inquiry. Again I knocked at the door: all continued silent; and Juliet murmured, "Perhaps he is not here? It may be below that he intended to meet us?"

"Perhaps," I said: "but still this uncertainty is intolerable!" I added musingly to myself.

I stooped down, and peeped through the key-hole. The first glance showed me the confused paraphernalia of a laboratory, just as it is usually described in books or as imagination is in the habit of depicting it. There was some horrible reptile of the alligator species, suspended to the ceiling; there was a death's head grinning from a little shelf of jars and phials; other shelves, as well as the table, were covered with chemical implements of strange shapes and names unknown to me, but suddenly conjuring up ideas of the philosopher's stone, the elixir of life, and all the wondrous mysteries of a lost science, as alchemy was supposed to be. There was the furnace too: there was an immense arm-chair in which the aged Professor Steinbach might have appropriately reposed his enervated form—but which scarcely seemed suitable for an individual in all the vigour of youth, as Frederick Ravenscliffe was. There were huge bottles—some green and some red—bearing upon them those cabalistic characters which may be seen on the bottles of coloured waters in chemists' windows. I caught a glimpse likewise of a galvanic battery, and of other articles the details of which I have now forgotten. But on the floor there seemed to be a strange confusion. I beheld a chair overturned: near it there was a dressing-gown, seeming to define something like the shape of a human being: there was a large tub;—while a cap and several garments lay scattered about. What did all this mean? I closed my eye, for I was wearied of concentrating its gaze through so small an aperture.

"What do you see, Ellen?" inquired Juliet, full of anxiety and suspense.

"It is the laboratory—and there is the furnace," I responded, again peeping through the key-hole; "and there——But, good heavens! that dressing-gown must be upon a human form!—the form itself is lying along——Yes, yes—I see! I follow the outline——"

"Ellen?"—and Juliet gasped vainly for the power of further utterance.

"Yes—good heavens! I comprehend it all!"—and it was with a cry of affright I sprang up from my crouching posture at the door. "He is motionless! he is dead!"

My fingers seized the handle of the door: but it was fastened inside. I threw myself against it with all the impetus and energy I could possibly give to my form: the door was burst open—for it was only held by a small brass bolt at the top. Juliet and I rushed in; and Oh! what a spectacle met our view! For there, lying forward—enveloped in a dressing-gown—his face completely immersed in a tub full of a sickly-smelling pungent liquid—was Lord Frederick Ravenscliffe!

"Good God! he has drowned himself!" shrieked Juliet, clasping her hands in horror and affright.

"Unhappy man!" I exclaimed: and I also was a prey to the wildest horror, as I felt that a ghastly paleness had seized upon my countenance—my bonnet was flying off my head—and my whole aspect must have been that of one who was frenzied.

CHAPTER LXXXIV.

THE VISCOUNT.

NEVER, never can I forget the scene which thus burst upon my view. Though an instant back I had been more or less prepared for it, by the glimpse I had obtained of Ravenscliffe's posture in reference to that tub—as well as by certain reminis-

cences of the past—yet was it as hideous and as frightful as if there had been no such presentiment at all. There he lay, his face downward,—and that face immersed in the contents of the tub; so that in a moment it became evident to my comprehension that he had at length realized one of the appalling projects which in the excruciation of his mental anguish he had so passionately enunciated to me at River House.

"Oh! you know not what horribly fantastic ideas have at times taken possession of my brain! What if I were to journey to Naples or to Sicily, and plunge headlong into the crater of Vesuvius or of Etna? or what if I were to dip my head into a bath of burning vitriol?"

These were the terms in which that wretched young nobleman had spoken on the occasion whereunto I refer: and how terribly had he now fulfilled one of the menacing predictions he had thrown out in reference to himself! For the tub

No. 66.—PERCY.

was filled with some corrosive fluid, which, as the deposition given by a chemist at the Coroner's Inquest afterwards proved, consisted of the most potent acids that could possibly be combined.

Juliet staggered back and sank into the armchair to which I have before alluded. I approached the body to assure myself that life was extinct; for otherwise I should as a matter of course have at once taken measures to render assistance. But when I touched the hand which rested upon the floor, I found that it was perfectly cold. A moment's impulse was on the point of making me drag the countenance of the corpse away from the tub: but the next instant a thought stayed my hand. Why was the face buried in that corrosive fluid? Was it not to disfigure the entire countenance, so that the particular mark of the brand across the brow should not be seen? It would therefore have been an act of cruelty towards the memory of the deceased to have done that which otherwise would have been an act of humanity—or in other words, to stand the chance of withdrawing the countenance from the corrosive fluid before complete disfigurement had taken place.

Yet must not such disfigurement have been instantaneous? No doubt it was; or at all events the work of destruction to the outline and symmetry of those lineaments was speedily accomplished. But I was at that moment too much agitated and horrified to weigh all these matters deliberately: I thought only of the wretched young nobleman's object—and I was resolved that it should be accomplished.

But I must mention a little incident. As I was approaching the horrible spectacle in the middle of the apartment, with the first impulsive idea of ascertaining if Lord Frederick were really dead, I trod upon a large graduated glass measure which was lying on the floor close by the tub. It broke to pieces beneath my foot. I did not pause at the instant to think of the occurrence; but a few moments afterwards, as I stood by the arm-chair into which Juliet had thrown herself—and as we were both in awful silence contemplating that horrible scene—a strange and fearful idea began to steal into my mind. Had the young nobleman taken poison before his face came in disfiguring contact with the corrosive fluid? Yes!—methought such appeared to be the case. There was a chair thrown down just behind: it was on the very spot where he might have been seated in such a manner that if he fell forward his head would necessarily become immersed in the tub. My imagination soon arranged it all. The unfortunate Frederick Ravenscliffe might have placed himself on the chair in front of the tub—his right hand might have held the glass of poison—scarcely had he poured that poison down his throat when its effect was accomplished—from his hand dropped the glass upon the ground—forward he fell—the chair rolled away from behind him—and perhaps at the very moment that the vital spark was extinguished, did the branded countenance plunge into the corrosive fluid! Thus might it possibly have all been; and there was the awful conviction in my mind that I had rightly conjectured the whole tremendous truth.

A thousand considerations however made me understand that the deceased nobleman had studied with all his art so to arrange and combine circumstances as to avert the suspicion that he perished as a suicide. Yes!—the letter written to Juliet proved this: the manner in which he had for the last six weeks affected to be busied with chemical experiments, also proved it. His death was to seem the result of an accident; for he had doubtless calculated that when thus found with his head half immersed in the tub of corrosive fluid, it would never strike any one to examine the measure-glass that might lie near him upon the floor. Or perhaps he had fancied that the glass itself would break when dropping from his hand. At all events, whatsoever his ideas on all these points might have been—and whether he had in the first instance taken poison, or whether this belief of mine was erroneous, and he had veritably trusted only to the stifling effect of the corrosive fluid to kill him at once without pain—nevertheless, be all this as it might, two facts were certain enough. The

first was that he *had* committed suicide: the second was that he had laboured with all his ingenuity to prevent the world from entertaining the suspicion. I was therefore glad that I had, although by accident, crushed the measure-glass under my feet; for at least it could betray nothing now;—and snatching up a brush, I swept the pieces to the vicinage of the table. Juliet, recovering her self-possession, seemed to comprehend all that was passing in my mind; for she rose from her seat—and accosting me, she took my hand, saying in a low deep voice, "The world must believe it was an accident, dear Ellen!"

"Yes," I responded: "it is our duty to throw as much as possible a veil upon the past. Society will not be benefited by the return of a verdict of *Felo de se* instead of *Accidental Death*, nor by the refusal of Christian burial. But on the other hand an immensity of injury would be inflicted by the publication of the entire truth: the feelings of yourself, as his wife, would be outraged!—the feelings of his parents and his brother would likewise be outraged!—the memory of the dead himself would be unnecessarily desecrated, and this would be a posthumous cruelty as abominable as it is needless!"

Juliet pressed my hand in recognition of the kindness which thus prompted me to conjure up as many arguments as possible against the necessity of suffering the world to learn the stupendous secret which the unhappy suicide had studied so carefully to conceal; and we now hastened down from the apartment. The alarm was quickly given to the old people: they were seized with consternation and dismay; and for some minutes they sat staring at us both with mingled horror and stupor. At length they began to recover themselves: but I had to repeat the terrible announcement before they seemed rightly able to understand it thoroughly. Then they ascended the stairs: Juliet remained below—but I accompanied them. I bade them be careful how they spattered themselves with the corrosive fluid; for they were now about to lift the corpse from its present position. They did so. It was a fearful task which I was imposing upon myself; and nothing but my strong affection for Juliet would have permitted me to drag myself through such an ordeal. But I knew that she was anxious to know everything, even to the minutest detail; and it was under this conviction that I acted. I therefore compelled myself to fling one look upon the countenance of the suicide, as the Jansons, with murmurs expressive of horror—with quivering forms and with trembling hands—dragged him away from that contact with the dread fluid contained in the tub. Yes!—I glanced at that countenance. Just heaven, what a spectacle! But enough——I can say no more upon the subject!

Pale as death—sick—ill—my limbs failing under me—I staggered down the staircase, and rejoined Juliet. She did not require to put a question to the effect whether her miserable husband's stratagem had succeeded, and whether the brand was now utterly obliterated from his brow?—she saw by my looks that the wretched Frederick's aim had been only too fearfully accomplished!

It is not necessary to enter into the very minutest details in respect to the remainder of this frightful episode. I will therefore only fling a passing glance at the excitement which prevailed in the neighbourhood when the news spread—the mingled interest, sympathy, and curiosity with which Juliet and myself were surveyed when we returned to the inn—or the difficulty which I experienced in keeping away from the garrulously inclined landlady, who I saw was most anxious to have an opportunity of overwhelming me with questions. I must however observe that early on the following day we received four or five notes or visits from genteel families residing at a little distance and who kindly invited Lady Frederick Ravenscliffe and myself to stay with them. These invitations we however declined, as it was our purpose to return to London as soon after the Coroner's Inquest as possible. A communication had been sent to the Earl and Countess of Carshalton, Lord Frederick's parents, announcing his death: but they came not to the scene where the tragedy had occurred. The Earl was ill: the Countess could not or would not leave him. But Viscount Ravenscliffe, the deceased Lord Frederick's elder brother, arrived at the village in the course of the forenoon of the day following the sad occurrence: but he did not condescend to hold the slightest communication with Juliet. He sought to obtain an interview with myself; but this I declined, on the ground that his sister-in-law was the more proper person from whose lips he should seek explanations,—though indeed I was glad of any plea to avoid such an encounter, for I was by no means anxious to be questioned in reference to the details connected with Lord Frederick's death.

The Inquest took place at the *Leather Bottle*—the little public house up the road leading to the Manor—at about three o'clock in the afternoon of the day following the tragic occurrence itself. Old Janson and his wife were first called as witnesses. From their testimony the Coroner and jury were impressed with the following ideas—that the deceased, having wilfully quarrelled with his wife, separated from her and sought the solitude of Willowbridge Manor, a person of the name of Humphreys having recommended it to him as a nice quiet abode where he might harbour until it was sold or let—that the deceased was passionately attached to chemical pursuits, and that the fact of a laboratory being at Willowbridge had proved his chief inducement for going thither—that on the previous day the ladies had called at the Manor House—that after they had departed, deceased inquired who they were—that on hearing that one was Miss Percy, he in an excited tone demanded a description of the other—that when he had received it he became terribly agitated, and hurried forth to overtake the ladies—that on his return he had announced his real name to the old people, he spoke of a reconciliation with his wife, he ordered a festival to be prepared, and he intimated his intention of leaving Willowbridge, with his wife and the other lady, in the evening of that very same day.

Juliet was compelled to attend as a witness: but she was overwhelmed with grief, and not a single question was put to her. She handed to the Coroner the letter which she had received from her husband; and this letter was read to the jury. It completely corroborated all the evidence given

by the Jansons. Was there a doubt to be entertained by Coroner or jury as to the verdict that was to be returned? Assuredly not! And then too, a chemist proved the nature of the corrosive fluid, and sagaciously suggested three or four different experiments for which such a large quantity of such a liquid might be used. Finally a surgeon came forward, who clearly demonstrated that the unfortunate young nobleman, when seated in the chair close by his tub of corrosive liquid, had been seized with a fit—doubtless produced by the strong exhalation thereof—and that he had fallen forward, to meet a horrible death, and to be found in the position described by the Jansons. As for myself, it was not deemed necessary to examine me at all, and I was very glad that I escaped so unpleasant an ordeal. Everything seemed to be most terribly clear: no suspicion of suicide could be possibly entertained on the part of one who was so rejoiced at being reconciled to his wife—who intended to return with her to River House—who promised to behave so well for the future—and who had actually written a letter of penitence that she might hold it in her possession as a talisman against any fresh demonstration of unkindness or cruelty on his part. Therefore a verdict of "Accidental Death" was returned; and immense was the sympathy displayed towards Lady Frederick Ravenscliffe. The Viscount kept himself so retired during these proceedings, that it was not generally perceived by those around that he treated his sister-in-law Juliet with such utter neglect,—completely ignoring her as it were, and behaving as if not the slightest regard need be paid by his high and mighty aristocracy for the feelings of a young lady who had just lost her husband. Juliet of course regarded it as a very happy release: but the Viscount being ignorant how his brother had been branded, knew not what the widow's feelings might thus secretly be—and therefore if her affliction were ever so poignant she would have experienced no consolation or sympathy at his hands.

The inquest was over—Juliet and I were alone together in our little sitting-room at the inn—and we were holding a discussion previous to making up our minds whether we should at once order the postchaise to return to London. I should observe that the first thing in the morning of this day of which I am writing, and which followed that of the tragedy at the Manor, an undertaker had been sent for from the nearest town, and the preparations for the obsequies had therefore already commenced. But it now remained for Juliet to learn whether it was the wish of the Carshalton family that her deceased husband should be deposited in the vault belonging to that family—or whether, as he had been cast off when alive, he was now equally rejected and repudiated when dead? The mode of ascertaining this point formed the topic of the little discussion that was taking place between myself and Juliet. I counselled her to pen a note, couched in a coldly polite style, to Viscount Ravenscliffe, who still remained at the inn,—requesting to be informed of the family's wishes and intentions: but Juliet, feeling hurt and indignant at the conduct of her brother-in-law, objected to hold any communication with him.

"He may think," she said, "that it is an overture on my part towards a correspondence, and that I am displaying an anxiety to be received into the Carshalton family."

"No, my dear Juliet," I answered; "you shall so word your note that it shall be as coldly reserved and as calmly dignified as possible; and it will therefore serve as the best rebuke that could possibly be offered to that young nobleman for his conduct."

Juliet consented: the note was written, and entrusted to the landlady to be delivered to the Viscount. In a few minutes the hostess reappeared, with an intimation to the effect "that his lordship would wait upon the *ladies* if they gave him permission."

I looked at Juliet, who made me a sign to imply that I might do exactly as I thought fit in the matter; and I therefore said to the landlady, "Let Lord Ravenscliffe be introduced."

The Viscount quickly made his appearance. He was a few years older than his deceased brother, but not near so prepossessing in his personal appearance. He could not even be called handsome: in figure and height he was insignificant; and his habitual air was that of cold insolent hauteur. There was also a slight tinge of coxcombry in his manner, principally arising from the habit which he had of carrying a quizzing-glass stuck in the socket of his eye; and as perhaps he was really near-sighted, he screwed up that particular eye which had the effect of distorting his countenance for the while into a grimace. Altogether Viscount Ravenscliffe was by no means an interesting personage, so far as outward appearance went; and I had already seen enough of his disposition to have but an indifferent opinion of his heart's qualities.

On entering the room, he bowed slightly to Juliet—but with greater formality, and indeed more respectfully to myself. We both acknowledged the salutation with the utmost coldness. Juliet would not speak; and it was therefore I who had to request his lordship to be seated.

"You are perhaps surprised," he said, as he took a chair, and thrusting his glass into his eye, began steadily to contemplate Juliet—"you are perhaps surprised that I should seek a personal interview with you, Miss Norman—"

"My lord!" ejaculated Juliet, the rich blood suddenly mantling upon her handsome countenance, while she drew up her fine form to its full height: "you have either addressed me by that name through mistake, for which you will of course apologize—or else with a deliberate intention to insult me, for which unmanly act of cruelty I should not envy your feelings."

"Ah! I thought that when actresses had married noblemen," said the Viscount, with flippant insolence, "and when the husbands died, the widows had the decency to resume their maiden names."

"My lord," interrupted Juliet, her eyes flashing fire, "I see that you *have* come with the deliberate intention of insulting me!—and I demand that this interview may immediately terminate."

"And I also, my lord," I interposed, "desire that you quit the room immediately; for conduct more gross than this which you are displaying, has perhaps never been witnessed. Depart, my lord!—there is the door!"

"Ah, ha!" he said, laughing superciliously;

"a couple of actresses giving themselves these airs!"

"Begone!" cried Juliet furiously.

"Pacify yourself, my dear friend," I said; "and you, my lord, remain for a few moments that I may tell you something which it were as well that you should hear. You use the term *actresses* as if in taunt: you think that you are humiliating and vilifying us; and even if it were so, your conduct would be that of the veriest dastard that ever dared insult a woman, but would shrink from the glance of one of his own sex. Well, my lord, we *are* actresses!—or at least we have been so. But have the actresses in whose presence you now stand, had naught to do with your own family that might at least render you civil and polite? My lord, the life of your own father was saved by me, Ellen Percy—otherwise Miss Trafford, the tragic actress——"

"But all the memory of that good deed was wiped away," ejaculated the Viscount, "by your conduct in assisting your friend Juliet Norman to inveigle my brother into a marriage with her: for of course you *did* so assist her——"

"Silence, insolent person that you are!" ejaculated Juliet. "Say anything you will to *me*: but accuse not my friend Ellen, the best and purest-minded of women! And as for your thinking to upbraid us because we have been actresses, let me tell you that the daughter of the proudest peer might envy Ellen's reputation as that of the greatest tragedian of modern times——"

"And perhaps Miss Norman," interjected the Viscount, with a mocking laugh, "considers herself to have been the most accomplished danseuse after Elssler and Taglioni! But come, we will put an end to all this nonsense. I only came for mere curiosity's sake—just to see what sort of person my self-styled sister-in-law might be——"

"And since you are here," exclaimed Juliet,—"since for a purpose so insolently avowed you have sought our presence,—you shall remain to listen to a few words which I have yet to speak. Know then, that in espousing your brother Lord Frederick, I married one who was destitute of all resources: it was upon my own income that he lived—it was in the house which belonged to me that he dwelt! He had not a shilling nor a foot of ground that he could call his own: he was therefore indebted to me for the bread that he ate! It was even my money which he took away with him when he left me upwards of two months back—my money therefore which has maintained him during his residence at the mansion where he has met so terrible a death! Thus you see, my lord, that the aristocrat may be indebted to the actress——though God knows that not for worlds would I have alluded to these circumstances in reference to the unfortunate deceased, were it not for the purpose of giving an answer to the cowardly malignant taunts which you have flung out!"

It was evident that the Viscount winced a little under the infliction of this speech: but still as his object was to humiliate Juliet, and perhaps myself likewise, he returned to the attack.

"Ah, well," he said, with the same insolent flippancy as at first, "the advantage was all your own; for you shone for a little while in the borrowed light of aristocracy—and if you had possessed as many thousands as you possessed hundreds, you would still have owed an immense obligation to my brother for having given you his name. So now, my good girl, take my advice—drop the Lady Frederick Ravenscliffe—become plain Juliet Norman once more——"

"Ah, my lord!" exclaimed Juliet bitterly, "if you knew everything, perhaps you would not proffer this advice, because you would conceive that I should be only too glad to adopt such a course of my own accord! Yes, my lord—I say if you knew *all*," continued Juliet, with increasing bitterness, "you would not think any honour has been conferred on me by the bestowal of the name of Ravenscliffe!"

"Juliet, enough!" I said, stepping forward, and laying my hand upon her shoulder: "that solemn secret must be religiously kept!"

"Ah! a secret?" said the Viscount: "what mean you?"—and his curiosity was now evidently piqued.

"A secret, my lord," answered Juliet, "the proclamation of which would fill the minds of all the members of your family with consternation and horror! Therefore be you upon your guard, my lord—let all the members of your family likewise be upon their guard, how they goad, taunt, or aggravate me——"

"Enough, I say, Juliet! enough!" I exclaimed.

"By heaven, there is some mystery in all this!" cried the Viscount, now looking anxious and full of suspense,—"a mystery which must be fathomed! Speak, Lady Frederick——"

"Ah! you give me my proper title now," ejaculated Juliet, with a certain air of triumph. "But no, my lord—I will not speak! The secret to which I allude is mine, to be disposed of as I think fit—to be treasured up or to be proclaimed according to circumstances——"

"But if there be any mystery attached to my unfortunate brother," said the Viscount, perplexed, afflicted, and even frightened, "I beseech you to reveal it. Yes—there must have been a mystery in his life—perhaps also in his death!—for it was not natural, that complete seclusion into which he retired—that sudden abandoning of himself to a scientific pursuit for which no one had ever previously heard that he had any taste——"

"I would advise you, my lord," I said, "to abstain from seeking to penetrate into these mysteries. Let it be sufficient for you to learn that if you or any of your family attempt to throw the slightest slur upon my friend Lady Frederick Ravenscliffe, she has it in her power to take a signal vengeance by making a frightful exposure—which as a matter of course she would be exceedingly loth to do, as a blight would thus be thrown upon the memory of her own husband. But still, if in self-defence she be compelled to snatch up such a weapon——"

At this moment there was a knock at the door of the apartment: I suddenly ceased speaking—and Juliet, who was nearest to the door, opened it.

"Please, your ladyship," said the hostess of the little establishment, "a gentleman of the name of Singleton begs for the honour of an interview. He is a surgeon living near Dover——"

"Ah!" ejaculated Juliet. "Yes—let Mr. Singleton be introduced:"—then as the landlady retired, Juliet said to the Viscount, "Perhaps your lordship will presently signify to me by means of a letter or message what steps are to be taken towards the interment of your deceased brother?"

Viscount Ravenscliffe was evidently about to give some answer; but at that moment the door again opened, and Mr. Singleton made his appearance. The Viscount bowed and withdrew; and the surgeon, shaking hands with Juliet and myself, said in a voice of condolence and sympathy, "It is a remarkable coincidence which brought me this evening into this neighbourhood."

"You have only just arrived, then?" I said, inquiringly.

"I have only just arrived at this inn," answered Mr. Singleton. "A relative of mine, living at some little distance, has been taken very ill—I was summoned from River—I reached his house at about two this afternoon—the rumour of the tragedy at Willowbridge Manor was wafted thither—and I deemed it my duty to come and offer my condolences to Lady Frederick Ravenscliffe."

Juliet expressed her gratitude; and then she said, "You, Mr. Singleton, know everything—Ellen has already told me so—I mean the terrible fact of the brand that was impressed upon *his* brow—that mark which rendered him a second Cain upon the earth—which drove him almost to madness——"

"Juliet, Juliet," I said, "do not thus refer to the past! Console her, Mr. Singleton—console her!" I added; and I then hastened from the room.

I must explain this abrupt departure. It struck me that I heard a strange sound, as if of a half-suppressed ejaculation, coming from the landing outside at the moment when Juliet with a revival of bygone passion had spoken of the brand impressed upon her deceased husband's brow. A suspicion at once seized upon me; and I therefore hurried from the room in the manner I have just described.

As I opened the door of the apartment, the door of a room opposite was at the same instant closing. I shut the door of the room from which I was issuing; and then I beheld the door opposite slowly move upon its hinges. Some one looked forth: it was Viscount Ravenscliffe!

"Miss Percy," he said, advancing upon the landing—and I saw that his countenance was as pale as death,—"one word! I beseech you, one word in private!"

I stepped forward to the door of his apartment—a glance flung into the interior showed me that it was a sitting-room—and I therefore hesitated not to enter it.

"Miss Percy," continued the Viscount, in whose manner a complete change had taken place—for he looked distressed, affrighted, and humiliated,—"Miss Percy, I know not how to preface what I have to say—I am cruelly embarrassed——"

"Perhaps I can assist you, my lord," I said: and then after a pause, I added, not with the accents of inquiry, but in the manner of an accusation,—"You listened at the door of the opposite apartment!"

"I confess it, Miss Percy—I confess it! The truth is, the last words that were spoken in that room just before Mr. Singleton was announced ——I refer to all that yourself and your friend said in allusion to some terrible mystery connected with my deceased brother——those words agitated me fearfully—inspired me with a harrowing curiosity——"

"No wonder, my lord! it was natural enough!" I interrupted him. "But why came you for the purpose of insulting two defenceless females,—one your own sister-in-law—the other myself, who had never done you the slightest injury?"

"Do not fall back upon accusations and reproaches," interrupted the Viscount; "do not, I entreat you! I listened at the door——do not be angry with me——But it suddenly struck me that to the friend who was thus admitted so readily—to this Mr. Singleton the surgeon—the fullest confidence would be shown, and that therefore I might hear something — I might glean some clue——"

"To the elucidation of the mystery?" I interjected. "Yes—and you *have* gleaned it!"

"My God, Miss Percy! horrible words met my ears! Oh, I shudder—I shudder!"—and the countenance of the nobleman was ghastly pale, while his form trembled visibly. "Cain! my brother likened unto Cain? No! for Frederick never raised a hand against a brother!"

"My lord, seek not to penetrate further into this mystery," I said; "for I warn you that it is terrible!—nay, more—it is horrible!"

"Suspense will kill me!—this fearful uncertainty —this hovering betwixt the wildest imaginings and the most excruciating uncertainties! No, no —Miss Percy! I could not endure it! For God's sake let me know the whole truth—or I shall do something rash and mad to discover it! Tell me, then—the brand impressed Cain-like upon my brother's brow——"

"Alas, my lord, it was so!" I responded: "but I will not enter into particulars—nothing shall induce me. Suffice it for you to learn that for a crime which ruined the peace of a family—a fearful private vengeance was wreaked—and a searing iron left its indelible, its appalling mark——"

"O horror!" groaned the miserable Viscount, clasping his hands together; then, as a light seemed suddenly to flash in unto his brain, he looked with a ghastly significance up into my countenance, saying in a low sombre voice, "I understand it all now! My brother died not—no—he died not by accident——It was as a miserable suicide!"

I answered not a word, but my look, full of gloomy meaning, conveyed an eloquent response. Again did a long deep groan come from the lips of the Viscount: he then turned aside, covering his face with his hands; and for nearly a minute there was a profound silence in that apartment. At length the nobleman turned again towards me; and as he removed his hands from his countenance I saw that his features had a fixed rigid look of mingled woe and horror; and I could not help thinking that insolent self-sufficiency and flippant pride never had sustained so complete a humiliation!

"Miss Percy," he said in a voice that was sombre even to sepulchral gloominess, "there is indeed a fearful secret within the knowledge of yourself, and Lady Frederick, and that surgeon who has just arrived,—a secret which if proclaimed, would redound with dishonour and disgrace upon the entire family of Carshalton! Branded and a suicide! Oh, my miserable brother! But can you pardon me, Miss Percy —and can my sister-in-law pardon me—for my gross, vile, cowardly conduct——"

"Yes, my lord," I said; "we can pardon you! And now, as this interview is most painful, let it at once terminate. Answer me therefore: what is your intention with regard to the interment of your deceased brother?"

"He shall be buried with all due honour and solemnity in the family vault of the Carshaltons," rejoined the Viscount. "If Lady Frederick Ravenscliffe will come to Carshalton House until——"

"It is not usual for ladies to attend at funeral obsequies," I said; "and therefore Juliet will not desire to follow her husband's remains to the grave. Neither does she experience any inclination to force herself upon the notice of a family which has hitherto repudiated and ignored her. Thus though it be unusual for a wife to separate herself from her husband's remains until the arrival of the last moment, yet will the widow in the present instance adopt an exceptional course. To you, my lord, be now assigned the charge of superintending your brother's funeral: Juliet will accompany me to London. Farewell."

Having thus spoken, I quitted the apartment. On returning to the room where I had left Juliet and Mr. Singleton, I found them conversing together; and in a few words I described what had just taken place betwixt myself and Viscount Ravenscliffe. Juliet was satisfied with the arrangement which had been made in respect to the funeral. Mr. Singleton shortly took his departure, to return to the abode of the relative on account of whose illness he had been summoned from such a distance; and as it was now past eight o'clock in the evening, Juliet and I resolved to set off at once for London. The postchaise was ordered to be got in readiness with all possible despatch: the account was settled with liberality; and we were about to ascend into the vehicle, when Viscount Ravenscliffe suddenly made his appearance, and in silence proffered his hand to assist us. We took our seats—the Viscount bestowed upon us the most courteous salutations —and the equipage drove away at a rapid rate.

"At the last moment," observed Juliet, with a certain degree of bitterness in her tone, "he thought it better to sustain appearances and seem to be on friendly terms with me. Ah! he feels that the less scope there is given for gossip and chit-chat, the better—and that the sooner all the circumstances connected with the tragic occurrence shall die out of the memory of the dwellers in this neighbourhood, the more satisfactory will it be."

"It is very certain, my dear Juliet," I responded, "that an overweening aristocratic pride has within the last hour received a most signal discomfiture, and patrician insolence has been taught a lesson which it will not very readily forget."

———

CHAPTER LXXXV.

A MYSTERY.

THE visit to Willowbridge had been attended with circumstances calculated to produce the strongest impressions alike upon the mind of Juliet and myself. Undertaken for a comparatively trivial object, this journey had led us to a destination where the most important events were to ensue. It all seemed to be perfectly providential,—something which if read in the page of romance would be looked upon as strained, exaggerated, and unnatural — but which thus happening amidst the circumstances of real life, only tended to illustrate most forcibly the poet's aphorism that "truth is stranger than fiction." Lord Frederick Ravenscliffe was no more: the young nobleman whose treatment of Juliet, in all its various phases, had so signally influenced her destinies, had ceased to exist. He had perished as a suicide,—the deed of self-destruction being the result of a plan which was evidently laboured, well-weighed, and executed in a manner displaying a horrible clearness of mind. The letter he had penned in the last hour of his existence, proved how keenly calculating and how shrewdly foreseeing he was even in the supreme moments when Death, obedient to his own invitation, was staring him in the face. And this letter served a twofold object: it not merely averted suspicion from the fact that he was a suicide—but it also constituted to some extent an atonement towards Juliet, inasmuch as it eulogized her character and was well calculated to place her in an admirable position before the world. In respect to what Juliet herself felt for the loss of her husband,—I may state that when the influence of the first shock was past, she could not experience any great amount of grief and affliction; for, as I have before said, the death of Lord Frederick Ravenscliffe was a happy release, and it would have been the veriest affectation to regard it in any other light.

It was about ten o'clock at night when the postchaise drew up in front of my house in Great Ormond Street. We alighted: Beda hastened forward to receive us—and in a few hurried words I whispered to my faithful dependant the intelligence that extraordinary adventures had occurred at Willowbridge, the leading incident being the death of Lord Frederick Ravenscliffe. Beda was astounded and shocked: but there was not at the moment any time for explanation. Juliet was very much fatigued and exhausted with the excitement through which she had passed; and she was anxious at once to retire to her own chamber.

"Beda, you had better attend upon her ladyship," I said. "But where is Miss Glentworth?"

"She is out, Miss," replied Beda.

"Indeed?" I said: and a misgiving seized upon me—for it was past ten o'clock: but without choosing to display any particular emotion, I said, "I suppose Miss Glentworth left a message in case I should return?"

"Miss Glentworth simply said that she herself should return by seven or eight o'clock," rejoined Beda: "but she has not as yet been back. It was at six o'clock—immediately after dinner—that she went out."

"In the carriage?" I inquired.

"No, Miss—on foot," was the reply.

"Well, attend upon Lady Frederick Ravenscliffe, Beda," I said; "and I will await Miss Glentworth's return."

Juliet overheard this little colloquy—but she thought nothing particular of it; for she was in ignorance of those circumstances the recollection of which was only so well calculated to excite misgivings in my mind on account of the present occurrence. Juliet retired to her chamber; and I proceeded to the drawing-room. I was very uneasy; I had a vivid recollection of how Mary Glentworth had behaved in reference to the young Marquis of Dalrymple—how studiously she had concealed from me the clandestine interviews with that young nobleman—and how she had even condescended to falsehood to veil her proceedings and avert my suspicions. Only two months had elapsed since the memorable scene in the jeweller's shop when Mary flew into the arms of the Duke of Ardleigh, and which incident was followed by a complete exposure of all circumstances that regarded her. Could she during these two months have formed any fresh acquaintance producing an impression upon her heart? It was scarcely to be believed. Had any accident befallen her? or had she become the victim of any treachery?

As the reader may suppose, I was much bewildered and distressed as I asked myself these questions. I looked at my watch: time was gliding away; it was half-past ten o'clock—and Mary had not returned. At length I heard a vehicle drive up to the door. In my anxiety and suspense I could not wait a moment to see whether it were really an arrival at the house; but I flew down the stairs. There was a knock at the door: I hastened to open it—and Mary Glentworth crossed the threshold just as the cab which had brought her thither drove away.

"Thank heaven, you are returned, Mary!" I exclaimed, embracing her the instant I had closed the door. "You know not how uneasy you have rendered me!"

"Uneasy?" she repeated; and methought it was in a strange, vague, listless manner—while instead of returning my embrace, she seemed only to tolerate it, and her form was quite inanimate in my arms.

Seized with affright, I stepped back a pace and looked at her. Her cheeks were of marble paleness: from her lips also had the colour fled; her eyes had a fixed but vacant stare. Yet she seemed to display no emotion: her entire air was that of an inanimate coldness. I could not understand it. There was something awful in her appearance—more awful and more appalling than if there had been a violent outburst of emotions or a tornado of passion.

"Good heavens, Mary!" I exclaimed, seizing her by the hand and pressing it with fervour in the hope of infusing some degree of life's warmth and friendship's animation into her heart; "what is the matter with you, Mary? What has happened? It seems as if something terrible——"

"Happened?" she repeated, with a strange vacancy. "Nothing has happened:"—and she was moving through the hall towards the foot of the staircase.

"Mary," I said, catching her by the arm, "have

I offended you? Have you no kind word for me? —Have you forgotten that I have been absent from home since yesterday morning——"

"Ah, indeed! I had forgotten it," said Mary. "I am glad to see you, dear Ellen:"—and she kissed my cheek with as much coldness as if it were a marble statue that had been inspired with a single moment's life in order to bestow that kiss; and the mere contact of the glacial lips froze the blood in my veins.

I did not say another word then and there. I saw that there was something horribly, fearfully wrong. I was afraid of engendering a conversation which might be heard by the domestics, and which it would be most undesirable that they should hear. I therefore followed Mary in silence up the staircase. She actually did not seem to be aware that I was behind her; she took no notice of me—she looked not to the right nor to the left —she appeared to be walking mechanically as if it were in a dream. My heart kept tightening and tightening; my brain too felt as if there were a cord being drawn around it: my mind experienced a hideous suspense—an appalling conviction of some stupendous calamity having overtaken the unhappy girl in whom I was so deeply interested. She walked straight up to her bedchamber: she had no light in her hand—but I had brought a lamp which had been standing on a table on the drawing-room landing; and as I placed it on the drawers, Mary's eyes rested upon me.

"And have you bought the estate, Ellen?" she asked, as she put off her bonnet and mantle; and her tone was cold, level, monotonous, as if there were completest apathy in her heart, and as if the question were only put because it was the first that rose to her lips, and not because she experienced any interest in what she was saying.

"No, Mary," I answered, "I did not go to purchase it—I merely went to look at it in the first instance."

"Ah, true! I recollect now," she said.

"But it is not my intention to purchase the property," I continued. "In the first place it is not eligible: in the second place a dreadful occurrence has taken place there——"

"Ah, indeed! a dreadful occurrence?"—but cold as ice was the tone.

"Yes, Mary; and I am sure that you will be very much astonished when I tell you that we encountered Lord Frederick Ravenscliffe at the very house which we went to inspect——"

"Ah, Lord Frederick Ravenscliffe — Juliet's husband. Yes—I know him."

"And he is dead, Mary," I continued: "he died a horrible death——"

"Poor man! A horrible death!"—but it was an ice-statue that was speaking.

"Frightful—terrible!" I ejaculated with vehemence. "But good heavens, Mary! what is the matter with you? Oh, do, do tell me, I beseech you! Surely, surely you will not keep a secret from the best and dearest friend that you have upon the face of the earth?"

Mary had just begun to loosen her apparel as a preliminary towards undressing herself: she now desisted—and sat down upon an ottoman by the side of the bed, her gaze fixed upon me as if with the vacant expression of a person that was wondering who I was and why I was there. And yet there was not anything like idiocy in her gaze: it rather struck me as being the fixity of silent rigid despair. Good heaven! what awful calamity could have fallen upon her head within so short a time?—or what could she have done that might possibly produce a grief so hopelessly profound—a desperation that could dream of no redemption?

"Mary," I said, gazing fondly and entreatingly up into her countenance, "I conjure you to speak to me! Tell me what ails you?"

"Nothing, Ellen—I am perfectly well," was the answer given in a voice of ice.

"And yet you are deadly pale, Mary—there is no colour on your cheeks—your lips are ashy——"

"And yet I am quite well," she said: and she was still speaking in that cold, level monotony of voice which seemed to indicate the completest apathy, and as if neither the heart nor the imagination had anything to do with the words that were uttered from the lips.

"Mary," I said, "do not afflict me thus! Something has happened! All this is most unnatural! You were never so before!—no, not even when you lost your mother—nor when you found that Herbert Dalrymple was your half-brother!"

I said these things in the hope of exciting Mary Glentworth; for I felt that it would be even better to plunge a dagger into her heart, so to speak, in order to startle her from this apathy, than to leave her thus entombed in it. It was with this same view that I had previously told her about Lord Frederick Ravenscliffe in the hope of galvanizing her feelings: I was now repeating the attempt, but in a stronger manner and through a more powerful medium. All was useless. There she sat, motionless as a statue—looking the picture of silent, ineffable despair. Yet there was something about her—I can scarcely describe what—but a *something* which convinced me that her mind was not altogether shattered— that the lamp of reason had not been extinguished in the sanctuary of her brain!

"Mary, Mary," I passionately cried, seizing her hands and pressing them in my own; "tell me what has happened, my dear friend!—tell me, dearest Mary!—I adjure you by everything sacred to tell me!"

"I have nothing to tell you, Ellen," she answered: and withdrawing her hands, she placed them one above the other on her knee—her form slightly inclining forward—her eyes bent down— and the expression of her countenance still that of mute ineffable despair.

"Shall I hasten for medical assistance?" inquired a whispering voice from the other side of the bed; it was Beda who spoke, and who having glided into the room, was not immediately perceived by me.

"I do not know—I am bewildered what to think, to say, or do:" and then I glanced at Mary: but finding her motionless and apathetic as before, I again caught her vehemently by the hands, exclaiming, "Mary, this cannot last! You alarm— you frighten me! Are you ill, my dear friend? Speak! Are you ill? Will you have medical advice?"

"Medical advice:"—and it was with a smile icily scornful that Mary repeated the words: the next moment the smile was gone—her countenance was rigid as before.

I saw the absolute necessity of rousing her by some means—I scarcely knew how—scarcely even cared indeed, for she was driving me to perfect desperation. So I exclaimed, as if in an excited manner, "Run, Beda—run, and fetch a physician! —two physicians, if necessary! We will have a consultation! My poor friend Miss Glentworth is very ill."

"Leave me—leave me, Ellen," she now said, speaking petulantly and impatiently, but likewise with another scornful smile as if to give me to understand that she knew I was not serious in sending for the medical practitioners, and that the stratagem was too flimsy to deceive her. "Leave me, dear Ellen," she repeated: "I wish to be alone."

She now rose up from the ottoman—but it was only to stand like a statue before me. Yes—there she stood, like a marble statue—pale as one —the very effigy of despair itself! I made a

No. 67.—ELLEN PERCY.

sign for Beda to retire: I hastened to secure the door behind her; and then throwing my arms about Mary Glentworth's neck, I exclaimed, "Oh, deal not with me so reservedly, my friend! Tell me the cause of your affliction! If it be aught whereof in the presence of any other you would be ashamed—yet with me, dearest Mary—with me who love you so well, and whom you ought to treat like a sister—there need be no secrets!"

Still Mary Glentworth gazed upon me in the same vacant manner as before; and resuming her seat she began playing with her kerchief as if the state of her mind were now bordering upon idiocy. I almost wrung my hands in despair at the apparent impossibility of extracting a syllable from her lips. I looked at her with the most earnest attention—I contemplated her with the closest scrutiny: I did not think she was going mad—but I felt convinced that her mind had received a shock and that some great calamity had befallen her.

That she had willingly gone astray in any sense I could not conceive : for I naturally supposed that if such were the case she would make every endeavour to conceal the remorse and regret which followed, instead of betraying a perturbed state of mind.

"Mary," I said, again taking her hand and pressing it to my lips, "once for all I conjure you to tell me what has happened and what is the matter with you! It would be cruel—very cruel of you, Mary, to leave me any longer in the terrific suspense which I now experience!"

She seemed struck by these words : she suddenly raised her countenance somewhat—she bent her full blue eyes upon me—she seemed to reflect for a few moments ; and then she said ; "I would not for the world distress you, Ellen! Leave me now, my sweet friend! I can assure you I am more collected and composed!"

"Ah! then, something *had* occurred to distress you?" I exclaimed.

"Do not press me for an explanation now, Ellen," rejoined Mary Glentworth. "To-morrow I will tell you all. Good night, my dear friend."

"Good night, Mary," I said. "But are you sure that you would not like me to remain throughout the night with you?—or will you have Beda?—for you might be seized with indisposition——"

"No, Ellen," answered Mary ; "I prefer being alone. Do not be uneasy on my account : I shall immediately retire to rest. A good night's repose——"

But here she stopped short ; and an expression of indescribable bitterness appeared upon her countenance, as if it were a hideous mockery to suppose that she could expect to enjoy a good night's rest. She saw that my own looks denoted anguish as I observed that expression on her features ; and hastening to throw her arms round my neck, she exclaimed, "For heaven's sake do not press me now, dear Ellen!—suspend your judgment—wait until to-morrow! I will then tell you all! But Ah! when I think of it, let all this lay between you and me—do not tell Juliet that anything extraordinary has occurred! As for Beda, we know that her discretion is to be relied upon ; and if you tell her to think no more of what she may have seen this evening, she will obey you implicitly."

"And you insist, Mary," I said, in a half reproachful tone, "that I shall leave you for the night?—and you will not tell me what has occurred?"

"Wait, wait until to-morrow!" she said, almost petulantly : and her present excitement contrasted strongly and strangely with the glacial apathy of look and manner that she had just now worn.

"Yet answer me one question—only one question!" I said; for a terrible idea was haunting me. "You have not seen *him?*—you surely know whom I mean?—your half-brother——"

"What, Herbert Dalrymple?" ejaculated Mary. "Oh, no! no! I have not seen *him!* And now good night, Ellen!"

She embraced me—she gently pushed me towards the door—and I was compelled to leave the room. I repaired to my own chamber, where I found Beda waiting for me : she did not ask any question :—indeed it was almost invariably her habit to wait until I thought fit to enter into discourse with her ; for of all beings in the world she was the last to display any undue curiosity, and yet the first to take a lively interest in any topic which at all engaged my own feelings or sentiments.

"I have received no explanation from Miss Glentworth's lips," I said. "She has promised to deal with me to-morrow in the spirit of a friendly frankness. Meanwhile, Beda, say nothing to a soul—not even to Lady Frederick Ravenscliffe——"

"Even without this injunction, Miss," answered Beda, "I should have held my peace in reference to Miss Glentworth."

After some little conversation—in the course of which I gave Beda a few particulars relative to the incidents that had occurred at Willowbridge —I dismissed her to her own room. I lay down to rest : but it was long ere sleep visited my eyes —for I was cruelly perplexed and bewildered on Mary Glentworth's account.

In the morning, immediately upon quitting my chamber I proceeded to Mary's room. I found that she likewise was up and dressed : and it struck me that there was a certain decisiveness in her looks—a resoluteness of expression which I had never noticed before, and which I therefore concluded to be associated with the mysterious mood of the preceding evening. It was with a certain sedateness that she greeted me, although with affectionate kindness ; but methought her spirits had now utterly lost all remnant of their pristine exuberance, and were toned down into a seriousness that might be deemed more appropriate for one of far maturer years. Indeed, it struck me that Mary's disposition had undergone a still greater transition towards gravity and pensiveness than even when all the discoveries in respect to the Ardleigh family had produced so strong an effect upon her; and I experienced a feeling of sadness at the idea that the buoyancy of her nature, as I had first known it, should ever have been checked or weighed down by the untoward circumstances of life.

"Now, Mary," I said, "you will fulfil your promise of last night——"

"My dear Ellen," she interrupted me, taking my hand and retaining it in her own—but rather holding it as if unconsciously and unwittingly, than pressing it with any degree of warmth emanating from the heart,—" I beseech you to throw a veil over the scene of last evening! If you love me, as indeed I know you do, you will grant me this boon!—you will not press me for a single syllable of explanation! Ellen, it is *my* secret!"

"After the manner in which you have just spoken, Mary," I said, "it would be rude and discourteous on my part to press you for explanations. You are putting friendship out of the question—you seem to think that I cannot entertain on your behalf such a degree of interest as will leave me a prey to the acutest suspense on your account——"

"Yes, Ellen—I know all that you feel for me," answered Mary ; "and it is to this very love itself that I am now appealing when I beseech and implore——"

"Enough, Mary," I said : "you have declared that it is your own secret—and it shall remain so!"

I was about to add something more: indeed I was on the point of saying, "And heaven grant that you have no reason of which you need be ashamed, for thus making it your secret!"—but I checked myself. I neither sought to irritate nor to grieve—neither to chafe a spirit that might be already wounded, nor to appear to entertain any feeling of bitterness on account of the reserve that was maintained towards me: I therefore said not another syllable upon the subject—and we quitted the chamber together. At the breakfast-table Mary's demeanour was about the same as for the last two months it had been, with the exception that perhaps her speech was the least thing more deliberate and her tone a shade colder. What—Oh! what, I asked myself, could be passing in my young friend's mind?—what secret could be locked up in the sanctuary of her heart? what mystery was entombed in the profundities of her soul?

Immediately after breakfast a dressmaker arrived to prepare deep mourning for Juliet, who was now to wear widow's-weeds in order to sustain appearances before the world, although in her own heart she considered her husband's death, as I have already stated, to be a happy release. The newspapers gave a lengthy account of the tragedy at Willowbridge as well as of the inquest which had been holden; and the impression calculated to be left upon the public mind after a perusal of the narrative, was entirely that which the Coroner and Jury had themselves received—namely, that it was a case of accidental death. The whole of Lord Frederick's letter was printed in the journals; and its effect was to place the character of my friend Juliet on the highest possible pedestal in public estimation. A few days passed away—at the expiration of which interval Mr. Norman returned from the Continent, where a letter from Juliet had reached him, communicating the catastrophe at Willowbridge. He stopped at River House, whence he wrote to inform his daughter that he should remain there for the present; and she, thinking that her father would be dull if left there alone, made up her mind to rejoin him. Thus, instead of spending some weeks with me as was her original intention, she tarried but ten days; for now that her mind was no longer unsettled in respect to the fate of her husband, she longed to get back to the seclusion of her own rural abode, afar from the din and bustle of the metropolis.

During these few days which thus elapsed, Mary Glentworth's manner continued the same as I have last described it; and not another syllable in reference to the past fell from her lips. Occasionally there was a slight embarrassment in her look when our eyes met,—as if she felt that the same implicit confidence did not reign betwixt us as heretofore—as if some slight shock had been sustained by our friendship—as if the sisterly bonds which had previously united us had been loosened—and she herself the cause of all this! But heaven knows that I felt towards her just as affectionately as ever; and it was on account of this very love and interest which I experienced on her behalf, that I trembled lest her conduct on that memorable night should have left behind it any source of regret and remorse.

A fortnight had now elapsed since my cousin Henry went to Paisley to settle matters with Mr. Macdonald. At the end of the first week I received a letter from Henry, telling me that he could not complete the business so speedily as he had anticipated, and that he might possibly be detained another week by the affairs which were then engrossing his attention. In the meanwhile I had not been unmindful of a certain request that was made to me by William Lardner. This was to the effect that I would give him my advice in reference to a proposal which had been made him. It appeared that on board the East Indiaman which had brought him home from the Cape of Good Hope, William Lardner had attracted the notice of a certain Sir Robert Temple—a Colonel in the East India Company's service, and who was reputed to be a gentleman of considerable wealth. During the voyage Sir Robert Temple had suffered severely from illness: his own body-servant was likewise laid up the whole time; and William Lardner had proved unremitting in his attentions towards them both—so that the young gipsy-sailor completely won the favour of the veteran nabob. On arriving in England, Sir Robert offered to take William Lardner as a page or confidential servant,—promising however to treat him more as a friend than a menial, and to have due regard for his future welfare if he should conduct himself in a proper manner. It was whether he should avail himself of this opportunity that William Lardner desired to consult me. I therefore granted him an interview one morning that we might discuss the subject.

"You see, Miss," said William, "I had taken a fancy for a sailor's life; and it would only be the hope of improving my position in some other capacity that could induce me to abandon the sea."

"The offers of Sir Robert Temple are most generous and most tempting," I said; "and I should have no hesitation in advising you to accept them if I were acquainted with the character and disposition of the gentleman himself. But you can surely judge whether Sir Robert be a man who acts by caprice, and who is at all likely to disappoint the hopes which he now holds forth——"

"It is this very point, Miss," exclaimed William, "that makes me undecided how to act, and which has determined me to consult you. I know that Sir Robert is a good-hearted man at bottom—generous and liberal: I saw plenty of proofs of all this on board the ship. But then he is a strange temper—irritable and capricious—difficult to please—apt to give way to abusive language—very dictatorial——"

"Really, William," I said, "you are depicting a character which frightens me on your account; for if you were to abandon the life of a sailor, which is a certainty in respect to income, for the position of a valet in this gentleman's service, the tenure of which place may be most uncertain——"

"Ah! that's what I have reflected upon, and what I have represented to Beda!" exclaimed William. "It would be hard to give up a certainty for an uncertainty. But then, on the other hand, Sir Robert Temple really seems to possess a very good heart, and to be incapable of allowing his irritability or ill-temper to lead him into an act of downright cruelty or injustice. A sailor fell from the mainyard and fractured his thigh—the limb had to be amputated—a subscription-list was sent round amongst the passengers — some gave a guinea—others half a guinea—others five shillings —and so on. Sir Robert Temple put down his name for ten shillings——"

"And you tell me," I exclaimed, "that he is really rich and naturally generous?"

"Stop, Miss, if you please!" said William Lardner. "Sir Robert Temple put down his name for ten shillings in the subscription-list; and privately he sent the poor man ten guineas. This I know to be a fact, for the simple reason, Miss Percy, that I was made the almoner of Sir Robert's bounty; and he particularly charged me not to mention the circumstance to any one except the poor sailor himself."

"Without another moment's hesitation, William," I said, "accept the proposal of Sir Robert Temple! Yes—this advice I emphatically give you! Any one who could act in the way you have described, must be a good man. I do not think that you will ultimately have occasion to regret the course I recommend you to adopt. Sir Robert Temple will study your welfare, if you only continue to deserve his good opinion—as I am convinced that you will!"

"It shall be no fault of mine, Miss Percy, if I do not keep my situation with Sir Robert: and I had already made up my mind that if I did take it, I would put up with all his whims and caprices —I would avoid irritating him——"

"But you must not be too servile, William," I said, with a deprecating smile.

The rich blood mantled upon the youth's handsome countenance, and his dark eyes flashed for a moment, as he exclaimed, "No, Miss Percy! it is not in the nature of one of my race to be too servile! But to conduct myself with a proper forbearance—to study to the very utmost to avoid all cause for irritation—to anticipate his wants—to show myself grateful, in a word, for the favour bestowed upon me——"

"Yes, William," I interrupted him, "behave towards Sir Robert Temple as Beda behaves towards me, and you cannot fail to secure his esteem. Therefore, all things considered, William, you had better signify your intention of accepting Sir Robert's offer. Where does he reside?"

"He gave me his address," responded Lardner; "it is at a West End hotel—but I believe that Sir Robert's intention is to take a house in some cheerful neighbourhood of London: for he is an old bachelor, Miss Percy—and I almost think, from certain things he used to say to me, that he has no relatives for whom he cares, even if he has any relations at all; so that he stands all the more in need of faithful attendants——and such will I be towards him! Besides, Miss," added William, now suddenly seized with bashfulness, "it will of course be more pleasant to remain altogether in England—in the neighbourhood of London too— than to be carried in a ship to the end of the world—to be months and months away from one's native land, without knowing what may happen during one's absence—for of course, Miss, you know that I take a great interest in Beda——"

"I know it, William," I said, smiling good-naturedly at his increasing bashfulness and embarrassment: "you are fond of each other—and some of these days you may think of marriage;

but for the present you are both very young. However, a long life of happiness may probably be stretching before you,—and bear this in mind, William — that while you on the one hand are doing your best to earn a competency, Beda is pursuing the same course on the other hand. She has already certain prospects——But no matter! the time is not yet come for me to be more explicit!"

I was alluding to the sum of one thousand pounds which the Earl of Carshalton had placed in the funds to the name of Beda Robinson, under the trusteeship of myself, and of which bequest I held the documentary proof. I had never breathed a syllable on the subject to Beda—but I was now about letting out the secret to her lover, when I suddenly checked myself; for I still thought it better to allow the matter to remain in the background for at least a little longer, and until the young couple should be somewhat older.

In the afternoon of that same day William Lardner returned to the house, and requested another interview with me. This I at once granted. On entering into my presence, he hesitated, and looked confused and embarrassed, until I encouraged him to speak.

"The truth is, Miss," he said, "the old Colonel desires to call upon you; for I happened to tell him that you knew something about me, and if it were necessary could speak a word in my favour——"

"To be sure!" I exclaimed: "nothing will please me more, William, than to be enabled to render you a service! By all means let Sir Robert Temple call upon me. I shall be glad to form the acquaintance of any one who promises to be kind and good to you."

William Lardner was overjoyed at the permission thus accorded him to acquaint Sir Robert Temple that he might pay his respects to me; and in the course of the evening I learnt that I might expect a visit from the wealthy nabob on the morrow, between two and three o'clock in the afternoon. I must observe that Beda was greatly delighted at William's present prospects: she was glad that he was to remain in England, and that he had abandoned the dangers of a seafaring life.

On the following day, at about two o'clock, I took my seat in the drawing-room, prepared to receive the expected visitor. Mary Glentworth was in her own chamber,—where, I should observe, she had recently been much in the habit of secluding herself. It was about half-past two when I heard an equipage stop in front of the house: then the usual summons was given at the front door—and I heard that door duly opened by one of my domestics. I waited for the appearance of the nabob: it struck me that he was a very long time in making this appearance; and I remembered that I had not heard the front door close again. I got up from the sofa where I was seated; and went to peep through the window. A large yellow barouche (evidently a hired one) was standing opposite the house: a footman in livery, and William Lardner in his sailor's attire, were assisting an infirm old gentleman to ascend the steps of the front door. That glance was sufficient to decide me how to act. I was almost angry with William for not having informed me that Sir Robert was scarcely able to walk, and that it would be therefore preposterous to expect he could ever mount the stairs to the drawing-room. I hastened forth from that room—I descended the staircase—and I hastily said to my parlour-maid as I passed her in the hall, "I will receive Sir Robert in the dining-room."

On entering that apartment, I left the door ajar; and I now caught the ejaculations which in a hoarse voice and with irritable accents, the nabob was addressing to his lacquey and to William Lardner.

"Now, then, the left foot! Come—lift it, can't ye? There! there! gently now! Stop! let me lean on you, William. Perdition take the fellow! what an awkward brute it is! Now for my poor gouty leg! Mind, Reuben—mind! Do you hear, sirrah? By Jove, if you don't take care, I'll pack you off with a flea in your ear! Oh! oh! Hang the fellow! how awkward he is! Come, you try, William——"

"Beg pardon, Sir Robert," humbly interjected a voice, which I afterwards discovered to be that of Reuben the lacquey: "I'm doing my best——"

"Don't answer me, you scoundrel!" exclaimed the nabob, with awful fierceness. "You did it on purpose, sirrah! You owed me a spite—you resolved to wreak it—you knew exactly where the gout lay—you pinched my toe—I felt it through the bandage! You are a scoundrel, sirrah—an infernal scoundrel!"

The old nabob had a habit of grunting at the end of every short sentence; and a curt sharp grunt it was—not of that kind which is usually expressed by the term "ugh!"—but the nearest method of conveying the accurate sound is by speaking it "hur!"

"Now, then, over the threshold! Hur! William you rascal! let me hold on to your shoulder! Hur! hur! Reuben, mind what you're up to! What the deuce—hur!—possesses the fellow! I'll—I'll play vengeance with you, you scoundrel!—hur!"

I am describing as well as I can the pleasant and agreeable process by which the old nabob got himself into my house—or rather I should say by which he was conveyed into the house. At length he was brought into the dining-room, where he lifted off his hat and made a sufficiently courteous bow.

"Take me to the sofa—the sofa, hur!" he grunted out. "Hold me up, Reuben! You see, Miss Percy, this precious scoundrel of mine—hur!——There! take care of the right leg!——This scoundrel, I say, does it on purpose to plague me! As for William—hur!—hang you, William! why don't you turn me round so as to get properly on the sofa? There! hur! hur! Now, that's right! There!—hur!"

And thus, in the midst of a succession of irascible ejaculations and grunts, with divers contortions of the countenance as the gouty toe twinged him, Sir Robert Temple managed to settle himself upon the sofa at last.

"Get out, Reuben!—hur! Begone, William! —hur! hur!"—and in this summary manner did the nabob dismiss from the room the lacquey already in his service, and the valet whom he meant to take into it.

I beheld before me a tall thin man, of about sixty-five—who neither looked like a bilious East Indian nor a gouty subject. So far from being bilious, he had a very red face:—his profile indicated that he had once been handsome, for it had all the remains of aquiline symmetry; but it was wrinkled with age, and bore the effects of mingled good living and pain—the latter being the natural consequence of the former. His eyes were somewhat watery; his hair was thin and grey; and he had lost several of his teeth. He had a stern aspect, as one who was accustomed to command authoritatively and to be obeyed implicitly. In his costume he was somewhat of an old beau: he had a blue surtout with a velvet collar—a buff waistcoat—and black kerseymere trousers. One foot had a patent leather boot—the other an enormous great list shoe, distended with the crossed and quadrupled bandages beneath. A double eye-glass was suspended to his neck by a black ribbon: a handsome gold chain, with a bunch of massive seals, depended from his fob. He wore light-coloured kid gloves; and having seated himself on the sofa, he wiped the perspiration from his countenance with a delicate cambric kerchief. I should add that there was a strange admixture of courtliness and roughness in his manners,—brutality being quickly succeeded by urbanity, and the habitual sternness of his countenance occasionally relaxing into a smile which seemed to imply that its expression might once have been naturally affable enough—but that must have been many years ago!

"Beg pardon, Miss Percy, for all the disturbance I make—hur!—and all the trouble I give. But this cursed gout——beg pardon, Miss, for swearing!—enough to make an angel swear!—hur! hur!"

"Pray do not vex yourself, Sir Robert," I said, pitying the poor man; for I saw how his features every now and then had a flitting paroxysm of anguish passing over them. "Will you permit me to offer you some refreshment?—a glass of wine and a biscuit?"

"Wine indeed!—hur! hur! What would Doctor Strychnia say?—hur! No, no, Miss! I'm allowanced to three glasses a day!—hur! But still if I might be so bold—and if you had such a thing—hur! just one glass of Madeira."

I immediately rang the bell; for it fortunately happened that I had in the house some very fine old Madeira, which my friend the Countess of Belgrade (Lady Cecilia Urban that was) had sent me, together with some other choice wines, at the time when I commenced housekeeping for myself. The Madeira was accordingly soon brought in, in company with a cake, some sandwiches, and some biscuits: the salver was placed upon a little table, which was stood opposite to the Colonel; and he helped himself to a glass of his favourite wine.

"Good!—hur! very good! 'Pon my word—hur!—I don't know when I've tasted better! Quite mellow!—hur! Old East India!—hur! Wonder what my friend Strychnia would say if he could just peep in? But he can't—thank God, he can't!"—and Sir Robert chuckled gleefully, as if it were a glorious thing to cheat his physician, though he himself stood the chance of being the sufferer from the pleasant little fraud.

I handed him a piece of cake: he looked up

smiling, and said, " 'Pon my soul, Miss Percy—hur! a very handsome young lady! Don't blush—hur! I'm old enough to be your grandfather. Why, if you went out to India you'd marry a Rajah—or a Nizam—or a Sultaun—hur! Better not, though!—all rascals—hur!—precious rascals!—arrant scoundrels, I can tell you! India a fine country though, Miss—capital shooting in the jungles—hur!—rather dangerous though! Was once under a tree, with a tiger in front—a boa constrictor up in the boughs—and a cobra close at my feet—hur! Pleasant that—hur! wasn't it?"

"It was a predicament, Sir Robert," I said, "from which I should think that you must have experienced some little trouble in escaping?"

"Not a bit of it, Miss!" he replied. "Rifle ready levelled at tiger—hur! Double-barrelled—one shot at tiger—down he fell! Up went the rifle—second shot into the tree—down came the boa constrictor!—hur!—sixty feet long! No lie, this, Miss Percy!—Skin in Madras museum—whole story well known in India—hur!"

"But what about the cobra di capello?" I inquired, willing to humour the old gentleman for the worthy young William Lardner's sake.

"Ah, cobra?—hur! Cobra didn't like the way his friends were despatched—deuced sharp work he thought it!—glided away—hur! Snake-charmer came by at the very moment—hur! Got the snake—snake danced for ten years afterwards on his tail, to the sound of a pipe. Died—preserved in a jar—spirits of wine—hur! Got him with me at my hotel—bought him of the snake-charmer—hur! Very fine girls in India, Miss Percy," he added, almost in the same breath: "nautch girls—devilish fine!—hur!"

"And were you long in India, Sir Robert?" I asked.

"Thirty years, Miss: that must be at least ten more than your own age. Brought home the rupees—hur! hur!"—here he chuckled pleasantly: "but left my constitution behind!"—here he made a wincing grimace. " 'Pon my soul, this Madeira's so good—hur!—and that infernal scoundrel Strychnia not being here—must have another glass! Don't know though—hur! What do you think about it?—hur! Well, here goes! In for a penny they say—hur!—you know the rest?"

He accordingly helped himself to a second glass, taking care to fill to the very brim; and as he drank it, his countenance became more rubicund and his eyes more watery.

"About that young fellow, Miss—hur!—William what's-his-name?"

"Lardner," I suggested.

"Ah, Lardner!—hur! Good name that!—great philosopher bore it—Doctor Dionysius! Read his Cyclopædia—hur!—could point out, though, plenty of mistakes!—hur! About that boy again—likely looking chap—swarthy—gipsy cast—none the worse for that, if the gipsy vices are weeded out of him—hur!—lying, thieving, and all that sort of thing—eh, Miss Percy? eh, Miss Percy?"

"I can assure you, Sir Robert," I said, "that to the best of my knowledge, William Lardner is an excellent young man. I have had opportunities of putting his good principles to the test—I can answer for his honourable feelings—his fidelity towards those whom he undertakes to serve——"

"Not another word!—hur! hur!" and he tapped his stick with violent satisfaction upon the carpet. "I'd take him blindfold on such a recommendation! I've already got—hur!—a very good fellow—that rascal Reuben—attentive as man can be—civil and obliging—hur! I blow him up at times—in fact I'm always blowing him up; but I don't mean it—and he knows it, the scoundrel!—he knows it—hur! You see, Miss Percy, I'm very infirm—and that's the truth of it. I want more than one faithful dependant—hur! Accustomed to dozens in India—hur!—find I can't do without them here—hur! You see, Miss Percy—eh, Miss Percy?—hur! So I shall take William—they won't quarrel—Reuben isn't jealous—and William is too young to be. He shall have a good master—hur!—but he must put up with all my nonsense; for I tell you what, Miss Percy—I'll give you a practical receipt, which you can mention amongst your friends. If any of them get the gout, let them have some one to blow up—hur! There's nothing affords such relief as giving a fellow a good blowing-up. It can't hurt him—and it does a wonderful deal of good—hur!—to the sufferer. 'Pon my soul, this Madeira—I really think—hur!—I shall trespass on your hospitality for another glass—hur! hur! Oh! bother take Strychnia! Let him go to the—the——Beg pardon, Miss Percy!—was going to mention a name which mustn't be breathed to ears polite—hur! hur!"

Sir Robert Temple filled his third glass; and as he imbibed it with infinite gusto, his face became fiery and the water ran out of his eyes.

"Ah!" he said, with a long sigh of pleasure, as with trembling hand he deposited the empty glass upon the salver, "I wish I dared finish the bottle. It's nectar for the gods!—hur! Hah! hah! how I've cheated old Strychnia!—got my three glasses here—and shall have them again in the evening after dinner—hur! But now, Miss Percy, that I've had the honour of making your acquaintance and tasting your beautiful wine—hur! hur!—I hope it won't be the last time—for with your permission I shall now and then drop in, just to tell you how William gets on—hur!—for I mean to take him—he is evidently a good youth—hur!—and he shall have good wages—good food—Does he like curry, do you know? Hur! hur! Ah, that you can't tell!—but we shall see. However, it's a bargain; I take the boy! I've hired a house up in the Regent's Park: the upholsterers—hur! hur!—are all at work—great rascals, Miss Percy, these fellows! precious scoundrels!—hur! Want constant looking after! Got a beautiful carriage building—hur! Carriage-builders great rogues—try to take you in—hur!—but it won't do with me!—and I shall very soon let them see it—hur! hur! Now, with your permission—hur!—I'll make my bow."

I rang the bell: Reuben and William made their appearance: Sir Robert shook hands with me; and then commenced the process of getting him back to the yellow barouche. This was even more difficult than his introduction into the house: for the three glasses of Madeira seemed to have aggravated the pain of the gout, and to have rendered him more irritable than ever. It did indeed appear necessary that he should have some one to blow up; and of the present opportunity he fully availed himself. However, when once he was seated in the yellow barouche, his irritability seemed to leave him; and with an urbane expression of countenance he made me a polite bow, as I stood in the hall until the equipage drove away.

CHAPTER LXXXVI.

THE PARTNERSHIP.

IN a few more days Henry Wakefield returned to London; and I need scarcely state that our meeting was of the most tender description. I inquired how he had settled matters with Mr. Macdonald? —and he explained to me exactly how the affair then stood, and which on account of certain events that are to follow, I must also make clearly apparent to the comprehension of my readers. It will be recollected that deeds of partnership had been signed between Mr. Macdonald and Henry immediately upon the landing of the latter at Liverpool on his return from the United States. The partnership was established for fourteen years, with all the usual conditions and restrictions; and it gave Henry a third share in the business. There was in the deed of partnership a clause to settle the mode of procedure in case either of the partners should be desirous to dissolve the connexion at any time previous to the lapse of fourteen years; and the clause specified how notice of such desire and intention was to be served upon the other partner, and how thirty days were to elapse from the date of such service until the dissolution itself could be finally effected. Such was the nature of the agreement, the minute details of which had not dwelt in Henry's recollection at the time when he first told me of the partnership:—in fact he had signed the documents so hurriedly at Liverpool, that he had failed to take special note of some of the minor terms and conditions.

"And therefore you see, my dear Ellen," he now said, "the partnership is not as yet dissolved: but it will be in due course,—the notice having been given according to the prescribed formality. Mr. Macdonald would have released me from the necessity of giving the month's notice; but as the deed had been drawn up and signed between us, there was no alternative except to abide by the strict letter of its provisions."

"And when was the notice given, Henry?" I inquired.

"To tell you the truth, Ellen," he answered, "the notice was only given a few days ago. When I got to Paisley Mr. Macdonald would not hear of our separation: he had so many reasons to advance against it! He declared that notwithstanding the riches which you, my dear Ellen, possess, it would be infinitely better that I should have a business or profession to occupy me, if only for an hour or two in the day. I told him that you had an objection to my continuation in business—and moreover, that I could not possibly suppose you would like to fix your abode at such a place as Paisley, so far beyond the reach of all your friends and acquaintances. Then Mr. Macdonald suggested the opening of a branch house in the metropolis, the entire superintendence of which might be entrusted to me. This idea I also had to combat; and it was

with difficulty that I at length succeeded in convincing Mr. Macdonald that on no conditions and in no circumstances could our partnership continue. Several days however were thus wasted; for he was constantly begging me to consider and re-consider each proposition emanating from himself and each decision of my own. I could not act churlishly nor abruptly towards the worthy man who took me by the hand when I required a friend and who first enabled me to eat the bread of independence; and thus for very gratitude's sake I delayed pressing the business unto a conclusion that might have seemed too abrupt——though believe me, dearest Ellen! my heart was yearning to fly back to London that I might be with you again! And then too, there were numerous details into which it was necessary for me to enter in reference to the new connexions I had founded for Mr. Macdonald in the United States——"

"Enough, my dear Henry," I said: "I can full well understand that there was plenty to occupy your time during your fortnight's absence. In respect to Mr. Macdonald, we must ever think of him with gratitude; and if circumstances were otherwise with us, it would have proved a fortunate thing for you to be accepted as junior partner in such a house. But as it is, it becomes needless to maintain that connexion."

Henry took a lodging in the neighbourhood, in order that he might be with me as much as possible; and when he pressed me to name the day on which I would accompany him to the altar, I proposed that our union should take place in six weeks. I thought that during this interval there would be leisure to make several arrangements that were requisite, and some of which I am about to particularize. In the first place we were anxious either to purchase or hire a mansion in the country, with a little domain attached; and this was not a matter which could be decided in a single day. In the second place, it was my intention to divide my fortune, and present at least two-thirds to my intended husband, so that when accompanying me to the altar, it should not be as one who was dependent upon my purse. To carry out this arrangement marriage-settlements were requisite; and Mr. Wilkinson, the worthy lawyer, had to be consulted. When I communicated to Henry my design in respect to this method of disposing of my fortune, he was almost overwhelmed by his feelings: he declared that he had no wish to be made independent of me—that such was his love towards me, such his conviction of a reciprocal attachment, and so great his trustfulness in the generosity of my character, that to him it was perfectly indifferent whether the control of our entire fortune remained in my hands or whether it were divided. But I was determined to pursue the course which I had sketched out: my father approved of it; and Henry was therefore constrained to submit. In respect to Mary Glentworth I besought her to live with me as heretofore: I could not endure the idea of parting from her—I felt as if I were discarding one whom I had learnt to love as a sister, and whom as a sister I was bound to treat! But Mary's mind was positively made up—her determination was irrevocably taken: she would therefore live by herself. I offered to make her a present of the lease of the house in Great Ormond Street, as well as to give her likewise all the furniture it contained : but she said that the establishment was too large for her—that she likewise coveted a more secluded spot—and that she should hire some neat little villa in the neighbourhood of London.

Henry and I (generally accompanied by my father) visited several country-seats within a range of twenty or thirty miles of the metropolis; and at length we found one which we thought would suit our views, inclinations, and resources. I need not however enter into many details upon the point: suffice it to say that Mr. Wilkinson was instructed to take measures for the purchase of the freehold, to examine the title deeds, and to conduct the business with the least possible delay.

Three weeks had elapsed since the return of Henry Wakefield from Paisley; and the preliminaries for our bridal were being settled. In three weeks more would dawn the day which was appointed for that ceremony! It was not to be solemnized with pomp or *eclat*: on the contrary, it was to be as private as possible. Mary Glentworth and two other young ladies of my acquaintance were to officiate as bridemaids; Mr. Norman and Lady Frederick Ravenscliffe were to arrive from Dover to be present at the ceremony; Major Gower and his beautiful wife Aline were also to be with us on the occasion. My father (still passing before the world as an uncle only, and bearing the name of Forsyth) was to give me away;—and in addition to those already named, the Marquis and Marchioness of Campanella and the Countess of Carboni were to favour us with their company. I might mention some other little details in connexion with the preparations for the wedding—but it is unnecessary: indeed it were needless to have given any such explanations at all, if it were not to show the reader how matters were progressing, and to what an extent the fond hopes and anticipations of Henry and myself were by circumstances encouraged.

Three weeks, I said, had elapsed since Henry's return from Paisley; and it wanted but a couple of days to the expiration of the period over which the notice ranged for the dissolution of partnership. On the particular morning of which I am now about to speak, I was sitting in the library, at about ten o'clock, with my father, who had called early—indeed he had arrived at breakfast time, that he might communicate some tidings of a favourable character in reference to the little domain which Mr. Wilkinson had been directed to purchase. For not many minutes had I been there closeted with my father, when there was a loud and apparently an impatient double-knock at the front door; and in a few moments Henry burst into the library. Distress was depicted on his countenance, and his manner was much excited. I was alarmed: my father also was terrified; and flying towards Henry, I besought him to tell me what was the matter.

"Poor Mr. Macdonald," exclaimed Henry, "he is ruined!—irretrievably ruined!"

"Ruined?" I ejaculated. "Oh! indeed, Henry, this would prove afflicting intelligence!—for never, never shall I forget how kind and good a friend he was to you!"

"Yes," proceeded my cousin, "I fear that he is ruined! Indeed, I am sufficiently acquainted with his affairs——and then too the loss at Paisley itself——"

"But what could have produced this sudden and terrible catastrophe?" asked my father.

"The great American house of Rawlins and Sydney at New York, with its branch at Liverpool, has stopped payment—literally gone to pieces, it is believed, without the prospect of paying a single shilling in the pound! And then too——"

"Yes—I remember to have heard you speak of that firm before, Henry," said my father. "You thought it a very wealthy one?"

"And so did everybody!" exclaimed Henry. "But this is not all!—misfortunes never come alone! There has been a tremendous conflagration at Mr. Macdonald's principal factory—by some unaccountable oversight Mr. Perkins his head clerk had omitted to pay the insurance-premium which fell due a few days previously; and thus——"

"These are indeed dreadful tidings!" I exclaimed: "but still, my dear Henry, perhaps after all you need not despair on your kind friend's account?"

"Alas!" exclaimed Henry, with anguish depicted upon his countenance; "look at these letters!—one written by himself—the other by the very clerk whose culpable neglect has entailed so frightful a loss! Yes, yes—the unfortunate Macdonald is a ruined man! Oh, to think that a property so immense as this was the other day, should suddenly fall in like a house of cards!"

"Ah! while pitying poor Macdonald and his family," I exclaimed, "yet must I sincerely congratulate you, my dear Henry, that you have escaped the ruin in which you might have become involved, and which indeed would have been inevitable had that partnership continued!"

"Ah!" suddenly ejaculated my father, who had caught up and was reading the letters which Henry had flung down upon the table; "what does this mean? Did you note the postscript to the letter written by Perkins, Mr. Macdonald's clerk?"

"What postscript?" asked Henry. "I scarcely read the letter through! I was so distressed—indeed I felt half distracted on poor Mr. Macdonald's account, when having read the letter announcing the failure of Rawlins and Co., I opened this second letter—I mean the one from Perkins—— But what says the postscript?"

"Henry, recollect!" cried my father vehemently, "on what day was it that you signed or served the notice for the dissolution of partnership?"

"I recollect perfectly!" exclaimed Henry, with a sudden start as if he were galvanized by a presentiment of evil. "It was the tenth of July."

"And this," exclaimed my father, "is only the seventh of August! Oh! Henry, Henry!"

"Father," I cried, smitten with affright, "you do not apprehend—you do not conjecture——"

"Good heavens! can it be possible?" moaned Henry. "No! no!—such a horrible calamity——"

"Alas!" ejaculated my father, "I fear the very worst. Yes!—there is no doubt upon the point!—for you, unhappy boy, are to all intents

and purposes still a partner in that house which is now bankrupt, and which involves you in its own ruin!"

"No, no, my dear father!" I cried; "it were impossible! There would be no justice——"

"Ah, Ellen!" said my sire, compassionately, "law is not always justice—and I fear me that in this instance the law is utterly against poor Henry. See! what says Perkins in his hurriedly written postscript?—'*Poor Mr. Macdonald is almost distracted; but he fails not to think of you, my dear Mr. Wakefield; and he feels deeply for you!*'—Alas, what meaning can be attached to this postscript——"

"It were better," I said, "to see Mr. Wilkinson at once, and ascertain the exact position in which Henry is placed. Come! let us all set off together!"

I hurried up to my chamber—put on my bonnet and scarf—and sped down-stairs again. We did

not wait to order the carriage: a cab was quickly fetched—and in a few minutes we were at Furnival's Inn. Suspense was most strong and painful in the hearts of all three; we felt as if we were possibly looking a very grave and serious calamity in the face. It was with no very enviable emotions, therefore, that my father, Henry, and myself ascended the staircase to Mr. Wilkinson's office. The lawyer, being disengaged, received us immediately; and the letters which had communicated such terrible catastrophes were placed in his hand. The case in respect to the notice for the dissolution of partnership was then fully explained; and Mr. Wilkinson said, without a moment's hesitation—for the point was, alas! only too clear,—"To all intents and purposes, Mr. Wakefield, you are still a partner in the firm of Macdonald and Company; and therefore you are involved in its present calamity."

Henry's countenance, previously pale, now became of a deadly pallor. I seized his hand, and pressed it hastily,—whispering some encouraging words in his ear.

"And do you mean, Mr. Wilkinson," he said, "that if the house of Macdonald becomes bankrupt, I also shall be declared a bankrupt?—that my name will be paraded in the *Gazette*—that I shall have to undergo an examination in a public tribunal——"

"My dear young friend," interrupted Mr. Wilkinson, "no possible blame can attach itself to you—nor indeed for that matter to Mr. Macdonald either, so far as we at present understand the business——"

"But the disgrace! the disgrace!" ejaculated Henry with vehemence.

"The most fastidious or scrupulous person in the whole world," rejoined Mr. Wilkinson, "could not consider, much less proclaim that any disgrace would attach itself unto you. Besides, your tale will be very soon told, and the facts will be rendered apparent. You have never been veritably a partner—you have never exercised the authority of one—you have never received any share of the profits: indeed a bill might be filed in Chancery——"

"But in the meantime," exclaimed Henry, "my name may be paraded in the *Gazette*——"

"That is really so small an evil," said the lawyer, "in comparison with others that might have presented themselves——"

"What mean you?" demanded Henry. "Surely this evil is sufficient!"

"I mean, my young friend," replied the attorney, "that if the marriage settlements had been already signed, two-thirds of Miss Percy's fortune, being made over to yourself, would become liable for the debts of the firm of Macdonald and Co.:—and if the country seat and domain were already purchased, that property likewise might have been held liable!"

"Oh! good heavens, Ellen!" exclaimed my cousin, his countenance expressing dismay at the bare idea of these contingencies which Mr. Wilkinson was suggesting: "from what perils have you escaped!—you might have been ruined on my account!"

My father now rose from his seat; and taking the hand of each of us, he said, "My dear Ellen—my dear Henry—pray take my advice. Go out and walk together—or return home; and I will speedily rejoin you. I wish to consult with Mr. Wilkinson."

I understood my father's meaning: I saw that this was a matter which must be conducted without excitement, and must be envisaged by a becoming calmness. I therefore at once complied with his recommendation; and Henry accompanied me from the lawyer's office. We began to walk slowly towards Great Ormond Street, I leaning upon my lover's arm.

"In all this, my dear Ellen," said Henry, "you do not blame me?"

"Blame you, Henry?" I ejaculated, with fervour: "it is impossible! In entering into partnership with Mr. Macdonald, you were acting for the best—you were pursuing that laudable career of industry in which you had embarked——"

"And if my name, Ellen, should appear in the *Gazette*, associated with that of Macdonald, as an insolvent or a bankrupt," said Henry—and I felt his form quiver as I held his arm,—"would not you——"

"Oh, Henry!" I exclaimed, conjecturing what was passing in his mind; "how can you think of putting such a question to me? Have you received no proofs of my love and devotion?—are there no additional proofs which I may yet afford?" I asked, in pursuance of a certain idea that was floating in my mind. "But let us not now say another syllable upon the subject;—let us wait until my father rejoins us! We shall then understand the precise position in which you are placed."

We reached Great Ormond Street; and there we remained not long in suspense, for my father soon made his appearance. We both saw that his countenance was grave and serious, as he said to us, "Now, my dear children, listen with calmness and fortitude to the statement which I have to make."

We all three sat down; and my father continued speaking in the following manner:—

"There can be no doubt, Henry, that you are involved in all the difficulties and embarrassments of the firm of Macdonald and Company. If Mr. Macdonald succumb beneath the blow, you will be deemed a bankrupt with him; and you will be subjected to all the same inconveniences and consequences as if you had been a partner for as many years as you have been for days only—and though the public may sympathize with you, yet can the law make no exception in your favour. Scarcely had you both left Mr. Wilkinson's office, when an eminent barrister happened to call in; and this was the opinion that he expressed. But on the other hand, Mr. Macdonald may be enabled to overcome the difficulties wherein these failures have placed him——"

At this moment there was a double knock at the front door; and the servant speedily entered the room, to intimate that a gentleman from Paisley—Mr. Graham by name—desired to see Mr. Wakefield, whom he had ineffectually sought at his lodgings.

"Ah, Alexander Graham!" ejaculated Henry: "Mr. Macdonald's nephew! He is doubtless come concerning this business——"

"You had better go and see him alone in another room," I said; "for he may consider the affair to be of a private nature——"

"No, my dear Ellen!" exclaimed Henry; "he shall speak in your presence—in the presence of my uncle likewise! I have no secrets from you.—Let Mr. Graham be introduced to this room," added Henry, turning towards the domestic.

In a few moments Alexander Graham made his appearance. He was quite a young man, of about Henry's own age—namely, two-and-twenty—tolerably good-looking, of slender figure and genteel address. His countenance indicated a sorrowful condition of mind; and taking Henry's hand, he wrung it with much fervour, murmuring, "My dear Wakefield, my uncle has sent me to you—do not misjudge him!—I beseech you not to misjudge him!—for he is innocent of any evil design towards yourself!"

"I am sure of it!" exclaimed Henry: "I know that Mr. Macdonald is an honourable man! But tell me everything, Alexander—speak out candidly!

This is my cousin Miss Percy—you must recollect her—you saw her at Paisley. And this is my uncle Mr. Forsyth. Speak therefore candidly—I have no secrets from my beloved relatives."

"You must prepare yourself, Wakefield," said Alexander Graham, " to hear the very worst. The conflagration at my uncle's principal factory inflicted a blow which would have been surmounted with comparative ease, serious though it were, if it had not happened simultaneously with the failure of Rawlins and Sydney. You know the faith my uncle reposed in that house——"

"And which was doubtless strengthened," interjected Henry, "by the statements which I from time to time transmitted from New York; for in that city the credit of the firm stood on the highest eminence. But tell me, Alexander, in one word —what will be the result? Can your uncle survive the blow? or will he succumb?"

The answer might be immediately read in Alexander Graham's countenance, even before he spoke the words which were to leave no doubt as to the desperate condition of Mr. Macdonald's affairs.

"My uncle," he said, in a tremulous tone, "sees ruin staring him in the face. It would require an enormous sum to save him from perdition and enable him to retrieve his affairs: but whence could he obtain such a sum? where could he find it? In a few days——Alas! my dear Wakefield, my uncle is half distracted at the thought—and I also am poignantly afflicted——"

"I understand what you mean, Alexander," said Henry, in a sombre tone: "ruin—bankruptcy —exposure—and disgrace!"

"Believe me, Wakefield—believe me," cried the young man, "my uncle was incapable of wilfully injuring you! The other day he was rich and flourishing, when with the most benevolent intentions, as well as with a feeling of thankfulness for the services you had rendered him, he made you his partner. It is true that there might have been this much of selfishness in his views, that he sought permanently to avail himself of the zeal, the perseverance, and the aptitude for business which you had all along displayed. At all events, on the day when you signed those deeds at Liverpool, my uncle had every reason to believe himself a man of wealth and property. Therefore, Wakefield, he did not wilfully wrong you—calamities have suddenly smitten him—they struck him blow upon blow! Who could have foreseen that on the very occasion when through the negligence of a clerk the assurance-premium was left unpaid, the fire would break out and its ravages extend to so fearful a degree? Or who could foresee that one of the greatest American houses established at Liverpool, and which every one believed to be as safe and as solvent as the Bank of England itself, would suddenly suspend its payments, with the startling development of the fact that it had been virtually bankrupt for years and that it does not possess assets sufficient to promise a dividend of a shilling in the pound?"

"Say nothing more in extenuation of your uncle," exclaimed Henry; "for as my cousin and my uncle will tell you, I have from the very first proclaimed my conviction that he is an honourable man, suffering from circumstances over which he had no controul."

Young Graham pressed Henry's hand in ac-knowledgment of this assurance; and I said to my father, "Let us now leave them for the present: they may have various details of business to talk over."

My sire saw that I had some motive for inducing him to leave the room with me; and he accordingly followed into another apartment.

"Now, my dear father," I said, "what is to be done in this case?"

"What would you do, Ellen," he ejaculated, for a moment surveying me uneasily, as if he conjectured what was passing in my mind and was very far from approving of it. "No positive harm can happen to Henry—he has no property to be seized —the twelve or fifteen hundred pounds which reverted to himself as commission and profits on his year's transactions in America, were all left in Mr. Macdonald's hands, and therefore have become merged in the common ruin. Henry cannot be put into prison—and I repeat, he has no property to be taken from him. He may suffer the inconvenience of having to go to Scotland to pass some examination, or whatever the process may be, according to the Scotch law of sequestration or bankruptcy, whichever they call it——"

"But the disgrace, father—the disgrace!" I exclaimed. "Do you not see that the bare idea of all this has pierced like iron into Henry's soul? Ah! and I can well understand it! He feels that at the very outset of life, when only having recently entered on the career of manhood, his name has a stigma thrown upon it——"

"But in such a case as this, Ellen," interrupted my father, "it is a fastidiousness amounting almost to an affectation——"

"Not so!—for in such cases everything depends upon the degree of sensitiveness of the individual! It is useless, my dear father," I continued, "to argue whether or not this sensitiveness be justified or whether it be overstrained,—still it cannot be helped! I know—I feel the blow will be struck at Henry's happiness——"

"Then if such be your idea, Ellen," exclaimed my father, "for heaven's sake follow the bent of your own generous impulses!—for I see that there is some idea now floating in your mind."

"Yes, father," I said; "and my resolution is taken. Henry is the very personification of honour; and Oh! I love him because he is so high-minded and so well-principled! Yes—I love him for his mental qualities even more than for his good looks! No blight shall seize upon such a soul—no evil influence shall be shed upon it!— No!—better far that in poverty we should wed, or that our marriage should be postponed—that I should return to the stage and that he should go forth into the world again."

"Noble-minded girl that you are!" exclaimed my father; "I was first of all disposed to be angry when I suspected what was passing in your mind; but now I cannot give utterance to a single word of blame!"

"And, therefore, my dear father," I said, seizing both his hands, and looking up into his countenance, "you will assist me in the course which I have resolved to pursue?"

"Yes, my dear girl," answered my sire: "I will to the best of my ability second your admirable intentions!"

We then consulted together for about a quarter

of an hour, at the expiration of which interval Henry joined us.

"You see that Mr. Macdonald," he said, "not satisfied with having written me that letter conveying the terrible intelligence, deemed it to be his duty to send off his nephew to enter into more detailed explanations—as well as for another purpose——"

"And that other purpose, Henry?" inquired my father.

"You know that the money which was due to myself in the shape of salary, commissions, and profits, amounted to about fifteen hundred pounds. Not requiring the money, I left it in Mr. Macdonald's hands, intending to draw a cheque for it when I might need the sum——"

"And that money is lost, Henry?" I said. "But no matter!—do not despond!"

"Oh, I am not grieving for the loss of my money!" he exclaimed: "but I was about to tell you how considerately and thoughtfully poor Mr. Macdonald has behaved. He has sent me by his nephew Alexander the entire amount which is due to me: but I would not take it! I said, 'No, it is neither Mr. Macdonald's to give nor mine to receive: it belongs to the creditors of the firm, and to them only must it be given.'—So I have refused to accept it, and Alexander will take it back to Paisley. Thither must I accompany him——"

"Yes, my dear Henry," I said; "it were well for you to depart with the least possible delay and ascertain for yourself precisely how matters stand."

To be brief, Henry Wakefield made his arrangements to leave the metropolis in the course of that day: and when the moment came for us to bid each other farewell, he said to me in a tremulous voice, "Alas, dear Ellen! how short-sighted are mortals! How easy it is for them to propose on the one hand, but with what fatal opposition to their designs does heaven dispose on the other hand! When I returned from Scotland the other day, we thought that we were meeting to part no more——"

"Henry," I murmured—for my voice was nearly choked with the violence of my emotions, "be courageous—gather all your fortitude to your aid!"

"Oh, dearest Ellen, if it were a calamity of some other kind," he cried, "it would be far more tolerable. If for instance it were the loss of wealth, entailing the necessity of hard-toiling industry upon myself, I should not complain! No! —methinks I should rejoice to be enabled to earn a competency for you!"

"Go, Henry—go, my well beloved!" I said: "proceed to Paisley—and perhaps everything will not turn out to be quite so bad as you apprehend!"

"At all events," he responded, "my absence shall not be a moment longer than circumstances render necessary; and therefore we shall soon meet again, dear Ellen."

"Yes, Henry," I said: "we shall perhaps meet sooner than you now expect."

He looked at me for an instant as if he thought that I had some ulterior view, or that there was some hidden significancy in my remark. And Oh! when I beheld those handsome dark brown eyes gazing with love and tenderness upon me—

and when I beheld a pensive sadness mingling with the animation of ardent affection which beamed upon the nobly beautiful countenance of my cousin—I felt that I could make any sacrifice, so far as I myself was concerned, in order to relieve the heart of that beloved one from a pang!

"Now go, Henry," I said; "and sustain your courage. Remember that even if adversity should shed upon you its direst afflictions, my love will continue constant and imperishable, knowing no decrease. But adversity will *not* follow you, dearest Henry—for there is justice in heaven, and your life has been too pure and good to permit that same heaven to do aught beyond bringing you through a temporary ordeal. I have faith in the future; and it is in no thoughtless spirit that I proclaim my conviction that prosperity and happiness will constitute the main tenour of our lives."

Cheered and encouraged by these words, Henry took his departure, in company with Alexander Graham, for Paisley. My father had in the meanwhile obtained an interview with young Graham alone; and he had ascertained the sum that would be absolutely needful to retrieve the affairs of the firm of Macdonald and Co., and save it from bankruptcy. For the remainder of that day my father was busied in transacting a certain business with which I had entrusted him; and he passed the night at my house—for on the morrow we were to set off on a long journey together.

CHAPTER LXXXVII.

MR. MACDONALD.

BEDA saw that something unpleasant had occurred; and as the faithful girl was to a very considerable extent admitted to my confidence in all things, I afforded her a certain insight into the cause of these new troubles that had arisen. She was greatly distressed; but with characteristic fortitude she conquered her own emotions in order to be the better enabled to administer consolation unto me. I assured her that my mind was nerved with the utmost fortitude—that having now looked the calamity in the face, I had already become resigned to it—and that indeed I rejoiced at being enabled to avert its worst effects, which was the aim I had now in view. Beda at first desired to accompany me on the journey which I was to undertake on the morrow; but I begged her not to press the wish—for I said, "I would rather, Beda, that you should remain at home, so as to be enabled to pay your attentions to Miss Glentworth."

Beda understood what I meant; and she at once yielded. She knew that I was more or less alarmed on account of Mary Glentworth's altered state of mind, and by the recollection of that scene which had occurred on the evening of my return from Willowbridge, when Mary had gazed upon me with such an expression of strange, cold stupor. In plain terms, Beda knew that I wished her to keep to a certain extent a watch upon Mary Glentworth,—not with any undue impertinence of espial, but in the spirit of purest and most disinterested friendliness. And here, speaking of Mary Glentworth, I may add that I had afforded her some insight into the misfortunes which had overtaken my cousin Henry; she showed much real sympathy and distress—she spoke most kindly and affectionately to me; but all this friendly concern appeared soon to die away—not exactly into apathy—but to be absorbed as it were in that inward contemplation on which Mary Glentworth always now seemed bent, as if her heart cherished some secret that was serving as the focus for all her own sentiments, emotions, thoughts, and feelings.

On the following day my father and I set off on our journey; and it was late in the evening when we reached Paisley—for *that* was our destination, and thither we proceeded without stopping. We took up our quarters at an hotel; and so soon as we had partaken of refreshments, we retired to the chambers that were respectively provided for our accommodation. We did not make any communication to Henry nor to Mr. Macdonald that evening: indeed it was our purpose to keep our presence in Paisley a secret from Henry until after certain matters should have been transacted with the manufacturer himself.

On the ensuing morning, after breakfast, my father penned a note which he despatched by a messenger, who was charged to deliver it privately and secretly into the hand of Mr. Alexander Graham. The messenger set off; and in about half-an-hour young Graham made his appearance at the hotel. He was astonished on beholding me; for my father in his note had not mentioned my presence in Paisley.

"Where is Henry now?" inquired my father; "and have you followed the injunction given in my letter?"

"Implicitly, Mr. Forsyth," answered Graham: "I have not mentioned to a soul your arrival in this town. As for Henry Wakefield, he has gone to see my uncle's attorney, who is charged to lay before him a complete statement of the affairs——"

"Then there is every prospect," said my father, "that Henry will be engaged at the attorney's for some hours?"

"No doubt of it," rejoined Graham. "But Oh, Mr. Forsyth! what made you come to Paisley? and you too, Miss Percy? Think you that my poor uncle, afflicted and humiliated as he is, will feel pleasure in looking you in the face, when he must think that you regard him as the author—though the involuntary one—of Henry Wakefield's misfortune in becoming involved in the disgrace of the impending bankruptcy?"

"Is the state of Mr. Macdonald's affairs generally known throughout Paisley?" I inquired.

"Alas, yes!" replied Alexander. "Do not evil news ever travel fast?—and the instant it was known that the house of Rawlins and Sydney had stopped payment——"

"To be sure!" interjected my father: "such circumstances are sure to be known. And now, Mr. Graham, with regard to our presence in this town, it can be barely necessary for me to give you the assurance that we come not to reproach your uncle—but on the contrary, to sympathize with him in his misfortunes. Nor perhaps is that all! But you shall know everything presently. Have the kindness to procure for us an interview

with your uncle as speedily as possible—arrange it so that we may be alone with him—or at least that only yourself may be present in addition to us—while every precaution must be taken to keep our presence in Paisley a secret from Henry Wakefield until we ourselves shall say that the time is come to reveal it."

Alexander Graham gazed upon us with curiosity and wonder: he knew not what to think concerning our visit to Paisley; and he at length said, "My uncle is now in his counting-house—I left him busied with his books. He is alone—he has given orders that he is not to be disturbed——"

"But he will see us, Mr. Graham?" said my father; "for I can assure you that we shall not idly nor unduly trespass upon his time."

"Come with me," said Alexander; "and you shall see my uncle. Miss Percy, it is only a twelvemonth since you were last at Paisley; and *then* you beheld in Mr. Macdonald a man who had every reason to rejoice in his riches and whose prosperity was indicated by his looks. Now all is changed! He is ruined in his fortunes—and in the course of even a few days since the blow struck him, he has become changed in countenance and in gait. He is pale—he stoops—— alas! you will pity him; for I know that you are incapable of blaming him!"

"And Mrs. Macdonald—and the daughters," I said; "do they bear up against the calamity?"

Alexander Graham's eyes filled with tears: he gave no answer—and I was sorry that I put the question.

"Come," I said to my father; "let us accompany Mr. Graham: there is no time to lose!"

We proceeded to the factory in which Mr. Macdonald's counting-house was now situated; for he possessed two or three different establishments in Paisley. Alexander Graham entered the office first, to assure himself that his uncle was alone; and then he made a sign for us to advance from the ante-room where we had tarried for a few moments.

"Alexander," said Mr. Macdonald, "what means this?—who comes? Did I not say that I desired to be left alone? Am I not overwhelmed with accounts——"

"Pardon me, my dear uncle," said Alexander deferentially; "but when you see who it is that——"

"What! is it possible? Miss Percy!" exclaimed Macdonald, now hastening forward to greet me. "Ah! I can scarcely say that I am glad to see you——"

"And yet, Mr. Macdonald," I interrupted him, in a kind tone, "you must not be displeased that I have thus obtruded myself upon you. Permit me to introduce my uncle Mr. Forsyth, of whom no doubt Henry has already spoken to you."

"He has, Miss Percy," said Mr. Macdonald, as he bowed to my father. "Ah, poor Henry! it is the severest pang of all!—I feel it quite as much as the blow which has smitten my wife and children, and perhaps made beggars of them!"

"No, Mr. Macdonald," I said, "it is impossible that such a fearful calamity as this can overtake the family whom you so fondly and dearly love!"

"Alas, Miss Percy," responded the manufacturer, in a faltering tone, "you do not suspect the extent to which my affairs are involved. The loss of my factory, with all the goods it contained, was equivalent at least to eighty thousand pounds: the failure of the American house involved me to the extent of seventy thousand pounds; and there are two other houses which having been ruined by that same stoppage, are now unable to meet their engagements with me. In a word, Miss Percy, when everything has been taken by my creditors, the whole of my liabilities will yet remain unsettled! In such circumstances what hope does there exist for my family?"

"Do you not believe, Mr. Macdonald," I asked, "that where misfortunes are unavoidable, and have not been brought down by any fault on the part of the sufferer, it is probable that heaven may send assistance in some form or another?"

"If heaven sent assistance at all, Miss Percy," replied the manufacturer, "it would be through the medium of an angel, like yourself! And Oh! believe me, I thank you—cordially and sincerely thank you for the sympathy which you are displaying towards me!"

"Mr. Macdonald," I answered, "I have every reason to experience a feeling of friendship for you. You know how I am situated with my cousin; and therefore all the sense of obligation which he harbours towards you is shared by myself. You took the fatherless youth by the hand and gave him the means of earning his bread: you were kind to his mother, my own revered aunt:—when she died, you came forward as the adviser and the consoler—you showed confidence in Henry, when still a mere youth—you despatched him to America—in a word, Mr. Macdonald——"

"Why recapitulate this, Miss Percy?" said the worthy manufacturer, wiping away the tears from his cheeks. "I only performed a Christian duty; and if I had the same opportunities, and the same circumstances were to arise, I would pursue the same course over again. Ah, Miss Percy! I have studied to be a kind husband, a good father, and a stanch friend—I have never wilfully injured any one—and yet in my old age misfortunes enter my house like a ravaging army!"

"Oh, my dear uncle!" exclaimed Alexander Graham, clasping his hands and giving way to his affliction.

"No, no!" I interjected, "do not despair! Believe me, Mr. Macdonald, things are not so bad as you apprehend! Indeed, your wife and family will *not* miss a single comfort which they have hitherto enjoyed!—your own credit, Mr. Macdonald, will be saved—and Henry will at the same time and for the same reason be spared——"

"Miss Percy, what mean you? what mean you?" asked the manufacturer, surveying me with bewilderment,—instinctively prompted to hope for something, yet daring not to give way to so wild an idea. "It is kind—most kind of you to shape in the form of assurances the wishes of your heart! But, alas——"

"Uncle!" ejaculated Alexander Graham, with a species of prophetic enthusiasm on his good-looking countenance, "do not despond! Rest assured that Miss Percy has come hither for some purpose, and that she is the angel whom heaven has sent to raise you up in the hour of your bitter need!"

My heart was swelling with emotions: the tears were flowing down my cheeks. I had been endeavouring to break gradually that intelligence which I feared to communicate too abruptly; and now, unable any longer to restrain my feelings, I gave vent to them amidst broken murmurs and gasping sobs—saying, "You are saved, excellent man! you are saved!—you who took compassion upon my fatherless cousin, heaven has now taken compassion on you—and I the humble instrument!"

The manufacturer was quivering with suspense as well as with other emotions: he saw that some stupendous change was about to take place in his position—but he scarcely comprehended what. My father now handed me some papers from his pocket-book; and proffering them to Mr. Macdonald, I said, "Here my dear sir, are cheques, bills, and bank receipts, for the sum that will redeem you. Take it—it is yours!"

The manufacturer gazed upon me for a moment in stupid astonishment: then bursting into tears, he turned round to his desk, buried his face in his hands, and wept aloud. As for Alexander Graham, he staggered against the wall; and there he likewise wept profusely. Need I say that my father was deeply affected—or that I experienced one of the most delicious moments of my life?

And now, all of a sudden, Mr. Macdonald, starting up from his seat at the desk, took the bank-receipts and other securities which I had brought with me from London: he hurriedly glanced over them—he scanned them with the keenest, most eager scrutiny, yet with a feverish celerity:—he was evidently taking the step to convince himself that it was not a dream, but that it was a reality! And when he found that it was really no vision, but that the money was there—bills, cheques, and bank-receipts, representing the vast sum which would reinstate his credit in a moment—he sank on his knees at my feet, exclaiming with the very wildness of passionate joy, "Yes—you are an angel! You have saved me! But, Oh! upon what terms dare I accept this amount?"

"On your own terms," I answered, my voice still tremulous; for I was yet revelling as it were in the luxury of performing a good action of such stupendous magnitude. "I shall take no acknowledgment at your hands—not a line of writing shall pass between us! Rise, Mr. Macdonald, I beseech you!"

He pressed my hand to his lips: he rose up from his suppliant posture; and said, "But years must elapse before I could ever hope to pay this money back again! years must even elapse before I can make a beginning! No, no, Miss Percy—I must not take such a sum as this! I knew that you were rich—Henry told me so: but such an amount as *that*—why, it must be all your fortune!"

"Mr. Macdonald," I said, "that money is intended for your use, and you will receive it. Let me deal candidly with you, for I am not quite so much the angel as you think; but you will find that there is a vast amount of the selfishness of the human being in my conduct. Henry would die of a broken heart if the disgrace of your failure redounded upon himself! I love Henry—and I would rather sacrifice all my fortune that he should live to make me some day a happy bride, than that he should perish because I chose to remain rich. Therefore, my dear sir, you see that I am selfish——"

"Oh," exclaimed Mr. Macdonald, "if the world knew no other selfishness than this, what a paradise would earth be!"

"And now go, my dear sir," I hastily said,—"go to your wife and daughters, and tell them that your long life of goodness and respectability is not to be tarnished and rendered wretched towards its close! God bless you, my dear sir! and may you henceforth prosper!"

I turned hastily away to avoid any farther expression of gratitude on the part of the manufacturer; and said to Alexander Graham as I flew to the door, "Come with us!"

He followed my father and myself; and when we were in the street, I said to him, "Be so kind as to repair to your uncle's lawyer—tell Henry that I am in Paisley—that I wish to see him—and that he is to come to me at once. But in the first instance break to him what I have just done—or at least afford him an insight into it—for I do not wish to be compelled to give all the explanations from my own lips."

"I will go at once, Miss Percy!" replied Alexander. "Oh, believe me! I would go to the end of the world to serve you!"

Away he sped; and I accompanied my father back to the hotel. We walked on in silence: my own heart was now again too full of emotion to allow my lips to give utterance to a word—while my father was naturally lost in the contemplation of the enormous sacrifice which I had made, and which though he had been fully prepared for it, was still sufficient to bewilder and astound him.

We reached the hotel; and my father understood that it was now my wish to be left alone to tranquillize my feelings and prepare myself for the approaching interview with Henry. But not long did I remain alone; for presently hasty footsteps were heard ascending the staircase—then the door was burst open—and Henry Wakefield entered with a half-wild expression of countenance.

"Ellen, my beloved!" he at once exclaimed, taking me by the hand; "tell me, is this true? is it indeed all truth that I have been told?"

"Whatever Mr. Graham may have communicated to you, Henry," I said, "is undoubtedly correct——"

"Ellen, you are an angel!" and he folded me in his arms. "Oh, my beloved! is it possible that you have made this tremendous sacrifice?"

"No sacrifice, my dear Henry!" I said, as we sat down together. "Your name will exist untarnished—the magnanimous sensitiveness of your disposition will not be wounded——"

"Ah! and thus it was for me—and for me only," he exclaimed, "that you have done this?"

"For whom else would you have me do it? Certainly no sentiment of friendship or gratitude towards Mr. Macdonald would have been powerful enough——"

"Oh, no! you have done it all for me, Ellen!" he cried, almost with wildness. "But my God! am I worthy of it? Oh, if the illimitable love which I bear you, Ellen—if the resolve which is imperishable in my heart, to make your happiness

the study of my life—if to cherish you as never woman was before cherished,—Oh! if all *this*, with its infinite variety of pure and ennobling influences, be sufficient to render me worthy of the immensity of your own love—Oh! then, Ellen, I do indeed deserve it!"

"Henry, such language as this from your lips," I said, "is more than an adequate reward for any little sacrifice I may have made. And indeed it is no sacrifice! That fortune which came to me so suddenly and unexpectedly, can scarcely be missed when it has departed in a similar manner."

"Oh! but, Ellen dearest," ejaculated Henry, "you have not parted with it *all*?"

"Yes—all!" I answered: "it is exactly sufficient to make up the sum which would save Mr. Macdonald from the ruin and the disgrace that would redound upon yourself."

"All your fortune, Ellen?" cried Henry, with a look of wild affright.

"Compose yourself—do not be excited," I said. "Yet—it was *all* my fortune: and why not?"

"Then, by heaven! this shall not be!" he ejaculated: "it is too much! Macdonald shall at least give back a part!"—and Henry was rushing frantically, when I ran after him and held him back.

"Stay!" I said; "and listen to me! Let Mr. Macdonald keep all or none; for it is only the entire sum which can save you both—and if you are not to be thus saved, it were needless to fling away a portion only. Now, Henry, will you be led by me? will you suffer me to have my own way?"

"Ellen, I feel distracted at the thought! You have made a sacrifice for me——"

"Answer me, Henry," I interrupted him; "would you not, if need were, lay down your life for me?"

"Oh, you know that I would!" he enthusiastically exclaimed: "you know that I would, Ellen!"—and he pressed me to his heart.

"Well then, Henry," I rejoined; "and if you would lay down your life for me, as I would assuredly lay down mine for you—what in comparison is this surrendering up of so much dross?"

"Ah, Ellen!" cried my cousin, "if it were I who had made the sacrifice, I should glory in it! But, Oh! for you—you, who have made so many sacrifices on my account—you who have rejected the offers of titled nobles when they have proposed to lead you to the altar——"

"Hush, Henry—hush!" I said. "Do I not love you? and is there any merit in following the inclinations of my own heart?"

"Adorable being that you are!" exclaimed Henry: "by heaven I feel as if I could kneel down and worship you! Beautiful, beautiful Ellen! you are a veritable angel in my path! Oh, I cannot explain the feelings which now possess me! I am mad in my love for you!—mad in my grief that you should have made this fearful sacrifice!"

"But you must not be afflicted, Henry," I interrupted him. "Your heart ought to be light and buoyant; and it is thus that I wish to know that you are. As for money, Henry, it does not constitute happiness; and I ought to thank heaven that there is a profession open to me——"

"Ah!" ejaculated Henry, as if thus suddenly

reminded of something which had not before struck him: "a profession? Oh, Ellen! Ellen! do you, do you mean me to understand that you will be compelled to return to the stage?"

"To be sure, Henry," I answered him, quietly, as if it were altogether a matter of course. "And you know very well that I did not abandon the stage through any distaste——"

"Ellen, I will labour day and night—I will work like a slave," exclaimed Henry vehemently, "rather than that *you* shall again have to toil after having been so immensely rich——"

"Rich for a few weeks," I said, smiling. "Believe me, dear Henry, I had not become so accustomed to riches as to stand the slightest chance of missing them now that they are gone. Yes, I shall return to the stage——"

"Ah, then, I may still continue a partner in the house which you have saved from ruin! I also shall obtain a competency——"

"Indeed, my dear Henry," I said, "I think that you must have had quite enough of partnerships! For heaven's sake dream not again of such connexions! All the prudence of one individual may be neutralized by the incautiousness of another—in the same way that ability may be neutralized by ignorance. I do not say it is so in the present case: heaven forbid that I should throw the slightest slur upon Mr. Macdonald! But in one word, Henry, profit by this dreadful experience——"

"Ah, Ellen!" he exclaimed, suddenly starting up from his seat; "I *will* profit by it! Your words shall not be thrown away! But tell me," he continued, taking me by the hand, holding it tight, and looking me fixedly in the face, "are you determined to go back to the stage?"

"Dearest Henry," I replied, throwing my arms about his neck, "be not angry with me for the decision: but there is no alternative! There are no other means of subsistence——"

"I tell you that I will work and toil for you!" he cried passionately.

"But when I have a profession which will produce us a handsome revenue," I said, "would it not be a veritable sin——"

"There, Ellen, I see that you are decided! And, Oh!" he added, for a moment wringing his hands bitterly, "I see likewise that an interval must again elapse ere we may proceed to the altar! Ah, accursed destiny!—but there is no help for it! No, no!—and if such be indeed our destiny, we must accept it! I will fulfil mine. Courageous girl that you are! You, the heroine, inspire me with the courage of a hero! Oh, I will acquire riches, Ellen—yes, immense riches! Believe me that the wealth you have this day lavished for the noblest and most generous of purposes, is but as nothing in comparison with the almost fabulous treasures which may be had for the seeking! Yes — treasures unheard of before! — treasures such as throw eastern tales into the shade! And these treasures will I make mine!"

I gazed in consternation, dismay, and affright upon my cousin: I thought that his brain was turning—I feared lest the excitement through which for the last two or three days he had been passing, should have driven him mad.

"Good heavens, Henry—my best beloved!" I exclaimed: "what means——"

"Ellen, you think me mad?" he cried.

"Pray, pray be calm, Henry dearest——"

"Oh! calm, Ellen? I am wild with joy, now that the idea has struck me——"

"Henry, I beseech you to sit down—tranquillize yourself! You are frightening me, dearest—and Oh! it is more than I can endure!"

I now wept outright: Henry seized me in his arms—kissed away my tears—lavished caresses upon me.

"Ellen, my beloved," he said, "I am not mad! But there is gold——"

"Oh! again that idea!" I ejaculated, almost impatiently. "Pray, pray be rational! Continue to look your position in the face as hitherto you had regarded it——"

"Dearest Ellen," said my cousin, "I am incapable of trifling with your feelings! I implore you to listen to me!"

"Speak, Henry," I said: "let us both be calm!"

"Do not therefore again interrupt me, Ellen dearest," resumed Henry, looking entreatingly in my countenance, "when I approach the same subject—No, do not!—believe me, I am most sane —most serious—for there is in America, Ellen, a region where gold is abundant——yes as abundant as the sands on the sea-shore——"

A wild cry now issued from my lips, for I felt convinced that poor Henry's brain was in reality turned.

"Good God, Ellen!" he exclaimed, "why will you not believe me?"

"Yes, yes, I believe you, Henry," I said, now thinking it necessary to humour him—and I felt as if my heart was about to break. "But let us turn to another topic——"

"Is it possible you think——"

"What shall we talk of, my dear Henry? Come, sit down quietly——"

"In the name of God, hear me, Ellen!" he cried. "I am not mad—I am not even excited unnaturally! When I was at New York I heard accounts of this gold region—I listened only with the interest which one bestows on intelligence of a curious nature, but with which there is no selfish concern——"

"And you do not believe, Henry——"

"I firmly believe, Ellen, that there is a region——"

"Oh! where is my father? Henry, Henry dearest——"

"Ah! I must indeed seem to be dealing with fables—with romances — with oriental legends!" exclaimed Henry: "but, by heaven! Ellen, I am telling you the sober truth after all! Do listen—I ask you not to believe until you shall have heard! Will you hear me, Ellen? But first of all look at me well—and tell me, do I *seem* as if I were going mad?"

I gradually became more tranquil as I gazed upon Henry's countenance and saw that it was beaming with the animation of intelligence the most lucid, of candour the most open, and of love the most devoted. The *mind* shone in the depths of those handsome brown eyes: there was no vacancy nor aberration in those marvellously handsome orbs. Full of delight, therefore, at the conviction which now seized upon me that his brain was *not* affected—but full of a wild wonder as to what

could be the meaning of all he had been saying—I flung my arms about his neck, exclaiming, "Proceed, dearest Henry!—proceed!"

"I must repeat what I had already begun to explain," he said, now resuming his seat by my side on the sofa and placing his arm round my waist. "There is in America, Ellen, a region which is as yet but partially explored, and concerning which the most exciting reports recently arrived at New York. I speak of California. At first I treated those rumours with indifference: then I grew interested and asked questions; and I ascertained beyond the possibility of doubt that these rumours were based on strictest truth. Just before I left New York, a party of adventurous young Americans set off to visit the gold regions of California. Amongst them were two or three with whom I was intimate; and they proposed that I should accompany them. But I declined, with a smile at the thought that the bare idea

No. 69.—ELLEN PERCY.

could have been entertained that I should yield to such a temptation. No: I had *then* the affairs of Mr. Macdonald upon my hands—and moreover, dearest Ellen, I was anxious to return to you! But now—but now——"

Henry stopped short and averted his countenance to conceal the emotions which were now agitating him. I threw my arms about his neck, exclaiming, "You shall not go, Henry!—it would be madness for you to set out upon an enterprise which may terminate only in illusion and disappointment!"

"Oh, Ellen—dearest Ellen!" he replied, in a tremulous voice; "if I were to consult only my tenderest feelings and most selfish inclinations, I should not *go*—I should never leave you again! But I am now the slave of circumstances——In a word, dearest Ellen," he cried, starting up from his seat, "I beseech you to use neither argument nor remonstrance—neither entreaty nor persuasion: for here, before heaven I vow that I will make this attempt to acquire riches—and there is a voice speaking in my soul which gives me the assurance that I shall succeed!"

But notwithstanding the vow which Henry had just taken—notwithstanding his earnest supplication that I would not seek to dissuade him from his purpose—I *did* argue and entreat; and never did I find so much eloquence at my command for the purposes of persuasion. At length Henry threw himself at my feet, exclaiming, "Command me, Ellen, and I will obey you!—but beware how by breaking the heroic spirit of enterprise that is within me, you cast a blight upon my happiness altogether! Now, Ellen, decide! How is it to be?"

I saw that the crisis was a most serious one: I perceived that my cousin was fully bent upon the expedition in search of riches; and I now beheld a new phase in the magnanimity, the fearlessness, and the energy of his character. Could I crush such a disposition?—dared I say the word which should bid him remain? And yet it was almost with a breaking heart that I spoke that other word which bade him go!

CHAPTER LXXXVIII.

THE DEPARTURE.

IT was thus decided; and forth upon the wide world my cousin—the object of my love—my affianced—was to go as an adventurer in search of gold! When my father was made acquainted with Henry's decision, he at first seemed alike afflicted and astonished: but he soon became grave and thoughtful—and for some hours he sat in meditation scarcely opening his lips to speak unless he were spoken to. In the course of that day Mrs. Macdonald and her daughters called at the hotel to thank me for what I had done; and a most affecting scene it was. They embraced me—they wept while proclaiming their heartfelt gratitude—they almost knelt at my feet to worship me. But I will not dwell upon this portion of my narrative: suffice it to say that on the following day I set out with my father and Henry on our return to London; for it was agreed that my cousin should pass at least a week in the metropolis before he bade me adieu to set off on his Trans-Atlantic enterprise.

During the journey from Paisley to London, my father continued to be pensive and abstracted, until at length I began to fancy that there must be something else in his mind apart from his grief that I should have lost my fortune, that my marriage was to be indefinitely postponed, and that my *intended husband* was to set out upon this wild romantic enterprise. But I awaited another opportunity to question my father on the subject: for I did not like to speak of it in the presence of Henry.

We reached London in safety; and Mary Glentworth received me with a greater display of affection than for some time past she had shown; while from Beda's lips I presently learnt that no incident worthy of note had occurred during my absence. I had now to break to Mary Glentworth and to Beda the intelligence that I had disposed of all the fortune I had recently obtained—that my marriage was not at present to take place—and that Henry was to leave England very shortly on a speculative expedition to California. Both Mary and Beda were afflicted and astonished; but I could not help observing that the latter displayed more feeling on the subject than the former. And now likewise to those friends who had been invited to the bridal, was it necessary to make excuses,—the young ladies who were to be the bridesmaids—Major Gower and his beautiful Aline—the Marquis and Marchioness of Campanella—and the Countess of Carboni. Yes—and letters had to be written to Mr. Norman and Juliet at Dover; and let me assure the reader that all these were by no means pleasurable tasks. No!—and while penning the several epistles which communicated to all the above-mentioned friends the tidings which could not fail to surprise and grieve them, I felt a sad tightness at my heart, and the tears trickled down my cheeks. Oh, yes!—and I will confess still more than this—I frequently desisted from my occupation to bury my face in my kerchief and give vent to the full tide of my affliction. But my mind has ever been naturally strong, and I have found that there is no calamity in this world which when it has occurred or is occurring, is really so terrible in its experience as it had been in anticipation. If any one had said to me a week back, "Your bridal will not take place; you will have to surrender up all your fortune; and your handsome cousin, instead of conducting you to the altar, will set off to another hemisphere, perhaps never to return!"—if any one had thus prophesied to me, I should have answered, "Such an assemblage of calamities would be crushing and overwhelming!" But now all these misfortunes had come upon me—I was looking them in the face—and yet I succumbed not: for though bitterly, bitterly afflicted, yet on the whole I bore up courageously against them. Oh! it was through no deficiency of feeling on my part: for heaven knows how much I loved my handsome, elegant, high-minded Henry, and with what thrilling joy I should have accompanied him to the altar! Oh, no! I was not callous, nor apathetic, nor indifferent! But the fact is that every misfortune is more terrible when threatening from a distance than when its actual visitation is made. Imagination exaggerates everything that is as yet unknown or unfelt: it exaggerates all its ideas of approaching happiness as well as all its ideas of coming misery. The heat of the Indian clime is not so burning as the untravelled fancy conceives it to be; nor is there so keen an intensity as imagination conjectures in the ice-wind of the poles.

Reverting however to my own particular case, I must repeat that I was enabled to bear up better than I could have anticipated against the misfortunes which had combined to pour themselves upon my head. I saw that Henry was elate with hope, and that he entertained an heroic confidence in the success of his intended enterprise. That he should set out in such a frame of mind, nerved with so much self-reliance, and sustained with so much mental fortitude, was an immense consolation for me. And now I began to fathom the cause of that pensiveness into which my father was so often plunged since the Californian affair was first mentioned to him at Paisley. The inclination had seized upon him to accompany Henry: it had been growing stronger and stronger within him, until at length it developed itself sufficiently to be fathomed by me. I remember that it was on the third day after our return to London, and on an occasion when I happened to be alone with my father, I said to him, "You have something upon your mind; and I think—at least I fear I can surmise what it is."

"Ah, Ellen!" he said, with an abrupt start: but instantaneously becoming calm and collected again, he added, "But why should you *fear?*—because if you do indeed divine what is passing in my thoughts, you might perhaps be rather inclined to look favourably upon the project: for should I not be a friend and protector for him whom you love so well?"

"Ah, then I am right!" I ejaculated; "and you do really dream, my dear father——"

But without being able to finish the sentence, I burst into tears.

"Weep not, dear Ellen—weep not!" said my sire, affectionately embracing me. "The period is at hand when great sacrifices of feeling must be made by each and all of us; and believe me, it will prove for the best! You have abandoned your magnificent fortune—and you are about to return to the stage. Henry is on the point of setting out for a far-off land in quest of a fortune to supply the one you have so nobly ceded; he is very young to go alone—it is far different from a mere commercial visit to New York——In a word, dearest Ellen, I have made up my mind to accompany him!"

"Oh! my dear father!"—for I could not bid him go, and yet on the other hand I dared not bid him remain and thereby deprive Henry of his companionship.

"Ellen," continued my father, in a lower and still more serious tone, "I owe everything to you. You have raised me up from the mire and dirt, to place me in a position of comfort: you have rescued me from peril—you have done everything but the single act which you could *not* perform—and this is to redeem my name from infamy! But in every other sense you have been my saviour and my good angel. In our case the usual circumstances of the world are reversed; and instead of the daughter owing everything to the father, it is the father who owes everything to the daughter."

"Oh, speak not thus!" I said. "Wherefore use this language?"

"Listen, and I will tell you, Ellen," resumed my father;—"and I am all the more anxious to give you certain explanations, because while they develop my own views, they are also calculated to infuse hope and comfort into your soul. In the first place, dear Ellen, I have the firm conviction that Henry is pursuing no phantom, but that he is on the track of a substantial reality. Yes—I am certain that the little American peninsula bearing the name of California, will prove a veritable El Dorado—not of romance, but of history! Well then, Ellen, Henry will become rich—and I also may enrich myself; and sweet will it be for me to possess the means of lavishing those bounties and charities that may go far to make a complete atonement for the past! But these ideas,

Ellen, are puny in their selfishness, and miserably insignificant in juxtaposition with the other motives which are now inspiring me. For have I not told you, and do I not feel, that I owe you everything?—the bread I eat, the garments I wear, the personal safety I enjoy, the experience of the sweet happiness of knowing that there are yet beings in this world who care for me! Well then, Ellen, how illimitable is the debt of gratitude which I thus owe you!"

"Enough, dear father!" I exclaimed; "how can a parent veritably owe anything to his child? I have but fulfilled a duty——"

"The case is not as you put it, Ellen," interrupted my father. "You can owe me no duty, for I never performed mine towards you; and as I never showed you any kindness, you owe me no debt of gratitude. On the other hand, I owe you everything!—and all the more so because a parent has no right to expect aught at the hands of his children. It is he who should give to them, and not they who should give unto him. Well, Ellen! ——do not interrupt me, my dear girl——you see that I feel the immensity of the obligation which I owe you; and now an opportunity presents itself for me to prove that I am not ungrateful, but that I am only too ready and anxious to do a service unto my daughter. Listen, Ellen! He whom you love so well—your future husband—is about to visit a far-off land, in search of treasures which are not to be won without encountering toil and peril, difficulty and danger. I will go to watch over him. I will follow in his footsteps, Ellen!—I will be ever vigilant to warn him of the approach of danger—and I swear to you that if it present itself, I will throw myself in front of Henry so as to shield him from harm! When he lies down to slumber, I will remain like a wakeful sentinel at his post to watch over and protect him. I will succour him in all his undertakings: I will be his servant—his slave, if needful——a faithful friend and adviser—not merely a relative, but a father! In a word, my darling daughter, I shall hold myself bound, if heaven spares my life, to bring back Henry safe in due time to England, saying to you, "Ellen, I never left him! By night and by day did I keep my promise: I watched over him for your sake!'—And this is the principal reason for which I have resolved to accompany Henry to California."

I threw myself into my father's arms, thanking him most sincerely for the kind feelings which he was thus demonstrating towards Henry and myself. I assuredly thought it hard to lose my parent and my lover at the same time: but not for a moment did I outwardly repine—not a syllable did I utter that could have the slightest effect of deterring my father from his purpose. No!—it seemed to me as if he would prove a safeguard to my Henry, and that there were now a thousand additional guarantees for the success and security of him who was dearer to me than life itself. My father's project was speedily communicated to Henry, who assented to it with joy when he found that I had already given my concurrence.

The reader will remember that I had presented to my father the entire sum of three thousand pounds which Mrs. Oldcastle had left me about a year back. With this amount he had purchased an annuity; and as one of the preliminaries to his departure he gave me an authority to receive his income during his absence, enjoining me to make what use of it I thought fit,—which I promised to do in order to avoid discussion, though in my own mind I was resolved to leave it to accumulate against his return. There was another little pecuniary matter which was also brought under my attention, and which it is necessary I should explain somewhat in detail. It will be borne in mind that Henry had left in the hands of Mr. Macdonald the amount of fifteen hundred pounds which belonged to himself. This amount Mr. Macdonald—with more generosity towards Henry than good faith towards the general body of his creditors — had sought to repay when bankruptcy was staring him in the face. But Henry had then refused to receive the money. Subsequently, when I had placed my whole fortune at Mr. Macdonald's disposal, and when Henry had decided upon going out to California, the Paisley manufacturer begged him to take the money that was his due. But Henry would only on that occasion accept the sum of five hundred pounds, as being necessary for his expenses and also as a provision in case of disappointment in the New World. Before leaving Paisley, he had however addressed Mr. Macdonald in the following terms:—"If after having settled your liabilities with the money which my cousin Ellen has placed in your hands, you find that you have the sum of a thousand pounds standing over, you may appropriate it for the liquidation of the balance due unto myself. In this case, Mr. Macdonald, you will be so kind as to remit that sum of a thousand pounds to my cousin Ellen. I shall not mention the circumstance to her until the very eve of my departure, for fear lest she should endeavour to force upon me that sum, which I do not require, and which in all reason and justice ought to revert to herself, for she has surrendered up her entire fortune and is about to go back to the stage for the means of obtaining her existence!"

It was thus Henry had spoken at Paisley to Mr. Macdonald; and it was not until the parting hour came—the hour of sad farewells—that he mentioned the incident to me. I was too wildly afflicted—too forlorn and desolate in my grief—to pay much attention to pecuniary matters; and I hurriedly promised to receive the money if it should happen to be sent, and to use it for my own purposes—though I secretly resolved to deal with it in the same manner as I proposed to treat my father's annuity. Ah! very, very bitter, and full of anguish, was that parting! First I clung frantically to a father—then distractedly to a lover —there were moments when I was almost inclined to fall down upon my knees and entreat that they would not depart. But no! my spirit was not abased, nor my despair so profound as all that! Were I to group together all the most pathetic language which the English tongue may afford for such a purpose, I could not convey an adequate idea of the anguish of those parting moments. At length the last embrace was taken —the last farewells were said—the door closed behind two forms that were retreating with heartrending emotions, afraid to trust themselves another instant with me; and I threw myself upon

the sofa, burying my face in the cushion, sobbing and weeping as if life itself were ebbing away in the gush of mental agony to which I was thus giving vent. It was evening when they departed; and soon after they had left the house I sought my chamber. I lay down to rest, thinking however that it was impossible I could sleep: but mental exhaustion prepared the way for the slumber which stole over me.

I slept soundly until the morning, and arose with my feelings tranquillized and my soul resigned—although I cannot say that I was happy. No!—but I felt that sensation which must have been so well comprehended by him of old who wrote of what his mental equanimity was when " the bitterness of death was past." I knew that there was now a necessity for the exercise of all my fortitude and for the summoning of all my courage. Letters, written in a hopeful and cheerful strain, which I received from Liverpool, and which were penned by my father and lover at the moment when they were preparing to bid adieu to the shores of England, contributed to my solace and encouragement.

I was never one of those persons who, to use a common phrase, " suffer the grass to grow under their feet ;" or postpone until to-morrow what may be done to-day. Neither did I conjure up futile reasons, pretexts, or excuses for delaying the performance of a task or a duty. Thus I was not now at all inclined to be dilatory in renewing my engagement with Mr. Richards: I did not seek to persuade myself that I required time for the recovery of my mental equilibrium; on the contrary, I knew very well that the sooner I found occupation again, the more completely would my mental equanimity be established. Mary Glentworth, having returned to the stage after the vacation, was pursuing her career with considerable success: indeed she was amply fulfilling all the promises made by her debut.

It was a week after the departure of my father and Henry, that I one evening informed Mary of my intention to accompany her to the theatre, as I purposed to have some conversation with Mr. Richards. On reaching the establishment I found that Mr. Richards was absent dining with some friends, but that he was expected to return between nine and ten o'clock. I accordingly resolved to wait for him; and in the meanwhile took my place in a private box. The house was crowded—Mary Glentworth surpassed all her former displays, and achieved a most brilliant triumph.

It was verging towards ten o'clock when one of the underlings of the theatre came to announce that Mr. Richards had just returned, and that he would either wait upon me in the private box or receive me in his own room. It was not convenient to converse on matters of business in the box; and I therefore preferred the other course. In a few minutes I was in the manager's room, which only but a comparatively short time back I had fancied that I should never enter again! Mr. Richards received me with his usual demeanour of courteous politeness; and if he really had any suspicion of what my object might be, he was careful not to betray that such was the fact. Placing a chair for my accommodation, he at once began speaking of the success which my friend Mary Glentworth was achieving, and which even surpassed all his most sanguine expectations. Having conversed on general topics for a few minutes, there was a brief pause—which was broken by myself; for suddenly settling my countenance into the seriousness of a business air, I said, "And now, Mr. Richards, I am going to make an announcement which may or may not astonish you—but which perhaps will surprise many who have heard that it was my intention to retire altogether from the stage."

"Ah!" said Mr. Richards, with a smile of satisfaction upon his countenance: "is it possible that the dramatic sphere is again to be lighted by its most brilliant constellation?"

"All flattery and pleasantry apart, Mr. Richards," I said, "I am indeed serious in the hint which I have thrown out. Yes—to speak plainly and positively, I am induced by circumstances to return to the stage!"

"While in one sense rejoicing at this announcement," observed Mr. Richards, "yet in another sense believe me, my dear Miss Trafford, I should be distressed to learn that any unpleasant circumstances——"

"I am very much obliged to you, Mr. Richards, for your kind feeling," I interrupted him; "and I think it right to inform you that the fortune which I had expected to hold, has slipped out of my grasp. This circumstance has led to the postponement of my marriage with Mr. Wakefield my cousin, which I should have otherwise contracted."

"I sympathize with you, Miss Trafford. But herein the old proverb specially finds an illustration, that it is an ill wind which blows nobody any good. Pardon me if you perceive any little levity or selfishness in this remark: and permit me to add that you bear your reverses with the most marvellous fortitude."

"It is useless to repine," I rejoined, "at that which cannot be helped. But what I have told you is in confidence. It was not generally known that I had any good pecuniary prospects—still less generally could it have been known that I was on the point of marriage. Therefore although I have given these explanations to you——"

"I shall use them discreetly," interjected the lessee; "and where I am questioned shall just say sufficient to account in a becoming manner for your return to the stage."

"That is just what I require. And now," I added, with a smile, "I suppose you will not refuse to give me an engagement?"

"Assuredly not. And upon your own terms! But you will not be too hard upon me?"

"I had already made up my mind in respect to the terms which I had thought of proposing. For the last two seasons I received forty pounds a week: I think that I might now ask fifty."

"Well, Miss Trafford," said the manager, looking rather serious, and evidently disposed to drive a bargain, although but a moment back he had told me I might stipulate my own terms: "things are not flourishing in the theatrical world——"

"Yet you have a crowded house, and my friend Miss Glentworth is bringing gold to your treasury."

"True, Miss Trafford!—but the expenses are enormous! The committee of the theatre are particularly hard upon me——yet if you persist, and those are your terms——"

"Circumstances are rendering me more mercenary than I was," I interrupted him. "I am compelled to utilize my profession, so to speak, as much as possible. This is but fair."

"Not another word, Miss Trafford!" exclaimed Mr. Richards: "it is a bargain! The terms are agreed upon—and to-morrow my solicitor will send you the drafts of the usual documents. I think you do not take a benefit?"

"No—I waive that condition. And now, Mr. Richards," I continued, "as this little matter is settled between us, I shall return to my box: for Miss Glentworth is very anxious to see your new ballet, and I have promised to remain with her for the purpose."

I issued from the manager's room, and proceeded to join Mary Glentworth in her own dressing-chamber. I told her of the arrangement which I had effected with the lessee; and when, having put off her theatrical costume, she was apparelled in her own attire, we repaired together to the private box that was at our disposal. The curtain was still down; and the audience were waiting for the ballet. I glanced forth from behind the curtain of our box; and the first person on whom my eyes rested was Edwin St. Clair. Apparelled with his usual elegance, he was seated with several other gentlemen in a box, in the centre of the house, exactly facing the stage. Turning towards Mary, I said, "You remember Mr. St. Clair?—one of the members of the Government whom we heard make that brilliant speech the night we went to the House of Commons?"

She first glanced in the direction of the box to which I have alluded; and she said with that coldness which of late had characterized her speech, "Yes — I remember Mr. St. Clair; and I had already recognised him in the house."

As my eyes wandered round the tiers to see if there were any other persons whom I knew, I beheld two ladies sitting alone together in a private box, which I perfectly remembered to have been well-filled, as indeed every compartment of the theatre was, during the progress of the drama in which Mary Glentworth had appeared. It was therefore evident that the other persons who were previously in this particular box had departed at the fall of the curtain, they not choosing to remain to see the ballet. But of these two ladies who did remain, I immediately recognised one to be Lady Lilla Essendine. I had not seen her for a long while: I had not even heard of her. I now looked at her attentively for upwards of a minute: and though it was a considerable distance across the vast theatre and the blaze of light was dazzling, yet it struck me that she looked exceedingly sickly and delicate, as if she had only recently recovered from an illness. But beautiful was she even then, with that sweet interesting external loveliness which concealed the revolting ugliness of her soul. Neither Edwin St. Clair nor Lady Lilla Essendine noticed me; for it was only cautiously from behind the drapery of the box that I thus peeped forth.

The curtain now rose upon the commencement of the ballet, of which I had read brilliant descriptions in the newspapers. And certainly it was well worthy of the eulogiums thus passed. The scenery was beautiful; and Mr. Richards had congregated an excellent amount of Terpsichorean talent. But as my eyes wandered over the principal dancers, to ascertain whom I might recognise, I was suddenly struck by beholding Melissa Harrison. A year had elapsed since the occurrences connected with the Marquis of Tynedale, which had revealed in its true light the infamous character of the young woman; and as immediately after those incidents she had become the mistress of the Marquis, she had left the stage to live as a fine lady and ride in a carriage. Thus for a long period I had lost sight of her, until she now appeared upon that stage again; and therefore I concluded that she had separated from the Marquis and was necessitated to fall back upon her old profession. She was one of the "stars" of the ballet: but she was not without a rival there. Indeed she was equalled, if not eclipsed, by a new *danseuse* of whom I must speak. I had read of her *debut*, which was only very recent; and the journals had spoken most admirably of her. She was said to be an English girl; but she figured in the playbills as Mademoiselle Angeline. She was about two-and-twenty years of age, possessing a very handsome face and a remarkably fine person. Indeed, with the splendid contours of her charms, she reminded me of Juliet; and if I remembered right, the newspapers had already compared her to that accomplished *artiste*.

Not many minutes after the ballet had commenced, the door of our box opened, and Mr. Richards made his appearance.

"May I come in for a few moments?" he inquired. "I wish to speak to you, Miss Trafford, in order to settle the evening of your reappearance upon the stage."

"By all means come in," I said, "and tell us something about this new acquisition of your's, who is really *deserving* of all the praises bestowed upon her by the journals. It is only two months or ten weeks at the outside, since I thought of retiring altogether from dramatic life; and during that interval I have not once visited the theatre until this evening. You must therefore treat me as a stranger, and humour my questions."

"Cheerfully," replied the manager, as he took a seat behind Mary Glentworth and myself in the box. "You allude to Mademoiselle Angeline?"

"Precisely," I answered. "Who is she?—for of course we know that she is English. Indeed her looks prove it."

"It is a singular story," said the lessee; "and if you have patience to listen, I will tell it. It must have been as near as I can remember a couple of months ago—very shortly after your secession from the stage—that I formed the acquaintance of her who now bears the name of Mademoiselle Angeline. The story is however confidential, for reasons that will presently be obvious. I must tell you that I was one evening passing through some poor and obscure street which served as a short cut from a place where I had been dining to the theatre, when I beheld a young female suddenly flit by me and disappear within the side door of a pawnbroker's shop. The gaslight had revealed to me a countenance which struck me as being remarkably handsome; and you may judge by looking at Mademoiselle Angeline whether my opinion was correct and my taste was good upon the point. I was moving on, when a feeling of interest in that young woman detained me linger-

ing about the spot. Presently she issued forth; and now I beheld tears glistening upon her cheeks. Indeed she was sobbing bitterly. I addressed her in the kindest manner, begging her at once to understand that I was not a man who would insult a young lady, much less one who was in affliction. I addressed her as *a lady*, not merely from a motive of courtesy, but likewise because her appearance indicated something superior to the condition in which I found her. I do no mean that she was well dressed, because it was the very reverse—she was poorly clad: but there was a certain air about her——In a word, you can look at her as she now is, and fancy whether a mean apparel would altogether subdue that gentility of manner which distinguishes her."

"She is certainly lady-like," I remarked; "and there is an air of modesty about her. But pray proceed, Mr. Richards. I am already interested in her."

"When I addressed her in the manner already described," continued the lessee, "she suddenly wiped her eyes and looked at me earnestly for a moment, as if to assure herself that my conduct corresponded with my words; and then in a low tremulous voice, she thanked me for my sympathy and passed on. I should add that her countenance had become scarlet, as if with a sense of shame and humiliation at the idea of being seen issuing from a pawnbroker's shop. I dared not detain her: it appeared to me as if it were a case of genteel poverty whose only consolation was to shroud itself from the eyes of the world. But when she was out of sight I entered the pawnbroker's shop, and put a few questions. I learnt that the young female had brought some trifling article of raiment, on which she begged the loan of ten shillings, but it was only half this sum that the shopman thought himself justified in advancing. She was evidently much disappointed and distressed: but she took the amount, gave a name and address, and quitted the place. It was through no impertinent curiosity that I inquired that name and address. The latter was in some street at no great distance: the former was Jane Smith. I thought to myself that some pressing want—perhaps the payment of rent—had to be supplied, and that the poor creature might be reduced to the utmost distress in consequence of the disappointment she had experienced. I therefore proceeded to the address which had just been made known to me,—arranging in my mind by the way the manner in which I should again introduce myself and the most delicate method of proffering succour without appearing to have—as indeed I had *not*—a sinister motive. But when I reached the particular street, I found that there was no such house there, for the numbers did not run so high; and therefore I concluded that the name of Jane Smith was likewise fictitious. I came back to the theatre, vexed and angry with myself for not having detained her in conversation when I met her emerging from the pawnbroker's shop."

"All this was very kind of you, Mr. Richards," I said: and the compliment was not idly passed, for I had at different times heard several little traits of a charitable nature in connexion with the lessee. "But your history must have a sequel—or else Mademoiselle Angeline would not be here."

"It has a sequel—and a singular one," continued Mr. Richards. "The very next day, when I was here at the theatre, at about one o'clock, to attend the rehearsal of a new piece, I was informed that a young female requested to speak to me on some professional business: I desired that she might be shown to my room; and there I presently joined her—for I was on the stage at the time."

"Ah, I see!" I exclaimed: "a little event suitable for the pages of a romance?"

"Exactly so, Miss Trafford," rejoined the lessee. "You may conceive my amazement, blended likewise with joy, when I at once recognised my Jane Smith of the preceding evening. I say joy, because I now felt that I had an opportunity of relieving her wants if need should be. Her amazement was as great as mine—but it was blended with the utmost confusion. I desired her to sit down and compose herself; I saw that for some little while she struggled hard against the emotions that were convulsing her; and I affected to be busy with the arrangement of some papers on my desk, in order to afford her leisure to regain her self-possession. Then, when I thought she was sufficiently composed for discourse, I gently spoke a few encouraging words. She said that as we had met before, and under peculiar circumstances, it would spare her the pain of a preface to describe how her necessities were such as to compel her to seek an engagement upon the stage. I assured her of my readiness to forward her views to the utmost of my power, and inquired in what capacity she thought of going upon the stage? She replied, with some degree of hesitation, that she entertained the hope she was not without qualifications for the ballet. I said that of course I was to suppose she had never been upon the stage before? She answered in the negative—but added that she had always been passionately fond of dancing; and so far as the boarding-school accomplishment went, had been considered proficient. I intimated the necessity of her giving me, in the presence of the ballet-master, a proof of her abilities; and I presently arranged that this should take place after the rehearsal and when the company had dispersed. She was at first very diffident: but M. Duprez"—here Mr. Richards alluded to the ballet-master—"and myself encouraged her, so that she acquired confidence. We then perceived she did indeed possess a marvellous talent; and M. Duprez whispered to me aside that the training of a few weeks would enable her to become an accomplished danseuse. I had therefore no hesitation in promising her an engagement. But how to assist her in the meanwhile? I endeavoured to elicit something of her circumstances: I could obtain nothing beyond the announcement, made with an outburst of weeping, that she was in the deepest distress. In as delicate a manner as possible, I placed money in her hand, and inquired her name. She hesitated for a moment—blushed—and faltered forth 'Jane Churchill.' I thereby knew that either she was now using, or on the previous night had used, a fictitious surname; indeed methought that both might be fictitious, and that her real one was still unknown to me. I was about to ask her place of residence: but I did not like to put the question; and having expressed her grati-

tude in a few words, but those most sincerely spoken, she took her departure. She studied for seven weeks; she was unremitting in her labours, and Duprez declared that he never felt so much pleasure in teaching any one as he did Miss Churchill. A week ago she made her public appearance, under the name of Mademoiselle Angeline;—and you know with what effect."

"And beyond the details you have given," I said, much interested in the new danseuse, "you are ignorant of all circumstances connected with her?"

"Entirely so," replied Mr. Richards. "She has volunteered no explanations—and I have asked for none. Ah, by the bye! I should observe that within the last three or four weeks she has moved to a humble but respectable lodging in Long-acre; for of her own accord she gave me her address, in case there might be any sudden necessity for communicating with her. Where her former abode was I know not."

"And have you not told her of the inquiries you made of the pawnbroker?" I asked. "But no!—of course you have not! It would have been useless, and might have humiliated her."

"For that very reason I have kept silent upon the subject," rejoined Mr. Richards.

There was a pause, during which I reflected upon all that I had heard; for I felt interested in Jane Churchill, alias Mademoiselle Angeline. At length I said, as if in a careless conversational manner, "I see that you again include Miss Harrison in the ballet."

"Yes,—she came back to me the other day," responded Mr. Richards, not knowing that I had any particular reason for thinking evil of her, beyond the fact that was generally known, that she had been the mistress of the Marquis of Tynedale. "I suppose that she quarrelled with a certain nobleman—or else he became wearied of her. At all events it answers my purpose sufficiently well that circumstances should have placed her in need of an engagement."

A little more conversation ensued between Mr. Richards and myself, chiefly in reference to my reappearance on the stage, the date for which he might advertise me, and the piece that should be presented for the occasion. Mary Glentworth and I departed some few minutes before the conclusion of the ballet—the carriage was in waiting—and we returned to Great Ormond Street.

CHAPTER LXXXIX.

REAPPEARANCE ON THE STAGE.

GREAT was the excitement not merely in the theatrical world, but also with the public generally, when it became known that I was about to return to the stage. The newspapers teemed with the most flattering paragraphs; and there was every indication that my reappearance would be attended with an immense success. I selected the character of Lady Macbeth; and on the night of the representation the theatre was crowded to excess. As on many former occasions, hundreds and hundreds were utterly unable to obtain admittance; and nothing could exceed the enthusiasm with which I was welcomed by the audience.

As I was proceeding from the stage to my dressing-room, during an interval between the Acts, I observed a tall distinguished-looking man, standing at a little distance. He was about forty years of age; and as he held his hat at the moment in his hand, I saw that he had dark hair which though very full at the sides, was somewhat worn away just above the forehead, but only sufficiently to have the effect of giving greater height to that brow without verging on what might be termed baldness. He had a pale complexion and a pensive look: his features were regular and somewhat delicately chiselled: altogether he was decidedly a handsome man. He was dressed with the utmost elegance, and yet without the slightest foppery or pretension: indeed his entire air was that of the strictest gentility. How it happened that I observed so much of him at the moment, was because he not only stood back to make way for me, but he took off his hat to bestow a salutation that was alike profoundly respectful and replete with the evidences of good breeding. It was in turning to acknowledge his politeness, that I saw sufficient of him at the moment to note as much as I have already placed on record.

I proceeded to my dressing-room, where I was speedily joined by two or three of the principal actresses, who congratulated me on the immense success that was attending my reappearance on the stage. As we were conversing together, I learnt from an observation which fell from the lips of one of the *artistes*, that the tall distinguished-looking gentleman whom I had just seen in the "wings" of the stage, was a baronet bearing the name of Sir Hugh Ward.

"I thought that you, Miss Trafford," said one of the actresses, "expressly stipulated that on the evenings when you appeared, no idlers nor loungers should be admitted behind the scenes?"

"I have invariably been in the habit of specifying to Mr. Richards that such is my wish," I said; "but I have never made it the subject of a special clause in our contracts."

"Oh! but don't you know," exclaimed another actress, "Sir Hugh Ward is a member of the committee of the shareholders to whom the theatre belongs?—and thus Mr. Richards could not very well prevent him from coming behind the scenes once in a way."

"It is indeed only once in a way," remarked another; "for I do not think that Sir Hugh has been near the theatre for the last three years. I have heard it said that he had been residing altogether on the Continent—and he only returned to London a day or two back."

Here the conversation was interrupted by the necessity of separating to reappear upon the stage; and on my way thither I again passed Sir Hugh Ward, who was now conversing with Mr. Richards. He had evidently acquired the Continental habit of excessive politeness towards ladies; and he again took off his hat as I passed—so that I was again compelled to acknowledge his courtesy by a slight inclination of the head. His dark eyes were fixed upon me with an expression of the most respectful admiration; and indeed there was nothing that could possibly offend in that mute but eloquent homage to my tragic fame. The perform-

ances progressed; and at the conclusion of the tragedy I was saluted with one of those demonstrations of enthusiastic applause which were by no means strange nor rare in my professional career.

Mr. Richards had arranged that I and Mary Glentworth should play on alternate nights; so that Mary had no cause to be jealous or mortified on account of my splendid triumph of this particular evening, inasmuch as she would reap the reward of her own exertions on the following one. Besides, notwithstanding the change which had of late come over her, there was really naught of any jealous or envious feeling in Mary's disposition; and her character was naturally too generous to be imbued with the spirit of rivalry. She therefore felicitated me on the triumph which I had achieved; and methought there was a return of her old cordiality as she expatiated for a few minutes upon the effect my performance had produced upon her while she viewed it from a private box.

On the following day I read with unfeigned satisfaction the eulogies which the dramatic criticisms in the morning journals passed upon me; and I folded them up in order to send across the ocean to my father and Henry. While I was thus engaged, between eleven and twelve o'clock in the forenoon, the parlour-maid entered bringing me a letter. It was addressed to *Miss Percy*; but the handwriting was unknown to me. I opened the letter, and found that it contained naught but a Bank of England note for a thousand pounds.

"Ah, at last," I ejaculated within myself, "it is come! I really think that Mr. Macdonald has taken his time to send it——for it is just three weeks since Henry and my father left England. However, I suppose the poor man wished to assure himself that his circumstances would really permit him to spare this sum at the present moment. Ah! perhaps the person who brought it may be waiting?"—for the missive had been delivered by hand, and not through the medium of the post: moreover as there was no letter of advice, nor a single syllable written inside the sheet of paper which had contained the bank-note, the idea suddenly struck me that either Mr. Macdonald himself or one of his family had come to London and was waiting to see me.

I rang the bell—the parlour-maid reappeared —and I inquired, "Is anybody waiting?"

"No, Miss," answered the servant.

"Indeed!" I ejaculated, somewhat surprised. "Who delivered the letter?"

"A tall, good-looking young man," rejoined the parlour-maid; "with light hair, I think—though I did not take particular notice of him——"

"Do you think he was that Mr. Alexander Graham? You remember——"

"What! the young gentleman who called just before you went to Scotland, Miss—about five weeks ago? Well, really, I cannot say—it might be——"

"No matter!" I interrupted her. "I dare say it was; and Mr. Graham, thinking that it was too early an hour to disturb me, lost no time in leaving the letter, but purposes to call again."

I waited till three o'clock in the full expectation of seeing Mr. Graham; for I was tolerably sure that it must be really he who had called in

the forenoon to deliver the letter at the house. But he did not make his appearance—indeed no one called; and the carriage came round to the door to take me into the City, according to an order I had given. For as I have said on a previous occasion, I was determined not to use Henry's money: indeed, I was very far from wanting it—and I therefore resolved to invest it in the Funds in his name. The business was soon transacted; and the note for a thousand pounds was paid into the Bank of England, whence it had originally issued.

On returning to Great Ormond Street, I expected to learn that Alexander Graham had called; but he had not made his appearance. A week or ten days passed, and there was neither visitor nor any other communication on the part of Mr. Macdonald.

"Well," I finally said to myself, at the expiration of a fortnight, "Mr. Macdonald must have

sent the letter by some friend's hand to London, instead of trusting it to the post, so as to assure himself that it would be safely delivered. But it is quite evident that the messenger was neither Alexander Graham nor any other member of the manufacturer's family; or else I should have been favoured with a call. At the same time I do really think it would have been more consistent with courtesy—to say nothing of gratitude—if Mr. Macdonald had penned but a single line conveying his compliments. Yet I must not be vexed or offended with the poor man!—for his brain can scarcely have recovered from the shock produced by all the tremendous troubles through which he has passed!"

Having come to this conclusion, I sat down and penned a few lines to Mr. Macdonald, acknowledging the receipt of the thousand pound note, according to an intimation which I had received from my cousin previous to his departure from

London. I transmitted my kindest regards to Mrs. and the Misses Macdonald, and concluded by apologizing for the delay of a fortnight in writing, on the score that I had been expecting that some one might possibly call on Mr. Macdonald's behalf. This letter was duly sealed, addressed, and sent to the post.

I have now to speak of certain incidents which occurred three or four days later than the date of which I have been speaking. It was my turn to appear at the theatre in the evening: Mary Glentworth pleaded indisposition as a reason for not going to see the performances; and I by no means thought it a frivolous excuse on her part, for she looked sickly and ill. I therefore went alone, or rather, I should say, accompanied by the servant-maid: for I left Beda in attendance upon Mary Glentworth. The performances took place; I appeared in one of my favourite characters, and experienced a most flattering reception. When the curtain fell at the close of the drama, I hastened as usual to my dressing-room, to change my apparel and get to the carriage as speedily as possible; for as a general rule I sought to avoid late hours. But on entering my dressing room, I found Beda waiting for me, in company with the other maid-servant. The motive of Beda's presence there was quickly explained. Mary Glentworth had been seized with fainting fits: Beda had sent for medical attendance—but Mary seemed to be getting worse: and the faithful girl had therefore availed herself of the return of the carriage to the theatre to fetch me, in order that she might urge my immediate hastening back to Great Ormond Street.

"For I thought," added Beda, "that it was just possible—although most unusual,—still I say it was *possible* that you might stop to see the ballet; and I was really afraid——"

"Good heavens, Beda! is she so very ill?" I exclaimed.

"She has fainted several times; and Mr. Doveton"—thus alluding to the surgeon who had been summoned—"shakes his head so mysteriously, and looks so ominous——"

"Perhaps, Beda, Mr. Doveton is uncertain and undecided what to think of the case? He may wish for a consultation with some physician?"

"Very likely," said Beda. "But come quick, dear Miss——"

"Hasten you home first, my dear Beda," I interrupted her; "it will be a quarter of an hour before I can leave—and every minute is precious where life is concerned! Go, take the carriage—I will return home in a cab——"

"And why should I not take a cab, Miss?" asked Beda.

"Because there is always a trouble to get one amidst the mass of private vehicles—and because the carriage will take you more quickly! Listen, Beda! You must go and fetch Doctor Manvers of Lincoln's Inn Fields; and if he be not at home, hasten and summon Doctor May of Bedford Square. Here, take my card, Beda! and be sure you procure the assistance of one of those eminent physicians!"

"I will, Miss!"—and she was hurrying away when suddenly recollecting something, she exclaimed, "Ah! here are some letters that came by this evening's post——I thought I would bring them!"

Throwing the letters upon the toilet-table in my dressing-room, away sped Beda: and let the reader comprehend that so hurried was the excited colloquy which had just taken place that it had not occupied as many moments as it has required minutes to describe it. I was much grieved at the intelligence of Mary Glentworth's illness, which I knew could not have been exaggerated; for Beda would not have come to hasten my return unless she had seen that the case was serious. I did not tarry to read the letters which had been brought, but hurried my toilet as much as possible; and the moment my theatrical costume was superseded by my private apparel, I secured the letters about my person, and hastened forth, followed by my maid-servant. On emerging into the street I cast my looks up and down in search for a cab, or some hanger-on to procure me one,—when a livery-servant stepped up to me, and touching his hat, said, "Here, Miss Percy, at your service!"—at the same time pointing to an equipage which stood in front of the stage-entrance.

"Ah!" I exclaimed, fancying that I at once recognised the livery: "you belong to the Marquis of Campanella?"

"Yes, Miss—the Marquis of Campanella," repeated the man, somewhat sententiously.

"Then, as the case is urgent, I know that I can take a liberty and use this carriage."

I unhesitatingly stepped into the vehicle, the door of which was immediately closed upon me.

"But there is my servant!" I exclaimed from the window of the vehicle.

"Oh, one moment, Miss!" she said. "I forgot in the hurry your jewel-casket!"

She turned and disappeared in the stage-entrance of the theatre: the footman sprang up behind the carriage in which I was seated—and the equipage at once rolled away. But my maid-servant? I could not thrust my head out of either of the windows, for crowds of vehicles were passing on both sides; and as for making my voice heard from the interior, such an idea would have been preposterous amidst the *fracas* and din which always prevail in the neighbourhood of a great theatre towards the close of the performances. There was no check-string: the carriage was speeding onward—and my maid-servant was left behind!

At length it was at such a distance that when by this time I might have thrust my head forth from the window, I thought it to be too late; and I said to myself, "She has doubtless already taken a cab to follow me home!"

Up to this moment I had conceived it to be entirely a mistake or an oversight on the part of the domestics belonging to the equipage that my maid-servant had been left behind. There was much noise and confusion prevailing near the stage-entrance at the time, so that perhaps the announcement in respect to my jewel-case that was left behind in my dressing-room, was either unheard or misunderstood. It was thus I thought. But now as the equipage dashed along, the idea rapidly grew up in my mind that it was not pursuing the direction of Great Ormond Street; and then a sudden suspicion of some treachery flashed through my brain. Obedient to the first exciting impulse, I thrust forth my head and called loudly to the coachman to stop. The equipage at once drew up in the street where this scene took place: the footman leaped down from behind, and came up to the window, touching his hat.

"Does the coachman know the way?" I inquired.

"What, Miss?" asked the man, as if struck with stupid amazement: "know the way, Miss?"

"Yes—that is what I said. Does he know the way, I repeat?"

"Of course he does, Miss," was the lacquey's prompt rejoinder. "He could not possibly fail——"

"Ah! I feared that you were taking the wrong route," I said, "because I did not exactly recognise——"

"I can assure you, Miss, it is the right one," interjected the footman: "but of course, if you would prefer, Miss, that any other route should be taken——"

"No, no," I ejaculated; "it is all right! I am sorry to have given this trouble and to have stopped the carriage. Pray proceed!"

Again the footman leapt up behind—the coachman touched his horses with the whip—and away sped the equipage, while I sank back ashamed and mortified at having suddenly given way to suspicions which I felt to be so unfounded. On we went: several minutes elapsed—and now I said to myself, "Surely Great Ormond Street ought to be reached by this time?"

Scarcely had I made this reflection, when on looking forth from the window, I perceived that we were in a street of very different appearance from that where I dwelt; for it was larger and handsomer, and seemed to be in a more fashionable quarter. The equipage dashed up to the door of a fine house; and there it stopped. Down leapt the footman; he opened the door of the carriage and lowered the steps with the haste and *fracas* which always accompany these proceedings, and which lacqueys seem to think is an indispensable portion of their duty.

"But where am I?" I asked in bewilderment, though scarcely with any degree of terror—for I thought simply that some egregious mistake must have been made, and I saw that my personal freedom stood not for a moment the slightest chance of being compromised by coercion, as several persons were passing in the street, and there was a policeman standing near a lamp-post at a little distance.

"Where are you, Miss?" repeated the footman, again with an air of stupid amazement, as if he knew himself to be all right in his own proceedings and fancied that it was I who was in confusion about mine. "Why, Miss, at home."

"At home?" I ejaculated. "Not my home! not in Great Ormond Street!"

"No Miss—to be sure it! it's master's."

"Your master's house?" I said, growing impatient. "But is not your master the Marquis of Campanella?"

"Yes, Miss—the Marquis of Campanella," repeated the footman, giving it out loudly and sententiously, as he had ere now done at the entrance of the theatre, as if for the behoof of the passersby.

"Then your master has moved very recently?" I exclaimed, in continued bewilderment.

"Oh, yes, Miss," responded the footman: "he has only been here for the last few days."

"Extraordinary!—and I to know nothing about it! But the Marchioness and the Countess Beatrice?"

"Oh, yes, Miss!" said the footman promptly.

"They are here?" I demanded.

"Oh, yes—to be sure, Miss!"—and again he glanced around upon the passers-by as if proud of being in any way connected with the parade of all these high-sounding names.

"But it is impossible I can alight now," I said: "you have made a mistake—you thought that by the fact of my at once accepting the use of this carriage, I wished to be brought here! Ah! by the bye," I suddenly demanded, "since the Marquis and his family are here, at this house—for whom was the carriage waiting at the theatre?"

"Why, for you, Miss, to be sure!" responded the footman, with an air of the most ingenuous wonder that such a question should be put; and he really began to survey me by aid of the gaslight as if he thought I was taking leave of my senses.

"Well," I said to myself, "all this is very stupid on my part!—the whole affair becomes as clear as daylight! Beatrice or the Marchioness—but most likely Beatrice—must have been at the house, or else at the theatre—or must have met Beda—or something of the kind——at all events they must know of poor Mary's illness and that my carriage was in use in conveying Beda from place to place; and they have sent their own equipage to be placed at my service. It was all my fault for not telling this footman that I wanted to be taken to Great Ormond Street: and so, as I gave no special instructions, he naturally supposed the carriage was sent to bring me here—and hither I have accordingly been brought."

Thought travels infinitely more quickly through the brain than a pen on the paper; so that the reader must comprehend that all these reflections which have taken me some minutes to write and will take him some moments to read, flitted through my imagination in the space of half-a-dozen seconds. I fancied I saw it all as clearly and lucidly as possible!

"Well," I said, "I must alight for a moment: it would be most rude and discourteous to do otherwise! But pray remain here at the door, for I shall have to depart in a few moments again!"

"To be sure, Miss," replied the footman, touching his hat: and then he held his arm for me to descend from the carriage.

I tripped lightly out—the front door already stood open—and another footman was stationed there. The gas-lamp suspended inside illuminated a spacious and handsome hall and revealed a superb marble staircase. I hastened into the house: the second footman to whom I have alluded closed the front door, and hastened to lead the way up the grand staircase. Statues, vases, pictures—in a word, all the evidences of wealth, good taste, and luxury met the eye on every side: but the house with its appointments was totally different from the one where I had last seen the Marquis and Marchioness of Campanella and Beatrice di Carboni. This circumstance appeared to me to be utterly insignificant; for if the Marquis had moved it was from one ready-furnished mansion to another, because when he had first come to London it was only to stay a limited time—and though he had now far exceeded the period to which his

sojourn was at the outset intended to be circum-
scribed, yet he had by no means the idea of making
England his permanent home, and had not therefore purchased furniture.

Thus I was ascending the stairs with the fullest
conviction that this change of dwelling from one
furnished house to another was completely recon-
cileable with all circumstances,—when it suddenly
struck me that the livery of the footman who was
preceding me was not precisely the same worn by
the Marquis of Campanella's domestics. True, it
was light blue turned up with silver, and black
pantaloons; but the arrangement of the lace was
different—these buttons were plain, whereas those
of the Campanella liveries had the crest of the
Marquis stamped upon them—and those black
pantaloons had two thin red stripes, while on the
other hand the Campanella liveries had not. Yet
otherwise there was so great a similitude between
the two that it was no wonder if in the dusk of the
streets and in the excitement of my feelings, I had
failed to notice those little details in respect to the
livery of the carriage-footman, which I now discovered in reference to the dress of the valet who
was preceding me. For a moment a slight suspicion flashed to my mind; but I at once banished it, saying to myself, "The Marquis may have
partially altered his liveries in the same way that
he has altogether changed his domicile."

A spacious and handsome landing was now
reached; but the footman, instead of throwing open
the door which was in front, and which I supposed
led into the principal drawing-room, opened a side
door, announcing in the usual ceremonial manner,
"Miss Percy."

He stood aside with a respectful demeanour to
suffer me to pass: I crossed the threshold—the
door closed behind me—and I found myself in
an exquisitely furnished apartment, where a
gentleman rose from his seat at the table to receive me.

I stopped short, utterly confounded with mingled amazement and terror; for it was Sir Hugh
Ward whom I beheld before me!

CHAPTER XC.

SIR HUGH WARD.

THE room, as I have said, was elegantly furnished; and the light of gas, mellowed and soft-
ened by globes of thick ground glass, was diffused
through that apartment. The Baronet himself
was in elegant evening costume,—black dress-coat
and pantaloons—patent leather boots, shining re-
splendent—a snowy white waistcoat, with a gold
chain festooning over it. The diamond studs of
his shirt, and a ring with a single brilliant, threw
forth their vivid jets of light in luminous reflection of the beams of the gas. An expression of
mingled pleasure and admiration, somewhat subdued by an evident sentiment of respectful courtesy, appeared upon his countenance. But he
came forward to accost me with an air which increased my surprise, even so much as to render it
superior to my indignation; for he seemed as if
perfectly confident of being cordially met by me,
and therefore as if he were utterly unconscious

and veritably innocent of any treacherous deed
perpetrated with an express view to beguile and
inveigle me thither.

"At last, my dear Miss Percy!—at last!" he
said. "I have waited with a pleasurable impatience—for I knew that I might entertain the
hope which is now at length fulfilled!"

Good heavens! what did I hear?—was this a
cruel mockery of my position? was it an odious
levity, over which the well-bred and courtly man
of the world knew how to throw the gloss of a
seemingly exquisite politeness? or was it some
fearful mistake under which he was labouring?
For an instant I felt my brain whirl and reel,
until suddenly startled to a sense of my position
by the contact of his hand as he endeavoured to
take my own. I snatched my hand away—I recoiled a pace or two—I felt the flush of indignation rush burning up to my countenance—and I
exclaimed, "Stand back, sir—and insult not one
who has come hither under a deplorable mistake
on her part!"

"A mistake, Miss Percy?" he ejaculated, his
features all in a moment displaying an amazement
which indeed looked most genuine.

"Yes—a mistake!" I repeated emphatically;
"and circumstances lead me to conclude that I
am the victim of some deep-laid and subtle
treachery on your part."

Sir Hugh Ward gazed upon me in speechless
astonishment for upwards of a minute; and I
could not help keeping my eyes riveted upon his
countenance, in order to ascertain whether all this
wonder on his part were real or simulated.

"Treachery—a mistake—Miss Percy?" at
length he said. "I confess that I am utterly at
a loss to comprehend you."

"Then it is not worth while, sir," I answered,
"to enter into explanations. Suffice it for you
to know that though willingly I came hither, yet
I knew not whom I was destined to meet—the
meeting is disagreeable—and you will permit me
to depart?"

Again Sir Hugh Ward literally stared at me
with amazement; and then, as if a sudden idea
had smitten him, an ironical smile appeared
upon his lips, revealing a very handsome set
of teeth of the possession of which he was evidently by no means unconscious; and he said,
"The only mistake, Miss Percy, which can by
any possibility exist, is that you came to meet
some other person whom you took to be me——
though, by heaven! under all circumstances I
cannot for an instant suppose such to be the
case!"

Again did the hot blood burn upon my cheeks,
and I veritably stamped my foot with a fierce impatience, as I thought that the Baronet, either
with the most refined wilfulness, or else labouring
under the most egregious error, was levelling the
ignoblest taunt at my character.

"This is too much, sir!" I exclaimed: "I
flatter myself that repute proclaims me to be
virtuous and well conducted—and what I seem in
public, believe me, that I am in private!"

"Then tell me, Miss Percy, once for all," demanded Sir Hugh Ward, "why you adopted a
course which at least proves you to be intensely,
wickedly, and dishonestly mercenary? and why,
having taken that step, you now come hither?"

I was enraged—I was half maddened; and yet I was bewildered. What on earth could he mean? There was a seriousness in his tone, an earnestness in his look, and a conviction in his manner, which forbade the idea that he was bantering me.

"It is for you to explain yourself," I cried: "for I have no explanation to give—and all these proceedings are utterly incomprehensible! But no!" I ejaculated; "I will neither wait to receive explanations nor to give them! I will depart! I need not the use of your carriage—I will go hence on foot!"

Thus speaking, I turned towards the door, to which I was nearer than he. For an instant I thought—exultingly thought—that my freedom was not molested; and my fingers grasped the handle of the door. But the next moment he was by my side; and placing his foot against that door, he said with a strange mingling of gentleness and firmness, "We cannot part thus, Miss Percy. I am incapable of wilfully and without previous aggravation committing an outrage upon the feelings of a lady: but my own pride and sense of dignity will not suffer that I should permit myself to be outraged, duped, and probably laughed at."

"Good heavens! what do you mean?" I exclaimed, now cruelly affrighted and bewildered. "Listen to me, sir! A young friend of mine lies dangerously ill—perhaps at the point of death! I must go to her——"

He shook his head; and again that ironical smile, but yet so calm and polished—a smile of the gentlest sarcasm—wavered upon his lips.

"I regret to perceive," he said, in a tone of real sorrow, "that a young lady of whom I entertained a different opinion, should have recourse to such poor and paltry duplicity. But it will not serve your turn!"

"Do you not believe me, sir?" I indignantly demanded. "What reason have you to think that I am deceiving you?"

"Alas, every reason!" replied the Baronet. "In the first place, if this tale, so readily invented, happened to be true, you would not have been at the theatre at all."

"But the tidings were only brought to me at the very last!" I passionately exclaimed.

"Then you would have at once gone home from the theatre to the sick couch of your friend," rejoined Sir Hugh Ward, "and you would not have come hither."

"Oh, heavens! where is the key," I cried, "to the elucidation of this odious mystery?"

"I previously knew much of human nature," said the Baronet, mournfully shaking his head; "but I had yet to learn that to be an actress was to be *altogether* an actress, and that the artificialities displayed upon the stage were to be carried permeatingly through the circumstances and intercourses of private life. I am not naturally a bad man—though perhaps not over nice nor particular in some things: but you begin to make me think so ill of human nature that I shall end by not caring if I become as bad as all the rest!"

I listened with a species of shuddering dismay to this speech. It was not the language of a man who was indulging in a cruel and prolonged system of banter: it was that of one who was evidently speaking from the depth of his convictions. I was smitten with a sense alike of the impropriety and inutility of displaying passion in the presence of such a man; and controlling my agitated feelings as well as I was able, I said, "You misjudge me most cruelly and outrageously! Explain the grounds upon which you build such odious theories and apply them to me!"

"Oh, Miss Percy, this is really going too far!" ejaculated the Baronet; "and I begin to lose all patience. But no!—I will be calm:" and he was instantaneously calm again. "When I look in your countenance," he went on to say, "I really can scarcely bring my mind to conceive——And yet you are an actress!"

"Ah! is this meant for a taunt?" I ejaculated, —"a taunt thrown out against one who in order to earn her bread, uses the little talent which God has given her—and who has always so used it that the breath of scandal has never yet dared——"

But I could not finish the sentence; and I burst into tears.

"Ah, you well-nigh disarm me!" exclaimed Sir Hugh Ward. "But yet, when I think of everything, these tears cannot be genuine!"

"Sir," I suddenly ejaculated, dashing away those tears, "there is a mystery to be cleared up; and even though my friend be perishing, my reputation must not be trampled in the mire. Say, why did you expect me?—for that you *did* expect me here is only too evident."

"Why did I expect you? Oh, Miss Percy!"— and once more that mild gentlemanly smile of half-subdued irony passed over his lips; "will you again descend to subterfuge and artifice? If you had intended to add to your treasures the offering I sent—to laugh at me for my pains—and thereby punish me for my temerity, you need not have come hither *now*: you might have kept my offering and treated me with silent contempt! You would *then* have only incurred the imputation of a mean dishonesty and a detestable shabbiness. But as it is, I have a right to think that you came hither with the intention of yielding to my overture—but that suddenly seized with some unaccountable whim—perhaps prudery—perhaps disgust for my person——for I can assure you that I am not particularly vain, and I know that aversions are often thus abruptly taken——but it was under some such influence as this, I say, that you all in a moment repented of the step you had taken, and you are now studying to beat as decent a retreat as possible!"

Again did I listen in the stupor of bewilderment to a speech which evidently emanated from the deep convictions of the man. I was fearfully mystified: it seemed as if there were a horrible tangled web to be unwoven, but I knew not where to take up the first thread of the complicated skein. All in a moment my thoughts settled upon one particular point of his speech; and I ejaculated, "You allude to an offering? Good heavens, what offering did you ever make to me, or that I ever accepted?"

"What!" he cried, as if likewise struck by an idea; "is it possible that you may not have received it? But no! no! it could not be intercepted by another!—for if so, you would not have come hither now!"

"Then, sir," I responded emphatically—and my cheeks were again burning,—"if you ever dared send—yes! I use the word *dare!*—if you ever dared send, I repeat, aught in the shape of present, gift, or intended bribe to me, it has never reached my hands, and it must have been intercepted!"

For a moment Sir Hugh Ward seemed staggered: but returning into the midst of his incredulity, he shook his head, asking, "Then, if that gift never reached you, how knew you that I entertained such hopes and ideas——"

"Good heavens! I never knew it," I indignantly exclaimed, "until the hour that is passing!"

"Oh, this is too much! Then how was it, Miss Percy," he demanded, raising his voice in an anger that was now getting the better of him,—"how was it that you came hither in my carriage?"

"The explanation is simple," I at once replied. "I sent my own carriage away with a faithful attendant who accompanied it, to seek eminent physicians for my sick friend. I was changing my toilet at the time. When this was accomplished, I left the theatre. I was seeking for a cab, when a livery-servant addressing me by name, offered me the equipage to which he belonged. I thought that I had recognised the liveries of my friends the Campanella family: I mentioned that name—the domestic readily repeated it as if it were that of his noble master and mistress—and I unhesitatingly entered the equipage. I thought I was going home—I presently discerned the contrary—I spoke to your footman—he gave me answers which were satisfactory, though heaven can tell how they were intended!—and I was brought hither. I thought my friends the Campanellas must have changed their abode since I last saw them;—and to be brief, I imagined when I entered this room I should find myself in their presence. This is my tale. Go, question your footman as to what took place between him and me——yes, and especially at the very door of your house ere I alighted from the carriage: and if the man speak truly, he will confirm all that I have just said!"

Sir Hugh Ward listened to me with an air of the deepest interest,—his looks also expressing uncertainty and astonishment as I went on speaking. We were still standing close by the door of the apartment; but he had withdrawn his foot from it—he no longer seemed to be bent on retaining me a prisoner there, or else he knew that at the first attempt which I might make to leave the room he had but to stretch out his hand and hold me back.

"Pray sit down, Miss Percy," he presently said, "and let us talk over this matter deliberately."

"I trust, sir, that it will not be needful for our interview to be prolonged many moments," I said, "for you will confess that you have laboured under some error—that there has been a great and signal mistake somewhere——"

"We have not yet arrived at that point, Miss Percy," interjected the Baronet. "But let us be seated."

"Thank you, sir—this will do," I said, declining the hand which he proffered as if to conduct me to a seat; and I took a chair that was close by the door. "Now, on your side, you have only to explain——"

"Stop, Miss Percy!" he cried, as he took a seat at a short distance from where I had placed myself: "you are now hurrying on as if you wished to have everything your own way—as if you thought you could bewilder me and throw me into such a confusion of ideas that I should adopt any tale which you might choose to tell, or catch up any belief it may suit you to propagate! Now, in plain terms, the story you have told me is all very well:—the only misfortune is, Miss Percy, that I cannot put faith in it!"

"Sir Hugh Ward!" I ejaculated, starting up indignantly from my seat; "you are resolved to outrage me in the most flagrant manner!"

"Stop, Miss Percy," said the Baronet, also rising from his seat—but he spoke with an air of calm resolution. "Since you are determined to assume such high ground, I must at once adopt a similar position and assume as it were a posture of defence. I am not to be denounced by implication as being either ungentlemanly or a coward: nor will I consent to become the butt of your merriment—to be laughed at by you—perhaps to be made the sport of your conversation when you are with companions of the same disposition as yourself. Ah, no, Miss Percy! ye shall not play the Merry Wives of Windsor and make me your Falstaff!"

"Again this extraordinary delusion of some kind!" I ejaculated. "But my patience is worn out——"

"You shall not leave this house, Miss Percy!" interrupted the Baronet, with a stern, decided expression of countenance: "I have bought you—and you are mine! Were it veritably a mistake, I should respect you: but all circumstances tend to prove that there is no error, and that your conduct is base, mean, and hypocritical to a degree which astounds me! I have bought you, I say —you have accepted the price—and mine you shall be!"

The countenance of Sir Hugh Ward now indicated a fierce resolution as well as the flaming-up of strong passions within his breast. He approached me; and with a shriek I exclaimed, "Stand back, sir!—dare not lay a hand upon me, or I will scream for assistance!"

"Ah! think you that I shall observe any measures of delicacy with such as you?" demanded the Baronet. "No! no! Doubtless all your outward rectitude of conduct has been an hypocrisy and a delusion—and perhaps this very interval of prudery is for the purpose of making me esteem more highly the final surrender! But the game has been played to a degree that has well-nigh nauseated me!"

"Good heavens, Sir Hugh!" I ejaculated, "what can I do to convince you——"

"Enough! enough!" he exclaimed; "let this scene finish!"—and springing forward, he endeavoured to seize me in his arms.

Light as a fawn I bounded towards the window; and tearing aside the curtain, I saw that it looked upon a little garden at the back of the house. I tried to push up the window—but it was fastened. I thrust my hand against one of the panes, and broke it.

"Now," I said, "beware how you touch me!—I will cry for assistance! Let me leave your house, Sir Hugh Ward!"

"Yes, leave it!" he ejaculated, with an air of ineffable disgust and contempt; "for by heaven! though you possess the beauty of an angel, I have no farther fancy for you! By all means go!"

I was bounding towards the door, indifferent up to this point in respect to the taunts and abuse which he was levelling against me: but I suddenly stopped short, as he added, "Go—and to-morrow all London shall ring with the report that Miss Trafford, the celebrated tragic actress, sold herself to me for a thousand pounds!"

Yes—I stopped short as if a thunderbolt had suddenly fallen at my feet! I felt that I suddenly became ghastly pale, and my limbs were sinking under me. That threat so horrible—so diabolical—was overwhelming!

"Ah! have I touched you at last?" exclaimed the Baronet, with a fierce malignant expression of triumph in his usually mild and intelligent eyes. "Yes, Miss Percy—or Miss Trafford—or whatever you call yourself—you may have made me a dupe: but I will expose your character and tear the mask from your countenance! *My* conduct may have been daring in the first instance; but *your's* was nothing short of robbery. In a word, you might have scorned the overture—but in that case you should have returned the bank-note!"

A half-stifled scream burst from my lips.

"The bank-note?" I exclaimed. "I never received a bank-note from *you!*"

"Not a bank-note for a thousand pounds—nearly three weeks back——"

"Good heavens! what does this mean?" I exclaimed, now actually writhing with the torture of suspense and bewilderment. "Nearly three weeks back, do you say—a bank-note——"

"Yes," exclaimed Sir Hugh, with a smile with more than a genteel irony in it: it had a veritable sardonism: "and the note was not sent back to me! And what is more, I know that it was paid into the Bank of England; for I went and asked the question—and the reply was an affirmative. My own valet delivered the enclosure at your house!"

"My God! what have I done?—into what a fearful error have I been led!—what a tremendous mistake has been committed!" and I tottered to a seat, on which I fell almost annihilated by the announcement that had just been made.

"What! another phase in your drama of hypocrisy?" ejaculated Sir Hugh, again speaking with disgust and impatience. "I should have thought you were now sufficiently unmasked——"

"As I have a soul to be saved, Sir Hugh Ward," I interrupted him, "I am innocent of all you would impute to me!"

"Answer me!" he vociferated, now stepping forward and seizing me forcibly by the wrist: "are you not tired of playing the fool? are you not ashamed of yourself for having played it so effectually? You acknowledge that you received the bank-note for a thousand pounds which I sent you in a blank envelope nearly three weeks back——"

"Yes—hear me, Sir Hugh!"—and I forcibly drew my hand away: "yes—hear me!—it is true—I received a bank-note at that time——"

"To be sure! I thought it could not have been

intercepted and used by any one else! I knew it had been paid into the Bank; and I had the strongest conviction that it was *you* who must have so paid it. A truce therefore to all argument or recrimination!—you are thoroughly beaten at every point—and heaven only besides yourself can tell why you should have waged this protracted but ineffectual contest. I have indeed a right to be angry," continued Sir Hugh, in a softening tone; "but if you will only smile and look pleased, and come of your own accord to throw your arms about my neck——"

"For God's sake spare me, sir!" I exclaimed, almost maddened by my feelings. "Amidst all the confusion that is in my brain, I comprehend just sufficient to show me that circumstances have combined in a most extraordinary manner to render me their victim——"

"What! not enough of prudery and folly yet?" ejaculated the Baronet; "and I who was good-naturedly offering to forgive you for this half-hour of the idlest and silliest scene that ever was conjured up by woman!"

"Oh, heavens!" I exclaimed, wringing my hands: "circumstances are so terribly against me that even if I were to tell you all the tale you would not believe me! But Oh, Sir Hugh Ward! I entreat you to listen!"—and I clasped my hands imploringly.

"All this is idle, and even nauseating to a degree," he impatiently exclaimed. "You received my bank-note——"

"By heaven, I swear," I cried, with the most passionate vehemence, "that I knew not it came from *you!* No note or message accompanied it——"

"But my name and address were written on the back!" ejaculated Sir Hugh, "as legibly and plainly as writing could be rendered! It was a new bank-note—that was the only writing at the back—indeed I flattered myself I was managing everything in the most delicate way possible—and most assuredly my conduct ought to have been otherwise appreciated!"

"Sir," I answered, well-nigh overwhelmed by my horrible feelings, "a tremendous mistake has been committed. Alas! I now see it all! For heaven's sake be not incredulous—do not at every step set me down as a cunning hypocrite endeavouring to deceive you: but believe me when I declare, as I have a soul to be saved, that by a coincidence I was at that very time expecting the remittance of precisely that same sum; so that when I received a bank-note for the amount in a blank envelope, it never occurred to me to read the writing at the back——Indeed I never do——But I went to the Bank itself—I paid in the money—not to my own name——"

"A truce to all this verbiage!" interrupted Sir Hugh. "You enhance a thousand times all that is blameable in your conduct, and the insult you put upon me becomes all the more galling and intolerable, by the fact that you seem to take me for a senseless idiot to be duped and deluded by any rhodomontade!"

"And yet I declare," I vehemently cried, "it was all as I have told you! Yes—and to prove it, I will pay you back the money, Sir Hugh——"

"Another idle tale!" he ejaculated; "for if you have invested it in the name of another, you cannot draw the sum out again from the Bank. Good heavens! to what artifices do you have re-recourse that you may cling to this thousand pounds!—how polluted in soul must you be to receive it for a meritricious purpose!—but how infamous of you not to complete the bargain, although it be in reference to the sale of your own person!"

The indignant blood rushed to my cheeks; and stamping my foot with violence upon the carpet, I exclaimed, "You *shall* hear me! Listen, then, while I tell the tale which will account for this strange coincidence! I have a cousin—Henry Wakefield by name—who recently quitted England. At the time he was taking leave of me, he intimated that I should in a little while receive the sum of a thousand pounds from a manufacturer named Macdonald at Paisley. Conceive therefore what I must have thought when one day a letter was brought to me, and in a blank envelope I found a bank-note for precisely the very sum I was expecting——"

"What! delivered *by hand*, when you expected it from Paisley?" cried Sir Hugh sarcastically.

"Ah! methought it had been delivered by a friend or relation of Mr. Macdonald. I inquired of my servant for a description of the person who brought it—I was told it was a tall, slender, fair-haired young man——"

"Yes—my valet," said Sir Hugh, with quiet irony. "And doubtless your Mr. Macdonald had some relation whom this description of my valet would in every sense suit,—so that whichever way you turned, you could not possibly fail to have a salve for your conscience!"

"Oh, how bitter are your words! how cruel, how cutting is this incredulity! You presuppose a falsehood for every word that issues from my lips! Yet all I say is truth——and not the least portion of it is the fact that the personal appearance of your valet, as hastily sketched by my maid-servant, corresponded with a certain Alexander Graham, the nephew of Mr. Macdonald."

"And now let me tell you, Miss Percy," said Sir Hugh Ward, "that I do not believe a single syllable of this tale of your's—which has not even the merit of being specious and possessing the air of possibility! But this is the flimsiest and most trumpery contrivance——"

"Oh, I will convince you of its truth!" I exclaimed. "I have written to Mr. Macdonald—doubtless my letter will elicit an answer in a day or two——"

"That will not suffice, Miss Percy," interrupted the Baronet. "You owe me a debt—and it shall be paid to-night. I am implacable and merciless as Shylock himself. You sought to make me play Falstaff to you as one of the Merry Wives of Windsor: but the whole shall result either in the Taming of a Shrew or Turning the Tables."

It was with bitter irony and fierce resolution that Sir Hugh Ward thus spoke: indeed his whole manner and appearance had undergone a remarkable change within the last quarter of an hour; and whereas at first he was so exceedingly polite and gentlemanly, even in his accusations and reproaches, he was now curt, bitterly cutting, and even brutal in some of his taunts and invectives.

"I will depart!" I exclaimed. "And believe me, Sir Hugh Ward! my reputation shall yet be cleared up!"

"You shall not depart!" he vociferated. "I have bought you—and you are mine!"

He sprang towards me—he threw his arms round my waist—he endeavoured to approach his own lips to mine: but by a desperate effort I disengaged myself from his embrace. The front of my dress was however disordered in the struggle; and a couple of letters which I had thrust into my bosom, fell upon the carpet. These were the letters which Beda had brought with her to the theatre, but which I had not then time to read, nor even to glance at, and which until this present moment I had forgotten.

Baffled and discomfited by the desperate resistance I had offered—pale with the rage of disappointment—Sir Hugh Ward stood at a little distance: but his natural good feelings triumphed sufficiently over his darker passions to prevent him from immediately repeating the attempt and having recourse to a more brutal violence than he had already exercised.

"Well, go!" he said in a tone of as much disgust and contempt as if he were speaking to some loathsome object. "You have been here long enough—too long indeed! I hate and loathe you, base swindler—mean robber—dirty larcenist, that you are!—and rest assured that I will have a signal vengeance!"

My spirit was well-nigh broken, although I had just proved so successful in repelling the attack made upon me: I felt exhausted by the scene—I had no strength nor power left for further argument or self-vindication. To beat a precipitate retreat and leave all the rest to chance was now my only thought. Stooping down, I hastily snatched up the two letters that lay upon the carpet: but ah! an ejaculation burst from my lips as I recognised Mr. Macdonald's handwriting and beheld the Paisley post-mark.

"Oh!" I said, my entire form now vibrating with suspense and joyous hope; "it is perhaps possible that I may be enabled to prove the truth of all my statements!"

I tore open the letter; and the first object that met my eyes, was the printed form of a cheque. I hastened to glance over its contents: it was a draft upon a London banker, payable to me or my order, for one thousand pounds sterling. A cry of joy thrilled my lips; and then I hastily ran my eyes over the letter which contained the draught. The epistle was worded as follows:—

"Paisley, September 27th, 1843.

"My dear Miss Percy,

"Your letter at first caused me the utmost astonishment, and then inflicted upon me the keenest pain. It astonished me, because it spoke of the safe reception of a bank-note for a thousand pounds forwarded by me—whereas alas! no such remittance had been made from my office. But then supervened a sense of the deepest affliction; for I at last comprehended what your letter meant. It conveyed a severe reproach for my failure to keep the promise which I had made to Henry Wakefield. Oh, Miss Percy! from *your* hands I must receive everything with submission; for you are my saviour—you have

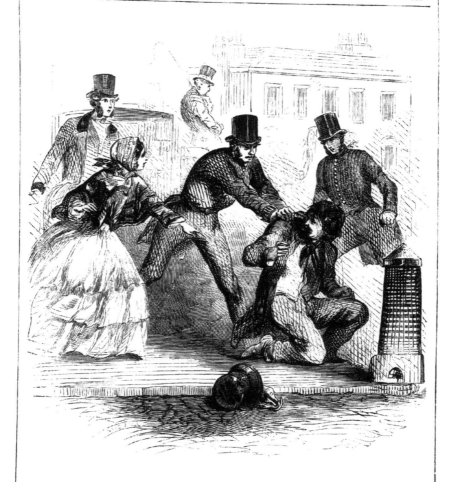

rescued me from ruin, bankruptcy, and degradation! But still, Miss Percy—*still*, let me ask
why write such a letter as that? Ah! it was the
most terrible of satires! To acknowledge the receipt of something which had not been sent—to
apologize for the delay of a fortnight in making
that acknowledgment, when there was nothing
really to be acknowledged—to thank me for something which I had not done—to tell me that you
had invested that which you had not to invest—and
then to wind up with assurances of friendship towards myself and transmissions of love to my wife
and daughters—Oh, Miss Percy! from first to last
your letter did indeed constitute a terrible satire!
Yet I repeat—I submit with all due humility; for
I am under obligations which make me your slave!
"Let me add a word in my justification. Your
cousin—as noble-hearted and as generous a youth
as ever lived—desired me to liquidate all my lia-

No. 71.—ELLEN PERCY.

bilities before I thought of remitting the sum of a
thousand pounds to you. I supposed therefore
that there was no immediate hurry in the matter;
and I was waiting until the books were fully made
up to ascertain whether a sufficient surplus would
remain to me after the liquidation of my liabilities,
to remit the thousand pounds. Your letter came
at the very moment when the accounts were being
balanced, and I was rejoicing at the fact of being
enabled to remit the amount. Thus, Miss Percy,
by this very same post you would have received the
enclosed draft even though your own letter had
not reached me!

"May heaven bless you, my dear young lady!
You have proved my saviour and my good angel;
and if the heartfelt prayers of one's fellow-creatures ever avail in this world, you assuredly have
those of

"J. MACDONALD."

Such were the contents of the epistle which contained the draft for a thousand pounds; and though for an instant I was cruelly shocked at the impression produced upon poor Mr. Macdonald by my letter, yet was all sense of annoyance speedily absorbed in a feeling of wild tumultuous joy as I found that I held in my hand the means of completely vindicating myself to Sir Hugh Ward. With rapidity did my eyes glance over Mr. Macdonald's letter: the Baronet must have seen that a change was coming over my countenance—and he must have observed likewise that I held in my hands a draft for a sum of money while I was perusing the letter which had contained it. Thus, when I raised my looks towards his countenance, I perceived that it wore an expression of interest, curiosity, and suspense.

"Ah, Sir Hugh!" I exclaimed, with triumphant accents, "you will not henceforth deny the possibility of the strangest coincidences!—because *here* perhaps is an event the most extraordinary of all! Throughout an hour of accusations and recriminations, of chargings and fendings, of distress and insult for me, and of bewilderment for both, have I unconsciously possessed about my person the means of clearing up everything in a moment!"

"Ah! is this possible?" ejaculated Sir Hugh.

"Possible?" I repeated; "it is done! it is accomplished!"

"No, no, Miss Percy!" he said, with a sudden alteration of the countenance; "this is another stratagem——"

"Enough, sir!" I imperiously interrupted him. "You ere now boasted of some good feeling—you declared that you would not wilfully outrage a female: prove that it was no idle vaunt on your part! There—read, Sir Hugh Ward!—and render me an act of justice!"

I handed him the letter, which he literally snatched with avidity; and he rapidly ran his eyes over its contents. I saw that his countenance quickly underwent a change: the remnant of supercilious irony which had lingered there, yielded to seriousness—which in its turn merged into interest and respectful admiration as he raised his eyes towards me when he had finished the perusal of the letter.

"And here," I said, "is Mr. Macdonald's draft for a thousand pounds; and this, sir, belongs to you: for, thank God! I am at once enabled to repay the sum which I so innocently and unconsciously appropriated from your purse!"

Sir Hugh Ward was naturally a generous man; and though somewhat of a libertine, yet he possessed many excellent qualities—and he was never dishonourable in his amours. This was the character that on subsequent occasions I heard of him. He now stood before me with a sorrowful and contrite look: he was not confused nor embarrassed—but his demeanour expressed the frankness and candour of one who recognised at a glance how unwittingly he had been led on to assume the most insulting attitude towards a virtuous woman, for which he was now ready to demand pardon.

"Miss Percy," he said, "I humbly crave your forgiveness. I have outraged you in a manner that would be the grossest and the most abominable, were it not that I have sinned in ignorance of the fact that I was thus sinning!"

"Not another word, Sir Hugh!" I interjected.

"Under all circumstances you were justified in acting as you have done."

"And yet, Miss Percy, I again and again crave your pardon! It has been a Comedy of Errors mingled with more or less of Tragedy. If this were the time of the Caliphs, and these adventures happened at Bagdad, the reigning monarch would order the narrative to be written in letters of gold. But pardon me for a few moments, Miss Percy! I have a duty to perform! It is to hasten at once and inform my domestics——But no matter what I shall say!" he suddenly interrupted himself. "Rest assured that I shall place your conduct in the most refulgent light! I shall do you ample justice, Miss Percy!"

The Baronet bowed respectfully and quitted the apartment, leaving the door partly open, doubtless as a signification that I was free to avail myself of the means of egress if I thought fit. But I had no fear now; and I resolved to await his return. I had confidence in him: I felt certain that he would prove a man of honour when placed in those circumstances which demanded honourable action on his part.

In five minutes he came back to the room; and on presenting himself again, bowed with the utmost respect.

"My carriage still awaits your orders," he said; "and I have spoken to my servants in such terms as cannot fail to enhance, and not depreciate, the character of Miss Percy in their estimation. They know me well, and are aware that I should not attempt to deceive them. Besides, it is fortunate, Miss Percy, that the footman belonging to the carriage should have been addressed by you in such terms as now fully prove to him that you came here entirely under a mistake."

"One word more," I said, "ere I take my departure! How was it that I came here at all?"

"I think that I can satisfactorily explain the point, Miss Percy," replied the Baronet: "but you must suffer me to give a few little prefatory details, at which I will however glance as lightly and delicately as possible. I will commence by informing you that for some few years I have been travelling abroad. When on the Continent, I heard of your fame in England; and I longed to behold you. I therefore was not likely to delay this pleasure when my return to London afforded me the opportunity of enjoying it. Being a member of the committee of the theatre, and one of the largest shareholders, I thought I might usurp the privilege of passing behind the scenes. I saw you close; it was sufficient! I was struck by your beauty——But on this point I suppose I must say no more! I got into conversation with Richards: I will candidly confess that I dropped a hint of something that was passing in my mind—an idea I had formed—a hope I had entertained——But he assured me that it was all useless. In a word, Miss Percy, if I had depended only on what Mr. Richards told me, I should never have made any overture towards you at all; for if he were your father or brother, he could not have spoken in higher terms of your character. It was not from his lips that I gleaned the fact that your real name was Percy; but it was a whisper which I accidentally caught up, I scarcely know where. As for your place of abode, that was of course easily ascertained; and then, Miss Percy, I had sufficient vanity—sufficient egotism——No! it was not that, for on my soul I am not inordinately vain! However, without dwelling on the point, I resolved to make a bold attempt—while at the same time I studied to invest the proceeding with a degree of delicacy that might gloss over its audacity. Hence the idea of the transmission of the thousand pound note. Ah, Miss Percy! I now feel humiliated and ashamed—and yet after all it was only the course which any man of the world——"

"Pray proceed with your explanations, Sir Hugh Ward," I interrupted him; "and spare all comment."

"As I was informing you, Miss Percy, I adopted the idea of transmitting the bank-note, with my name and address written upon the back of it. Otherwise it was utterly unaccompanied by any sign or evidence of what my purpose was or what my hope might be. I naturally concluded that on receiving such a missive you would wonder who the note could come from, and you would seek to learn, so that either in your indignation you might restore it to the source whence it emanated, or that in a softer and less virtuous mood you might be enabled to communicate with the bestower of the gift. In a word, Miss Percy, I felt as confident that you would behold the name and address upon the back of that bank-note, as that I am a being of flesh and blood having the honour of this moment addressing you! Who could have dreamt of such a coincidence as that you at the self-same time should be expecting precisely a similar sum, neither more nor less, from another quarter! However, I see that you are getting impatient——"

"I have told you, Sir Hugh Ward, that my friend Miss Glentworth is ill. Besides, my absence will alarm the household—I am anxious—I am nervous for many reasons ——"

"I will detain you, Miss Percy, but a few minutes longer. For my own sake I hope that you will consent to remain for that short space, and listen to the rest of my explanations; because although I am not over nice nor particular, as I just now observed, — yet on the other hand I would not rest willingly under the imputation of performing an outrageous or atrocious deed against a young lady who for so many reasons ought to be enabled to command chivalrous treatment on the part of the male sex."

"I will remain and listen to you for a few minutes, Sir Hugh Ward," I hastily rejoined. "And now I beseech you to proceed."

"Well, Miss Percy, the note was sent," continued the Baronet; "and I can assure you that throughout the remainder of that day and the next I was full of suspense to see whether it would be kept or returned to me. It was not returned; several days passed, and still the bank-note came not back to my hands; but still all was silent likewise on your part. What did it mean? Did you purpose to keep the bank-note and treat me, the donor, with contempt? No! I could not think it. Richards had assured me that you were the very paragon of virtue: but yet, I thought to myself, a paragon of virtue would assuredly scorn the idea of keeping the bank-note under any consideration whatsoever. Then likewise methought that since you had kept it, you must be mercenary: and if mercenary, you could scarcely be virtuous; or if still virtuous, that you must have

your price. Pardon me for entering into these details—but you must acknowledge, Miss Percy, that when I found the bank-note did not come back, it was natural enough that I should thus deliberate with myself. Then I thought it was just possible it might have been intercepted, and that it had fallen into other hands. I made certain inquiries, and I found that the note had been paid into the Bank of England: but whether by you, or any other person, I could not of course ascertain. Nevertheless, I indulged in the hope that it was yourself who had thus made use of it: and I moreover flattered myself that you were merely awaiting some favourable opportunity to honour me with an interview. Time was however passing on, and you made no sign—all was still—a profound silence on your part! Then, after some reflection, I said to myself, 'I have been very remiss and neglectful: Miss Percy studies to keep up all possible appearances; and perhaps, afraid to take the initiative upon herself, she is waiting for me to afford her an opportunity of honouring me with her presence.'—I must inform you that the young footman who is attached to the carriage, was taken into my confidence in respect to my designs and hopes in this particular matter. So I bade him attend at the theatre with the carriage on each evening when you appeared; for it naturally occurred to me that you could not fail to perceive that it was thus constant in its attendance—that you would understand what it meant—and that you would therefore avail yourself of the equipage. Something to all this effect did I tell the young footman; and I bade him act with vigilance and discretion. I knew that on all these points he was thoroughly to be trusted. But to be brief, Miss Percy, you now understand how it was that my domestic, acting entirely in accordance with my instructions——"

"Yes—I perceive—I comprehend it all!" I exclaimed. "He thought that I was voluntarily entering your carriage, with a perfect consciousness of whose it was——"

"And thus, when at the door of the theatre, and again likewise at my own door," rejoined Sir Hugh Ward, "you spoke of the Marquis of Campanella, my domestic naturally imagined that you were making use of that name in order that the passers-by should hear it, and that every species of injurious suspicion should thus be averted from yourself. My servant therefore—as he has just informed me—proclaimed that name aloud, inwardly chuckling at the idea that he was skilfully taking up a cue which you were giving him, and that he was playing out the game according to your prompting. Now, Miss Percy, I have no more to say—unless it be to reiterate my regret, as well as the sense of humiliation and shame which I experience——"

"Enough, Sir Hugh Ward!" I interrupted him, "I might have been rendered the victim of circumstantial evidence and of strange coincidences: but thank God! everything has been elucidated at last. There, sir, is the cheque for the amount which is your own."

"Miss Percy," said the Baronet, "if I only dared implore you to retain that cheque ——Ah! do not start indignantly! I am incapable of offering you additional outrage or insult! But if you would retain that amount, and expend it on

charitable purposes according to your own discretion—perhaps in the theatrical world—amongst
your poorer brethren and sisters in the profession——"

"No, sir!" I emphatically said; for I felt as if
this were merely a delicate way of making me a
present of the thousand pounds. "There is your
money, sir!—and I thank God that from my own
resources I am enabled to dispense a few little
charities from time to time. I shall now take my
departure."

Thus speaking, I bowed to Sir Hugh Ward, and
at once issued from the room. There was a footman in the hall, who immediately opened the front
door. The carriage was still waiting opposite the
house; and the very moment that I made my appearance on the threshold, the expert and trustworthy young footman who thought he had been
playing his master's game so nicely, opened the
door of the vehicle for me to take my seat therein.
But quickly drawing down my veil, I hastened
away, without taking the slightest notice of that
obsequious attentive lacquey. I was fortunate in
obtaining a cab at a little distance; and I hastened
home to Great Ormond Street.

———

CHAPTER XCI.

THE SURGEON'S ANNOUNCEMENT.

It was long past midnight when I reached my
dwelling; and on arriving there I was glad to find
that my absence had not produced so much uneasiness or consternation as I had been anticipating. The maid-servant who had attended me at
the theatre, went back to my dressing-room to
fetch my jewel-casket which she had forgotten;
and when she came forth again, she looked vainly
around for what she believed to be the Marquis of
Campanella's equipage. She concluded that I had
not chosen to wait for her, on account of my
anxiety to see Mary Glentworth;—and she accordingly took a cab home. When she found that
I had not arrived, she informed Beda of what had
occurred to separate us at the door of the theatre;
and they were both surprised at my absence. But
it was not until the lapse of about an hour that
this surprise began to grow into uneasiness; for
they feared lest I should have been taken ill at the
Marquis of Campanella's mansion,—whither they
had no doubt that I had gone. Indeed, they were
just thinking of sending off to make some inquiry,
when I arrived in the cab.

Under these circumstances I did not consider it
necessary to enter into a long explanation of all
that had occurred: I therefore suffered my depen-
dants to believe that I had really been with my
friends the Campanellas; and I hastily threw out
some sufficient excuse to acquit myself of the imputation of heartlessness in having apparently
neglected my friend Mary Glentworth.

But now in reference to Mary herself. Beda,
on hastening away from the theatre in my carriage, had proceeded at once to Lincoln's Inn
Fields, where she was fortunate enough in finding
the celebrated Doctor Manvers at home. He at
once consented to accompany her: but when he
and Beda arrived in Great Ormond Street, Mary

Glentworth was out of all danger, and had sunk
into a serene slumber. Mr. Doveton, the surgeon,
acquainted Doctor Manvers with the particulars
of all that had occurred; and the eminent physician, having delivered his opinion, took his
departure. Mary had remained wrapped in
slumber from that moment: Mr. Doveton had
gone home: and thus I found the house more
tranquil than I had expected. I retired to rest—
after having stolen on tiptoe into Mary's room to
assure myself that she was sleeping tranquilly; and
slumber was not long in visiting my own eyes, for
I was thoroughly exhausted in mind and body. I
nevertheless rose at a tolerably early hour in the
morning: and I hastened to Mary's chamber.
Beda, having slept in her room, was already up;
and Mary, who had been awake for a few minutes,
was conversing with her.

"My dear friend," I exclaimed, embracing Miss
Glentworth, "you were very ill last night!"

"But I am quite well this morning," she answered somewhat quickly. "Indeed, I think my
illness must have been a great deal exaggerated——"

"Miss Glentworth fancies," said Beda, "that
it was perfectly unnecessary to call in the medical
men — that it was a mere common fainting
fit——"

"Oh, my dear Beda!" exclaimed Mary, "I know
that everything was done for the best; and not
for a moment must you make me seem thankless
or ungracious in Miss Percy's eyes!"

"At all events you feel much better this morning," I said, "and that is the essential!"

"Much better!" ejaculated Mary: "I feel perfectly well! Yes—I can assure you, I never
felt better in my life! I suppose, Beda, that the
physician whom you fetched——what was his
name?"

"Doctor Manvers," interjected both myself and
Beda.

"Yes—Doctor Manvers," resumed Mary Glentworth. "I suppose that he did not stay a minute,
when he found that I had recovered from the fit
and had gone quietly off to sleep?"

"Oh, yes!" responded Beda: "Doctor Manvers
remained for at least twenty minutes in conversation with Mr. Doveton."

"Where?" asked Mary.

"In the drawing-room, after having visited you
for a moment in this chamber. But you were
sleeping——"

"Now, my dear Ellen," interrupted Mary
Glentworth, suddenly turning her eyes upon me,
and speaking almost with a degree of petulance,
"I do not want to have these doctors visiting me
again! I dislike doctors—I have no confidence in
them——"

"Hush, my dear Mary!" I said: "you must
not talk in this manner! The public at large are
under the greatest of obligations to the medical
profession——"

"It may be so," said Mary curtly: "but I for
one——However," she suddenly exclaimed, "I am
quite well! I am just going to get up and dress
for breakfast—and therefore so far as I am concerned, I do not want to have any more to do with
doctors—neither do I wish to see them if they
call."

I now left Mary Glentworth's chamber, rejoiced to perceive that she was so much improved in health, and thinking very little of her petulant and even ill-tempered remarks: for as I have before stated, her disposition had undergone a considerable change during the last few months, ever since the discovery of her parentage, her mother's shame, and the fact that she had been bestowing her heart's affections upon her own half-brother.

She presently came down to breakfast; and she looked very well, considering the severity of the illness of a few hours which she had experienced on the preceding evening. Her cheeks were slightly pale, and there was a faint bluish tint, just perceptible around the eyes. But in other respects she seemed better than usual—for there was more gaiety in her tone—she appeared to converse with a lightness and a blitheness which for months past she had not displayed. Yet it once or twice struck me during the breakfast-hour, that there was something forced in this manifestation of good spirits on Mary Glentworth's part, and that she was affecting a gaiety which she did not altogether feel in reality. Scarcely, however, did a suspicion of this sort enter my mind, when I banished it; for it was grateful to my heart to be enabled to entertain the idea that my friend was recovering somewhat of her lost spirits — while on the other hand it was painful to harbour the thought that she had any new source of trouble or annoyance which she was endeavouring to conceal.

After breakfast, Mary Glentworth hastened up to her own chamber—desiring Beda, whom she happened to encounter in the hall, to tell Mr. Doveton, if he called, that she was so completely restored to health as to be enabled to dispense with his services. It did not seem to strike her that there was something impolite, rude, and most unladylike in this method of dismissing a medical attendant: and as I was determined that Mr. Doveton, who was a very excellent and kind-hearted man, should not be treated with so much disrespect, I gave instructions that when he called he was to be conducted into my presence. Not many minutes after I had issued this order, the surgeon arrived at the house; and he was shown to the room where I was seated.

"How is my patient this morning?" he inquired, as he took the chair which I indicated.

"Miss Glentworth declares that she is quite well," I answered.

"Indeed? and yet it may be so! But at all events I had better see her——"

"Not unless you think it absolutely necessary," I rejoined. "We all have our peculiarities—and my friend Mary entertains a prejudice on a point to which I will not more particularly allude."

Mr. Doveton looked very hard at me for a few moments; and I could not help thinking that there was something more or less significant in the way in which he thus regarded me. Indeed, methought that he was studying to ascertain if there were any ulterior motive or hidden thought in my own mind in connexion with what I had just been saying.

"Of course, Miss Percy," said Mr. Doveton, at length breaking silence, "if it is Miss Glentworth's wish that I should discontinue my visits—and if you likewise——"

"My dear sir," I exclaimed, "I can only have

one wish upon the subject; and this is that your visits shall be paid to Miss Glentworth as long as you may deem them necessary. But I thought perhaps that this little malady was entirely past——"

But here I stopped short; for again I observed that Mr. Doveton was contemplating me with a singular expression of countenance. A suspicion struck me that there was something he wished to reveal, or else something in reference to which he desired to question me. I knew not which it was; —but that there was something behind that strange look on his part, I was thoroughly convinced.

"Surely, Mr. Doveton," I said, "you do not apprehend any return of these fits on the part of Miss Glentworth?—you do not fear that the seeds of serious indisposition are taking root in her constitution? Or perhaps you think the stage——".

The surgeon gave a dry cough; and again looking me very hard in the face, he said, "Then, in reality, Miss Percy, you have no knowledge of anything which might possibly account for that kind of illness which so abruptly seized upon your friend?"

"I? any particular knowledge! No, Mr. Doveton! You alarm me! What can you mean?"

"I know not, Miss Percy," he said, "whether this conversation ought to be prolonged—whether I might not be violating——"

"Violating what?" I exclaimed. "Confidence do you mean? Has Miss Glentworth told you anything——Ah, poor girl! her mother dropped down suddenly and died with frightful abruptness! Perhaps Mary fears——"

"Miss Percy," said Mr. Doveton, "your friend Miss Glentworth has told me nothing! Indeed, last evening, during the intervals between the fits, she would scarcely give utterance to a syllable; and now, as you have informed me, she declines to receive my visits. To that decision I bow; and I am not offended. But I consider it my duty, after a little reflection, to acquaint you as the young lady's friend—indeed for her own sake the fact ought to be made known to you——for I see that you are indeed ignorant of it——"

"Good heavens! you alarm me, Mr. Doveton!" I exclaimed. "What do you mean? what secret is this which ought to be made known to me? Keep me not in suspense!"

"Miss Percy," answered the surgeon, in a slow and deliberate manner, "I hope for her own sake that your friend is privately married——"

"What!" I faintly ejaculated: for though it was now something more than a suspicion which agitated in my mind, yet did I strive to repel the conviction of the fatal truth.

"Do you not understand me?" asked the surgeon, with a look and tone which showed that he compassioned me on account of the shock which he felt I must sustain when the last remnant of the veil should be torn away from the truth. "Your friend Miss Glentworth ought to bear another name——and unless her happiness is to be wrecked, that name should be the one which a father can honourably bestow upon the babe which in due time——"

"Mr. Doveton! no—impossible!" I murmured, in a faint tone. "You are mistaken!"—and I felt that I looked aghast as I sank back in my chair.

The surgeon shook his head, saying, "I scarcely think that I am mistaken, Miss Percy. Dr. Manvers himself entertains a similar opinion."

"No! I cannot believe it!" I murmured, in a fainter tone than before, and likewise with a much fainter hope that the opinion of the medical men would prove to be erroneous.

· "It is true, Miss Percy," said Mr. Doveton; "or else never was I so deceived in all my life! But I am *not* deceived—I am confident, backed as I am by the opinion of that eminent man, Doctor Manvers. Yes, Miss Percy, your friend is already three months at least in the course of maternity."

"Three months!" I ejaculated; for I was suddenly smitten by the coincidence of dates in association with the remembrance of an occurrence that was floating in my mind.

For it was precisely three months ago that on my return from Willowbridge I had found Mary absent from the house, and that when she came back it was in a mood so strange and with looks so full of the stupor of despair as to be indicative of some calamity that had overtaken her, or of some misdeed that was followed by its remorse. Yes—precisely three months, day for day: for this was the thirtieth of September of which I am now writing, and it was on the thirtieth of June that Mary Glentworth had returned home in that state of mind which had filled me with misgivings that had never since been completely subdued nor set at rest.

"Three months!" I had ejaculated, as this comparison of dates sprang up vividly in my mind; and it was with that kind of start which one gives when an event that has hitherto been involved in the deepest mystery, seems all in a moment to receive an elucidation.

"Ah!" said Mr. Doveton: "then, from your manner, Miss Percy—from your looks, which were even affrighted—from the ejaculation which has burst from your lips, I must suppose that your unfortunate friend Miss Glentworth has been the victim of villany, and that a conjecture has arisen in your mind pointing to her seducer?"

"No," I exclaimed, terribly distressed: "if that poor girl have indeed been made the victim of treachery, I am utterly at a loss to conceive who could have been the author of her ruin. But let us not continue this discourse now: and may I hope that the secret—— "

"The secret is a professional one, Miss Percy and it is sacred," interrupted Mr. Doveton. "I should be willing to offer my services as a friend, were it not that I might be deemed selfish—— And yet this is impossible!" he added, with a sudden assertion of manly dignity; "for you ought to know that I am too high in my profession and too independent in my means——"

"I know it," I said.

"Therefore," he at once continued, "when I spoke of proffering my services as a friend, I meant that as you two ladies live alone together —and as I know that your society is limited and select—I would offer myself as one who would see the seducer of Miss Glentworth — remonstrate with him—appeal to him—if, alas! it be not useless—— for she is exceedingly beautiful, and

young persons of her attractive description, especially on the stage——Pardon the observation, Miss Percy—but *your* character is above even the slightest breath of suspicion——Yet as I was about to observe, there are many unprincipled men of rank and distinction — even married men——"

"I know all this, Mr. Doveton—I have not been nearly three years upon the stage without becoming aware of the truth of all you are saying. I thank you most sincerely for your kind and friendly proffers; and if I should need your generous intervention on Mary's behalf, I shall avail myself of it."

The surgeon now rose; and without renewing his request to see Mary Glentworth, he took his departure. The moment the front door had closed behind him, my first impulse was to hasten up to Mary's chamber and beseech her to give me her confidence; but a second thought held me back. I remembered that her disposition had become changed, and that of late the same frankness as formerly had not existed between us—at least from herself towards me. I resumed my seat, and gave way to my reflections. Five months had elapsed since the explosion in respect to her parentage,—five months since the fatal truth was revealed to her that the Marquis of Dalrymple was her own half-brother! Since that date the young nobleman had been abroad; and I felt convinced that Mary had not become *his* victim. No! And therefore I fixed my thoughts upon that memorable occasion three months back, when she had returned home in so strange a state of mind. But how could she have fallen?—by whom could she have been beguiled within so short a time after her heart's affections were blighted in respect to Herbert Dalrymple? I could think of no one who might be the author of this calamity.

I was bewildered how to act. Might the medical testimony be wrong? Alas, no! I scarcely dared indulge in such a hope! But if it were right, was it not my bounden duty as Mary's friend to learn the exact truth as soon as possible, and ascertain if it were practicable to save her reputation by means of marriage? And then the wild idea shot through my mind that by some possibility she might have been wedded in secret. No!—this hypothesis I was compelled to abandon; for I felt convinced that if there were any foundation for it, she would not have kept that secret at least from one whom she knew to be her best and most devoted friend. Then what was I to do? Ah! a thought struck me. I would wait a few days: I would conceal everything that had taken place between the surgeon and myself: I would keep watch at the theatre and elsewhere — and ascertain, if possible, whether there were any person on whom her regards were particularly bent— any one who by the external evidences of his own conduct might demonstrate a special interest in the beautiful and rising actress?

When my mind was made up to this mode of action, I composed my looks—I settled my ideas, so that I might be completely on my guard when in Mary's Glentworth's presence. About an hour after Mr. Doveton had taken his departure, Mary descended to the room in which I was seated; and presently she asked, as if in a listless indifferent way, whether either of the medical gentlemen had been? I was pretending not to notice her particularly—though in reality I was scrutinizing her countenance with attention; and I observed a slight glitter of uneasiness in her looks.

"Mr. Doveton has been," I said: "but I told him that you were quite well—and he took his departure."

"And did he say anything?" asked Mary, now affecting to be glancing over the columns of a newspaper which she had just taken up: "did he, I mean, think that there was anything at all serious——"

"Perhaps if he had thought so," I responded "he would have urged the necessity of seeing you —which he did not."

I then turned the discourse into some other channel, and for the remainder of the day Mary Glentworth continued to affect that same gaiety which she had forced herself to maintain during the breakfast hour; but I now knew for a certainty that it was unnatural—and from the bottom of my soul I commiserated the poor girl who thus felt herself constrained to veil her secret beneath the hideous mockery of an artificial cheerfulness. In the evening I accompanied her to the theatre. No one unconnected with the business of the stage was admitted behind the scenes when I was there,—though I knew perfectly well that this regulation did not prevail when I was absent. Thus, on the present occasion, I had no opportunity of judging whether the individual who had rendered Mary his victim, or to whom she might have voluntarily abandoned herself, was in the theatre at all. For if I cast my gaze over the male performers, my eyes could settle on none who did not treat her with the utmost respect, or whom she did not keep at a proper distance. And if I scrutinizingly sent my regards travelling round the tiers of boxes, I could single out no person who contemplated her with that degree of significancy which might serve as an elucidation to one who already possessed a partial knowledge of the young lady's secret. We returned home,—Mary in seeming good spirits as before, but I myself as much at a loss as ever to conjecture who could have been the author of her undoing.

On the following day I was compelled to go and make certain purchases for a new costume in which I was shortly to appear at the theatre: for perhaps I need hardly inform my readers that I invariably supplied my own dresses, and never availed myself of the theatrical "properties" except in reference to those insignia which had nothing to do with actual articles of raiment. I had called at several shops; and I was issuing from the last one where I had purchases to make—I was just about to enter my carriage—when a man in shabby attire, was brushing hastily past me. The recognition was instantaneously mutual; for an ejaculation of horror burst from my lips, while the man himself started and stopped short for a moment as if irresolute how to act, and then rushed onward at a rapid pace.

"Stop him!" I exclaimed: "it is Luigi, the Italian assassin!"

My servants took up the cry: my footman (for I had recently added this domestic to my establishment) rushed after him; and a couple of policemen seized him at a little distance. He made a desperate resistance: the officers hurled him upon the pavement—he was overpowered and captured. I had sped mechanically to the spot; and I exclaimed, "It is Luigi, the murderer of Mrs. St. Clair!"

The fellow darted upon me a look of diabolical malignity; and I feel convinced that if the constables had not retained him in a firm grasp, he would have sprung forward to do me a mischief. But when he found himself completely in their power, he maintained a moody silence—he folded his arms, and seemed to resign himself to his fate.

"Is there anything I can do?" I asked of the officers: but I was fearfully agitated, and scarcely knew what I was saying.

A crowd had collected around—the whisper had already circulated, "It is Miss Trafford!"—and the constables likewise showed by their respectful manner that they knew me.

"No, Miss," answered one of them; "it is not necessary for you to come to the police-office now. We shall be able to identify the man from a description we have. At all events we could state enough to procure a remand; and if it's required, you can attend at the next examination. We'll let you know, Miss."

With these words they hurried the criminal off, a portion of the crowd following; but truth, rather than any sentiment of vanity, compels me to add that by far the greater portion of the spectators attended me to my carriage—which I was very glad to reach, for I felt faint with the reaction following upon the agitation and excitement attendant upon the scene I have just described.

I ordered the equipage to drive at once to the Marquis of Campanella's residence. The Marquis and Marchioness were out; but Beatrice di Carboni was at home. I informed her that the law had at length fixed its grasp upon the assassin of her husband — the twofold murderer who had rendered not only the Count of Carboni his victim, but likewise Mrs. St. Clair. Beatrice expressed her satisfaction,—not because she could possibly entertain any sympathy on account of her deceased husband, but for the reason that in the rectitude of her principles she was pleased that a great criminal should meet the retribution of justice.

I returned home, earnestly wishing that I had not to appear that night at the theatre—for I felt indisposed after the occurrence of the day; but still I was not sufficiently ill to justify me conscientiously in making an apology for my absence; and I never was one of those professionals who on the slightest pretext had recourse to a medical certificate to avoid the fulfilment of a duty. Therefore, at the usual hour, I repaired to the theatre, accompanied by Mary Glentworth; for though it was not her turn to perform this night, yet she went with me—as was indeed her custom. When under those inspirations which gave me the enthusiasm, the power, and the nerve, as well as the complete self-possession which contributed so much to my dramatic success, I lost sight of the salient incident of the day; and I performed my part in a manner to elicit the wonted meed of applause. While upon the stage, I was casting my eyes around the tiers of boxes, when whom should I behold seated together, and having the mutual demeanour as if no vindictive hate had ever raged between them, but Edwin St. Clair and Lady Lilla Essendine! I was astonished at this circumstance;

for knowing—or at least suspecting so much as I did, of their fearful secrets, I had thought it scarcely possible that, unless for some purpose of wickedness, they could thus come together with a friendly mien in public.

When the performances were over, I retired as usual to my own dressing-room to change my costume; and I wondered that Mary Glentworth did not join me there, as was her wont. Therefore, when I had resumed my private raiment, I sought her in the stage box where she had been seated throughout the performances; and I was at once struck by her appearance. She did not seem to notice me. She was leaning back in the box, pale as a ghost: all her limbs appeared to be rigid, as if labouring under a species of tetanus. Her lips were apart: they were blanched, and gave a ghastly gleaming to her beautiful teeth which usually shone with so brilliant an effect. In a word, her whole appearance was precisely as if her vision had suddenly encountered some hideous spectacle, the effect of which was transfixing and paralyzing. Yet the drapery in front of the box was so disposed in reference to the position in which she was seated, that her eyes could embrace naught but the orchestra and the stage.

I stood for a few moments on the threshold of the box, almost as much stupified and dismayed as Mary herself appeared to be: but as I regained my self-possession, the thought struck me that this was neither the time nor the place to ask for an explanation. I therefore advanced into the box as if I had observed nothing peculiar; and then I noticed that Mary regained her own presence of mind with a sudden start. This circumstance likewise I affected not to perceive; and taking my seat by her side, I said as if quite in an indifferent manner, "You did not come to me in my dressing-room."

"Ah! no! I forgot!" she said, with another start, as if thus reminded of an inadvertence which might tend to betray some secret that she was bent upon concealing.

"I did not think that you wished to see the ballet this evening," I went on to observe; "and therefore I ordered the carriage to be here at the usual hour. But if you desire to wait——"

"Yes!" said Mary, with a strange abruptness and with something even of fierceness in her tone: then instantaneously recalling the idea, she added somewhat more collectedly, "No! I will go with you at once! And indeed I feel the atmosphere to be particularly oppressive to-night!"

We accordingly left the theatre; and during the short ride homeward, Mary Glentworth endeavoured to force herself to converse with some degree of cheerfulness; but she could not—and the effort was evidently a painful one. I however affected not to notice it; and I went on discoursing as if there were nothing to trouble my mind. But all the while I was deliberating within myself whether I should seize upon this opportunity to question my friend in respect to the *one* serious topic that was uppermost in my thoughts:—and yet I knew not how to give the conversation the requisite turn.

We reached Great Ormond Street. Supper was always laid, though neither Mary nor myself were as a rule accustomed to partake of that repast, nor to sit up to a late hour. The moment we entered the dining-room and I glanced at my companion, I was shocked on perceiving that her countenance still retained the same ghastly death-like pallor which had so much dismayed and appalled me at the theatre. There was also a certain wild fierceness in her looks,—a species of vindictive glare in those eyes that were wont to be of such melting, amiable softness. I was again on the point of questioning her, when she suddenly said, "Good night, dear Ellen. I shall go to bed at once—for I do not feel very well to-night. Not unwell," she instantaneously added; "but tired—exhausted—I scarcely know how."

Words of questioning were about to burst from my lips, when I felt that I dared not give utterance to aught that might all in a moment evoke the wild grief that was evidently pent up in Mary's bosom. I therefore held my peace, and bade her good night. We separated—she retired to her chamber—but I, feeling no inclination for slumber, sat down in the dining-room to give way to my reflections.

——

CHAPTER XCII.

THE CONFESSION.

THOSE reflections were painful enough; for the appearance of Mary Glentworth when I joined her in the box at the theatre, had denoted a condition of mind which was even fearful to think of. That scene too struck me as being in some sense an inevitable result, or at least a sequence of the former condition of mind to which I have so frequently referred—I mean that cold stupor of despair, that dull apathy of utter desperation, which she had displayed when returning to the house on the same night that I got back from Willowbridge.

"Poor Mary!" I thought to myself: "there must be a very terrible agitation in your soul! Oh, that you would treat me with confidence, and tell me everything! At least I might endeavour to console you, even though it might be impossible for me to aid in rescuing you from degradation and dishonour!"

As I went on reflecting, I thought of all the former circumstances of Mary Glentworth's life—of how she and I first grew acquainted, and how she had become my companion and dwelt with me. Though she was about my own age, yet I could scarcely help regarding her as an elder sister might look upon a younger one: I even considered that to a certain extent she was under my protection, and that her orphanage gave me a sort of guardian's authority and right over her,—especially when I took into consideration the circumstance that at her mother's death she found a friendly asylum through my intervention, and she had seemed like a desolate one to cast herself in full reliance upon me.

"Ought I therefore," I asked myself as the result of all these reflections, "to leave her thus uncomforted and unconsoled?—ought I to wait until accident may reveal something, or she herself may choose to speak, and thus afford me an opportunity for holding serious discourse with her?—or ought I not at once to make this the opportunity? Ought I not when we stood here together, imme-

ANGELINE.

diately after entering the house, to have caught her in my arms and entreated that she would once more regard me as a sister and give me her confidence? And how do I know but that the unfortunate girl may be even now weeping bitterly in her chamber—that she may be yearning to speak to me—yet that she may dare not?—that she may feel herself utterly forlorn and desolate—more than ever an orphan—without a living soul to breathe the language of sympathy in her ears?"

It was thus that I exclaimed to myself; and under the impression of these thoughts, I hesitated no longer how to act; I stole up to Mary's chamber. The door was locked : I tapped gently—and Mary's voice from the inside inquired, "Who is there?"

"It is I, Mary dear," I said : "I wish to speak to you for a moment."

The door was unlocked; and on entering I

No. 72.—PERCY.

found that Mary was only half undressed, although nearly three quarters of an hour had elapsed since she retired to her chamber.

"What !" she ejaculated, "you have not yet gone to bed?"

"No, Mary—I could not sleep: I felt that I could not !" I answered. "I wished to speak to you !"

As her face was now turned towards the toilet-table on which the lamp stood, I was startled and shocked by the ghastly expression of that countenance; and the traces of recent weeping were upon her cheeks. It was almost with a cry of anguish that I flung my arms about her neck, exclaiming, "Oh, for heaven's sake, my beloved friend, tell me everything! Let me console you—let me advise you! But do not, do not treat me as if I were the veriest stranger—or as if you thought that there was a diminution of affection on my part towards you !"

"Ellen, you are very kind," said Mary,—"very, very kind, my dear friend," she continued in a voice tremulous with emotion: and then, as her accents grew firmer and she evidently regained her self-possession, she added, "But why, dear Ellen, should you think that there is anything so very serious——"

"Mary, I do not merely think," I answered—"but I *know* beyond the possibility of doubt that you are cherishing a terrible secret—that the time will come when you will stand in need of all the assistance of friendship——"

"Ellen!"—and it was now a ghastly look which Mary fixed upon me as she was thus suddenly thrown off her guard. "Ellen!" she repeated: but then she could say no more, for her tongue evidently clave to the roof of her mouth.

"Oh, the time for secrecy is past!" I ejaculated. "I must tell you all I know, Mary! I must invoke your confidence by all possible means! —I must solicit it even perforce, since voluntarily you will not give it to me! Mary," I added, looking her earnestly in the face, "you are in a way to become a mother!"

She had seen that this accusation was about to flow from my lips—she perceived that I was acquainted with her position even before the words had fallen from my tongue; and the blush of shame was glowing upon her cheeks as those words were spoken. No syllable of denial came from her own lips: that tell-tale glow was spreading over her neck, her shoulders, and her bosom; and as her head drooped upon my breast, the deep convulsive sobs which agitated her entire frame indicated how much she felt.

"My poor Mary," I said, straining her again and again in my arms, "did you not know that from me you would receive all sympathy and consolation—and that even if you had been weak and frail, I should have abstained from harsh reproach?"

She started from my arms—she stood before me in the middle of the chamber, her countenance still glowing, but now with some other feeling beyond that of shame. Raising her finely modelled arm, she exclaimed, "I swear to you, Ellen, that the diabolical treachery of another, far more than any weakness or frailty on my part, has led to my dishonour and my degradation! To some little extent I was wrong—but not to so fearful an extreme! Oh, no, no!—and if you knew all——"

"And why should I not know all, Mary?" I asked, taking her by the hand, and making her sit by me on the ottoman which was close to her bed. "It is three months, Mary, since we thus sat together, in this very spot—and I then implored you to reveal the cause of your despair——"

"No—I could not!" exclaimed Mary. "Besides, I was in that state of mind so fearfully unnatural —balancing between suicide on the one hand and murder on the other——"

"Good heavens, Mary!" I ejaculated: "what means this dreadful language? Murder——"

"Yes!—the murder of the villain who rendered me his victim!" rejoined Mary. "Can you not therefore understand that my mind was in a state which rather shunned than courted confidential intercourse with a friend, and which was beyond all the consolations of sympathy. Do not think, Ellen, that towards you I was ungrateful or un-

kind: but Oh! my soul had received such a shock —my whole disposition was altered—it seemed as if I had gone to sleep the same being that I always was, and had then awakened with utterly different instincts and with entirely another nature!"

I shuddered as I listened: but I was nevertheless bestowing the caresses of tenderest sympathy on my afflicted friend.

"And it was on that evening, then, Mary," I said, "when you returned home in that mood of sombre gloom and cold stupor—it was on that evening that treachery made you its victim——"

"It was so," responded Mary. "Oh, Ellen! I can scarcely bring myself to reveal the particulars of the hideous history! But to-morrow or next day, when my mind is more calm——"

"Do you not remember, my dear Mary," I asked, "that on the former occasion—the one to which I have alluded—three months back—when we sat here together, and I entreated and implored that you would give me your confidence—you assured me that if I would only have patience until the following day——"

"True, dearest Ellen!" interrupted Mary: "but, Oh! circumstances were so different *then!* My shame was as yet unknown to you: but *now* it is no longer a secret! Then I shrank from revealing it: now it is revealed—the most painful portion of the ordeal is past—and a few details will put you in possession of everything! Nevertheless, if you desire it, Ellen—if you fear that I shall yet again treat you with reserve and want of frankness, I will at once enter upon the history. Yes—and better too!" ejaculated Mary; "far better that I should yield to the influences of a mood which is so very different from any that I have known for many weeks past?"

"Proceed, my dear friend," I said,—"proceed;". and we sat together upon the ottoman, I having one arm thrown round Mary's neck, and her head half reclining upon my shoulder.

"I must revert," she said, after a brief pause, "to that memorable date of my existence when the circumstances of my birth were cleared up, and when the horrible truth was revealed to me that my affections had been unconsciously won by my own half-brother. You know the shock that my soul received — you know how implacable I became against the Ardleigh family?—you know that even against Herbert himself a species of hatred occupied the place of love in my heart?"

"But you are not going to tell me, Mary," I shudderingly asked, "that anything of all this subsequently changed—that you and Herbert Dalrymple met again——"

"Good heaven, no!" ejaculated Mary, starting with affright at the bare idea which had prompted the question on my part. "Oh, no! no! But if I am now referring to those incidents, Ellen, it is only to remind you of the impression which they produced upon me—to recall to your recollection the effect that they left upon my mind——"

"Oh, yes—now I understand, Mary!" I said, breathing more freely. "You suffered much, I know, my poor friend!—all the best affections of your heart were blighted—you were made to feel as if you were an object destined to become the focus of all possible calamities—and in your despair you proclaimed to me that the power of love was dead within you!"

"Yes, Ellen," resumed Mary; "and it was precisely to this condition of mind on my part that I was desirous of recalling your attention. A few weeks passed—I appeared upon the stage—not without a certain promise of success; my heart began to grow somewhat more warm towards the world—and when I read in the public journals all the flattering eulogies which were passed upon me, the idea that a full measure of happiness might yet be in store for me stole into my mind. Then, shortly afterwards, Henry Wakefield returned to England: I saw how delighted you were—I comprehended how much pure and holy felicity was then within the range of your experience. You possessed the love of a handsome, elegant, noble-hearted young man: and I rejoiced that the prospect of so much happiness should be in store for you as that of becoming the bride of one so well worthy to possess you. My soul grew still warmer towards the world; and I began to ask myself whether it were right, reasonable, or natural that I should entomb my own heart in the grave of perished affections, and that the past should constitute a huge stone to seal it like a sepulchre, instead of suffering it to be once more lighted up as the temple of love's chaste and holy worship!"

"Yes," I interjected; "your mind was recovering a healthy tone—the morbid influences of the past were subsiding——"

"Oh! if that auspicious process had gone on unchecked — unmarred," exclaimed Mary, "I might now be a different being! But listen to my story. It was just at the very time when this improvement began to take place in the state of my mind, that one day—I remember it well—it was the day after Henry Wakefield's arrival—you were out together—and I also went out to take a long ramble and give way to those new ideas which were arising in my mind. I sought the Regent's Park; and while walking there, I presently became conscious of the fact that I was the object of marked attention on the part of a gentleman, whom I at once recognised—yes, recognised as one of the most distinguished personages of the day—a statesman of brilliant talent——"

"Mary!" I ejaculated, starting as if galvanized by the sudden idea which swept through my brain: "is it possible that you are alluding——"

"To Edwin St. Clair," she responded. "Oh! I know, Ellen, that you have often let fall from your lips certain words which have proved that you thought most indifferently of his character—that you believed him to be unprincipled—and it has even struck me at times that you knew more of him than you chose to admit——"

"Yes, Mary," I exclaimed, my blood boiling within me and all my veins tingling with indignation; "I know Edwin St. Clair to be the most unprincipled of men! And if, Mary,—as I now more than half suspect—if, as I shall doubtless hear from your lips, he be the author of your undoing——"

"It is he, Ellen! it is he!" ejaculated Mary: "he is the treacherous villain by whom I have been undone!"

"And thus, my dear friend," I said, gazing upon her with illimitable compassion, "as if the catalogue of Edwin St. Clair's misdeeds were not complete—as if his crimes had not already swollen into a volume of sufficient bulkiness—he must superadd iniquity upon iniquity, until he numbers you in the catalogue of his victims—and your honour, my poor Mary, is immolated to his depravities! But there shall be an end of all this!—and though too late to save you, my sweet friend, yet in time to ensure the safety of others whom he may have marked out for his victims!"

"Oh! show me how to be avenged upon that man!" exclaimed Mary Glentworth, with fierce eagerness; "show me how to inflict some terrible punishment upon him—and believe me, my heart will quail not! It is upon this idea that I have been feeding myself,—I may almost say that it is for this purpose I have consented to live during the three months past since the fatal moment when I became a disgraced and dishonoured being!"

"We will not speak of punishment or vengeance now, Mary," I said: "let this topic be reserved! But answer me," I continued, as an idea now flashed to my brain: "was it because you beheld Captain St. Clair this evening at the theatre——"

"Yes—with a young and beautiful lady—you once pointed her out to me—I mean Lady Lilla Essendine——"

"Ah! and it was because you beheld them together that you were filled with a vindictive rage at the moment when I joined you in the box?"

"Oh, yes!—a fierce vindictive rage!" replied Mary; "and yet it may seem strange to you, because full well I know that Edwin St. Clair would not do me an act of justice by leading me to the altar and giving a father's name to my babe when it shall come into the world. But I have wandered away, Ellen, from the thread of my story; and now I will resume it. When the sad narrative is completed, you will better comprehend the nature of those feelings which agitate in my heart."

"Yes—proceed, dear Mary," I said; "and take up the thread of your recital from the point where I interrupted it. You were telling me that while walking in the Regent's Park you became aware——"

"That I was the object of attention on the part of Edwin St. Clair; and I must confess that a feeling of pride seized upon me at the thought that one of the most eminent and brilliant men of the present day should thus deem me worthy of such marked notice. This was no doubt a weakness on my part — it was a moment of silly vanity: but, alas! all of our sex, Ellen, are not as perfect as yourself. Moreover, you have promised not to chide me; and I on my part have undertaken to reveal the whole truth frankly and without suppression. Yes—I admit that my pride was flattered when I beheld that man so eminent for his intellectual qualifications—of such god-like beauty of person—bestowing his earnest attention upon me! My brain grew dizzy as I beheld him following in my footsteps and evidently seeking an opportunity or an excuse to address me. But then, all in a moment I remembered my past adventures —the unguardedness with which I had formed the acquaintance of Herbert Dalrymple—the counsel you, dear Ellen, had given me never again to suffer strangers to accost me without the most sufficient reason; and my good genius was rapidly reasserting her empire. But then my evil genius whispered in my ear that Edwin St. Clair was no ordinary man—that he must not be treated as any common stranger—and that if he honoured me with his notice, it would be most preposterous and ridiculous for me to reject that which was a flattery and a compliment. In a word, my dear Ellen, I suffered Edwin St. Clair to accost me; and when once the ice was broken, I did not on that occasion regret my weakness—no, nor would I even to myself confess at the time that there was weakness in it at all. For, Oh, Ellen! you who know him can understand the effect which those powers of conversation, alike so insinuating and so brilliant—that courtly elegance of manner—that winning address—that facility of conveying a compliment in a strain the most insidiously flattering for the very reason that it appears not to be flattery at all——"

"Yes, Mary—yes!" I said; "I can indeed understand what an effect all these powers and influences must have produced upon one who was so little on her guard! But proceed. I have promised I would say nothing which may seem to savour of reproach."

"St. Clair walked by my side for some little while," continued Mary; "and at length he gradually, and with an appearance of the utmost delicacy, introduced the topic of the loss of his wife. I know not how he framed his speech—I cannot repeat his language: but suffice it to say that he gave me to understand I had made an impression upon him—that when he had seen me on the stage he was ravished with my beauty—and that he had longed for an opportunity to speak to me, to form my acquaintance, to know me better—and, in a word, to assure himself that I really possessed those good qualities and amiable traits for which he gave me credit. Oh, Ellen! I cannot tell you all that he said: but perhaps you may conjecture——"

"Dwell not, Mary," I said, "upon this portion of your narrative; for I have already granted that the language of Edwin St. Clair is endowed with a seductiveness and that his manners possess a fascination most dangerous to those female hearts that are not completely on their guard."

"You are very kind to make allowances for me, Ellen," responded Mary Glentworth. "And now I will candidly confess that I was even more dazzled by Edwin St. Clair's brilliant accomplishments than I could have previously conceived that it was possible for me to become. You remember that you once took me to the House of Commons; and on that occasion, although my mind was then filled with the image of him whom at the time I only knew by the name of Beauchamp, yet did it seem to me as if even on that occasion St. Clair's eloquence shed a secret spell upon me. Thus, when he accosted me in the Park—when he glided into conversation with me in a manner which had so little of libertine insolence in it, but so much of an exquisite refinement—when he went on discoursing to me with an ease that was alike friendly and respectful—I was dazzled and bewildered. Then, as I have already hinted, he complimented me on my dramatic triumphs in a strain which was so utterly different from gross palpable flattery—insinuating rather than boldly couching his phrases—applauding me indirectly rather than directly—by inference and implication rather than by an overt eulogy which might have

savoured of fulsomeness,—I could not help thinking within myself that I had seldom met a more agreeable companion. Then, with that ease which he displayed in gliding into all topics—conducting you unconsciously and insensibly into them rather than abruptly taking you by the hand as it were and leading you into some new conversational pathway—he so delicately gave me to understand that with the exception of his deceased wife I was the only person who had ever made an impression upon his heart. I felt my own heart palpitating; and I was credulous enough to lend a willing ear to his speech. For, Oh! although I had some while back assured you, dear Ellen, that the power of love was dead within me, yet I had deceived myself at the time, and it was only in the morbid condition of my feelings that I had conceived such an idea or had embodied it in the language which I addressed unto yourself. I am telling you all these things, Ellen, because I wish you to understant that if in some sense I were weak and feeble, yet that it was under the influence of a fascination which was irresistible; and it seemed to be as if I was after all formed to love and to be beloved! But if with these details I weary you——"

"No, my dear Mary," I interrupted her; "you do not weary me. On the contrary, I wish you to tell me everything, so that I may be enabled to estimate the full extent of St. Clair's wickedness. Proceed, therefore, in your own manner—and suppress not a single tittle of whatsoever you may have to say. Ah! I should ask you, did St. Clair speak of me?"

"Yes: he knew that I was living with you—and upon that topic he likewise with a species of natural transition turned the discourse. Oh! it is with such an easy dexterity that this man leads the mind from one subject to another! and it is no wonder that he possesses within the walls of the legislature such a power over the minds of his audience! He spoke of you—he eulogized your talents in the most enthusiastic terms. He then said that he was about to communicate a great secret to me. He went on to explain that when you first appeared upon the stage, he thought there would be something brilliant in the achievement of making you his wife——"

"Ah! he said this?" I exclaimed.

"Yes—and he moreover told me that he proposed to you, and that you refused him. He said, with an air of the utmost contrition, that he had urged his suit with a pertinacity which gave you offence—that you had repelled him haughtily—that harsh words had ensued betwixt you—and that from that moment you had never spoken to him nor recognised him when you met."

"Yes—he did indeed make me a proposal of marriage," I said, with some degree of bitterness; "and his conduct to me was altogether of the most outrageous description. I have never told you the story, Mary—because when unpleasant adventures are passed and ended, I dislike to recall them—and I have always had an abhorrence to rendering myself the heroine of my own discourse. Besides, when once Edwin St. Clair was married to my friend Zarah, whom you knew, I was naturally inclined to bury as much as possible in oblivion whatsoever would have told to his discredit. But to return to the topic of your own narrative,—did it not strike you as somewhat singular that he should confess to you the circumstance of having sought my hand in marriage, just after he had been telling you that you were the only one of the sex who, with the exception of his wife, had ever made an impression upon his heart?"

"Oh! Edwin St. Clair," exclaimed Mary, "is by no means the person to contradict his own discourse, or leave the mind impressed with the idea of contradictions and inconsistencies on his part. He went on at once to inform me——Ah! now, Ellen, you will not think that I am attempting to glorify myself at your expense; but you will understand that I am merely telling you the exact truth, in order that you may comprehend all the duplicities which that man brought to bear upon my mind——"

"I understand you, Mary," I said; "and again I beg you to tell the tale after your own fashion."

"I will, Ellen. He went on to say that he did not really love you as he felt he had loved his lamented wife, and as he knew that he would love me——"

"The detestable hypocrite!" I ejaculated. "Oh, such love as that which he bore for his wife! If you knew all, Mary——But no matter! Another time I may perhaps initiate you more deeply into many secrets and mysteries connected with Edwin St. Clair. Proceed, my dear friend—and excuse me for this interruption."

"Yes, Ellen—he told me that he had not really loved you, but that he thought it would be a glorious triumph if he could carry off a prize concerning whom there prevailed a sensation amounting to a positive *furor* in the fashionable world at the time. And all this he explained in a manner so natural—in terms that appeared to be so unquestionably invested with truth and sincerity—that I believed him: yes, I believed him!—and when I now look back upon my credulity, I feel as if I could go mad with rage and indignation at myself! But you may easily conceive—indeed you have already shown that you full well conjecture, why he should have turned the conversation upon yourself. It was his aim to devise some pretext in order to prevent me from mentioning to you the acquaintance I had formed. But I comprehended not his object and his purpose at the time. Thus it was with a credulous ear I listened to him as he went on to suggest how inconvenient and impolitic it would be to suffer you to learn that we had thus met—that he had expressed so deep an interest in me—and that he ventured to intimate the hope we should meet again. I gave him a half-promise to this effect; and we separated. Afterwards, when I was alone, and when I had leisure to reflect on all that had taken place, I asked myself whether I ought not to look with mistrust and suspicion upon the language and conduct of that man—whether I ought not to think of all the good advice you had given me—and whether it were not even my duty to tell you everything that had occurred? But no! my evil genius got the better of me again. I thought to myself that I was a being formed to love and to be loved; and when I beheld how happy you were in the love of your handsome and noble-minded Henry, I exclaimed, 'And why should not

I know the bliss of love likewise?'—and then too I was dazzled by wild hopes: I pictured to myself the brilliancy of an alliance with the eminent statesman Edwin St. Clair! I knew that I should not be the first actress who had risen from the stage to a higher rank; and, in a word, I was intoxicated with all the vain and foolish thoughts that entered into my mind!"

"Oh, if you had spoken to me, Mary," I ejaculated, "how different would it all be now. But it is useless for me to give vent to these bitter sayings, which even savour of a reproach,—and I who have already pledged myself to abstain from reproaches altogether!"

"You may now conjecture, Ellen, what I am about to relate," proceeded Mary. "We did meet again! A couple of days afterwards Henry Wakefield took his departure; and it was on that same day I met St. Clair a second time. He spoke more openly to me of his love: he pointedly spoke of marriage also. When we parted, it was with but little hesitation I promised to meet him again. On the ensuing day I pretexted the necessity of going on a shopping excursion: that was on the same day on which you were visited by the poor dramatic author, of whose interview with you, my dear Ellen, you subsequently gave me so graphic a description. And all the time the egotistical Mr. Jingleton was inflicting his absurdities upon you, I was walking with Edwin St. Clair in one of the most secluded portions of the Regent's Park,—listening to the language of love, and credulously confiding in all that flowed from his lips. Ah! in order to render my narrative as complete as possible, I should remark that although on occasions I had heard something drop from your lips detrimental to the character of St. Clair, notwithstanding the usual reserve which you maintained with regard to him,—yet pardon me if I thought that you were in some sense prejudiced, or that you had been misled. And Oh! when a young woman blindly loves, it is so easy for the object of her affections to persuade her of the existence of his own immaculate character! Yes —for though I have since perceived that it was a mere infatuation on my part, by no means insignificantly fostered by my own insensate ambition, I did verily imagine at the time that it was love with which Edwin St. Clair had inspired me. But to continue my narrative. On the following day you went to Willowbridge; and I met St. Clair again. He then asked if I would bestow my hand in marriage upon him?—and when overcome with joy rather than with confusion, I faltered out an affirmative, he seemed to be inspired with the sincere delight of one who entertained the most honourable intentions. He then expressed a wish to introduce me to two or three female relations whom he represented as staying at his house; and all this he said with so much seeming delicacy and with such an appearance of good faith, that I was completely deluded. I assented; and we separated, after having made an appointment for the morrow. And now, Ellen, I come to the fearful portion of my narrative!"

Mary paused for nearly a minute; and when she again spoke, it was in a lower voice and with a sombre tone.

"It was in the evening that I was to meet St. Clair again in the Park, where he proposed to be walking with his female relatives that he might have the pleasure of introducing to them his intended bride. If I had not been blinded by my infatuation, I should have seen that there was something suspicious and sinister in this arrangement: but credulity, as well as every other sentiment or passion, merges at seasons into the wildest extremes. Accordingly, after a hasty dinner on the day of which I am speaking—and having informed Beda that I should be home before dusk —for it was the last day of June, and the days were at their longest—I set off. On reaching the place of *rendezvous*, I found St. Clair waiting for me; but he was alone. He had a specious tale ready devised for the occasion: he assured me that the ladies, his relatives, were anxiously expecting me at his house—that they objected to the idea of meeting me in the Park, as it would seem as if there was something clandestine and stealthy in such a proceeding, and as if they were ashamed that an actress should visit at the place where they were temporarily abiding. But all this St. Clair said in language so delicate and in a manner seemingly so considerate, as to be impossible to wound my feelings; while that very allusion to my position as an actress gave a colour to the excuses he was devising in order to induce me to accompany him to his house. I was completely blinded; and I proceeded with him thither. His dwelling, as you well know, Ellen—for you visited it to see poor Zarah on her death-bed—is in the immediate vicinage of the Regent's Park. We arrived there; and I was at once conducted up into the handsomely furnished drawing-room. No ladies were in that apartment: but St. Clair observed, with his wonted air of sincerity, that they would join me in a few minutes. I sat down: he placed himself on a chair near me; and he directed my attention to different objects of curiosity and *vertû* which were profusely scattered about upon the table. Amongst other things there was an elegant little rosewood box——"

"A rosewood box?" I ejaculated, the allusion suddenly and vividly conjuring up in my mind a fearful reminiscence connected with the death of Zarah: and now I more than suspected the nature of those details which Mary Glentworth was about to give me.

"Yes—a little rosewood box," she resumed. "But why, my dear Ellen, do you seem startled——"

"Go on, Mary—ask me no questions! Another time——But pray proceed!" I ejaculated: "for, Oh! my poor friend, I must not keep you lingering over these details!"

"My attention was directed to that little rosewood box," she continued; "and St. Clair at once began to tell me some tale with regard to it—some legend which he doubtless invented for the purpose. While thus conversing, and keeping my thoughts engaged upon the topic,—which with all his subtle art he knew how to render so interesting,—he took a key from his pocket: he opened the box—it contained naught but——"

"Naught but——" and then I checked myself: for I did not wish to have the appearance of knowing or suspecting too much on an occasion when it was not my purpose to account for such knowledge or such suspicion.

"It contained naught," continued Mary, "but a white rose."

"Miscreant!" I mentally ejaculated, while a strong shudder swept through my form.

"But Oh that white rose, Ellen," proceeded Mary, not observing my emotion, "simple as the object itself may seem, yet was it the fatal cause of my undoing! But here let me declare that if that man had only attempted to take the slightest liberty with me—if by a single libertine look he had made me suspect the dark purpose of his soul —the veil would have fallen from my eyes, I should have rejected his overtures with scorn and indignation, I should have overwhelmed him with reproaches, and should have fled! This doubtless he knew: he had well studied my disposition and character—he had seen that I was not one who would willingly and wantonly abandon myself to a dishonourable course, and that therefore my ruin must be accomplished by a foul stratagem. And it was so. St. Clair smilingly bade me inhale the fragrance with which that artificial rose was fraught. I took it from the box—I approached it to my nostrils—and then all in a moment consciousness abandoned me."

Again did Mary Glentworth pause for nearly a minute: and then she added in a gloomier and more sombre tone than before, "When I recovered my senses, I was in a chamber——St. Clair was with me——my destruction had been accomplished!"

"Just heaven!" I murmured, "that such hideous iniquity should be perpetrated!"—and then folding Mary in my arms, I faltered out in a voice trembling with emotion, "You spoke truly, my dear friend, when you said that though weak, feeble, and indiscreet to a certain extent, yet that you were indeed very far from meriting the full amount of blame for this dread catastrophe!"

"No, Ellen," she responded: "it was as foul a crime as ever was perpetrated against the honour and virtue of a woman! I cannot depict the feelings with which I became aware of the mighty wrong thus done me. I did not rave, nor shriek, nor cry out: I was plunged into blank despair. This afforded leisure and opportunity to the villanous author of my ruin to address me in terms which showed—if any proof were now wanting—the utter heartlessness of his character. He represented that for my own sake I must keep the seal of silence upon my lips, and forbear from breathing a syllable which would proclaim my dishonour and degradation. He gave me to understand that it was entirely on my own account that he proffered this advice—for that he himself was perfectly indifferent to the exposure of the whole proceeding—that indeed he should rather glory in it—and that he should be looked upon as a fortunate man by his friends and acquaintances for having secured so charming a prize. He went on to intimate that if I thought fit, I might become his pensioned mistress — that the whole matter might be kept secret—that all I should have to do would be to represent to you, Ellen, that I preferred having a separate establishment — and that from you likewise might the real truth be thus hidden. I heard all that was said, though I did not voluntarily listen to it. I repeat, my soul was plunged into the stupor of blank despair: it seemed as if an awful consternation were upon me!—as if I had been smitten down by the storm of heaven, and was now waking again to hear the stupendous thunder continue to reverberate around me! Edwin St. Clair endeavoured to elicit from my lips a response to the propositions which he had been addressing unto me: he therefore lavished caresses upon me—or rather he attempted to do so; but I sprang away from him. Then, as he entreated me to be pacified, and as he appealed to the strength of his passion as an excuse for the treachery he had committed, I cut him short by telling him that I loathed and abhorred him—that I would sooner find myself a wretched mendicant in the streets than accept the gilded splendour which he offered me—and I concluded by declaring that all he could now do to mitigate, if possible, the atrocity of the outrage was to keep the secret, and not compel me to have recourse to suicide as the only refuge from degradation and disgrace. This prayer on my part that he would keep the secret, was in entire consonance with his own views and wishes; and indeed he himself had been recommending that course, as I have already stated. Then, Ellen, I left the house—and I returned hither. You had just come home from Willowbridge: I need not recapitulate all that took place between yourself and me. You can judge what was the state of my mind! But at one time I really did purpose to make you my confidant, and to reveal everything on the morrow. When the morrow came, however, I had not the courage. No!—I shrank from the idea of proclaiming to you how weak, how credulous, and how foolish I had been—and how this folly of mine had led to my ruin! When I looked up in your face, Ellen, and knew that you were pure and chaste, I could not bring my mind to confess that I was polluted and contaminated. I knew not how to act; there was no excuse which I could devise—no tale that I could tell you, to account for that mood in which I had returned home; and therefore I was compelled to shut myself up in that reserve which must doubtless have seemed so unkind and so ungenerous towards you. Oh, dear Ellen! believe me that I have not loved you less than I had been wont to do: but you can make allowances for the horribly afflicted state of my mind—for the mingled shame and despair which had possession of me!"

"Alas, my poor Mary," I exclaimed, "I can make every allowance! Oh, what a history of villany and iniquity is this which has just flowed from your lips! And you have cherished a desire for vengeance, Mary?—you have not once felt your love for that man reviving?"

"Oh, no!" cried Mary: "love for *him?*—it is impossible! I never loved him in reality: it was a fascination—a bewilderment of the mind at a moment when that mind was beginning to recover from the morbid influence of past circumstances, and was therefore perhaps more than ever susceptible of certain impressions. No! I never loved St. Clair as I loved Herbert Dalrymple: and Oh! even if it were the reverse—even if I *had* adored and worshipped the very ground upon which St. Clair trod—everything would have become changed within me by the foul treachery which he practised! It seems to me that true love can only associate itself with an idea of that which is noble

and magnanimous and high-souled, and that it must suffer annihilation in the presence of the unmasking of cold-blooded villany. But as I have already assured you, Ellen, whatsoever sentiment I in the first instance experienced for Edwin St. Clair, was not genuine love; and therefore it survived not the blow which was dealt to my feelings on that fatal day. The hope of vengeance has ever since been cherished in my heart!"

"And supposing, Mary," I said,—"only supposing for an instant, that Edwin St. Clair might be induced by coercion, by menaces and threats, to make you his wife——"

"No, Ellen!" interrupted Mary Glentworth; "I could not accompany that man to the altar! Oh, I would surrender up ten of the best years of my life to regain that diadem of purity which has been snatched from my brow; and you may believe me when I declare that immense are the sacrifices I would make in order to cover my shame with a gloss of virtue and stand before the world as a wedded wife! But to be the wife of *him*—No, no! it were impossible! I could not so far play the hypocrite as to kneel at the altar by the side of the man who has so foully wronged me! I would sooner want bread than receive it from such a source! Yes!"—and here Mary's naturally soft and amiable eyes glistened with an expression of fierceness,—"and I would sooner that the babe which I bear in my bosom should be born in shame and nameless, than that it should inherit that name which henceforth must to me be ever held accursed,—a name which I shall never breathe except in company with a malediction flowing from the heart!"

"There is something terrible in the very strength of your language, Mary," I said; "but it at least proves to me that on no consideration would you espouse the man who has so deeply wronged you."

"Never!" replied Mary emphatically. "Not once since my ruin has been accomplished have I ever entertained such an idea, nor experienced the scintillation of such a hope. I have not appealed to him to do me an act of justice—I have not once made the slightest attempt to communicate with him. I seem to be devoting myself to the idea of vengeance, if ever circumstances should place it in my power to inflict condign punishment upon Edwin St. Clair. Do you remember that evening ——it was about five or six weeks ago—when you went to the theatre to announce to Mr. Richards your intended return to the stage——we remained to see the ballet——"

"I remember it perfectly," I said; "and that very same evening Mr. St. Clair was present in the theatre."

"Yes—it was to this very incident I was about to allude," responded Mary Glentworth. "It was the first time he had been to the theatre since his iniquitous conduct towards myself——or at least it was the first time that I had seen him there——"

"But when I pointed him out to you," I interjected, "little suspecting how well you knew him—and even considering it possible that you might have forgotten who he was since the night you saw him in the House of Commons,—you seemed to be as calm and self-possessed, or rather as cold and indifferent——"

"Yes—I know it," said Mary; "and I experienced at the time a species of stern satisfaction at the thought that I could thus exercise so much control over myself. Then more than ever was I convinced that at no time had I entertained the slightest scintillation of genuine love for Edwin St. Clair ; for from the box in which I was seated by your side, Ellen, I could look upon him with the coldness of an implacable hatred, — that hatred which needed not to excite itself, because it could bide its time in the fierce stern hope that sooner or later its craving would be appeased and it would be enabled to gloat over a vengeance terrifically wreaked !"

"But this evening, Mary," I said—"this evening, when I entered the box and beheld you leaning back in your seat — your countenance pale as marble—your limbs rigid—your eyes glaring unnaturally——"

"I have already told you, Ellen," interrupted Mary Glentworth, "that I had discerned St. Clair seated by the side of the beautiful Lady Lilla Essendine. I must frankly confess that at the moment an unaccountable feeling of jealousy sprang up in my heart. All the hatred which had previously been concentrated against Edwin St. Clair, seemed to take Lilla Essendine within its ominous scope. I thought to myself that if he were paying his addresses to her, it would be with a really honourable intention, and that he would make her his bride, because *she* was a lady by social position and by title, and it might be for him a brilliant alliance. Therefore rage took possession of my heart at the thought that as I was an actress, it was for this reason I had been made a dupe and a victim; whereas if I had been a titled lady, St. Clair's suit would have been honourably intended !"

"My dear Mary," I said, "do not rely too much upon the notions and opinions you may form in reference to Edwin St. Clair. He is swayed by no considerations of decency or propriety whatsoever, in any details of his conduct. He no more sacrificed you simply because you were an actress, than he would marry Lilla Essendine or any other patrician lady merely on account of the possession of a title. But you speak of the jealous rage which seized upon you this evening——"

"I am not quite sure, Ellen," said Mary, "that I have properly explained my sentiments. Of Lady Lilla Essendine I could not exactly be jealous—inasmuch as if Edwin St. Clair had risen straight from her side to offer me his hand and beseech that I would accompany him to the altar, I should have rejected the proposal with loathing and abhorrence. Therefore I could not look upon Lady Lilla Essendine as a rival who was receiving certain attentions which were coveted by myself: for none such did I covet! But as I looked at Lady Lilla Essendine, my thoughts seemed to apostrophise her with great bitterness, as if I were thus speaking:—'Ah! because you are a lady of rank and title, he would not dare to perpetrate an outrage against you. No!—whatsoever word he may breathe in your ear, will be truthful in the sense which it conveys; and if he whisper the language of love, it will not be intended as a snare! Thus, *you*, proud lady, have immunities and privileges which are denied to the actress, who in his eyes exists but as a being to be made the toy of his pleasure and serve his fantasy !'

—It was thus that my thoughts flowed as I regarded Lady Lilla Essendine; and I included her in the hatred which I experienced for St. Clair."

"It was a strangely morbid state of mind, Mary," I observed; "for whatever Lady Lilla Essendine may be towards others——and observe! I am passing no opinion upon her!—— she at all events has done nothing to injure you."

"I know it, Ellen. But there are certain moods," continued Mary, "in which passions and prejudices blind the soul against all reason and justice,—causing the hatred which should attach itself only to one, to be reflected on another,— filling the mind with false ideas, and making the mental vision view every object through a still falser medium."

"Yes—it is so," I observed. "And now, my poor Mary, that you have unbosomed all your secrets to me, let me entreat that you will retire to rest. You know that in every sense you have in me something more than a friend—you have one who loves you as if you were a sister! You demand vengeance on the man who has so cruelly wronged you; and I cannot fly in the face of human nature itself by telling you *not* to seek for such vengeance. No!—were I in your position, I also should yearn to be avenged! Therefore, Mary, it is even possible that as your friend—as your pledged sister—I may assist you in your vengeance—I may perhaps find the means or indicate the way——"

"Oh do this, Ellen," ejaculated Mary Glentworth, "and you know not how illimitable will be my gratitude! But understand me well, Ellen! What I mean by the word *vengeance* is something that I may do to that man without having the blow redound upon myself. I do not wish this blow to be twofold—to strike *him* and to strike *me* at the same time. I will not render myself a martyr to my own vengeance. These are my ideas. If they were otherwise, I need not have waited for the opportunity to wreak a vengeance : I need not be still waiting, and prepared to wait for weeks and months—perhaps even for years, before my aim can be accomplished. No!—because I might have lain wait for him with a loaded pistol in my hand; and I might have taken his life. Ah! but I should have thereby sacrificed my own life—I should have given it up to the law, the gibbet, and the executioner! This would have been sorry vengeance. The vengeance I crave, dear Ellen, is that which can be inflicted without injuring a hair of my own head——"

"And it is such a vengeance as this, Mary, that you shall wreak," I answered. "Trust to me, my dear friend! The career of that man's infamy has already lasted too long!—it must draw to a close! And now good night, Mary—and remember that in me you have a friend and a sister !"

We embraced each other tenderly. All that reserve, and even cold diffidence, which for some little time past had characterized Mary Glentworth's bearing towards me, now disappeared :— there was no secret which she kept from me, and consequently there was no barrier betwixt the sympathies of our souls. She was once more the affectionate, confiding, frank-hearted Mary Glentworth towards me :—but Oh! how different was the position of the poor girl from what it used

to be in the days of her artless innocence, when she was a dweller at the picturesque cottage in the neighbourhood of Dover, and had never known what love was—had never been subject to temptation—had never experienced a dark feeling of hatred—and had never from her red lips fiercely breathed the word *revenge!*

CHAPTER XCIII.

ANGELINE.

On bidding Mary Glentworth good night, I retired to my own chamber, where I found Beda sitting up for me. I had quite forgotten that the faithful girl would be sure thus to await me; and on beholding her, I was much concerned at my

neglect in not having dismissed her long ago to her own bed; for it was now close upon two o'clock in the morning.

"My dear girl," I said, "to think that you should have been sitting up for me!"

"It is not only my duty, but also a pleasure, dear Miss," responded Beda. "Do you know that I always look forward with so much delight to this half-hour when I am alone with you in the privacy of your own chamber, before retiring to rest?"

"And why so, Beda?" I asked, surveying her beautiful countenance with an affectionate interest.

"Because," she responded, "it seems that the hour for retiring is also that of the outpourings of confidence. If ever you tell me anything of a private and secret nature, my dear Miss, it is generally when we are alone together on the occasion of your night-toilet; and therefore it always appears as if it were the moment when you bestow especial marks of your kindness upon me."

"And therefore, Beda," I said, smiling, "if I were now to bid you at once retire to your own chamber, instead of remaining to assist me at my toilet, you would be sorry?"

"Oh yes! I would rather remain with you," she exclaimed. "Look, dear Miss! do I seem at all sleepy?"—and she gazed with her large black luminous eyes up into my countenance.

I sat down before the mirror; and Beda began combing out my hair. I was forcing myself to assume an aspect as composed as possible, for fear she might think that I had remained so long in Mary Glentworth's chamber on account of the discussion of unpleasant matters;—and in order to touch upon a cheerful topic, I said, "I was very glad to hear from William Lardner, when he called upon you this morning, Beda, that he continues to be so happy and comfortable in his situation with Sir Robert Temple."

"Oh, yes!" exclaimed Beda: "William is as happy as the day is long. Sir Robert Temple is at bottom a very kind-hearted man, though so eccentric and peculiar; and as William has now been with him exactly two months and a half——"

"So long as that?" I said. "Heavens! how time slips away! It seems that it was but the other day Sir Robert called upon me to inquire what I knew concerning William."

"It is two months and a half, Miss," interjected Beda. "It was in the middle of July when William accepted the situation: it is now the first of October. But have I happened to mention to you, Miss," continued Beda, "that William frequently sees an old employer of his?—a gentleman whose name," she added, in a lower tone, "it is impossible to breathe without a shudder at the wickedness of his character, and a deep regret that it should be so."

"You mean——"

"I mean Captain St. Clair—or Mr. St. Clair, as I believe he has called himself ever since he became a Cabinet Minister and a Right Honourable, —as if he wished to be thought of only as the statesman and without any reference to the fact of his having ever been a military man. But as I was observing, Miss, William frequently sees Mr. St. Clair—nearly every day indeed——"

"Ah, I remember," I ejaculated, "that Sir Robert Temple's house is in the Regent's Park: but I am not aware in which quarter it is situated."

"It is the very next house to Mr. St. Clair's," rejoined Beda.

"Ah, the next house?" I said. "And does Mr. St. Clair seem to recognise William?"

"I believe not, Miss," replied Beda; "at least if he recognise William, he does not choose to show that such is the fact. But it is now, you know, upwards of fifteen months since William left Mr. St. Clair's service; and he has grown more manly since then — his appearance has altered——"

"Depend upon it, Beda," I said, "Mr. St. Clair *has* recognised him. All the circumstances connected with the yacht at Ramsgate, are too deeply impressed on St. Clair's mind not to main-tain in his memory the countenance of William Lardner. Besides, my dear Beda," I added, smiling, "William's face is not an ordinary one— it is quite good-looking enough to make an impression—especially when the duskiness of the complexion is taken into consideration."

"Well then, Miss," said Beda, "let us suppose that Mr. St. Clair *has* recognised William: he is nevertheless too proud to acknowledge any former acquaintance—or perhaps he thinks that it would be more convenient to bury all the circumstances of the yacht as much in oblivion as possible."

"Perhaps so," I said in a musing tone; for it struck me the coincidence was somewhat singular that William Lardner's name should be mentioned in connexion with that of Mr. St. Clair at a moment when I was revolving in my mind how and where I could find a faithful and trustworthy individual to undertake a task requiring more or less astuteness and delicacy of management.

"William," continued Beda, little suspecting what was passing in my mind or how suggestive all her observations were gradually becoming, "frequently speaks to Mr. St. Clair's domestics; and there is an old housekeeper at Mr. St. Clair's abode, who has taken a very great liking for William, because she says that he resembles a nephew of whom she was very fond, but who died at an early age, of some malignant fever."

"And what is the name of this housekeeper?" I asked, in a musing manner, as I still revolved the point which Beda's words had suggested.

"Mrs. Holman," answered the young girl. "But methinks, dear Miss, there is something in your mind?—something which is occupying you, apart from the present topic of our discourse——"

"Not so completely apart from it as you might fancy, Beda," I responded. "On the contrary, it seems to me to be something more than a mere coincidence that William Lardner should be dwelling next door to Mr. St. Clair—that he should have formed an intimacy with his servants—that he should have attracted the favourable notice of the very domestic who if she choose can invite him into the house——"

"I now comprehend," exclaimed Beda, "that you desire William Lardner to undertake some special task which you are willing to entrust unto him. You know, my dear Miss, that he will go through fire and water to serve you—and I need not add that such service would be faithfully rendered."

"Yes, Beda," I rejoined, in a solemn voice, "there *is* indeed a service which William can render me—but not merely to myself alone; it is a service that he will be rendering to society in general! In a word, Beda, I may tell you this much,—that the knowledge of fresh misdeeds on the part of Edwin St. Clair has reached me; and if I any longer permit him to make use of the terrible weapons which he has in his possession, I shall look upon myself as an accomplice in his crimes. The career of that man must have an end!——yes, a speedy ending!— and William must assist us in bringing it about."

"He will do so, dear Miss," responded Beda. "You have at all times only to speak, and both William and myself are prepared to obey you implicitly."

"I know it, my faithful Beda," I replied. "And

now listen to my instructions—or rather let me tell you what it is that I require; and then I shall leave it to the ingenuity of William—perhaps with some little suggestions from yourself," I added, smiling, " to accomplish the desired aim. There is in St. Clair's house a small rosewood box of curious workmanship. It is no doubt for the most part under lock and key; and perhaps it is usually secured in some safe place in his own bed-chamber. That little box, Beda, to which I am alluding, contains a white rose; and it is for this reason that I must obtain possession of the box. When once the evidence of all St. Clair's guilt is in my hands, I may be enabled to dictate any terms to him —in the first place compelling him to make atonement where he has offended and where such atonement would be accepted—and afterwards compelling him to quit for ever a land which has become the theatre of so many misdeeds on his part. Or if from a certain quarter," I continued in a musing strain, " a still darker vengeance be demanded—if it be required that this man's life shall be given up to the offended laws of his country—then shall even this extreme measure be adopted, and retribution in its direst form shall meet Edwin St. Clair face to face!"

" But to accomplish any of these purposes," said Beda, " you require the rosewood box; and I can only too well understand that it is a poisoned flower which it contains. Ah, dear Miss! never shall I forget that fearful occasion when at the hut in the neighbourhood of Petersfield, the vile old hag Dame Betty rendered you insensible with the white rose! And Edwin St. Clair possesses a similar weapon!—for a weapon indeed it is! But rest assured that William shall procure it. To-morrow I will see him——"

" To-day you mean, my dear girl," I exclaimed, glancing at my watch; " for it is now close upon three o'clock in the morning."

I then dismissed my faithful dependant to her own couch, while I sought mine. In the dreams which visited me the images of Mary Glentworth and Edwin St. Clair were conspicuous : and my fancy represented the former as swooning away from a white rose which the latter was thrusting into her countenance.

In the course of the day following the night of Mary Glentworth's confession, Beda sought an interview with William Lardner, and communicated to him the desire which I had expressed that he should undertake a special service. He readily agreed : the nature of the affair was explained to him; and he vowed that he would accomplish the task. At the same time, though expressing himself thus confidently, he begged Beda to represent to me that there might be some little delay previous to the effectual carrying out of the project, as it was one which must be managed with caution and with delicacy—opportunities must be watched for—and, in short, the enterprise needed tact, vigilance, and sound discretion. Beda reported to me the result of her interview with her lover William; and I was well pleased to learn that he spoke so confidently in respect to the issue of the affair—while I bade her enjoin him the next time they met, that he was by no means to endanger the success of the issue by haste and precipitation.

Some few days after the occurrences which I have just been relating, I had occasion to call at the theatre at about the hour of noon. An author of some promise had written a drama which Mr. Richards felt disposed to produce, provided the character which was cast for myself should experience my approval. The author was to meet us there at the time of which I am speaking, and was to read to me some of the principal speeches which he had put into the mouth of the heroine. I was somewhat too early for the appointment; and proceeding towards the stage, I paused to gaze upon the *danseuses* who were practising under the auspices of M. Duprez—the ballet-master. This was the first occasion on which I had seen Angeline Churchill in her private apparel. I now beheld her in a plain modest garb; and methought that it became her infinitely more than the gauzes, the tinsel, and the trumpery which constituted her professional costume. I have already said that she was about two-and-twenty years of age, possessing a handsome face and a fine person. She was genteel in her bearing, and seemed unexceptionally lady-like in her manners. From the very first I had been interested in her; for it was now nearly six weeks since I had learnt from the lips of Mr. Richards the manner in which he first became acquainted with her. It was not only in consequence of the tale of misfortune which I then heard, but likewise on account of her modest and well-behaved demeanour, that I felt interested in Angeline. But strange to say I had not as yet spoken to her on any single occasion: we had never been thrown together; and two or three times when I had endeavoured to fling myself in her way I had failed to accomplish my aim. It had once or twice struck me that she purposely strove to avoid me; and yet I banished this idea almost as speedily as it was formed: for what earthly reason could she have for such conduct? However, to be brief, I had never once exchanged a syllable with Angeline; and yet for the past six weeks I had felt so much interested in her!

But if, as I have already said, I had thought her exceedingly good-looking when dressed in the ballet costume, I was infinitely more pleased with her on now beholding her in her private apparel. It suited so well with the natural modesty of her appearance; while on the other hand the placid and somewhat melancholy expression of her countenance seemed to be mocked by the meretricious garb of the ballet-dancer. Angeline had dark brown hair, shining with a natural gloss: her eyes were of violet blue, and not particularly large; her nose was perfectly straight—her mouth was beautifully formed—and her chin in its configuration completed the perfect oval of the countenance. Her forehead was not high; and this might by some critics be considered a fault— though I myself am of a different opinion; for if the Greek statues are to be taken as the types and models of true feminine beauty, they assuredly for the most part furnish an argument that low foreheads are the standard of perfection. I may be permitted thus to record my opinions, inasmuch as being possessed of a very high forehead, I cannot possibly be accused of seeking excuses for what the world might deem a defect if belonging to my own countenance. Speaking however of Angeline Churchill, I should add that the face suffered not in the slightest degree from the lowness of the forehead—but seemed as open, frank, and candid as if the brow were of the loftiest dimensions.

She was tall and possessed of a fine figure; indeed I have already said that in this respect she reminded me of my friend Juliet—and the newspapers had recorded a similar sentiment. If she danced with exceeding grace and lightness, there was an equal amount of elegance in her walk when clad in plain clothes; and if there were something which was no doubt deemed by the male sex to be fascinating and ravishing in her appearance when on the stage, there was assuredly a still more interesting and prepossessing air about her when viewed in her own plain, modest, but neat raiment.

I was now determined to speak to Angeline Churchill. She did not appear to be altogether happy; and I thought that possibly she might be friendless in the great metropolis. Besides, the circumstances attending her first introduction to Mr. Richards, proved that she must have been acquainted with no small amount of misfortune. Perhaps she required a friend?—perhaps even though now rescued from the iron grasp of poverty, she nevertheless might have other sorrows which could be consoled with the sympathy of friendship? These were the thoughts that passed through my brain; and at all events I determined to speak to her.

But while I was thus contemplating the proceedings of the ballet-dancers, my looks being chiefly riveted upon Angeline, I beheld Melissa Harrison emerge from one of the opposite "wings" and take her place amongst the troupe. The instant her eyes caught mine, they were averted; and I saw that the colour deepened upon her countenance. She had never once attempted to speak to me—she had never dared even to approach me, since we had both happened to return at about the same time to the stage.

I should observe that Melissa was exceedingly jealous of Angeline, by whom she was assuredly equalled if not eclipsed. Some little gossip in respect to this feeling on Miss Harrison's part had reached my ears; and now as I stood contemplating the two, I saw enough to convince me that the rumour was perfectly correct. When in the presence of the audience, Melissa would not of course have dared to display her irritable feelings: but now that it was merely a rehearsal, she was not compelled to put any such restraint upon herself—nor did even the shame which she felt in my presence induce her to study the proprieties of demeanour.

"That is not your place, Miss Churchill!" exclaimed Melissa angrily.

"I beg your pardon, Miss Harrison," answered Angeline, with a lady-like calmness and self-possession: "I believe that this is my place—and if we appeal to M. Duprez——"

The ballet-master at once settled the question by declaring that Miss Churchill was perfectly correct.

"Oh, of course!" ejaculated Melissa, with a contemptuous toss of the head; "if Miss Churchill were wrong, M. Duprez would swear that she was right!"

"Silence, Miss Harrison!" ejaculated the ballet-master; "your words would be an insult, were they not beneath contempt!"

"Ah! beneath contempt—are they?" ejaculated Melissa, now unable to restrain her rage. "Then I tell you what, M. Duprez,—you may report me to the manager if you like, and get me my dismissal! The sooner the better! I won't dance any longer in company with Miss Churchill! She is constantly putting me out—she usurps my place —she thrusts herself forward as if to receive all the applause of the audience—in a word, she is a conceited minx!"

Here M. Duprez stamped his foot impatiently, and then began scraping away vehemently at his fiddle, or rather kit. The storm seemed to have passed over—at least Melissa now remained silent; but I noticed with feelings of mingled indignation and sorrow that Angeline Churchill looked very much distressed at the treatment which she had sustained. And now there came a part in the new ballet which was being rehearsed, where Angeline had to go forward and dance alone for some minutes. This spectacle was more than Melissa Harrison could endure; and with a sudden ejaculation which had a sort of screaming accent in it, she cried, "It is my place you are taking—and you shall not supplant me!"

"Silence, Miss Harrison!" ejaculated M. Duprez.

"Not for an old fool like you!" she vociferated. "Of course there is something between you and Miss Churchill, with all her modest looks! The stillest water runs the deepest! I don't like your modest people! Prudery is a mask——"

Here she was interrupted by cries of "Shame!" from the lips of several of the other dancing-girls; while M. Duprez had gone off in a rage to seek for Mr. Richards.

"Who cries Shame?" ejaculated Melissa. "I say it is all true!" she added, fiercely, and assuming a sudden air of defiance. "Let Churchill deny it if she can! I'll take my oath any day that she is the mistress of that old French rascal Duprez!"

At this juncture I was hastening forward in the hope of being enabled to wield my own authority and rescue poor Angeline Churchill from the abuse and invectives which Melissa was throwing forth, —when at that moment Angeline exclaimed, "It is false, Miss Harrison!—it is false! It is a vile malignant calumny——"

But here Angeline suddenly stopped short—her face became deadly pale—I saw her stagger as if she were about to faint—I sprang forward, and caught her in my arms. At that same instant consciousness abandoned her; and it was an inanimate form that I was sustaining.

"For shame of you, Melissa! It is shameful! it is infamous!" ejaculated the surrounding ballet-girls. "Miss Churchill gave you no offence!"

"Why does she put herself forward to supplant me?" demanded Melissa, trembling with rage.

"Help me to bear Miss Churchill to my own dressing-room," I said. "The conduct she has experienced is most abominable!"

As I thus spoke, I bent a withering glance upon Melissa. She seemed for an instant as if she were inclined to hurl back defiance at me, and even burst forth in some abusive attack against myself; but doubtless a second thought made her reflect it would be more prudent for her to hold her tongue —for I could have told a tale in reference to a certain cheque and a certain Marquis which would have for ever branded Melissa with infamy.

Miss Churchill was conveyed to my own room, where I laid her upon the sofa, and began to administer restoratives. Two other ballet-dancers had helped to support their companion thither. It was only a few minutes back that I had been longing to speak to Angeline, and had resolved to throw myself in her way; and now accident had flung us together! I wished to be alone with her; and I said to the two girls, "You would perhaps do well to leave your companion to my care. She has been grossly insulted, and her nerves have been strongly acted upon. See! she is recovering! the presence of several persons may excite her —— leave her alone with me, that I may console and soothe her."

The two *danseuses* accordingly retired; and scarcely had the door of the dressing-room closed behind them, when a strange incident took place. Angeline Churchill at that instant opened her violet eyes; but no sooner did her gaze meet mine, when all languor and faintness suddenly abandoned her—and with an ejaculation which struck me as being full of mingled terror and aversion, she sprang from my arms,—for though lying upon the sofa, yet her head was pillowed upon my bosom.

"Good heavens! what is the matter, Miss Churchill?" I exclaimed. "You are not with an enemy!—you are with a friend!"

"A friend?" ejaculated Angeline, in accents so singular that I was hurt, affrighted, and bewildered; for her voice seemed to indicate the bitterness of hatred mingled with scorn and contempt.

"Is it possible," I ejaculated, involuntarily giving audible utterance to the thought which now suddenly flashed to my mind!—"is it possible that her brain is turned?"

"No, Miss Percy," she responded, having caught the words which had thus issued from my lips: "my brain is not turned!"

I started when she addressed me by my proper name of Percy; for though it was pretty generally known in theatrical circles, and even beyond them, what my real name was, yet no one except private friends ever addressed me otherwise than as Miss Trafford—especially when at the theatre.

"Yes," repeated Angeline Churchill, with what appeared to me to be a renewed bitterness of tone, and with a look of hatred flashing out of her violet eyes,—"I never was more sane in my life; but I would rather be mad than by the lucid possession of my reason be enabled to comprehend that I am placed under an obligation to *you!*"

Astonishment for a few moments held me silent: I was confounded and bewildered. At length drawing myself up to the fulness of my tall stature, I said with a cold dignity, "It were a charity, Miss Churchill, to believe that you are insane, in order to acquit you of the grossest and most unaccountable breach of good manners which I ever had the misfortune to contemplate."

"I care as little for the evil as I do for the good opinion of Ellen Percy," retorted Angeline,—whose nature which I had hitherto believed to be so gentle, seemed to be transformed into that of a tigress—or rather to be developing qualities of evil and capacities of hatred which methought must have lain strangely dormant before.

"At all events, Miss Churchill," I said, still speaking with a dignified coldness—though actually I found it difficult to prevent myself from bursting into tears; for I was cruelly hurt, shocked, and afflicted, by the conduct of Angeline towards me,—"but at all events, Miss Churchill, you will perhaps explain in what manner I have been unfortunate enough to offend you; for I can assure you that I am not so indifferent as *you* affect to be to the good or evil opinions of my fellow-creatures—and as I am utterly unconscious of having done aught that might provoke your rancour——"

"You have done everything!" ejaculated Angeline wildly; "you have reduced me to what I am!"—then throwing herself upon the sofa, she burst into an agony of tears.

"Good heaven!" I thought within myself; "after all the poor creature is demented!—and I have been treating her so coldly and haughtily!"—then advancing towards Angeline, I said in a mild soothing voice, "No, no! I am incapable of doing you an injury! On the contrary, I experienced a feeling of interest towards you from the very first moment I beheld you——"

"Ah! a feeling of interest in *me?*" ejaculated Miss Churchill, suddenly removing her hands from her countenance, and looking up at me with her violet eyes which still expressed fierce hatred even through the tears that were standing in them: "a feeling of interest in *me!* But do you know me?" she abruptly demanded.

"Know you?" I said, again smitten with astonishment, and also with a cruel misgiving in respect to her sanity. "I know you as Angeline Churchill—a name which perhaps is not your own any more than mine is really Trafford——"

"But by any other name do you know me?" she demanded, with sudden fierceness, as she riveted her eyes upon my countenance; and her white teeth gleamed between her quivering lips which were almost as white themselves.

"No," I responded—but not without a sensation of affright lest she should suddenly burst forth into a maniac violence and spring furiously upon me.

"Ah! I thought not!" muttered Angeline: and then she was moving towards the door, when she turned as if a sudden thought had smitten her, and she exclaimed with renewed fierceness and violence, "Ah! you felt an interest in me? Could it have been that in your soul there was a presentiment that I was a being who had suffered on your account—yes, a presentiment which made you feel that you had wronged me, although you still remained in utter ignorance of who I really was! Oh, away with all pretended feeling and interest! You have no pity and no compunction! Have you not reduced me to what I am?—is it not through you that I have become a ballet-dancer?—through you therefore that I have been compelled to submit to the insults of that impertinent young woman whose tainted reputation renders it horrible and loathsome for me to come in contact with her? Now do not think I am mad, Miss Percy! *You* are not more sane than I! But enough. Perhaps the time will come when you may know more! At all events deem not that you have laid me under an obligation to you:—I would kill myself if I thought for a single moment that it was so!"

Having thus spoken, Angeline Churchill quitted the dressing-room, closing the door behind her, and leaving me a prey to the utmost perplexity, astonishment, and even dismay. Could the unfortunate young woman be really mad? — was she labouring under some extraordinary monomania in reference to myself? I assuredly had never seen her until within the last few weeks—at least not to my knowledge; and as for having in any way consciously injured her, it was entirely out of the question. How was it possible that I could have been the means of reducing her to the position of a ballet-dancer? Truly, the idea of monomania seemed the most probable theory to account for her conduct;—and yet I was not altogether satisfied that this was the correct explanation of the mystery; for her looks had not been those of one whose brain was disordered: on the contrary, there was a terrible saneness—a fearful collectedness, in the fierce looks of hatred with which she had regarded me. But if not insane, how was her behaviour to be possibly reconciled to all circumstances that were within my knowledge? And Oh! in any case, it was distressing to think that one whom I had looked upon as being so meek and mild, could all of a sudden develop such strong capabilities for aversion and hatred; for scorn and contempt! Ah, methought that her feelings must have been cruelly warped; and who could tell what misfortunes and calamities she had known previous to obtaining her bread by the profession of a ballet-dancer,—that profession which she evidently so much loathed and abhorred!

While I was giving way to these reflections—bewildering myself with conjectures — thinking that something ought to be done, yet knowing not what I should do—the door again opened, and the object of my painful thoughts reappeared. Yes—Angeline Churchill stood upon the threshold: her face was now perfectly calm, though very pale—and her violet eyes were fixed steadfastly upon me with the completest lucidity of expression. Indeed, as I have already said, even in their very fierceness there had been naught rabid in their look. I fancied that the period of monomania having left her, she was repentant for her conduct, and that she came to apologize. I rose from the chair on which I had remained seated in deep and painful meditation; and I advanced to take her hand, thinking that I could anticipate her purpose by the assurance that she was completely forgiven. But she drew back with a cold hauteur amounting almost to a repelling disdain; and she said, "Miss Percy, if you consider that I am under the slightest obligation towards you, I may as well ask something which will enhance that obligation. I beg therefore that what has taken place between us may be kept entirely secret. I do not say I am actually sorry for whatsoever has transpired; but I confess that I was taken off my guard—and perhaps I said more than I intended——perhaps I betrayed my feelings too far. Therefore, I repeat, let the seal of secrecy rest upon your lips. You are all-powerful here; and a word from your tongue would cause my dismissal. You would thereby be depriving me of my bread. Heaven knows I often eat it in bitterness when I think how it is earned!—but it were still more bitter to have none to eat—espe-

cially as there is one dependent upon me. I say no more. I know that if you have made up your mind to complain to the lessee, nothing will divert you from your purpose: but I know on the other hand that if you say the secret shall be kept, your word will not be forfeited."

I could scarcely any longer imagine that the person who thus spoke collectedly to me was really wrong in her mind; and therefore I exclaimed, "There must be some frightful mistake, Miss Churchill! What injury do you suppose that I could ever have done you?"

"No matter, Miss Percy," she responded. "This is not the time for explanations. Perhaps that time will never come! At all events let us be strangers to each other for the future;—and I repeat, it depends upon yourself whether I lose my bread!"

"Whoever you may be," I ejaculated,—"and whatsoever deplorable error you may be labouring under, you have nothing to dread from any vindictiveness on my part! From all that I can now perceive or imagine, you deserve my pity—my sympathy—my commiseration!—and therefore it is by no means probable that I shall attempt to persecute you."

"Your pity!" she ejaculated, in a tone of ineffable contempt and scorn, again mingled with the strongest aversion: but instantaneously altering alike her tone and look, she added in a much milder voice, "Well, your pity!—be it so! I am sufficiently inured to everything which this world can inflict, that I can now even support that! Well then, I repeat, be it so!—Your pity! and now for pity's sake," she added with a slight tincture of irony in her tone, "let the veil be dropped upon this scene which has taken place between us."

Having thus spoken, Angeline Churchill again disappeared from my presence. I was so much excited and bewildered by everything which had occurred, that I could not immediately leave my dressing-room: I remained there to compose myself, and likewise to reflect. But my reflections flowed in the same channel as before; and again was I painfully balanced by conjecture between the idea of her saneness and that of her madness. At length I issued from my room; and I speedily learnt the issue of the scene which Melissa Harrison had that day in her jealousy excited. She had received a prompt dismissal from Mr. Richards: she had not thought fit to make any apology—she had not requested permission to remain—but she had shut herself up in a sullen reserve and a moody silence. In this humour she had left the theatre.

The dramatic author had sent an apology for his non-appearance, — alleging a sudden and very severe indisposition which prevented him from attending according to appointment; and I was by no means sorry that this had occurred, inasmuch as I was now in no mood to listen to the reading of any drama or portion of one. But while still thinking of the strange scene which had taken place betwixt myself and Angeline, I said to Mr. Richards, as if in quite a casual way, "Have you ever heard anything more respecting the circumstances which compelled Miss Churchill to seek an engagement with you?"

"Never," he responded. "I know no more of her private history than I did at the outset; and I believe that I narrated it all to you one night in a private box——"

"Yes," I said: "I remember. But do you not happen to know whether Miss Churchill lives with her family—father, mother, brothers, and sisters——"

"I know absolutely nothing about her," interrupted Mr. Richards; and I felt convinced he was speaking the truth. "She seems to be a very nice young lady—quiet, modest, and well-behaved; and really there was not the slightest ground for the base insinuations thrown out by Miss Harrison! Duprez was very indignant——"

"By the bye," I said, "you know, I believe, where Miss Churchill lives?"

"Ah, I understand you, Miss Trafford!" ejaculated Mr. Richards; "your good heart is ever prompting you to act kindly towards your fellow-creatures. You think that poor Miss Churchill may require the consolations of friendship after the gross insult she has received——"

"But if I were to take it into my head to call upon her," I interjected, "you will keep the matter secret, Mr. Richards?"

"Why, of course!" he exclaimed. "It would not do for Miss Trafford the great tragedian, courted and looked up to as she is—more thought of than any peeress in the land—a lady riding in her own carriage—to be suspected of making calls upon a ballet-dancer. No! no! Do you pursue your charitable course; and rest assured that the secret shall be well kept by me."

As the reader may thoroughly understand, nothing was further from my purpose than to consult my pride in the matter; and indeed I had no such pride at all; for it was scarcely an hour since I had determined upon making friends with the ballet-dancer and inviting her to my house. But I suffered Mr. Richards to remain under this delusion, because I did not wish him to mention that I had in any way questioned him in reference to Angeline Churchill, for fear lest it should reach her ears that I had been making inquiries concerning her.

"Ah!" I said, "you have now forgotten to tell me where she lives."

"Oh! that information can be soon supplied," ejaculated the lessee; "for I think I have already told you that very shortly after Miss Churchill obtained an engagement at the theatre, she voluntarily gave me her address, in case she might be at any moment wanted. Have the goodness to step with me as far as my room. I know the address is somewhere in Long Acre—but I have forgotten the number."

I accompanied Mr. Richards: he seated himself at his desk, which was completely smothered with correspondence, playbills, manuscripts of dramas, and documents of various descriptions. But still there was a certain order in all this seeming confusion; for he was a man of method and regularity—and it was owing to these qualities, as well as to the vast sums which I had been the means of bringing into his treasury, that he kept his head so well above water while so many other theatres were continuously entailing bankruptcy upon their lessees. He therefore knew in a moment where to lay his hand upon his address-book; and he copied upon a slip of paper the abode of Angeline Churchill.

I now at once returned home to Great Ormond Street, having made up my mind how to act. I had simply promised Angeline that the scene which had occurred betwixt us should remain a secret; but I had not pledged myself to abstain from making any inquiries concerning her. These inquiries I was resolved to institute; and in this course I was impelled by no mere idle curiosity—on the contrary, I was anxious to ascertain if there were any ground for the supposition that she had ever sustained any ill at my hands, or if any circumstances could by a possibility have led her to such a belief. For I could not rest easy under the imputation; and I was determined to satisfy myself whether it were the raving of a monomaniac, or whether in perfect saneness she might be labouring under some deplorable error. The point once ascertained, I should know how to act. If by any chance an unremembered inadvertance, or an involuntary act of unkindness on my part, had directly or indirectly furnished ground for the accusation, I was resolved to study the best means of making ample atonement; but if it should prove on inquiry that in some aberration of intellect she had formed erroneous and delusive notions with regard to me, I would do my best to disabuse her.

Accordingly, on reaching Great Ormond Street, I once more had recourse to my faithful fairy-like Beda. I simply told her that I had reasons for instituting particular inquiries in respect to a certain person: and the girl never displayed any curiosity, or asked more than I chose to tell her. I bade her use the utmost discretion and tact in performing the part entrusted to her. I intimated that there was some one who lived in dependence upon Miss Churchill; I knew not who this some one could be—but could only presume that it was a parent, or a young brother or sister. I instructed Beda to commence her inquiries in the evening when Angeline should be at the theatre; and I gave the faithful girl the address which I had received from Mr. Richards.

It was not my evening to appear at the theatre; but I accompanied Mary Glentworth. When we returned home, I retired to my chamber almost immediately; for I was anxious to learn the result of Beda's expedition. It was completely unsatisfactory.

"I went to Long Acre, as indicated on the slip of paper," she said; "and I passed by the house specified as Miss Churchill's address. It is a small jeweller's shop. I presently entered, and intimated to an old man who stood behind the counter that I wished to make a small purchase. He showed me some lockets which I asked for: I bought one—and as I paid the price, I inquired, as if casually, whether he knew of any cheap and respectable lodgings to be let in Long Acre? He reflected for a few moments, and then said that he did not; but that doubtless in some of the neighbouring streets I should find what I required. I then said that it struck me I had once seen a bill announcing lodgings to let in his window. He assured me that I must be mistaken—for that he never let lodgings: he had been in the house twenty years, and had occupied it solely for the use of his family and two or three workmen, as he was a working jeweller. I was already prepared with fresh observations in case of emergencies: but in order to avert suspicion, and account for my lingering in the shop, I proceeded to purchase another little article. While settling for this, I began speaking of the theatre; and still as if casually, I inquired if he ever went thither? He replied that he did occasionally; and he spoke of you, dear Miss, in terms of the highest eulogy. I asked him if he admired Miss Harrison as a dancer? I named one or two others who are favourites in the ballet; and then I mentioned Mademoiselle Angeline. I do not know whether it were mere fancy on my part—I really cannot tell—but it struck me that he glanced singularly up at my countenance for a moment; and then he said in the same quiet way as before, that he had seen Mademoiselle Angeline once at the theatre, but that he was no admirer of the ballet. I dared say no more: I was afraid of exciting suspicion, in case he knew of circumstances which he was purposely suppressing,—and I left the shop."

"This is strange!" I observed. "But you are sure that you went to the right address?"

"As sure as that I am here," responded Beda. "But I have not quite told you all. I was determined not to be defeated if there were possibly a means of gaining my point. I accordingly stopped at a book-stall a few doors off; and while purchasing a volume, I got into conversation with an old woman who keeps the shop, while the boy was serving me. I guardedly asked such questions which elicited information perfectly corroborative of what the old jeweller had told me. She said that her neighbour had lived there for upwards of twenty years, and that he had no lodgers, his family and his workmen only occupying the house. I said, as if quite conversationally, that I supposed as he sold a great many nice trinkets, and as it was near the great theatres—moreover as a number of the inferior actors and actresses and ballet-dancers lived in the vicinage—he experienced a good custom on their part? The old woman laughed at what she thought was my ingenuousness; and shaking her head, she observed that if the old jeweller placed much reliance on such custom, he might shut up his shop to-morrow. I took my leave of the old woman; and was proceeding along the street, wondering what I could do next, when I met a policeman. I slipped half-a-crown into his hand, and told him I wanted to ask a question of quite a secret character—but I had a particular motive—and that indeed I was employed by a gentleman for the matter which I had in hand. The constable was civil, and the touch of the coin was evidently by no means disagreeable. He bade me speak. I asked him if he knew Mademoiselle Angeline by sight? He replied that he ought to do, for he was frequently on duty inside the theatre where she danced. I then asked if he knew where she lived? He responded in the negative. I said that I thought it was somewhere in Long Acre; and after a little reflection he observed that now I mentioned it, he remembered to have met her occasionally in the day-time in that street, but he did not know whether she lived there. I asked if he knew any particular shop which she was in the habit of frequenting?—and he again replied in the negative. Then he ejaculated, 'Stop! now I think of it, I have seen her go two or three times to the old jeweller's on the other side of the way: but it could only be for some little article of pur-

chase.'—This was all I could glean from the constable; and this is all, dear Miss, that for the present I am enabled to report to you."

I commended Beda for the tact and ability which she had displayed in conducting the inquiries; but I was considerably bewildered by the result. Could Angeline have given so completely a fictitious address to Mr. Richards that not even any letter or message sent to the jeweller's would be received on her behalf? I knew not how to act: but at length I made up my mind to question Mr. Richards further on the morrow, and ascertain from him whether he had ever had occasion to send a note or message to the address which Angeline had given him.

Accordingly, on the following day, I went to the theatre; and I said to the lessee, "Are you sure that you gave me the right address?—for Miss Churchill does not lodge there."

He referred to his book: he showed me the entry—and it was correct.

"She is here now," he said; "and I will go and ask her——"

"That is precisely," I interrupted him, "what I do not wish you to do! If there be so much mystery connected with her abode, it would be indiscreet for me to attempt to fathom it. But perhaps you can recollect——"

"Ah! now I remember," ejaculated Mr. Richards, "she did request at the time that if ever I had any communication, it should be sent in writing, and not by a verbal message: but to the best of my knowledge there has never been any need to send any communication at all, for she has been most regular in her attendance both at rehearsal and performance. But I tell you what we will do! We will presently put the matter to the test. Can you return a little after three o'clock, Miss Trafford?—or shall I tell you the result in the evening?"

"Oh! you may tell me the result in the evening," I responded; for I did not wish to seem too anxious on the point.

I went away; and in the evening I proceeded to the theatre a few minutes earlier than usual.

"The test has answered," said Mr. Richards. "The bills containing the new ballet were brought in to me between three and four o'clock: I sealed a copy in an envelope—addressed it to Mademoiselle Angeline—and despatched it by a messenger to the jeweller's. The jeweller received it, saying it was all right; and the messenger returned. Now I have satisfied your curiosity," added Mr. Richards, with a smile; "and you will perhaps tell me why you yourself are observing so much mystery—and why you cannot express to Miss Churchill at once your wish to call upon her?"

"Because," I replied, "the mystery which she herself observes, forbids such an overture. I beg you therefore to keep silent in reference to all these proceedings."

"I see!" said Mr. Richards: "there is a proper pride on both sides!—the pride of the ballet-dancer who conceals her lodging because it is humble—and the pride of the great tragedian who does not think it becoming on her part to go point blank at the matter and demand the address of the mysterious abode."

I only smiled, and left Mr. Richards to his own

solution of the subject. But when I had leisure for reflection, I thought that it would be inconsistent with propriety for me to adopt underhand means to fathom a secret which Miss Churchill evidently took so much pains to conceal. I therefore intimated to Beda that she need not prosecute her researches; and I said to myself, "I must leave it to the chapter of accidents to develop an opportunity for me to come to some explanation with Angeline."

<hr />

CHAPTER XCIV.

LUDOVICO MARANO.

A WEEK passed away without any incident worthy of notice. William Lardner was progressing in the good graces of the old housekeeper of Edwin

St. Clair: but he had not as yet found an opportunity of obtaining possession of the little rosewood box. In respect to Angeline Churchill, nothing more had transpired. We seldom met, as I now never stayed to witness the ballet: but if we did happen to encounter each other, we did not speak —and she appeared not to notice me.

I am now about to speak of the murderer Luigi. I must first observe that on the day when he was captured, he was taken before the magistrate; and sufficient evidence was adduced to procure his remand for a week on the charge of having caused the death of Mrs. St. Clair by throwing a corrosive fluid at her. On being again examined at the police-court, he was remanded for another week,— it being intimated that when he should be again brought up, evidence would be forthcoming to show that he was likewise the murderer of the Count of Carboni; and a police-constable gave the Countess and myself due notice that we must attend at the court on the day to which the case was adjourned. But during this second week of Luigi's remand the most serious reflections occupied my mind. I asked myself whether the man could actually and positively be deemed the murderer of Mrs. St. Clair? It was true that by throwing the vitriol he had ruined her beauty and destroyed all her taste for life, so that she had been led to commit suicide; yet it was *not* literally Luigi's act which had in a direct manner deprived her of life. How, then, could I suffer the man to be condemned to death for the extreme crime which after all he had *not* committed?—because I knew sufficient of the law to be aware that for the mere throwing of the fiery acid—and supposing that Zarah had recovered—he would only be condemned to transportation for life. Then, in respect to the murder of the Count of Carboni, neither Beatrice nor myself were positively certain that Luigi was the author of the deed. It was mere suspicion on our part; we could not swear it was the Italian valet whom we had seen through the darkness of the night precipitating the unfortunate Count from the cliff at Dover. Therefore, if this second case should break down—as I felt assured it would and must—I was compelled to revert again to the question, "Could Luigi be permitted to remain under the extreme imputation of having directly and positively, by his own deed alone, sent Zarah out of existence?"

From the bottom of my soul a negative was emphatically given forth. I could not possibly become a party to the condemnation of that man for a crime of which he was not actually culpable. *Morally* he might have been guilty of Zarah's death: but *legally* he was not. I carefully reviewed all the circumstances attending her last hours and her dissolution; and the longer I retrospected upon those painful scenes, the more was I convinced that, while the physicians at the time had relied confidently upon the vigour of Zarah's constitution to surmount the effects of the injuries she had received from the vitriol, she herself was resolutely intent upon suicide. She knew that her beauty was ruined—she had naught left that was worth living for—and she had chosen to die. She had perished by her own hand: the white rose from the curiously carved box had proved the means of her destruction. She had voluntarily inhaled its poisonous perfume—and when she was no more, it had been found by the maid upon her bosom! To me therefore it was as clear as daylight that Mrs. St. Clair had committed suicide. Morally, Luigi was the author of her death, inasmuch as he had done that which rendered her life distasteful: but legally, if all the facts were known, he could not be doomed as her assassin. Now, was it not my bounden duty to proclaim those facts? Yet, on the other hand, I had solemnly pledged myself to Zarah, that I would keep the seal of inviolable secrecy upon my lips in respect to all the circumstances which attended her death. But could I at present regard such an oath?—would it even be perjury to break it?—was I not bound by every law human and divine to go forward as an impartial witness? True, I might not be summoned to furnish any testimony at all in reference to the case of Mrs. St. Clair: but acquainted as I was with particular facts, was it not imperative upon me to step voluntarily forward and detail them in the presence of the dread tribunal? No doubt Luigi had committed crimes which rendered him worthy of death: but unless the law should hold him liable for capital penalties, was it for *me* to assume the office of a judge, and say, "Let him die! for even though he be not strictly guilty according to the indictment, yet he is a wretch unfit to live!"

All these were painful reflections; and I felt I was placed in a very awkward position. But still there was my sense of duty; and I was bound to perform it. But now another consideration entered my mind. I was by this time resolved to accomplish the duty to which I have alluded; and I saw that it would entail ulterior consequences. It would implicate Edwin St. Clair. A searching investigation would take place: Zarah's lady's-maid would be brought forward, and she would have to describe all the particulars of the last moments of her mistress.

Then it would inevitably transpire that St. Clair was an accomplice in his wife's suicide, and that he was actually privy to the fact of her inhaling the poisoned fragrance of the white rose. He would be taken into custody; and heaven could only tell how hardly it might go with him, or how the first step in the development of his iniquities might lead to the elucidation of all his other crimes. But this was no consideration of a nature to hold me back. On the contrary, it was perhaps a reason why I should pursue my own special course, as dictated by every possible sense of duty. Besides, it was only very recently that I had come to a decision to put an end to this man's career of crime: I was actually employing an agent, (William Lardner) to get into his possession the substantial proof of those crimes—I had even resolved that if Mary Glentworth should insist upon St. Clair's being handed over to the grasp of justice, I would throw no obstacle in the way. Thus, everything considered, I saw that my own path was clear; and I felt that I was standing upon the threshold of grave, solemn, and awful events.

While I was thus one day seriously reflecting, just at the time when it was necessary to make up my mind to the pursuance of some particular course, I received a note from Beatrice Carboni, requesting me to call upon her. I was at the very instant thinking of paying her a visit, and conversing with her very seriously in respect to Luigi—perhaps even revealing to her the many circumstances connected with Zarah upon which I had been meditating: and therefore I lost not a moment in setting out for the mansion of the Marquis of Campanella. It was about the hour of one in the afternoon when I reached it; and on inquiring for the Countess of Carboni, I was informed that she was at home, that she was engaged with a visitor, but that doubtless she would see *me*—for all the domestics at the house knew that I was very intimate with Beatrice. I was accordingly shown up to the drawing-room, where I found her seated with a gentleman whom by his appearance I at once took to be a foreigner. He was about five-and-twenty years of age—a little above the medium stature—slightly but symmetrically built —and of exceedingly prepossessing demeanour. His complexion was rather dark: he had very fine black eyes—regular features—and a profusion of black hair shining with a rich gloss, and curling naturally. His whiskers were trimmed with precision; and the two sable lines of a small moustache, pointed and slightly curled at the corners of the mouth, threw out in vivid contrast the vermilion of his lips as well as his pearly teeth. He was elegantly dressed, and had an unmistakable air of distinction about him.

He rose from his seat to bow to me with the habitual politeness of a foreigner, while Beatrice hastening forward, clasped my hands with the wonted fervour of friendliest pressure. Then for an instant there supervened a slight embarrassment in her manner—the colour went and came on her beautiful cheeks—she glanced towards her companion—she again bent her eyes upon me—and suddenly recovering a complete self-possession, she said, "Allow me to introduce to you Signor Ludovico Marano."

I started at that name of *Marano*:—and well I might! Well also might Beatrice for a few moments have felt a conflict of strange emotions within her, as she presented the foreigner! For Marano was the name of the young Italian officer whom she had so sincerely and devotedly loved—whom she had seen so foully murdered before her eyes—and whom she had beheld suspended, by the diabolical vengeance of her husband, to the ceiling of that apartment in which she was kept for several mortal days in hideous captivity! Who, then, was this Ludovico Marano? Must he not be a relation of the perished Angelo? Such were the questions which I rapidly asked myself; and Beatrice, perceiving the start which I gave—no doubt observing likewise that the colour now went and came upon my own cheeks—took my hand once more; and pressing it with a species of spasmodic violence, said in a low voice, "Ludovico is the cousin of the unfortunate Angelo!"

The Italian understood what was thus said; for he at once observed in tolerably good English, "We were speaking of you, Miss Percy, at the very moment when your name was announced; and the Countess was telling me that you are acquainted with all the secrets of her life,—and what is more, she told me how immense are the obligations under which she lies towards you."

"Yes," interrupted the Countess, with a tone and look of deep feeling; "it was through my dearest friend Ellen, that my complete innocence was brought to light, and that I was reconciled to my sister and brother-in-law!"

"Permit me," said Ludovico, in a most courteous manner, "to add the meed of my own gratitude for the noble part which you played in convincing the Count of Carboni that his wife and my deceased cousin were innocent. I loved Angelo as if he were my brother: and his sudden disappearance from the theatre of the world caused me the deepest affliction. I knew not how to account for his disappearance: I knew not to whom I could address myself for information! Circumstances brought me the other day to England—where indeed I have occasionally sojourned before. I yesterday met the Countess of Carboni, whom I had formerly had the honour of meeting in Florence: I requested permission to call upon her—and within the last hour she has revealed to me the whole frightful narrative which is only too well known to you."

We sat down; and Beatrice said, after a pause, "I wish to speak to you, dear Ellen, in reference to the miscreant Luigi."

"And I also was desirous of having some serious discourse with you, Beatrice, concerning that man."

"You may speak in the presence of Signor Marano," said the Countess; "for he will naturally be only too glad to hear of the certainty of that doom which now awaits the wretch whose iniquities caused so monstrous and deplorable a tragedy!"

"Yes!" ejaculated Ludovico Marano vehemently; "for as I have already told you, Miss Percy, I loved Angelo as if he were my brother—and it can be no unchristian feeling which induces me to proclaim my sincere hope that Luigi will not escape his righteous doom!"

Though the Italian's words were in one sense fraught with a meek deference to higher powers, yet was there a strong bitterness in their accents, and his dark eyes shot forth a bright vindictive fire. But all this seemed to me natural enough, considering what must be passing in his mind, and considering likewise that the hot Italian blood rolled in his veins.

"I do not think it is quite so certain," I said, "that Luigi will be condemned to the extreme penalties of the law."

"What!" ejaculated Beatrice, with a start of astonishment: "that wretch escape?"

"By heaven, no!" exclaimed Ludovico Marano, also with a start, but even still more vehement than that which the Countess had given.

"If he were to escape his righteous doom," added Beatrice, "I should say that there was no justice in heaven!"

"And I should proclaim," cried Marano, "that your English tribunals, the rectitude of which is so much vaunted, were utterly deficient in the sterling principles of justice in a retributive sense!"

"Wherein exists your doubt?" inquired Beatrice.

"I will tell you," I said, finding myself at length able to thrust in a word after the ejaculatory expressions in which the astonishment and indignation of the Countess and Ludovico had found a vent. "You know, Beatrice, that in respect to the dreadful scene upon the cliffs, you and I can only give but the vaguest testimony; and we must not suffer our feelings or our prejudices to urge us on to the utterance of a word in addition to the statement that we gave to the authorities at Dover. Upon such evidence as this no English tribunal will condemn Luigi."

"All this I had foreseen," ejaculated the Countess. "I was ere now telling the same to Signor Marano——"

"Yes," interjected Ludovico; "but there is the other case, which is sufficiently positive—the throwing of the vitriol at the English lady, Mrs. St. Clair——"

"Certainly!" said Beatrice: "she died from the effects of the outrage—and the murderer will be condemned to death!"

"Now, it is precisely on this point," I said, "that I have been most seriously reflecting, and that I wish to hold discourse with you, my dear Beatrice. There are certain facts and circumstances within the range of my knowledge—for you are aware that I was well acquainted with the unfortunate Mrs. St. Clair——"

"And those circumstances?" said Beatrice hastily: "to what can you possibly allude?"

I hesitated to speak further, and glanced towards Ludovico Marano.

"Oh! do not fear to express your thoughts in his presence," cried the Countess. "I am confident that we must all three entertain a common object—which is to see that a great criminal shall not escape the hand of justice!"

"I must inform you," I resumed, after a few moments of reflection, "that from these facts and circumstances which are within my knowledge, and which must in due course be made known in the presence of justice, Luigi cannot—will not—and must not be condemned for a crime which he did not commit."

"How! a crime which he did not commit?" ejaculated Beatrice impatiently. "Did he not throw the vitriol at Mrs. St. Clair?"

"Yes," I answered: "beyond all doubt he perpetrated that atrocity."

"And did she not die from the effects thereof?" exclaimed Beatrice.

"No," I responded, looking her steadily in the face.

"What, Ellen!" she exclaimed. "But all the world is convinced of the fact which you alone deny!"

"All the world," I calmly and deliberately rejoined, "is not acquainted with those circumstances that came to my knowledge at the time."

"Good heavens! what can you mean?" exclaimed the Countess.

"If I thought that justice was to be defeated," interjected Ludovico, "I would——"

He stopped short abruptly: but there was a fearful menace in the expression which at the moment seized upon his countenance—though the next instant it died away into a sombre gloom.

"Ellen, you are speaking in enigmas!" said Beatrice; "for you cannot possibly have any ulterior motive for saving one whom you know to be an assassin! No, no, my dear friend! you are as incapable of double-dealing as an angel in heaven itself!"

"Do not press me for explanations now," I said; for I did not choose to speak more openly in the presence of Signor Marano—though I had previously been quite prepared to admit Beatrice into my confidence. "You know me, my dear friend—and you are aware that I never speak without a certainty of the facts which I may proclaim. Hear me, therefore, while I say this much,—that as sure as I am sitting here, evidence will be proffered to show that Luigi is not altogether so culpable as public opinion now believes in reference to Zarah's death. In a word, Beatrice—and you likewise, Signor Marano—if you now wish to deliberate upon the circumstances environing Luigi, you may take it for granted that he will not be condemned to death in the case of Mrs. St. Clair—but that he will be sentenced to the minor penalty of transportation. Then, in respect to the fearful tragedy of the cliffs, there will be an acquittal for want of sufficient evidence."

"Does the matter really stand thus?" inquired Beatrice, looking aghast at the statements I was making: "and must the author of so many hideous calamities—the perpetrator of so many black iniquities—escape with his life?"

"He will—he must," I responded. "Believe me that I am telling you the truth!"

"For such a wretch to live," exclaimed Ludovico, "is to rob me of all the gratification of beholding my poor cousin Angelo's fate fearfully avenged! What can be done? Surely, surely, your ladyship can prove," he added, turning to Beatrice, "that it was Luigi whom you beheld in the act of hurling your husband from the cliff?"

"No, Signor!" I at once ejaculated: "her ladyship can prove nothing of the kind! Truthfulness must be observed even in the case of a villain so iniquitous as Luigi! The first deposition made by Beatrice and myself in the presence of the Mayor of Dover, positively affirms that we only entertained a suspicion—for the night was dark—we were at a distance——"

"Oh! but when you made that deposition," exclaimed Marano vehemently, "you were both under the influence of wildly harrowed feelings! Since that period you have had time to reflect—you have gathered your recollections—you have remembered other incidents——"

"Signor," I interrupted him, with all the vehemence of indignation, "I am surprised at you! You must not attempt to put words into our mouths, nor dazzle us with a false light: for even though it is the case of such a wretch as Luigi, yet must he have the fullest measure of justice done him according to the letter of the law. And that law commands witnesses to be sincere and impartial in giving their evidence. In a word, Signor, neither Beatrice nor myself can be induced——"

"No, no, my dear Ellen!" said the Countess hastily, and with agitation; "we will not swerve from the strict line of truthfulness. But you must make allowances for Signor Marano's feelings, embittered as they are on account of the horrible fate of his beloved relative Angelo:"—and she sighed deeply as she mentioned the name.

"Miss Percy," said Ludovico, in a contrite tone and with a humbled look, "I do indeed beseech you to make allowances for me! I would not insult either yourself or the Countess by the supposition that you are capable of exaggerating your testimony to the prejudice of even a wretch so vile as Luigi!"

"Enough, Signor!" I said: "I forgive you. Yes, I can indeed make allowances for your feelings!"

Marano bowed, still in a contrite and humble manner; and then he said, "I believe it is to-morrow that Luigi again appears before the magistrate?"

"Yes," I answered: "and then the case of Mrs. St. Clair will be thoroughly gone into—afterwards he will doubtless be charged with the murder of the Count of Carboni; and if so, your attendance, Beatrice, and mine will be required. Indeed, I have already received a notification to this effect——"

"And I also," rejoined the Countess. "But Ah! when I bethink me, have you yet seen to-day's paper, Ellen?"

"I saw the *Times*," I answered: "but it said nothing fresh of Luigi."

"I have not as yet seen to-day's journal," remarked Beatrice: "we do not have it until luncheon time."

At this moment a domestic entered, bearing a newspaper, which he placed upon the table; and he then retired. It was the *Morning Post.*

"There is the journal!" exclaimed Beatrice. "It is not the same which you have seen, Ellen—and there may perhaps be something in it concerning the criminal, or in reference to the anticipated proceedings of to-morrow before the magistrate."

"It is scarcely probable," I said, "for no one can as yet be aware of the nature of the testimony I shall give in reference to Mrs. St. Clair's case."

"Ah!" ejaculated Beatrice, who had taken up the newspaper; "there is a long account of Luigi's demeanour in prison! His moods alternates betwixt intervals of sullenness and others of deep dejection—— "

"The very thing I should have expected on the part of such a wretch!" ejaculated Ludovico. "But proceed, my lady. What else does the newspaper say?"

"It says," continued Beatrice, as her eyes were glancing over the statement, "that there was an interval yesterday when he was more than usually dejected. Ah! and he asked the turnkey whether according to the English laws it made any difference in the punishment if an accused person confessed fully and frankly."

"And what did the turnkey reply?" inquired Ludovico.

"It does not say whether the official gave any answer," continued Beatrice: "but the paragraph goes on to state that immediately after Luigi had put the question, he seemed to repent of it: he was perhaps carried away by the utter despondency of his feelings at the moment—and he affected an air of hardihood and indifference."

"Is that all?" asked Ludovico, who seemed to follow with a deep, sombre, sinister interest everything that related to the criminal.

"No—there is another paragraph," responded Beatrice. "Ah! the wretch's courage is evidently giving way: for it appears that later in the afternoon of yesterday he again sank into a mood of deepest despondency,—and he expressed a wish to be attended by an Italian Catholic priest, if such could be found. Ah! and then again he assumed an air of hardihood, declaring that he did not mean what he said, and endeavouring to carry it off with a ferocious gaiety, which was however most unnatural. And now that's all."

Beatrice laid down the newspaper; and Ludovico Marano gradually fell into a profound meditation. I felt that I had nothing more to say on the present occasion; and indeed, after the turn which the discourse had taken previous to the newspaper being brought in, I was rather anxious to cut short the interview. I accordingly rose to take my leave; and Beatrice said to me, "Perhaps you will come again in the evening, my dear friend; for if I remember correctly, you have no engagement to-night at the theatre?"

"I will come," I said: for I thought it probable that Beatrice might wish to see me alone, and that she might suspect I should have spoken more frankly in reference to the case of Mrs. St. Clair if Ludivico Marano had not been present.

I bowed to that gentleman, who started somewhat abruptly from his profound meditation on finding that I was about to depart; and I issued from the room.

Having descended the staircase, I had reached the threshold of the front door, and was on the point of entering my carriage, when I found that I had left my kerchief up in the drawing-room; and being affected with a slight cold at the time, I could not dispense with it. I hastily ascended the stairs again; and just as I approached the drawing-room door—which was standing ajar—my ear caught the voice of Ludovico Marano, ejaculating vehemently, "By heaven I will accomplish it! The villain shall not escape the gibbet!"

I pushed open the door: the Italian started—Beatrice likewise looked confused—and I at once said, "I have returned for my kerchief. I was no willing listener; but I could not help overhearing what you, Signor, just proclaimed from your lips."

"You mean, Miss Percy"—and he looked embarrassed,—"you mean——"

"I mean the words you uttered, to the effect that Luigi shall perish upon the scaffold."

"They were spoken in the heat of passion!" said Beatrice; and I could not help thinking that she was somewhat too ready in interposing on the Italian gentleman's behalf.

"Yes—in the heat of passion," he said, at once recovering himself,—"just as a person is sometimes in the habit of declaring as something positive that which he merely wishes to see accomplished."

"At all events, Signor," I said, in a serious tone, "it will be only discreet and honourable on your part to abstain henceforth from urging the point for which you besought my forgiveness ere now. I know enough of the Countess of Carboni," I added, looking impressively at Beatrice, "to be aware that she is as incapable as I myself am, of torturing, exaggerating, or colouring her testimony in respect to the scene on the cliffs, for any sinister purpose."

"Oh, Ellen, believe me," exclaimed the Countess, with an air of the utmost sincerity, "you only do me justice in this opinion which you entertain of me!"

I then took my departure, fully satisfied in respect to Beatrice—but not without misgivings to the effect that Ludovico Marano, carried away by his impetuously vindictive feelings, was capable of straining any point in order to procure the capital conviction of Luigi. But on the other hand I knew that a British tribunal was not to be trifled with or easily misled—and that therefore whatsoever sinister intents Ludovico might harbour would in the long run prove impotent and ineffectual. During the drive home in my carriage, I congratulated myself on having maintained a certain degree of reserve in the presence of Ludovico, and for not having fully explained the grounds on which I so positively asserted that Luigi would not be found guilty of the murder of Mrs. St. Clair.

In the evening, between seven and eight o'clock, I called at the Marquis of Campanella's mansion; and I found Beatrice alone. The Marquis and Marchioness had gone to dine with the Earl and Countess of Belgrave. Beatrice was invited also—but she preferred remaining at home to receive me.

"I am afraid, my dear Ellen," she said, after the interchange of some few observations on different topics,—"I am afraid you were rather shocked and angry at Ludovico Marano's vehement and even intemperate language of the afternoon: but you must remember that the Italian disposition is quite different from the English. It is more mercurial and excitable, like that of the Frenchman: it wants the calmness, sedateness, and phlegmatic self-possession which characterize the Saxon."

"To what profession does Signor Marano belong?" I inquired.

"He also was in the army, as well as his unfortunate cousin—whose name," added Beatrice, in a lower tone, "I can never breathe without emotion, and of whose image I can never think without feeling as if there were lightning gushing through my veins. Ah! can you wonder, my dear Ellen, that in his anxiety to behold the punishment of the wretch Luigi, Ludovico Marano should be hurried away by his feelings, even so far as for a few moments to lose sight of the strict course of probity and truthfulness?"

"And yet as a military man," I observed, "he ought to be so very punctilious and particular——"

"I believe that in all respects he is a most honourable man," interrupted Beatrice: "but vengeance, my dear Ellen, is particularly dear to the Italian heart—and in order to accomplish it, or see it accomplished, the extreme nicety of scruple is sometimes set aside. But I should inform you that Signor Marano is no longer in the Tuscan army. A distant relation of his family has recently died, and bequeathed his wealth to Ludovico. If the unfortunate Angelo had lived, he would have become the possessor of these riches. But I hope, my dear Ellen," proceeded the Countess of Carboni, "that you have entertained no prejudice against Signor Marano?"

"I hope that of a prejudice I am incapable," I replied, "but I should certainly have been better pleased with the Italian gentleman if he had displayed less anxiety to induce you and me to exaggerate and misrepresent the facts in reference to the fatal scene upon Dover Cliffs. And then too, Beatrice, I cannot forget that even after he had seemed by his contrite air to acknowledge that he was in error—and after he had besought my forgiveness—I overheard him giving vent to vehement ejaculations in your hearing, when you were alone together."

"Yes—but I assured you at the time—I mean when you so suddenly reappeared," interjected the Countess, "that it was a mere impassioned utterance on his part; and he gave you a similar explanation. But why do we linger upon this topic?"

"It is you yourself who have introduced it, Beatrice," I replied. "It was not my intention to say another word upon the subject. On the contrary, I meant to confine my own discourse to an explanation of the statements which I made in the afternoon——"

"Yes—I remember!" exclaimed Beatrice; "you are alluding to the case of Mrs. Clair. Tell me, my dear Ellen, how is it that you are enabled to speak so positively when you assert your conviction that Luigi will not be condemned to death on that indictment?"

"To-morrow I shall explain to the police-magistrate that which I am about to explain to you, Beatrice," I answered. "The truth is, a terrible secret was by accident brought within my knowledge; and if I have not hitherto proclaimed it, I can assure you it has been from motives of delicate consideration for the memory of the deceased Zarah. But believe me, my dear friend—believe me, when I assure you that Zarah did not die from the effects of the vitriol that was thrown at her—nor of the shock that was sustained by her constitution!"

"Good heavens! what strange secret is this which you are about to reveal to me?" asked the Countess, displaying the most suspenseful curiosity. "Would you have me believe that Mrs. St. Clair was assassinated by some other hand? or that she committed suicide?"

I did not immediately answer the question: but I looked significantly at Beatrice—and then I said in a low solemn voice, "Yes — the unfortunate Zarah committed suicide: and what is more, her husband was privy to the fact! Aye, he was an accomplice in it! There will be an exposure, Beatrice!—this is now inevitable!—and the deceased Zarah's principal maid will be summoned and brought forward—and her evidence will afford a clue to everything!"

"Ah! I knew that there was foul play!" ejaculated a voice, coming from the door.

Both Beatrice and myself started up in astonishment and alarm at the interruption. I had not immediately recognised the voice; for it was altered from its natural tone by deep concentrated passion: but as I started up to my feet and flung my look towards the door, I beheld upon the threshold the unmistakable form of Dame Betty. Yes—there was the wrinkled hag, her countenance looking more hideous than ever I had before seen it. She was tolerably well dressed—just as a respectable tradeswoman might be, with nothing of the gipsy to characterize her costume. She stood motionless on the threshold, leaning on her stick, and the doorway forming as it were a frame in which the ghastly living full-length portrait was set.

"Who are you, woman?" demanded Beatrice, in a moment recovering her presence of mind.

"She can tell you who I am," responded the dame, extending her stick towards me. "She knows whether I loved Zarah in spite of all her haughty disobedience — the imperiousness of her conduct towards me — and her frequent interference with my plans! Yes, Ellen Percy can tell whether I loved Zarah!"

Beatrice looked towards me for some explanation of this strange intrusion; and I said to Dame Betty, "What are you doing in England? Know you not that it was the wish of that deceased granddaughter whom you declare that you loved so much——"

"Her wish that I should live abroad in a foreign land? This is what you mean, Ellen Percy—is it not? Well, well," continued the hag, shaking her head as she advanced into the room, leaning on her stick; "let me avenge Zarah's death—and then I will return to France—to die there! But vengeance I must have! I came to see your ladyship," she continued, now turning to Beatrice; "for I presume that you are the Countess of Carboni. I came to tell you that I am the grand-mother of that Zarah whose beautiful countenance was disfigured by the wretch Luigi; and as you are the widow of the nobleman whom he hurled from the cliff, I thought that there would be sympathy between us—because we have both sustained losses from the same criminal hands——"

"Sympathy, my good woman?" said Beatrice, somewhat astonished: "and what did you wish that I shall do for you? If you are in distress"——and Beatrice extended her hand towards her purse, which lay upon the table.

"No! no!" ejaculated Dame Betty: "it was not your gold or silver that I coveted! In a word, all that I *did* need has been obtained—and so there's an end of the matter."

"What mean you?" asked Beatrice with renewed astonishment. "I know of nothing that you have obtained——"

"Yes, yes," responded the harridan, with a sinister slyness of look: and then with a guttural chuckling of triumph, she added, "I have obtained the information that I sought."

"Do you understand her meaning, my dear Ellen?" asked Beatrice, in a low voice: and then in a still more subdued tone, she inquired, "Do you think the unfortunate old creature is demented?"

"No, no—I am not mad!" cried Dame Betty, whose ears with astonishing keenness had caught the sense of the Countess of Carboni's latter query. "But you want to know, lady, what I mean—and I will tell you. I always thought there was something strange and unnatural about Zarah's death,—the more so that I had very excellent reasons for knowing that her husband St. Clair was not the most honourable and virtuous of persons:"—here the hag glanced significantly at me. "I came over to London—Miss Percy saw me—she knows very well where I did her a great service——that night, you remember, my dear," she continued, addressing herself thus familiarly to me: "it was the night of the eleventh of May——"

"Yes, yes—I know full well to what you allude!" I exclaimed: and not choosing to disguise my aversion for the wretched woman, I added, "Proceed with your explanations—and appeal not to me."

"Why, you do not cherish rancour *now*?" ejaculated the dame. "Poor old Gilderoy assured me that if I gave my evidence on the memorable night to which I have alluded, I myself should be held utterly harmless, and that you would forgive all the past so far as I myself was concerned with it."

"If the unfortunate Gilderoy gave you those pledges," I said, "they shall be held sacred by me! But proceed——and remember that the Countess of Carboni can have no interest in the discourse which you have just now been addressing to me; for it is replete with mystery for her "

"Well, well," said the dame: "then I will continue——"

"And use despatch, for heaven's sake!" I interjected—for it did me harm to find myself in the company of that wretch whom I knew to have been a remorseless and unscrupulous poison vender.

"As I was saying," she resumed, "I suspected

that there was foul play in respect to poor Zarah; and I came over to England to investigate the matter. But Gilderoy got hold of me—he had me in his power—and he packed me off again to the Continent. Well, well, I thought to myself it was my destiny to die abroad, and so I resolved to yield with a good grace. Then five months passed away, and all was quiet and tranquil enough, until the other day, when lo and behold! I was startled by reading in an English newspaper that the villain Luigi—that detestable thrower of vitriol—had been arrested. Ah! then I thought to myself it was high time to return to London again and see what would turn up. When once in this great metropolis, my mind was pretty soon decided how to act. I knew that you, Miss Percy, were about the last person that ever saw poor Zarah alive: the newspapers said at the time that you had been summoned to her death-bed. Well then, I thought to myself that you might have your suspicions—or you might even be able to tell a tale which for some reason or another you might not have chosen to make public. But then, how was I to get at you? I had reckoned upon the assurance which Gilderoy had given me of forgiveness on account of the past: but still I could not suppose that you would admit me to your house. Well, then, what was I to do? My presence here explains the course which I adopted. I knew that you were intimate with the Countess of Carboni. So to the Countess of Carboni I accordingly came, to seek her kind intervention with you, Miss Percy, that you would grant me an interview—or at least communicate through her ladyship whatsoever you might know in reference to poor Zarah's death. Well, I find my way to this house—I inquire for the Countess—I am told she is engaged with Miss Percy. 'Nothing can be better!' I ejaculate to myself: 'the Countess will sympathize with me on poor Zarah's account; Ellen Percy will relent; and all will be well!' So I coolly told the lace-bedizened lacquey that I was expected at the conference which was going on between you two ladies——"

"You dared say that?" exclaimed Beatrice, who by this time was more than disgusted by the air of familiarity which the dame was gradually assuming.

"Why, yes, I did, my lady," responded the harridan, with the most cool insolence; "for I thought it was the only way of getting into your presence. And when the lacquey had reached the landing and indicated the door, I told him he need not trouble himself any further. So I opened the door for myself; and at that very instant I caught the words that were flowing from Miss Percy's lips. So you see that I then and there obtained all in a moment the very information which I was seeking!"

I scarcely know how it was that Beatrice had patience to listen to this long tirade; but I myself suffered the hag to go on speaking, for I was more or less anxious to learn whatsoever she might choose to reveal in reference to her own proceedings. Scarcely had she finished her narrative, when the door of the drawing-room opened; and a servant entering, said to Beatrice, "If you please, my lady, Signor Marano has called."

The Countess flung a look upon Dame Betty, as much as to imply how provoking her presence was at such a moment: but I at once said in a low hurried voice to Beatrice, "Go and receive Signor Marano in another room. I wish to say a word or two alone to this old woman!"

"Where is Signor Marano?" inquired Beatrice of the footman.

"Thinking that your ladyship might be engaged, I showed him into the dining-room," was the answer.

"I will proceed thither," said Beatrice: and she accordingly issued from the apartment.

I was now alone with Dame Betty; and as I turned somewhat abruptly towards her, I perceived that she trembled and quailed slightly, at the same time fixing upon me a half searching, half mistrustful look.

"What do you mean by this, Miss Percy?" she asked: "why have you just manœuvred to be alone with me? I suppose there is no treachery——"

"Treachery?" I quickly ejaculated. "Such a word applied to me!"

"Well, well, Miss—I didn't mean to offend you," interposed the hag, "but I hope it is all fair and straightforward, and that you haven't forgot the promise made to me by poor old Gilderoy, and which you just now renewed?"

"Be not afraid," I said. "I hold myself bound to respect Gilderoy's promise, even though it was made on my behalf entirely without my consent."

"Of course you would not harm me," continued the dame; "for I gave the evidence that night in Gilderoy's presence—and Parks refunded you your fortune; so that it was with some little astonishment I learnt you were still upon the stage, when I arrived in London this afternoon."

"That fortune I never received. You know that there was a conflagration the same night——"

"And poor Gilderoy perished," ejaculated Dame Betty. "He used me harshly enough on that occasion; but still I respected him as a gipsy-chief—and I have since mourned his loss. But you say that you did not receive your fortune?"

"I did not," was my response. "Alas! I fear that Mr. Moss, the clerk, who acted so friendly a part, perished in the conflagration: but whether Mr. Parks himself likewise perished, or whether he escaped——"

"Then all is mystery!" said the dame; "and during the five months which have elapsed since that date, I have been moping on the Continent, so that I literally know nothing, and am unable to give you the slightest particle of information! I would if I could. I have no longer any enmity against you—for I know that poor Zarah loved you—and besides I was always the tool of others in anything that I did——"

"I know it but too well," I interrupted the dame. "And now let us change the topic: let us divert our attention from the affairs which concern me, to those which concern you."

"Me? Well, yes—to be sure!" said the harridan. "Poor Zarah's death——"

"Ah, woman!" I ejaculated, "if you had even the most ordinary sensitiveness of feeling, you would now sink down overpowered by the intelligence which I have to communicate. Oh, you have prepared poisons——"

"Miss Percy—these walls may have ears!" said the dame quickly.

"Yes—you have prepared poisons," I continued, heedless of the interruption, "to a fearful effect!"

"Oh, my dear young lady—pray, pray be cautious!"—and the hag looked frightened. "Speak in a low tone—and don't tell me—no—pray don't tell me—that—that——"

"Could you suppose, woman," I demanded, "that the white rose should never be scented by any nostrils save those of an enemy?"

"What!" gasped the wretched hag, staggering as if smitten a blow. "You do not mean—you do not mean," she repeated, becoming more and more aghast as her horrible suspicions were strengthening into a conviction,—"you do not mean——"

"Yes! I mean that your grand-daughter committed suicide—that her husband was the accomplice—and that immediately after her death, the maid who entered the chamber found the white rose upon the bosom of her mistress!"

The dame stared at me with eyes so full of horror that by her looks she seemed as if she were going insane. It appeared as if she must burst forth into some violent outpouring of rage or grief, or of both blended: but then all in an instant a calmness that was terribly sombre, seemed to take possession of her; and she said in a low hollow tone, "This is retribution! But there shall not the less be vengeance!—yes, vengeance on St. Clair!—for perhaps he was more than a mere accomplice in a case of suicide!—far more probable is it that he was a downright murderer!"

"No—he was but an accomplice," I replied. "But what do you purpose to do?"

"Denounce St. Clair to the authorities of justice!" replied the hag.

"And he," I said, "will at once turn round and accuse you as the compounder of the poison with which the white rose was imbued."

"Let him do it," answered Dame Betty with a sombre tone and look. "I care not! I have lived long enough! But even if I still clung to life, yet would I have vengeance upon that man!"

"Remember," I said, "that you have made up your mind to set the first spark to a train of fearful magnitude, and which will cause a tremendous explosion. That you will be involved in the common ruin, there can be no doubt. I do not speak from any feeling of sympathy—because sympathy in this case I can have none! But I give you warning, because you may not at the present moment foresee the consequences——and as it is for the sake of avenging poor Zarah that you are about to act——"

"I care not for the consequences!" ejaculated the dame vehemently.

"Then I assuredly can have no interest in staying or checking you," I said. "It is quite clear that events of fearful import are about to ensue."

"Yes!—and if the flame spreads," said Dame Betty, "there will be a terrific crash, and more than one person will go down to destruction! Ah! ha! it will be an exciting spectacle; and you can look on in safety and behold it!"

With these words Dame Betty turned abruptly towards the door. I did not detain her—I had not another word to say—and she went forth from my presence.

ANOTHER PORTRAIT OF ELLEN PERCY.

Almost immediately afterwards Beatrice returned to the drawing-room, exclaiming, "I have strange tidings for you, dear Ellen! Luigi will not escape!"

"What mean you, Beatrice?" I demanded. "Has Signor Marano succeeded in making you promise——"

"Signor Marano has done nothing that I know of, except bring me the tidings which he has learnt out of doors, and which I was about to communicate to your ears if you had permitted me." And Beatrice assumed a certain coldness of tone and distance of manner as she thus addressed me.

"Pardon me, my dear friend," I exclaimed, hurt and vexed to think that I had wounded her feelings: "but I certainly was afraid that Signor Marano had over-persuaded you in reference to the testimony which you will have to give——"

"I shall have to give no testimony—neither will

75.—ELLEN PERCY.

you, Ellen," interrupted Beatrice. "We need not appear at the police-court to-morrow."

"You surprise me, Beatrice!" and I confess that for the moment I apprehended some trickery on Marano's part, and of which Beatrice had been made the dupe.

"The explanation is easy," she said. "This afternoon the criminal Luigi was visited by a Catholic priest; and the result was that the miserable man summoned the governor of the prison and made a full confession of his crimes. Yes—he has avowed himself the assassin of the Count Carboni—he admits that it was he who precipitated my husband from the cliffs at Dover; and this confession he will repeat to-morrow in the presence of the magistrate."

"Ah, then," I said, "the wretched being doubtless hopes to make an atonement to heaven—and he will yet die upon the scaffold! But if he remain firm to his purpose, and if he do really confess to-morrow the murder of your husband, Beatrice, it will be indeed unnecessary for either you or me to appear at the police-court."

"And thus," said Beatrice, "you will be spared the pain of revealing everything, you know in reference to your deceased friend Mrs. St. Clair."

"Yes," I rejoined : "I shall be spared that pain, provided that the wretched man do really confess the other crime—I mean the murder of your husband. But, alas! I fear that even though I myself may remain silent in respect to a deed which would throw a shade upon poor Zarah's name, and make bigots regret that she should be buried in consecrated ground,—I fear, I say, that there is another who will proclaim that tale."

"You allude to the gipsy woman who has just been here ?" said Beatrice inquiringly.

"I do," was my answer. "But let her take her own course. I was prepared to perform my duty ; and if there be now no necessity to pursue that painful path, I may rest contented with the knowledge that I did not shrink when circumstances seemed to be urging me on. And now farewell, Beatrice. It is getting late—and I promised to join my friend Mary Glentworth at the theatre by ten o'clock."

CHAPTER XCV.

THE ROSEWOOD BOX.

On the following morning I anxiously awaited the arrival of the newspapers; and when they were delivered, I searched with much suspense for any paragraph that might contain information in respect to the criminal Luigi. Nor did I search in vain ; for I speedily beheld at the head of an article, the following words—" CONFESSION OF THE ITALIAN ASSASSIN."

It appeared from the statement of the journal, that in consequence of the publicity previously given to Luigi's express wish to be visited by an Italian Catholic pastor, a reverend gentleman called at the prison on the preceding day between three and four o'clock. He was immediately admitted into the presence of Luigi ; and they were closeted together for an hour. "Of course," continued the newspaper statement, "it is not known what passed between the Italian priest and his wretched fellow-countryman,—whether it were the criminal's own spontaneous desire to confess, or whether this confession were the result of the religious admonitions, entreaties, and representations of his holy visitor : but certain it is that at the expiration of the hour the presence of the governor was requested. A full confession was then made ; and the wretched man avowed that it was he, as suspicion had already indicated, who had hurled the unfortunate Count of Carboni from the cliffs at Dover about a twelvemonth back." The newspaper went on to assure its readers that the governor of the prison had duly warned Luigi that his confession would be used as evidence against him ; but the criminal seemed to have completely made up his mind how to act : his language was most contrite—his demeanour most becoming. "It can only therefore be as a mere

matter of form," added the journal, "that he will appear this day before the magistrate according to the period of the second remand ; for if he repeat his confession—as there is little doubt that he will —he will be at once committed to Newgate for trial at the next session of the Central Criminal Court."

Such was the statement made by the newspaper ; and I was certainly glad to receive this corroboration of the intelligence communicated by Beatrice on the preceding evening. The turn which circumstances now appeared to be taking, would absolve me from the necessity of any active intervention therein ; and I could not help feeling that if ever the punishment of death ought to be inflicted, it was in the case of such a wretch as Luigi. Therefore on this ground I was well pleased to think that justice would not be cheated of its due.

I was wondering whether it would be necessary for me to appear at the police-office so as to be in readiness to give my testimony in case Luigi should change his mind and refuse to repeat in the magistrate's presence the confession which he had made to the priest and the governor, when a police-officer called at the house. This was one of those who had arrested Luigi a fortnight back— the same one who had promised to give me all necessary information, and who had brought me the summons to appear as a witness on this particular day. I ordered that he should be shown into the dining-room, for Mary Glentworth was getting somewhat nervous and restless on account of her peculiar condition ; and I did not therefore choose that a constable should be shown into the apartment where we were seated together.

"I am happy to inform you, Miss," began the police-officer, when I repaired to the dining-room, " that there is no need for your attendance to-day at the court ; and I have sent one of my mates to give the same notice to the Countess of Carboni."

"I have just been reading," I said, "in the newspapers, that the murderer has made a full confession——"

"And so much the better, Miss, for you !" replied the policeman ; "for it will save you a world of trouble and annoyance. Police-courts ain't the places for young ladies to appear in. But this confession-business is rather a bad job for me and my mate which is my pardner in getting up the case."

I could not for the moment comprehend what the officer meant by " pardner," until the next instant it struck me that it was a malpronunciation of the word " partner." I therefore said, " How does it so materially affect your interest ?"

"Why, you see, Miss," answered the constable, smoothing down his beaver hat with the sleeve of his coat, "it's sheer money out of our pocket. The more we have to do in getting together witnesses, watching the case before the magistrate, and then attending it at the Old Bailey when the trial comes on, the more we are off regular duty—which is a blessin' in the first place ; and then the better fees we get on the day of trial, which is an advantage in the second place."

I was about to remind the officer that he ought rather to rejoice that the criminal should have been led to such a sense of his duty as to make as much atonement as he could by means of confession, when it occurred to me how vain it was to remonstrate with a man who evidently regarded the whole affair in a mere business view and selfish light. Then remembering that he had been civil and attentive to me, I placed half a sovereign in his hand, saying, "Perhaps this will in some way indemnify you for the loss you fancy you sustain. But tell me," I continued, thus cutting short his thanks, "what if the prisoner should change his mind and *not* presently make the promised confession? Should I not in this case be required to attend? Besides, for certain reasons I would rather do so."

"Why, Miss, in that case," responded the officer, "we should ask for another remand; and as it is three weeks to the next sessions, there is plenty of time to get up the case properly. At all events I can assure you that there is no need for your attendance to-day."

I reflected for a few moments. I was anxious to learn whether Dame Betty would avail herself of the forthcoming proceedings to make any statement and carry her threat into execution in reference to St. Clair. I therefore said, "If you have time after the examination I should like to know the result."

"I will call, Miss," responded the officer. "The case will be taken first immediately after the night charges; and if the confession is made—as I have no doubt it will be—it will only be the work of an hour, taking down the depositions and everything. I shall therefore be able to call between one and two o'clock, if that hour is convenient to yourself."

"I shall be at home," I rejoined: and the officer then took his departure.

I need not say that during the interval I experienced some little degree of suspense as to how matters might progress: but there was the certain presentiment in my soul that the web was closing rapidly in around Edwin St. Clair,—that web which his own iniquities had woven! I had seen on the preceding evening that Dame Betty was resolved to bring about a crash, even though she herself should go down with it. And then too I thought that apart from the measures that I myself was taking to put an end to the criminal career of St. Clair, other circumstances would transpire and other agencies were at work to bring about his downfall, as if heaven itself were resolved that his course of crime should be now forthwith arrested. And furthermore, as I reviewed all those bygone matters into which I had obtained an insight, and of which I had something more than a bare suspicion—though I was utterly without evidence to prove them in a court of justice—I felt convinced that the exposure of St. Clair's guilt would in a particular sense involve Lady Lilla Essendine; and I could not help shuddering when I reflected how probable it was that a being with whom I had once been on terms of intimacy, might at no very distant period be arraigned for her own turpitude in the presence of a criminal tribunal!

It was about two o'clock in the afternoon when the officer returned. I again received him alone; and he at once said, "It is all over, Miss. The Italian has confessed—and he has been committed for trial."

"And what were the circumstances?—I mean did anything particular transpire?" I asked, somewhat falteringly; for I was full of nervous suspense.

"Nothing very particular, Miss," replied the officer. "The Italian looked very demure and penitent—but still he had a vile hang-dog aspect, and I thought that if ever any one deserved going to the gallows, it was him. First of all the business about poor Mrs. St. Clair was entered into; and the Italian at once said he would give no trouble in the matter, but would admit that he had thrown the vitriol. He went on to say that he supposed it was wondered why he could have done such a wicked thing; but he would rather not give any explanation—he had privately confessed everything to a priest, and that was sufficient. The magistrate of course told him that he was not bound to say any more than he thought fit. Ah, Miss! the fellow speaks English uncommonly well! I only wish I could speak Italian half as glib; for who knows of what use it might be to one?"

"And in reference to the other case?" I inquired.

"Oh, that was also entered into—and then the Italian went on to make his promised confession. He said that he had been a long time in the service of the late Count of Carboni; but that in the month of March of last year, events transpired which compelled him to leave his lordship's service. He was driven mad, he said, by this and other circumstances, which he did not however explain. Some months afterwards—that is to say in October, also of last year—he was at Dover, when he saw the Count, who was living privately at a little villa in the neighbourhood of that town. Luigi was in distress, and asked the Count to relieve him; but his lordship spurned him from his presence. Then Luigi was determined to be avenged. He watched the Count—he dogged him on the cliffs at nightfall—he again accosted him—a few sharp angry words ensued—Luigi sprang at his lordship—there was a tussle—and all was soon over."

"And was this the entire explanation which the criminal gave?" I asked.

"He only added that he was very, very sorry for what he had done," replied the police-constable; "and that during the year which had elapsed since that fatal night, he had not been in his right senses. It was therefore, he said, in a species of madness he had done the diabolical deed of throwing the vitriol at Mrs. St. Clair. That was all. The magistrate thereupon committed Luigi for trial at next month's sessions of the Central Criminal Court. There is no doubt, Miss," added the police-officer, "that when the sessions come on the Italian will be arraigned only for the Carboni case, as that is the simplest—and, as the clerk of the court just now said, the murder was direct and positive upon the man's own confession, requiring no corroborative evidence of any kind."

"And this was all that took place?" I inquired, wondering whether anything would now be said in reference to Dame Betty.

"That was all, Miss," rejoined the constable. "The Italian was removed; and by this time he is in Newgate. The sessions come on on the sixth of next month; and his business will soon be done for."

I gave the constable another fee; and he took

his departure. I was again rejoiced to think that circumstances should have so progressed as to save me the necessity of going forward to make those statements which would have thrown a slur upon the memory of the deceased Zarah: but I wondered that Dame Betty should have been absent from the police-court—or at least that she should have abstained from taking any step in pursuance of the menaces she had so emphatically held out. I thought that she must have cooled over the matter, and must have preferred consulting her own safety to the adoption of a course which would have involved herself in ruin along with others.

Three weeks now passed away; and during this interval I neither heard nor saw anything of the old gipsy-woman. I told Beda that I had reason to believe that she was in London: but my faithful dependant also failed to encounter her. I saw Beatrice three or four times: I learnt that Signor Ludovico Marano was remaining in the British metropolis; but I did not again fall in with him during this period. I however could full well guess—though I did not mention my idea to Beatrice—that he was anxious to behold the condemnation and execution of the man who had been the cause of his beloved cousin's dreadful death. In reference to Luigi himself, I read occasional paragraphs in the newspapers. He continued most contrite and devout, according to those statements; and he was frequently attended by the Italian Catholic priest who had in the first instance urged him to confession.

But during this interval of three weeks, an occurrence took place which seemed partly to corroborate my recently formed idea that Edwin St. Clair's star was on the wane. There was a sudden breaking up of the Ministry to which he belonged; and he was ejected from office. It was then said that gross mismanagement and favouritism had been displayed in the department over which he had presided; and though some few journals defended him, alleging that his enemies were now bestowing a coward kick upon the dead lion, and his conduct had been unimpeachable,—yet the great majority of the public prints animadverted severely upon his Ministerial conduct, and declared that when parliament should meet again there must inevitably be a strict investigation into it.

And now the sessions of the Central Criminal Court commenced, on a Monday morning as usual. The Recorder, in making his charge to the Grand Jury, alluded to the case of Luigi. His lordship's observations were however brief; for he said that the Grand Jury would have no difficulty in finding true bills on the prisoner's own confession. These bills were found accordingly. The trial—if such it could be called, when a culprit intended to plead guilty—was to take place on the Wednesday morning; and again I wondered whether Dame Betty would seize that occasion to take any step in pursuance of her menace, or whether she had altogether abandoned the idea in regard to her own safety.

It was about nine o'clock on the Tuesday evening—and I was seated alone in the drawing-room, Mary Glentworth being at the theatre—I was thinking how the events of the morrow would pass off,—when Beda came rushing into the apartment, followed by William Lardner. The looks of both

were troubled; and by the general excitement of their manner I saw that something had happened.

"Oh, dear Miss!" exclaimed Beda: "the rosewood box——"

"What of it?" I demanded, glancing towards William; but not perceiving it in his hands, my suspicion of some mishap was confirmed.

I should here observe that it was about five weeks since William had undertaken the task of procuring the rosewood box, and that he had hitherto failed in accomplishing his design.

"Pardon me, Miss Percy!" he said, with a troubled countenance: "but I did my best,—and if I have been forestalled by another——"

"Forestalled?" I ejaculated. "What do you mean, William?"

"I mean, Miss," he mournfully responded, "that what I have failed in seven weeks to do, an old gipsy has done in a single day—nay, almost in a single hour!"

"And that gipsy!" exclaimed Beda, "is Dame Betty! I am sure of it by William's description!"

"I thought so," I remarked, "the moment I heard the statement made!"—and now I was smitten with the conviction that the wily old hag had been merely biding her time, and that something was pending for the morrow. "But explain yourself, William. I am sure you are not to blame—and I shall not be in haste to accuse you of neglect."

"Oh, thank you, Miss!" he said, in accents of fervour. "What I have to tell you is but short. In the first instance, as you know, Mrs. Holman, Mr. St. Clair's housekeeper, took a fancy to me and treated me with kindness. I soon got a footing in the house, taking great care however to avoid encountering Mr. St. Clair himself—which was not very difficult, for he is so seldom at home. I devised every plan—I watched every opportunity. I pretended to admire the furniture and the pictures in the different rooms, and to be always anxious to go over the house. Mrs. Holman used to humour me, as she fancied she was doing: but I never could catch a glimpse of the rosewood box. I tried to draw her into conversation upon the subject of the numerous curiosities which were lying about,—hinting that there might be others locked up, and which I should like to see. She did open several cabinets and cupboards, displaying a variety of curious things—but never the one for which I was so anxiously on the look-out. Indeed, I never could get her to take me into her master's bedroom—where, from the information you originally sent me by Beda, Miss, I thought the rosewood box must most probably be secured. Thus the time has passed until now."

"Proceed, William," I said. "You have done all that you could in the matter; and less than ever am I disposed to blame you for failure."

"I am now going to speak of to-day, Miss," resumed Lardner. "Mr. St. Clair went out shortly after eleven o'clock in the forenoon; and I called as usual upon Mrs. Holman. As I was coming out of the house, I saw an old gipsy woman standing at a little distance, in earnest conversation with a girl whom I at once recognised to be Mr. St. Clair's housemaid—Emma by name. She is a good-looking young woman—fresh from the country, for she has only been in the service some few weeks; and while on the one hand I had noticed that she was very vain and conceited, on the other hand I had found her to be equally credulous and silly. The gipsy-woman's back was turned towards me—and so I did not recognise her: for otherwise I should have known who she was, as I have on two or three occasions seen Dame Betty. She was dressed in a mean shabby style, with an old brown cloak, and a stick: but I had not an idea who she was,—for I only know the bag slightly. It immediately struck me that she was pretending to tell Emma's fortune; and I was half inclined to go and interrupt the proceeding—when it struck me that I had no business to interfere—and besides which, that Emma in her mingled pride, conceit, and vanity, would be sure to take it in ill part and bid me mind my own business. Then I thought of re-entering the house and mentioning the circumstance to Mrs. Holman, so that she might gently remonstrate with Emma and prevent her from foolishly parting with her money in future. But then I reflected that the housekeeper was a strange-tempered woman, and that she might dismiss Emma from the service; so that I should have been sorry to become the cause of the poor girl losing her place. Thus I did nothing in the matter, but returned into my master's own house. I soon ceased to think of the affair—hours passed on—and it was between four and five o'clock when Sir Robert Temple sent me to the post-office with his letters. At a little distance from Mr. St. Clair's house, I beheld two figures through the dusk which was beginning to close in; and I again recognised Emma and the old gipsy. But still I knew not it *was* Dame Betty; for on perceiving a person coming, Emma gave the gipsy something—I could not distinguish what. The crone thrust it under her cloak—and they separated: the dame hastened off in one direction; and Emma, being compelled to pass me on her way to the back gate of her master's house, uttered an ejaculation on recognising me. 'Don't say that you saw me talking to an old gipsy!' she entreatingly exclaimed; 'for Mrs. Holman would be so angry, and would turn me away!'—I promised that I would not say anything unnecessarily to do her an injury; and I was beginning to remonstrate when she flippantly ejaculated that 'it was her business,' and glided away from me. I proceeded to the post; and perhaps half-an-hour elapsed before I returned as I had other little commissions to execute, one of which was for Mrs. Holman herself. Therefore on my way home, I called at Mr. St. Clair's; and on entering the servants' hall, I found the domestics in great excitement and consternation. But Emma was not there. Before I could utter a single syllable of inquiry, the parlour-bell rang furiously twice. That was a signal for Mrs. Holman. The worthy woman was greatly troubled; and she rushed up-stairs. I asked what was the matter? One of the footmen told me that his master, on returning home about ten minutes back, had retired to his chamber to dress for dinner, and that he had quickly discovered the disappearance of a curiously carved rosewood box from a cupboard in his dressing-room. It further appeared that when this announcement was made in the servants' hall, Emma had changed colour, and had looked altogether so exceedingly frightened that attention was imme-

diately riveted upon her. Mrs. Holman demanded if she knew anything of the box? She threw herself shrieking upon a chair, exclaiming something about a gipsy. This was reported to Mr. St. Clair, who immediately summoned Emma up into the parlour, where she had been but for a few minutes when the bell rang for Mrs. Holman, as I have just described. I did not say anything about having beheld Emma with the old gipsy; but it struck me that the very object which I had seen the girl give the crone, was of a size and appearance to correspond with that box; and I wondered at the strange coincidence that another should have been intriguing to obtain that which I myself had for six or seven weeks been labouring to procure. In a few minutes down came Mrs. Holman, crying bitterly and saying that Emma had confessed to the circumstance of having been cajoled by the gipsy into procuring the box by aid of false keys which the crone had given her for the purpose of opening the different cupboards till she should find it. It furthermore appeared that the gipsy had held out all kinds of brilliant promises, about a lord for a husband, and a carriage and four, and all kinds of nonsense of that sort, to induce the girl to procure the box, which the crone had promised to return on the morrow. Emma said that she was overawed by the fact that the gipsy should possess the knowledge of such a box being in the house at all; and when she found that box—answering, as it did, the exact description given of it by the crone—she was more than ever convinced that she was gifted with preterhuman powers. Mrs. Holman had been inclined to discharge the girl on the spot: but Mr. St. Clair suddenly seemed to make light of the matter—promised Emma his forgiveness——and expressed his wish that nothing more might be said on the subject—while as for putting it in the hands of the police, he could not think of bringing such a ridiculous scandal upon his household. There the matter ended; and I hastened away to bring you, Miss Percy, the information which I feared would vex you very much. But again I assure you, Miss Percy, that it has not been through——"

"And I again assure you, William," I interrupted him, "that it is by no means necessary for you to make so many apologies or afflict yourself upon the point. And now tell me—did you happen to hear whether Mr. St. Clair exhibited any particular emotion on receiving a description of the gipsy woman?—for such a description he was certain to demand——"

"I can give you no information, Miss, on the subject," rejoined Lardner. "Mrs. Holman did not breathe a syllable in allusion thereto. But this she *did* say, that it was quite astonishing how suddenly her master's manner changed, and how from the excitement of furious anger his mood altered all in a moment into the calmest composure, when he insisted that nothing more should be said upon the subject. And now tell me, Miss Percy—is there anything I can do for you? are there any means by which I may still testify my zeal and devotion towards you?"

"No, William," I responded: "there is nothing now which you can do for me."

I expressed my gratitude for his good intentions; and I bade him remain to pass the rest of the evening with Beda. When I was alone, I reviewed all that I had just heard from William's lips; and I thought to myself, "St. Clair endeavoured to carry off the matter with a cool indifference in the presence of his servants when once they began speaking of the intervention of the police. But at this moment he must be a prey to the most poignant terrors! Doubtless he suspects only too well who the old gipsy crone was; and perhaps he is wondering why she turns against him. In what horrible uncertainty must his mind be plunged!—how he must be racking his imagination with wild bewildering conjectures in reference to the use that Dame Betty can mean to make of the rosewood box and its contents! But will he remain in England? or will he fly? Will he admit to himself that the web is closing in around him? or will he still remain in the infatuated belief that the favourable stars of his destiny can never cease to shine? Ah! not for all the treasures of the earth would I endure the mental excruciations which at this moment that wretched man must be suffering!"

I was still pursuing the same course of meditations, when I retired to rest. I awoke at an early hour in the morning; and when Beda made her appearance to assist in my toilet, I said to her, "I entertain a presentiment that the day will not pass without some event of signal importance in reference to Edwin St. Clair."

"In was an evil moment for him," remarked Beda, "when Dame Betty turned round upon him. She is horribly vindictive!—and in the pursuit of her vengeance she would even sacrifice her own safety—or at least boldly disregard it."

"But still I am at a loss to conceive how she will act in the present instance," I observed, "and what course she purposes to adopt: for as Luigi is is to undergo no trial, there can be no investigation into the causes of the late Mrs. St. Clair's death."

It would be however a mere waste of time for me to place on record all the ideas which passed through my imagination after I had risen in the morning of that memorable day. I was full of suspense in reference to what might occur at the Old Bailey; and I will confess that I longed to be present in the court and contemplate the proceedings. But inasmuch as I am by no means desirous that the reader should be kept similarly in suspense, I will hasten to pursue the thread of my narrative.

I remained at home, expecting that from some source or another I should receive tidings of whatsoever was passing; and indeed I had reason to suppose that William Lardner intended to be a spectator of the proceedings in the Central Criminal Court. The time-piece upon the mantel in the drawing-room was just proclaiming the hour of noon, when I heard footsteps come rushing up the staircase—the door of the apartment was literally burst open—and William made his appearance, exclaiming, "Ah, what a scene, Miss! what a scene! He is in custody!!"

"Who? who?" I demanded: "who is in custody?"

"Mr. St. Clair!" was the answer.

At the same moment a carriage drove rapidly up to the front door of the house: I hastened to the window—and I beheld the Countess of Carboni alighting. It instantaneously struck me that she had been present at the proceedings at the Old Bailey,—though on the last occasion when I saw her she had not dropped the slightest hint that such was her intention.

"And you say that Mr. St. Clair is arrested?" I exclaimed in an excited tone, as I again turned towards William Lardner.

"Yes, Miss!—and he has been carried off to the police-office to be examined before the magistrate! And old Dame Betty has gone as his accuser—and there is Emma—and poor Mrs. St. Clair's maid——"

"Then hasten you, William, to the police-office," I said: "learn the result—and bring the tidings hither. Ah! I had almost forgotten to ask about Luigi?"

"Condemned to death, Miss."

"Yes—condemned to death!" repeated the voice of Beatrice, who at this moment entered the room.

"And you were there, doubtless?" I exclaimed to my friend, who thus made her appearance as William Lardner was departing to execute the commission with which I had charged him.

"Yes—I was in the Central Criminal Court," replied Beatrice. "And, Oh, what a scene! But doubtless you have already learnt——"

"Yes—that St. Clair is arrested," I said.

"Arrested as the murderer of his wife," ejaculated Beatrice,—"or else as the accomplice in her suicide. You cannot conceive, my dear Ellen, the astonishment and dismay—the wonder and excitement——In short, I never beheld such a scene!"

"It must have been most startling!" I exclaimed. "But do tell me, Beatrice——"

"Then, you are as yet acquainted with no particulars?" said the Countess of Carboni.

"With none," I replied. "I had just learnt that St. Clair was arrested when your carriage drove up to the door. And now tell me what took place."

"I must enter somewhat into details," said the Countess of Carboni. "It was not until last evening that I even thought of being present in the Central Criminal Court to-day——"

"And perhaps," I interjected, "Signor Ludovico Marano suggested the idea?"

"Yes, he did, Ellen—and it is useless to deny it. Besides," added Beatrice, with a certain display of dignified independence, "why should I not follow the bent of my own inclination?"

"You have a perfect right, my dear Beatrice," I responded. "Well, last evening you formed the idea——"

"But I did not make up my mind," resumed the Countess, "until this morning, when Signor Marano called again—and though my sister and brother-in-law somewhat objected——"

"Yet you went, Beatrice," I said, somewhat impatient for the forthcoming narrative.

"Yes—I went under the escort of Signor Marano. To tell you the truth, Ellen—and I do not think you will altogether hate me for the confession—I longed to hear the death-sentence pronounced upon the wretch whose iniquities had caused the death of Angelo Marano. But I see you are impatient! Well, then, I accompanied Ludovico:—we found a great number of persons collected in the narrow thoroughfare of the Old

Bailey—and when we alighted from the carriage and inquired our way to the gallery of the court we were at first assured that it would be impossible for us to find room, for it was already so much crowded. However, by dint of feeing the officials, we succeeded in obtaining seats in the gallery, which as well as every other part of the court, was excessively thronged. The proceedings were just commencing: the Judges had taken their seats—the Jury were being sworn. The prisoner was not as yet in the dock. I accordingly had leisure to glance around; and I caught a glimpse of the Right Honourable Edwin St. Clair, in the body of the court. I saw two or three persons in the neighbourhood of where I was sitting pointing out St. Clair to their neighbours: and one of those individuals said, 'It is only natural that he should come to hear sentence of death pronounced upon the wretch who was the cause of his wife's death.' —It struck me that St. Clair was exceedingly pale; and I observed that he kept looking all around as if to ascertain who were present. But at the time little did I suspect why he was so uneasy! Presently the prisoner was introduced into the dock——"

"And what was his demeanour, Beatrice?" I inquired.

"It seemed firm and collected—but mournful —deeply mournful," answered Beatrice, speaking slowly as if she had to search for words in order to express her meaning adequately. "But I could not obtain a very good view of his countenance," she continued, speaking more quickly; "for where I sat in the gallery, his back was for the most part turned towards me as I looked down into the dock."

"And the proceedings quickly commenced?" I said inquiringly. "But Ah! I forgot to ask—was the Italian Catholic priest present?"

"Yes—no—I am not sure," responded Beatrice, with what seemed for an instant to be a slight degree of confusion: but I quickly forgot the little incident in the excitement of the narrative on which she forthwith entered. "The Clerk of the Court," she hastily went on to say, "read the deposition of the prisoner's confession made at the police court three weeks ago—— "

"The confession of both crimes do you mean?" I asked.

"No," replied Beatrice,—"only the confession in respect to the fearful scene upon the Dover cliffs; and when the Clerk had finished reading, he asked whether the prisoner purposed to plead *Guilty* likewise in the presence of that tribunal? He answered in a firm voice that he did. There was some little conversation carried on in a whisper between the Judges; and then they were about to put on the black caps, when a shrill screaming voice yelled out, 'Is there not to be any inquiry into the other matter?'— All was astonishment and excitement in the court; and the Clerk cried, 'Silence, woman!'—I looked, and I saw an aged female, tolerably decently dressed, leaning upon a stick, making her way through the crowd; and then the next moment I beheld Mr. St. Clair endeavouring to force a still more rapid *exit*. At the moment I had not the slightest idea that there could be any connexion between the two incidents,—I mean the presence of the old woman and the attempted retreat of St. Clair: but the

next instant an announcement was made which electrified the whole court."

"An announcement by that old gipsy?" I anxiously asked.

"Yes," responded Beatrice: "for forth from her lips pealed the screaming, shrieking words—'Seize upon St. Clair! arrest him! he was the murderer of his own wife!'—Of course everybody fancied that it was some unfortunate madwoman who had found her way into the court; and a couple of constables had already seized upon her, when she yelled out, 'Unhand me, or I shall serve you as St. Clair served my grand-daughter, his unfortunate wife! This flower is poisoned!' she vociferated, at the same time producing from a small rosewood box something that looked like a faded white rose. You cannot conceive, my dear Ellen, how acute was the suspense displayed by every fixed look and by every suspended breath throughout that hall of justice; and all that I am telling you passed with an exceeding rapidity. The police constables fell back at the terrible announcement of the flower being poisoned: the crowd opened likewise, recoiling in alarm: and the hag made her way straight to the barristers' table. Even the learned gentlemen themselves seemed to dislike the contiguity of the hag with the flower which she had announced to be poisoned: for they shrank back from her presence. 'Ah! I see that you do not doubt it!' ejaculated the dame: 'but still you shall have proof!' "

"Proof? What in the court?" I exclaimed. "What proof could she give?"

"You shall learn. All in a moment," continued Beatrice, "she took from a basket which she carried beneath her shawl, a couple of small rabbits, which she tossed quickly one after another upon the table. Then, quick as the eye can wink, she thrust the faded white rose at each rabbit— and ejaculations of mingled surprise and horror burst from the lips of the nearest bystanders, for the little animals at once turned over on their backs, stiffened quickly, and were dead. It was the work of a moment!—death was in the white rose!—that was clear enough! But I cannot explain the effect of this strange spectacle, which became absolutely appalling when associated with the terrific charge which had pealed forth from the woman's lips against Mr. St. Clair. And that effect was most powerfully enhanced when the woman shrieked forth, 'This was how his wife died!'—and then she pointed with her long lank finger towards St. Clair, exclaiming, 'Why did he want to fly when he saw me enter the court?'— Yes, it was astounding!"

"The scene must have indeed proved most fearfully interesting," I said. "But what prevented St. Clair from escaping?"

"I looked to ascertain that point," responded Beatrice; "and I perceived that three or four stalwart-looking gipsy men had their hands upon his arms, while he was endeavouring to assume a look of scornful contempt for the accusation levelled against him. Then the old gipsy-woman again raised her voice, screaming forth, 'I have my witnesses! Here is a girl who can prove that this box was until last night in the possession of her master St. Clair!—and here is the deceased Mrs. St. Clair's confidential maid who can prove that when her mistress died the faded white rose was found lying on her bosom! And who was last with her? Her husband! Her husband, Edwin St. Clair!'—Indescribable was the effect produced by these words," added Beatrice.

"And St. Clair himself?" I asked.

"He was as pale as a ghost," responded Beatrice; "and as I swept my eyes round upon the assembled mass of spectators, I could tell that the tide of opinion was rolling most strongly against St. Clair. I should again observe that the scene which it has taken me so many minutes to describe, passed in an incredibly short space of time,—scarcely any one attempting to interrupt it, and the very Judges themselves sitting in the silence of stupefaction. But at length the senior Judge began to speak. I could not catch all he said; but I heard something about ' a strange and most unparalleled interruption '—' very wrong for the old woman to adopt such a course '—' case for a magistrate in the first instance '—and words to that effect. By this time an inspector of police had made his way towards the spot where Edwin St. Clair was standing: something was said to the old woman about 'charging St. Clair;' and she replied vehemently, ' I do!'—Then the inspector formally took Edwin St. Clair into custody; and he left the court, followed not only by the old woman and her two female witnesses, but likewise by no inconsiderable portion of the crowd; for the circumstances which had just transpired seemed to have rendered St. Clair more attractive in respect to morbid curiosity than the prisoner in the dock himself."

"Ah! the prisoner in the dock!" I interjected. "We have absolutely lost sight of him!"

"And really, for the time being," replied Beatrice, "he was almost lost sight of in the court itself; for no tongue can afford you an idea of the excitement which prevailed during the brief space occupied by those extraordinary proceedings. When St. Clair was borne off in custody, all those persons who remained behind gazed at one another as if to demand whether it were a dream which had just passed before them, or if it were a reality? At length the Chief Judge began to make some observations. He said ' that whatever might be the result of the extraordinary accusation just made against Mr. St. Clair in reference to his deceased wife—and in whatever manner that lady might have met her death, whether from the effect of the corrosive fluid thrown at her, or whether from any other cause—all this had nothing to do with the present case. The prisoner in the dock was not now arraigned for the murder of Mrs. St. Clair: he stood there to receive sentence for the crime of murdering an Italian nobleman, the Count of Carboni.'—The Judges then put on their black caps; and the senior functionary passed sentence of death in a most solemnly impressive manner."

"And how did the wretched culprit bear himself while the awful ceremony was in progress?" I inquired, shuddering at the bare idea.

"I could not see his face," responded Beatrice. "But when the sentence was pronounced—— However, I suppose you will see it in the newspapers, Ellen—it is sure to be there——"

"See what, Beatrice? You can tell me, surely?" I said, somewhat surprised at the manner in which she so suddenly interrupted herself.

"Oh, to be sure! When sentence was pronounced," continued Beatrice, again speaking slowly, and seeming to measure her words, as she had done during a former part of the discourse, "the miserable wretch fell down upon his knees, and implored mercy on the ground that he had made a full confession. The Judge shook his head —and observed that the criminal could expect no mercy, and must not entertain the slightest hope of a commutation of his sentence."

Beatrice paused for nearly a minute; and then she added, "A terrific yell burst from Luigi's lips; and he was borne out of the dock. Thus terminated the terrible scene, Ellen. And now that I have told you everything, I must take my leave."

"Wherefore are you in such a hurry, Beatrice?" I inquired: and then, as a sudden thought struck me, I exclaimed, "But perhaps Signor Marano is in your carriage?—And I have been guilty of the most flagrant discourtesy in not inviting him to walk in!"

"No, my dear Ellen," answered Beatrice: "Ludovico Marano is not with me. He—he is waiting—I mean to say he went in another direction——to keep some appointment——I know not exactly what. And now adieu, dear Ellen."

Beatrice pressed my hand, and hurried off—assuring me that her sister the Marchioness of Campanella would be most anxious for her return.

An hour afterwards William Lardner returned to the house, with the announcement that Mr. St. Clair had been charged before the police magistrate with having murdered his wife, or else having guiltily connived at her own self-destruction; and he had been committed for trial on the latter charge.

CHAPTER XCVI.

LUIGI'S LAST CRIME.

MARY GLENTWORTH was secluded in her own chamber during the hours that were passed in the manner which I have been describing; and now that I had ascertained how serious indeed was the predicament in which Edwin St. Clair was placed, I hastened to communicate it to her.

"You have yearned for vengeance, Mary, against the villain who ruined you," I said; "and you will now behold a terrible chastisement inflicted upon him—although it will be retribution from another source and for another crime! St. Clair is in Newgate, charged with having been accessory to the self-destruction of his wife!"

"Oh, is this possible, my dear Ellen?" exclaimed Mary Glentworth, the fierce fire of gratified malignity flashing forth from those eyes that were habitually so mild in their expression.

"It is possible, Mary. Nay, more," I said, " it has actually happened!"

"Heaven be thanked!" she exclaimed, clasping her hands as if in gratitude for some immense benefit.

"Hush, Mary! hush!" I said: "it is blasphemy to thank heaven in such a sense!"

"And yet I do thank heaven," she replied, with fierce emphasis, "for having brought down destruction upon the head of the villain who ruth-

lessly and deliberately destroyed my honour and happiness!"

But I will not dwell upon the discourse which took place on that occasion between Mary Glentworth and myself. Suffice it to say she was terribly vindictive in respect to St. Clair: but really this was not to be wondered at, when the immensity of her wrongs was taken into consideration.

Three weeks passed away; and, according to the newspaper paragraphs, the Italian Catholic priest was most assiduous in his visits and attentions to the doomed Luigi. In pursuance of the established custom, the Sheriffs had appointed the second Monday after the session of the Central Criminal Court, as the day on which the law was to be carried into execution. In the interval no commutation of the sentence was announced—no mitigation of the extreme penalty seemed at all likely to occur.

No. 76.—ELLEN PERCY.

The time drew fearfully short; and on the Saturday previous to the Sabbath which was now the only intervening day ere the morning of doom,—the grisly preparations for the execution commenced. William Lardner happened to be passing that way; and he beheld workmen putting up the barriers to break the pressure of the crowds which were certain to assemble to witness the execution. But it was not until early on the Monday morning that the gibbet was brought forth from the place where it was habitually kept in the press-yard. For this piece of intelligence I must assure my readers that I am indebted to the newspapers: for William Lardner possessed not that morbid curiosity which could alone have induced him to repeat on the Monday morning that visit which he had paid to the Old Bailey on the Saturday night. But the daily journals gave a painfully minute description of the scene presented to the view in front of Newgate on that Monday morning. The crowds were gathering fast—pouring in from all directions to secure good places for witnessing the execution; and masses of juveniles of both sexes watched with eager interest the proceedings of the workmen who were engaged in connecting the stout wooden barriers with the huge black gallows that had been drawn forth.

But the gibbet was destined to be disappointed of its prey; and at about half-past seven o'clock on that Monday morning, the rumour began to be whispered that the Italian had committed suicide.

"Impossible!" exclaimed one of the loungers outside: "the fellow could have had no chance!"

"The turnkeys have never left him since sentence was passed," observed another.

"At least they ought not to have left him," said a third: "but I did hear it stated two or three days ago——"

"What did you hear stated?" asked several voices eagerly.

"Why, that when the Italian priest has visited the murderer, they have been allowed to remain alone together—because, you see, Catholics have to make secret confessions——"

"Well, but when the priest was not there, then the turnkeys were—or ought to have been; and so I proclaim that the Italian could not have committed suicide—and we shall presently find it is all a hoax!"

"Well, I certainly should not like to be disappointed," said another; "for I've walked six miles this mornin'—me and my old 'ooman here—just to have a look at the hangin'——."

"Oh, don't be afraid!" cried the foremost speaker, dogmatically; "you won't be disappointed, my good fellow!"

This conversation was overheard by one of the newspaper reporters; and it was duly recorded in the columns of a Sunday journal. But in spite of the dogmatism with which one individual had denied the possibility of the occurrence, the report was nevertheless true—and Luigi had committed suicide!—so that the man who with his wife had walked six miles to witness the execution, was disappointed after all! In order that the reader may thoroughly understand the circumstances of this act of suicide, it is necessary that I should transfer to my pages a portion of the evidence given before the Coroner in the afternoon of that same day. For little delay was allowed to ensue before the inquest took place; and the greatest excitement prevailed throughout the neighbourhood of the prison. A number of strange rumours were afloat,—some to the effect that the turnkeys had connived at the wretched man's self-destruction—others declaring that the Italian priest had disappeared most singularly:—in short there were all the wild speculations, reports, and gossipings that usually attend upon anything of importance and of mystery. Indeed, it was not until I received a second edition of the evening paper, that I could obtain anything like an accurate version of the morning's transactions; and it was this journal to which I refer that contained the full account of the Coroner's Inquest whence I am about to make certain quotations. Here is the first extract:—

"THOMAS GILBERT deposed as follows: I am a turnkey of Newgate prison, and have held my present situation for some fourteen or fifteen years.

The deceased Luigi had been about six weeks in Newgate from the date of his committal for trial. He has been constantly attended by an Italian Roman Catholic priest who was called Father Maffeo. It has been customary to leave the priest and the prisoner alone together since the latter was condemned to death, because it was supposed that the prisoner might have to make confessions according to his creed, and which he would not do in the presence of a third party. Properly speaking, a prisoner condemned to death should never be lost sight of by the authorities of the gaol: but in such a case as this an exception was made for the reason which I have stated. The object of keeping a personal watch over a convict is to prevent him from laying violent hands upon himself; therefore we of course supposed that the presence of the priest was effectual for this purpose. It was my duty to share with another turnkey the task of sitting with the prisoner day and night; but when Father Maffeo arrived, I was in the habit of retiring into the court-yard and waiting till the priest reappeared. There is a long passage from the court-yard towards the condemned cell; and that passage branches off into another,—so that if the door at the entrance of the first-named passage is left unfastened, it is quite possible for any one to pass by the second-named passage into the condemned cell without being seen by a person standing at the entrance into the court-yard. This must be borne in mind, as it will explain something that I have presently to say. But first of all I have some other little particulars to mention. Yesterday being the Sabbath as well as the last day the prisoner had to live, Father Maffeo passed many hours with him: and as usual they were left alone together. I was on duty a part of the while. I walked in the court-yard as usual, until relieved by my fellow-turnkey. Then I again went on the same duty for a couple of hours in the evening. I was in the cell when Father Maffeo left the prisoner for the night. The prisoner knelt and seemed to pray fervently, as far as I could judge, not understanding the Italian language. Both the priest and the prisoner could speak English; and the priest inquired of me at what hour he could be allowed to return on the following morning—that is to say the morning of this day. I told him he must consult the governor upon the point. While we were yet speaking, the governor came to make his usual round; and Father Maffeo received the assurance that he might present himself for admission at any hour he thought fit. The priest accordingly said that he should be with the prisoner at four o'clock in the morning. He departed, and I went off duty at the same time, being relieved by a turnkey named James Coppin."

The second extract from the evening papers is as follows:—

"JAMES COPPIN being now called, spoke to this effect: I went on duty in the prisoner's cell last night about ten o'clock. The prisoner seemed restless and nervous, and I recommended him to go to bed and endeavour to sleep. He said that he would follow my advice; and undressing himself got into bed. He presently asked me whether reprieves or pardons ever came in the middle of the night? and I said I did not think they did. I was not much surprised at the question, because I knew that the prisoner had all along cherished the hope of being treated mercifully in consequence of making a confession. Still I thought it my duty to tell him it was my belief that there was very little chance of his life being spared; and I asked him whether his clergyman Father Maffeo had not told him the same? I thought that he looked at me in a strange manner for a moment; and then he said, 'I know very well that you turnkeys will not reveal the fact until a particular moment, even though you should have the reprieve in your pocket!'—He then turned round as if he were composing himself to sleep; and the conversation dropped. He lay quiet for two or three hours; he then complained of thirst, and I gave him some water. He asked me how long I had been connected with the gaol?—and when I told him sixteen years, he inquired whether I had ever experienced the pleasure of communicating the tidings of a reprieve or pardon? I told him that I never had, for it was the duty of the chaplain or the governor to announce so important a fact to a prisoner. I saw that he was harping upon a reprieve; and I thought it very wrong to suffer him to indulge in a hope which I felt convinced would be disappointed. I therefore again recommended him to put aside all thoughts of this life, and prepare himself thoroughly for the next. He again surveyed me with a singular expression of countenance: I cannot describe it—but it seemed as if he thought that I was wilfully deceiving him, and that I knew more than I chose to say. Then he observed, in a significant manner, 'Ah! you little think what interest is making on my behalf!'—I was surprised at the observation, for I wondered who would interest himself for such a being. Yet I said nothing; for as a matter of course I could not contradict the statement he had made. He again turned round, and either composed himself to sleep, or at all events he lay quiet for a considerable interval. Then he inquired what o'clock it was? I told him that it was half-past three. He started up, ejaculating in English, 'Then in another half-hour I shall know my fate!'—From this observation it immediately struck me that the Catholic priest must be the person who was interesting himself in the prisoner's behalf, or else communicating with other friends in the background. Therefore, as I was ignorant of all particulars on the point, I abstained from any additional remark—neither choosing to encourage nor destroy a hope which was based upon grounds whereof I had no knowledge. Shortly afterwards Father Maffeo arrived; and at the same time I was relieved by Thomas Gilbert."

At this point it will be better to resume the quotation of Thomas Gilbert's evidence, in order to give a continuity to the narrative. Gilbert proceeded to depose in the following terms:—"It was about four o'clock this morning when the Reverend Father Maffeo arrived at the gaol; and I at once introduced him to the prisoner's cell. James Coppin came out of the cell at the same time; and we left the priest and the prisoner together. We walked for a few minutes in the court-yard; and then James Coppin said he should go and have a bit of a nap for an hour or two. I asked him when he should return? He said at seven o'clock. I replied that I hoped he would, if it was only for a few minutes, as it would give

me an opportunity of going and getting a mouthful of breakfast. This, as I have said, was at four o'clock. I walked up and down in the court-yard to keep myself awake; and so the time passed. I heard seven o'clock strike by St. Sepulchre's, St. Paul's, and other churches. A few moments afterwards Father Maffeo appeared at the door leading into the court-yard, and asked me to let him out,—adding, ' The other turnkey has gone in to the prisoner.' — Not for a single moment did I suspect that this was otherwise, because I remembered James Coppin's promises, and I thought that he must have entered by the passages while I was taking my walk in the court-yard. Thinking it was all right, I led the priest towards the gate of the prison, and I could not help saying, ' I suppose your reverence will return presently to accompany the unfortunate man to the scaffold?'—' Yes,' answered Father Maffeo; ' I am merely going to obtain some little refreshment, for I am nearly exhausted.'—He then issued forth from the gaol, and I went to get my own breakfast, feeling confident that my mate James Coppin was with the prisoner. Half-an-hour afterwards I thought I would go to the cell and see whether Coppin himself wanted to be relieved, and how matters stood; for it was drawing towards the fatal hour, and the Sheriffs as well as the executioner might be soon expected. I entered the cell, and was instantaneously struck by perceiving no one there except the prisoner. Then a second glance at the prisoner himself, showed me the whole truth. He was dead!"

The other turnkey, James Coppin, stated in addition to the evidence which has already been quoted, that he did not return to the cell according to his promise, from the simple fact that he overslept himself; and thus he was not with the prisoner for a single minute during the interval from seven till half-past when Thomas Gilbert fancied that he must be there.

A turnkey who was on duty at the entrance of the prison, deposed as follows: "I remember the Reverend Father Maffeo leaving the gaol at a few minutes past seven. Thomas Gilbert brought him as far as the lobby. I heard Gilbert inquire whether his Reverence did not mean to return? and the priest replied that he should not be long, as he was only going to obtain some refreshment. He was in a plain suit of black. On all occasions he wore a cassock and bands: but he said that he had left them behind in the prisoner's cell to avoid the inconvenience of being recognised by the crowd so densely assembled in front of the gaol. When he had gone, I said to Thomas Gilbert that I thought it rather odd he should leave his fellow-countryman even for a few minutes at such a crisis: but Gilbert remarked that the Italians were queer people and did things different from the English. He then went off to get his breakfast. Father Maffeo did not return; and at about half-past seven I first learnt from Gilbert that the prisoner was dead. Father Maffeo has not since appeared at the gaol."

A surgeon deposed that he resided in the neighbourhood of Newgate, and that at about half-past seven he was sent for. He was introduced into the condemned cell, where he found the prisoner quite dead. He had opened a vein in his right arm, and had bled to death! It was with a sharp-pointed nail that he had effected his object. There was a large pool of blood upon the floor. The prisoner was lying partially up in the bed, with his head leaning forward upon his breast; so that it seemed as if he had pierced his arm when in a sitting posture, and had then either thrown himself back, or else had gradually sunk into that semi-recumbent position in proportion as life was ebbing away. There could be little doubt that the punctures in the arm were effected by the prisoner himself, from the posture in which he was lying, and the fact that whereas the vein was opened in the right arm, the sharp-pointed nail was still held tightly between the finger and thumb of the left hand. The surgeon expressed his opinion that Luigi could only have just expired at the moment when Thomas Gilbert must have entered the cell. Now, as this was at about half-past seven, and the priest had left at seven, the question was whether Luigi had punctured his arm while Father Maffeo was still with him, or immediately upon finding himself alone?—or, in other words, whether half-an-hour was sufficient for the suicide to bleed to death? The surgeon spoke guardedly on the point: for though on the one hand the time was short enough for the fulfilment of the tragedy itself, yet on the other hand he had discovered by post-mortem examination that Luigi's frame was so fearfully emaciated and attenuated as to render the threads which held body and soul together very easy of severance.

The Coroner demanded if Father Maffeo were in attendance?—and he was answered in the negative. Further questionings on the part of this functionary elicited the following facts,—that none of the officials of Newgate were acquainted with Father Maffeo's place of abode—that they had never thought of asking him—that when he had presented himself at the prison, announcing who he was, he at once obtained admittance. The ecclesiastical costume which he had left behind in the prisoner's cell, was produced; but it in no way afforded any clue to the solution of the mystery which now seemed to envelope the Italian Catholic priest. It is but justice to the Governor of Newgate, in order to acquit him of any charge of negligence or of slovenliness in the performance of his duty, to state that he deposed as follows:—"Before the deceased Luigi was transferred to Newgate, he was in the House of Detention. It was there that he expressed a wish to be visited by a priest, and there that Father Maffeo accordingly first called upon him. This I read in the newspapers. Therefore, when Luigi was committed to Newgate, I had not the slightest hesitation in allowing the continued attendance of the priest whose ministrations he had received at the former place of incarceration."

The Governor of the House of Detention deposed to the following effect:—"Luigi was in the first instance in my custody. I remember it was on the fourteenth of October—that is to say, about six weeks back—between three and four o'clock in the afternoon, a gentleman called upon me, representing himself to be an Italian Roman Catholic priest, and saying that he had come in consequence of an intimation which appeared in the newspapers of that day, to the effect that Luigi had expressed a wish to be attended by a pastor of his own creed and his own country. The

individual announcing himself as Father Maffeo, produced several papers, which he represented to be credentials or testimonials: but on glancing at them, I observed that they were written in a language which I could not understand; and moreover, even if it had been otherwise, I should not have read them. I should have conceived that it would be an insult to a respectable and reverend person. If at any time a gentleman came and represented himself as a minister of religion, I should take it for granted that he was telling the truth—that is to say, provided his personal appearance seemed to corroborate the statement, as it fully did in the instance to which I am specially alluding."

I have now recorded the salient points of the Coroner's Inquest—or at least as much of them as it is necessary for the reader to become acquainted with. A verdict of *Felo de se* was returned; and the corpse of Luigi was ordered to be interred at midnight, without the funeral service, within the precincts of Newgate. The Coroner, on summing up, had made some strong observations to the jury upon the suspicious conduct of the Catholic priest: but still, as that functionary observed, there was no evidence of a direct nature to inculpate Father Maffeo as an accomplice in his fellow-countryman's suicide.

As I have already said, it was in the evening paper that I read this account of the Inquest; and I could think of nothing else for the remainder of the night. Indeed, after I had retired to rest, the whole affair continued to haunt me: and I can scarcely tell how it was, but several vague suspicions and misgivings kept flitting through my mind. They were too indefinite to be deliberately envisaged—far too unsubstantial to be studied or analyzed; and yet they seemed more or less to point in a particular direction, so that I was rendered restless and uneasy by the sensation that there was a mystery to be cleared up, and by a presentiment that the elucidation would prove more or less painful for me.

On the following day, at about one in the afternoon, I proceeded to the Marquis of Campanella's mansion to call upon Beatrice. On alighting from my carriage, I found the front door of the house standing open, as the hall-porter was receiving letters which the postman was delivering. I learnt that the Marquis and Marchioness had just gone out, but that the Countess of Carboni was in the drawing-room; though whether she were disengaged or not, the hall-porter did not know. He however added that he was tolerably sure her ladyship was alone. He was about to ring a bell to summon a lackey to conduct me up-stairs, when I declined giving the trouble,—saying, "I can find my way very well."

The hall-porter knew that I was intimate at the house, and that I might therefore dispense with ceremonies. He bowed, and I passed on. I ascended the staircase—I approached the drawing-room door—I perceived that it was ajar—and voices were speaking within. I at once recognised them: they were the voices of Ludovico Marano and Beatrice di Carboni. I was instantaneously on the point of throwing open the door, when I was riveted to the spot by certain words which struck my ears.

"We are both terribly avenged, dear Beatrice!"

said Ludovico Marano,—"I on behalf of the cousin whom I loved as a brother!—you on behalf of that same Angelo whom you at one time loved so tenderly, and who perished so prematurely and so fearfully! Yes, Beatrice—it is done! and all that I promised to do I have accomplished! So well has everything been managed, that detection is impossible! And now, dearest Beatrice, tell me if I may at length fall at your feet and implore that you will bestow this fair hand upon me?"

"Yes, Ludovico," responded the low tremulous voice of the Countess of Carboni: "I will accompany you to the altar! Yes—I feel that I can love you!—for you are like your cousin Angelo—and what is more, you have avenged him! Oh, revenge is sweet, Ludovico!—and I, though English by birth, nevertheless feel as if Italian blood rolled in my veins when I think of revenge!"

"Yes, dearest Beatrice—revenge is sweet when it is the all-absorbing passion," rejoined Ludovico: "but afterwards—Oh! how infinitely sweeter is love! Revenge is the fierce passion which intoxicates as with brandy; but love is the sentiment which produces a dulcet ebriety as if with delicious wine! And Oh! I, Beatrice, after having experienced the former, am now tasting of the latter! Say, dearest—how is it with you?"

"With me likewise, Ludovico. Now leave me," murmuringly answered the voice of Beatrice; "for I must reflect upon all you have said—and I must think upon the terms in which I shall break to my sister and my brother-in-law the intelligence that I have accepted the offer of your hand."

I now heard the sound of kisses; and suddenly seized with affright on account of my position at that door—fearful of being taxed with the meanness and baseness of wilful eavesdropping —remembering too that on a former occasion I had shown how I had overheard something which passed at the time between these self-same persons —I attempted to beat a precipitate retreat. I rushed to the top of the stairs: I descended half-a-dozen of them—I was perhaps never so completely deprived of all self-possession, so confused and bewildered! The conversation itself which I overheard had first of all thrown me into a perturbed and excited state; and then came the sudden dread of being caught in the act of playing the eavesdropper. But when I had descended those half-dozen stairs, I stopped short—I regained my fortitude—I said to myself, "My carriage will be seen at the door: it is now too late to retreat—I must return and see Beatrice!"

I accordingly began at once to retrace my steps; and on the top of the stairs I encountered Ludovico Marano, who was just issuing from the drawing-room.

"Ah, Miss Percy!" he said, bowing with that profound courtesy which is adopted by all foreigners: "I have the honour to salute you."

I had not once seen Signor Marano since the day of my introduction to him; and now, as I glanced at his countenance, I was struck by the conviction that he was changed in some respect or another:—he did not look like the same being I had previously seen. Indeed, I might have even passed without recognising him if he had not first addressed me. I started—I again looked at him; and now methought that he himself was trembling with confusion and becoming over-whelmed with embarrassment. An idea smote me with lightning rapidity; and I perceived how and where he was changed. That profusion of black hair, shining with a rich gloss and curling naturally, was gone: it was all cropped close! The whiskers that had been trimmed with such precision, and which had seemed to serve as an ebon frame for the dusky-complexioned countenance,—those whiskers were likewise gone! And the moustache, pointed and slightly curled at the corners of the mouth—that had likewise disappeared! No wonder that I should have deemed him altered! But why was it? Oh! I literally started as if galvanized when a thought struck me. Ah! and that thought instantaneously became a conviction. I understood it all! — Ludovico Marano had played the part of the Roman Catholic priest to the wretched Luigi!

"Ellen, dearest Ellen—is that you?" exclaimed the voice of Beatrice, who having heard Ludovico Marano address me, now came forth from the drawing-room.

But I could not answer. There I stood gazing with mingled horror and consternation upon the Italian; and I felt that my face must be as ghastly as that of a corpse. He himself, having previously looked confused, could no longer doubt that there was something wrong; and turning hastily towards the Countess of Carboni, he said something in Italian, which from a certain trifling knowledge I had obtained of the language, I felt assured was to this effect—"I go at once! Let us meet in Paris!"

He bowed, and endeavoured to pass me hastily: but I caught him by the arm, saying in a low voice and with painful utterance—for I was almost overwhelmed by all that was in my mind—"Stop, Signor! you cannot depart thus! You have a crime to answer for! Complicity in a man's suicide is by the law of England *murder!*"

His somewhat dusky countenance became of a dead sallow paleness, and his naturally handsome eyes suddenly gazed upon me with a hollow haggard expression.

"No, no, dearest Ellen! you would not do this!" murmured Beatrice, in an imploring tone. "For God's sake let him depart! He is to become my husband; and—and—I love him!"

My hand dropped from its grasp upon Ludovico Marano's sleeve! I could not resist that appeal so piteously and so earnestly made by the soft tremulous voice of Beatrice. Ludovico Marano flung upon me a look of indescribable gratitude; and he hastily descended the stairs, while I slowly followed Beatrice into the drawing-room.

CHAPTER XCVII.

THE TWO TRAVELLING-CARRIAGES.

IT was slowly that I thus followed in the footsteps of Beatrice: for I could not help feeling that I had been guilty of a weakness, and had, so to speak, proved unfaithful to the cause of rigorous justice in suffering Ludovico Marano to escape. There was a shade of melancholy upon my countenance, doubtless appearing akin to the languor of my footsteps; and I felt that a gulf had opened betwixt Beatrice and myself—that there was no longer between us the same friendship as heretofore; for she stood an altered being in my eyes. I regarded her as the accomplice of Ludovico Marano!

She, on her own side, seemed to understand what must be passing in my mind; for on entering the drawing-room, she looked round timidly at me, and then she flung her arms about my neck, exclaiming, "Oh! is there any loss of friendship between us?"

"Beatrice," I said, in a cold voice, as I disengaged myself from her embrace, "I now comprehend it all! The beardless countenance of Signor Marano and the cropped hair tell the tale only too legibly! The vindictiveness must have been terrible which could thus triumph over even all the personal vanity of a young man; and I know that this vengeance has been horrible!—for after all, notwithstanding his black and numerous crimes, Luigi has been rendered a victim!"

"A victim of what, Ellen?" said the Countess, looking at me with mingled deprecation and the pride of angry feelings.

"A victim of misrepresentations," I responded, "which never ought to be made even to a criminal—but which are doubly infamous when masked under the cloak of religion!"

"Infamous?" echoed Beatrice. "Do you apply this term, Ellen, to Signor Marano?"

"Yes—to Signor Marano," I rejoined. "Oh! do not think to trifle with me, Beatrice! I understand it all! The only wonder is that I did not comprehend it as the fearful drama was progressing!"

"And what do you understand? what do you conjecture, Ellen?" asked Beatrice, trembling and quivering, and evidently putting the question fo the purpose of ascertaining precisely how much I might know, and to what extent either she herself or Ludovico Marano might be in my power.

"I fathom your purpose, Beatrice," I responded, somewhat bitterly; "but still I will explain my meaning. There was a vengeance to be wreaked on Luigi by both of you!—vengeance on Marano's part for the death of his cousin Angelo! vengeance on your part for the same cause, and likewise for the reason that he was the author of the whole dismal tragedy at the Chateau of Carboni! I do not wonder that the hearts of both of you should have yearned for vengeance: that was natural enough!—but Oh! the vengeance itself ought to have been of a legitimate character! Let me analyze the circumstances. I came to you one day, and I told you two distinct things. The first was that Luigi could not be convicted of a capital crime in the case of Mrs. St. Clair; and the second was that our evidence would not be sufficient to condemn him for the assassination of your husband. You feared that he would escape the gallows; and to the gallows you were determined to send him. How did events progress? Signor Marano was present on the occasion—the newspaper arrived—and you read therein that Luigi, either in his remorse or his hypocrisy, had asked for a priest. The circumstance gave Signor Marano an idea which I can only characterize as horrible and hideous—an idea such as an Italian vengeance could alone dream of!"

"Ellen!" ejaculated Beatrice, her countenance flushing and her eyes flashing with anger. "Ellen!" she repeated, but deprecatingly and entreatingly.

"Oh! I will do you no harm, Beatrice!" I said. "You know that I have had the opportunity of doing you so much good in my time, that I should now be sorely grieved to injure you! But still you shall hear me while I prove that I have fathomed all the purposes of your soul!—and this shall be your punishment! Yes—well do I remember how ominously pensive was Signor Marano on that occasion when he learnt from the columns of the *Morning Post* that Luigi had demanded a priest. And moreover, did I not by accident catch the vindictive words which he uttered?—those words the significancy of which I now see that you yourself must have only too well understood, and which involved a scheme of vengeance as dark as any Italian imagination could have conceived! And that very day, within two or three hours of the resolve being taken, did Ludovico Marano present himself as a priest at the House of Detention; and he persuaded Luigi that confession would obtain a mitigation of the punishment. So the man confessed that crime which could not otherwise have been brought home to him——I mean the assassination of your husband!"

"And do you regret," demanded Beatrice, somewhat sarcastically, "that a murderer should have been thus punished?"

"No, Beatrice," I solemnly answered: "I do not regret that a murderer should have been punished; but I deplore that the vilest of agencies should have been used for the purpose: I lament that in order to bring *one* criminal effectually to justice, *two* other persons should likewise have rendered themselves criminal! And Oh, Beatrice! now I full well understand why you were confused—why you spoke strangely to me, when you came to tell me the particulars of Luigi's trial—and why you also suppressed a circumstance at the time!"

"And that circumstance?" demanded Beatrice quickly.

"You told me that on receiving sentence," I continued, "the miserable wretch fell down on his knees and implored mercy on the ground that he had made a full confession. You told me likewise that when the judge shook his head and declared that the criminal could expect no mercy he gave vent to an appalling cry. But then you did *not* add that the criminal demanded mercy *as a right* on the ground of his confession—and that thus vociferating, he was hurried away from the dock. You feared lest by your manner you should betray something! I subsequently read that incident in the newspapers; but I thought little of it at the time, because my suspicions were very far from being excited in reference to yourself and Signor Marano. *Now*, however, I comprehend everything. Yes!—and the proceedings at the Coroner's Inquest—the testimony of the turnkeys—prove how Luigi had been buoyed up by the hope of pardon until the very last! Who thus buoyed him up? Marano, in the guise of a priest!—Marano who doubtless told him that he had interest sufficient to obtain a reprieve!—Marano who was thus executing a cold-blooded vengeance,—exciting the wretch with false hopes in order that he might enjoy the moment when they should be all scattered to the winds! O Beatrice, this is a horrible tale—and terribly does it grieve me to think and to proclaim that you have been an accomplice in the whole! What took place yesterday morning when the miserable man resolved upon self-destruction, I know not——I scarcely dare even venture to guess!"

"I will tell you, Ellen—I will tell you!" exclaimed Beatrice, now looking and speaking wildly; and she was evidently not the mistress of her thoughts or actions—or else perhaps she would not have revealed the details of the catastrophe. "All that you have said is true: but you deal harshly with me!—you deal harshly with Marano likewise! For, Oh! was it not natural that there should be a craving for vengeance in such circumstances? Yet listen! Ludovico went early to the gaol yesterday morning: he told Luigi that he had done everything which man could do to obtain a reprieve, but that he had failed. And then Luigi sank into the deepest despondency;—and thus two hours passed. Ludovico dreamt not that he would commit suicide: he did not mean it—he did not intend it—he wished to see him suffer upon the scaffold. But presently he became aware that Luigi was doing something mysterious; he tore down the bed-clothes—and he saw that the wretch had punctured his arm so violently that the blood was welling forth in a cataract. Then Ludovico was afraid—he was seized with a powerful terror. Luigi implored him to let him die without making any endeavour to save his life long enough that he might go upon the gallows: and Ludovico fled. That is precisely everything which took place; and though Luigi went not forth upon the scaffold, yet did he die a despairing, miserable wretch—and our thirst for vengeance has been appeased!"

"And if Signor Marano should tell the tale," I said, "he will glory in it as an Italian only can glory in his vengeance! Alas, no! I am wrong! I am speaking to one in whose veins rolls English blood—and *she*, I regret to find, loves vengeance likewise!"

"Oh, you are very, very bitter, Ellen!" said Beatrice; "but if you yourself ever sustained such deep wrongs as those which resulted to me from the villanies of Luigi, you would not remain so strictly scrupulous and punctiliously conscientious as you now are! Remember, it was Luigi who purposed to ruin me in the estimation of my husband—Luigi who sent Angelo to my chamber where he met his death—Luigi who gave such a colour to all the most trifling circumstances that my husband believed me to be deeply criminal! And it was Luigi who brought the food to the apartment where I was imprisoned with the hanging corpse of Angelo,—Luigi who subsequently painted the hideous picture which my husband carried about with him as a memento of the diabolic vengeance which he himself had wreaked! Oh, did I not receive fearful lessons in the schools of vengeance? And yet how you blame me, —*you* who best know how deeply I have suffered!"

Beatrice now sank upon a sofa weeping bitterly. I must confess that I was touched by the spectacle: and I said in a milder voice than I had been hitherto using on the present occasion, "Beatrice, if you value my friendship, as you seem to do——"

"Oh, can you doubt it, Ellen?" she exclaimed, amidst her sobs: "can you doubt it?"

"No—I will not doubt it, Beatrice," I replied. "Let me, then, in the name of that friendship conjure you not to link your fortunes with such a man as Ludovico Marano!"

"What, Ellen!" and the Countess started, at the same time dashing the tears away from her eyes. "You know——"

"Yes, Beatrice," I interjected; "I will confess that I again this afternoon became an unintentional listener to something that was being said! I could not help it: the words that met my ears riveted me to the spot! In short, Beatrice, I know that you have pledged your hand to that man——and Ah! now I recollect! did you not proclaim that you loved him?"

Beatrice remained silent; and a gloomy shade came over her countenance. At length she said, "Ellen, while valuing your friendship, I cannot permit you to be the arbitress of my destinies. I beseech that the subject may here terminate."

"Oh, no!" I exclaimed with vehemence: "friendship has its privileges——"

"Enough, Ellen!" interrupted the Countess. "Your sentiments and mine differ on many, many points; and though you still speak to me of friendship, yet full well am I aware that you think far less of me than but a few hours back you did. Leave me for the present, Ellen, and come to-morrow. We will then resume the subject."

She gave me her hand: but scarcely had I touched it when she withdrew it quickly, as if she thought that I was about to receive it with reluctance and that I now regarded her with aversion. She hastened away into an adjoining apartment; and I issued from the house with sorrow in the depths of my soul. It was indeed with reluctance that I *had* touched that hand; for it had seemed to me as if there was blood upon it,—the blood of Luigi's last crime—the blood of self-destruction! For the reader must not think that because I had appealed to her in the name of friendship to avoid a step which I feared would prove the crowning misery of her life, I still felt towards her the same as before. No!—friendship was gone: she stood in another light in my estimation—she was not the same Beatrice whom I had previously known and loved! Yet would I have done a last generous act towards her; for I could not abandon her to what I foresaw must be an unhappy fate.

On the following day, at precisely the same hour, I called at the Marquis of Campanella's mansion. Beatrice had left in the morning for the Continent: the Marquis and Marchioness of Campanella had gone to accompany her as far as Dover. I therefore saw that the infatuated Beatrice was intent upon linking her fate with the man whom I looked upon as little better than the vindictive assassin on whom his own vengeance had been wreaked! For a moment I thought of writing a letter to the Marchioness of Campanella: but the next instant I said to myself, "No: I have done enough! There is a point at which even the most friendly intervention in the affairs of another becomes an impertinence and a gross impropriety;—and into this extreme I will not run."

I have now to speak of other matters. Precisely five months had by this time elapsed since the unfortunate Mary Glentworth became the victim of Edwin St. Clair's villany. As the reader knows, she was in a way to become a mother: but it was yet easy to conceal her position from the eyes of the world. It was however different within the circle of our own household; and the prying gaze of a domestic might detect that secret which it was so desirable to veil. Besides, Mary's health was suffering; and the excitement produced by her own vindictive feelings—gloating as they did over the fallen condition of her betrayer, Edwin St. Clair—was telling upon her constitution. She could no longer invoke her natural energies for performance upon the stage; and she feared lest by a falling off in her acting she should impair the good reputation she had won. In a word, I saw that she needed change of scene and quietude; and I was resolved that she should have both. While I was thinking how her engagement could be broken off with Mr. Richards, and how a sufficient excuse could be made for her disappearance from the stage for a few months without engendering suspicion in reference to the real cause, a catastrophe occurred which suddenly furnished the opportunity. It was at the end of the month of November of which I am now writing, that the name of Mr. Richards appeared in the list of Bankrupts. All his engagements were therefore brought abruptly to a close; and the theatre was shut up.

Everybody was astonished: for the universal opinion had been that the lessee was not only doing well, but even making a fortune. This idea was fully justified by the overflowing houses which he had enjoyed during the two years and a half that I had appeared upon the boards of the theatre; and it seemed to be corroborated by the fact that he paid his way with the utmost regularity. But the whole truth now came out. He had borrowed a very considerable sum of money four or five years back, when he first took the theatre; and of this amount he had paid nothing off. He had lived luxuriously; and if he had created few additional debts, he had done naught towards the liquidation of the old one. The person who had lent him the money died; and the executors threatened to put in force the warrant-of-attorney which Mr. Richards had given as a security for the loan. To save himself from prison he got himself made bankrupt. Immediately upon the occurrence of the catastrophe, he addressed very courteous and friendly letters to Mary Glentworth and myself,—expressing his sorrow at the severance of the engagements, but venturing to hope that this severance would only prove temporary, as he felt confident that in a few weeks he should be clear of his difficulties and in a position to resume the lesseeship of the theatre, and thereby secure our services again. We replied in suitable terms; for his conduct had always been most liberal, straight-forward, and honourable towards us.

A compulsory holiday was now forced upon myself; for there was no other theatre where at the time I thought fit to accept an engagement: while in respect to Mary Glentworth the circumstance was really a favourable one. I proposed to her that as she was acquainted with the secret of Juliet having become a mother before she was a wife, she should treat her with an equal degree of confidence; for I well knew that she would gladly afford Mary an asylum during the time that she might wish to seclude herself from the world. Mary assented: I accordingly wrote to Lady Frederick Ravenscliffe full particulars respecting the villany of which poor Mary had become the victim; and we received the kindest answer from Juliet. Her father was upon the Continent; and she therefore declared that she should be glad of the proposed companionship. I resolved to pass about a month at River House, and so spend my Christmas there. I did not choose to take Beda with me, for the simple reason that Mary Glentworth was particularly anxious to veil her shame from every one beneath my own roof. I therefore told Beda that I desired her to remain in London, to watch over the interests of my own establishment; and I moreover hinted that as she was constantly receiving the visits of William Lardner, I should not like to deprive her of the pleasure which she naturally experienced from the circumstance. Beda was always docile and obedient to my wishes; and thus this little matter was easily arranged.

It was in the commencement of December that Mary and I arrived at River House, where we were most cordially received by Juliet. The weather was superb: the autumn had been unusually beautiful—the hand of winter had not as yet seemed to touch the landscape scenery—many of the trees still preserved their foliage, though the leaves were all displaying those varied and beautiful tints which in their perishing state they disclose, just as the chameleon puts forth the most vivid and varying hues in the hour of its death. The sun shone brightly, and even powerfully; and it veritably appeared as if it were the commencement of spring, instead of the approaching extinction of the current year. Need I say that from Juliet Mary experienced the utmost sympathy on account of the hideous treachery of which she had been rendered a victim?

On the very day after our arrival at River House, an accident occurred which not merely for its own sake, but for that of the circumstances which grew out of it, must find a place in my narrative. It was at about eleven in the forenoon —the weather being still as beautiful as on the preceding day, and all nature smiling as if in defiance of the approach of winter,—when, as Mary and I were conversing in the drawing-room together, Juliet being at the moment in some other part of the house, we heard the sounds of some equipage dashing along; and then the next moment there was an awful crash. We rushed to the window, and instantaneously discerned the cause. A nobleman's travelling-carriage, as we could tell by the blazonry on the panels, had upset in a ditch on the opposite side of the road. Ejaculations of terror burst from the lips of Mary Glentworth and myself: but these were instantaneously succeeded by other cries—namely, of astonishment—as we both at the same moment recognised the liveries of the domestics. It was the Duke of Ardleigh's equipage to which the accident had happened.

"Good heavens!" cried Mary: "there will be broken limbs there!"

"Let us remain," I said; "for whatsoever may be the results, our presence might perhaps be unwelcome."

We now saw the servants hastily open the door that was uppermost; and the Duke of Ardleigh himself was first dragged forth from the interior of the vehicle. He at least did not seem to be much hurt; for he was gesticulating vehemently;—but it soon appeared to be different with a lady who was next extricated from the overturned equipage. She was dragged out in an evidently senseless condition—her garments in disorder—her long dark hair hanging down.

"The Duchess!" I exclaimed: and I was about to flee to render her assistance, when I beheld Juliet issue forth from the house, accompanied by one of her maid-servants. Then I decided upon remaining where I was, at least for the present—for I was anxious to prevent a meeting between Mary Glentworth and the Ardleigh family. There

was evidently no other person inside the carriage: but while the unconscious Duchess was being borne into the house, another equipage dashed up to the spot. This likewise belonged to the ducal family, as we could again discern by the liveries; so that Mary and I watched from the window, but keeping ourselves concealed by the curtains, to see who would now alight. Down leapt the lacquey—the door of the carriage was opened—and out sprang the Marquis of Dalrymple.

A presentiment which had already seized upon my mind, to the effect that something of importance would arise from the accident to the Ardleigh travelling-carriage, now seemed to receive its fullest realization. It was this presentiment which had retained me at the window, and prevented me from hastening from the room to render assistance; for I somehow or another deemed it most expedient to keep close by Mary.

"Ah!" she ejaculated, as she beheld Herbert

Dalrymple alight from the second equipage: but it was in a low tone that the ejaculation was given forth, and the expression of her countenance at once became sombre and gloomy.

Now, the reader must bear in mind that it was exactly seven months since that memorable scene in the jeweller's shop which had led to such startling revelations for Mary Glentworth, — seven months since she learnt that the Duke of Ardleigh was her father, — seven months since she discovered that in the person of Clarence Beauchamp she had loved her own half-brother, the Marquis of Dalrymple!

What unlucky stars had combined their malignant influences to bring all these personages at the same time beneath the same roof? I saw in a moment that the Ardleigh family would be sure to learn presently that myself and Mary Glentworth were there; for it must transpire in the course of conversation with Lady Frederick Ravenscliffe, as she was ignorant that there were any reasons why the fact had better be concealed. Mary understood what was passing in my mind; and she said coldly, "Do not annoy yourself, my dear Ellen, on account of this occurrence; for the Ardleigh family is nothing to me. I have told you as much before. I shall keep my own room, and take care to avoid a meeting during the hour or two that they may perhaps remain beneath this roof."

"At all events, my dear Mary," I said, "as Juliet is acquainted with so much that concerns you, why not suffer her to know the rest?—why not let her be taken entirely into your confidence? If you assent, I will speed and whisper in her ear that there are most special reasons why your name should not be mentioned in the presence of the Ardleigh family; and on another occasion we will tell her the whole truth."

"Do as you like, Ellen," responded Mary: "and perhaps it would be better for you to act as you have suggested."

Mary Glentworth now hurried up to her own chamber, while I proceeded down stairs to ascertain to what extent the Duchess of Ardleigh was injured, and likewise to whisper a few hasty words in Juliet's ear. On reaching the hall I found that much confusion prevailed: the Duke's domestics and the servants of River House were running hither and thither, or else were conversing in low mysterious whispers. I hastened to the dining-room, to which the Duchess had been borne; and I beheld her stretched upon the sofa—her husband, her son, and Juliet bending over her, while her own lady's-maid and Juliet's were removing her bonnet and shawl.

"I hope that her Grace is not seriously injured?" I asked in a whisper of Juliet.

Lady Frederick Ravenscliffe shook her head ominously,—at the same time replying in a very low tone, "She is evidently much hurt: but we know not as yet to what extent. We have sent for Mr. Singleton."

The Marquis of Dalrymple now observed me; and at once taking my hand, he pressed it with the fervour of true friendship, at the same time looking both amazed and pleased to find me there. The Duke was also astonished at recognising me; and he whispered, "This is a bad business, Miss Percy: I don't know how it will end. The idea

of an unfenced ditch by the side of a public highway! I should as soon think of having an uncovered well next to my drawing-room! But I wish that fellow Peaseblossom had been here——"

"See, my lord!" I interrupted him; "her Grace moves! She groans—she is in great pain——"

"Ah, poor creature! no wonder!" responded the Duke; "for her head came in violent concussion with the frame-work of the carriage door as it fell over."

I now seized an opportunity to draw Juliet aside for a moment; and I hastily whispered, "Do not mention the name of Mary Glentworth in the presence of any of these personages! I will give you sufficient reasons on another occasion."

Juliet bent upon me a look of intelligence, as much as to imply that my wish should be complied with, whatsoever its motive might be; and we returned to the sofa whereon lay the Duchess of Ardleigh. In a few minutes Mr. Singleton was announced; and he at once proceeded to examine the Duchess of Ardleigh's head. As I watched his countenance, I perceived that it gradually lost much of the ominous seriousness which it at first wore; and at length he said, "The injury is great; but so far as I can now judge, it is by no means necessary that it should prove fatal. The Duchess must be conveyed to a bed-chamber; and it is probable that for several days—it may even be for weeks—she must be kept as quiet as possible beneath this roof."

"Do you not think it better," inquired the Duke, "to move her Grace up to London—to our own mansion?—One word aside with you, if you please, sir!"

I had noticed that Mr. Singleton was looking very hard at the Duke; and I now all in a moment comprehended why it was that his Grace suddenly took him aside. Mr. Singleton was the surgeon who had been called in on the night of Mrs. Glentworth's death: he had then seen the Duke of Ardleigh, whom he however believed to be only plain Mr. Glentworth, the deceased lady's brother-in-law. Now, all in a moment he had recognised that same self-styled Mr. Glentworth in the Duke of Ardleigh who stood before him! It was therefore no doubt for the purpose of giving some few syllables of explanation that the Duke drew Mr. Singleton aside in the manner which I have just described.

"And now about the removal?" said the Duke, when their hastily whispered colloquy of a few minutes was over.

"Impossible, my lord!" answered Mr. Singleton: "it would be the death of her Grace!"

"The hospitalities of River House," said Juliet, "though no doubt humble and insignificant to a degree in comparison with the princely magnificence which prevails at Ardleigh House, shall be most cordially afforded——"

"Oh, I have no doubt of that, Lady Frederick," replied the Duke: "but I only thought——"

"Father," interrupted the Marquis of Dalrymple, in that tone of reproof which he not unfrequently adopted towards the Duke, for whom he scarcely experienced very much respect, "Lady Frederick Ravenscliffe has spoken most kindly and generously; and all our gratitude is her ladyship's due."

"Oh, to be sure!" exclaimed the Duke; "and of course I am very much obliged to her ladyship."

Herbert Dalrymple bit his lip with vexation; for he saw that his father's conduct was superciliously rude and flippantly impertinent. But Juliet, taking no farther notice of the Duke, began to issue orders for the ensurance of the best and kindest treatment in respect to the Duchess. Her Grace was moved up to the principal chamber; and Mr. Singleton then desired that she should be at once undressed and got to bed. I was about to remain with Juliet and the maids, in order to render my assistance, when Mr. Singleton hastily whispered in my ear, "I wish to say a few words to you, Miss Percy."

I accordingly accompanied him from the chamber. The Duke of Ardleigh and the Marquis of Dalrymple were shown to the drawing-room: I repaired with Mr. Singleton to another apartment.

"And so that is the Duke of Ardleigh!" he said, with a certain degree of abruptness the moment we were alone together.

"Yes," I replied; "and I saw how you recognised him. You started——"

"Yes, yes," interjected Singleton; "I did indeed start!—and no wonder! for it was not so much on account of the abrupt discovery that the person whom I had supposed on the night of the poor lady's death to be *Mr. Glentworth*, is none other than *the Duke of Ardleigh*,—but it was because a most singular secret came to my knowledge only yesterday; and I should have this very day called upon Lady Frederick to inquire if she knew where I could communicate with Miss Glentworth——"

"Indeed?" I ejaculated. "Did you not know that Miss Glentworth was living with me?"

"I knew that she was some time ago," responded Mr. Singleton; "but I was not sure whether circumstances might not have altered——"

"I will tell you a secret, Mr. Singleton," I said; "because I fancy from the turn the conversation has taken, you must know or at least suspect something—for immediately after mentioning the name of the Duke of Ardleigh, you began speaking of Mary Glentworth."

"Aye, to be sure!" ejaculated the surgeon: "and no wonder! for the intelligence I obtained yesterday——Ah! but first of all tell me what is this secret which you were just going to reveal?"

"Simply that Mary Glentworth is at this moment at River House," I responded.

"Ah!" ejaculated Mr. Singleton; "this is strange!—perhaps in some sense fortunate—— but all that is just as it may be——"

"You are speaking in enigmas," I said. "But perhaps you do not know exactly what I know——"

"Or perhaps I know a little more," interjected the surgeon, with a good-tempered dryness. "You imagine that Mary Glentworth——"

"Hush!" I said, as a sudden thought struck me. "Whatever I may know of Mary Glentworth, the secret is not my own; and without her consent I dare not touch upon the subject."

"I both admire and approve of your discretion, my dear Miss Percy," said Mr. Singleton. "Perhaps it would be better that I should explain myself in the first instance thoroughly to you. I will tell you all that I know in reference to Mary Glentworth——"

At this moment we became aware that the door was open, and Juliet's lady's-maid was entering to announce that everything was ready in the invalid chamber for the presence of Mr. Singleton. At the same instant I caught sight of the young Marquis of Dalrymple crossing the landing; and I asked myself, "Was the door opened at so inopportune a moment as to allow his ears to catch what Mr. Singleton was saying to me? I hope not!—for it is better that nothing should transpire to excite a fresh interest in the mind of Herbert Dalrymple with respect to his half-sister."

"We will meet again presently," hastily whispered Mr. Singleton to me. "And now," he added aloud, "let us go together to the invalid's chamber."

CHAPTER XCVIII.

THE OLD GARDENER'S DISCOVERY.

THE Marquis of Dalrymple had traversed the landing without noticing me and Mr. Singleton— or at least without appearing to observe that we were at the same time issuing from an apartment adjacent to the drawing-room which he had just left; for he did not turn round, but kept straight on his way towards the chamber to which his mother had been conveyed. The Duke had reached it before him; and this I thought rather singular, for I fancied that Herbert's naturally affectionate and generous disposition would have led him in all possible haste to the couch of his invalid mother; so that I again said to myself, "Is it possible that he could have tarried on the landing to overhear anything that was passing betwixt Mr. Singleton and me?"

I looked furtively at the young Marquis as this thought crossed my mind on entering the invalid chamber; and I could discern an expression of uneasiness and anxiety upon his countenance, which was also very pale. But there were no evidences to corroborate the misgiving which was floating in my mind; for the condition of Herbert's mother was sufficient to account for the mental distress he might be experiencing.

The Duchess still lay in a state of unconsciousness: she had not even so much as groaned or moaned since she had been conveyed up-stairs to that chamber. Mr. Singleton desired every one to leave the room with the exception of Juliet and myself; and his wish was of course complied with. I need not linger upon this portion of my narrative; suffice it to say that Mr. Singleton carefully examined the injury sustained by the Duchess of Ardleigh, and the result was such as to corroborate the opinion he had formed in the first instance— namely, that though the injuries were serious, they need not necessarily prove fatal; and that it was not merely possible, but even probable that there would be an eventual recovery.

"And now, Miss Percy," he said, "you yourself may go and report this opinion of mine to the

Duke and the Marquis; for they are of course most anxious to learn the result of the examination."

I accordingly quitted the chamber, and proceeded to the drawing-room, where I found the Duke of Ardleigh and his son Herbert. I made the report with which I was entrusted; and the Marquis of Dalrymple, clasping his hands fervently, exclaimed, "God grant that my dear mother may survive!"

"At all events the affair looks better than I had expected," said the Duke. "I hope there is no injury to the skull? Perhaps you can tell me Miss Percy, whether Mr. What's-his-name—— Ah, I recollect! Singleton!—said anything about trepanning or trephining. You are doubtless aware, my dear Herbert, that there is a great deal of difference between the two; and as I was one day explaining to Peaseblossom——I remember, the rascal had fallen asleep after I had condescended to play him half-a-dozen tunes on the violin——Eh! and by Jove," ejaculated the Duke, thus suddenly interrupting himself, "I wonder whether my dear old cremona got smashed in the upsetting of the carriage!"

Considerably excited by his apprehensions on the point, the Duke rushed from the room; and the Marquis glanced after him for a moment, with a half-contemptuous, half-melancholy expression upon his lips.

"And thus, Miss Percy," said Herbert, now turning to me, as we found ourselves alone together, "we meet again! And in the first instance allow me to renew the assurances of my gratitude for all the kind things you said to me on that memorable day, exactly seven months ago, when in Mr. Wilkinson's office——"

"I remember full well, my lord," I interrupted him, "all that then took place. You declared that the words I spoke, the advice I gave you, and the well-meant things I said to you, were seed that should not fall upon barren ground."

"And I told you truly!" exclaimed Herbert. "When I left England seven months ago, I thought it would be for a long, long period. I remember that I said to you that if we should ever meet again, you should not blush to know me. I did not then think we should so soon encounter each other as destiny has thus led us to do. My parents came to me in Paris—they besought me to return and at least spend the Christmas holidays with them, even though immediately afterwards I should go abroad again. Miss Percy, I was overruled: I did not wish to return to England—at least not for a long, long time to come. It was far from my desire to incur the chance of meeting——"

He stopped short, and suddenly averted his countenance: then he took three or four hasty strides across the room; and returning to me, he asked, with a pale face and an agitated, suspenseful look, "How did *she* bear the calamity which smote us? does she think of me as a sister thinking of a brother? And if—and if—by any accident we should happen to meet——"

"My lord, cannot you turn the discourse upon some other topic?" I inquired, terribly apprehensive lest we were approaching dangerous ground.

"Yes!" he exclaimed; "there is a topic which I ought to touch upon, Miss Percy!—and this is to give you the assurance that the kind words you spoke to me ere I left England, were not thrown away. I have become an altered being—or at least I have returned to be what I was when you first knew me! Oh, yes, my kind good friend!—for so I must call you, and so I must ever regard you!—I am telling you the truth!"

"I believe you, my lord," I replied: for there was an unquestionable sincerity in the young nobleman's words and looks.

"Ah! there is one further observation I must make!" he ejaculated; "and this is to convey the assurance that although in one sense I regretted poor Mary should have gone upon the stage, yet that since she resolved to embrace that profession, I rejoiced unfeignedly when I read of her success."

The Duke of Ardleigh now abruptly returned to the drawing-room, exclaiming, "My old cremona! my favourite violin! it has ceased to exist! It is smashed to atoms! Good heavens! what distressing calamities to be compelled to communicate to one's friends! My wife nearly smashed to pieces!—and my fiddle completely so!"

I availed myself of this opportunity to glide forth from the drawing-room; and I was about to proceed to Mary Glentworth's chamber to communicate all that had happened, when I met Juliet upon the landing. She beckoned me into a neighbouring apartment; and when we were there alone together, she asked, "What meant you, my dear Ellen, by that earnestly whispered injunction, to the effect that I was not to breathe the name of Mary Glentworth in the presence of the Ardleigh family?"

"It is a strange and exciting tale which I have to tell you, Juliet," I responded; "and if these particulars have hitherto been withheld from your knowledge, it has been through no want of confidence, but simply because there is involved in Mary's history one of those secrets which it is always expedient to keep narrowed within the most limited compass."

With this apologetic preface I proceeded to give Juliet the outlines of all that I myself was acquainted with in respect to Mary Glentworth,— her parentage, the discovery which she had made that the Duke of Ardleigh was her father, and the inauspicious love she had conceived for the Marquis of Dalrymple. Juliet listened with interest and astonishment; and when I had concluded, she exclaimed, "Alas, poor Mary! she has known troubles as great as any that I myself ever experienced! But will not these present complications prove very embarrassing for her? It is quite evident that the Duchess must remain some time beneath this roof—all the laws of hospitality compel me to bid the husband and the son stay here likewise——and yet on the other hand the asylum which I have offered and promised to Mary——"

"It is indeed embarrassing!" I interrupted Juliet. "I know not what I can do—unless it be to depart stealthily with Mary to some other place for the present——"

"Had you not better see what she herself says?" inquired Lady Frederick Ravenscliffe.

"Yes—of course she must be consulted. But Mr. Singleton has some communication to make to me; and it is concerning Mary Glentworth. I do not know what it can possibly be. It would prove strange indeed if it should in any way alter her position towards the Ardleighs!"

"Indeed, why do you think it may?" inquired Juliet.

"I do not know—I have no particular reason, unless it were that there was something so strangely significant in Mr. Singleton's words and manner——"

"I will at once go and send him to you," said Juliet: "he has doubtless by this time finished his ministrations to the Duchess. Her Grace was beginning to rally the least thing when I just now left the chamber; but I fear that it must still be many hours, if not even days, ere she will regain her consciousness."

Juliet now quitted the apartment; and in a few minutes Mr. Singleton made his appearance.

"Again we are alone together, Miss Percy," said the worthy gentleman; "and now we will have some serious discourse. I do not know whether you happen to remember the old gardener who used to be attached to the picturesque little cottage yonder——"

"To be sure!" I ejaculated: "I remember him well! Yes—and what is more, I know likewise that he was much attached to Mary. He had known her from her childhood."

"I am about to speak of that same man," resumed Mr. Singleton; "you know that the unfortunate Count of Carboni lived for awhile in that cottage: but of course you know all this full well! because you were at Dover at the time when the unfortunate nobleman met his death. Since that tragic event the cottage has only been let for a short period, to some elderly female, who did not like its loneliness and therefore left it. Now it is expected that a very excellent tenant may take it; and accordingly the landlord has ordered the whole premises to be thoroughly embellished and repaired. Thompson, the old gardener, was instructed to get the house in readiness for the reception of the painters and other workmen. He was yesterday going over the place, when his attention was drawn to the wainscot of the principal chamber——"

"The very chamber," I ejaculated, "in which poor Mrs. Glentworth died!"

"The same," rejoined Mr. Singleton. "Well, as I was saying, old Thompson's attention was drawn to what appeared to be a large crack in the wainscot: but on a closer examination he found that it was occasioned by a sliding panel which had become partially moved out of its setting. Perhaps you will think, Miss Percy, that all this looks very much like a scene in a romance: but I can assure you that it is strictly true——"

"Do you suppose I doubt, my dear sir?" I exclaimed. "Pray proceed."

"Thompson opened the panel completely," resumed Mr. Singleton; "and he found that it served to conceal a recess which must have been just behind the head of the bedstead that poor Mrs. Glentworth used to occupy. Thus, for a place of concealment for papers nothing could possibly be better. And papers, my dear Miss Percy, were discovered there!" added the surgeon, with a significant look.

"Papers?" I said inquiringly: "papers of importance?"

"Yes—papers of the utmost importance," rejoined Singleton. "Old Thompson cannot read; and therefore he came straight off to me as one whom he had known for a number of years, and in whom he could put trust. He told me of the discovery he had made; and he placed the papers in my hand. I said I would look over them, and if they should prove to be of any importance or value, he would be sure to receive a reward from some quarter or another. In the meantime I bade him say nothing upon the subject to any other person; for even before I had glanced at the documents, I conceived it to be unquestionable that they must be really of more or less value to have been so carefully concealed."

"I am dying with curiosity, Mr. Singleton," I said; "for I perceive that I am about to learn something which must in some sense or another affect my friend Mary Glentworth's position."

"I again repeat that is as it may or may not be, according to circumstances," replied Mr. Singleton. "But I will at once tell you the main point which is now brought to light: I will give you the details afterwards. In a word then, Mary Glentworth is *not* the daughter of the Duke of Ardleigh!"

"Good heavens!" I ejaculated in wild astonishment: "not the daughter of the Duke of Ardleigh?"

"No—nor even the daughter of her whom she always looked upon as her mother!"

I was astounded and stupified: it seemed to me impossible. I gazed in vacant bewilderment upon the surgeon's countenance: but I saw nothing therein to induce me to believe that he could have any sinister motive for making a misrepresentation—while I knew that he was incapable of so sorry a jest.

"It is true, Miss Percy," he said,—"as true as that you are there! Mary Glentworth was only the niece of her whom she regarded as her mother: but the aunt evidently loved the girl as much as a mother herself could have done. It is a strange, wild, romantic story!"

"It must be," I murmured, scarcely able to emerge from the surprise which had seized upon me, but feeling as if I were groping my way out of the dark mazes of a dream.

Then a thought swept like vivid lightning through my brain. Good heaven! if this were true, Herbert Dalrymple and Mary might after all have gone to the altar—there was no impediment of a moral tie nor in the shape of kinship's bond to prevent them! It was not a half-brother loving a half-sister: everything was different—Oh! so different from what had been proclaimed and supposed!

"I see that you scarcely yet believe the truth of the statement I have made unto you," resumed Mr. Singleton. "But the papers which I have in my possession form a complete corroboration. Not only is there a full narrative in the handwriting of Mrs. Glentworth herself—but there are likewise various letters from her sister——"

"Her sister?" I said inquiringly.

"Yes—her sister Jane, Mary's mother. There is likewise the certificate of Mary's birth, with the names of her parents, showing that in lawful marriage was she born—or at least justifying the belief that such was the fact."

"Oh, Mr. Singleton!" I exclaimed, " these are indeed important papers which have fallen into your hands! I know that Mary feels the stigma of illegitimacy as the most frightful misfortune ; and now that I am enabled to assure her that she was born in wedlock——"

"Ah! but wait a moment, my dear Miss Percy," said Mr. Singleton. " The query is whether Mary would rather look up to the Duke of Ardleigh as her sire, than be compelled on the other hand to acknowledge the paternity of a humble clerk in a counting-house ?"

"Infinitely sooner would Mary acknowledge the humblest of individuals as her father in an honourable sense, than the proudest duke in a dishonourable one! In a word, Mr. Singleton, Mary at present hates and loathes the Duke of Ardleigh, although she believes him to be her father: and this aversion is so strong because she looks upon him as the betrayer of her mother. And she is now concealing herself in her own chamber," I continued, " that she may not incur the chance of encountering either the Duke or his son——"

"Well, then," interrupted the surgeon, " if the feeling of aversion is so strong as you describe, it will evidently prove a relief to Mary to know that she is honestly born, though of a humble father. But now there is another question—and it is a pecuniary one——"

"Ah! I understand you, Mr. Singleton!" I ejaculated. "You wish to know whether Mary Glentworth receives an income from the Duke of Ardleigh—and whether, if such be the case, she would hesitate to sacrifice it by proclaiming that she is *not* his daughter?"

"Yes," responded the surgeon: "this is the question I would fain ask."

"Then the reply is easily given," I said: "for Mary's hatred and aversion—her prejudice and her rancour, have been too strong to permit her to receive a single shilling from the Duke of Ardleigh for a long time past. It was to maintain herself in independence that she went upon the stage; and I believe that she would sooner starve than accept a shilling from the bounty of the Ardleigh family."

"Now I understand the actual position of affairs," said Mr. Singleton; " and you can at present comprehend why I declared just now that the revelation might or might not prove agreeable to Miss Glentworth, according to circumstances."

"You see, therefore," I responded, " that in every sense it will prove agreeable, and that there is not the slightest reason why the secret should be kept from her. Shall I go and impart it ?"

"Yes—if you think fit, Miss Percy," replied the surgeon. " But have you no curiosity to hear a history as singular as it is romantic ? I do not think I should detain you very long : moreover I wish to while away half-an-hour or so, ere I return to the chamber of the Duchess ;—and inasmuch as for some twenty or one-and-twenty years or thereabouts, Mary Glentworth has remained in ignorance of the true secret of her birth, it can matter but little if the truth be now delayed for half-an-hour longer."

"True," I said; "and you may easily understand, Mr. Singleton, that I do experience the liveliest curiosity to learn a history which cannot fail to be of a deep romantic interest."

"I will give it you in a consecutive narrative form," said Mr. Singleton, "just as if I were an author telling a tale, without reference to notes or authorities as he proceeds."

We had all the time been standing in the window-recess of the room where this conversation took place: but now we sat down; and Mr. Singleton commenced his narrative in the following strain :—

" In some obscure village of a midland county, lived the Reverend Mr. Latimer for a great number of years. He was the vicar of the village ; but it was a poor living—about a hundred and twenty pounds a year. He was a widower, and had two daughters—both of whom were of highly prepossessing appearance. They had lost their mother early ; and thus, although their father did his best, considering his limited means, to give them a decent education, yet there was wanting that continuous inculcation of moral principle which can only take place under a mother's auspices and receive its inspirations from the source of a mother's affectionate carefulness. Mr. Latimer was a good man, but somewhat indolent—of an easy disposition—satisfied so long as everything went well—and not choosing to anticipate evils for the future. Thus, when death carried him off somewhat suddenly at the age of about fifty-five, it was found that he had not made the slightest provision for the future maintenance of his daughters, and that the sale of his furniture would only just liquidate the funeral expenses and his debts. The orphan sisters, who were then respectively about eighteen and nineteen, consoled each other as well as they were able : they fancied that because in their humble village they were paragons of scholarship and learning, they were really of high education and accomplishments, and that they had only to seek in order to obtain the situations of governess. With the few pounds which remained to them after the settlement of the accounts in the village, they proceeded to London. I must here inform you that the Latimers were related to a family in a position even more humble and far less genteel than their own. The name of this family was Glentworth. It consisted of a widow, three daughters, and a son. The three daughters had all married small tradesmen, and were scattered in different parts of the country : the son, William Glentworth, was a clerk in a mercantile counting-house. The two sisters, on their arrival in London, went to the house of their Aunt Glentworth. By her they were not received with any particular cordiality; for she was not only poor, but likewise mean and selfish. The sisters therefore resolved to exert themselves to the utmost to obtain situations without delay : but they soon began to find that it was by no means so easy as they had fancied when setting out from their distant country village. In short, when their qualifications came to be inquired into by the ladies to whom they appealed, it was found that the education they had received was only just a decent one, and sufficient to qualify them for the post of mere nursery-governess. But weeks passed while the poor girls were being thus gradually and gradually let down from the high pedestal of their hopes and deposited at the base. Meanwhile Aunt Glentworth was growing impatient and looking sullen; but William Glentworth was a good young man, and vowed that his cousins should never want a home so long as he by his industry could give them one. At length Mary, the elder sister, obtained the situation of a nursery-governess with a wealthy family dwelling in the country, a couple of hundred miles from London. It was heartbreaking for the sisters to separate; but it was necessary. Not long after Mary, the *elder* sister, obtained a situation, Aunt Glentworth died; and so soon as a decent interval had elapsed, Jane Latimer, the *younger* of the two sisters, became the wife of William Glentworth. Mary obtained a temporary leave of absence from the family in the country in order to be present at the wedding; and it was with the most unfeigned sincerity she wished her sister all possible happiness,—not merely on account of the love which subsisted between them, but likewise because poor Mary herself was drinking deeply of the gall of unhappiness! The situation she had accepted was scarcely tolerable. Tyrannized over by her master and mistress—teased and worried by the children—and scorned by the domestics, she was in that false position in which young women of her class invariably find themselves. Therefore, after her sister's wedding, she returned into the country, only to find her situation less endurable than ever. Can it be wondered if she soon began to listen with some degree of attention to the overtures which were made to her by a nobleman who occasionally visited at the mansion where she was? This nobleman was then called Lord Dalrymple, belonging to the ducal family of Ardleigh. To be brief, Mary Latimer fled with him—placed herself under his protection—became his mistress. A few weeks afterwards William Glentworth was killed by an accident, leaving his widow totally unprovided for and in a way to become a mother. Mary Latimer, being amply supplied with money by her protector, failed not to furnish pecuniary aid to her unfortunate sister. Mary likewise became pregnant; and Lord Dalrymple seemed to be delighted at the idea of such paternity, though he was already married and had a son. The political party to which Lord Dalrymple belonged, suddenly coming into power, his lordship was appointed to one of the minor embassies on the Continent; and he was compelled to set off with the least possible delay. He took an affectionate leave of his mistress Mary Latimer, with whom he left an ample supply of money; and he departed to the capital of the petty Italian State to which he was accredited. I must now observe that ever since the marriage of Jane, the two sisters had corresponded only by letter—they had not met; for Mary was ashamed to look her sister in the face. Yet when she found that this younger sister refused not the pecuniary gifts which she forwarded, she took courage, and at length ventured to call upon her. The meeting was an affectionate one; and Jane uttered not a syllable of reproach against Mary for her fall from virtue. On the contrary, she sympathized with her, and seemed to think that it was scarcely possible she could have done otherwise. Jane was very sickly—her health was failing—and she apprehended the time of her *accouchement*. Mary endeavoured to reassure and console her, and promised that if anything should

happen to her, she would prove a mother to the expected babe. Jane was confined of a daughter, which she christened Mary in honour of her sister."

"Ah!" I exclaimed; "then the Mary Glentworth who is now beneath this roof, bears her own proper name?"

"Yes—you are right," rejoined Mr. Singleton. "The babe to whom I am alluding, has grown up into your friend Mary Glentworth! But let me resume the thread of my narrative. Not long after the birth of the little Mary, her mother died. The infant's aunt, Mary Latimer, at once fulfilled the promise she had made to her deceased sister, and resolved to become a mother to that child. Now, I have already told you, that Mary Latimer was pregnant by her paramour Lord Dalrymple; and it was only a month after her sister's confinement and death, that she herself was taken in labour. She was delivered of a dead infant; and thus she was all the better enabled to become a mother to the little Mary her niece. A couple of years elapsed before Lord Dalrymple returned to England: the little Mary was presented to him as his own daughter, and he entertained not the slightest suspicion that it was otherwise. In the meanwhile, Mary Latimer had adopted the name of Glentworth, so that she might avoid bringing disrepute upon her own family name—and also perhaps because this name fitted with the one in which the little Mary had been christened. Lord Dalrymple in due time became the Duke of Ardleigh,—the Duke who is now beneath this roof! Do you require to be informed why the secret respecting Mary's parentage was so religiously kept by her whom she looked upon as a mother?"

"No," I answered; "those reasons are intelligible enough. The unfortunate lady received an income from the Duke of Ardleigh, who supposed that Mary was his own child; and moreover Mrs. Glentworth—as I suppose we must continue to call her—cherished a hope that the Duke would continue his paternal succour so long as Mary should live. But if those reasons be intelligible enough, I am on the other hand at a loss to comprehend for what purpose Mrs. Glentworth should have left a narrative behind her——"

"Her objects are explained," answered Mr. Singleton, "at the close of the narrative itself. She knew not what destiny might be in store for her daughter: she knew not whether circumstances might not some day or another arrive which would render it desirable for the girl to become acquainted with all her past history. There might be the scruples of some eligible suitor to satisfy—to prove to him that she was not born in shame, but that she was the offspring of a lawful wedlock. And then, too, Miss Percy—does it not strike you that Mrs. Glentworth may have thoroughly comprehended all the most intricate depths of her adopted daughter's character?"

"True!" I exclaimed; "and she may have been inspired by the presentiment that the day would sooner or later come when Mary would learn sufficient to make her wish to learn more; and that if in the first instance she should acquire the belief that she was illegitimate, she would be crushed with a sense of shame, from the abyss of which she would be afterwards lifted by the subsequent discovery

that she was born in honourable and sacred wedlock!"

"All your reasoning is excellent, Miss Percy,"
said Mr. Singleton. "And then too, does it not
occur unto you that a woman of remorseful feelings, as Mrs. Glentworth evidently was—a woman
whose sense of bygone guilt and shame had traced
its melancholy expression upon her countenance,
furrowed her brow with untimely wrinkles, and
given her a haggard careworn look,—do you not
conceive, I ask, that such a woman was the very
one who was the least likely to go out of the world
carrying an important secret with her?   Indeed,
such a woman would have looked upon it as something awful and desecrating to allow a human
being to remain in eternal ignorance of his or her
parentage; and she was sure to devise some means
by which it should be sooner or later made known.
Doubtless it was from affectionate motives that she
preserved the many letters that she received from
her sister Jane; and therefore she had these to
annex in after years, as corroborative evidence, to
the narrative which in her compunction and remorse she was finally led to pen.   And it is easy
to perceive by the tone of this narrative, that its
authoress was a strict believer in religious truths:
she had hopes in heaven, and entertained fears
of hell: she was even superstitious in her sentiments.   But I have now said enough, Miss
Percy," added Mr. Singleton, "to account to you
for the motives which could have induced the unhappy lady to pen the narrative of her degradation and her shame."

"And perhaps she intended on her death-bed,"
I observed, in a mood of mournful musing, "to
place those documents in the hands of Mary, or to
tell her where they might be found after her
demise: but alas! she little foresaw that she was
doomed to perish so suddenly and so prematurely.
But now, Mr. Singleton, with your permission, I
will go and reveal to Mary Glentworth this intelligence so startling and so romantic, as well as so
well calculated to infuse joy into her heart."

"And I will revisit my patient," said the surgeon: then looking at his watch, he added, "We
have been together an entire hour, I declare!"

Mr. Singleton and I now left the apartment
where the preceding explanations had taken place;
and I thought that it would be but seemly to enter
the invalid chamber with him, if only for a moment, to ascertain how the Duchess of Ardleigh
was progressing.   I did so, and found that her
condition was slightly improved,—though, as a
matter of course, this improvement was very
trifling, considering the serious injury she had
sustained.   Juliet was seated by her bedside; and
I just whispered to her, "As I foresaw, the revelation is most important.   I will tell you everything
presently."

I then issued from the chamber; and I was about
to commence the ascent of the second flight of stairs,
which led to Mary's bed-room, when lo and behold!
she herself came tripping down that flight.

"Ah!" she ejaculated, the least thing impatiently: "it is lucky that I have at last fallen
in with a human being!"

"What in heaven's name do you mean?" I demanded.   "But stay not out here on the landing!   Come hither with me!   I have something of
the utmost importance to say to you!"

"Indeed?" she ejaculated, as she at once followed me into the room where I had previously
been conversing with Mr. Singleton.

At the same moment I heard another door
open on the landing; so that I hastily dragged
Mary into the apartment with me, and closed the
door as quickly as possible.

"What did you mean, my dear Mary," I now
asked, "by saying it was fortunate that you at
last fell in with a human being?"

"Why, do you know, Ellen," she exclaimed,
"that two mortal hours have elapsed since the
accident in the road!"

"I could not come to you before, Mary," I interjected.   "Circumstance followed circumstance
in quick succession——"

"But how could I know all this?" she asked.
"I am sorry if I just now displayed any petulance:
but somehow or another I have got irritable and
restless of late.   I did not like to be for two
hours alone up in my chamber—seeing no one—
ringing the bell without getting a servant to attend upon me——"

"Oh," I exclaimed, "they have all been so
occupied!"

"But you forget that I continued in utter ignorance of what was going on," she said.   "You
did not come near me—I even grew alarmed—
though I scarcely know at what——"

"Well, well, my dear Mary," I interjected:
"you need not say so much to excuse yourself."

"Yes—but I feel it is necessary, because I do
not like to seem to be irritable with you, dear
Ellen.   I really did not know whether the Ardleighs
were here still or not: so I thought that at any
risk I would come down to see what was the
matter."

"The Ardleighs are still here," I said; "and
the Duchess is very ill.   She is most seriously injured—there is concussion of the brain——"

"I presume therefore," interrupted Mary,
"that they are now all going to stay here for
some time?—and therefore I at least must find
another asylum——"

"Be not impatient," I said, assuming a most
solemn look and tone.   "Before you decide on any
step, listen to what I have to tell you.   I have an
important revelation to make!"

"Indeed?" ejaculated Mary: "an important
revelation?   But I hope it is not concerning these
Ardleighs——"

"It will afford you pleasure, Mary, because it
will remove the stigma which you believe to affix
itself——"

"To my birth?   Oh, Ellen!—dear Ellen—if this
be so——"

"It is, Mary—it is!" I exclaimed.   "Listen——
be not too much excited——But—but—you are
not the daughter of the Duke of Ardleigh!——
You were not born in shame!"

A wild cry of joy burst from Mary's lips; and
she flew into my arms.   But at the same instant
the door of the apartment was thrown violently
open—and Herbert Dalrymple rushed in, exclaiming in a tone as wildly joyous as was the cry
from Mary's lips, "Oh, God be thanked! Mary,
dearest Mary, you may now become mine!"

He was about to fling his arms around her,
when she sprang back, and gazed upon him for

a moment with an indescribable expression of countenance : then suddenly pressing her hand to her brow, she gave vent to a moan of deepest despair and sank senseless into my arms.

CHAPTER XCIX.

THE MARQUIS AND MARY.

THE Marquis of Dalrymple looked as if stupified with astonishment and consternation when Mary Glentworth started backward to avoid his embrace, and when she gazed upon him in that strange peculiar manner which seemed to indicate that there was an ineffable despair in her soul.

"Good heavens! what does it mean, Miss Percy?" he demanded, as I bore Mary to the sofa. "Is it joy? is it grief? is it madness?"

No. 78.—ELLEN PERCY.

"Give me water, my lord, to sprinkle upon her countenance!" I interrupted him. "There! there! that decanter!—now pour some on my kerchief!"

"Shall I summon the surgeon?" asked Herbert quickly.

"No, my lord," I replied: "there is nothing dangerous——at least I believe and hope not! But perhaps you had better withdraw——"

"Oh! do not send me from the room, Miss Percy!" he exclaimed, in an imploring tone. "Good heavens! I should have thought that the announcement which you just now made to Mary, would have filled her with joy! But Oh! perhaps she never, never loved me!—for Ah! that look which she just now fixed upon me, was one so singular—so incomprehensible——"

"Do not excite yourself, my lord," I said. "See! she is about to recover——But, Ah! it were as well that I should at once warn you most earnestly and most solemnly to entertain not a single hope—to indulge not in a dream which can lead to naught but disappointment!"

"My God, Miss Percy!" murmured Herbert, becoming deadly pale, and trembling visibly under the influence of his emotions: "you do not mean ——Oh, no! you cannot mean that she hates me!"

"Ask me not for a single syllable of explanation," I rejoined, cruelly bewildered how to act or what to say: "it is a subject which must never be revived again!—and you, my lord, ought not to have come back to England so soon!"

"Miss Percy," he said with a look and tone of the most mournful reproach, "such words from your lips? I should not have thought it! Does it not seem as if providence itself had brought me back to England at the time when my presence was to be needed at the couch of a suffering mother—perhaps at her death-bed——"

"True, my lord!" I said, humbled as well as pained by the reproach conveyed in the words which he had uttered. "I did not think of that circumstance at the moment! Indeed, I feel so confused and bewildered——But tell me," I abruptly ejaculated, by way of changing the conversation, "how came you to burst into the room at such a moment?"

"Oh! I will tell you, Miss Percy," exclaimed Herbert; "and you will not blame me. While my poor mother was being got to bed, my father and I were shown to the drawing-room——you repaired with Mr. Singleton to another apartment. When my mother was undrest, a domestic came to inform us that we might proceed to her chamber. But as my father and I were traversing the landing, the lady's-maid was opening the door of another apartment; and I heard Mr. Singleton say that he would tell you all he knew in reference to Mary Glentworth."

"Ah!" I ejaculated: "then my suspicion was correct! I fancied that you overheard something that was thus said——"

"Yes," continued Herbert: "and Oh! you may imagine Miss Percy, how excited at once grew my feelings—how ardent became my curiosity! What, I asked myself, could Mr. Singleton have to tell you in reference to Mary which you knew not before? Oh! how I longed to watch and listen—to play the eavesdropper—to hide myself behind a curtain or under a sofa—anywhere! so that I might obtain an initiation into these mysteries! But I did nothing so unhandsome. I suspected that you were to have a private interview with Mr. Singleton; and I resolved that when it was over I would implore you to admit me into your confidence, if this could be done without indiscretion. I therefore kept watch only so far as to ascertain when your next private interview with Mr. Singleton should be over. At length it terminated——or at least I judged so, when I saw you upon the landing. I was about to accost you, but Mary was making her appearance. I retreated into the drawing-room until I had seen you both enter here together. Then I approached the door—I was about to open it—when words, which for the moment riveted me to the spot, caught my ear,—words which told me that all the previous supposition was wrong—that Mary is not my half sister—that there is no stigma upon her birth——and then, wild with joy, I burst into this apartment!"

While the Marquis of Darymple was giving me these explanations in a hurried and excited manner, but in a subdued tone, I was still continuing my ministrations to Mary Glentworth. I was sprinkling water upon her countenance, chafing her hands, and putting back the luxuriant masses of her hair from about her forehead. She seemed to be giving signs of reanimation—but they were faint and feeble; and I began to apprehend lest I should be compelled to send for the assistance of one of the female domestics. But this I was anxious to avoid, for I did not wish that the veil of secrecy, hitherto drawn over the present scene, should be lifted.

"See, my lord—see," I said, "what your indiscretion has done! You first of all give way to your curiosity—then you cannot curb your feelings—you burst abruptly into the room—and here is the consequence!"

"Ah? do you apprehend any danger?" exclaimed Herbert, with an anguished expression of countenance. "Oh for heaven's sake let me hasten and fetch hither Mr. Singleton!"

"What?" I said; "from the side of your mother's couch?—that mother whose life may possibly depend upon the constant care and attention of the medical attendant?"

"Oh!" exclaimed Herbert, with wild vehemence of tone and impassioned gesture, "do I not love Mary as well as my mother? O God! I feel that both are equally dear to me!"

"Speak not thus, my lord," I said, with the most solemn emphasis: "for henceforth Mary Glentworth can be nothing more than a mere stranger to you! Believe me, I am telling you the truth!"

"Oh, no! it cannot be!" ejaculated Herbert in accents still more impassioned than before: "it is impossible! Mary, Mary!" he continued, sinking upon his knees by the side of the sofa on which she lay; "speak to me, dearest!—tell me that I am not hateful to you! Open your eyes—look upon me—Oh look upon me, dearest Mary! with those beautiful blue eyes of thine! Oh, you once loved me—and it is impossible that you can now hate me! Have mercy upon me, dearest Mary!"

He had taken her hand—he was pressing it to his lips—the tears were falling fast from his eyes and bathing that hand. It is bad enough to see a woman weep; but to behold a man dissolve in tears, is a spectacle calculated to melt the sternest heart. I experienced an illimitable compassion for that unhappy young man: I felt the tears now trickling down my own cheeks. I essayed to speak—I wished to conjure him to leave the apartment, for I thought that Mary would soon recover; but my power of utterance was choked. And now a deep convulsive sob came forth from Mary Glentworth's throat, making her bosom heave and fall tumultuously; and the next instant, before I could stretch forth a hand to prevent it, Herbert's arms were thrown about her neck. To my astonishment, Mary's arms were flung round him in their turn; but it was with murmurings and moans expressive of the deepest mental agony that she received his caresses.

"Oh, Mary! dearest Mary!" he exclaimed, "you do not hate me!—no, no, you do not hate me! You love me!—and, my God! I love you more tenderly and more passionately than ever!"

Deeply affecting was this scene: but all in a moment it experienced a wild and startling change.

"Enough! enough!" literally shrieked forth Mary Glentworth, in a voice the utter misery of which cannot possibly be explained in words. "Talk not to me of love, Herbert!—talk not to me of love! It is a tale which I must not hear! And yet, O God! if it were otherwise——"

Here the wretched girl threw herself upon the sofa whence she had started up, and began sobbing and weeping as if her heart would break.

"Good heavens! I shall go mad!" exclaimed Dalrymple. "What does all this mean? I am loved—and yet I must not speak of love! The tremendous barrier which we fancied to oppose our union, exists no longer—it has become suddenly dissolved—it has melted away like the snow—and yet I am to infer that my love is as hopeless as ever! What does it mean, I ask. Tell me, Miss Percy!"

I could not answer a word: I turned away, covering my face with my hands, and the tears streaming like rain-drops between my fingers.

"Oh, this dreadful suspense! this horrible mystery!" exclaimed Herbert, stamping his foot upon the carpet, and looking as if he were half-frenzied. "Mary, I conjure and entreat you——"

He stopped suddenly short: he had again sunk upon his knees—he had endeavoured to throw his arms about her once more; but she repulsed him in a manner which might appear to him to be with a sort of horror, though it was in reality with the vehemence arising from her own distracted state of mind.

"My God! what have I done to deserve this?" exclaimed the young Marquis, as much bewildered as he was afflicted. "Caresses at one moment—repulses the next! First the testimonials of love—then the evidences of hate! Oh, these inconsistencies! What do they mean? Is there aught connected with your history, as you have ere now been led to read it, different from the way you were wont to understand it?—is there aught that can have embittered you more against my family?"

"No, no, Herbert!" responded Mary, in a half-choking voice; "your family is now nothing to me!"

"My family is nothing!" exclaimed the Marquis. "But I, Mary—I, who love you so tenderly and devotedly—am I nothing?"

"You?"—and it was with a species of enthusiasm that she spoke, as much to imply that with him it was very different: but all in a moment checking herself, she simply said, "I beseech you not to question me. Leave me! Let us part—and—and this time——" but here her voice seemed to fail her, and she appeared to be seized with a suffocating sensation, until with an almost preterhuman effort she added, "And this time, let it be for ever!"

Herbert Dalrymple dashed his open palm against his forehead as if he were labouring under a maniac excitement; and then rushing towards me, he exclaimed in a voice the accents of which appeared to be full of frenzy, "What does all this mean, Miss Percy? Oh! if there were ever the slightest

sentiment of friendship on your part towards me ——and you *did* once assure me of your friendship!—I beseech you to explain the meaning of all this! Leave me not a prey to such excruciating suspense! It is cruel—it is inhuman——"

"My lord," I interrupted him, "pray, in the name of heaven, exercise some command over your feelings! Circumstances have occurred——but no explanations can possibly be given now——indeed, they never can be given! You must accept Mary's decision as final—you must not indulge in hope——"

But I here stopped short; for I was floundering deeper and deeper in a quagmire of excuses and evasions which instead of improving matters, were only calculated to render them much worse. But perhaps upon no occasion in which the affairs of others were concerned, did I so completely lose my self-possession and presence of mind.

"Ah, I see that from your lips I can obtain nothing satisfactory!" exclaimed Herbert, in a tone of the bitterest reproach; "and this is conduct which I little expected from you, Miss Percy! Now, Mary," he continued, turning abruptly away from me, and accosting Miss Glentworth, "I will make one last effort to obtain an explanation from your lips! I should have a right to demand it after everything which has taken place between you and me—but I will only entreat it. Yes—bid me go upon my knees, and I will do so!"

"No, no!" ejaculated Mary: "kneel not to me, Herbert!"

"This wildness of tone—this desperation of manner—this passion amounting almost to distraction,—good God! what does it mean? But Ah!" he continued, "if you are thus excited, it is all the greater reason why I myself should endeavour to become reasonable! Yes, yes—I will be cool! Now therefore, Mary," he continued, "I conjure you to answer me this question—do you still love me?"

"Love you?" she ejaculated, starting up with a look that seemed to imply that to have her love suspected were tantamount to an accusation of crime which she was bound at once to repel. "Love you?" she repeated at the interval of but a few moments—and her entire appearance showed how much she did really love Herbert Dalrymple; for there was an inexpressible tenderness in her looks—there was the most eloquent animation on her countenance—there was the strong palpitation of the bosom—and there was even the very attitude which seemed to show that she was ready to spring forward and cast her arms about his neck, but that some strong feeling of quite an opposite character held her back.

"Ah! then you *do* love me?" exclaimed the Marquis, his accents thrilling with joy; "and this point is no longer for a moment dubious!"

And he on his part seemed ready to wind his own arms about the form of Mary, when a gesture, half-peremptory and half-deprecating, which she made, kept him riveted to the spot.

"Hear me, however, Herbert," she said, now speaking with a composure such as she had not before manifested from the commencement of this painful scene,—"hear me, and interrupt me not! You ask me whether I love you? My looks even more than my words—my tears and my despair, must have already most eloquently answered that question! Oh, for months past—yes, for upwards of seven long months since you and I parted—you remember that day——"

"Oh, yes, yes!—it was a dreadful day!" interjected Herbert, shuddering: "a day that never can be forgotten!"

"No, never!" rejoined Mary. "Well then, ever since that terrible day I have not known the real state of my own heart—I have not comprehended the true sentiments of my own soul. At one time methought I hated you—at another time there was tenderness in my bosom as your image was conjured up to my mental view! But Oh! I endeavoured to persuade myself—I tried to persuade Ellen likewise—that I hated you—or at least that everything would inevitably be at an end betwixt you and me even if circumstances were altogether different! But now, Herbert—but now—Oh! I feel that in reality I have never ceased to love you! I have deceived myself—my mind has been in a morbid condition——yes, more morbid than I can possibly explain! It has been mad! yes, mad!—it has yielded to a fantasy which now makes me the wretched, wretched being that I am!"

"A fantasy?" murmured the young Marquis, at first in a manner of vacant inquiry. "A fantasy?" he quickly repeated, as a suspicion evidently sprang up in his mind. "Good heavens! what can you mean, Mary?"—and he looked frightened and full of the most painful suspense.

"Nothing! nothing!" ejaculated Mary, shivering from head to foot. "Do not question me!—let our interview here end!"

Herbert Dalrymple paced thrice to and fro in the apartment; and I watched him with the most painful interest and curiosity—while Mary sat upon the sofa, her looks bent downward, her breathing quick and excited, her bosom heaving and falling rapidly, and her hands quivering as if the fingers were agitated with spasmodic convulsions. At length Dalrymple stopped suddenly short close by the sofa; and he said, "Mary, if you mean me to understand that since we parted you have seen another whom you think you can love—if in a moment of desperation, or in one of those moods when you believed that you hated me—or if with the idea of snatching at some change, in the belief that it was what your diseased mind needed—or to fill up a supposed void in your bosom—if in any of all these circumstances, I say, you listened to the love-suit of another, I will forgive you, Mary!—Oh! I will pardon you! In a word, the whole past, whatever it may be, shall be buried in oblivion—and this day shall be regarded as the era of a new and happy existence! Speak, then, dear Mary——"

"Oh, such kind words as these!" she ejaculated in accents of despair. "Oh! wretch that I am! what amount of happiness have I lost!"

"For mercy's sake tell me what you mean, Mary!" cried Herbert: "tell me—tell me——"

"No, no!—just heaven, no! it were impossible!"—and the poor girl again shuddered visibly: she was labouring under the most fearful excitement.

"Yes—but you must tell me!" said Herbert, whose suspense was evidently most excruciating.

"You do not mean me to understand, Mary, that—that——you are married?"

The burning glow of shame mantled upon her countenance; and at the same instant she burst into tears, which streamed down upon her crimson cheeks like a shower upon a peony.

"My God! what would you have me suspect?" ejaculated Dalrymple, now starting as if a serpent had stung him. "Must I think——But no! no! it were impossible! As soon could I believe that snow itself might turn black—as soon believe that the lily might change to the hue of jet—as that you, Mary—you——"

"Enough, Herbert!" moaned the wretched girl. "I would have kept the truth from you," she continued, in a voice broken and half suffocated by her feelings; "but you have gone on until at length you have drawn forth my fatal secret!"

"O God! then it is so!"—and Herbert dashing his open palm against his forehead, staggered back and sank upon a chair.

At the same instant Mary Glentworth cast upon me a look of ineffable misery—a look so forlorn and woe-begone, that methinks I behold it now even as I pen these lines some years after the occurrence itself,—and she said in a hollow tone, "Tell him what you like, Ellen—tell him what you think fit—but conjure him so to act that we may never meet again! I go to my chamber: you will join me there as soon as possible—will you not, dearest Ellen?"

"I will, Mary," I responded, pressing her hand in my own, and flinging upon her a regard fraught with the deepest sympathy.

She glided from the apartment; and as the door closed behind her, Herbert Dalrymple sprang up from his seat. The words which Mary had said to me were spoken in a tone too low for his ear to catch them; and as he bent a haggard despairing look upon me, he said, "She is gone!"

"Yes—my lord," I answered. "And Oh! let me conjure you—as she herself through me entreats—that henceforth you will act as if there were no such being in the world as Mary Glentworth!"

I stopped short; for the young Marquis turned away from me with so strange an abruptness that I thought he was about to leave the room and hasten after the object of his unfortunate love. I bounded towards him; for I dreaded lest there should arise a scene in the house. I perceived, however, that he was merely about to take three or four turns to and fro in the apartment; and I regarded him in silence. At length he accosted me as abruptly as he had a few moments before turned away; and he said, "May I know the history of this dread misfortune? I cannot suppose that Mary was capable of willing weakness: the conviction is strong in my mind that she was a victim."

"She was!" I answered. "Oh, believe me that she was——"

"Enough, Miss Percy," he interrupted me. "I know that nothing but truth ever comes from your lips. Ah! even this is a relief, to know that she fell not by her own fault, but by the villany of another! And may I ask, Miss Percy, who is the miscreant——"

"If he were at large in the world, I would not

tell you, my lord," I responded; "because I should tremble lest you might seek to avenge in a duel the dishonour of her whom you love. But inasmuch as the law has fixed its strong hold upon him——"

"The law?" ejaculated Dalrymple, his countenance suddenly expressing astonishment and affright. "What! has Mary appealed to the tribunal of justice?—has she been mad enough to expose her own dishonour?"

"No, my lord," I said. "But let me mention a name, and you will understand what I mean. It is the name of Edwin St. Clair!"

"Ah, the villain!" ejaculated Dalrymple: "'tis well for him that the walls of Newgate constitute a barrier betwixt us! But tell me the history of all this, Miss Percy—show me how Mary became his victim—and—and——But proceed!" he exclaimed, thus abruptly checking himself.

I gave him a brief outline of the narrative which I had received from Mary Glentworth's own lips: and when I described how she had been rendered insensible by a poisoned rose, Herbert exclaimed, "Ah! then, that tale so strange and wild which the old gipsy told in the court of justice, must have been true! The unfortunate Mrs. St. Clair must have been murdered by her own husband!—and he will assuredly go to the scaffold!"

"You have now learnt," I said, "how Mary was rendered the victim of that villain! She is here, beneath a friendly roof, to conceal her shame——"

"Miss Percy," interrupted the young Marquis, with a strange suddenness, "you are the friend of both of us. Will you go and bear a message from me to Mary Glentworth?"

"Proceed, my lord," I said, without pledging myself positively to an affirmative in reply to this question.

"Go, Miss Percy," he said—and it seemed to me that there was a strange, unnatural, desperate, calmness in his look, tone, and manner, or at all events he spoke with the resolution of one who had made up his mind to act with an inexorable firmness. "Go to her, Miss Percy—and say that Herbert Dalrymple still regards her as his betrothed; and this proof he gives her of the illimitable love which his heart cherishes towards her. Tell her that for the present we will not meet—but that some months hence, when she may again appear before the world, I shall be ready to conduct her to the altar."

Astonished and amazed—indeed even confounded by the language thus held to me—I was unable for upwards of a minute to give an answer. At length I said, "My lord, I cannot become the bearer of such a message. Much as I love Mary Glentworth, yet must I have some little consideration for yourself——I mean that I cannot allow a generous heart to be led astray by a momentary enthusiasm——"

"I understand all the upright punctiliousness of your conduct, Miss Percy," said the Marquis of Dalrymple; "but if you will not carry the message, you will at least permit me to be the bearer of it myself. Therefore have the kindness to show me where I may find Miss Glentworth."

There was still the most steady calmness in the young nobleman's voice and manner, so that I had now no longer any doubt concerning the fixity of the resolution to which he had come. But still I said, "Your lordship had better reflect for a few hours."

"It is unnecessary, Miss Percy," he interrupted me in a tone of serene determination. "I love Mary—and I am convinced that she loves me in return. I will accomplish her happiness. Under other circumstances it would be an act of the greatest indelicacy to speak or to think of marriage when my mother is lying in a state of unconsciousness,—perhaps upon a bed of death. But these are no ordinary circumstances—and mine therefore must be no ordinary conduct. And now to another point. With all your experience of the world, you doubtless distrust the decision to which I have come—you think that it is a passing enthusiasm which will yield to reaction, and that sooner or later the time must come when I shall repent of the course which I am adopting. Fear not this result. Believe me, it will not ensue. My mind never was more clear than at the present moment!—never more competent to embrace the range of all circumstances—to calculate all consequences! Is this sufficient? Will you now do me the favour which I ask? or must I again demand permission to be the bearer of my own decision to that poor girl who has recently left us?"

I was deeply affected by the language which the young nobleman thus held towards me on my young friend's behalf. I looked upon him with that friendly admiration with which I was wont to regard his character during the earlier portion of our acquaintance; and I thought to myself that he did indeed possess the most chivalrous disposition, so that it was an immense pity his natural good qualities should have at any time been warped or obscured. But still I could not help thinking that there was a certain degree of folly in the path which he resolved to pursue; and I resolved to make one final effort to persuade him to take time for reflection. I conceived this to be my duty, so that hereafter he should have no reason to reproach me as having in the slightest degree led him onward to a step whereof he might repent. But when I commenced a new remonstrance, he at once cut me short with a courteous firmness; and he said, "Miss Percy, do what I ask—or suffer me to do it for myself."

"Then I will go, my lord," I said. "But remember that if at any future time——"

"Entertain no apprehension, Miss Percy, that I shall reproach you:"—and he spoke with the calm deliberation and tranquil firmness of one who was positive and decided how to act.

I could not help saying in a voice tremulous with emotion, "Oh, my lord, this is generous—even *too* generous!" and then I quitted the room.

CHAPTER C.

ANGELINE'S LODGINGS.

I PROCEEDED to Mary Glentworth's chamber, considering that I had now no longer a right to hesitate—that I had accepted a mission, and that I was bound to accomplish it. I opened the door of her apartment: I found her seated upon a chair at the toilet-table, on which her elbow rested, and her head was supported by her hand. In the other hand there was a kerchief saturated with tears: she had evidently been weeping copiously since she had sought her chamber; but now her eyes were dry—and as I entered, it was a look of forlorn and blank despair which she fixed upon me.

"Oh, Ellen," she said, in a voice of profoundest mournfulness, without moving from her seat—without even changing her position—so that it was easy to perceive that the tremendous excitement which she had passed through had been succeeded by a languor—almost a complete prostration, which she could have wished to droop still farther down so as to enable her to hail the presence of death itself,—"Oh, Ellen, what happiness might have been in store for me if I had never lent an ear to the wiles of Edwin St. Clair: for then, instead of being a lost, ruined, and dishonoured girl, I should have been able to present my hand to Herbert Dalrymple, and say, 'Yes, I will accompany you to the altar!'"

I sat down by her side. I said a few consolatory words—then I spoke encouragingly—then I went on to breathe language still more hopeful; and at length I revealed to her the message with which I was charged. She gazed upon me with such an indescribable expression of happiness on her countenance—with the animation of such an ineffable joy—that never did she seem more beautiful in my eyes. But I awaited the moment when some terrible reaction should ensue; for I was almost confident that though for an instant she was bewildered and dazzled, delighted and enraptured by this proof of Herbert's love and generosity, she would nevertheless deem it expedient to reject the proffer as a wrong-doing towards himself.

"Tell me, Ellen," she suddenly exclaimed, "what has transpired—what has come to your knowledge—to make you aware of those important circumstances which you just now mentioned to me?—I mean in reference to the mystery of my birth?"

I accordingly proceeded to recite to Mary Glentworth everything which I had learnt from the lips of Mr. Singleton; and it may easily be supposed with what absorbing interest she listened to the narrative. She frequently shed tears as I spoke of her mother and her aunt; and when I had finished, she reflected in profound silence for some minutes. At length she said, "And all this, therefore, can be fully corroborated by documents that are unquestionable?"

"Everything can be thus corroborated!" I answered; "and furthermore I can take it upon myself to say that in the course of the day, Mr. Singleton will place all the papers in your possession."

"Heaven be thanked," she exclaimed, "that the stigma of illegitimacy no longer rests upon my birth! Ah, my poor aunt! you were indeed to me as a mother!—and so tender and steadfast was your affection that never for a single instant could I suspect otherwise than that you were my maternal parent! I shall not love nor reverence your memory the less for this discovery! No!—I shall ever cherish it, as if I were still unde

the same belief as heretofore! And now, Ellen, in reference to Herbert, I accept——"

"You accept, Mary?" I ejaculated, not altogether able to conceal my astonishment.

"Yes—I accept a proposal which is dictated by the tenderest love as well as by the loftiest generosity!" she enthusiastically cried. "What! do you doubt it, Ellen? Oh, I have experienced unhappiness sufficient to make me covet a period of felicity! And that will come! Yes!—go to Herbert, and tell him that my liveliest gratitude as well as my most devoted affection——"

"And you do not require time for consideration, Mary?" I said. "Remember——"

"Consideration?" she ejaculated. "No! no! It were utter madness—it were suicidal to reject such an offer as this! But Ah! there is one thing which you must now do for me! This is to communicate with the least possible delay to the Duke of Ardleigh the fact that not in the slightest degree do I owe him the allegiance of a daughter. Go and do these things for me at once; and then almost every care—almost," she repeated, as she doubtless thought of her position, "will be lifted from my mind!"

I quitted the room, certainly somewhat surprised that Mary should have so readily accepted the Marquis of Dalrymple's offer; for I could not help fancying that there was a certain degree of selfishness in her conduct, and that while thinking too much of her own happiness she was not sufficiently studying that of the young nobleman. But matters had reached such a point that I could no longer with delicacy or propriety interfere to prevent their progress according to the will of the principal parties concerned; and I therefore resigned myself to my position of intermediary or simple bearer of messages.

I found the Marquis of Dalrymple in the apartment where I had left him; and the moment I entered, I looked stedfastly at his countenance. The first glance was however sufficient to convince me that his resolution was in no way changed; and I communicated the result of my interview with Mary. It was calmly and without enthusiasm that he expressed his satisfaction; so that I still feared there might be a certain amount of generous self-sacrifice in his conduct;—but I urged not another remonstrance nor put another question upon the point. I proceeded—as I deemed myself in duty bound to do—to acquaint him with all the facts that had transpired in reference to Mary Glentworth's birth; and he agreed with Mary's wish that no time should be lost in communicating them to his father. I now therefore went in search of the Duke. It was by this time past one o'clock in the afternoon; and on inquiring where his Grace was, I learnt that he was partaking of refreshment in the dining-room. Thither I repaired; and I found the Duke doing most ample justice to a cold pheasant, as well as to a bottle of sherry with which the dish was flanked.

"You see, Miss Percy," he at once said, "although I am terribly distressed on account of my beloved wife—and likewise in consequence of a violin which no money can replace—I am nevertheless bound to sustain my physical strength, so as to meet all these heavy calamities. Can I have the pleasure of assisting you to a wing——"

"No, my lord, I thank you," I answered: "I have something of importance——"

"Ah! if Peaseblossom were here," exclaimed the Duke, "he certainly would not refuse——"

"But as Mr. Peaseblossom is not here," I said, somewhat angrily, "I must beg of your Grace to devote a few minutes' attention to the humbler individual who is now addressing you."

"No—not humbler, Miss Percy!" he exclaimed, filling a bumper of sherry; "for you know the fair sex——"

"Do listen to me, my lord!" I interjected: "it is something which closely concerns you—— In short, I wish to speak of Mary Glentworth."

"Proceed, Miss Percy," said the Duke. "If Mary requires a cheque, I cannot forget that she has certain claims——"

"It is just this very point, my lord," I again interrupted him, "on which I wish to disabuse you. In short," I added, thinking it better to come to the point at once, "Mary Glentworth has no claim whatever upon you—as indeed you have none on her;——for she is not your daughter!"

"Ah! what?" ejaculated the Duke, with so sudden a start that he upset the glass of sherry into the dish of pheasants. "Not my daughter?"

"No, my lord. There is a strange history which you have to learn; and when you are in possession of all the details, you must not blame the memory of the deceased lady——"

"I have no inclination to reproach the memory of any one who is dead," observed the Duke; "for I cannot see what earthly good it would do me. But you astonish me in respect to Mary! If she is not my daughter, of course she must be somebody's——and perhaps you will tell me——"

"Your Grace shall know everything," I interrupted him. "Indeed, it is by Mary's special request that I have lost no time in making this revelation."

"Pray continue, Miss Percy," said the Duke. "I will take this other wing and refill my glass, while you go on talking."

I gave the Duke the necessary particulars,—making my history however as short as possible. The nobleman continued to eat and drink; and the first excitement of suspense being over, it was with no very considerable display of emotion that he listened to the narrative. When I had concluded, he said, "Well, this is one of the strangest histories I ever heard in my life; and yet I am convinced it is true because all the parts fit in so accurately and nicely. But Ah! I hope it will be kept secret from my son Herbert—or else he will now perhaps be for making a fool of himself——"

"With that business, my lord, I can have no concern," I said: "but it is now my duty to add that Mary Glentworth is beneath this roof; and I give your Grace the information inasmuch as it is scarcely possible you can avoid meeting her."

"Ah! she is here?" ejaculated the Duke. "Well, then, the best thing to be done is to send Herbert off directly. Yes—I can easily devise an excuse: he must go up to London to break to his younger brothers and sisters the sad tidings of this accident which has befallen their mother——"

"Yes, my lord," I said; "that will be the better plan."

I then sped from the room, in order that I might have an opportunity of saying a word or two to the Marquis of Dalrymple before his father saw him. I found him in the drawing-room; and I hastened to say, "You just now expressed your desire that Mary and yourself should not meet again under existing circumstances—that is to say, not for the next few months. An excuse for your immediate departure will be presently furnished by your father himself. He knows that Mary is beneath this roof——"

"Does he know that we have met?" inquired Herbert, but with an air of more or less indifference; for notwithstanding his natural good qualities, it was impossible he could entertain much filial respect towards such a father.

"His Grace does not know that you have met," I answered: "indeed, I dropped not the slightest hint to his lordship of anything which has this day occurred in reference to Mary and yourself. And now, my lord, it were well if you were to delay not in taking your departure."

The Marquis of Dalrymple proceeded to the sick chamber, to ascertain precisely the condition in which his mother then was; and to his joy he found that Mr. Singleton was now enabled to give a much better account of his patient than might have been anticipated. Herbert had therefore all the less hesitation in taking his departure at once and leaving his mother there.

The two travelling-equipages had been taken to the little inn in the village of River, so that they might be put up there until they were required, and that the requisite repairs might be effected to the one which had been upset in the ditch. Orders were now sent off to get the other carriage in immediate readiness, as the Marquis of Dalrymple proposed to continue his journey to London without delay. To be brief, he took his departure without again seeing Mary Glentworth; but on bidding me farewell, he whisperingly reiterated the assurance that his resolution in reference to her would never be changed, and he begged that he might from time to time be permitted to correspond with her.

I had now leisure to seek an opportunity of being alone with Juliet. I had as yet everything to make known to her,—the same tale in reference to Mary Glentworth to tell over again. But I had more to reveal to her than I had done to the Duke of Ardleigh; for I hesitated not to acquaint Juliet with the exceedingly generous conduct of Herbert Dalrymple towards Mary, and the engagement which now subsisted between them. Juliet was naturally much astonished at the statement which thus met her ears; but she was much rejoiced on Mary Glentworth's account.

After this interview with Juliet, I repaired to the drawing-room, where I found the Duke of Ardleigh. I was going to speak to him on a particular subject; but he at once anticipated me by exclaiming, "Ah! I am glad you have come, Miss Percy! I was just thinking at the moment how I could get to speak to you again; for I do not feel altogether comfortable beneath this roof——"

"You mean, my lord," I said, "on account of Mary Glentworth?"

"Exactly so," he replied. "I intended no imputation against the hospitality of your friend Lady Frederick Ravenscliffe,—for that is unexceptionable—the house is comfortable—every attention has been shown my dear wife—and I am sure nothing could be better than the pheasants or the sherry. But don't you see, Miss Percy, it would be awkward and embarrassing for me to run against Miss Glentworth—she would feel it just the same—she knows her aunt was my mistress——"

"All this, my lord, constitutes the very subject," I said, "upon which I purpose to speak to your Grace. Lady Frederick Ravenscliffe would rejoice that you should make her house your home as long as circumstances render it necessary: but Mary must be considered——"

"I know what I will do!" ejaculated the Duke: "in fact, I had already made up my mind just before you entered the room. I will go to the hotel at Dover——it will be much better——I can stay there as long as the doctor may think it needful for the Duchess to remain beneath this roof. I can call every day—and if I name a particular hour, Mary can keep her own room just at that period——"

"All this can be easily managed, my lord," I said: "and I think you have adopted a most prudent resolution in repairing to the hotel at Dover."

Matters were thus settled; and in the course of the afternoon the Duke took his departure from River House, so that only the Duchess and her confidential maid remained there. Her Grace continued unconscious of all that was passing around her; and though she opened her eyes, yet there was no intelligence in them—it was upon vacancy that they looked. Mary Glentworth now suddenly expressed to me a desire to visit the bedside of the Duchess; and as a matter of course there was not the slightest objection to the gratification of her wish. But when once in that chamber, Mary vowed that she would take her turn in performing the part of nurse towards the patrician lady; and I had no difficulty in comprehending that it was for Herbert's sake she thus demonstrated so much kind solicitude on behalf of the mother. All her rancour against the Ardleighs was gone; she had no longer any reason to cherish it against any scion of that family. If she thought of her own mother, it was not now as the degraded and dishonoured mistress of the Duke: it was only of her aunt that she could thus think; and it was evident that this aunt had willingly accepted her destiny at the time as the nobleman's paramour—so that it was not for such a reason that Mary could continue to bear rancour against the Duke; though on the other hand it was of course deemed expedient, considering all past circumstances, that they should, if possible, avoid a meeting. Mr. Singleton placed in Mary's hands the documents which had been discovered at the cottage; and a liberal reward was forwarded, through the agency of the worthy surgeon, to the old gardener.

On the following day two physicians came down from London, they having been despatched by the Marquis of Dalrymple. They fully approved of everything which had been done by Mr. Singleton; and they declared that it would be dangerous to remove the Duchess for the present. But I must now divert the reader's attention from this topic for the present, and speak of other matters.

It was on the third morning after my arrival at River House with Mary Glentworth, that I received a letter from Beda, containing two pieces of intelligence which were of more or less importance. The first was that she had discovered the residence of Mademoiselle Angeline Churchill the ballet-dancer; the second was that the humpbacked dwarf whom I had seen at Gilderoy Hemp's establishment, had been to the house to inquire for me and had left word that he should call again. I had hitherto fancied that the dwarf must have been included amongst the victims of the terrific conflagration at Gilderoy's abode; and I was therefore startled and amazed when I read that announcement in Beda's letter. I was naturally anxious to see the humpback. Perhaps he could give me some information that might be important; for there was always in my mind the doubt as to whether Parkes had actually perished in that conflagration or not. When coming to River House, I had made up my mind to remain there altogether for a month or so; but my resolution was now suddenly altered, and I determined to go back to London—at least for a few days—so that I might see the humpback. I represented to Juliet and Mary that some urgent business had unexpectedly transpired to take me back to the metropolis; and I set off accordingly.

It was between four and five o'clock in the afternoon when I reached Great Ormond Street; and I at once sought from Beda's lips the details of those matters which she had mentioned in her letter.

"And first of all relative to the humpback," I said; "because that is of the greatest importance. Here is a man whom for the last seven or eight months we have supposed to be no more, suddenly reappearing——But tell me all about it, my dear Beda!"

"Indeed, my dear Miss," she replied, "I have very little more to tell you than was communicated in my letter. When I was out yesterday, a person called, answering exactly the description of the dwarf,—a hideous old man, about three feet in stature, with a head leaning all over on one side—a mouth all awry—grey hair and shaggy overhanging brows——"

"Yes—it must have been the very same!" I ejaculated.

"It could be none other," rejoined Beda. "He asked for Miss Percy. It was Susan who answered the door; and she told him that you were not at home. He simply said that he would call again; and turning on his heel, he hastened away. Susan had not time to ask him his business: indeed, as she has confessed to me, she was somewhat frightened at the appearance of the strange being——"

"Ah, then, at least it is fortunate," I exclaimed, "that he was not told that I had gone out of town for a month; as he will now doubtless call again in a day or two. He must have something to communicate,—unless you think, Beda, he may be poor and in want, and therefore remembering me——"

"I should rather suppose that he has something to communicate," replied Beda. "If he had thought of drawing upon your purse, he would not have allowed all these months to elapse."

CHARLOTTE TREMAINE.

"Well, we shall see when he calls again," I interjected. "And now, Beda, in reference to Mademoiselle Angeline? You have discovered her abode——"

"Yes," replied the faithful girl. "I went out yesterday afternoon to make a few purchases; and as I was passing along Holborn, I beheld in front of me a female figure which I thought was not altogether unfamiliar. She presently stopped for a single moment to glance in at a shop window: I caught a glimpse of her countenance—it was Angeline Churchill! I continued to follow her: she proceeded along Holborn, until she reached Little Queen Street, down which she passed. Along Great Queen Street she went,—I still in the track, but taking good care to avoid suffering her to perceive that she was thus followed. Al-
No. 79.—ELLEN PERCY.

though you told me some time ago that I need not make any further endeavour to ascertain her place of residence, yet as this opportunity seemed to present itself, I thought there could be no harm in rendering it available——"

"And you did right, Beda," I ejaculated. "But proceed."

"As Mademoiselle Angeline was pursuing her way, I thought to myself," resumed Beda, "that it would be singular after all if she were going to the jeweller's shop in Long Acre—for she was bending her course in that direction. And so it proved, sure enough! I watched from the opposite side of the street: she remained but a couple of minutes inside the shop; and when she came forth again, she had a letter in her hand. This however she quickly concealed amongst the folds of her dress; and then she hastened along the thoroughfare. Yes—she walked very quickly; and I believe that she is a young person of the strictest propriety of conduct—for two or three times while I was following her, I beheld her turn abruptly aside and evidently with much indignation as some foppish individual bent his insolent looks upon her, at the same time giving utterance to some words which were no doubt offensive to her ears. On she went towards the Strand — Waterloo Bridge was reached—she traversed it. I continued to follow her; and, to be brief, I traced her to a house in a street leading out of the York Road. The appearance of the house is quite respectable; and I have no doubt that Angeline *does* live there—for I remained upwards of half-an hour watching, and she did not come forth again. Besides, I am almost confident that I caught a glimpse of her face at a window on the second floor; and she had no bonnet on. But I instituted no inquiries in the neighbourhood—for I thought she might probably hear of them; and at all events I preferred waiting until I should have communicated with you."

"You did well, Beda," I answered; "and to-morrow I will go and call upon Angeline."

Yes—I was resolved to avail myself of the discovery which was thus made. I had now more than one reason: I was not only anxious to come to an explanation with Miss Churchill, and ascertaining from her, if possible, the grounds upon which she had levelled such singular charges against me, two months ago, in my own dressing room at the theatre; but I was desirous also of seeing if I could be of any assistance to her. I felt confident that the poor girl laboured under some error in reference to myself, and for which she was to be pitied not blamed: I therefore harboured no anger towards her; but on the contrary, all my best sympathies continued to be engaged in her behalf, as I could not forget the painful history which I had received from the lips of Mr. Richards, and which showed how great her distresses must have been ere she procured an engagement at his theatre. Since he had been bankrupt I had not seen Angeline's name announced in the advertisements of any other theatrical establishment. Perhaps she had failed to obtain such an engagement as she might choose to accept?—perhaps the hand of poverty might once more be pressing heavily upon her? It was thus that I thought; and I was resolved to avail myself of the present opportunity of offering the succour of my purse, if it should be needed. For the reader must bear in mind that I had at the outset become interested in Angeline Churchill as much from her modest and well-behaved demeanour, as on account of her misfortunes, her personal beauty, or her artistic talents.

I bade Beda remain at home that she might be sure to see the dwarf when he should happen to call again; and between eleven and twelve in the forenoon of the day after my return to London, I alighted from a hack cab at the commencement of the York Road, near the foot of Waterloo Bridge. In a few minutes I diverged out of that thoroughfare into the street which Beda had mentioned; and I knocked at the front door of the house which she had specified. The door was opened by a servant-girl of about six-teen, and who evidently belonged to the class of drudges known as maids-of-all-work.

"Does Miss Churchill live here?" I inquired.

"Miss Churchill? No, ma'am," was the girl's answer, so readily given that I scarcely dared suspect its sincerity.

"Are you sure?" I nevertheless asked. "Miss Jane Churchill—or perhaps Mademoiselle Angeline is the denomination?"

"No such lady here, ma'am," responded the maid-of-all-work. "There's Mr. and Mrs. Parsnip—a very quiet old couple which lives on the first floor——leastways they ain't at home now—they're gone into the country to spend Christmas with some friends at Woking——"

"But I speak of a young lady——"

"Ah, well! there's Mr. and Miss Smith which lives on the second floor—father and daughter. She's a nice young lady—though I don't like the genelman much;"—and here the maid-of-all-work lowered her voice to the softest whisper, so that I had no difficulty in concluding that Mr. and Miss Smith were at home in their lodgings at the time.

That name of *Smith* was the one which Angeline gave at the pawnbroker's, as Mr. Richards had discovered: but then Smith was a common name, and from this very fact it was the most frequently assumed by persons using a fictitious nomenclature. Thus, after all, I reflected within myself, the fact that the young lady had used that name at the pawnbroker's afforded no positive ground for believing that it was the name she passed by elsewhere.

"Have the goodness," I said to the maid-of-all-work, slipping some money into her hand, "to describe this Miss Smith."

"Well, ma'am, I should think she is about two or three and twenty years old—very handsome—dark brown hair—yes, and dark blue eyes—tall—fine figure——"

"It must be the same!" I mentally ejaculated: "and then too, Beda is almost positive that she saw her at one of the second floor windows of this very house! At all events I will risk an intrusion upon Mr. and Miss Smith; for if there be any error I can but apologize."

Having thus made up my mind, I said to the girl, "Have the goodness to conduct me up-stairs; for I am tolerably certain that I am acquainted with Mr. and Miss Smith."

"Well, to be sure!" ejaculated the girl: "if this isn't the very first time they've even so much as had a soul to see them! But do tell me, ma'am, if you think it's true that——"

"What?" I asked, perceiving that the maid-of-all-work was artless and ingenuous, with all the uncouthness and familiarity of a girl fresh from the country.

"Why, that Miss Smith," she responded, "is a theatre-going young lady?"

"Ah!" I ejaculated, now thoroughly convinced that there was no mistake and that I was on the right track. "But what makes you think——"

"Oh! pray don't say a word, ma'am," interjected the girl, looking half frightened; "but two or three times I've seen Miss Smith working at such thin queer-looking dresses—mere skirts——no, frocks I mean!—made of gauze-stuff——"

"Do not ask questions about other people's

business, my good girl," I said. "And now have the kindness to show me up-stairs."

"Lor, ma'am! it's quite easy to find the way!" cried the servant. "Go straight up the stairs—the second floor—door facing you—"

"Enough!" I said: and I began ascending the staircase, wondering what effect my presence would produce upon Jane Churchill—for this, be it remembered, was the name which she had given Mr. Richards as her real one.

On reaching the landing of the second floor, I hesitated for an instant whether to proceed any farther; for I feared lest my conduct should savour of an impertinent intrusion. But then I recalled to mind all the reasons which I had grouped together as a motive for the adoption of this course: I hesitated no longer, but knocked at the door.

"Come in," said a voice which I instantaneously recognised as that of Miss Churchill.

I opened the door: but at the very moment that I appeared on the threshold, I was transfixed with the wildest degree of astonishment; for in the man who suddenly started up from a chair near the fireplace, I recognised Mr. Parks!

CHAPTER CI.

EXPLANATIONS.

WHAT words can express the wonderment which thus seized upon me? Yes—there he was, that man of unmistakable appearance,—ugly and sinister-faced—his red hair mingled with white—his cheeks covered with freckles, as they were always wont to be! He had on spectacles:—he always used to wear them during the earlier years of my knowledge of him; he had then left them off for an interval; but now it seemed he had taken to them again. Yes—there was Mr. Parks the attorney!—the man concerning whose fate I had for many months past been altogether dubious,—wondering whether he had perished in the conflagration, or whether he had survived it!—but now having this uncertainty dissipated all in a moment—for there stood that man!

A half-stifled shriek had indicated the sudden surprise, and perhaps apprehension, of the young lady; but it was a scarcely audible ejaculation which had burst from the lips of Mr. Parks himself. I should observe that it was a tolerably decent room on the threshold of which I had stopped short; but while thus describing it, I am speaking comparatively. What I mean to be inferred, is that it was a sufficiently respectable apartment for a ready furnished lodging in a somewhat poor street leading out of the York Road. There was a certain evidence of feminine taste in the room,—a neatness which struck the eye at a glance. There is an expressive though somewhat commonplace English word which will better convey my meaning: it is the word "tidiness." There was a large nosegay of artificial flowers in a plaster of Paris vase: and a bird was chirruping in a cage girt with a piece of yellow muslin. At the moment when I entered, a pink gauze dress—the unmistakable transparent garment of the *danseuse*—slipped from the hands

of Mademoiselle Angeline, as she started on beholding me and gave vent to that half-stifled shriek to which I have already alluded. I heard the servant girl come rushing up the stairs: for though that shriek was low, yet it had met her ears, the house being so small and the sound therefore having so short a distance to travel. But instantaneously recovering my presence of mind, I stepped back upon the landing, exclaiming, "It is nothing!—merely the suddenness of recognition!"

I then entered the room, closing the door behind me.

"Miss Percy," cried Angeline, hastening towards me, half in consternation and half with a look of ill-concealed rage, "if you still possess the power or the inclination to injure my unhappy father——"

"Your father?" I ejaculated, in renewed astonishment: and I flung a look upon Parks, doubting whether it could possibly be the fact: but I saw that he was all pale and trembling, as miserable and woe-begone a wretch as on that memorable night when he stood in the presence of Gilderoy Hemp, in the midst of the awful tribunal which had reminded me of the dark inquisitorial chambers and vehme-gerichts of the middle ages.

"Yes, my father!" said Angeline—or rather Jane Parks, for this was indeed her proper name.

"No, no! Miss Percy will not hurt me!" said Parks, in a tremulous tone and with looks of the most abject entreaty. "She promised Zarah that she would not—Gilderoy himself told me so! She likewise pledged herself to that stern old man! They were vows solemnly taken! I performed all the conditions imposed upon me; and if she did not recover possession of her fortune, it was not my fault."

I was astonished at the words he had last spoken; and I exclaimed, "But as you survived the fire, was it not *you* that received the money?"

"I? No!" he ejaculated. "Do I look like a man possessing wealth? Ask my poor daughter to tell you what we have suffered! She knows it—she has felt it all! *She* has earned the bread which for some little time we have eaten with a comparative degree of comfort!"

A light darted in unto my brain. All the reproaches, so bitter and yet so mysterious, which Angeline had levelled against me, two months back in my dressing-room at the theatre, were now completely intelligible. She had looked upon me as her father's unrelenting and remorseless enemy—the authoress of his ruin—the cause of his misery. This was now comprehensible enough; and it was not difficult to conceive that he had given his own version of past transactions and had told a tale after his own fashion.

"You, Miss Parks," I therefore at once said, "have wronged me by the evil opinion which you have entertained; but that is a matter which can be cleared up presently. In reference to yourself, Mr. Parks, I do not hesitate to admit that I gave to Zarah the pledge of which you have spoken—I renewed the same vows to Gilderoy. I flatter myself that I am a woman of truth; and even though I thus made pledges which had the effect of cheating the laws of my country of their due, yet shall they be regarded with the strictest honour and integrity."

"Ah, Miss Percy," he exclaimed—and it was evident that an immense weight was lifted from his mind,—"this was only what I expected from *your sense of justice!* Good heavens! I have suffered enough! and I beseech you to prove forbearing in the presence of my dear daughter! Do not give vent to accusations too terrible for her to hear!"

I understood what the wretched man meant: he was significantly imploring me not to charge him in his daughter's presence with the murder of my grandsire Mr. Forsyth. I was at once struck by a sense of what must have been all the filial conduct of that excellent young woman towards her unhappy father: I remembered her poverty, as I had heard the tale from the lips of Mr. Richards —how she had visited the pawnbroker's to pledge some trifling article of raiment, and how great had been her distress when she found that she could not raise precisely the sum that she required. Then I *recalled to mind* how in my dressing-room at the theatre she had implored me not to use my influence with Mr. Richards to deprive her of her bread as there was some one who was dependent upon her, and this *one* I now found to be her father! Everything told a tale of a daughter's struggles to maintain an impoverished sire—of deep filial regard for a fallen parent! Could I say or do anything to plunge a dagger into the heart of this admirable young woman? No—I could not!

"Miss Parks," I said, turning towards her, and speaking in a tremulous voice, for my soul was filled with emotions, "I do not wish to render this scene more unpleasant to you than I can possibly help. But you and I must have no misunderstanding between us. You must know me well! You must learn to believe that I had naught but the kindest feelings when I endeavoured to display my sympathy towards you! Your father must now tell you in my presence that I have never done him an undeserved wrong. Has he not already confessed that he surrendered up my fortune?— does he not therefore prove by his own words that he had deprived me of it?"

"Yes, yes—it is true!" said Jane Parks, evidently staggered and even dismayed by this appeal to her common sense as well as to the stubborn presence of facts. "Oh, Miss Percy, if I have wronged you——"

"You have," I said; "and though not for a single instant did I suspect who you could possibly be at the time when you levelled such strange accusations against me in my dressing-room at the theatre,—yet was I amazed and bewildered, as well as confident that you were labouring under some error; for I knew that there was no being in the world whom I had wilfully or wantonly injured to an extent justifying one-thousandth part of the complaints which found their vent from your lips."

"Ah, Miss Percy!" said the young woman, "I do indeed begin to fear——"

"Nay—but you must be convinced!" I ejaculated. "Mr. Parks, we will not enter into particulars in the presence of your daughter. For the sake of this admirable young woman I am only too willing to spare you. But the truth you must confess, that I may be disabused in her estimation! Say, then, have I ever done you an undeserved injury? Speak, sir! I insist upon your answer!"

"Say no more, Miss Percy," interjected Jane, bursting into tears. "My father's looks only too well corroborate the truth of your averments. Accept, therefore, the humblest and most contrite apologies from one who is incapable of doing you or any other living creature a studied injustice! Permit me to take your hand."

I at once gave her my hand, and I pressed hers with warmth and effusion. The tears were raining down her cheeks, and her bosom was convulsed with sobs. It went to my heart to behold this spectacle of grief on the part of one whose conduct I knew to be most exemplary; and as she took and pressed my hand to her lips, I stooped down and imprinted a kiss upon her forehead.

"Now, Jane," I said, "have the kindness to withdraw for a little while. It is absolutely necessary I should have some discourse with your father——"

"But tell me, Miss Percy—relieve my mind from suspense!" she said; "for I am now haunted with horrible fears. My father has debts—if his creditors knew where to find him——"

"Ah, I understand!" I exclaimed. "You wish to know how I discovered your residence?"

"Was it through the jeweller?" she inquired: "is it possible that he has proved treacherous?"

"No," I responded: "it was not through him that I was directed hither. A young servant of mine followed you the day before yesterday from Holborn——"

"Ah!" she ejaculated: "there was a moment when I thought that a young girl with a dark veil over her countenance, was watching me as I issued forth from that jeweller's shop: but I afterwards fancied that it was a false alarm——"

"Yet your surmise was correct," I rejoined. "That was my servant."

"And did she call at the jeweller's shop," inquired Jane Parks, eagerly, "about two months ago—a day or two after that scene in your dressing-room?—and did she put questions to that jeweller,—questions which though not actually pointed, nevertheless rendered him suspicious——"

"Yes—it was my servant," I responded. "But the jeweller said nothing to betray you."

"And why did you seek my abode?" she quickly inquired.

"I wished to come to explanations with you—to learn the cause of those charges which you levelled against me—to assure you of your error—to offer you my friendship! In reference to my visit here to-day, I need only add that my servant followed you the day before yesterday, and tracked you to this house. My object in seeking you was still the same; for little did I suspect who you really were, or whom I should meet here:"—and I glanced towards her father.

"I, in my turn, must give you a few words of explanation," said Miss Parks. "That jeweller had received large sums of money from our family; and although in our poverty his niggardness prevented him from opening his purse for our succour, he consented to receive any letters which might be addressed to his abode for me. The letter which your servant must have seen me reading the day before yesterday, was one from the lessee of a theatre, giving me an engagement, which is to commence next Monday:"—and she glanced at the gauze dress which she had tossed over the back of a chair.

"I am rejoiced," I said, "to hear that you are still prospering in the profession which you have chosen. And now leave us, Jane, for I have matters whereon it is absolutely necessary I should speak to your father."

Miss Parks again took my hand, and pressed it with fervour. Then, advancing to her sire, she said, "Father, I do not seek to penetrate into any of these mysteries—for mysteries I see that there are! I hope that the result of your interview may be such that I may never again hear of anything wrong between yourself and Miss Percy. Let me conjure you to treat her with frankness and candour in whatsoever dealings ye may now have together. Oh, father! fail not to keep my words in mind!"

It was thus with earnest entreaty that she spoke; and then she hastened from the room.

"Mr. Parks," I said, as the door closed behind her, "you possess a daughter whose example ought to have a beneficial effect upon you! You saw that I was forbearing in her presence. I know not what tale you may have told her, but it is evident she suspects not the full amount of your misdeeds. I could not find it in my heart to strike the terrific blow which would have been dealt her by proclaiming all that you are! And now listen to me. You have recalled to mind the pledges which I gave the deceased Mrs. St. Clair and the venerable Gilderoy Hemp. Those pledges were given by me on a certain condition. The condition was that my fortune should be restored to me; and that being done, I held myself bound to take no further step to deliver you into the hands of human justice, but to leave you to your own conscience. Now, then, prove to me that your portion of the compact was performed on that night when you signed the documents making me over the heritage of which I had been dispossessed!—prove to me that it was not you, nor any one connected with you, that subsequently obtained possession of the whole amount standing in your name in the Bank of England!"

"By heaven, Miss Percy," ejaculated Parks, with vehemence, "I can advance no better argument than that which I just now put forward. Look at my position——"

"It is true," I said, "that you are evidently poor: but how do I know that you did not take possession of the money and by some means lose it? Did not your wife flee away from her home, with all the valuables of the house, the very morning after that memorable night——"

"Ah!" he exclaimed with bitterness; "and tell me, if you can, where she is gone!"

"What?" I cried; "are you in ignorance upon the point? And the children with her!"

"All our children, except our eldest daughter," he rejoined, with a half-stifled sob,—"that daughter whom you find here! But the villain Moss——"

"What?" I ejaculated; "your clerk, Mr. Moss? Is it possible? Did he not then perish——"

"No, no, Miss Percy," exclaimed Parks; "he saved himself—and it was he who obtained pos-

session of thirty-eight thousand pounds standing in my name in the Bank of England."

"Good heavens! is this the fact?"—and I was confounded. "But the proofs! the proofs, Mr. Parks! The tale seems so extraordinary——"

"Ah, well it may!" he interjected: "and Oh, Miss Percy! if I have sinned terribly, I have been as terribly punished!"

"I cannot understand how all this could have been," I said, shaking my head dubiously: for I knew how well the man could dissemble, and I loathed the idea of being in the presence of such a wretch. "You must not think, Mr. Parks, that because I am a woman I have no head for business-affairs. There seem to be contradictions in your tale—or rather I should say in the tale which you would have me infer from what you have already said. On that night at Gilderoy Hemp's, you signed transfer-documents for £36,300; and those documents bore the date of the 11th of May. They were in possession of Gilderoy. But the very next day the whole £38,000, belonging to you, were sold out by a Mr. Jenkinson, and by virtue of papers which bore the date of the 8th of May. Now, these papers having your signature affixed, were not the same which by any possibility could have got into the possession of Mr. Moss, supposing that he had by some means procured the documents which Gilderoy held in his hands."

"Hear the explanation," said Mr. Parks: "it is simple and easy. It will prove that I am not deceiving you—it will prove likewise that it was not my fault that you did not obtain the sum of £36,300 according to the assignment I made for your use on that memorable night."

"Proceed," I said: "but pray do not trifle with me. You may perhaps find me more keen and shrewd than you imagine in detecting any inconsistencies in your tale."

"Judge for yourself," he resumed, "whether I am disposed to tell you the truth. I have one point to prove—and I will prove it. This point is that I acted fairly towards you in respect to that transfer of the money; and that being proven, you will adhere to your own pledges,—those pledges which you made alike to Mrs. St. Clair and to Gilderoy Hemp. I must begin by informing you that in consequence of all the proceedings of yourself and your father with a view to recover your fortune, I had grown frightened. I had succeeded in overreaching you by means of the cheque written with the sympathetic or disappearing ink, and by means of the documents you had signed: but still I was restless and unsettled. I knew that your father was persevering, shrewd, and keen-witted: I felt persuaded that neither of you would let the matter drop, if you had a chance of reviving it——and, in short, I fancied that accident might still place me more completely than ever in your power. My wife knew that I had dispossessed you of your heritage——"

"And did she know," I asked, "how my poor grandfather met his death?"

"Hush! hush! for heaven's sake, hush, Miss Percy!" ejaculated Parks, but in the low half-subdued tone of terror. "No! she knew it not! That was a secret which I thought rested only with myself so soon as the grave had closed over my mother! Well, as I was saying, Miss Percy,

I was frightened lest your turn to triumph would come, and that the day of retribution would arrive for myself. I partially revealed my fears to my wife: we deliberated—and we decided upon flying to a foreign country. I had some debts, which I could however have easily paid out of the money that I possessed; but I thought that this was useless, as it would only diminish the capital I should have to take with me. Therefore we resolved to decamp secretly; and for this reason we did not sell off the furniture and take those measures which would have shown that we were breaking up our establishment. This was our plan—to depart suddenly some fine morning, with all the plate and valuables, and such things as could be packed up in a moment—and of course with the money which was to be sold out of the funds. Our arrangements were thus definitively settled. I should observe that our daughter Jane was on a visit to some friends in Paris; and we wrote to her to come over to us at once, without however stating for what reason. All the other children were at their different schools; and we sent for them, under pretence of being present at a grand juvenile entertainment which we purposed to give. And now mark well the facts which I am about to explain! When everything seemed ready for the carrying-out of the enterprise, I obtained a number of Bank transfer-papers in order to fill up the requisite forms for the sale of the funded stocks which I possessed. I suppose, judging by dates, I must have prepared and duly signed those papers on the 8th of May. I remember that for the next two or three days I was anxiously awaiting the arrival of Jane, and I did not think it prudent to sell out the money until she should be with us. In other words, I was deferring this last important step until we were altogether ready for departure, for fear lest the circumstance should get abroad, and my creditors suspecting my purpose to decamp, should suddenly pounce upon me and thrust me into prison. This delay was fatal to me. In the evening of the 11th of May, that old woman—you know whom I mean—she is generally known as Dame Betty—called and said that I must accompany her as she had business of a most important character to consult me upon, or else some secret to communicate—I now forget the exact excuse that was made. You are aware, Miss Percy—for it transpired at what may be termed the trial, and therefore why should I attempt to conceal it?—you are aware, I repeat, that this old woman and I once had certain dealings together, and therefore I did not for a moment imagine that she meant to do me a mischief. I accompanied her—she took me to Gilderoy's establishment—and there I found myself a prisoner. I need not remind you of what followed; for, as I subsequently learnt, you and your servant Beda were concealed the whole time behind a curtain in the spacious room——"

"And who told you this?" I inquired.

"I will tell you presently, Miss Percy," responded Parks. "To pursue the thread of my explanations in a continuous manner, I must remind you that when the trial was over, the gipsy-guards conducted me away from the room. I was plunged into a cellar—or I may more properly call it a dungeon: for the guards assured me that it was absolutely necessary I should remain in closest custody until Gilderoy gave the mandate for my release. A lantern was left with me—sufficient provisions were likewise furnished; but the door was fast locked and bolted, and I was as much a prisoner there as if I had been within the walls of Newgate. You may suppose, Miss Percy, that my thoughts were not very pleasant: but I pass over all this—for if my reflections had been fraught with anguish while I was pondering on the loss of the fortune I had possessed, what must my mental horror have been as the conviction gradually dawned in upon me that the premises were on fire? Miss Percy, if I were endowed with all the eloquence and all the powers of language that ever belonged to the most accomplished orators and writers, I could not do justice to all that I then felt. No!—it is impossible for words to describe the agony of mind—the appalling horror which I endured! First of all it was the smell of fire which came upon me: then the cries of wild alarm which were raised smote my ears; and I could no longer endeavour to persuade myself that it was a mere delusion. And full soon the sound of the raging element itself reached me, even in that deep subterranean,—that gushing noise which always accompanies fire—sweeping and roaring and rushing onward like the wind itself! I flung myself against the door—I beat it with all my force —I shouted for assistance—and then I gave vent to the most piteous cries. Again I say that no language can possibly convey an idea of what I then felt. My brain seemed to be turning: the idea of perishing by the most horrible of deaths would have been sufficient to make intellects of even a stronger order than mine reel upon their seat! And then the din of falling masonry—the sounds of cross-beams giving way—joists and rafters snapping, breaking, and crashing, — all these evidences served to prove that the conflagration was gaining ground and that it was immense. But was I forgotten? was no one coming to deliver me? was I to be abandoned to the most hideous of deaths? The thought was insanity itself. Again and again did I dash my form against the door: I even sought in my madness and desperation to claw down the very masonry with my nails——until at length consciousness utterly abandoned me!"

Here Mr. Parks paused, shuddering visibly as he recalled to mind the incidents of that horrible night; and I felt assured that he was in no sense exaggerating them.

"When I slowly began to recover my senses," he presently resumed, "it seemed to me as if I were awaking out of a horrible dream. Total darkness environed me where I was. I stretched out my hands:—they encountered walls of solid masonry. A sense of the reality of all the horrible things that were floating in my mind, rapidly seized upon me; and, to be brief, in a few minutes I thoroughly comprehended my position. I was still in the dungeon, where the light had gone out. All was quiet: a dead silence prevailed. What had happened?—had the fire been extinguished? had my terrors exaggerated its ravages at the time? and was it sufficiently insignificant to render it needless for those who held me in their custody to think of liberating me from that dungeon? Such was the conclusion to which I came; and exhausted by my painful reflections, I fell asleep upon the pallet which was provided for my use in that cellar. How long I had been unconscious, I knew not:—how long I next slept, I knew not!—but when I awoke I was very hungry. I groped my way to the little table on which the provisions had been placed; and I made a hearty meal. My fingers encountered a bottle: I placed it to my lips—it contained brandy—and in the hope of drowning my cares, at least for the time-being, I swallowed the contents, which might be very nearly a pint. Then I again slept. I knew not how long: but I was awakened by sounds which I could not immediately understand. It seemed as if a quantity of heavy materials were being agitated or moved about in the neighbourhood of the door. Then I began to think that probably my dungeon was buried beneath the ruins of the building, and that persons were coming to my assistance. My blood ran cold at the idea that I had probably been even nearer death than I had suspected; and I anxiously listened to the sounds which were approaching nearer and nearer. At length my ear caught human voices speaking to each other just outside the door: then followed the heaving-away of some bricks and rubbish—and then the drawing back of the bolts and the unlocking of the door. A cry of joy which burst from my lips, convinced those who came to release me that I was alive. They were three of the gipsy-guards who had consigned me to that dungeon: and one of them bore the appellation of Black Ned."

"Ah!" I ejaculated; "I know the man! But proceed, Mr. Parks."

"Ah, Miss Percy! what a tale had I then to learn! Nearly four-and-twenty hours had elapsed since I was first thrust into that dungeon!—the remainder of the memorable night itself—the whole of the ensuing day—and it was then between ten and eleven o'clock on the second night when succour thus came to me! I was astounded on learning that so much time had passed: I was prepared to hear that there had been the lapse of half-a-dozen hours or so—but I was amazed at the tidings that nearly four-and-twenty had gone by! I could only account for my utter ignorance on the point by the supposition that I must have remained in a state of unconsciousness for a much longer time than I had at first supposed,—probably from the narcotic effect of the smoke which had penetrated into the dungeon. However, be all this as it might, certain it was that the sun had risen and gone down over my head while I was entombed in the dense darkness of that place. As you may suppose, Miss Percy, I put a thousand questions on being released. Where was Gilderoy? He had perished in the conflagration. Where was Moss? It was not known; but it was supposed that he likewise had met his death amidst the fury of the flames. Then, by an ejaculation from Black Ned's lips, I learnt that you, Miss Percy, and your servant Beda had been present in the large room where the trial took place; for Black Ned said something to the effect that it was fortunate for you and the girl that you had taken your departure at the time you did. As I looked around me on emerging from my dungeon, by the light of the moon I saw that all was a heap of ruins. Black Ned gave me

some brandy and likewise some food; and I began to recover from the exhausting influence of my captivity. While I was thus refreshing myself, he said 'that during the rage of the fire it was everybody shifting for himself, and that I was forgotten; that when all was over and daylight broke upon the smouldering ruins, those gipsies who had survived did not like to appear upon the scene or to hang about the place, for fear lest I might be discovered, either dead or alive, in the cellar, and they should consequently be arrested to answer any charge which might be brought against them on my account; thus they therefore remained away from the ruins throughout the day, but when night came Black Ned and two or three others resolved to ascertain my fate.' Such were their explanations—and I was thus indebted to them for my release from that horrible prisonage; for if they had not come, I should doubtless have perished of starvation—because the dungeon, it appeared, was completely heaped over by the masses of fallen masonry and half-burnt timbers, so that there was not the slightest clue to lead the police or any other persons visiting the ruins to the supposition that there was a human being buried beneath that pile. However, I escaped — and I regarded my deliverance as something next to miraculous."

Again Mr. Parks paused; and I said to him, "You have looked death as it were in the face: I hope that the influence of such a recollection will not be lost upon you?"

"Misfortunes, Miss Percy," he responded, "are invariably accompanied by the sternest moral teaching. But you would not believe me if I were to declare that henceforth I shall be an altered man?"

"You will be judged by your deeds, Mr. Parks," I said, somewhat laconically: for I knew how consummate a hypocrite he was, and I was determined not to be duped by any maudlin sentimentalism on his part. "Proceed with your narrative—or rather bring it to a conclusion, for I should imagine that it must be nearly terminated."

"Yes," he resumed, "I have not much more to relate. On taking leave of the gipsy-men, I hastened away from that neighbourhood. As you may suppose, my mind was in the wildest uncertainty in respect to what might have happened at home during my absence,—yes, and in the wildest uncertainty in reference to the fate of the transfer-papers which I had signed at Gilderoy Hemp's. Perchance they were burnt along with Gilderoy himself?—perchance Moss had obtained possession of them and had escaped from the conflagration? My mind was acutely tortured with suspense. I made the best of my way towards my own residence. I beheld no lights in any of the windows; and I was smitten with alarm. I knocked at the door. It was presently opened by an old charwoman, who was accustomed to assist the servants occasionally in their work. She seemed to be stupified with astonishment on beholding me, and still more so when I inquired how my wife and children were? Then I learnt that they were gone! But I will not attempt to describe what my feelings were, Miss Percy: I will confine myself simply to a narrative of the facts. It appeared that my wife

was very uneasy when she found that I did not
return on the preceding night, and she resolved to
sit up for me. It was about two o'clock in the
morning when Mr. Moss drove up to the house in
a cab; and my wife flew down-stairs to see what
was the matter the moment she recognised his
voice. He made some statement to my wife—but
what it was did not transpire to the knowledge of
the domestics or the charwoman. Moss then
went into my private office, where he remained
for about half-an-hour; and the charwoman knew
that he was engaged in turning over all the
papers in the drawers of my desk, because she
found him at this work when, by my wife's in-
struction, she took him in some refreshment. At
the expiration of that half-hour, Mr. Moss departed, after another interview of a few minutes
with my wife. It then appeared that for the remainder of the night—or rather the four or five
next hours of early morning, my wife was engaged in packing up all the plate and valuables,
—making some excuse to the charwoman and the
servants to the effect that important business had
called me to the Continent, and that she was about
to join me there. She paid all the domestic-
servants their wages, presenting them likewise
each with a liberal pecuniary gift as a compensation for the suddenness with which they were
about to be discharged. Then, a little before
nine o'clock that morning, my wife and children
took their departure: but my eldest daughter
Jane had not arrived from the Continent. Such,
Miss Percy," continued Mr. Parks, "was the intelligence which I received from the charwoman.
Ah, no! it was not all! I should add that my
creditors, on hearing of the family's decampment,
had at once made an irruption into the house—
the servants had all left—the charwoman was
about to leave likewise, but they desired her to
remain for the purpose of taking care of the furniture until law proceedings should finally dispose
of everything."

"But how did you know, Mr. Parks," I inquired, "that it *was* Mr. Moss who obtained possession of the money?"

"Oh, can there be a doubt of it?" exclaimed
the lawyer. "Listen, Miss Percy! Scarcely had
I received all those particulars from the charwoman,
when I rushed into my private office: and there I
found that all the drawers of my desk had been
forced. Who had forced them? Mr. Moss!
Who, then, had found the papers therein duly
signed—duly drawn up—with all forms completed
—for the selling out of the thirty-eight thousand pounds from the Bank of England? Yes,
yes—it was Moss—and none other that did this!
On the following day I went into the City and
made inquiries: I entertained the last desperate
hope that my money might still be safe. No—it
was gone! It had been sold out by some person
giving the name of Jenkinson. This was not
Moss: the personal descriptions differed;—but it
was no doubt a friend of that villain's who transacted the business on his behalf."

"But how know you, Mr. Parks," I inquired,
"that it was not your wife who had taken possession of the transfer-papers and who sold the
money out of the funds?"

"I am convinced that it was *not* Mrs. Parks,"
responded the attorney. "In the first place we

had no such acquaintance of the name of Jenkinson · and it was therefore very unlikely that
Mrs. Parks would have entrusted so important
an affair to any stranger with whom at the moment she had accidentally fallen in. In the second
place, if Mrs. Parks had really got possession of
the papers, she would have gone *in person* to the
stock-broker to make sure of the business and to
accelerate it. In short, Miss Percy, there are
countless considerations which I need not now
enumerate, to prove that it was Moss who obtained possession of the money."

"Yes," I said, after a few minutes of reflection:
"I am now inclined to entertain the same
opinion. And since that date——"

"I have heard nothing of my wife," interjected
Parks,—"nothing of my children! Whither they
could have gone, I know not. What tale Moss
could have told my wife on that night when he
arrived so suddenly at the house, I cannot conceive. Perhaps be represented that I had fled—
or that I had perished—or that I was plunged
into the abyss of some frightful calamity,—in
order that he might have a pretext for looking
amongst my private papers. But I cannot tell!
—it is all beyond conjecture! No letter arrived
at the house; for the charwoman promised to
watch for the postman and convey to me any
correspondence that might be addressed to my
name. My creditors made me a bankrupt—but
I did not surrender—I concealed myself: I have
ever since been playing at hide-and-seek; for what
tale could I have told to account for the loss of my
fortune? Everything which my wife had left at
the house was sold off——In short, Miss Percy,
I became a ruined man,—my creditors taking all
they could lay their hands upon—the decree of
bankruptcy still remaining in force against me—
and the officers of the court ready to seize upon
my person and thrust me into gaol for not having
surrendered to the *fiat*, as the legal expression
terms it."

"And your daughter came to England?" I
said, thinking compassionately of Jane Parks.

"Yes—my daughter came to England," replied
the attorney, "a few days after the hurricane of
startling incidents which overwhelmed me. The
Tremaine family, with whom she had been staying in France, were absent from Paris at the time
when the letters I had written to urge my
daughter's return, were transmitted. It was not
until her return to Paris with the Tremaines that
Jane received the letters. Then she hastened to
London. But heavens! what tidings awaited
her! The home broken up—a charwoman receiving her mysteriously, and then conducting her
stealthily to the lodging where I, her father, was
hiding myself—her mother, her brothers and
sisters, gone—and no one knew whither!—my
fortunes beggared—my purse empty——"

"Yes—it must have been a terrible blow for
your unfortunate daughter!" I said. "But did
you not make any inquiries to discover, if possible, a trace of your wife?"

"Yes," murmured the attorney. "I made all
the inquiries that in my impoverished condition I
could possibly institute: but I could obtain no
clue to the elucidation of the mystery."

"And if your wife should write," I asked inquiringly, "where——"

"The letters will be delivered at the jeweller's in Long Acre," rejoined Parks. "The post-office authorities have received instructions to that effect. But as so many months have now elapsed since the disappearance of my wife, I can only conjecture that she must have suddenly resolved upon going on a very long voyage, and that therefore there has not yet been time for any letter to reach me from the place of her destination. And now, Miss Percy, I think that I have nothing more to relate or explain to you. I hope—indeed I am sure that I must have convinced you——"

"Yes, Mr. Parks," I interrupted him, "I do assuredly believe that you lost all the money which stood in your name in the Bank of England; and indeed it little matters, so far as I am concerned, who retained possession of it. Suffice it, therefore, for me to add that I hold myself bound to keep the pledges which I made to the late Mrs.

No. 80.—ELLEN PERCY.

St. Clair and to Gilderoy Hemp. Henceforth you and I will be utter strangers to each other."

With these words I rose from my seat and abruptly quitted the room; for I felt that in no other way could my interview with such a character terminate. I could not bid him farewell, nor give utterance to anything resembling a courteous word at parting; for did I not know that he was one of the authors of my grandsire's death? and could I even consider that his crime was expiated by the fearful catalogue of sufferings he had endured?

As I went forth upon the landing, I closed the parlour door with some degree of violence, so as to make Jane Parks aware that my interview with her sire was ended. As I had conjectured, she was in the back room of that floor; and she at once made her appearance on the threshold. I saw that she was very pale, and that she had evidently been weeping: but inasmuch as it was a profound sorrow that was expressed upon her countenance, and not any degree of horror or excitement, I felt convinced that she had not listened at the door of the front room, nor had obtained any deeper insight than she before possessed into her father's misdeeds.

"Come out with me for a walk, my dear Jane," I said. "You and I must have a little conversation together—and I would rather not remain here any longer."

"In one minute, Miss Percy," she responded, "I will be at your service!"

Her bonnet and shawl were soon put on: she just looked into the front room to tell her father that she should not be long; and then we left the house together.

CHAPTER CII.

CHARLOTTE TREMAINE.

SILENCE prevailed between us for two or three minutes after we were in the open air. We passed along the street—we entered the York Road—and then it was that my companion said with a certain degree of timidity, "I hope, Miss Percy, that my father treated you at last with that candour and frankness——"

"Let us not say another syllable upon the subject, Jane," I interrupted her. "Suffice it for me to inform you that I was so far satisfied with the explanation he gave as to induce me to declare that at my hands he need apprehend nothing for the future, no matter what my power might be to do him an injury. But we are likewise to remain utter strangers to each other——I mean your father and myself; for it is quite different with respect to you, my dear Jane!"

"And do you mean," she tremulously asked, "that I may consider you my friend?"

"Yes—assuredly!" I exclaimed. "Such is my meaning! such is my intention!"

At this moment we reached the corner where the York Road joins the Waterloo Road; and ejaculations expressive of recognition and amazement burst forth from the lips of Jane Parks and from those of a young lady whom we at the instant encountered. This young lady was of medium stature, and of very genteel figure. She was dressed with a certain neatness and plainness of style which were perfectly consistent with the most refined taste. In other respects her appearance at once struck the beholder as something even more than lady-like; for it was elegant. She was not handsome:—she was not even pretty—though she was likewise very far from being ugly. Her age was about my own—that is to say midway between twenty and twenty-one; and before I leave this passing description of her, I must add that though possessing no strictly critical claims to personal beauty, she had nevertheless fine hair and good teeth. But there was something which seemed bold in the expression of the large blue eyes, which by some persons however might have been considered handsome.

I have already said that ejaculations of recognition and surprise burst from the lips of my companion Jane and the young lady whom we thus encountered. They shook hands with every demonstration of fervid affection: I believe that they would have embraced each other if the meeting had not occurred in the public street and in the middle of the day.

"Dearest Jane! is it possible?"

"Dearest Charlotte! is it indeed you?"

These were the ejaculations that marked the moment of the encounter; and then, so soon as the first feelings of excitement had subsided, Jane introduced the young lady and me to each other, so that I now learnt her name to be Charlotte Tremaine. Jane Parks presented me as Miss Percy: but I saw that Miss Tremaine regarded me with considerable attention; and at length she said, hesitatingly—almost diffidently, "I have seen portraits of Miss Trafford, the celebrated tragedian; and you, Miss Percy, bear a most striking resemblance——"

"May I tell the secret?" inquired Jane Parks in a half-whisper, which was not however low enough to escape Charlotte Tremaine's ears.

"There is but little of a secret in the matter now, Jane," I responded, with a smile; "for it is pretty generally known——"

"Ah! then," ejaculated Charlotte Tremaine, with an enthusiastic expression of countenance, "it is Miss Trafford to whom I have the honour of speaking!—and Miss Trafford and Miss Percy are identical! You must know," she continued, "that I have been a great admirer of your's from all that I have read concerning you; for, as you may suppose, I never beheld you until this moment. But I have lived so much upon the Continent—indeed altogether for the last three or four years—and therefore I have had no opportunity of beholding you upon the stage. But now I am delighted to form your acquaintance!"

I made suitable acknowledgments for the compliments thus bestowed upon me; and there could not be the slightest doubt in respect to the sincerity with which the young lady spoke.

"Not only am I so great an admirer of your's," she continued, with an utterance the rapidity of which received its impulse from the enthusiasm that had taken possession of her,—"my parents—my sisters likewise—we have all entertained the greatest interest in your behalf! My friend Jane here can tell you this much——"

"Yes, it is perfectly true," said Miss Parks. "When a long time ago I told them that you had some acquaintance with my family, they overwhelmed me with questions: but these I was ill able to answer, because I never saw you until a few months back, Miss Percy——I also had been absent from London for some three or four years——"

"But though we could learn so little from our friend Jane respecting you," continued Charlotte Tremaine, "we have always devoured with avidity everything that the newspapers said concerning you."

"At all events it is quite clear," I observed, bending a smiling look upon Jane Parks, "that whenever you may have spoken of me to your friends, you abstained from mentioning my real name."

"Yes, Miss Percy," rejoined Jane; "for when I first learnt——I think it was through the medium of a letter from one of my sisters—that you were going upon the stage—I was at the same time informed that you did not wish your real name to be known; and therefore I considered it a secret which I was bound to keep even from friends so dear and so intimate as Charlotte and her family."

This was another good trait which I had just discovered in the character of Jane Parks; and I could scarcely help wondering that so unprincipled a father should possess so excellent a daughter.

"I hope, Miss Percy," said Charlotte Tremaine, "that you will do me the favour of calling upon me. I assure you I shall esteem it an honour—— my parents and sisters likewise will be glad to give you the most cordial welcome!"

I could not possibly resist a courtesy and a kindness which expanded indeed into the most friendly demonstrations towards me: and I said, "It will afford me great pleasure to call upon you, Miss Tremaine, and to be presented to your relations. But you will likewise allow me to have the satisfaction of seeing you at my own house?"

I named my address in Great Ormond Street; and Miss Tremaine intimated her own present place of abode, which was in some fashionable street at the West End of the town.

"But you, my dear Jane," she ejaculated, now turning towards Miss Parks,—"what has become of you for the last eight months?—how is it that I never heard from you—that my own letters were returned through the post? Oh, my dear Jane! you know not what uneasiness you have caused us all!"

"Alas, Charlotte," said Miss Parks, bursting into tears, "it is a long and a painful story——"

"Good heavens! what can have bapppened?" ejaculated Miss Tremaine. "The rumour reached our ears that your family had all left England— we of course supposed that you had accompanied your father and mother——But Ah! you are weeping! I see that I have touched some painful chord——"

"Perhaps it were as well," I here interjected, "if I were to leave you together; for you have doubtless much to talk about——"

"No—do not leave us, Miss Percy!" cried Charlotte Tremaine. "I am sure we can have no secrets from you. Nay—I do implore that you will stay with us! Indeed I will walk in whichever direction you may think fit to pursue! The object which brought me into this part of London can be accomplished another time. It was to call upon an old nurse who was in our family many years ago—she lives somewhere in the neighbourhood of the Blackfriars Road—I have a few little presents for her—but I will take another opportunity of calling upon the worthy old creature."

"When did you arrive in London, Charlotte?" inquired Miss Parks, who had now considerably recovered her self-possession.

"Only the day before yesterday," replied Miss Tremaine. "Yesterday I passed by the house where you used to live; and I saw that it was shut up. I therefore knew that the report which reached us some months ago, that your family had quitted England, must be true. And is it not so, Jane?"

I saw that Miss Parks scarcely knew how to

reply; and I said, "Yes, Miss Tremaine—it is true that our friend's mother, and brothers and sisters, have gone abroad——And perhaps you may suspect by this time that her father has experienced misfortunes——"

"Alas! some idea of this kind did certainly enter my head," said Miss Tremaine, "when I found that you did not write, Jane—that my own letters were returned through the post——But travelling about the Continent as we were, we so seldom received tidings of anything that happened in England——"

"Ah! I *did* write to you, my dear friend," said Jane. "I wrote to you twice; and—and—receiving no answer, I feared lest I had lost the friendship of your family—— for my father's name figured in the Gazette——"

"Good heavens, Jane!" ejaculated Charlotte; "could you form such an opinion of myself or any one connected with me? We never heard of this misfortune which overtook your father; and as for the letters which you declare that you wrote to me, they must have miscarried. But such miscarriage is by no means a rare thing with the French post-office, when letters follow you about from place to place and are re-directed half-a-dozen times. Now let us think of a few dates, my dear Jane," continued Charlotte. "It was about the middle of May when you left us in Paris, to return to England in pursuance of letters received from your parents. A fortnight afterwards we went to Rouen——"

"And it was about that time that I must have written to you in Paris," interjected Jane.

"From Rouen we almost immediately proceeded to Havre," resumed Miss Tremaine, "and thence to Dieppe. We crossed to Jersey for a week or two—and on our return to Paris, I made sure that I should find letters from you at the post-office. There were none. It was then that I wrote to you, my dear Jane——the letters were returned after some weeks through the post-office, with an intimation that you were not to be found at that address. Then my uncle Colonel Tremaine arrived in Paris; and he mentioned a rumour which he had heard to the effect that you and your family had all gone abroad."

"How singular—and Oh! how ungrateful," exclaimed Miss Parks, "must my conduct have appeared!"

"No," replied Charlotte; "we did not judge you hastily. You know that my father never forms an opinion precipitately, and always endeavours to prevent those around him from being hasty in their judgments. We all said that we would wait—that time perhaps would solve the mystery and bring letters from you——"

"Ah, this was most kind! most generous!" murmured Jane, much affected. "And I wrote a second time to you——that was in the month of June. I do not hesitate to confess, Charlotte," she continued, in a tremulous voice, "that I was very, very poor——I ventured to appeal to your friendship——"

"Oh, heavens! that you should have been poor!" cried Miss Tremaine; "and that I should have remained ignorant of the fact! You know that I am incapable of telling a falsehood on the subject; and therefore I can only say that there was a strange fatality about these two letters of yours. They never reached me; or else, Jane——"

"Oh, I know your goodness of heart!" cried, Miss Parks: "and I was wrong——yes, very very wrong to suspect that you and your family could have been purposely and intentionally reserved towards me on account of my father's misfortunes. But Oh, my dear Charlotte! when people are brought down in the world, they are taught so many rude lessons in adversity's school that their minds become warped—their vision grows jaundiced—they suspect their best friends——"

"As you have done in this case, my dear Jane," interjected Charlotte, speaking with the utmost kindness. "Did you not know that you always had a home to which you could return wheresoever my parents dwelt?—did you not feel convinced that the slightest hint to the effect that money would help you was certain to receive instantaneous attention?"

"I ought to have known all this," rejoined Jane Parks; "but Oh! when I found that my letters remained unanswered what could I think?"

"I am sure," I observed, now breaking in upon this discourse, "enough has been said upon the subject. The miscarriage of letters on the one hand, and the return through the post of those written on the other hand, are clearly established and require no further demonstration."

"Tell me," said Charlotte Tremaine, with that generous enthusiasm which seemed natural to her, —"tell me, my dear Jane, is it now too late——"

"I am eating the bread earned by my own industry," interrupted Miss Parks. "Accept my sincerest gratitude, Charlotte, for the proffer which I see that you are about to make me; and believe me that should I unfortunately need the succour of a friend at any future time, I shall not hesitate to apply to you. And now I will give you a proof of the reliance which I place upon your friendship. I will not attempt to disguise anything from you—I am sure that you will not scorn and repel me when I tell you that I also have betaken myself to the stage——"

"You?" ejaculated Charlotte Tremaine, with a look of ineffable amazement. "Is it possible?"

"But in a far humbler sphere," proceeded Jane Parks, "than that in which my friend Miss Percy so gloriously shines. In short, Charlotte, you who are always reading of dramatic matters, — you must doubtless have fallen across the name of Mademoiselle Angeline—although it has been but for so short a time before the public——"

"Yes—I have heard of it!" cried Miss Tremaine. "But you do not mean me to understand——"

Jane Parks looked deprecatingly at her friend for a moment; and then she said, "Yes—I mean you to understand, Charlotte, that I am Mademoiselle Angeline!"

"And sincerely—most sincerely, my dear Jane," said the young lady, with all the fervour of her impulsive disposition, "do I congratulate you on the success which you have achieved! If I deplore anything, it is that there should have been a necessity for you to betake yourself to the stage. It is however done; and we will not touch upon the past more painfully than is absolutely necessary. I know, Jane," added Charlotte empha-

tically, "you will experience at the hands of my parents and my sisters as hearty a welcome as you ever received from them in other times—the welcome which is bestowed on a dear, dear friend!"

Jane Parks could not give any verbal response to the words that were so kindly spoken: she was overpowered by her emotions: but taking her friend's hand, she pressed it warmly. I should here observe that while engaged in this conversation, we had reached Waterloo Bridge—we proceeded slowly along it—and the variations of feeling and excitement which accompanied the discourse had little need to be checked through fear of being observed: for as those of my readers who dwell in the metropolis well know, there are never half-a-dozen passengers seen at any one time upon that bridge.

"I daresay," cried Charlotte Tremaine, after a pause—and she now spoke with the evident intention of turning the discourse into a different channel, so as to relieve Jane's mind from any painful impressions that might have been left upon it,—"I daresay you are anxious to know all about our own proceedings and movements. As I just now told you, we only arrived in London the day before yesterday after an absence of nearly four years from England. We are temporarily staying with my uncle, Colonel Tremaine; and it is at his house that I shall expect to see you, my dear Jane —and you likewise, Miss Percy. But we shall not remain for more than a week in London: we are going to the old Hall in Staffordshire."

"Tremaine Hall!" ejaculated Miss Parks. "How often have I heard you speak of that beautiful place!—how often likewise have I heard your father describe the home of his ancestors!"

"You are aware, my dear Jane," resumed Charlotte,—"indeed my father has never made any secret of it——for the necessity was not entailed upon him by any extravagancies of his own, but through the enormous expenses of a lawsuit which was forced upon him and which dragged its slow length through the Chancery Court,—it is no secret, I was about to say, that my father was compelled to go abroad for a few years to economise, and what is called to 'nurse the estate.' But the lawsuit has recently been settled—not with any very great advantage to himself—yet in a manner which enables him to return to his native country and go back to live at the old Hall and in the midst of his tenantry in Staffordshire."

"Most sincerely do I congratulate you, upon this happy occurrence," said Jane: "and may you, my dear Charlotte, and all with whom you are connected, experience many, many years of bliss and prosperity."

It was now Miss Tremaine's turn to press with fervour the hand of her friend: and as a modest blush overspread her countenance, and she suddenly cast down her eyes with an air of some little confusion, she said, "The return of the family to the old Hall will be celebrated by an event——a bridal——"

"Indeed?" ejaculated Jane, in mingled astonishment and delight. "May I hope—dare I venture——"

"Yes — my dear friend, your conjecture is right," said Miss Tremaine, with a deepening blush upon her cheeks and an enhanced confusion of the looks. "Circumstances have occurred——"

"Now," I interrupted her, "I must insist upon leaving you alone together. You are old friends—there may be subjects concerning which you have given each other your confidence——"

"There is no topic, Miss Percy," said Charlotte, "upon which I need hesitate to touch in your presence. Therefore, if you would really afford me a proof that you desire my acquaintance and wish that it should ripen into friendship——"

"I cannot commence such an acquaintance or such a friendship by intruding on your secrets," I said. "Besides, I have really some calls to make," I added, as an excuse for separation: "and you must suffer me to depart."

"On this condition," exclaimed Charlotte, "that you will call upon me to-morrow or at your earliest convenience? Pray do!" she added urgently. "I shall long to see you again, Miss Percy!"

I gave the promise that was solicited; and before I left the two young ladies together, I said to Miss Parks, "If you can call upon me in the evening, Jane, I should be glad, as I wish to see you."

She answered in the affirmative; and I proceeded towards the Strand, leaving Charlotte Tremaine and Jane Parks upon Waterloo Bridge. As the reader may suppose, I had ample food for reflection in all that I had heard from the lips of Mr. Parks, and in the discovery that his clerk Moss was after all most likely to be the person who had plundered me of my fortune. But I will not trouble the reader with my meditations on this subject: what their nature must have been can no doubt be easily imagined.

On reaching Great Ormond Street, I anxiously inquired of Beda if the humpbacked dwarf had called during my absence: but I was answered in the negative. I then told the astonished Beda the particulars of my visit to the house in the street leading out of the York Road,—how Mademoiselle Angeline had turned out to be Miss Parks, and how she was living there with her father. Other particulars I gave, relative to the explanations I had received from the lips of Mr. Parks; and Beda, at the conclusion of my narrative, exclaimed, "Although I am prepared to be astonished at nothing in this world, yet I must confess that I did believe Mr. Moss to be an honest and well-meaning young man and faithfully devoted to your interests!"

"Such also was my impression," I responded; "but you see, my dear Beda, how in this world we may be deceived. And now I am anxious to see the humpbacked dwarf; for it is possible he may have something to tell us in reference to this Mr. Moss——although I have utterly abandoned every hope of regaining a single fraction of that fortune whereof it would seem that by fatality's self I was to be deprived!"

In the evening, at about seven o'clock, Jane Parks made her appearance. She again expressed the liveliest gratitude for the forbearance which I had shown towards her father—whom however she merely looked upon as the plunderer of my fortune, while she remained in utter ignorance that he was an accomplice in the murder of my grandsire.

"And now, Jane," I said, "I wish to have a few explanations in reference to yourself. How long was it that you had until this day entertained so evil an opinion concerning me?"

"Listen while I enter into a few details," answered Jane. "I must tell you that from the time that I left school I never was a particular favourite of my mother——"

I could not help here thinking in my own mind that Mrs. Parks might have conceived a dislike for her eldest daughter for the simple reason that there was an immense dissimilitude between herself and all her brothers and sisters,—not merely in person, but also in disposition; for whereas Jane was good-looking, amiable, and well principled, the rest of the Parks tribe were (so far as I knew anything of them) ugly, ill-conditioned, bad-tempered, and most unloveable beings. Now, inasmuch as in these respects they perfectly resembled their mother, it need not for a moment astonish the reader to conceive that she should bestow all her affection upon the tribe of offspring who so much resembled her, and all her antipathy upon the well-favoured exception. But after this digression I must suffer Jane Parks to continue the explanations which I did not positively interrupt at the time by any remark from my lips.

"I never was a particular favourite of my mother," she said; "although my father was sufficiently kind to me. My home was an unhappy one; and I longed to leave it. I fell in with an old school-companion — Charlotte Tremaine: she asked me to go abroad with her family—an arrangement to which her father, who is very indulgent in most respects, at once assented. I travelled with them for a twelvemonth. During this interval I formed the acquaintance of another family in which there were several young ladies, and whose name was Mountford. From them likewise I received an invitation to pass a few months in their company; and that period was happily spent at Brussels. Then I returned to the Tremaines at Paris; and I accompanied them into Italy. After our return to France, I again received an invitation from the Mountfords; and another period of some months was spent with them. They went out to India, and almost persuaded me to accompany them; but Charlotte Tremaine wrote to beg that I would return to her—and as I regarded her as the best friend I had in the world, I complied with her wishes. I remained with the Tremaines until summoned to England by my father's urgent letters in May last. You already know under what circumstances my father and I then met. Until that period I had always entertained a high opinion of you, Miss Percy; and I was therefore grieved and astonished to learn from my father's lips——But I will not tell you what he said!"

"I think you had better tell me everything with candour, Jane," I replied, "in case there should still be anything for me to explain away."

"Since you desire it, your wishes shall be obeyed," she answered: then in a slow and mournful manner, she went on to say, "My father assured me that you had proved the author of his ruin—that you had advanced claims to which you had no right—that you had availed yourself of legal quibbles under the advice of some unprincipled attorney——Oh, Miss Percy! how can I continue this narrative so painful — so humiliating—"

"Finish it, Jane, and it will at least be something off your mind. Doubtless your father gave you to understand that I persecuted him remorselessly——"

"Yes—such was the assurance he did indeed give me! He told me such tales—he bewildered and horrified me! I fancied that you had compelled him to surrender up his own fortune by means the most iniquitous—by threatening to accuse him of fraud and forgery—and therefore a deadly rage against you took possession of my soul! And now you can understand wherefore I spoke so bitterly on that occasion in your dressing-room——"

"Enough, my dear Jane!" I interrupted her: "all that is atoned for and forgiven. But did you not hesitate to apply at the same theatre for an engagement?"

"If you had continued upon the boards of that theatre, I should *not* have applied," responded Jane: "I should have dreaded to come in contact with you——I would rather have starved! But it was immediately after your secession from the stage that I made my application to Mr. Richards. Then, it was not until after I had made a successful *debut* as a *danseuse*, that you returned to the sphere from which you were after all only a few months absent. Conceive what my feelings were the very first time I saw you, and some one whispered to me, 'That is Miss Trafford!'—But I conquered my emotions so far as to avoid the betrayal of them; I could not then abandon the stage—I had a chance of earning my bread by the profession which I had embraced—and I preferred the alternative of coming in frequent contact with you, painful though it would be, to that of wilfully seeking starvation alike for my father and myself. But Oh, Miss Percy! let us now quit this painful topic—and let me assure you that, strong as my other feelings have been, those of gratitude are not now less potent: for I at length recognise all the noble generosity of your disposition—I understand it—I appreciate it! Of my father," she added, in a low tone and with a sudden mournfulness of manner, "I shall say nothing more. The decree has gone forth from your lips!—you and he are to be strangers for the future!"

"Yes," I rejoined: "but this is no reason, my dear Jane, wherefore you and I should not be excellent friends!"

"Oh! no, no, Miss Percy!" exclaimed Miss Parks, her countenance suddenly brightening up with joy.

CHAPTER CIII.

CHARLOTTE'S LOVER.

THERE was a brief pause, which was broken by Jane, who said, "And now tell me, my dear Miss Percy, what do you think of my friend, Charlotte Tremaine?"

"Do you not remember, my dear Jane," I asked, "what she herself said of her own father?—that he was never precipitate in delivering opinions or coming to conclusions:—and you must admit that

the principle is a good one. However, so far as I could judge of your friend Miss Tremaine, she is generous-hearted and amiable—I should say that she is totally deficient in foolish pride—without the slightest affectation or conceit. She no doubt entertains a great friendship for you; and you will permit me to observe that the circumstance of having secured the good opinion of such a family as the Tremaines speaks immensely in your favour."

"Miss Tremaine has conceived a great liking for you," said Jane Parks; "and she sincerely hopes that you will favour her with a call to-morrow. Indeed, she bade me assure you that she should wait at home from three to five in the hope of having the pleasure of receiving you. The family are temporarily staying, as I think you heard her say, with a bachelor uncle, Colonel Tremaine, who is very well off and possesses a fine house in South Street. I may add for your information that Charlotte has five sisters——"

"Six sisters in all, and no brothers?" I asked.

"No brothers," rejoined Miss Parks. "Mr. and Mrs. Tremaine never had any more children; and these were six girls. It is a fine old family, so far as I have at different times learnt; and amongst Mr. Tremaine's ancestry there have been peers and baronets—but by some means or another none of these titles has descended unto himself. As for the old Hall in Staffordshire——But perhaps, Miss Percy," ejaculated Jane, thus suddenly interrupting herself, "I am troubling you with matters in which you have not the least concern nor interest?"

"On the contrary," I answered: and then I added with a smile, "Although I just now deprecated any haste in giving an opinion relative to a lady in whose company I was not more than half-an-hour, yet I will frankly confess that I saw quite enough of Charlotte Tremaine to be interested in her. Proceed therefore, my dear Jane, in giving me the information you think fit in reference to this lady's family."

"I was about to speak of the old Hall," resumed Miss Parks. "I have seen a picture of it—and a fine spacious building it is,—almost completely embowered amidst trees of such a size that they seem to be the growth of centuries. Some portion of the edifice dates as far back as the time of Queen Elizabeth: but the principal frontage belongs to the age of George the Second. The old Hall has not escaped the common fate of such structures in a district where the peasantry are imbued with many traditionary superstitions; and thus it has its haunted room and its ghost—though Mr. and Mrs. Tremaine have often assured me with a smile that they have occasionally slept tranquilly enough in the former and never encountered the latter. It is to this mansion that the family are now returning after an absence of about four years; and the first fortnight or three weeks of their arrival at home, will be signalized by a wedding——the bridal of the eldest daughter of the Tremaines."

"And that eldest daughter," I said, "is Charlotte?"

"Yes," returned Jane; "and I have no doubt that the marriage will be a happy one. There are certain romantic circumstances connected with the loves of Charlotte and her intended husband, a portion of which came under my personal knowledge, and the whole of which I am at liberty to communicate."

"Be sure not to violate any confidence, Jane," I said; "because I never choose to pry into other people's affairs—and indeed I have no curiosity in that sense."

"Miss Tremaine begged me to communicate her intended marriage in formal terms to you," answered Jane, "because she is most anxious that you should pass a week at the Hall in Stafford shire, so as to be present at the bridal."

"However flattered I may be by such an invitation," I said, "I scarcely see how I can accept it on the part of perfect strangers."

"Oh, you will not regard them as strangers!" exclaimed Miss Parks: "you will find yourself on friendly terms with them immediately! But you will call to-morrow in South Street—will you not?—and then you will receive from Miss Tremaine's own lips the most cordial assurance of welcome. I was going to enter into many particulars relative to the attachment of herself and her intended husband: but I see," continued Jane with a smile, "that you are so afraid of being deemed unduly curious—and I respect you all the more for the feeling—I will only give a rapid sketch. I must begin by telling you that some two years and a half ago I accompanied the Tremaines into Italy. I think I stated that much just now. We remained for four or five months at Milan; and there, amongst others, we formed the acquaintance of a young subaltern officer in the army of one of the petty Italian States. He was on leave of absence and was staying at Milan. An attachment sprang up between himself and Charlotte; and when this Italian gentleman proposed to Miss Tremaine, she consulted her parents. I have already given you to understand that Mr. and Mrs. Tremaine are kind and indulgent to their children; but still they are persons who can be firm when they conscientiously deem that decisiveness is necessary. Mr. Tremaine spoke to the young officer; and in every point he was satisfied with the exception of one, which eventually constituted an apparently insurmountable difficulty. His connexions were good—his family was highly respectable—his own character was unimpeachable—his honour was untarnished—his conduct was steady and regular: but his pecuniary resources were exceedingly limited—and though there were members of his family who were wealthy, yet his own prospects of inheriting any of their riches were remote and uncertain. At that time Mr. Tremaine knew not how his lawsuit might terminate; for on the one hand the gain of it could not increase his own possessions—whereas on the other hand the loss of it might impoverish him, as it involved the defence of his estates against the claims and pretensions of others. There was consequently the chance of his inability to bestow upon his children anything beyond the most moderate income at his death. All these circumstances were duly represented to the young Italian, as well as to Charlotte herself; and although the lovers were convinced that they could subsist happily upon the barest competency, Mr. and Mrs. Tremaine, with the natural caution of parents, thought otherwise. Then was it that they exercised the conscientious firmness of their cha-

racter; and the lovers were compelled to bow to their decision. I am extending this narrative beyond the limits which I first prescribed myself——"

"Proceed, Jane," I said: "it does indeed become interesting; and since you are permitted to give me these particulars, there is no harm in my listening to them."

"Immediately after the decision of the parents was made known," resumed Miss Parks, "the disconsolate lover quitted Milan—while the Tremaine family proceeded to Venice. Two years and a half have passed away since that period. The other day the lawsuit was decided in Mr. Tremaine's favour; and he therefore keeps possession of his estates. These are not entailed; and at the death of their parents the six sisters will find themselves in possession of some ten thousand pounds a-piece. But this is not all. Colonel Tremaine, who is very infirm and feeble and who expects he has not long to live, has made his will, concerning which there is no secret. He is worth about sixty thousand pounds: he has appointed his six nieces his heiresses; and thus they will each inherit an additional ten thousand pounds. But we are speaking specially of Charlotte. You see, Miss Percy, she will have as a fortune twenty thousand pounds. You know the old adage, that it never rains but it pours——"

"It is as true," I said, "in respect to instances of good fortune as in those of evil fortune."

"And in the present instance," continued Jane, "it is all in the sphere of good fortune. The Tremaine family were returning home to England to pass a short time with the Colonel in South Street, Park Lane—and thence to proceed to the old Hall in Staffordshire,—when at Calais, three or four days ago, whom should they meet but the young Italian officer? He presented himself to Mr. Tremaine, representing that fortune had recently smiled upon him, the death of a wealthy relation having bequeathed to him a considerable property. Now, the sequel of this tale of real life is precisely what it would be if it were a mere fiction penned by a novelist. The lovers are to be married: the bridal is to take place at the old Hall—and Colonel Tremaine is going into Staffordshire with his relatives to be present on the occasion. There is the whole story. It is simple in its facts; and yet, as you yourself have said, it is far from being devoid of interest. And now, my dear Miss Percy," inquired Jane, after a brief pause, and with a slyly good-natured smile, "do you know wherefore I have inflicted the narrative upon you? It is that I might so far enlist your sympathies on behalf of these faithful lovers, to induce you to accept the invitation which is given you to be present at the bridal. I am assured—and I feel convinced, that all parties concerned will deem themselves honoured by the presence of one whom they, together with the rest of the world, look upon as the greatest tragedian of the age!"

"And are you to be present, my dear Jane?" I inquired. "But of course you are! It was foolish of me to ask the question!"

A shade came over the countenance of Miss Parks; and she said in a voice that was slightly plaintive, "No, Miss Percy—I shall not be present at this bridal. I have received an invitation ——Oh, of this you may be assured!—and it has pained my friend Charlotte that I should have declined it. But I was firm in giving that decision. I am not so conceited or so foolish as to blind my eyes to my own position. There is a wide distinction *between the eminent tragedian*— affluent, living in good style and courted by everybody, as you are,—and the mere ballet-dancer, living in obscurity! But this is not all. With a father situated as mine is—bankrupt—liable to be arrested at any moment for his debts,—and with the great grief that is in my mind on account of the uncertainty that prevails in reference to my *mother, my brothers, and my sisters*——No, Miss Percy!" said Jane, thus abruptly but decisively interrupting herself, "every sense of delicacy and proper feeling prevents me from entertaining the idea for a single moment of accepting this invitation!"

I could not help acknowledging to myself the soundness and potency of the reasons thus adduced; and my looks more than my words expressed my commendation of Jane's conduct. Indeed, I did not choose to say too much on a matter that was alike delicate and painful. We continued to converse together until about ten o'clock, when Miss Parks took her leave—but not before I had obtained from her the promise that she would be a frequent visitress at my house.

On the following day, in the course of the morning, I received a note the address of which was in the well-known writing of the Marchioness of Campanella. Her ladyship therein requested me to favour her with a call in the course of the afternoon, as she was very uneasy on account of her sister Beatrice, and wished to consult me on the subject. Accordingly, at about two o'clock I entered my carriage and drove to the Marquis of Campanella's mansion. On alighting, I was at once conducted to one of the sitting-apartments, where the Marchioness was waiting for me. I found her alone; I saw that she looked unhappy, though she smiled with her wonted affability as she advanced to greet me.

"What evil tidings has your ladyship," I asked, with exceeding anxiety, "in reference to Beatrice?"

"I scarcely know how to answer you, my dear Miss Percy," replied the Marchioness. "When Beatrice came back——"

"Came back?" I exclaimed. "When did she return?"

"Ah! then, you are ignorant," cried the noble lady, "that Beatrice came home the day before yesterday?"

"Your sister," I said, with a slight tincture of coldness in my tone, "departed with great abruptness so far as I was concerned; and she has not thought fit to favour me with any announcement of her return to England:"—but even as I thus spoke, I was bewildered and perplexed, for I wondered whether anything had arisen to cause her unhappiness in respect to her contemplated union with Ludovico Marano, or whether indeed that match were altogether broken off.

"You look offended, my dear Miss Percy," exclaimed the Marchioness. "I hope in the name of heaven that Beatrice has not proved ungrateful to you who have been her best and dearest friend—a more than sister towards her!"

"The Countess of Carboni," I responded,

"asked me to call upon her on the thirtieth of November——it was on the preceding day that she gave me the appointment——and when I came at the time specified, I found that she had departed that same morning for the Continent, —the Marquis and your ladyship having accompanied her for the purpose of being her escort as far as Dover."

"Yes—we accompanied her to Dover," said the Marchioness. "She informed us that she purposed to repair to Paris, and there seclude herself for a while in the bosom of some quiet family, or else to retire for a time into a convent; for her mind was so unhinged by the excitement of recent occurrences,—the arrest and death of Luigi,—these circumstances having so vividly conjured up the memory of past sorrows!"

"Ah! those were her intentions?" I said, thus perceiving that Beatrice had evidently kept her sister and brother-in-law entirely in the dark in reference to her matrimonial project.

"Yes—those were her intentions," continued the Marchioness, with an air of surprise. "Is it possible that she did not communicate them to you?"

"No," I answered laconically: and though deeply vexed at the deception which Beatrice had practised towards her relatives, I still did not choose to betray her secret.

"We offered to accompany her to Paris," continued the Marchioness; "but she begged that we would part from her at Dover. We yielded to her request, thinking it would be unadvisable to vex or perturb her mind more than it was already troubled. The day before yesterday, after about a week's absence, she suddenly returned home in the evening. Her looks were strange and wild; and in reply to our anxious questions, all we could obtain from her was that she had altered her mind and that she preferred continuing to sojourn beneath the roof of her sister and brother-in-law. All day yesterday I endeavoured to obtain from her the cause of the new sorrow that has smitten her; for that she *has* sustained some additional affliction I feel perfectly convinced! At length in my despair I wrote to you, knowing how deep is the regard she entertains for you, and believing that you wield a great influence over her."

I reflected for a few moments; and then I said, "Yes—I will see Beatrice, if she will receive me."

"Receive you? Oh, can you doubt it?" exclaimed the Marchioness. "Go to her chamber—you know it—she is there."

I accordingly ascended to the Countess of Carboni's room: I knocked at the door—the voice of Beatrice was plaintively heard bidding me enter—and as I crossed the threshold, she slowly raised her eyes as if expecting only to behold her sister or a female domestic. Then she gave a quick start,—and ejaculating, "Is it you, Ellen?" she gazed upon me with a species of mingled stupor and affright.

There was a strange sinister light in those eyes of deep grey which were wont to be full of a mournfully serene softness; her face was exceedingly pale—and with the beautiful fairness of her complexion, it seemed as if this pallor were that of death itself. She was dressed in a morning *déshabillée*, and her long brown tresses were floating over her half-naked shoulders.

SARAH BARRON.

"Beatrice," I said, in a kind soothing voice—for her appearance was such as to deprive me o all resentment — "in heaven's name, what has happened?"

She did not immediately answer me; but slowly rising up from her seat, she fixed her eyes stead-fastly upon me for a few moments—and then said in a low deep voice that seemed to be full of con-centrated bitterness and despair, "You were right, Ellen! your forebodings were only too true! ——Ludovico Marano is a villain!"

"Ah!" I said, the suspicion which was pre-viously in my mind being now fully cleared up. "But what has he done, Beatrice?"

No. 81.—ELLEN PERCY.

"He has basely trifled with my feelings," she rejoined, in the same tone as before: "he has abandoned me for another!"

"Frankly, Beatrice," I said, "I cannot regret that you have not espoused this man. But is this all that he has done?—has he taken no advantage of your weakness——"

"Ellen!" and the Countess gazed upon me with mingled amazement and anger. "Do you think I am capable——"

"I only dreaded," was my answer, "that such strong feelings as those under which you now evi-dently labour, could only have been excited by some great and signal outrage."

"And is it not outrage sufficient," she asked bitterly, "to be jilted by a man—to be treated with scorn and contempt——"

"Rather than give way to this rage and despair, Beatrice," I said, "go down upon your knees and thank heaven that you did not accompany such a person to the altar !"

"Your words, Ellen," she answered, after a long pause, and with a look altering favourably, "have infused new ideas into my mind. Yes, yes! I ought to be grateful! But tell me—have you revealed anything to my sister?"

"Nothing," I rejoined. "Yet she will expect me to tell her something—it was she who sent for me to come hither——and Oh, Beatrice! the duplicity with which you have acted——"

"Do not blame me—do not upbraid me !" cried the Countess vehemently; "I am already suffering enough! For heaven's sake keep my secret! Leave me now, dear Ellen! I shall grow calm presently—your visit has already done me good—and it shall be with more composed looks, that I will next meet my sister. Come to me again in the evening—and I will tell you everything that happened."

She pressed my hand; and I left her. Returning to the Marchioness, I simply said, "Beatrice is more tranquil now—her mind is growing settled. Go to her—do not harass her with questions—but speak soothingly and kindly. Your ladyship will perceive that her mood is changed."

The Marchioness expressed her fervid gratitude for the assurances I thus gave her: and I took a temporary leave of her ladyship, informing her that I was to call in the evening. On re-entering my carriage, I proceeded to visit some shops where I had purchases to make, until it was about five o'clock, when I ordered the coachman to drive to South Street, Park Lane. The equipage stopped in front of a house of imposing aspect ; a servant in a superb livery opened the front door; and on my inquiring for Miss Tremaine, he requested me to follow him. He threw open the door of a handsomely furnished apartment on the ground floor : but he did not announce my name,—probably because he had been ordered to show me thither at once on my arrival, or else because he did not at the moment know that there was any one in that room at all. He stepped aside—I crossed the threshold—two persons were within that room —but so absorbed were they in their own interesting conversation that they evidently had not heard the opening of the door. I stopped short in amazement, and with what other commingling feelings the reader may possibly imagine better than I can describe them, when in the young man who had his arm thrown round Charlotte Tremaine's graceful form, and up into whose countenance she was tenderly gazing, I at once recognised Ludovico Marano.

I do not know whether any ejaculation escaped my lips—but I remember perfectly well that the Italian was the first of the two lovers who perceived me; and instantaneously withdrawing his arm from about Charlotte Tremaine's waist, he said, "Ah, Miss Percy! Have I indeed the honour of meeting you again ?"

It struck me for a moment that there was in his looks something more than the mere confusion produced by this surprise : but if so, it disappeared almost immediately ; and with the completest self-possession he advanced with extended hand towards me. I was completely astounded by the effrontery of this conduct on his part : but still I was so far the mistress of my own actions as to avoid giving him my hand in indication of friendship.

"For heaven's sake, be good and generous towards me, Miss Percy !" was the hasty whisper which emanating from Ludovico's lips, now fell upon my ear.

"My dear Miss Percy," immediately afterwards exclaimed Charlotte Tremaine, now hastening forward and taking me by the hand, which she pressed warmly, "a thousand welcomes! I was waiting at home to receive you according to the message which I sent by our mutual friend Jane Parks! I see," she continued, with a slight blush upon her countenance, "that it is unnecessary to present Signor Marano to you, as you have evidently met before."

"Did I not tell you, Charlotte," inquired Ludovico—and I perceived that his eyes flashed an uneasy glance towards me,—"did I not tell you that I had the honour of meeting Miss Percy—on one or two occasions—at the Marquis of Campanella's——"

"No, Ludovico !" ejaculated Miss Tremaine: "I am sure you said not a syllable upon the subject when we met the other day in Calais; and you know that during the ten minutes or quarter of an hour we have now been together, the discourse has been on another subject."

"True !" said Ludovico. "But rest assured that though I did not mention to you, Charlotte, that I had met Miss Percy and that she and the celebrated Miss Trafford were one and the same person, I had not the less appreciated the honour of her acquaintance—I had not the less felt proud——"

"Oh, if you had told me the other day at Calais," ejaculated Charlotte, "that you knew Miss Trafford, I should have overwhelmed you with questions ! But, as Miss Percy herself is aware, it was not until yesterday that I learnt how the name of Trafford was but an assumed one, and that she was privately known to her friends as Miss Percy."

While Charlotte was thus speaking with her wonted enthusiasm, Ludovico Marano was bending upon me a look which I could well understand : it was significant of a hope that I would say nothing which could in any way prejudice him in the mind of Miss Tremaine. He was evidently uneasy : he saw that he ought to take his departure and leave me and Charlotte together; but on the other hand he did not like to abandon us to a tête à-tête in which he thought that I might perhaps give utterance to certain truths which would not be very agreeable to the young lady's ears.

"May I ask, Miss Percy," he inquired, "whether you have recently seen our mutual friends the Marquis and Marchioness of Campanella ?"

"Within the few past hours I have seen her ladyship," was my response : and then, looking the Italian steadily in the face, I added, "And I have likewise seen the Countess of Carboni."

"Ah!" he ejaculated with a sudden start—but still it was so slight that only I myself perceived it; for he possessed an immense amount of moral courage. "Is — is — the Countess in England? Methought from Calais she went on to Paris——"

"She is in England, signor," I said, with a pointed emphasis which rendered the Italian still more uneasy and made it every instant more difficult for him to conceal his apprehensions in the presence of a third person.

"Ah! the Countess of Carboni?" said Charlotte Tremaine, musing for a few moments over the name. "That is the lady concerning whom you spoke to me once, Ludovico, in connexion with that horrible affair of the murderer and suicide Luigi, I think——though, to tell you the truth, my dear Miss Percy, I am never fond of reading the newspaper-accounts of such atrocities. —But dear me! here am I keeping you standing in the dining-room, when my parents, my uncle, and my sisters, are all up in the drawing-room, anxious to be introduced to you!"

"Take Miss Percy with you at once, my dear Charlotte," said Ludovico; "and I will repair to my hotel and change my toilet for dinner. The Colonel dines punctually at half-past six, I believe?—and I shall be here to the minute."

I felt myself to be most painfully situated: I was in a condition of the utmost embarrassment and perplexity. Should I denounce Ludovico Marano as a person utterly unworthy the hand of Charlotte Tremaine?—or ought I first of all to speak to Beatrice upon the point and discover whether she chose to have her name mentioned in connexion with the matter—or whether, with a natural sentiment of feminine pride, she would rather conceal the fact of having been deceived and jilted, if I may use the term, by a heartless, unprincipled individual? But all of a sudden it struck me that I ought *not* to pause for the purpose of consulting Beatrice in the matter. It was sufficient for me that the happiness of a young lady was involved; and taking into consideration all I knew in reference to Ludovico Marano, I saw that it would be a sin to allow Charlotte Tremaine to go, without being thoroughly cautioned and forewarned, in the company of such a man to the altar. Besides, I now saw in the bold effrontery with which he was on the one hand endeavouring to carry off the sinister peculiarity of his own position, and yet on the other hand maintaining a look of deprecation and entreaty fixed upon myself—I saw in all this, I repeat, an additional proof of the consummate duplicity and unprincipled nature of his disposition. Thus, after a few instants' hesitation and reflection, my mind was made up how to act.

"One moment, Signor Marano!" I exclaimed, as with a low and obsequious bow he was on the point of passing me.

"At your service, Miss Percy," he ejaculated, abruptly turning back. "Always at the service of a lady whom it is impossible to help regarding with the highest admiration!"

He kept on bowing as he thus spoke: there was a certain significancy in his accent—and his looks were full of the most earnest appeal. It struck me that Charlotte Tremaine now began to fancy that a scene was passing around her which she could not altogether comprehend; and she flung quick glances first at her lover—then at me—and back again at Ludovico. The door had been left

ajar as I entered the room; I now proceeded to close it—and this circumstance, appearing to herald something serious or important, struck Charlotte Tremaine with something more than mere curiosity; for I saw that she was even seized with uneasiness. As for Ludovico Marano, he was now very pale—his lips were quivering uneasily—and he was evidently a prey to a growing terror.

"Miss Tremaine," I said, with a grave countenance, and in a voice that was of corresponding solemnity, "I am placed in a position the painfulness of which you will presently understand and make allowances for——"

"Oh, if Miss Percy intends to reveal a certain secret," interrupted Ludovico, "relative to the part which I have acted at the instigation of the lady to whom we have already alluded——I mean the Countess of Carboni—she is welcome to tell the tale. There is little or nothing in it of which I need be ashamed!—but whether it be a generous proceeding on Miss Percy's part——"

"Heavens! what means all this mystery?" ejaculated Charlotte, much afflicted and bewildered. "Tell me, Miss Percy, I beseech you! As for you, Ludovico, I am of course well aware that you are incapable of anything which you need blush to acknowledge!"

"Yes—believe that it is so, Charlotte!" exclaimed the Italian. "You and your family know me far better than Miss Percy knows me: Mr. Tremaine made every species of inquiries concerning me between two and three years ago——"

"I am making no accusation, signor," I interrupted him, "against the repute which as an honourable man you may have borne in your native land, and at the time to which you are alluding. But your own conscience——"

"Of what do you accuse him, Miss Percy?" demanded Charlotte Tremaine. "This scene is becoming most painful! Little did I imagine, when anticipating the pleasure of meeting you, Miss Percy——"

"And little did I imagine, Miss Tremaine," I interjected, "that I, on accepting your kind invitation, should be placed in a position so awkward as that in which I now find myself. But it is a duty——"

"Let me tell the tale," exclaimed Ludovico Marano, whose cheeks for the last minute or two had ceased to be pale and were flushing feverishly. "That miscreant Luigi of whom we just now spoke, was the cause of a terrible tragedy wherein a beloved cousin of mine became a victim: and I cherished the deadliest hatred against this Luigi!"

"But all that is natural!" ejaculated Charlotte, who was listening with the intensest interest. "Oh, Miss Percy! you cannot blame him!"

"Let not this painful scene," I said, "be unnecessarily prolonged. And Oh! for me it is indeed bitterly painful that I should be compelled to perform the part of an accuser! Yet so it must be! Signor Marano," I ejaculated, turning towards the young Italian, and addressing him with a look and tone which I intended should bring him at once down from the pedestal of defiance and hardihood whereon he had again been endeavouring to establish himself,—"dare you deny that you personated a Catholic priest—that you assumed the name of Father Maffeo——"

"But this is ridiculous!" ejaculated Charlotte.

"I now remember reading of that man Luigi's suicide about a fortnight ago—and I recollect that the name you have just mentioned——"

"Father Maffeo," I interjected.

"To be sure!" cried Charlotte: "it was he who attended the wretch in his cell——"

"It is he who stands *here!*" I said, pointing to Ludovico. "Let him deny it if he can!"

"Oh, he will deny it, Miss Percy!" exclaimed Charlotte; "because it is outrageous! it is preposterous!"

"It is true!" I cried. "And again I say, he dares not deny it!"

Charlotte bent a look of most anxious, suspenseful inquiry upon Marano: his face told the tale but too plainly—his aspect confirmed my words—he saw that a cry was about to burst forth from Charlotte's lips—and snatching hold of her hand, he said, "For heaven's sake do not prejudge me!——let me tell you the whole tale!—and though it is little generous on the part of Miss Percy——"

"Oh, signor!" I ejaculated, "do not attempt to throw back upon my head one single particle of the blame which attaches itself entirely to you! But put this history apart—lay it aside——"

"Oh, perhaps he can explain it so as to satisfy you, Miss Percy!" cried Charlotte, trembling with nervous uneasiness. "Let him continue!"

"It is unnecessary," I said: "we will turn our attention to another point. Oh, Miss Tremaine! it is only in your interest that I am speaking; for very, very painful is this scene to me! But you are confiding and generous-hearted—you are frank and trustful—and I dare not suffer you to be duped and deceived! Yet duped and deceived you are! Oh, Charlotte, I pity you—and it rends my heart to proclaim the fatal truth!—but the vows of that young man were the other day plighted to Beatrice di Carboni—and at this very instant she is writhing under a sense of the wrongs which she has sustained at his hands!"

A half-stifled cry now came from the lips of Charlotte Tremaine: she thrust Ludovico away from her—she bent a look of anguish upon me—and she sank upon a chair. But consciousness did not abandon her: it was evident she had sustained a blow which for the moment stupified and overwhelmed her, closing the fountains of an affliction the outburst of which would have at once proved a vent for her wounded feelings.

"Signor Marano," I said, hastening towards the Italian, who stood riveted to the spot, the very picture of mingled dismay, rage, and discomfiture, "I have only performed a duty!—and now I enjoin you to leave this house without delay!"

Ludovico started, as if smitten with the conviction that everything was indeed over in respect to Charlotte Tremaine: his countenance became ghastly pale—a diabolical expression seized upon his features—and he said to me in a low hoarse voice, "By heaven, Miss Percy, I will be avenged! You know me!—I will be avenged!"

"Ah!" ejaculated Charlotte, starting up from the chair on which she had sunk down a few moments previously: "you have now revealed your own character, Ludovico, in a manner which I cannot possibly mistake! Depart, signor!—depart, I command you!"

The Italian bent for a moment a supplicating look upon Charlotte: but he read naught in her features that was indicative of a yielding weakness on her own part, or that could encourage him to make one more desperate attempt to recover his lost ground;—and therefore, as if suddenly making up his mind how to act, he rushed precipitately from the room. Then Charlotte Tremaine flung her arms about my neck, crying, "Oh! from what an abyss of sorrow have you saved me!"—and she burst into tears.

CHAPTER CIV.

ANOTHER JOURNEY.

PAINFUL as was the part which I had been compelled to perform, I still could not look back upon it with regret: indeed I was now rejoiced that I had with such stern perseverance obeyed the dictates of duty. In this sense I spoke to Charlotte Tremaine; and she said, "Yes, Miss Percy—I give you credit for the best possible feelings! But, Oh! to think that there should be such duplicity in human nature!"

"The Ludovico Marano of the present day," I said, mournfully shaking my head, "is evidently much altered from the Ludovico Marano to whom your love was first given!"

"But this Countess of Carboni?" said Charlotte, inquiringly; "are you sure that she is not some intriguing syren who may have beguiled and fascinated Ludovico—thrown her spells about him——"

"Not so!" I responded. "Believe me, Ludovico Marano was faithless to your image when he told a tale of love to the ear of Beatrice di Carboni—and then to her he proved faithless also when suddenly encountering you again!"

"But Oh, my friend!" interrupted Charlotte, "ought I not to look upon this conduct on his part as a proof of the strong love he entertains towards me?"

"I beseech you, Charlotte," I said, now addressing her in the kindest spirit of entreaty, "not to waver in the resolution to which you ere now came when you bade Ludovico Marano depart! It is utterly impossible that you can accompany to the altar a man in whose veins rolls the fiercest Italian blood—whose instincts are as ferocious as those of the wild beast—and whose ideas of vengeance are as terrific as those of the Malay or the Red Indian! Listen, Charlotte! It is a tale which I thought and hoped I should never be called upon to repeat: but under existing circumstances it is necessary to give you some details."

I then told her sufficient with respect to the recent proceedings of Ludovico Marano under the disguise of Father Maffeo, to convince Charlotte that she must indeed abandon all idea of accompanying such an individual to the altar. She listened with a profound attention; her face was very pale—her eyes were fixed, and no tear moistened them. It was evident that in proportion as I developed the details of Ludovico's dark vindictiveness, she was nerving herself with the courage necessary to proclaim her resolution as being finally taken. Therefore, when I had finished, she said in a calm collected voice, "You are right, Ellen—for henceforth I shall call you by your Christian name, because circumstances have suddenly established an intimacy between us! Yes, you are right! I must think no more of Ludovico Marano—everything is at end between him and me! And now come—let me introduce you to my parents and my sisters."

"Would it not be advisable," I asked, "to postpone this introduction? Do you not now require leisure for reflection—to retire to your own chamber——or else to communicate without delay to your parents——"

"Come with me, Ellen, I repeat!" exclaimed Charlotte. "I must introduce you to my sisters ——they are expecting you! I can whisper a word in my mother's ear—she will accompany me from the room—and I will then reveal to her what has occurred."

I offered no further remonstrance, but accompanied Charlotte, who was now displaying a degree of fortitude and self-possession which surprised me, but which I was nevertheless glad to find that she could thus bring to her aid. She led the way up to the drawing-room, where I was introduced to the Tremaine family, from whom I experienced a most cordial reception. Mr. and Mrs. Tremaine were both short, stout, good-natured looking personages—perfectly genteel in their manners, but with a warm affability and frankness which seemed to repudiate all useless forms and to thaw the coldness of whatsoever ceremony was indispensable. Colonel Tremaine, though a younger brother, looked at least a dozen years older than Mr. Tremaine: but then the soldier was tall, stooping in his gait, and suffering from bad health. Charlotte's five sisters—the youngest of whom was thirteen—were all good-natured, affable, kind-hearted girls, partaking of the disposition of their parents; while in respect to personal appearance, they were good-looking, showy, and genteel, without deserving the epithets of either handsome or beautiful.

But there was another young lady present in that room—and *she* really was most exquisitely lovely. Never had I beheld a female countenance which more completely fascinated me at the first glance than that of Sarah Barron, for such was the young lady's name; and I found that she was the governess of the two younger girls, whose ages were respectively thirteen and fifteen. Miss Barron was even more lady-like in appearance than any of the Misses Tremaine,—and she was infinitely superior in personal attractions. She seemed to be considered on a perfectly equal footing with themselves, and was introduced to me in due course. I liked her the moment I saw her; and, when at parting, we shook hands, I thought to myself, "There is one with whom I could become intimate immediately despite the caution which the world's experience has taught me!"

But I must not linger to speak more of Sarah Barron for the present: nor is it now my intention to enter into any lengthened description of the Tremaine family; for in the course of this narrative I shall have yet to devote more than one chapter to incidents of a startling and thrilling nature connected with this family and their old ancestral Hall in Staffordshire. Therefore, to continue the thread of my tale, I should proceed to observe that Charlotte continued to maintain the most perfect composure and self-possession. When I had been in the drawing-room about ten minutes, I saw her rise from her seat, approach her mother—but as if quite in a casual and indifferent manner—and whisper a few words in her ear. Mrs. Tremaine rose; and as she was about to follow her daughter from the room, she stopped opposite me, and said, "I hope, Miss Percy, that you will remain to dine with us? I can assure you that Charlotte stayed at home on purpose to receive you: or else she would have fulfilled a promise she made to dine with her godmother, Mrs Milnes."

"I am truly sorry," I said, "that Miss Tremaine should have declined any agreeable engagement on my account: but you must really excuse me this evening—for I myself have an engagement to keep."

"Well, if that be so," returned Mrs. Tremaine, "we must look for this pleasure on a future occasion."

She then followed Charlotte from the room; and I remained in conversation with Mr. Tremaine, the Colonel, and the young ladies. In about a quarter of an hour a man-servant entered the apartment, and whispered something to Mr. Tremaine, who thereupon rose from his seat and withdrew. I thought to myself that he had been thus sent for by his wife and eldest daughter to confer upon the subject which now so closely concerned them; and in a few minutes I rose to take my leave. Colonel Tremaine—evidently having heard of the invitation which had been given me to proceed into Staffordshire to be present at the bridal, and little suspecting how this marriage was now broken off—said, as he shook hands with me, "I hope we shall see you again in London, Miss Percy, before we all go into the country: but if not, we shall at all events have the pleasure of greeting you soon in Staffordshire."

I simply expressed my gratitude for the Colonel's kindness; and having shaken hands with the young ladies, I descended from the drawing-room. A bell was rung in order that a domestic might escort me to my carriage; but as I was passing through the hall, Mr. Tremaine came forth from the dining-room—and with an off-hand cheerfulness, which evidently was assumed to prevent the servant from suspecting that there was anything wrong, he said, "Do not go, Miss Percy, before you have bidden farewell to my wife and Charlotte."

I accordingly followed him into the dining-room, where I found Mrs. and Miss Tremaine. Both had evidently been weeping; and the mother held the hand of her daughter fast locked in her own, in that mode of imparting a tacit encouragement and solace which mothers only know how to convey.

"Miss Percy," said Mr. Tremaine, addressing me in kind tones, but with a grave expression of countenance, "accept our sincerest thanks for the part which you have this evening performed. Fortuitous circumstances have enabled you to render an immense service to my daughter, by saving her from becoming the bride of a man whom, after all I have recently heard, I should be sorry to acknowledge as my son-in-law. You have had a delicate and a painful task to accomplish; but you have not shrunk from it. In a day or two we shall all leave London. I have a favour to ask. It is that you will in a short time pay us a visit in Staffordshire, and there pass with us a few weeks?"

"Most sincerely do I support Mr. Tremaine's request," said Mrs. Tremaine, now rising from her seat and warmly pressing my hand.

"And I, my dear Ellen," added Charlotte, "hope that you will afford me this additional proof of friendship?"

I assured my new friends that an invitation which was so warmly given did not require an instant's deliberation in respect to the answer that was to be returned; and we parted, with the understanding that Charlotte was to write to me in the course of a few days and name the time when I was to proceed into Staffordshire,—I on my side holding myself bound to obey the summons, provided no unforeseen incident of importance should in the meanwhile arise to prevent me.

On leaving South Street, I returned to my own abode, as my dinner was waiting for me: but slight was the inclination that I experienced for food, as my mind had been considerably harassed by the scenes which I have been describing. At about eight o'clock I repaired to the Marquis of Campanella's mansion. The Marquis and Marchioness received me with the warmest demonstrations of friendship; and they gave me the assurance that my visit in the afternoon had worked a considerable change in the mood and humour of Beatrice—for that though she had not become absolutely cheerful, she had at least displayed a more healthy temperament since my intervention was invoked. She had dined with them —she had remained in their society until within a few minutes of my arrival—and she had only retired to another apartment, in the expectation of my coming, as she wished to see me alone. I accordingly proceeded to the room where Beatrice thus awaited me: and as I entered, she exclaimed, "Oh, Ellen! after everything that has occurred, can you thus continue to befriend me?"

"There are certainly, my dear Beatrice," I answered, "many points in your conduct during the last few weeks, which have greatly distressed me —and which, I do not hesitate to add, gave a shock to the strength of those friendly feelings that I had experienced towards you. But you have been so severely punished——"

"Ah! if by being thus chastened, I have regained your friendship, Ellen," interrupted Beatrice, with an unmistakable depth of sincerity, "I shall not regret——no, I shall rather rejoice that I have been so punished! And now, sit down, and let us converse more at length upon those matters which were too painful to be deeply probed when you were here in the afternoon."

"Rest assured, Beatrice," I responded, "that my feelings shall be the same towards you as ever, if I find that you yourself are changed and altered in those respects where such amelioration is desirable. And now tell me whatsoever you may choose to communicate."

"You know, Ellen," resumed the Countess of Carboni, "that about ten days ago I left London with the intention of becoming the wife of Ludo-

vico Marano. We were to meet in Calais, where our hands were to be joined in marriage by the priest, according to the Catholic rites. I devised some tale to account with my sister and brother-in-law for my desire to leave England: I feigned a wish to proceed to Paris. I know not how it was, but I dared not tell them that I intended to marry Ludovico Marano. Perhaps it was that there was something in my conscience which told me I was doing wrong to reward with love a vindictiveness so fearful as that which he had wreaked on the miserable Luigi:—or perhaps it was that I dreaded being questioned too closely on the subject, and that your remonstrances had touched me somewhat. However, certain it is that I resolved to maintain the secret for the present, and write the intelligence of my marriage after it should have been accomplished. My sister and the Marquis accompanied me as far as Dover, and thence I proceeded to Calais. There I took up my quarters at one hotel—Ludovico being at another. A few days passed, during which the necessary arrangements were being made for the bridal ceremony; and I, infatuated creature that I was! persuaded myself that I loved Ludovico as much as I had ever loved his cousin Angelo. One day he came to me; and I saw by his countenance that something was wrong. I soon learnt the truth. He confessed that he had some time ago loved another—that he had just met this other— that his former passion was suddenly revived— and that he now found that he was about to commit a deplorable error in respect to myself. Indignant words burst from my lips—a scene ensued, with the details of which I will not weary your patience, Ellen——and we separated."

"Did you tell him you should return to London or proceed to Paris?" I asked.

"Ah! now I recollect, I said something about proceeding to Paris. It was in my mingled rage and grief—I spoke of burying myself in a convent ——But why do you put the question, Ellen?"

"I have a reason," I returned: "I will explain it presently. Continue, Beatrice."

"I have nothing more to add," said the Countess,—"except that I returned to London, utterly broken-hearted, as I fancied, with mingled shame and rage, wounded pride and fierce vindictiveness?"

"Oh, do not—do not always talk of revenge, Beatrice!" I exclaimed. "This is the point on which I chiefly wish you to curb your emotions and command your passions! There is a certain extent to which vengeance may always reach, because it is a natural feeling and cannot be altogether controlled. But when it passes just limits——"

"Ah! why did I not always listen to you?" exclaimed the Countess. "So long as I regarded you as my guide, and followed your counsel, I always found myself in a straightforward path! Henceforth I will continue to be led by you—— Oh, believe me, Ellen, I will!"

"Now you are speaking as I like to hear you speak," I said: "and I shall enter with all the more confidence upon that which I have to communicate."

"You have something to tell me, then?" ejaculated the Countess, with an unavoidable display of nervous suspense.

Without specially noticing it, I went on to say

"Now, Beatrice, if I tell you that in respect to Ludovico Marano you are already sufficiently avenged, will you promise me that there shall be no gloating over this vengeance—no morbid craving for the infliction of a greater amount of chastisement?"

"I promise you, Ellen," she answered, "that the excellence of your advice and the genial influence of your example shall not be lost upon me:"—then, after a pause, which was evidently meant to convince me that she was striving to discipline her feelings as much as possible, she said in a voice which was only slightly tremulous, "But am I really to understand that Ludovico Marano is already punished for his conduct towards me? If this be the case, whence does the chastisement come? and whose hand has dealt it?"

I proceeded to explain to Beatrice that it was only on the previous day I had fallen in with Miss Tremaine—that I heard she was engaged to be married to an Italian gentleman—but that it was only in the afternoon of this particular day, after my visit to Beatrice, I had discovered who the Italian was. I frankly informed her that I had explained a sufficiency of his vindictive conduct in respect to Luigi, to set Charlotte and her parents completely against Ludovico Marano, and that the engagement was broken off:—but I assured the Countess that I had carefully abstained from compromising her name in reference to those special transactions. I saw that her form quivered with a certain degree of satisfaction as I went on speaking: I saw by the heaving of her bosom, the dilation of her eyes, and the quickness with which her breath came, that the serpent of vindictiveness was lifting up its head in her heart:—but on the other hand, I saw that she was exerting almost preterhuman efforts in order to crush the reptile beneath the heel of her own strong will. I argued favourably instead of unfavourably from all these signs—because I knew that human nature cannot conquer its thoughts or amend its failings in a single moment, and that the effort to do so is the strongest indication of eventual success.

"And now, Beatrice," I said, "you understand why I just now inquired whether at your last interview with the Italian in Calais, you informed him of your intention to proceed to Paris? For when I first met him this evening in South Street, he had a certain air of assurance: he evidently thought that you were indeed far away from London—he suspected not that I had seen you— it was far from entering his mind that I could possibly be aware how he had duped and deceived you. He certainly trembled and felt uncomfortable at my presence in the midst of the Tremaine family—because he feared lest I should tell the tale of his proceedings in respect to Luigi, or that I might even have said something in reference to his recently contemplated marriage with you: but still he evidently hugged the hope that if he could not altogether cajole me into silence, he should at least be enabled to make some counter-statement that would avail with the loving Charlotte. But when he heard that you were in London, and that I had seen you, he grew more and more uneasy——and then came the catastrophe, as I have already explained it."

I remained in conversation with Beatrice until past ten o'clock, when my carriage came to fetch me; and I returned to Great Ormond Street, leaving the Countess of Carboni in a frame of mind which gave me every hope that the happiness of her future years might yet be ensured.

On the following day, at about noon, I received a visit from my friend Mrs. Gower, whom perhaps the reader will better remember as Aline Marcy. Six months had elapsed since she became the wife of Major Gower; and during this interval they had chiefly resided at their country-seat; but I had seen them on three or four occasions when they visited London. On this present occasion they had arrived in the metropolis on the preceding day; and Aline, as the reader may observe, had lost no time in affording me a fresh proof of her friendship. She was looking more beautiful, if possible, than ever; and she spoke in modest yet fervent terms of the tender love which her husband displayed towards her. He would have accompanied her on this visit to Great Ormond Street, but the business which had brought him to London, detained him at the Horse Guards; for he was making arrangements to obtain his Lieutenant-Colonelcy. Aline inquired most affectionately after her friend Mary Glentworth; and I informed her that she was staying with Lady Frederick Ravenscliffe near Dover, where I had left her three days back.

After having chatted for some little while on various subjects, I said, "And how is your amiable friend Lady Kelvedon?"

A shade came over Aline's beautiful countenance, as she replied, "Alas! Hermione's health has been lately declining——"

"Good heavens!" I ejaculated, as a fearful suspicion smote me at the very instant. "Her ladyship's health is declining?"

"Yes—for the last six weeks," rejoined Aline.

"Six weeks?" I mechanically repeated, now struck by the thought that if what I surmised should be true, this period was almost sufficient to carry the unfortunate victim to the very verge of the grave. "And where is she? Doubtless at Kelvedon Hall?"

"Yes," replied Aline: "she has been there for the last four or five months."

"I saw her," I rejoined, "in Eaton Square just before she was returning with her husband to the Hall: but I did not know whether they might not have since revisited the metropolis."

"No—not once," answered Aline. "I proposed to the Major to go and visit the Hall—I wrote to Hermione to that effect: but she delicately represented to me that her husband is so eccentric and peculiar—loving an almost total seclusion——"

"And—and," I asked, "do you happen to know, Aline, where the nephew, Mr. Collingwood, is at the present time?"

"No," replied Aline: "but I dare say he is an occasional visitor to Kelvedon Hall, as usual. Had you any particular motive for asking the question——"

"Tell me something more," I interrupted Aline, "about poor Lady Kelvedon! I am quite concerned on her behalf! Doubtless in her letters, Aline, she has explained her feelings and sensations?—because it seems so strange that a young lady at her time of life—not yet four and twenty years of age—possessed of every luxury and comfort—surrounded by all the elements of happiness which wealth can purchase—should give way——"

"Did I say, then, that her spirits were suffering as well as her body?" asked Aline, gazing at me for a moment with some little degree of astonishment. "But doubtless I must have said so——"

"It occurred to me that you did," I rejoined—for a moment however seized with no little degree of confusion, as I saw that I had been saying too much and had laid myself open to be questioned.

"Hermione has certainly written to me in a desponding strain," resumed Aline. "At first, when she experienced a slight indisposition, she thought nothing of it—she fancied that it was an affair of two or three days, and far too insignificant to necessitate the summoning of the medical men. But the indisposition did not pass away so quickly — Hermione gradually grew more and more languid——"

"Ah!" I ejaculated—and I felt a cold shudder creep over me. "She grew more and more languid, did you say, Aline?"

"Yes—and then came loss of appetite—which, you know, is always a bad sign with persons who may yet be called quite young——"

"Oh, yes, a bad sign indeed!" I exclaimed: and still colder grew the shudder that crept over me. "But I suppose—I hope, I mean—that her ladyship continued to take her wonted exercise——"

"No," interjected Aline; "that is another ominous sign in connexion with one who was so fond of being in the open air."

"Ah! from all you are telling me," I cried, with increasing horror and alarm in my soul, "I fear that poor Lady Kelvedon must be very, very ill——"

"Oh, no, my dear Ellen! that is not the term!" exclaimed Aline. "neither is the matter so bad as all that. It is not a regular illness—she is not confined to her bed—the doctor himself thought and spoke very lightly of it in the first instance —though perhaps now——"

"Ah!" I again ejaculated: for every fresh detail which Aline thus gave me, seemed to be but an additional corroboration of the horrible suspicions which had fastened their vulture-claws on my brain: but still for many reasons I exerted every possible effort to veil my emotions as much as I could. "And now, what does the physician say?"

"The last time I heard from Hermione," rejoined Aline, "she said that the medical attendant gave it as his opinion that it was only a nervous affection, arising from a derangement of the liver or heart——"

"Oh, all this is very serious, Aline!" I exclaimed, now scarcely able to control my feelings sufficiently to prevent them from betraying themselves. "I always tremble," I hastened to add, "when I hear of a patient at first becoming slightly indisposed — then gradually growing more languid, with an increasing loss of appetite, an indisposition for exercise——"

"Ah! and I forgot to observe," exclaimed Aline, thus interrupting me as I was mechanically repeating those words which had been indelibly impressed upon my memory—the very same words which I had overheard Dame Betty speak to Mr.

Collingwood in the midst of the ruins of the farmhouse near Petersfield,—"I forgot to observe," said Aline, "that in addition to all these details, there seems to be a gradual falling away——and you know, my dear Ellen, what a beautiful figure Hermione had—how superbly modelled were all the contours of her shape! Oh! it would indeed be a pity if that fine form were to become emaciated with sickness."

"Yes—a pity indeed, Aline!" I exclaimed. "Do you know that I have a very great mind to set off at once and see Lady Kelvedon? I feel quite unhappy on her behalf! You are aware I always liked her——"

"And Hermione has always spoken to me in the highest terms of yourself, my dear Ellen," rejoined Mrs. Gower. "I am sure she will be delighted to see you! It will be quite a different thing for you to go alone to the Hall, than for me and my husband to proceed thither! His lordship would scarcely object——"

"At all events, Aline," I interrupted her, "I will risk his lordship's displeasure; for I feel so much concerned about his poor wife that I have made up my mind to pay her a visit."

Aline encouraged me in the idea; and as it was now only an hour past noon, I resolved to set off at once; for I calculated that I could reach Kelvedon Hall at a decent hour in the evening, as it was about six miles on this side of Petersfield. Aline left me to make my arrangements,—but not without desiring me to convey to Lady Kelvedon the warmest assurances of friendship and love on her behalf.

The moment she was gone I sent out to order a post-chaise; and I summoned Beda into my presence. To this faithful girl I gave certain explanations relative to the motive of my hurried visit to Kelvedon Hall; and I likewise addressed to her some particular instructions, which I charged her to lose no time in obeying. She promised implicit obedience to my orders—and I knew very well that her pledge would be fulfilled: but the matter was so grave and serious that it naturally rendered me all the more precise in my instructions, and all the more anxious to make myself completely understood.

I set off alone on my journey into Hampshire: but there was a delay in obtaining post-horses at two of the towns through which I passed—and it was not until a late hour in the evening that I drew nigh to Kelvedon Hall. I then reflected that it would be indiscreet to call at that hour; it would seem as if I came with the predetermination of stopping for the night, and thus taking a liberty which would be only too well calculated to anger the old nobleman and to excite strange comments throughout the entire domestic establishment. Besides, I thought within myself that the lapse of some twelve hours would make no very important difference in the business which I had in hand;—therefore, everything considered, I resolved to proceed as far as Petersfield and visit the Hall on the following day. This plan was adopted. I arrived at Petersfield and took up my quarters at the same hotel where eight or nine months back I and Beda had stayed while undertaking the expedition in respect to Dame Betty. The servants remembered me:—there was the same garrulous waiter who on the former occasion had first given me so much in-

formation relative to Lord and Lady Kelvedon and Mr. Collingwood. I again questioned him—but, as a matter of course, in a seemingly casual and indifferent manner. He spoke of Lady Kelvedon's indisposition, but did not know half so many details as I had already received from Aline. I inquired if Mr. Collingwood had been in the neighbourhood lately? and the waiter exclaimed, "Oh, no, ma'am! Mr. Collingwood has not been here for some months past. They say he is upon the Continent——how true this may be I don't know——but I have heard it whispered that his circumstances have lately got so embarrassed it is inconvenient for him to appear in public either in this part of the country or in London."

I gleaned no other particulars from the waiter; and after having partaken of some refreshment, I retired to rest.

No. 82.—ELLEN PERCY.

CHAPTER CV.

KELVEDON HALL.

AT nine o'clock on the following morning I left Petersfield, and in something less than an hour came in sight of Kelvedon Hall. It has already been slightly glanced at in a former chapter, as a very large mansion, with a modern front, standing on an eminence, in the midst of a spacious park. I need not elaborate this description—and will therefore content myself by simply adding that the Hall constituted the principal feature of a scene which was picturesque even in the winter time, but which was of exceeding beauty, as I recollected to have beholden it, when passing it by in the spring season of the year, on the occasion of my visit to Petersfield in company with Beda.

The post-chaise rolled into the park, the lodge-keeper having flung open the iron gates at the entrance; and up a noble avenue it proceeded until it stopped in front of the portico of the principal entrance. I had already decided upon giving the name of Percy, and not that of Trafford; for her ladyship knew me by the former as well as by the latter—and I was averse to what I may term exciting a sensation amongst the domestics of Kelvedon Hall by parading myself, so to speak, as the popular actress. I was first of all conducted into a small elegantly furnished room on the ground-floor: but I was not there kept waiting many minutes—for the door opened, and Lord Kelvedon himself made his appearance. He seemed to be in the enjoyment of good health—for my looks were at once riveted upon him to ascertain *this* point, and to discover whether he betrayed any of those symptoms which in respect to his wife had filled me with so much horror and consternation. His lordship was enveloped in a handsome dark flowered silk dressing-gown; and he wore a black skull-cap. He looked not a whit more decrepid than when I had last seen him some months back; and it even struck me that there was a little more colour upon his cheeks in the fresh air of the country, than when he was breathing the somewhat less pure atmosphere of Eaton Square in the metropolis. He accosted me with far more urbanity than I could possibly have anticipated: he took my hand—pressed it with the apparent warmth of an old acquaintance—and at once said, "You are welcome to the Hall, Miss Percy. It is strange—but Hermione was speaking of you this very morning—yes, and last evening likewise——she expressed a desire to see you —I do verily believe that if you had not thus come of your own accord, the day would not have passed without her writing to say how gratified she should be if you could possibly find the leisure to pay her a visit!"

I was as much surprised as rejoiced to hear the old nobleman talking in this strain: I dreaded lest I should find him reserved, morose, and distant—but on the contrary, I was receiving from him a welcome that was actually cordial.

"I am highly flattered, my lord," I said, "at thus finding myself borne in mind by her ladyship; and I am well pleased to discover that my presence is no intrusion——"

"Intrusion indeed?" he ejaculated: "nothing of the sort! I tell you that Hermione will be pleased to see you——"

"I learnt from Mrs. Gower that her ladyship was suffering in her health—I reflected that as her ladyship had some little while back, when I saw her last in London, expressed a desire to cultivate my friendship, I ought to lose no time in manifesting my concern at her indisposition——"

"I will go and tell Hermione everything you say," interjected Lord Kelvedon, "and prepare her to receive you. She is so low, and nervous, and dejected——"

Here his lordship abruptly averted his countenance, doubtless to conceal the emotion which was excited within him as he thought of the ailing condition of the young wife whom he loved so tenderly and who was indeed the old man's darling.

"But I shall order your post-chaise to be put up," he resumed, turning back from the door which he had just reached; "and you must stay with us——yes, you must stay with us as long as ever you can! I know Hermione will be glad to have you—and if, poor dear creature! we can do anything to rally her spirits——However, we shall see! we shall see!"

Lord Kelvedon now left the room: but in a few minutes he returned, and there was an expression of joy upon his countenance as he exclaimed, "Your presence, Miss Percy, has already worked wonders! Hermione is longing to see you!"

I followed the nobleman from the apartment: he conducted me up the staircase, and led me into an elegantly-furnished room, which I cannot better describe than by denominating it a boudoir. There I found Lady Kelvedon, half reclining in an easy chair, supported by immense cushions. She looked very ill,—Oh! very different indeed from what she was when I first beheld her riding in her carriage through the streets of Petersfield! —very different too from when we had last met at the town mansion in Eaton Square! She was pale —her face was thin—her features had an air of being what is termed peaked: her form had fallen away—and the hand which I pressed was lean, if not actually emaciated. The animation of delight which appeared upon her countenance as her husband conducted me into her presence, rendered her wanness all the more visible; and I burst into tears as I beheld the wreck which this once superb creature was becoming, and the cause of which physical ruin I could only too well conjecture!

"Ah, my dear Ellen," she said, "I must be indeed much changed that you are thus affected at beholding me! Perhaps I am even more altered than I myself fancied——"

"No, my dear," interrupted Lord Kelvedon: "I am sure Miss Percy will tell you that you are looking better than she could possibly have expected to find you after all the afflicting accounts she received from your friend Aline! Is it not so, Miss Percy? Don't you think her ladyship looks better than—than——" and he nodded his head significantly.

"It is very kind of you, my lord," said Hermione, "to endeavour to set my feelings at rest by these little devices and well-meant duplicities. But Miss Percy cannot possibly support you in the tale," continued Lady Kelvedon, speaking in a languid voice, which also denoted that it required an effort to give utterance to her words. "Some months have elapsed since she has seen me —and therefore my altered condition at once struck her as if it were with a blow—and in her friendship for me she wept!"

"But though you are now ill and suffering," I said, "let us hope that a change will take place——"

"Ah, no, Ellen! this cannot be!" said Lady Kelvedon, mournfully shaking her head. "I feel as if I were gradually sinking—slowly, slowly— yes, very, *very* slowly—and yet perceptibly! My life is gradually oozing out of me—I have no energy left! Even when the sun is shining on these beautiful December days which we have recently had, I feel no inclination to go out into the fresh air—no, nor even to cross the threshold of my apartment!"

"But, my dear girl," exclaimed the old nobleman, "you feel better now? Yes—I know you are better at this moment? Miss Percy's presence has revived and cheered you; and when once the energies thus receive an impulse, they continue to gather a healthful tone——"

"At least, my dear husband," said Lady Kelvedon, speaking in a stronger voice, and smiling sweetly, "our friend Miss Percy shall not have any reason to suppose by my countenance that I am not rejoiced to see her. But now leave us alone together——we have a thousand little things to say——And, Ah! by the bye, I wish you to go out and take some exercise this fine, frosty, healthful day."

"Well, well, my dear," rejoined the old nobleman, "I will leave you and your friend alone together. Only mind——mind, Hermione!" he added, with uxorious playfulness, as he tapped his young wife's cheek, "I must find you quite gay and in good spirits on my return."

With these words Lord Kelvedon left the boudoir; and when the door had closed behind him, Hermione took my hand—looked with an expression of anguished earnestness in my countenance—and said, "Tell me frankly and truly, Ellen—do you not find me very, very much altered?"

"I will not attempt to deceive you, my dear Lady Kelvedon," I answered: "you are indeed looking ill: but——"

"Oh, my dear friend!" she exclaimed, "I fear that I shall never recover from this illness, so strange—so mysterious, which has been creeping upon me——"

"Do not despair!" I said. "Perhaps——"

"Oh, Ellen! it is kind of you to speak hopefully; but there is something within my own heart which tells me that I am doomed! The physician is perplexed and bewildered—I see that he is, although he studies to avoid betraying what he thinks and feels! And when the physician is thus baffled and at a loss—when he, on being questioned, is compelled to take refuge in vague generalities or downright sophistries, instead of proving that he possesses the ability to grapple with the insidious disease,—what hope dare I entertain? But tell me, Ellen——and pray forgive me for asking the question if there be anything indiscreet in it——but do you think that those lozenges which you gave me some eight or nine months ago, could have produced any prejudicial effect upon me?"

"Good heavens, no!" I vehemently exclaimed: "it is impossible! Believe me, my dear Lady Kelvedon——"

"Enough, Ellen!" she interrupted me: "it is useless to say another syllable upon the subject! The question was rather prompted by a light passing idea than by any other motive. Besides, after all, you yourself have frequently used those pink lozenges for beautifying your complexion, although heaven knows you could little require such auxiliaries——"

"Tell me, my dear Lady Kelvedon," I said, thus interrupting her, "how long is it since you first experienced the slightest warning of this indisposition?"

"It is impossible to answer the question, Ellen," she replied: "it came upon me by degrees—it stole insensibly on me. If you look back to the earliest period of your existence, you cannot tell when the power of reflection commenced: you cannot form nor convey an idea how the mind took its initiatory steps, nor how memory first began to exert itself. Now, all that I have just said, though perhaps hyperbolic and far-fetched, nevertheless well illustrates what I mean you to understand, when I say that this indisposition of mine stole upon me imperceptibly at first, so that it was only by a gradient process the thought crept into my mind that I was not so well in health as I was wont to be."

"Our mutual friend Aline," I said, "has communicated to me certain symptoms which you have experienced:"—and I then proceeded to detail them,—the gradual languor—the increasing loss of appetite—the indisposition for exercise—and the gradient falling away, so that it seemed as if attenuation must in process of time merge into emaciation. "Has it been thus with you?" I inquired: "and has Aline rightly informed me?"

"There is an accuracy—a painful accuracy in the details as you have given them!" replied Lady Kelvedon. "But really, my dear Ellen," she exclaimed, forcing herself to smile, "one would think that to all your other accomplishments you add that of medical skill!"

"Believe me, my dear lady," I answered, with a sufficient gravity to show that I was speaking neither idly nor carelessly, nor for the mere sake of saying something, "I have a purpose in view. Do not excite yourself—suffer me to ask a few questions——"

"Anything you please, Ellen," rejoined Hermione. "I know the excellence of your motives: but alas! I fear——"

"I neither wish you to hope nor fear anything," I interrupted her. "Suffer me to put a few queries—and do you respond to them as if you attached not the slightest importance thereto. I myself know not whether they will lead to anything—but be patient, and we shall see."

"Proceed, my fair catechist," said Hermione; "and I will answer you in the spirit which you suggest."

"Is there any particular food which you are accustomed to take?" I inquired, feeling the necessity of shaping my queries as guardedly as possible.

"No," replied Lady Kelvedon. "I have lately lost my appetite—and I am compelled to pamper it with whatsoever strikes my fancy at the moment."

"And his lordship, perhaps, does not take his meals with you, now that you are an invalid?"

"Yes—every meal. His lordship is all attention. He has his peculiarities—but he is a warm-hearted man; he scarcely ever leaves me! The only instance in which perhaps he ever dictates a will of his own, is in his desire to dwell in perfect seclusion here. Oh! I longed to have some friend—I thought of Aline—but then she must have come with her husband—and I knew that his lordship would not like to have guests staying at the house, whom it would be necessary for him to entertain at table in one room while I was confined to another."

"Not exactly confined to this room?" I said inquiringly; "because you can walk about if you choose——"

"Yes—but I have no energy, Ellen!" interrupted Lady Kelvedon. "It is not that I have lost the use of my limbs. No! I have still a certain degree of strength left. See!"—and rising from the easy chair, she walked across the boudoir: but on returning to her seat, she threw herself into it with a certain visible air of languor, almost bordering upon exhaustion. "The truth is, I have no energy—no spirit——"

"And your handmaidens," I said,—"are they attentive? Do you know them well——"

"Oh, yes," she responded: "they are the same whom you saw in London. They have been with me ever since my marriage, nearly two years ago. But why do you put such a question?"

"No matter," I rejoined. "I have already said that it is something more than mere casual conversation——"

"Yes—Ellen!" ejaculated Hermione, as if a light were dawning in unto her mind: "you have indeed a special motive! Perhaps you think that I am being unfairly tampered with?"

"Oh, Lady Kelvedon!" I cried; "is it possible that such an idea has ever entered into *your* thoughts?"

"Frankly speaking," returned Hermione, "the idea *has* on two or three occasions floated in my brain——But it is a horrible notion, and one which I ought not to mention, inasmuch as it implies an accusation of a terrific nature against some or all of those persons by whom I am surrounded."

"Nevertheless, tell me what you think," I said. "We are speaking within four walls—no one can overhear us—and whatsoever you communicate is a secret between ourselves."

"On condition that you regard it in this light," proceeded her ladyship, "I must not hesitate to unbosom myself freely to you. When I have contemplated this strange malady of mine I confess that the idea has stolen into my brain that perhaps——But no! I cannot tell you!"

"Let me interpret your thoughts for you," I said, taking her hand and looking earnestly in her countenance. "You conceive it possible—we will not say probable—but you conceive it *just* possible that—that—poison——"

"Ah! you *have* interpreted my idea!" said Hermione, with a shudder. "But no! I discard it! It is only in my most morbid moments——"

"Let us entertain the idea for an instant," I said. "Think, my dear Lady Kelvedon!—reflect! Is there a soul amongst all the domestics by whom you are surrounded, on whom your suspicions could for a single instant alight?"

"Not one!" she emphatically exclaimed. "Ah! now I comprehend wherefore you just now asked me whether my husband took his meals with me—whether my handmaidens were kind and trusty? Ah, then, the same idea must have struck you, Ellen! But I beseech you to banish it; for I again tell you that it is an utter impossibility!"

"Well, we will not talk any longer upon the subject," I said. "But now tell me, my dear Lady Kelvedon, why did you wish to see me? You have friends far more intimate—you have relations—you have parents and sisters——"

"Yes—but I have no friend," she fervently interjected, "whom I esteem more highly than you! Think you that I can ever forget, my dear Ellen, how kindly you behaved to Aline when she was poor—dependent—but honourably and bravely seeking a means of independence,—when in compliance with my wish you took her by the hand—you instructed her without fee or reward—you enabled her to make a brilliant *debut*—you gave her the opportunity of earning a livelihood when she fancied that she needed it? Or think you that I can forget your generous conduct to Major Gower, in surrendering up so large a portion of the wealth the whole of which you might have claimed? Yes!—that conduct was noble indeed; for it enabled him to conduct Aline to the altar; —and you know how deeply interested I have always been in Aline. Therefore," continued Lady Kelvedon, "you cannot wonder that I should have esteemed and valued you as an excellent friend, short though our acquaintance were, and little as we had seen of each other. But beyond all these feelings," she went on to say, now speaking with some little degree of hesitation, "I will frankly confess that there was an idea floating in my mind, when I more than once expressed the fervid wish to see you——"

"And that idea?" I asked, with some degree of suspense.

"Ah, Ellen," responded her ladyship, "I thought that perhaps the French chemist of whom you once spoke to me, and who was so skilful in compounding certain sovereign remedies——"

"Ah! you allude to the pink lozenges?" I ejaculated. "By the bye," I asked, as if quite carelessly, but with a vivid hope springing up in my heart, "do you happen to have any of them left?"

"Not one," she replied: "I used them all. Ah! and now I bethink me," she continued, as that evanescent hope died within me, "I was more than ever wrong to inquire just now if they could possibly be deleterious; for his lordship partook of the same beverage in which they were mixed—it was always in our coffee—and he has in no way suffered. But I was about to observe, Ellen, that perhaps the French chemist who proved himself so skilful in one respect, might possibly be acquainted with some sovereign elixir —some remedy unknown to the generality of the medical profession, which would reach my case? It is this idea that has floated through my mind, and has conjured up your name more than once to my lips: but I dared give no explanations to his lordship, for I never forgot that I had pledged myself to an inviolable secrecy——"

"And since you have proved thus mindful of your promise, my dear Lady Kelvedon," I interrupted her, "I will give you a proof that such good faith may not be altogether without its reward. Listen to me! It was not a French chemist who compounded the lozenges which I presented to you some months ago. Pardon the little deception: but I did not then deem it advisable to tell you a tale of mere gipsy charms and spells——"

"Oh! is it possible that you know any one, Ellen," exclaimed Hermione, "who is skilled in any art which could by a possibility reach my case? I am so young to die!"—and the poor creature shuddered convulsively.

"No! you shall not die yet," I exclaimed, "if

it be within the scope of human means to raise you up to health and vigour once more! And of this I do not despair. No! But do not excite yourself!—you must not indulge too exultingly in hope! And yet there *is* hope——"

"Oh, Ellen! is this indeed possible?" reiterated Lady Kelvedon, and the reader may imagine with what a degree of anxiety and suspense she put this question—for it doubtless seemed a matter of life and death to her!

"Listen to me," I said, again taking her hand and pressing it warmly: "but I implore you to exercise as much control as possible over your feelings! I *am* acquainted with a gipsy-woman, who is skilled in arts that are not generally practised—*and heaven be thanked that they are not!*" I mentally ejaculated. "I believe that I can find this woman—and that very shortly too: and if so, she must come hither to see you—at least it is probable that she may wish to judge for herself——"

"Let her come, my dear Ellen——Oh, let her come!" exclaimed her ladyship, the excitement of her feelings bringing back the colour to her cheeks and pouring a flood of light into her eyes.

"Yes—she shall come, if it be necessary," I rejoined: "but how is this to be managed? The whole proceeding must be wrapped in the deepest mystery—the veil of secrecy must be thrown over it—and not even your own husband must be made acquainted with the circumstance of your receiving a visit from this gipsy-woman."

Lady Kelvedon reflected for a few minutes; and then she said, "It must be contrived—yes, it must be contrived by some means or another!"

"But how?" I inquired; "for I must leave you presently to ascertain if this woman can be found: and before we part we must make some arrangement according to which I shall be enabled to bring the dame hither at any moment."

"I see a plan, Ellen," said Lady Kelvedon, "if you yourself can so conduct your own arrangements as to make them correspond therewith. The dusk now closes in by four o'clock—the evenings are thus very long. If the appointment could be made, therefore, for the evening part of the day——"

"It shall be so," I replied. "Proceed."

"You could come to me alone in the first instance," continued Lady Kelvedon, "leaving your gipsy-companion at a short distance from the house. I can then manage all the rest."

"It shall be so," I rejoined. "But pray bear in mind that I am not positively sure of being enabled to discover this old crone. The chances are however in favour of the affirmative: but still there is the possibility of failure."

"First of all I put my trust in heaven," replied Lady Kelvedon solemnly; "and then, my dear Ellen, in you!"

I hastened my departure from Kelvedon Hall, because I was most anxious to return with the least possible delay to London. His lordship was astonished and annoyed when he heard that I was going after only remaining a couple of hours at the mansion: but I assured him that it was in order to make some purchases in the metropolis to please her ladyship, and that I should be back again in two or three days. This pretext satisfied

him: he was pleased to learn that his wife had energy sufficient to think of making any purchases whatever; and in delicate terms he offered to supply me with a liberal cheque upon his banker: but I of course declined the proposal, as I had in reality no purchases to make.

During the journey to London, I had leisure to reflect maturely and deliberately upon the main features of this very difficult case which I had now taken in hand. The first question which suggested itself, was whether Lady Kelvedon was really suffering under the influence of a slow poison—or whether she were not? I believed that she was. All the symptoms were precisely the same as those which Dame Betty had detailed to Mr. Collingwood amidst the ruins of the farm-buildings when she sold him her venomed lozenges, and when accompanied by Beda, I overheard their discourse. But if Hermione were really suffering under that terrible influence, who was administering the poison? who day by day was driving as it were a fresh nail in her coffin? Not Collingwood himself: he had been for many months absent from the neighbourhood. It must therefore be some creature whom he had bribed—some domestic beneath the roof of that mansion. How could I possibly lay my hand upon this particular individual, when Hermione herself had so vehemently declared that she could suspect no one? And then too, I dared not breathe a syllable of accusation against Collingwood; for the reader cannot have forgotten the oath which I took in the ruins, to the effect that I would never say anything which should compromise his safety on account of the discourse which I had overheard between himself and the old woman. The situation of affairs was therefore altogether complicated; but I believed and hoped that I should be enabled to unravel the tangled skein most effectually, if I could only fall in with Dame Betty.

CHAPTER CVI.

DAME BETTY.

THE moment I alighted from the post-chaise at my house in Great Ormond Street, the front door was opened; and the faithful Beda, welcoming me home, hastily whispered, "I have succeeded!"

I knew what she meant; and an ineffable sensation of joy took possession of my heart. Hastening with her into the dining-room, I shut the door, exclaiming, "You have found her? you have seen her?"

"Yes," responded Beda; "and she holds herself at your orders and disposal. I assured her that if you should happen to require her services the recompense would be large——"

"Yes—it is as I foresaw, Beda!" I ejaculated. "I do indeed require the woman's services! Most fortunate was it that before I left London I so earnestly conjured you to use every effort to discover the abode of the hag—to bid William Lardner likewise exert himself——"

"And yet it was neither William nor I, who, in a direct manner, so to speak, made the discovery. Perhaps we should have both still been prosecuting a tedious, if not useless search——"

"Then how *did* you discover the dame's abode?" I hastily inquired.

"The humpbacked dwarf called yesterday afternoon," responded Beda, "about a couple of hours after you had left——"

"Ah, indeed?" I ejaculated. "And he gave you the information? This was indeed most providential!"

"Yes—he happened to know where Dame Betty might be found," replied Beda. "Your surmise was perfectly correct—the dame *is* waiting in London for the trial of Edwin St. Clair——"

"And the dwarf?" I interjected, with some degree of anxiety: "did he hint at the nature of the business which led him to seek an interview with me?"

"Yes," rejoined Beda: "but it is now of little consequence or import. It happened that a few days ago he was in the neighbourhood of the York Road——I should observe, by the bye, that it was between ten and eleven o'clock at night——when to his ineffable astonishment he recognised Mr. Parks, carefully muffled up though he was. The humpback had all along fancied that the lawyer had perished in the conflagration; and therefore he was smitten with amazement: but he neither accosted Parks, nor suffered him to perceive that he was thus recognised. But the dwarf imagined that the information might be useful to you, dear Miss; and therefore he called for the purpose of giving it. I thought it better to tell him that you were already acquainted with the fact, but that you had quite done with Mr. Parks, and that he had become an object of indifference to you."

"That was right, Beda," I interjected; "for you thereby prevented the humpback from molesting or interfering with the wretched man. But did you reward him?"

"I gave him two sovereigns," answered Beda, "for his thoughtfulness in calling upon you in reference to Mr. Parks, and for affording me the information in respect to where I could find Dame Betty. I told him that he might call again in a few days, when perhaps you would do something more for him. William Lardner and I went to Dame Betty's lodging—we saw her—she was at first cold and reserved towards us, until I began to speak of Zarah, and reminded the dame that I had been her grand-daughter's friend—that I had helped her to escape from the madhouse—in short, that Zarah had loved me. Then the crone melted; and for the same reasons she began to speak well of you, dear Miss. You may conceive how rejoiced I was when I found her mood thus turning. I told her that you might possibly require her services, for which you would most liberally remunerate her—and that as a kind of retaining fee, I was authorized to place twenty guineas in her hand. Everything has thus terminated satisfactorily; and Dame Betty is entirely at your disposal. If you wish to see her, William Lardner happens to be here at the moment," added Beda, with a slight blush upon her beautiful face: "and he shall at once hasten and fetch her. In an hour she shall be here."

"By all means let him hasten away!" I exclaimed; "for I can assure you, Beda, that it is indeed a matter of life and death with the unfortunate Lady Kelvedon!"

William Lardner was accordingly despatched in quest of Dame Betty; and during the hour which elapsed ere the arrival of the hag, I explained to Beda the circumstances of my visit into Hampshire, and the course which I intended to adopt with the old gipsy-woman. The faithful girl fully approved of my plan, as I sketched it forth; and she declared her conviction that Dame Betty would fall into my views and bend herself to my purpose.

The hag arrived—she was conducted into my presence. I made a sign for Beda to retire: I thought it better to be altogether alone with the dame. She wore an air of confidence and patronising familiarity: she had no further rancour against me—she knew that I was not purposing to do her any harm—she probably felt proud at finding that her services were at length necessary even unto *me*—and she was assuredly rejoiced at the prospect of reaping a golden harvest according to the promise held out to her by Beda. I should add that she was dressed just in the same style—that is to say, like a respectable tradeswoman—as when I had seen her about two months back, on the occasion of her abruptly breaking inupon my interview with Beatrice di Carboni.

"Sit down," I said, adopting a tone and manner which were calculated to repel any impertinent familiarity, and yet at the same time to sustain within her a feeling of confidence in my good faith with respect to the present transaction. "I am desirous of speaking to you on a subject most grave, serious, and important."

"Proceed, my dear," answered the dame. "Through your intelligent deputy you have sent me some gold and offered me more. I will do everything for gold except abandon my purposes of revenge against Edwin St. Clair;—and *that* I know," she added, with a grim smile, "is a sacrifice which you are about the last person in the world to ask me to make."

"It was not my intention to make the slightest allusion," I said, "to that wretched man, unless you yourself had spoken of him. "I wish to concentrate your attention on one subject only; and I beg that you will answer me as succinctly as possible—that you will avoid all unnecessary digressions—and that you will likewise bear in mind that your reward is to be proportionate to the truthfulness, the despatch, and the efficacy with which you may be enabled to serve me."

"An excellent preface, my dear," said the dame; "and every point shall be borne in mind. Proceed: I am entirely at your service."

"Between eight and nine months ago," I resumed, "you sold ninety poisoned lozenges for the sum of fifty sovereigns to a person of the name of Collingwood."

"True," answered the dame. "You knew it at the time—you overheard my discourse with Collingwood—I told him so—and then he exacted the oath from you and Beda——"

"Which oath we do not intend to violate," I rejoined. "But listen to me! For the last six weeks Lady Kelvedon—the young wife of the old lord who is Mr. Collingwood's uncle—has been suffering with all the symptoms which you yourself detailed on that very same occasion to Mr. Collingwood."

"Well then," said the dame, "perhaps he is administering the lozenges."

"No—not *he*," I ejaculated: "he is on the Continent. But are you aware of any person beneath the roof of Kelvedon Hall, who may at present be employed as his agent?"

"I am not acquainted with a single soul within those walls," answered the dame,—"at least not to my knowledge. Collingwood never told me when nor how he meant to use the drugs, nor for whom they were intended—though perhaps I might have made a guess upon this latter point, for I knew that he had an old uncle who had married a young bride, and that by either cutting off the one or the other—or perhaps both—he would as a matter of course materially advance his own interests."

"Well," I said, "no matter as to how the poison is being administered. There is, alas! little doubt that the unfortunate lady is suffering under it! For six weeks she has complained—she has now an almost total loss of appetite——"

"The appetite requires much pampering?" said the dame inquiringly.

"Yes," I replied. "She is growing gradually more and more languid—she has lost all inclination for taking exercise——"

"She has no energy?" asked Dame Betty.

"None: and she says that her spirit is likewise broken. Still she has not entirely lost her strength: she rose up in my presence and walked across the room——"

"And then she threw herself into her chair as if completely exhausted?" interjected the dame, still speaking interrogatively.

"Exactly so!" I cried. "Oh, I see from your manner, and I judge from your words, that the worst is to be apprehended!—I mean that the unfortunate Lady Kelvedon is indeed suffering under the influence of poison!"

"No doubt of it," responded the dame. "But there is an antidote——"

"Ah! thank God!" I ejaculated. "Then it is not too late——"

"I hope not—since you likewise hope it, and since I am now to consider myself temporarily in your service——"

"You hope not?" I interrupted her: "but tell me likewise that you *think* not? Oh, for God's sake do not deceive me! Now I remember full well every word you spoke to that villain Collingwood when you met him amidst the farm-ruins near Petersfield. You said that there were ninety lozenges in the box that you gave him—that it was a supply for *three* months, reckoning one a day—but that if he wanted to kill his victim in *two* months, he must administer one lozenge a day for the first month, and two a day for the second. Oh, I shudder as I reflect——"

"You shudder at what?" asked the dame, exhibiting but little emotion.

"Six weeks have elapsed," I rejoined—and my voice sounded hoarse in my own ears,—"six weeks have elapsed since Lady Kelvedon first experienced a sense of indisposition——"

"And perhaps," interjected the dame, with what struck me to be a diabolically wicked smile, "she had been taking the poison for at least a week before she even began to think within herself that it was quite possible she was not so well as she used to be."

"Just heavens! what do I hear?" I exclaimed,

now seized with the direst affright. "At least seven weeks may have elapsed since the venom was first infused into her system? Perhaps this may be the eighth week?—and Oh! if your dreadful suggestion should have been followed—I mean that of killing the victim in two months——Oh! in this case she is already tottering on the very verge of the grave—and it may be too late to save her!"

"Then why do you send for me?" asked the dame bluntly.

Oh! for an instant how I loathed, abhorred, and even hated, that vile wretch!—how vehemently I could have denounced her as the atrocious vender of poisons—the infamous murderess—the demoness to whom might indirectly be attributed the death of my grandfather—the hag whose detestable compounds had no doubt worked even a larger amount of mischief than I could possibly suspect!

"Are you going to treat me with a piece of play-acting, my dear?" asked the vile harridan, with a half supercilious, half familiar smile. "How you seemed to flame up all in a moment! How vehemently you dashed away those masses of glossy black curls from the sides of your beautiful countenance!—how the two rows of pearls gleamed betwixt the vivid vermilion of your Grecian lips! How the pink-tinted nostrils of that faultlessly chiselled nose dilated!—how those magnificent large eyes shot fire!—and how your fine full bosom swelled as if actually about to burst its prisonage of corset!"

"Silence, woman!" I angrily ejaculated: but all in a moment hope sprang up in my heart—and I cried, "Ah! there is a certain assurance about you!—a certain confidence! Yes—you are doubtless very skilful——"

"So, my pretty dear," interrupted the hag, with a cold sneering sarcasm, "you can loathe me one instant—but you can fly to me the next?"

"Tell me," I exclaimed, "that you can save the life of Lady Kelvedon, and five hundred guineas shall be your recompense!"

"Ah! do you really mean this?" cried the hag, her reptile eyes gleaming with delight.

"I mean it! I repeat the pledge! Most solemnly do I swear to you——and you best know whether I can keep an oath!—you can tell whether I have been faithful to the one which the villain Collingwood extorted from me——"

"Yes, yes—and also the promises you made to Gilderoy on my account," rejoined the dame. "But five hundred guineas——"

"You think a large sum?" I ejaculated. "I will show you my banker's book——"

"No, no, Miss Percy—your word is sufficient," interjected the dame. "But the process of curing Lady Kelvedon will be almost as slow as that other process—the one of poisoning, I mean—which has brought her down to her present perilous condition."

"No matter how slow," I exclaimed, joyous hope expanding in my heart, "provided it be sure!"

"It is as sure, my dear girl," replied the old woman—and though I recoiled from her familiarity, yet I greedily drank in the assurance which she was giving me,—"it is as sure as that every poison has its antidote, and that I am acquainted with the antidote of the poison which by a gradient process has been carrying Lady Kelvedon to the very verge of the grave!"

"Ah! then, you think," I said, with a strong shudder, "that her ladyship has indeed been brought so near to the final confronting of death——"

"And from all you have told me," interrupted the dame, now speaking with more gravity than she had hitherto adopted throughout this interview, "that in three days more she would be beyond the point from which it is possible to snatch her back to life—and in a week or ten days she would be a corpse!"

"And you *can* snatch her back from the verge of the grave?" I demanded, with anxiety.

"Yes—provided that no time be lost in the administration of my remedies."

"It is indeed my wish that no time should be lost!" I cried. "When shall you be prepared?"

"Unfortunately at this moment," muttered the harridan, more in a musing strain than for my behoof, "I have none of the pink lozenges—— But there are the drugs which could be otherwise administered——"

"Oh delay not, I conjure you!" I exclaimed.

"No, no, my dear—there shall be no unnecessary delay," rejoined the dame. "To-morrow I will call and bring you certain drugs——But Ah!" she suddenly interrupted herself, "what guarantee am I to have for the payment of the sum when the lady is cured?"

"You have my sacred word of honour," I answered; "and it is a pledge which has never been falsified! But methinks I have omitted to mention something—which indeed is a stipulation——"

"Proceed," said the dame.

"It will be absolutely necessary for you to accompany me to Kelvedon Hall, that you yourself may see her ladyship——"

"But I can cure her without seeing her!" interjected Dame Betty.

"I know it," I said: "but still it is requisite that you should accompany me. I have spoken to her of my acquaintance with a gipsy-woman—— In short, she already expects you."

"Indeed?" cried the dame; and for a moment she looked upon me with some degree of suspicion and mistrust.

"Yes," I responded: "for how was it possible that I myself could undertake to administer drugs or medicines?—how could I pretend to fathom her malady?—how could I——"

"You have told her she is poisoned?" inquired the dame, fixing her regards scrutinizingly upon me.

"No—heaven forbid!" I exclaimed; "and she need never know it!"

"Five hundred guineas," said the harridan, "are a bribe sufficient to render me faithless to the cause of Mr. Collingwood, who gave me but fifty. But still I should be loath that any evil overtook him; exposure in one case means exposure in another——"

"And is my conduct," I asked, "that of one who purposes to bring about an exposure?"

"No!—true!" said the dame: and then she added with a chuckle, half sarcastic, half triumphant, "For when the immaculate, the high-principled, and pure-minded Ellen Percy is thus holding familiar intercourse with an old poison-vender——"

"Ah, well, dame," I interjected, "since you yourself have said it, let the argument stand as a proof of my good faith. But Oh!" I went on to say, speaking solemnly, "do not allude with jest or levity to your antecedents as a poison-vendor: for remember that the white rose was the cause of Zarah's death—the means of her suicide!"

"True," said the dame: and she became humbled.

"There is one more point," I resumed, "concerning which I am desirous to speak. Pray listen with attention. Now, it is evident that some one within the walls of Kelvedon Hall, has been for weeks past administering poison to the noble lady of that mansion. You are about to provide an antidote——"

"One word will suffice!" interrupted the dame, with a smile of confidence upon her lips; "for I can fathom what is passing in your mind. Make yourself easy on that score! The drugs I am about to prescribe will prove a restorative from the effects of poisons hitherto administered, and an antidote against all poisons that may be administered during the time the drugs themselves are being taken."

Thus far my conversation and my arrangements with the old harridan were completely satisfactory; and I now addressed her in the following terms:—

"You remember that some time ago——fear not, I am not going to reproach you—for as much as possible I will fling a veil over the past, in consideration of the good you are at this present time about to accomplish——But I was going to say that some time ago you gave Beda two boxes of lozenges——"

"Yes—I remember—it was when I met her in Birmingham—she came with me to my cottage——"

"Never mind the particulars," I said. "You gave her the two boxes, one containing the brown or poisoned lozenges—the other containing the pink——"

"Which is the antidote," ejaculated the dame.

"I know it:—and those pink lozenges I kept for whatsoever emergency might occur. The brown ones I destroyed."

"And what became of the pink?" asked the dame, hastily, and with a visible start of uneasiness.

"Do not think," I said, at once comprehending what was passing in her mind, "that I have it in my power to forestall or dispense with your aid in reference to Lady Kelvedon. No. Those pink lozenges have been disposed of. Some months ago—when dreading lest through Collingwood's villany Lady Kelvedon should be poisoned by means of the brown lozenges supplied by your hands—I called upon her ladyship; and under a certain innocent pretext I presented her with the box of pink lozenges which I had in my possession. I said nothing of poison—I simply flattered her vanity and gave her to understand that it was a specific for the complexion which I was thus proffering her. She has now been informed that those lozenges emanated from a gipsy-woman;—and if I at present tell you all these particulars, it

is that when you appear in her presence you may know how to shape your replies to any question she may put, or frame your observations upon the topics she may initiate."

"I shall play my part in this respect according to your instructions," replied the dame.

"And now," I continued, "you will the better comprehend the motives which led me to stipulate that you are to present yourself before Lady Kelvedon as a gipsy-woman, and therefore in the gipsy garb."

"That is easily arranged," replied the barridan. "You say that I am to accompany you? Perhaps you will be ashamed——"

"If you would undertake to meet me," I said, "in the neighbourhood of Kelvedon Hall—you being habited in your gipsy costume—it would be more suitable as well as more convenient."

"I will do so," rejoined the woman. "You see, Miss Percy, that I give you the best possible

proofs of my good faith in these matters, as well as of my willingness to meet your views in every respect."

After some little farther conversation, it was arranged that Dame Betty should meet me on the road near the gate of Kelvedon Park, at five o'clock in the afternoon of the ensuing day. I gave her ten guineas, alleging that the sum was for travelling expenses, but intending it to serve in reality the purpose of sustaining the excitement of her avaricious feelings and securing her fidelity all the more completely in the present instance. She took her departure, apparently very well pleased with the result of the interview; and this was not to be wondered at—for I had promised her a reward of a magnitude doubtless far exceeding the recompense which she could ever at any one time have received from her criminal employers. But would the circumstance exercise a beneficial influence upon the dame's disposition and future dealings?—would it lead her to reflect that the wages of virtuous deeds might possibly be greater than those of crime? Who could tell?

CHAPTER CVII.

THE SECOND JOURNEY TO KELVEDON HALL.

WHEN I informed Beda that Dame Betty had entered completely into my views, and that I was going to meet her on the ensuing day at Kelvedon Hall, the faithful girl looked anxiously in my countenance as if in painful uncertainty whether she was to accompany me? I at once comprehended what was passing in her mind; and I said, "It is perfectly needless for you to come with me, my dear Beda. I have now no fear of any treachery on the part of the old woman. It was St. Clair who used to urge her on to make attempts upon my life; but now she is pursuing him with even a greater degree of implacability than ever she pursued me. Besides, she no longer dreads anything at my hands—but on the contrary, she has an immense reward to win by her fidelity and good conduct."

"True, my dear Miss," answered Beda; "all these calculations had passed through my own mind before you enumerated them."

"Then what do you apprehend, Beda?" I asked.

"I apprehend nothing positive nor definite," rejoined the young girl: "but I always feel more happy when I am with you—and if there be any danger, latent or apparent, I would rather share it with you."

I caressingly patted Beda's cheek; but I said, "No—it is really useless for you to come with me. If it were to any other mansion I was going, I should be pleased to take you: but to Kelvedon Hall it is otherwise. His lordship is so peculiar in his humour—so singular in his moods—and so eccentric in the prejudices that he conceives——"

"Not another word, dear Miss!" interjected Beda. "If you have reasons against taking me, it is quite sufficient."

Here therefore the conversation ended; but I recognised therein another proof to be added to the million previously existing ones, of the tender and devoted interest which Beda experienced in my welfare and safety.

On the following day I ordered the postchaise to be at my house at such an hour in the forenoon that I might calculate as nearly as possible upon reaching the neighbourhood of Kelvedon Hall at about five o'clock in the evening. My travelling-toilet was completed by the time the equipage arrived: I had already descended from my chamber, and was waiting in a front parlour as it drove up to the door. Beda, who was with me, hastened to fling a glance from the window to assure herself that it was the expected equipage which had arrived; and then I heard the ejaculation, "Ah!" fall from her lips—but in a low tone, so that it was involuntarily uttered and not intended to direct my attention to any particular object.

Nevertheless, I asked, "Is anything the matter, Beda?"

She seemed to hesitate for a moment what reply she should make; and then she said, "You will perhaps think me very silly, dear Miss—and doubtless I am wrong to say a single syllable to excite apprehension or that may seem to be of evil augury: but—but——"

"But what, my dear Beda?" I hastily inquired.

"I saw an ill-looking man pass the house. Indeed, he stopped for a moment—looked at the postchaise—then turned round and stared up at these windows; but on catching a glimpse of me, he continued his way with rapidity."

"Was he a gipsy-man, Beda?" I inquired.

"No," she rejoined. "Ah! I can conjecture what is passing in your mind!—Dame Betty would act only with the agency of men of her own race! True!—and I again repeat, I do not apprehend any treachery at the hands of Dame Betty——"

"Well then, my dear Beda," I interrupted her, "it is not the accidental coincidence of an ill-looking man passing the window at the moment, that must make us tremble. It is your kind interest on my behalf that renders you nervous and anxious on the present occasion. But fear nothing, Beda: you will soon see me again."

I kissed the cheek of the affectionate girl; and binding her "good bye," proceeded to take my seat in the postchaise. The equipage rolled away; and it was just turning the corner of the street, when a cab dashed past at a rapid rate: yet it proceeded not too quick to prevent me from catching a glimpse of the countenance of Lady Lilla Essendine who was seated in the vehicle.

I had thought nothing of the little incident of the ill-looking man mentioned by Beda: there was to me naught in the slightest degree ominous or threatening in that occurrence: but I must confess that a partial change took place in my mind the instant I caught that glimpse of Lady Lilla Essendine's countenance. I could not account for the change that smote me,—or rather, I ought to say that I was smitten with no positive idea of danger—I did not feel at all justified in entertaining the slightest apprehension: I felt that I might just as well treat the sudden appearance of this lady as an accidental coincidence as I had treated that of the ill-looking man in front of my own house. But still I could not look upon the matter thus lightly: my feeling was that of a superstitious yielding to an evil augury. I felt ashamed of myself: I strove to conjure up every other possible topic to chase that disagreeable one from my mind; but I found this to be no easy task. I thought of my beloved Henry and of my father, who four months back had set off on their voyage to the far-off gold region which I fervidly hoped would turn out to be no fable: but still the image of Lady Lilla Essendine would persist in rising up along with those dearer images whose presence I was voluntarily and eagerly courting. And then too, that very incident in respect to Lady Lilla's abrupt appearance in the cab gave a sort of significancy to that *other* incident of the ill-looking man which I had at first regarded as utterly devoid of any sort of consequence.

As time passed on, however, and the postchaise rolled farther and farther away from London—and as on occasionally looking through the little circular window behind, I saw that I was not followed—my superstitious apprehension grew weaker and weaker, until at length it was totally lost in the sense of burning shame which I experienced for what I now conceived to be the outrageous and unpardonable folly of my conduct. At the places where the chaise stopped to change horses, I looked to see if there were any persons of suspicious aspect hanging about, or whether the successive postilions had an air at all calculated to make me uneasy. But in every respect I found the circumstances to be totally devoid of all suspicion, so that my courage was completely restored, and I beheld the dusk approaching without any return of uneasiness.

At the last posting-town I learnt, upon inquiry, that it was likely to be as close as possible upon five o'clock when the chaise would arrive in the neighbourhood of Kelvedon Hall; and I bade the postilion stop in the road when he came to within a couple of hundred yards of the park-gate. This he promised to do; and I slipped a liberal fee into his hand, as I thought he might otherwise look strangely upon the circumstance of my being about to encounter an old gipsy woman, and I knew very well that the coin would effectively induce him to keep his opinion to himself.

The chaise halted at the spot which I had already designated; and a glance thrown at my watch by the aid of the lamps, which had been lighted at the last posting-town, showed me that it was ten minutes past five o'clock. The evening was dark; and as I stepped out of the chaise, I could see but a short distance along the road, as I flung my regards to and fro. Scarcely however had a minute elapsed, when I became aware of a dark form at a little distance; and as it emerged from the surrounding obscurity, I recognised the bowed figure of the old gipsy woman, enveloped in a dark cloak, the hood of which was drawn over her large white cap. She carried her crutch, but did not tap it hard upon the ground; for she doubtless thought it prudent to make as little noise as possible.

"How long have you been in the neighbourhood?" I inquired in a whisper which was inaudible to the postilion.

"About an hour," was the answer.

"And have you looked to see whether you can enter the park otherwise than by passing through the gates?" I demanded; "for if not, you must get into the chaise, and this will entail the necessity of telling the postilion some tale and of ordering him to stop again in the middle of the park for the purpose of setting you down——"

"Dear me, Miss Percy!" interrupted the crone, "how ready you seem to be to meet difficulties half-way! There is no necessity for me to get into the chaise in order to ride through the park-gates. I have discovered a gap in the fence which will answer my purpose. And now tell me whereabouts I am to await your farther bidding—east, north, south, or west of the Hall? how far off? and in what kind of hiding-place?"

"On the southern side of the main building," I responded, "you will find there is a shrubbery of evergreens. There is a small grass-plat between the shrubbery and the building itself; and in each corner of the grass-plat there is a vase. Now I wish you to hide yourself in that part of the shrubbery which is nearest to the vase standing at the south-western corner of the grass-plat."

"Good!" responded the dame. "Have you any further instructions?"

"None," I replied,—"at least not for the present. Ah! by the bye, I ought to inform you that I cannot possibly tell how long it may be after I have set foot in Kelvedon Hall, that I shall come to fetch you from your place of concealment. It may be a few minutes—it may be half-an-hour—it may be even an hour——"

"No matter, Miss," answered Dame Betty: and then she added with a low chuckle. "Have you not bought me for the present, body and soul? Let me see? The price——"

"Five hundred guineas," I emphatically ejaculated.

"Ah, true!" rejoined the dame. "I thought it just as well to mention the amount once more, so that there might be no possibility of a mistake."

Having thus spoken, she hobbled away, speedily disappearing from my view in the surrounding obscurity. I had taken good care that the postilion should not overhear a single syllable of whatsoever passed between us: but still I thought it better to say something to the man as an additional precaution beyond the bribe I had given him.

"It is most probable," I said, "that I shall set out on my return to London to-morrow morning: at all events it is next to a positive certainty that I shall leave some time in the course of the day. I can give you the assurance in advance, that Lord Kelvedon will permit you to put up your horses in his stables, and to mingle with his domestics during the period of my sojourn here. Now, it suits me that not a syllable be spoken in reference to the interview I have just had with a certain woman, who has brought me particular information that I required——"

"It's no bisness of mine, Miss," interjected the postilion; "and I'm ready to take my 'davit that I didn't see no o'oman and nothink whatsomever."

"That is right," I rejoined. "If you drive me as fast to-morrow as you have done this evening, you will have the same reward I have already given you."

This was a delicate way of holding out to the man the prospect of an additional bribe for the maintenance of secrecy in respect to my interview with the gipsy crone: and resuming my seat in the vehicle, it speedily reached the park-gates. The lodge-keeper came out—the gates were thrown open—up the avenue dashed the equipage—and in a few moments it stopped at the entrance. Lord Kelvedon happened to be traversing the hall at the very instant when the front door was opened and I crossed the threshold of the mansion. He hastened forward to give me a cordial welcome, and I was thus rejoiced to find that his humour had in no way changed towards me, but that I stood as high in his good books as on the preceding day. I inquired after the health of Lady Kelvedon?—and he responded with a mournful shade upon his countenance, "I am afraid that she is much worse since yesterday morning when you left her."

"Worse?" I ejaculated: and then I thought within myself, "Perhaps my presence here may have induced the miscreant, whoever he or she may be, that is administering the poison, to make haste and finish the fearful work lest I should return and put a stop to it. If so, thank heaven that I *have* returned so speedily!"

"Yes—worse, I am afraid," said the old lord, thus answering the ejaculation which had burst from my lips,—" more languid—more deficient in energy—experiencing a diminished appetite—— But perhaps your presence will revive her again ! Ah, by the bye, Miss Percy, have you brought the purchases which my dear Hermione instructed you to make in London ?"

"How can you ask me, my lord ? Do you not know it was almost solely for this purpose that I went up to London ? The parcel is in my box—or rather the small portmanteau which I have taken the liberty of bringing——"

"Liberty ? why, what do you mean ?" exclaimed Lord Kelvedon. " Don't you know you are welcome ? Here, James !"

"Yes, my lord," said one of the liveried lacqueys, stepping forward in obedience to his master's summons.

"Get Miss Percy's portmanteau—tell the postilion he can put up his chaise and horses here—and see that the man himself is made comfortable. Now, Miss Percy, let me escort you. You know the way — but I long to have the pleasure of seeing a smile come back to Hermione's lip; for I know she will be very glad to see you. Ah, here is Matilda!"

The young person to whom Lord Kelvedon alluded, was one of his wife's maids; and she gave a respectful curtsey on seeing me, for she knew me well by sight.

"See that Miss Percy's luggage is taken up to one of the best spare-rooms," said the nobleman. "And perhaps, Miss Percy," he continued, turning towards me, " you will give Matilda your key so that she may get out the parcels which are intended for Hermione ?"

"Oh, certainly," I replied: for, as the reader may suppose, I had failed not to bring some presents from London for Lady Kelvedon, that I might thereby maintain to her husband the tale in reference to the purchases.

Matilda took the key; and I now followed Lord Kelvedon to that same elegantly furnished boudoir where I had before seen her ladyship. She was evidently delighted to greet me again ;—for a moment I was shocked at beholding how much paler she was than when I had left her in the forenoon of the preceding day. However, I veiled whatsoever emotion I thus experienced,—though I inwardly shuddered lest the diabolic wickedness of the secret poisoner should have proceeded to an extent which would baffle all Dame Betty's art and all the power of the antidotes which she might employ.

"Here is your friend, my dear Hermione !" exclaimed Lord Kelvedon ; " and she has brought you a lot of things from London !"

"Yes, my dear Lady Kelvedon," I said with a significant look ; "I have fully succeeded in all you wished and desired."

"Oh, how kind of you to take so much trouble, Ellen !" said her ladyship, pressing my hand with the most grateful fervour; for she comprehended the intelligence I meant to convey.

Matilda now entered the room, bringing two or three parcels which I had ordered Beda to pack up and put into the portmanteau :—and the young female was about to withdraw, when Lady Kelvedon said, " Stop a moment, Matilda ; I have some orders to give you. You must desire that dinner be served up for Miss Percy as soon as possible. We have dined, my dear Ellen," she continued, turning towards me ; "for as I am an invalid, it renders us somewhat unfashionable in our hours —and his lordship is kind enough to accommodate his hours to mine. But Matilda shall immediately see about your dinner, Ellen——"

"Thank you," I interrupted her ladyship; " I stopped on the way and took all requisite refreshment—I will now wait till your coffee is served up."

Matilda, upon hearing this decision to which I came, withdrew; and as the door closed behind her, I bent down towards Lady Kelvedon, as if merely to place the parcels in her lap, and I hastily whispered, " Pray get rid of his lordship!"

"In a few minutes," was the equally hasty whisper given by Hermione in response. "Come," she added, speaking audibly to her husband, as I unfastened the strings and wrappers of the packages : "look at these beautiful satins which Ellen has bought me ! and these laces ! Ah, and this cachmere !"

"Exquisite ! lovely !" ejaculated the old nobleman. "And now, my dear Hermione, cheer up ! you will soon get better !—you will wear these beautiful satins and laces ; and this cachmere will become you so when you ride out in the carriage !"

"Yes—you will wear them all," I quickly whispered to Lady Kelvedon: and whereas I had hitherto seen that she was a prey to the utmost suspense and anxiety, her countenance now all in a moment became animated with joy and hopefulness, and she pressed my hand with the most affectionate fervour.

"My dear husband," she said, beckoning the old lord towards her with smiles upon her lips, " I do indeed already feel so much better that I have the presentiment your kind presage will be fulfilled. You see how much good my dear friend Ellen's visit does me !"

"Heaven bless you, Miss Percy !" exclaimed the old nobleman, seizing both my hands, and pressing them with a violence which almost hurt me, though it was the spectacle of his strong affectionate emotion on behalf of his darling wife which brought the tears into my eyes. " I don't know what I can do for you—I must think of something ! If I were the King of England I'd make you a duchess: but by Jupiter ! you shall be well rewarded somehow or another ! Don't think I mean to say anything to offend your pride, my dear young lady—for we all know that in these matters you are as proud as Juno !"

"Well, well, my lord," I said, laughing, " let us first wait and see whether my presence will really continue to have so good an effect as you seem to hope and believe—and then rest assured that I shall put your kindness to the test in some way or another."

"And now, my dear husband," said Hermione, " you must leave me and Ellen alone together."

"Yes," I interjected : " for if I am to be doctoress, I must have my own way. But, joking apart, I have a great deal of little chit-chat for her ladyship: and then, amongst other things, we must discuss how these dresses are to be made up—for I have brought all the newest fashions with me. Ah, here they are!" I added, taking a French Fashion-book out of one of the parcels.

"Well then, I will leave you together," said the old nobleman, who would have leapt over the moon if he were able and if he had been told to do so—or he would have stood on his head, or performed any feat, no matter how hazardous or ridiculous, to testify his joy at the prospect of his darling's recovery.

"And pray do not think of coming back to us," said Hermione, "until I send Maltilda to fetch you: for I mean to have a very long, long confidential chat with my dear friend Ellen."

"Anything you like, young ladies," rejoined the old nobleman: and he hastened from the boudoir.

The moment the door closed behind him, Lady Kelvedon threw her arms about my neck; and in a paroxysm of ineffable emotions hitherto pent up, but now finding vent, she exclaimed, "Oh, dearest Ellen? I know you have brought me the tidings of recovery, life, and health! I understood your meaning just now!"

"Yes," I said, "my dear lady, the gipsy woman is here—and she promises everything. In a word, I have every hope that she will be enabled to cure you!"

Lady Kelvedon was now weeping softly, as her head was pillowed upon my bosom; and my own tears mingled with hers—for there was an ineffable joy in my heart to think that a creature so young in years, so amiable in disposition, and so exquisite in beauty, had every chance of being again restored to health and happiness.

"And now let us delay not," I said: "the gipsy woman is close at hand! You are to manage her introduction to this room?"

"I promised you that this should be easy," rejoined Hermione: and then she gave me certain instructions which the reader will immediately comprehend by following me in the course which I at once proceeded to adopt.

I took a key from the mantel-piece; and I passed into an inner room, which was her ladyship's bedchamber. Beyond it there was a dressing-room, and this communicated with a bath-room. Outside the bath-room there was a little landing, with a private staircase. There was no other means of communication with this landing except by the way which I was now pursuing. At the bottom of the staircase there was a door, which I opened with the key; and I took good care to lock it behind me. I was now in the open air—in a garden at the back of the house. The evening was getting somewhat lighter; for the stars were coming out, and the moon, which was close upon its full, was rising. I turned along a gravel walk to the left—passed through a gate in the boundary-wall—and entered upon the grass-plat to which I had alluded in my instructions to Dame Betty. A glance quickly flung around, convinced me that the coast was clear; and I sped in the direction of the large vase at the south-western corner of that grass-plat. There was immediately a rustling amongst the neighbouring evergreens:

I said in a low voice, "It is all right!"—and the gipsy woman came forth from her hiding-place.

"How go matters indoors?" she quickly asked me.

"Her ladyship is worse," I responded—"an increase of languor—a total failure of the appetite——"

"It is serious!" said the dame: "but still as long as she has been able to keep up and not take to her bed——"

"No, no, she is up and dressed!" I interjected.

"So much the better!" rejoined the woman, with the emphasis of confidence. "And now lead the way."

It is needless to recapitulate the avenues by which we passed to gain the boudoir; suffice it to say that while retracing the way I had previously taken, I conducted the dame, and unobserved we reached the apartment where I had left Hermione. She flung a quick glance upon the crone, who threw back the hood of the cloak; and Lady Kelvedon was now seized with a sudden faintness—she was well-nigh overpowered by her feelings, as she doubtless looked upon that woman as the arbitress, so to speak, of her life or death. I hastened to support Hermione in my arms; and the dame, seating herself in a chair opposite, began contemplating her ladyship with the most earnest attention. There was a bottle of salts upon the table; and by the aid of these Hermione was soon recovered—for she had not fainted outright.

"Compose yourself, my dear friend," I whispered; "for this woman may possibly require to ask you some questions."

Dame Betty continued to gaze upon Lady Kelvedon for two or three minutes,—a short space when the words themselves which denote it are idly and flippantly thrown off from the tongue or the pen, but a perfect century for those who are suffering anxiety and suspense! Never did Dame Betty's countenance seem to be so thoroughly inscrutable as during these two or three minutes: I could deduce naught from it—neither hope nor fear; but a cold terror was growing upon me. At length the dame spoke; and she began asking Hermione a multitude of questions, relative to symptoms, sensations, and feelings—but so carefully wording her queries as to leave her ladyship totally unsuspicious of the fact that she was labouring under the influence of poison. Indeed, I could not help giving Dame Betty credit for the tact, the delicacy, and the ingenuity with which she shaped her interrogatory. Then, as I continued to watch her countenance I saw that it grew a trifle brighter—and hope once more expanded in my soul.

"Well, my lady," said the dame at length, "I think I can promise——yes, I will venture to declare that you shall be cured!"

A cry of joy burst from Hermione's lips; and she exclaimed, "Fulfil your promise, my good woman, and your reward——"

"That point," I interjected, placing my fingers upon Lady Kelvedon's lips, "is already settled. It is not for you to trouble yourself on the subject —at least not for the present."

"I leave myself, Ellen, entirely in your hands," said Hermione.

Dame Betty had in the meanwhile risen from her seat; and she drew forth from her pocket a small common wooden box, about four inches long, two wide, and an inch and a half deep. It had a sliding lid: and when this was opened, it revealed a number of little packages in different coloured papers.

"Are we sure to be free from interruption?" inquired the dame, glancing around.

"Yes," responded Hermione: "I locked the door of the boudoir while Miss Percy came to fetch you."

"And now I require," continued the gipsy-woman, "a bottle or decanter, some water, and a tea-spoon."

Hermione intimated that I should find the things that were needed in her dressing-room: I hastened to procure them, and returned to the boudoir. The dame took a little pair of scales from the bottom of the box, together with some diminutive weights such as are used by chemists and druggists; and she accurately measured four distinct powders, which she put into the decanter. This she filled up with water, and shook it for several minutes. Then she placed the decanter on the table: the water was all clouded, and it occupied nearly five minutes for the powders to become completely dissolved, so that at length the water was of pellucid clearness as before, and there was not even so much as the slightest sediment at the bottom.

"Two wine-glasses," said the dame.

These were quickly forthcoming; and the woman filled one of the glasses. She slowly drank off its contents; and this I considered to be not so much an essay on her part as to whether the mixture was properly made, as it was meant to be a studied proof that she was veritably and truly administering an antidote, and therefore something perfectly innocuous so far as she herself was concerned. Then she filled the second glass: and this she handed to Lady Kelvedon. Under any other circumstances, Hermione, rendered fastidious by illness, would doubtless have shrunk in loathing from the shrivelled dirty hand that was stretched out to her; but now she greedily accepted the proffered draught, which she at once swallowed.

"It is almost tasteless," she said, as I received the glass from her hand.

"And now, my lady," said the crone, "you have taken the first step towards recovery. To-morrow morning, an hour before breakfast, you must take another glass; and likewise to-morrow afternoon before your dinner. At what hour do you dine?"

"At four," was the answer.

"Then take the dose at three," rejoined the dame. "I must return and see you to-morrow evening—that is to say, if I can possibly get back to London to-morrow night, or any time before the dawn of the next day; for I have urgent business in the metropolis."

I knew to what she alluded: it was the trial of Edwin St. Clair which was fixed for the next day but one.

"You shall have my postchaise," I said. "Rest assured, therefore, that immediately after you have seen Lady Kelvedon to-morrow evening, arrangements shall be made for your departure."

"Enough, Miss Percy!" ejaculated the crone: "that is all I require."

"But to-night where will you sleep?" asked Lady Kelvedon, uneasily. "Had I not better take his lordship into our confidence?"

"No—not for the world!" cried Dame Betty. "The secret is between ourselves——Miss Percy knows it must be so!"—then, as I made a sign of assent, she went on to say, "Trouble not yourself, my lady, on my account. I know an ale-house on the road about a mile and a half hence; I do not care for a little walk—the evening is beautiful—it is a full moon—and the stars are shining."

I now proceeded to conduct Dame Betty out of the mansion, by the same avenues through which I had introduced her. But when we reached the bath-room, I stopped short, caught her by the arm, and said impressively, "Tell me, I conjure you! have you spoken truthfully?—will she be saved?"

"I swear it," answered the dame: "but the case is indeed a serious one—and. two or three days later it would have been *too* late! She must have a vigorous constitution. The poison has been at work for at least two months——"

"Oh, if I could but discover the miscreant who is administering it!" I ejaculated.

"What? to give him or her up to justice?" returned the dame quickly; "and thus perhaps bring about a total exposure?"

"No," I answered; "my promise has been solemnly given to the contrary. But you see the influence which I exercise over Lady Kelvedon; and it would not therefore be very difficult for me to procure the removal of so dangerous a person under some pretence or another."

"Keep your eyes open, and watch!" returned the dame.

We then issued from the mansion together; and at the garden-gate I said to her, "To-morrow evening, at six o'clock punctually, I will seek you in the shrubbery again. Arrangements shall then be made for your journey to London."

"And perhaps you will have to accompany me," rejoined Dame Betty.

"Indeed?" I ejaculated. "And why so?"

"Because, I will tell you frankly, this case is even worse than I had anticipated from the description you had previously given me. Nay, start not! I have no doubt as to the result! I only tell you that it is a grave and serious matter. But I stake everything as to the success of my treatment! Keep back the reward if you will until the end. There!—does that satisfy you?"

"Perfectly," I responded. "But why do you think that I shall be compelled to accompany you to London?"

"Because there is a certain drug which I had not time to procure, and with which indeed I thought I should have been able to dispense. It has nothing to do with the antidote against the poison: *that* is already in the lady's possession. But it is a restorative——"

"Say not another word," I interrupted her: "I understand you!—you wish me to become the medium of placing it in her ladyship's hands—and you may command me. I will therefore hold myself in readiness to accompany you, if needful, to-morrow evening. But one word more! Is her ladyship suffering under the influence of the poisoned lozenges which you sold to Mr. Collingwood?"

The dame did not immediately answer: but at length she said, "Come! There must be all frankness between us; for you are liberal, and you keep your promises. Well then, I reply, *Yes!* Lady Kelvedon is suffering under the influence of the brown lozenges manufactured by me. For the rest you must draw your own conclusions."

With these words she hobbled away; and I began to retrace my steps, my heart beating with joy at the positive assurances I had received in respect to the final recovery of Lady Kelvedon; for I felt confident that Dame Betty knew her business too well to incur a chance of failure after all she had said.

Having threaded the avenue in the garden, I reached the door at the bottom of the private staircase,—when all in a moment it struck me that I had inadvertently omitted to lock that door on issuing thence a few minutes back with the old woman. How I could have been so forgetful I cannot possibly conceive: but such was the fact—and it is useless to pause for the sake of explanation or excuse. The key was in the lock on the inner side; so that when passing that way just now with the gipsy-woman, I had merely closed the door behind me.

I was excessively angry with myself; but still as I found the door shut and no one was to be seen in the rear of the premises, I caught at the idea that my negligence had produced no evil effect. Now, therefore, taking the most particular care to lock the door, and to try it to assure myself that it was completely secured, I ascended the staircase. I had left a light burning in the bath-room; and as I reached the landing, a shadow was thrown across it from just within the threshold of that room, the door of which stood open. The next moment a female form appeared: and my first impression was that it must be Lady Kelvedon herself who had come to meet me for some purpose or another. But the next instant I saw that it was one of her ladyship's attendants, who bore the name of Agatha. She was a young woman of about eighteen, tolerably good-looking, but with a somewhat reserved expression of countenance.

"I beg your pardon, Miss," she immediately said, with the most perfect self-possession: "I did not know that it was you."

"Why should you beg my pardon?" I asked, advancing into the bath-room, so that I might bring the young woman herself within the rays of the wax-light which I had left there.

"I meant, Miss," responded Agatha, "that I did not know it was you who had gone out by the private door."

"Ah!" I said: "then you just now came up the private staircase?"

"Yes, Miss," was Agatha's response; and still she maintained the most perfect calmness and self-possession.

"Are you accustomed to use that staircase?" I inquired. "But stop! I will tell you why I ask. I had a headache—I wished to take a turn or two in the garden—and Lady Kelvedon gave me the key of the door at the bottom of the staircase, telling me that I had better lock it on going out. This I forgot to do; and now you may perhaps understand that I am more or less surprised to find this little inadvertence on my part should

in the short space of five minutes be taken advantage of."

Agatha listened to me with an unmoved expression of countenance,—an expression which I did not altogether like, for methought that there was a sort of stubborn sullenness in it, and that this was likewise the cause of the steady patience with which she remained silent until I had finished.

"I do not understand, Miss," she now said, "what you mean by taking advantage of your inadvertence."

"I mean that the private door was shut, though not locked," I rejoined. "You must have tried it to see whether it were fastened or not."

"Of course I did, Miss," answered Agatha, with a cool unconcern which I fancied to savour very much of a dogged insolence, and which increased my dislike for the young woman. "I did not for a moment pretend that I had not tried the door: I did not want you to believe such a thing; and if you had asked me the question point-blank, I should have at once told you that I *did* try it."

Agatha was looking steadily at me as she thus spoke; and I was gazing fixedly upon her. For an instant it struck me that her manner was nothing more nor less than the calm composure of complete innocence: but the next moment suspicion again sprang up in my mind as I caught the sullen expression of her countenance, and as I remembered that beneath the roof of that mansion there must be some one who for the most fearful reasons had become an adept in the art of dissimulation and hypocrisy.

"And might I ask, Agatha," I said, "why you happened to try the door?"

"To be sure you may ask," she responded; "and I might, if I chose, refuse to answer you; for I do not acknowledge you as my mistress, nor have I yet been told that you are installed as her ladyship's deputy. But as I have done no wrong, I will explain what I *have* done. You see that here is a bath: but there is no cistern. When the bath is to be used, the hot water has to be brought in pails from the kitchen and carried up this private staircase! Now, I, too, as well as yourself, Miss Percy, happened to have a headache this evening——"

Here she blushed, stammered, and for a few moments looked so confused that I thought she was about to break down in the midst of excuses. But I was wrong: for she quickly regained her self-possession, and proceeded in the following manner:—

"So like yourself, Miss Percy, I went out to get a little fresh air. I saw a light in this room; and it at once struck me that her ladyship must be going to take a bath. I wondered I had heard nothing of it, because whatever instructions are given either to Matilda or myself, we generally communicate to each other, as we are the two principal maids. So I came to see whether the bath was really being prepared: the door was unfastened—I ascended the stairs—I looked into this room—I had not been here a moment before you made your appearance. That's all, Miss Percy:—and perhaps you will now tell me whether there is anything extraordinary in it?"

I was bewildered what to think, or how to answer. Suspicion was strong in my mind; but on the other hand, I was always full of alarm at the idea of yielding unjustly to first appearances and receiving erroneous impressions to the prejudice of individuals who might be perhaps altogether innocent. I had never taken my eyes off the young woman while she was speaking; and though I still disliked the expression of her countenance, yet there seemed to be a certain consistency in her story, every tittle of which might possibly be the exact truth. Therefore I resolved to give her the benefit of the doubt and thus adopt the safer side—so that I might guard against wronging her by acting on an unjust suspicion.

"No, Agatha," I said, "there is nothing at all extraordinary in your explanation: and granting it to be true, I do not hesitate to express my sorrow if I have treated you with harshness."

"To tell you the truth, Miss," rejoined the young woman, "I *did* think you spoke to me in a very peremptory style: but a single word of kindness from your lips is sufficient."

Her voice trembled for a moment as she gave utterance to these concluding words: but still there was the same unmoved, reserved, or perhaps even sullen expression of countenance, which did me positive harm to gaze upon it.

"Now, Agatha," I said, "you can withdraw."

"To be sure, Miss:"—and she was passing on towards the dressing-room, with the evident intention of traversing the whole suite, so as to issue forth from the boudoir door.

All of a sudden I recollected that Lady Kelvedon had locked the boudoir door—she might not perhaps have unlocked it—it was most probable that she would wait for my return ere she did so—and thus it would seem strange to Agatha if on threading the boudoir, she found the door fastened. Besides, it also struck me that Lady Kelvedon, in her delicate state, might experience a sudden excitement amounting almost to a shock, if Agatha should make her appearance so unexpectedly.

All these considerations flitted through my mind in a moment: and I ejaculated, "Stop! Which way are you going?"

"It is quite immaterial, Miss," responded the young woman: "only I thought that I heard you lock the door at the bottom of the staircase, and you have the key in your hand. I feared that it would be troubling you to let me out that way, as well as indeed being perfectly unnecessary—for it is just as easy to pass through these rooms."

Again I regarded the young woman steadfastly as she spoke: I strove as it were with all my mental energy, to discriminate whether there was an under-current of cool dogged insolence in her bearing, tone, and language—or whether it was all mere mannerism on her part. But it was impossible to determine the point with any degree of certainty; and I felt that the secret impression left on my mind was against her.

"No," I said; "it is no trouble for me to let you out of the private door: and it will be better not to run the risk of disturbing her ladyship, for she was sleeping when I left her."

I proceeded down the private staircase, followed by Agatha: I opened the door, and she passed out. Again locking the door, and taking the key with me, I reascended the stairs. While returning to the boudoir, I decided upon saying nothing to Lady Kelvedon in reference to this little incident with

regard to Agatha; for I was fearful of exciting in her ladyship's mind the idea that I suspected, or positively knew, that she was being unfairly tampered with by somebody beneath that roof. But the reader will not be surprised to learn that my mind was more or less agitated by misgivings in reference to Agatha.

CHAPTER CVIII.

A DAY AT KELVEDON HALL.

IT must not however be thought I had arrived at any positive and settled conclusion in respect to Agatha, or that I was completely convinced that she was the wretched agent of Mr. Collingwood's dark iniquity. I bore in mind the words of Dame Betty, that I must keep my eyes open and watch; and I resolved that during the short time I should be beneath that roof I would keep the strictest look-out on every one who approached her ladyship, and that every circumstance which might occur, however apparently trivial, should be carefully envisaged and considered.

On returning into the boudoir, I told Lady Kelvedon that it was possible I should be compelled to return to London on the following evening. She was vexed and annoyed at this piece of intelligence: but she ceased to deplore the subject when I assured her that it was for her own benefit.

"And therefore," I said, "as it is now probable that I may have to visit you again with the least possible delay, you had better affect to be whimsical and capricious in the presence of his lordship—you want more things from London—and I must go to procure them for you. Do you understand?"

"But what trouble I am giving you, my dear Ellen!" said Hermione, with a look of deep concern.

"Not another syllable upon the point!" I ejaculated. "And now let us secure this decanter in some safe place—and I will unlock the boudoir door—and then we must send for his lordship; or else he may think it strange that we keep him away from us so long."

These matters being settled—and my bonnet and shawl (which I had hitherto kept on in consequence of having to go into the garden) being laid aside—and Lord Kelvedon being again seated in the boudoir, we rang for coffee. A large silver salver was presently brought up by Matilda; and upon it, in addition to the usual tea-apparatus, there were dishes of sandwiches, cold chicken, and other little delicacies which had been ordered on my account. I should here observe that Matilda was some three or four years older than Agatha—that she likewise was tolerably good-looking—but that she possessed a countenance the frankness and openness of which were remarkably prepossessing. Her attentions were bestowed not merely with a respectful readiness, but likewise with that appearance of good-nature and hearty willingness to oblige which render the services of some domestics so much more agreeable than those of others.

Matilda stood at a side-table, on which she placed the tray; and there she poured out the tea

WALL SC.

or coffee according to our respective tastes. I noticed that both Lord and Lady Kelvedon took coffee, which was as a matter of course served to them from the same coffee-pot. Matilda waited while these refreshments were being partaken of; and then she withdrew, carrying away the tray. I remained chatting with Lord and Lady Kelvedon until about ten o'clock, when I bade them "Good night," and Matilda was summoned to conduct me to my chamber. There I found a cheerful fire burning; and I perceived that everything had been done to administer to my comforts, so that I warmly thanked Matilda for all her thoughtfulness on my behalf. I retired to rest; and being wearied after the day's journey and the exciting incidents of the evening, I soon fell asleep.

When I awoke in the morning, Matilda was prompt in answering the summons of the bell. She came accompanied by the housemaid to light

the fire; and though I declared that I never allowed myself such luxurious habits at home, the attentive Matilda would persist in having her own way, good-naturedly observing to me that it was much colder in the country than in London. I inquired how Lady Kelvedon was that morning? —but Matilda replied that she did not know, for it was not her turn to wait upon her ladyship that day: it was Agatha's duty. I then incidentally learnt that although there were four lady's-maids, Matilda and Agatha performed the principal duties, and were, so to speak, most especially attached to her ladyship's personal service.

When my morning toilet was completed, I repaired to the boudoir, where I found Lady Kelvedon up and dressed: but she was reclining upon the sofa or lounge, where I had previously seen her. She was alone; she greeted me with affectionate warmth; and in reply to the first anxious question which I put, she said that she did perhaps feel the least thing better, but to so trifling an extent that it might be only the effect of imagination. She was however more cheerful than for a long time past she had been when getting up in the morning; but this of course might be attributed to my presence.

"I am not worse, dear Ellen—*that* is very certain!" she said, with a sweet smile; "and it would be ridiculous to suppose that I could feel very much better after the lapse of only a few short hours, and having only taken two glasses of my medicine."

Lord Kelvedon presently made his appearance; and the bell was now rung for breakfast. The tray was brought in by Agatha, and placed upon the side-table, just as it was by Matilda on the preceding evening. A round rosewood table in the centre of the room was spread with a snowy white cloth, and furnished with the substantial materials for the morning's repast. As I was a guest, Agatha bestowed her first attentions upon me, by asking which I was pleased to take, tea or coffee? I decided upon the former; and I was served accordingly.

"Which will your ladyship please to take this morning?" added Agatha.

"Coffee, as usual," answered Hermione.

I pretended to be deep in the process of cutting a cold chicken that was before me; but I scrutinisingly watched the proceedings of Agatha—as indeed I had studied those of Matilda on the previous evening: but I could not detect the slightest circumstance of a suspicious character — not the slightest movement—not the slightest look that tended to confirm my misgivings in respect to the young woman. She at once poured out the coffee from the silver pot without turning aside—without any shuffling with the hands,—in a word, without affording the faintest ground for supposing that by any skilful manipulation or dexterous legerdemain, she had slipped anything into the cup of coffee which she now proceeded to hand to Lady Kelvedon. Then his lordship decided on taking coffee; and I saw by the answer he gave that it was likewise his *usual* beverage, and that indeed the question of choice was merely put to the nobleman and his wife as an ordinary matter of form. To be brief, the morning repast was disposed of without the slightest incident transpiring to corroborate any suspicion which I might have previously formed in respect to Agatha.

Lord Kelvedon went out riding on horseback, leaving me and Hermione alone together, according to the expressed wish of her ladyship. She begged me to go and take a walk, or else a drive in the carriage, as the weather was of a beautiful frosty freshness and clearness, and she was considerately afraid that I might suffer for want of exercise. But I had resolved to remain upon the watch—I was determined not to quit Hermione throughout the day, unless it were absolutely necessary; and I therefore assured her that so far from needing exercise, I was only too glad to have a good rest after my journey of the previous day and with the prospect of another journey in the evening. I therefore remained in the boudoir: and I conversed in the most cheerful strain, so that I might keep up Lady Kelvedon's spirits.

Shortly after the hour of noon, Agatha entered the boudoir to inquire what refreshment her ladyship would take for luncheon? I saw that the idea of food almost produced a nausea on Hermione's part; and I had noticed that a single piece of muffin was all the solid material she had taken for breakfast. She now turned to me, saying, "I feel that I ought to take something; and indeed I have more or less forced myself to swallow whatsoever food has entered my lips for weeks past. But I am now sick of broth—and gruel—and beef-tea—and gravy-soup——"

"And yet you must take something," I said, entreatingly.

"Yes, I know it," rejoined her ladyship. "Well, Agatha," she added, with a melancholy smile, "I suppose it must be a little beef-tea,—which is the refreshment I most usually take."

Agatha retired; and in about a quarter of an hour she reappeared, bringing the massive silver tray on which were the materials for a substantial luncheon; and amongst them a breakfast cup about half full of strong beef tea. Again did I watch the young woman's countenance—but it was calm and collected, with that settled expression of reserve or sullenness which I had before noticed. I attentively studied all the details of her bearing and demeanour towards her master and mistress, as I had done in the morning (for Lord Kelvedon now made his appearance, having returned from his ride). I could not help coming to the conclusion that the young woman's general deportment was precisely the same towards Lord and Lady Kelvedon as it had been towards myself on the preceding evening. She spoke coldly: with coldness too she performed whatever services were required of her: there was no hearty willingness nor good-natured anxiety to oblige, as there was on the part of Matilda. But, on the other hand, there was assuredly no studied hypocrisy — no grovelling servility towards some while reserve was being maintained towards others; for, I repeat, her conduct towards her master and mistress was precisely the same as it had been to me. I therefore concluded that it was mere mannerism, and that it altogether ceased to be disagreeable or even to be noticed with those who were accustomed to it.

After luncheon Lord Kelvedon went out again; and I now resolved to turn the discourse with Lady Kelvedon upon her principal handmaidens—but in the most delicate and cautious manner, so as to keep faithful to my plan of avoiding the chance of exciting any suspicion that I had an ulterior motive for so doing.

"Matilda," I said, "seems to be a very nice young woman? I can assure you she has studied her best to render me as comfortable as possible."

"No doubt of it, my dear Ellen," responded her ladyship; "for such is Matilda's disposition. She is good-nature personified! I must not however be unjust towards Agatha. It requires to know this young woman to appreciate her good qualities. Perhaps you would not think it—but she is quite as good-natured as Matilda——only she displays it in a different manner. She is reserved, quiet, and inobtrusive: yet she anticipates all my wants just the same as the more hearty and agreeable-mannered Matilda."

"In that case," I said, "your ladyship has two valuable servants:"—and I made the remark as a salve to my own conscience, which reproached me for having entertained unjustifiable misgivings and unwarrantable suspicions in reference to Agatha.

Soon after three o'clock, Lord Kelvedon reappeared; and it was now that his wife began playing the part which I had suggested—namely, the expression of a desire to have several articles of dress which she knew very well could only be obtained in London. She spoke with that air of capriciousness and whimsical levity which are so often displayed by invalids; and then her countenance brightened up when I offered to procure everything she required.

"But you would not have Miss Percy set out for London this evening?" ejaculated the old nobleman, who naturally saw something outrageous in such a proceeding according to the view which he took of it.

"Indeed, my lord," I hastened to say, "I have urgent business requiring my presence in the metropolis; and if I do not return to-night, I must set out to-morrow. It shall be made to depend upon her ladyship, and how she finds herself presently."

Agatha now entered the boudoir to lay the table for dinner. A couple of the footmen brought up the dishes; but they did not remain to wait at table—it was Agatha who performed this duty; for ever since the commencement of her illness Lady Kelvedon had chosen to be attended as much as possible by her own handmaidens, for she complained that the footmen were too noisy.

The dinner passed off without any incident worthy of mention—without the occurrence of the slightest reason to resuscitate against Agatha all those suspicions which had died away after hearing the character which her mistress had given of her. And now, when the table was cleared and Lord Kelvedon had partaken of two or three glasses of wine, it became necessary to think of getting rid of his lordship for the present, as the hour was approaching when Dame Betty would be waiting for me in the shrubbery. I made a sign to Lady Kelvedon: she acknowledged it by a look which showed me that she knew what was passing in my mind; and in a few minutes she began to suffer her head to fall back slowly over the cushion of the sofa, while her eyelids were seen gradually to droop.

"Her ladyship feels sleepy," I whispered to Lord Kelvedon.

He understood the hint: it was intended for him to retire; and he rose from his seat accordingly.

"I will keep watch by her ladyship's side," I said; "and when she awakes I will send and let you know."

The nobleman withdrew from the boudoir; and as the door closed behind him, Hermione opened her beautiful eyes, smiling at the success of the stratagem which she had adopted. I then fastened the boudoir door; and consulting my watch, I found that it was a quarter to six o'clock—close therefore upon the hour when Dame Betty would be expecting me in the shrubbery.

I put on my bonnet and shawl, which I had purposely left in her ladyship's apartments since the preceding evening: I took the key of the private door—and I set out on my little expedition. The reader may be well assured that on this occa-

sion I was specially careful to *lock* as well as shut the door at the bottom of the staircase; and on emerging into the open air, I plunged my looks in every direction to assure myself that I was unobserved. The heavens were dark with black clouds that were floating high above; and I could not see to any very great distance around. But I listened—and all was still. I glided along the avenue in the garden: I was approaching the door in the boundary-wall, when I suddenly stopped short, for it struck me that I caught the sound of a footstep at a little distance. Yes—there was no doubt of it!—'twas the footstep of a man's heavy boot upon the gravel walk rendered hard and crisp by the frost. Another moment, and I heard voices speaking in a low tone,—a man's voice and a woman's voice; and then my ear could follow the lighter steps of a female in conjunction with the heavier ones of a man. The sounds were approaching the spot where I stood: they were coming along a diverging walk. Something must be done on the instant! Noiseless as a snake gliding in the grass, I slipped amongst the evergreens; and crouching down, I listened with suspended breath.

"Well, you know," I heard the man now say, "he told us to beware of this Ellen Percy, for she got upon the scent of what he meant to do some months ago—and that's the reason that made him hold off so long. He would have held off longer too, only his circumstances were growing so desperate——"

The female voice then said something; but I could not catch what it was. Indeed the voice itself was so indistinct that I was not even able to judge by its tone whether it were one that was known to me.

"Of course she must suspect!" rejoined the man: "or else what the deuce has she come again to the house for, after having been two or three days ago?"

The female voice again said something, but as indistinctly as heretofore.

"I couldn't come last night, my dear girl," said the man: "or else of course I should have done so. You know that I love you—don't you?"

There was a murmuring sound of a female voice, and this was followed by the noise of several hearty kisses which reached my ears. The loving couple—for such they evidently were—retraced their way along the walk; and some minutes elapsed before they returned near enough for me to catch another syllable of what was passing between them.

"I wonder whether it was only an excuse on Miss Percy's part?" said the man, when his voice once more came within the range of my hearing; "or whether she really had a headache and went out for the fresh air?"

The female voice said something, this time in a somewhat louder tone, though I was still unable to catch the sense of what she *did* say: but it struck me that it was the tone of Agatha's voice. The man again spoke—but I only caught the words "private door"—"unlocked"—and "bath-room:" and then there was a low but merry laugh on the part of the female. For an instant I was struck by bewilderment, for the laugh sounded as if it were Matilda's voice—whereas all other circumstances had been com bining to establish in my soul the conviction that it was Agatha who was walking with her lover in the adjacent pathway. And then, as if it were decreed that this bewilderment on my part should be only momentary, I heard the man speak the name of *Agatha*; and I said to myself, "Yes—he is addressing her by that name! It is *she*; and after all, my original suspicions were not erroneous; for *she* is the fiend in female shape who has administered the poison to her mistress!"

"What will I do?" said the man, when I again caught the sound of his voice:—"why communicate without delay to Mr. Collingwood, to be sure! What would you have me do?"

The female voice said something: and here again I felt more than ever convinced that it was the tone of Agatha which I heard.

"No proof of anything?" ejaculated the man. "Why, if Miss Percy knows so much as it seems she *must* from what master told you and me, all her suspicions must be excited——What? Ah! the oath! Well, but it will not do to leave matters in any sort of doubt. Master must be informed—and then he can do as he likes."

The female voice spoke; and I just caught the words, "write"—"post"—"messenger."

"Oh, the post will do!" replied the man: "there's no money for special messengers. And now, like a good girl, go and scribble me this letter. Ah, what a cursed thing it is that a chap of my sagacity can neither read nor write!—and yet here I am employed in the most delicate matters!"

The female voice again interposed something.

"To be sure, my love!" pursued the man: "you shall continue to be my little secretary as well as my pretty little wife when all this business is settled. My secretary you are already—and as good as my wife too, for that matter, barring the parson's blessing and the marriage lines—which shall all be right enough before——'

Here a "hush! hush!" was distinctly wafted to my ear; and then followed the sounds of more kissing. For two or three minutes the conversation that ensued was too indistinct for me to hear more than a few syllables, because the couple were again retiring farther along the walk: but I did two or three times catch the names of "Agatha," and once that of "Matilda:" but I felt convinced that the *former* name was applied in tender ejaculation to the young female by her companion.

"And now go and write this letter to master," were the words I next heard spoken, as the couple again drew near the spot where I was concealed. "The same address as last time, mind! How long shall you be? But stop! I shan't be able to wait—and it's dangerous too for me to risk being seen hanging about the premises when everybody supposes I have gone abroad with master. And then too there's my horse down under the hedge at the end of the field——"

There was now a rustling of the wind amongst the evergreens, and I therefore lost the reply which his female companion gave him, and which I should otherwise on this occasion have certainly caught, for they came nearer than they had previously done to my place of concealment before they turned to retrace their way.

"Well, let me see—it's now about six o'clock," said the man; "and I may possibly come back in about an hour. But we won't risk another meeting to-night. Depend upon it this Miss Percy will have eyes for everything! I tell you what you can do. Go and write the letter at once—and then you can watch your opportunity to steal out of the house, and slip it into the stone vase—you know, dearest——the same one where you used to leave flowers for me as a sign when we could meet? But you know all about it!—so go like a good girl! Ah! while I think of it, just lay a stone on the top of the letter so that it shan't blow away; and if you put it into the vase presently, I can come back for it at my leisure. I'll however take good care it shall be in the post before the morning at Petersfield."

A few more words were exchanged—but these I could not catch; and then the lovers separated. The man passed out of the premises by that garden-gate which I was about to seek ere I hid myself amongst the evergreens; and I most sincerely hoped that he would not by any accident be led to enter the shrubbery where I had no doubt that by this time Dame Betty was concealed. As for the man's female companion, she flitted along the gravel-walk at a rapid rate; and though she passed very close to the spot where I was concealed, I could not obtain a sufficient view of her to convince myself that it was really Agatha—though indeed I had scarcely any doubt in my mind upon the point.

When all was still, and I had allowed as I thought a sufficient time for the departure of the man, as well as for the entrance of the young woman into the mansion, I stole towards the garden-gate. I opened it, and plunged my looks into the obscurity which lay beyond. I could discern no human form; but I proceeded slowly and cautiously towards the shrubbery; and when the vase at the south-western corner of the grass-plat was reached, I said in a low tone, "Dame Betty, are you there?"

There was a rustling amongst the trees; and the gipsy crone speedily came forth.

"Is everything right?" she asked.

"Yes," I responded; for I did not choose to say a syllable, at least for the present, in reference to the track upon which I had got towards the complete discovery of the agents employed by Collingwood in his detestable plot. "Come along! her ladyship awaits you! Do you still think it probable, on reflection, that I shall be compelled to accompany you to London?"

"I cannot possibly answer that question until I shall have seen her ladyship. As for me, my dear, you know it is absolutely necessary that I should speed to London: for the trial of that villain St. Clair takes place to-morrow."

"My promise shall be kept," I replied. "If I go with you, I shall leave in the postchaise, and take you up where we met last night. If I do not go with you, I shall pretend to dismiss the postchaise, and I will privately tell the postilion that you are to be his passenger and that he will find you at the spot to which I have just alluded."

"No possible arrangements can be better, Miss Percy," answered the dame; "and they are precisely those which I foresaw you would make. So, you see, your young head is as wise as my old one."

I led Dame Betty into the back garden—I unlocked the private door—and when we had entered I carefully relocked it. In a few moments we were in the boudoir. Lady Kelvedon bestowed the kindest welcome upon the old gipsy-woman, and replied with cheerfulness to the questions that were put to her. The dame was very minute in these queries; and I could presently judge by the answers that the crone would resolve upon taking me to London to become the means of conveying the new drug that was required, into the possession of Lady Kelvedon. Nor was I wrong in my conjecture; for after having finished her catechising, Dame Betty said, "Yes, it is as I thought! The work is already sure enough—but it will alike be surer and quicker under the influence of the drug that is now wanting. I won't undertake to send it by post, or yet by parcel——"

"I have already declared my willingness to accompany you," I said. "We will set off presently; and if I cannot immediately return to Kelvedon Hall, I will send a faithful messenger" (thus alluding to Beda), "to whom her ladyship will give ready access."

"Oh, but you must return, my dear Ellen!" exclaimed Hermione: "you must come in person, and not by deputy!—for you know how dull I shall be without you!"

"I will come, if possible," was my answer. "And now about the postchaise——"

"Your ladyship will continue to take that draught," said Dame Betty, "which I prepared last evening. I hope to be enabled to see you again at the end of a week: but if you should chance to have emptied the decanter before my arrival, you must make yourself a fresh supply. Here is a little box of ingredients; and a slip of paper which I have placed inside, indicates the quantities to be used. I shall send special directions with the other drug which I am about to procure in London.—I have now nothing more to say. What o'clock is it?"

"Half-past six," I said, looking at my watch.

"Well," rejoined Dame Betty, "in an hour we ought to start. I will be at the appointed spot, Miss Percy; and I must trespass on your goodness to take me all the way up to London. It is night-time—and therefore no one need perceive that you have got an old gipsy as your companion."

I now conducted the dame out of the boudoir; but when we reached the private door at the bottom of the staircase, I peeped cautiously forth into the garden ere I suffered the dame to cross the threshold; for I feared the young woman who had promised to write the letter, and who I had no doubt was Agatha, might be flitting to the spot where she was to deposit the correspondence until it should suit her lover to return and fetch it away. But the coast was clear; and Dame Betty emerged from the premises under my escort, without any incident to molest or alarm us. I waited near the garden-gate until her form was completely lost in the surrounding obscurity; and then with a heart palpitating with suspense, I sped to the nearest vase. I thrust in my hand: no letter was there! I then sped forward to the next vase—but still no letter. The third vase to which I proceeded, was the very one which has before been mentioned in reference to the instructions I had given to Dame Betty. I thrust in

my hand. Yes!—there was a paper package lying beneath two or three stones at the bottom of the vase.

I unhesitatingly took possession of the packet, and speedily retraced my way to the private door, which I reached unobserved. In a few moments more I was in the boudoir, the door of which I at once unlocked; and ringing the bell, I said to Hermione, "I am forced to depart, you see: but it is for your good. The old woman is cautious and will trust to no means of transport or conveyance except the hands of a friend in supplying you with the additional drug which is now alone required to render your cure certain."

Agatha answered the bell; and I said to the young woman, "Have the kindness to order the postchaise to be ready in about three quarters of an hour." .

"Yes, Miss," she answered, and then withdrew.

I had watched her attentively; but there was not the slightest change in her countenance, and a stranger would have thought that it was to her a matter of the most perfect indifference whether I went away or whether I stopped.

"Good heavens!" I mentally ejaculated, "what consummate hypocrisy!"

I now proceeded to my own chamber under pretence of making some little change in my toilet previous to my departure—but in reality to have an opportunity of being alone for a short space. But scarcely had I entered that room when Matilda made her appearance, exclaiming, "Oh, Miss! this is really quite unexpected, this sudden departure! Allow me to pack your portmanteau——"

"Thank you, Matilda," I answered; "you shall pack it presently for me. I wish to be alone for a quarter of an hour or so," I added in a kind tone.

The young woman retired. I then locked the door, and drew forth the brown paper packet which I had secured beneath the folds of my dress. I found that the brown paper was merely to protect the letter which it enclosed from getting damp or soiled at the bottom of the vase, for there was no writing upon that envelope. The letter itself was addressed to Mr. Collingwood, at the *Hotel du Nord*, Boulogne. The writing was that of a woman, but evidently feigned—a fact which was all the more apparent from the circumstance of the letters being made to lean the wrong way, as if the pen had been held in the left hand. I unhesitatingly broke the seal of the letter, and proceeded to scan its contents. These were brief, and were penned in a similar fashion to the writing of the address. They ran as follow:—

"December 14, 1842.

"Ellen Percy is at the Hall. She first of all paid a flying visit the day before yesterday in the morning; then she went away and came back again yesterday evening. I do not know how long she means to stop; but I don't think it will be for any length of time, as she keeps the postchaise, horses, and postilion there. There is nothing else to say. Everything *at present* goes on as usual. The sick one is no better. But whether the visit of E. P. will make any difference—or what it may lead to—or what it means, is more than I can say.

I await your instructions. Please, sir, to write to me as before.

> "Your Humble Servant,
> "R. B."

These were the contents of the letter; and they showed me that the visits of the old gipsy remained totally unsuspected. But it scarcely required a moment's reflection upon the nature of that letter's contents: my mind was instantaneously made up how to act. I took from my trunk my writing-materials, with which I always made it a rule to travel; and with the other letter before me as a model for the penmanship, I hastened to indite the following lines:—

> "December 14, 1842.

> "I am sorry to say that everything stands a chance of being immediately discovered at the Hall; for three or four eminent physicians have been called in from London, and they have said enough to put matters in a very awkward position. So please to send money at once to all concerned, that we may get away out of the neighbourhood: for though I am stanch, yet I will only answer for myself. Don't fail to attend to this, as it's the only means which I can see to prevent the danger of certain parties peaching. You understand me.
> "Your Humble Servant,
> "R. B."

This note I folded up, and addressed in precisely the same manner as the one which had served me as a model so far as the penmanship was concerned. I hesitated for a moment whether I should destroy the model, or keep it against any contingencies that might arise; and I decided upon the latter course. I therefore secured it in my portfolio. It had been stamped with some common seal with a flower upon it; and I stamped mine with a blank stone that was set in the top of a pencil-case. I may incidentally observe that I had every reason to flatter myself upon the accuracy with which I had imitated the sort of left-handed writing and configuration of the letters afforded me by my model.

I enveloped my newly fabricated letter in the piece of brown paper; and having carefully locked up my portfolio, so that its contents might not be peered into, as it contained the model letter, be it understood—I hastily put on my travelling-dress. I then unlocked the door and rang the bell.

"Matilda," I said, when this young woman made her appearance, "you may now pack up my trunk for me;"—and at the same time I slipped half a sovereign into her hand; for I was much pleased with her attentions, and in my own thoughts I agreeably contrasted her good-natured agreeable disposition with the morose sullen demeanour of Agatha, who, I felt assured after all, must be the veriest of hypocrites since she had succeed in impressing Lady Kelvedon with the idea that she was in her heart well-meaning, kind, and considerate.

I now returned to the boudoir, where I found Lady Kelvedon alone. This was precisely what I wished; for I was thinking on my way thither that I had committed an oversight in not letting her know that I did not desire her husband to be present when I returned to her. I had still some

thing to do: it required a little tact to manage it —but I had no fear of succeeding, for Hermione was simple-minded, credulous, and artless as a child. I therefore again locked the boudoir door; and I said, "You must lend me the private key once more. The gipsy-woman will have to revisit you at the end of the week; and I must indicate to her another place of concealment—for the shrubbery is somewhat too remote. Indeed there is no reason why she should not at once enter the side gate of the garden the next time she comes. If I mistake not, there is a knot of evergreens where she could more conveniently conceal herself; and I will just run down and take another survey of the place, so as to be enabled to give her the minutest instructions."

"Do so, my dear Ellen," said Lady Kelvedon, fully believing everything I told her.

I hastened to the private staircase—descended it —and issued forth from the private door, which I locked behind me. The moon was now breaking through a cloud—the clouds themselves were dispersing upon the face of heaven—and it promised to be a beautiful night. Away I sped to the garden-gate: another moment and I was skirting the pathway of the lawn, bending my hurried steps towards the particular vase which now acquires a certain fame in my narrative. Therein I deposited my letter enveloped in the brown paper; and I dropped three or four stones upon it. I then hurriedly retraced my way; and re-entering the garden, closed the door as cautiously as possible. I was gliding along the path, when again I heard voices and footsteps; and in the twinkling of an eye I was once more in my old place of concealment amongst the evergreens.

"What new adventure can this be?" I mentally ejaculated. "Is it again Agatha with her lover? If so, are all my well-laid plans baffled? Has he returned sooner than I had anticipated to seek the letter in the vase? and not finding it there, has he sought and managed to obtain this second interview with the girl?"

Such were the reflections which I hurriedly made, but all the while listening with suspended breath. I still heard the sounds of voices; but not a syllable that was uttered could I catch. The footsteps continued along the same gravel-walk as that where I had heard them on the previous occasion. I was indescribably vexed and annoyed; for I felt assured that the project I had devised for the purpose of removing such darkly dangerous characters from the sphere of their iniquitous proceedings, stood every chance of being completely upset.

"Good night, dear Richard," at length said the well-known voice of Agatha, now speaking in quite an audible tone; and then kisses were exchanged.

Richard! Yes *that* was the name by which she had addressed her lover: and the initials which appeared at the bottom of the letter written on his behalf to his master were R. B. But scarcely had she spoken that "Good night," when there was a strong rustling of the wind, which was rising, amongst the trees; so that whatsoever response he gave was lost to my ears. Immediately afterwards I heard the garden-gate open gently; and almost at the same time a female form passed in front of the evergreens in the midst of which I was concealed. The moon was now shining gloriously: its beams fell completely on that figure—and I recognised Agatha. I could even distinguish her countenance; and a smile of tender pleasure predominated over the natural reserve and sullenness of its expression.

"Ah, wicked girl!" I thought to myself: "even though I may now be in some way baffled in the design which I had formed, yet will I assuredly discover some other means very shortly to remove you from about the person of the amiable mistress whom you have been killing by inches! Fortunately it matters not for a few days that you should still retain your post; for she possesses the antidote—while on the other hand your poisons must by this time be very nearly exhausted!"

Agatha passed rapidly along the walk: but I remained two or three minutes in my place of concealment until I felt assured that she must have re-entered the mansion. I then emerged from amidst the evergreens, and speedily regained the boudoir.

"Have you taken a good survey of the premises?" inquired Lady Kelvedon.

"Yes," I answered; "and now I must make haste to depart:"—for as I spoke I heard the sounds of the postchaise drawing up in front of the mansion.

I unlocked the boudoir door, and then rang the bell. Agatha quickly made her appearance; and methought for a moment that she looked slightly flurried: but if my surmise were correct, she the next instant regained her usual self-possession, with her wonted reserved coldness of look.

"Have the kindness to tell his lordship," said Hermione, "that Miss Percy is about to take her departure. I believe that the postchaise is at the door?"

"Yes, my lady," was the response: and Agatha left the room.

In a few minutes Lord Kelvedon entered. Something more was said about the purchases I was supposed to have to make in London; and then I bade Hermione farewell. The nobleman escorted me down to the chaise; and as he handed me into it, he said, "Pray make haste and return, Miss Percy; for no one can do Hermione any good but yourself!"

CHAPTER CIX.

ANOTHER STARTLING ADVENTURE.

THE postchaise drove away: and as it was proceeding through the park, I wondered within myself what would now be the fate of the letter I had left in the vase?

"If this Richard," I thought, "went thither and found no letter, and then sought that interview with Agatha and told her so, how great must have been the consternation of both when on comparing notes they found that it was gone! Who can tell but that this circumstance may accomplish the very aim which I originally had in view, by causing them to take to flight without delay—perhaps during this very night—with the idea of saving themselves from an exposure that they may deem imminent. However, we shall see!"

The chaise continued its way—the park-gates flew open—and the equipage rolled into the road. It stopped at the place where I was to take up Dame Betty; for I had already given the postilion instructions to that effect; and the gipsy-woman was there in readiness. She took her seat in the vehicle, which immediately proceeded at a rapid pace.

No discourse of any consequence took place between us; and we had gone about a couple of miles from the spot where I had taken up the woman, when all of a sudden the chaise came to a dead halt. The horses plunged—there was a cry of human distress—and scarcely had I put down the window which was nearest to me, when an ill-looking fellow appeared at the door. This he immediately opened; and in a gruff voice exclaimed, "Come, get out, both of you—and don't delay a minute, or it will be the worse for you!"

My first impression as the chaise stopped was that this was some new treachery on Dame Betty's part; and I was not even reassured when she began crying in a voice which really seemed to be full of terror, "What's this? what's this?"—but then I thought that the old crone was only getting up a little bit of tragedy, to avert my suspicions from herself, for fear lest in my desperation I should turn round and wreak some sudden vengeance upon her.

"Who are you?" I demanded: "and by what right," I added, "do you dare stop us? If you want my purse——"

"Hang your purse!" ejaculated the ruffian, who I saw was a most ill-looking fellow; but he had nothing of the gipsy about him.

At the same moment two other men came up to the door of the chaise; and a glance showed me that they were likewise of a demeanour different from that of the vagrant race at whose hands I had on former occasions suffered outrage and violence.

"Come, get out, Miss—or I shall have to pull you out," exclaimed the man who had first made his appearance.

"But who are you?" demanded Dame Betty: "don't you see the young lady offers you her purse?"

"Oh, well, if there's to be all this talk," growled the fellow, "here goes!"—and he seized me forcibly by the wrist.

"Unhand me!" I ejaculated; "and I will alight:" for I saw that it was utterly useless to offer any further resistance.

I accordingly descended from the chaise; and then I beheld the postilion lying senseless, or dead, upon the ground—so that there was no longer any doubt as to the lips from which the cry of distress had emanated.

"Don't offer to move," said the ruffian who was first alluded to; "or else I shall be forced to lay a tight hand upon you."

"But I won't get out! I will have nothing to do with you!" cried Dame Betty; "you may do your worst!"

"Wretches!" I ejaculated; "you have killed that man!"—and I pointed towards the postilion.

"Killed?—not he!" cried one of the men: "he'll be all right enough presently.—Once for all, dame, will you alight?" he fiercely demanded, as he turned towards the chaise.

"No!" yelled the gipsy-woman; and by this time I was confident that it was really no treachery on her part; while to my mind vividly rushed certain circumstances which for many hours I had utterly lost sight of—namely, the lurking ill-looking man whom Beda had seen in front of my house in London, and the presence of Lady Lilla Essendine in the cab which had dashed past the postchaise at the outset of my journey.

But I had no leisure to reflect upon these matters, nor to conjecture how they could be possibly dove-tailed into the incidents which were now passing; for these incidents were following each other with a rapidity which engrossed all attention. The foremost ruffian of the three sprang into the postchaise and dragged Dame Betty out. At first she screamed; but the wretch hurled her upon the ground, and with horrible oaths bade her hold her tongue. The dame was terrified into silence; and the moonbeams showed that her countenance was hideously ghastly with alarm.

"Now, what do you want?" I demanded of the men. "Is it money? If so, state your views——"

"Come along with us at once, both of you!" exclaimed the foremost: "and if you don't——"

"Where are we to go?" I asked. "Surely this is some mistake?"—but my heart told me that it was not, though I was utterly at a loss to conceive what it could mean.

"Oh, bother all this talk!" growled another of the men. "Come you along, Miss!"—and he caught hold of me.

I struggled desperately—my bonnet and shawl were torn off—and the ruffian raised a bludgeon to deal me a blow, when fearing that I should be murdered, I cried, "Strike not, and I will go with you!"

"That's sensible," said the man: and allowing me to pick up my bonnet and shawl, he hurried me away.

I glanced over my shoulder, and saw that another of the men was now making Dame Betty accompany him; while the third was raising the postilion from the ground; and in the midst of my own terror and affliction it was some solace to perceive that the unfortunate postboy was showing signs of life.

The place where this adventure had occurred, was at the corner of a lane; and it was down this lane that the gipsy-woman and I were being hurried by the two ruffians who had us in their power. My custodian had not his hand upon me; and I glanced rapidly to the right and the left, to see if it were possible by a sudden spring to save myself by flight. The fellow's eye was however keener than I thought; for at once divining my purpose, he said, "You'd better not, Miss!" and then he brandished his club threateningly.

"A hundred guineas," I cried, "if you let me escape!"

"Make it five hundred, Miss!"

"Well, five hundred!" I said, "and you shall have a cheque for it!"

The fellow burst out into a laugh, exclaiming, "You surely don't take me to be such a fool? The hangman's noose is perhaps what you call a check!"

"No—by heaven, I am sincere!" I ejaculated, thinking in my desperation that any pecuniary terms would be cheap for the purchase of my liberty. "Come—what say you? My freedom and that of the old woman——"

"I rayther think not," responded the man, with another mocking laugh.

"You mistrust me?" I ejaculated, with feverish anxiety.

"Why, do you think that I warn't warned that some such dodge as this would be played?" he coarsely responded.

"Offer them money, Miss Percy!" shrieked Dame Betty from behind.

"Silence, you hag! or I'll dash your brains out!" I heard the voice of her custodian growling fiercely.

"And you, too, had better be silent," said the man who had me in his power: and again he brandished his club. "Whatever you may offer, even if you meant to keep your promise, we shall be better paid by refusing than accepting it. And now hold your tongue."

This mandate was spoken in the most peremptory fashion; and I therefore saw that it was useless to attempt to gain any advantage by means of bribery. In a few minutes more we came suddenly upon a sort of covered chaise-cart, which was waiting at a bend in the lane; and a man was standing at the horse's head. The brilliant moonlight enabled me to perceive that this individual might be classed in the same category as the other three ruffians—namely, that he was ill-looking enough, but that there was nothing in his appearance to indicate that he belonged to the gipsy tribe.

Dame Betty and I were now ordered to ascend into the chaise-cart; but I thought that I would make one more effort on behalf of freedom—and I therefore exclaimed, "Remember that punishment must sooner or later come for such an outrage as this! Be reasonable! be wise! I offer five hundred guineas to any one who will effect the release of myself and this aged woman!"

The man who had all along taken the lead in the present proceedings, here stopped me short with a terrible imprecation; and I was compelled to ascend into the vehicle. Dame Betty, who was muttering unintelligibly between her thin sunken lips, followed me; our two custodians jumped in after us; and then the driver ascended to his seat. There was a sort of curtain of some coarse material which was now drawn over the front or opening of the head of the chaise-cart; and the vehicle drove rapidly away. The horse was evidently a good one: and notwithstanding that the load was somewhat heavy for a single animal, its capacities were more than equal to the task.

"What do you think all this can mean?" I whispered in the lowest possible tone to Dame Betty.

She did not however give any response: she was still muttering to herself—she was rocking her form to and fro—she was evidently the prey to a deep affliction; and I therefore wondered whether she could form any conjecture relative to the motive of this outrage, or whether she had obtained into it that insight of which I myself was utterly deficient. I scarcely knew whether my question was put in too low a tone for her to hear it, or whether she was too much absorbed in her own painful reflections to pay any heed to me;

and I was afraid to repeat my words in a louder tone, for fear of provoking some brutality on the part of the ruffians who had us in their power.

Upwards of an hour passed from the moment when the vehicle had started; and it had the while pursued its course with undiminishing rapidity. The men maintained an almost total silence; and when they did speak a few words, it was only in a low tone amongst themselves. The dame had gradually ceased to mutter and rock herself; and she now lay back in a corner of the vehicle, so motionless that one might have taken her to be dead, were it not for some faint sound of breathing which came from her lips. I should observe that throughout this journey of upwards of an hour, I had not the slightest idea of the direction that was being taken; for the curtain continued to be closed, and there was only a little circular window at the back of the head of the chaise-cart, but in the position in which I sat I could not see out of

it. Even if it were otherwise, it would have been of little or no consequence, for if I had seen that we were passing through a village or hamlet, I should not have dared to cry out, for I knew that I was in the power of a set of desperadoes who would think nothing of silencing me by means of a blow dealt from a heavy bludgeon.

At length—while I was becoming more and more lost in wonder in respect to what our destination could be, and when we should reach the end of the journey—and while, too, all kinds of painful misgivings were floating in my mind concerning the fate that might be reserved for us—the driver opened the curtain and said something to the men who were sitting just within it. For the moment I obtained a glimpse of the scene which the broad round moon was illuminating: I saw a collection of buildings—and in the midst of them there was one object which at once struck a chord in my memory. This was a sort of round tower with a pointed roof; and I could scarcely keep back an ejaculation at all the varied and painful reminiscences which were thus suddenly excited in my brain; for I had now scarcely a doubt that I was once more to find myself a prisoner in the ruins of the farm-buildings near Petersfield! At the same instant Dame Betty gave an abrupt start as she herself caught a glimpse of the same outline of buildings; and she nudged me with her knee, as much as to imply that our destination was about to be reached.

And it was so: for in a few minutes the vehicle stopped at the entrance into the ruins; and the two ruffians who held the dame and me in their custody, commanded us " to alight—to be quick about it—and not to make any more talk, as we had done at the outset, for that it would be all useless and a mere waste of time."

I was determined not to afford these brutal persons any pretext or opportunity for treating me with violence; and I therefore at once obeyed the mandate which was given, and descended from the chaise-cart. But while doing so—and likewise after having alighted—I surveyed the countenance of the driver with more attention than I had at first bestowed upon him, in order to ascertain if it were one which might be supposed to give promise of good feeling or of personal selfishness, if either could be by any means appealed to. But I saw that the first impression I had received in reference to this man was correct, and that he was altogether as ill-looking an individual as the other persons concerned in the outrage. It was therefore with a deep though subdued sigh that I found myself compelled to abandon every hope in that quarter. As for Dame Betty, she now spoke not a word, but followed me out of the vehicle; and as the moonbeams played upon her countenance, they showed that its expression was that of the fiercest and most diabolically vindictive rage that ever was pent up in the human breast.

The moment she had alighted from the chaise-cart, the driver handed down a basket to the two men who remained with us: and bidding them " good night," he whipped his horse, and the equipage rolled away. I flung a hasty glance around, with the last wild hope that some wayfarers might possibly be in sight: but the reader will bear in mind that the neighbourhood of these ruined farm-buildings has on a former occasion been described as exceedingly lonely—and not a human being now met my eyes except Dame Betty and the two ruffians who had us in their power.

"This way, if you please," said the man who had all along acted as spokesman and chief; and he began leading me into the midst of the ruins.

I do not mean that he placed his hand upon me; but he made me keep very close behind him: he was evidently maintaining the strictest watch over me; and I saw that the slightest attempt to escape would draw down his vengeance upon my head. On the other hand, as I glanced behind, I perceived that the second ruffian did keep a firm grasp upon Dame Betty; but this was most probably to overcome her reluctance to proceed, rather than because the man was actually afraid that such a poor decrepid old creature could have the slightest chance of saving herself by flight.

We passed into the midst of the ruins; and the men conducted us towards that out-building which has been before described in the course of my narrative, and which evidently once served as an oast, or place for drying hops. We entered it: we ascended the rickety wooden staircase leading up to the room where the open trapdoor was in the ceiling; and there we halted for a few moments, while one of the men struck a light, for which purpose he had the requisite materials about him. A candle being lighted, was stuck into a bottle which happened to be lying on the floor; and then the two ruffians led me and Dame Betty into the adjoining room,—the very one which between eight and nine months back had served as a place of imprisonment for myself and Beda!

"Now, here you are to remain for the present," said the man who acted as leader. " I can't tell you exactly to a day or an hour when you will be set at liberty; but this much I promise—that if so be you keep yourselves quiet and don't give me and my mate here no manner of unnecessary trouble, you shan't be rendered very uncomfortable. As for your lives, nobody wants anything to do with them; and so you may make yourselves easy on that score. Look! there's wood to light a fire with; and you shall have food so soon as me and my pal here have unpacked the basket."

Having thus spoken the fellow quitted the room, followed by his companion; and then the sound of a bolt being driven into its socket reached my ears.

"Do you understand what it all means?" I now quickly demanded of Dame Betty; for I was full of the most painful suspense. "Can it possibly be that Mr. Collingwood has returned to England——"

"No, no, Miss!" interrupted the crone, with bitter accents: " the present affair has got nothing to do with Mr. Collingwood! It's very different altogether!"

"What!" I ejaculated: "you understand it? you comprehend it all?"

"The more I strain my eyes to look, the clearer it all becomes," said the dame. "At first, I confess, Miss, I was utterly at a loss to conceive what it meant; but in a very little while a suspicion began to steal into my mind—and while we were pent up in that chaise I reflected more and more——"

"Well, well," I ejaculated; "and you say that you can now fathom the mystery?"

"Yes," rejoined the crone; "and the words which that fellow has just spoken, confirm all my suspicions. He cannot tell us to an hour or to a day how long we are to be confined here!—our lives are not in danger! No! no!—it is not our lives, you see, young Miss, that these villains want! it is only our liberty that is for a while suspended!—it is our persons that are detained!"

"But why—why?" I demanded impatiently; for I thought that Dame Betty, who was speaking with exceeding violence and fierceness, would never come to the point.

"Oh! don't you see?" she ejaculated; and it was almost a veritable yell of rage which burst from her lips: "you do not understand it! Oh, how blind! how stupid!"

"And how insensate of you," I cried, "to continue in this strain—still keeping me in the dark——"

"Oh, don't you see," she exclaimed, "that it is all to prevent us from giving evidence to-morrow at the Old Bailey!"

"Ah!" I ejaculated, as a light now suddenly burst in upon my brain; and I at once recognised the probability of the dame's explanation. "Yes, yes—it must be so! That ill-looking man—and then Lady Lilla——"

"What do you mean, Miss?" quickly demanded Dame Betty. "Speak, speak!"—and she almost stamped her foot with feverish impatience. "Has Lady Lilla dared to interfere——"

"I can only tell you this much," I answered,—"that just as I was on the point of setting out yesterday morning, an ill-looking man was seen loitering about in front of my house——"

"Well, well! was it one of these men?" demanded Dame Betty.

"I do not know," I responded: "I did not see the man yesterday morning: it was Beda—the faithful and sagacious Beda—and she had her misgivings——"

"But what concerning Lady Lilla?" asked the dame.

"A few minutes after I had left the house," I rejoined, "a cab swept past the postchaise in which I travelled; and Lady Lilla Essendine was in that cab. It might have been nothing but a coincidence——"

"No! no!" interjected Dame Betty: "there are no such things as coincidences in matters of this sort! I never knew that suspicious circumstances turned out to be mere coincidences! But there used to rage a fierce hatred betwixt St. Clair and Lady Lilla——"

"Ah!" I interrupted her; "surely your sagacity must make you aware that crime has its expediency and its policy; and there are bonds which hold together hearts that otherwise throb with mutual hatred. It is not three months ago that I myself beheld St. Clair and Lady Lilla seated together in the same box at the theatre——"

"Oh! it is now all apparent enough!" ejaculated Dame Betty, again with a ferocious expression of rage upon her haggard, shrivelled countenance: "it is all clear enough!—that fair-haired Lilla and the handsome St. Clair are again friends! Oh!—and am I to be cheated of my vengeance——"

"Peace!" I interrupted her; for she was now giving vent to her fury in accents that were half vociferating, half screaming. "You know what those men told us—and therefore if you value your life you will forbear from creating a disturbance! I am sure the wretches are capable of every atrocity; and if it was from Lady Lilla Essendine that they received their instructions, these will have been of no mediocre character. But tell me, why did you say just now that the words which one of the men had spoken, confirmed your previously existing suspicion that we have been carried off and imprisoned here to prevent us from appearing at the trial of Edwin St. Clair?"

"Because it is not quite sure that the villain St. Clair's trial will come on to-morrow in London. It might be by some accident postponed——and therefore the intimation has been given to us that the term of our captivity cannot be indicated to a day or to an hour. Oh, it is all intelligible enough!" added the dame with a cry of rage; "and Zarah will go unrevenged! The villain St. Clair will escape!"

"Are you confident of this?" I asked. "Were you not bound over as a witness to appear at the trial?—and if you do not answer to your name, will not the process be ordered to stand over——"

"Ridiculous!" interrupted the dame, with an accent of angry contempt. "How ignorant you are upon such points? However, now you are enlightened a bit; for I tell you that St. Clair will get off—he will be discharged *without a stain upon his character!* The judge will take care to tell him *this,*—because he belongs to the patrician order—an ex-Minister—a leading statesman—a man of reputed wealth——"

"Hush!" I interrupted the crone, whose voice kept rising to a higher and higher key until it threatened to rend the very walls themselves with a pealing scream; and I was really afraid lest the anger of the two ruffian guards might be excited. "Pray be more cautious!—for we are in the power of lawless wretches, and the threat which was just now held out is not the first that ever met my ears in this room. It was here that Mr. Collingwood gave vent to the most horrible menaces; and if I then believed—as in truth I did—that he was capable of putting them into execution, how much more readily ought I to believe the same of these wretches in whose hands we now find ourselves!"

"They may as well kill me at once as interpose between me and my vengeance!" shrieked forth the dame, so that I now thought she was going mad. "What else was I living for?—what for weeks and weeks past has been my hope by day and my dream by night? Ah! and now to have it disappointed!—Oh, it is more than I can endure!"

I was on the point of rushing towards her, to compel her by some means to hold her peace—perhaps even to place my hand upon her mouth—when the door opened, and the two men reappeared.

"Hold your cursed row, beldame!" said the junior of the two.

"Here's bread, and meat, and butter, and tea," said the other, who usually acted as spokesman; "and you must manage to make yourselves as comfortable as you can. But if we hear any more screaming or shrieking, my good dame——"

"Let me go, wretches!" she vociferated; and she produced upon my mind the impression of some wretch rendered insane by the reactionary influence of her own diabolic spells.

The foremost ruffian aimed a blow with his cudgel at the dame's head; but she fortunately shrank back in time;—and I, rushing forward, exclaimed, "Coward! you would not strike a woman!—an aged one, too, such as she!"

"Let her hold her tongue, then," growled the fellow, with a sombre, sullen fierceness. "Why does she go on with her aggravating ways?—But I see you haven't lighted your fire! Well, you can do as you choose on this point: it's no business of our'n."

The articles of food which the men had brought were duly deposited upon the ricketty old table; and then they retired—but not before they had bent another menacing look upon Dame Betty, as much as to remind her of the prudence of holding her peace. We heard the bolt spring into its socket; and I whispered to the crone, "That bolt has been put up since Beda and I were imprisoned here: for *then* the door was fastened by means of a bar and a piece of rope."

"And most likely the bolt was put up in the course of this very day," rejoined the dame; "for the whole affair was evidently planned beforehand—and it was all settled and arranged where you and me were to be locked up."

"And heaven help me," I thought within myself, "at the prospect of having such a vile wretch as you as my companion for this night, and perhaps all day to-morrow!"—and I shuddered at the idea.

"However," said the dame, who was now speaking in a subdued and muttering tone—for the recent conduct of the ruffian with the clubstick had evidently terrified her,—"however, I will sooner or later have vengeance upon St. Clair—and vengeance upon Lilla Essendine! Oh, yes! I must yet see that man mount the scaffold!—I must see whether the white night-cap will as well become his head as those masses of light brown auburn hair! I must see also the perfidious Lilla mount the scaffold,—she with her blonde hair and beautiful complexion—with the dazzling whiteness of the neck and shoulders——".

"Silence, woman!" I ejaculated; "you shall not give way to such language in my presence! It may be right and proper to desire that the vengeance of the law shall overtake great criminals: but there is something shocking in the idea of gloating in this savage manner——"

"What! do you mean to say," interrupted the dame, with mingled scorn and contempt in her accents, "that you have any pity for that man or that woman——"

"No!—I have assuredly no earthly reason to bestow any pity upon them," I interrupted the crone: "I know that they have proved the source of much rancorous persecution against myself,—persecution, too, of which *you*, dame, have been the principal agent—"

"Well," she interjected: "and now too, at this very moment you are a prisoner on their account and at their instigation! St. Clair is in danger of having all his iniquities exposed; and Lilla Essendine trembles lest the same storm-cloud should burst over her own head. Therefore she now befriends him;—and the result is that you and I are disposed of here. Yes!—they had every reason to get rid of *me*," continued the dame, with the most intense acrimoniousness; "but it certainly is not quite so clear why they should have included *you* in the business. For surely by this time they have had enough proofs to convince them how meek, and mild, and forgiving you are!—how energetic, bold, and decisive in some respects—how feeble-minded, sentimental, and maudlin in others!"

"Because I do not gloat implacably over ideas of vengeance as you do?" I exclaimed, somewhat angrily: and then still more annoyed to think that I should have suffered myself to be irritated by the crone's taunts, I said, "But no matter!—you may think what you choose of me; for your opinion is really of the utmost indifference."

"Well, at all events," interjected the crone, now affecting to chuckle for a moment, "those two—I mean St. Clair and Lady Lilla—seem to consider you to be an object of alarm, since they have taken so much trouble to put you out of the way as well as myself. But of course I can understand their calculations," continued the dame, more seriously: "they apprehended a thousand things in reference to you! You could tell certain tales of the white rose; and they feared that because you had not gone forward, it was no reason why you should not appear as a witness at the twelfth hour. And then, too, they said to themselves that though you are so kind and good-hearted, yet that a sense of duty ——But what on earth is the good," the crone interrupted herself, "of indulging in this sort of speculation? Ah! the fellow told us that we ought to light the fire—and he was right: for I am perishing with cold!"

"Then light it," I said; and I might have added that it was the sinister fire of the woman's evil passions which had hitherto rendered her insensible to the icy cold which prevailed in that room.

And I too was now suddenly reminded of the existence of this glacial atmosphere which was environing me: but I had hitherto failed to perceive it in consequence of the excitement of my feelings,—an excitement which had been sustained by the rapid colloquy with the old woman. She now lighted the fire: and seating herself on an old garden-basket which was in the room, and which she turned upside down in order to make it serve as a stool, she stretched forth her skinny fingers to catch the genial warmth which the fire gave forth.

CHAPTER CX.

THE BILLET.

THUS was it that I again found myself a prisoner in this apartment belonging to the ruins of the farm-buildings! But on the former occasion what a different companion had I!—the amiable, the faithful, and the beautiful Beda! Now my companion was a horrible ugly old harridan who so far from having aught loveable in her character, had everything that was detestable. She was a woman stained with crime; and though within the last forty-eight hours she had been serving my purposes in a good cause, yet this was far from sufficient to atone for all her past iniquities, or to subdue the sense of loathing which for so many reasons I experienced at having such a companion.

As for the room itself, the reader is already aware of the miserable nature of its appointments, —an old bedstead, an old ricketty table, a couple of chairs, only one of which was now serviceable;—and the aspect of the place seemed very little different from what it was when first I saw it between eight and nine months back. There were the two windows, both barred—one still having the wooden trap-door which Black Ned had put up against it to serve as a shutter—and the other having a little dingy piece of green baize hung up to perform the part of a curtain. The walls all soiled and stained with the damp—the ceiling breaking in from the same cause—the dirt collected upon the floor—

and the cold draughts which penetrated from every side, all combined to render the room as utterly cheerless as possible, and to aggravate the intense misery that I experienced from finding myself placed in such a position. For even if I averted my eyes from those walls, or from that wretched bedstead, or from the windows—the one with the wooden shutter, and the other with the green blind—what object met my view? The hideous hag, Dame Betty, sitting over the fire, giving way to her reflections, and perhaps forgetting at the time that I was present there at all!

I had very little doubt, if any, that the crone had hit upon the right solution of that which was at first so deep a mystery, and that she had accurately conjectured the cause of our arrest and detention. I therefore entertained little or no fear for my life: I did not think that *this* was in any peril. But my liberty—Ah, that might be suspended for two or three days! It seemed a perfect age!—and to be passed in such a place, and in such companionship! Besides, poor Beda would be full of anxiety and suspense at neither seeing nor hearing from me; for I had promised to write if I did not return within a certain time. And then too, the tidings of the outrage committed on the high road might be conveyed to Kelvedon Hall; and in what an agony of suspense would Hermione be plunged! Oh, for numerous reasons apart from any selfish personal considerations, I bitterly deplored this loss of my liberty!

Some time had passed after Dame Betty had lighted the fire, and she at length slowly turned her regards towards the table on which the men had left the provisions.

"Well," she muttered, in a tone that was just audible, though she did not seem to be purposely addressing her speech to me, "there's no use in starving oneself. Famishing will not give me my vengeance one hour the earlier, or procure my liberation one moment the sooner. Do you mean to eat, Miss?" she inquired, now turning her regards upon me.

"No," I replied: "I have not the faintest appetite."

"Perhaps you dined later than I did," responded the crone; "and no doubt you dined better at the Hall than I did at the ale-house. I say, Miss "—and now her voice sank to the lowest possible tone that could be heard,—"do you think there is a chance of making our escape? You did it once, you know——"

"Yes—but it was under different circumstances," I responded. "There was only your adherent Black Ned to deal with in the first instance; and then too, Beda was a most valuable assistant——"

"Yes, yes—and I am useless!" interrupted the dame, with accents of irritability and petulance: "I am a hindrance rather than a help! But the windows, Miss?—the windows? Do bestir yourself!"

"If I thought there was any use in bestirring myself," I said, "rest assured that I should not remain sitting listlessly here. As for the windows, you ought to know full well that they are barred—for it was you who sent me and Beda into captivity here——"

"I know it—I know it," ejaculated the crone; "and you seem to talk, Miss Percy, as if you

fancied that this was a very just retribution which has now befallen me."

"I certainly might enunciate such a moral in respect to yourself," I answered. "Our evil deeds very often redound upon our own heads, and we suffer the same penalties which we have unjustly and wickedly inflicted upon others. It is however useless for me to preach seriously to you in your present state of mind. You have suddenly begun to dream of an escape; but as if all your own sagacity and ingenuity were paralyzed, you appeal to me."

"Yes: you are young—you are vigorous—you are full of strength and intelligence," interjected the dame: "you surely could do something!"

"What can we do? Did you not trust to these walls and these bars when you sent me and Beda as prisoners hither? And if we had been watched by two men instead of one, we never could have made our escape. Now there are two men here——"

"I have been listening," said the crone, "in order to ascertain, if possible, whereabouts in the building they are. It is my opinion they are in the room below."

"And that likewise is my belief," I said; "because I distinctly heard them descend the staircase after they left us just now; and there seems to be an odour of tobacco ascending from below."

"The very circumstances which led me to suspect," cried the dame, "that they are down stairs!"

"And rest assured that they are upon the alert," I said. "We cannot force this door—we cannot break away the bars from the windows—we are utterly without the means of escape!"

Dame Betty made no answer; but I saw that an expression of deep concentrated rage came over her countenance,—thus showing with what strong feelings she was compelled to admit unto herself the truth of my observations. She resumed her seat, from which she had arisen when first speaking of an escape; and again she hung over the fire, her lean hands extended and her fingers all stretched out separately. A considerable time once more passed in silence,—during which I made a variety of reflections upon the circumstances of the present adventure. Amongst other facts I could not help noticing this one,—that no attempt had been made to rob me of my purse nor of the jewellery that I had about my person. The ruffians had not as yet shown themselves as robbers; but I had much rather that they should have done this and left me my liberty. And then, too, I could not help thinking of the unwavering steadfastness with which the bribe I had offered was refused by the man who had me in his custody. No doubt the desperadoes had been assured that whatsoever bribe I might offer would only be intended as a snare; but still I felt convinced that a very heavy reward indeed must have been ensured to them for their present proceeding in order that so stern a negative should have been proclaimed in answer to my proposition. And there was another subject which forced itself upon my thoughts: namely, that it was indeed a most righteous retribution that Dame Betty should now find herself a captive in the very place where she had caused Beda and myself to be imprisoned and where for several hours we were actually in terror for our lives!

But I will not dwell at unnecessary length on the various topics of my meditations during another long interval of silence which now prevailed. At length Dame Betty, who had apparently forgotten her previous intention of having something to eat, rose from her position in front of the fire, and approached the table. She cut herself a slice of bread, mumbling something all the time; and I fancied that what she said chiefly consisted of maledictions against Edwin St. Clair and Lady Lilla Essendine. Returning to the fire-place, she began to toast her bread; but I still experienced not the slightest inclination for food—and I remained seated at a distance from the crone, for I loathed her too much to give the slightest indication of an approach to that familiar companionship which under other circumstances—I mean if the woman herself had been different from what she was—would possibly have been established between us by the nature of our position. I looked at my watch: it was now midnight. The time had passed away more rapidly than I had anticipated. It was nearly eight o'clock when the outrageous attack was made upon the postchaise; it was past nine when the covered cart brought Dame Betty and myself to the ruined farm-buildings. Upwards of two hours and a half had therefore elapsed since our introduction into the wretched room where I now found myself in company with that harridan.

I was seated near the window: it was that window which had the little dingy curtain, and which, as I well remembered, looked out upon the court-yard and the straw-yard at the back of the premises. Not many minutes after I had looked at my watch, the idea began to steal into my mind that I heard some very low yet just perceptible sound in respect to that window to which I am alluding. I turned my head and listened—but without immediately lifting the curtain. And now, as I held my breath suspended, I acquired the certainty that the window (which consisted of two small frames, whereof one was made to slide over the other) was being moved in its setting. Now, what could this mean? For an instant I was seized with a cold tremor: but it immediately passed away as the conviction smote me that treachery could scarcely be presenting itself through such an avenue. If the men wanted to murder us, there was the door for them to enter: and besides, the window was barred. If they wanted to listen to our discourse, they might have crept up to the door: it was not so deficient in chinks nor so well adjusted in its framework as to prevent those villains from becoming either eye-witnesses or ear-witnesses of what was passing within. Then, inasmuch as I was now assured that no treachery was likely to be impending from the region of the window, the thought struck me that some friendly intervention might be at hand. I looked round: I became aware that the curtain had not been so completely closed over the window as to prevent any one who had climbed up thereto, from seeing into the room. And if some one had indeed clambered up, the individual, whoever it might be, could discern Dame Betty as well as myself; and all the precautions which were now being taken might be for the purpose of communicating with me only, and not with the old gipsy harridan.

As these reflections passed through my mind—and as at the same time a conviction was now established within me that the window was really being slowly and carefully moved sideways in its framework, especially as I felt a cold draught coming in upon me—I resolved to shape my own actions in accordance with what I believed to be the prudential course that was being adopted by the operator without. And then an idea struck me. Perhaps it might be one of the two ruffians, who now felt himself disposed to come to terms with me and accept the bribe, but who was acting unknown to his companion, and who also wished to keep the matter secret from Dame Betty? As for the crone herself, she continued to be engaged in making toast in front of the fire; and she was so seated that she did not observe me nor the window against which I was placed.

Immense and very acute was the suspense which for some minutes I endured; for I was utterly unable to settle my mind to any positive conjecture as a solution of the mystery that was now passing. At length the curtain was pushed aside, and a hand was thrust in at the window. That hand held a note, which I quickly took; and the hand was instantaneously withdrawn. I rose from my seat, and paced three or four times to and fro in the room, so as to divert Dame Betty's attention from any sound that she might possibly have heard, inasmuch as it was with a somewhat unguarded movement—a start of joyous hopefulness, that I had almost snatched rather than calmly taken possession of that note. But the dame kept her position at the fire, and evidently had not been disturbed. The candle was burning in a bottle upon the mantel; and having taken those few turns, I approached the table on which the food was placed, as if for the purpose of helping myself to some of it. By these means I placed myself with my back towards the dame, and yet in such a position as to be enabled to read the billet by the light shed from the mantel. With what a beating heart did I now proceed to examine that note! It was written in pencil; the hand was a bold round one; and on glancing at the name, I was still more agreeably surprised, and startled with a still more thrilling joyousness than before, on beholding the signature—WILLIAM LARDNER. The contents of the note were as follow:—

"I am here, Miss Percy, ready to assist you to the best of my ability, and if needful, to risk my life in your service. There are three men in the room below. There were two at first; but a third has just arrived. I listened without being perceived; and I overheard him say to his companions, immediately on his entry, *that it had been made all right with the postilion.*

"I do not know whether the old woman, Dame Betty, is put up in the room to watch you, or whether she is as much a prisoner as you are. Neither do I know whether matters so stand that you would like me to go off at once and procure the assistance of the constables at Petersfield; or whether it better suits your views that I should labour by some other means to effect your rescue. Therefore, I have taken this course to ascertain what you desire. If you wish me to go off at once to Petersfield, be so kind as to lift the window-blind up suddenly and drop it again: I shall understand the signal. But if, on the other hand, you wish me to adopt some other means so as to effect your release without the chance of noise and exposure, be so kind as to lift up the corner of the curtain gently three times. Or again, if you wish to give me a few whispered instructions (in which case I shall suppose that Dame Betty is a prisoner along with you, and therefore will help rather than hinder) be so good as to wave your kerchief out of the window for an instant. I will manage to creep up again with but little risk of discovery on the part of the three men in the room below.

"Your humble but devoted servant,
"WILLIAM LARDNER."

Such were the contents of William Lardner's note; and my heart was filled with joy at the certainty of such friendly aid being nigh at hand. I hastily deliberated with myself for a few instants in respect to the course that I should adopt; and then I decided on communicating to Dame Betty the incident which had just occurred.

"Hush!" I said, advancing towards her; "do not give vent to any loud ejaculation! There is hope! This billet has just been thrust in at the window. Read it!—it explains itself!"

The dame for a moment surveyed me with astonishment; but her countenance quickly brightened up—she snatched the billet from my hand and greedily ran her eyes over its contents.

"William Lardner?" she said. "Why, that must be the young man at Ramsgate——"

"Yes—who saved my life," I interjected, "when St. Clair planned and prepared the diabolical stratagem in reference to the yacht. But of that no matter! You may judge whether the youth is trustworthy by that letter, which he has written doubtless by the aid of the moonlight—and by the risk he is running at the hands of these ruffians below."

"Yes, yes—he is faithful! that is evident, Miss Percy!" said the dame. "And what do you mean to do?"

"For my part," I answered, "I think the best and the shortest mode is to make the first signal——"

"That he may fetch the constables from Petersfield?" interjected Dame Betty. "Yes, yes! to be sure! The shortest plan is the best! Anything so that I may be enabled to get up to London in time——"

"Enough!" I said. "It is agreed, therefore, that the first signal shall be made."

Scarcely had I thus spoken, when a sudden ejaculation on the part of one of the ruffians down stairs reached the ears of Dame Betty and myself. It was a terrible curse, coupled with the words, "A spy!"—and then there was a rush of several footsteps from the doorway forming the entrance into the oast.

"He is discovered!" I cried, almost frantic and desperate with alarm: and I rushed to the window.

Tearing aside the curtain, I looked out. The moon was shining gloriously; and I could distinctly perceive some one—who I felt assured must be William Lardner—leaping over the gate leading from the court-yard into the road that separated it from the straw-yard. The three men were in full pursuit. Dame Betty was quickly by my side; and she ejaculated, "Oh, they will take him! they will take him!"

"No!—look how he runs!" I cried. There! he speeds along the road!—he is gaining ground! he will outstrip his pursuers!—Oh, no! he will be taken, and we are lost!"

"Perdition!" muttered Dame Betty in a low but concentrated voice of mingled rage and disappointment; and she struck her crutch forcibly upon the flooring of the apartment.

The sudden turn which was so disastrously given to the hopeful prospects of our cause, arose from William Lardner falling headlong all in a moment, as if he had tripped over something in his path, or else been smitten a blow by an invisible hand. There he lay—I knew not whether he had stunned himself by the fall, or whether he had been stricken down by apoplexy! But certain it was that there he fell, and there he lay motionless; and in a very few instants the pursuers were upon him. They raised him up: the flood of moonlight enabled me and Dame Betty to perceive that he lay like one dead in their arms; and they evidently examined him attentively for nearly a minute. Then they carried him hurriedly along the road, retracing their way to the gate; and as they entered the court-yard, I cried out, "Let me minister to the unfortunate young man! Surely you will not let him die——"

"You hold your tongue, Miss!" growled forth the individual whom I have all along denominated the spokesman of the trio. "This is serious enough, I can tell you; and if you don't remain quiet, you'll find that it's no child's play that we are engaged in, and that some of the threats we held out just now will be put into execution."

"I care not for your threats!" I cried; "you may do your worst! I will not remain here without raising a voice when a fellow-creature is perhaps dying for want of the services that we can render!"

"Let her talk on!" exclaimed another of the men: "she must know it's all of no use—and if she don't know it, she'll very soon find it out."

"At all events," I said, now recovering sufficiently from the excitement of my feelings to perceive how utterly useless it indeed was to beat the air with words which had no other effect than that of irritating the ruffians,—"at all events I beseech you to treat that young man with kindness—to show him such attentions as he may require——"

"Oh, he's all right enow!" growled the principal ruffian: "he'll come to soon enough. And precious lucky he tripped at the moment he did; for I was just on the very point of sending a brace of bullets after him."

"And I had got my barkers ready," added another of the desperadoes.

"Wretches!" I inwardly ejaculated.

As they approached the building, I strained my eyes to obtain a view of William Lardner's countenance as he was being borne onward by the three men; and now a cry of horror burst from my lips as I caught sight of a dark stain upon his forehead—a stain which instinct even more than my own vision at once told me was blood.

"He is wounded!" I ejaculated: "he has hurt himself seriously! Perhaps he is killed! I beseech you to let me attend to him for a few minutes! I do not ask to be set at liberty——I will make no attempt to escape——"

"I suppose the young chap is the lady's lover?" said one of the fellows; and his two comrades joined in his own coarse laugh at the brutal jest.

"He is a worthy youth in whom I am certainly interested!" I indignantly exclaimed; for I felt that in my agitation and alarm on his behalf I had gone too far in avowing a knowledge of him to be able to retract or to use any subterfuge with the slightest chance of being believed. "But you may think what you choose, provided that you will only for a few minutes play a humane part——"

"I think, Miss Percy," answered the spokesman, in a mocking tone, "me and my mates will prove quite good enough nurses for the young chap; and so you needn't be under any alarm, I can assure you."

They now passed with their burden into the doorway on the same side of the building where the window was situated from which I was looking; and the unconscious form of poor William Lardner was lost to my view.

"That chance of escape is over!" I said, with a profound sigh, as I turned towards Dame Betty.

Her whole countenance was distorted with rage, disappointment, and grief: she literally wrung her hands as she ejaculated, "Everything goes against us! It is destined that Zarah shall be unavenged, and St. Clair shall escape!"

"It is indeed most unfortunate!—most unfortunate!" I murmured to myself. "What a fatality! But Ah! William's note must be burnt!"—and I hastened to commit it to the flames.

"How could he have found," inquired Dame Betty, as if suddenly inspired by another hope, "that you were here?"

"I know not," I responded. "But one thing is very certain,—and this is that I may behold in his presence the forecasting prudence and precaution of my faithful Beda."

"And perhaps Beda herself may be at hand somewhere?" ejaculated the dame; "perhaps she may be in the neighbourhood? and there is yet another chance! What do you think, Miss?" and the old woman was quivering with impatience and suspense.

"No," I rejoined, after only a very few moments' reflection: "it is by no means probable! Beda would not have come alone with William—she is too prudent and modest. She evidently sent him to be upon the look-out——"

"Ah! then all is lost!"—and Dame Betty, returning to her seat before the fire, rocked herself to and fro, giving utterance to low moans and mutterings, until at length her head fell completely forward on her bosom, as if she were a child sobbing herself to sleep.

I thought that she might fall into the fire: I accordingly touched her upon the shoulder, and bade her lie down. She adopted my advice—hobbled to the bed — threw herself on it — and drawing the coverlid over her, was soon buried in a sleep in which all her sense of rage and affliction was for the time doubtless lost.

I returned to the window and listened; but I could not hear the sound of any human voice. The cold night air of December was penetrating like a succession of ice-shafts, and the chill seemed to enter into the very marrow of my bones. I closed the window—drew the curtain over it—and went and sat down before the fire, painfully wondering how it fared with poor William Lardner.

Time passed on—all continued silent—and I still sat in front of the fire. Fortunately there was ample fuel to replenish the grate; and I therefore suffered no longer from the cold. Every now and then I rose and walked a few times across the room to give exercise to my limbs: but the greater portion of the remainder of that night was passed in the chair in front of the fire. I did not once close my eyes in slumber: I did not even so much as experience the slightest drowsiness; but broad awake did I remain while the old dame continued to slumber soundly upon the bed. At length the dawn of the wintry morning began to glimmer: I drew back the little window curtain; and Dame Betty presently woke up. She at once asked if anything fresh had occurred; but I answered in the negative.

"And now," she said, with a strange fierceness of look, as if she were almost prepared to wreak her spite upon me, "I care not what happens or what becomes of me—or of you—or any one else; for my enemies have prevailed, and this day will St. Clair go forth into the world again—acquitted—discharged with unblemished character—"

"Be not so hasty in rushing to conclusions," I said; "for though your language and demeanour seem now to be but little conciliatory towards myself, I will nevertheless remind you——"

"Ah, my dear young lady!" interrupted the old crone, "you must forgive me! I felt almost beside myself—I did not mean to offend you——"

"Well, say no more upon the subject," I observed, with more or less good-nature in my tone and look; for much as in my heart I loathed her, I nevertheless wished to keep on what might be called a good understanding with the dame on account of the work which was yet unfinished in reference to Lady Kelvedon. "Do you not reflect that the moment you are liberated hence, you may repair to London—you may address yourself to a magistrate—you may circumstantially narrate the reasons which prevented you from attending at the Old Bailey this day?—and inasmuch as a foul conspiracy has been entered into in order to defeat the purposes of justice, measures will no doubt be taken to bring the guilty St. Clair again to trial, and with perhaps a very different result!"

Scarcely were these words spoken, when an ironical laugh—but one that was full of the strange sweet music of that voice which was so familiar to my ear—rang through the room. Both Dame Betty and myself started and flung our looks in the direction of the door, towards which our backs had been previously turned; and Lady Lilla Essendine stood before us. We had not heard the door open: the bolt had evidently been drawn back with the utmost noiselessness, so that her ladyship might thus play the part of an eavesdropper—which she had done; for as that musical laugh rolled away, she said, as if speaking in a tone of the most good-tempered raillery, "No, no, my dear Ellen!—we are not quite so

ELLEN PERCY AS PORTIA.

foolish and short-witted on *our* side as to allow such advantages to be retained on *your's*."

I had already assumed an air of cold haughty indignation; and when Lady Lilla addressed me thus familiarly by my Christian name, I felt the blood glowing upon my cheeks—and I was on the point of giving vent to some angry rebuke, when it struck me that I had better for the present play altogether the part of a listener, and hear what she might have to say. And before I continue a description of this scene, I must observe that never perhaps had Lady Lilla Essendine appeared to greater advantage than on the present occasion. She wore a dark velvet bonnet, which contrasted with the long luxuriant ringlets of that light hair which I have previously described as flaxen mingled with pale amber, and shining with that rich gloss which generally belongs only to the auburn hue. She was handsomely dressed in all respects, and

No. 86.—ELLEN PERCY.

wore costly furs. There was a sunny light shining in her large beautiful blue eyes; smiles were upon her lips of vivid vermilion;—and altogether she looked as if she were come upon some errand of benevolence, humanity, and goodness, instead of for any purpose connected with the outrages which had been perpetrated against the old gipsy-woman and myself. And there she stood,—near the threshold of the door,—her tall form full of elegance and grace, just as if she were paying a visit of the kindliest courtesy, and as if she expected to be greeted by friends whom her presence enlivened and rejoiced! Her self-possession was immense: the ease with which she threw the gloss of the most lady-like gracefulness over her hardihood—the facility with which she rendered her very effrontery agreeable, so to speak, by an air exquisitely well-bred,—all served to astonish and almost to bewilder! And then, too, as she stood

there, it really seemed scarcely possible to believe
that the being who was alike so handsome and so
beautiful — and in whose countenance there appeared to be so much genuine sweetness of expression—it seemed impossible, I say, to believe
that this woman of transcending attractions was
a very fiend of wickedness, possessing a heart
capable of every iniquity! Such however I knew
her to be; and therefore it was only for a moment
that I was dazzled by her appearance as she burst
upon my sight, more superbly handsome with her
aquiline profile and grandly sculptured form than
she had ever before seemed,—at the same time
that she was more surpassingly lovely, in the
blonde delicacy of her beauty and with her daz-
zlingly fair complexion, than I was even wont to
fancy her to be!

"No, my dear Ellen," she went on to say, in
the same tone of good-tempered raillery as before
—and her pearly teeth shone between the vivid
vermilion of her well-cut lips—"I do not think
that this good woman here"—and now she bent a
half supercilious, half mischievously sly smile upon
Dame Betty—"will have the opportunity of taking
any such wise and sagacious steps as you were
recommending at the moment when I entered the
room."

I continued to hold my peace. The gipsy-
woman had given a sudden start as if about to
say something; and then it seemed as if she
likewise were smitten with the propriety of becoming a listener at the outset, instead of questioning or recriminating : and she therefore held her
peace. Lady Lilla did not seem to be prepared
for this :—for an instant she bit her lip, and I
saw a slight flush sweep quickly over her countenance. But immediately regaining a perfect command over herself, she said in a somewhat taunting tone, but still with a perfect lady-like grace,
"Oh, I see that it is for me to initiate the topics
of conversation, and to start subjects for our discussion. Well, be it so."

She then closed the door behind her; and the
next moment bending on Dame Betty a look which
a stranger would have fancied to be fraught with
the most exquisite sweetness, she said, "Oh! I am
not afraid to trust myself with you both, I can
assure you! But even if it were otherwise, I
might incur the venture, because there are those
within call who are accustomed to do my bidding to
the letter; despite the inordinately liberal offer of
a bribe of five hundred guineas by cheque on a
London banker :" and here her ladyship laughed
with every appearance of the most joyous, hearty,
ingenuous merriment.

I of course perfectly well understood the allusion : but my countenance underwent not the
slightest change — and I preserved a cold calm
dignity, as well as a continued silence.

"As for you, my good woman," proceeded Lady
Lilla Essendine, again turning towards Dame Betty,
"you have been particularly unreasonable of late :
but I think I can convince you of the propriety
of being reasonable for the future. In the first
place your bitter vindictiveness against Edwin St.
Clair has been misplaced and unjustifiable ; for
Zarah perished as a suicide, and was not murdered
by her husband. This you must know well ! But
it is not worth my while to argue the point. Suffice it for you to know that you are baffled in the

revengeful aim which you were pursuing. At ten
o'clock this morning, Edwin St. Clair stands before his judges *only* for a few moments, and *only*
for the purpose of being at once discharged, inasmuch as the prosecution falls to the ground. Now,
therefore, my good woman, it is high time that
you should be reasonable—unless you choose to
run the risk of counter-accusations that may be
levelled against you. For it can be proved that
you have been cunning in the manufacture of
white roses——"

"Ah! but you would not dare to tell that
secret!" ejaculated Dame Betty, with an accent
that was fierce, though her looks expressed uncertainty and bewilderment, as if she were at a loss to
comprehend how it was that Lady Lilla could be
taking such a high ground, and assuming that
calm air of defiance and self-possession which
denoted a perfect sense of security.

"You are mistaken, my good woman," responded her ladyship : "I should dare to accuse
you or any one else whom I might know to be a
dabbler in poisons—a follower in the footsteps of
the Exilis, Tophanas, and Brinvilliers of other
times."

I cannot explain how astounded I was at the
manner in which Lady Lilla Essendine thus took
the high position of one who in the strength of
conscious innocence was prepared to turn round and
accuse the guilty! It was the most insolent hardihood and the most brazen-faced effrontery that
ever were known; but yet over all there was the
gloss of so sweet a courtesy—the polish of so well-
bred an air, that the effect was to bewilder and
stupefy the imagination.

"Yes," continued Lady Lilla, now emphasizing
the words significantly, "there is the most perfect
understanding between Captain St. Clair and myself. All past differences are settled. In those
differences there was weakness :—in our present
union there is strength. I have no doubt, my
good woman, that in your malevolence you might
proclaim charges and accusations against St. Clair
and myself : but they would fall to the ground—
no one would lend them a hearing—and you would
only be exposing yourself to be dealt with by the
law as a base slanderer, or else as a rampant
lunatic."

I looked at Dame Betty, and I perceived that
Lady Lilla's words were producing a strong impression upon her. I could have told the dame
that it was only in the utter desperation of their
position and circumstances that St. Clair and Lady
Lilla had resolved to put the best face and the
boldest front upon matters, and assume the high
ground of terrorism and coercion in order to intimidate and overawe those who might do them a
mischief. I might also have reminded Dame
Betty that Lady Lilla was interfering so actively
on St. Clair's behalf, because she felt that the same
influence which brought down the thunder-cloud
upon the head of one, would cause it to explode
over the head of the other,—in short, that their
interests had that frightful identity which could
not fail to be associated with a corresponding identity of guilt. But it was not for me to stir in the
slimy depths of a morass where naught but poisonous reptiles were agitating ;—it was not for me to
direct one of the envenomed creatures to avoid
the snares that were set for it by another!

therefore still remained silent, and even affected to turn away from listening to a topic which had such loathsome associations.

"You must not think, my good woman," continued Lady Lilla Essendine, "that I have come hither to entreat you to adopt a particular policy—or to make terms with you—or to threaten you because you deserve to be considered an object of apprehension. Nothing of all this! It is from motives of pity that I address myself to you in the present terms. An opportunity is afforded you of atoning for the wanton and unjustifiable mischief which you have inflicted upon Edwin St. Clair. Here is a paper, confessing that your charges were unfounded—your accusations malevolent. Sign this paper."

"I will not sign it!" exclaimed the old woman in a determined voice. "Do your worst!"

"You would not wish me, dame," responded Lady Lilla, with a remarkable sweetness of look and voice, "to take you at your word. Here!—look for one moment at this paper!"

I glanced towards Lady Lilla Essendine, who had now approached close up to the dame and was displaying a paper, the size of a sheet of foolscap, before her eyes.

"Well—and what is there here?" demanded Dame Betty.

"Look!—read *this* portion attentively," rejoined Lady Lilla Essendine: and she pointed towards the paper which she held.

Then there was silence for nearly a minute. I again glanced towards them: Lady Lilla was still holding the paper before the dame's eyes:—the dame herself was looking dubiously as if there were a strong struggle of some nature taking place in her mind.

"I have brought pen and ink with me," said Lady Lilla; and in a moment she produced a very small morocco case containing a gold pen and a little ink-bottle. "You see, my good woman, I require nothing but your signature here; and——"

She stopped short: but as I again glanced towards her for an instant, I caught an expression of deep significancy just as it was vanishing from her countenance.

"Well then, give me the pen!" said Dame Betty suddenly.

Lady Lilla drew the old woman towards the table; and then within a few moments the document was signed. But at the same instant I beheld Dame Betty hastily thrust something into her pocket; and methought that the action was accompanied by the rustling of paper.

"Ah! I forgot to ask," she exclaimed, "when I shall be set free from this place?"

"Within an hour after I myself have left it," replied Lady Lilla; "and the moment when I *shall* leave it now depends upon the result of a little conversation which I am about to have with Miss Percy, if she will be kind enough to grant me her attention."

Thus speaking, Lady Lilla crossed the room from the vicinage of the table to the spot where I was standing upon the other side; and the expression of her countenance was that of the most lady-like courtesy, and of the sweetest affability, as if we were bosom-friends without a hostile thought between us. I however bent upon her a look

which showed how well I knew her, and how deeply I abhorred her character. For an instant a flush crossed her countenance; but the next moment she said with a sweet smile, "While dealing with the old woman, I had no objection that you should hear what took place between us: but now that I have to deal with *you*, we will converse in whispers if you think fit."

"I have no secrets of any kind with Lady Lilla Essendine," I said, stepping back a pace or two.

"Oh, very well," she observed, without the slightest change of tone or manner. "Then, as you have no objection for this worthy dame to hear what may transpire between us, I will speak out. You have heard me tell her that this morning at ten o'clock Edwin St. Clair goes forth free again into the world, and doubtless with a compliment from the presiding Judge at the Old Bailey. Ah! it is now nine o'clock," she continued, looking at her watch: "in another hour he will be at liberty!"

"Might I inquire wherefore you address these observations to me?" I asked.

"Simply to show you," replied Lady Lilla, "that whatsoever design *you* may have had——"

"I can answer for it," exclaimed Dame Betty, "that Miss Percy had no design of the sort: for she would not even have left Kelvedon Hall last night if it had not been for me."

"Nevertheless," resumed Lady Lilla, "Miss Percy may feel indignant at having been detained a prisoner in this place all night—she may be inspired with vindictive feelings—old rancours may have revived; and therefore it is to guard against the consequences——"

"You must not expect, Lady Lilla Essendine," I said, "to intimidate me, nor to work upon my mind as by some strange unknown means you have contrived to render your influence paramount over this woman. I will sign no paper."

"No, Miss Percy," answered Lady Lilla, "the highest compliment is about to be paid you. All that you have to do is to pledge your most solemn word of honour that you will keep the seal of silence upon your lips in respect to everything which has happened since last night—and you also shall be set at liberty. Indeed I might even dispense with enjoining this stipulation at all; for I think that under all circumstances, you, Miss Percy, would be little likely to apply to a justice of the peace, or indeed to give publicity——"

"And wherefore should I not seek to punish those who have perpetrated such an outrage against me?" I inquired.

"Because you would have to tell, Miss Percy," rejoined Lady Lilla, with the self-sufficient smile of one who is about to adduce an unanswerable argument,—"because you would have to tell how you went to Kelvedon Hall accompanied by a gipsy, whom you introduced under circumstances of stealthiness: for as you may now comprehend, you have been watched——"

"Ah!" I ejaculated, as I felt my cheeks glow with indignation.

"Oh, be easy on that score, my dear Miss Percy!" responded Lady Lilla. "I do not wish to pry into any of your secrets, provided that you will leave mine alone. I do not know why you went to Kelvedon Hall—and I do not care to know: but I am very certain that there is something connected with your visit thither which demands secrecy, or at least forbids exposure. You see therefore that I am already in possession of something which is almost as good as a guarantee that even of your own accord you would be inclined to place the seal of silence upon your lips. Therefore it is really a mere trifling matter of form for you to give the pledge which I have just now demanded."

I at once saw how impolitic it would be on my part to allow Lady Lilla Essendine to suppose that there was really something so very secret and important in my visits to Kelvedon Hall, and that therefore she had really gained a certain advantage over me by the shrewdness of a guess. I accordingly said with an air of indifference, "Your ladyship is mistaken. The whole world may know for what purpose I sought Kelvedon Hall; and without incurring the imputation of arrogance or vanity, I may add that I am not accustomed to do anything which I should blush to have known."

"Oh! but persons may have motives for doing good actions in secret," ejaculated Lady Lilla, with a look that showed me she was not my dupe in respect to the indifference with which I had affected to treat the allusion to Kelvedon Hall. "However, on that score I need say nothing farther. I leave it to yourself to weigh in your own mind whether you think fit to give me the pledge I have demanded as the price of your liberty at the expiration of an hour; or whether——"

"Yes—speak the alternative," I said, perceiving that she hesitated.

"Or else you will remain here for some two or three days longer," continued Lady Lilla,—"indeed until there be time for me to write a letter from Calais or Boulogne, to order my myrmidons to set you at liberty. You see, therefore, there is no disguise in my intentions; and I really leave you, my dear Miss Percy, the arbitress of your own fate."

"And you," I said, feeling the indignant blood boiling within me, "have dared to treat me in this outrageous manner!—to make me pass the night in this vile place!—you who ought to go down upon your knees before me and thank heaven that no accusing voice was raised against you when nearly two years back, in the drawing-room at the Normans' house in Hunter Street, you meant to lay me dead at your feet! But heaven preserved me *then*, as it had watched over me before, and as it will continue to watch over me still! Go then! You shall obtain no pledge from my lips. And now address me not in another syllable."

"Insensate that you are, Ellen!" ejaculated Lady Lilla Essendine, now losing her self-possession and suddenly displaying all the evidences of the fierce rage that had been excited within her. "Know you not that you are in my power? One word from my lips will seal your doom!"

"And one word from my lips," I responded, "will render you all ghastly and quivering with terror: for I tell you that you are a *murderess!*"

"Wretch!" ejaculated Lady Lilla Essendine; and she did indeed become ghastly, and she was indeed quivering from head to foot,—her whole appearance being so changed that it seemed an impossibility to believe she was the same lovely and fascinating creature who a few minutes back had stood there.

I retreated three or four steps; for the idea struck me that she might have a white rose about her person, as I knew that there was more than one in the world; and for that fleeting moment indeed I was surprised at my own audacity in flinging the terrible name of murderess at her.

"Now listen to me, Ellen Percy," she said, speaking in a low voice, but the accents of which denoted a deep concentrated rage. "You have alluded to an occasion nearly two years ago, at the house of your friends the Normans in Hunter Street. Do you not remember what on that occasion I told you?—that not to be my friend was to be my enemy! This was no idle saying—nor did it imply a futile menace on my part, as I may yet teach you to your cost! Keep to your hostility if you will—proclaim it openly if you think fit, instead of contenting yourself with pursuing it stealthily! I will show you whether you would gain much by such a course. Now I leave you. You are too independent to give a pledge; I am too independent to demand it again from your lips."

"Ah! is it so?" I ejaculated: and the next instant my hands were at the throat of Lady Lilla Essendine.

So sudden and so powerful was my attack, that she was completely overpowered in the twinkling of an eye; and she fell upon the floor.

"Let her go, Miss Percy!—don't be a fool!" ejaculated Dame Betty. "Those ruffians will come up and murder us!"

"Be quiet, dame!" I said, in a most peremptory manner. "Listen!"

And we did both listen, while my hands were still upon Lady Lilla's throat,—my looks showing such stern determination that she evidently thought I should strangle her outright at the first indication of an attempt to cry or to resist. For several moments we listened; and still all was silent.

"Now," I said, "you see, Lady Lilla, that thus the victory is my own, and the momentary conflict has not reached the ears of your myrmidons. Answer me!—for you see that I am desperate, inasmuch as my position was rendered desperate by your menaces. Tell me in what part of the building is the young man confined, who was captured by your ruffians in the middle of the night? Beware how you deceive me; for I must inform you that this is not the first time I have been a prisoner in these ruins, and I am familiar with their situations and details."

"That young man," said Lady Lilla, who was just enabled to speak in a whisper as I loosened to the slightest degree the gripe which I had upon her throat,—"that young man is a certain William Lardner——"

"Yes, yes—I know it!" I ejaculated: "he was a sailor on board the yacht where you used to meet Edwin St. Clair and plot your horrible schemes for my destruction. I demand to know where he is now confined: for doubtless these ruffians told you on your arrival?"

"They have him down below," replied Lady Lilla: "he is along with themselves."

"Now, dame," I said, hastily addressing myself to the old woman, "go boldly down stairs—say that you are free—that you have come to terms with her ladyship—and tell Lardner that he is to walk up. If the men offer to accompany him, say that it is needless, for that I likewise am free, and that William Lardner is only required to give a certain pledge in order to be restored to liberty also."

"Yes, yes," said Dame Betty: "but first of all let me get back the paper I signed just now——"

"We will have it presently!" I hastily interrupted her: "for you must return to this room with William Lardner. Yes—be sure and return, that it may give a colour to a proceeding which would otherwise look suspicious."

The dame accordingly quitted the room, closing the door behind her; and I said to Lady Lilla, "Your life is at my mercy. A few moments' pressure of my thumb, and your life is extinct! Remain perfectly tranquil therefore, while I thus suffer you to breathe; for you see that my eyes are fixed keenly upon you, and at the faintest motion of the lips which may seem to herald an attempt to send forth a cry, my fingers shall fasten upon you as if this hand of mine were an iron vice."

Lady Lilla Essendine gazed up at me with an expression of countenance which I can scarcely define;—it was vague, and almost vacant under the influence of consternation—for she evidently thought that I was fully nerved to desperation, and therefore capable of fulfilling the threats to which I had just given vent. And desperate I indeed was, though I do not know that I should have gone to such an extent as to take her life, even though it were to prevent her from screaming out and thereby imperilling my own. The minute or two which followed were full of acutest suspense; and when I heard footsteps beginning to ascend the ricketty staircase, I felt as if all my energy must melt away in a moment and that I must shriek out for mercy; for my first impression was that they were the hurried footsteps of the excited ruffians which were thus ascending. But I was soon relieved of this cruel uncertainty; for the door opened, and the dame reappeared, followed by William Lardner. There was an abrasion upon his forehead—but I was infinitely rejoiced to perceive at a glance that it was by no means serious; and William himself testified his delight and astonishment at beholding the position which matters had now assumed.

"Are the men below thrown totally off their guard?" I hastily inquired.

"Yes—perfectly," replied William. "The appearance of the dame satisfied them in a moment; and indeed, one said to his companions that 'he knew it would be all right the instant her ladyship came.'"

"And you think that you can walk out unmolested, William?"

"I am certain I can," rejoined Lardner, with an air of unmistakable confidence.

"But let me go away first!" interrupted the dame. "I have particular reasons—very particular——"

"Be silent!" I interrupted her peremptorily. "Before you had got fifty paces from the ruins the whole proceeding might be discovered—you would be pursued and caught—whereas William

will speed at a rate baffling all pursuit—he will hasten to Petersfield——"

"Yes, yes," said William: "tell me what I am to do!"

"Petersfield," I said, "is about two miles distant. How long will you be——"

"How long?" ejaculated Lardner. "In twenty minutes I will be there."

"Good!" I said. "But tarry you there precisely one hour after reaching it; and if at the expiration of that time you do not see me appear in safety at the hotel, lose not another moment in giving the requisite information to the authorities—and say that Lady Lilla Essendine is the authoress or the instigatrix of whatsoever evil may be discovered within the walls of these ruins!"

"I will depart at once," said William. "Your commands, Miss, shall be executed to the very letter!"

"Ah! but one word more!" I ejaculated. "Here, Dame Betty—thrust your hand beneath her ladyship's shawl. There! draw forth the paper which you just now signed! No, no! you are not to keep it! Give it to William!—it will be an evidence——Be quiet! I warn you!" and I bent a menacing look upon Lady Lilla; for I thought on the instant that she was on the point of screaming out. "There, William!—secure that paper in your pocket!—and now depart!"

Lardner issued from the room, closing the door behind him.

"Watch from the window, dame," I said; "and see that he issues forth in safety from the ruins."

The old woman accordingly took her post at the window looking upon the back premises; while I, still with one knee upon the prostrate form of Lady Lilla Essendine, kept both my hands about her throat as if thus griping it in an iron vice. I retained likewise my looks keenly bent upon her eyes—flinging my regards down into their depths, as if therein to fathom the very purposes of her soul. In a few moments Dame Betty ejaculated, "He is safe!"—and then I began to breathe more freely.

CHAPTER CXI.

LADY LILLA AND ELLEN.

YES—I breathed more freely, for I felt that an immense advantage had been gained: but I did not relax my hold upon Lady Lilla's throat. Ah, that beautiful throat!—I may here parenthically observe that it was destined to bear for several days the black and blue marks imprinted by my fingers; for so soft was the skin that it was easy of discolouration.

"Keep watch, dame!" I said. "Is he pursued?"

"No—it is all right," she responded. "There! he has leapt the gate!—he is now proceeding along the road between this yard and the next! Ah! now he begins to run!—he is proceeding at a tremendous pace!"

"And there is no pursuit?" I inquired, with increased exultation.

"None," rejoined the dame.

Still I kept my fingers menacingly upon the

throat of the prostrate lady, for I was determined to give William Lardner as much opportunity as possible of distancing the chances of a pursuit: but still I felt that I could not for many minutes longer keep in my present position; for my arms were getting benumbed and my fingers were growing stiff. Yet in my soul there was a sense of ineffable joy to think that I had thus triumphed over this lady whose very courtesy had at first been a supercilious insult, whose softly glossed self-sufficiency was a most galling arrogance, and whose menaces at the last had proved still more chafing to my spirit; for I possessed my own pride as well as anybody else.

"He is out of sight!" said the dame, at the expiration of about three minutes.

"Now, Lady Lilla," I said, "I am about to release you. Whether you choose to raise an alarm and bring up those ruffians to assassinate myself and this old woman, it is for you to decide. At all events you see the precautions which I have taken—and you will therefore act at your peril. Now rise."

Thus speaking, I relinquished my hold upon her throat,—at the same time hastily stepping backward in order to avoid any sudden attack which in her infuriate rage she might think fit to make upon me. I thus reached the table, and took up a knife which lay there, to show her that my energies still continued firm and resolute. But there was no need for these precautions: Lady Lilla strove to rise—she gasped—a gurgling sound came up from her throat—and she fell back in a state of insensibility. I hastened to her assistance: I raised her in my arms; and I bade Dame Betty sprinkle water upon her face. Several minutes elapsed before she recovered her consciousness; and thus there was a still further interval gained to ensure the unpursued flight of William Lardner.

"Where am I?" asked Lady Lilla, as she opened her beautiful large blue eyes; and then, as a train of recollections evidently swept with the velocity of a whirlwind through her brain, her countenance became convulsed with the agitation of all the direst passions that could possibly find a place in the human heart.

"I do not wish to triumph ungenerously over you," I said; "but you *must* see that you are now in my power. Perhaps you would do well to listen to me ere you think of summoning assistance."

Lady Lilla flung upon me a look of indescribable hatred, as she rose up from my arms and tottered to a seat. I resumed possession of the knife, and rushed to the window to assure myself that the dame had not been deceived by her own eyesight. Not a soul was in view; and my heart leapt as I thought that ten good minutes had now elapsed since the faithful gipsy youth had fled from the ruins—and in another ten minutes he would be at Petersfield.

"You have conquered, Ellen," said Lady Lilla Essendine; "and now will you come to terms?"

"It is not for you to dictate terms," I answered: "it is for me to proclaim my own stipulations."

"And what are these?" asked Lady Lilla.

"That you immediately intimate to the men below that they are to suffer this woman and myself to go hence unmolested. Perhaps you will

tell me that our lives are in your power," I continued. "Yes!—no doubt it is so, with foes as wicked as yourself and as desperate as your myrmidons! But on the other hand remember that William Lardner can tell a tale which would send you and those men to the scaffold, if you dare have recourse to extreme measures towards us!"

Lady Lilla appeared to reflect for a few moments; and then she said, humbly and submissively, "I must confess, Ellen, that I am thoroughly vanquished. I know you are not malignant—I know you are not revengeful. If you will consent to bury this present adventure in oblivion, you shall never hear of me again: and I will undertake to promise that you shall never more hear of Edwin St. Clair either. I am promising in reference to the latter nothing more than I can perform."

I felt that I had achieved a grand triumph, and that it was all the more signal inasmuch as whatsoever the contents of the foolscap sheet of paper might be which Dame Betty had signed, it was as good as in my own possession, and was almost sure to constitute some hold upon Lady Lilla and St. Clair, and strengthen the power which former circumstances had given me over them. I also reflected that by refusing terms I might goad her to desperation, and provoke her to run any risk; for I could not forget that she had three desperadoes in her service. I therefore said, "I am satisfied, Lady Lilla, with the triumph I have accomplished and the lesson I have taught you. Being a heroine upon the stage, I do not seek to render myself a heroine in real life. Besides, my time is valuable, and I have no desire to waste it in proceedings before the local magistrates. Suffer me and this woman to depart without further molestation; and I promise you that I have on hand business of a more important character than to seek for any additional revenge for the atrocity of your conduct."

"Prepare to depart," replied Lady Lilla; "and from the head of the stairs I will call to the men, bidding them suffer you and this woman to issue forth unmolested."

"Be it so," I said. "But remember, if you hear any report in reference to this outrage, you must attribute it to other sources: for not even to such a one as *you* would I wilfully break whatsoever might savour of a promise. The postilion, for instance, may have told the tale——"

"No—he is silenced," answered Lady Lilla.

"What?" I ejaculated: "was he bribed?"

"Not *before* the attack took place," rejoined her ladyship. "But very soon afterwards I was on the spot; and I can assure you that beyond a few bruises the postilion was uninjured. He was stunned, but soon brought back to consciousness; and then a liberal reward placed a seal upon his lips."

"My house in London had been watched—was it not so?" I asked, determined to glean all particulars, if possible.

"Yes—your house was watched by one of the men down stairs. Dame Betty had long been looked for: she was seen entering your house the other evening—and then the day before yesterday you were both seen to leave London by different means of conveyance."

"And you were on the alert," I ejaculated, "at the time I was leaving my house in a postchaise:

for I caught a glimpse of your countenance in a cab."

"Yes: and I saw you likewise," rejoined Lady Lilla. "And now perhaps it may be as well for me to tell you, Dame Betty, that notwithstanding the paper which you have signed, has passed out of my possession — though you still retain the bank-note for a thousand pounds——"

"Yes, yes—and I mean to keep it!" cried the dame, querulously, as she placed her hand upon her pocket: "for I signed the paper—and it is not my fault if you have not still got it. Besides it is a part of the present conditions that I keep the bank-note—is it not, Miss Percy? is it not?"

I made no answer; and Lady Lilla Essendine at once said, "Yes, keep it, dame—keep it; and let there be peace between us. But I was about to observe that in reference to the trial of this morning, such a host of witnesses are now gathering—yes, at this very moment — to serve the cause of Edwin St. Clair,—such immense exertions have been made—and so many influential friends induced to come forward to speak to his high character,—while so many damnatory circumstances are ready to be adduced against yourself, that even if this stratagem to keep you away had failed, and even if now by some magical process you could transport yourself into the witness-box of the court, the chances are ten to one that you would experience the most signal failure. I have nothing more to say; and I am ready to fulfil my part of the compact by emancipating you both."

On my side I had no inclination to hear any more even if there were more to tell; and I had nothing more to ask. I therefore put on my bonnet and shawl: the dame enveloped herself in her cloak—and we prepared to take our departure. I had little fear that Lady Lilla would develop any fresh phase of treachery; for all the odds were now so tremendously against her. Nor was I deceived; for as we descended the stairs, she cried from the summit, "It is all settled—and you can suffer them to depart."

The three men were smoking in the lower room; they took but little notice of us; and we issued forth from amidst the ruined farm-buildings. As the reader may suppose, I was considerably rejoiced to breathe once more the fresh air of freedom; but I felt wearied and indisposed by the long restless night which I had passed and the anxiety of mind I had suffered. Indeed I longed to reach the hotel at Petersfield, not merely to assure William Lardner of my safety, but likewise that I might obtain those refreshments which were so necessary.

For upwards of five minutes Dame Betty and I walked together without a word being exchanged between us; we were both absorbed in our own thoughts. At length I said, "What was the nature of the paper you signed?"

"I have no more idea, Miss, than you yourself can possibly have," replied the woman.

"Ah! I understand," I exclaimed: "you saw the bank-note, and that was sufficient for you?"

She chuckled and placed her hand upon her pocket,—the horrid laugh and the movement constituting her only reply.

"And thus," I could not help observing, "after all your terrible hatred against Edwin St. Clair —after all your cravings for vengeance—after your almost sanguinary thirst for the very blood of that man—you suffered yourself to be bribed in a single moment!"

"Ah, my dear Miss, when you have lived as long as I have in the world," interjected the crone, "you will know how to make the best of a bad job. Why should I refuse a thousand pounds in my old age?"

I could not help thinking that she would perhaps have sold even Zarah for half the sum—or that she would now sell me in Lady Kelvedon's case, if Mr. Collingwood were to offer her a trifle more than the five hundred pounds which I had promised. As I have said on a former occasion, it was now my interest to conciliate the woman; and I therefore did not make any farther observations in respect to the bribe she had received from Lady Lilla Essendine.

"What do you propose to do?" I inquired.

"I have now nothing to do," she answered, "but to attend to your business. Perhaps, my dear young lady, I may procure at Petersfield the drug which I require."

"If so," I ejaculated, "it will be all the better; for now it is quite clear that you have no particular need to hasten to London."

"We will separate, Miss," responded Dame Betty, "as soon as we reach the outskirts of the town: and if in about three hours you send William Lardner to a certain public-house"—here she named it—"I will either give him the drug, or else I will let him know that I have failed to procure it—in which case I will make some other arrangement."

"And remember that in a week you are to see Lady Kelvedon again," I said.

"This day week, at six o'clock in the evening punctually, I will be in the shrubbery close to Kelvedon Hall. But you are going to the hotel in Petersfield. What about your luggage?"

"Ah! I forgot to speak upon the subject!" I exclaimed. "But no matter! I shall doubtless recover my portmanteau when passing through the town to which the postilion belonged."

I and Dame Betty now separated; and I entered the streets of Petersfield. I felt somewhat embarrassed at the idea of reaching the hotel on foot without any luggage,—not because I feared that I should be looked suspiciously upon in respect to the means of payment, but because I feared that the circumstance itself might expose my character to some animadversion. While I was reflecting on the point, I beheld William Lardner lounging about in the neighbourhood of the hotel: he at once caught sight of me, and hastened towards me.

"Thank heavens, you are safe, Miss Percy!" he ejaculated. "Oh, how anxious I have been! In twenty minutes more, I should have gone to the Mayor——"

"And now, William," I said, "it is unnecessary to make any exposure upon the subject. Follow me. We will presently find an opportunity of conversing upon the incidents that have just passed."

I proceeded to a shop where portmanteaus were sold, and purchased a small one. I then visited two or three other shops, in order to procure toilet articles and other little necessaries for immediate use; and at the best mercer's in the town

I bought some silks, gloves, and other things, as a present for Lady Kelvedon. The portmanteau was thus stocked—William Lardner carried it upon his shoulder—and I had now no longer any hesitation in proceeding to the hotel. Then how comfortable was it to perform my ablutions in a chamber with a cheerful fire blazing—and afterwards to sit down to an excellent breakfast. When this repast was concluded, I desired that "my servant" (thus alluding to William Lardner for the sake of appearances) might be sent to me.

"In the first place, William," I said, "let me thank you most earnestly for your intervention on my behalf. Tell me, how came you to find out that I was imprisoned at the farm-buildings?"

"Immediately after you left London on the morning of the day before yesterday," replied William, "Beda came to me and urged me to set off at once to be upon the look-out, for she was full of anxiety and feared lest some treachery were intended. I accordingly obtained leave of absence from my master, and took my departure. I stopped at a way-side public-house in the neighbourhood of Kelvedon Hall ;—and who should take up her quarters at the same place but Dame Betty ? I was careful to keep myself out of her sight; for I thought that if she were really behaving faithfully towards you, it would be useless to annoy her by letting her perceive that she was watched—and on the other hand, if she were behaving treacherously it would be all the more easy for me, when unseen by her, to discover and baffle her perfidy. Last evening she went out at about five o'clock—and I followed her at a distance. She entered Kelvedon Park by means of some opening in the fence : I did not like to follow her into that enclosure ; and I remained lurking about in the neighbourhood. After a while she reappeared, and proceeded along the road. Now again I dogged her movements ; and at the expiration of a short time a postchaise came out of the park. It stopped and took her up. I was concealed at no great distance from the spot : but then I scarcely knew how to act. I felt almost convinced that you were in the vehicle—that you were returning to London—that everything was right and straightforward—and that Beda's apprehensions were therefore unfounded. I accordingly made up my mind to get back also to the metropolis. I had paid my little score at the public-house, and I had about my person the few necessaries which I had thought fit to bring from London ; so that there was no need to retrace my steps to that way-side inn. I continued walking along the road, hoping that some conveyance would overtake me, or that when I got to the nearest town, I should find one. I proceeded tolerably fast ; and presently—it might perhaps have been about a mile and a half from Kelvedon Park—I saw a postchaise stopping in the middle of the road. On going up to it, I was struck with the idea that it was the one which I had seen halt to take up Dame Betty. At the same time I heard the sounds of another vehicle rolling along the road at a distance——"

"It could not have been the chaise-cart which took me and Dame Betty," I thought to myself ; "for that was too far down the lane to be heard in the road. But, Ah! it was doubtless the equipage which bore Lady Lilla Essendine : for

she told me that she was on the spot almost immediately after the postilion had been restored to consciousness."

"I hastened to the postchaise," continued William Lardner : "a glance thrown inside, showed me that it was empty ; and I put some questions to the postilion. He was reluctant to answer and guarded in his replies ; but I used threats—and after some trouble I elicited from him that there had been an attack—that a young lady and an old woman were carried off—but he did not know where. All he could tell me in addition was that he had received an assurance to the effect that their lives were quite safe, and that it was for some great law-business or another the proceeding took place. The postilion then mounted his horse and drove off, after having offered me a lift—which I however declined. I could not for the life of me comprehend whether Dame Betty was a principal in the plot and that she had suffered herself to be carried off for the sake of appearances—or whether she had now veritably become the victim of some treachery in her turn. I did not however waste any time in useless conjecture : I thought of the farm-buildings, and I fancied that if you were a prisoner anywhere in that neighbourhood, it would be at those buildings. I should tell you, Miss, that during the daytime I had ascertained, from inquiries at the public-house, exactly where they were situated ; and I have a pretty clear head in reference to the position of places —for this is one of the peculiarities of the gipsy race, and moreover as a sailor I know something about the points of the compass. Well, Miss, off I set to walk in the direction of those buildings ; and I reached them at length. I saw lights in one or two of the windows : I was then tolerably well convinced that I had followed up the right track. I crept stealthily towards a room on the ground-floor where one of those lights was burning : I listened to the discourse of two men who were there —but they were talking on matters which had no concern with their captives. I made a tour of the buildings ; and while engaged in this survey, I beheld the arrival of another person. He joined his companions : I again listened—but I could learn nothing of any consequence. I however need say no more—for you know the rest."

"I know, William, that your conduct has been most admirable !" I exclaimed ; "and you will be well rewarded. Those men kept you a prisoner amongst themselves from the instant of your capture to that of your deliverance ?" I added inquiringly.

"Yes : but they treated me well enough," answered William : "they did not bind me—they gave me food—but they signified very plainly that if I made the slightest attempt to escape I should have a pistol-bullet through my brains, for they were all provided with fire-arms."

"And now let me see that paper," I said, "which was taken from about the person of Lady Lilla Essendine."

"Ah, here it is !" replied William : and he produced it.

The document was drawn up in a legal style— the penmanship seemed to be that of a lawyer's clerk—and the phraseology had the same technical savour. It was to the effect that "the undersigned" (meaning Dame Betty) did thereby, of

ELLEN PERCY AS JULIET.

her own free will, confess the wicked falsehood of the imputations which she had advanced against the Right Honourable Edwin St. Clair; that having failed in an endeavour to extort money from that gentleman, she had devised those accusations, partly in a spirit of vindictiveness, and partly with the idea that even at the eleventh hour they might have the effect of so intimidating Mr. St. Clair as to accomplish a drain upon his purse; that she now deeply regretted the iniquitous course she had so adopted; that being aware of the intimate acquaintance, and indeed kinship, which existed between the Right Honourable Edwin St. Clair and Lady Lilla Essendine, she had applied to her ladyship to learn how she was to act in order to display her contrition, and yet save herself from the consequences of perjury, slander, and defamation; that Lady Lilla Essendine, having taken legal advice, decided upon obtaining the

signature of the repentant woman to this present document, with the understanding that if need were, the undersigned (meaning Dame Betty) should appear before a magistrate and confirm by affidavit the statements made in the said document.

Such was the tenour of the paper which I now perused; and I resolved to keep it in case it should ever prove useful in the bringing of St. Clair and Lady Lilla to that condign punishment which I felt assured must sooner or later prove their doom. I now instructed William Lardner to repair to the public-house named by the old gipsy-woman, and during his absence I walked out into the town.

As I was proceeding along a street, I met a young lady whose countenance at once struck me as being far from unknown; for it was assuredly one of the most lovely faces that ever my eyes had rested upon. She evidently at once recognised me: she accosted me by name—and then the next instant I recollected her as Miss Barron, the governess in the Tremaine family.

I greeted her cordially; for I had conceived a liking for her, even during the brief half-hour that I had been in her company five or six days back; and I inquired if by any accident Mr. and Mrs. Tremaine and her family had come to Petersfield?

"No, Miss Percy," replied Sarah Barron; "they left London for Tremaine Hall in Staffordshire the day before yesterday. But I have obtained a week's holiday to visit my relations, who live in this town. I have not seen them for two years—I had been upon the Continent with Mr. Tremaine's family——"

"And doubtless therefore, Miss Barron," I said, "your relations were delighted to see you?"

"Ah, my poor mother was indeed rejoiced!" responded Sarah Barron, as the tears were sent up by the emotions of the heart to the brims of her beautiful blue eyes. "And my brother Reginald too——Ah, Miss Percy!" she ejaculated, thus interrupting herself; "it is really singular that I should have met you in Petersfield!"

"Singular?" I said, surprised at the observation; "and why is it singular?"

She blushed—looked confused for a moment—and then, with a smile of the most amiable sweetness, she said, "Those who are celebrated in the world, know not in what nooks and corners their names may be idolized or their talents admired. But have you half-an-hour to spare? Oh, you might render me the greatest possible service!"

"Rest assured, Miss Barron," I said, "if it be in my power to oblige you, I should do so with the utmost pleasure. But excuse me," I added with a smile, "if I remind you that your observations are full of mystery."

"Do come with me, Miss Percy, and the mystery will be cleared up! I can promise you a little surprise, which I am certain cannot give any offence—though it may assuredly fail to please as a compliment, accustomed as you must be to homage of every species. But pray come with me, Miss Percy!" cried the amiable Sarah, with a smile indescribably sweet. "My mother's house is close at hand—and she will be overjoyed to see you!"

"With pleasure will I accompany you," was my answer.

We accordingly walked on together; and I had now an opportunity of contemplating Sarah Barron more at my leisure than hitherto. She was not as tall as myself: indeed she was only of the medium stature—but her symmetry was perfect. The head was well poised upon the neck; the neck itself arched with a swan-like gracefulness, which gave alike elegance and dignity to the young lady's bearing. Her features were regular: the nose was perfectly straight—the mouth small and well-formed—the chin delicately rounded, and thus completing the oval of a matchless countenance. Her eyes were not large, but they were of a beautiful blue, soft in their expression, yet intelligent. Her age was about two-and-twenty; she dressed with considerable neatness, though in a plain unassuming manner; but her entire bearing bespoke good-breeding and gentility.

I was just speculating how it was that Sarah

Barron had been compelled to go out into the world as a governess, when she said to me, "I flatter myself, Miss Percy, that you will like my mother. She has known great misfortunes, but she has encountered them all with a true Christian resignation, so that her looks indicate a placid contentment and a mind at ease, instead of wearing a dejected or careworn expression. My father was a Colonel in the English army; but he accepted a General's appointment under Don Pedro's banner, and lost his pension, but not his rank, in the English service. I do not exactly know how all this was; but it is nevertheless as I tell you. Don Pedro owed my father about ten thousand pounds, in English money, and never paid him a shilling. Harassed and spirit-broken in the vain endeavour to prosecute his claims to a successful issue, my poor father died when I was still quite young; and my mother found herself a penniless widow. Some friends, compassionating her position, obtained in her behalf a pension of eighty pounds a year from the English Government, in consideration of the services of my father previous to his entrance into the Portuguese army. Upon that pension," added Sarah Barron, in a voice that was low and tremulous with emotion, "my mother subsisted respectably——she herself educated me entirely, for she is highly accomplished——and she fitted me to fill the situation of a governess. I owe everything to that kind and excellent mother!"

"And your brother, Miss Barron?" I said. "I think you just now spoke of a brother?"

"Yes," she answered; "my dear brother Reginald! You will see him. He is two years older than myself. His education was provided for by an old friend of our family—a celebrated painter, who took Reginald to live with him: but alas! he died suddenly when my brother was only about fifteen or sixteen; and thus the hopes which had been entertained——"

"I understand you, Miss Barron," I said, perceiving that she hesitated; "it was supposed that this kind friend would provide for your brother or give him some profession?"

"Yes," responded Sarah. "My brother had already conceived a taste for the fine arts; and the death of his kind friend was a great blow to his hopes and prospects. It is true that another friend took him by the hand and had him to reside with him in London at different times, especially on several occasions within these last two or three years. But alas! it turned out that his friend made promises which he never meant to fulfil, and in other ways deceived those hopes which he had excited in my poor brother's breast. So for the last six months Reginald has resided altogether at home with my dear mother; and this is one respect is more pleasing to me, because I know that it prevents her from feeling lonely—but in another respect it is to be deplored, inasmuch as in the metropolis only can my brother hope to make his way.—But here we are."

Miss Barron thus checked herself at the door of a small but neat-looking house, in a street which had an air perfectly respectable although narrow and retired. The door was opened by a neatly dressed modest-looking servant-girl; and Sarah introduced me into a little parlour, which was comfortably and genteelly, though plainly furnished. Her mother was there—a lady of about fifty years of age, with a serene and benevolent expression of countenance, and still with the lingering traces of a beauty which must have been great in her earlier years, and which her daughter had fully inherited. The moment I entered the room, I saw that Mrs. Barron surveyed me with earnest attention: then she gave a sudden start—she flung a look of inquiry upon her daughter—and again she fixed her eyes upon me.

"Oh, I know you!—yes, I recognise you!" she now exclaimed, hastening forward to welcome me: " the likeness is truly wonderful! Ah, my daughter told us that she had met you in London the other day—and we cannot tell you how much we longed to form your acquaintance likewise! Oh how rejoiced Reginald will be!"

At this moment the door opened; and a thin, pale, interesting young man, about four-and-twenty years of age, made his appearance. He was good-looking certainly, but not so handsome as a man as his sister was beautiful as a woman;—for this was Reginald Barron. The instant he saw me, he gave vent to a wild cry of delight—joy flashed in his eyes—a kindred animation glowed on his cheeks—he was the very personification of enthusiasm at that moment!

"My dear Miss Percy," said Sarah Barron, "I am afraid that all this must be more than mysterious to you!—it must even be annoying, and may appear rude! Come, let us explain it all in a moment!".

Thus speaking, she led the way up-stairs to a room on the first floor; and as she threw open the door, I perceived that it was an artist's *studio* to which I was being introduced. I crossed the threshold—I found myself face to face with a portrait which made me start: I glanced around—likeness upon likeness met my eyes—and on four distinct pieces of canvass was my countenance represented, just as if I beheld it reflected in so many mirrors!

CHAPTER CXII.

THE ARTIST.

YES—there were the portraits representing me in four of the principal characters which I was in the habit of personating on the stage. As Portia in the " Merchant of Venice " I was depicted with the forensic cap and gown; and the likeness instantaneously struck me as being most admirable. Next I contemplated myself in the character of the heroine in "Romeo and Juliet:" but on this piece of canvass there were two heads—for I was drawn in the act of discoursing with the old nurse, this latter face being an imaginary one. The third picture represented me as Lady Macbeth, when, as a somnambulist, she walks with a light in her hand. The fourth picture represented me as Mrs. Beverley in "The Gamester;" and this portrait was as perfect as the rest. On raising my eyes from the contemplation of the series, my looks encountered those of Reginald Barron; and I felt a blush rise up to my cheeks at the intentness with which he was regarding me. For it instantaneously struck me that it was not only with the studying gaze of an artist that he was surveying my features in order to catch any peculiar expression, but that he was inspired with another sentiment. Yes—I felt the colour glow upon my cheeks; and quickly averting my face, I affected to be again contemplating the portraits.

"Oh! now do you understand, my dear Miss Percy," exclaimed Sarah Barron, "when I said that you could do me a favour? My brother was anxious to survey you close—to catch the expression which might best be transferred to the canvass——"

"And I am sure Miss Percy cannot be annoyed or offended," cried Mrs. Barron; "for her talents have no worshipper more devout than Reginald!"

"And will Miss Percy pardon me my boldness," said Reginald meekly, " in having dared thus to make these poor attempts to transfer her countenance to the canvass?—will Miss Percy forgive me, I ask, that I should have taken such a liberty without in the first instance beseeching her consent?"

"Every one," I said, " has a perfect right to employ his talents according to his inclination or ability. You have taken no liberty, sir."

"And you are not offended with me," interposed Sarah, "for having brought you to the house for the purpose which I have named? Reginald was not satisfied with his portraits. Pardon him his vanity—but he declared that if he could only be in the same room with you for a few minutes, he could render his work so life-like——"

"Mr. Barron might have called upon me for such a purpose," I said: " other artists have done so; and I have assisted their labours to the utmost of my power. I hold that every public character must submit to certain claims that can be made upon him or her; and perhaps I shall not incur the imputation of vanity while confessing that if there must be portraits, engravings, and lithographs taken of my countenance, I would rather they should be as true to nature as possible, than owe anything to the imaginations of the designers."

While I was thus speaking, I addressed myself particularly to Miss Barron and her mother: yet for courtesy's sake I glanced once or twice towards Reginald, so as not to have the appearance of ignoring his presence altogether: but my looks were quickly averted again, for his eyes were fixed upon me with a most impassioned ardour. When a woman is the object of such a gaze, and comprehends the feeling which inspires it, she may notice it much more speedily than any casual bystanders might do: and thus I verily believe—indeed I am perfectly sure, that Mrs. Barron and her daughter did not comprehend the true meaning of Reginald's looks. They fancied that he was merely surveying me with that admiration for my talents which they supposed to have been the sole and simple motive for painting me in so many different styles.

"Yes—I might have called upon you, Miss Percy," said Reginald: " but how could I tell in what manner I should be received? I had no means of obtaining an introduction to you; and I feared to intrude as a stranger without a warrant for presenting myself. I might have told you that I was an artist and explained my object: but obscure and utterly unknown as I was—and still am

—how dared I hope that you would even receive me at all? It was all these considerations, Miss Percy, which prevented me from intruding myself upon your presence: but now that I have had this supreme happiness"—here his voice trembled for a moment—"you will see how it has inspired me!"

He took up his brush; and for about a minute he applied it to the face of the portrait which represented me as Portia.

"Now look!" he exclaimed, standing aside from the front of the canvass which rested upon an easel.

If it had not been for the discovery which I had made in respect of the young man's real feelings towards me, I do verily believe that an ejaculation of astonishment would have burst from my lips at the first glance which I flung upon that portrait. It had wanted but a touch to render it perfect as a likeness: that touch had been given—and it was indeed now perfect! I was always fond of the fine arts, and have ever been considered to possess some little taste in respect to paintings. I had now the deep conviction that these paintings were of a very high character: they did not merely give promise of future excellence—they were masterpieces in themselves. It was my duty to speak candidly on the point to the mother and daughter, as well as to the artist himself: but I did so in a manner to convince him that the homage which he had paid to me through the medium of his pencil, could exercise no influence beyond that of winning my gratitude and inspiring me with a feeling of interest in his future success.

While I still remained in the *studio*, Reginald Barron put the finishing stroke to the other three portraits; and I purposely tarried thus to afford him the opportunity of rendering his works as perfect as possible. Yet the task was a somewhat unpleasant one to me; for every time that Reginald Barron turned his eyes upon me, I observed in his regards that expression of impassioned ardour which had already more than once brought up a blush to my cheeks.

I descended into the parlour with Mrs. Barron and Sarah,—Reginald remaining behind in his *studio*. The moment I was alone with the two ladies, the mother threw her arms about my neck, exclaiming, in a voice full of emotion, "It is as if an angel had entered our house; for you have infused hope and joy into every heart!"

"Oh, yes!" murmured Sarah, much affected; "hope and joy into every heart!"

"The hope," I said, impressively, "that your son, my dear madam, may succeed!—the hope, Sarah," I added, in an equally emphatic manner, "that in your brother you may one day hail a great artist!"

"And now that his pictures are completed," said Mrs. Barron, "could you give me the slightest hint, my dear Miss Percy, in respect to the mode which he ought to adopt for their disposal?"

"My dear mother," interjected Sarah, "it is not exactly to Miss Percy that you ought to put the question. She has already proved so kind and good—besides I will ask Mr. Tremaine——"

"I myself should be glad to purchase one of those pictures," I said: "but I am delicate in making the proposition. I know not what value

to set upon it. And understand me well—understand me *well*," I repeated, "I would not for the world give less than any other purchaser might be disposed to offer."

"Reginald has no idea," said Mrs. Barron; "for several times when I have spoken to him about selling those four portraits, he has given me no satisfactory answer—he has turned the discourse into another channel——"

"I leave the matter in your hands, my dear madam," I said; "and at any time when you choose to communicate with me on the subject, I will remit you a cheque for the amount."

"And which portrait," inquired Mrs. Barron,—"which of the four, my dear Miss Percy, would you prefer?"

At that instant the parlour-door opened, and Reginald Barron made his appearance. He was paler than before; and it struck me that he staggered somewhat as he entered the room; so that I threw a second glance at him to ascertain whether he was really labouring under some strong feelings or not?

"Mother, what are you talking about?" he demanded, almost angrily. "My pictures are not for sale."

"Not for sale?" cried Mrs. Barron, in amazement, and likewise with affliction depicted upon her countenance. "Why, what on earth do you mean, Reginald?—for what have you toiled? Have you not adopted a profession by which you hope to live?—and was it not just now causing so much happiness to your sister and myself, because we heard from the lips of one who is a judge, the assurance that you *do* possess the talent and that you *will* shine?"

"Nevertheless, mother," said Reginald, taking a seat, "those four pictures are not for sale. I will at once begin to paint others—I will transfer to canvass the portraits of other celebrated persons ——Oh! I will work day and night to afford you pleasure, dear mother—and likewise you, my dear sister! God knows that if I could render you both rich and independent, it would be the happiest moment of my life to proclaim that you were so! But these four portraits," he added slowly and emphatically, "shall never be disposed of for gold."

"How silly of you, Reginald, to talk thus!" said Mrs. Barron. "You must not think that you are paying a compliment to Miss Percy by such conduct; because it is no compliment. Miss Percy knows perfectly well that an artist paints to live."

"You must now permit me to take my leave," I said; for I was anxious to get away from the midst of the scene which had so unexpectedly arisen.

"No, no—do not leave us immediately, my dear Miss Percy!" said Sarah Barron, who looked much distressed. "These little family matters ought to be reserved for discussion when we are alone together. You will dine with us—you will pass the day here——"

"I can assure you," I said, "that I must now take my departure. I am about to leave Petersfield to pay a visit to Kelvedon Hall——"

"And in a short time," ejaculated Sarah, "you will be at Tremaine Hall in Staffordshire, and I shall have the pleasure of meeting you there! Farewell, Miss Percy, if you *must* leave us."

I again made apologies for the necessity of taking my departure: I shook hands with Mrs. Barron and her daughter—I bowed with polite courtesy to Reginald—and in a few moments I was wending my way through the streets, back to the hotel,—thinking of all that had just occurred, and pitying the young artist for the infatuated passion which he had evidently conceived towards me.

On entering the hotel, the waiter said to me, "If you please, ma'am, a person has left a portmanteau addressed to you. I said you were out: he answered that it was all right."

"I daresay it is," I responded, instantaneously comprehending that this was my portmanteau which was in the postchaise at the time when the attack took place.

I ascended to my apartment, to which the portmanteau had been borne; and I found that my surmise was perfectly correct.

William Lardner returned at about two o'clock; and he placed a little paper package in my hand, observing that Dame Betty had given it to him to be delivered to me. I had now nothing more to detain me at Petersfield: but still I scarcely liked to return at once to Kelvedon Hall; for as it was not my purpose to say anything in reference to the adventures of the past night, I saw that I should be compelled to pretend that I had been to London and that I had thus returned so soon again. Lord Kelvedon himself might begin to think there was something strange in these rapidly successive comings and goings; and the domestics would assuredly entertain that opinion. Besides, I was very much fatigued through having been up the whole of the past night, and through having spent it so wretchedly. Therefore, all things considered, I determined to sojourn at Petersfield until the ensuing day: but I also purposed to keep entirely within the walls of the hotel in the meantime, so that the Barrons should not learn that I had remained in the town, and thereby have reason to feel offended at my having refused to partake of their hospitality. Having thus made up mind to tarry at the hotel until the next day, I thought it better to send William Lardner back to London; for I felt tolerably confident that I should not stand in any further need of his services. I accordingly dismissed him with a liberal reward—bidding him thank Beda for her kind consideration on my behalf, and to tell her that it would not be long ere I should return home again.

William Lardner took his departure: half-an-hour elapsed—and I was seated in my room at the hotel, reading a book which I had purchased, when the door opened and the waiter announced Mr. Barron.

I started for a moment: I felt the colour come and go in quick transitions upon my cheeks. I was both indignant and surprised; but I saw the necessity of instantaneously resuming an air of calm self-possession. The waiter withdrew: Reginald Barron stood before me. He was in a sort of artist's *deshabillée* when I had just now seen him at his mother's house: he then wore a *blouse*, his collar was turned down, and his hair was in disorder. Now he was apparelled in the raiment which was evidently his best—a genteel suit of black. His hair was well arranged; and altogether he

certainly appeared to much better advantage than when I had just now seen him. I comprehended the truth in a moment :—he had studied to look his best at this interview.

As if considering that it was quite an ordinary matter that we should have called upon me, I said with a polite courtesy, which was slightly cold, "I suppose, Mr. Barron, you have brought me some message from your mother or from your amiable sister?"

"No, Miss Percy," he answered: "they do not even know that I have called."

"Then might I at once inquire," I said, "what is the business that has brought you hither?"

"I could not have rested another hour," ejaculated Reginald vehemently, "until I had given you an explanation! Pray therefore listen! You spoke to my mother of purchasing one of my pictures——"

"And if I therein did wrong, Mr. Barron," I said in a somewhat peremptory manner, "you have my excuses. I now request that nothing more may be said on the subject; and you will be kind enough to leave me."

"I cannot leave you!" he cried, with the same impassioned vehemence as before. "There must be an explanation!"

"But I ask for none, sir," I said, with a look and tone of rebuke.

"But there are positions, Miss Percy," he quickly rejoined, "where explanations may be given when they are not sought. This is now *our* case. I who was so bashful, so trembling and shrinking, that I dared not venture to knock at your door in London to beseech a moment's interview with you,—am now bold enough to force myself into your presence! Yes—for 'tis you yourself that have made me bold!—you yourself that have given me this courage: for you have spoken hopefully and encouragingly *to* me and *of* me! Ah! take care, Miss Percy, that you have not driven me mad and wild with the intoxication of joy!"

"Now, Mr. Barron," I said, "if you be thus speaking with the enthusiasm of an artist elated by the honest opinion that has been passed upon his pictures, I can forgive you—I can even understand it. But if in any other sense you are addressing me, I must desire—nay, command, that you at once take your departure."

"No, no!—you must and shall hear me!" he exclaimed, with vehemence of gesture. "Do you know why I have painted so many representations of your matchless beauty?—do you know why I would not sell those pictures for all the gold that the earth's mines could produce? Do you know why my cheek is pale—why my form is attenuated—and why illness has fastened its claws upon me?—consumption perhaps——I know not——but something that is tearing at my very vitals! And I have said nothing of all this to my poor mother or my fond sister; for why should I render them unhappy? I have suffered in secret—in secret I must still suffer! I know that what I aspire to is hopeless: I see that your love can never be mine! But, Oh! Miss Percy, you need not have treated me with scorn and contempt at one moment—with that freezing, glacial politeness at another! You might have been more merciful!"

I should have interrupted the young man—I

should have commanded him to be silent and to leave me—I should have pursued the same peremptory course with which I had commenced, were it not that I was afraid of creating a scene in the hotel, and bringing up the domestics to listen at the door, even if they did not burst into the room itself to ascertain what was the matter. Thus I had suffered Reginald Barron to continue speaking,—hoping that when he should have given full vent to his feelings in a volume of words, he would become more temperate.

"Be reasonable," I said. "You do not reflect how you may compromise me in this place. Your behaviour, sir, is not generous. You accuse me of treating you with scornfulness:—I utterly deny the imputation. I behaved to you with a suitable courtesy, considering that our acquaintance was altogether of scarcely an hour's duration."

"But I have known you for the last two years!" exclaimed Reginald Barron. "I have been the first to arrive at the theatre, and the last to leave it on the nights when you performed! I was there early to watch for your appearance, and gloat over the idea that I was breathing the same atmosphere with yourself. In imagination I sent my regards penetrating through curtain and scenery — aye, and through walls likewise — to seek you out where you were arraying yourself for the character which you had to perform:—and, Oh! this was a bliss ineffable! Then who applauded you more loudly than I?—who was more enthusiastic——"

"Cease, Mr. Barron!—cease!" I said, entreatingly: "in the name of heaven cease! You terrify me!"

"No, no! I must continue until the end!" he ejaculated: and it now appeared to me as if he was actually experiencing a fierce pleasure in compelling me to listen to him, because he saw I was afraid of a disturbance being created in the hotel. "Yes—I will speak on to the end! I have told you why I was early at the theatre on those nights when you performed: I will tell you why I was also one of the last to leave. It was because I loved to look upon the spot where you had been—the boards where you had trod! Again was imagination at work; and it depicted you there, all glowing in your grand beauty——"

"Sir, I will hear no more!" I exclaimed, now driven by indignation to adopt a peremptory course once more. "Your language is such that I cannot listen to it! Know, then—for I am not ashamed to tell you—that my heart's affections are fully engaged, and that my hand is pledged to another. Now, sir, I appeal to you as a gentleman, —will you continue to address me in a strain which amounts to a persecution? Ah! I remember something which you said just now, and to which I ought to reply. You accused me of adopting a glacial demeanour towards you. I tell you again that I treated you with that amount of politeness which was due from a lady to a gentleman when they met for the first time. How inconsistent has been your conduct! You just now thanked me for having given you words of hope——"

"Hope as an artist!" ejaculated Reginald Barron; "but not that hope which would have proved the most delicious that could have been infused into my soul! I tell you, Miss Percy, that you have nearly driven me mad! For heaven's sake

take compassion on me! No one will ever love you so dearly——"

"Sir," I interrupted him, "it is impossible this scene can last! What would your mother say if she beheld you thus outraging one who had expressed an interest in your success?"

"I cannot now think of my mother!" interjected Reginald: "I can think only of you!"

"Oh! but this is too much!" I said, cruelly bewildered. "You love your sister—do you not? She is amiable and good: I also love her—I would seek to make her my friend—I am sure that she entertains friendly feelings towards myself! But what would she think if she knew that you had sought me here—defenceless and unprotected as I am at the moment—to heap these insults upon me?"

"I cannot pause to think of my sister!" he exclaimed. "I tell you that I am mad! Every additional instant that I stand here gazing upon your transcendant beauty, my soul seems fired with flames that are consuming my very vitals! You shall be mine! There is a tyranny which even the most devoted love can exercise!—indeed it is love's last resource!—and such a tyrant am I now becoming towards you: for I am driven to desperation! Yes—by heaven! it is impossible to remain here in your presence——"

"Be calm!—be calm, I conjure you, Mr. Barron!" I said: for he was growing so excited, his speech was so vehement, and his eyes were flaming upon me to such an extent, that I was frightened that if he did not raise an alarm in the hotel, he would on the other hand attempt some violence against myself. "Be calm!" I repeated. "Sit down—suffer me to retire for a few moments that I may tranquillize my own feelings—and then I will return and converse quietly with you on all these points."

He reflected for a few moments; and then he said, with the air of one who felt that he had all the advantage on his own side, "Well then, be it so! Withdraw for a few minutes. Perhaps I have been too vehement—perhaps I have given way too much to my feelings! But come back soon—and you shall find me more reasonable."

I gladly availed myself of this opportunity to quit the apartment. In order for the better understanding of what is to follow, I must explain that there was a little landing at the head of the staircase: my sitting-room opened on the right hand—my bed-chamber was exactly opposite. But facing the stairs there was a third room, of very small dimensions—which I had noticed, when the door was accidentally left open, to be likewise a bed-chamber. The reader will be pleased to bear these circumstances in mind.

On issuing from my sitting-room, I hastily crossed the landing in order to seek my bed-chamber. I had closed the door of the sitting-room behind me: but at the very instant that I was entering my chamber, Reginald Barron looked out of the apartment where I had left him, saying in a rapid whisper, "For heaven's sake be not too long! You have inspired me with hope—and you shall find me reasonable!"

He instantaneously re-entered the sitting-apartment, closing the door; and I precipitated myself into the chamber. I had already made up my mind how to act. I hastily put on my bonnet and shawl—stole forth from the room—glided down the staircase — and passed into the street. I felt assured that the young man was half demented. It would have been easy for me to summon the waiters, or place myself under the protection of the landlady of the establishment: but, as the readers are aware, I had always entertained an unconquerable dislike to render myself the heroine of a scene that might provoke gossip and scandal. I therefore thought that the best plan would be to go out and walk for an hour, so that the insensate young man might have leisure for cool reflection—in which case he might possibly be brought to a sense of the impropriety of his conduct and take his departure. If he should act otherwise, I thought to myself, and persist in remaining in my apartment at the hotel, it would then be time enough to adopt stringent measures on my return. There were other reasons why I was loath to take extreme steps unless driven to them as a last resource. I knew that if he created a disturbance in the hotel, he would be given into custody; and I wished to save his mother and sister the consequences of such an ignominy. It was this consideration which now prevented me from proceeding straight to their house, and invoking their aid to shield me against further persecution on the part of Reginald.

It was all very annoying indeed. I seemed to be no sooner freed from one disagreeable adventure, than I was plunged headlong into the midst of another. But still I hoped that the step I was now taking would have the desired effect—and that when the young man should find he had been outwitted, he would become humiliated and crest-fallen, and retreat from the quarters where I had left him.

I walked about the streets of Petersfield for an hour—taking care to avoid the neighbourhood in which Mrs. Barron's house was situated. The dusk was closing in at about four o'clock—for it was the middle of December—when I retraced my way to the hotel. The weather was fine: I had walked rapidly — my spirits were cheered — my mind was invigorated; and I resolved to act with the utmost firmness in case there should now arise a necessity for the adoption of such a course. I ascended the staircase — the gas was already lighted upon the landing—and I noticed that the door of the chamber facing the stairs stood half open. A light was burning in that room: a lady was standing in front of a mirror, in the act of gazing upon a necklace of pearls which she held in her hand. She was in evening costume, with a low body and short sleeves: she had a beautiful head-dress formed of pearls; and her figure struck me as being fine and symmetrical. Her back was towards me; and why the door should be open while she was thus engaged in her toilet, I could not at the moment understand. However, she was dressed, and there was consequently nothing indecent in her appearance—though the fact itself was either indelicate or thoughtless. On hearing footsteps at the head of the staircase, she called out in a somewhat petulant tone, "Come, chambermaid! do make haste with that band-box!"

Her words at once revealed to me how it was that she was thus standing there with the door open; and her voice was instantaneously recognised by me: for this elegantly apparelled personage was none other than Melissa Harrison.

At the same time she turned round, and caught sight of me. I should observe that it was upwards of two months since I had seen her—the last occasion being on the night when she so grossly insulted Miss Parks at the theatre,—since which date she had disappeared from my view. But here she was suddenly turning up again, at the hotel at Petersfield—elegantly dressed—and looking, I am bound to confess, handsomer perhaps than I had ever before known her!

"Ah, Miss Percy!" she said; "is it you? I thought it was that stupid girl of a chambermaid, who understands nothing, and is awkward at everything!—leaving the door wide open——"

I was passing into my own chamber, without taking any further notice of Melissa, when she came rushing after me, exclaiming, "Let us be friends! Surely you must have forgiven me by this time for any ill I have ever done you?—and you know that I always liked you!"

"If you are really sorry, Melissa," I said, in a somewhat severe tone, "for any injury you have ever done me, I will not say that I cannot forgive. But as for the revival of friendship between us, it is impossible; and I beseech that our interview may end here."

I entered my bed-chamber; and was about to close the door, but Melissa followed me.

"Is it possible," she cried, "that you can bear me so much ill-will: I did not think you were vindictive!"

"I am not vindictive, Melissa," I said, still speaking with a calm severity: "but there are offences which cannot so easily be forgotten. Pray do not let us dispute. I will not in any way interfere with you—I have no wish to do so: pray do not interfere with me."

"Oh, well," she cried, tossing her pearl-bedizened head, "if this is the style in which you are disposed to treat an old friend, you may as well proclaim downright hostility at once. I tell you what it is, Miss Percy! I am not now in a position to put up with any of your airs, as I have done on former occasions. You can play the great lady, I know full well: and so can I——for I value money no more than you do—and perhaps not half so much!"

I made no answer—but flung upon the depraved young woman a look of pity and contempt, at the same time keeping my stand near the door as if I desired her to quit my chamber that I might close it after her. But she only seemed to become more irate, as she drew her really fine form up to its full height, exclaiming, "Ah! then it is to be war between us! Well, let it be so!—and see if I don't find an opportunity of being revenged on you! I only made offers of friendship just to try you. You are a prude——and I hate you!"

With these words she flaunted out of the room, banging the door behind her. At the same time I heard footsteps ascending the staircase; and I soon knew that it was the much-abused chambermaid who was waiting on Melissa: for the latter began giving vent to her ill-humour in a vehement tirade against the unfortunate domestic.

"This is a pretty hotel!" exclaimed Miss Harrison. "First of all I am thrust into this wretched little chamber, where there is no fire-place! Then you neglect me—you are an hour in bringing up my things——"

"I beg your pardon, ma'am," answered the chamber-maid meekly: "but you were told when you arrived just now, that the house was full and that this was the only chamber you could have for the present. You shall be put in possession of the best that next falls vacant;—and as for not waiting on you quick enough, I beg to observe that we are short of hands, and I have got to answer a dozen rings at the bell——"

"Well, then, cut yourself into a dozen pieces!" retorted Melissa. "Here! give me the band-box! Now then," she continued in a milder tone, "you are a little more on the alert; and if you behave better I shan't scold you. Do you know the lady in the next room?"

"Yes, ma'am: it is Miss Trafford, the celebrated actress, I'm told. She has been here several times before: she is a good customer and always pays well."

"And how long does she mean to stay here?" demanded Melissa.

"I don't know, ma'am, but she never stays long at a time. I think she must have some friends in the town or neighbourhood she comes to see. Perhaps she will be off to-night—perhaps to-morrow."

"Well, then, I will have her chamber when she goes," returned Melissa. "But I must have a sitting-room likewise——"

"The sitting-room opposite, ma'am," said the chamber-maid, "will become vacant at the same time; for it is also occupied by Miss Trafford."

"Ah, indeed!" ejaculated Miss Harrison. "Then who was that tall, handsome, pale young gentleman, dressed in black, that I saw just now coming out of that sitting-room?"

"I don't know, ma'am—I did not see him. Perhaps it was a friend," suggested the chamber-maid,—"a gentleman who may have called——"

"No doubt it was a gentleman who called!" interjected Melissa: and methought there was a certain degree of maliciousness in her accent. "But look at my watch! What o'clock is it?"

"It is close upon five, ma'am," responded the domestic.

"And you have ordered the fly for five—have you not?" asked Melissa. "Well, that is all right. I am very nearly ready—though I am half perished with cold, dressing in this wretched room, without fire, and with the December wind blowing through the chinks of this bow-window!"

"By the bye, ma'am, I forgot to ask you something," said the chamber-maid. "Missus presents her respectful compliments——"

"And pray who is missus?" inquired Miss Harrison, contemptuously accentuating the ill-pronounced word.

"Missus, ma'am?" exclaimed the chamber-maid, evidently in astonishment that the term should not have been understood. "Why, that's Mrs. Peters, the landlady, to be sure."

"And what message has Mrs. Peters sent to me?" demanded Melissa.

"Oh! it's only about the chaise, ma'am," returned the chamber-maid. "Missus wants to know how far it is going—and whether it's to stop and put up at the place—or whether it's to

be sent back to fetch you at any particular hour?—because then missus will know what instructions to give the coachman."

"Perhaps you can tell me," said Melissa, "how far off Escott Court is—the seat of the Marquis of Tynedale, you know: for I am a perfect stranger in Petersfield and all its neighbourhood."

"Ah, indeed, ma'am! you are going to Escott Court—are you?" said the chamber-maid, speaking in a voice which was more profoundly respectful than ever. "It's a beautiful place—I mean of course in the summer time: but even now, in the middle of winter——"

"Yes—I have no doubt it is a very fine place," interjected Miss Harrison. "But I am accustomed to live in fine places," she continued, in a tone of self-sufficiency. "You have not yet told me how far off it is? About three miles—or something of that sort—is it not?"

"Exactly so, ma'am," rejoined the chamber-maid. "You are acquainted with the Marquis of Tynedale, then?"

"It would appear as if I were—would it not," asked Melissa, "since I am going to a banquet which he gives there this evening? But we were speaking of the chaise. I shall keep it at Escott Court; for I do not exactly know at what hour the party may break up. It is however most probable that I shall be back in good time—for the Marquis keeps very early hours."

"Then I will tell missus that the chaise is to put up at the Court," said the chamber-maid. "Ah, there it is! I hear it driving round to the portico at this moment."

"And I am ready!" exclaimed Melissa. "Just one more peep in the glass! I think I look pretty well—eh?"

"Quite beautiful, ma'am," responded the chamber-maid.

"Well! after all, you are a well-meaning, good-tempered, civil girl," said Miss Harrison; "and if I was just now rather impatient with you—Is my hair all right?"

"Nothing could be better, ma'am; and it sets off those pearls in such grand style!"

"Really you are a judge!" ejaculated Melissa. "Now where are my gloves—my handkerchief? Ah! and here is my purse! There are five shillings for you. And now my shawl! There! Gently over the shoulders! That's right! You can attend me down to the chaise. I really scarcely regret now that I left my own maid in London behind me."

Here the conversation ended; and I heard Miss Harrison descend the staircase, followed by the chamber-maid.

CHAPTER CXIII.

THE TWO BED-CHAMBERS.

THE partition between Melissa's bed-room and my own was so thin that I could not help over-hearing every syllable of this discourse;—and most probably the chamber-maid had forgotten that the partition was thus slight—or else she was unaware that I had re-entered—or perhaps

ANOTHER PORTRAIT OF MELISSA HARRISON.

(which is most probable) she was completely in-different as to whether the conversation might be listened to or not. At the outset I was taking off my bonnet and shawl with no studied intention to catch anything that might be said in the ad-joining room: but when Melissa began to speak of my own self I listened—and then I tarried in my chamber until she had descended to the chaise: for I thought that after the threats she had held out, and the malignant spirit she had demon-strated towards me, it would be just as well if I could obtain some little insight into her present position, her movements, her intentions, and the

grounds upon which she had so vauntingly pro-claimed her disregard for money, thereby inti-mating that she was well supplied with funds.

As the reader may have observed, I learnt from Miss Harrison's discourse with the chamber-maid that Reginald Barron had left my sitting-room opposite. I had not failed to notice the malicious tone in which Melissa had alluded to himself and me; but this was something which I thought I could afford to treat with thorough contempt. Indeed, I congratulated myself on the success which had attended my proceeding in respect to that young man; and I mentally said, "Doubtless he saw that he was *outwitted*: he felt mortified and humiliated—and he departed in a different spirit from that in which he had arrived!"

I now flattered myself that I should pass the evening in peace and comfort, without any farther annoyance or interruption. Reginald Barron was disposed of—Melissa had gone to the Marquis of Tynedale's country seat—and I felt that my mind was relieved. I ordered dinner, which was presently served up; and amongst the various subjects which now engaged my thoughts, was this new phase which had just developed itself in Melissa Harrison's career. I knew that some months back her connexion with Lord Tynedale was broken off, and thence the necessity of her returning as a *danseuse* to the boards of the theatre. But was this connexion already renewed? or was it about to be resuscitated?—or was the Marquis merely entertaining a party of gay females at Escott Court, and for old acquaintance' sake had invited Melissa to be amongst them? But if she were not again the mistress of the Marquis, how came she to be in good feather, possessing an elegant toilet, jewels of no mean description, and boasting of her ability to throw money about in all directions without regard to its value? Perhaps she had found another protector, but nevertheless had her own reasons for visiting the Marquis of Tynedale? As a matter of course, I could not arrive at any positive conjecture on these conflicting points; and I can assure the reader that I did not waste very much time in deliberating upon them. I again had recourse to my book, which was a very amusing one; and throwing *myself into* an easy chair close to a cheerful fire, I soon became absorbed in the contents of the volume.

It must be borne in mind that I had been up the whole of the past night and that I had spent it in a manner which, physically and mentally, was both wearing and tearing. The reader will not therefore be surprised to learn that when I had partaken of a cup of coffee, an hour after dinner, a drowsy sensation began to steal over me—my eyelids grew heavy—and I could not retain the sense of what I was reading, or rather endeavouring to read. I started up to make an effort to throw off this sleepiness: I looked at my watch—it was barely nine o'clock, and therefore too early to retire to bed. I resumed my easy chair, flattering myself that I was now broad awake once again: but I soon found that the drowsiness was returning—that a heaviness was sitting upon my eyelids—and that my head was drooping forward on my bosom. This time I could not struggle against the sensation—I could not shake it off: I abandoned myself to it—and the mists of sleep gradually closed in around me.

When I awoke, it was with a sudden start, as if from the influence of a dream which had more or less affrighted me. Yet what was it that I had seen, or fancied that I had seen? Methought that the door of the apartment had slowly opened—that some one had looked in—and after pausing for a few moments on the threshold, had advanced a little farther into the room. It was the form of Reginald Barron! Then I fancied that he stood for two or three instants, as if irresolute and uncertain how to act—but that then, with the air of suddenly making up his mind, he hastily retreated

on tiptoe from the apartment, closing the door behind him. It was then that I awoke.

"Was it a dream? or was it a reality?" I asked myself. "It must have been a dream! If I had been awake—or only just sufficiently awake to be at all aware of his entrance, I should have instantaneously started up in mingled indignation and alarm. Yes! it must have been a dream! He would not dare return to the hotel, nor renew his unmanly persecutions, after the treatment he has experienced at my hands! But let me see how long I slept."

I referred to my watch: it was just ten o'clock. I had slept upwards of an hour. I rose from my seat, and was about to ring the bell for the chamber-maid to give me a candle, when I heard some one moving in the adjoining room—Melissa's chamber I mean; and I thought that this must be the chamber-maid. I accordingly opened the door for the purpose of calling her, when I caught a glimpse of the countenance of Melissa Harrison herself. She had her own door slightly ajar; and the gas on the landing revealed her features as she was thus peeping out. It also struck me that there was a very peculiar expression upon those features,—a mocking malice—a leering irony, which I could not understand. I instantaneously closed the door of my sitting-room, and returned to my seat, resolving to wait a little while before I passed into my bed-chamber; for the suspicion was in my mind that Melissa was ready to waylay me and pick a quarrel if possible.

"She must have returned," I said to myself, "while I slept in this arm-chair. Perhaps the depraved creature has partaken too freely of wine—she is excited, and determined to insult me if I afford her an opportunity? This I will not do!"

I accordingly remained in my sitting-room until all was still in the adjoining apartment. I had no longer any inclination to sleep; and therefore the sensation of drowsiness returned not upon me as I sat in that easy chair. At length I said to myself, "The footsteps have ceased in Melissa's room—no one is moving about there now—all is silent!"

I rose; and not thinking it worth while to summon the chamber-maid, I took up a wax-light from the table—stole gently across the landing—and entered my chamber. Bed-rooms at inns do not generally wear a very comfortable aspect; but it was different on the present occasion. A cheerful fire was blazing in the grate—the draperies were closed completely over the windows—the curtains were drawn entirely round the vast old-fashioned four-post bed, which looked like a room within a room. I locked the door—hastily put off a portion of my apparel—and stood before the fire to arrange my hair. Now I again felt tired and wearied—I longed to be in bed: I thought of the miseries of the past night—and I felt as if that long cold wretched vigil was only to be compensated for by a sound unbroken slumber on this present night. I therefore hastened to disapparel myself: I extinguished the wax candle, and proceeded to enter the bed. But scarcely had my head touched the pillow, when there was a movement by the side of me, and I was enfolded in a pair of arms which were instantaneously thrown around my form!

A scream was on the very point of bursting from my lips, as at the same time I made a desperate effort to release myself,—when a laugh in a well-known voice burst abruptly upon my ears; and the head which was now revealed from beneath the bed-clothes, was embellished with the long flowing hair of a woman. It was Melissa Harrison in whose arms I was thus clasped,—Melissa whose mocking laugh rang in my ears! The scream was therefore hushed at the very instant it was about to escape from the portals of the lips; and by a renewed vigorous effort I forced Melissa to loosen the arms that had fast encircled me.

"How dare you perpetrate so infamous a trick?" I demanded, sitting up in the bed at as great a distance from Melissa as possible, and at the same time dashing back the curtains so that the light of the fire was now more completely shed upon the scene.

Melissa continued to laugh with a heartiness that was unmistakable; and I was so enraged that I could scarcely refrain from inflicting summary chastisement upon her.

"How dare you," I again demanded,—"how dare you treat me thus, wicked creature that you are?"

"Ah, I can well understand all this rage and fury!" ejaculated Melissa, now desisting from her laughter, and addressing me with a species of taunting significance. "I almost pity your disappointment, my dear Ellen! *These* were not the arms in which you expected to be embraced!"

"Wretch!" I ejaculated, now springing from the couch; "what mean these infamous insinuations?"

"Ha! ha! my dear Ellen!" said Melissa, with the most insolent familiarity. "I have got eyes to see with, and a mind to understand what I *do* see. Oh, the virtuous Miss Trafford—the prude Miss Percy! Ah, I always thought the stillest waters ran the deepest; and now I have received a positive proof of it!"

What did the vile young woman mean? Ah, an idea struck me! I remembered with what a malicious significancy she had coupled my name and that of Reginald Barron when she was in conversation with the chambermaid: I was horrified and indignant—indeed I was almost boiling with rage to think that by the habit of judging others through the medium of her own depravities and profligacies, Melissa's prurient imagination should have conceived such an outrageous notion in reference to myself and that young man!

"Your conduct is abominable!" I said, quivering with rage from head to foot, as I stood in my night dress by the side of the bed. "You know in your heart that what you dare imply is a base slander—a vile calumny! Never has my private conduct belied the impression which in public it has made!"

"No, no, this will not do, Miss Percy! this is too strong, my beautiful friend Ellen!" cried Melissa. "It is no wonder that you succeed in keeping up your character when you play so cunning and deep a game. You have no lover in London; but that is no reason why you should not come to Petersfield for one! Yes, yes—you have friends in the town—you often visit the hotel—but you never stay long at a time! No, no! that wouldn't do!—it would excite suspicion!"

"Silence, base wretch!" I ejaculated, stamping my foot with a fury, a spite, and a feeling of hatred and vindictiveness such as I had never experienced before towards any human creature. "Every word that falls from your lips is an abominable falsehood! Your language is the slime of the snail on the leaf of the lily! But I will not vindicate myself to *you*. Leave this chamber!—rise—depart, I insist upon it!—the room is mine!"

"No wonder you are in a rage!" said Melissa with the most provoking coolness; "your disappointment is evidently dreadful! As for myself, I mean to remain here."

"What! remain in my room?" I exclaimed: and I felt that my eyes were literally flashing fire.

"Yes—to be sure! It suits me. I have my own reasons:" and here Melissa again burst forth into a laugh which sounded in my ears like the malice-mirth of a fiend.

"No, Melissa!" I said: "no, infamous wretch that you are!—this is too much! Rise, I command you! or I will pull the bell—I will raise an alarm——"

"Now, don't think, my dear friend," interrupted the provoking wretch, "that you will frighten me with any such threat! I know better. You don't dare do it. There now—am I right?"

I was bewildered and almost stupefied. The vague idea was floating in my mind that Melissa knew of something which I did not—or that in her devilish malice she was prepared to put upon some circumstance, otherwise trivial and innocent, a construction which might really be made to tell most seriously against my character. The image of Reginald Barron rose up in my mind:—how could I tell how much I was compromised by him? Ah, that dream, as I had taken it to be!—that appearance in my sitting-room!—was it a reality? Had he indeed stolen thither when I slept? had he been observed when stealthily beating a retreat? and was it all this that had put such dreadful ideas into Melissa's head concerning me? Ah! and now as all these thoughts were striking me as it were blow upon blow in rapid succession, I suddenly recalled to mind the fact that Melissa was peeping forth from her door when I looked out of my own sitting-room; and thus I comprehended in an instant that if Reginald Barron had really paid that late visit to the hotel, his stealthy movements might have been perceived by Melissa. Yes, yes—it must have been so!—and hence that peculiar expression of mocking malignity and ironical significance which I had caught upon her countenance!

All these remembrances and reflections trooped through my mind in as many seconds as I have taken minutes to record them. I was shocked, and almost appalled at the aspect which the whole affair was assuming: I saw that my character was at the mercy of a vile young woman, who, from the mere influence of her own depravities, was but too readily inclined to put the most abominable construction upon every circumstance that related to myself. Could I tarry there to reason with her?—dared I raise an alarm and summon the hotel domestics for the purpose of ejecting her from my chamber? No, no!—I dreaded a scene —I recoiled from the possibility of accusations which would receive a tremendous weight from circumstantial evidence: I was bewildered—I felt half wild—half mad! Again did the bitter, taunting laugh of the vile Melissa ring in my ears; and she exclaimed, "Ah, Ellen! instead of standing there shivering in your night-dress by the side of this bed, you expected to be clasped all warm and glowing——"

I tarried to hear no more: I felt as if every word the wretch was uttering fell like a drop of poison on my soul!—as if her very breath infected the atmosphere and diffused contamination around me! It was with a half-shriek that I sprang away from the side of the couch. I snatched up my garments, which I had thrown upon a chair near the fire: and unlocking the door, I rushed from the room. Melissa's voice called out something after me: I gave no heed to it at the moment—I sprang into the chamber which properly belonged to herself; and falling upon my knees by the side of the couch which was there, I burst into tears.

Long and passionately I wept; for I considered this to be one of the most frightful afflictions that had ever befallen me—at all events it seemed to be second only to that former occasion when my character was well-nigh shipwrecked at River House. I mean when holding Juliet's child in my arms, I was seen by Henry Wakefield. Yes, long and passionately I wept: perhaps for nearly half-an-hour I knelt by the side of that bed, sobbing as if my heart would break. But at last I began to experience a relief in the very violence of that weeping: it afforded a vent which did me good. I rose up from my kneeling posture: I sat upon the couch and I reflected. By degrees, my mind grew stronger: the whole affair began to look less and less terrible the longer I envisaged it; and I thought to myself, "I was wrong to yield to utter despair before I had in imagination exhausted every means of vindicating my character! There is one course that is open to me: I will appeal to Reginald Barron, through the medium of his mother and sister, to do me justice! He cannot be utterly depraved—he cannot entertain so rancorous an hostility against me as to assist in ruining my reputation!"

My resolve being thus adopted, my mind grew still calmer and calmer: and by the street-lamp which shed its rays in at the window, I smoothed my dishevelled hair before the looking-glass in the chamber. There was light enough to show me that I was very pale and that my eyes were red with weeping. I bathed them, for they smarted; and then I lay down to rest,—having first assured myself however that I had locked the door. And now I began to recall to memory the words which Melissa had vociferated forth at the instant when I was fleeing in horror and dismay from my own chamber. What were those words?

"Why, this is the best part of it all! You are mad! It is as ridiculous as it is amusing!"

These were the words to which she had given utterance. Has not the reader at times observed that something which passes almost entirely unheeded in the exciting moment of its occurrence, may subsequently be recalled with the most critical accuracy? It was so in this instance. Yes—those were the words which the tongue of Melissa had sent pealing after me—of which I had taken no heed at the moment—but which I now recollected and repeated likewise with the conviction that they were precisely those which had been uttered. Again and again did I ask myself what their meaning could be? I could conjecture nothing—unless it were that the vile young woman was expressing her triumph in being left to the usurped enjoyment of my comfortable chamber.

Sleep at length stole upon my eyes: but as I gradually awoke at an early hour in the morning, it was with a sense of tightness across the brain, and an inward sinking, so to speak—the sure indications of a recent period of powerfully wrought emotions having been passed through. It required but a very few instants to recall to mind all the circumstances which had so terribly harassed me. I started up in the bed, and looked at my watch. It was then half-past six o'clock in the morning. The heavens were still dark—it was by the glare of the gaslight that I was enabled thus to ascertain the time. I was about to lie down again, when methought that I heard the sounds of voices somewhere near. I listened. Yes!—there were assuredly voices speaking in a low hurried tone. Ah! and there were footsteps too! These were in the adjoining room,—not the sitting-apartment, but the bed-chamber!—my bed-chamber, which I had been forced to abandon to the usurping possession of Melissa Harrison! I continued to listen with suspended breath. The partition, be it recollected, was very slight: and to my illimitable surprise I caught the sound of a masculine voice—though it was speaking in too low a tone for me to recognise it, much less to comprehend the sense of what it was saying. Yes—it was a man's voice! But dared I conjecture whose it was?—and if so, what a new and startling phase did it seem to be developing in the history of the last few hours?

Still I listened—yes, listened with suspended breath! I now heard a sound as of a window opening,—but opening so gently that it was all but noiseless and would fail to be perceived by any one unless the faculties and senses were by circumstances inspired with so vivid a keenness as that which now characterized mine. In a few moments I could not any longer doubt that what I suspected was actually taking place, and that a window was being opened. What could it mean? Oh! this incident, coupled with the sound of a man's voice in the adjacent chamber, seemed to tell a tale which was only too easily understood!

I now glided from the bed, and I approached the window of the little chamber where I found myself. It fortunately happened that this was a species of bow-window; for it looked upon the top of the huge portico of the hotel. There was consequently a view to be obtained sideways; and the eye could sweep the street from one end to the other. This explanation will show how I was enabled to observe what was taking place, and which I am about to describe.

The form of a man was descending from the window of the adjacent room. He was dressed in black: he was tall: and now as his countenance was upturned towards that window, I recognised Reginald Barron. At this I was not surprised: my mind was already prepared for such a discovery. He was lowering himself by means of a blanket, or coverlid, twisted round into the form of a rope. The window was not very high from the pavement: there was another window immediately underneath it; and in a few moments the foot of Reginald Barron touched the sill of that lower window. Then the rope was instantaneously drawn up: Reginald kissed his hand, the gaslight again glancing upon his countenance;—and darting along the street, he was in a few moments hidden from my view.

All this I beheld, with the certainty that I myself was not perceived by Reginald Barron while thus peeping from the side of the bow-window. The street continued perfectly quiet; no early-riser—no neighbour—no police official had witnessed the proceeding: or at least no notice was taken of it, and no disturbance was made. I sat down upon the side of the couch, sick at heart—shocked and disgusted at the *denouement* of this episode of depravity. But suddenly I was startled as my thoughts collected themselves and I began putting all circumstances together. Reginald Barron must have been hidden in my chamber at the time when I was there—when I was undressing—when I entered the bed, to find myself clasped in Melissa's arms—when I stood in my night-gear by the side of that bed—when I was rendered almost infuriate by Melissa's vile insinuations—and finally when I burst forth from that chamber to seek refuge in the one where I now was. Ah! and there was no longer the slightest difficulty in comprehending all Melissa's allusions—all the insinuations she had thrown out, even to those very parting words which she had flung after me, as it were, when I was gliding from the room! It was altogether a series of incidents which I could scarcely bear to look upon, and which I could not review otherwise than with the keenest sense of loathing and disgust.

While I was giving way to my reflections, I heard the window in the adjoining room closing as gently as a few minutes previously I had heard it open; and I was just asking myself what course I should now pursue, when there was a gentle tap at the door of the chamber. I felt assured it must be Melissa. I hesitated to pay any heed to the summons—for I felt that the presence of the profligate creature would be loath-some to me; and after the discovery I had just made I could no longer apprehend that my character was in her power. But on a second thought I determined to see what notion she still entertained, or affected to entertain on this head: for it was important for me to acquire the certainty that she had not the slightest ground for aspersing my good name.

I therefore opened the door, and Melissa made her appearance. She had thrown on some of her clothing, and carried the rest over her arm; for it appeared that she had taken her raiment with her when gliding into my chamber on the preceding evening.

"Now," she hastily whispered, "you can go and resume possession of your own apartment."

I was just on the point of expressing a loathing and repugnance against the idea of again setting foot in a room which had been the scene of such profligacy, when it struck me that if it were discovered in the hotel that we had changed chambers, it would appear exceedingly singular. I therefore snatched up my own apparel: but ere moving to quit the chamber, I said, "Your conduct has been infamous, Melissa!—infamous to a degree! I

know more than perhaps you imagine——I know why the window in the adjoining room opened just now—and I saw who descended into the street!"

Melissa laughed, and said, "It is one of the raciest adventures I ever met with in all my life! On my soul, when I saw the young fellow glide into your chamber last evening—and you yourself almost immediately afterwards peep forth from your sitting-room—what on earth could I think but that you were secreting a lover?"

"And now," I said, my heart leaping with joy as I perceived that Melissa no longer entertained an opinion that was prejudicial to me,—"and now you find how you have wronged me?"

"Why, of course," interjected Melissa, who spoke with a certain degree of hardihood, as if she were now quite brazen and full of effrontery in pursuing her profligate career,—"why, of course, it would be ridiculous for me to tell you that I any longer suppose you were secreting a lover, since it seems you know that he has passed the night with *me*, and that therefore explanations have taken place between us. He is wonderfully sentimental, that young man!—and I am really surprised you were not moved by all he said to you yesterday: for he told me everything—he was very candid——"

"And did he tell you," I demanded, "how it was that he came to seek my chamber?"

"Yes. I really can scarcely help laughing myself into fits at the whole affair! It is most supremely ridiculous, and therefore highly diverting! I obtained a paramour when little expecting one; and he was forced to content himself with me while craving after you. The fact is, he meant to see you once again last night, to upbraid or entreat you—to threaten or to pray—I'm sure I don't know which. However, he called at the hotel at about ten o'clock. He stole up to your sitting room—he saw that you were asleep in your chair—he was advancing to awaken you—perhaps with a kiss—who knows, Ellen?—when a thought struck him. I don't know what nonsense he talked to me about loving and hating you at the same time—resolving to possess you that his passion might be appeased and at the same time that his vengeance might be sated——"

"Well, leave that subject alone, Melissa—and tell me quick what happened," I exclaimed.

"Ah! I almost forgot that we are both standing here shivering in the cold; but I can't help dwelling on the details of an adventure which is so exquisitely diverting. Well then, an idea struck him, I was saying——he knew which your bed-chamber was: he had seen you enter it in the day-time when you gave him the slip—you know—for he told me all about it—and bitterly vindictive he was! Well, he knew which was your chamber; and he glided into it. He little thought that I had heard footsteps stealing across the landing, and that I was therefore on the watch. He stole into your chamber—he concealed himself in that large wardrobe which you might have observed in the recess. Ah, by the bye, there's one thing, Ellen, I may tell you, which may perhaps be gratifying to your prudish modesty; and this is that the young fellow could not possibly catch the slightest glimpse of you while you were undressing yourself, or during any subsequent part of the pleasant little adventures that ensued betwixt you and me."

I confess that the assurance thus conveyed was grateful enough to my feelings; the more so that I had the certainty of its truth, inasmuch as I knew full well Melissa would not travel out of her way to invent anything of a nature calculated to afford me pleasure.

"No sooner had I witnessed that little circumstance so full ot suspicion," proceeded Melissa Harrison,—"I mean the stealthy gliding of that young gentleman across the landing to your chamber, when I said to myself, 'Oh, oh! so Miss Ellen has her little intrigues and her affairs of gallantry after all!'—Then almost immediately afterwards I saw you peep out—you at once retreated on catching a glimpse of me; and all this naturally confirmed the idea that you were dealing with a lover. So then a mischievous thought entered my head. I fancied that I would spoil your sport,—little foreseeing how the adventure was to terminate. I hastily disapparelled myself, but took my clothes with me in case of need; and I glided into your chamber. Scarcely had I ensconced myself comfortably in the couch, when you entered. As you did not approach the bed nor draw aside the curtains, I saw that my stratagem would succeed to the very last. You know what followed."

"I do, Melissa," I responded. "And now I think you have told me enough."

"No, no!—just one moment more!" ejaculated Miss Harrison. "If we are doomed to catch colds, a minute more or less standing here, will not alter the matter——and the whole business is so particularly amusing, it is really a delight to review the details."

"Well, then, proceed—and make haste," I said.

"Only conceive the feelings of that young fellow," continued Melissa, "cooped up as he was in the wardrobe! First of all, when I hastened into the room and proceeded to occupy the couch, he naturally thought it was *you*: he supposed that you had disapparelled yourself in some dressing-room adjoining or close at hand. But he did not mean to quit his hiding-place until you should be fast asleep. I have no doubt he was feasting his imagination—gloating over your rich charms——"

"I am going, Melissa," I said.

"Just one word more! It is really too good to be lost—and you ought to know all, because it so nearly concerns you. Well, not many minutes had elapsed before our young gentleman heard the door open again and some one else enter. This was *you*: but he did not know it. How could he? He thought that you were already in bed—he dared not peep forth, for the doors of the wardrobe made a grating sound. He was horribly perplexed and bewildered: nay, more—he was terribly alarmed. The only solution for the mystery which he could conjecture, was that you had some female attendant to sleep with you. Soon afterwards came the scene betwixt you and me. Then our young gentleman was perfectly astounded. Every moment he fancied that I should let out the fact that he was concealed in the room: for he saw full well that I knew it. And it really *is* a wonder that I did not say something far more pointed than I did to you, which might have

had the effect of at once bringing matters to an explanation: but as a matter of course I fancied that you were privy to a lover's concealment, and that therefore you understood the meaning of my allusions just as well as I did myself. You rushed from the room; and so soon as the door closed behind you, I said aloud, "Come forth, young gentleman, from whencesoever you are concealed!'—He made his appearance. I cannot tell you how immense was his agitation—how wild his excitement —at least as it was displayed in his looks. I enjoined him to be silent, or to speak only in whispers. Now, you must confess he is very good-looking, Ellen—he has beautiful eyes and teeth—nice curling black hair—he is pale and intellectual too—Indeed, I took a fancy to him—and I thought that the adventure was altogether so delicious——"

"I am now going, Melissa," I said; and in another moment the door closed gently behind me.

CHAPTER CXIV.

THE PORTRAIT.

I WAS again in my own chamber—but a chamber which I loathed the very atmosphere of, for it seemed to be feculent and contaminating. It was only as a matter of expediency that I had so far conquered my feelings as to return into a place which seemed to me to be so foul and polluted. But, as I have already said, I was anxious to avoid every occurrence that might be calculated to engender gossiping remarks; and moreover I was very far from desirous of having it known that I was at all acquainted with Miss Harrison, or whatever she called herself at the hotel; for I fancied that she would not remain there very long without causing her true character to be suspected. The reader can scarcely conceive how intense was the loathing with which I had remained in her company for the last ten minutes in the adjacent chamber: but beyond every other consideration was the desire to ascertain precisely what view she now took of my conduct in respect to Reginald Barron. This point I had cleared up: I found that I still stood as high as ever in the estimation of Melissa Harrison; for my virgin pride shrank from the idea of being suspected even by such a depraved and profligate creature as she.

As for what I thought of Reginald Barron himself, no words can describe the abhorrence and disgust which I experienced for that young man. Indeed, his avowals of love towards myself now seemed to me all the more insulting, inasmuch as he could have consented to become the passing paramour of a vile woman in whose way accident had thrown him. And then too, there was the base deliberate attempt which he had intended to make upon my honour,—concealing himself in my chamber for the purpose of outraging me in my sleep! It was an accumulation of infamies. Were they to go unpunished?—was I to tolerate such flagitious conduct? But how could I chastise him? Not by the invocation of the law's aid. No! I had already, as it were, consented to the hushing of the whole proceeding by not alarming the household. Besides, as I have repeated over and over again, never travelled out of my way to court publicity, or to render myself the heroine of adventures. What, then, should I do? Should I communicate to Mrs. Barron and to Sarah the iniquity of a son—the infamy of a brother! No, of what avail would this be? it would only afflict *them*, without recalling what was done—perhaps without rendering the young man himself either wiser or better. Besides, I felt that if I were in the place of a near relative of such a wretch I should be thankful for the generosity of any one who would conceal his crimes from my knowledge!

While giving way to my reflections, I commenced the performance of my toilet. My ablutions were finished—I was begining to dress, when the door opened, and Melissa thrust in her head, saying, "May I enter for an instant? There is something I still wish to say to you."

"Come in, and let your communication be brief. I do not wish to dispute with you; but your own good sense must tell you, Melissa——"

"Yes, yes! I can understand very well that we can never be good friends again! But I really bear you no ill-will, Ellen—— only I thought yesterday afternoon that you treated me in such a very imperious haughty way, that I was determined not to stand it."

"And now what do you wish to say to me?" I inquired.

"If you see this young Barron," resumed Melissa, "you must not let him think that I told you he passed the night with me: but you must let him know the truth,—that you saw him descend from the window by means of the twisted counterpane. I promised him most solemnly and sacredly that I would not of my own accord divulge that which he desired to keep a secret——"

"It is by no means likely," I said, "that I shall have any farther communication with Mr. Barron. If the contrary should happen, you may depend upon it that he shall know the full truth from my lips. And now, Melissa, let us separate."

"Just one word more!" she ejaculated. "Are you going to remain in Petersfield to-day?"

"Why do you ask?" I inquired, being resolved to ascertain the motive.

She hesitated for a few instants—and then said, "You know the Marquis of Tynedale—but I don't suppose you speak to him after everything that occurred about the cheque some time ago——"

"Tell me wherefore you have touched upon this topic," I interrupted her.

"Well, if you do happen to fall in with the Marquis—because he is very likely to call here to-day," continued Melissa, "you won't of course mention anything to my prejudice? Now do listen a moment! I will tell you exactly how I am situated—and I crave your merciful consideration. I renewed my connexion with the Marquis a few weeks ago. It was he who sought me; for there is more or less infatuation in that quarter. However, to be brief, I became his *chere amie* again. Now you understand," added Melissa with a smile, "the history of the pearls—the gold watch and chain — the handsome dresses — the well-filled purse——"

"Proceed, Melissa — proceed with the main object of your discourse," I said. "It would afford me a real pleasure to learn that you had obtained all those possessions from another and more legitimate source. But go on."

"Well, you must know that three or four days back, the Marquis and I had a little tiff. It was he who began the quarrel. He happened to see me conversing in Regent Street with a young officer of the Guards—a handsome young fellow certainly; and the old lord took umbrage. All in vain was it that I vowed and protested I had never seen the young Guardsman before in my life, and that I was only asking him my way. The Marquis was most unreasonable: he would not allow that I could possibly want to inquire my way in Regent Street; and, to be brief, he swore that our connexion was at an end. Well, off he comes to his country-seat in the neighbourhood of Petersfield. I let a day or two pass, thinking that he would write for me to come to him; but no such good luck! So then I wrote myself, to say that I should dine with him at Escott Court last evening at half-past five o'clock. It was a bold stroke: but I know his disposition well, and that he likes anything of a spirited character. Now you understand why I was all bedecked with my pearls and jewels last evening, and why I was in grand toilet. Of course I told the chambermaid a pack of stories, to the effect that there was going to be a splendid entertainment at Escott Court; because it would never have done to let her think that I was going to a *tête-à-tête* dinner with his lordship. It would have excited a suspicion at once!"

"And what was the sequel, Melissa?" I inquired; for I was anxious to put an end to the conversation.

"To tell you the truth, I did not exactly strike the grand successful blow which I expected. The Marquis received me with courtesy, but with shyness. There was an excellent dinner on the table —but a reserve in his manner. The upshot was that I could not induce him to say the word which would have kept me at Escott Court. I was too proud to humble myself outright and promise that I would never meet the young Guardsman again——"

"But the sequel, Melissa? the sequel?" I said impatiently. "You constantly diverge into details to which I do not care to listen."

"Oh, well, then—the sequel is this," rejoined Miss Harrison,—"that the old nobleman is coming to call upon me to-day. I am passing here as Mrs. Cavendish—husband abroad—lady's-maid ill in London—came in a hurry, and therefore took postchaise instead of using private carriage—and so forth and so forth. All this, you know, is to keep up my respectability at the hotel. But as for the Marquis, if you should meet him—and if he should speak to you—and you should speak to him in return, pray don't——"

"Now, set your mind at ease, Melissa," I interrupted her. "I shall leave the hotel soon after breakfast. You had better not appear to know me at all; so that if the Marquis should happen to call upon you before I have quitted the place, and if he should see me, I will pass him by as if I had never met him before."

"Thank you, Ellen! thank you!" exclaimed Melissa. "I do not ask you to forgive me——"

"Enough!—and now let us separate."

The next moment Melissa Harrison disappeared from the room, to my infinite relief; for I loathed her presence: I saw that she added hypocrisy and dissimulation to profligacy the most depraved. She would not have pretended that she had never been unfriendly towards me, if it were not that she wished to put a seal upon my lips in reference to the incident of the past night, in case I should fall in with the Marquis of Tynedale and choose to enter into conversation with him.

My toilet was now completed—the servants were by this time all astir in the hotel, for it was eight o'clock; and on proceeding to my sitting-apartment, I found the fire lighted and the breakfast cloth laid. By the help of the morning meal and a local newspaper which was brought to me, I whiled away an hour. It was then nine o'clock: but it was still too early to set off for Kelvedon Hall, which was only six miles distant — for I meant on arriving there to pretend that I had come from London, so as to avoid the necessity of any explanations in reference to the incidents which had occurred since I left that country-seat the evening but one previous. I was thinking whether I had not better wait till about eleven o'clock before I gave the orders for my departure, when one of the waiters entered, bearing a box, or packing-case, about two feet and a half long, two feet wide, and six inches in depth. It was addressed to me as Miss Trafford; but I was perfectly unfamiliar with the handwriting. I asked who brought the box?—the waiter replied that it was a man having the air of a porter, and that he departed immediately. I could not conceive what the case could contain, nor from whom it could come. It was therefore absolutely necessary to open it without delay, that I might see whether there were a letter inside. The waiter procured a chisel—the lid of the packing-case, which was carefully nailed down, was forced off—and behold! there was the portrait representing me as Portia, set in a handsome gilt frame!

I started for an instant as if a reptile had stung me, so strong was the feeling of indignation which seized upon me,—an indignation in which even surprise itself was absorbed; for I had not the slightest doubt that it was a present from Reginald Barron, made in the hope of propitiating and conciliating me. There was a letter; but this was addressed to me as Miss Percy:—the case was otherwise directed, because he knew that I was passing at the hotel as Miss Trafford.

"Ah, now I know what it is," I said, assuming a careless air in the presence of the waiter.

The man—whose looks, as he flung them on the portrait, and then instinctively threw them upon me, certainly paid a high though involuntary homage to the talent of Reginald Barron—withdrew from the apartment; and I hastened to open the letter. Its contents ran as follow:—

"December 16, 1849.

"How can I venture to address you, Miss Percy, after my conduct of yesterday? It was most outrageous! It would be unpardonable on the part of any earthly woman: but you are an angel, and therefore may I yet hope to be forgiven! I was mad—I was as much intoxicated by the state of my feelings in consequence of having seen you, as ever a person was inebriated by the influence of wine. I know that if an individual commit an outrage, an offence, or a crime, when under this latter species of intoxication, he cannot appeal to justice to recognise therein an extenuation of his guilt, because the law declares that it is an aggravation. But in reference to the ebriety of the feelings—the intoxication of the brain, produced by a sentiment or a passion over which the individual has no control, is there not an allowance to be made? Yes!—and here the law itself is merciful: for if the individual perpetrate an offence under the influence of a sudden passion only, apart from the artificial stimulant of wine, it is held that he is deserving of consideration. It is thus—to illustrate my point—that what is murder in one case becomes only manslaughter in another. Is not all this true, Miss Percy?—and will not you therefore, who are more merciful than justice, and who have in your composition naught of the sternness of human law—will you not make an allowance for me?

"You came unexpectedly to the house—you burst upon my sight like a beautiful vision. The angel that I was worshipping at a distance, stood before me all in a moment! The goddess of my devotion, whom I believed to be in a far-off place, was there in my presence without an instant's warning! Oh, can you wonder that my brain reeled with the bewilderment of feelings which no tongue can proclaim and no language can depict? I was maddened—and I acted as a madman. Maniacs have frequently assailed those whom in their sane moments they most tenderly loved, and for whom they would rather die than injure even to the extent of a hair of the head. And in such a case those maniacs become the objects of commiseration and of sympathy—not of loathing and aversion. It is this forbearance which I claim—this lenient feeling to which I appeal. There is a doctrine that it behoves us to control our passions as much as possible—and that if we fail to do so, we must take the consequences of our derelictions. But is not this the straining of the sternest morality to the very utmost, inasmuch as human nature is known to be frail and fallible, and from every pulpit we are taught the cause of our fall? Or again, is it not a doctrine which may be speculatively put forth from the lips of those who practically are incapable of judgment? In other words, is it not, I will ask, the doctrine of beings pure and immaculate as yourself, who, acknowledging the sway of no turbid passion and no hasty sentiment, believe that the rest of humanity possess principles as excellent as themselves?

"This is a long letter, Miss Percy: but my offence is a grave one, and requires much pleading to enforce its claim to extenuation. I do not think that to you I shall appeal in vain. I do not ask you to see me—I do not suppose that when once the impression of yesterday's scene shall have worn away, you will ever bestow another thought on the poor artist who dared to love you from a distance, and who was driven wild by ineffable feelings by your presence! But I ask you to forgive me. Yes—I know that you will vouchsafe this pardon—if not for my sake, at least for that of my mother and my sister, both of whom love, and admire, and respect you. Do not therefore refuse the humble tribute which

accompanies this letter—the portrait of yourself: It is the one on which I bestowed the utmost care: it is the one to which I devoted the greatest pains. I beseech you to accept it. By so doing you will restore somewhat of peace of mind to one who is now immeasurably wretched.

"Permit me therefore to subscribe myself

"Your most humble servant,

"REGINALD BARRON."

I had scarcely patience to peruse this letter. Three or four times I tossed it down indignantly upon the table :—three or four times, while yet unfinished, I was on the very point of tearing it into countless fragments to be consumed in the flames. I knew it to be the effusion of the vilest dissimulation and the grossest hypocrisy : yet I *did* contrive to conquer my feelings so far as to read on to the end,—partly because I wished to see to what extent the impudence of this young

NO. 89.—ELLEN PERCY.

man could reach, and partly that I might judge how I was to deal alike with the epistle and the picture. And as I continued the perusal of that specious pleading—that well-disguised sophistry—I thought that if it were possible for anything to have enhanced the disgust—the loathing—almost the abhorrence, which I felt for Reginald Barron's character, it was this precious composition. That it was well written—that it was eloquent, and logically composed in its very speciousness—I did not attempt to conceal from myself. The greater, therefore, was the pity that a young man with such talents should be so thoroughly, and I believed hopelessly, depraved !

He evidently fancied that I remained in total ignorance of the main incidents of the past night. He alluded only to the scene which had taken place between us in the afternoon: he thought that I was unaware of everything which subsequently followed. He flattered himself that I knew not of his revisit to the hotel in the evening —his concealment in my chamber—the diabolical intentions which he had harboured—the fact that he was there hidden when I was embraced in Melissa's arms—the circumstance that he had remained throughout the night in her company— and the means by which he quitted the hotel at an early hour in the morning. But inasmuch as all these particulars were known to me, how could I do otherwise than look upon him as one of the basest and vilest of men? I shuddered as I thought that at this moment I might have possibly become a dishonoured and polluted being—robbed of the virtue which I had maintained throughout so many temptations and through so many trying circumstances—unworthy ever again to look my beloved Henry Wakefield in the face—doomed to mourn the blight of all my heart's best and purest affections! Yes—I shuddered! for I knew that I had escaped the utmost peril on the part of one of the most unprincipled of beings. Can the reader wonder, therefore, if I adopted the course I am about to describe?

I took a pen-knife, and cut the canvass of the picture out of its frame. I folded it up into the smallest possible compass—enveloped it in two or three sheets of paper, so that the contents might not easily be discovered by the touch of the hand —and carefully sealed the package. I then addressed it to Mr. Barron, at his residence. This being done, I rang the bell, and when the waiter made his appearance, I desired him to send me a messenger. The porter presented himself; and I said to him, "You will take this parcel to its address. Inquire for Mr. Barron—see him alone —and place it in his hands. If he be not at home at the time, say that you will return presently: but explain your business to no other person."

The porter promised to do my bidding, for which I gave him a liberal fee: and he took his departure. The delicacy with which I was conducting this portion of the arrangement, was in order to prevent the transaction from becoming known to his mother or sister: for I have already said that it was no part of my purpose to act unkindly or maliciously towards them. If they knew that Reginald had sent me the portrait (as indeed they *must*) I could only leave it for him to make some excuse for the absence of any letter of thanks or acknowledgment from my hands: I could not take universal precautions——in a word, I could not conduct the proceeding otherwise than I was doing.

I now ordered a chaise to be got in readiness to take me away from the hotel. I broke up the picture-frame, and packed the fragments in one of my portmanteaus, to be burnt at some convenient opportunity. The chaise was speedily announced to be in waiting; and I hastened to take my seat in it. I did not see anything more of Melissa Harrison: but I had overheard the chamber-maid announce to her, while I was seated at breakfast, that there was now a suite of apartments, comprising a sitting-room, at her disposal.

In about an hour I reached the gates of Kelvedon Park; and a few minutes afterwards I alighted in front of the Hall. I had already paid the driver of the vehicle; so that the instant my baggage was delivered to the servants who hastened forward to receive me, the man mounted the

box and drove away; and by this little piece of management I trusted to avoid the discovery that instead of having journeyed from London, I had only arrived from Petersfield. And now the first thought that struck me, was whether I should still find Agatha beneath that roof?

"It would be indeed strange," I said to myself, "if she and her lover Richard should have the audacity to remain in this place after they *must* have discovered that their letter was taken out of the vase on the grass-plat. But we shall see!"

Matilda came forward, with her smiling good-humoured countenance, to welcome me back again to Kelvedon Hall; and my first question was concerning her mistress.

"Her ladyship seems a little better—but not much," replied Matilda. "She will be glad to see you, Miss Percy! She was saying to me this morning that she hoped you would return soon; and his lordship is most anxious——But here is his lordship!"

The old nobleman at that moment made his appearance; and he gave me a cordial welcome.

"I had a presentiment that we should see you to-day, Miss Percy," he exclaimed: "and what do you think? Hermione has just told me—not ten minutes back indeed—that if you *did* come, she would descend from her boudoir in the afternoon, and take her place at the dinner-table."

"Indeed!" I exclaimed, in accents of the most unfeigned joy. "Then her ladyship must feel much better!"

This conversation took place in the entrance-hall, at the foot of the great staircase, up which Matilda was already proceeding, accompanied by a lacquey who carried my portmanteaus. I turned to follow; and at that instant my eyes fell upon the countenance of Agatha, who was standing near. I gave an involuntary start; for it struck me at the moment that the young woman's features looked more reserved and even sinister than they had ever seemed on any previous occasion. She evidently noticed that start—as indeed well she might, for it was the strong recoil of one who beholds a reptile suddenly prepared to spring. She spoke not a word of greeting, and was passing on her way, when I could not help saying to her in a peculiar tone, "So I hear that her ladyship is better, Agatha?"

"Yes, Miss," she replied, with the most perfect self-possession—indeed with a countenance so unmoved that I was again forcibly struck with the idea that she must be the veriest hypocrite that ever walked upon the face of the earth.

She passed on her way, for she was traversing the entrance-hall at the time; and Lord Kelvedon said to me, "Now make haste to your chamber, my dear Miss Percy; and then come to Hermione —for she will be full of suspense and anxiety until she sees you!"

I sped up the staircase, and reached my chamber—where Matilda, who was all attention as usual, was lighting the fire, which was ready laid in the grate. I speedily dismissed her for the present; for I did not wish her to be in the room while I unpacked my portmanteaus, inasmuch as I had a certain little parcel that I was resolved should escape all observation, even on the part of one whom I did not in the slightest degree mistrust. The reader can easily imagine that I allude to the little packet of drugs which Dame Betty had sent me at Petersfield.

I found Lady Kelvedon in the boudoir; and though in external appearance she was but little changed, yet her spirits were evidently better than when I was last there—and she gave me the assurance that she felt as if the treatment of the old gipsy-woman was beginning to do her good. This was only the fourth day of her taking her medicine, and therefore when I heard her thus speak so cheeringly, I felt certain it could not be without the evidence of her own sensations. Now, therefore, that I was in possession of the drug on which Dame Betty had so especially counted and which was to make sure doubly sure, I felt completely at ease in reference to Hermione's case. The packet contained a scrap of paper on which instructions were written for the mode of using the drug: no time was accordingly lost in following the prescription—and Hermione smiled with a real gaiety as she spoke of "the old gipsy-woman's elixir of life."

The various presents which I had brought from Petersfield, but which were supposed to have been obtained in London, were spread out upon the sofa; and when Lord Kelvedon presently entered the boudoir and beheld these things, he reiterated the expression of his gratitude for all the trouble I had taken.

"It is you — and you alone, my dear Miss Percy," he exclaimed, "who have wrought a beneficial change in Hermione! I do not know how it is," he went on to observe, more slowly; "but I have recently entertained fears that you are too much secluded:"—and he now addressed himself direct to his wife; — "perhaps you have not enough gaiety—I have kept you too much out of society—I have been selfish! You perceive——"

"No—do not blame yourself, my dear husband!" exclaimed Lady Kelvedon; "for I can assure you that you have no cause. I have experienced a perfect distaste for all society——"

"But now that feeling is passing away," interjected the nobleman; "and perhaps Miss Percy will agree with me in thinking that your mind ought to be aroused?"

"I do think so, most decidedly!" I said, recollecting that Hermione entertained the greatest friendship for Aline, and knowing likewise that nothing would delight Mrs. Gower more than to pay a visit to Lady Kelvedon. "I am very glad your lordship has mentioned the subject, to which I should have certainly taken the liberty of alluding——"

"Do what you like in the matter, Miss Percy!" exclaimed his lordship: "every arrangement you may make will be sure to please me. Fill the Hall with guests, if you think fit! And now I shall leave you both together, that you may discourse on the subject and settle your proceedings."

The old nobleman accordingly withdrew; and Hermione said to me, "Here indeed is a change, my dear Ellen! If only a fortnight back I had thrown out the slightest hint indicative of a desire to have Aline or any one else to stay with me, there would have been objections——Indeed, as you already know, it was only *your* name which in this sense found favour with my husband. Ah!

by the bye, I received a letter this very morning from a friend of mine with whom you are well acquainted. I mean the Countess of Belgrave."

"Oh, yes!" I exclaimed: "I know her ladyship well."

"She mentioned your name in her letter," resumed Lady Kelvedon, "and speaks in the most affectionate terms of you. You knew her, I think, when she was still Lady Cecilia Urban?"

"Yes," I responded, "I have known her more than two years—and she has only been married a year."

"Now, if I chose to avail myself of his lordship's permission," continued Lady Kelvedon, "here is an opportunity for having a most agreeable guest, who is as intimate with you as she is with me. Her husband, the Earl of Belgrave, has gone on a visit of two or three weeks to a near relation of his own who lives in Paris: but Cecilia did not feel inclined to undertake the journey at this season of the year."

"By all means," I said, "invite the Countess of Belgrave to stay a few days here, if you experience the inclination. And Aline?"

"I will write to them both," answered Lady Kelvedon. "Not to-day!—but to-morrow. To-day I must have the full enjoyment of your society, which shall not be broken in upon even for the purpose of penning these two notes of invitation."

I was rejoiced at the idea of Hermione receiving guests: for the circumstance indicated a favourable change in the state of her mind—and therefore the depressing influence of the poison which for weeks had been administered to her, was evidently falling off. But perhaps the poison itself was being no longer administered at all, and therefore Dame Betty's medicine was proving all the more effective, its power being condensed in the process of working a cure, and none of that power being as it were intercepted for a mere antidotal purpose.

In the course of the afternoon the London morning papers were delivered at Kelvedon Hall; and everything which Lady Lilla Essendine predicted in reference to the proceedings connected with Edwin St. Clair at the Old Bailey was fulfilled to the very letter. In the absence of the *one* material witness for the prosecution—namely, the old gipsy woman—his acquittal had been at once pronounced, and the judge assured him that he left the Court without the slightest stain upon his character. But upon this subject I need not now dwell at any greater length, because I shall have yet much to say relative to Edwin St. Clair in future chapters of my narrative.

I seized an opportunity, within an hour or two after my arrival at the Hall, to walk out for a few minutes into the grounds: and I examined the stone vase to see if by any chance the letter which I had written in a feigned hand and deposited there, should be still in that place. No letter was in the vase:—but though it had disappeared, I was still uncertain as to what had been its fate—whether it had been consigned to the post, or whether it had been destroyed by the wretches connected with the murderous plot which I was now so successfully engaged in frustrating.

Lady Kelvedon fulfilled her promise by descending that day to the dining-room; and on the following morning she still further rejoiced both her husband and myself by appearing in the breakfast parlour. The habit of taking her repast in the boudoir was thus given up; and the lady's-maids no longer waited at meal times upon their mistress. Two or three days passed—and Lady Kelvedon was now improving visibly and undoubtedly under the influence of the peculiar drug which had been added to the other ingredients of her medicine. I should observe that the invitations had been sent to the Countess of Belgrave and to Major and Mrs. Gower—they had been accepted on the part of both the ladies—but business unexpectedly took Major Gower to the north of England, so that he did not propose to accompany his wife on the occasion to Kelvedon Hall.

———

CHAPTER CXV.

MATILDA.

I AM now about to speak of incidents which occurred on the fourth day after my arrival at Kelvedon Hall. It was the 20th of December; and it was on the 13th that Hermione had begun to take the old gipsy-woman's medicine: the lapse of a week had beyond all doubt done much for this amiable lady—and I had not the slightest misgiving left in reference to her eventual cure.

It was about noon, and I was seated with Lord and Lady Kelvedon in an elegantly-furnished apartment called "the morning room," and which was situated in the front part of the house. Presently, a young man on horseback was seen approaching along the avenue; and Lord Kelvedon remarked in a casual manner, "It is young Brownlow."

"Ah, indeed!" ejaculated Hermione; "this reminds me of something. I am sorry to say I shall shortly lose Agatha."

"How so?" inquired his lordship: and it may be easily conceived by the reader how I myself was suddenly rendered an interested person in this discourse.

"She has told me very candidly," continued Lady Kelvedon, "that she is going to settle herself by marriage. She has therefore intimated her desire to leave me at the expiration of a month; and the young woman spoke very feelingly, I can assure you—for you would not think by her countenance that she possessed such a good heart as I know that she does."

"But how does the appearance of this young Brownlow, the tax-gatherer's son," added Lord Kelvedon, "put you in mind that Agatha has given you warning? Do you mean that——"

"Yes," replied Hermione, with a smile: "I mean precisely what I see that you already more than half conjecture; for it is this very identical Richard Brownlow that Agatha is going to marry."

I started: but as my kerchief at the same moment fell from my lap upon the carpet, it seemed as if this were the cause of that abrupt movement on my part, and thus it passed without farther notice.

"Ah, indeed," said Lord Kelvedon: "so Agatha is going to marry young Brownlow? Well, she is a fortunate girl. His father is tolerably well off, and the young man himself seems to be industrious. I have noticed for the last twelvemonth that he has gone about collecting the assessed taxes; so that I suppose old Brownlow has delegated the office of collector to him."

While Lord Kelvedon was thus speaking, I was surveying Richard Brownlow from the window. He was advancing on horseback, at a moderate pace; and I therefore had a full opportunity of thus studying his appearance. He was a good-looking young man, about five and twenty years of age: he was neatly dressed, without any pretension; and there was nothing in his countenance to justify the suspicions which I entertained concerning him. And then an idea struck me. How could he be a tax-collector if he were unable to write, and was compelled to get his mistress to perform the part of secretary? But then the next moment another thought occurred to me,—which was, that the receipts might be already filled up and signed by his father—so that he himself had nothing to do but to deliver them on receiving the respective amounts.

The young man rode up to the entrance of the mansion; and just at the moment Lord Kelvedon remarked, "He rides a very nice nag."

"Yes," I said: "so far as I am a judge, it seems a nice horse."

I hastened to avail myself of the excuse thus afforded for approaching the window; and under pretence of looking at the horse, I was in reality studying the proceedings of its rider. The hall-porter was standing on the steps; and Richard Brownlow was looking over one of those long narrow-shaped books containing the printed forms used by tax-collectors. In a few moments the young man found the receipt for which he was searching; and he mentioned a sum to the hall-porter. This official counted out the money from his own pocket; and then I beheld Richard Brownlow filling up the printed form with a pencil as he still maintained his seat on horseback.

"Perhaps," I thought to myself, "he may just be enabled to write his name, and that is all?"

The receipt was handed to the porter, and Richard Brownlow rode away. In a few moments a footman brought the receipt into the morning-room; for Lord Kelvedon was always very particular in respect to his accounts.

"Are the taxes heavy in this part of the country," I inquired, longing to obtain a sight of the document which the old nobleman now held in his hand.

"Look, Miss Percy," he said: and he tendered me the paper.

I took it:—the entire form had just been filled in with pencil-writing,—the date, the sum, and the young man's own name, all being written in the same hand—and this a good fluent hand; so that I was lost in astonishment as I compared the present fact with my previous impression that the man was utterly incapable of writing at all!

"And so you think this will be a good match for Agatha?" I said to Lord Kelvedon.

"A very good one," responded the nobleman. "Young Brownlow is steady: he belongs to a respectable family—perhaps you may have noticed that he is by no means bad-looking—and his father gave him a good education."

I was more and more astonished.

"A good education!" I thought within myself; "and yet he professed to Agatha to be unable to read or write! Was it some deeper piece of wickedness on his part, for the purpose of shifting all the responsibility, in case of detection, from his own shoulders to that of the young woman who loves him? Yes—it must have been so! Unless indeed there is an extraordinary mistake somewhere or another? But no! how can this be? R. B. stands for Richard Brownlow. Yes!—and did I not hear the unmistakable voice of Agatha address him as *Richard*, the other evening when I was returning from depositing the letter in the vase?"

I was much bewildered with the incident that had thus occurred: but it is needless to swell out my narrative by a record of all the reflections and meditations that passed through my brain upon the occasion. Indeed, my attention was presently diverted to other subjects; for between one and two o'clock a carriage with four post-horses drove up to the entrance of the Hall. This was the Countess of Belgrave's barouche: she had just arrived from London—and she had brought Mrs. Gower with her. Warm were the greetings that now ensued: indeed the Countess was specially delighted to meet me at Kelvedon Hall; while both she and Aline were rejoiced to learn that Hermione's health was improving.

After luncheon we went out for an airing in the carriage,—Lord Kelvedon riding on horseback; and this was the first time that Hermione had been outside the front door for the last three weeks. She was in excellent spirits: the presence of her friends combined with the exhilarating influence of the clear frosty atmosphere to produce this effect. We proceeded nearly as far as Petersfield; and I beheld the ruined farm-buildings where I had so recently been a prisoner in company with Dame Betty. As we were returning home, a very elegant equipage dashed past us: a female was seated therein—and I at once recognised Melissa Harrison; so that I had no difficulty in conjecturing that she had succeeded in making her peace with the Marquis of Tynedale. Although the glimpse which I had of her was so transitory, it was nevertheless sufficient to show me that she was magnificently dressed, and reclining back in the splendid equipage with the fastidiously insolent air of a great lady.

We returned to Kelvedon Hall; and as the dinner-hour approached, I repaired to my chamber to perform my evening toilet. Matilda was quickly in attendance, and she lavished on me her usual assiduities.

"So your fellow-servant Agatha," I said, "is going to leave her situation in this establishment?"

"Yes, Miss," replied Matilda. "Agatha is going to be married."

"I heard her ladyship intimate the fact," I responded. "The person whom she is going to marry is named Brownlow, I think?"

"Yes, Miss; and he is a very respectable young man," said Matilda. "I have known for some months past that he was courting Agatha, though she did not like to mention it to her ladyship till this morning; for you know my lord is very particular, and will not allow the servants to have any followers."

"And yet I heard his lordship speak very favourably of Richard Brownlow," I remarked.

"Of course, Miss," rejoined Matilda; "because his lordship could not possibly speak in any other way of the young man: but for all that, his lordship would be dreadfully angry if he knew that Richard Brownlow had ever visited Agatha here by stealth. Perhaps you might have seen, Miss, that the moment Richard collected the tax to-day, he turned and rode off?"

"Yes—I noticed it," I answered. "But did I understand you that this Richard Brownlow has visited Agatha stealthily?"

"Ah, Miss, you know it!—or at least you must have suspected it!" cried Matilda; "and on that very account poor Agatha thinks you have taken a dislike to her."

"Explain yourself, Matilda," I said, now feeling that the discourse was every moment becoming more and more interesting.

"Why, Miss, the other night, you know," continued Matilda,—"it was the second time you came to the Hall—on the 13th of this month—I remember the date very well,—you went into the garden because you had a headache—you left the private door unlocked—and Agatha went up the staircase——"

"Yes—all this is true, and I remember the circumstance," I said.

"Well, Miss," continued Matilda; "Agatha told me that she met you on the occasion—she said it was in the bath-room, and that when you questioned her you looked at her so very hard that she fancied you suspected something."

"And what did she suppose I suspected?" I inquired.

"That she had stolen out into the back garden for the purpose of meeting her lover—which was really the case; and poor Agatha said she felt all of a tremble in your presence—she stammered, blushed, and looked confused, for she told you a story—she said that she, like yourself, had gone out to get the fresh air on account of a headache, while in reality it was because she had expected to meet young Richard for a moment that she might exchange a word with him. But he did not happen to come that evening."

"And so Agatha fancies," I said, "that I have conceived a dislike towards her? Is this idea based upon no other ground than that which you have just explained?"

"Not that I know of, Miss," answered Matilda. "This is all that Agatha told me. She is of rather an independent spirit—though I believe she possesses an excellent heart——"

"At all events," I interjected, "I am quite prepared to hear you tell me that she has conceived a dislike towards myself."

"No!—I don't think that, Miss," responded Matilda: "but she certainly thinks that you have once or twice spoken rather harshly to her—and she has therefore shown the independence of her disposition in return. Perhaps she considers it rather hard that you should have questioned her so closely and looked at her so suspiciously on that evening to which I just now referred; because, as she says, she was really doing no harm—and if now and then she *did* stealthily meet a young man to whom she was honourably engaged, it was only because she was not allowed to receive him in the servants' hall. I told Agatha that I was convinced you had no ill-feeling towards her, Miss——at all events you never mentioned to her ladyship that you suspected she had met her lover——"

"But if I held my peace upon the point, Matilda," I said, with some degree of emphasis, "it was only because poor Lady Kelvedon was at the time too ill to be troubled with such matters; or else perhaps——yes, indeed——I am speaking deliberately when I say that I might have mentioned certain things to her ladyship——"

"Indeed, Miss?" ejaculated Matilda, with a startled and frightened air.

"Do not be alarmed," I said, with a reassuring smile: "for you know very well that it is not about yourself I could tell any tales."

"Ah, no, Miss!" exclaimed Matilda. "I was not afraid of that; for I have never done anything wrong. But you were speaking of Agatha. I suppose——"

"Has not this Richard Brownlow succeeded in obtaining a very great influence over Agatha?" I inquired.

"I don't know, Miss: I can scarcely tell," responded Matilda. "But might I ask what makes you think——"

"Do you happen to know whether Richard Brownlow is a person of good education?" I inquired: "has Agatha herself ever spoken to you on the point?"

Matilda reflected for a few moments; and then she said, "No, Miss—I don't think she has. She is a very reserved girl—she does not talk much to her fellow-servants——"

"Now I was surprised," I said, "to hear his lordship to-day speak of Richard Brownlow as a well educated young man; whereas I had some reason for fancying that it was the exact reverse and that Richard Brownlow was a young man of no education at all."

"Indeed, Miss?" exclaimed Matilda. "But I really cannot say how the truth may be—I know very, very little of Richard Brownlow—I have never spoken to him but twice in my life——But still I should think he must be a person of at least some education; for he is now collecting the taxes, you see—and he is promised the situation of under bailiff to the Marquis of Tynedale."

"Ah, indeed?" I said. "A bailiff must have some knowledge of accounts as well as of reading and writing; and therefore it is tolerably clear that Richard Brownlow must be a person of some decent education. But if you know nothing of his mental qualifications," I continued, "you at least know something relative to those of your fellow-servant, Agatha?"

"Oh, yes!" exclaimed Matilda. "Agatha is rather a clever girl. She writes a very good hand——"

"And perhaps you know her handwriting," I said, now determined to take a particular step as the opportunity presented itself.

"Of course I do, Miss," rejoined Matilda, surveying me with an air of surprise mingled with a growing perplexity.

"But suppose," I continued, "that Agatha was to disguise her handwriting——"

"What! disguise it?—how so, Miss? what do you mean? I don't understand——disguise her writing, Miss?"

"Yes, Matilda," I said: "the question I put to you is plain enough. Suppose that Agatha had disguised her handwriting to the utmost of her power, do you think that you would be enabled to distinguish it?"

Matilda looked more and more perplexed at the turn which I was giving the discourse: she reflected and hesitated for some time—and at last she said, "Yes, I think that I should know her handwriting."

I opened one of my portmanteaus and drew forth my portfolio. Thence I produced the letter which I had taken from the stone vase; but I did not suffer Matilda to see the envelope, which was addressed to Mr. Collingwood, at the *Hotel du Nord*, Boulogne. Unfolding the letter itself, which contained no indication of its being intended for Mr. Collingwood, I said, "Is that Agatha's handwriting?"

Matilda received the letter, and having glanced at it, she raised her looks towards my face, asking in a low and even hollow voice, "What does all this mean, Miss? what is it to lead to? Do you—do you mean——"

"Look at the letter again, and read it if you like," I said. "It is very generous and good-hearted of you to be so much concerned on behalf of your fellow-servant: but be so kind as to put all these considerations out of the question while you tell me whether this is Agatha's handwriting or not."

"Ah, Miss, do inform me in the first place," said Matilda, with the deepest anxiety exhibited in her tones, looks, and manner—indeed her countenance was very pale, whereas it was usually tinged with the hues of buxom health,—"do inform me how this letter fell into your hands, and what makes you suspect——"

"Do not ask me any questions, Matilda," I interrupted her: "there are reasons why I cannot answer them—at least not for the present. Perhaps the day may come when you will know everything."

"Ah! not for the present?" ejaculated Matilda. "Then is there something dreadful?"

"I must not be questioned," I said. "On the other hand, you must really answer me the query which I have put. Is that the handwriting, though artfully disguised, of Agatha?"

"Oh, Miss!" cried Matilda, "if I were to say *yes*, what would you do? what do you intend?"

"Nothing for the present, I repeat! But if you think fit——Answer me first however: is that Agatha's handwriting?"

Matilda took the letter close to the lamp which was burning on the toilet-table; and methought that she was examining the writing with a carefulness and an attention best calculated to ensure the most guarded answer—for she was at least two or three minutes before she gave me her response. Then she slowly turned towards me, and flung a timid glance of entreaty or inquiry on my countenance.

"Speak out boldly, Matilda," I said: "no possible harm can happen to you—and if you are delicate in being considered a witness against your own fellow-servant, I will faithfully promise that your name shall never be mentioned."

"Oh, thank you, Miss!" cried Matilda, her features brightening up. "Well then, I have no longer any hesitation in saying that this is most assuredly so very much like the handwriting of Agatha, purposely disguised——"

"Enough, Matilda!" I said, taking the letter from her hand. "I had little or no doubt upon the point; but still I wished to obtain confirmatory evidence, if possible."

"But how came that letter, Miss, to fall into your hands?" asked Matilda.

"I tell you that this is my secret," I responded. "Now, if you choose to whisper in the ear of Agatha that I do not consider her to be a proper person to remain attached to the service of Lady Kelvedon——"

"She has given a month's notice, Miss," interjected Matilda.

"I am aware of it," I rejoined: "but not even so short a period as another month ought she to remain beneath this roof. No!—she must not. You may whisper in her ear, therefore, that I have obtained a clue to certain facts——"

"Yes, yes, Miss! I will tell her!" cried Matilda. "But whatever it may be, you will not mention it to his lordship or her ladyship? you will be merciful? you will not destroy a poor young woman——"

"Do as I have suggested," I interrupted Matilda, "and you will spare me the necessity of telling anything to Lord and Lady Kelvedon. In a word, you must induce Agatha to leave this house! It would be better if she and her intended husband were to leave the neighbourhood altogether——aye, or even to leave the country!"

"In how short a time?" asked Matilda. "What is the delay that you will accord, Miss Percy? for perhaps I cannot all in a moment——"

"Within three days Agatha must have left Kelvedon Hall," I rejoined. "And now let the subject drop."

"Ah! but tell me," said Matilda, "what you have discovered or what you suspect? It is evidently something dreadful! That letter says—— Ah! what does it say?—something about *the sick one being no better;* and then it goes on to say that *whether the visit of E. P. will make any difference, is more than can be foreseen.* Now the sick one must doubtless——or at least I should think the phrase must mean Lady Kelvedon; while the initials E. P. most certainly allude to yourself, Miss."

"Let us not discuss the subject, Matilda," I said. "It is a painful one, and you are a good young woman, with a feeling heart——"

"Oh! but I hate these dreadful mysteries," cried Matilda. "You see, Miss, everything now leads me to suspect that there is something very terrible in all this. It is evident that your presence here has made a difference in respect to her ladyship:—within the last eight days there has been a gradual and visible improvement. Ah! it is you that have done this, Miss Percy! But what would you have me to understand? Oh! I beseech you to tell me, Miss!—because how do I know whether circumstances may not——"

"Enough, Matilda!" I ejaculated: "whatever these circumstances may be, rest assured that they can never implicate you! And now let me make haste with my toilet; for it is close upon half-past five o'clock."

It was to this hour that the dinner-time had been altered for the last few days, and the repasts were always served punctually at Kelvedon Hall, for his lordship was very particular upon these points. I locked my portfolio again in my trunk, and I secured the keys about my person: but I watched an opportunity to do so when Matilda's back was turned, for I did not of course wish to wound her feelings by allowing her to imagine that I supposed her capable of possessing herself of the letter in order to save the character of a fellow-servant in case the day of threatening exposure should ever come.

I proceeded to the drawing-room, where I found Lord and Lady Kelvedon, the Countess of Belgrave, and Aline, all ready assembled. The three ladies were all in full evening costume, as I myself was; and exceedingly beautiful did they appear. The day's ride had imparted a slight tint to the cheeks of Lady Kelvedon: her eyes were brighter than they had recently been; her long brown wavy hair fell in a heavy mass, so to speak, upon her back. In one of the earlier chapters of my narrative I have described the Countess of Belgrave. She was now twenty years of age, of a fine tall commanding figure. Her dark hair displayed the most luxuriant profusion; her eyes were truly magnificent; she carried her head proudly upon the long stately neck; and the whole expression of her countenance was that of a haughty beauty. In strong contrast was her appearance with that of Aline, whose blue eyes were so mild and soft in their expression, whose looks were so replete with the most winning amiability, and whose movements, gestures, and attitudes were associated only with elegance and grace, while those of Cecilia produced the impression of a superb queenliness and haughty majesty. Yet be it remembered that the Countess of Belgrave in reality possessed a very good heart; and with those towards whom she did choose to unbend she proved a most affable and agreeable person. Still she was one of those with whom it was impossible to feel on precisely the same terms of intimacy as with Lady Kelvedon or Aline; for even in her most amiable moments there was always a certain manifestation of conscious dignity which repelled that exceeding warm gush of feelings which flowed from the heart towards the other two.

Dinner was quickly announced; we partook of the sumptuous repast; and in due time we rose from the table and again found ourselves in the drawing-room. There we remained conversing until Lord Kelvedon joined us; and then coffee being served, I took my seat at the piano in compliance with the request of my friends. I sang and played two or three airs: I was then succeeded by the Countess of Belgrave, who was a grand musician. Afterwards Aline took her turn: and thus the evening passed until about ten o'clock, when I proposed that we should retire to rest, for I was afraid lest Hermione should sit up too long. We bade his lordship "Good night," and accompanied Lady Kelvedon to her boudoir, that we might have a last few minutes' chat before separating.

For the better understanding of the incidents which are to follow, the reader will permit me to remind him that her ladyship's suite of apartments consisted of the sitting-room or boudoir—

next the bed-chamber—then a dressing-room—then a bath-room—beyond which was the landing at the head of the private staircase. I must further observe that since Lady Kelvedon's illness, her handmaidens had taken it by turns to occupy a couch which was made up in the dressing-room adjoining her ladyship's own chamber. This duty was generally shared between Matilda and Agatha. It was Agatha's turn to occupy that couch on the present occasion; but she had not yet made her appearance,—it being Hermione's custom to ring when she required the presence of her handmaiden for the night.

"Come, let us sit down and talk for ten minutes," said Lady Kelvedon, "before we separate. I am so glad to have you all with me that I can scarcely even afford to part with you until to-morrow morning!"

"And you feel so much better, my dear Hermione—do you not?" asked Aline.

"Oh, infinitely better!" responded Lady Kelvedon. "It seems," she added, with a quick glance of significancy flung towards me, "as if the lapse of the last week had begun to give me a new lease of life. I have now energy and spirits: to-morrow we will again take a long ride in the carriage—I even promise myself a little walking exercise; and in a few days, if I go on thus improving at the same rate, I shall astonish you all by taking a canter across the park."

"Nothing could afford me greater pleasure," said the Countess, "than to hear you talk in this cheerful strain. But it is our friend Ellen who has performed the miracle. His lordship assured me just now at dinner that it was her presence only which had wrought the cure——"

Just at this moment we were all four startled by a crashing sound, which seemed to emanate from somewhere within the suite of apartments. It was an abruptly occurring and quickly passing din, just as if some heavy object had fallen or something had given way.

"Good heavens! what can it be?" ejaculated Lady Kelvedon; and all the colour had now fled from her cheeks.

"Do not be alarmed," I said: "depend upon it, we shall find that nothing very serious has happened! It seems as if it were a portion of the ceiling that had fallen in one of the inner rooms. But we will soon ascertain:"—and I took up a wax taper.

"My dear Ellen," exclaimed Lady Kelvedon, seizing me by the arm, "let me ring for some one! —let us summon assistance!"

"Oh, no," I said: "it is unnecessary. Hark! the noise has ceased?"

"We will at least go with you, Ellen," said the Countess of Belgrave, preparing to follow Lady Kelvedon and myself.

"And I am not to be left behind," said Aline, bringing up the rear.

We passed in this manner from the boudoir into the bedchamber,—I myself carrying the light, Hermione hanging to my arm, Cecilia and Aline following close behind. There was nothing in the bedchamber to account for the sound; and we passed thence into the dressing-room.

"Ah!" I ejaculated, "the atmosphere is thick with dust! You will find that my mode of accounting for the disturbance was not very far from the correct one. Something has given way."

But it was not in the dressing-room, nor yet in the bath-room which lay beyond, that we could discover the cause. I now opened the door leading upon the landing: but I immediately recoiled for a fearful chasm appeared to be yawning at my feet. At the same time an ejaculation of terror burst from the lips of Lady Kelvedon, as she caught me by the arm to pull me back.

"Good heavens!" she cried; "the flooring has given way!"

"The flooring!" exclaimed Cecilia and Aline, as if they were both speaking in the same breath.

"Yes, indeed—it is so," I responded. "But there is no danger of this floor"—alluding to the one on which we then stood—"giving way likewise. It is the upper part of the staircase which has fallen out, as it were, from the wall; and the landing, losing its main support, has fallen in."

Yes—the case was as I have represented it: the whole of the landing and the three or four upper steps of the staircase had disappeared from the view—or rather lay in a confused jumble of broken woodwork, lath, and plaster on the ground-floor beneath!

CHAPTER CXVI.

THE CHASM.

LADY KELVEDON, though improved in health and spirits, was yet very far from being strong enough to encounter this incident without emotion; and I therefore lost not an instant in speaking to her in the most reassuring manner,—characterizing the affair as one of those little incidents which might be expected to take place in new buildings as well as in old. I however closed the door that looked upon that chasm as quick as possible, and got Lady Kelvedon back into the boudoir with the least possible delay.

"Let us send for his lordship!" said Hermione. "Indeed I think we ought to let the whole household know——"

"Oh, pray tranquillize yourself," I said: "there is not the slightest necessity for doing anything of the kind!"

"No—not the slightest," said the Countess of Belgrave, who thoroughly understood what my purpose was: namely to avoid any additional causes of excitement, and to let the matter pass over as smoothly as possible, for the sake of Lady Kelvedon's nerves, which would be incapable of enduring any severe play upon them.

"But I dare say," said Hermione, "the whole household is by this time alarmed!—the din must have been heard in the servants' offices!"

"Take my word for it," I said, "the noise was not heard at all—or if so, it was attributed to some other cause. Remember, that private staircase is enclosed within four very thick walls; and between it and the servants' offices there are the store-rooms. Besides, if the sound had been really heard, we should by this time have had all the domestics flocking hither to ascertain what is the matter."

"And you really think, my dear Ellen," cried her ladyship, "that it is useless to inform my husband?"

"Useless until to-morrow," I answered. "If the household generally remain unconscious of the event, there is no use in spreading the alarm. No good could be done to-night: there are no masons at hand to commence the work of reparation; and even if there were, you could not be annoyed by the sounds of their labour while you want to sleep."

"But are the contiguous apartments all safe?" asked Hermione.

"As safe," I responded, "as if they stood upon a solid rock!"

The Countess of Belgrave and Mrs. Gower echoed this assurance which I had just given; and Lady Kelvedon began to regain her lost self-possession. She however looked at me in a manner as if she had a request to make, but which she

scarcely liked to proffer; and I quickly comprehended what was uppermost in her mind.

"My dear Hermione," I said, "I will pass the night here with you. Yes—it will be better; and this will at all events convince you of my firm conviction that there is nothing to be apprehended."

"Oh, then, pardon my foolish fears!" exclaimed Lady Kelvedon: "but I accept your kind offer, Ellen—and you will not find that I shall trouble you any more with my nervous apprehensions."

Cecilia and Aline now prepared to bid us "good night;" and as they were issuing from the boudoir, I whispered to them, "It will be better for you not to mention to your maids to-night what has occurred; or the report might circulate and an alarm would be excited in the house——which would prove most detrimental to the health of our dear friend Hermione."

The two ladies made me a sign to signify their

compliance with my hint; and they took their departure to their own respective chambers.

"Whose turn is it," I asked, when they were gone, "to sleep in the dressing-room to-night?"

"Agatha's," was Lady Kelvedon's response.

"Ah! I remember! so it is!" I ejaculated. "But if you like, we will dispense with her services altogether for this present occasion——"

"Oh, no! let us have her near us!" cried her ladyship: "for though I really do not anticipate the slightest danger—and moreover, as I am not so foolish as to imagine that even if it threatened us, it could be warded off by her presence,—still there is that superstitious idea which in all things prompts us to have faith in numbers when assembled together."

"Well, be it so," I responded: "but do not send the girl out of the room when once she shall have entered it; for we have already agreed, you know, that the accident is not to be generally communicated until the morrow."

"You shall have your own way in all things, my dear friend," rejoined Hermione.

I now rang the bell as a summons for Agatha; and this young woman almost immediately made her appearance. As the reader has seen, I could have wished to dispense with her presence; for I thought it very likely that Matilda might in the meantime have communicated to her on the subject of her leaving the house within three days—and I did not therefore wish to have in such close vicinage a person who might have learnt how she was suspected by me. But I did not combat Lady Kelvedon's wish to have Agatha's attendance, for fear of being closely questioned as to the causes of my own disinclination. Besides, I thought to myself that however malicious, spiteful, or ill-intentioned Agatha might be, I would adopt the proper precautions to prevent her from doing any harm, either to her mistress or myself. When Agatha entered the boudoir, I looked at her attentively, but without appearing to be thus intent on the study of her countenance. I saw that her features were calm and placid as usual—unmoved in their somewhat sullen and sinister expression; and I said to myself, "Matilda has not yet found an opportunity of touching on the point;—and perhaps it is all the better under existing circumstances."

"Agatha," I said, "come with me for a moment into the adjoining room."

I took up a taper; and she immediately followed me with that cold air of reserved and distant respect which she maintained towards me as well as to her noble master and mistress. I led her on as far as the bath-room; and then I said, "An accident has occurred close by this evening: but do not be alarmed. The whole flooring of the landing-place has fallen in!"

"Indeed, Miss?" —and now Agatha seemed somewhat excited above her wonted mood of frigid imperturbability.

"Yes," I continued; "but for obvious reasons I have thought it better to suffer no noise to be made upon the subject until to-morrow. Thanks to the operation of the inscrutable ways of Providence"—and here I looked her very hard in the face—"your mistress is improving in health; but all unnecessary excitement must be avoided."

"No doubt of it, Miss," answered Agatha, who by this time had relapsed into her cold phlegmatic manner, and whose countenance underwent not the slightest change as I riveted my regards so fixedly upon it.

"I am going to pass the night with Lady Kelvedon," I continued; "for she is somewhat nervous on account of this accident: but you will occupy the couch in the dressing-room all the same."

"Yes, Miss," she responded.

We then returned into the boudoir, where Hermione almost immediately commenced the details of her night-toilet by the assistance of Agatha.

"I must go to my own chamber for a few minutes," I said; "and then I will return."

I proceeded to my room, where I found Matilda awaiting my presence. She had made up a good fire, as was her custom; and she was warming herself by it when I entered.

"Have you yet spoken to Agatha," I inquired, "relative to that matter which I mentioned this afternoon?"

"No, Miss," answered Matilda: "I have not yet found an opportunity."

"Well, it is of no consequence," I said: "tomorrow will do just as well."

When she had unfastened my dress, I dismissed her for the night; for I was not accustomed to engage her attentions any farther in my preparations for retiring to rest. I thought that she lingered in the chamber and fidgetted about somewhat, as if she desired to speak to me ere she took her departure: but I said to myself, "In the goodness of her heart she wishes to intercede for Agatha. It is well-intentioned and praiseworthy on her part; but I will not afford her the opportunity!"

She bade me good night: and left the room. A few minutes afterwards I put on a morning wrapper, and returned to Lady Kelvedon's boudoir. Hermione was nearly ready to seek her own couch: I sat down, and conversed with her until her night-toilet was completely finished and Agatha had retired into the dressing-room. I then proceeded to disapparel myself; and in a short time I occupied my share of Lady Kelvedon's bed. She did not converse many minutes before slumber stole upon her eyes; and by half-past eleven o'clock she was asleep. I lay awake, thinking of the occurrences of the day—but for no very great length of time; and at midnight I also was sinking into a profound repose.

But this was not destined to last for any considerable period. I was awakened by a sound which reached my ears; it struck me that I heard a window opening at no very great distance. I listened with suspended breath:—all was still, and I thought my imagination must have deceived me. I was composing myself to sleep again, when I was once more startled—and methought that it was by a similar sound. But again, when I listened, everything was once more still, and the most solemn silence appeared to be reigning throughout the spacious habitation. Nevertheless, as my suspicions were so strongly excited against Agatha, I was determined to assure myself that there was nothing wrong. I therefore descended with the utmost gentleness from the bed; for Lady Kelvedon was sleeping soundly by my side. I listened at the door of the dressing-room; but all continued perfectly still. Yet I was resolved to leave nothing to mere surmise or conjecture: I therefore opened that door of communication, but in so noiseless a manner that in this respect it was the same as if I had not opened it at all. I peeped in—the light was extinguished there: but a taper was burning in the chamber which I occupied with Hermione; and by its beams I could discern that Agatha was fast asleep—or at least she was lying in her couch with her eyes shut, and with the appearance of one who slumbered profoundly. I glanced at the window: the draperies were closed almost completely over it; but through the slight opening that there was in the middle, I could see that the window itself was shut and that the fastening was secure. Closing the door as noiselessly as I had opened it, I crept back to my place by Hermione's side.

I did not immediately endeavour to compose myself to sleep again: I lay thinking and listening. If any one had been there to put the question to me whether I now believed that I had heard a window opening, I should have been inclined to answer at once in the negative; but still there was in my soul a lurking idea—a species of vague apprehension, to the effect that it was not altogether an illusion on my part. Not more than five minutes had elapsed after I had thus returned to bed—the most solemn silence again appeared to be prevailing throughout the mansion—when all in a moment, suddenly as the trumpet of doom may be supposed to send forth its pealing blast when the great final day shall come, that stillness was fearfully, horribly broken in upon! Not more terribly does the appalling cry of " Fire!" come upon the ears of those who are startled up from their slumber,—not more hideous could the yell of "Murder!" be, when all in a moment pealing through the silence of night,—than was the manner in which the stillness of Kelvedon Hall was now broken! First one tremendous ejaculation of mortal terror!—then another! the latter following as closely upon the former as two pulsations of the heart, or two strokes of a bell that is being rung violently! Thus they smote upon the ear! Thus they rang horribly through the mansion! —and they were accompanied by the sounds of two heavy bodies falling one after the other just as quickly as the two cries that indicated the mortal pain of some horrible catastrophe!

I started up all shuddering and quivering: Lady Kelvedon sprang up in a similar manner by my side: then there was instantaneously the sound of Agatha leaping from her own bed in the next room.

"Good God!" cried Lady Kelvedon; "is it a horrible dream?" and she sank back gasping with affright and terror, on her pillow.

" For heaven's sake compose yourself!" I said: "but it is no dream!"—and in the twinkling of an eye I sprang out of bed.

At the same instant there was a violent knocking at the door leading into the dressing-room, and which door I had locked after peeping in upon Agatha.

"Open, open! for God's sake!" cried that young woman's voice. "Something terrible has occurred close by!"

I opened the door with the utmost despatch; and as the light streamed upon Agatha's countenance, the beams showed that it was as pale as that of a corpse.

"Good God! Miss Percy!" she murmured, clasping her hands; "what can it be? The sounds came from *there!*"—and she pointed in the direction of the bath-room, or rather of the private staircase which lay beyond—for I instantaneously comprehended her meaning.

I threw my morning-wrapper over my shoulders—caught up a light—and rushed towards the bath-room. Nothing unusual was there to be seen; and the window was closed; but it was with an awful shuddering throughout my entire form, and with the horrible presentiment of being about to make some terrific discovery, that I opened the opposite door of that bath-room—the door which now overhung the chasm where a landing once had been! At the same instant a strong gust of wind blew in upon me, nearly extinguishing the light which I carried; but I instantaneously shielded it with my hand. Agatha was behind me in her night-dress: but I had not time at the moment to think of her, nor to pause to reflect how she might possibly be connected with all the horrible things that were progressing at Kelvedon Hall.

And now I stood upon the threshold of that doorway which overlooked the chasm: the window was open—the curtains were blowing with the strong current of air. Yes—there I stood above the wreck of the fallen floor! I plunged my eyes down into the abyss; dark objects lay there— human shapes—yes, unmistakable forms of men —but motionless as if dead! No, they were not dead!—for moans of intense agony were heard; and I ejaculated, "There is life in those wretches! and whoever they are, they must receive prompt ministration!"

I was about to step forward upon the staircase, so as to descend and see what could be done for the miserable beings lying at the bottom—when Agatha caught me by the arm, exclaiming, "For God's sake, Miss Percy, take care what you do! Those steps will not bear you! all their support is gone!"

I instantaneously recognised the truth of what Agatha said. I felt at the moment that she had actually and positively saved my life; and it struck me as singular indeed that I should owe my life to her who I should have thought would perhaps have been only too glad to take it or to see it sacrificed.

"Go and unlock the outer door, Agatha," I said; "for there is a loud knocking at it—and it is doubtless his lordship who is alarmed!"

Agatha at once retired; and I stooped as far over the chasm as in safety I dared—to discern, if possible, who were the men that were lying below. But as it was only a taper which I had in my hand, I could not throw the light in such a way—or rather I should observe, with sufficient power to obtain a view of the countenances of the individuals at the bottom. They were two men; and they seemed to be very coarsely dressed, so that I could not form the slightest conjecture who they were. It was only for a moment that I thus lingered over the abyss; and then I sped back into the bed-chamber.

Lady Kelvedon had fainted: the Countess of

Belgrave and Mrs. Gower were bending over her: they had only just thrown on some loose articles of apparel—they had been alarmed by those terrific cries which had swept like the yell of murder through Kelvedon Hall. And now I myself flung on a shawl which I caught up—and I thrust my feet into slippers—and I sped towards the outer door of the boudoir, at which there was renewed knocking; for Agatha had locked it again after giving admission to Cecilia and Aline. It was now his lordship who entered: he was terribly alarmed—he asked a thousand questions—but I did not pause to answer one. I left the Countess of Belgrave and Aline to respond to them as best they might; for I had just hastily explained to them that a frightful catastrophe had occurred at the private staircase. Snatching up the key of the door at the bottom of that private staircase, I rushed from the boudoir, exclaiming, " Come with me, Agatha ! I insist upon it that you come !"

The young woman had also thrown on a few articles of apparel: she flung upon me a look which seemed to be full of astonishment; and then she said, " Most decidedly, Miss Percy, I am prepared to go with you ; and such peremptory language is not necessary."

I was just upon the point of telling her that such bold words would not serve her turn, when I thought it useless to waste a moment of precious time in bandying observations; and I rushed out of the boudoir — thinking however to myself, " Something has unquestionably happened which has brought matters to a crisis; and Agatha will be unmasked—or perhaps she will fall upon her knees and confess !"

By this time the entire household was alarmed, and all the domestics were flocking from their respective apartments. In a moment I was assailed by a dozen questions.

" What is the matter, Miss Percy ? What were those cries, Miss ? Was it his lordship ? Is her ladyship worse ? Is she dead ? Are there robbers in the house ? What is it ?"—and so forth.

" Come with me," I cried; " and you shall see !"

" In the name of heaven, Miss Percy, what is the matter ?" asked Matilda, who now came rushing down the stairs, as pale as death, and only half dressed—as indeed were the generality of the servants.

" Come with me ! come with me !" I ejaculated: " there is no time for explanations !"

We rushed down the principal staircase—we gained the domestic offices: I flung open one of the back doors—and we passed out into the premises in the rear of the mansion. It was a singular spectacle. There was I, holding in my hand a taper, followed by a crowd of half-dressed domestics, some three or four of whom also carried lights; and a species of wild dismay was depicted upon all countenances.

Thus did we burst forth into the open air; and then I sped straight to the private door to which allusion has been so often made in recent chapters. Some one, looking up, ejaculated, " The window is open !"

" Yes," answered Agatha: " it was there that they came in !"

" Who came in ?" demanded half-a-dozen voices. " What ! robbers ?"

At this moment I turned the key in the lock, and I flung the door wide open. The whole spectacle revealed itself completely. The flooring that had fallen in—the broken balustrades—the staircase that jutted out, as if without support, from the wall—the mass of ruins on the ground—and two human forms stretched there, motionless, in positions which made them seem as if they had been flung there by giant hands—or what was still more natural, and was also strictly correct, as if they had fallen from the open window above ! And now a wild scream rang through the night-air, and one of the half-clad female domestics sprang past me, threw herself upon one of the forms which lay prostrate there, and gave vent to all the horror of her feelings in another long loud scream of agony. It was Matilda !

" Poor young woman !" I ejaculated: " the scene has turned her brain !"

" Oh ! wretch, wretch that I am !" she cried, in accents that I shall never forget, and which even as I now write seem to be ringing in my ears still. " Kill me! slay me! take me to prison! hang me on the highest gibbet !—for my crimes are immense ! Robert ! Robert ! speak, speak! Are you dead ? Oh, pray speak—if only for a moment !"

I was literally staggered by this scene: I was stupified—I was astounded. What! Matilda thus accusing herself ? What did it mean ?

" Why, this is Robert Burton !" exclaimed one of the footmen, as he lifted up the individual on whose form Matilda had thrown herself, while a couple of the females took charge of Matilda herself; for the wretched young woman had suddenly fallen into a state of unconsciousness.

" And who have we here ?" ejaculated another of the footmen, raising the second individual. " Why, is it possible ? Mr. Collingwood !"

" Collingwood !"—and the name was echoed by every tongue.

" Bring them forth !" I said ; " see if there be life in them !"

" Mr. Collingwood is a corpse, Miss ! Yes—his day is over !" exclaimed a footman.

" And 'tis the same with Burton !" cried the other footman.

" Robert Burton !" I ejaculated: " is that the man's name ?"

" Yes, Miss—that's the name."

I looked upon the countenance, and it was utterly unknown to me. A tremendous revulsion of feeling was now taking place in my mind with a violence that was almost overwhelming. Robert Burton! that name answered to the initials at the bottom of the letter which I had taken from the stone vase! Good heavens! was it possible that after all I had wrongfully suspected Agatha and her lover Richard Brownlow, while Matilda and Robert Burton were in reality the guilty persons!

" And who is Robert Burton ?" I demanded: " or rather I should ask, who was he ?"

" Why, Miss, didn't you know ?" exclaimed the butler. " Mr. Collingwood's servant."

There could be no longer a doubt: everything was now apparent—and it was with the greatest difficulty I could restrain myself from seizing Agatha by the hand, pressing it warmly, and imploring her to forgive me.

"Are you sure they are both dead?" I inquired, averting my eyes from the ghastly spectacle of the two corpses.

"There's no doubt of it, Miss," was the answer given by three or four tongues.

"Nevertheless," I said, "let some one mount a horse immediately, and run and fetch the surgeon. All this is most serious—and everything must be done in a consistent and proper manner. Meanwhile remove the bodies to some convenient place—let restoratives be at once applied——"

"The heart of Mr. Collingwood, Miss, will never beat again," said the butler solemnly; "and I much fear that in his lifetime it was a bad heart when it did beat!"

"As for his valet," said one of the footmen, "he is stone dead!"

"Nevertheless," I said, "let my instructions be attended to; for there's often a lingering spark of life when it seems to be extinct. Where is Matilda?"

"They have taken her indoors, Miss," answered one of the servants. "Ah, good heavens! strange things are about to come out!"

"And it was true, you see, Jem," ejaculated one of the footmen to another, "that I did meet Bob Burton lurking about the place t'other night, when everybody thought he was in France along with his master!"

"Yes, yes—it was true enough, no doubt! And look at them—master and man—disguised as labourers! Ah, perhaps the illness of our poor mistress——"

"No doubt of it!" ejaculated several voices, as suspicion all in a moment flamed up into conviction. "Ah, that wretch Matilda!"

"Come with me, Agatha! come with me!" I said; "and let us hasten back to her ladyship!" but I now spoke with such marked kindness and friendship towards the young woman that she again gazed upon me with astonishment.

We re-entered the domestic offices; and meeting one of the servants who some few minutes back had taken charge of Matilda, I said, "Where is the wretched young woman? and how fares it with her?"

"We have taken her up to her own chamber, Miss," was the reply: "she is still in a state of unconsciousness—and I have come down to get some vinegar."

"And when she recovers," I said, "keep a strict watch upon her: she may attempt to commit suicide, or to escape——"

"We will look after her, Miss," replied the servant.

I hastened up the stairs, followed by Agatha; and on reaching the landing, I paused for a moment to say another kind word to her.

"What a shocking scene—was it not, Agatha?" I remarked, throwing into my look and voice as much friendliness as possible.

"Oh, dreadful, Miss! But I feel as if I were almost overwhelmed with consternation and dismay!" continued Agatha—and she looked deadly pale; "for Oh! what must we think of Matilda? what must we think of dear Lady Kelvedon's illness? Oh! now a thousand little circumstances rush to my mind, fearfully proving that Matilda is the vilest of all vile creatures! But, Ah! Miss!" ejaculated Agatha, as a light seemed suddenly to flash in unto her brain, "you have suspected it from the first! Ah, my God! and you have suspected me also!"

"Agatha!" I said, taking her hand and pressing it warmly, "I have suspected you, I confess it!—yes, with sorrow and almost with shame do I confess it! Forgive me! I declare to you that a number of circumstances——"

"Oh, Miss," said Agatha, the tears trickling down her cheeks, "you are so ready to speak kindly where you think that kindness ought to be shown, that you win every heart! Say no more, Miss—unless it is to tell me that you do not suspect me now!"

"Heaven forbid, Agatha!"—and again and again I pressed her hand with the heartiest warmth. "Now let us return to your mistress."

We entered the boudoir. Lady Kelvedon was only at that very instant opening her eyes; and the old nobleman was calling upon her in the most piteous manner to look upon him and to speak to him.

"Leave us, my lord," I said, "for a few minutes: leave us, I beseech you!"—for I saw that by his entreaties and whinings he was only pursuing a course that was calculated to excite Lady Kelvedon even more than other circumstances would tend to play on her nerves. "Go, my lord, I beseech you! withdraw into the boudoir! Agatha will tell you the fearful discoveries that have been made!"

Lord Kelvedon accordingly retired: and by the time the door had closed behind him, his wife had completely regained her consciousness.

"Ah! then," she said, "it is not all a dream! Night!—tapers burning! You, dear Ellen—you, Cecilia—and you, Aline—half-dressed, about my bed! Then something dreadful has happened? Yes, yes! I remember the landing falling in! But Ah! those fearful, shocking cries! Ellen, I beseech you to tell me what dismal tragedy has occurred beneath this roof to-night?"

I will not endeavour to spin out my narrative by recording all I said for the purpose of preparing Hermione to receive the intelligence which I had to impart: suffice it to say that I presently revealed to her the facts that her husband's nephew Collingwood, and the valet Robert Burton, disguised in the coarsest apparel, had endeavoured to enter the mansion stealthily by the window over the private staircase—that ignorant, in the darkness, of the fact that the flooring had fallen in, they had thought to let themselves down easily, one after another, upon the landing—but that they had gone headlong down to the very bottom. Lady Kelvedon's senses seemed for awhile to be so paralyzed by this astounding intelligence that she made no remark and gave no verbal expression to her thoughts. Leaving her in the care of the Countess of Belgrave and Aline Gower, I passed into the boudoir, where I found Lord Kelvedon still questioning Agatha in reference to the circumstances which had so recently transpired, and of which she had been giving him the horrified and excited account.

"Good God, Miss Percy!" said the old nobleman, quivering nervously from head to foot; "to think that my own nephew——Oh, the villain! it is only too clear! only too palpable! And I who used to love him!—and who made a will leaving him an income that would have placed him far beyond want! But Ah! do you think——Good heavens! I can scarcely find language wherein to shape the question——But do you think, Miss Percy, that he came to assassinate me—or my poor dear wife? And do you think that her illness after all——"

"My lord," I said, "it is useless now to bewilder yourself with conjectures! Everything will be made apparent shortly."

At this moment a female domestic knocked at the door of the boudoir: she came to announce that the surgeon had just arrived, and that he was examining the two bodies which had been conveyed into one of the rooms down stairs. Almost immediately afterwards the surgeon himself made his appearance; and Lord Kelvedon at once demanded with nervous haste, "Well, what of that graceless nephew of mine? what of the unhappy man?"

"Whatever injury he may have done, or sought to do you or your's, my lord," answered the surgeon solemnly, "is now to be accounted for in another world. Mr. Collingwood ceases to exist!"

"My lord," I said, "I wish to say a few words to you alone immediately!" I spoke in a whisper; and then turning to Agatha, I said, "Let the medical gentleman see Matilda next. Lady Kelvedon does not now require his assistance."

In a few moments I was alone with his lordship; and then addressing him in a solemn manner, I spoke as follows:—

"Nearly nine months have elapsed since circumstances rendered me acquainted with certain villanous designs which your nephew, Mr. Collingwood, harboured either towards your lordship or towards Lady Kelvedon. He got me into his power; and under the most terrible threats of death he extorted from me a solemn oath, that during his lifetime I would keep silent upon the subject, and would do naught to compromise him. He is dead—and I am released from that oath! I may now speak out. Learn therefore, my lord, that your wife has been perishing under the effects of a slow and subtle poison, administered by the wretched Matilda at the instigation of this Robert Burton who has met a violent death at the same time as his master. But your wife is progressing towards health; for through my agency she has procured the antidote!—through my means she is in possession of the medicaments which will effect a cure! Now, my lord, I should imagine that you would not wish a greater amount of publicity than is absolutely unavoidable to be given to all these affairs. As a matter of course, there must be an inquest on the two bodies—and the wretched Matilda will perhaps have to be dealt with by the hand of justice. Let us therefore be guided by circumstances: but let us not of our own accord do anything to add to the notoriety which these frightful proceedings must, even as it is, only too assuredly attain."

"My dear Miss Percy," answered the old nobleman, "your wishes shall be attended to in every respect. Indeed, I myself will say nothing—no, not even to Hermione! I will only speak when you give me leave, and only say just what you suggest!"

At this moment the door again opened; and Agatha made her appearance, saying, "Miss Percy, will you come quickly? Matilda beseeches and implores that you will! I think she is dying —she is assuredly very bad—and the medical gentleman himself requests that you will lose no time in repairing to her bedside!"

"I will do so, Agatha," I responded: and I at once issued from the boudoir.

I ascended to Matilda's chamber: the surgeon and an elderly female domestic were there. The wretched young woman seemed to be lying in an exhausted state: her countenance was deadly pale —her cheeks looked sunken—her eyes seemed hollow—it actually appeared as if she had experienced an illness of many weeks. As I made my appearance the surgeon and the domestic moved towards the door; and Matilda exclaimed in a species of half-maniac tone, "Yes—go, go, I beseech you! leave me alone with Miss Percy! It is to her only that I will make confession of my enormities!"

The medical man and the servant accordingly issued from the chamber: but now it seemed as if a paroxysm of mingled shame and horror seized upon the wretched young woman—for she covered her countenance with her hands and burst into tears. I sat down by the side of the couch, saying, "If your crimes have been so great, Matilda, remember that your penitence must be proportionate!"

"Oh, yes—my crimes have been immense!— and you know them all, Miss Percy," she exclaimed wildly and passionately: "yes, you know them—because I am guilty of everything of which I felt sure that you suspected Agatha. But I must confess my wickedness to you just the same as if you were ignorant of it; for it seems to me as if this is the only means by which I can demonstrate my contrition, or remove a portion of the tremendous weight which now rests upon my soul!"

"Proceed, Matilda," I said. "Confession has ever been held as a proof of salutary sorrow and repentance!"

CHAPTER CXVII.

CONFESSION.

THERE was a pause, during which Matilda appeared to be collecting her ideas as well as she was able; and presently I observed that a strong shudder swept over her form, for the very bed shook beneath her. I comprehended what was passing in her mind, and what terrible scene was conjured up to her recollection; because she turned her haggard eyes towards me, and asked in a hollow voice, "It is true, then, Miss Percy—and my fancy is not deceiving me?—it is true that Robert Burton is no more?"

"It is true, Matilda," I answered.

"Oh, that heaven would now put a speedy end to my own existence!" she cried; "for I cannot bear to live! You know not the wretch that I altogether am! But Ah, Robert made me his victim!—and when he had seduced me from the path of virtue——yes, Miss Percy! when he had seduced me—for I am a fallen and degraded crea ture——and, Oh! my God! the babe that I bear in my bosom——"

"Matilda, compose yourself," I said; for she had started up in a wild paroxysm of despair, and I dreaded lest she should suddenly lay violent hands upon herself.

"I will be as calm as I can, Miss Percy," she replied. "But, Oh! what a wicked wretch have I been! and in what horror must you hold me! Yes—it was I who administered the slow poison to that good kind mistress who ever had a friendly word for me!—it was I who continued day by day to administer the fatal lozenges,—ruthlessly beholding her pining, fading, and perishing before my eyes! Yet not altogether *ruthlessly;* for, Oh! there have been bitter, bitter moments when remorse has seized upon me as if it were a vulture fastening its claws upon my heart!"

"And you tell me," I said, "that it was day by day you administered the slow poison? But tell me how you did this."

"Oh! when it was my turn to attend upon her ladyship," rejoined Matilda, "it was so easy for me to slip a lozenge into the coffee or the chocolate at breakfast-time—I mean into her own cup—or else into the basin of soup or beef-tea which she took for her luncheon."

"And upon those days," I said, "when it was Agatha's turn to wait upon her ladyship?"

"Oh! when once a person has entered upon the ways of crime," exclaimed Matilda bitterly, "the imagination becomes horribly ingenious for the carrying out of its nefarious aims! On those days, for instance, when Agatha waited upon her ladyship, I used to be upon the watch for her when she came into the kitchen to order whatsoever her ladyship preferred for luncheon; and then I would either officiously assist to prepare it—or I would take upon myself the entire task, bidding Agatha go and do something else; so that this readiness on my part was set down to that character for good-nature which I have always borne. Ah, Miss Percy! rest assured that when people make up their mind to commit crimes, the ways are only too easy and the opportunities are only too great! My God! would that it had been otherwise! I might then have hesitated—I might not be the wretch that I have become! But, Oh! believe me, it was not without a severe struggle in the first instance that I yielded to the representations—the mingled threats and entreaties—of Robert Burton! He had seduced me; I dreaded the consequences—he promised grand things—we were to be married—we were to be enriched whenever his master should be enabled to reward us——"

"Enough, Matilda!" I said; for the narrative was a very shocking and painful one for me to listen to. "I can understand all the motives which triumphed over the weakness of your own disposition and nature. But tell me—there is one point which I can scarcely understand. How was it that Mr. Collingwood sought to bring about the death of Lady Kelvedon, when it was by the death of his lordship that he might have chiefly hoped to profit?"

"Oh! his calculation, Miss Percy, is easily explained," answered Matilda. "It is true that if he had consigned his uncle to the grave, he would have inherited the title of Kelvedon: but of what use would the mere name have been without the family estates? Those estates are not entailed; and therefore Lord Kelvedon could bequeath them unto whomsoever he thought fit. Now, Mr. Collingwood, knowing how dotingly attached the old nobleman is to his young wife, thought it most probable that he had made a will bequeathing the great bulk of his property—perhaps indeed the whole of it—to her ladyship. Then of what use to put Lord Kelvedon out of the way under such circumstances?"

"Ah! now I begin to comprehend the deep and cunning calculations of the villain Collingwood!" I exclaimed. "He thought that he would send her ladyship as speedily as possible to the grave, and then his uncle would once more look upon him as his sole heir, and he might in due course make certain of succeeding not only to the peerage of Kelvedon, but likewise to the estates!"

"Yes, Miss Percy—those were the calculations of Mr. Collingwood," answered Matilda.

"You perhaps little suspect," I said, "that one evening I was a listener to some conversation which passed between yourself and a man in the garden. It was just about a week ago—indeed, the same evening on which I left the Hall. But strange to say I could not once catch a glimpse of either of you—nor did I hear *your* voice sufficiently clear to recognise it. I thought that you were Agatha, and I subsequently thought that the man who was with you, must be the bearer of the Christian name of Richard—Agatha's lover, indeed."

"Ah, Miss," said Matilda, "now I begin to comprehend how it was that you possessed yourself of the letter which I wrote on Robert Burton's behalf, and which I put into the vase——"

"Yes—I took it from the vase," I said. "I then penned another letter——"

"Oh! now I understand it all, Miss," rejoined Matilda; "and it was that letter which brought Mr. Collingwood secretly from France, to inquire into the position of affairs. He could not comprehend it. The letter was of a nature sufficient to fill him with consternation, and yet to be more or less ambiguous—because he thought to himself that if it were so urgent for Robert and me to get out of the neighbourhood, we surely had enough money for such a purpose without waiting for a remittance from him. To be brief, he came to England: he found to his astonishment that Burton had never caused such a letter to be written; and then, Miss Percy, suspicion fell upon *you*. Though how the letter which I had deposited in the vase could have been changed for another, utterly defied all our conjectures."

"And you held a consultation, doubtless?" I said inquiringly.

"Yes—last evening," responded Matilda.

"But tell me," I said, "was it suspected that Lady Kelvedon was getting better through my agency?"

"Yes—oh, yes!" answered Matilda. "Mr. Collingwood said it was plain enough that you suspected what was going on, and that you were administering an antidote. Well then, all his dreams and visions, so grand though so iniquitous, became suddenly threatened with annihilation; and he was reduced to despair: he knew not how to act. He resolved to take some little time to consider; and it was agreed that I should meet him and Robert Burton again this evening in the garden. And now, Miss, I must remind you of what took place in your own chamber this evening, when you were performing your dinner-toilet——"

"Yes, Matilda. I produced a letter which you in reality had written, but which I attributed to the penmanship of Agatha."

"And so I saw, Miss, that you were firmly convinced Agatha was the guilty creature who had been administering poison to a good kind mistress! Conceive the emotions I experienced during that scene! Heavens! how I trembled lest every instant I should betray myself!—and when you placed the letter in my hand, I turned away under pretence of approaching the lamp—but it was in reality to conceal my countenance from your view. Ah! you remember how I questioned you, Miss—how eager and earnest I was to obtain from you a single syllable which might serve as an explanation——"

"I recollect the scene full well, Matilda," I interrupted her. "And now proceed. What have you next to tell me? You doubtless met Mr. Collingwood and Robert Burton, according to the appointment of the preceding evening?"

"Yes, Miss Percy," responded Matilda: "and I told them how your suspicions had fallen upon Agatha. But this had nothing to do with the resolve which Mr. Collingwood had already taken: for indeed I found that his mind was made up, and he was determined to risk everything on the cast of a single die—to strike one last blow——"

"And that blow," I said, with a cold shudder, "was to have been stricken to-night?"

"Yes," rejoined Matilda. "Alas! it was at my instigation that after a brief debate Mr. Collingwood resolved to make his entry, along with Robert Burton, through the window overlooking the private staircase, and to which it was easy to climb up by means of the grape-vine which extends its branches all over that part of the building. Oh, heaven! now again the scene—the awful scene presents itself vividly to my view!"

She sank back as if about to faint. I sustained the wretched young woman; and I held a glass of water to her lips. She drank some, and soon revived.

"Tell me, Matilda," I said,—"for you remember that your confession is to be complete—what was the manner of proceeding which the villain Collingwood had sketched out for himself and his wretched follower to adopt? That it was murder, I have no doubt——"

"Oh! God forgive me! Yes, it was murder!" moaned the wretched Matilda: and again she shuddered visibly.

"But how did the assassins purpose to execute their diabolical object?" I inquired: and I kept on experiencing a succession of cold tremors as I listened to these hideous details.

"Mr. Collingwood had provided himself with a phial of deadly poison," continued Matilda, "a single drop of which let fall betwixt the lips, proves fatal! Oh, heavens! my strength seems to fail me! No! it is but a passing weakness! I will proceed.—If Agatha and her ladyship slept, well and good!—but if otherwise, then there were two strong men ready to overpower them both!"

"But was it purposed to kill Agatha likewise?" I asked.

"No—not unless the crime became an absolute necessity," was the reply. "And Oh, Miss Percy, here again is it that my own conscience tortures me so terribly: for, alas! I was all the time consoling myself with the idea that whatever might ensue, suspicion never would be attached to me—that I therefore was safe—and that under all circumstances, especially with the impressions dwelling on your mind, it would be Agatha against whom the whole weight of accusation would rest. And thus was it that I recommended the two intending murderers to enter by that window; for I thought that if they were discovered, it would be supposed they had been in collusion with Agatha, as it was Agatha's turn to sleep to-night in the dressing-room. Thus you see, Miss, that all my own thoughts were selfishly bent on calculating how in every possible contingency I must be safe!"

"Am I to understand, then," I asked, "that Mr. Collingwood's calculation was to accomplish his crime so secretly and cunningly that all suspicion would rest upon Agatha as the authoress of the foul deed?"

"Yes—such was his main calculation: but after all, it was a bold stroke that he was playing, leaving a great deal to the chapter of accidents."

"And if it had succeeded," I said,—"and if Agatha had been accused of murdering her mistress—and if she had told the tale of how two persons entered by the window and perpetrated the crime——"

"Who would have believed such a tale?" asked Matilda. "Nothing would have been stolen; and Agatha must have represented the men as two common-looking fellows coarsely dressed, with masks upon their countenances—for with these were they provided. Then who would believe that two low ruffians would have stealthily entered that chamber to poison a lady for the mere sake of committing a crime, and without the object of plunder! Ah! rest assured, Miss, that poor Agatha would have been deemed guilty—and even you yourself would have suffered her to go with but little sympathy to the scaffold, for you would have been convinced of her iniquity."

"Alas, yes! it must have been so!" I murmured.

"But this was not all," resumed Matilda: "there was yet another calculation. Suppose that Agatha had slept soundly—suppose that Mr. Collingwood had penetrated unheard and unperceived into her ladyship's chamber, and that she also was sleeping soundly—the fatal poison would have been dropped between her lips—and then let us suppose that the murderers succeeded in effecting a retreat as noiseless as their entry had been. Well, Miss Percy, what would have happened? In the morning Lady Kelvedon would have been found dead in her bed; and there was the chance that her death might have been attributed to natural causes!"

"What!" I exclaimed; "Mr. Collingwood calculated upon such a chance when he knew that I was at Kelvedon Hall, and that my mind was filled with suspicions?"

"Ah, Miss Percy! he scarcely knew what to think in reference to the policy you were pursuing. There was however one thing which was as clear to him as the sun at noon-day,—which was that you

were religiously and faithfully adhering to a solemn oath which he had once exacted from you."

"True, Matilda!" I said: " to that oath I did indeed adhere—but it was because I found that I could not merely keep my pledge, but likewise baffle his nefarious projects at the same time. But understand me well!" I emphatically added. " If matters had ever come to that point at which it was necessary for me to decide between violating an oath on the one hand and suffering Collingwood to murder Lady Kelvedon outright on the other hand, I should not have hesitated a single moment as to what alternative it was needful to adopt: I should have violated that oath—I should have proclaimed everything, and should have invoked the aid of the law for the punishment of the wretch! But it has so happened that I have been enabled to keep my oath, and yet frustrate his designs! Indeed, Matilda, there are many points connected with all these incidents,

No. 91.—ELLEN PERCY.

from first to last, which prove to me that the hand of providence itself——"

"Oh yes, Miss!" ejaculated the young woman, with terror depicted on her countenance, " I feel that the hand of God has indeed been made apparent in much that has taken place! and Oh! I am not fit to die!—and yet it seems to me as if the hand of death were upon me!"

"You must resign yourself, Matilda," I solemnly rejoined, " to the dispensations of that providence which has so signally manifested itself in recent events. The falling-in of that flooring doubtless prevented murder's work being done. Oh! how short-sighted are we mortals! At first I looked upon the occurrence as savouring of the character of a misfortune, because I feared lest it should impede the progress of Lady Kelvedon towards the recovery of her health. But now what am I to think? That it was a means adopted by providence itself to arrest the stealthy footsteps of the wicked—to save them from the perpetration of great crimes—and to inflict upon them condign punishment for their past offences! Yes all these objects were achieved at one and the same moment!"

"All!" murmured Matilda.

"And it was doubtless the inspiration of providence," I continued, "which prompted me to suggest that the accident should be concealed until the morning. I did not tell you, Matilda, that I meant to pass the night in her ladyship's room: I did not breathe a syllable to you of the falling-in of the landing. I dismissed you to your own chamber; and you thought that I purposed to remain in mine."

"And, Oh, Miss! how far was I from suspecting," moaned the wretched Matilda, "that a chasm was yawning to receive into its depths the two men who were bent upon a midnight deed of crime! Oh, you cannot conceive how fearful was the agitation which seized upon me when those appalling cries pealed through the mansion: for I knew them to be the cries of men—they were not female voices which sent forth those awful yells of agony! I declare to you, Miss Percy, that for all my wickedness I believe I was almost sufficiently punished during the few moments that elapsed from the instant that I rushed forth from my chamber, to that when consciousness abandoned me in the presence of the horrible spectacle that I was destined to behold!"

"And do you now assure me, Matilda," I asked, "that you are completely contrite?"

"Would to God, Miss Percy," she ejaculated, "that I could live over again the last three months of my existence! But tell me—Ah! tell me—and do not deceive me! What is now to be done——"

"Do you mean in reference to yourself, Matilda?" I asked. "You had better not think of worldly matters —— bend your ideas upon heaven——"

"Oh, my God! what do you mean, Miss Percy?" cried the wretched young woman. "If I should be mistaken—if I have not received a shock which will in a few days or a few hours prostrate me as a cold corpse—if I should *live* —— Oh! then you mean me to understand that I must be consigned to a gaol and that I must perish on the gallows!"

"Matilda," I said, very seriously and very solemnly, "I should be wrong to deceive you in any way. Your wickedness has been great; and there is no extenuation for it. You have not sinned under a sudden impulse; but it has been a deliberate—and I must even say a cold-blooded perseverance in the most diabolical iniquity. Moreover, this wickedness of your's is now known to many persons——"

"Yes, yes, Miss Percy! it is all true—all too true!" ejaculated the wretched young woman, clasping her hands in all the wildness of despair. "I must be handed over to the grasp of justice—I see that I must!—nothing can save me!"

"Be tranquil, Matilda!—be composed!" I said: "or else I shall doubt the penitence and contrition which you have been professing. It was my duty to make you comprehend the immensity of your wickedness: but now I may be permitted to give you an assurance that you have to deal with those who are mercifully inclined. That you will have

to answer for your conduct before a public tribunal, there can be no doubt: but that every intercession which mercy dictates shall be made on your behalf, I can safely promise. You will not lose your life ignominiously; but you must make up your mind to meet some severe penalty —and the resignation with which you bear it, will prove more effectually than words can do your sorrow and contrition for the past."

After having said all I could to settle the young woman's mind into what I considered to be a suitable state of composure, I issued from the chamber. The elderly female domestic to whom I have already alluded, at once returned thither; and I now sought an opportunity of having a few words of conversation with the medical man. He informed me that Matilda was certainly in a very bad state—that she had received a fearful shock, and that she might sink under it—unless on the other hand she should live on as a wretched maniac. He said that he should see her again before he left the house, and that he meant to charge the woman who was now with her not to lose sight of her for a single moment.

I now returned to the boudoir. I found that Lady Kelvedon was considerably tranquillized in mind, but that she had been expressing her wish that I should return to her. I desired the Countess of Belgrave and Aline to withdraw to their respective chambers: I likewise requested Lord Kelvedon himself to leave me alone with his wife; and I begged Agatha to seek her couch again in the dressing-room. When alone with Lady Kelvedon, I gradually broke to her all those details in connexion with her own case whereof she had hitherto remained in ignorance; for I thought it better that she should know everything at once, than labour under any suspense. I found that I had adopted the right course; for though she was deeply, deeply affected, yet the vent which her feelings found in tears seemed to do her good. She flung her arms round my neck—she wept upon my bosom—and I breathed everything I could think of that was cheering and consolatory in her ears. At length we retired to rest again; for it was now past two o'clock in the morning, and the household had become quiet once more—though I question whether many eyes were closed in slumber after the horrible incidents which characterized that night of tremendous memories!

There is a point upon which I should here touch for a moment, in case the reader should not have comprehended one special portion of the explanation of past events. I allude to that particular evening when I overheard what took place in the garden. It was now evident enough that the first couple who were walking about there while I remained concealed amongst the evergreens, were Robert Burton and Matilda—though I had been strongly impressed at the time that it was Agatha's voice of which I had occasionally caught a whispering murmur. The man had mentioned the name of *Agatha;* but he was only speaking *of* her, and not *to* her. In short, I was altogether deceived. Then the second couple whom I had heard walking in the garden, were really Agatha and Richard Brownlow. As for the note, it had after all been taken from the vase by

Robert Burton and sent off to Mr. Collingwood at Boulogne; so that everything was actually progressing at that time in respect to the letter which I had written in a feigned hand, precisely as I had hoped and intended,—though such were the complications which seemed to ensue from the confusion of persons and circumstances, that I had remained uncertain as to the fate of that letter.

Lady Kelvedon soon slept by my side: but slumber did not revisit my eyes: it was scarcely possible indeed that I could compose my mind sufficiently to woo the presence of balmy repose after the horrible incidents which had that night occurred. It was altogether one of the most fearful and startling dramas in which I had ever played a real and veritable part, and which were so different from the fictitious scenes that are enacted upon the stage!

But if I myself were unable to sleep, it was equally so with Agatha; and shortly after seven o'clock in the morning, I heard her moving about in the adjoining-room. I rose and went to her, and she said to me, "Did that unfortunate young woman make a complete confession of her iniquities?"

"Yes, my dear Agatha," I answered; "and there is not the shadow of a suspicion resting against yourself! I sincerely hope that you will be happy with the young man who in due time is to become your husband; and you will permit me to make you a little present of a hundred pounds as a dowry—for you shall not go an empty-handed bride to the altar!"

Agatha returned me suitable thanks; and as I now proceeded to my own chamber to perform my morning toilet,—leaving Lady Kelvedon still buried in a profound sleep,—I said to myself, "Never again will I judge by outward appearances! The morose-looking Agatha is a well-principled, excellent-hearted young woman!—the seemingly good-natured, buxom, happy-looking Matilda was all the while capable of any iniquity—false, perfidious, and vile!"

On reaching my own chamber I rang the bell; and the summons was answered by one of the female-servants. I sent her to inquire after Matilda; and on her return she informed me that the wretched young woman had become quite delirious, and that she was crying out for a clergyman that she might make a confession of all her sins. I inquired if the medical gentleman had arrived—for he had promised that he should be at the Hall at an early hour: but I found that he had not as yet made his appearance. I sent the young woman to bid the female who was in charge of Matilda take most especial care of her; for I feared lest in her delirium she might lay violent hands upon herself. I proceeded hastily with my toilet, that I might be enabled to see the surgeon the moment he should arrive, in order to consult him as to the actual condition of Matilda, and whether he considered that her intellects were sufficiently clear to render it worth while or expedient for a minister of the Gospel to be sent for to attend upon her.

The toilet-table in my chamber stood against one of the windows, so that the looking-glass upon that table might occupy a convenient position for the use of any one who might have to consult it. I was standing before this glass, hastily arranging my hair, and at the same time reflecting most painfully upon all the horrible things which had occurred at the mansion,—when suddenly a piercing scream thrilled through my brain—then in the twinkling of an eye it appeared as if a dark cloud passed before the window—and then there was the noise of something falling upon the ground beneath. An ejaculation of horror burst from my lips: a suspicion of what it was had flitted through my brain in a moment! There was a rush of footsteps overhead: I tore open the casement and looked out. My suspicion was confirmed!—there lay a human form in a night-dress on the ground beneath the window—it was motionless—and I recognised the countenance of Matilda!

I shrank back from the casement with a sickening sensation at the heart, a feeling of the brain, and a faintness coming over me; for horror was succeeding upon horror with a frightful rapidity and with an almost overwhelming force. Good heavens! this was in some sense a kindred sequence to the appalling incidents of the past night!—punishment and retribution were coming fast and thick upon the perpetrators of iniquity!—accident and suicide were clearing the criminals away from the stage of their monstrous proceedings!

A few words of explanation will suffice to dispose of this last tragedy. Matilda had gradually ceased from her delirious ravings—her head had fallen back upon the pillow—she had closed her eyes—and the female-servant who was with her, naturally fancied that being mentally exhausted, she was sinking off into slumber. The woman peeped forth from the door to see if she could find any other female domestic to come and relieve her for a little space: she saw a housemaid on the landing below—and she was passing down the staircase to speak to her, when all of a sudden the window in the room which she had just left was heard to open—then pealed forth that frightful scream which had so pierced my brain—and the tragedy was complete. The wretched young woman had terminated her career with the crowning guilt of a distracted suicide; and the surgeon just arrived in time to pronounce that the spark of life was extinct!

<hr>

CHAPTER CXVIII.

MYSTERIOUS TIDINGS.

I TREMBLED for the consequences of this accumulation of horrors in respect to the death of Lady Kelvedon. Matilda's suicide could not be concealed from her, because the rending scream of the wretched young woman had penetrated to Hermione's chamber and startled her up from the sleep in which I had left her plunged about half-an-hour previous. I had again a difficult task to accomplish in soothing her ladyship; and it was not until she had given vent to her horrified feelings in a flood of tears, that she became in any degree tranquillized. The Countess of Belgrave and Aline assisted me most affectionately and tenderly in the ministrations which I thus paid to Lady Kelvedon; and I left Hermione in their charge, for I was now determined to adopt a particular course without any further delay. I sent to inform Lord Kelvedon that I wished to speak to him immediately in the library, where I was waiting for him. He soon made his appearance: he was quivering and trembling all over with a pitiable degree of nervousness, on account of the new horror which had just occurred beneath the roof of his mansion.

"My lord," I at once said, "you have been kind enough to intimate your readiness to place implicit reliance on my judgment under existing circumstances——"

"Yes, yes, Miss Percy!" he answered; "do what you will—suggest what you think proper! But, Oh, heavens! does it not seem to you as if this house were actually accursed?—as if the vengeance of heaven itself were falling upon it?"

"Heaven's vengeance is only overtaking the guilty, my lord," I answered: "but still these horrors are indeed too much for your wife to sustain. They are striking her blow upon blow!—her nerves cannot possibly endure such excitement—and she must be removed from the scene. Yes! she must immediately leave a spot where hideous ideas and frightful thoughts are enveloping her, and where everything is now seen through an atmosphere as horrible as a blood-mist! With your permission, my lord, I will at once take her to London."

"Yes, yes, Miss Percy! immediately—without delay!" answered the nobleman. "I think as you think—it will prove too much for Hermione to remain here any longer."

"Yes—far too much," I rejoined. "There will be all the confusion and excitement attendant upon the Coroner's inquests—the removal of the bodies—the re-building of the floor above the private staircase——"

"Yes—there will be all that!" said Lord Kelvedon, trembling as if he were afflicted with the palsy. "Depart immediately if you will! I suppose I must remain here for the present?"

"Yes—you must remain here, my lord," I answered. "Do you know the Coroner? I mean are you intimately acquainted with him?"

"He is a tenant of mine," responded the nobleman; "and he is indebted to me for the appointment."

"You will take care, my lord," I said, "that my evidence may be dispensed with. I shall accompany her ladyship. It is of infinitely more consequence that I should proceed with her to Eaton Square than that I should tarry here to attend the Coroner's investigation."

It was accordingly agreed that the departure should take place the moment the requisite preparations could be effected; and when I informed Hermione of the arrangement which I had thus made, she cordially gave her assent thereto. She was most anxious to leave Kelvedon Hall, for it was now indeed the scene of horrible associations from which the strongest mind shudderingly recoiled, and from which therefore the more sensitive feelings of an invalid revolted with a still greater loathing. As for the Countess of Belgrave and Aline, they were only too glad to regulate their movements according to the convenience and the welfare of their friend Hermione; and it may also be supposed that they had no very particular inclination to remain beneath a roof where in so short a space so many frightful incidents had occurred.

In less than a couple of hours everything was ready for the departure. Agatha was to accompany her mistress: but I was considerate enough for the excellent young woman's feelings to desire that she should leave a letter to be sent to her lover Richard Brownlow, in order that he might not fancy himself in any way neglected or slighted by her.

We reached the metropolis in the afternoon; and I was glad to observe that Lady Kelvedon sustained the impression of recent occurrences with a greater degree of mental strength than I could have supposed she would have been able to exert. But she was supported, and in a manner tranquillized, by the conviction that her restoration to sound health was being effected; for I had said everything soothing and encouraging to her on this important point. On arriving at the mansion in Eaton Square, Hermione begged me to remain a day or two with her; and I readily gave my assent—for indeed I had purposed so to do. The Countess of Belgrave and Aline perceived the necessity of Hermione enjoying as much tranquillity as possible: they therefore took their leave, and returned to their own respective homes.

I had now an opportunity of entering more fully than I had previously done into a series of explanations in reference to the proceedings of the past. In giving those explanations, I made Lady Kelvedon a confidant of many of the most salient episodes of my own life; for it was more or less necessary to do this, in order to explain how it was that I had first of all become acquainted with Dame Betty—how I had learnt anything in reference to the poisoned lozenges—how I was enabled to furnish her ladyship with an antidote some time back—and how I had been led to suspect Mr. Collingwood's iniquitous intentions. On all these points I gave Hermione the minutest details—for I now considered myself bound so to do; and the reader may imagine with what a degree of interest she listened to the revelations that were thus wafted to her ear.

"One of the principal reasons," I said, "which induced me to recommend that you should at once come to London, is that this woman Dame Betty may call upon you here or at my house. She must see you—the week has nearly expired for that purpose—and I know that when she hears of everything that has happened at Kelvedon Hall, she will not think it very prudent or safe for herself to proceed thither again."

Hermione left herself entirely in my hands in respect to the old woman; and I resolved to lose no time in communicating with her. Accordingly, after having dined with Lady Kelvedon in Eaton Square, I repaired to my own house in Great Ormond Street. My arrival at home was quite unexpected by Beda, who was therefore all the more rejoiced to see me; for I had now been precisely a week absent. And during that week how many things had happened! how much had I to relate to my faithful Beda! how much gratitude to express for her affectionate forethought in sending William Lardner to watch over my safety in Hampshire! And with what an awful interest was it that Beda listened to my narrative of the recent proceedings at Kelvedon Hall! I bade her lose no time in seeking for Dame Betty, and making an appointment for the old woman to be at my house at some hour on the following day, so that Lady Kelvedon might meet her there. Beda promised to execute my mandates forthwith; and when I had read several letters which had arrived for me during my absence, I returned to Eaton Square.

On the following day Beda came to Eaton Square with the information that she had seen Dame Betty, who would be at my house in the evening between eight and nine o'clock. This appointment Lady Kelvedon and I accordingly kept; but her ladyship met the dame with very different feelings from those which she had formerly experienced towards her—for now she knew that this woman possessed the diabolic knowledge which had proved the source of her almost fatal illness, as well as she was endowed with that other species of knowledge which had furnished the antidote. But Lady Kelvedon threw a veil over her feelings as much as possible; and Dame Betty had no reason to suspect that I had found it expedient to deal so candidly with her patient. She asked her ladyship a number of questions: she was completely satisfied with the responses; and she declared that there was no doubt nor indeed any longer a difficulty in respect to Hermione's cure.

"Foreseeing—or at least hoping that this would be the case," said the hag, "I have brought with me an adequate supply of the medicaments, which your ladyship must continue to take. There need be no change; and in six or seven weeks from the present time you will feel that you are altogether a different being."

Thus speaking, the old woman laid a packet upon the table in the room where the interview took place; and I then conducted her out of Lady Kelvedon's presence. I bade her follow me into another apartment; and when we were there alone together, I said, "Beda told you everything which has occurred at Kelvedon Hall?"

"Yes — everything," answered the dame,— "everything! I mean to leave London to-night, and England to-morrow. After all, Miss Percy, France is the safest country for me: for who can tell how that fellow Collingwood may have spoken to any one?—or how my name may be mentioned in any letter that might now possibly turn up? In short——"

"Yes—you had better leave England," I said, well pleased to hear that the hag had arrived at that very decision which I had made up my mind to suggest to her. "You were promised five hundred guineas for effecting the cure of Lady Kelvedon. Here is half that sum; and the other half shall be paid in six weeks from the present time, provided that the result shall prove as favourable as you have led us to expect."

I counted down two hundred and fifty guineas in bank-notes and gold upon the table; and the harridan's eyes glittered as she beheld that sum, while her fingers literally trembled with a kindred sensation of pleasure as she gathered up the notes and the coins.

"You will let me know," I said, "in the course of a few weeks, where you are to be found in France, so that I may make you the promised remittance which shall complete the stipulated sum."

The dame expressed her gratitude: but instead of taking her departure, she lingered—looked at me in a peculiar manner—and seemed as if she had something to say of high importance to say to me.

"Have you anything else to impart," I inquired, "relative to Lady Kelvedon?—is everything being done that can be done?"

"Yes, everything, my dear Miss!" answered the dame; "and there is nothing else to be done. Lady Kelvedon will in six or seven weeks be as well and healthy as you are. But you see that I have something to say; and so I have. Yet I little thought that the time would ever come when I should be saying something to you that would tend to your advantage—or else to that of your family—as I believe it will——"

"What can you mean?" I asked, much surprised at the turn which the conversation was thus taking.

"Answer me a question or two," resumed the dame. "Had you not some relations of the name of Wakefield who lived at Sheffield a few years ago?"

"Yes—an aunt and a cousin," I ejaculated. "The aunt is dead——"

"And the cousin?" inquired Dame Betty.

"But are you really asking," I said, "from a good motive?"—and my heart was palpitating violently as I feared lest there should be something sinister beneath the hag's present conduct towards me.

"What earthly motive can I have except a good one," she ejaculated, with a slight show of petulance, "since I myself am so little acquainted with the matter that all I can do is to furnish a clue which it is for you to follow up."

"Indeed?" I exclaimed. "Then if by suspicion I have wronged you, I beseech forgiveness."

"You have forgiven me enough, Miss Percy," said the dame emphatically, "to induce me to forgive you. Besides, you were a friend of Zarah's— and whenever I think of that, it makes me doubly regret that I should have ever displayed any hostility towards you. But your cousin——"

"He is absent from England," I answered: "he is far away. Nevertheless, I can communicate with him if there be anything of importance——"

"Ah, well! at all events he is alive," interjected the dame. "Now, from a few words which I heard a while ago from the lips of a woman at Stafford, I think this cousin of your's may possibly be entitled to something handsome if he knew how to look after it."

"This is very extraordinary!" I said; "and I am almost inclined to think that you must be making a mistake. There is assuredly no fortune in the family which has hitherto escaped our knowledge; for my cousin's father—my uncle Mr. Wakefield—died in a state of insolvency."

"Ah! but had he not a brother?" inquired Dame Betty, "or at all events some relation through whom there might have existed a claim?"

"Yes—I think that I have heard of another Mr. Wakefield," I said, striving to gather my recollections; "but I am not sure."

"I myself know very little about it," said Dame Betty: "for I had no particular curiosity at the time—and even if I had, the woman did not seem inclined to gratify it. She only spoke vaguely—because she was asking me some questions about a gipsy family named Robinson——Why, that very family, to be sure! to which your Beda belongs!"

"Indeed?" I exclaimed, imagining that from the very fact of this dovetailing together of incidents there must be something real and tangible at the bottom of Dame Betty's present discourse. "But you know Beda's father and mother are dead."

"Don't I know all about Beda," demanded the dame, "since she lived with me at one time? Ah, that was just before she went to you. And didn't Beda's parents receive an annuity for having restored a child to its home from which it had been stolen?"

"Yes!" I ejaculated. "But what has this to do with the circumstances to which you are alluding?"

"Oh, simply because the woman Sturton—the woman of Stafford, I mean—was asking me about that Robinson family; for she knew them well—and she had no liking to them, either—for if I mistake not, she had something to do in the stealing of the child——or at least her parents had—but I really forget the particulars now."

"Well," I said, "but the inquiries which this woman Sturton instituted relative to the Robinsons, had nothing to do with the Wakefield family?"

"I don't know," responded Dame Betty: "all I can tell you, is that she spoke of the two things in the same breath; and she said that if she only knew where to find out any of the Wakefields of Sheffield, she should not perhaps be in such poverty as she was at the time when I saw her."

"This is most extraordinary!" I cried: "and I cannot possibly understand it! Is she a gipsy-woman?"

"Yes, by birth," replied Dame Betty: "but she married out of her tribe—just as my poor dear Zarah did."

"And how came you to know," I asked, "that I was related to the Wakefields of Sheffield?"

"Have I not known something about you for several years past?" inquired the dame: "have I not known that you lived with your grandfather Forsyth at Leeds?—did I not know Parks?"—and here she smiled with a grim significancy.

"Ah, true!" I said. "And therefore when the woman Sturton spoke to you of the Wakefield family——"

"I did not tell her," rejoined the dame, "that if she applied to you she might possibly procure some information concerning those Wakefields. Because I had no love for you at the time when I saw the woman Sturton; and I thought that if it was to put anything in the way of your relations it would be benefiting you likewise; and so as I did not want to benefit you, I held my peace. But now that I entertain different feelings towards you—and that you have not betrayed me in this Collingwood affair—and you are behaving so honourably towards me with regard to the money for her ladyship's cure——"

"But how do you know that the woman Sturton is still at Stafford?" I inquired.

"Because poverty is for the most part stationary," responded the dame; "and because likewise her husband was a native of that town, so that she may have a few friends there."

"Then she is a widow?" I asked.

"She was a widow when I saw her a year or two ago," rejoined the dame; "and unless she has married again——"

"But where could I find her in Sheffield?" I demanded.

Dame Betty mentioned a particular address, which I at once committed to paper. I then asked her if she had any more information to give me on the point? I begged her to tax her memory, in case she should have omitted to mention any particular that might be of importance: but she assured me that there was nothing to add, for that it was more by the woman Sturton's mysterious manner and significant looks than by actual words that she (Dame Betty) had been impressed with the idea that there was something of a real importance at the bottom.

The old woman now took her departure; and I returned to the room where I had left Lady Kelvedon. I accompanied her home to Eaton Square; and I remained with her until the next day. Lord Kelvedon then arrived from Hampshire. The Coroner's inquest had taken place: verdicts of "Accidental Death" had been returned in the case of Collingwood and Burton, and "Temporary Insanity" in that of Matilda. The impression made by the evidence on the Coroner's jury was that the crime of murder had been contemplated by Collingwood and his valet, and that Matilda was their accomplice: but nothing was said in reference to the poisoning. Indeed, his lordship had induced the Coroner to cut short the proceedings as much as possible, —which that functionary effected by telling the jury that when once they were satisfied as to the cause of the deaths of the three persons, there was no necessity for them to descend more deeply into particulars.

I now prepared to leave Eaton Square, for I was all impatience to journey into Staffordshire. Lord Kelvedon endeavoured, through the medium of his wife, to make me accept of a cheque upon his banker for two thousand guineas: but I would not listen to the proposal:—all that I would suffer in a pecuniary sense was that his lordship's purse should be the source of Dame Betty's reward. I made Agatha a present of a hundred guineas; and the young woman overwhelmed me with assurances of gratitude. As for Lord and Lady Kelvedon they seemed to think they could not say enough to express their own kind feelings towards me; and Hermione in particular wept bitterly when I took my leave—for as she knew I was going to stay with the Tremaines in Staffordshire, she feared lest two or three weeks might elapse ere we should meet again.

It was exactly a fortnight since I had left River House near Dover; and though throughout several recent chapters I have not once alluded to the inmates of that dwelling, it must not be supposed that I myself had been unmindful of them —but I have thought it better not to interrupt the thread of my narrative for the purpose of referring to any incidents that were passing elsewhere. Besides, have really very little to mention on this particular topic. The Duchess of

Ardleigh had been pronounced out of danger, and continued to improve, though very slowly: the Duke sojourned at the Ship Hotel at Dover: and the young Marquis, be it remembered, had taken his departure before I myself left River House. Mary Glentworth continued unremitting in her attentions to the Duchess: her Grace was made acquainted with the real circumstances attending Mary's birth; and therefore, when she found that the young lady was not actually her husband's daughter, she experienced no disinclination to be attended upon by her. On the contrary, after a little while the Duchess evidently began to receive Mary's ministrations with favour and satisfaction: but she did not mention her son's name in Mary's presence. The Duke called every day at River House; but Miss Glentworth always contrived to be in her own chamber at the period of his lordship's arrival; and thus they had not met once during the whole time. It was alike from Mary and Juliet that I received these particulars; for both had written me several letters during the fortnight which had elapsed since my departure from River House. Indeed, amongst the letters which I had found at home on my return from Kelvedon Hall, there was correspondence from those two dear friends of mine. But there was another letter to which I must make a passing allusion. It was from the Marquis of Dalrymple himself; and it contained a letter addressed to Mary Glentworth, which he requested me to forward to her. In his epistle to me he said that although he had now experienced a sufficient interval for deliberate reflection on the resolve to which he had come when at River House, in respect to the espousal of Mary at a future period, he still remained firm to that resolution; he beheld not the slightest reason to regret it—he perceived not the slightest motive for recalling it. He sincerely thanked me for the many kindnesses that I had shewn him, and declared that through me, in a variety of ways, he had become the altered being that he was. The letter he had written to Mary Glentworth was left unsealed that I might peruse it; and I was much touched by this proof of confidence and delicate consideration on his part. I *did* read the letter, because I thought that under all circumstances I was in duty bound to do so. It was couched in the most affectionate terms: it made not the slightest allusion to the reason of the temporary separation of some few months betwixt himself and his intended: but it breathed all the fervour of a manly love, without sickly sentimentalism or maudlin triviality. I therefore had no hesitation in sending this letter to Mary Glentworth; and I penned a few lines to the young Marquis to let him know that his request had been complied with, and likewise to show him that I appreciated the frank and generous method of his procedure.

I had some curiosity to ascertain what had become of Edwin St. Clair and Lady Lilla Essendine. I learned through William Lardner that St. Clair had not returned to his residence in the Regent's Park after the trial at the Old Bailey. He made further inquiries at my instigation; and he ascertained that both St. Clair and Lady Lilla had gone abroad—but he could not discover to what part of the world they had betaken themselves.

The day after I left Eaton Square—and while I was making my preparations for a journey into Staffordshire, as I had received the promised letter from Charlotte, inviting me to pass some time with her family at Tremaine Hall—a large box arrived at the house; and on opening it, I found that it contained a magnificent present of plate from Lord Kelvedon. It was a complete dinner service, fitted for the entertainment of twenty-four persons,—silver dishes, side-dishes, soup-tureens, sauce-boats, and plates, all complete—with my initials engraven on every article. There was likewise a splendid set of diamonds from Lady Kelvedon; and this superb gift—or rather assemblage of gifts, was accompanied by a most friendly letter from his lordship, and a most affectionate one from Hermione.

As the reader may suppose, I was very glad to find a letter from Charlotte Tremaine, inviting me to stay at her father's mansion; because it was at no great distance from Stafford, and I was anxious to prosecute my inquiries in that town after the information I had received from Dame Betty. That anxiety was all the greater on account of the very vagueness of the information. I could scarcely conceive how there was a possibility of my cousin Henry Wakefield having any prospects with which he was previously unacquainted. I nevertheless remembered that his mother, my deceased aunt, had always avoided speaking about her departed husband, or making any allusion to family affairs; and this I had attributed to her grief at her husband's untimely death, which had been produced by his financial difficulties. Still I thought that if she had been aware of the existence of any chance by which her beloved son's circumstances might at any time be improved, she would scarcely have failed to leave some parting instructions on the subject. However, I was determined to investigate the business without delay; and thus I lost no time in making my preparations for a journey into Staffordshire. On this occasion I resolved to take my faithful Beda with me; while she rejoiced at the prospect of again travelling in my company.

We set out in the morning of the third day following the one on which I had taken leave of my friends in Eaton Square; and we arrived at Stafford in the evening. We took up our quarters at the best hotel in the town; and I resolved to lose not a moment in entering on my inquiries in respect to the woman Sturton. I should observe that I had mentioned all the circumstances to Beda; but she had no recollection of the name—she was unable to throw the faintest additional light upon the mystery. She was, however, most anxious to conduct the present inquiry on my behalf; and accordingly, on our arrival at Stafford, she issued forth from the hotel to proceed to the address specified by Dame Betty. I should have accompanied her; but I felt rather indisposed after all the excitement I had recently undergone—and moreover I fancied it would seem strange if the instant I arrived at the hotel I went out to visit some poor neighbourhood, as I had no doubt the district where the woman Sturton resided must prove to be; whereas, on the other hand, Beda could institute inquiries without attracting any particular attention.

She was nearly two hours absent, during which

time I experienced no small degree of anxiety. At length she returned; and I at once saw by the expression of her countenance that she had no good news to communicate. Her explanations were soon given. She had called at the address specified by Dame Betty: a woman named Sturton, with two or three children, had lived there for a while, until a year back; but she had left, being impelled by the direst destitution to seek refuge in the workhouse. To the workhouse Beda had repaired: the object of her inquiry was not there; and after some difficulty she succeeded in ascertaining that Mrs. Sturton and three children had only been for two months in the workhouse—that they had then left—but Beda's informant knew not whither they had gone. The porter of the workhouse-gate recollected, however, that there was a certain woman in the establishment at the same time, with whom Mrs. Sturton was intimate; that woman had also left, and the porter knew where she lived. Away Beda sped to continue her inquiries; and she had succeeded in finding the woman thus referred to. It appeared that she had quarrelled with Mrs. Sturton, and had lost sight of her for a long time until a few weeks back, when she happened to meet her in quite a different part of the town from that in which she herself resided. They had not then spoken; but Mrs. Sturton had the appearance at the time of being plunged into very deep distress. This woman to whom I am alluding, promised Beda that she would make inquiries and institute a search after Mrs. Sturton—my faithful young dependant promising a handsome reward if success should crown the woman's endeavours; and she told her to write to me at Tremaine Hall.

This was all that could be done for the present; but I hoped that matters were put in a train for some more satisfactory development.

On the following morning I proceeded in a chaise to Tremaine Hall, which was a few miles distant from Stafford. I found that it realized the description which Miss Parks had given me of it, according to a picture which she had seen. It was a very large edifice, presenting two or three styles of architecture, with a comparatively modern frontage. It was almost entirely surrounded by trees, some of which were of enormous growth; but they were now nearly all denuded of their foliage, for it was close upon the end of December that I visited it. It stood in the midst of its own ample domain; and I could readily comprehend that in the summer time the entire scenery must have a very beautiful appearance.

It was two or three days after Christmas-day that I thus arrived at Tremaine Hall; and most cordial was the welcome that I received. There was something truly parental in the affectionate manner with which Mr. and Mrs. Tremaine greeted me: Colonel Tremaine was there—and he expressed his joy at meeting me again: Charlotte and her five sisters crowded round me; and I felt just as if I were an old acquaintance who had known them all for several years. Such indeed was evidently the feeling with which they sought to imbue me:—in the frank generosity of their dispositions they sought to place me at my ease at once, and overstep in a moment all the barriers of a cold formality. I looked round for Sarah Barron; but I did not see her. I won-

dered whether she had yet arrived at the Hall—and if so, of what nature our meeting would be —whether she had discovered that I had returned in so strange a manner the portrait which her brother had sent me—or whether, on the other hand, she remained altogether unsuspicious of the existence of anything peculiar between himself and me.

I was conducted into an old-fashioned parlour, where luncheon was presently served up; and after the repast Charlotte offered to show me the chamber that was allotted for my reception. I accompanied my warm-hearted friend thither; and I found that there was an ante-room which was to be occupied by Beda. I thanked Charlotte for this arrangement, as I liked to have my faithful dependant near me. I then inquired after Miss Barron; and Charlotte exclaimed, "Oh, she will be here this evening. You know she is staying with her mother and brother at Petersfield; for she wrote to us the other day, and in the letter she said that she had just experienced one of the greatest pleasures which she could possibly be permitted to enjoy—for that you had called upon her. As she had not seen her mother for so long a time, my parents gave me permission to write and tell her that she need not hurry in coming hither; and thus she has extended her visit to Petersfield a little longer than she originally purposed. But she is sure to be here this evening; for we are going to have a few friends, in honour of your arrival—and I know that Miss Barron would not miss the opportunity of testifying, along with others, her joy at your presence. But come, my dear Ellen! let me show you over the mansion!"

I accordingly accompanied Charlotte: she took me through the different rooms—and I was much interested in many of the objects which she pointed out to me. There were several fine old pictures by eminent masters: there were some curious relics, such as armour, vases, drinking-cups, and other articles of the Elizabethan age, to which period the existence of the greater portion of the dwelling owed its date: and there was a choice library, the arrangements of which had been completely modernized, and the shelves of which were filled with all the works of the best authors.

"But there is still something," I said, with a smile, "which you have not yet shown me, but of which I received a hint from our mutual friend Jane Parks."

"Oh! I'll be bound to say I know what you mean!" ejaculated Charlotte. "It is the haunted room—is it not?"

"Yes," I responded: "and I see that you do not treat the matter so seriously and gravely as if you really believed in the fact?"

"When I was a little girl, it was different, my dear Ellen," rejoined Charlotte. "But I do really believe that Lavinia and Emilia"—thus alluding to her two young sisters, whose ages were respectively thirteen and fifteen—"are foolish enough to entertain a superstitious dread of the haunted apartment. But come! you shall see it!"

Miss Tremaine led the way along a passage which we had before threaded, and which communicated with a small landing-place and a staircase. I had noticed this landing and this staircase before, for we had already passed that way in going over the house. Indeed, there were three stair-

cases——one in the centre, which was of course the principal—and one at each extremity of the building. This one to which I am now referring, was at the western end of the mansion, where all the servants' offices were situated : and it was the landing of the second floor to which Charlotte Tremaine was now conducting me. Four rooms opened thence ; and I now observed that on previously passing that way, Charlotte had taken me into three—but she had not entered the fourth. I now mentioned this little circumstance to her—adding with a smile, " I am almost inclined to think, my dear Charlotte, that you purposely passed by this room just now ?"

" Yes—I did," she responded ; " because it has become a sort of habit amongst the entire household to leave it unvisited. The servants perhaps have some little superstitious feeling with regard to it. In fact, dear Ellen, I know they have.

No. 92.—ELLEN PERCY.

Before we went upon the Continent, my father and mother slept in that room several times, for the express purpose of convincing the domestics that it is a mere idle rumour which had become associated with it : but all of no avail!—and therefore the task of beating the superstition out of their heads has been given up as a hopeless one. The peasantry on the estate all cherish the legend, if I may use such a term ; and they would as soon think of doubting the gospel itself as the story of the ghost—or rather ghosts, I should say —for there are two—of Tremaine Hall. Then, you see, inasmuch as the generality of our female-servants are taken from amongst the daughters of the peasantry, the belief continues inveterate ; and the consequence is that the room has been left just as if it had no existence in the mansion at all. This was the case for the last three or four years before we went abroad ; and this is the case now. But since you wish to see the room, there is not the slightest reason why your curiosity should not be gratified."

Thus speaking, Charlotte Tremaine took down a key from a corner where it hung upon a nail; and she opened the door of the haunted room. My first idea was that I was about to enter a gloomy looking apartment, with the shutters closed, and the curtains drawn over the windows. But nothing of the kind! It was a large airy room, well lighted, and of cheerful aspect—about the very last indeed which according to superstitious prejudice one would be inclined to associate with anything supernatural!

"There is an inner door, I perceive," I said, after looking around this really comfortable chamber.

"Yes—that is the dressing-room," answered Miss Tremaine: and she threw open the door.

It was a convenient toilet-chamber, lighted by means of a window on the roof; for it was so situated in the interior of the dwelling as to be unable to be provided with a window in the side wall.

"Well," I said, "if this be your haunted apartment, Charlotte, I would just as soon occupy it as that which you have assigned to me; and I know that Beda would be quite as happy and contented in the little dressing-room as in the ante-chamber where she is to sleep next to my own room."

"But as there is no necessity, my dear Ellen," said Charlotte, laughing, "for you to run the slightest risk of frightening your own imagination or that of your pretty black-eyed servant, we will not talk any more of your occupying these rooms."

"Oh, certainly," I rejoined, "it would seem like a piece of foolhardiness on my part to volunteer such a thing! But suppose, for instance, that on arriving here I had found the mansion crowded with guests, and only this apartment with the little dressing-chamber unoccupied, I would have most cheerfully accepted these accommodations for myself and Beda. You were telling me, however, just now, that there is a legend connected with the room, and that vulgar superstition, not contented with bestowing upon it one ghost, has bounteously endowed it with a second——"

At this moment we heard the clear musical voice of Lavinia, exclaiming along the passages, "Charlotte! Miss Percy! where are you? Here is Miss Barron arrived!"

"Ah! let us go and see her!" ejaculated Charlotte. "You must restrain your curiosity, my dear Ellen, about the ghosts. But it shall be gratified another time!"

We accordingly quitted the Haunted Chamber; and Lavinia joined us on the landing.

"Oh, Charlotte!" she cried, with a half-frightened look; "how could you take Miss Percy there? Suppose something dreadful presented itself to your view——"

"Do not be foolish, Lavinia," interrupted Miss Tremaine. "So you say that Miss Barron is arrived?"

"Yes—she has just come. She got here earlier than she expected—and she is asking for both of you. Oh, I am so glad she is come!"

"We are glad, my dear Ellen," said Charlotte,

turning to me, "to welcome Sarah back again; for we do not treat her as a mere governess, you know—we look upon her as one of ourselves, she is so amiable and good—so lady-like and pretty!—and then too, she has been with us for some years, and has always taken such an interest in everything which relates to the family!"

We proceeded along the passage; and on the landing of the principal staircase we met Sarah Barron. She immediately embraced Charlotte: then she took me by the hand, pressing it most fervently,—her truly beautiful countenance being all wreathed in smiles. By her demeanour towards me I presumed that she had heard nothing in reference to the affair of the portrait, which was at all calculated to produce any restraint or embarrassment in her feelings with regard to the terms on which she should stand towards me.

As the day was exceedingly fine—bright and frosty—Mr. Tremaine proposed that we should all sally out for a good walk through the park; and to this a general assent was given. I walked principally with Charlotte; Miss Barron devoted herself specially to her two charges, Lavinia and Emilia. A couple of hours were agreeably passed: we reached the house at three o'clock; and then we sat conversing in the drawing-room until dinner was announced at five. Afterwards we separated to our respective chambers to dress for the evening party.

At about eight the carriages began to drive up to the entrance of the Hall; and the "few friends," as Charlotte had represented them, turned out to be some fifty or sixty guests; so that the drawing-room, as well as the apartments devoted to cards and to music, were speedily filled. I found myself the object of general interest and attention; I was treated with the utmost courtesy, friendliness, and respect; and I found that my profession of an actress exposed me not to a single mortification beneath that hospitable roof, nor amongst the friends whom the Tremaines had gathered around them. Mr. Tremaine requested me to sing; and a young baronet with whom I had just been dancing, conducted me to the piano in the music-room. He himself was a good musician; and he turned the leaves for me. Mr. Tremaine sat close by: Mrs. Tremaine and Charlotte stood behind me; and the moment the rumour spread throughout the rooms that I was about to sing, all the guests came crowding into the apartment where I was thus seated. I cannot speak of my own performance further than to remark that it seemed to give the liveliest satisfaction, amounting in some parts of the room to a perfect enthusiasm; and amongst those who afterwards complimented me in terms of the most fervid admiration, was Sarah Barron.

All of a sudden there was a visible confusion at the doorway of the apartment — voices began ejaculating something—the words "flood" and "canal" reached my ears; and now all attention was directing itself towards the entrance of the room.

"There is something the matter, Mr. Tremaine!" I said, in a hurried tone to the master of the mansion, who had taken up the music-book from which I had just been playing.

"Oh, papa!" cried Lavinia, making her way through the crowd and rushing with affrighted countenance towards her father: "the park is all overflowed! the waters are rising!"

"Ah!"—and Mr. Tremaine started up to his feet; while, at the same time, a footman who had been communicating the intelligence on the landing just outside the apartment, hastily approached his master to confirm the tidings which had issued from Lavinia's lips.

CHAPTER CXIX.

THE FLOOD.

THE report was not a false one. There was now a general rush towards all the windows of the suite of apartments which had been thrown open for the entertainment; and I cannot find words to convey an idea of the singular impression made upon my own mind by the spectacle which met my view. It appeared as if by the waving of an enchanter's wand Tremaine Hall had suddenly been transported into the midst of some little island; for a vast sheet of water spread its expanse before the eyes; and the feeling of amazement which the scene conjured up, was naturally mingled with terror. Indeed, screams and ejaculations indicative of affright, burst from the lips of many of the ladies, as they caught the first glimpse of the flood from the windows of the brilliantly-lighted saloons: but Mr. Tremaine and the other gentlemen present hastened about from one terrified group to another, affording the assurance that no actual danger was to be apprehended, though possibly some inconvenience might ensue. Mr. Tremaine sent out some of his domestics to ascertain to what height the waters had risen about the elevated ground on which the mansion stood; so that he might learn whether all the roads in the neighbourhood were closed by the waters, or whether there were any issues yet left free.

Presently several of us hastened to look forth from the back windows of the Hall: thence we sped to the extremities of the long passages, so that we might extend our survey from the side windows; but all around the mansion the white surface of flood was shining like quicksilver in the pure brilliant starlight. It was a strange spectacle!—it seemed as if it were an immense sea dotted with countless little islands, and with numerous trees towering high above the surface. The hedge-rows defined long straight lines: cottages stood like portions of a miniature Venice, as if purposely built in the midst of vast lagunes. At the rear of the premises the flood had not as yet approached nearer than about half a mile; and thus no parts of the kitchen-gardens, the orchards, or the shrubberies, were submerged. Towards the sides of the mansion the flood had approached nearer; and in the front the waters were within a hundred yards of the portico, so that almost the entire park was converted as it were into one huge lake. Such was the aspect which the flood presented at about eleven o'clock at night, some half-hour after the first warning of its presence had been given at the mansion.

It appeared that the canal at some short distance, had for a long time past been considered in a very dangerous state; and several of the inhabitants had predicted that unless certain measures were adopted it would some day break down a sort of dike which served as one of its banks, and would overflow the country. There was consequently now no difficulty in surmising that this had happened: but as the whole of that district was exceedingly level, the waters had glided rapidly rather than rushed furiously, and the whole neighbourhood was submerged stealthily rather than violently. Indeed, when the first feelings of excitement were over at the Hall—when even the most timid ladies were comparatively tranquillized, and the gentlemen were enabled to deliberate calmly upon the occurrence—it appeared to be one that was really only calculated to produce inconvenience, and not to be fraught with any more serious evil. It was estimated that the ground-floors of those cottages which stood lowest, could scarcely be more than a foot under water; and little apprehension was entertained that the flood would approach close up to Tremaine Hall; for, as I have already hinted, it stood upon a slight eminence, rising in an almost circular form in the very midst of the domain. Thus, in a generally comprehensive view of the whole case, little danger was to be dreaded in respect to human life, and none at the Hall. But on the score of *inconvenience*, it assuredly might be different; for the very part which lay lowest, and where the waters were consequently sure to be the deepest, was the main road skirting the park railings. How were the guests to take their departure? Some few of the gentlemen, more adventurous than the rest, declared that the flood should not bar the progress of their carriages; for that if their coachmen were afraid, they themselves would mount the boxes and drive the equipages. But the ladies who belonged to these somewhat boastful-speaking gentlemen, protested loudly against any such proceeding. Then arose an argument on the practicability of it; and several estimates were at once made of how much lower was the road than the highest point to which the water had yet attained in the park. The most contradictory calculations were thus put forward,—one gentleman declaring that the water would not be found to rise to the height of a foot in the road, and another expressing his conviction that it would be found up to the horses' stomachs. At length Mr. Tremaine interposed by ejaculating, "It is all very well, gentlemen, for you to argue in these contradictory terms: but most of you seem to have lost sight of the descent of the road to the bridge at one corner of the park, and that awkward hollow at the other."

"True!" cried several voices.

"I have not the slightest doubt," continued Mr. Tremaine, "that the water is at least five feet deep in the hollow; and as for the bridge—why, you would not be able to find it at all!"

"Then we are indeed hemmed in as it were!" said several of the disputants who had just been arguing vehemently on the brighter side of the question.

"But what of our prospects in the rear of the premises?" asked an elderly gentleman, who began to look rather glum at the idea of being kept away from his home.

"I have just been making a survey in that direction," exclaimed the young baronet to whom I have alluded, and who just now entered the drawing-room from which he had been for some little while absent. "There is no chance in that direction. I have spoken to some of your men, Mr. Tremaine—and they have satisfactorily proved to me that the two lanes which alone might be reached from that quarter, must be absolutely impassable."

"Let me go and hear the reports of those I have sent out," said Mr. Tremaine, "and who have doubtless by this time returned."

During the discussion of the subjects which I have thus briefly noticed, the ladies were not merely attentive listeners, but they likewise threw in observations of their own; and many blank faces and anxious looks might have been observed when the conclusion of the argument seemed to indicate that there was no alternative but to make up the mind for a sojourn at Tremaine Hall throughout the night, and perhaps even for a longer period. Not that anything else except the kindest hospitality was to be anticipated beneath that roof; but there are always many reasons why persons do not like to be detained away from their own homes. As for Mrs. Tremaine and her daughters, they manifested the kindest feeling, in hastening amongst their guests and distributing the fervid assurances that everything should be done to conduce to their comfort: but though the habitation was a spacious one, I could not help thinking that it would be found somewhat difficult to provide accommodation for such a number of persons.

Presently Mr. Tremaine returned to the drawing-room: three or four gentlemen had accompanied him while he went to ascertain from his domestics the precise aspect of affairs; and therefore there was now more than one voice to explain how matters stood. Each gentleman became the centre of a little group: but the general tenour of the tidings was of course the same. Mr. Tremaine's servants had been in every direction—some on horseback: and according to the reports it was deemed decidedly unsafe for any attempt at departure to be made by the guests that night.

Now that the worst was known, the company speedily resigned themselves to a position that was unavoidable; and Mr. Tremaine begged the gentlemen to get up another dance, in order to cheer the spirits of the ladies. The excellent band which had been hired from Stafford, struck up in the drawing-room; and dancing was resumed accordingly. Afterwards supper was announced; and we all proceeded to the dining-room where an elegant banquet was spread. Mr. Tremaine sent the champagne circulating freely; and the gentlemen were more than usually assiduous, if possible, in their attention to the ladies on account of the peculiar position in which they were all placed. Presently the ladies retired to the drawing-room; and then I beheld Mrs. Tremaine, Charlotte, and Sarah Barron, speaking apart, with countenances which indicated some little degree of perplexity, if not of annoyance. I immediately conjectured what the subject of this discussion was; and as a sudden thought struck me, I advanced towards the trio.

"You are perplexed, my dear madam," I said to Mrs. Tremaine, "how you are possibly to dispose of so many guests?"

The affair was really a serious one. All the carriages had been put up at the Hall: there were consequently all the servants attendant upon those carriages; and in addition to these there were between fifty and sixty guests.

"Every room—every nook and corner, must be put into requisition!" said Mrs. Tremaine. "I suppose, my dear Ellen, that you will not object to share your chamber with Charlotte? Your pretty maid-servant can take Lavinia or Emilia into her own couch——"

"Oh, most certainly!" I exclaimed: "deal with my room as you think fit. The chamber you have given me is a large one: why not make up an extra bed there?"

"Ah, how kind and considerate on your part, my dear Miss Percy!" said Mrs. Tremaine—"I really think we shall be compelled to do so; for, as I and Charlotte and Miss Barron were making our calculations, it was clear that every room in the house must not only be occupied, but also made the most of."

"Except of course the haunted room," interjected Charlotte.

"Yes—except the haunted room," said Mrs. Tremaine. "There *was* a time when I and your father——But no matter! I suppose as we get older we become more nervous."

"And why not let that particular room be occupied?" I at once asked. "Suffer me and my maid to change our quarters thither ——"

"No, no, Miss Percy!" interrupted Mrs. Tremaine: "I would not permit such a thing! What? you, a guest, to be treated in such a manner! No, no! If anybody slept there ——"

"Now pray do me a favour, my dear madam," I said: "suffer me and my faithful Beda to occupy that chamber and that dressing-room to-night! I told Charlotte to-day that I should not have the slightest objection to sleep there. I appeal to her if I did not? Therefore it is no sudden access of hardihood on my part;—and in plain terms, I should like to have my wish gratified all the more especially, for the sake of convincing your domestics that no faith need be attached to the superstitious rumours pertaining to that apartment."

"Have you heard the legend connected therewith?" inquired Mrs. Tremaine.

"No," I responded; "and I would rather not hear it to-night. The imagination sometimes plays strange freaks, and reproduces scenes that have been told or read, with all the vividness of a fearful reality. If I know nothing connected with the haunted apartment, as you call it," I added, with a smile, "my imagination cannot receive a feverish impulse therefrom: but if, on the other hand, I do hear or see anything which bears an analogy to the details of the legend, then may you safely arrive at the conclusion that the apartment is in reality haunted after all."

"I have a great mind to offer to bear you company, my dear Ellen," said Charlotte. "Would you, Sarah, if I agreed?" she inquired, turning towards Miss Barron.

This young lady turned pale:—indeed methought that she was already pale, and that she now became still more pallid; so that I at once said, "Do not ask your friend such a thing, Charlotte! And as for you yourself, you confessed to me to-day that a few years ago there was a tinge of superstition in your character."

"And now I wish to convince myself practically and effectually," interjected Charlotte, "that I am free from that taint."

"No, my dear friend," I responded with a smile; "I will not have your company. I have made up my mind that I and Beda will be alone together in the occupation of the haunted room. So it is settled, my dear madam," I added, turning towards Mrs. Tremaine; "and I shall proceed to give Beda orders accordingly. Ah, by the bye! pray let the matter rest for the present as a secret between ourselves—do not suffer it to be whispered amongst the guests—do not even let Mr. Tremaine know it until it be at least too late for him to interfere! And do not tell your sisters, Charlotte!—while upon your silence, Miss Barron, I equally reckon!"

I was compelled to use some additional arguments and entreaties to induce Mrs. Tremaine to give her assent to my proffer: but it is unnecessary to record any more of the conversation. Suffice it to observe that I gained my point; and stealing forth from the drawing-room, I went and gave the requisite instructions to Beda.

By the time that I returned to the drawing-room, the gentlemen were proceeding thither from the apartment where the banquet had taken place; and dancing was now renewed. To be brief, it was between two and three o'clock in the morning when the company separated for the purpose of retiring to rest. The best arrangements which were possible under the circumstances had been made for the accommodation of so numerous a party; and while the words "Good night" were being uttered in every direction, and doors were closing all over the house, I glided towards the haunted chamber, followed by Beda.

According to the instructions which I had given her, the faithful and intrepid girl had already been there and had lighted a fire, which was now blazing cheerfully in the grate. She had placed wax lights upon the toilet-table, and we had brought a taper with us, which I desired her to keep in the dressing-room. I locked the door, saying to Beda, "At all events, my dear girl, no mischievously inclined person shall have an opportunity of playing us a trick, even supposing that it has by any possibility been whispered that we are going to sleep here. I will not insult you by asking if you are at all frightened, or if you regret the willing assent you gave when I just now asked whether you would agree to share with me the occupancy of the haunted room?"

"Oh, no, my dear Miss!" replied Beda, "I do not for an instant regret the answer that I gave; and as for being frightened, I never entertain any fear when I am with you."

"You have not heard the story connected with this room, Beda?" I said. "I think you told me so just now?"

"I have not heard it, Miss," was her answer, "and I am rather glad of it—for it is just possible that the fancifulness of a dream may reproduce it with a vivid semblance of reality."

"The same idea struck me, Beda," I ejaculated, "when I ere now proposed to Mrs. Tremaine to occupy this apartment. But you must not think, my dear Beda, that my offer was made through any foolhardiness on my part: it was simply because I knew that the offer would prove a real accommodation to our kind hostess under existing circumstances—and as I have no superstitious fears, I thought that it would be absolutely selfish and egotistical on my part *not* to make such an overture."

"I am glad that you did, Miss," observed Beda. "There must be really something very silly to believe that such a beautiful cheerful-looking room as this could be haunted!"

"This was also the same idea which struck me to-day, my dear Beda. It is not that I altogether disbelieve the existence of preternatural visions, because religion itself makes us aware that in the olden time there must have been such spectacles. But what I doubt is that heaven will permit innocent and unoffending persons to be terrified by any hideous visitation from the other world. Such a proceeding would be useless as well as cruel; and heaven does nothing uselessly or cruelly. But if on the other hand the visitation should prove a beautiful spirit, and its object should be one of utility and benefit,—then, in *this* case, there can assuredly be no reason to dread it."

"So that altogether," interjected Beda, "you are devoid of apprehension, Miss?—and that is precisely the same feeling which I entertain."

"In short, Beda," I added, "the whole question may be summed up in a few words:—we do not doubt the possibility, but we doubt the probability of supernatural appearances."

While this discourse was taking place, Beda was assisting me to disapparel myself; and when my night-toilet was completed, I said, "Now, my dear girl, in order that we may not stand the risk of being terrified or startled by any strange sound, we will endeavour to convince ourselves so far as we may be enabled, that there are no means whence such sounds should arise."

We made a complete investigation of the two rooms—looking under the beds, as well as in the cupboards and the chest of drawers: but there did not seem to be so much as a board that creaked under our feet, or anything else that was likely to startle or alarm us.

We now sought our respective couches—I occupying the one in the larger chamber, and Beda taking possession of the one in the little dressing-room. The tapers were burning on the toilet-table; and Beda had the chamber-candlestick in the next room. I should add that the door of communication between the two rooms was left open.

It was nearly four o'clock before we had got to bed; and then I lay awake for at least half-an-hour, thinking on divers matters, and every now and then opening my eyes to glance around the room; for though I can positively assure the reader that I was not in the least degree frightened; yet there was some feeling—I can scarcely explain it—which made me thus glance about the place as if it were to reassure myself that I *was* perfectly justified in keeping superstitious ideas at a distance. At length a sensation of drowsiness began to steal over me—my eyelids grew heavy—my thoughts were falling more and more into confusion—and I slept. But I was soon awakened—and it was in a most startling manner. There seemed to be a rush of something through the room; yet the sound had altogether ceased when I sat up, broad awake, and listened. For several minutes did I thus listen with suspended breath; but all continued silent, until I was made aware by a movement in the dressing-chamber that Beda was also awake.

"Cannot you sleep?" I inquired in a kind voice.

"I was asleep, dear Miss," she responded; "but ——but——in short, I awoke."

"Yes—I awoke likewise after a slumber," I said; then consulting my watch, which lay upon a table at the side of the bed, I added, "It is only a little past five o'clock; and therefore we have not slept very long."

"Let us compose ourselves to sleep again," answered Beda.

"Yes," I said: and then silence prevailed—for I thought to myself, "Perhaps it was all imagination on my part, and there was really no particular sound heard?—or else Beda considers it more prudent to say nothing on the subject?"

I lay down again; and at the expiration of about another half-hour I once more sank into slumber. But again was I destined to be startled up; I was once more broad awake—and there was upon my mind the impression that I had heard the same sound as before, like the gushing passage of some invisible body through the apartment, or the hurricane-like rush of unseen wings. That I had been awakened in terror, was pretty certain; for not merely was the sensation in my mind, but the cold perspiration had broken out upon my forehead—and the front part of my hair felt all damp from the same effect, as I raised my hand to still the violent throbbing of my brows. My heart was palpitating furiously: I had indeed been tremendously frightened, either in a dream or by some startling reality—I could not tell which.

I listened, and all was again still for some minutes—until another movement in the next room convinced me that Beda was once more awake. This time it was she who spoke first to me; and she inquired in a voice which methought was slightly tremulous, "Can you not sleep, dear Miss?"

"I have again been asleep, Beda—and again am I awakened. And you?"

"The same with me," she responded after a few moments' silence—no doubt the silence of hesitation.

"Did you hear anything, Beda?" I asked.

She now came gliding forth from the dressing-chamber; and seating herself on the side of my bed, she fixed her superb dark eyes with inquiring earnestness upon me, saying, "Did you hear anything, dear Miss?"

"Yes—methought I did," I rejoined. "But tell me first of all, what you fancied that you heard?"

"I can scarcely tell—I can scarcely describe it," answered Beda: and I now observed that her bosom was palpitating quite as violently as my own had just before been doing from the furious pulsations of the heart. "And yet it seemed to me," she continued, "as if it were something like a rushing sound which passed rapidly through the room—Yet I know not exactly where, or in which direction—whether it was above or below —from your room into mine, or from mine into yours——And then it ceased all in an instant."

"This is exactly what I fancied, Beda," I responded. "Twice——"

"Yes, twice, dear Miss!—both times it was the same! But on the first occasion I did not like to express what I fancied or feared, lest you should think that I was suddenly becoming a coward——"

"There was assuredly such a noise as you have described, Beda," I interrupted her; "and on both occasions did I hear it as well as you. There is no cowardice in acknowledging that we heard the sound: the cowardice would be in imputing it to preternatural causes. No!—there are often strange noises in old buildings—timbers creaking, or suddenly bursting—rats rushing underneath the boards——"

"And doubtless this last explanation will serve," ejaculated Beda, "to account for what we have heard!"

"Yes—this is very probable," I said. "And now, my dear Beda, return to your own bed, and let us see if we shall be permitted to obtain a few hours repose; for we were up very late, and these fitful slumbers which we have hitherto caught are tantalizing and exhausting rather than soothing or refreshing."

Beda accordingly sought her own couch; and silence again prevailed in the two chambers. But I could not again woo the presence of slumber very readily—though I lay perfectly still to avoid disturbing Beda in case she might be more fortunate than myself in respect to the advance of sleep. At the expiration of a short time I heard a sound as if of the rattling of something; and I confess that the idea which at once struck me was that the noise resembled precisely what the rattling of human bones must be. I will even make another confession, and admit that a sudden terror seized upon me: it was a cold tremor—the perspiration bathed my forehead like the chill dew of death—and my heart was again palpitating violently. But this paroxysm of affright quickly passed away: I grew calm and collected—I listened —there was silence for upwards of a minute—and then the sounds were renewed. They were the same as those which had just disturbed me: they seemed like the rattling of bones somewhere upon the floor, at a part to which the carpet did not extend—but I could not exactly tell where. I now again raised myself in the bed and listened; and gradually the idea crept into my mind that the sounds proceeded from a cupboard in the corner of the room. I glided from the bed—I advanced towards that cupboard: the noise continued—but the instant my fingers touched the handle of the door to open it, the sounds ceased.

"What can it possibly be?" asked the voice of Beda, who was now close behind me; and so noiselessly had she glided from her own chamber, that I was startled by her presence.

"I cannot conceive," I answered. "Have you been awake long, Beda?"

"I have not been to sleep, Miss, since I sat by your bedside: and I more than suspected that you were remaining awake likewise."

"And you heard those sounds, Beda?" I asked.

"Yes," she responded. "And do you know what it struck me they were like? Methought they resembled the rattling of human bones!"

"And such also was my fancy," I rejoined.

"But as we just now agreed between us, there are often strange noises in old houses : sometimes they concentrate themselves in one particular room, which thence obtains a reputation for being haunted. It may be so here."

"It may be so," answered Beda. "If you are not frightened, dear Miss, I am sure I shall not be. No ! I could not be frightened where you are !"

I patted her caressingly on the face ; and then I said, as I held the cupboard door open, " Look, my dear Beda—this place is empty ! The sounds, whatever they were, must have come from underneath the boards—or else from behind the wainscot ; and again must we recur to the presence of rats as the solution of the mystery."

Thus speaking, I closed the door of the cupboard ; and we again sought our respective couches. I was almost inclined to tell Beda that she might share mine : but I was afraid that if I did so, the very circumstance itself might excite or increase her fears by seeming to indicate that I myself was frightened. Sleep came upon my eyes more quickly than I could possibly have expected ; and I slumbered on uninterruptedly until past nine o'clock. Beda was up and just completing her toilet. I smiled as she came forth from the dressing-chamber ; and I said, " Well, my dear girl, how did you sleep after all ?"

"I slept soundly," she responded, " after that last fright——I mean, after the last time we were startled."

"And I also," I said. " But let us see whether the floods are subsiding."

"I sprang from the bed : we drew back the window-curtains—and as we surveyed the country from that side-casement, it struck us both that the waters had diminished to some little extent.

"In reference to those little circumstances which startled us, Beda," I said, " I think we had better not make any special mention of them ; for if we do so, it will only be encouraging the superstitious belief which already prevails amongst the domestics. Perhaps I may privately mention to Mr. Tremaine my notion that there are rats under the boards, or behind the wainscot : but further than that——"

"Rest assured, dear Miss," interrupted Beda, "that from my lips nothing shall go forth. I shall simply declare that we passed the night quite comfortably, and that the idea of the chamber being haunted is something only worthy of ridicule."

"I do not know whether it be that the daylight renders me courageous," I said, " but according to my present feeling, I should not at all object to pass another night in this chamber, even if it were only for curiosity's sake, so as to ascertain whether those sounds would be repeated. For now that we are prepared for them, Beda, we should be enabled on a second occasion to judge of them more calmly and dispassionately—and perhaps to arrive at a better conclusion what they really are."

"Well, Miss," said Beda, " if the floods have not subsided sufficiently to allow the guests to depart, we must sleep here another night : for of course it would not do for you to say that you decline. It would be either tantamount to an admission that you had seen or heard something to alarm you—or else that you were afraid to try the experiment a second time."

"True !" I observed : " but from the appearance of the flood I should scarcely think that it can have subsided sufficiently for the guests to be enabled to take their departure."

My toilet was completed ; and I now descended to the breakfast-parlour.

Only Mrs. Tremaine, Miss Barron, Charlotte, and her two youngest sisters were as yet there. Charlotte at once raised her finger to her lips, at the same time significantly pointing towards Lavinia and Emilia, as much as to give me to understand that they were unacquainted with the fact that I had slept in the haunted chamber. I noticed that Miss Barron looked very pale : I inquired if she were not well ?—she pressed her hand to her brow, complaining that her head ached dreadfully, and attributing it to the late hour to which she had sat up.

"And you, my dear Ellen," asked Charlotte Tremaine, looking hard at me,—"have you slept well ?"

"So well," I responded, " that I feel completely refreshed, and have no sensation as if I had not retired to rest until three o'clock in the morning. But what of the floods ?"

"They seem to have subsided somewhat," answered Mrs. Tremaine ; " and I hope that such may prove to be the fact. Mr. Tremaine and several of the gentlemen have ridden out to make a survey, so that when they return they may be enabled to report progress. I did not tell him," she whispered in my ear, as she took me aside, " that you slept in the haunted chamber : for I thought that it might only annoy him that I had permitted you to do so——and indeed, I was afterwards very sorry to think that I had allowed myself to be overpersuaded by you. But it was really very kind of you !"

At this moment the door opened ; and a number of the lady-guests entered the breakfast-parlour. Others shortly afterwards made their appearance one by one ; and finally the gentlemen returned from their excursion. They were as a matter of course assailed by questionings from all sides ; but the answers they had to give were far from satisfactory. The flood had certainly subsided a little, and the waters were decreasing gradually ; but the main road still continued impassable. It was blocked up as it were at two distinct points : namely, at the two angles of the park ; and thus all egress beyond those two points was prevented. The bridge, to which Mr. Tremaine had on the preceding evening alluded, had fallen in or given way in some manner—but it could not at present be exactly conjectured how. At all events no equipage could pass that way. Then, as for the other point, it was the hollow to which allusion had likewise been made by the master of the mansion ; and there the water proved to be deeper than he himself had estimated.

"In fact, ladies," said Mr. Tremaine, " from all we have been enabled to gather from my servants and labourers, as well as from the country-people, who are wading either on horseback or on foot through the deluge, there is no chance of a subsidence sufficient to allow the hollow to be passed or the bridge to be repaired until to-morrow. You must make up your minds to tarry another day at the Hall. Expresses shall be sent off to the houses of those who desire to forward any such messages homeward; and we will send into Stafford for such letters as the postman may not have been enabled to deliver. More I cannot do, beyond offering you the most cordial hospitalities of my abode."

Such was Mr. Tremaine's speech; and as a matter of course, expressions of gratitude emanated from the lips of all. But I could see that there were many whose looks as plainly as possible interpreted the annoyance and vexation which filled their hearts,—those looks being as much as to say, "I wish, in the name of heaven, that I for one had not on this occasion crossed the threshold of Tremaine Hall!"

There was a moral lesson to be gained from the study of the countenances, the conduct, and the demeanour of the multitude of guests now gathered at the breakfast-table. Those who had been blithest on the preceding evening, were now the most dispirited; those who had seemed the most ready to enjoy themselves in the ball-room, were now the very first to feel the influence of *ennui*; those who had looked most gay, now appeared the most jaded: while, on the contrary, those who had seemed to enter the least into the light-hearted spirit of the preceding evening's entertainments, were now the foremost in exerting themselves to cheer the tempers and exhilarate the moods of those around them. I furthermore observed that those who were most flattering and complimentary towards the hostess and their daughters on the preceding evening, were now the most reserved and distant—as if in the sullenness of their ill-conditioned minds they actually ascribed the fault of the flood to their entertainers, and instead of thanking them for their hospitality, were almost ready to turn round upon them and savagely demand, "Why, in heaven's name, did you ask us here at all?"

Oh, the false gloss which society so often wears! —Oh, the littleness of mind, the paltriness of character, the churlishness and selfishness of disposition, which particular circumstances are calculated to display! Oh, the hypocritical smiles which are worn as a mask!—Oh, the unseemly wrinkles which the true light of day lays bare! And then I thought to myself, as I contemplated a shaded-silk dress which an old dowager wore, "Society is like shot-silk: it must be viewed from all points and in all lights, as well as in all situations —or else its colours will assuredly deceive us!"

But to continue the thread of my narrative. The company were doomed to pass another day at Tremaine Hall; and I felt myself destined to pass another night in the haunted chamber. I can hardly tell how the forenoon was whiled away until luncheon-time; but I remember that billiards and bagatelle were rendered available—a party of four dowagers made up a rubber of whist, the effect of which was to render two of them more savage than ever because they lost, and to console the other two because they won— some of the younger ladies betook themselves to embroidery or other fancy work—and divers books of prints were languidly turned over and over again. But there was an improvement in the state of affairs at luncheon-time; for not only did the repast itself cheer the spirits of the depressed and the desponding, affording an excuse for drinking wine, cherry-brandy, and bottled stout, but the

same period beheld the arrival of the letters and newspapers. There happened to be a very piquant elopement-case; and by the aid of this, together with a murder and a burglary reported at great length, the company got on very excellently until dinner-time.

It was not until the hour of dressing for this repast, that I had an opportunity of speaking to Mrs. Tremaine or to Charlotte in reference to my intention to pass another night in the haunted room.

"I cannot think of it, my dear Miss Percy," said Mrs. Tremaine, emphatically.

"But your embarrassments and perplexities on account of your guests," I replied, "are just the same as they were last night; and it is a perfect matter of indifference to me where I sleep."

"Mr. Tremaine would never permit it!—the Colonel would be most indignant!" ejaculated the lady of the house; "and if it were known that I had suffered you to do such a thing——"

"Do listen to what mamma says, Ellen!" interjected Charlotte. "We can make other arrangements for you: you can have back your own room —Lavinia and Emilia can occupy it with you— and Miss Barron shall share my chamber, along with Lydia and Phœbe;"—thus alluding to two others of her sisters.

"What is this?" inquired Miss Barron, who at the moment entered the back drawing-room where the little colloquy was taking place between myself, Mrs. Tremaine, and Charlotte.

"Miss Percy is making up her mind to be obstinate," said Mrs. Tremaine, but with a good-natured smile. "She will not listen to reason— she persists in sleeping again in the haunted room."

"Ah!" ejaculated Miss Barron. "Really, Miss Percy——"

"All remonstrance is vain," I interrupted her: "I am determined! And why should I not? You, my dear madam," I continued, turning to Mrs. Tremaine, "have occupied that chamber, with Mr. Tremaine; and without arrogating to myself any very exalted amount of courage——"

"Oh, we know you are courageous, Ellen!" interrupted Charlotte: "we require no additional proof of *that!*—and therefore if you have no other reason to sleep in the haunted chamber, pray do as mamma requests you."

"But I *have* another reason," I rejoined, with some degree of emphasis. "There is a little discovery which I wish to make——"

"A discovery?" ejaculated Charlotte. "Do you mean that you really wish to see the ghosts?"

"No—I could scarcely be so foolish as to wish to see them," I replied, with a smile; "even if I were foolish enough to believe in them. But I tell you again that there is a little discovery I am desirous of making; and it refers to the cupboard in the corner farthest from the door. However, it is no use for you to question me any further——"

But I stopped short; for I was struck by the singularity of the look which all the three ladies now wore; and then Charlotte suddenly said, "Have you heard the tale from any source?"

"No," I replied; "and I do not want to hear it—at least not for the present. Do bear with me—let me sleep in that room to-night—and to-

morrow I will take possession of my proper quarters. Ah! and while I bethink me, let the same silence be maintained in reference to my occupation of that room to-night as there was last night."

I did not wait for any answer: but I hurried out of the back drawing-room, and glided down the staircase. It yet wanted an hour to the dinner-time; my evening toilet would not occupy above twenty minutes—and I had noticed a particular dramatic work in the library which I was desirous to consult. This reference I therefore thought of making during the leisure that I should have till dinner-time. I accordingly repaired to the library,—which was already lighted up, for it was past four o'clock, and the season of the year, be it remembered, was at the close of December. I advanced up to the shelf where I knew that I should find the book I required; and I was just taking down that volume, when it

No. 93.—ELLEN PERCY.

struck me that I heard the sounds of footsteps in the immediate vicinity of a large screen which stood near. I turned hastily round—for the footsteps appeared to be stealthy; and at the instant I fancied that I beheld the form of a man, muffled in a cloak, gliding behind that screen. I rushed in the same direction: but I beheld no one. I looked to see what means of egress there were: there was an inner door behind that screen, and I did not know with what part of the house it communicated. I caught hold of the handle—it turned in my grasp—the door opened—and the cold evening air blew upon my face. That door opened into the back garden. A deep obscurity there prevailed; and amidst it I beheld no dark form gliding on. My first impulse was to raise an alarm by summoning the domestics from their adjacent offices: but a second thought restrained me. Was it not all imagination on my part?— who would go rushing about the premises, at that hour, muffled up in a cloak, at the risk of being encountered by some of the numerous occupants of the mansion? As for thieves and evil-disposed persons, did not they choose different hours for the prosecution of their nefarious aims? Yes—assuredly so. I therefore closed and locked the door; and taking the book with me, I ascended to the haunted chamber,—where I found a cheerful fire blazing in the grate, the wax-candles lighted, and Beda waiting for me; for she knew that this was about the time when I should ascend thither for the purpose of my evening toilet.

CHAPTER CXX.

THE HAUNTED CHAMBER.

BEDA was already aware of my determination to pass another night in the haunted chamber; for she knew that the guests were still confined by the pellucid barriers of the flood to the limits of Tremaine Hall. I thought that there was a slight shade of seriousness upon her countenance as I entered the room: but it almost immediately vanished—and I knew not whether it were dispelled by an effort on her part, or whether it was a mere transitory pensiveness which flitted away of its own accord.

"My dear Beda," I said, "I hope you are not vexed to find yourself in these quarters still?"

"Oh! how can I be vexed," exclaimed the beautiful girl, her large eyes being full of animation, "when I am along with you?"

"And yet I fancied, Beda, that when I entered the room—as the door opened softly and you did not immediately observe me—that there was a shade upon your countenance."

"Oh! I was only thinking," she quickly interjected, "of what I had just before heard! But it was nothing, my dear Miss——nothing that vexed me, I mean!"

"And what was it that you heard, Beda?"—for I could not help suspecting that it was something in reference to the haunted apartment itself.

"What did I hear? Oh! nothing, dear Miss! Only the gossip of two or three of the domestics in the servants' hall. But come—let me assist at your evening toilet! Oh, I like to help to apparel you!—you are so beautiful! All the servants declared that Miss Percy was the belle of the room a thousand times over!"

"You have always kind words for me, Beda," I said; "and I appreciate those observations from your lips, which from the lips of others would be only regarded as vain and idle compliments. But tell me, what was all this gossip about in the servants' hall?"

I now noticed that Beda's large luminous eyes were thrown furtively in the direction of the cupboard to which allusion has before been made; and methought that at the same time an expression of half-affright, half-horror passed over her countenance.

"Oh, nothing!—do not ask me, Miss!" she replied, now affecting to bustle about and prepare everything for my evening toilet.

"Nay—but do tell me," I said; for my curiosity was now piqued. "I am convinced you have heard the tale which belongs to this room!—and if so, I may as well know it likewise."

"It is a very horrible story, Miss," answered Beda; "and I do beseech and implore that you will postpone until to-morrow——"

"I understand what you mean, my dear girl!" I interrupted her. "You are afraid that I should be frightened to-night when sleeping in this room? Ah, generous creature that you are! You see that the legend is something only too well calculated to scare the mind: and yet you yourself will risk the encounter of all these terrors rather than separate from me! Ah, I am almost sorry, Beda, that I have volunteered to pass another night in this room!—yes, sorry for your sake!"

"Do not think of me, dear Miss," cried the faithful girl. "I am sorry that you yourself—— Because really, after all I have heard—and remembering those strange sounds——"

Here she stopped short, as if angry with herself for having said too much: and then she again glanced with mingled furtiveness and terror towards the cupboard.

"Tell me, Beda," I said, "what you have heard. If you keep the history from me, my imagination will perhaps only set itself to work all the more actively to conjure up every kind of unreal horrors."

"True, Miss!" exclaimed Beda: "and therefore it is after all better that I should tell you what I have heard! I was down in the servants' hall just now—some of the domestics belonging to the guests were there; and they were conversing with three or four servants of the establishment. Of course it had been whispered amongst the domestics generally that you and I had occupied the haunted room last night. The servants asked me whether I had seen or heard anything particular—and I replied in the negative. Then the conversation dwelt on the topic; and the old laundress told the tale. She has been a great number of years at Tremaine Hall—she was here when the incidents of the legend occurred——"

"Oh, then, the date of the tale," I exclaimed, "is not very remote."

"Only about fifty years," answered Beda; "and the laundress was a young girl of sixteen or seventeen at the time. Of course the present Mr. Tremaine was only a mere child then. He was an only son—and he had lost his mother in the first few months of his existence. His father was a fox-hunting, jovial squire; and thus his grief for the loss of his wife did not last very long; and in the course of a few months—sooner a great deal than such things should have taken place—the Hall was filled with company once more. Amongst them was a distant relation of Mr. Tremaine's—a Captain Cautley, who had recently returned from India with considerable wealth, although he was still a young man, being not more than two-and-thirty years of age. He was very handsome, and endowed with most fascinating manners. He had gone into the army when sixteen: he had been abroad for nearly the same number of years: he went away a boy—he came back a man; and there was one whom he had left as a pretty prattling girl, who in the meantime had grown up, and whom he found when he came back to be a most beautiful woman. This was his cousin Arabella Ravenscliffe."

"Ravenscliffe?" I ejaculated, surprised at this mention of a name that was so familiar to me.

"Yes—Ravenscliffe," rejoined Beda; "for it appears that there is some distant connexion between the Tremaines and Lord Carshalton's family—though I know not exactly how or in what degree; and moreover I believe, from what I heard, the two families are estranged—knowing nothing of each other, and not caring to know anything."

"It is strange, Beda," I observed, "how certain names have been recently mentioned in my hearing,—as if they were really destined to be grouped altogether in the end, for the purpose of developing some important result! But proceed with your narrative."

"I am telling you a tale, dear Miss, of half a century back—when Squire Tremaine, as he was always called, was the master of the estate and mansion. I was telling you likewise that it was here, beneath this roof, that Edmund Cautley, on his return from India, encountered his cousin Arabella Ravenscliffe. She was now a superb woman of five-and-twenty, in all the glory of a most magnificent loveliness. As I heard the tale from the old laundress, it was scarcely possible to perceive any poetry in the description: but still her language is graphic enough to enable the imagination to conceive all the poetry for itself. And so, without any very great mental effort, I could picture the tall, slender, elegant-shaped Captain Cautley—with his countenance slightly bronzed by the sun of an Indian clime—his dark eyes, his finely-pencilled black moustache—and his air of the finished gentleman,—meeting beneath this roof the superb and queen-like Arabella, whose light brown hair fell in myriads of ringlets upon snowy shoulders—whose complexion was of the purity of the lily, imperceptibly blending with the softest blush of the rose—whose large blue eyes were full of languor and tenderness—and whose form, above the usual stature of woman, was remarkable for graceful symmetry and softly rounded proportions."

"Indeed you are poetic, my dear Beda!" I exclaimed, with a half-smile. "But are you sure that you are justified in using such terms after the description received from the lips of a menial?"

"In her own plain, but sensible and graphic style," rejoined Beda, "she succeeded in making the portraits of her characters stand out as it were with life-like effect from the canvass of her word-painting. I am but expressing the same ideas in other terms."

"Proceed, my dear girl—and pardon me the interruption."

"The tale is not a very long one," resumed Beda. "Arabella Ravenscliffe had lost her father; and her mother, who had been a very beautiful woman in her day, was almost completely blind. Thus Arabella was compelled to be a constant attendant on her afflicted parent; for their means were very limited indeed—all her resources being pretty nearly swallowed up by a long and disastrous lawsuit, in which her branch of the family was plunged with some other branches,—a terrible network of legal difficulties which the old laundress herself dared not attempt to unravel in the form

of an explanation. Well then, considering the poverty of Mrs. and Miss Ravenscliffe, it was quite a godsend for them when Squire Tremaine invited them to come and take up their abode altogether at the Hall soon after the death of his wife; for he thought that though the mother was nearly blind, yet that by the assistance of the daughter, or by the aid of the two together, his housekeeping affairs might be comfortably superintended. And then came Captain Cautley, as I have already said. There was plenty of company at the Hall for a while; and so far as the old laundress can recollect, nothing particular was thought in reference to the Captain and Arabella, until the guests had taken their departure and there was a species of lull after a long round of pleasure;—and then it was observed that the handsome Captain and the beautiful Arabella were frequently seen whispering together—evidently snatching moments to be apart from the Squire and the half-blind lady—sometimes walking in the garden and the shrubberies—but chiefly in the most secluded spots; so that there was not much trouble in conjecturing that they were lovers. But after a little while Captain Cautley was suddenly ordered to join his regiment, which was stationed in Ireland, where troubles had broken out. After his departure a visible change took place in Arabella Ravenscliffe: her natural gaiety seemed to have fled, though she strove to maintain a forced animation in the presence of the Squire and her mother. As for the Squire, his life seemed to be divided into three parts:—one was spent in the saddle, the second at the table, and the third in bed. He was fond of his bottle—he drank very hard; and when he was not tipsy or asleep, he was out hunting. Of course such a man was but little likely to notice any change that took place in the young lady; and if she had turned from the fair creature that she was, into an Ethiopian, he could scarcely have perceived it. Then as for Mrs. Ravenscliffe, she was becoming more and more blind, and could discern nothing. The servants had their eyes open—they began to have their suspicions of something: but it was not for them to speak a word, unless it were whisperingly uttered amongst themselves;—and even in this they were diffident and cautious, because Miss Arabella was a great favourite, and very good to them. But what they did suspect was that the poor young lady had been betrayed and abandoned by Edmund Cautley—and that she was in a way to become a mother!"

Here Beda paused for a few moments, while a blush stained her cheek; for such was the exceeding purity of the young girl's soul, that it shocked her, even in her discourse with me whom she regarded in the light of a confidential friend, to be compelled to allude to such a subject.

"No more company now visited at Tremaine Hall," continued Beda; "but how this was prevented, the servants knew not,—whether it were that the Squire himself had become indifferent on the point—or whether Arabella succeeded in influencing him and her mother to that extent. The fact however seems to be as I am relating it. At length, after the expiration of six or seven months from Captain Cautley's departure, he suddenly reappeared at the Hall. His arrival was almost immediately followed by certain little changes in the interior arrangements, which must be mentioned. Hitherto Mrs. Ravenscliffe and her daughter had occupied the same chamber: but now Mrs. Ravenscliffe moved to another one, which had an almost equally large bedroom adjoining. They are situated in the eastern wing of the building. The old laundress who tells the tale, but who was then quite a young girl of seventeen or eighteen, was appointed to attend by night upon Mrs. Ravenscliffe, and to sleep in the chamber adjoining her own. Miss Arabella removed into this room,—*this* room, my dear Miss Percy, where you and I are now seated!"

There was another brief pause; and then Beda continued in the following manner:—

"All these arrangements took place upon grounds which appeared to be quite natural and proper. It was alleged that Arabella's health was suffering through the constant attentions she bestowed upon her mother; and that therefore if she devoted her days to that mother, she had a right to enjoy an adequate amount of rest at night. The mother said the same thing: the Squire was utterly indifferent as to what was being done, so long as his own accustomed course of enjoyment remained uninterrupted. Again were Edmund Cautley and Arabella Ravenscliffe seen frequently walking together, or whispering apart; and what is more, the young lady was often seen in tears, though she evidently did all she could to conceal them. But at the expiration of two or three weeks, Arabella was represented as being indisposed: she kept her chamber for a few days—she would not receive the visits of any professional man—but the mother used to go and sit with her for nearly the whole day. The servants whispered amongst themselves, wondering whether their former suspicions were true—and if so, how matters would be suffered to progress. To their surprise, however, Miss Arabella left her chamber at the expiration of a few days: she looked very pale, languid, and thin; and there was wonderment amongst the domestics—but they fancied that they must have been mistaken, and that the young lady could *not* have been in a way to become a mother. A few weeks passed—and Captain Cautley again absented himself; but this time it was only for about a month—and it was said that he had been to London to effect his retirement from the service, either by selling his commission or going on half-pay, I know not exactly which. He returned to the Hall; and just at that time the Squire was laid up in bed from a serious accident, he having broken his collar-bone by a fall from his horse. And now I come to the tragic part of this most dismal story. A few days after Captain Cautley's return to the Hall, he and Arabella were seen walking together in the shrubbery; high words were passing between them: the sounds could be heard—but the sense could not be distinguished. It was conjectured that Arabella entreated and threatened, and that Edmund Cautley spoke to her in harsh unfeeling terms. Beyond this nothing more was known of that interview. This was not however the only event of significancy—indeed I may say of importance, which occurred that day; for very shortly after the scene in the shrubbery, there was another scene in the drawing-room—where the mother, the daughter, and Captain Cautley

were present together. One of the servants endeavoured to listen: but all that could be gleaned was that the mother virulently reproached Captain Cautley for something which could not be understood—though it was surmised because he refused to espouse her daughter. At the end of that interview the Captain took his hurried departure from the Hall, without even seeing the Squire—who, as I have already observed, was lying ill of a broken collar-bone. The hours passed away; and at the usual time in the evening the inmates of the Hall retired to rest, little suspecting the nature of the horrors that were to occur during that memorable night. A gardener, who lived in one of the outhouses, returned home at about eleven o'clock; and as he was passing along the back of the mansion, he was suddenly startled by beholding a person enveloped in a cloak, who was just disappearing through a door which opens into the library."

"Ah!" I ejaculated, smitten by a strange feeling which I must candidly confess was one of uneasiness, if not actually of terror. "Do you mean a door which is of glass half-way down, and has a shutter to put up over it?"

"Yes—the same," replied Beda, surveying me with the intensest curiosity. "But why do you ask the question? and why do you turn so pale, dear Miss? What has affected you?"

"Nothing, nothing!" I rejoined. "I will tell you presently. Proceed, Beda."

"The gardener caught a glimpse of that cloaked figure," continued Beda, "and rushed after the individual. He caught him by the mantle; and then the gentleman turned round, and the gardener saw that it was Captain Cautley. He began making excuses: the Captain gave him a guinea, and desired him to say nothing of the circumstance. The gardener pursued his way with the guinea in his pocket,— and wondering what the circumstance could mean,—why the Captain, in short, should be thus stealthily entering the Hall. In the morning Miss Arabella did not descend to the breakfast-table at the usual hour; and after a while her mother, becoming alarmed, sent one of the servants to inquire if she were ill. No answer was returned to the summons at the door of the chamber,—*this* chamber, my dear Miss! The door itself was locked: but it was soon forced open—and then what a spectacle met the view!"

Beda shuddered—rose from her seat—flung a rapid uneasy look around her—and then said in a low deep voice, "Captain Cautley was lying stretched upon the floor, weltering in his blood—a long sharp knife having inflicted the wound! There he lay, enveloped in his cloak—and he had been dead many hours! But that was not all. For *there*—in that dressing-room where I slept last night, — *there*, my dear Miss Percy, the wretched Arabella was found suspended to the cord by which the skylight is opened or shut! She had on nothing but her night-dress and a morning-wrapper: she was thus all clothed in white, as if she had apparelled herself purposely in garments which might seem to be those of the grave!"

Beda again paused, her looks full of horror; and I felt that horror was also in my own countenance —for I not only thought of the tragic story which I had just heard, but likewise of that cloaked figure which I had seen, or fancied that I had seen, in the library, and which had appeared to have passed out of the glass door leading into the back garden.

"Mrs. Ravenscliffe, the wretched mother, gave way to the wildest grief," continued Beda: "but she recovered her self-possession by the time the Coroner's Inquest was held. In answer to a question which was put to her with all befitting delicacy, she positively denied that her daughter had become a mother: but she proclaimed it was the truth that Arabella had been most cruelly trifled with and disappointed by Edmund Cautley in respect to her heart's tenderest affections. Mrs. Ravenscliffe further said that on the day when Cautley had left the house after the interview at which all three were present, he had been solemnly adjured at that interview to fulfil his promise to Arabella—but that his replies were evasive, that his heartlessness was therefore apparent, and that after some angry words he quitted the place. Then whether it were that Arabella herself had privately communicated with him and appointed a last meeting, or whether it were that he himself had sought such an interview, could not be determined and was left to conjecture. Little however did it matter how the actual facts of the case might veritably be: it was only too evident that Cautley had perished by the hand of Arabella, and that she had put a period to her own existence. A suitable verdict was accordingly returned—the bodies were interred in the village churchyard—but the rites of Christian burial were not afforded to the remains of Arabella Ravenscliffe."

"This is indeed a most dismal tragedy, my dear Beda," I observed. "But perhaps you have more to tell me?"

"Immediately after the inquest," proceeded my faithful dependant, "Mrs. Ravenscliffe left Tremaine Hall; and the Squire was thus abandoned to the care of menials. The report soon began to spread that the apparitions of the deceased had been seen about the premises: no one would enter *this* chamber, which acquired the reputation of being haunted; and that gardener to whom I have already alluded, declared that as he was one evening passing along the gravel walk communicating with the back door leading from the library, he beheld the figure of Edmund Cautley which sped rapidly past him, and enveloped in a cloak just as he was on that night when the same man saw him stealthily entering the mansion. And since then it has been said that the ghost of Captain Cautley has frequently made his appearance—but only in two spots: either in the neighbourhood of that back door leading into the garden, or else at this haunted chamber. And rumour likewise declares that the apparition is always that of a man muffled in a cloak, so that the countenance is not visible, hastening on at a quick gliding pace, and disappearing the very instant it reaches the door leading from the library into the garden, or else the door of this room. Then, in reference to the unfortunate Arabella, it is said that her spirit wears precisely the same appearance as on that night of murder and of suicide, when she was clad in the white muslin wrapper as if she had purposely assumed a garb that should most closely resemble the apparel of the grave!"

While Beda was giving me these explanations, I had some trouble to compose my countenance sufficiently to prevent her from suspecting that something strange was passing in my mind: but I confess that I inwardly shuddered as I thus heard how the shade of Captain Cautley was reported to haunt the premises, enveloped in a cloak, and how the apparition had been principally seen in the neighbourhood of that glass door leading from the library into the garden. Could it be possible that the report was indeed founded in fact?—and that I had beheld the apparition? Was it not singular that before a single syllable of this tale had reached my ears, I should have seen something which appeared to give its superstitious part so terrible a confirmation?—how could I have *imagined* the figure of a man muffled in a cloak, and disappearing at that very door which was so intimately connected with the circumstances of the legend? It was strange!—it was remarkable!—and again must I confess that I shuddered inwardly as I thought of it: but I resolved to place a seal upon my lips, so that I should not add to whatsoever sentiment of alarm there might already be in the mind of Beda.

"Continue," I said; "if there be anything more to relate."

"Yes, my dear Miss," resumed Beda; "there is indeed something more to relate—and it corresponds frightfully——No! I will not speak in this manner!—I mean to say that it really does seem to give a sort of corroboration to one of the circumstances of last night. But you shall hear and judge for yourself," she somewhat briefly ejaculated. "Squire Tremaine continued in an invalid state for some few years after the tragic incidents which I have been relating; and at length, in compliance with his repeated demands and entreaties, Mrs. Ravenscliffe consented to return to the Hall to superintend the household affairs. But not long had she been here when she was seized with a grievous illness which smote her as if all of a sudden; and in her delirium she raved of frightful things. In a word, my dear Miss, it would have appeared from what she thus unconsciously said, that she had perjured herself when before the coroner: but it was certainly in some sense excusable, for a parent is naturally anxious to screen the honour of a child, whether living or dead. Yes—it would seem, from the wild delirious exclamations of the unhappy woman, that her daughter had become a mother at the time when the fact was suspected. And what is more, dear Miss——what is more——"

Here Beda paused, and looked up into my countenance with her large dark eyes so full of a strange mysterious significancy, that I felt convinced it must be something fearfully striking indeed which could thus move one whose mind was naturally so strong, whose intelligence was so clear, and whose soul was so intrepid.

"Speak, my dear girl," I said; "it is useless to keep anything from my knowledge."

She glanced towards the cupboard in the furthest corner of the room: she pointed with her beautifully-shaped hand in that direction; and she said in a low deep voice, "It was there—*there*, dear Miss—beneath those boards—according to the revelation made by the wretched Mrs. Ravenscliffe in her delirium—it was *there* that the corpse of the infant was concealed; for it is supposed to have been born dead!"

I felt a cold shudder creeping over me; it was a glance of mingled horror and terror which I threw in the direction of that cupboard; and Beda, perceiving that her narrative had made a strong impression upon me, hastened to exclaim, "Oh, but we will not give way to idle fears, dear Miss! There are coincidences for which it is difficult to account; and that noise last night in that very place—Oh! it must have been caused by the rats!"

I saw that the good-hearted girl was endeavouring to sustain my courage because I had undertaken to pass another night in the haunted chamber; and I saw likewise that she more or less repented having told me the tale. I was resolved not to recall the overture I had made to occupy that chamber again. I had a certain pride which prevented me from proclaiming myself to be a coward; but at the same time I regretted that I should have compromised Beda in the matter.

"My dear girl," I said, "if you have any hesitation in sharing these rooms again with me to-night——"

"Oh, dear Miss," she ejaculated, "how can you suspect me of such pusillanimity? Granting everything to be true which is alleged by superstitious rumour, what have we to fear,—we who have done no harm, and whose consciences are pure! Wherever you remain, Miss Percy, I also will remain; and therefore not another syllable on the point! I have a few words to add to make the sad, dismal tale complete. The severe illness which so suddenly overtook Mrs. Ravenscliffe proved fatal at the expiration of a few weeks; and she perished in the midst of a raging delirium."

"And that cupboard, Beda," I said,—"was it ever searched?"

"No, Miss—never," was Beda's reply. "I do not exactly know what importance might have been attached to the ravings of the unhappy mother—whether it was supposed that truth really lurked at the bottom of them, or whether it was surmised that her disordered fancy had taken its impressions from the questions put to her at the inquest, I cannot tell: but certain it is that no one sought this chamber for the purpose of investigation or of search; and the local authorities doubtless concluded that they had nothing more to do with the matter—or else the details of the wretched woman's death were so hushed up that naught transpired beyond the walls of the mansion. The Squire died soon after Mrs. Ravenscliffe was consigned to the tomb; and the present Mr. Tremaine—then a minor—succeeded to the possession of the property."

Beda ceased speaking; and almost immediately afterwards the dinner-bell rang. My toilet had been delayed while I was conversing with Beda and listening to the tale which she told me: I therefore now made haste to finish it; and little more passed between us on the occasion. I descended to the drawing-room, whence there was an almost immediate adjournment to the dining-room; and the appearance of a splendid repast seemed to put even the most ill-tempered dowager of the company into a good humour.

When the ladies retired from the banqueting-apartment and gathered by themselves in the drawing-room, Mrs. Tremaine found an oppor-tunity to entreat that I would alter my intention in reference to the haunted chamber; but I positively declined to do so—and implored that she would still keep the secret, so that no step might be taken by Mr. Tremaine to prevent me from executing my design. Charlotte likewise spoke to me on the subject: and I said to her, "How is it, my dear friend, that you seek to dissuade me from my purpose? I thought you told me that when you were a little girl you were superstitious, but that since you have grown up——"

"And what I told you was true, Ellen," interrupted Charlotte. "I do not believe in the existence of apparitions; but still I think that the imagination may sometimes play strange and dangerous freaks when subjected to particular influences. And besides, there is something so inhospitable and even apparently so cruel in suffering you to occupy that chamber——"

"On this score you need not blame yourself," I said, "inasmuch as it is all my own doing, and I have wilfully and steadily opposed your mother's well-meant dissuasions."

"Well," interjected Charlotte, "as for any actual cause of apprehension I do not believe that it exists. No one has ever seen the ghosts except those who are determined to believe in them; and those are amongst the most uneducated and superstitious of the domestics. You know that my parents more than once slept in the haunted apartment: they neither heard nor saw anything to alarm them. When we first went upon the Continent—that was four years ago, you know—Lavinia and Emilia were too young to travel and have their studies neglected; they were then only nine and eleven respectively:—and so they remained behind at the Hall."

"But not alone?" I ejaculated.

"No:—Miss Barron was of course with them," answered Charlotte; "and during the period that they were thus together beneath this roof, Miss Barron never heard nor saw anything to terrify her—though I do not think," added Charlotte, with a smile, "that she possesses so much courage as yourself, Ellen, or would like to sleep in the haunted apartment. But do tell me one thing! What did you mean just now, before dinner, by saying that there was a little discovery you were desirous of making, and that it referred to the cupboard in the corner that is remotest from the door?"

"When I made that remark, Charlotte," I answered, "I was utterly ignorant of the particulars of the legend attached to the haunted room; and I was struck by the singularity of the look which your mother, yourself, and Miss Barron suddenly wore."

"And have you since heard the tale?" inquired Charlotte hastily.

"Yes," I replied. "And now I comprehend wherefore you all three regarded me in so strange a manner when I spoke of that cupboard. Now, if you promise, Charlotte," I continued, "to keep the seal of silence upon your lips, I will tell you something which will serve to explain the meaning of my words when I said that there was a little discovery I wished to make in the cupboard."

"I promise you to keep the seal upon my lips," replied Charlotte, her looks expressing a deep curiosity.

I proceeded to tell her how both Beda and myself had fancied that we heard sounds like the rattling of bones, either in the cupboard or else in its immediate vicinage. Miss Tremaine listened with looks that gradually expressed a feeling of dread, while her countenance became paler.

"If you had been alone there," she said, "I should have attributed it to the imagination: but you and Beda together——"

"Oh! that we heard the sounds, I have not the slightest doubt!" I said; "but that they are to be accounted for in more ways than one, is equally certain. Now I beseech you not to say a syllable on the subject. Ah!" I ejaculated, "there is Miss Barron close by! Do you think she overheard what we were saying?"

"No," returned Charlotte: "you see she has her back towards us—she is contemplating her two pupils Emilia and Lavinia, of whom she is so excessively fond. If she had heard us discoursing on this subject, she would have doubtless at once joined us; because in the natural goodness of her disposition she would be more than ever inclined to associate her entreaties with mine, to the effect that you will not occupy that room tonight."

Charlotte and I had withdrawn into a windowrecess—the draperies were half-closed over it—and it was one of those curtains which had prevented us from observing the approach of Sarah Barron in that direction. She was not half-a-dozen yards from us when I so suddenly perceived her on happening to thrust aside the folds of the drapery. But as she did not turn to join us, I concluded, with Charlotte Tremaine, that she had not overheard what I said.

"Not that it would particularly matter if my words had reached her ears," I said to Charlotte; "for she would keep the seal of silence upon her lips just as well as yourself. And now not another syllable in reference to the haunted chamber!—for I am determined to pass the night there; and in the morning I will tell you how it has fared with me."

While speaking of Charlotte Tremaine, I should perhaps observe that she did not once make the slightest allusion to Ludovico Marano: there was in her general demeanour a certain serenity and tranquillity which proved that she had resigned herself courageously to the fate of a disappointed love, and that if on the one hand she felt that her affections had received a shock, yet that on the other hand there was consolation to be derived from the thought that she had escaped an alliance with one who was not worthy of her love. As for Sarah Barron, I had not as yet found an opportunity of being with her alone—or rather, I should say that circumstances had not once thrown us alone together; and thus I had no means of judging what she knew in reference to the picture her brother had sent me, and which I had returned to him.

The gentlemen presently rejoined the ladies in the drawing-room: but as we had all been up so very late on the preceding night, there was a general disposition to seek an indemnification by retiring early on this occasion; and therefore, at about eleven o'clock, the company began to disperse to their respective chambers; and again was it while the words "Good night," were being uttered in every direction and doors were closing all over the house, that I glided towards the haunted chamber.

———

CHAPTER CXXI.

SECOND NIGHT IN THE HAUNTED CHAMBER.

I FOUND Beda in the apartment: the wax tapers were lighted—a cheerful fire was blazing in the grate—and, as I have before observed, the appearance of the apartment was the very reverse of melancholy or gloomy.

"Now, my dear Beda," I said, "we will sleep together in the bed in this room—we will shut the dressing-room door, so that no sound may reach us from the skylight—for the wind is moaning somewhat without, and it may have a peculiar noise when penetrating from above. We will lock the chamber door, as we did last night——"

"I cannot think how it was," interrupted Beda, "but I am really very much afraid that to my negligence it is to be attributed——"

"Negligence, my dear girl?" I ejaculated. "No! it is impossible! You were never guilty of negligence! But of what are you thus so foolishly endeavouring to prove yourself culpable?"

"I cannot conceive what I have done with the key of the door," answered Beda.

"Do you mean this door?"—and I pointed to the one communicating with the dressing-room.

"No, dear Miss: that key, as you may perceive, is in the lock: but the other one—that door opening on the landing——"

"Ah!" I ejaculated; "is the key gone? How is this?"

"That is the very point I am at a loss to clear up," returned Beda. "After you left the room at dinner-time, I made sure that I locked the door—and I am almost convinced that I hung the key on the nail in the corner of the landing, according to custom. At least all this was my impression: but perhaps it was a very erroneous one, and I may not have locked the door at all, but I may have taken the key in my hand and left it down in the servants' hall."

"Why should you surmise that you did this?" I inquired.

"When I came up at about nine o'clock to look to the fire," continued Beda, "I could not find the key upon the nail: but on trying the door, I found that it was unlocked. I have been ever since bewildering myself as to how this could be. I have searched everywhere for the key—but in vain: I have asked the domestics if they have noticed a stray key lying about: but no!"

"Now, my dear Beda," I said, "do not trouble yourself any more upon the point; for to me it is all perfectly intelligible."

"Indeed, dear Miss?" she ejaculated. "And how?"

"When we separated at dinner-time, we were both more or less pensive and thoughtful—our minds were abstracted. It was natural enough—and in such a mental state the ideas get confused and the memory fails to register incidents with its usual accuracy. Therefore was it that on leaving this chamber, you fancied you locked the door and hung the key upon the nail in the landing; whereas it is now evident that you merely took the key with you in some listless mood, without locking the door at all—and you must have dropped or laid the key somewhere, but where you cannot now recollect."

Beda reflected for a few moments; and then she said, in a deliberative and uncertain manner, "It may be so—it must be so: but still—but still—it does indeed seem to me very, very strange——"

"Yes," I hastened to interject; "it seems strange, my dear Beda, that you should do anything which at all savours of neglectfulness,—you who are invariably so discreet, so regular, so punctual, and so accurate! But no matter! We need not lock the door at all—no one will come to disturb us. And now, dear Beda, let us retire to rest."

While we were disapparelling ourselves, I purposely talked in a gay strain, without making the slightest allusion to the incidents connected with the haunted room. Beda comprehended my purpose, and she followed my example. We knelt down together and said our prayers: we then sought the couch: we conversed for a little while —we bade each other "Good night"—and silence prevailed in the chamber.

I had read in old romances of haunted rooms in ancient castles—I had a vivid recollection likewise of Walter Scott's description of such an apartment in "The Betrothed," and likewise of his fearfully graphic tale, "The Tapestry Chamber:" but little had I ever foreseen that I myself should make personal acquaintance with a haunted room, or for two consecutive nights become the inmate of one. Yet so it was. And now I asked myself whether I had been foolhardy in my conduct, and whether I deserved to be punished for what I was doing? But I was really enabled most conscientiously to acquit myself of all blame in this sense. Not so easy was it to answer the question, whether there was really anything to apprehend? I had seen a muffled and cloaked figure pass out at a particular door at a time when I had actually known nothing of the legend which related to such a cloaked and muffled figure, or to the reason why the apparition should be supposed to haunt the vicinage of that particular door. But this was not all! I had fancied that I had heard the rattling of bones in a particular spot before I had ever heard a syllable to direct my attention to that spot or to engender in my imagination the idea which had so smitten me. Could all this be accounted for by the theory of coincidence? Could the gliding figure in the muffled cloak have been a creation of the fancy? Possibly so:—but, on the other hand, the sounds resembling the rattling of bones could *not* be similarly disposed of; for Beda had heard them as well as myself!

I endeavoured to avoid bewildering myself with these questions: I strove to turn my thoughts into another channel: I shut my eyes, and did my utmost to woo the presence of slumber. But all was of no avail. I felt restless and uneasy: there was an anxiety in my mind—a sort of readiness to be influenced by the first circumstance that might arise to change that anxiety into absolute terror. I could have kept on turning and tossing about in the bed—but I feared to disturb Beda,

though I could scarcely fancy that she was slumbering. At length, as I did gently turn round towards her, the dear girl's large dark eyes opened; and we both smiled as we thus looked at each other, for we mutually comprehended what was passing in our minds.

"You cannot sleep, dear Miss?" said Beda.

"No—nor you," I answered. "Come, let us resolve to shut our eyes—not look at each other—but do all we can to woo the advance of slumber.. Everything is quiet—there is not a sound—and therefore let us sleep!"

Beda assented to my proposition: we turned from each other, and shut our eyes. Half-an-hour might have passed away, and sleep was stealing over me—all ideas were growing dim in my brain—the loss of consciousness was almost complete,—when all of a sudden an ejaculation burst from the lips of Beda. I started up; and then the same sounds as on the preceding night met my ears,—those sounds which resembled the rattling of human bones!

"Now," said Beda, springing from the bed, "we will see, dear Miss, what this really is!"

"How do you propose to act?" I inquired, instantaneously gathering courage from the example of intrepidity which she was now setting me.

"Look!" said Beda: and she produced from under the bed, a chisel, a mallet, and a tolerable-sized iron wedge, all of which articles she had taken from a store-room in the course of the evening.

I was glad that she had done this: those sounds had been plainly heard again; and though they had suddenly ceased after lasting for merely a few moments, yet was their impression too strong upon my brain to be mistaken. Neither of us had any desire for slumbering immediately: we were both broad awake; and as I looked at my faithful companion, I saw that her lips were slightly compressed with the feeling of resoluteness that inspired her.

We opened the door of that cupboard which has been before so frequently mentioned; and first of all we carefully examined the boards by means of one of the wax-lights. The floor of the cupboard, or closet, was not a continuation of the planking of the room itself, as is the case in most modern houses: but that flooring had been evidently laid down in quite a distinct manner. In short, there were two boards placed lengthways at the bottom of this cupboard.

"I think you will first of all be compelled to remove a piece of the skirting-board," I said; "and then you may easily force up the plank."

"We will see," answered Beda. "Where are the nails which fasten down these boards? Ah! here is one! But it is quite loose! See! with the slightest effort it comes out!"

And sure enough, by a very trifling touch with the edge of the chisel, the nail sprang out of its setting.

"I do really believe, dear Miss," said Beda, looking up with mysterious gravity into my countenance, "that these boards have been tampered with, and have at some time or another been raised since they were first laid down. Yes!—look! here is this piece of the skirting board which is all loose! Ah, it easily comes off!"

At that instant we heard some sound behind

us in the chamber: we both started up from our kneeling posture on the threshold of the cupboard; —and there, in the shade thrown by the curtains of the bed, and close by the room communicating with the dressing-room, stood the figure of a female clothed in white!

I am free to confess that an ejaculation of terror was on the very point of bursting from my lips—perhaps indeed it *did* find vent—but in the twinkling of an eye Beda bounded forward and seized upon the object of my transitory terror. I cannot find words to describe the rapidity with which all this took place: it was the work of a few seconds! A moan came upon my ears; and whom should I behold before me, pushed or dragged forward by the firm grasp of Beda, but Sarah Barron!

"Good heaven!" I ejaculated; "what can this mean? Beda, unhand Miss Barron!—she could not come to frighten us!"

"I unhand Miss Barron at your bidding, Miss," responded Beda: "but if ever I beheld guilt of some kind or another depicted upon human countenance, it is on this young lady's!"

And it was so: for as I now concentrated my regards on Miss Barron's face, I saw that it was perfectly ghastly. There was something terrible in the eyes that were fixed and in the features that were rigid! She tottered forward—she clasped her hands—her lips were ashy white: she endeavoured to say something, but she could not—and she staggered towards an arm-chair, into which she fell.

"She has fainted, Beda!" I said. "Hasten, dear girl! some water!"

We bathed Sarah Barron's forehead; but she gave no sign of returning consciousness. She was more than half-dressed: that is to say, she had only taken off the evening dress that she had worn; and had enveloped her person in a white muslin wrapper. She therefore had on her corset; and I desired Beda at once to loosen it. This she did: at the same time she felt that some object was secured about the young lady's dress: it was the key—the missing key of the haunted apartment!

Here, then, was a proof that a stealthy visit thither had been intended and prearranged in Miss Barron's mind; and there was every necessity for such proof, inasmuch as it was totally impossible to conceive what earthly object she could have in adopting such a course. Not for the mere childish purpose of frightening myself and Beda: for Sarah Barron was too sensible and too intelligent—too delicate and too ladylike in her habits, to condescend to a silly trickery.

"This is most extraordinary, Beda!" I whispered.

"Incomprehensible!" answered the faithful girl. "She does not recover! Shall I go and procure other restoratives?"

"No—it is not necessary. Look! her lips begin to waver!—life is flaming up within her!—Ah! her eyelids also move!"

She slowly opened her eyes: beautiful blue eyes they were—so soft in their expression and yet so intelligent!—but they quickly acquired a startled and affrighted look as they evidently recognised the two countenances over which their regards travelled.

"Good heavens, Miss Percy!" she murmured, "what have I done? and what must you think?"

She burst into tears: for some minutes she wept passionately—she moaned and sobbed piteously—she lamented as if her heart were about to break. Both Beda and myself were as much affected as astonished: we besought her to tranquillize her feelings; and I said, "Explain your conduct, Miss Barron: and doubtless there will be an end of it —for it is next to impossible that you could have done or meant anything serious!"

"Ah, Miss Percy! ever kind—ever generous—ever disposed to be forgiving!" ejaculated Sarah, seizing my hand, and pressing it to her lips. "And you too, Beda—you are doubtless kind of heart!—for it is impossible that you could have done otherwise than take the best of examples from the best of mistresses!"

"What can you mean, Miss Barron," I asked, "by addressing us in such a strain? What have you to implore? what have you to plead for?"

She threw her shuddering glances around the haunted room: it struck me that they lingered with an enhanced and peculiar horror upon the cupboard, the door of which stood wide open; and then covering her face with her hands, she remained motionless as a statue—absorbed in a reverie which no doubt was as painful as it was profound. Thus, for upwards of a minute a dead silence prevailed in the chamber,—a silence so deep that a pin might have been heard to drop. But all of a sudden that silence was broken. The rustling sound which Beda and I had heard on the preceding night, was revealed: it seemed to be passing under our feet—rapid as a whirlwind; and then it closed with the rattling as of bones beneath the floor of the cupboard. The ghastliest paleness overspread the countenance of Sarah Barron: she started wildly—her looks were swept around—she abruptly wrung her hands as if it

were a paroxysm of frenzied, maddening grief that seized upon her:—and then in a voice which was half stifled, yet piercing, she cried, "My God! the very vermin make sport of the bones of my poor child!"

And then consciousness again abandoned her. But Oh! what revelation was this for Beda and myself! Though the picture required filling up with details, yet it seemed all in a moment to present to the mind's comprehension a perfect explanation of Sarah Barron's singular conduct. Beda flung upon me a look which was full of affright and horror; and I whispered, "Alas! this poor creature has doubtless suffered immensely—and we will not be hasty in judging her!"

Nearly a quarter of an hour elapsed before Sarah Barron was again brought back to consciousness. She then threw herself at my feet, saying, "I beseech and implore you, Miss Percy—and you likewise, Beda—to respect the fatal, the terrible secret which in my anguish and agony I have revealed to you! You shall know all tomorrow! I will tell you everything—or now if you insist upon it!"

"No, no—I insist upon nothing!" I said. "But tell me—answer me only one question! Do you know of a man, muffled in a cloak—perhaps that he may be taken for an apparition if meeting with any of the credulous servants—Are you privy, I ask, to the stealthy visits of such a person within the walls of this mansion?"

"I! No! As God is my judge I know nothing of that whereof you are speaking!" exclaimed Sarah. "Tell me, Miss Percy—why do you ask? What has made you——'

"Nothing! nothing!" I ejaculated. "I will explain myself to-morrow."

"Oh! do you really believe," inquired Sarah, "in any single detail of all those things which superstitious terror alleges——"

"No——at least I scarcely know what to say ——but I think not. However, let us quit the subject. You have appealed to us, Miss Barron——"

"Let me assure you, Miss Percy," she exclaimed, starting up from her knees, whence I had previously been vainly attempting to raise her; "let me assure you that mine has been weakness and not guilt; and even if the entire tale be known to the world, I can only be scorned and shunned, but not execrated!"

"Enough, Miss Barron!" I said, now addressing her in the kindest possible tone. "I pledge myself—and Beda will join me in the vow—that we will wilfully do naught to injure you; and so far as your secret may be safely and consistently kept——"

"Nothing more is needed from your lips, Miss Percy!" interrupted Sarah. "To-morrow you shall know everything. You will then pity me!—you will scarcely blame me! And now permit me to retire. Ah! I perceive that the key is in your possession! I was about to restore it——it was I who took it from the nail where it hung on the landing—and I unlocked this door. But I will tell you everything to-morrow."

The poor creature spoke with difficulty: she was weighed down with the deepest affliction—she seemed completely crushed and overwhelmed—she scarcely dared look Beda or myself in the face. She drew the muslin wrapper around her form; and bidding us "Good night," with an air of perfect humility, she stole from the chamber.

"We now know, Beda," I said, "what bones there are beneath the flooring of that cupboard; and we will pursue our researches no further. Lock the door, my dear girl—and let us retire to rest again."

We laid down accordingly; but little more conversation passed between us ere sleep visited our eyes—and we slumbered on undisturbed till the morning. We arose; and as we were performing our toilets, I said to Beda, "It is evident that the hurricane-like sound which so much startled us, is caused by the rush of rats under the flooring or inside the wainscot of the room; and the existence of that lofty skylight on the roof of the adjacent chamber, imparts a peculiarity to that sound—making it ascend and giving it the effect of something invisible sweeping through the room. As for that *other* noise, Beda," I added, in a lower and more solemn voice, "the confession of that unhappy young woman has made us aware what it is. The less we speak of it the better!"

But though I had now satisfactorily accounted in my own mind for the sounds which had at first startled me, there was still *something else* to be explained; and this was the presence of that cloaked figure which I had seen glide forth by the glass door of the library, or at least disappear behind the screen which led to that door. How was *this* to be accounted for? I knew not: but I did not feel disposed to put faith in anything supernatural at a moment when I was clearing up other mysteries by natural means.

On looking from the window of the haunted apartment, I perceived that the flood had almost totally disappeared, at least in that direction; and on presently leaving the chamber and peeping forth from other windows, as well as making inquiries, I ascertained that the waters had subsided to a degree which opened all the means of communication with adjacent parts. The guests were accordingly enabled to take their departure after breakfast,—much to the gratification of most of them, though there were of course some who appeared to regret the necessity of leaving the hospitalities of Tremaine Hall.

Miss Barron did not appear at the breakfast-table; and it was stated that she was very unwell. I could not help pitying her sincerely, although I now knew enough of her antecedents to be aware that she was far from being a guiltless creature; yet still I commiserated her, and I would not for the world prove the cause of harrowing her soul with any additional or unnecessary tortures. I therefore hastened to her chamber when I fancied that I should find her alone there; she was much confused and distressed on beholding me—but I at once said to her, "I do not come to seek explanations from your lips at present. Tranquillize your mind—compose your feelings—and endeavour to cast off this excitement which is fevering your blood. You shall take your own time and choose your own leisure to give me the promised explanations. Indeed, it will suit me better that you should postpone them, at least until to-morrow; for I have received a letter this morning which compels me to visit Stafford on some little busi-ness. Let me hope that when I return in the afternoon or evening, I shall find you in a more tranquil and comfortable state of mind."

Miss Barron wept: she pressed my hand, in order to convey her gratitude for the kind words I had spoken; and I quitted her chamber.

The letter I had received was from the woman whom Beda had directed at Stafford to make inquiries concerning the residence of Mrs. Sturton. The woman to whom I have first alluded, had succeeded in the task allotted to her; and I was now acquainted with the abode of the female from whose lips I was to receive some useful if not valuable information,—that is to say, supposing reliance could be placed upon the representations made to me by Dame Betty in London.

It was merely necessary for me to intimate to Mr. and Mrs. Tremaine that I wished to go to Stafford on some little business of my own, in order to induce them at once to place one of their equipages at my disposal. I should observe that Charlotte and Mrs. Tremaine had inquired how I had passed the night in the haunted room? — and I had assured them that neither Beda nor myself had been alarmed by anything of a supernatural character.

I set off for Stafford, accompanied by Beda; and as the distance was only a few miles, and the carriage was drawn by a splendid pair of horses, the journey was soon accomplished. We repaired to the hotel at which we had stopped on our arrival at Stafford; and we lost no time in bending our steps towards the address indicated in the letter which I had received that morning. As we were walking through the streets of Stafford, a recollection struck me.

"My dear Beda," I said, "I remember full well that Dame Betty intimated something to the effect that this Mrs. Sturton bore no good will towards your family——"

"And I recollect likewise that you told me this before, Miss," answered Beda. "It was because my parents restored the child which this woman's parents had stolen. Well, there is no necessity that I should accompany you; for she might suspect who I am—or she may have even heard that I am in your service——"

"Yes—it will be better that I should go alone," I observed. "Ah! by the bye, you in the meantime, my dear Beda, can go and remunerate the woman who sent us the information."

We accordingly separated; and I pursued my way (which I ascertained by occasional inquiry) towards the address indicated in the letter. I was not long in reaching a miserable street in the very poorest and vilest quarter of the town; and of all the houses in that street, the one at which I was about to call was the very worst. A horrible-looking old woman was standing at the door, gossiping with the baker's boy; and she dropped an obsequious curtsey as I accosted her. I asked if a female bearing the name of Sturton lived in that house? The answer was in the affirmative; and the old hag, shaking her head, added, "Ah, ma'am, she is very, very poor, and got three children. I do think they are all starving; and if you are come to assist them——"

"That is my object," I said, cutting short the woman's observations. "Be so good as to show me the room."

The house only consisted of two floors—it was a mere cottage: and it was in the back room of the upper floor that I found the object of my search —the woman Sturton. Good heavens! what a spectacle met my view! A wretched creature, haggard and emaciated—with three miserable-looking children, more than half naked, squalid, lean, with famine written upon their countenances,—a room utterly denuded of furniture, with some straw and rags on the floor,—this was the shocking *tableau* that met my vision!

The appearance of a well-dressed lady in the abode of poverty, naturally excites some hopeful idea in the minds of its wretched inmates; and thus the three children gave vent to ejaculations of joy—and the mother hastening forward, said, "Oh, ma'am! if you are come to assist us, God bless you! for we are starving!"

The tears started into my eyes: I was almost choked with the emotions which appeared to rise up into my very throat; and thus I could not immediately speak. Such a picture of wretchedness —of gaunt, stark, squalid, hideous, famine-stricken misery—had never before met my eyes!—a misery which had worn away the flesh down to the very bones—a misery which showed the ribs through the skin of the starving children—a misery which gave an expression of wolfish hunger to their countenances!

"My poor woman," I at length said, "I am come to assist you. Have you heard that anybody was inquiring after you?"

"No, ma'am. But who are you that you take any interest in such poor forlorn wretches as we are? Oh! if you had not come, this very day should we have returned to the workhouse! Yes! ——we were there once before——but Oh, the horrors of that place!"

"Well, well," I said, "you shall not go back to the workhouse—at least if I find you in any way worthy of the relief that I propose to offer. But no more for the present! Here—take this money —procure food for yourself and your children— and tell me how long it will be before you can presently render yourself decent and respectable so as to come to me at the hotel where I am staying?"

I placed five sovereigns in the hands of the woman; and it was a cry—almost a shriek of joy which burst forth from her lips when she beheld the gold. The three children instinctively fell upon their knees; and altogether the spectacle was a most affecting one. But, to be brief, Mrs. Sturton informed me that she had some decent apparel, which she could presently redeem from the pawnbroking establishment where it was pledged, and that she would be with me in a couple of hours at the hotel.

I quitted the house; and I was slowly retracing my way towards the hotel—mournfully reflecting upon the scene of ineffable misery which I had been contemplating—when I suddenly heard my name mentioned by an individual who stopped short as I was about to pass him when turning the angle of a street.

"Ah, Miss Percy!" he ejaculated: "is it possible that I behold you in this part of the world?"

I at once recognised him: it was Viscount Ravenscliffe who had thus stopped short on beholding me. The reader will recollect that we had formerly met at Willowbridge, on the melancholy occasion when his brother Lord Frederick committed suicide in so dreadful and extraordinary a manner. That was precisely six months previous to the date of which I am now writing; and the Viscount was still in mourning. I have on a former occasion observed that he was by no means good-looking—that he was short in stature and of insignificant personal appearance—but that he habitually had an air of cold insolent hauteur, with a tinge of coxcombry in his manner—and that he was very fond of using a quizzing-glass, which he would keep for some minutes at a time stuck in the socket of his eye. Towards me he was however now most courteous and polite; for be it remembered that the closing scene at Willowbridge had humiliated him and had almost brought him to his knees in the presence of Juliet and myself, when he found how completely the honour of his deceased brother's name was in our keeping.

"And is it indeed possible," he repeated, after I had returned his salutation, "that I meet you, Miss Percy, in this quarter of the world?"

"And wherefore," I asked, with a smile, "should I not have business at Stafford as well as other people? But my visit hither is merely a flying one: I am staying in the neighbourhood——Indeed I believe that the family is somewhat connected with your own——"

"Ah! do you mean the Tremaines?" ejaculated the Viscount.

"Yes—I am staying at Tremaine Hall," was my rejoinder.

"And a beautiful place it is," resumed Viscount Ravenscliffe. "Of course you are aware that our family-seat of Carshalton is only about thirty miles from here—in the neighbourhood of Embledon?"

"I knew that your family's country-seat, my lord, could not be very far distant, inasmuch as Staffordshire and Warwickshire join: but I was not aware it was quite so near as I now learn it to be."

"And so the Tremaines have returned to their own ancestral home?" ejaculated the Viscount. "Ah! what disputes, quarrellings, and lawsuits has that family seen in its time! And our's likewise—and the Wakefields also——"

"The Wakefields?" I ejaculated, in astonishment at the sudden mentioning of the name.

"Oh, yes," answered the Viscount: "the Tremaines, the Ravenscliffes, and the Wakefields were all more or less connected some half-century or century ago. But relationship dies out, as it were——"

"What Wakefields were those to whom you allude?" I asked.

"I really can scarcely tell you, Miss Percy," replied the Viscount: "many long years have passed since the Wakefields have been enabled to claim any kinship with us, or to have their names mentioned in Lodge's *Peerage* as being connected with even the most distant branches of the Carshalton family. But I have heard that there was a time when all three families—the Tremaines, the Wakefields, and the Ravenscliffes—were at loggerheads to dispute the Carshalton peerage; and then, as this point could be no longer questioned, the grounds of the quarrel were shifted, and litigation was carried on in reference to the Carshalton estates. Well, then the Ravenscliffes brought counter-suits against the Tremaines and claimed the Tremaine estates: and thus there was the most singular but at the same time one of the most costly legal entanglements that ever the world beheld. It was no doubt a fine game for the lawyers, but a ruinous one for the litigants."

"And what became of the Wakefields," I asked, "in the midst of all these legal conflicts and embroilments?"

"Oh, they were routed in every sense — they were extirpated—they died out of existence—and I believe the family has long been extinct. Ah! by the bye, if I recollect right, I have heard that some twenty or five-and-twenty years ago there was a man who put himself forward as a lineal descendant of the *great Wakefields of Warwickshire*, as the family was really entitled to be called a century or two ago: but the fellow was a mere impostor——"

"Do you recollect any of the circumstances of his claim, my lord?" I inquired, with an air as if I was merely sustaining a conversation and had no ulterior object in view.

"I have heard my father speak of the subject," replied Viscount Ravenscliffe; "but I really have taken little note of what he has said—for no one has of late years ventured to breathe even so much as a hint to the effect that the Carshalton peerage and estates are not vested in the right family. I think however that I have heard of this Gerald Wakefield——Yes, to be sure! I recollect now! his name *was* Gerald!—and I believe that he was some needy adventurer who thought probably to extort money from my father. But he suddenly disappeared, and was heard of no more."

"And thus," I observed, "the three families were almost immemorially at legal warfare?"

"Oh, yes," answered the Viscount: "and a mint of money must have been expended in their insane quarrels. You must understand—that is to say, if you really take any interest in the subject, Miss Percy——"

"Oh! being intimate with the Tremaines," I interjected, "and having the honour of being acquainted with your family, my lord, I am of course interested in the subject—as a matter of passing conversation."

"Well, then, I will give you a few more particulars," resumed the Viscount,—"though I tell you candidly I am by no means well versed in the history of these quarrellings and squabblings, which always seem to me to constitute a web most difficult to unravel. But there was a period—some two centuries ago perhaps—when the titles of Carshalton and Ravenscliffe were separated, and a Tremaine bore the title of Carshalton. Then, too, there was a baronetcy in the Tremaine family, which somehow or another became extinct, I cannot tell you how;—and the Wakefields were baronets also a century and a half ago——"

"Indeed!" I ejaculated, more and more surprised at everything I heard in reference to the Wakefields. "Then these titles have been lost?"

"The Baronetcy of Wakefield is extinct—yes, and likewise that which was in the Tremaine family," answered the Viscount: "but as for the two titles of nobility, they have for a long time past been entirely in my own family. Thus my father is the Earl of Carshalton; and the second title is that of Viscount Ravenscliffe—as I need scarcely inform you, Miss Percy," added the nobleman with a smile.

"It is singular," I observed, "that I never once heard your deceased brother Lord Frederick speak of these subjects—no not even the one of the latest date—such, for instance, as the claims of Gerald Wakefield——"

"They are not within the personal recollection of the younger branches of our family," rejoined the Viscount. "Indeed my father himself gets into a complete fog if attempting to explain how in his own earlier years he had to litigate with Squire Tremaine; and if he only goes farther back to unravel the legal feuds, claims, pretensions, counter-claims, and counter-pretensions, of the Tremaines, the Wakefields, and the Ravenscliffes, he finds himself so utterly bewildered that he always gives it up as a bad job. My brother never troubled himself on the point; and I myself, as I have already told you, know very little about it."

I now made a movement as if about to take leave of the Viscount and pass on, when he said to me in a serious tone and with a significant look, "I am not unmindful, Miss Percy, of the secrecy which you have so generously maintained relative to the deplorable circumstances which were so closely connected with my unfortunate brother. I should do myself the honour of calling on you at Tremaine Hall; but for years the two families have been at variance."

"And you, therefore, my lord, have perhaps never set foot in Tremaine Hall?" I said. "It is a handsome and interesting country-seat——"

"Oh, yes! I have been in it, Miss Percy," interjected the Viscount. "I had the curiosity some time ago to visit the mansion: but it was when the Tremaines were abroad—and therefore pray do not mention the circumstance in their hearing."

"No, I certainly would not do so," I answered: and taking leave of the Viscount, I returned to the hotel.

Beda was already there,—she having speedily acquitted herself of the task which I had assigned her while I went and sought out Mrs. Sturton at her miserable abode. I told Beda all that had just taken place with Viscount Ravenscliffe: she listened with the deepest interest and attention—and when I had finished speaking, she asked, "And what do you think of this, dear Miss?"

"I have no doubt," I replied, "that the Gerald Wakefield to whom Viscount Ravenscliffe just now alluded, will prove to be the one of whom Dame Betty spoke—most probably the elder brother of Mr. Henry Wakefield's father. But we shall see, Beda! For myself I am determined to subdue the spirit of conjecture as much as possible, and not abandon myself to dreams or ideas on Mr. Henry's behalf, which may perhaps be disappointed. Besides, I will tell you candidly that though I shall of course push this investigation to the very utmost, I do not see how it can possibly result in any advantage to Mr. Henry."

———

CHAPTER CXXII.

MRS. STURTON'S EXPLANATIONS.

PUNCTUAL to the appointment which she had made, Mrs. Sturton came to the hotel a couple of hours after I had left her at her own wretched abode; and her appearance was now indeed much changed. She was of course still thin, pale, emaciated, and sickly-looking: but she was clean and respectable—she wore decent raiment—and there was an expression of hope, and thankfulness, and even joy upon her countenance. She seemed to be about forty years of age—though I presently learnt that she was really not more than five-and-thirty. She was of gipsy origin, and for more than half her life she had dwelt with her tribe in the true gipsy fashion,—until she had married out of that tribe, as I learnt from Dame Betty. Her husband had been a hawker of Sheffield and Birmingham goods: he did a good business, and maintained his wife and family in comparative comfort and respectability, until his death which happened suddenly. The woman endeavoured to carry on the business—but she failed: then her husband's relatives set her up in a little shop in Stafford—but here she still experienced a complete want of success, so that she sank down into poverty. Her friends died off or went elsewhere—and for the last two or three years her existence had been of the most wretched description.

When she came to me at the hotel, I received her alone in my sitting-room; for I thought it better that Beda should not be present. I told her who I was—what I had heard from Dame Betty in London—and wherefore I had now sought her in Stafford. I told her likewise that I had a cousin named Henry Wakefield, who had gone to America: and when I had given all these particulars, I said, "Now tell me what you have to impart; and whether it be serviceable or otherwise, you shall be rewarded. But of course your recompense will ultimately prove in proportion to the value of the information itself."

"You already know, Miss," said the woman, "that I was a wandering gipsy living with my parents; and our tribe chiefly frequented these midland counties. What I am now going to tell you happened about twenty-two years ago——".

"I will take down memoranda of what you narrate," I said; for I had writing materials before me. "Twenty-two years ago?"

"Yes, Miss," resumed Mrs. Sturton. "I was then a mere girl of about thirteen or fourteen; but I recollect the circumstances well—and I afterwards heard my parents speak of them very frequently. We were in Warwickshire at the time; and we were encamped close by Embledon. One evening an elderly gentleman, between fifty and sixty years of age, came and took my father on one side; and they spoke for a considerable time together. The gentleman gave my father money, and went away. I presently heard all about the matter—for I listened while my father told my mother: indeed he spoke freely and openly in my presence. He said that the gentleman was a Mr. Wakefield——"

"Do you know his Christian name?" I inquired.

"Oh, yes, Miss!" answered Mrs. Sturton. "It was Gerald."

"I thought so," I said. "And now proceed."

"It appeared that Mr. Gerald Wakefield had persuaded and bribed my father to seize and carry off the younger child of Lord and Lady Carshalton, whose country-seat was at no great distance. This child was then about a twelvemonth old, or barely so much; and his nurse was accustomed to take out the babe every day in the park when the weather was fine. The child was stolen accordingly, and in a manner which plunged the Carshalton family into the utmost uncertainty as to what its fate could be. The nurse placed the child, enveloped in a shawl, upon a shady bank ——for the infant was fast asleep—while she strayed to a little distance to gather primroses and violets, it being in the Spring season. Then my mother, who had been upon the watch, crept towards the place and bore away the child, unperceived by its nurse. Have you taken down all these particulars, Miss Percy?"

"I have made memoranda sufficient for my purpose," I answered. "Proceed."

"I am now about to begin what may at first seem to be quite a different story," said Mrs. Sturton; "but you will soon find, Miss, how it will all fit in along with the rest. There was a gipsy family of the name of Robinson, that frequented the same midland counties as we did; but for some reason or another there was a jealousy betwixt our family and the Robinsons. Well, Miss, it seems that Mr. Gerald Wakefield went to the Robinsons just about the same time that he came and sought out my father; and he proposed something to the man Robinson. This was nothing less than that he should engage the assistance of some of his confederates for the purpose of waylaying a postchaise which was expected to pass along the road from Birmingham to Carshalton at a particular hour in the evening. The occupants of that postchaise would prove to be a gentleman and a boy; and both were to be murdered on the spot!"

"Good heavens! can this be possible?" I ejaculated.

"I am telling you, Miss, all I have heard and all I know," replied Mrs. Sturton. "I have no other means of convincing you of the truth of the statement. It may seem incredible—but it is not the less true on that account."

"And who were that gentleman and that boy," I asked, my blood running cold at the time, "who were thus to be intercepted and brutally murdered?"

"The gentleman—or rather nobleman," replied Mrs. Sturton, "was none other than the Earl of Carshalton himself; and the boy was his elder son, the Viscount Ravenscliffe, then about five years of age."

"And Mr. Gerald Wakefield was monster enough," I exclaimed, "to plan these tremendous crimes? God grant," I mentally added, "that he may, after all, prove not to be a relation of my dear cousin Henry!"

"Yes—he planned these crimes," answered Mrs. Sturton; "and there can be no doubt that when he employed my parents to carry off the infant Frederick Ravenscliffe, it was with the intention that this child should be made away with in case the other and greater crime succeeded."

"And how did it fail?" I asked. "Were the Robinsons too well principled to listen to such hideous and demoniac proposals?"

"Either it was this," responded Mrs. Sturton; "or else it was on account of the spite they had against us—so that they would rather resign all chance of emolument for themselves, than allow my parents to remain in a position to reap a fine reward."

"Rest assured," I exclaimed, somewhat indignantly, "the natural good feelings of those Robinsons predominated above every such petty vindictive personal feeling as this to which you have been alluding. But no matter! Proceed— and tell the tale in your own way."

"The Robinsons pretended to fall into Mr. Gerald Wakefield's views: but they acted in quite a different manner. The postchaise which was bearing the Earl and his son from Birmingham to Carshalton, passed along the road unmolested: and that same night the infant was stolen from the keeping of my parents. I need scarcely tell you, Miss Percy, that it was the Robinsons who thus got possession of the child—the little Frederick Ravenscliffe; and he was forthwith restored to his parents. The Robinsons were well rewarded: it was even said they received a pension from the Earl of Carshalton until their deaths,— but how true this may be I do not know. They did not however breathe a syllable calculated to betray either my parents or Mr. Wakefield. Gipsies never turn round upon each other—no, not even those between whom a feud is raging; and thus I daresay that the Earl of Carshalton never suspected for what purpose his infant had been carried off, nor how Gerald Wakefield had been ramifying such a tremendous plot."

"And what were Gerald Wakefield's motives in forming such an atrocious design?" I inquired. "But I need scarcely ask!—for the whole matter speaks for itself. He considered himself entitled to the earldom and estates of Carshalton in the event of the Earl and his two sons being put out of existence?"

"There could be no doubt, Miss Percy," replied Mrs. Sturton, "that in such a case he would have been the heir to the title and estates of Carshalton. He was descended from a family which in former times had litigated the possession of the honours and property with the *then* holders thereof: in short, I often heard my father say that there could be no doubt as to the position of Mr. Wakefield towards the Carshalton, or Ravenscliffe, family. But all these points might be perhaps cleared up, if it were worth while, by means of the papers——"

"What papers?" I inquired.

"The papers, Miss, I am about to place in your hands," rejoined Mrs. Sturton: "that is to say, if you think it worth while to take possession of them."

At the same time she produced a small brownpaper parcel, tied round with a piece of string and sealed with wax. It was dirty and greasy: and the woman said, "I am really almost ashamed to bring it to you in this state, Miss Percy: but I came away in a hurry to keep my appointment with you——"

"You need offer no excuses," I interrupted her, as I took the packet and placed it on the table before me: and then I asked, "How came it in your possession?"

"I must finish the narrative, Miss, which I have previously been telling you," resumed Mrs. Sturton. "When Mr. Gerald Wakefield found out that he had been deceived by the Robinsons, he was like a madman. He did not blame my parents for any neglect on their part in losing the child after having stolen it; because, in truth, the possession of that child for any purpose whatsoever was useless so long as the father and elder brother remained alive. Therefore, even if the infant Frederick had *not* been so taken by the Robinsons, he would have been restored all the same, for the reasons I have just stated. Mr. Wakefield had concealed himself in a hut midway between Embledon and Birmingham; it was at that time in the possession of some old gipsy women—it has since fallen into the hands of that very Dame Betty of whom you have spoken——"

"Ah!" I ejaculated; "I know that cottage! Yes—I have been there! But proceed. Mr. Wakefield, you say, was concealing himself there——"

"And when he learnt the failure of his plans, he was either seized with a sudden and fatal illness," continued Mrs. Sturton; "or else he took poison—I cannot tell you which. However, he died. My father was with him in his last moments; and—and——"

"I understand you," I observed, seeing that the woman hesitated. "Your father took possession of everything he found about the person of the accomplished villain, and perhaps suicide, Wakefield?—and thus was it that those papers fell into your father's hands?"

"Your conjectures are correct, Miss Percy," replied the woman; "and I may add that as Wakefield died so suddenly, the old gipsy-women in the house were afraid that they might be accused of foul play with regard to him; so that he was buried quite secretly in the little garden behind the cottage. As for those papers," continued Mrs. Sturton, "they proved to be valueless to my father; and they afforded no indication of any relatives that Mr. Wakefield might have possessed. My father would have destroyed them; but my mother considered it better to keep them in case by any accident they should ever prove of the slightest use to any person, and thus become the source of reward to us for giving them up. I have kept them with the same hope since my parents' death: — through all my misery and poverty have I kept them—and now, Miss Percy, I have given the packet into your hands."

"And can you form an idea," I asked, "whether this Mr. Gerald Wakefield was really any relation to Mr. James Wakefield, who many years ago died in insolvent circumstances at Sheffield?"

"I have no positive means of making any assertion on the point, Miss," replied the woman. "But still——"

"Dame Betty told me," I interrupted her, "that when she saw you some time ago, you made use of an expression, to the effect that if you could only find the Wakefields of Sheffield you should not be so badly off as you were."

"I will explain this observation on my part," said Mrs. Sturton. "It was about two years ago that I happened to hear from some old factory-operative that a long time back he had worked for a Mr. Wakefield at Sheffield, and that this Mr. Wakefield was supposed to have been descended from some younger branch of the great Wakefields of Warwickshire. The operative further told me that the Mr. Wakefield to whom he alluded was dead, but that he had left a family behind. I went to Sheffield; and there I learnt that Mrs. Wakefield and her son had moved to Paisley. I could not journey to Paisley—I had not the means; but an acquaintance of mine was shortly after going to that town—and I got him to make inquiries. In process of time I learnt that Mrs. Wakefield was dead and her son had gone abroad to some foreign land. Now you understand, Miss Percy, why I said to Dame Betty that if I could only find the Wakefields of Sheffield I might be enabled to do some good for myself: for I have always entertained the hope that some day or another these papers might be purchased from my hands by a member of the Wakefield family——though I certainly do not see how the possession of them can prove of any material benefit under existing circumstances. For there is the Earl of Carshalton—and there is the Viscount—and he may marry and have children——"

"And more than that," I added, "the Wake-field claims may be really valueless, even if it should transpire after all that my cousin Henry is actually the lineal representative of the great Wakefields of Warwickshire. But no matter. I accept these papers from your hand. If they in any way regard my cousin Henry, he will of course keep possession of them: if they do not regard him, they shall be restored to you. And now let me ask in which manner I can best serve you? You have failed in business:—is it worth while to set you up in it again? You best know your own capacities."

Tears were running down the woman's cheeks as she faltered forth her thanks; and then she said, "I know why I failed before, Miss Percy. It was because my own expenses were too great. But adversity has taught me terrible lessons; and rest assured that if I had an opportunity I should profit by them. A very few pounds would suffice to set me up in a little business which would enable me to earn a comfortable livelihood for my children and myself."

"How large a sum?" I inquired.

Mrs. Sturton hesitated: then she fumbled in her pocket—she drew forth a piece of a newspaper —and at length she said, "This paper enveloped some little article which through your bounty, Miss Percy, I was able just now to purchase. It is a piece of yesterday's local journal—and there is an advertisement that happened to meet my eye. It is a small business to be disposed of—I know it well——But Ah! fifty pounds! 'tis a very great deal of money!"

"Come to me in an hour," I said; "and we will see what is to be done. Remember, I do not at all promise you that I shall advance this amount: but I shall think over it."

"And whether you do or not, Miss Percy," replied the woman, "heaven bless you for what you have already done for me!"

She then took her temporary leave of me; and so soon as she had departed, I summoned Beda, to

whom I communicated all that I had heard. I then opened the packet which Mrs. Sturton had left behind her; and I found that it contained a number of papers, most of them soiled and greasy —some of them torn—but all in a legible condition. They consisted of *memoranda* indicative of where genealogies were to be traced and title-deeds to be consulted—of how research was to be made in such-and-such volumes in the British Museum, in such-and-such wills at Doctors' Commons, and in such-and-such records at the Herald's Office. Then too, there were marriage and baptismal certificates; and there were copies of pedigrees; and there were notes indicative of the particular newspapers in which advertisements had at certain times appeared for special objects, all connected with the great Wakefield lawsuits of by-gone times. There were likewise *memoranda* of the different suits which had been so brought, and the journals in which reports were to be found of the arguments adduced in the pleadings, and the judgments rendered in the Chancery Courts or the Judicial Committee of the House of Lords. The papers showed that they had belonged to Gerald Wakefield: but there was no mention of any younger brother. And what was more extraordinary, there were no certificates, allusions, or *memoranda*, to connect this Gerald himself with the Wakefield family of Warwickshire. Therefore, not merely was everything still in doubt as to whether my cousin Harry were in any way connected with the family—but it was equally uncertain whether the documents now in my possession would be of the slightest service to any human being at all.

"Nevertheless, Beda," I said, "the woman has given them up readily and of her own accord—spontaneously and unasked; and I will give her the recompense which I contemplated when I bade her return in an hour. Go and make proper inquiries relative to the shop indicated in the advertisement."

While Beda was absent upon her errand, I reflected upon everything which had this day come to my knowledge; and I said to myself, "If it be worth while at all to pursue the investigation, there are two necessary steps to be taken as preliminaries. One is to ascertain whether my deceased uncle James Wakefield of Sheffield had an elder brother named Gerald; and if so, the other preliminary is to discover whether they could claim connexion with the family that was evidently once so great and important in Warwickshire. Now, who in the absence of my father and cousin can satisfy me on the first point?"

At that moment the name of Mr. Parks flashed to my memory; and I at once penned the following letter :—

"Stafford. December 28, 1842.

"My dear Jane,

"Circumstances have transpired which enable you to render me a service—or at least I believe that it is possible for you to procure information on a point where it is very desirable. You know that I had an uncle named James Wakefield, who was a manufacturer in a small way of business at Sheffield, and who died of a broken heart many years ago, in consequence of pecuniary misfortunes. Can you learn for me whether this uncle of mine

BEDA.

possessed a brother?—and if so, what the brother's Christian name may have been? And supposing that you should find that there was such a brother, would you also endeavour to ascertain whether he ever claimed to be the lineal representative of a great family of the name of Wakefield which was famous in Warwickshire a century ago?

"Though I direct this letter from Stafford, yet you must send your answer to me at Tremaine Hall. Your friends there are all in good health; and Charlotte was speaking most kindly concerning you this very morning.

                              "Yours sincerely,
                                        "ELLEN PERCY.
"Miss Parks, London."

By the time this letter was finished, Beda returned; and she informed me that the inquiries she had instituted were altogether favourable. I accordingly said to her, "You, my dear Beda,

No. 95.—ELLEN PERCY.

shall receive this woman Sturton when she comes back presently: you shall tell her who you are—and you shall place in her hands my draft upon London for fifty pounds."

I drew the cheque accordingly: and then retired to another room. In about a quarter of an hour Beda came to me with tears in her eyes,—saying, "Oh, if you had seen that poor woman, dear Miss, you would have rejoiced at the possession of the power to bestow such a boon upon her! As for myself, she pressed my hand to her lips—and she said that it was because my parents had been worthy people and had done good actions, that I myself was allowed by heaven to enjoy so much prosperity!"

It was now three o'clock in the afternoon: we took our seats in the carriage, and returned to Tremaine Hall. As all the guests had departed, and there were numerous chambers now empty, there was not the slightest need for me to volunteer to occupy the haunted apartment; and thus I and Beda took up our quarters in the rooms originally intended for my reception. I dressed for dinner; and the evening passed away without any incident worthy of mention. Miss Barron still kept her chamber: but I learnt that she felt much better, and that she had positively declined to receive any medical advice.

CHAPTER CXXIII.

THE LIBRARY.

IT was about half-past ten o'clock when the family separated for the night; and I was about to ascend to my own chamber, when I suddenly recollected to have seen in the library a compendious history of Warwickshire, with an account of all the leading families that in times past or present had any connexion with the county. I determined to procure the volume: and I retraced my way for the purpose. So completely was everything which had that day occurred now uppermost in my mind, that I entirely forgot the incident of the cloaked figure in the library, until my fingers grasped the handle of the door leading into it. I confess that I suddenly stopped short: but the next instant I was ashamed of myself for this pusillanimous hesitation; and I mentally ejaculated, "I will not deserve the name of coward even in my own secret thoughts!".

I therefore boldly opened the door, and entered the library. Rapidly were my looks swept around; but no one met my eyes. There was the screen occupying its usual place, and so situated as to protect any one who might be in the library from the draught of the glass door opening into the garden. Determined not to be overcome by any superstitious feeling, I advanced with steady and firm gait towards that screen, and glanced behind it. No one was there; but I nevertheless started—for the sound of the rustling of a window curtain close by, had assuredly fallen upon my ear. Instantaneously was my look flung in that direction. It was a window in a species of recess beyond the ranges of shelves in the library; it was in the same wall as the glass-door itself—it therefore looked likewise upon the back garden. Yes—that curtain was still moving!—it had evidently been agitated——but might it not be by the wind?

I was about to turn away, upbraiding myself for the transient terror which had seized upon me, when methought that if I wished to restore my credit in my own estimation, I ought to go boldly and look behind that curtain in order to assure myself that there was really nothing there.

"Yes—I will do it!" I said; and accordingly forthwith towards the curtain did I advance.

Scarcely however had my hand touched it, when it was thrust aside by some one behind; and thence forth glided a tall figure, completely muffled in a cloak, just as I had seen it on the preceding evening. A cry was on the very point of bursting forth from my lips, and the taper was nearly dropping from my hand,—when I caught sight of a countenance which at once struck me as being not altogether unfamiliar. All my fortitude revived in a moment: I knew that it was no ghost—and I sprang towards him, tearing his cloak off his shoulders, and crying, "Stop, I command you!"

"For God's sake, have mercy upon me!" were the imploring words that now fell upon my ears; and the individual, taking off his cap, revealed his countenance completely.

It was that of Ludovico Marano, as I had already suspected.

"Have mercy?" I ejaculated indignantly. "Mercy on whom? On an intruder?"

"Oh, Miss Percy! you cannot possibly think," exclaimed Ludovico, "that I should have come hither for any improper purpose!"

"To steal into a private mansion — to creep hither as the burglar comes!" I angrily rejoined: "to penetrate like the gliding thief——".

"By heaven, Miss Percy, these are strong terms which you are using!" interrupted Ludovico; and I perceived that a demoniacal expression of rage flitted over his countenance, reminding me of that diabolical look which he wore when about a fortnight back he had said to me at Colonel Tremaine's house in South Street, Park Lane, "Miss Percy, I will be avenged! You know me! I will be avenged!".

For an instant therefore I was seized with alarm, as I remembered that I was alone in that room with a man who had already in the case of Luigi given such frightful evidence of his terrible vindictiveness.

"Signor Marano," I said, "you cannot be surprised if strong terms should come from my lips when I encounter you here!"

"Now, hear me, Miss Percy! hear me!" he said, in a tone of voice which was full of pathetic entreaty. "I love Charlotte—and I seek one last interview with her! You must suffer me to behold her for the last time! Oh, pray do not refuse me!—but rather assist me in my design!"

"I assist, Signor Marano, in such a proceeding?" I ejaculated, my indignation again getting the better of my prudence or my terror. "Tell me in one word, how did you obtain admittance hither?"

"It is easy to conceal oneself in this place of an evening," he replied; "and as for that glass door, no one seems to think it strange if it be found unlocked in the morning. I will deal frankly with you, Miss Percy. I have heard the legend connected with Tremaine Hall——"

"Ah!" I said. "And you think that——"

"Let me explain!" he interrupted me. "I thought it possible that Charlotte might happen to come hither alone—to fetch a book—or to give way to her thoughts, if she still loves me. And then this guise," continued Marano, "would have served me well in case I had happened to run against a domestic. Ah! and by the bye, Miss Percy, I think that you yourself were yesterday evening inclined to believe that you had seen the spirit of Captain Cautley——"

"A truce to this idle discourse, signor," I exclaimed. "Learn from my lips the assurance that Charlotte Tremaine does not continue to think of you—at least not with love! And therefore be persuaded by me—act a prudent, I will even say a generous part—and seek not to persecute that young lady! If I have now abstained from raising my voice and crying for assistance, it is because I would not take a step that should create a scandal in the house, or afford scope for gossip and tittle-tattle. Pray therefore depart! I entreat and conjure—nay, more, I command you!"

"Ah!" he ejaculated, his entire air and manner changing all in a moment, and his countenance again wearing that look of diabolical malignity to which I have before alluded : " you dare address me in these peremptory terms ?—and all my own courtesy is thrown away ?"

At the same instant he drew forth a pistol from his pocket : a glance showed me that it was a double-barrelled one—a cry rose up to my lips—but I held it back, for at the same moment he exclaimed, " Speak not !—utter not a sound !—or by heaven I will fire !"

The double-barrelled weapon was within two feet of my face as those terrible threats smote my ear ; and I was transfixed with terror. I knew how fearfully vindictive the man was : I knew also that he was one of the worst specimens of the Italian disposition ; and I was therefore stricken with the horrible conviction that he was quite capable of fulfilling his diabolic threat. And thus there I stood, holding the taper in one hand, and having dropped from the other the cloak which I had torn off him and which I had been mechanically retaining in my grasp. Yes—there I stood, statue-like, with an awful consternation on my mind. I felt as if I were looking death in the face—because that pistol might explode by accident, or through the sudden deepening of the malignant feeling which the man entertained against me !

" Now, Miss Percy," he said, " you are in my power—and perhaps it is for *me* to command ! Down on your knees, and swear to perform whatsoever I am about to dictate ! I know that if you take an oath you will keep it, however repugnant its fulfilment may be to your own feelings."

" I will not swear," I answered, as I felt my presence of mind returning. " No !—you may kill me—but I will not have an oath extorted from me by such means as these !"

There was an instant when so truly diabolical and fiendlike was the expression of Ludovico Marano's countenance, as I thus addressed him, that I already felt as if that instant was to be my last, and that there would be a sudden flashing before my eyes, a sudden din in my ears, and that by an abrupt transition of scenes I should awake to the consciousness of another world. I remember that this idea—this truly awful idea—swept vividly through my brain ; for never did any man seem more fully capable of perpetrating a villanous action than did Ludovico Marano at that moment !

" You will not swear ?" he said. " We shall see ! But I tell you that you *will* swear !—and for these reasons—that in the first place it is nothing so very outrageous to your feelings which I am about to demand of you—and in the second place because I swear by everything sacred in heaven and everything terrible in hell, that I will mercilessly blow out your brains if you do not !"

I shuddered from head to foot : as glacial a sensation swept through me as if I had been all in a moment lifted up from the spot where I stood and deposited amidst the ice of the northern pole.

Again was I on the point of crying out : the impulse to send a scream pealing throughout the mansion was almost irresistible : but even amidst the very wildness and poignancy of my terror, there was a certain degree of presence of mind which made me say to myself, " He will assuredly shoot me if I do!"

" Give me that light," he said ; for doubtless perceiving the tremor which swept over me, he dreaded lest I should drop the taper and that we should be left in darkness.

I gave him the candlestick ; and as he took it, the formidable weapon came still closer to my face. Again I shuddered : again did the horrible apprehension seize upon me lest that instant should be my last !

" Now listen to me, Miss Percy," he said, as he deposited the taper upon a neighbouring chair. " I am determined to see Charlotte Tremaine—and you shall help me in the accomplishment of that object. All I ask is to see her ! I do not believe that she could have all in a moment divested herself of the love that for a long period she had entertained for me ! It is impossible ! All my strong attachment was not to be recompensed by so much heartlessness on her part ! It was a momentary prejudice to which she yielded !—and you, Miss Percy, excited it ! *You* therefore shall now become the means of destroying it ! You shall bring us together ! It is all that I ask ; and if Charlotte Tremaine now assures me that after a period of calm and deliberate reflection she still desires that everything is to be at an end between us, I will bow to her decision. But this decision I am determined to have ! Now, Miss Percy, will you swear to do my bidding ?—will you go and bring Charlotte Tremaine hither ?—will you faithfully promise you will raise no alarm—warn no one except Charlotte of my presence here—and take no step that may in any way interfere with my plans ? If you swear, I shall believe you. If you refuse——"

" Signor Marano," I interrupted him, " is it possible that you—a gentleman by birth—belonging to a nation once renowed for its chivalry and its magnanimity—is it possible that you can stand here with a loaded weapon in your hand and give way to the most horrible threats to a defenceless female ?"

" Such pleading as this is vain and useless, Miss Percy !" he ejaculated. " I am resolute and determined ! You have done me much wrong : you shall now put it right !"

" I have never done you any wrong, Signor Marano, that you yourself did not deserve," I responded. " Oh, let me appeal to your better feelings in the present case ! Or I would even ask if you are not afraid of the course which you are pursuing—in the first instance seizing hold of the tale which superstition tells, as a means to render a particular disguise available for your sinister purposes——"

" Enough ! enough !" cried Marano impatiently. " Take your course !—decide quickly !—or by heaven I swear——"

" Be cautious," I ejaculated, " how you give utterance to such fearful oaths ! For if ever there were a case in which a miracle might be worked to save a defenceless female——"

" What mean you ? what mean you ?" demanded

Ludovico vehemently. "Come! this is child's play! Do you fancy," he asked, with a scornful sneer upon his lips, "that the real ghost of this library will make its appearance to save you——"

"Ah!" I cried, with a sudden start. "Look behind you!"

The Italian also started: he was galvanized with a panic terror; and turning his head quickly, he *did* look behind. Then I flew at him with all the strength and energy that I possessed:—with one hand I struck the pistol upward—with the other I at once clutched it. Marano fell backward by the violence of the attack; and I tore the pistol from his grasp. At that very moment the door of the library opened—some one entered—and in the twinkling of an eye Beda came gliding upon the spot where this strange scene was taking place.

"Ah, this is indeed providential!" I exclaimed. "Silence, Beda! The wretch is in our power! Do you know him? It is Ludovico Marano! And you, signor," I added, now touching his forehead with the muzzles of the pistol-barrels, "dare to show any resistance, and you will see that I know how to follow up my victory!"

The Italian's eyes glared like those of a hyena as he lay upon his back on the carpet, and my knee rested upon his chest: his lips were ashy white—and as they quivered with the emotions of rage and disappointment and mortification which he experienced, the white teeth, closely set, gleamed betwixt them.

"Beda," I said, "go quickly and tell Mr. and Mrs. Tremaine what has happened. It is needless to alarm the household—they will act as they may think fit."

"My God, Miss Percy!" said Marano, "pray do not take this step!"

"I shall take it, signor. Go, Beda!" I cried: for she was lingering as if with the idea that the Italian's entreaty might perchance induce me to alter my mind.

"No, no!" he cried; "you will not do it! Mr. Tremaine may hand me over to the grasp of justice!"

"He can take whatsoever course he thinks fit, signor," I replied, as I heard the library door close behind Beda. "I would have spared you this ignominy and danger; but you would not accept the terms which I offered. You have only yourself to thank for the issue which the present adventure is now taking. Beware how you attempt to move, signor!—for you must know that if I am rendered desperate, it is by your own conduct!"

I spoke with a degree of stern resoluteness that seemed suitable to the position in which I found myself placed; and I continued to hold the pistol in a threatening manner at the Italian's head.

"Release me," he said,—"release me, I conjure you! I will at once take my departure! I swear that I will never approach these premises again—I will never molest Charlotte nor yourself——"

"Silence, signor! silence!" I said in a peremptory tone. "It is useless for you to entreat or implore. I am decided and determined!"

So terrible grew the Italian's looks at this instant that I really fancied he meant to make some desperate effort to shake me off. But he did not; yet his eyes were glaring up at me in a manner only too well calculated to fill my soul with terror. There was a minute of profound silence,—a minute of acute suspense on my part: but this feeling was suddenly put an end to by the opening of the door—and again did Beda glide towards me. She was accompanied by Mr. and Mrs. Tremaine, neither of whom had begun to undress when she had knocked at their chamber-door to summon them. I now suffered Ludovico Marano to rise up from the carpet; but hastening to the glass door, I leant with my back against it, keeping the pistol in my hand. Mr. and Mrs. Tremaine were very much excited: they both however flung looks of gratitude and admiration upon me, as if thanking me for my conduct; and then bending their regards upon Ludovico as he stood before them, they exclaimed in a breath, "Villain! what are you doing here?"

"A very few words of explanation will suffice," I said, taking it upon myself to answer for the culprit. "He does not believe that your daughter Charlotte has finally renounced him: he seeks an interview with her—he swears that he will hear the decision from her lips only! After everything that has passed, I could not take it upon myself to bring Charlotte and this person together; therefore did I send Beda to fetch *you*—Charlotte's parents—that you may act according to your own discretion in the matter."

"Signor Marano," said Mr. Tremaine, making a sign for his wife to be silent, "you are adopting a course which cannot possibly be justified! My daughter has declined to receive your addresses——"

"She is coerced!" exclaimed Ludovico passionately: "she is coerced! I will not believe it can possibly be otherwise! For two years and upwards had we loved each other—for two years and upwards had I cherished your daughter's image!—and from her own lips had I received the assurance that mine was equally dear to her?"

"Dare not to talk of love, signor," ejaculated Mr. Tremaine sternly, "when you cannot deny the fact that you made overtures to another lady—to Beatrice di Carboni——"

"It was a momentary infatuation!" cried the Italian, stamping his foot with the enraged excitement of one who thus endeavoured to enforce a preposterous assertion.

"It is useless to argue this point," ejaculated Mr. Tremaine: "my daughter has ceased to look upon you otherwise than as a man utterly unworthy of her regard. And even were it not so, both her mother and myself—aye, and all our friends—would strenuously and inexorably set our faces against the bare idea——"

"Ah, I knew that she was acting under coercion!" exclaimed Ludovico. "I must see her! I will hear from her own lips that she loves me no longer!"

"And what," asked Mr. Tremaine, "if Charlotte repeats the assurance which I have already given you? Will you act as a man of honour? are you capable of doing so? will you pledge yourself that you will henceforth abstain——"

"Ask Miss Percy," demanded Ludovico Marano, "whether I have not already given promises to this effect? Look you, Mr. Tremaine! I am no needy adventurer seeking your daughter's hand for the sake of any fortune which you may be enabled to give her——"

"Enough, signor!" interjected Mr. Tremaine; "this is the only reason which induces me to treat you with a certain degree of consideration, after everything which has come to our knowledge concerning you. Yes—you shall hear the decision from my daughter's lips."

Mr. Tremaine made a sign to his wife: he also whispered a few words in her ear—and she quitted the library.

"My dear Ellen," said Mr. Tremaine, advancing towards me and speaking in a hurried whisper, "tell me exactly what happened betwixt yourself and this man."

"The explanation is soon given," I answered. "I came into the library to fetch a book—I caught the Italian playing the part of Captain Cautley's ghost—I tore his mantle from off him—and there it lies! He threatened me—I did all that I could to avoid disturbance and noise in the house —it is his own fault if I found myself compelled to send for you."

"But your own heroism, Ellen?" ejaculated Mr. Tremaine. "How was it that you discomfited him?"

"I seized him unawares — or rather I succeeded in throwing him off his guard," I replied; "and then I snatched the pistol from his grasp."

"Brave girl!" ejaculated Mr. Tremaine, taking my hand and pressing it warmly. "But give me this weapon, which is not fitted for such delicate fingers as these:"—and he accordingly took the pistol from me, at the same time adding in a whisper, "A thousand thanks, my young friend, for your endeavour to settle the matter amicably and quietly. But no coercion is necessary now— the Italian has accepted terms, and he must abide by them."

I moved away from the door; and, accosting Beda, I whispered, "Most fortunate, dear girl, was your entrance at that moment. How happened it?"

"I met Miss Tremaine on the stairs just now," answered Beda; "and she told me that you were just coming up, and that you had only gone to the library to procure yourself a book. When several minutes had elapsed and you appeared not, a vague apprehension stole over me——"

"And so you came to look for me, my faithful young friend?" I rejoined. "But here is Miss Tremaine!"

The Italian had in the meanwhile been leaning against the wall of the room with his arms folded across his chest—with a fixed expression of countenance, and with a sinister gleaming of the eyes. As I heard the door open, and at a glance perceived that Mrs. Tremaine was now returning, accompanied by her daughter, I looked hastily towards Ludovico; and I at once noticed that he was now a prey to a degree of suspense that was evidently great. How was it that this man, who had offered to lead Beatrice di Carboni to the altar, could now *act*, and doubtless *feel* likewise, as if his life's happiness depended on the decision that was to issue from the lips of Charlotte Tremaine? It was because he did really love the latter; while in respect to the former his feelings had been attracted towards her at the time by that horrible identity of vindictive interests which had prevailed in respect to Luigi.

Charlotte had begun to arrange her hair when her mother so unexpectedly appeared in her apartment. She had not been able to gather up the masses of that brown hair again: she had therefore left it flowing all dishevelled over her shoulders: and this gave her a certain wildness of appearance not altogether unsuitable to the singular melodramatic scene that was occurring. I have before said that Charlotte was not handsome—she was not even pretty: but still she was naturally interesting, and even prepossessing. Now, however, she did seem absolutely handsome,—of a fearful beauty too—with that dishevelled hair, a loose muslin wrapper enveloping her form, her cheeks very pale, her lips slightly apart with the suspenseful nature of her feelings, and the ivory teeth shining between!

"Here, Signor Marano," said Mr. Tremaine, "is my daughter——."

Ludovico bounded towards her—threw himself upon his knees—and clasping his hands, exclaimed passionately, "Have pity upon me, Charlotte!— do not renounce me! do not give me up! I swear that I love you—and *you* only! Oh! do not let one fault separate us for ever! You are dearer to me than life! I take God to witness that——."

"Hush, Signor Marano!" said Charlotte, speaking in a firm tone: "beware of such oaths! Rise also, I beseech you! It is not for you to kneel in my presence!"

"Oh, tell me that there is hope!" cried Marano, in a tone that was alike pathetic and rending; "tell me that there is hope—and *then* bid me rise! But if there be none, then may you as well take that weapon from your father's hand and therewith smite me dead upon the spot!"

"Heaven forbid!" ejaculated Charlotte, with a visible shudder. "Rise, signor!—I will not speak to you while you remain in this suppliant posture!"

"Every word of yours is a law with me," rejoined the Italian, as he rose from his knees. "But Oh, Charlotte! dearest Charlotte!"

"Hush, signor! hush!" she interrupted him; "that language must not emanate from your lips! Heaven knows I wish you no ill; and may you find happiness elsewhere!—but between you and me everything is at an end! Yes!—do not force me into further explanations: they would necessarily be painful,—but I repeat, between you and me all is at an end!"

"And now, signor," said Mr. Tremaine, turning towards the Italian, "may I request that you will fulfil the pledge so impressively given, and depart hence."

Ludovico Marano gave no response: there was something sinister, ominous, and even terrible, in his appearance. His complexion, naturally of an olive hue, was of a ghastly sallowish white: his lips were compressed, but in such a way that it was easy to perceive the upper teeth were fixed upon a portion of the lower lip, which they were biting as if the volcano agitating in the young man's breast could be thereby kept down. His chest was rising and falling rapidly: he looked like one who was capable of all in a moment starting from that position and doing some desperate deed.

"Signor," said Mr. Tremaine, evidently smitten with some misgiving to the same effect as that which I have just mentioned, "I appeal to you as a gentleman——"

"Sir, I am rejected cast off—refused by your daughter!" exclaimed Marano, turning abruptly towards Charlotte's father. "Think you that I can tamely endure——"

"Sir, I beseech you," interrupted Mr. Tremaine, —"I implore that you will treat the matter with fortitude and magnanimity! You cannot complain of want of indulgence on our part, considering how you have this night introduced yourself into the house——"

"Charlotte," demanded Ludovico, in a hoarse voice, as he turned abruptly away from Mr. Tremaine, "is it your decision that everything is to be at an end between us—that forgiveness is impossible——"

"For heaven's sake," replied Charlotte, "let us argue the point no further! I have said that I wish you no ill—but on the contrary, I earnestly hope that you will experience happiness elsewhere——"

"Happiness?" echoed Marano, with the most scornful irony of accent: "happiness? Oh, the idea is preposterous! What happiness can there be for *me*? It is gone for ever!—and the person who has destroyed it—the one who has been to me as an evil genius—is *you*, Ellen Percy!—*you*! And thus do I avenge myself!"

Quick as thought—quick indeed as the eye can wink—the Italian snatched the pistol from the hand of Mr. Tremaine, and levelled it at me. I started back with a scream of terror. At that instant the explosion took place! But at that very instant also, the door of the library opened, and a female figure appeared on the threshold—and with a wild shriek this figure sank down there, in the open doorway! And in a moment the bosom of the white dress that she wore was dyed with the gushing blood.

"Wretch!" thundered Mr. Tremaine: and he sprang towards Marano.

The pistol was double-barrelled; and one barrel was still charged. It was again quick as thought —again quick as the eye can wink, that the weapon was pointed at me; and I caught the fierce lightnings of terrific hatred and demon-like vindictiveness which the eyes of the wretch darted forth. Towards him bounded Beda; and at the very instant that the second explosion took place, her hand struck the pistol upward. The bullet penetrated the ceiling—the Italian flung the weapon upon the carpet—dashed Beda away on one side and Mr. Tremaine on the other—and bounded towards the screen. The next instant we heard the glass door open and close with a crashing sound.

Nothing could exceed the wild excitement which prevailed in the library—the cries and ejaculations of horror which were bursting forth— Mr. Tremaine rushing in pursuit of the Italian— Mrs. Tremaine and her daughter flying to raise the form that had sunk down upon the threshold —and I half fainting in the arms of Beda, who by her presence of mind had undoubtedly saved my life by striking the pistol upward at the moment when it was a second time levelled at me! But who was the unfortunate victim of the first shot? —who was bursting into the library at the very instant when the winged messenger of danger was issuing from the muzzle of the weapon? Alas, poor creature!—it was Sarah Barron!

The whole household was now alarmed: the reports of the double-barrelled pistol had rung throughout the mansion—the cries and screams were likewise heard—and Mr. Tremaine was now exclaiming in a most excited state, in the back garden, "Murder! Haste in pursuit of the murderer! Help to catch the assassin!"

The domestics, male and female, flocked towards the library; and Charlotte's sisters came speedily thither likewise. Colonel Tremaine was not the last to appear upon the scene. But there was now no longer a possibility of throwing a veil over Ludovico Marano's visit to the mansion and its object. Everything was told—though necessarily in a hurried manner; and several men-servants sped forth in pursuit of the Italian.

But what of Sarah Barron? She had fainted; and as I have already said, the front part of the morning wrapper which she had put on ere leaving her chamber, was dyed with blood. It was quickly ascertained that the bullet had penetrated somewhere in the right shoulder, just below the collar-bone; and as a matter of course a messenger was instantaneously despatched on horseback to procure medical assistance. Sarah was removed to her own apartment, and Mrs. Tremaine dressed the wound to the best of her ability. At all events, the blood was stanched; and this was naturally considered a great point gained. Slowly and with difficulty was Sarah brought back to consciousness: she at first seemed to be awakening from some wild and horrible dream; but when she raised her hand to the wounded part, the sensation of pain which she evidently experienced gave an impulse to her memory—her ideas were speedily collected —and she came to the knowledge of what had happened. Mrs. Tremaine, Charlotte, and myself, who were now in the room with her, all three said the most consolatory things that we could possibly think of; and we explained everything which had occurred—for Sarah was naturally most anxious to be enlightened on this head. She told us in her turn, that first of all she was struck by hearing voices speaking in an excited manner—then she heard Mrs. Tremaine ascend to Charlotte's chamber to fetch her down stairs—and fancying that something was wrong or that something unpleasant was taking place, she had risen from her couch, she had thrown on a wrapper, and she had descended to the library. It was no wonder that Sarah should have heard the unusual sounds of voices in the library at that hour, inasmuch as her chamber was precisely overhead.

The pursuit after Ludovico Marano proved ineffectual; and the domestics returned without having been enabled to get upon his track. But long before the menials came back with this intelligence, medical assistance had arrived; and the surgeon at once proceeded to extract the bullet. The operation was a painful one: it occupied some time—but he succeeded in accomplishing it. Sarah asked him with much anxiety whether he thought that there was any danger? He hesitated to answer: she pressed him—he spoke evasively; and then she said that so far as she herself was concerned, she was resigned to whatsoever might be her fate; but that she had a mother and brother who ought to be made acquainted with her position if it were one that menaced her life. Then it was that the surgeon threw a look of painful significancy upon Mrs. Tremaine, Charlotte, and myself: we understood what he meant—and Mrs. Tremaine hastened to say, "It is impossible we can conceal from ourselves, my dear Sarah, that there is always danger in a case of this kind—although thanks to your excellent constitution, your youth, and the care which shall be taken of you, there is every reason to hope in a happy issue. Nevertheless, as it would no doubt be a comfort to yourself to have with you those whom you love best, I will send off a messenger to your mother in the morning; and most welcome shall that worthy lady and your brother be at Tremaine Hall."

Sarah Barron expressed her acknowledgments for the kindness of which she thus found herself the object. The medical man took his leave, promising to return at an early hour in the morning; and Sarah then earnestly entreated that we would seek our own chambers, for she now felt easy and would be contented if one of the maid-servants remained with her. Mrs. Tremaine would not hear of this proposal: I likewise offered to sit up with Miss Barron; but Charlotte carried the point on her own behalf by the plea which she urged.

"It was on account of me," she said, "that the assassin Marano came to the house:—through me therefore that our poor Sarah has been wounded; and I insist upon my right to remain with her."

The argument was considered conclusive: so that Mrs. Tremaine and I withdrew to our respective apartments. On reaching my own room, I embraced Beda tenderly, declaring there could be no doubt she had saved my life; and we sat up for an hour, discussing the occurrences of the evening, ere we retired to rest. But even when I had lain down in my own bed, it was some time before I could close my eyes in slumber; for not only did all the incidents which I have been relating reproduce themselves over and over again in my mind, but there was one circumstance which troubled me peculiarly. Sarah Barron's mother and brother would shortly be at Tremaine Hall! How could I possibly meet that brother of the unfortunate young lady?—how could I consent to live for an hour beneath the same roof with the hypocrite and dissembler whom I knew to be an accomplished villain? Yet on the other hand how could I find an excuse for precipitate departure? or if I resolved to remain, how could I avoid showing by my demeanour, that I abhorred and loathed the sight of Sarah's brother? And there was another consideration. Even if for poor Sarah's sake, and in the presence of all circumstances, I controlled and veiled my own feelings, how could I suffer such a wretch to enter amidst the pure society of Mr. and Mrs. Tremaine's daughters? And yet on the other hand, how was I to take any decisive step without giving poor Sarah a shock which might prove most detrimental, even if not fatal, in the position in which she was placed? All these were bewildering questions which I was compelled to put to myself: and sleep came upon me before I had succeeded in arriving at any settled plan of proceeding in the midst of my perplexities.

I awoke at an early hour in the morning, and at once despatched Beda to the invalid's chamber to make suitable inquiries. The surgeon had already been; he had as a matter of course spoken encouragingly to Sarah herself; but privately to Mrs. Tremaine he had intimated that there was much to be apprehended in respect to the issue. The greatest grief was spread throughout the mansion on Sarah's account; for she was a universal favourite. As for Charlotte and her sisters, they were deeply distressed, — especially Emilia and Lavinia, the unfortunate young lady's pupils. So soon as I was dressed, I proceeded to visit Sarah. I found Mrs. Tremaine and Charlotte with her; but I soon observed that Sarah made a pretext to get rid of them,—without however suffering them to perceive that it was her desire to be alone with me. At length we were thus alone together; and then Sarah grew excited—she took my hand and pressed it to her lips—she also moistened it with her tears. I conjured her not to think of anything that was at all calculated to distress her, for I judged what was uppermost in her thoughts.

"My dear Ellen," she said, "there is a heavy weight upon my mind—I must and will give you certain explanations! Pray listen to me! Oh, I beseech you to listen!—and I shall be much easier if you will!"

Again I remonstrated, assuring her that no explanations were necessary, and that I had ceased to think of everything in connexion with herself, except the injuries she had received and the hope I entertained that she would recover.

"No, my dear Ellen," she answered, "I shall not be pacified nor tranquillzed by such assurances as these, kind though they are. When there is a weight, heavy as if it were of lead, pressing upon the soul, relief must be sought for. Listen, then! —listen, I beseech you!—and if there be anything which can aid the surgeon's skill in ministering to my advantage, it will be the unbosoming of my secrets to your ears. I shall be restless, uneasy, and full of painful anxiety until this be done."

Sarah spoke so earnestly, and with so much entreaty, that I saw it would do her more harm to refuse than it could possibly do her an injury to allow her to have her own way. I therefore assented; and I saw at once that there was a gleaming of satisfaction on her countenance — though it was almost immediately succeeded by an expression of mingled pain and seriousness, as she prepared to enter upon the explanations she thus insisted on giving.

"Perhaps you have heard," she began, "that about four years ago, when the family first went upon the Continent, I remained here at the Hall, to superintend the education of Emilia and Lavinia. There is no harm in stating that Mr. Tremaine went abroad to economise—he having at the time a lawsuit that was almost ruinous in its cost, and which, if its issue were a failure, would tend to impoverish him exceedingly, if not involve him in absolute ruin. Therefore you will not be surprised to learn that the establishment at the Hall was placed upon the most economical footing, and all those servants were discharged who were not absolutely necessary in the positions which they occupied. So few people in so vast a mansion made it seem like a deserted place, and the impression upon my mind was somewhat a gloomy one. I necessarily fulfilled the duties of mistress of the establishment while I was thus left in charge of it. In the performance of these duties I generally had to go about once a week to Stafford, to make such purchases as were required. Sometimes I would take my young pupils with me if the weather was fine; but if otherwise, I left them at home in the charge of an old nurse who was a most trustworthy person. I am not going to make my story a long one—I do not wish to weary you with details; nor is the topic so pleasant as to induce me to dwell upon it. Suffice it therefore to say that on the occasion of one of those visits to Stafford, I encountered an individual with whom accident rendered me acquainted—a nobleman bearing a name which has often and often exercised an influence upon the destinies of persons beneath this roof."

"Whom can you possibly mean?" I asked, suddenly smitten with a suspicion that the young nobleman thus alluded to was not altogether unknown to me.

Sarah Barron wiped away a tear from her eye; and she said, "I mean Viscount Ravenscliffe."

"Ah!" I ejaculated—for my suspicion was confirmed. "This very day I met him!"

"You met him?" said Miss Barron, with surprise and anxiety depicted on her countenance. "What! you know him?"

"Yes — slightly," I answered. "His brother Lord Frederick, who died about six months ago, was married to my most intimate friend——"

"Miss Norman!" ejaculated Sarah. "Ah, yes! —so I remember reading in a newspaper when I was upon the Continent. But you met the Viscount to-day? Did he know where you were staying?"

"Yes," I replied. "I happened to inform him that I was visiting my friends at Tremaine Hall."

"And did—did he ask any other question?" inquired Sarah: "did he by any accident mention my name?"

"No," I rejoined. "I only spoke to him for a few minutes. I must tell you that I am not very well acquainted with him—we had only met once before—and that was under painful circumstances —the occasion of his brother's death. Besides, Sarah," I added, "whatever may have taken place betwixt himself and you, a proper feeling of delicacy would no doubt prevent him from putting any question to a third person that might engender a suspicion."

"True!" said Miss Barron. "And then too," she went on to observe, "I have long ago discovered that he really cares nothing for me. I do not believe that he really ever loved me! No, no! it was impossible !—or else he would not—no! he would not have acted as he did !"

"I beseech you, Sarah," I said, "not to give way to repinings and regrets——I mean do not excite yourself—say no more upon the subject now——"

"Oh, yes! I must tell you everything!" she interrupted me; "and then my mind will be comparatively at ease! I was saying that I met Viscount Ravenscliffe at Stafford :—that was four years ago, when I was barely eighteen. I was inexperienced in the world; and when on the next four or five successive occasions that I visited Stafford, I met the Viscount, I could no longer think it was accidental—but I felt flattered and pleased by the idea that he was purposely seeking me. And then I began to listen to the tale which he breathed in my ear; and when he spoke of an

honourable love and marriage, and the certainty of being enabled to overcome the prejudices of his parents, my heart bounded with exultation : for I naturally thought how proud and grand a thing it would be for me to become a nobleman's wife,— a Viscountess at once—a peeress at a future time ! Those meetings grew more frequent : they did not take place only at Stafford, but in the neighbourhood of the Hall; and I, believing that he was honourable and loving—affectionate and faithful— incapable of deceiving me,—alas ! I was too full of confidence——and—and—I fell !"

Sarah Barron paused and covered her face with her hands: but she did not now weep—neither did she sob—no, nor did so much as a sigh agitate her bosom. But there she lay for two or three minutes, perfectly motionless—buried, so to speak, in the very trance of thought itself.

"Now, my dear Sarah," I said, when she at length moved her hands from her face, "you have told me enough—I can divine all the rest. Of what need to revive the most unhappy memories ?"

"Ellen," she answered, in a firm tone, "I have said that I would tell you everything; and I am determined to do so. I wish you to see whether I have been adequately punished for the weakness of which I have been guilty."

"I am sure you must have been !" I replied; "for even my own conjectures concerning your case can supply sufficient to prove that you have passed through an ordeal which though serving as a chastisement from heaven, may nevertheless entitle you to the sympathy of your fellow-creatures upon earth !"

"Oh, what kind words flow from your lips, my dear Ellen !" murmured Sarah. "Yes—mine was indeed a terrible ordeal !. But then I deserved it ! —Oh, I deserved all the agony of mind that I endured ! for was I not very deceitful towards those who had left me in charge of their children ? On two or three occasions I introduced the Viscount secretly into the mansion——"

"Ah, I remember !" I ejaculated : "he told me he had visited the Hall during the absence of the Tremaines. But then we were only speaking at the time of the traditionary feuds and animosities which had subsisted between the families. And now proceed, Sarah; and bring your tale to a quick ending."

"In a few months after the commencement of my acquaintance with Viscount Ravenscliffe," continued Miss Barron, "I was in a way to become a mother. Oh! you may possibly be enabled to picture to yourself how passionately I entreated the Viscount to fulfil his pledges and make me his wife! It was then that the excuses and pretexts he advanced began to open my eyes to the dreadful truth !—to the fearful comprehension of the fact that I was betrayed ! I can conceive the deep horror, the consternation, and the growing agony of mind, with which in oriental climes the doomed wretch first begins to feel the dread idea creeping into his soul that the plague has taken hold of him; and of a kindred nature was the feeling which then took possession of me! I strove to cling to hope as to an element that was necessary to my existence: but it grew more and more phantom-like before me—more and more impalpable—more and more vapoury, until it vanished

altogether! For the Viscount pretended—as a pretence I am sure it *was*—that he was compelled to go upon the Continent on some business for his father. He promised to write: I did receive some few letters at distant intervals—but I could not shut my eyes to the fact that they were all so cautiously worded as to contain no promise of marriage. Not that I would have availed myself in a legal sense of any such promise, even supposing one to have been made: but it was no longer possible for me to doubt that I was utterly and completely betrayed. Time wore on—and I continued to conceal my position from the few servants who were in the house. To be brief, I veiled it altogether: I am convinced that it was never once suspected. At length the dread moment was advancing—the hour of woman's direst extremity was drawing near. I knew not what to do: my mind was in a horrible state of uncertainty—I was

in a constant condition of bewilderment—it was a prolonged and hideous consternation. Some preparations I made; but to no ear did I breathe my secret—the aid of no surgeon did I invoke against the coming trial. And that hour came! It was in the early part of the night—a night of storm and tempest without—a night of horror and of agony for me! How was it possible that I could conceal my shame and disgrace any longer? In the midst of my almost mortal throes of mind and body, an idea struck me. In the haunted room I should be safe! No one would penetrate thither, whatsoever groans might be heard! To the haunted room therefore I dragged myself; and there did I become the mother of a male child which came not into the world alive. In the morning I was found as usual in my own chamber: I complained of a passing indisposition—I nursed myself for a few days—and then I was again at my post, conducting the affairs of the household and superintending the education of the children. And no one suspected what had happened!"

Sarah Barron paused for a minute or two; and then she continued her narrative in the following manner:—

"But how to dispose of the remains of the infant? I had deposited the corpse in the cupboard farthest from the door; and I had taken the key with me. One night I revisited the room, with the intention of fetching the dead infant and burying it somewhere in the garden. But as I stooped down in the cupboard, I noticed that the flooring was loose; and I was struck with certain details of the legend which attaches itself to that apartment. It might have been true, then, after all (I thought to myself) that Arabella Ravenscliffe had become the mother of a child which was concealed in that very self-same spot! The idea was horrible—and yet it was suggestive. I found that the boards could be raised with but little difficulty in that cupboard, for the nails only fitted loosely and could be easily extracted. And thus, my dear Ellen, to be brief, it was there—as you learnt the night before last—that I concealed the dead infant!"

There was another pause; and this time tears did trickle forth from the eyes of Sarah Barron. At length she continued :—

"Soon afterwards I was summoned to the Continent, with my two young charges Lavinia and Emilia. I had previously written to the Viscount: he sent me a brief answer, pleading the pressure of business for the brevity of his communication—but concluding with the wish that I might enjoy all possible happiness; and this was expressed in a way as if it were a farewell he was taking of me. I wept bitterly; but my pride prevented me from writing to him again. Time passed on: I need not tell you, Ellen, how there have been moments when in the solitude of my own chamber I have wept bitter burning tears as I thought of my degradation and dishonour; for though the world was ignorant of my secret, yet in my own estimation—just heaven!—how low had I been brought! Let me however pass over all this. I come back to Tremaine Hall: and what happens? That all of a sudden everything connected with the haunted chamber is most vividly brought back to my recollection! Not that my memory could ever prove faithless," continued Sarah Barron bitterly, "to incidents of such a nature: but together with those recollections dread fears were also excited. What do you suppose were my feelings when the day before yesterday you said in the presence of Mrs. Tremaine, Charlotte, and myself, 'that there was a little discovery you were desirous of making, and that it referred to the cupboard in the corner farthest from the door?' Good heavens! what could you mean? This was the question I asked myself. Had anything transpired to make you suspect my secret? or did you purpose to investigate that nook through any other impulse? No! for you assured Charlotte that you had not learnt the particulars of the legend. I was half maddened—I knew not what to think or what to do. But a few hours later on that same evening I heard something which certainly relieved me from suspense, but which only enhanced my hideous terrors a

hundred-fold. I saw you and Charlotte retire into the window-recess of the drawing-room when we came up from the dining-room; and I felt convinced you would converse together of the haunted chamber. You did. I listened—I overheard all that passed. Oh, heaven! how cold the blood ran in my veins when you declared that Beda and yourself had fancied on the preceding night you heard sounds like the rattling of bones either in the cupboard or in its immediate vicinity! Ah, then I comprehended what was the nature of the discovery you had to make! And then too a thousand times more wild and horrible grew the terrors that haunted me:—my guilty conscience enhanced the veriest trifles into the most important circumstances, just as the microscope magnifies hairs into cables. What if you were really to discover bones in that cupboard? There would be an inquiry and an investigation—and anatomical evidence might prove that so far from the bones being those of a child placed there half a century ago in the time of Arabella Ravenscliffe, the date of those infant relics might be ascribed to a period of only four years back! And then methought that circumstances would so combine against me—tittles of evidence unobserved at the time would be remembered, collated, and amassed, to bring home everything unto myself! All these reflections swept maddeningly through my brain; and I gave myself up as one lost. I heard you ask Charlotte if she thought that what you had been saying together had reached my ears: I heard her reply that 'it was by no means probable, as my back was towards you and I was contemplating my two pupils Emilia and Lavinia?' But I had overheard every syllable; and no words can by any possibility describe the effect which your revealings to Charlotte Tremaine had produced upon my mind!'

"I can well understand it," I said, in a compassionating tone, and with a look of kindred sympathy; for how was it possible to help pitying the unfortunate young lady?

"Have you ever heard or read, Miss Percy," proceeded Sarah Barron, "or has it ever occurred to you, that when persons are driven almost to distraction and desperation by the imminence of some tremendous danger, they often have recourse to the most silly, absurd, and puerile means in the hope of warding it off? Yet such is the fact. And now, therefore, you will not be surprised to learn that a similar folly took possession of me in the midst of the mental desperation to which I found myself reduced. In a word, I thought to frighten you and Beda out of the haunted chamber. For this purpose I purloined the key: I knew that there was no bolt or other fastening whereby you could secure the door inside, and I did not pause to reflect whether you might care about the key being missed and ask for it—or whether you would take other precautions, such as by placing chairs or piling furniture against the door. Oh! you may judge how attenuated was my mind—how morbid was its condition, and how ridiculous were my ideas in the midst of their horrible distraction! If I had been calm and rational—if I had only possessed a glimmering of my wonted reason and common sense—I should have known that you, Ellen, were of all persons the least likely to be affrighted or scared by the bare suspicion of a ghost without taking some means to assure yourself upon the point."

"Do not dwell upon this subject, Sarah," I said. "Indeed, I can now understand it all! You entered the room in a white dress——"

"Yes—I stole in," rejoined Miss Barron, a visible shudder passing over her form; "and I beheld you both—yourself and Beda—kneeling down at the cupboard,—that cupboard in which lay the remains of my dead infant!"

Sarah covered her face with her hands; and now the tears gushed forth betwixt her fingers. I entreated her to be composed: I reminded her that if she thus gave way to the excitement of her feelings she might prevent the healing process in reference to her wound; and I also bade her recollect that Mrs. Tremaine and Charlotte might at any moment return to the room. These representations succeeded in inducing her to exercise a strong control over her emotions; and I left her with the promise that I would revisit her chamber soon after breakfast.

———

CHAPTER CXXIV.

THE WALK BY THE SIDE OF THE CANAL.

THE incidents of the preceding night had produced a most painful effect upon all the inmates of the mansion. That Sarah Barron was in great danger, was of course generally known; and as she was universally beloved, a gloom was thrown upon the spirit of even the humblest menial in the establishment.

After breakfast—when I was thinking of fulfilling my promise and returning to Sarah's chamber—I was informed by Charlotte, who had just been thither with her mother, that the patient had fallen into a deep sleep, and that the surgeon, who had again come to see her, had strictly enjoined that she should not be disturbed. I was glad of this opportunity of seeking fresh air—of being by myself, and giving way to my reflections without restraint. I accordingly rambled forth into the grounds; and I reviewed everything which I had heard from the lips of Sarah Barron. That she had been cruelly deceived by Viscount Ravenscliffe, was only too apparent: that her innocence and her confidence had been most shamefully taken advantage of, was beyond all doubt. But nothing could be done in her behalf! I knew that it was utterly ridiculous to suppose that an appeal to the Viscount would move him to do her an act of justice. And as I thus gave way to my reflections on the point, I could not help mentally ejaculating, "How many instances of aristocratic profligacy and heartlessness have come to my knowledge! And that name of *Ravenscliffe*,—does it not seem to be indissolubly associated with everything that is evil? Alas, poor Sarah! it might almost be considered for you a happy release if the hand of the assassin Marano shall have dealt thee thy death; for if thou livest on, it will be to deplore to the end of thy days the heartless treachery of one who bears the name of Ravenscliffe!"

There was another subject which occupied my thoughts; and this was one to which I have already alluded—namely, how I was to act in reference to the probable visit of Sarah's mother and brother to Tremaine Hall. But again was I bewildered by the conflicting ideas which were conjured up on this point; and I was utterly unable to arrive at any fixed and definite determination. Indeed, I was in the midst of my perplexing meditations on the topic, when I began to think that I had wandered far enough from the Hall; and that I ought to be retracing my way thither; for if poor Sarah Barron should awake, she might inquire after me, and she might possibly consider that it was unkind on my part to be absent when she had solicited my presence. Indeed, I had rambled farther than I had intended; and I was now pursuing a path which lay along the bank of the canal that had so recently overflowed. The particular spot where I was thus walking, was more elevated than elsewhere, and had not been submerged during the flood, so that it was now quite dry. I was just turning to retrace my way to Tremaine Hall, but my attention was suddenly caught by some object floating in the canal at a little distance. I looked again; and even before the idea had formed itself as it were in my mind, an instinctive shudder swept through me. Yes—it was a corpse that was floating in the water!

I swept my gaze around, and I beheld a couple of labouring men working at a little distance. I hastened towards them: they soon noticed me—and I waved my kerchief for them to come. I told them what I had seen; and they sped to the spot in the direction where I had beheld the body floating; but I myself remained at a little distance, for I had a horror of looking upon the dead. It naturally occurred to me that it was some unfortunate person who had been drowned during the recent floods; and I thought that it must be a gentleman, or at all events an individual of the middle class of life, for the garments which clothed the corpse were evidently of broad-cloth.

But though I did not approach the spot where the men were now wading into the canal to drag forth the dead body, yet I remained tolerably near in order to learn if there were any letters or cards about the person of the deceased that might establish his identity. In a very few minutes I saw that they were dragging the corpse up the bank, and I averted my eyes. A few more minutes elapsed, and then I heard footsteps advancing from behind; for one of the labouring men was now coming to speak to me.

"We have got him out, ma'am," he said; "and he seems quite fresh, as if he hadn't been in the water many hours. He looks quite the gentleman too——"

"You had better search the garments," I said, "to see if there be any papers or a card-case—also if there be any valuables; and you can let me know, for I will tell Mr. Tremaine—who, being a justice of the peace——"

"There's a gold chain round the gentleman's neck, ma'am," interrupted the labourer; "and there's a handsome watch in the waistcoat pocket. He looks like a foreigner."

"A foreigner?" I ejaculated: "and what makes you think so?"

"Because of the hair on the upper lip," answered the man. "What's the name of it again? My mate yonder called it——"

"A moustache!" I exclaimed. "But is the complexion of the deceased——"

"It must have been dark, ma'am, I should say by the look of it," replied the labourer. "He is a young man——"

"Then it may be the same!" I ejaculated, as a certain suspicion was every instant growing stronger and stronger in my mind. "Ah! unhappy wretch, if it were so!"

Conquering my repugnance to look upon the dead, I hastened towards the spot where the corpse lay. The first glance which I flung upon the countenance was sufficient:—it was that of Ludovico Marano!

Although I had for the last few moments suspected that this was the discovery I was about to make, yet did I experience a shock when it *was* made. I felt that the colour fled from my cheeks, and a cold shudder swept throughout my entire form. Guilty though the wretched man had been, and worthless as a member of society—nay, more than worthless—absolutely pernicious and hurtful, like a venomous reptile—yet was there something horrible in the reflection that one whom but a few hours back I had seen in the full vigour of life and health, should now be stretched—stiff, stark, and cold—a corpse there! And how came he by his death? Was it by accident or by suicide? I could not even form a conjecture.

"Cover the body up decently with something," I said to the men when they had given me an account of the effects found about its person; "and bear it to some neighbouring cottage or public-house. I will return to the Hall and acquaint Mr. Tremaine with the discovery."

Towards the mansion I accordingly retraced my steps, but in a far more hurried manner than when I had ere now strolled thence in a leisurely and thoughtful mood. The tidings I had to impart were quickly circulated throughout the mansion,—though I took care that they should be delicately broken to Charlotte, for fear lest there might be any lingering remnant of affection in her heart towards the unprincipled Italian who within the last few hours had ceased to become an item in this world's busy hive.

Before proceeding to touch upon any other subject, I will finish the episode in reference to Ludovico Marano. An Inquest was held in the afternoon of that same day at the public-house to which the corpse had been borne. Mr. Tremaine was under the disagreeable necessity of giving evidence on the occasion, and of stating that the deceased Ludovico Marano had at one time been a suitor for his daughter's hand, but that for certain reasons his addresses had been rejected. It was also mentioned in evidence how the Italian had stealthily introduced himself into Tremaine Hall on the preceding evening, and how he had dangerously wounded a young lady living in the capacity of governess beneath the roof. But Mr. Tremaine was not the only witness examined on the occasion in addition to the two labourers who had dragged forth the body from the canal. A fourth person gave important testimony, which served to guide the Jury in their deliberations ere coming to a verdict. I will here transfer to my own narrative the evidence of the witness thus alluded to, precisely as it appeared at the time in a Staffordshire newspaper:—

"My name is George Stokes, and I work for Farmer Bentham of Maypole Grange. I was at the *Three Compasses* alehouse last night until about half-past eleven o'clock; and then I left. To reach my cottage the nearest way is to keep along the bank of the canal on the further side from Squire Tremaine's grounds. Just as I reached the wooden foot-bridge, I saw some one leaning over the railing, and looking down into the water. I knew it must be a gentleman, because I could see he had good clothes on, and he had a gold chain that was shining in the starlight. I don't think he heard me approach, because when I stopped and said, 'Good night, sir,' he started and seemed quite bewildered. I could see his countenance plain enough, as the moonbeams were playing upon it. He had a moustache. I have no doubt the deceased was the gentleman that I thus saw on the bridge. To continue what I was saying, he seemed immediately to recover himself, and answering my salutation, he at once inquired whether the water was deep there? I told him it was. He asked how deep? I said that it might be about six or seven feet deep for at least a couple of hundred yards above and below the bridge. He asked me whether people who happened to be found drowned in the canal, were buried in a churchyard or in unconsecrated ground? I thought the question rather singular, and I told him so; but he said that he was a foreigner, that he did not know anything about the laws and customs of England, and that he was only asking for curiosity's sake. So I told him that if people were drowned by accident, they were of course buried in a churchyard. He then asked me if a person accidentally shot another with a pistol, whether the punishment would be death according to the law of England? I told him that if it was an accident there would be no punishment at all—or if so, only a very slight one; but that if there was any malice in the deed, it would be very different, although it might be made to appear that it was an accident. He then asked, 'Supposing a person aimed a pistol at one individual, but happened to hit another, what would be done to him?' I told him that I did not know much of the law, but that I should fancy a person in such a case would be treated just as any common murderer, because when he fired the pistol his object was to commit murder. But I thought all these questions so singular that I asked the gentleman who he was and why he was out at that late hour on the canal bridge. He told me that he was an intimate friend of Mr. Tremaine—that he was staying at the Hall—that he had been out to dinner in the neighbourhood—and that perhaps he had partaken of a glass or two more than usual. Of course this explanation seemed completely satisfactory; and I offered to see the gentleman as far as the Hall. But he only laughed, assuring me that he was not tipsy; and he gave me half-a-crown for my civility. He then went off the bridge in the direction of the Hall; and I continued my way along the canal to my own cottage."

After the evidence thus given, the Jury had but little difficulty in coming to a conclusion. It was clearly a case of wilful self-destruction, in order to avoid the legal consequences of a great crime which had been committed; and a verdict of *Felo de se* was returned. The corpse was buried in some obscure place, without funeral rites; and thus ignominiously terminated the career of Ludovico Marano. Charlotte Tremaine experienced a slight shock when the intelligence of his death was first communicated to her; but she quickly rallied—and she said that it would be a miserable affectation on her part if she were to seem to grieve another minute for one whom she had ceased to love, and had learnt to despise and almost to hate, from the very instant when she had first discovered that he was so utterly unworthy of her affection.

It was in the afternoon of the same day of which I have been writing, that I again found myself alone with Sarah Barron in her chamber. She was no worse since the surgeon had made his report in the morning—but on the other side, she was no better. She might sink or she might rally: her fate was at present scarcely within the range of prophecy; for if on the one hand the old adage applied, "that where there was life there was hope," yet on the other hand it was impossible to blind oneself to the fact that a straw thrown in the scale would turn it completely to her disadvantage. Her mother and brother had been sent for; and the medical man had recommended that her mind should be kept as tranquil as possible.

I was again alone, I say, with Sarah Barron. I sat down by the side of her couch; she took my hand—she looked plaintively into my face—she besought me "to grant her one more favour, in addition to the many boons she had already received from me." These were her own words; and I hastened to reply, "Rest assured, my dear Sarah, that if with propriety I can grant your request, it shall not be made in vain."

"Ah, my dear Ellen," she murmured, "there is a qualification in your answer! I know not whether you will consider my request to be fraught with impropriety; but alas! I fear that most probably you will do so! So no more upon the point! And yet," she added bitterly, "it were hard to die—my God! it were hard to die and to leave those bones——"

"Sarah!" I interrupted her "I comprehend what you mean! Yes!—now I understand you! Your request shall be granted."

A gleam of ineffable joy and gratitude overspread the poor young woman's countenance: she took my hand and pressed it to her lips. It was some time before she could speak; and at length she said, "If I die, Ellen, it will be in blessing your name! and if I live it will be to cherish the holiest sense of gratitude for all your goodness towards me. And Oh!" she added, "if anything can save my life, it is not the surgeon's skill, but it is the infusion of a balm into the gaping wounds of my heart! And this office of the ministering angel you are performing towards me!"

"Say no more, my dear Sarah," I replied. "During the coming night everything shall be done according as I may best interpret the wishes which I suppose to be floating in your mind."

And behold! during the night which followed, Beda and I again paid a visit to the haunted room. Upon this occasion Mrs. Tremaine and Charlotte were in total ignorance of our design: Sarah Barron only was acquainted with it. It was verging towards midnight when my faithful young dependant and myself stole into that chamber. It was not a pleasant task which I had undertaken to perform; but it was nevertheless with a mournful willingness that I entered upon it, because I knew that its fulfilment would infuse consolation into the soul of an afflicted fellow-creature. Beda and I raised the boards in the cupboard, and we collected a few particles of tiny infant bones; there were also the remnants of some garments in which the infant had been wrapped. We had brought with us a small box to receive these remains; and on leaving the haunted chamber, we stole down into the library. Thence we passed out into the garden; and choosing a secluded spot, we buried the box in the earth. It was under the shade of some lilac-trees now withered beneath the cold hand of winter, that we interred those remains; and on the following morning, when I described to Sarah Barron exactly what we had done, she wept softly and plenteously as she gave murmuring expression to the thought that the flowers would in the spring-time bloom over the spot where those relics lay buried.

In consequence of the exciting events which had occurred in reference to Ludovico Marano, I had not hitherto been enabled to carry out an idea which I had formed: namely, to speak to Mr. Tremaine in reference to the Wakefield family. But now I found leisure so to do; and in compliance with a hint I gave him to the effect that I wished to have some little discourse with him, he conducted me to an apartment where we were alone together.

"I believe, Mr. Tremaine," I said, "that the name which I am about to mention has been so unpleasantly mixed up with the traditions of your family, that it will not prove pleasant to your ears."

"You must either allude to the name of Ravenscliffe or Wakefield, my dear Ellen," answered Mr. Tremaine; "and if you have a special purpose in mentioning either, I am sure that it can only be a good one; and therefore will I endeavour to conquer all prejudice on the point."

"It is the name of Wakefield," I answered.

"A name that was once a proud and a great one in the Midland Counties," replied Mr. Tremaine. "Proceed, Ellen."

"An aunt of mine married a Mr. Wakefield," I continued; "and something has recently come to my knowledge which renders it of the utmost importance that I should obtain all possible information in respect to one particular point: that is to say, whether my deceased uncle Mr. Wakefield was a descendant of the great Warwickshire family."

"I had long believed the Wakefields to be extinct," answered Mr. Tremaine; "but even if it should prove otherwise, their claims could not possibly injure me. The quarrels between the Tremaines and the Wakefields were long ago settled in the Chancery Court. If there be any renewal of litigation, it must be between the Wakefields and the Ravenscliffes. Now, my dear Ellen, I am totally unable to afford any information towards the solution of the query which you have put to me; and indeed, I scarcely see how you are to obtain it, unless at a great expense and by searching parish registers—for as a matter of course you have failed at the very point where you must have set off——"

"I have as yet failed in nothing, my dear sir," I answered; "for the simple reason that I have attempted nothing."

"What?" ejaculated Mr. Tremaine:—"then you are inquiring about the Wakefields of Warwickshire, and you have not examined the registers at Embledon?"

"Embledon?" I echoed, struck with the coincidence that the name of this place which had at one time been so often uppermost in my thoughts, should now again be forcibly presented to my contemplation. "No! Are there any particular registers at Embledon?"

"Most assuredly," answered Mr. Tremaine. "You are not far from thence—only about thirty miles or so. You are welcome to take the travelling-carriage — and a pair of post-horses will speedily convey you thither."

"The business of searching the registers," I said, "may detain me more than a few hours: I might even be kept some days at Embledon. I will take a postchaise; and as it is really a matter of the greatest consequence that I should ascertain this point with the least possible delay, will you kindly excuse my absence for a short time——"

"Do as you like, my dear Ellen," interrupted Mr. Tremaine: "make this house your home—come and go as you think fit! You need mention your business to nobody: it is sufficient that you have something to do at Embledon for a few days. As for the travelling-carriage, you had better take it——"

"No—I would rather not," I answered. "It is my wish to transact this business secretly and quietly for the present; because if my inquiries should turn out to be unfavourable, then no one need know that any hope of a particular character had been entertained. Permit me therefore to travel by the less ostentatious means of a hired postchaise."

"Be it as you will, my dear Ellen," answered Mr. Tremaine; "and remember that if in any way I can assist you in your proceedings, you may command my services."

A valid excuse for leaving Tremaine Hall at that particular crisis, was what for the last four and twenty hours I had been endeavouring to find; and now it presented itself all in a moment. I should thus avoid the painful embarrassment of encountering Reginald Barron. A servant was despatched to a village in the neighbourhood where a postchaise might be procured; and by the aid of Mr. Tremaine I was enabled to make such excuses to his brother, his wife, and his daughters, for my sudden departure, as to prevent them from considering it to be associated with either strangeness or rudeness. I bade farewell to Miss Barron, earnestly expressing the hope that on my return at the expiration of a few days I should find her rapidly progressing towards convalescence; and I then took my departure, accompanied by the faithful Beda.

CHAPTER CXXV.

THE HUNTING PARTY.

WHEN we were seated in the postchaise together, I proceeded to examine the contents of the packet which I had received from Mrs. Sturton. I had previously looked over them at Tremaine Hall as well as at the hotel at Stafford; but I had found no baptismal certificates from the parish of Embledon. Now however that I examined some of the *memoranda* with greater minuteness than I had hitherto done, I found occasional references made to certificates which might be seen in the registers of marriages, baptisms, and deaths, in that parish. Thus Mr. Tremaine's information was confirmed: but still I wondered why amongst this packet of papers there should be such a complete absence of every possible document that could in any way connect the late Gerald Wakefield with the Wakefields of Warwickshire.

"I almost fear," I said to Beda, "that I am bent on a fruitless journey to Embledon; for if the registers there had been enabled to furnish Gerald Wakefield with certain certificates, they would doubtless be found amongst the contents of this packet."

"With due deference to you, dear Miss," replied Beda, "it does not at all follow. Mr. Gerald Wakefield may have lost certain certificates —or they may have been amongst other papers— or he may have known where to procure them so readily that it was quite as natural he should be without them as that you yourself, Miss Percy, are now travelling without yours."

"It is not quite the same thing, Beda," I answered, with a smile, "considering that Mr. Gerald Wakefield had to make out a particular lineage—which I have not. However, we shall see."

The postchaise drove on; and presently it entered, from a maze of lanes, upon the broad route which led direct towards Embledon and thence to Birmingham. At the expiration of about three hours and a half, after leaving Tremaine Hall, we reached the brow of a hill whence the first glimpse might be obtained of the little village which was situated in the depth of the valley. When first I had seen it exactly two years and three months back—namely, in the autumn of 1840—it was embowered in verdure, and the rivulet meandering through the vale looked like an irregular line of quicksilver. But now, in the middle of winter, the trees were denuded of their foliage—the hollow wind moaned through the skeleton boughs—and there was the ice-spell upon the stream. My heart swelled with emotions as I recollected that it was *there*—in that village—I first learnt that I had a father still living, and that I was clasped in the arms of that parent, for whom I had since done so much, and who had so completely repented of the misdeeds of his past life! I had now very few secrets from Beda; and the subject to which I have just alluded was known to her. She therefore comprehended why the tears were trickling down my cheeks: she took my hand and pressed it; she gazed affectionately upon me—and upon her own ebon lashes were the teardrops now hanging as if they were liquid diamonds. She loved me as if she were a sister: she smiled when I smiled, or she wept when I wept—there was a marvellous sympathy on the part of that beautiful young girl towards myself.

It was about three o'clock in the afternoon as we entered the village of Embledon. I had already told the postilion to drive to the principal tavern:

but I had however previously made up my mind not to stop longer at the miserable public-house which was so vividly depicted in my recollection, than should be necessary to procure a lodging at some respectable tradesman's house. But when the postchaise stopped, it was *not* in front of the public-house which I thus remembered: neither was it a miserable old man nor a blear-eyed woman who came forward to receive us. The spirit of enterprise had penetrated into Embledon since I was last there; innovation and improvement had rendered the place barely recognisable. For there, instead of the public-house, stood a small but neat and well-built inn; and instead of a crazily swinging sign, with a daub to represent a green dragon, there were the words indicating the name itself in gilt letters along the *façade* of the building. The landlord and landlady, who made their appearance, were a young couple of most respectable demeanour, and neatly dressed; and when Beda and myself were introduced into a private apartment, we at once abandoned the idea of seeking lodgings elsewhere. The dusk was setting in, for it was in the very midst of winter; and therefore I determined to take no step in the business which had brought me thither until the following day.

In the morning, after breakfast, I proceeded to the vicarage, attended by Beda; and I inquired for the Reverend Mr. Croft. Again, for the second time, did I find myself in the presence of the short stout gentleman with a very red face, who exercised the spiritual control over that district: and the moment I gave him my card, he exclaimed, "Miss Percy! Miss Percy! Why, surely I have had the pleasure of seeing you before?"

"Yes," I answered: "two years ago I called upon you for some little information."

"I remember!" he ejaculated. "You wanted to see another Mr. Croft who resided in the village?"

"And now, sir," I hastened to interrupt him, "my business is of quite a different character."

I explained it; and he said, "You shall see the registers immediately. It will give me much pleasure to assist your researches to the utmost of my power. I was told by my predecessor, when I first came to Embledon about twenty years ago, that there used to be in his time a constant hunting and searching after particular entries connected with the great Wakefields of Warwickshire——"

"But during *your* time, sir," I interjected, "I presume that spirit of inquiry has completely died away?"

"Yes, in reference to the Wakefield family," rejoined the clergyman. "I do not remember that any one has been to me for such a purpose before to-day. But come, Miss Percy — and you shall enter upon your investigation at once."

Still accompanied by Beda, I proceeded to the church; and there several hours were passed in looking over the registers—but without any satisfactory result. At length I gave up the investigation, convinced that it was useless to pursue it: but I contrived to recompense Mr. Croft for his trouble by placing five guineas in his hand and begging that he would dispose of the amount in any way that he thought fit for the benefit of his parish. When I was again at the *Green Dragon*, I deliberated with myself upon the course that I should now pursue. For reasons that are known

to the reader, I did not wish to return immediately to Tremaine Hall; and I had nothing to keep me any longer at Embledon. I thought of returning to London and writing some efficient excuse to my friends in Staffordshire. Upon this course I resolved; and I ordered a postchaise to be in readiness on the following morning after breakfast, to take Beda and myself to Birmingham, whence we might proceed by the railway to the metropolis.

But how true is the proverb that "while human beings propose, heaven disposes!" Who could have foreseen or anticipated what was to occur to alter the plans which I had formed? Let me however pursue the thread of my narrative in due order.

The morning dawned, gloomy, misty, and damp; and as the landlord, who acted as his own waiter, accompanied his wife to bring in some of the materials for breakfast, he remarked that "the scent would be capital," and that "the fox-hounds were to meet at the Whitestone Edge close by." Little interested indeed was I on such a subject; but for courtesy's sake I made some remark; and the landlord proceeded to observe, "I daresay the Viscount will be with them to-day. He is greatly attached to the sport! The Earl his father used to be one of the best riders in the whole county, I've heard: but ever since he had a paralytic stroke about eighteen months ago, he has not crossed a horse."

Beda and I glanced at each other; for the garrulous landlord little thought how much we could tell of the Earl of Carshalton's sudden illness in the railway train, and that instead of being paralysis, it was apoplexy with which he had been smitten at the time. However, we said nothing; and having finished our breakfast, we took our seats in the postchaise. Away we went; and Embledon was soon three or four miles behind us. All of a sudden we heard the postilion give a loud and joyous "Halloa!"—and glancing out of the window, we beheld a corps of hunters in their red-coats dashing across an adjacent field at a tremendous rate. In less than a minute another cry burst from the postilion's lips: but this time it was one of terror—and the vehicle dashed on at a quicker pace than before. I looked forth from one window—Beda from the other; and we perceived that some accident had occurred at the turnpike-gate a little way ahead. We were speedily upon the spot; and the truth was quickly ascertained. There were cross-roads at that place: and the foremost individual of the hunting party had in a moment of ungovernable excitement, or else of most preposterous bravado, ridden his horse at one of the gates. A terrible accident was the consequence: the adventurous rider was thrown; and the utmost consternation prevailed amongst all who had gathered upon the spot. But who was the individual that had thus become the victim of his own foolish vanity or mad audacity? It was Viscount Ravenscliffe!

Could it be possible that within so short a space after I had heard the narrative of his treachery to Sarah Barron, I was destined to become the witness of what might be looked upon as heaven's chastisement for the nobleman's misdeeds? At least such was the reflection that struck me at the very instant I learnt the name of the personage to whom the accident had occurred.

"Open the door!" I exclaimed to the postilion, who had dismounted from his saddle.

I alighted, followed by Beda; and one of the hunting party immediately exclaimed, "Good heavens, Miss Percy! is it you?"

This was the young Baronet whom I had met at Tremaine Hall, and to whom I have before alluded. It happened, moreover, that there were two or three other gentlemen amongst the hunting party who knew me by sight; and they saluted me with the utmost courtesy.

"Is his lordship much injured?" I asked, advancing towards a group in the midst of whom the sufferer now was.

"He is unconscious—but life is not extinct," was the reply. "We must remove him home at once."

"This postchaise is at your service," I exclaimed. "Is Carshalton far from hence."

"Only about a couple of miles," replied the Baronet. "Ah, Miss Percy! if we might ask such a favour of yourself, and your young attendant here——"

"Speak! what can I do?" I exclaimed. "But suffer me to see the unfortunate Viscount! Ah! you have done well! you have loosened his neckerchief—you have bathed his countenance with water! Have you any vinegar?" I inquired, thus addressing myself to the keeper of the turnpike.

Vinegar was almost immediately forthcoming: I moistened my kerchief with it, and placed it upon the Viscount's forehead.

"No limbs seem to be broken," said the Baronet. "I think the injury is done to the head."

"The sooner he is now got home the better," I observed. "Tell me candidly, what were you just now about to ask of myself and my companion?"

"That you would have the kindness, Miss Percy," responded the Baronet, "to accompany the Viscount to Carshalton. Ladies can minister more effectually to the wounded and the sick than we uncouth beings of the ruder sex. Besides, the postchaise is roomy enough——"

"If it is desired that we should accompany the Viscount," I answered, "most assuredly we will do so."

The inanimate form of the nobleman was conveyed into the postchaise: Beda and I entered also, and bestowed such ministrations as we were enabled to afford during the short journey. We bathed his temples and chafed his palms—but all in vain; we could not restore him to life—and yet the vital spark was not extinct. At length we drew near to a spacious mansion—the gates of a park were thrown open by the porter at the lodge—and the man was sadly afflicted upon hearing what had happened to the Viscount. As far as this point the chaise had been accompanied by the hunting party, whose sport was turned into mourning by the occurrence: but now the young Baronet requested that the postchaise should proceed in advance, so that the anxiety of the inmates of the mansion need not be prematurely excited by beholding a large cavalcade advancing through the spacious park.

In about ten minutes the vehicle stopped in front of the Earl of Carshalton's country seat: the hall-porter came forth—and I communicated to him in a few hurried words what had occurred.

"For heaven's sake, ma'am, go up first of all and break the news to my lord and her ladyship! Her ladyship is a great invalid——"

"I know it," I interrupted him: for it was not the first time that I had performed the painful task of communicating evil intelligence to the Countess of Carshalton.

I was shown upstairs to the drawing-room, where I found her ladyship alone. The reader will recollect that I have before described her as a thin sickly-looking woman; and she was now about fifty-two years of age. She was habitually cold, reserved, and distant; but on the few occasions that I had seen her, she had always unbent towards me on account of my conduct to the Earl when he was seized with apoplexy in the railway train. However, since the date of the marriage of her son Lord Frederick with Juliet I had not seen the Countess of Carshalton: and I did not exactly know how she might now receive me,—whether she might think that I had been an accomplice in persuading, inducing, or compelling her younger son to enter into that alliance—or whether she might be ignorant of the main details. But it was of little consequence (I thought within myself) what opinion she might entertain of me; for all her ideas, poor woman! would soon be concentrated upon another object.

It was somewhat to my surprise that the moment I entered the drawing-room the Countess of Carshalton started up from her seat, exclaiming, "Dear me, Miss Percy! is it indeed you? It is an age since I have seen you! Did you think there was a coolness on our part towards you on account of a certain circumstance? Alas! if there were, rest assured that all such feelings were buried in the grave of my poor dear Frederick! And I should add that your name has been most favourably mentioned to me in reference to the closing incidents of my poor boy's career!"

I knew that the Countess was alluding to her elder son, the Viscount, as the one who had made favourable mention of my name to her; and I said, "Alas, my lady, it grieves me again to be the bearer of evil intelligence!"

"No, no! you do not tell me so!" she said, her pale face becoming still more ghastly in its pallor, and her thin spare form quivering with a strong spasm that shot through it. "Speak!—quick! Keep me not in suspense! The Earl—my husband——"

"No, my lady," I said: "it relates not to his lordship. But I am distressed——"

"My son! my son!" shrieked the unhappy Countess, as a suspicion of the truth flashed in unto her mind. "He has been out hunting——"

"Prepare yourself," I interjected, "for something terrible: but put your faith in heaven, for the evil may not be beyond redemption!"

"My son! where is he?"—and never shall I forget the wild thrilling anguish with which the cry pealed forth.

I now told her everything; and the unhappy mother precipitated herself down the stairs to meet her first-born. The Viscount had been borne into the hall: the servants were collecting—consternation, dismay, and confusion were already spreading throughout the mansion. The Earl of Carshalton, who had been walking in the grounds, was speedily fetched; and nothing could exceed

the grief of both the distracted parents, as they beheld the almost hopeless condition of their son. The Viscount was conveyed to his chamber; and medical attendance soon arrived—for some of the hunting party had ridden in several directions, to order the medical men of the district to proceed to the mansion, so as to ensure the quick arrival of at least one of them. And now came that interval of stupendous suspense—that fearful period—during which surgical skill was employing itself to detect the extent of the injury, so that a report might be made accordingly. That interval of suspense was as terrible to the afflicted parents as is the deliberation of a Jury to the trembling culprit who stands in the dock. But at length the report of the surgeons was made—and, alas for those distressed parents! it was utterly hopeless.

No. 97.—ELLEN PERCY.

CHAPTER CXXVI.

CARSHALTON.

YES—utterly hopeless was that report. The surgeons spoke conscientiously—but it was with pain and grief that they did so. The Viscount had sustained a most terrible fracture of the skull; recovery was impossible: his days—indeed his very hours might be numbered! But parental affection cherishes hope until the last:—indeed it hopes on in desperation's despite;—and it therefore invokes every possible agency which can be thought of to bring about the issue it desires. In the present case expresses were sent off to Birmingham that the most eminent practitioners of that town should be despatched to Carshalton; and the speediest measures were likewise adopted to procure the first physicians from the metropolis.

I should observe that so soon as some semblance of order began to arise out of the chaos of agitated feelings and proceedings engendered by the accident, I intimated to the Earl and Countess that I was about to bid them farewell. But her ladyship entreated me to remain. She declared that it seemed as if it were destined by heaven that I should be mixed up with the affairs of the Carshalton family. I had saved the life of the Earl in the railway-carriage—I had behaved with kindness in reference to the closing incidents of her son Frederick's career—and I had now been upon the spot to minister to the elder son when it was the will of heaven that a fearful accident should overtake him. It was in this strain that the Countess of Carshalton spoke; and it was impossible I could prove deaf to the entreaties which were so vehemently and passionately addressed unto me. The Earl likewise implored me to remain; and drawing me aside, he whispered in an excited manner, "If the worst should happen, who would be here to sustain the Countess if you go away? For heaven's sake stay, Ellen!—stay, I beseech you! I do not know how it is, but it seems as if you were a being who appears amongst us when your presence is most necessary!"

"I will stay, my lord," I answered: "but it is on condition that you permit me to share the duties of a nurse with the Countess, whose strength is not equal to the exigencies of such a position."

"Do what you will," rejoined the Earl, "for I know that whatsoever is done by you must be right."

I sat with the Countess by the couch of her perishing son: I breathed in her ear language that was more consolatory than hopeful, and which appealed to her sense of religion rather than to the more worldly side of the question. In short, without giving any shock to her feelings, I delicately and cautiously prepared her for the worst that might happen. The physicians came from Birmingham: they could recommend little more than the surgeons of the district had already accomplished. The day passed—and in the evening a couple of celebrated physicians arrived from London: but these in their turn could recommend little more than their predecessors in the sick-room had already done. Throughout the night did I share the duties of nurse with the Countess of Carshalton. The Earl would have remained with us; but the medical men had insisted upon his retiring to rest. As for the unfortunate Viscount, he lay in a state of unconsciousness of what was passing around him,—now and then moaning in a low plaintive manner, which indicated that he suffered some pain—occasionally opening his eyes, but not with the faculty of sight, or at least not to exercise it with the power of recognition—but only to look vacantly and with glazing eye-balls.

"Good heaven!" murmured the Countess to me, as towards morning the patient seemed to be sinking, "what a frightful catastrophe if this old and time-honoured house should cease to exist!—if the mighty race of the Carshaltons should become extinct! Alas, alas! it is hard that both

sons should go!"—and here the voice of the unhappy Countess was lost in suffocating sobs.

I saw that the affliction of a mother was not altogether unblended with a certain degree of family pride, and that while the Countess of Carshalton was deploring the probable loss of an only remaining child, she thought also with grief and bitterness of the fact that the name of Carshalton might die out of the peerage. But to do her justice, the more worldly-minded phase of her reflections did not last very long—or at least did not display itself visibly; for all her ideas seemed to be again concentrated in the course of a few minutes upon the sufferer who was perishing before her eyes. She whispered to me her alarm that he was sinking: I expressed a similar fear—and the physicians who had been kept in the house, were called up.

Two hours later—while the grey misty dawn of a wintry morning was struggling to make its way through the clouds of darkness that seemed to cling tenaciously to the heaven of this hemisphere, it was considered expedient to summon the Earl of Carshalton from his chamber; and on his arrival in the room of his dying son, I made a movement to retire. But the Countess, catching me by the hand, threw an appealing look upon me. I knew what she meant—and I remained. It was a painful scene—Oh! most sad and painful, to witness the grief of those parents who only six months back had been bereaved of one of their sons, and who were now doomed to sustain the loss of the other! But I will not dwell upon the subject—suffice it to say that at about nine o'clock in the morning of the day following the accident, Viscount Ravenscliffe breathed his last!

The Countess of Carshalton fell back fainting into my arms; and I bore her from the chamber. For hours she was like a distracted creature: she gave way to the wildest lamentations—and I feared her reason would be altogether wrecked. I had never passed through so painful a scene; but I exerted myself to the very utmost in order to tranquillise and console her; and at last I succeeded to a certain extent. To be brief, during the next four or five days I was almost constantly with the Countess; and when I was not in attendance upon her, my faithful Beda took my place. We were to her as two daughters might be to their mother; and the Countess deeply felt the attentions which we thus bestowed upon her. As for the Earl, he was terribly cut up: he remained much secluded in his own apartment—but on several occasions he said that he should not thus withdraw himself from the society of his wife, if he were not fully aware that I was much better enabled to soothe, console, and tranquillise her mind than he himself could possibly be.

I wrote to Tremaine Hall to inform my friends there of the reasons of my protracted absence; and I requested Charlotte to write and let me know how Sarah Barron was getting on. By return of post I received communications from the Hall: Sarah's mother and brother had arrived there; and a very favourable turn had taken place in the condition of the wounded young lady.

By the request of the Earl and the Countess of Carshalton, I wrote several letters to the most intimate friends of the family, informing them of the accident which had caused the death of the Viscount, and inviting them to attend the funeral. In the course of a few days, therefore, several guests arrived at Carshalton; and the preparations for the funeral were conducted to a very considerable extent under my superintendence; for both the Earl and Countess seemed more and more inclined to trust everything to me. At length, exactly one week after the accident, the funeral took place; and the remains of Viscount Ravenscliffe were consigned to the family vault in Embledon Church.

It was the day after the funeral—the guests took their departure—and I was seated in the drawing-room with the Earl and Countess of Carshalton, when the latter said, in that low half-whispering voice which she had adopted ever since the catastrophe, "I wonder whether there were any papers of importance in the drawers or writing-desk of—of——"

She could not bring herself to allude more significantly to her deceased son, but as a matter of course both the Earl and myself understood very well whom she meant.

"Some one must see to it," said the Earl; and he glanced towards me.

"I think, my lord," I said, in a tone of kind and mild remonstrance, "that you, as the father, ought to perform that duty. It is hardly one which I could venture to undertake."

"True! true!" said the Earl: and he quitted the apartment.

He was absent for about an hour; and on his return it was easy to perceive by his countenance that he had passed through a very painful ordeal. But it also struck me that the process had left something more than a mere general impression on his mind: I fancied there was something he wished to communicate, but that he scarcely knew how to shape the prefatory words.

"Do you wish to speak to me alone, my lord," I asked.

"No—it is not necessary that I should speak to you alone, Ellen," he replied. "It is a subject which I think ought to be mentioned in her ladyship's presence; for if there be any means of making an atonement or a reparation wheresoever any human being may have suffered through our lamented son——"

"Speak, speak!" said the Countess: "what do you mean? Ah! doubtless amongst the private correspondence of—of——"

"Yes—I have discovered a clue to something which must be investigated," resumed the Earl. "Tell me therefore at once, my dear Ellen," he continued, turning towards me,—"do you know anything of a young lady named Sarah Barron, who was once governess in the Tremaine family——"

"She is still governess there," I answered: and now I all in a moment comprehended what discovery it was which the Earl had made in reference to his deceased son, and why he spoke of reparation and atonement.

"Ah! then you know her?" he exclaimed.

"But this is the secret of her honour which I am confiding to you, Ellen!"

"It is no secret to me, my lord," I replied. "I am already well acquainted with all the particulars of that unfortunate connexion which subsisted four years ago between your lost son and Sarah Barron."

We had some further conversation on the subject; and at length the Earl said, "It is for you, Ellen, to tell us how we can possibly make any reparation——No! that is scarcely possible! I will therefore ask how we can make any *atonement* on the lost one's behalf?"

After some little reflection I suggested a means—which I need not however specify in this place, as I shall shortly have occasion to take more particular notice of it.

Another week elapsed; and at the expiration of that period I received fresh communications from Tremaine Hall. There was a very kind letter from Charlotte; and there was one from Sarah Barron herself, written as a proof that she was progressing towards complete convalescence. She informed me therein that the first intimation she had received of the death of the Viscount, was by hearing Mrs. Tremaine and Charlotte allude to it when they were in her chamber: she pretended to be asleep at the time—and thus she avoided the betrayal of any emotion. In the course of the billet which she thus wrote me, she alluded most emphatically to the kindness of Mr. and Mrs. Tremaine in permitting her mother and brother to continue so long at the Hall, that she might enjoy their society; and she added that inasmuch as she was now so completely out of danger, those beloved relatives of her's were about to take their departure.

I was glad to receive this concluding piece of intelligence; for circumstances rendered it desirable that I should return to Tremaine Hall, and I could not have possibly thought of proceeding thither with the chance of meeting Reginald Barron. But now I no longer hesitated; and taking a temporary leave of the Earl and Countess of Carshalton, I set out, accompanied by Beda. During the journey we reviewed everything that had lately happened; and amongst other topics which arose, was the letter I had written to Jane Parks. More than a fortnight had elapsed since she must have received that letter; and no answer had reached me. I felt assured that she was incapable of an ungrateful neglect; and therefore I concluded that she had removed from the lodgings to which I had addressed the communication—or else that she was absent from the metropolis. Beda inquired what I intended to do in reference to the investigation of the Wakefield concerns?—and I told her that it was my purpose to speak candidly on the subject to Lord Carshalton, when, after the lapse of a little time, his mind should have so far recovered its natural tone that it would not be indelicate on my part to broach such a topic.

It was about two o'clock in the afternoon when Beda and I arrived at Tremaine Hall; and most cordial was the greeting which I experienced from Mr. and Mrs. Tremaine, who hastened forth to receive me. Charlotte and her sisters had all gone for a walk, as the day was beautifully fine: Colonel Tremaine had returned to London, whither some particular business had called him. I inquired after Sarah Barron; and Mrs. Tremaine was about to give some answer, when the young lady herself appeared upon the landing above, — saying, "I heard your voice, Miss Percy, and I could not help coming forth to welcome you!"

"Oh! what will the doctor say, Sarah," cried Mrs. Tremaine deprecatingly, "if you thus expose yourself to the draughts on the staircase?"

"I will join you, Sarah," I exclaimed; and I hastened up the flight to the first landing.

Miss Barron embraced me; and we passed together into the back drawing-room where, as it appeared, she had been accustomed to sit for the last two or three days, since she was enabled to leave her own chamber.

"I am glad that we immediately find ourselves alone together," I said; "because I have something of the greatest importance to communicate to you."

Sarah turned pale; and becoming much agitated, she said, "Is it possible that the Viscount thought of me in his last moments?"

"No, Sarah," I replied; "he never once regained his consciousness from the moment when he was hurled from his steed. But not to keep you in suspense, everything is known to his afflicted parents——"

"Everything?" echoed Sarah, with a start.

"No, no—I do not mean everything to the very uttermost detail! But the Earl and Countess know that you became a mother, Sarah—and that the offspring of your fatal connexion with their son did not survive its birth. Two or three letters of your's to the Viscount were discovered amongst his private papers——"

"Oh! is my secret safe?" demanded the unfortunate young lady.

"Could you dream that it would be otherwise," I exclaimed, "in a quarter where I possess any influence, or on the part of those parents who have now to deplore the cruel treachery of which their son was guilty towards you? Oh! you will be convinced of their generosity and their goodness, Sarah," I continued, "when I tell you that they have studied and striven to make all the reparation and atonement which under the circumstances may be possible. The very day after the remains of their son were consigned to the tomb, and while the hand of affliction still lay so heavy upon his soul, the Earl of Carshalton devoted his best attention to your case. He wrote several letters to influential members of the Government —others to the Portuguese Ambassador in London——"

"Oh!" ejaculated Sarah, as an idea of the actual truth now struck her: "is it possible that there is a chance of my poor mother recovering the fortune which it broke my father's heart in vainly seeking?"

"Yes, Sarah," I replied; "there is not merely the chance—there is the certainty! Here is a letter from the Portuguese Ambassador to the Earl of Carshalton, informing his lordship that he (the Ambassador) recognises on the part of his Government your mother's claim——"

"Oh, what joy! what joy!" ejaculated Sarah: "my poor mother will be rich and independent!"

"I have not quite told you all," I resumed. "The Portuguese Ambassador furthermore declares that within three months from the present date the whole amount, of ten thousand pounds sterling in English money, shall be forthcoming, provided that your mother consents to waive all claim to any accumulations of interest. He does not deny the right to such accumulations; but the Portu-

guese treasury is at a low ebb; and by asking too much——"

"Oh, my dear friend!" cried Sarah, "if my dear mother were here, she would go down upon her knees to pour forth her gratitude! But she will be here presently——"

"What?" I ejaculated—for I was literally startled at her words: "is your mother here still? I thought she was to have taken her departure for the south of England——"

"Yes—but Mr. and Mrs. Tremaine," interjected Sarah, "insisted upon her remaining a few days longer."

"And your brother?" I asked: and I felt that a species of cloud came over my countenance as I put the question.

"He also is here," rejoined Sarah. "But, Ah, how strange you look! Now I am convinced that it was not mere fancy on my part——"

"What do you mean?" I asked.

"To tell you the truth, Ellen," continued Sarah, "I was surprised when we first met at the Hall, that you never said a single syllable to me in reference to my mother or brother, and that not once did you even so much as allude to the picture— although heaven knows it gave us all the greatest pleasure to forward it to you at the hotel at Petersfield!"

"Ah!" I said. "Then you were aware that the picture was sent?"

"Aware of it?" she exclaimed: "how could I have been otherwise? But, Oh! stranger and stranger still become your looks! Tell me, Ellen —you were not offended?—for Reginald acted with the concurrence of his mother and myself."

"Did he tell you," I asked, in a cold tone—for I saw that the crisis of explanation was inevitably approaching,—"did he tell you in what manner I acknowledged the receipt of that picture?"

Sarah reflected for a few moments; and then she exclaimed, "Now that I bethink me, he said very little on the point——simply that you had written him a letter of courteous acknowledgment——"

At this moment the door of the back drawing-room opened, and Mrs. Barron made her appearance. I am not one of those persons who visit the sins of individuals upon their relations; and especially in this case I felt assured that the mother ought to be held irresponsible for the misdeeds of her son, even as I had considered the sister free from any taint entailed by a brother. I therefore welcomed Mrs. Barron with the utmost cordiality; and she expressed her delight to meet me again.

"But Oh, my dear mother!" exclaimed Sarah, "you know not what happiness is in store for you! You cannot possibly form a conjecture with regard to the immensity of the obligation under which you lie to Ellen Percy!"

Mrs. Barron bent her wondering looks upon me —while her daughter continued to exclaim, "You are now rich, dear mother!—for, thanks to our kind friend here—yes, thanks to the interest which she has exerted on your behalf, your claims are recognised!"

"Oh, is this true? is this possible?" murmured Mrs. Barron; and as a faintness came over her, she sank upon a seat.

At that very instant it struck me that I heard a movement at the door. I glanced in that direction: it was standing ajar—and methought that the sound of a supressed sob was now wafted to my ear. I instantaneously conjectured what it was: I was anxious to avoid a scene; and exclaiming, "Look to your mother, Sarah!" I abruptly quitted the room.

My suspicion was fulfilled; for on the landing outside I found myself face to face with Reginald Barron. He had listened at the door: and nothing could now exceed the air of profound contrition, of remorse, of shame—aye, of the deepest humiliation, which his countenance wore. He seemed like one who was ready to sink into the earth; and most assuredly he felt as one who must at the instant have wished that he might be snatched away from my sight!

I beckoned him to follow me into the front drawing-room, where there happened to be no other persons at the time; and when we were there together, he stood before me, all trembling, like a culprit.

"Mr. Barron," I said, "you have doubtless heard of the change which has taken place in your mother's circumstances?"

"I have heard enough to convince me," he said, sinking upon his knees, "that you, Miss Percy, are an angel, and that I have been the vilest and most wicked of mortals!"

"Rise, sir—rise, I command you," I interrupted him. "I need no compliments nor flatteries from *your* lips! I love your sister, and I respect your mother. For *their* united sakes I have interested myself in a certain quarter: and I have succeeded in obtaining the recognition of your mother's rightful claims. Now, Mr. Barron, you will leave Tremaine Hall with the least possible delay. You may make your own excuse—which perhaps will not be difficult considering that the sooner your mother repairs to London to sign the necessary documents at the Portuguese Ambassador's mansion, the sooner will it facilitate a settlement of the matter. But depart, I say!—it is my command!"

"And it shall be obeyed, Miss Percy," interjected Reginald Barron. "But tell me—tell me, I beseech you—has my sister spoken to you in reference to that portrait?"

"Your sister, Mr. Barron, suspects that there is something strange or peculiar in my bearing when your name is mentioned. I have given no explanations."

"And you will give none?" ejaculated Reginald vehemently. "Oh! I beseech you not to betray me! My dear sister Sarah is so high-minded and well-principled!—she is virtue's self! she is purity personified!"

"Enough, Mr. Barron," I interrupted him. "I have not betrayed you to your sister—and I will not betray you if you will depart immediately."

"In one hour, Miss Percy," he rejoined, "my presence shall be no longer a source of annoyance to you beneath the roof of Tremaine Hall. But one word before I depart!—and this one word you *must* hear, for it is nothing that can be construed into an insult!"

"No—I will hear nothing from your lips," I exclaimed. "Depart, sir!"

"Whatever evil were to happen to me," cried Reginald, his cheeks flushing and his eyes flashing with a strange glow,—"even though you were to expose all my past villany to my mother and my sister—yet will I proclaim that which is now uppermost in my thoughts! For you are the noblest-hearted of women; and though your own great talents have given to your name an undying reputation, yet shall your beauty also be immortalized on the painter's canvass! This is the task to which I now devote myself: the portraits you have already seen, are as nothing in comparison with the *one* grand work of art which I feel myself capable of achieving! And when that task shall be accomplished, death may come—and consumption, the inexorable enemy that is now working slowly but surely within, may crown its own process of destruction!"

Having thus spoken, with a volubility and an enthusiasm which defied all interruption, Reginald Barron rushed from the apartment, leaving me in a singular state of bewilderment; for I knew not whether to look upon him as more madman than hypocrite. And yet, notwithstanding the strong reasons which I had for regarding him as an unprincipled dissembler, it was impossible to shut my eyes to the fact that there was more or less the fervour of sincerity in what he had just been saying—as if there were times when the intuitive promptings of genius rose far superior to the dictates and impulses of evil passions.

I now hastened to meet Charlotte and her sisters, who had just returned from their walk; and they were all delighted to see me again. Presently it became known that Mrs. Barron and her son were on the point of immediately leaving the Hall for the purpose of proceeding to London; and the reason given was legitimate enough. Through my kindness, it was said, Mrs. Barron had procured the recognition of her rights, and she must now lose no time in adopting certain measures which this important *first step* rendered requisite. Mrs. Barron departed, having warmly embraced me as the authoress of the prosperity which she was speedily destined to enjoy: but I managed to avoid another meeting with Reginald, and he had the good taste not to seek it.

After dinner I again found myself alone with Sarah Barron for an hour or so. She gazed at me in a peculiar manner; and then she said, diffidently and hesitatingly, "My poor brother, Ellen, is deeply penitent for the offence that he gave you when at Petersfield. He has now told me everything——"

"Indeed!" I ejaculated, as a vivid blush crossed my countenance. "He has told you everything?"

"Yes—everything, I repeat," rejoined Sarah,—"how he called upon you at the hotel and avowed his mad presumptuous love,—how, when you gave him an answer which he ought to have at once taken as definitive, he persisted in pleading his suit until his conduct passed the bounds of courtesy——in short, dear Ellen, he told me how you commanded him to leave your presence. And then all night long he wandered about like one distracted."

"Ah! he has been telling you all this?" I said, now comprehending that Reginald had in reality only told a portion of the tale, and had given it more or less a colouring to suit existing circumstances.

"Oh! it is no wonder that you should have been

offended with him, Ellen," continued Sarah ; " for I know how enthusiastic is his disposition, and I can easily comprehend how he may have suffered the glowing fervour of his love and admiration and worship to carry him away ! But believe me, there is not a better principled young man—no, nor a loftier-minded one on the whole face of the earth ! It is not because he is my brother——"

" Enough, my dear Sarah !" I said : " we will not pursue this topic."

She instantaneously changed the subject ; and nothing further occurred between us on that occasion to require mention in the pages of my narrative.

When I retired to my own chamber for the night, I could not help mentally ejaculating, " What singular beings are we mortal creatures !—how capable of dissimulation is mankind ! and how little able are some individuals to read the hearts of others ! Here are a brother and sister who entertain the highest opinion of each other, and yet both of whom are more or less fallen creatures ! The brother places his sister on the very highest pedestal of virtue :—Oh, if he could draw away the veil and read the secrets that lie behind, what would he think ! How bewildering would be his consternation if he were to learn that this sister whom he deems so pure and chaste, is in reality a degraded and dishonoured young woman ! Or, on the other hand, if she herself could but penetrate into the mysteries of her brother's heart, and read all the dark passions which agitate therein—if she could fathom all the profundities of his soul and discern the iniquities of which he is capable,—how terribly would the blow strike her ! and what a fearful shock would her confidence in human nature experience ! Oh, after all, it was a wise dispensation of the Creator that it should be thus difficult for the eyes of one individual to penetrate into the heart of another !"

Having stayed two or three days at Tremaine Hall, I returned to Carshalton, accompanied by Beda. I found the Earl and Countess impatiently awaiting my arrival ; for it seemed as if they could scarcely now exist without me ; and such indeed was the assurance which I received from their lips. They spoke to me of living with them altogether : they vowed that I had been to them as a daughter during the period of their bitter distress ; that it was therefore as a daughter they loved me, and they besought that I would never think of again returning to the stage. I was almost on the point of seizing that opportunity to speak to the Earl and Countess in reference to the Wakefield matters : but I thought it was yet scarcely time, because their thoughts were naturally still full of the immense bereavement they had so recently sustained. I thanked them for all the kind things they said to me ; but I gave no pledges in respect to taking up my abode altogether with them. I treated the subject with what may be termed a species of delicate evasiveness.

It was on the day after the return to Carshalton from Tremaine Hall, that the incident which I am about to describe took place. It was the hour of noon : Beda and I were together in a sitting-apartment which was specially appropriated to my own use when I chose to retire thither ; and we were discussing some of the most recent events that had occurred, when the sounds of a vehicle advancing towards the mansion, reached our ears. On glancing through the window, we

beheld a postchaise dashing along the avenue ; and in a few moments the equipage drew up at the front entrance.

" It seemed to me to contain but one person," I said ; " and that was a lady."

" The same idea struck me," answered Beda.

We retired from the window, thinking that the arrival could in no way concern ourselves ;—and I should observe that by the position of the casement it was impossible to obtain a view of any person who might alight at the front entrance. Scarcely a minute had elapsed when the door was thrown open ; and who should make her appearance but Jane Parks ! With an ejaculation of joy I bounded towards her ; for that joy was twofold. In the first place her presence promised to clear up the mystery of her protracted silence in reference to the letter I had written to her ; and in the second place I was smitten with the hope that she had some good tidings to communicate.

" My dear Ellen," she exclaimed, embracing me fervidly, " did you think that I had neglected you, or that I had proved ungrateful ?"

" No, no ! I felt convinced that you had not !" I replied. " I thought that you might have been absent from London—or that you had changed your lodgings——"

" Neither the one nor the other !" interrupted Jane. " I received your letter at the proper date——"

" And perhaps you answered it," I said, " and your letter may have miscarried ?"

" No—I did not answer it by letter," she rejoined. " I am answering it now personally ! Oh, I will not keep you in suspense ! I have obtained all the information you desire ; and heaven grant that the result may turn out as my father now feels assured that it will !"

" What mean you, dear Jane ? what mean you ?" I inquired, with feverish impatience.

" Look, Ellen !—look ! Read for yourself !" she ejaculated ; and she produced a small packet sealed and directed to me.

I tore it open : a few minutes sufficed to glance over the documents it contained ; and throwing my arms round my friend's neck, I embraced her warmly,—murmuring, " Dearest Jane ! you have rendered me a service which I never, never shall forget !"

" Oh ! did I not owe you the deepest, deepest debt of gratitude, Ellen ?" exclaimed Miss Parks ; " and did I not rejoice when the arrival of your letter appeared to furnish me with the means of testifying my devotedness towards you ? My father declared to me, on perusing your letter, that he thought he might possibly discover a clue towards the elucidation of the two points that had to be cleared up. He remembered to have heard your grandfather say something in reference to the Wakefields many long years ago ; but it had lain dormant in his memory until your letter revived the recollection—and he promised me to set to work at once. To be brief, he did so : but the task was a longer one than he had at first anticipated. And Oh ! should have written to you, Ellen !—I kept blaming myself day after day for keeping you in suspense : but I thought to myself that if my father should succeed, it would be such a happy, happy moment for me when I might surprise you——"

"And you have done so, Jane!—and this happy moment you are enjoying!" I interrupted her: "for you have indeed rendered me an immense service! Look, my dear Beda!" I cried, turning towards the faithful girl: "look at these documents!—and inasmuch as you know everything connected with the matter, you may be enabled to judge of their importance."

"I have been to Tremaine Hall to seek you, my dear Ellen," continued Jane Parks: "you were not there—the Tremaines pressed me to stop—they offered to send the packet to you hither—but I would not linger a moment—I was resolved to give it into your hand! And you see how careful I was in respect to its contents: for I addressed the envelope to you, in case by any accident the packet itself should be lost. There is one word which I must add," said Jane, her voice sinking to a low deep whisper;—"and this is that my father gave himself up to the task with the most unwearied assiduity: for, Oh! it was a relief to his mind, Ellen, to be enabled to do anything that might prove his gratitude towards you!"

Some more conversation passed between myself and Jane: but it is unnecessary to dwell any longer upon the subject—for I am now about to transport the attention of the reader to another apartment within the walls of that spacious mansion.

It was a couple of hours later, on this same day of which I have just been writing; and I was now seated with the Earl and Countess of Carshalton. We three were alone together; and I communicated to my noble host and hostess the circumstance of a young lady-friend of mine having arrived to see me.

"Your friends must be our friends, Ellen," said the Countess; "and I pray you to bid this young lady remain with you as long as she may think fit, or as you may choose to have her."

"She must return to London to-morrow," I replied; "but in the interval she will avail herself of your ladyship's hospitality——"

"No, Ellen," said the Countess; "that is too formal a term. This house is your home; and you must make your friends welcome here. For have you not promised that you will henceforth live with us altogether——"

"I do not think that I exactly gave such a promise," I answered, with a smile. "Not but that I am deeply grateful——"

"Ah! I noticed that Ellen would not give any promise!" exclaimed Lord Carshalton. "But she shall not leave us—unless indeed——"

He stopped short, and looked at me: then he slowly turned his eyes upon his wife, and said, "Ellen is a very handsome young lady; and it is almost impossible that her hand and heart should be disengaged."

"I never thought of this!" said the Countess, with a mournful look. "God knows, I wish you all possible happiness, my dear Ellen!—but already does the bare idea of ever losing you smite me with the force of a new affliction!"

"It is true," I said, while I felt a blush flitting across my countenance, "that my hand is engaged. But——"

"Speak, Ellen! speak!" ejaculated the Earl of Carshalton. "If you are only waiting until your intended husband—whoever he may be—shall acquire a sufficiency to maintain you both, that cause of delay need exist no longer. The Countess and myself owe you an immense debt of gratitude: we never can altogether pay it—but we may at least acquit ourselves of a part of the obligation."

"My cousin," I said, "to whom I am engaged, is not in England. He is gone to America."

"To America?" cried the Earl. "Then it may be yet some time before he will return to this country—and we shall not lose you quite yet!"

I saw that the features of the Countess brightened up somewhat—that is to say, as much as they possibly could, considering how deep a shade of melancholy had settled upon them.

"What is the name of your cousin?" inquired the Earl; "and what profession does he follow?"

"His name is Henry Wakefield," I replied.

"Wakefield?" echoed the Earl. "How singular!" and he looked significantly at his wife. "What I mean is this, my dear Ellen," he continued, again turning towards me, —"that the young man whom we are already prepared to welcome and to love for your sake, bears a name the mere mention of which has been wont to grate harshly against my nerves. Nevertheless I may thank heaven that this kind of prejudice has for a long time past been dying out——"

"I am rejoiced to hear it, my lord!" I replied; "for my cousin Henry could not help the circumstance of having been born with the name of Wakefield, any more than he can help being descended from a particular family of Wakefields."

Both the Earl and the Countess started, as if they fancied that it was not a mere random remark which I had just made, but a significant hint which I had purposely thrown out.

"Do you mean to say," ejaculated the Earl, "that your cousin is descended from the great Wakefields of this county?—a race which we considered to be extinct, when Gerald disappeared some two and twenty years ago!"

"But Gerald Wakefield had a brother named James," I remarked.

"Ah! was it so?" cried the Earl. "I never knew much of Gerald Wakefield: I never even believed that he had the power of substantiating his claims. But he had a brother, you say?"

"Yes, my lord," I rejoined: "and that brother left behind him a son—my cousin Henry."

"If I had entertained ten thousand prejudices against the name of Wakefield," said the Earl, "I would crush and stifle them all for your sake, Ellen!"

"And I echo the sentiment," said the Countess of Carshalton, as she caressed my cheek with her thin pale hand.

"I am all the more rejoiced," I said, "to hear such generous language flow from the lips of you both, inasmuch as I have now the most important matters to submit to your consideration, and to which all that I have been saying for the last few minutes has been merely intended as a preface."

I proceeded to narrate to the Earl and Countess of Carshalton everything which I had heard from Mrs. Sturton at Stafford; and it was now for the first time that they learnt how the stealing of their son Frederick by the gipsies two and twenty years ago, was an act far more significant than they could possibly conjecture at the time; and how, instead of being an isolated piece of wickedness, it was in reality a link in a tremendous chain of iniquity, designed and fabricated by Gerald Wakefield. Nor less did the Earl and Countess now become aware of the fact that the obligation under which they lay towards Beda's deceased parents was infinitely greater than at the time they had conceived, inasmuch as the Robinsons had not merely proved the means of restoring to them their lost child, but likewise had prevented murder's work from being done! It was with a deep and awe-felt interest that the Earl and Countess listened to these details; and when I concluded the narrative which I had originally received from Mrs. Sturton's lips, I produced the packet which she had given me. All the documents were carefully looked over by the Earl of Carshalton; and finally I displayed the additional papers which Jane Parks had that same day brought me. The Earl produced from his strong-box in the library a quantity of old documents, to which he referred, and betwixt which and those that I had placed before him he instituted a comparison.

But it is not my purpose to dwell on this subject at the present stage of my narrative. Suffice it to say that on the day following the one of which I have been writing, the Earl and Countess of Carshalton accompanied me to London; for the matter which I had submitted to his lordship's consideration, was considered to be so momentous as to render it expedient that he should immediately consult his solicitor. We brought Jane Parks up to London with us; and I need scarcely add that the faithful Beda did not remain behind in Warwickshire.

Before I separated from Miss Parks, I took an opportunity to say to her, "You have rendered me a service, Jane, which may perhaps be immense; and believe me when in all sincerity I declare that I consider your father has done somewhat towards making an atonement for the past."

The grateful young woman pressed my hand fervidly; and she departed to her humble lodging, happy at being enabled to bear such a message from myself to her sire.

CHAPTER CXXVII.

AT HOME AGAIN.

The Earl and Countess of Carshalton would only permit me to return to my own house on condition that I promised to spend the greater portion of every day with them; and that when circumstances and leisure would permit, I would return with them to their country-seat in Warwickshire. I was glad to get home again: I had passed through a period of considerable excitement for the last few weeks, commencing with the date of the episode which so vitally concerned Lady Kelvedon. I therefore needed repose and rest; and moreover I had many letters requiring my attention. On calling upon Lady Kelvedon, I found that she was progressing most favourably — that the bloom was coming rapidly back to her cheeks, and that the appearance of emaciation was yielding to a healthy plumpness of the form.

At the expiration of a few days Lord Carshalton's attorney made a certain report to his noble patron in reference to the matters which had been submitted to him. This report possessed all the importance which I had foreseen; and it was now considered expedient that my cousin Henry Wakefield should be sent for. It was five months since Henry and my father had taken their departure for the great Western World. I had heard from them when they arrived at New York; and they had subsequently written from two other stages of their route towards that El Dorado whereof they were in search. It was now necessary to send off a messenger after them, as I knew not how to address a letter in such a manner that it would reach them:—indeed I was waiting for fresh intelligence from them to learn their exact whereabouts before I could forward another written communication. But now, as I have hinted, it was expedient to act promptly; and a messenger, alike intelligent and trustworthy, must be despatched in pursuit of my sire and my cousin. Who was to go? The Earl's lawyer had suggested one of his own clerks: but I did not like the proposal: I wished the emissary to be a person who had some feeling of interest in the matter apart from mere business-views. Indeed, I seriously thought of undertaking the voyage myself; and I went so far as to speak to Beda on the subject and inquire whether she would like to accompany me.

"Yes, dear Miss," she exclaimed; "I would go to the end of the world, either with you or without you, in order to serve you! But it is impossible that you can embark on such an enterprise! I know who will do it!"

She glided away from my presence: she would not heed me when I called her back—for I more than half suspected what she was now on the point of doing. She sped to her own chamber, put on her bonnet and shawl, and rushed past me on the stairs where I vainly endeavoured to intercept her.

"Beda! Beda!" I cried; "do nothing rash! be not precipitate, I implore you!"

She now gained the front door: she looked back at me with a smile of good-natured triumph on her lips; and then she disappeared from my view.

Nearly two hours elapsed, at the expiration of which time Beda returned into my presence, introducing her lover William Lardner.

"There, dear Miss!" she exclaimed; "there is the messenger who will go for you across the Atlantic, and who has sworn to me that he will waste not a moment in accomplishing the mission which you are about to entrust unto him!"

"Yes, Miss Percy," said William Lardner, with a certain decisiveness of look and tone; "Beda has told you the truth! I am ready to depart!"

The tears came into my eyes, for my heart was filled with emotions at this demonstration of the enthusiastic devotedness which the young couple entertained towards me.

"No! no!" I said; "I cannot accept such a self-sacrifice on your part, William! Besides, your master—or rather I may call him your *friend*, Sir Robert Temple——"

"Everything is settled, Miss Percy!" interrupted William.

"Settled?" I ejaculated, with astonishment. "You do not mean to tell me that you have already spoken to Sir Robert Temple?!"

"I have not only spoken to him, Miss Percy," rejoined William Lardner; "but I have received his permission to undertake this voyage."

"And let me add," interjected Beda, "that I was present on the occasion; and though Sir Robert grumbled and swore very much at first, yet when he heard that it was on your behalf, Miss Percy, he changed all in a moment and gave his assent. So William does not lose his situation."

"And never, never shall he be a loser," I cried, "for such generous conduct as that which he is now displaying towards me! It cuts me to the very quick to think of separating you, because I know how dear you are to each other! But inasmuch as I see that you are resolute,—you, William, in undertaking this enterprise—and you, Beda, in permitting him to undertake it,—I shall not refuse

to avail myself of the great and signal service which may thus be rendered. And, Oh! on your return, William," I added, "it will perhaps be in my power to display my gratitude more signally than—than——But no matter!" I ejaculated, thus suddenly checking myself. "You both know that I am incapable of ingratitude—and what is more, that I have your interests sincerely at heart!"

In the evening of that very same day William Lardner took his departure, having received from me the minutest instructions how he was to proceed, together with a liberal sum of money for his expenses. He was also charged with pecuniary subsidies for my cousin and father, as I knew not how they might be situated in this respect. I did not witness the parting between William and Beda: but for this much I can vouch, that when Beda joined me half-an-hour after her lover was gone, she wore a look that expressed something more than even a calm fortitude: there was a veritable happiness in it—for the noble-minded, devoted girl was rejoiced at being enabled to display her love and affection towards me. And thus was it that William Lardner set off on his enterprise!—set off with the most willing heart, and with a sentiment of honest pride at finding himself looked upon as the most trustworthy person whom I could possibly find for the important mission that had to be accomplished. I need scarcely add that I wrote a very polite letter to Sir Robert Temple, thanking him for his great kindness in suffering his favourite attendant thus to take so long a leave of absence on my account. The very next day the old nabob called upon me, with the assurance that he was only too happy to be enabled to render me a service; and he remained about an hour in conversation,—discussing at the same time a bottle of my old Madeira, despite the urgent counsel of his medical adviser, Doctor Strychnia, that he should allowance himself in respect to alcoholic beverages.

It was on the second day following the departure of William Lardner, that on calling at Carshalton House at the West End of the town, I found the Countess was alone,—the Earl having gone to his solicitor's on some business. Her ladyship appeared very low-spirited and mournful: I had fancied that for the few previous days she had begun to rally somewhat; but I was now grieved to observe that she was as distressed and desponding as within the first week of her bereavement. Placing myself by her side on the sofa, I took her hand and besought that she would continue to exert a Christian fortitude in respect to the heavy affliction under which she was suffering.

"It is impossible, my dear Ellen," she answered, "that I can ever think of that severe dispensation of heaven without being reminded at the same time of my obligations as a Christian. Oh! the loss of a beloved child, Ellen, teaches the sternest lessons! It makes me reflect whether I have done my duty in many, many ways;—and now—I will confess it—there is a regret in my mind—a remorse —I scarcely know how to express myself—but it is a dread lest there were duties which I have left unfulfilled!"

"Ah, my dear Lady Carshalton," I said, looking earnestly up into her countenance, "if I dared venture to hope that your mental regards are now fixed in one particular direction——"

"Is it possible, Ellen," cried the Countess, with a start of surprise, "that you have fathomed what was passing in my mind? Oh! when I think of him whom I have lately lost, I think also of the poor boy who went before him!—and then, Ellen, my heart is ready to break as I remember how harsh was the conduct which the Earl and myself pursued towards him—how inexorably we refused to answer his letters——"

But here the Countess stopped short as she burst into an agony of weeping; and I, taking advantage of this moment of tender weakness on her part, exclaimed entreatingly, "Oh! if such be your feelings in respect to your lost son Frederick, why not make some little atonement by bestowing your kindness on the wife whom he has left behind him?"

"And do you think—do you think, Ellen," asked the Countess of Carshalton, in a low and scarcely audible voice, "that your friend Juliet would now receive any demonstrations of kindness from those who have hitherto treated her with so much scorn and contempt?"

My heart bounded with joy as I exclaimed, "Will you permit me, my dear Countess, to be the means of conveying an expression of kindness from the Earl and yourself to Lady Frederick Ravenscliffe?"

"Yes—do so," said the Countess. "And now no more, my dear Ellen! My heart is relieved of a load; but the very process of so relieving it is calculated to overpower me with emotions. Trust to me when I declare that the Earl will approve of the step which I am now taking."

When I returned to my own house, I wrote a letter to Juliet; and in the evening of the following day she made her appearance in Great Ormond Street. She had lost no time in obeying the summons contained in the letter: she had taken a postchaise—and attended by her maid, had come up to London. It was nearly two months since I had seen her. Yes—it was nearly two months since the accident had occurred to the Duchess of Ardleigh opposite River House. The reader must have begun to fancy that I had altogether lost sight of that episode; but we will now revert to it again. During the last few weeks I had received several letters from Juliet as well as from Mary Glentworth: I was therefore fully acquainted with all that had taken place at River House since I was last there; and the reader shall now be similarly enlightened in his turn.

When I had given Juliet a cordial welcome, and warmly expressed my delight at seeing her once more in Great Ormond Street, I inquired after Mary Glentworth. I learnt that she was quite well, and had sent the kindest messages to me. She was now within two months of the date at which she might expect to become a mother: Mr. Singleton the surgeon had been made acquainted with her secret; but Juliet assured me that it might still pass unsuspected by the world as far as Mary's personal appearance was concerned.

"She is happy and in good spirits," added Juliet: "she sketches forth in her mind a thousand bright plans for the future—and she unbosoms all her secret thoughts to me. She has likewise shown me the letters which she has received from the Marquis of Dalrymple, and which have been sent through your hands. They are replete with a manly affection; and I only hope that this generous-hearted young nobleman is not misinterpreting his own feelings, and that he will never repent the step which he has so solemnly engaged himself to take."

"That likewise is the aspiration which often goes up from my own heart," I said, "on behalf of Herbert Dalrymple and Mary Glentworth? But now that we have begun to talk on those topics you shall tell me everything concerning which I have any questions to ask, before we touch on other matters. Had you any suspicion that the intellect of the Duchess was giving way?"

"Not the slightest for three whole weeks," answered Juliet. "As I wrote and told you, her Grace progressed most favourably; and the medical men soon pronounced her out of danger. She appeared to conceive a strong fancy for Mary: she spoke as if she were quite sensible of Mary's unwearied attentions towards her——"

"But she never alluded to her son Herbert, I think you said," I inquiringly remarked.

"No: the Duchess never alluded to the Marquis—at least not in Mary's presence. It must have been from either a delicate motive, or else because she thought that everything was absolutely and positively at an end between the Marquis and Mary. Indeed there was everything to encourage this supposition on her part. The abrupt departure of Herbert so very speedily after the accident—the circumstance that he did not return—and then the fact that Mary herself never breathed his name nor made the slightest allusion to him in the presence of the Duchess——"

"Yes," I said; "all these circumstances were well calculated to impress her Grace with the idea that everything was at an end between them, and that their hearts had received a shock in respect to their first love, from which no recovery was possible. And thus the Duchess may have conceived that it was from the purest and most disinterested feelings of kindness that Mary proved so attentive by her bedside, alike by day and by night——"

"Until all of a sudden," added Juliet, "the unfortunate Duchess of Ardleigh became incapable of any rational reflection, and her mind was entombed in darkness, like a person visiting a sepulchre where the lamp abruptly goes out."

"And thus," I said, still in a tone of inquiry—for though I was previously acquainted with the main facts, yet there were many little details which it had been impossible to convey through the medium of epistolary correspondence,—"and thus the intellect of the Duchess did not give way by degrees, but broke down suddenly as it were?"

"Yes: and the medical men," replied Juliet, "declared that they seldom witnessed so abrupt a catastrophe in the psychological sphere. I remember that I entered her Grace's bed-chamber a little before midnight, to assure myself that she wanted for nothing: she then appeared as sane and lucid as you are now, my dear Ellen! An hour afterwards Mary Glentworth came knocking at my door, entreating me to hasten to the Duchess at once; for that she was like a mad woman. I went, and found her Grace raving in the arms of the nurse, who was scarcely able to hold her. After a while she became tranquillized; but her reason was gone. Although it was between two and three o'clock in the morning, I thought it was only consistent with propriety to send off for the Duke at once. You know he had taken up his quarters at the Ship Hotel at Dover? He certainly lost no time in coming to River House; but as he crossed the threshold, he exclaimed 'that if her Grace had lost her reason, that was the very reason why it was no use to send and disturb him!' I do not know whether he meant to make some pun or to play upon the words: but it struck me that his conduct was characterized by the most wretched bad taste—and I could not help administering a very sharp rebuke."

"He is heartless as well as foolish and thoughtless," I observed. "And then it was upon this occasion, I think you told me in one of your letters, that he and Mary met for the first time since the accident?"

"Yes: they met at last," said Juliet; "and the Duke first called her 'Mary'—then 'Miss Glentworth'—and then said he was bewildered in what

terms to address her, but that he should write up on the morrow and consult a friend of his——".

"Mr. Peaseblossom?" I interjected.

"Yes," rejoined Juliet, "that odious Pease blossom, who did make his appearance a couple o days afterwards, when it was determined to remove the poor Duchess to the Continent, and place her under the care of some eminent physician in the South of France."

"And then Herbert sped to Dover," I said, "to see his poor mother? He wrote me a letter to that effect; but he promised faithfully to keep his vow and not call at River House to see Mary."

"And that vow was kept," observed Juliet. "I think I mentioned in one of my letters to you that Mary herself displayed the utmost fortitude, and did not once express a desire to see Herbert, nor a regret that he should so strictly adhere to his own resolution and abstain from calling on her. But of course you know that Herbert sent her a letter and a very handsome present of diamonds through me?"

"Yes," I said: "I heard it from three distinct sources. You wrote and told me of it; Mary mentioned it in her letters; and Herbert himself penned me a few lines to say what he had done, and to express the hope that the proceeding would not incur my displeasure. Indeed this was scarcely possible; for inasmuch as I value poor Mary's happiness—and as I see that this is now entirely dependent on the fulfilment of Herbert Dalrymple's pledge to make her his wife—I am rejoiced at every additional testimony of his love and devotion. But was it possible that the poor Duchess proved completely unconscious of Mary's attentions towards her at the very last moment—I mean when she was being borne from the house into the carriage that waited to convey her to Dover?"

"The Duchess of Ardleigh's look," responded Juliet, "was as vacant as that of a child! She knew no one. I repeat, my dear Ellen, what I have before said,—that it seemed as if her intellects, once so strong, had all been shattered in a moment. Only conceive the once brilliant, the superb and haughty Duchess of Ardleigh, being reduced to the condition of a helpless idiot! I only know of one spectacle that is equally remarkable at the present time; and that is," added Juliet, "that the Earl and Countess of Carshalton should have bowed so low beneath the yoke of calamity as to acknowledge the ex-danseuse of the ballet as their daughter-in-law!"

There was a slight bitterness in Juliet's tone; and I hastened to say, "We will discourse presently on that topic, my dear friend. We have not quite done with the other subject. You saw the Marquis of Dalrymple at Dover?"

"Yes. I accompanied the Duchess," continued Juliet, "to the Ship Hotel, by the Duke's particular request. The young Marquis was fervid in his expressions of gratitude towards me on account of the attentions I had shown to his mother; and I saw that he was filled with deep emotion when I told him how Mary Glentworth had passed the greater portion of every day and night for three whole weeks by her Grace's couch. The Duke made a very long speech in acknowledgment of his own gratitude; and then he bade Mr. Pease-blossom say something likewise: but I hastened away, and thus lost the speech of that most erudite personage. I think I mentioned in my last letter that the Duke sent me a beautiful gift of jewellery from Paris, accompanied by a note: but I am certain that it was Herbert's delicate taste which selected the present and dictated the *billet*."

"I have now to inform you, my dear Juliet," I said, "that this very day I received a letter from the Marquis of Dalrymple, in which he tells me that he fears his mother's is a hopeless case. The physician in the South of France has begged that the Duchess may be conveyed to Genoa, to be placed under the care of an eminent practitioner there. Accordingly, the family were about to set off for the kingdom of Piedmont at the moment when Herbert Dalrymple was closing his letter."

"The brain of the Duchess," said Juliet, "must have sustained a very peculiar shock from the accident which occurred. But now, my dear friend, let us talk of your own affairs. You quite amazed and surprised me when you wrote and told me of the circumstances which induced you to send off for your cousin Henry Wakefield. How singular that you should now be so intimate with the Carshaltons that they almost regard you as their daughter!"

"But they are not the less ready to receive *you* with open arms, my dear Juliet," I said, "and to greet you as their daughter. You are silent——you do not answer me?"

"I came to London, my dear Ellen," she said, "in compliance with your summons; and I will still further obey your wishes by accompanying you into the presence of the Earl and Countess of Carshalton. But I cannot forget how I have been treated by them,—ignored, scorned, contemned—looked down upon as the obscure ballet-dancer who dared to marry a peer's son!"

"All this is true, Juliet," I said; "and you might now take a signal revenge by refusing to go to that nobleman and his wife to assuage the pangs of remorse in their hearts! But you are incapable of such conduct, Juliet!—you would not seek for such poor and mean revenge as this!"

"No—not for worlds!" she enthusiastically exclaimed. "I will go with you, dear Ellen, when you think fit: I will speak kindly to them—I will prove docile and dutiful in my conduct towards them, in all respects save one——"

"And that one respect?" I asked.

"That I will receive no bounty nor gift of any kind at their hands—that I will not place myself under the slightest obligation to them! I am not rich—but I am independent; and never will I sacrifice this independence to the caprice of those proud aristocrats who disdained and spurned me when perhaps their countenance would have been considered kind and advantageous."

I could not possibly combat the justice which pervaded Juliet's remarks; and I therefore made not the attempt. I now inquired concerning Mr. Norman: Juliet answered that he was still upon the Continent, where he purposed to remain some two or three months longer, as he found that his health was improved as well as his spirits.

"And it is fortunate," added Juliet, "that my father does purpose to absent himself thus much longer:—otherwise he might be returning to England just at the very time when his presence at

River House would be particularly inconvenient so far as Mary Glentworth's secret is concerned."

Juliet was dressed in half mourning; and she looked exceedingly handsome. It was now exactly seven months since the death of her husband Lord Frederick Ravenscliffe by means of the tub of corrosive fluid; and she again wore her hair in ringlets—the style which best became her. I have so often alluded to her superb style of beauty that I need not reiterate any details on the point: but I may content myself with simply observing that I had certainly never seen her look better than she did on the present occasion.

After dinner I proposed to Juliet to visit the Earl and Countess of Carshalton that very evening; for I had promised her ladyship to lose no time in bringing Juliet to her after her arrival in London.

"I leave myself entirely in your hands," replied Juliet, with the most good-natured affability; "and I am ready to accompany you at once."

I ordered the carriage to be gotten in readiness: we soon took our seats therein; and we proceeded to Carshalton House. The moment the front door was opened, a footman stepped forward to escort me, as usual, to the apartment where the Earl and Countess were seated; and it never struck me to inquire whether they were alone and disengaged, inasmuch as I took it for granted that such would be the case, because they had so studiously refused all society since their bereavement. Presuming therefore as a matter of course that Lord and Lady Carshalton would be found alone in the drawing-room, I followed the domestic thither, Juliet being with me. The door was thrown open, and my name was announced. I led Juliet forward: the Earl and Countess were there—but there was a third person present. This was a tall, handsome, dark-complexioned young man, about thirty years of age—fashionably dressed, but with the most elegant taste—and having altogether a distinguished look. I stopped short on perceiving the stranger; but the Countess of Carshalton at once came forward, saying, "Welcome, my dear Ellen!"—and then with much emotion, she added, "And a kind welcome to you also, Juliet!—*dear* Juliet! as you must permit me to call you."

The Countess kissed Juliet's cheek: then the Earl came forward—and he greeted her with a similar ceremony.

"I need not tell you, Count," said Lady Carshalton, turning towards the tall dark-complexioned gentleman, "that this is Miss Percy; for you were observing to me just now that you had seen her a year ago on several occasions."

"And I am therefore all the more delighted to have the honour of forming Miss Percy's acquaintance," said the Count, with a polite bow; and I noticed that he spoke the English language fluently, with but a very slight accent.

I observed likewise that he had given a slight start on catching the first glimpse of Juliet's countenance; and he was now surveying her with some degree of attention—but with a manner of the most perfect respect.

"And this, Count," said Lady Carshalton, "is my daughter-in-law, whom I think you have also seen before——Lady Frederick Ravenscliffe."

At the same time the Countess took Juliet's

hand, and with the most lady-like composure presented her to the foreign nobleman, whom in due course she introduced to us as Count Teleki. I immediately recognised the name as that of a Hungarian noble who frequently visited the British metropolis, and who I knew moved in the very best circles of fashion. It was evident that in Juliet he had at once fancied he recognised the lately celebrated *danseuse*; but nothing could be more politely respectful, nor more consistent with the breeding of the polished gentleman, than the manner in which he bowed to Juliet. It seemed as if it were quite sufficient for him that a lady should be introduced beneath that roof and under such auspices, in order that he should at once receive her as an acquaintance on an equal footing with himself. In a few minutes he retired; and then the Countess of Carshalton hastened to whisper in my ear, to the effect "that the Hungarian nobleman had been a very intimate friend of her lately deceased son the Viscount, and hence the exception which was made in his favour from the rule which excluded all other visitors from within the threshold of Carshalton House."

Turning from me, the Countess proceeded to take Juliet's hand again; and making her sit down by her side, she said in a voice that was tremulous with emotion, "You are welcome, my dear girl, beneath this roof!"

Juliet faithfully fulfilled the promise which she had made to me: she received all the endearments and caresses of the Earl and Countess of Carshalton with a species of affectionate duteousness. The Earl smoothed down her dark hair: the Countess surveyed her with attention, and evidently seemed surprised that she was so remarkably handsome as she really was. They had both of them seen her on the stage, but neither had ever beheld her so close as they now were. Indeed, Lady Carshalton subsequently told me that she had not preconceived the idea of so handsome a young woman; much less had she fancied that any ballet-dancer could possibly be so lady-like in her manners and so genteel in her deportment.

"My dear Juliet," said the Earl, after some conversation on general matters, "we are meeting this evening as if everything had always been complete friendliness between us. Let us suppose that it was so. Here is something which I hope you will keep as a memento of the affectionate regard which from this day forth will be entertained towards you by the Countess and myself."

At the same time the nobleman produced a casket, which he presented to Juliet. At first I trembled for what the result might be, when I recollected the positive declaration she had made to the effect that she would not be placed under an obligation to either the Earl or the Countess:—it was therefore a relief to my mind when I saw her take the casket with a calm unruffled expression of countenance. In the same mood too was it that she opened the casket; and it was somewhat deliberately that she surveyed its contents. They consisted of several costly jewels and brilliant gems: there were necklaces, and ear-rings, and bracelets, and brooches, and three or four rings. Juliet's survey of this splendid assortment might have lasted for about two minutes; and I thought to myself, "Is it that her heart has relented towards this noble couple? or is it that she is

dazzled by the appearance of those jewels?"—and I was not altogether unjustified in the latter suspicion, for Juliet had a slight tincture of vanity about her—but perhaps no more than was inevitably associated with the character of an eminently handsome young woman who from the very nature of the profession which for a while she had exercised, had been the object of a thousand flatteries and adulations.

But I was wrong in supposing that Juliet's eyes were riveted on the brilliant contents of that casket, for either of the reasons which had sprung up in my mind. With her beautifully-shaped fingers she selected a ring: it was a valuable one, though the very plainest of the set; and she said, "My lord, I accept this with duty and with gratitude. But I beg to decline the remainder of the splendid gift with which your goodness tempts me."

"Decline it?" ejaculated the Earl: and the Countess also gave a quick start. "Why so?" he asked, in the kindest and most conciliatory tone.

"Because, my lord," she responded, in a low calm voice, "I am not yet out of mourning for your son; and I do not therefore wear jewellery."

"Oh! but you will keep the casket," he exclaimed; "and when the time shall come, you will wear the jewels."

"No, I thank you, my lord," she rejoined. "I am living in a very quiet and retired manner—I see no society—and I have no need nor desire to embellish myself."

"But a young lady like you," said the Countess, now mildly and softly interposing, "receives such gifts as these, and keeps them as mementoes or as private property, even if she do not wear them."

"Your ladyship will not take it ill of me," answered Juliet, firmly and decisively, but yet with the utmost respect, "if I decline to receive anything but this one ring:"—and she placed it upon her finger.

The Earl and Countess looked annoyed as well as sorrowful; and I saw that they more than half suspected Juliet's motive. They exchanged rapid glances; and then they flung their eyes upon me; but I bent my looks downward and said nothing.

"Well," cried the Earl, somewhat abruptly, "I see that we must become better friends together than we are at this first interview!"

"I do not think, my lord," answered Juliet, "that we can become better friends than we are at present:"—and there was likewise a significancy in this observation as well as in the preceding ones.

Again the Earl and Countess exchanged looks of annoyance; while I bent a glance of entreaty upon Juliet; and she hastened to exclaim with enthusiastic fervour, "You love my dear friend Ellen; and no amount of affection which you may shed upon her can possibly be too great!"

"At least, my dear Juliet," said Lady Carshalton, "you will come and stay with us a few days?"

"I should be willing to obey your ladyship," was the answer; "but I can only allow myself a sojourn of two or three days in London—and these I must devote to my dear friend Ellen. Besides, I am in haste to return to my own house near Dover, where I have another dear friend stopping, and whom I cannot long abandon."

"Then you will come and see us again before you depart?" said the Earl; and now it was with a certain coldness that he spoke.

"I will come and pay my respects to your lordship and her ladyship," replied Juliet, "before I leave London."

There was then an awkward pause—a pause which every one felt to be embarrassing enough. At length Lady Carshalton suddenly exclaimed, "Would you have the kindness to ring the bell, Ellen?—and we will have coffee."

The tray was accordingly brought in and handed round; but Juliet declined to take either tea or coffee. Lady Carshalton pressed her with more earnestness than I could have thought that one of her naturally cold and reserved disposition could have possibly displayed; but Juliet simply answered, "I thank your ladyship. We had coffee after dinner: and I never take it twice."

A few minutes afterwards she rose from her seat, and said, "You will excuse me, dear Ellen, for hurrying you away; but I am somewhat fatigued with my day's travelling, and should like to retire early to rest."

The Earl and Countess did not press us to remain; and we accordingly took our leave, the nobleman and his wife slightly kissing Juliet upon the cheek; and not another word was said in reference to the casket of jewels which she had rejected and which lay open upon the table.

When we were again seated together in the carriage, there was an interval of silence,—which was at length slowly broken in upon by Juliet, who, taking my hand, said, "I hope, my dear Ellen, you are not in any way offended with me?"

"I know all you have suffered, Juliet," I answered, "in consequence of the haughty pride of those who would not in times past acknowledge you as their daughter-in-law; and though I deplore the scene which has just now occurred, I cannot altogether blame you for it."

"Then we will say no more upon the subject," she responded; and there was another interval of silence. "Unless," she presently added, "it be necessary for me to assure you that I am not heartless: but we all have our little feelings—and I cannot help thinking within myself that if the Earl and Countess of Carshalton had never felt the weight of affliction's hand, they never would have shown any kindness to me, and I never should have been this day invited to their mansion."

The carriage pursued its way homeward: and the clocks were striking ten as the equipage turned out of Holborn into one of the streets leading towards the quarter in which I dwelt. It now occurred to me that a strange sound met my ears,—the confused murmuring and buzzing of voices and the rush of footsteps, growing louder and louder, and different from what those sounds usually are in even the most crowded thoroughfares. Juliet quickly noticed the same thing; and clutching me by the wrist, she ejaculated, "Hush! what is it?"

At the same instant the carriage relaxed its pace—the sounds rapidly approached nearer—it was evidently a multitude of people rushing onward! What could it mean? We both grew

alarmed: I let down the glass on my side of the carriage, and was about to look forth, when a living torrent began sweeping by—a surging flood of people rushing in evident excitement, and their confused ejaculations bursting forth all round. The equipage now stopped short altogether: it was fairly hemmed in by that ocean of human beings—enveloped by a swarming multitude! The whole street was thronged with a dense mass; and the footman, leaping down from his seat, made his way to the horse's head—for the animal, being frightened, was beginning to rear and plunge in a menacing manner.

"Sit fast, ladies! there's no harm!" exclaimed a hoarse voice at the open window. "You need not be frightened!"

"Stand by the horse, flunkey!" vociferated another.

"Hold hard, coachman!" roared a third.

"Clear the way for the carriage!" thundered another voice: and then I beheld a policeman actively engaged in an endeavour to force back the crowd from such close contact with the vehicle.

But it was all in vain: for the officer was hurled with violence against one of the wheels: and putting my head out of the window, I asked, "For heaven's sake, what is the matter?"

"Matter enough, ma'am!" replied the policeman. "There's murder done in a house close by—and suicide too, I believe from what I've heard; so that the whole neighbourhood is in this tremendous state of excitement!"

"Murder?" ejaculated both Juliet and myself, as if we were speaking in the same breath.

"Yes, murder!" replied the policeman. "But Ah! take care, coachman!"—and now he suddenly spoke with all the excitement of one who beheld some tremendous danger imminent.

"Let us out!" screamed Juliet, in the wild accents of terror.

"Sit fast, my dear friend!" I exclaimed, without losing my presence of mind.

But now it was veritably a fearful spectacle which met our view,—the gas-lights of the street and the lamps of my carriage illuminating the entire scene. The ocean of people was surging onward: they were scrambling and rushing—pouring on frantically, each individual endeavouring to force for himself the speediest passage, and all seeming most painfully intent upon escaping from some danger which now appeared to menace themselves. The wildest cries burst forth; but besides the horrid discord thus raised, there quickly came upon our ears the tramplings of galloping horses and the quick rumbling of heavy wheels. The cause of danger was soon visible. A railway carrier's van, drawn by three horses, but with only a moderate quantity of goods heaped up in it, was being dragged along the street at a tremendous pace. According to the account which I subsequently read in the newspapers, the three horses had taken fright on finding themselves suddenly enveloped by the torrent of human beings; the driver lost all control over them—and on they sped! It was indeed an awful scene; for many human beings were trampled to death beneath the hoofs of the infuriate animals, or crushed beneath the heavy wheels, or else hurled down and trodden upon by the panic-stricken multitude.

All that I am taking minutes to describe occurred in the space of moments. On came the immense van : my coachman lashed his horse furiously to get the carriage out of the way — the animal swerved abruptly—the vehicle was turned half round—then the horse backed suddenly—and the hinder part of the equipage was struck with tremendous violence by the huge wain as it thundered past.

In the twinkling of an eye the carriage was upset, wild shrieks of terror pealing from the lips alike of Juliet and myself. The carriage fell upon the side against which I was seated, so that the brunt of the concussion was actually borne by myself ; for my person formed as it were a cushion to break the violence of the shock experienced by Juliet. But fortunately I sustained no serious injury ; for the sides of the carriage were well stuffed, and the very instant that I felt it was going over I instinctively threw myself back into the corner, where the lining was thickest and softest. Scarcely had the accident occurred, when the door that was uppermost was opened : and a voice exclaimed, "For heaven's sake tell me, ladies, are you hurt ?"

Then assistance was promptly rendered to Juliet, to extricate her from her unpleasant position ; and almost immediately afterwards I was helped out of the carriage. The personage who was thus so prompt in rendering his assistance, was Count Teleki, the Hungarian nobleman to whom we had been introduced at Carshalton House.

CHAPTER CXXVIII.

THE MURDER AND SUICIDE.

THOUGH neither Juliet nor myself were at all injured by the accident we had experienced, yet our ideas were to a certain extent confused and bewildered, and our toilet was disordered.

"Let me get you out of the crowd !" exclaimed Count Teleki : for the neighbourhood of the carriage was still thronged by multitudes of people.

"But my servants ?" I ejaculated ; "are they safe ? I fear that the coachman must be injured !"

"No, Miss—I am all safe," said the coachman, now appearing in view ; and at the same time I caught a glimpse of the footman close by.

"Leave your servants to take care of the carriage," said Count Teleki ; "and pray let me get you out of this crowd."

Leaning upon his arms for support, Juliet and myself gratefully accepted the assistance which was thus proffered : the crowd made way for us— we got beyond its outskirts—and the inhabitants of several of the adjacent houses came forth to offer us their hospitality. But we declined it, as Great Ormond Street was at no considerable distance, and we were well able to walk homeward.

But now we put rapid and anxious queries to Count Teleki, in respect to the amount of injury that he supposed might have been done by the waggon and the affrighted horses ; and we likewise asked if he was acquainted with any of the particulars of the tragedy that had occurred in the neighbourhood and which had created so tremendous an excitement ?

"I ave heard nothing more on this point than you yourselves, ladies, seem to be acquainted with," he replied. "After leaving Carshalton House just now, I remembered that I had in the morning received an application from an Hungarian gentleman, who from unforeseen and unavoidable circumstances had become plunged into misfortunes. Having no particular engagement for this evening, I resolved to call upon my afflicted fellow-countryman ; and being well acquainted with London, I decided upon walking to the place of his abode, which is in this immediate neighbourhood. I paid the visit accordingly, and took my leave some ten minutes ago. On entering into this street, I suddenly found myself involved in the midst of an excited crowd. I inquired what was the reason of the commotion ; but all I could gather from the brief ejaculatory answers that were hurriedly given me, was to the effect that a gentleman had murdered some lady in the neighbourhood, and that he had immediately afterwards committed suicide."

"A gentleman and a lady ?" I ejaculated. "I had not an idea that the criminal and the victim belonged to that order of society. Did you hear their names mentioned ?"

"No—I heard nothing more than what I have just told you, Miss Percy," replied Count Teleki. "As for my own narrative, it may be quickly brought to a conclusion ; for scarcely had I become involved amidst the crowd, when that wain came thundering along the street, and the heavy equipage made its terrible crushing way amidst the flying and affrighted multitude, just like a huge ship ploughing its course amidst the heaving billows of the sea. I can assure you that I for one narrowly escaped destruction. I am neither very weak nor very short," continued Count Teleki, with a smile ; "and yet for a few moments I was as powerless as an infant in the midst of that living torrent which was pouring through the street. Vain was every attempt to battle my way ! I was lifted completely off my legs ; and for some moments—I think that I might almost say *minutes*, I was thus borne onward by the fast flowing waves of that excited stream of people. All of a sudden I caught sight of a carriage. I recognised it at once ; for on leaving Carshalton House I had stood to admire that superb bay horse of your's, Miss Percy. But scarcely had I thus caught a glimpse of the equipage, when the threatening wain drawn by the three frenzied animals, came thundering past—the cries that were already wild enough, burst forth with a still wilder peal—and it struck me that the din of the huge equipage was for a moment blended with another sound, as if a crash had somewhere taken place. The wain dashed onward ; but your carriage had disappeared from my view. The density of the crowd was now considerably relieved ; and I had comparatively little difficulty in clearing a path for the half-dozen yards which separated me from the scene of the accident which had occurred to your equipage. You know the rest."

Both Juliet and myself expressed our warmest thanks to Count Teleki for the prompt assistance he had rendered us ; and by the time his explanations were finished, the door of my house in Great Ormond Street was reached. I of course asked him to walk in, as an act of requisite politeness ;

but he, with a well-bred delicacy, declined,—alleging that the lateness of the hour must deprive him of that pleasure on the present occasion. He however requested permission to call and pay his respects on the following day: and he received the assurance that he would be welcome.

The intelligence that some terrible transaction had occurred in the neighbourhood, had reached my house a few minutes before Juliet and I arrived there. The maid-servant who opened the door, and Beda who came gliding down the stairs, were alike astonished and alarmed on finding that we had returned on foot, and on perceiving that our looks had a certain wildness in them, while there was also disorder in our toilets—for our bonnets were crushed and disfigured. The accident to the carriage was soon explained, and we hastened to our respective chambers to arrange our toilets. In about a quarter of an hour Juliet and I again met in the drawing-room; but we had not been seated many minutes there, when Beda came rushing in with a pale countenance and excited looks ; and she exclaimed, " It is indeed too true! a terrible crime has been committed ! You know the victim !"

"We know her ?" ejaculated both myself and Juliet.

"Yes," replied Beda ; " you know the unfortunate creature ! I mean Miss Harrison !"

" What ! Melissa ?" cried Juliet, horror-stricken as she started up from her seat.

" Melissa murdered ?" I exclaimed, equally affected.

"Yes—Melissa Harrison !" rejoined Beda. "The housemaid has just been to the baker's to glean what she could—and she has learnt this much."

" But the author of the crime ?" I asked. " Is it true that the murderer has laid violent hands upon himself ?"

" So they say," answered Beda : " but I could learn nothing in respect to him—not even so much as his name."

And nothing more was ascertained that night by any one beneath the roof of my dwelling. When the morning came I was naturally anxious for the arrival of the newspapers, that I might glean additional details in reference to a crime that had produced so tremendous a sensation in the neighbourhood. The moment the morning journals were placed in my hand, I searched for the particular intelligence which so much interested me; and the words in large capitals, " Shocking Murder and Suicide of the Murderer," met my eyes. But as I flung my regards over the article with that sort of shuddering curiosity which renders one anxious to embrace the whole contents of a particular statement at a glance, I encountered the name of Colonel Bellew! Another moment, and I discovered who the murderer was! Not merely the murderer, but the suicide also! It was the individual whom I have just named :—it was Colonel Bellew himself!

It appeared that some few weeks previous, a gentleman giving the name of Williams, had taken lodgings at the house where the tragedy had just occurred. This house was kept by an elderly widow named Mason. Mrs. Mason soon began to suspect that everything was not straightforward and honest with her lodger; for he seldom went out during the day-time—and when he did

leave the house in the evening, he was always muffled up as if for the purpose of disguise. For the first two or three weeks he paid his rent regularly; and then he fell into arrears. About a fortnight previous to the tragedy the lodger sent out a letter to the post; and Mrs. Mason happened to observe (for she herself took it) that it was addressed to Miss Harrison, Tynedale Lodge, Kensington. The very next day a street-cab stopped at the door of Mrs. Mason's house; a well-dressed and handsome young lady alighted, and inquired for Colonel Williams. Mrs. Mason's servant said that a Mr. Williams lived there, but that she did not know he was a colonel. The young lady said it was all the same: and she was introduced accordingly to the apartments of the lodger. She remained there about an hour, and then took her departure. Shortly after she was gone the lodger rang the bell and sent out a twenty-pound note to be changed. He then paid his rent, as well as some little debts which he had contracted in the neighbourhood. About a week afterwards he sent another letter to the post, directed to Miss Harrison; but this time it was not addressed to Tynedale Lodge, but to some post-office in Kensington, with instructions penned in the corner " that it was to be kept till called for." On the following day the handsome and well-dressed young lady called again, arriving in a public cab as on the former occasion. She had not been long with the lodger before their voices were heard in loud altercation; and Mrs. Mason had the curiosity to go and listen at the door. She gleaned these particulars—that her lodger was a man of ruined fortunes and desperate circumstances—that he had once been an officer in the Guards—that he was now lying concealed as it were in that lodging, not merely on account of debts, but likewise because there was a warrant against him for having obtained three hundred pounds from some money-lender under false pretences. It was this last-mentioned affair which he was most anxious to settle. Mrs. Mason heard him appeal to Melissa (as he called the young lady) to extricate him from that difficulty. He said he cared comparatively nothing about the debts if he could only get rid of the more serious affair, which would be utter destruction to him if it were not promptly arranged. Melissa Harrison replied that she could not possibly advance such a sum, and that he had no right to expect it of her. He then began to menace the young lady, and to say that he would let the Marquis of Tynedale know how she had visited him at that house. Melissa remonstrated and entreated; but finding that her words produced no effect, she threatened the Colonel in her turn. Then he became more tranquil, and besought her forgiveness. Melissa said that as he now seemed inclined to be reasonable, she would again go to the extent of assisting him with a few pounds. Mrs. Mason tarried at the door no longer; but she had heard quite enough to give her a deep insight into the character of her lodger, as well as showing her who was the young female that thus visited him; and she was resolved to give him notice to leave her apartments.

Now comes the sequel to this sad and fearful episode. It must be observed that the murder took place in the evening of the 3rd of February; and it appeared that on the previous day the

Colonel sent another letter to the post, directed to Miss Harrison, and addressed to the post-office at Kensington to which allusion has already been made. Mrs. Mason had given the Colonel warning to leave her house; and his time would have been up in a couple of days—otherwise she would have remonstrated against his again receiving the visits of a young person of such equivocal character. The last letter was sent on the 2nd, as I have said; and between eight and nine o'clock in the evening of the 3rd, Melissa Harrison again alighted from a cab at Mrs. Mason's house. The Colonel, who was addicted to drinking, had been indulging even more freely than usual during the day, but especially since partaking of his dinner. Mrs. Mason had a presentiment that some altercation would arise ; and she determined to be upon the alert so as to anticipate the outbreak of any disturbance that might tend to bring disgrace upon her house. All

was quiet for some time ; but as she passed by the door of the Colonel's apartments, she heard Melissa saying, "It is no use troubling me in this way. You have no claim upon me ! When I was ill and thought I was dying nearly three years ago, you left me to perish without a farthing—me and my child,—your child !" At that moment Mrs. Mason thought she heard her servant coming down the stairs ; and not choosing to be seen playing the part of eavesdropper, she retreated from the door of the Colonel's suite of rooms. Half-an-hour afterwards the din of altercation smote her ears : and no longer feeling any delicacy on the point, she summoned her servant that they might ascend together and insist upon Miss Harrison's leaving the house. But when they reached the landing, the storm seemed to be experiencing a lull ; and they listened. All of a sudden they heard the Colonel demand, " Will you or will you not do what I ask ?" Melissa replied emphatically that she would *not* The Colonel threatened to spoil her with the Marquis of Tynedale. She said that she defied his threats, for that she would tell the Marquis the whole truth, explaining why she had visited the house, and that his lordship would believe her. The Colonel became terribly exasperated, and swore that he would tell such a tale as should outweigh every representation she might make. "Then," exclaimed Melissa, "if this is your villanous design, and if there must be open war between us, the sooner I go and give a hint to the *officers* of justice where they may execute the warrant, the better!"—The landlady and servant, thinking that Melissa was on the very point of issuing from the room, began to make their way down stairs, when all of a sudden a terrific yell, like that of a wild beast, burst from the lips of the Colonel; and it was accompanied by a sound as of a tremendous blow being dealt, instantaneously followed by the falling of a person on the floor. A shriek also rang through the house. The landlady and her servant were paralyzed with terror: they were transfixed upon the stairs. Another shriek rang forth from the apartment; then another sound, as of a blow, was heard, accompanied by the crashing of glass—and all was for a few moments still! The servant-girl fainted on the stairs: Mrs. Mason, recovering her presence of mind—or rather, I should say, impelled by the horrible state of her feelings — rushed *into* the room. There a fearful spectacle presented itself. The unfortunate Melissa lay upon the floor; and the fragments of a broken bottle showed but too plainly how the hideous wounds which were seen upon the forehead, had been inflicted. Her skull was literally battered in! "Wretch!" cried Mrs. Mason; "you have murdered her!"—The Colonel looked like one who had just been awakened out of a horrible dream: there was a species of vacant consternation and dismay expressed upon his ghastly countenance. But it rapidly expanded into a vivid consciousness of the horrible crime that had been perpetrated; and with wild accents, he exclaimed, "No! no! she cannot be dead! Good God! I cannot have killed her!"—Mrs. Mason stooped down and felt Melissa's heart; but it had ceased to beat. When she raised her eyes, the Colonel was no longer in her presence; and at the same moment she heard the door communicating with the *inner* room, shut hastily. She sprang towards it—but the key was at the same moment turned in the lock. That inner room was the Colonel's bed-chamber. The turning of the key was almost instantaneously followed by the report of a pistol, and then a heavy weight fell upon the floor. Mrs. Mason, in a state bordering on frenzy, rushed to the window of the sitting-room: she threw it open—and she shrieked for assistance. She was half maddened with the horror inspired by the double tragedy; and her cries alarmed the whole neighbourhood. Hence the concourse of persons which collected so quickly from all quarters, and in the midst of which multitude the accident had happened to my carriage.

I have now put the reader in possession of all the main facts connected with this appalling tragedy. I should add that when the police took possession of the premises, they found the wretched murderer weltering in the blood of a suicide, and stone dead. He had put the pistol in his mouth, and literally blown his brains out. It was through the medium of some papers found about his person, that the discovery was made of his name being Bellew instead of Williams.

And thus perished Melissa Harrison!—thus also died Colonel Bellew! The unfortunate young woman's life fell a victim to him who had in past years despoiled her of her honour! It transpired that the child which she had by Colonel Bellew, had died some time previous to the horrible tragedy which thus sent the mother herself to a premature grave. Melissa was the mistress of the Marquis of Tynedale at the time when she was unfortunate enough to renew her acquaintance with Colonel Bellew. Nevertheless, it was evident that she had not voluntarily renewed it—but that he had by some means or another found out where and with whom she was living, and had written to intimidate her into a meeting. Fatal meeting!—it had led to two others;—and the *third* of those inauspicious interviews had proved the last scene in the existence of Melissa Harrison!

It must not be supposed that all the details which I have laid before the reader, were afforded by the journals published on the morning that followed the evening of the tragedy. The main facts only were therein given: the minuter particulars subsequently transpired at the Coroner's Inquest;—but I have deemed it more expedient to collect the whole at once into a complete narrative, so as to avoid bewildering the reader with disjointed details.

Count Teleki called to pay his respects according to the permission he had received; and the favourable opinion which a first impression was calculated to engender with reference to this nobleman, was not impaired by a closer acquaintance. I have already said that he was handsome and gentlemanly: I may add that he was intelligent—that he had been well educated, and possessed a highly cultivated mind. His manners were polished and elegant, without affectation: they had the brilliancy of the well-bred foreigner blended with the more sterling qualities of the enlightened Englishman. He had known Juliet's husband as well as his elder brother, the Viscount; but it was only slightly that he alluded to them.

On the following day Juliet again accompanied me to Carshalton House, that she might take leave of the Earl and Countess. They received her with what may be termed a mild and serene friendliness of manner, without fervour on the one hand and without coldness on the other. On her part, Juliet maintained towards them a demeanour precisely similar to that which she had displayed during the first interview. The visit was not a long one; and when Juliet rose to take her departure, the Earl and *Countess* simply kissed her upon the cheek—but they gave her no invitation to return to their mansion. I was glad when the whole scene was over; for it was an ordeal quite as painful for me as for those who might seem to be the most deeply interested in it.

I prevailed upon Juliet to prolong her sojourn at my house for three or four days; and we saw the Hungarian nobleman on several occasions. I happened to learn from Lady Carshalton that he was immensely rich, and that he was unmarried: neither did she think that he was what is called "a marrying man," for he was always travelling about from one European capital to another, seldom settling himself anywhere for more than a few months at a time. I may add, while touching upon this topic, that the Earl of Carshalton threw in an eulogium upon the honourable character, good principles, and magnanimous disposition of Count Teleki.

Juliet returned to River House, having obtained a promise from me that I would soon pay her a visit there and pass some little time with herself and Mary Glentworth.

Lady Kelvedon progressed favourably and rapidly; and by the time six weeks had elapsed since the departure of Dame Betty for the Continent, her ladyship was altogether another being. The pledge, therefore, which I had given to the old hag was not forgotten; and I remitted her the remaining two hundred and fifty guineas to make up the sum of five hundred originally promised as her reward if she succeeded in effecting Hermione's cure. I now accompanied the Earl and Countess of Carshalton into Warwickshire for a month, my faithful Beda going with me; and on my return to London I was gratified by the reception of a letter from William Lardner, dated from New York, where he had arrived in safety. I need scarcely observe that the same packet contained letters for Beda, who was delighted to learn that her lover had got thus far on his expedition without experiencing the slightest adventure of an unfavourable character. At about the same time I received a letter from the Marquis of Dalrymple, informing me that his mother still continued in a hopeless condition so far as the skill of the Sardinian physicians was concerned; but that it was strongly recommended to consult an eminent practitioner at Naples, and that therefore a removal was about to be made from Genoa to the Neapolitan capital. And it was about this same time that I fulfilled my promise to Juliet by proceeding on a visit to River House: for the day was now close at hand when Mary Glentworth might expect to become a mother. Before concluding this chapter I will remark that Beda did not accompany me on the present occasion; for she was ignorant of Mary Glentworth's sad secret—and I considered that secret to be one the knowledge whereof ought to be confined to the narrowest circle possible.

CHAPTER CXXIX.

THE LAWYERS.

It was late in the afternoon, on a beautiful day at the close of March, 1843, that I arrived at River House. I was most warmly greeted alike by Lady Frederick Ravenscliffe and Mary Glentworth: but I had not been many minutes with them, ere I noticed that there was a certain gloom upon Juliet's countenance. At first I thought it might be through anxiety on Mary's account; but I was presently convinced that this was not the solution of the mystery. What secret grief could Juliet cherish? I was anxious to be alone with her that I might be relieved from suspense on this head. Accordingly, when I went up to change

my toilet after travelling, in preparation for the dinner-hour, I beckoned Juliet to accompany me; and when we were alone together, I exclaimed somewhat abruptly, "There is something on your mind, Juliet? For heaven's sake tell me what it is! Keep me not in uncertainty and doubt!"

"It is a letter that I received this morning, my dear Ellen," replied Juliet. "It is from my father——"

She stopped short, and the tears trickled down her cheeks. I was now seriously alarmed. I thought to myself that Mr. Norman must be ill at some distant place upon the Continent; and therefore I was smitten with wonder that Juliet did not offer to depart immediately and fly to the bedside of her sire. She seemed to divine what was passing in my thoughts; for she said, "Do not be under any alarm, Ellen, on account of my father's health. It is not *that* which grieves me!"

"Explain yourself," I cried, becoming more and more frightened. "What means this hesitation, Juliet? Has your father become involved in any trouble or embarrassment on the Continent?"

"It is something of this kind which threatens him," replied Lady Frederick. "I will be frank with you, at once, Ellen; and if for a moment I hesitated to explain everything, it was through no want of confidence—because you and I are as sisters together——"

"And you know, my dear Julie," I interrupted her, "I have every reason to love and respect *your* father as if he were my own! You have relieved me of my fears in reference to his health. But what embarrassment can menace him? Is it of a pecuniary character?"

"Yes," rejoined Juliet: "and it is this circumstance that made me delicate in explaining myself to you; because I know that your means cannot at present be very ample."

"But without another syllable of preface, Julie," I interjected, "pray tell me what is the nature and the extent of your father's embarrassment."

"You know, my dear Ellen," resumed Lady Frederick, "my father never was celebrated for great steadiness or regularity in pecuniary matters. Since my poor mother died fifteen months ago, my father has not earned a single shilling by his profession. You may remind me that he had a thousand pounds left him by Mrs. Oldcastle, and the produce of the sale of his furniture:—but the outstanding debts and the funeral expenses made some inroad upon those aggregated amounts. And then too, one cannot travel over the Continent without a well filled purse——"

"I can very well understand, Juliet," I interrupted her, "that your father's resources must be verging towards exhaustion—because you have omitted to mention that generosity of disposition on his part, which makes him open his purse at the very first syllable of a tale of distress, or at the very first glimpse of a picture of misery. And it is not difficult to conjecture how upon the Continent he may have met a number of his fellow-countrymen, in circumstances calculated to evoke his kindest sympathies."

"Such has indeed been the case, Ellen!" observed Juliet; "and I thank you, my dear friend, for thus doing your best to screen my father from the imputation of wanton extravagance. The generosity of his heart has led him into the em barrassment which now threatens to become even more serious. But I will explain it. For the last few weeks my father, as you are aware, has been staying at Strasburg. He there fell in with an old professional friend, who first made an inroad upon his purse, and then induced him to become security for him to a considerable amount."

"Good heavens!" I ejaculated; "can it be possible your father is menaced with a prison?"

"Alas, it is so!" rejoined Juliet, weeping. "His professional friend was himself threatened with a gaol; and my father, to save him from it, put his name upon a bill of exchange for eight hundred pounds. His friend assured him that he had certain expectations which could not possibly fail to be realized, and that therefore no risk was incurred by the proceeding. You know, Ellen, that my father is ever credulous where his generosity is involved and his sympathies are appealed to by a tale of distress;—and thus it is that he stands every chance of becoming the victim of his goodness towards this perfidious friend."

"Ah! then, the friend has really deceived him?" I ejaculated.

"From certain facts which have come to my father's knowledge," proceeded Juliet, "he has every reason to apprehend the worst. His friend has left Strasburg on pretence of coming to England to look after certain moneys that are due to him; but there is too much ground to surmise that this was a mere excuse for the purpose of getting away from the place and avoiding the very predicament in which my poor father has become involved."

"And what predicament is that?" I asked; "for you seem to speak, Julie, as if something more than a mere prospective danger had arisen to annoy and afflict your father."

"It is so, Ellen," she responded. "My father is a prisoner in the town of Strasburg."

"A prisoner already?" I exclaimed in amazement.

"Yes, already!—though not actually in a prison. The bill to which he has lent his name will be due in a fortnight; and according to the severity of the French laws applied to foreigners, my father's passport has been stopped to prevent him from leaving the town until the debt shall have been paid."

"But this is monstrous!" I ejaculated, now indignant as well as annoyed.

"It is nevertheless true," answered Juliet. "He is not actually in prison: but he is unable to leave the town. In short, he is is as completely under the *surveillance* of the police as if he were a felon having committed some heinous crime! He has little hope that his perfidious friend will come forward with the money to pay the bill at maturity; and if he do not, my poor father will be inevitably consigned to a French prison. You now know the history of my griefs, Ellen. Of course I will do everything I can to assist my father——"

"But how can you obtain eight hundred pounds all in a moment, Juliet?" I asked. "Your income is under a thousand a year; it is chiefly derived from the rents of houses in Dover; and if I mistake not, there was a special clause in Mrs. Oldcastle's will providing against the mortgage, sale, or alienation of your property in any shape or way. Was this not so?"

"Yes," replied Juliet; "and for that very reason my affliction is all the greater. I went to consult Mr. Mansfield, the solicitor, in Dover this morning; he says that I can do absolutely nothing. Indeed, my poor father has strongly urged me to make no sacrifice on his behalf: he likewise enjoined me to keep his misfortune a secret from you. He admits that he has been very foolish and overconfiding: and he says that he must now take the consequences."

"It is quite clear, Juliet," I said, "that you are utterly powerless to assist your father in his present dilemma. You live up to your income, and you cannot have much money at your banker's?"

"I have nearly two hundred pounds at the banker's," said Juliet. "I can raise money on the furniture as a security: there is nothing in Mrs. Oldcastle's will to prevent *that*. But the worst of it is, as Mr. Mansfield said, the furniture is so old-fashioned——"

"I understand," I exclaimed: "you could only raise a very moderate sum upon it?"

"Perhaps I might muster four hundred pounds altogether," said Juliet.

"And impoverish yourself for some time to come!" I ejaculated. "Now listen to me, my dear Juliet. I myself have been extravagant and have lived far beyond my means——"

"*You,* Ellen?" she exclaimed, with unfeigned surprise.

"But understand me!" I resumed: "I have not a single shilling of debt! You know that precisely eight months ago I surrendered up the handsome fortune I inherited from Mr. Gower——"

"Yes—to save Henry Wakefield's name from being dragged down into the vortex of dishonour, along with Mr. Macdonald of Paisley!" exclaimed Juliet.

"And when that sacrifice was made," I continued, "I had but a few hundreds of pounds left. It is true that Mr. Macdonald sent me a thousand pounds a short time afterwards: but this I regarded as my cousin Henry's money, and I invested it in his name accordingly. Well then, my dear Juliet, you know that I was compelled to return to the stage; and though I received a very handsome income for my professional engagement, yet it only lasted a few weeks: it was put an end to by that unfortunate bankruptcy of Mr. Richards. I ought then to have contracted my expenses and to have given up my carriage: but circumstances induced me to postpone this retrenchment. In short, to be candid with you, Julie, I was afraid that if I *did* retrench it would wear the aspect of a species of tacit appeal to the many kind friends whom I possess; I foresaw that I should be overwhelmed with offers to make use of the purse of Lady Kelvedon, the Countess of Belgrave, Mrs. Gower, and others—while Lord and Lady Carshalton would have insisted on becoming my bankers. Indeed, as it is, I have experienced the greatest difficulty in preventing the Earl and Countess from laying me under a considerable pecuniary obligation to them. You may think that I am independent, Juliet; and so I am in money matters. I might have carried this independence to the point of returning to the stage; for you know that when Mr. Richards, having got through all his troubles, opened his theatre again last month, he made me the most brilliant offers: but you are also aware what consideration it was that induced me to remain off the stage."

"Yes," responded Juliet: "the prospects of your cousin Henry——"

"But if I have inflicted upon you this long tale, my dear friend," I resumed, "it is simply to account for the statement I am about to make in reference to myself. My resources were almost exhausted by the large sum of money I placed in William Lardner's hands when he left England two months back; and *now* they are completely drained. I do not think that I have twenty pounds left in my banker's hands. Thus you see that if I do not all in a moment proffer you pecuniary assistance, my dear Juliet, it is because I am utterly without the means of doing so."

"I felt assured, Ellen," said Lady Frederick, "that your income must be limited for the present; but I was far from suspecting, my dear friend, that your fortunes were at so low an ebb."

"Nevertheless, Juliet," I continued, "something shall and must be done on your father's account! I will do for him that which I assuredly would not do for myself: I will write to some friend and borrow the amount which is required."

"If you have any scruple in adopting this course, Ellen," said Juliet, "there is a means by which we could raise the sum. Mr. Mansfield the lawyer told me that if I gave him some collateral security, he would furnish the money. I know that he would take your security——"

"But I am not quite twenty-one yet," I interposed, with a smile: "I am not of age—and my signature is not valid."

"Oh, it will be found valid enough!" ejaculated Juliet. "You are your own mistress—your furniture is very handsome and valuable——In short, I know that there will be no difficulty. And Oh! you cannot tell how great is the relief which my mind now experiences! I did not tell poor Mary that I had any cause for affliction; for I thought that as the hour of her ordeal approaches, she ought to enjoy as much mental tranquillity as possible."

"There is no reason why she should be at all enlightened on the subject," I said. "But let us now hasten to rejoin her—or she will suspect that there is something strange or mysterious attendant upon my arrival at River House."

On the following morning, soon after breakfast, I took an opportunity to say to Juliet, "You must remain with Mary, for she does not seem at all well. I will go into Dover, and will call upon Mr. Mansfield. If it be possible to effect an arrangement with him, it shall be accomplished: but I fear you are somewhat too sanguine, Juliet —and if there should be any disappointment in this quarter, I will write to either Lady Kelvedon or the Countess of Carshalton."

Juliet pressed my hand in token of fervid thankfulness; and I set off to walk into Dover. As I passed the cottage where I had first made the acquaintance of Mary Glentworth nearly two years back, I could not help thinking to myself, "How many strange incidents have come to my knowledge in reference to this dear friend of mine! How singular has been her connexion with many circumstances which have so intimately interwoven themselves as it were with the thread of my own

history! She has become the victim of that same Edwin St. Clair who so often sought to make me his victim!—she has likewise become the object of the love of that young Marquis who first of all bestowed his love upon me! She is now about to become a mother in seclusion and in secrecy, as my friend Juliet likewise became a mother in seclusion and in secrecy beneath the very same roof!—yes, within those self-same walls of River House! And I am here as the friend of Mary, in the same way that I was here as the friend of Juliet!"

Thus musing upon a variety of circumstances and coincidences which were connected with the name of Mary Glentworth, I pursued my way into the town of Dover. On arriving at Mr. Mansfield's office, I was informed that the lawyer was disengaged and would see me at once. I did not however give any name, but said that it was unnecessary inasmuch as Mr. Mansfield was unacquainted with me. In a few moments I found myself in the presence of the lawyer, who was a middle-aged man, with a cold calm expression of countenance, sufficiently polite in manner, but with an air as business-like as the aspect of his office itself. At the very first glance at Mr. Mansfield's countenance, I felt persuaded he was a man who would not deviate one hair's-breadth from the ordinary routine of business through any mere motive of generosity, and that Juliet had indeed been too sanguine in her expectations that he would advance any money without the most ample security. I should observe that Mr. Mansfield had succeeded to the business of the professional gentleman who had managed the affairs of the deceased Mrs. Oldcastle; and who, it appeared, had retired from practice some few weeks previous to the date of which I am writing.

Mr. Mansfield requested me to be seated; and when I mentioned my name, his countenance expanded somewhat from its air of cold politeness.

"Happening to know, Miss Percy," he said, "that you are a friend of Lady Frederick Ravenscliffe's, I need scarcely ask where you are staying in this neighbourhood."

"And perhaps, Mr. Mansfield," I said, "you may also surmise the nature of the business which has brought me to your office?"

"I presume, Miss Percy," he replied, "it is the business concerning which Lady Frederick did me the honour to consult me yesterday?"

I answered in the affirmative; and then I inquired, "Are there any means by which the requisite sum can be raised? I hesitate not to confess that at the present moment my own resources are peculiarly limited. I have friends who would cheerfully lend me the amount; but I dislike the idea of becoming a borrower."

"You must really know, Miss Percy," said Mr. Mansfield, "that if you stand upon any delicacy in making an appeal to friendship in matters of this kind, you will have to regard it as a purely business affair when addressing yourself to a professional man."

"In other terms, sir," I observed, "I must offer you security?"

"I have already told Lady Frederick Ravenscliffe," replied Mr. Mansfield, "that if she have any friend of undoubted solvency and respectability who will join her in a bond, I have not the slightest objection to recommend a client of mine to advance the desired amount. I presume, from your preceding observations, that you are quite ready and willing to lend your name for the use of Lady Frederick?"

"I am quite willing," I answered.

"But pardon me, Miss Percy," continued the lawyer, "there are certain little preliminaries which must be observed. You will satisfy me that you are a householder possessed of a certain amount of personal property—such as furniture, plate, jewels——"

"I can of course give you these proofs, Mr. Mansfield," I rejoined, somewhat coldly and distantly; "but if so much formality be requisite, I think that I had better apply at once to my own lawyer, Mr. Wilkinson, of Furnival's Inn."

"Mr. Wilkinson of Furnival's Inn?" ejaculated Mansfield. "Is he your attorney?"

"Yes," I answered, astonished at the sensation which my words had suddenly produced. "Why do you ask?"

"Because, singularly enough," replied Mansfield, "Mr. Wilkinson of Furnival's Inn is my London agent!"

"Then, after all," I interjected, "as he must know it one way or another, you may as well take the business in hand at once; and I authorize you to refer to Mr. Wilkinson on the points you have named."

"This can be speedily done, Miss Percy," rejoined Mr. Mansfield: "for I was about to remark that it is not only a singular coincidence that Mr. Wilkinson should be my London agent, but it is still more singular that he should be in Dover at this very minute!"

"Mr. Wilkinson in Dover?" I ejaculated.

"Yes:—he arrived late last night," returned Mr. Mansfield. "I have not yet seen him; but he sent me a note just now, to tell me of his arrival, and likewise to inform me that he had some little business to transact of a private nature which would occupy him for an hour or two, but that he would be with me at noon precisely."

I looked at my watch: it was now a little past eleven o'clock; and I said, "With your permission, Mr. Mansfield, I will return at twelve, so that I may see Mr. Wilkinson?"

The lawyer bowed an acquiescence to my proposal; and I quitted his office. I rambled towards the pier: I felt somewhat dejected, low-spirited, and humiliated. That I should be reduced to the necessity of mortgaging or pledging my furniture, plate, and personal property, for a few hundreds of pounds, was enough to mortify me, when I reflected that in the zenith of my professional success I could always command a handsome balance at my banker's. I was almost inclined to return at once to Mr. Mansfield's office, and tell him that I would rather let the affair drop at once, so far as he was concerned, and write to Lady Carshalton for the required amount,—when the whole business was for an instant driven out of my head, by the sudden and most unexpected encounter with a personage who has been recently mentioned in my memoirs.

I was walking towards one of the quays, when the passengers were landing from a steam-vessel which had just arrived from Calais. All in a moment some one ejaculated, "Ah, is it possible? Miss Percy!"—and Count Teleki stood before me.

The Hungarian nobleman had a cloak richly trimmed with fur, thrown over his shoulders: two domestics in livery, and a valet in plain clothes, were following him with such little portable articles of luggage that were not necessary to pass through the Custom House.

"I am delighted to see you, Miss Percy," he said: "and may I ask after your friend, Lady Frederick Ravenscliffe? Ah! I am charmed to hear that she is in good health!" he continued, when I had replied to his question. "I have been abroad ever since I saw you in London two months ago. You will be surprised to learn that I am the bearer of letters for Lady Frederick——"

"Indeed, my lord?" I ejaculated with amazement.

"Yes," he continued, "I happened to pass through Strasburg——"

"Ah, then, you saw her father?" I interrupted him.

"Yes—I saw Mr. Norman; and a very nice gentleman he is," proceeded Count Teleki. "It was not however my intention to deliver in person the letters which I have for Lady Frederick. I am desirous of reaching the metropolis with the least possible delay; and though, as I am aware, her ladyship's residence is on the high road only a couple of miles or so out of Dover, I shall be unable to stop. Do not however suppose, Miss Percy," he added, with a smile, "that it is through any want of respect or friendship to your friend Lady Frederick: but my time is really so precious that I must defer until a future occasion the pleasure of paying my *devoirs* personally at River House."

"Perhaps your lordship will permit me," I said, "to save you any further trouble in respect to those letters, by becoming the bearer of them to Lady Frederick?"

"Oh! if I might so far trouble you," he exclaimed, "I should be rejoiced; because I should then know that the letters had fallen into the hand of a trusty messenger!"

The nobleman thereupon drew forth his pocket-book, and gave me a small packet addressed in the well-known writing of Mr. Norman, to Lady Frederick Ravenscliffe. I promised that immediately on my return to River House it should be delivered to Juliet; and we separated. I continued my way towards the pier; and as I passed the steam-vessel, I observed that one travelling-carriage was already landed, and that another very handsome barouche was at the moment being lifted off the deck by the huge crane. From some observations which met my ears, I learnt that these carriages belonged to the Hungarian nobleman from whom I had just parted; and I saw that three or four other servants in the Count's livery were standing by to witness the operation of landing the carriages.

"It is strange," I said to myself, "but I certainly thought when first Count Teleki was introduced to Juliet, she had made a certain impression upon him. Indeed I felt convinced that he was smitten with her beauty! But now he passes by her house without even delaying his journey for a single instant to deliver the letters wherewith he was charged! Perhaps it was even in a semi-satirical vein that in speaking of Mr. Norman just now he remarked to me that he was a very nice gentleman indeed!"

The longer I thought of Count Teleki's conduct in respect to that packet of letters, the more deeply was I convinced that if it were not actually a studied slight towards Juliet, it was at all events a very unmistakable intimation that he did not care to renew his acquaintance with her. I felt piqued and mortified on her behalf; and I was angry with myself that I had not displayed the most haughty coldness towards the Hungarian nobleman. Indeed I was in one of those moods—so rare with me however—in which one is inclined to look upon everything with a jaundiced eye, and to behold slights, mortifications, and even insults, in the most trivial actions on the part of others.

"The other day," I thought to myself, "I was in the possession of an income averaged at twelve thousand a year!—and now I am compelled to have recourse to the most humiliating means to raise a few paltry hundreds? Not that I repent of the sacrifice that I made of my fortune!" I hastened to ejaculate: "for it was to save thy name, my well-beloved Henry! from degradation and disgrace!"

I endeavoured to reason myself out of the despondency and dispirited condition into which I had fallen, but I could not,—and it was with a slow heavy step, with a clouded countenance, and with a deep heartfelt mortification I again crossed the threshold of the lawyer's office just as the church-clocks were proclaiming the hour of noon.

I was at once introduced into the inner room where I had previously seen Mr. Mansfield: and I again found myself in the presence of this individual. He desired me to be seated,—observing, "You are punctual, Miss Percy—which is more than I can say of Mr. Wilkinson, for he has not yet made his appearance."

Scarcely however were these words spoken, when the door was thrown open, and Mr. Wilkinson literally bounded into the inner office.

"Ah!" he ejaculated, grasping my hand; "so I have found you at last!"

"Found me at last?" I exclaimed, with no inconsiderable degree of surprise. "But how could you possibly know that I needed your assistance? Ah! you have seen Lady Frederick Ravenscliffe perhaps?"

"Yes—I have seen her," responded Wilkinson. "She told me I should find you here. The coincidence is strange; for Mr. Mansfield and I are well acquainted!"

At the same time the London lawyer gave his hand to the Dover one; and the latter observed, "I suppose Lady Frederick told you why Miss Percy had called upon me?"

"No—she gave me no explanation," answered Mr. Wilkinson: "her ladyship merely informed me it was very probable I should find Miss Percy here."

"I wish Lady Frederick had been more explicit, Mr. Wilkinson," I said; "for it would have saved me the mortification of confessing that I wish you to help me in raising a sum of money——"

"Ah! ha!" cried the London lawyer, with a peculiar smile. "To raise a sum of money, eh? Well, this is strange!" he muttered, in a sort of chuckling way to himself: then he rubbed his hands; and looking with a smiling earnestness in my countenance, he repeated, "To raise a sum of money, eh?"

"Really, Mr. Wilkinson," I said, somewhat piqued by his manner, "if I did not know you better, I should think you were inclined to mock or laugh at me."

"My dear young lady," exclaimed Wilkinson, with fervour, "I know all the admirable feelings which possess you too well to make them the subject of ridicule! I would as soon hold the Bible itself in mockery! No, no!" and grasping my hand, he pressed it with a display of emotion which increased the amazement I was already experiencing at his extraordinary conduct.

"What have you to tell me?" I hastily inquired. "You were seeking after me?"

"I came from London especially to see you," replied Mr. Wilkinson. "I called at your house in Great Ormond Street yesterday at about noon: I was told you had come down into Kent—I took a post-chaise as soon as I could arrange to leave my office—I got down too late last night to call at River House——"

"Oh, keep me not in suspense!" I interrupted him. "What have you to impart? Is it some intelligence of the Ardleigh family?"

"No, no—it is all about yourself!" ejaculated Mr. Wilkinson: then turning to the Dover lawyer, he said, "There, Mr. Mansfield, stands a young lady who some time since inherited a large fortune; and every shilling of this fortune she spontaneously gave to rescue certain honoured names from the imminency of the Gazette! Think you that such conduct could go unrewarded? No, no! Heaven itself is in haste to recompense it!"

"What mean you, Mr. Wilkinson?" I exclaimed, now seized with a nervous trepidation. "Is it possible that Henry—I mean Mr. Wakefield—is returned?"

"No," interrupted the London lawyer: "it is nothing of that sort which I have to communicate. But pray compose yourself, Miss Percy! You have indeed some startling intelligence to hear——it is not bad—on the contrary, it is very good. In a word, you have only to conceive that you are in just the same position as you were before the 9th of August of last year."

The 9th of August! That was the very day on which I had placed the whole of my fortune in the hand of Mr. Macdonald of Paisley! What could Mr. Wilkinson mean? A sensation of wild delight swept through me: I flung upon him a look of tremulous suspense—I dreaded lest my fancy was suggesting the impossible! But my doubts were soon set at rest; for, again taking my hand, and pressing it in his own, he said, "You have caught my meaning, Miss Percy! Or at least, if you have not, let me hasten to tell you that you are again rich, as all your well-wishers would desire that you should be! The sublimest generosity on your part gave a fortune to Mr. Macdonald; and the strictest principle of honour on his part restores that fortune to your hands!"

A cry of joy escaped my lips; and then a sensation of dizziness came over me. I sank down upon a chair—my eyelids closed—but yet complete consciousness did not abandon me.

"Water, water, Mansfield!" ejaculated Mr. Wilkinson: "she is about to faint!"

But by a strong effort I recovered myself; and then I expressed my sincerest thanks to the London lawyer for the intelligence which he had brought me,—intelligence that was as startling and amazing as it was fraught with bliss. His congratulations were most fervidly proffered; and Mr. Mansfield spoke to me in a similar sense. It appeared to me like a dream;—and again I felt as if I should fall overpowered by the weight of excessive joy—as a bird might sink down when having penetrated into some previously unknown isle where the atmosphere was oppressive with the fragrance of flowers—or as a bee might droop when too heavily laden with the honied burden stored beneath its wings!

But again I exercised a strong power of control over myself; and I asked Mr. Wilkinson how all this came about, and how it was that Mr. Macdonald had so suddenly found himself in a condition to return me the vast sum I had advanced him?

"Here is a letter which he has sent you, Miss Percy," replied Mr. Wilkinson: "and here is the far longer letter which he wrote to me as your lawyer, begging me to break the matter to you with the least possible delay, but with the utmost delicacy and caution."

I opened the letter which was addressed to myself; and when I had read it, I said, "This communication gives no particulars: it merely abounds in the most grateful expressions for the service which I have rendered Mr. Macdonald, and in the most earnest wish that I may live on in health and happiness to enjoy the wealth which he restores with interest to my hands. A more grateful letter never was penned!—never were nobler thoughts committed to paper! But Oh, Mr. Wilkinson! it seems almost miraculous! How was it that so sudden a return of prosperity has visited the worthy Paisley manufacturer?"

"There is his letter of particulars to me——"

"Nay, but I cannot read it now! My brain whirls—my sight is dazzled! Leave the letter for me to peruse it at my leisure: but tell me in a few words how all this has been brought about."

"You know the old adage, Miss Percy," said the London lawyer, "that it never rains but it pours. You remember how thickly did misfortunes hail down upon the head of Mr. Macdonald. Well then, now all the circumstances of prosperity are showering quite as thickly around him. In the first place, the great American house of Rawlins and Sydney, which was supposed to have gone so completely to pieces as not to be able to pay a shilling in the pound, has recovered itself with a rapidity as marvellous as its descent towards the vortex of destruction seemed to be last year. Every farthing due to Mr. Macdonald has been remitted by Rawlins and Sydney; and the money came with scarcely any previous notice. Well then, you know that there was that tremendous conflagration of Mr. Macdonald's principal factory——"

"I recollect! And Mr. Perkins, his head clerk," I continued, "had omitted to pay the insurance premium within the proper time."

"Well, about that," interjected Mr. Wilkinson, "there arose some little dispute. The notice-paper from the Insurance Company said that the premium was due on such-and-such a day, and that it must be paid within fifteen days afterwards.

It appears that Perkins mislaid the notice-paper, and totally forgot the affair until the afternoon of the fifteenth day. He at once ran off to the Paisley agent of the Company: the agent was not at home, and Perkins left the cheque in a letter. During the night that followed the factory was burned down! The agent returned the cheque in the morning; and the company contended that the premium had not been even tendered in time, much less received in time, and the payment of the insurance-money was consequently refused. Mr. Macdonald was advised by his lawyer that the Insurance Company was justified in its proceeding; and he decided therefore upon submitting to the loss. Subsequently, when through your bounty, Miss Percy, his affairs were put straight again and he had leisure to look round him, he consulted eminent barristers in Edinburgh and London; and he was advised to bring an action against the Insurance Company. He did so. It was agreed that the subject-matter of dispute should be referred to arbitration; and this private tribunal ultimately gave its decision in favour of Mr. Macdonald. This occurred almost simultaneously with the sudden arrival of the remittances from Rawlins and Sydney. But that is not all," continued Mr. Wilkinson. "Perhaps you know a certain Alexander Graham?"

"To be sure!" I ejaculated. "Mr. Macdonald's nephew!—a very nice young man."

"Well," resumed Wilkinson, "you perhaps also know that Alexander was engaged to one of his cousins?"

"Yes — Mr. Macdonald's daughter," I said. "Proceed, my dear sir."

"His father died the other day, leaving Alexander a considerable fortune. The elder Graham was a very near and close man, and would give his son nothing during his life time. Well, Alexander, on taking possession of the paternal bequest, consigned two-thirds of it to his uncle Mr. Macdonald as a consideration for being admitted into partership on equal terms."

"And thus Mr. Macdonald, in repaying me this enormous sum of money," I said, "is not in any way embarrassing himself?"

"Not in the slightest!" rejoined Mr. Wilkinson. "His own letter to me will enable you to quiet these apprehensions on your part. He is again rich and prosperous: he can hold his head high; and that he can do so, he may thank you, Miss Percy!—for if he had once gone into the Gazette it would have been death to a man of his scrupulous notions of honour. And now, once more permit me to congratulate you on reaping the reward of a good action: for again are you the possessor of the splendid income of twelve thousand a-year!"

CHAPTER CXXX.

A SCENE AT BOULOGNE.

HALF-AN-HOUR after these last words were spoken to me, but while they were still sounding in my ear, I was on my way back to River House. The moment I entered the hall, Juliet came forward, flinging an anxious look upon me, exclaiming, "You have seen Mr. Wilkinson, of course? I do

not think he could have had any evil tidings for you!—and yet his sudden arrival frightened me!"

"I can assure you, dear Juliet, there is nothing to be frightened at," I said; and then seizing her hand, I pressed it with convulsive violence; but my emotions prevented me from giving utterance to another articulate word.

"Oh, if whatever has happened be fraught with bliss," exclaimed Juliet, "most sincerely do I congratulate you! But tell me what it is? Has Henry returned? or have you received good tidings of him?"

"Oh! if I may put faith in present circumstances as auguries for the future," I ejaculated, "Henry will return in safety, and everything will be happy and prosperous for us all! Two hours ago, Juliet, I was wandering dispirited and desponding upon the pier—humiliated and mortified; and now my heart is elate! But it is not that I experience a

selfish pleasure in the possession of riches: it is because they enable me to do good to others."

"Riches, my dear Ellen?" exclaimed Juliet. "What do you mean?"

"I mean," I responded, "that Mr. Macdonald of Paisley is the most honourable of men, and that all my fortune is restored to me!"

A wild cry of joy and surprise burst from Juliet's lips as she threw her arms round my neck and embraced me tenderly. I then explained to her all that I had heard from the lips of Mr. Wilkinson; and concluded by observing, "He is going back to London this afternoon; and to-morrow he will make the requisite remittance to your father at Strasburg, to relieve him from his embarrassments. Indeed, my dear Juliet, it is a thousand pounds which I have ordered to be sent to Mr. Norman; and you must write in a post or two, and devise sufficient reasons for inducing your father to remain abroad for a month or so. It would not do that he should return just at this time, to learn poor Mary's secret! It would necessitate so many explanations, which it were better not to give; and it would likewise overwhelm poor Mary herself with shame."

"Trust to me," said Juliet: "I will write the letter. And, Oh! a thousand, thousand thanks, Ellen, for your kindness towards my dear father! How rejoiced will he be to hear of your renewed prosperity! But, Ah! I have something to tell you——"

"Good heavens!" I ejaculated; "and I had as completely forgotten something as if it had never occurred at all! Here is a packet of letters from your father"

"From my father?" cried Juliet in astonishment. "But how did they come?"

"Whom should I meet just now upon the quay, but Count Teleki——"

"The very name I also was on the point of mentioning!" ejaculated Juliet. "The truth is, I felt uneasy at your prolonged absence: I went out to the front gate to see whether I could discern you coming along the road, when two handsome equipages, drawn by post-horses, dashed past—and from the window of the foremost a very courteous bow was made to me——"

"I am glad you found it courteous, Juliet," I interrupted her; "for I presume you are speaking of Count Teleki? But really I think his conduct would have been somewhat more polite if instead of consigning this packet to me, he had stopped for a moment at River House to deliver it with his own hand. You see, your father has written in the corner, 'Honoured by the Count Teleki.'"

"And I also thought, as the equipages dashed past," said Juliet, in a lower tone than she had previously adopted, and with a slight flush upon her cheeks—"I also thought at the time that he might have stopped, if only for a moment! Because, you remember the last time we saw him in London, he asked so particularly about the situation of River House; and he gratuitously promised with so much apparent sincerity to call as he passed by on his return from the Continent."

"Think of him no more!" I said; "but see if those letters from your father bring any intelligence of importance."

Juliet opened the packet; but she had not perused many lines of its contents, when an ejaculation of mingled surprise and joy burst from her lips—and she exclaimed, "Good heavens, what noble conduct! Ah! your kind deed is anticipated, Ellen!"

"Anticipated? What! is your father relieved from his liabilities?" I asked.

"Yes," rejoined Juliet, her superbly handsome countenance now glowing with animation. "And who do you think is the kind friend——"

"You cannot possibly mean Count Teleki?" I ejaculated.

"I mean Count Teleki," returned Juliet; and deeper grew the blush upon her cheeks. "Oh, how noble, and how delicately done! And still more delicate too, if possible, was the Count's conduct just now, which would not permit him to become the bearer in person of letters announcing his own generous action!"

"Deeply do I regret that I should have mis-

judged him," I said: "but really it was not my own fault. How could I possibly have foreseen that this letter was about to reveal to you so noble an action on Count Teleki's part?"

And noble it indeed was! It appeared that Count Teleki fell in with Mr. Norman at the principal hotel at Strasburg; and having seen Mr. Norman on the stage, he at once recognised him. Rumour whispered in the Count's ear the peculiar situation in which Mr. Norman was placed through a too generous confidence in a perfidious friend; and the Count availed himself of a speedy opportunity to address Mr. Norman on the subject. Then, in the most kind and delicate manner, he forced upon him the sum sufficient to liquidate the obligation,—bidding him repay it at his leisure, but conveying this information in a tone that showed it was veritably a gift, and not a loan which he had bestowed on Juliet's father.

"And what think you, Ellen," asked Juliet, with a blush still glowing upon her cheeks, "of such generous conduct as this?"

I certainly had my own ideas upon the subject. I thought that the Count never would display such wondrous liberality towards the sire, unless he were more or less smitten with the charms of the daughter—and if this were really the case, I had too high an opinion of Count Teleki's honour, from all that I had heard of him, to suppose that he was harbouring any views insulting to the character and reputation of Juliet. But still I did not like to encourage in my friend's mind a hope that might be probably disappointed: and I therefore said in an indifferent and offhand manner, "Oh, this is just the line of conduct which a chivalrous-minded foreigner would be likely to pursue!"

I now sat down to write several letters, for the necessity of a somewhat extensive correspondence was suddenly entailed upon me by the restoration of my fortune. There were numerous friends who were deeply interested in me, and to them I knew that the tidings would prove most welcome. Thus I wrote to the Carshaltons—to Lady Kelvedon—to the Countess of Belgrave—to Aline Gower, and to Charlotte Tremaine; nor did I forget to communicate the joyous intelligence to my faithful dependant Beda. I must also observe that I presently received the warmest congratulations from Mary Glentworth, whose language was fraught with the most sisterly sincerity as she spoke to me on the subject. I must add that I wrote in the kindest possible strain to Mr. Macdonald, assuring him of my everlasting friendship and esteem, and expressing my conviction that all enterprises which were based upon such honourable principles as those which he displayed, must inevitably succeed in the long run.

The hour of Mary Glentworth's sore trial was approaching, and in the evening Mr. Singleton, the surgeon, was fetched. The nurse had already been sent for: and all the requisite preparations, in short, were duly made under Juliet's supervision. I presently found myself alone with Mr. Singleton; and he said to me, "Well, my dear Miss Percy, I think everything has been done that could possibly be contrived for the keeping of Miss Glentworth's secret."

"But you are aware, Mr. Singleton," I responded, "how vitally important it is that the secret should be thus kept, and that the mystery should be surrounded with all possible defences! For from *you* nothing has been hidden!—you who are already so well acquainted with everything relating to Mary Glentworth, were not to be kept in the dark in reference to this, although it is assuredly the most serious episode of her life!"

"And having been fully taken into Miss Glentworth's confidence," returned Mr. Singleton, "it has been my duty and desire to deserve it. Yes—the secret will be duly kept; and when the young lady goes forth into the world again, she may hold her head erect: and she need entertain little fear that when she becomes the bride of the Marquis of Dalrymple, there will be any looks fixed upon her calculated to remind her of the secret and to call up the blushes to her cheeks."

"I sincerely hope, Mr. Singleton." I said, "that all these presages on your part may be fulfilled."

"No doubt of it!" ejaculated the surgeon. "The domestics beneath this roof are all completely trustworthy. They are devoted to their young mistress Lady Frederick Ravenscliffe, and they will therefore do anything for her friend Mary. I do verily believe that not a whisper concerning the real truth has got abroad in the neighbourhood. If there were, it would be sure to have reached my ears or those of my wife."

"Certainly," I interjectingly said; "and therefore we must congratulate ourselves on the fact that the domestics beneath this roof are so little given to gossiping and tittle-tattle. But there is perhaps a still more important point of consideration; and this is the trustworthiness of the persons to whom the child, if it live, is to be consigned."

"Ah, my dear Miss Percy!" interrupted Singleton, surveying me with a mysterious look, "I see that you are not well instructed on the particular point. You must either have misunderstood Lady Frederick and Miss Glentworth — or else they cannot have touched upon the point at all."

"To tell you the truth, Mr. Singleton," I rejoined, "there were other subjects of so grave a character pressing on my attention—alike yesterday evening after my arrival, and throughout this day—that perhaps I have not paid quite as much attention as I ought to the details of the arrangements made for the assurance of my friend Mary's tranquillity and peace in reference to this momentous secret. But I know this much—that the child is to be disposed of a week or two after its birth, in a manner that is so far consistent with tenderness and humanity as the peculiar circumstances of the case will permit."

"Most assuredly," answered Singleton. "The child will be consigned to strangers, and will be brought up by them under whatsoever name they may choose to bestow upon it."

"And those persons *must* be trustworthy!" I interjected.

"Suppose we adopt a course," said Mr. Singleton, "which will render it quite immaterial whether they are trustworthy or not? I mean to say——"

"I begin to understand!" I said: "those persons are not to know whose child it is, nor from whence it comes?"

"Precisely so," answered the surgeon. "I have already made my arrangements. I have a brother, a clergyman, as you are aware: he has by some

means or another—without in any way compromising himself—found out a couple who will take care of the child, and adopt it on certain pecuniary terms which have been agreed upon. In about a fortnight—always supposing the child lives—my wife will take it up to London: an appointment will be made for the woman who is about to adopt the infant, to meet Mrs. Singleton on some particular spot at a stated hour:—the one will receive the child from the arms of the other—and everything will be thus settled!"

"Alas," I said, "it is a sad thing to reflect that a poor innocent little being is to be taken from its mother's bosom and conveyed amongst strangers!"

"But how can it be otherwise in the present case?" asked Mr. Singleton. "Not even you, Miss Percy, with all your rigidly scrupulous notions of propriety and virtue, could possibly argue that Mary Glentworth is bound to sacrifice herself completely on behalf of a child born under such circumstances! Very, very different would it be if this child were the offspring of a moment of weakness when love and passion induced her to yield to the temptation! But she became the victim of a villain, who struck her down, as it were, with a poisoned flower—and she awoke to find herself dishonoured! Nature implants strong feelings in the bosoms of mothers towards their offspring, even though these were the children of shame: but then that shame has been as it were a voluntary fault—and the love which the yielding woman felt towards her seducer, has survived the shock of his inconstancy, to live in the shape of tenderness towards the child. But how different is it in this case!"

"I know it, Mr. Singleton," I interrupted him. "I cannot for a moment blame Mary Glentworth that she should disown and abandon her child."

"You could not even be surprised," added Mr. Singleton, "if she were to hate it?"

I made no answer to this question, and he went on to say, "You know what feeling of bitter, burning hatred she entertains towards the author of her dishonour—a hatred so condensed and concentrated——"

"I know it! I know it, Mr. Singleton!" I ejaculated. "But let us not talk upon the subject."

"I was only about to mention one more fact," said the surgeon; "and this is, that the woman who feels so bitter and burning a hatred towards the father of the child, can scarcely fail to view the child itself with aversion."

Here the discourse ended; and Mr. Singleton repaired to the chamber occupied by Mary Glentworth.

My narrative is now on the point of taking a most extraordinary leap; or at least the reader may consider it to be so, though he will hereafter in due course discover the motive. But let us suppose three weeks to have passed away since the date of which I have just been writing,—three weeks since I received the intelligence of the restoration of my fortune,—three weeks since that discourse with Mr. Singleton which I have just placed upon record. And during these three weeks I returned to Great Ormond Street—I revisited my friends in London—I received their congratulations on account of the wealth that had come back into my hands. Yes—and I had seen the fine dark eyes of Beda light up with an expression of ineffable joy as she felicitated me upon being rich again!

But at the expiration of those three weeks where was I? I am about to explain.

It was verging towards the end of April; and I was an inmate of the principal hotel at Boulogne. I had been there a day or two: I was alone—I had devised some excuse for not bringing Beda with me: indeed she did not know but that I had again left London for the purpose of returning to River House. But why was I now at Boulogne? what business had taken me thither? whom did I expect to meet? The curiosity of the reader shall be satisfied without delay; for it was none other than Herbert Dalrymple whom I was to meet at that hotel in Boulogne on that particular occasion whereof I am writing.

Before I continue the thread of my narrative, I must likewise add that I had written to the Marquis, who was at Naples at the time, to meet me at Boulogne; and hence the appointment which was now being kept, was made by myself.

It was about the hour of noon, on the 23rd of April, when the young Marquis was introduced to the apartment which I occupied in the hotel. Scarcely even giving time for the waiter to close the door after having announced him, he sprang towards me, exclaiming, "For heaven's sake, Miss Percy, put me out of suspense! Why have you sent for me thus strangely and mysteriously? Tell me, I conjure you, has anything happened to poor Mary?"

"Now, my lord," I answered, "you have need of all your fortitude—if you have in reality entertained towards my poor friend that strong affection——"

"Good heavens! I read it all!" ejaculated the young Marquis, with a sudden outburst of passionate grief. "Mary is no more!"

I averted my countenance and said nothing. Herbert flung himself upon a sofa; and burying his face in his hands, remained profoundly still and silent for several minutes. At length he slowly rose from his seat, and taking my hand, he said, "When did this happen, Miss Percy? Tell me the date of the fatal calamity which has deprived us of her whom we both so sincerely loved!"

"It was nearly three weeks back—at the time when I wrote to you."

"But Oh! why did you write so vaguely? why leave me in such cruel suspense?" exclaimed the young nobleman. "I of course comprehended that something had happened, or that evil tidings were in store for me: but I could not conceive what it might be. I thought perhaps Mary's mind had altered;—occasionally the dread idea *did* flash across my brain that death had perhaps done its awful work; but I quickly repudiated the supposition as something too terrible to be true! Oh, why did you leave me, I ask, in that horrible uncertainty?"

"Do not blame me, my lord!—do not blame me, I conjure you," I said, "for the course which I adopted! It was from the best and kindest motives——"

"Oh, I know it! I know it!" cried the young nobleman: "but, Oh! my mind is in that state I feel as if it can only be relieved by throwing an angry blame upon some one! God knows, Miss Percy, that *you* ought to be the last person on earth to be made the victim of my capricious grief!"

"No apology is necessary," I interrupted him. "I can make every allowance for the state of your feelings."

"Alas! that poor Mary should have gone thus!" he moaned, in a voice of bitter lamentation: and now he pressed his hand to his brows.

"Be consoled," I said; "be consoled, my lord!"—and I voluntarily took his other hand in both mine own, as I gazed up into his countenance, where a real and unmistakable grief was expressed.

"You know, Miss Percy," he said, "how earnestly repeated have been my assurances from time to time that I loved Mary devotedly—that I would fulfil my promise towards her——"

"I know it, my lord," I interrupted him. "But Ah! perhaps it is more as an honourable man that you are now grieving, than as a disconsolate lover? —it is because death has deprived you of the power and opportunity of fulfilling the pledges which you made?"

"No, no, Miss Percy!" exclaimed Herbert, with sudden vehemence; "you wrong me by the words you have just spoken—although I am well aware that you had no studied intention to wound my feelings, and that the language which passed from your lips was intended to convey consolation. But you have misunderstood me! If I now pine for Mary's loss, it is because I really loved—yes, loved her truly and sincerely! Oh, could you possibly doubt it?"—and now the tears flowed thick and fast down his cheeks.

I again turned aside, for this scene was a very painful one for me; and bitterly did I repent having undertaken the task.

"Tell me," resumed Herbert, after a long pause, during which he dried his tears, "was Mary sensible in her last moments?—did she breathe my name? did she leave behind her any tender message for one who was little dreaming at the time of the fearful calamity which was destined to smite him,—ruining his hopes and wrecking his happiness?"

"My lord," I said, in a low and tremulous voice, "if I were to tell you that poor Mary in her last moments besought me to convey to you the assurance of her fondest and most devoted love— and if I have to add that she said she was happy in dying thus prematurely, because she feared that if she lived to become your wife your happiness would be compromised if not ruined altogether——"

"Did Mary say all this?" asked Herbert: and again was the white kerchief applied to his eyes.

"If I were to tell you," I continued, "that Mary declared her conviction that heaven itself had interfered for the express purpose of preventing you from making the most generous of sacrifices on her behalf—and if, in pursuing the narrative, I were to inform you that Mary died contented and happy, confident that her departure from this world would prove the means of securing your felicity in the long run by preventing you from making a sacrifice which sooner or later you could not possibly fail to repent——"

"Oh! if it were thus that Mary spoke upon her

death-bed," exclaimed Herbert, "it was most noble
—most magnanimous! and the more therefore do
I grieve at the loss of such a being! But tell me,
Miss Percy—tell me, I entreat and implore—did
Mary die in the assurance of my love?"

"Let us talk no more upon the subject," I said,
—"at least not now. Is it not a very painful one?
—painful for us both?"

"Very painful," responded Herbert: "but yet
it is a topic which we must not immediately abandon. You know not how wild and joyous were
the hopes which I had entertained and cherished
for the future! I used to think to myself that all
the troubles and sorrows endured by poor Mary
should be amply compensated for by the thousand
evidences of love by which I would surround her!
Nay, more—I will even frankly admit to you, Miss
Percy, that in respect to the deplorable state of
mental darkness into which my unfortunate mother
has fallen, I experienced a certain degree of consolation; because I was wont to say to myself, 'The
only real obstacle to my marriage with Mary might
have been presented in my mother's repugnance;
and now that barrier exists not!' Because, as for my
father," continued the young nobleman, "I could
have either cajoled him into giving his assent, or
else I should have altogether dispensed with the
ceremony of asking it. But Oh! of what avail is
aught that I am now saying? Alas! Mary is
gone; and all the hopes that I had cherished for
the future—all the plans that I had conceived, are
suddenly swept away!"

Herbert paced to and fro in the apartment for
several minutes—his features were agitated and
his fingers worked convulsively; for I most scrutinisingly watched all his movements, though I did
not appear to be doing so.

"And then, too, Miss Percy," he presently continued, "I had pictured to myself how Mary
would prove a ministering angel to my poor
mother—how she would resume and perpetuate
those attentions which she so kindly and generously commenced towards my afflicted parent beneath the roof of River House! And my imagination even went further still; for I said to myself
that if some day my poor mother should regain
her intellectual faculties—if she should awaken
from this state of mental darkness to a renewed
daylight of intelligence—she would learn that
Mary had proved the ministering angel—all her
pride and her prejudices would suddenly give way
within her—and she would rejoice that so tender,
so loving, and faithful a creature had become her
daughter-in-law."

"Ah, my lord," I said in a tone that was full of
emotion, "did you really entertain all these dreams
and cherish all these hopes?"

"Oh, can you doubt it, Miss Percy?" he
ejaculated. "No, no! you do not doubt it!—you
know that I am telling you the truth! Alas, poor
Mary!—that she should have died in the belief
that her death was necessary to ensure my happiness, when it was her *life* which would have made
my bliss perfect! Oh, when I think of her—when
her image rises up before me—my God! it scarcely
seems possible that she should have been taken
from me, and that there is now nothing left but to
deplore her!"

Again he paced to and fro in the apartment;
and at the expiration of a few minutes I accosted

him, saying in a low gentle voice, and with as
much kindness as if it were a sister speaking to a
bereaved brother, "You had better retire and be
alone for a few hours. I know what grief is! In
certain stages and phases it requires solitude!"

"Yes—I will retire," said the young nobleman.
"I feel that it would do me good to be alone; for
I will conjure up poor Mary's image—I will apos-
trophize it as if it were veritably a last interview
which was taking place between us—and this will
at least be a consolation!"

The Marquis then left me; and I went forth to
walk, for my mind was much agitated in consequence of the scene that had just taken place.
When I returned to the hotel, I received a message
from the Marquis of Dalrymple requesting another
interview with me. I immediately returned an
affirmative answer; and in a few minutes he
entered my sitting-room. He was very pale, and
there was a settled melancholy upon his countenance.

"Miss Percy," he said, "I have one last favour
to implore. It is that you will tell me where the
remains of our poor lost Mary have been deposited,
and that you will not oppose my wish to proceed
to the spot that I may shed a tear over her last
resting-place?"

"I shall return to England to-morrow morning," I replied; "and you, my lord, if you think
fit, can accompany me. I may venture to offer
you, on Lady Frederick Ravenscliffe's behalf, the
hospitalities of River House."

"From what you have just said," rejoined Herbert, "I gather that the remains of poor Mary are
buried in the churchyard of that picturesque little
village! Doubtless she slumbers in the same grave
with the kind aunt who passed as her mother, and
who performed all the duties of the most tender of
parents? Yes—I will accompany you to-morrow!
But it will not be for many hours that I shall
avail myself of the hospitalities of River House.
I could not endure to linger amidst scenes which
would so vividly and painfully conjure up the
image of poor Mary. No! I will weep over her
grave—I will kneel and pray there,—and then
away again to the scene where my presence may
be required—away to Italy to attend upon my
poor afflicted mother!—for now that my hope is
destroyed that Mary would become the ministering
angel, it will behove me to redouble all my own
attentions. Ah, Miss Percy!" he continued, "you
know not how severe is the blow which I have
sustained! If it had come upon me suddenly, it
would have been completely overwhelming: but I
was more or less prepared for it——or if not for
this, at least for some great calamity—by the
tenour of the letter which you wrote me—so fearfully vague—so mysterious—and yet foreshadow-
ing as it were something of the dread truth! Oh,
during the rapid journey which I have accomplished by travelling day and night from Naples,
I have bewildered myself with conjectures—I have
been a prey to the most painful uncertainty! But
that uncertainty has terminated in the profoundest
grief!"

In a similar strain did Herbert Dalrymple continue to speak for a considerable time, until I at
length availed myself of a pause in the discourse
to ask whether there were any hopes of his mother
regaining the possession of her mental faculties?

"I scarcely know what to think," replied Herbert. "At first we had great hopes from the Genoese physician; but those hopes were disappointed. Then we were led to expect great things from the Neapolitan physician: but alas! I begin to fear that the result will prove the same as it was elsewhere."

"And your lordship's father," I said,—"how does he bear himself under this calamity which has overtaken her Grace?"

"You know my father well enough, Miss Percy," answered the young Marquis, "to be aware that he has not a heart ample enough to feel as he ought to do in such a case. It is a shocking thing that a son should be compelled to confess that there are times when he is disgusted with the frivolity of his own parent: but so alas! it is. He has got his friend Mr. Peaseblossom with him; and perhaps, after all, he is to be envied in respect to that absence of sensitiveness which prevents him from feeling the misfortune which has overtaken my poor mother."

It happened that the apartments which were allotted to the Marquis of Dalrymple at the hotel, were immediately above my own. Thus during the night which followed the day whereof I have been writing, I heard him pace to and fro for hours in his room ere he finally retired to rest. I therefore knew that he did indeed deeply feel the intelligence which I had communicated to him.

CHAPTER CXXXI.

THE FOLDING-DOORS.

Soon after breakfast on the following morning, I embarked on board the steam-packet for Dover. The Marquis of Dalrymple accompanied me. He looked pale and ill: he spoke in a voice of profound melancholy; and several times during the passage he said to me, "It appears to be all a dream! a vague and terrible dream!"

I surveyed him very earnestly on the third or fourth occasion when with a species of abruptness he made this remark to me; and I said slowly and hesitatingly, "Perhaps, my lord, the time may come when you will look back to this period and say to yourself that everything happened for the best! Nay, do not interrupt me—but listen for a few minutes!" I continued, my tone gaining firmness as I went on. "You will some day become Duke of Ardleigh: one of the proudest coronets of England will rest upon your brow! You may then think to yourself that after all it is fortunate that circumstances did not compel you to fulfil the promise which at a period of the most magnanimous generosity you had made! You may haply reflect that the Duchess of Ardleigh ought to be a lady taken from the ranks of the aristocracy—so that by position, or perhaps by wealth also, she might constitute a suitable match for one occupying your proud eminence. If all this should be the case, my lord, you will not repine that heaven should have taken poor Mary so prematurely! but you may congratulate yourself on having been shielded and saved from becoming the victim of your heart's own mistake!"

"By heaven, you wrong me, Miss Percy!"

ejaculated Herbert vehemently. "I am surprised at you—and your words add to my grief! You will not give me credit for a pure, sincere, and holy love for your deceased friend Mary!—you return again and again to harp upon a string which vibrates so painfully to my heart's core!—and if you had not proved to me the sincere and kind friend that you have been on so many, many occasions, I should be unable to answer you with ordinary patience. You wrong me! To any other person I should also say that I am insulted! My heart has made no mistake. It has truly and faithfully loved Mary Glentworth: it now mourns for her with the deepest grief. This love of mine was not the fleeting caprice of the moment—it was not the passion of an hour: it has been tried by the lapse of time;—and this you know, Miss Percy! Ah, I see that because there was a period of my life which seemed so little creditable to me —when you discovered that I was growing dissipated and a gambler—it is for this reason that you have never since entertained any real confidence in me!"

"You are wrong—you are wrong, my lord!" I said; "and I should not be justified in leaving you for another moment in such an error. By your conduct subsequent to the period to which you have just alluded, you have regained my good opinion—and of this you are aware."

"Then why address me in these terms, so full of suspicion?" exclaimed the young Marquis reproachfully: "why mistrust the strong love I felt for Mary? You did not thus speak to me when some months ago you consented that I should look upon her as my intended wife. And is it now when the grave has received the lamented object of my love, that this love should become the subject of distrust? Or is it that you think I am unworthy to kneel, to weep, and to pray above the resting-place of the departed?"

"No, no, my lord!" I said, deeply affected. "I do not think so——and pardon me, I implore you, if my language may have seemed too severe!"

"At all events," rejoined the young nobleman, seriously, "if ever I had thought it worth while to play the hypocrite, it is not now that poor Mary is gone and that she is insensible to any word or deed on my part!"

This discourse took place in the cabin of the steam-packet, where we were alone at the time; and in another half-hour we landed at Dover.

"If you have no objection, Miss Percy," said Herbert, "we will set out and walk. I should like to tread the path for the last time, which has been so often trodden by poor Mary—to look upon the picturesque cottage where so large a portion of her existence was spent—to wander through the fields where she has so often strayed——and then," he added, sinking his voice to a low and scarcely audible whisper, "to enter the churchyard and perform the duties which have now brought me to England!"

"We will walk," I said: and I averted my countenance, for I was under the influence of emotions which I will not now pause to describe.

We continued our way in silence, until the picturesque cottage was reached; and then Herbert stopped short, leant upon the gate, and surveyed the scene.

"It was in that summer-house," I whispered to

him, "that I first beheld poor Mary. This was two years ago. She was sitting at work,—her light brown ringlets showering upon her shoulders —the rose-hues of health upon her cheeks—her countenance expressing the purest thoughts——"

But I stopped short; for Herbert Dalrymple was now groaning audibly, and it did me harm to hear him. The tears streamed down his cheeks: he leant upon the gate—he buried his face in his hands, and sobbed violently.

"My lord!" I said; "my lord! pray forgive me for having touched a chord which has excited such painful feelings!"

"Oh, you have no need, Miss Percy, to ask for my forgiveness," he said. "I wish you to talk of Mary! Yes—speak of her in that tender strain ; for it does me good to weep for her!"

"Oh, then," I said, "you did love her very, very sincerely? Yes—I am sure of it!"

"Would to God," he passionately exclaimed, "that by surrendering the half of my own existence I could restore life to her whom I loved and whom I have lost! Yes—speak of her, Miss Percy! tell me of her as she was when you first knew her!"

"We will not now go to the churchyard," I said, as we moved away from the front of the picturesque little cottage. "Let us go on to River House. Lady Frederick Ravenscliffe will be anxious to see me—and she will speak to you of Mary. Besides, she may be desirous——"

"Yes, yes—I comprehend!" interjected Herbert: "she may be desirous to accompany us to the churchyard. Your suggestion shall be obeyed, Miss Percy: we will go first to River House. Indeed it is after all a suitable and proper act of courtesy which I owe Lady Frederick after her generous and hospitable conduct towards my poor mother."

River House was soon reached; and as the front door stood open—for Juliet had beheld our approach from a distance—I at once conducted Herbert up to the front drawing-room. I there requested him to remain for a few minutes;—and it was only for a few minutes that I left him there alone. When I returned to him, he was leaning against a window-recess, absorbed in such profound thought that he did not hear the door open ; and I paused to contemplate him for a moment.

"My God! my God!" I heard him murmur, in a tone of the bitterest lamentation; "that I should have come hither to weep for Mary's death, instead of to claim her as my bride!"

I advanced towards Herbert: he turned—and beholding me, said, "Where is your friend Lady Frederick Ravenscliffe?"

"She will be here presently," I responded. "Does it still appear to you as if it were a dream?"

"Yes—all a dream," rejoined Herbert, in a tone profoundly mournful. "I know that it is true!—as a matter of course I have a perfect conviction that all which you have told me has happened!—but still I feel a difficulty in realizing it in my own mind. Good heavens! if instead of coming to this house to gaze as it were upon the vacant places which were once occupied by Mary, it were to behold her bounding forward to receive me, how happy should I be!"

"Can your imagination depict such a scene?"

I asked. "Come—let us sit down together, and you shall tell me to what extent the fancy may reach under such circumstances."

"Oh, Miss Percy," answered Herbert, "you desire me to do something which would only be followed by the most painful feelings! You ask me to imagine a picture fraught with delight and bliss ; whereas, O God! it is one—it is one"—and here his voice was almost choked by his emotions —"of darkness and sadness and woe! Ah! heard I not some one else lamenting in the adjoining room?" and he glanced towards the folding-doors which separated the two apartments.

"Yes—there is some one sobbing there," I answered,—"some one whose bosom is at this moment so agitated——"

"You mean Lady Frederick Ravenscliffe?" interrupted the young nobleman. "Ah! she was likewise deeply attached to poor Mary! But now I bethink me!" ejaculated Herbert, turning his gaze suddenly upon me, and I might even say sharply upon me ; "it did not strike me before!"

"What mean you?" I asked.

"You, Miss Percy," pursued the Marquis, "have not displayed so much sorrow for the loss of your dear friend as I could have expected! Not once—no, not once have I heard from your lips such sobbings as were just now audible from the adjoining room! How is this? You, so sensitive!—so kind-hearted—not to have been more deeply afflicted than you are! And then too, you are not in mourning, Miss Percy! Yet how often have you told me that you loved poor Mary as if she were your own sister!"

"Is it not in the power of heaven," I asked, "to turn mourning looks into smiles?"

"Oh, Miss Percy! a smile upon your lips," exclaimed Herbert, "when the earth has only closed so recently over the remains of your friend! But what mean you? Oh, there is something strange in your look! Ah, that smile again! What? instead of tears—instead of sobbings and lamentations, your countenance is lighting up with joy!"

"Oh! and smiles shall be upon your face also," I cried, in an exulting voice ; "and there shall be no mourning!—and when you visit the church, it shall not be to kneel over the grave or weep over the tomb of a perished and lost one—but it shall be to conduct a bride to the altar!"

"Ellen!—Miss Percy! what mean you?" and Dalrymple sprang up from his seat, gazing upon me in utter bewilderment — as well indeed he might!

"I mean—I mean," I ejaculated,—"that you have been put to a test—a cruel and a severe one perhaps—yet necessary——"

"Just heaven! is this true?"—and the words pealed forth from Herbert's lips in a tone that was as much as to implore that he should be kept no longer in suspense. "No, no! you would not trifle with me! Tell me—tell me—I beseech you!—tell me! Mary—Mary—is—is——"

"Mary lives!" I answered : "she lives!"

At that moment the folding-doors opened; and Mary Glentworth made her appearance. But instead of bounding forward to welcome her faithful and constant lover, she was suddenly transfixed to the spot: a deadly pallor overspread her features—she tottered and would have fallen but that Herbert, darting towards her with a wild cry of indescribable joy, caught her in his arms. And then her arms were thrown around his neck—the sensation of faintness passed off—and she wept and sobbed for very happiness! I lingered for a few moments to gaze upon the scene; and then I glided from the room, leaving the lovers together.

In reference to the stratagem which had been practised towards the Marquis of Dalrymple, a few words of explanation must be given. It was originally suggested by Lady Frederick Ravenscliffe; and it was caught at with avidity by Mary Glentworth. It was no wonder that the experiences of Juliet's life should have prompted the idea of putting the young nobleman's love for Mary to the severest test; nor was it astonishing that, peculiarly situated as Mary herself was, she should have sanctioned a course the result of which would be to show her whether it were wise to bestow her hand on Herbert Dalrymple, or whether it would be more prudent for her to release him altogether from his engagement. I confess that at first I did not fall very readily into the plot, because I dislike all duplicities, deceptions, and misrepresentations of every kind. But when I came very seriously to contemplate the plan thus proposed for my co-operation—and when I duly weighed the importance of the result that was to be obtained —I certainly came to the conclusion that if ever there were a stratagem which though based on falsehood, appeared venial and justifiable, it was this. Having been led to adopt that view of it, it will be no longer surprising to the reader that I should have yielded to Mary Glentworth's entreaties and Juliet's representations, and that I became the principal actress in carrying out the scheme. My own opinion in reference to the result may be gathered from the following explanation which I gave to Juliet so soon as I had left the Marquis and Mary together:—

"I can assure you, my dear Juliet, that I tested Herbert in every possible way. At one time I bade him divert his attention from the topic: but he insisted upon coming back to it. I directed his thoughts towards the future years of his life, and spoke to him of the period when he would become Duke of Ardleigh: but nothing that I thus suggested seemed to engender the slightest selfish consideration nor to render worldly-minded motives dominant over the heart's affections. On the other hand, I addressed myself to his tenderest sensibilities: I spoke to him of Mary as she was when first I knew her; and then you should have seen how the tears gushed forth from his eyes and how convulsive were the sobs that rent his heart!"

"The experiment has therefore succeeded," exclaimed Juliet; "and the happiness of our dear friend Mary will be all the more complete! Did the Marquis ask you any questions——"

"Do you mean in reference to Mary's recent confinement?" I inquired; and then, as Juliet intimated an affirmative, I went on to say, "The Marquis put not a single question upon the point. I suffered him to understand that the child lived —that it was of the female sex—and that the little infant had been consigned to the care of trustworthy persons. And now that Herbert has discovered that the tale of Mary's death was a mere fiction —now that he is rendered supremely happy, and

that he will shortly lead her to the altar—he will doubtless breathe an inward vow never more to allude to that one past incident in her life!"

"Think you that he will never speak to her of the child?" asked Lady Frederick,—"that he will not out of very generosity propose something sooner or later for the child's welfare?"

"Oh! this is a question, my dear Juliet," I exclaimed, "on which we need not now speculate! It belongs to the future. The child is provided for under all circumstances."

Here the conversation dropped: but in reference to the remark which had just fallen from my own lips, I ought to observe that all the moneys of which Mary Glentworth could dispose, were appropriated for the purpose alluded to. She had the legacy of five hundred pounds bequeathed her by Mrs. Oldcastle; and she had some savings which she had made during the short time she was upon the stage. These amounts, together with a sum which I had insisted upon adding from my own newly acquired riches, constituted a handsome fund for the maintenance of the child, which had been consigned to the care of strangers.

Need I inform the reader that Herbert Dalrymple speedily forgave us all for the stratagem which had been practised, and of which he even approved? Indeed he felt proud at having been put to such a test, painful to his feelings though at the time it had been. He remained a week at River House; and at the expiration of that interval he set off again for Naples.

Mary Glentworth and Juliet now accompanied me to London, to stay with me at my own house in Great Ormond Street. Mary's health was completely restored; and Beda declared that she thought the trip of a few months to the neighbourhood of the sea-side had made Miss Glentworth look handsomer than ever.

Count Teleki now became a very frequent visitor in Great Ormond Street; and it was by no means difficult to perceive where the attraction lay. The idea I had formed some time previously on the subject seemed to be fully justified: the rich Hungarian nobleman was enamoured of Lady Frederick. Mr. Norman now returned to England, in better health and spirits than he had been since his wife's death. I need hardly state that it was with the most unfeigned pleasure he beheld the attentions which Count Teleki was bestowing upon his daughter; and I may add that in a little private discourse which took place between Mr. Norman and myself, I was enabled to inform him that Juliet had confessed to me she was very far from insensible to the handsome person, fascinating manners, and many excellent qualities of the Hungarian nobleman.

Upwards of two months elapsed from the date of the stratagem practised towards the Marquis of Dalrymple; and now this young nobleman himself returned from Italy. I had suggested that it would be expedient for him to obtain, if possible, his father's sanction to his marriage with Mary Glentworth—or at all events to communicate to his ducal sire his intentions on the point. He had the tact to enlist on his side the interest of Mr. Peaseblossom; and this gentleman used his influence with the Duke so effectually as to obtain his sanction to the alliance. The Duke would not however consent to come to England to

be present at the ceremony : but he gave his written concurrence therewith,—in the same document pledging himself that he would continue to make a handsome pecuniary allowance to his son. He moreover agreed to receive and to recognise Mary as his daughter-in-law. Thus his refusal to be present at the wedding—a refusal which was in reality a mere ridiculous caprice—threw not the slightest damp upon the spirits of the bridegroom and his bride nor any of their friends ; for it had all along been wished and agreed that the nuptials should be celebrated without ostentation or display.

The reader will remember that at the time when Mary Glentworth fell in with the Duke of Ardleigh at the jeweller's shop, and when she likewise discovered that the lover who had been wooing her under the name of Beauchamp, was really the Marquis of Dalrymple—the Duchess of Ardleigh gave the sum of ten thousand pounds to

be laid out for Mary's benefit. But at that time the young lady was fearfully embittered against the Ardleigh family, and she would receive no boon at their hands. It will also be borne in mind that an arrangement was privately made on Mary's behalf, by Mr. Wilkinson and myself,—according to which that sum of money was bought into the Funds in the lawyer's name, but in trust for the use and service of Mary herself. It was now therefore for the first time that she became acquainted with the fact that this transaction had taken place : but the Duke of Ardleigh mentioned it in a letter which he wrote to her, declaring that she was heartily welcome to that sum as a marriage-portion. As a matter of course there was not the slightest hesitation on Mary's part to accept it ; and Mr. Wilkinson prepared a marriage-settlement accordingly.

It was on the 30th of June, of the year of which I am writing (namely, 1843), that the Marquis of

Dalrymple led Mary Glentworth to the altar. There was a small and select circle of friends assembled at my house to constitute the bridal party. Mr. Norman gave the bride away; Miss Wyvill (one of Lady Kelvedon's sisters) and myself acted as bridesmaids. Mary looked remarkably handsome; and the bridegroom seemed alike to be proud and fond of her. When the wedding breakfast had been partaken of at my house, the newly-married couple set off in a travelling carriage for Dover, whence they proceeded to the Continent that they might join the ducal family at Naples. It was on the same day that Count Teleki proposed to Juliet. Exactly a year had elapsed since the death of her first husband, Lord Frederick Ravenscliffe; and the Hungarian nobleman had with characteristic delicacy awaited the expiration of the full period of a widow's mourning before he thus avowed his suit. His offer was not refused; and Mr. Norman had the satisfaction of beholding his daughter engaged to a noble foreigner of the highest respectability and possessed of immense wealth

Count Teleki had already obtained from me a statement of the exact position of Juliet's affairs; and he now displayed the natural generosity of his disposition. He suggested that Juliet should make over River House and all the other property to her father, so that the latter might be placed in independence with an income of nearly a thousand a-year. In consideration of this proceeding on Juliet's part, Count Teleki voluntarily made a settlement of three thousand a-year upon her, besides purchasing in her name a splendid mansion in Belgrave Square—for the nobleman purposed to pass a considerable period every year in England.

Pecuniary matters being thus handsomely and eligibly settled, it was agreed that the marriage should take place at River, so that Mr. Norman might give his daughter away from the house which had now become his own abode. Besides, the honeymoon was to be passed upon the Continent; and Dover was close by for the purpose of embarkation. I suggested to Juliet that for more reasons than one it would be expedient, or at least proper for her to pay her respects to the Earl and Countess of Carshalton; for I represented to her that not only was she their daughter-in-law—but her intended husband, Count Teleki, was intimate with them; and moreover, they had expressed their approval of the match, and had spoken in very kind terms of herself. I likewise bade her observe that as the star of her happiness was in the ascendant, and she was about to become more brilliantly settled in life than ever she had yet been, it was an excellent opportunity for the renunciation of all old rancours;—and she made no difficulty in yielding to my arguments. She accordingly accompanied me to Carshalton House, where a very different scene took place from that which had occurred on the former occasion of the visit thither; for now every unpleasant feeling was laid aside, and the embrace in which she was folded by the Earl and Countess, was cordially returned. Many costly gifts were now bestowed by the Earl and Countess upon Juliet: they included the casket of jewels which on a former occasion had been so positively declined; but this time no refusal was offered—and on the contrary, it was with

the most friendly gratitude that Juliet accepted these various proofs of the noble couple's favour. As a matter of course, they were invited to be present at the bridal,—which, as I have already stated, was arranged to take place in Kent.

Accordingly about one month after the marriage of Herbert and Mary, a somewhat numerous party was assembled at River House. There were the Earl and Countess of Carshalton—Mr. Norman and Juliet — Mr. Wilkinson, the lawyer — Lord and Lady Kelvedon—Miss Wyvill—Colonel and Mrs. Gower—and myself. I had taken Beda with me;—and here I may as well observe that both Juliet and myself experienced every certainty that however the name of Mary Glentworth (now Marchioness of Dalrymple) might chance to be mentioned within the walls of River House, there was no fear of the secret transpiring which so nearly concerned her good name and repute.

Count Teleki had remained in London to settle some few little affairs; but he was to come down to Dover on the day following our arrival at River House; and he was to take up his temporary quarters at the Ship Hotel ere the nuptial ceremony would serve as the signal for his departure with his bride on their Continental tour. The Count came according to appointment; and happiness was depicted upon his fine handsome countenance, while smiles of love and joy irradiated the beautiful features of my friend Juliet. The Count dined at River House in the evening of his arrival at Dover; and little thought I when we sat down to the banquet, how memorable that evening was to prove in the annals of my own existence!

It was the 31st of July, 1843; and I had completed my twenty-first year. Heaven knows I was not envious of the happiness which Juliet experienced; but I could not prevent a feeling of sadness from coming over me, as I sat at the dinner-table. I strove to rally my spirits to the best of my ability; but I could not succeed—though I believe that I veiled this mournful sensation so as not to betray it. I would not for the world have thrown a damp upon the happiness of that scene which was taking place on the eve of a bridal! Besides, I myself was the object of so much kindness and consideration on the part of every one present,—such dear friends of mine were there—Juliet, Aline, Hermione—and then too there were the Earl and Countess of Carshalton, and the worthy Mr. Norman, who regarded me with a species of parental affection —that I felt I should be guilty of something that might even savour of ingratitude if I were to exhibit sadness and mournfulness while they were all in their turns saying kind and cheerful things unto me. But soon after the dessert had been placed upon the table, a sense of such deep depression stole over me that I felt as if I must inevitably burst into tears. I rose from the table, and left the room.

It was a little past seven o'clock in the evening —the weather was exquisitely beautiful—a gentle breeze was attempering the sultriness which had marked the sun's progress that day—and the loveliest flowers were still pouring forth their fragrance around me ere they folded their leaves to woo a dewy slumber. The scene produced a sudden tranquilising effect upon my mind, so that the tears which had a few minutes before flowed as it were to the very brims of my eyes, were held back. But why had I been so sad? and why was it that the spectacle of Juliet's happiness had excited that sorrow in my mind—though heaven knows that it was untinctured by envy! I could not help thinking to myself that the loves of all my friends and acquaintances seemed to prosper, while mine had hitherto experienced only disappointment and calamity. Aline had espoused the object of her heart's devotion—Mary Glentworth was equally signalized by Fortune's smile—the same was now to be said of Juliet: while I was in a state of painful uncertainty relative to the fate of my own well-beloved Henry Wakefield! It was nearly a twelvemonth since he and my father had set off for California; and months had elapsed since I had last received any intelligence from them. Six months had gone by since William Lardner had set off to America in quest of them; and only once had any intelligence been received from him—and this was when he first arrived at New York. And here was I, rich once more—the possessor of a large fortune—and there were bright prospects awaiting Henry Wakefield—and yet he came not! I knew not even whether he was still in the land of the living: for often and often when I had reflected upon the stupendous perils which must be encountered by those who journey across the whole immense region of North America, from the landing-place on the eastern shore to the littoral of the mighty North Pacific—I had shuddered and trembled on behalf of those who were so dear to me—my lover and my father! Oh, what had become of them? what had become of them? It was this question which had over and over again recurred to my mind while I was seated at the banqueting-table!—it was this bewildering conjecture which had overshadowed my soul with its gloom!

I paced slowly along the gravel-walk in the garden: the soft tranquillity of the scene infused a sensation of relief into my heart. I stopped short near an enormous vase; and there I fell into a deep reverie. I thought to myself that heaven would scarcely be so harsh and cruel as to sunder me for ever from those on whose safe return my happiness so entirely depended: I blamed myself for having yielded to Henry's mad scheme of seeking an El Dorado in the Far West; and then I mentally exclaimed, "But it was not my fault! he was resolute!—and after all, he was impelled by the most laudable spirit of independence!"

As I thought of my cousin, my recollections were slowly carried back to other scenes and incidents: I remembered him as I had first seen him —a tall, genteel, and slender lad; and I recollected how I had then thought to myself that his large brown eyes, shaded by their ebon lashes, were the most beautiful I had ever seen. Then I remembered how I had again seen my cousin Henry: it was at the time of my grandfather's death; and though I was overwhelmed with grief, yet even then I could not help thinking how genteel and agreeable he was growing! And next my reminiscence settled upon the period when I lived with my aunt and Henry at Sheffield; and I recollected how a consternation had smitten him, and how tears had started into his handsome dark-

brown eyes, when I announced my intention of going to London to seek my own bread! Oh, as I thus retrospected, I felt that I had long loved my cousin dearly—very dearly!—and the deeper grew this conviction in my mind, the stronger became the feeling also that if anything were to happen to Henry I could not survive the misfortune. No! it would be the same as dealing a death-blow unto myself, if I were to be told that the hand of the ruthless Destroyer had smitten down the object of my love—had turned into marble those Grecian features that were wont to beam with intelligence, and had dimmed the light that shone so luminously in the large brown eyes!

I was suddenly startled from my reverie at the moment when it was reaching its most painful crisis: I heard the front gate open and shut—then there were the sounds of footsteps. I looked up—and O heaven! what a cry of joy it was that suddenly pealed from my lips as I caught sight of those of whom I had been thinking! Yes—there was my cousin Henry! there was also my father! and between them was a third person. Ah! was this possible? did I indeed behold the countenance of Mr. Moss?

Towards my sire and my cousin I flew!—towards me they flew likewise!—and in a few moments I was folded in their arms. By turns they embraced me—that father and that cousin who were restored to me!—and I need not say how fervidly I embraced them in return. But in the midst of my own joy—in the vortex as it were of my own wild delight, I was not so selfish as to forget the happiness of another who was dear to me; and thinking of Beda, I inquired anxiously, "Have you seen William Lardner?"

"There! there!" ejaculated both my father and Henry; and glancing in the direction to which they pointed, I beheld the delighted Beda clasped in the arms of her faithful William.

But now another scene of exciting interest took place: for Moss, throwing himself at my feet, exclaimed, "They have promised that you will pardon me, Miss Percy! Oh, promise that you will do so!"

"This penitent young man, dear Ellen," said my father, "has come to restore you the fortune of which he plundered you. Yes! the whole of it—thirty-six thousand pounds and upward——"

"Whatever promises you have made," I replied, with a gush of joyous emotions, as I glanced from my father to my cousin, "I am only too happy to confirm."

"And thus you are rich once more, dearest Ellen!" cried Henry.

"Yes—richer far than you at present surmise," I exclaimed: "for Mr. Macdonald has restored me everything—wealth has come to me from that quarter also——"

"God be thanked!" ejaculated my father; while at the same time a cry of exultation burst from the lips of Henry.

"Yes," I said; "Fortune has reserved all her bounties to shower them upon me thick and fast."

"Oh! you are now rich, dear Ellen," cried Henry: "but we have no such favourable tale to tell! Obedient to your summons we returned; and if the hopes at which in your letter you vaguely and mysteriously hinted, be doomed to disappointment——"

"They will not, dear Henry! they will not!" I ejaculated, in a tone of thrilling joy: "for you are indeed the heir to the earldom and estates of Carshalton!"

CHAPTER CXXXII.

HENRY.

BY this time the intelligence had spread through the house that the wanderers had returned, and that those who had roamed far away to the wild regions of the Western World, had come back to bless with their presence those by whom they were beloved. And forth from the dining-room poured the entire company; and then there were introductions on the part of those who were not acquainted before; and I unhesitatingly presented my parent by his right name of Mr. Percy, and proclaimed him as my father. For I knew that the Earl of Carshalton, in pursuance of a promise that he had often made to me, would be the first to stand forward and grasp him by the hand. And so it indeed happened. But scarcely had I introduced my father and Henry to those with whom they were previously unacquainted, than some one whispered in my ear, "Miss Percy, one word—and I leave you!"

I looked round; and Mr. Moss was standing at my elbow.

"Here," he said, presenting a small sealed packet—and he spoke in a voice that was full of emotion,—"I vowed that with my own hand I would restore you your fortune; and my word is fulfilled. Take it! you will find the sum correct. Repeat the assurance that you forgive me!"

"You may safely do so, Ellen," my father now whispered in my ear. "I know that the sum is contained in that packet, and that it is correct."

"I forgive you, Mr. Moss," I said: "from the very bottom of my heart do I forgive you!"

"A thousand thanks!" he said: he then grasped my hand for a moment—and darting away, was quickly lost to the view.

Oh! now it was a perfect whirl and confusion of felicitations and rejoicings—of congratulations and explanations—hurried words and excited feelings—language itself losing its coherency in the intoxication of bliss! And now I flew across the lawn to embrace my faithful Beda and felicitate her upon her lover's return; and then I grasped the hand of William Lardner himself, and I expressed my fervid thanks for the zeal and fidelity with which he had accomplished his mission. And then I rushed back, like a wild giddy girl, to the happy group from which I had burst away; and now I heard Lord Carshalton saying, as he held Henry's hand clasped in his own, "Yes — it is needless to maintain any further mystery on the point! The great Wakefields of Warwickshire were unquestionably heirs to the Carshalton peerage in case of failure in the direct lineage of Ravenscliffe. And here is the last scion of that family of Wakefield—the sole living representative thereof! He is my heir; and when I go down into the grave, an Earl's coronet will sit upon his

brow. But while I live, he shall be as dear to me as the son whom I lately lost!"

The scene had now become affecting; and tears trickled down many a cheek.

"How wonderful is all this!" whispered my father to me.

"Did you never suspect," I inquired, "that such an event might come about?"

"Never, never!" he responded. "I know so little of James Wakefield whom my poor sister married—and I knew nothing of the family to which he belonged."

This colloquy of my father was quickly cut short; for the Earl of Carshalton, hastily accosting me, took my hand and said, "Need I tell those who are gathered around, that our dear friend Ellen is the pattern of her sex! And Oh! it is not in a slight degree that I rejoice for her sake that the titles and the honours that I now possess will descend to him to whom her heart is devoted and who will lead her to the altar!"

Thus speaking, he placed my hand in that of my cousin Henry; and Oh! what love, what joy, what happiness then irradiated the faultless Grecian features and beamed in the large dark brown eyes!

My heart was so full of blissful emotions that I scarcely recollected how it was Henry and I now became separated from the group, and how we presently found ourselves walking alone together in one of the shady avenues of the garden. It was then the soft witching period of twilight; and there was a silence and a serenity in the scene congenial with what the state of our own feelings now was. Oh, the deep luxury of those feelings!—a depth of happiness too great for utterance—an amount of bliss too immense to find expression in words! But as we gazed upon each other with a species of subdued rapture, our looks denoted all we felt: there was a transfusion of the spirit of illimitable affection! And as I gazed upon him, methought that he was handsomer than ever. For if the torrid sun of another clime had somewhat embrowned his cheeks, it had rendered his aspect more manly; and there was the same faultless chiselling of the Grecian features—the same ivory whiteness of the teeth—the same clustering of the dark glossy hair in natural curls—the same light of love and frankness and intelligence in the handsome eyes! And on the other hand I know that he thought I also looked more beautiful than ever; for often and often has he since whispered this much in my ear—and even now that years have elapsed since *then*, he tells me that he still beholds me before him as I was that evening when we met after so long a severance—with my full dress toilet, my long raven ringlets showering down upon my shoulders, and happiness dancing in the depths of my dark eyes! Ah, it was not the least source of the happiness which we mutually felt, that in this meeting each exceeded in beauty and personal attraction the image which the other had been depicting; so that as he appeared handsomer in my eyes than ever I had before thought him, handsome though he always was,—in the same manner did I seem more beautiful in his estimation, lovely though he had always deemed me!

Some of my readers may think that all that I have just been saying is poor and puerile—that it is maudlin and lovesick—and that it ought not to find place in a sober serious narrative such as this. But well assured am I that this portion of my readers will be but few in number, and will indeed constitute the great minority. For all who have loved in their life's spring-time when the heart is in its freshness, will understand and appreciate the feeling which influences me *now* to chronicle all that I *then* felt. Oh! after a twelve-month's separation to meet again without a single pang to mitigate the joy of such meeting—to look upon each other and to behold that whatsoever good looks we might possess had been improved rather than marred by the lapse of time,—for one to say to himself, "She is more beautiful than when we parted!" and for the other to whisper mentally, "He is handsomer than when I bade him adieu!"—and to remember that parting moment when the eyes were filled with tears and the lineaments were agonized with grief—to contrast that with the present, and now to read love and joy in each other's eyes, and to see smiles upon each other's lips, and to know when those lips meet in kisses that they are not the sad tender tokens of farewell, but the joyous evidences of a re-union that is not to be parted,—Oh! does not all this constitute a paradise or rapture which is well worthy of being depicted! Few, few indeed are those who will not thank me for imaging this elysium in contrast with the many, many dreary scenes which have occupied more than one chapter in the former portion of my narrative.

And so Henry and I walked slowly to and fro in the shady avenue, his arm circling my waist, and our hands clasped. And there was a deep sense of the permanency of our happiness: there was in our souls the rooted conviction that our trials were over, and that poetic justice was about to be awarded unto us, just as we read of it in a novel or a romance. There was I, the possessor of riches, so that it would be with a great dower that I should go to the altar!—there was he, heir to great riches, and to a title likewise, so that it was with every possible advantage that young man of three-and-twenty would shortly settle himself in the world, with me, his young bride of one-and-twenty! All this we knew and felt; and it was eloquently expressed in the looks that we bent upon each other.

And there we rambled in the shady avenue, until at length we began to enter upon mutual explanations of everything that had occurred since we parted a twelvemonth back. But still it was some time before we could so far compose our feelings as to to give continuity and consecutiveness to our discourse; so that I shall not attempt to detail that conversation, just as it occurred, in which we were thus mutually explanatory. But it must be in a narrative-shape that I will put the reader in possession of the facts which I learnt from my cousin Henry.

He and my father had arrived in safety at New York; and thence they had written to me some letters which I duly received. At New York they made the most searching inquiries relative to that El Dorado which stretched its peninsular length along the western shore of Mexico. Having acquired sufficient information to confirm all the reports which Henry had heard when previously he was in America, in respect to California, they

had set off to accomplish the immense overland route across the entire width of the American Union. They had followed as nearly as possible the forty-second or forty-third degree of latitude; and every now and then, at convenient places, they had written letters to me. Few of these had ever arrived: it was only the first two or three communications that had reached me. By every possible variety of mode of travelling had they progressed,—sometimes being hurried along by the whirling locomotive on the railway—at others ploughing in a stately steamer one of the mighty rivers of that Continent where everything is so grand, the features of nature as well as the achievements of man,—now making their difficult way, on horseback, through the vast primeval forests or over the almost illimitable prairies—at other times compelled to pursue their wearisome journey on foot; exposed to a thousand perils, until at last the region they sought was gained. But then came bitter disappointment! They found that though they had not been misinformed in reference to the Gold Country, they must abandon every hope of obtaining the precious metal for themselves; for tribes of barbarous Indians were in possession of those districts, and their lives would have been equally safe if they had lain to sleep in a morass swarming with reptiles. To be brief, after incurring some fearful risks (and I subsequently heard from my father's lips marvellous accounts of my lover's courage and chivalrous daring) they were compelled to abandon the golden land which they had with such difficulty reached, and with mournful hearts resolve to retrace their way towards New York. But if they had previously encountered hardships and perils and difficulties, their former experiences were as nothing to what they had now to endure; for they were plundered of the pecuniary resources which remained to them; and on foot were they toiling their wearisome way, when on arriving in one of the central cities of the Union, they accidentally beheld their names mentioned in a newspaper.

Here let me break off the thread of the narrative for a few minutes, to chronicle the proceedings, as rapid as they were sagacious, of William Lardner. On arriving in America, he had followed the track of my father and cousin so far as I had been enabled to direct him by means of the last communication which I had received from them. By a careful study of geographical circumstances and of particular lines of route — always keeping their ultimate destination in view—he had gone on; and in every important city or town which he reached, he had inserted advertisements in the newspapers which could not fail to be intelligible to them if happening to meet their eyes. Of course all this was done at random; for William knew not whether he might overtake them, should they have happened to linger long on the way—or whether they might be returning—or whether the particular journals themselves might not circulate in the remoter districts through which they were possibly passing, and the advertisements thus meet their view. And thus at length the plan succeeded; and they met in the centre of the Great American Union. Let the reader conceive the joy of my father and cousin on greeting that faithful messenger who had come from England and from me! He gave them the letters and the funds with which I had furnished him. I had only written vaguely and cautiously, because I was fearful of inspiring too much hope. And thus, to be brief, I had simply said that circumstances had arisen in reference to probable rights and claims to certain property, which were however sufficiently important to require the immediate return of my father and cousin to England. Gladly indeed did they obey the summons, and welcome were the pecuniary remittances, for they were then brought down to a low ebb. On arriving at New York, my father most unexpectedly encountered Mr. Moss, the absconded clerk of Mr. Parks, the solicitor. He found the young man a prey to the deepest remorse; and he had easily persuaded him to come back to England to perform an act of justice towards me, 'which, as both my father and cousin pledged themselves, should elicit my completest forgiveness. They had arrived in London; and there they learnt at my house in Great Ormond Street that I had only left the day before for Lady Frederick Ravenscliffe's residence near Dover. They had set off without delay; and the happy meeting has been already described.

And now let us say a few words in reference to Mr. Moss himself. The reader will recollect the scenes which took place at the house of Gilderoy Hemp on the memorable night of the trial and the conflagration. When Mr. Parks had signed the transfer-papers to the amount of £36,300, for my benefit, Gilderoy himself took possession of them, saying that he and Mr. Moss would superintend the completion of the business on the following day. Down to this moment not the slightest evil intention had been harboured by Moss:—indeed if it were otherwise, he might have previously availed himself of a certain fact which had come to his knowledge, and which was that Parks had already signed the necessary papers for selling out all the money which he had in the Funds. But the conflagration burst forth: he beheld Gilderoy perish amidst the burning mass—he was impressed with the conviction that Parks had perished also; and *then* Satan suddenly whispered the word of temptation in his ear. That temptation was irresistible; and he sped in a cab to Mr. Parks's house. There he told Mrs. Parks that her husband had just perished miserably, an utterly ruined man—and that if she wished to save from the creditors what little personal property was left, she would fly away from the country with her children with the least possible delay. Pretending friendship, he offered to look over her husband's papers while she packed up the effects: he accordingly went to the private office; and there, after some search, he discovered the transfer-papers which he required. He assured the miserable Mrs. Parks that he had found nothing of any consequence, beyond the sum of a couple of hundred pounds in bank-notes, which he gave her. Whither she went he knew not: but the next morning, by the aid of a friend who assumed the name of Jenkinson for the purpose, he procured the entire sum of 38,000*l.* from the Bank of England. He fled to America. But remorse had already seized upon him before he even crossed the Atlantic: he reflected that he had defrauded me of the large sum of money that was my due, and that he had defrauded Mrs. Parks

(whom he believed to have been made a widow by the conflagration) of the balance that would have been coming to her. On arriving at New York, he plunged into dissipation; but he could not stifle the whisperings of conscience. A thousand times did he resolve to return to England and make such amends as still lay in his power; but he had not the moral courage. Months passed;—he gave up the course of dissipation and endeavoured to apply himself to study; but his soul was still haunted by the sense of his guilt—and in this frame of mind was it that he one day encountered my father. He had not expended above a thousand pounds of the money he had so fraudulently acquired; and thus there was more than sufficient remaining to reimburse the amount of which I had been plundered by his nefariousness. Indeed, after having repaid me, he had still some hundreds left; but what his plans might be, after having restored my fortune into my hands, neither my father nor Henry could tell me.

Before I retired to rest that night, I wrote a letter to Jane Parks, conveying the intelligence of all that I had heard in reference to Mr. Moss; and I took care that a messenger should start off by the earliest coach in the morning to bear that letter to the lawyer's daughter, so that they might both be relieved of some degree of suspense in reference to the means which Mr. Moss had adopted at the time, some fourteen months back, to induce Mrs. Parks to leave the country with her children.

On the following day the marriage of Count Teleki and Lady Frederick Ravenscliffe took place. The holy ceremony was performed at the little village church, Miss Wyvill and myself acting as bridesmaids. An elegant breakfast served as an excuse for the usual amount of speech-making; and a blush was more than once conjured up to my cheeks by a good-tempered allusion to the prospect of there soon being *another* wedding at which Miss Wyvill's services would no doubt again be put in requisition. At length the moment for the departure of the bride and bridegroom came; and as I strained the Countess of Teleki in my arms, I whispered with a prophetic fervour, "*This* time, dearest Juliet, you will be happy in the marriage-state!"

The party broke up next day at River House; and we all three returned to London, leaving Mr. Norman duly installed there. Lord and Lady Carshalton insisted that my cousin Henry should make their house his home for the present; while my father resided with me. The Earl behaved most generously: he not merely facilitated all the legal proceedings which were necessary to prove Henry his heir—but he at once openly acknowledged him as such, and declared his intention of allowing him six thousand a year until his (the Earl's) death should put him into possession of the whole of the great wealth that was associated with the Carshalton peerage.

But before I travel on too fast in my narrative, I must here pause to state that on the very day after my return to London—and while I was deliberating how I could best reward William Lardner for the fidelity with which he had executed my mission— a handsome though somewhat cumbrous equipage drove up to the door; and as the drawing-room window was partly open in consequence of the heat of the weather, I heard the following ejaculations, which in a hoarse voice and with irritable accents told me who the visitor was.

"There now, you scoundrel! the left foot! Mind, you villain! mind! Hur! hur! What the deuce! —hang you, you rascal! there! put down my crutch! Now, Reuben, the right arm! Hur! hur! William, you blackguard! dare you come all the way back from America to vex and annoy me and put me out of temper!—hur! hur!"

"I am sure, Sir Robert," answered the clear frank voice of William, "I am doing all I can to spare you pain——".

"Well, well! Hur! I daresay you think you are using me very tenderly: but—but—plague on you! you are hurting me as much as you can! By heaven, you scoundrel Reuben!—Ah, now it's all right! William has done it at last! There! Hur! hur!"

By this time the nabob was got up the steps of the front door: and I hastened down into the hall that I might welcome him.

"Beg pardon, Miss Percy," he said, as soon as he caught sight of me, "for all the row I am making at your house: but—hur!—this infernal gout, which never leaves me!—and I do believe I have been much worse——Plague take the door-mat! I nearly tripped over it! Hur!—I have been much worse since William was away. And that confounded ass Strychnia —— beg pardon, Miss, for swearing—but by Jove! if you had such a gout as this, you would swear too!—hur — hur!"

"Pray sit down, Sir Robert," I said, as Reuben and William now got him into the dining-room: and then I rang the bell.

"Hur! hur! I know very well what that means!" exclaimed the nabob, now chuckling heartily: "the old East India—eh? Well, hur! hur! I suppose I must yield to temptation—hur! hur!—and if Doctor Strychnia takes it into his head to blow me up, I must knock him down with my crutch. There! that's settled!—hur! hur! And now begone, you precious pair of rascals!" added Sir Robert, turning round upon William Lardner and Reuben. "I don't want you to overhear—hur!—what I have got to say——least of all you, Master William, you scoundrel!— hur!"

The two young men retired; and my own footman now brought in a salver covered with refreshments for Sir Robert Temple's behoof, not forgetting a bottle of the old East India Madeira which was so particularly to his taste.

"You are very good, Miss," he said; "you are too good. Hur! hur! But I can't resist it. Now I'll tell you what I called about," he went on to say, as he sipped his first glass of Madeira with infinite gusto: "William Lardner has come back —and from what I understand—hur! hur!—this Madeira is really excellent!—capital!—hur! But I was going to say that from what I understand ——correct me if I am wrong, Miss—hur! hur! —William did all that was required of him—hur! —did it well—hur! hur! did it quick too—hur! hur! hur!"

"I can assure you, Sir Robert," I said, "that nothing can exceed the terms in which I am bound to speak in praise of William Lardner. I was just

thinking, at the moment when you arrived, how I could best reward him——"

"Come, Miss—hur! hur!—you needn't be coy or sly—hur! hur!—with an old man like me— old enough to be your grandfather—hur!—or your great grandfather for that matter! There's to be a wedding—isn't there? Come, out with the truth! Hur! Your cousin—hur!—handsome young man—and all that! Well, so much the better. You'll make the most beautiful bride— hur! hur!—that ever went to the altar. Orange blossoms—white veil—blushes—downcast looks— palpitating heart—hur! hur!—and all that!" and the nabob chuckled pleasantly as he poured out for himself a second glass of wine.

I smiled; for I knew that what he said was good-naturedly meant, and that with all his peculiarities he was a most kind-hearted man at bottom; and I said, "Yes—you are right, Sir Robert: I shall soon accompany my cousin to the altar."

"Well, well," ejaculated the nabob; "and why shouldn't we have another wedding?—hur! hur! —at the same time? I know all about it! My William Lardner—hur! hur!—and your Beda! They love each other—hur! hur! hur!—hur! hur!"

"They love each other very tenderly," I said; "and some such idea as that to which you are alluding, Sir Robert, had indeed flitted through my mind just before you came. But then they are so very young, you know! Beda is only a little more than seventeen—and William is not twenty-one yet. They are too young to think of settling in life——"

"Too young!" ejaculated the nabob. "Nonsense!—hur!—sheer nonsense! Hur! hur! I dare say—no offence, Miss—but if you were only just turned seventeen — hur! and your cousin Henry Wakefield—hur! hur!—was only a little past twenty—you wouldn't cry out that you were too young! Hur! Deuce a bit! Hur! hur!"

I smiled and blushed, and then I said, laughing, "Well, I confess, Sir Robert, it would require very little argument to induce me to speak to Beda on the subject."

"Speak to her then!" interrupted the nabob. "I'll give you a knock-down argument at once. Hur! hur! Now then, Miss Percy—I of course know you mean to take care—hur!—of your pretty gipsy Beda. Hur! you know what I mean —in a pecuniary sense—hur! Well, I tell you what, Miss—don't think—hur! that I want to show off, or that I'm under the influence—hur! hur!—of this Madeira —though it's very good— hur! and this is my third glass, by Jove! hur! hur!—yet I'm quite sober and serious when I say—hur!—that whatever dower Beda is to have —hur! hur!—I'll double the sum for William Lardner. Come, Miss Percy — hur! — what do you say to that? Hur! hur!"—and as if to clench the promise, he tapped his crutch-stick so violently upon the floor as to make the glasses rattle upon the table.

"What do I say to it, Sir Robert?" I cried, again laughing; "why, that I think you will find you have made a very rash promise."

"Rash fiddlestick!" ejaculated the nabob. "Explain yourself, Miss. Hur! hur! What do you mean—hur?"

"I mean simply that Beda will be richer than you fancy. She already has a thousand pounds settled on her — it is in the funds — under my trusteeship—it was given her by the Earl of Carshalton—she is as yet ignorant of the fact——".

"Well, let her know it then," exclaimed Sir Robert. "A thousand pounds — eh? Well—hur! that's not ruinous! Come, it's two thousand I give William. Hur! hur!"

"Oh! but that is not all," I exclaimed. "Depend upon it, Sir Robert, you will repent of the rashness of your promise——"

"I'll eat my crutch if I do!" he interjected, chuckling. "Hur, Miss! Hur! hur! You don't know me! A pledge—hur!—from Robert Temple is sacred—hur! hur! Proceed!"

"I was about to tell you that it is my intention to bestow a thousand pounds upon Beda:—that will make her dowry two thousand."

"Oh! ho!" cried the nabob, with the merriest possible twinkle in his eyes; "so you think you are going to make me—hur! hur!—a levanter from my promise. No such thing, Miss! Hur! hur! Give Beda your thousand—hur!—and that with the Earl's thousand will make two—hur! I'll give William four!—There!—hur Why, by Jove! if this isn't my fourth glass!"

"Never mind, Sir Robert," I said, with much emotion: "it is an occasion on which you may really afford to be gay, for you are acting with a degree of generosity——"

"Pooh, pooh, Miss! generosity!" interrupted the nabob. "Just a freak on my part—that's all! Hur! hur! Come! let's have the young couple in—hur! hur!—and tell them——But I say, Miss, let me manage it—hur! hur! I'm the best person in the world at making such communications! I remember—hur! hur!—when I was in India, a fellow-officer was seized with cholera—middle of a jungle—no doctor—no help—hur! Devil of a case! hur! hur! 'Break it delicately to my poor wife, Temple,' says he—hur! and then he died—hur! Well, off I go—reach the place where the lady was—hur! hur!—find myself in her presence —hur!—and say, 'Please ma'am, very sorry—hur! but your husband just killed by a tiger:'—then she gave a great scream. 'No, no,' said I, 'by an elephant.'—Another scream. Hur! hur! 'No, no,' says I; 'a snake!'—A louder scream still. Hur! I could'nt think what the devil was the matter with the woman. Hur! hur! She would'nt suffer herself to be let down easy; so I flew into a passion and cried out, 'Well, plague take it—hur! hur!—if you must have all the truth at once, he's dead of the cholera!' And then, Miss—hur! hur!—what the deuce do you think she says? Why, that it was a consolation to know he had died of that—hur! hur!—rather than the tiger, the elephant, or the snake!"

"Well, really, Sir Robert," I said, laughing, "I cannot compliment you on having been very happy in the mode in which you broke the truth on this occasion; but as there is really nothing of an adverse nature to impart—but on the contrary, everything calculated to fill their souls with rejoicing—I think there can be no harm in allowing you to act as spokesman to William and Beda."

I accordingly rang the bell; and when the footman answered the summons, I said, "Tell Beda to come hither; and also tell Sir Robert Temple's servant William that he is wanted."

Beda first came gliding into the room; and

almost immediately afterwards William Lardner made his appearance. They glanced at me; I had assumed a serious countenance while awaiting the promised speech from Sir Robert's lips; then they glanced at the Nabob himself; but he had pursed up his mouth in such an extraordinary fashion—looking half wise and half savage, as he reclined back in his chair, that the youthful couple were evidently at a loss what to think of the present proceeding.

"Hur!" began the nabob: "hur! hur!" and then he looked with a sort of comical fierceness from William to Beda. "Now, I just tell you what it is—hur!—hur!—I mean you, you scoundrel William! hur!—and you, you little minx, Miss Beda! I mean to discharge you, sir, from my service—hur! hur! and your mistress, little minx, means to discharge you also; so that what the devil you're both to do I don't know, unless you—hur!—hur!—agree to get spliced and console each other. Why, what the deuce—crying?"

Beda was at a loss to comprehend the nabob's meaning; and bursting into tears, she threw herself upon my bosom, murmuring, "What have I done? You will not send me away from you!"

William Lardner looked bewildered; but still he seemed to have a certain suspicion that no evil was intended, but on the contrary, some great good; for he knew the ways and eccentricities of his master better than Beda did.

"Oh, but we are serious though!" exclaimed the nabob, striking his crutch upon the carpet: "serious enough—hur! We mean to turn you both off,—hur! hur!—you, Beda, with a couple of thousand pounds—hur! hur!—you, Master William, with four thousand—and by Jove if you can't make both ends meet on that—hur! hur!—you ought to be——Eh, Miss Percy? hanged both of them—eh? Hur! hur!"

Meanwhile I had been hastily whispering a few explanations and reassuring words in the ears of Beda; and now sinking upon her knees, she took my hand and pressed it to her lips; and then weeping with joy, and her cheeks suffused in blushes, she threw her arms about my neck and embraced me with the most fervid affection.

"Holloa! what?" exclaimed the nabob; "kneeling to me, William? Hur! Fiddlestick! nonsense! hur! hur! You are a good youth—and I like you—hur! hur! Why, 'pon my soul! I do believe—hur!—my eyes are watering! Pooh! tears? Hur! nonsense! Come, fill that glass, William! Why—you young scoundrel, you!—hur! what do you mean by spilling it?"

"I see that I must fill your glass for you, my dear Sir Robert," I said; "for you have rendered this young couple so happy——"

"Oh! but you, yourself—hur! are crying," interjected the nabob. "Well, well, I suppose it must go the round—hur!" and then the worthy old gentleman whimpered like a child; but it was with joy and delight at the spectacle of the happiness to which he had so largely and generously contributed.

Thus was it agreed that William and Beda should be married; and it was arranged that the union should take place at about the same time as my own bridal was to be celebrated. But before those happy days came, certain incidents occurred which I shall now proceed to describe.

CHAPTER CXXXIII.

A DEATH-BED.

ONE morning, after breakfast — at the expiration of about a week from the occurrences which I have been recording—a billet was placed in my hand; and I started on recognising the writing of the address. I was almost inclined not to open the note, but a second glance at the superscription showed me that it was penned as if the hand were tremulous at the time, and I experienced a sudden curiosity to learn by what emotion the writer was influenced when thus seeking to communicate with me. I accordingly opened the billet; and on reading the very first line, an ejaculation burst from my lips. The contents of the missive were very short; and when I had perused them, I inquired, "Who brought this letter?"

No. 102.—ELLEN PERCY.

"A female servant, Miss," was the footman's reply; "and she came in a cab."

"Go and tell her," I said, "that I will be with her ladyship as soon as possible. And order the carriage at once."

I ascended to my chamber, where I was immediately joined by Beda; and giving her the note, I said, "Beda, my dear young friend!—read this!"

"Ah! dying!" ejaculated Beda, as she cast her eyes upon the billet : "her ladyship dying ! And craving your presence in her last moments! But are you going, my dear Miss?"—and there was a visible glistening in Beda's dark eyes as she turned them suddenly upon me.

"Yes—certainly, I am going, Beda!" I answered. "Would you have me disregard such an earnest appeal as this?"

"No, no! not for worlds — provided it be genuine!" cried Beda. "But—but—you know that on a former occasion—when you were going to set off alone on a journey——"

"You had your misgivings, my dear Beda—and they were well founded! But you shall come with me now."

The luminous eyes lighted up brilliantly with joy; and we hastened to get ourselves in readiness. In a few minutes our toilets were made; and we descended to the carriage which was waiting.

"There cannot be a doubt, Beda," I said, thus breaking a long silence which had prevailed from the time the carriage left the house until it was just entering the Regent's Park,—"there cannot be the slightest doubt that all which this letter contains is genuine. There is in my soul a species of presentiment that the period for my own fortunes being in the ascendant, is a signal for retributive justice to overtake those who have been my persecutors and my enemies. Besides, it is totally compatible with this wretched creature's disposition and character, that she should thus seek forgiveness of me in her last moments—for with all her terrible aptitude for crime there was a deep superstitious feeling in her soul, and she professes a creed which more than any other enjoins not merely the confession of sins upon the death-bed, but likewise the necessity of obtaining the pardon of those who have been injured through the medium of those sins."

"Ah!" said Beda, "is Lady Lilla a Roman Catholic?"

"Yes," I responded. "Do you not remember that some little time ago I described to you how I was staying with her at her house called Claremont Villa—that was before I knew you, Beda——"

"Ah, I remember!" she ejaculated; "and Claremont Villa was destroyed by fire—and you then discovered that Lady Lilla had secretly maintained a little oratory in her house, decorated with Catholic symbols——"

"Yes," I said; "and this showed that she must have had very strong feelings on the subject of religion."

"Oh, but for a religious person," ejaculated Beda, "to be so wicked!"

"It is to all appearance contradictory," I said; "and yet the world has presented to our view a thousand illustrations of the connexion of superstition and crime. Yes—no matter whether Catholics or Protestants, this is often the case; and the greatest criminals have been known to be constant and devoted in their religious exercises. As for Lady Lilla Essendine, she is a woman of very sensitive nerves and whose conscience is easily touched. I remember that when I was staying with her, I was terrified by her moans at night; and I recollect also that on one occasion at the theatre, when she beheld me play Lady Macbeth, she fainted and was borne out."

"Ah, then, dear Miss Percy," said Beda, "it is indeed a matter of little wonder that on her death-bed she should be so stricken with remorse as to send and implore your presence that she may obtain your forgiveness."

The reader will probably recollect that when Claremont Villa was destroyed by fire, Lady Lilla Essendine removed into another house in the same neighbourhood—namely, St. John's Wood. This was now our destination; and we soon

reached it. It was a detached habitation, standing in the midst of a garden filled with the most beautiful flowers. Most of the casements were open, showing the elegant curtains within the rooms; and altogether, as the sun shone upon the scene, the dwelling appeared to be so complete a picture of cheerfulness and comfort, luxury and beauty, that it was scarcely possible to settle the mind upon the idea that Death was already beginning to make himself busy within those walls!

On alighting from the carriage, I was greeted by an elderly female who introduced herself as Lady Lilla's housekeeper; and she escorted me into the handsomely furnished drawing-room, requesting me to wait there a few minutes while she went to prepare her mistress to receive me. Beda accompanied me; and indeed she kept close by my side; for the faithful girl was not altogether convinced but that some treachery was intended. Full soon however did we receive the proofs that this was not the case; for when we were conducted to the chamber where Lady Lilla lay, the first glance was sufficient to show that the hand of death was at no great distance and that the hour of her dissolution was approaching.

Conceive, in that beautiful August weather—in that chamber so elegantly appointed, where the atmosphere was sweet with the fragrance of flowers, and where the songs of birds were wafted through the open casements—conceive that *there* lay the once brilliant Lady Lilla Essendine, perishing in the very bloom of her womanhood—for her age was only five-and-twenty! The masses of her pale amber hair flowed all negligently over her neck and shoulders of dazzling whiteness: her cheeks were colourless as marble; and upon the forehead the blue veins might be seen with an almost painful transparency; for her's was one of those complexions which, always fair and clear, become wondrously diaphanous under the influence of the insidious disease which silently devours the very vitals. For it was of a rapid consumption that Lilla Essendine was perishing!

When I entered the chamber, followed by Beda, the dying lady turned her beautiful blue eyes towards us for a few moments; and then covering her face with her hands, she began sobbing violently.

"I have come," I said, "in obedience to your summons: I have come to give you the assurance of my forgiveness for all the injuries you have ever done, or may have sought to do me. For, Oh! I need not ask whether you are truly penitent——"

"Penitent, Ellen!" she murmured. "Oh, I am afraid to die! I am afraid to die! My crimes have been so great!"

"However great your crimes, Lady Lilla," I solemnly answered, "the mercy of heaven is still greater! If in the recesses of your own heart you experience a deep contrition——"

"I do, I do!"—and now the wretched woman drew a crucifix from beneath the pillow and kissed it with fervour. "But is it possible, Ellen," she went on to say, in a tone of doubt and anguish, and with a kindred agony expressed upon her features,—"is it possible that you can forgive me?"

"Oh, believe, Lilla," I answered, "there is no vindictiveness in my nature!"

"No—there is not!" she said; "or else you might have avenged yourself terribly against myself and *another!* But you did not do it. And yet you have for a long time known how great was the turpitude of which we had been guilty——"

"Shall I kneel and pray with you, Lilla?" I asked. "Beda also will pray!"

"Yes—we will presently pray together," rejoined the dying woman; and then clasping her thin white hands, she murmured with a strange wild fervour in her looks, "Oh, of a surety your prayers, Ellen, must avail on high, even for such a sinner as myself; for you are the best and purest being that ever breathed the air of this world! Oh! and great happiness is in store for you!—and believe me, Ellen, that so altered is now the state of my mind towards you, I rejoice—yes, rejoice infinitely at your glorious prospects! I have heard that you have recently acquired great riches—I have heard also that you are to wed your cousin, the acknowledged heir of the Earl of Carshalton—and that he is well worthy of your love. Oh, may you be happy! may you be happy!"

These words were repeated with a real fervour; and she went on to say, "But it is not in response to prayers or adjurations from such lips as *mine*, that heaven will shower blessings on your head! It is for your own sake—on account of your many virtues—as a reward for your many excellencies, that you will enjoy all the felicity which can possibly be known on this side of the grave!"

There was another pause, during which Lady Lilly closed her eyes and retained her hands clasped over her bosom; while the slight but continuous wavering of her lips showed that a prayer, mentally uttered, was passing behind them.

"And now give me your attention, Ellen," she at length said; "for I must speak to you of the past. To you I must confess all my wickedness, as I have already made confession to the priest!"

"Shall I now retire?" asked Beda, in a whisper, as she came gliding towards me.

"No—remain, Beda," said Lady Lilla Essendine; "remain," she repeated; "for I have heard of your devotion to your excellent mistress—and whatsoever I have now to say unto her, may be heard by you."

Beda retreated towards the casement, while I sat down by the side of the bed: and Lady Lilla Essendine, looking up into my countenance with those blue eyes which I had often thought were in their liquid clearness so exquisitely beautiful, said, "After all, what have I to confess that you do not already know? For even if you have never acquired the positive certainty——"

"I know to what you allude," I said, a shudder passing through me; "and for a long time past I have entertained no moral doubt——"

"No, no—you could not!" she said: "you could not! You knew that I was a murderess! O God! is not the word horrible—horrible? And yet the name is mine!—it applies to me! Wretch that I am! you know that I was an accomplice in the murder of my own husband!"

I saw that Beda's countenance was as pale as death: I felt that my own was so likewise; and I said to Lady Lilla, "Why—Oh! why refer to these horrors?"

"Because," she exclaimed, "you must know every detail connected with my iniquity!—how I was spellbound—fascinated—led on by a fiend in human shape—and that demon with the form of an angel——need I tell you?—it was Edwin St. Clair! I had never seen him before I married his uncle Sir George Essendine. Born of Roman Catholic parents I was educated upon the Continent—partly in France and partly in Italy; and it was in the latter country that in my girlhood accident threw me in the way of the old gipsy-woman Dame Betty. It matters not how," continued Lady Lilla, "that this acquaintance originated. Suffice it to say that a young lady with whom I was intimate, found it convenient to retire from the world and conceal herself at Dame Betty's lodging in Florence for a time; and I stealthily visited her there. Little did I then foresee—I, a girl of scarcely seventeen—that the hag who thus became known to me, would ever be more closely mixed up in the incidents of my life! It was in Paris that I attracted the notice of Sir George Essendine, who had recently returned from an East Indian command, in the exercise of which he had gained a fortune and lost his health. My parents were then dead; and I lived wretchedly with an old aunt of villanous temper, and who never trusted me out of her sight. It therefore naturally struck me that marriage would be synonymous with freedom; and I accepted the offer made by Sir George Essendine. I belonged to a noble family—but I was portionless: he was immensely rich; and it was considered that patrician birth and great beauty on my side, constituted a fair equivalent for the wealth which existed on his side. After a while we came to England; and then Sir George introduced me to his nephew, Edwin St. Clair."

Lady Lilla paused; and I perceived that her entire frame shook, as if with a cold shudder slowly passing over it.

"Ah!" she said, with a strange wild flashing of the eyes, "no wonder, Ellen, that I should recoil from the very mention of that name!—for he who bore it was the cause of my undoing! But for *him* I might have been happy—a loved and respected wife—free from crime—stainless in thought and deed even as you yourself are! But we met; and from that moment my fate was sealed. Yes—the very first instant that St. Clair's eyes encountered mine I had a presentiment that as our looks had then strangely blended, so would our destinies be as singularly entertwined. I loved him!—yes, from that very first moment I loved him—madly, passionately loved him! Oh! to all outward appearance he was the noblest and most god-like of his sex; and I need not remind you, Ellen, that his manners possessed—aye, still possess—an indescribable fascination. I loved him; and methought that he loved me as tenderly in return. Such a love as I—a wife—bore for that man who was not my husband, could not be innocent. No—nor was it. I confess that I was weak and yielding; St. Clair was unscrupulous. I fell! My passion for that man was a delirium—a madness—a very frenzy. If I had been standing upon the brink of pandemonium itself, and he had ordered me to plunge in as a proof of my devotion, I should have unhesitatingly obeyed him. Never did man exercise so powerful a control over a woman as that which St. Clair wielded over me! Think you that one so unprincipled, so unscrupulous as *he*, was likely to let slip the opportunity which that fatal passion of mine placed within his reach? He was dependent on his uncle; and he could not do otherwise than calculate that if my marriage with Sir George were productive of issue—or if my illicit amour with St. Clair himself resulted in the birth of offspring, there would be an end to all his hopes and prospects! Need I dwell upon this point? Need I expatiate upon it? No! no! Suffice it to say that St. Clair began to whisper insidious language in my ear: he did not shock me by revealing his purpose suddenly and throwing off the mask abruptly; but he advanced cautiously. Indeed, so dimly significant were his hints and allusions and representations at first, that I could barely understand them. But at length his speech grew plainer and bolder; and as it thus proved more intelligible, I only clung all the more closely to him; for with a devilish artfulness he made me believe that we were both trembling upon a precipice—that the discovery of our guilty love must be speedy as it was inevitable—and that the terrific ire of the outraged Sir George would be wreaked upon both! And then St. Clair spoke as if he had sacrificed everything for the love which he bore for me; and he painted that love in colours so affecting to my feelings—so ravishing for my heart—that I was led to fancy the world ought only to exist for him and me alone, and that wheresoever there was a barrier to our happiness it was the duty of one or both of us to remove it. In short, my love was everything—all-absorbing and engulfing—calculated to render me a fearless heroine for any purpose of evil! I have already told you, how in my weakness I fell: you can now understand how the same passion became a strong and irresistible impulse to urge me on to the darkest, deepest crime! For such a crime as that which I committed, demands all the most daring hardihood of the human mind for its accomplishment! It was the crime of murder!—the murder of my own husband!"

Here Lady Lilla Essendine again paused. I would fain have cut short a narrative so replete with horrors, and the principal details of which had been long ago surmised by me even if they were not positively and actually known. But I said naught to place the seal of silence on the dying woman's lips: for a moment's reflection made me comprehend that in her dreadful frame of mind, it was natural she should look upon this confession of her enormities as more or less an atonement, or at all events as a proof of her deep contrition.

"Alas, for frail humanity!" she resumed; "no sooner is a wickedness thought of, when the means suggest themselves for its early accomplishment! Satan does not merely whisper the words of temptation in the ear; but he places the weapon in the hand! Yes—no sooner was that crime resolved upon, when the old gipsy-woman crossed my path. And then methought at the time it was an accident—a coincidence; but I subsequently discovered that it was not; for St. Clair already knew her well—yes—for some time he had known her—and I have reason to believe that that same Zarah who afterwards became his wife, had been his mistress

even previous to the time whereof I am now particularly speaking. However, be this as it may, certain it is that St. Clair in the dastard selfishness of his nature, endeavoured to fix the greater amount of crime's responsibility upon my shoulders: for he left me to negotiate the dread business with Dame Betty. It was soon done. The woman earned her living by misdeeds of every description —crimes, duplicities, and treacheries: she was not therefore one who asked a single unnecessary question, or cared to trouble herself with details beyond those which it was absolutely requisite for her to know. In short, she provided the means— the fatal means of executing the fell purpose that was already resolved upon. It was a poisoned camelia which she placed in my hand! Oh, that I could retrace the last few years of my life!" exclaimed Lady Lilla, in an excited tone: "Oh, that I could retrace my existence to the eve of that fatal day on which a crime was perpetrated that gave so horrible a significancy to the phrase which I once entrusted, Ellen, to your keeping!—I mean the words, ' *Do you recognise the symbol?* '"

"Ah! and from the lips of another," I said, "did I also receive an intimation which was terribly significant in respect to the fatal flower !" —and then I slowly and shudderingly repeated the sentence—" *He who smells the white rose, sleeps the slumber of death!*"

But Lady Lilla Essendine did not hear what I was now saying: or if she did, she paid no heed to it; for she had covered her face with her thin white hands, and she was lying back on the pillow, absorbed in the deepest thought—plunged in reflections which must have been of the most painful and harrowing character!

"Yes—the deed was accomplished," she presently resumed, as she withdrew her hands from her countenance and again raised herself up to a sitting posture in the bed, so that the luxuriant masses of her pale amber hair flowed over her naked shoulders and her bosom, giving to her looks a certain wildness which was only too faithfully in keeping with the narrative that was issuing from her lips: "the deed was accomplished; and it passed utterly without suspicion, not merely by the world at large, but also by the very domestics beneath the roof of the mansion where we dwelt. The idea was that my husband had perished of apoplexy; and the family physician himself confidently proclaimed that it was so. He died intestate: his nephew Edwin St. Clair succeeded to his riches, and became the possessor of the enormous income of twenty-five thousand a-year. Oh! you may judge how utterly unselfish was my crime in a pecuniary sense, and how completely it had been instigated by the strong mad love I bore for St. Clair, when I tell you that I stipulated not for any portion of the wealth which I knew he must inherit as the result of this stupendous iniquity for which we perilled our immortal souls! No— the only reward that I expected was his love,— his continued and undivided love, as I fancied that I already possessed it. But in this dream I was fearfully disappointed. Not long had the crime been perpetrated—not many months had elapsed after the accomplishment of that fearful act of turpitude, when circumstances transpired to convince me that St. Clair loved me not. I found that he was faithless to me—that others had claims upon his affection—that he was gay and inconstant—and that he lightly regarded the love-pledges which he gave forth from his lips. Never shall I forget the horror which seized upon me when I found that I had steeped myself so deeply in guilt for the sake of a man who was utterly unworthy a thousandth part of the sacrifice! A horrible remorse seized upon me: all the magnitude of my guilt rose up before me like a hideous demon threatening me with destruction: it flamed upon me like the glare from pandemonium's pit itself: it enveloped me in its coils as if a huge serpent had wound itself about me! I was resolved to flee for ever from my native land, and to go and bury myself in some religous sanctuary upon the Continent. It was then—yes, then, in a state of mind bordering upon distraction, that I penned a letter to St. Clair,—a letter full of lamentations and reproaches, tears and bitterness—a letter which seemed as it were to be an expression and an echo of the deep groans and the wild anguished cries which indicated the tortures of my soul! Of that letter, Ellen, you accidentally found a fragment; and now, as memory reproduces those dread sentences in your brain, you may conceive that there is no hyperbole nor exaggeration in the picture that I am drawing!"

'"No, no!" I said, shuddering from head to foot as I thought of the contents of that fragment.* "I am well aware that such lines could

* The fragment was given in Chapter VII: but it is here reproduced for the purpose of immediate reference on the part of the reader:—

'"Therefore do I bid you an eternal farewell! Yes—it is eternal! Never, never again will you behold the wretched being around whose heart you wove your spells! Never, never again shall you hear of her whom a stupendous infatuation made your victim! Oh, tears—tears for the remainder of my life!—naught, naught but tears! Ah, will they wipe away the stain? May God have mercy upon me! I feel distracted. I am like a maniac imprisoned and chained in a cell, wanting to do something, but yet not rightly understanding what it is that the soul yearns to do. Oh! is it suicide which is thus sitting like a black shape of vagueness, yet awful and terrible, amidst the darkness of my thoughts? My soul is harrowed: vulture-claws are tearing at my brain: serpents are piercing my heart with their stings. The talons of the former strike deeper and deeper into that brain: the fiery snakes tighten their coils around that heart. My tongue is parched, as if ashes were in my throat. Oh, for water! No!—tears, tears, tears must be my portion for evermore! But again I say, will they wipe away this sense of crime? Oh, the power of love, that it should have made me what I am! Was there ever such a love as mine? Thou wast mine idol: I deemed thee an angel until thou didst reveal thyself as a fiend! Good heavens! that when methought I was listening in the soft ectasy of ineffable tenderness, to the beatific language of passion which you were breathing in mine ear, your words should gradually take a different meaning—so that I (unconsciously at first) found myself listening to such an insidious tale as none but Satan's breath could waft in unto the brain. And yet it was so!—and I yielded—God help me! I yielded! I who was first the victim of love, became the victim of crime! But thou, O man! what art thou now doing in the world? Art thou happy for all this? No, no! Even if thou art racked with one millionth portion of the horrible thoughts, feelings, and sensations which are preying upon me—tearing my brain, stinging my heart, poisoning my very life-blood at its source,—my God! if thou dost experience as much only of all these horrors as a drop is to the illimitable ocean, thou wilt—"

only have been penned by one who was suffering at the time the most horrible tortures that the human mind could possibly know!"

"I went abroad upon the Continent," resumed Lady Lilla, after a long pause, during which she moaned and lamented piteously; "and for nearly two years I wandered about like a troubled spirit,—not daring to carry out the intention which had originally taken me abroad—namely, that of seeking the seclusion of a convent. At length all of a sudden I thought that I should like to learn how it fared with St. Clair,—whether he were stricken with remorse as I was—or whether he were still holding his head high in the world, enjoying its pleasures, and plunging into its dissipations. Yes! —and I am also bound to confess that I was anxious to learn whether my image had been utterly effaced from his heart. The moment that I had thus a special purpose in view, my mind seemed to acquire a certain fortitude; and though remorse was not dead within it, yet were the whisperings of conscience lower and more subdued and its prickings were less painful than they had previously been. I returned to England; and then I learnt, on inquiry, that St. Clair was one of the gayest of the gay—that he was one of the stars of the fashionable world—and that he led a life of pleasure and enjoyment. Horrible vindictive feelings took possession of my soul: remorse seemed now completely stifled beneath the feelings of rage, hatred, and malignity that sprang up within my breast! I was resolved to punish him for the very heartlessness which he evinced: and you may easily comprehend, Ellen, how my jealousy likewise urged me to interpose betwixt him and yourself, when I fancied that he was seeking to render you his victim and when I as yet knew not that you possessed so much virtue and so much strength of mind. We met, you remember, at Mr. Parks' house. There I engaged you in private conversation; and I entrusted to your keeping the white rose to which we have already alluded: I gave it you as a talisman which methought might serve you in the hour of need. You may wonder that I should have had the hardihood and the recklessness to have given you that talisman,—that I should have dared to allude to the white camelia or rose, and have bidden you use the words, 'Do you recognise that symbol?' But in my rage against St. Clair I was blinded to all consequences; and I cared not whether my proceeding should put you upon the track to discover other things—I mean to penetrate into the secret of the stupendous crime which he and I had perpetrated!"

There was another pause; but it was shorter than any of the preceding ones; for Lady Lilla quickly resumed her narrative in the following manner:—

"It was no hypocritical pretence on my part, Ellen, when I declared that I had formed a friendship for you and when I asked you to stay with me at Claremont Villa. You had baffled St. Clair—and I would have loved you for that reason only; but it was impossible not to be attracted by your many endearing qualities. You remember that while you were there on that first visit, you fell in with the old gipsy and Zarah—they sent you to me with the white rose as a symbol—and I saw that your suspicions against me were more or less excited."

"Yes," I interposed; "and it was at that time, too, I beheld your handwriting; and I was struck with its resemblance to the fragment of the letter which I had found at St. Clair's house. But by various means all those suspicions were lulled at the time. Indeed, Lilla," I added, in a fervid tone, "I could not believe it possible that one with your angelic countenance could have been so deeply criminal!"

"Alas, how deceitful are appearances!" murmured the dying woman; and for some moments her bosom heaved fearfully with convulsive sobs. "But let me continue my narrative," she resumed. "It was on the occasion of the visit of that old gipsy-woman and her granddaughter, that from something which fell from the lips of the former I learnt that she had long known Edwin St. Clair; and then by something which Zarah said, as well as by her flashing eyes and flushing cheeks, I suspected that she had been St. Clair's mistress. These circumstances were only too well calculated to embitter me still more against the author of my own undoing—the tempter who had led me aside from the path of virtue—the destroyer of my peace alike in this world and the next! But to continue. You, Ellen, came a second time to Claremont Villa——"

"And then I beheld St. Clair and yourself together," I said; "and I was struck with amazement. I listened—I could not help it—and I heard him speak of peace and war——"

"Ah! I recollect full well that interview which took place betwixt him and me!" said Lady Lilla. "It was of his own seeking. He came to propose terms of peace if I would have them—or to threaten me that if I dared carry on war against him, he would wreak a terrible revenge, for that he would accuse me—yes, he, the wretch! declared that he would accuse me of murdering my husband! Oh, the agony of mind which I endured!—but Oh, the rage with which I was smitten!—and Oh, the scorn with which I bade him defiance!"

"Yes, yes," I exclaimed: "I remember how terrible were your looks at one moment on that occasion! But how came Edwin St. Clair to know that you were bent on carrying on a warfare against him?"

"Had you not baffled him in his iniquitous design against you?" asked Lady Lilla; "had you not paralysed him with horror on presenting him the flower and demanding whether he recognised the symbol?"

"Ah, true!" I said; "and thus he felt convinced that none but yourself could have given me the information which I had so abruptly and successfully used!"

"Precisely so," rejoined Lady Lilla. "Ah! you may suppose, Ellen, that my interview that day with St. Clair produced a tremendous effect upon my mind! Before you I dissembled; but in the secret depths of my own heart I was so wretched—so intensely miserable, that I resolved upon suicide. Yes!—you start; but can you not conceive how my feelings may have been wrought up to such a pitch that the agony was intolerable? For all the terrible past had been vividly conjured up to my mind!—and shall I confess it?—that man Edwin St. Clair, for whose sake I had imperilled my immortal soul, seemed to me on the occasion of that interview to be handsomer than ever! A thousand fiends were agitating in my breast;—rage, jealousy, remorse—blighted love and a fierce vindictiveness! Oh, existence seemed intolerable! I had a phial of poison in my possession. It was an Italian phial which I had obtained from the old woman on the day when she sent you with a rose to me. Yes—I had procured it of her because even then I dreamt of self-destruction! You remember that phial, Ellen, which was in the filagree case!"

"Oh, yes! yes!" I said, with a shudder. "How well do I remember the first time I ever perceived that phial! I recollect too the servant herself said to me that she had not seen it before. That was when you fainted, and when the phial got broken and the little lapdog was poisoned by its contents."

"Oh, how faithfully all those incidents are treasured up in your recollection!" said Lady Lilla. "You cannot therefore have forgotten the moans and lamentations which disturbed you at night and brought you to my chamber? Ah! that circumstance, Ellen, must prove to you how agonized was my mind! Yes—veritably I was half mad! In my remorse I would kneel and pray in my little oratory:—in my vindictive rage I would concert the direst plans of vengeance against St. Clair;—and in my utter desperation of mind I was wont to think of suicide! But time passed on—and I lived. Yet, Oh! what an existence! One night I had the courage to go and see you in Lady Macbeth: heaven alone can tell what strange feeling it was which prompted me to do so!—but I obeyed the morbid impulse; and Oh, what a terrible punishment did I draw down upon my own head! The victim writhing on the stake—the wretch ascending the steps of the gibbet—the war-prisoner about to undergo the fiercest and tensest of Indian tortures, — all might be accounted happy and blessed in comparison with me as I sat contemplating the stupendous personation of conscious guilt which you so vividly presented! I swooned: I was borne from the theatre. I had recently seen St. Clair again; and he told me that you had read a fragment of the terrible letter which I had written him previous to my departure from England. I began to dread that for a variety of reasons you would be inevitably led onward to fix upon me the suspicion of the direst crimes. That fainting at the theatre was, I feared, sufficient to confirm any previous misgivings you might have entertained. What was to be done? I was half-maddened by my terrors: the scaffold seemed to be looming before me. In the desperation of my soul I thought that if I found you really suspected me, I would either take your life, or I would put an end to my own miserable existence before your very eyes. I called upon you at the house of your friends the Normans in Hunter Street. Oh! need I remind you of what took place?"

"No, no!" I said, with renewed shuddering: "it is needless! it is needless!—Beda knows nothing of it!"

"But she shall know it!" exclaimed Lady Lilla, with a species of frenzy in her eyes: "she shall know it, because I have vowed that every detail of my iniquity shall be exposed within the hour that is now passing! Know therefore, Beda,—

know," she continued, with frantic gesticulations, "that I endeavoured to kill your beloved mistress! Yes—I struck her down in a state of insensibility by means of the rose that was in my possession; and it was not my fault—but it was heaven's own sublime will—that she did not perish then and there! Now you may judge, Beda, how wicked I have been! Yes—throw your arms about the neck of your dear mistress—strain her to your bosom—congratulate her that she escaped the death which methought I had dealt her! And, Oh, I thank God—I thank God!" added the wretched woman fervently, "that I was spared that additional crime, and that you, Ellen, were permitted to live!"

There was another long pause, during which the unhappy creature gave vent to fresh lamentations and renewed moanings: she pressed her hands to her brows—she also beat her bosom—and she heeded not the entreaties I addressed to her that she would have recourse to prayer rather than to such means as these to prove her contrition and her penitence. She tossed about the rich abundant masses of her hair—she was frenzied for the space of a few minutes.

"Ah, now you see," she at length cried,—"you see, Beda, how very very wicked I have been! Could you have supposed that so much iniquity could have existed in one of your own sex?"—and she fixed her eyes with almost an expression of fierce defiance upon my faithful young dependant, while her white teeth were gleaming between her ashy lips; so that lovely in person though she naturally were, her beauty was now of a fearful description.

"Oh, my dear Miss Percy," whispered Beda, as she again flew towards me, and again flung her arms about my neck, "put an end to this scene, I beseech you! It is dreadful—dreadful!"

"I know what she says!" cried Lady Lilla: "I know what she says!"—and it was with a species of maniac frenzy that she abruptly put back the masses of her hair. "She is horrified at me! She dreads me! She trembles at me! She recoils from me! It is natural enough! Were I a tiger-cat—or even the wild tigress itself—one would not have more reason to shrink from my presence! Were I the most venomous of snakes coiled up in this couch and preparing to spring——"

"Speak not thus, insensate woman!" I exclaimed. "Is it by such mad language as this that you hope to make your peace with heaven? If it do you no good—as assuredly it cannot—wherefore do you bewilder and horrify us both with these wild outpourings?"

Lady Lilla looked at me with a species of stupefied astonishment for a moment: and then she said meekly and humbly, "I was wrong, Ellen! I had no right to send and beseech you to come hither to shock and horrify you,—I who ought to spring forth from my bed—yes, even though it be the bed of death—and kneel at your feet to implore pardon for all my crimes towards you! Bear with me yet a little space—and I will make an end of what I have to say: but, Oh! forgive me for the violence of my language! Remember, remember—I am dying!—and I shall shortly have to appear before the Supreme Judge!"

There was something very awful in the language which the wretched woman thus addressed to me; and I hastily whispered to Beda, "Go and resume your seat near the window—and tranquillise yourself as well as you are able. Bad though she be, yet she is dying—and we are Christians Beda—and it is our duty to soothe, if possible, her, passage out of this world!"

"I have brought my narrative down to a memorable date, Ellen," she resumed, in a calmer and more level voice than that in which she had previously been speaking,—"yes, a date that was very memorable for me! For my monstrous attempt on your life failed; and though I *now* thank heaven that it was so, yet *then* I was filled with rage and bitterness and disappointment—yes, and with a renewed terror likewise; for I thought that even *your* patience, Ellen, must fail before the tremendous aggravations which you had sustained at my hands. I felt that if ever there were a time and a case in which you were likely to appeal to the laws of your country for protection, *that* was the period and *that* was the crisis! Again was I driven nearly mad by my horrifying thoughts. What was I to do? Much as I hated St. Clair, I summoned him to my counsels: for I felt that we had a common interest in your destruction. We deliberated——and we resolved that you must die!"

"Wretch!" ejaculated Beda, starting up from her chair, with flashing eyes and glowing cheeks.

"Peace, Beda, peace!" I said, in a somewhat peremptory tone; and then I added in a kinder and more solemn voice, "Remember she is dying!"

Beda resumed her seat; while Lady Lilla Essendine once more covered her face with her white hands; and so deep a sob convulsed her that I gave an abrupt start as I was smitten with the idea that life must have ebbed away in that expression of agony. But it was not so; and slowly removing her hands again, she went on to say, as she turned a hollow look upon Beda, "You are right to reproach me; for it is but just my punishment on earth should extend to the very extreme, before the penalty of eternity commences!"

"No," I said, in a tone of solemn adjuration; "I cannot permit you to speak thus despairingly; for your language is tantamount to a denial of the mercy of providence. There *is* mercy, Lilla, even for one who has been as guilty as yourself! Proceed——Beda will not interrupt you again."

"Then let me repeat," she said, "that your death was resolved upon; for even though you had again displayed the most astonishing forbearance, yet did we both feel that the slightest accident might elicit from your lips sufficient to cause the destruction of us both. And then too, St. Clair had told me that you had written a complete narrative of the past, and that you had entrusted the papers to the hand of some friend who was to open the sealed packet under particular circumstances. We scarcely knew whether to believe that you had really done so, or whether it was a mere threat on your part,—a menace which the particular circumstances of the moment had elicited from your lips. At all events we resolved to be upon the safer side; and Oh! St. Clair was implacable! I repeat it, Ellen—I repeat it, with the deepest agony of feeling—I repeat it with the wildest mental anguish that ever yet was known,—we took counsel together to accomplish your destruction! Need I tell you that the incidents connected with the yacht at Ramsgate followed from that decision so atrocious, so hideous, so horrible? And I joined St. Clair at that town—I watched the progress of the proceedings with a terrible interest—and when I saw how determined he was, I could not help loving him again. Oh! this is a horrible confession—is it not? But I must render it complete—and I must therefore reiterate my words, and say that I almost loved him again for the mental firmness which he exhibited! And then he proposed to me that we should forget our past animosity; and he represented that the terrible identity of interests which bound us together should constitute a tie of tenderness once again. And in the turmoil of my evil feelings—in the wild morbid state of my passions, I again fell! I once more became his paramour!"

I could not conceal a manifestation of disgust and loathing at this part of the wretched woman's narrative: she saw what agitated me—and she exclaimed in bitter accents, "Oh! you know not how easy it is to sin again when once the footsteps have erred into the pathways of guilt!"

"Hasten," I said, " to make an end of your narrative! Let me assist you. It is needless to say more of the transactions in reference to the yacht at Ramsgate, than that heaven saved me from your machinations; and through the instrumentality of this faithful girl and of the excellent young man who will shortly conduct her to the altar, I was delivered from the terrible fate you had reserved for me?"

"Ah, then, Beda," she said, "you are soon to become a wife? And may heaven grant that your's will prove a career of happiness as complete as mine has been one of wretchedness!"

Beda made no answer, but averted her countenance towards the casement—through which the sunlit atmosphere was streaming into the room, fraught with the fragrance of flowers on the parterres below. She told me afterwards that there was something in her which seemed to recoil from the idea that a prayer breathed by such lips could prove of any avail unto her.

"I have now little more to add," resumed Lady Lilla Essendine, whose voice was becoming more and more feeble, and who exhibited symptoms of exhaustion. "Yet inasmuch as there is another criminal phase in my fearful career to confess, I hasten to state that the failure of the satanic machinations in reference to the yacht served not as a warning to convince St. Clair and myself that you were protected by heaven, but merely led us to resolve at another discussion that different and more insidious means must be adopted to accomplish your destruction. And therefore we again had recourse to the agency of the old woman Dame Betty; and she endeavoured to make use of *you*, Beda, as the instrument of the diabolic conspiracy—I mean with respect to the poisoned lozenges. We knew not then that you, Beda, had been in the slightest degree instrumental in frustrating the scheme of the yacht; and the old crone thought that from your gipsy sympathies we might rely on you."

"And she was deceived—miserably deceived!" ejaculated Beda, with emphasis. "Ah! I have this day learnt many things which I did not know before; and I tell you, Lady Lilla Essendine, that my dear mistress must have been an angel of goodness and forbearance and mercy to have suffered you and the villain St. Clair to remain unscathed in the world after all the horrible endeavours you made against her peace and against her life!"

"I feel the truth of all you say, Beda," responded the dying woman; "and it is because the forgiveness of angels imparts such peace to the soul of the perishing one, that I have sent to implore the pardon of your mistress now. Yet stay! have I aught more to relate?"—and here Lady Lilla, slowly passing her hand across her brow, seemed to be striving to gather her recollections. "Ah! perhaps it may be as well that I should tell you how after having renewed my criminal connexion with St. Clair, some cause of dispute arose—we broke out into upbraidings and recriminations—and we separated. Then I suddenly learnt that he had married Zarah; and I longed to meet him that I might overwhelm him with a crushing sense of ridicule. For though the world at large believed he had married her through love, yet I felt assured that there must be some deeper reading of the mystery; and I attributed the union to a hold which Zarah must have obtained over him by the knowledge of those fearful secrets which she might possibly have gleaned from the lips of her grandmother. And one day I was riding in the Park——"

"I remember the incident," I said, "to which you are about to refer. I also was in the Park on the occasion. If I recollect right, I was walking with my friend the Countess of Carboni. St. Clair and Zarah were also on foot; and you dashed by on horseback, in company with several ladies and gentlemen, amongst the latter of whom was the wretch Colonel Bellew, who perished some little time ago by his own hand, after having murdered a young female. And on that occasion to which I allude, you levelled some mocking words at St. Clair——"

"Yes—I did so," answered Lady Lilla. "But little did I then foresee what a terrible tragedy was to ensue, and how the unfortunate Zarah was to perish by the hands of an assassin: nor yet did I foresee that my connexion with St. Clair was to be renewed. Yet so it was——"

"I saw you together in a box at the theatre," I said, "within a very few months after the terrible death of his wife. I certainly was surprised: I thought that such deadly hatred as you had experienced for each other—or at least as you had cherished towards him——"

"Oh! but the state of my mind, Ellen," interrupted Lady Lilla, "was such that I gladly sought the companionship of the only man with whom I could converse upon the dread topics, and from whose lips I could elicit the assurance that there was no longer anything more to fear from you, for that if you had purposed to do us a mischief you would not have so long remained tranquil! Well then, we came together again—and again the terrible identity of our interests made us cling for a while to each other, as if there had never been any hatred or misunderstanding. And thus you saw that when calamities and perils suddenly gathered in quickly around him, threatening to crush and

overwhelm him completely—when he was a prisoner in Newgate, and everything seemed to depend upon keeping Dame Betty away from the
tribunal of justice, and preventing you likewise
from proceeding thither if such were your intention—you saw, I say, how ready I was to act and
how zealously I bestirred myself on his behalf.
And I succeeded. You know the result. We went
abroad together: but after awhile new causes of
dispute arose. Then came fresh accusations and
recriminations — rage inflamed us — a horrible
scene took place—and it appeared as if heaven's
vengeance were destined to strike us both at the
same time! For on that occasion I broke a blood-
vessel and nearly lost my life——"

No. 103.—ELLEN PERCY.

"And St. Clair?" I inquired: "for methinks
you said that it seemed as if heaven's vengeance
struck you both?"

"Yes," rejoined Lady Lilla: "it struck us
both! For while I was thrown upon the sick
bed whence I could scarcely hope ever to rise
again, St. Clair was seized with a sudden aberration of the intellect."

"What?" I ejaculated: "he went mad?"

"For some days he was raving," answered Lady
Lilla,—"raving beneath the same roof where it
was thought that I lay dying! Often-times when
the doors of the chambers happened to be open,
the horrible things to which he gave frenzied utterance reached my ears; and I shuddered and

writhed—for it seemed as if we were both enacting the crimes of your past years over again, so vividly did he conjure them up in his wild delirium! But fortunately he raved only in the English tongue; whereas the keeper and the nurse, and all the other servants whom he had about him, were French people utterly ignorant of our language."

Lady Lilla Essendine paused, and again pressed her hand to her brow. Then she went on to say "My narrative is nearly ended, and even were it otherwise, I should be compelled to bring it to a speedy termination—for I feel that I am sinking!"

"Hasten then—hasten!" I said: "conclude your explanations at once; so that we may pray *with* you, and pray *for* you!"

"A few more words, and I shall have finished," said Lilla—and she spoke in a voice that was evidently becoming more and more feeble. "Where did I break off? Ah, I remember! I was telling you how St. Clair went mad and how he raved! But after a short time he ceased to be violent—he grew more calm and more collected, though his intellects did not entirely recover their equilibrium. He came and sat by my bedside, and talked to me in a strain which filled me with such horror that I began to fear that I should go mad likewise. His mind wandered over the past; and it was with a hideous coolness that he described incidents and recapitulated events of the most frightful character. And then he said that he should never rest until he had possessed himself of another white rose, for that the one he had purchased from Dame Betty was taken from him at the time he was accused of being accessory to his wife's death. The idea of that white rose seemed to haunt him. I implored and entreated that he would turn his thoughts to other subjects; but I might as well have endeavoured to divert a rapid flowing river from its course or to arrest the tide of the ocean itself! St. Clair's morbid mind settled itself more and more completely on the *one* topic: he was completely monomaniac with that idea. On other subjects he could speak rationally enough if he thought fit; but when once his lips pronounced those fatal words, 'The White Rose,' it was the maddest tirade that thereafter went flowing from his tongue. He said that he must go into Italy and discover some person who could manufacture for him the poisoned artificial flower, just as Dame Betty might have done if she had not turned against him and if he knew where to find her. At length, to my infinite relief, he disappeared: he departed abruptly; and as soon as I was sufficiently recovered to endure the fatigue of travelling, I returned to England. But that illness was destined to be the prelude to a malady which should prove fatal; and excitement of mind has doubtless helped to hurry forward the catastrophe!"

"Have you not since heard of St. Clair?" I inquired.

"Yes—once," answered Lady Lilla. "A letter reached me a few days ago. It is here. You can read it."

She thrust her hand under the pillow, and drew forth a letter which she presented to me. I hesitated to touch it: but she said, "Read it, Ellen—do not refuse to read it. It will show you how the once powerful mind of Edwin St. Clair has become enfeebled, and how that brilliant intellect which so recently commanded the admiration of the British Senate, has shrivelled and dwindled down into a wretched monomania!"

I accordingly took the letter; and as I retained possession of it, I am enabled to lay it verbatim before my readers.

CHAPTER CXXXIV.

THE WHITE ROSE.

THE letter which St. Clair had written to Lady Lilla Essendine, ran as follows:—

"Rome, July 10th, 1843.

"I take it for granted, my dear Lilla, that you have quite recovered your health—that you have left the Continent which you always hated—and that you are re-established in the seclusion of your own delightful villa, which you always loved. I therefore purpose to address this letter to you at St. John's Wood; but whether you will be pleased or not to behold my handwriting again, I of course am unable to tell. I do not exactly remember how we parted; but I recollect full well you enjoined me to be sure and provide myself with a white rose before I ever ventured to show my face again in your presence. You appointed me your knight-errant to go out into the world and obtain a certain talisman without which I must seek you no more. Ah! ha! what a talisman! Not of love—nor of happiness—nor of riches: but the talisman of death! It was a strange mission that you thus confided to me: but I accepted it—and at the very moment at which I am now writing, I expect the visit of a person who will, I think, be enabled to procure me the desired object. At all events, my dear Lilla, you may rest assurred that I shall leave no stone unturned and spare no expense in following up my present purpose. I am devoted to it. I think of it by day—I dream of it by night. It is my only idea. As I walk through the streets, I often wonder what other persons are thinking of, until at length I come to the conclusion that *they* likewise must be in pursuit of the White Rose. Ah, ha! if so, they are in pursuit of death! By the bye, I found myself laughing heartily when I awoke this morning. I had been dreaming that I saw thousands and thousands of persons, of both sexes and all ages, struggling up a difficult and rugged height, to pluck the flowers which grew on its almost escarped side. The higher they got the more numerous and the more beautiful were the flowers. But ever and anon I beheld a climber let go his hold and tumble backward into the vortex beneath. I could not immediately perceive what was the cause of this: but presently, after I had beheld at least a hundred fall, I discovered that each victim had plucked a white rose amidst the general scramble for the flowers which grew upon the side of the mountain. And so, as I awoke from this dream, I laughed heartily and merrily; for Death was evidently busy amongst that crowd of climbers—and the weapons he made use of were white roses!

"To turn to another topic, my dear Lilla, I must inform you that I have totally given up all society. I will have neither friends nor acquaintances: I will have no visitors of any sort. I have turned away my French valet for admitting a person I did not wish to see; and I am now going to ring the bell and discharge the German valet, for fear lest he should do precisely the same.

"I have done it: the fellow is gone. I have paid him his wages and sent him about his business. I will have no servants for the future. If they are unfaithful, they involve you in a thousand dangers: but if they are faithful they bore one to death with their zeal and their officiousness. I do not want their attentions: the servants of the hotel are sufficient. But as I was telling you, Lilla, I mean to give up all society utterly and totally: I will have nothing more to do with the world;—and I think it very likely the world does not want to have anything more to do with me. So there is no love lost between us. I have done with everybody except yourself, my dear Lilla; for you have given me a mission—and when I accomplish it, I shall return to you. Yes—you have my pledge to this effect. The moment I shall succeed in procuring the White Rose, I will come to you. But never until I shall have achieved such success, need you expect to behold me. And if I find it not in Rome, I will go elsewhere: I will seek, if necessary, the ends of the earth in my pursuit of the desired object. Like Sadak in the Eastern tale, when in quest of the Waters of Oblivion, I will plunge headlong into the vortex of hideous perils—I will dare all possible dangers—I will not retreat; for if baffled in the end, it shall be through no cowardice on my part. By the bye, do you remember the story of Sadak? It is in the *Tales of the Genii*. How splendid is the catastrophe! The Sultan sends Sadak to fetch the Waters of Oblivion: they are procured;—and they prove to be the Lethean draught of death itself! The Sultan drinks and dies. Would it not be strange if something of the same sort should happen in reference to the White Rose! Oh, fancy that if when I brought it to you, and, like a chivalrous knight placed it at your feet, you snatched it up, smelt it, fell back and died! I can scarcely avoid laughing at the idea. But I must now make an end of my letter; for I hear footsteps ascending the stairs, and perhaps it is my Italian friend coming to tell me that my wish shall be gratified and that the White Rose is already within my grasp.

"EDWIN ST. CLAIR."

When I read this letter, I passed it to Beda; and as she began to peruse it, Lady Lilla said to me in a faint voice, "What think you, Ellen? If that man had never been guilty of a crime, it would be terrible to contemplate the ruin of the once splendid intellect: but inasmuch as he has been deeply criminal—indeed one of the greatest of offenders—his present condition can only be looked upon as a most righteous retribution."

There was a pause, during which I reflected on the remark which Lady Lilla had made, and the justice of which I could not possibly do otherwise than admit. Beda read the letter; and then folding it up, she laid it upon the table, at the same time bending her looks upon me with a significancy that was as much as to imply, "He is most deservedly punished!"

"And now, Ellen," said Lady Lilla, in a gentle tone, "will you give me your pardon—freely and unreservedly? will you smooth the pillow of her who is perishing before your eyes?"

"Lilla," I said, in a firm tone, "I forgive you! —from the very bottom of my heart do I forgive you! That this pardon is complete I call heaven to witness!"

"Oh, thank! thank you!" murmured the dying woman, with an effusion that was unmistakably sincere. "Give me your hand."

Not for a moment did I hesitate; but I yielded to her request.

"Oh! again and again I thank you," she murmured, pressing my hand to her lips; "and that solemn assurance of your forgiveness has afforded relief to my mind. Yes—I feel easier!"

"And now therefore let us pray together," I said; "for I think, Lilla—I think that you have not long to live!"

"No—I have not long to live," she said mournfully, but without bitterness. "I feel that my strength is declining fast. I have a sense of sinking—nature is dissolving! Pray, Ellen—pray! I will follow your prayer!"

I made a sign for Beda to approach the couch; and we were both on the point of kneeling, when there was a sudden and startling sound of footsteps rushing up the stairs — the voice of the housekeeper was heard crying out something—but heedless of the remonstrance (for such it was) the individual came dashing on — the door of the chamber was burst open—and Edwin St. Clair appeared upon the threshold. Lady Lilla Essendine, who was lying upon the pillow at the moment when we were about to pray with her, rose up to a sitting posture—and a cry of terror burst from her lips.

"The rose! the rose!" exclaimed St. Clair. "I have succeeded! Behold it!"

"No, no!" shrieked Lady Lilla: and covering her face with her hands, she sank back upon the pillow.

"Unhappy man!" I said, in a severe tone: but I confess that I was more or less affrighted by his appearance—for his looks were wild, his toilet was negligent and disordered, as if he had just come off a long journey—and he carried in his hand an artificial white flower: "unhappy man! do you not see that she is dying?"

"Come away, sir! for heaven's sake come away!" cried the housekeeper, now appearing upon the landing just behind St. Clair, whose arm she caught hold of.

"Begone, foolish woman!" he said: "there is fatality in my presence! I am armed with all the powers of doom! Death has appointed me his agent in this world!"

The housekeeper recoiled in terror; and St. Clair, closing the door with violence against her, locked it and drew forth the key, which he consigned to his pocket. This he did with one hand, while the other still retained the white rose, which I had no doubt was poisoned.

All that had just taken place, occurred so rapidly that there was no time for either myself or Beda to interfere in order to prevent him from locking the door and making us prisoners along with himself. I have already said that his looks were wild: there was indeed a veritable frenzy in them—a maniac excitement; and I was smitten with a horrible idea that fatal consequences might ensue from the possession of so deadly a weapon as that white rose in the hands of a madman.

"I know you, Miss Percy!" he exclaimed. "I know you too, girl!" he added, flinging a fierce look rapidly upon Beda: "but I do not want to have anything to do with either of you. I have renounced the world, as the world has renounced me!"

"Edwin, have pity upon me!" moaned Lady Lilla: "have mercy upon me, I conjure you!—I am dying!"

"Dying?" he ejaculated. "Why, so that woman told me on the stairs: but I thought she spoke falsely, to prevent me from coming to see you."

"It is too true!" I said, now venturing to interpose again; "and if you ever entertained one spark of feeling for that poor penitent creature——"

"What, Lilla do you mean? Lilla?" demanded St. Clair, flinging his regards upon me with a maniac wildness and uncertainty. "Why, I have loved and have hated her!—then I have loved her again! But stop! let me reflect!"—and he placed one hand to his brow, while the other still grasped the flower.

At that very instant something on the part of Beda struck me. She was now standing by my side. I happened to glance towards her, and she was evidently about to spring at St. Clair. I comprehended her purpose in an instant: it was to snatch the poisoned flower from his grasp. A horrifying sensation seized upon me: I felt convinced that the moment she made such an attempt would be her last, for that the maniac St. Clair would strike her down with that weapon which dealt destruction swift as the lightning-shaft itself! I clutched her by the arm; and I saw by her look that her purpose was instantaneously overruled by that action on my part.

Lady Lilla Essendine again raised herself up in the couch—but it was with a visible feebleness and an evident painfulness. She looked at St. Clair: at first her eyes were dim and glazing—but gradually they grew brighter—they became illuminated with their wonted lustre—and they even seemed to flash vividly as she exclaimed, "Wretch! you will not even allow me to die in peace! My mournful entreaty has proved ineffectual! But now I command you to depart! Avaunt! thou art Satan himself! your presence makes my death-bed terrible! Answer me one word, St. Clair? Have you a single particle of sense and reason left?"

"Yes, yes!" he ejaculated. "I am not mad, though you may think I am—and there have been times when I have thought the same of myself. But no, no! I am not mad! What would you say to me, Lilla?"

"That if you were wise you would leave this house without an instant's delay—you would flee from England! I have confessed everything—our mutual crimes are known——"

"Ah!"—and then a sudden light appeared to flash in unto the mind of St. Clair. "You have confessed? Then to whom have you confessed? Why, to those whom I find here!"

"No, no, Edwin!" screamed forth Lady Lilla: "to the priest! to the priest!"

"The priest would reveal naught!" cried St. Clair. "There would be nothing to fear at his hands! But the danger that menaces me is here!"—and his maniac regards flamed upon Beda and myself.

"No! no!" shrieked Lady Lilla: "harm them not! harm them not!"

"They shall perish!" vociferated St. Clair: "they shall perish! Ah!—and at last, Ellen Percy, I am the conqueror!"

He sprang forward as he thus spoke, with the white rose in his hand. Quick as lightning the faithful and intrepid Beda threw herself in front of me, crying, "Leap from the window, Miss! leap from the window!"

A scream rang wildly from my lips as the conviction struck me that Beda's death was inevitable; for the wretched maniac was on the very point of thrusting the rose towards her face, despite the efforts she made to clutch at it. But at that very instant another cry rang through the room; and it was also with lightning speed that the dying Lilla sprang from her bed. Every remaining energy was suddenly concentrated in that effort! She threw herself upon St. Clair—she tore the rose from his hand—and she tossed it out of the window, close by which she at the moment fell down before either Beda or myself could save her.

A cry, resembling the savage yell of a wild beast, burst from the lips of Edwin St. Clair as he found himself thus suddenly and unexpectedly baffled. I and Beda hastened to raise up Lady Lilla Essendine: but her head drooped over my arm, and her eyes were fixed. I placed my hand upon her heart: she was dead. The look which I flung upon Beda conveyed the fact; and Beda said in an impressive voice, "In the moment of death she atoned for much that was evil in her past existence!"

"Yes—she saved your life, Beda, and perhaps mine also!" I answered. "May God have mercy upon her soul!"

"Amen!" murmured Beda: and we at the same time placed the corpse upon the bed.

"Wretched man!" I said, turning towards Edwin St. Clair, "there lies your victim! 'Twas you that led her from the path of virtue!—you who plunged her so deeply into crime! You made her life wretched and criminal; and you would not suffer her death to take place in peace! You have been her evil genius from the first unto the last! But the moment of retribution is at hand. Murderer of your own uncle! you shall not escape the doom which justice has in store for you!"

"What! would you dare seek to detain me?" he cried, his eyes again flaming with rage upon me.

"Yes, I! And, Oh! for such a purpose I feel that I shall be strong! Beda, shout from the window for help!"

"By heaven, there will be more of death's work here!" cried the half-frenzied St. Clair: and he rushed towards me.

I had caught up a chair as a weapon of defence: he tore it from me with as much ease as if I were a mere child—and he hurled it across the room. Beda in the meanwhile had cried out for help; and now she sprang from the neighbourhood of the window as if she were a young tigress: she darted at St. Clair just at the very instant that he was about to seize me with his infuriate grasp. Her hands were fixed upon his throat; and half-strangled, down he fell. Something dropped from about his clothes: it was the key of the door. Persons were already knocking there, and were even trying to force it. Snatching up the key, I flew to unlock the door; for St. Clair seemed to be utterly powerless in the firm grasp which Beda's delicate but vice-like hands had fixed upon his throat. All in a moment the scene changed. As the key was turning in the lock, Beda was hurled off St. Clair; and with a savage yell of triumph he sprang to the window. It was already open, be it remembered; and without a single instant's hesitation he leapt through it, disappearing from our view.

Alas! all this dreadful scene had taken place in the chamber of death; and there was something horrible—something appalling in the idea that so much desecration had fallen upon an occasion which ought properly to have been deeply solemn. And now, as the housekeeper and two other female servants rushed into the room the moment the door was opened, they beheld their mistress stretched a corpse upon the bed—and they stopped short aghast.

"Yes," I said, penetrating their thoughts; "her spirit has fled for ever—and it has been a hideous and revolting scene. That villain St. Clair——"

"What has become of him? where is he?" demanded the housekeeper.

Beda, who had sprung towards the window the moment St. Clair leapt thence, now turned towards the spot where I stood addressing the servants; and she said in a solemn tone, "If I mistake not, the guilty St. Clair is already in that world to which his victim"—and she pointed towards the dead Lilla—"had preceded him by but a few minutes!"

And so it proved to be. Beneath the window, upon a parterre of flowers lay the corpse of St. Clair. Unmaimed and unmangled was his body: he could not have harmed himself to the slightest degree by his descent from the window. It was not thus that he had died: there was not so much as a spot of blood nor a scratch upon his skin! Neither was the mode of his death at all mysterious; for the stiffened fingers of the right hand retained their grasp upon the White Rose, which Lady Lilla had tossed from the window, and which had no doubt caught St. Clair's eye at once as he alighted on that bed of flowers which likewise served as his bed of death!

Thus as a suicide perished St. Clair. He died at last by his own hand; and the career of turpitude which had taken murder as its starting-post, had finished in self-destruction! It was a day memorable in my history,—a day on which two persons whose proceedings had at various times so gravely affected my own interests, had perished! But Lady Lilla Essendine had given up the ghost in the very act of performing a good deed; while St. Clair had died impenitent, with no atonement made, and with all the tremendous weight of guilt upon his head. Need I say how deeply sensible I was of that new proof which Beda gave of her devotedness towards me, when in the midst of the horrible scenes in that death-chamber she had flung herself forward to meet the blow which was intended for myself?

When the excitement attending the discovery of the suicide of Edwin St. Clair had in the course of an hour subsided within the walls of the deceased Lady Lilla Essendine's habitation, I thought there was no need for me to remain there any longer. I had already given Lady Lilla's housekeeper a full description of all the circumstances attending the death of her mistress and the self-destruction of St. Clair; and I left my card with her that it might be presented to the officials of the Coroner in case inquiry should there be made in reference to the latter event. Meanwhile, a communication had been sent to the domestics at St. Clair's house, which was at no great distance, to inform them of the death of their master and to desire that they would adopt immediate measures for the removal of the corpse. This message was promptly attended to; and some of St. Clair's servants came up at once from the house to take charge of the remains of their master. I had told the housekeeper that she must be particularly cautious in disposing of the poisoned rose: her first impulse was to destroy it by throwing it into a fire: but I had bidden her by no means do so, as it was absolutely necessary that it should be preserved to undergo chemical examination,—or at all events to await the orders of the Coroner.

The body of St. Clair was fetched away upon a bier a few minutes before I took my departure; and I now thought I had done all I possibly could in the case. I had left the amplest instructions of every description with the housekeeper: there was not a single point on which such advice might be required that I had not fully entered upon. Before I ascended into my carriage I returned to the death-chamber and flung a last look upon Lady Lilla Essendine. She seemed to be sleeping serenely: her features were beautiful in death as they had been in life: the lids were closed over the eyes—but still the tracery of blue veins was lingeringly defined, yet gradually disappearing to be absorbed in death's marble monotony of whiteness. She was not yet laid out; and the luxuriance of the pale amber hair seemed to form a silken pillow whereon rested that beautiful head. But Oh! I knew that it was the form of a murderess I was gazing upon; and I shuddered as I thought of her future state, and wondered whether she had sufficiently made her peace with heaven to experience that pardon in the world whereunto she had gone, which I had so heartily accorded her in this!

I and Beda were now seated in the carriage; and I ordered the coachman to drive direct to the mansion of the Earl and Countess of Carshalton at the West End. For Henry, be it recollected, had established his quarters there: my father had gone to see him before I had received the summons to Lady Lilla's death-bed; and I was now naturally anxious to hasten and inform them all in that mansion of what had occurred. I did not recollect that the nearest way would be along the very avenue in which the house of the self-destroyed St. Clair was situated: I was too much absorbed in the painful reflections which the entire scene had left behind it, to have any thought for extraneous matters. But all of a sudden I exclaimed, "How foolish of Joseph!"—thus alluding to the coachman: "he is taking the very route which under existing circumstances I would rather avoid!"

"To be sure!" exclaimed Beda: "this is the place where Mr. St. Clair's house is situated! Shall I tell Joseph to turn back?"

"No," I said: "it is not necessary. Let him proceed. But Ah! what is this?"

The ejaculation was wrung from my lips by the spectacle of an old woman—clothed in rags, bowed so as almost to be bent double, and leaning upon a crutch-stick—who suddenly came forward to the carriage, making a sign for the coachman to stop. When I say clothed in rags, I mean that she was literally in tatters—a wretched tatterdemalion, presenting a spectacle of the most utter misery—to such an extent indeed that I failed to recognise her until Beda abruptly ejaculated, "Dame Betty!"

So imperative was the manner in which she motioned for the coachman to stop—so full of significancy was her look—that, as he afterwards told me, he felt so convinced it was no ordinary beggar who thus acted that he at once pulled up his horses.

"Miss Percy," ejaculated the hag, "I have been to your house!—they told me you had come up to the Regent's Park—I dragged myself here! For heaven's sake assist me!"

With the recollection of all I had heard in reference to this woman still strong in my mind—with all the vivid impression of the guilt of her own infamous career, and of the shocking things which had thence resulted—I naturally recoiled from the presence of the wretch. She observed the sense of loathing with which I was seized: she saw that Beda also revolted against her; and she said, "Ah! I am indeed very low down now! Misery has fastened its hold upon me—wretchedness and poverty! I am almost starving. I was robbed of the great bulk of the money you sent me. But look at me! My appearance tells its tale! Ah!" she added, with an extreme bitterness; "is not this aspect of mine eloquent enough in proclaiming to what I am reduced?"

"Wretched woman," I said, "I thought I should never encounter you again; and heaven knows I hoped it! Nevertheless it seems to be almost providential that you should have found yourself in this neighbourhood at such a crisis—to learn what has happened——aye, and to be stricken with remorse if you could be sensible of such a sentiment!"

"And what has happened?" she asked, looking at me with bewildered curiosity.

"If there were no such wretches as you in the world," I said, with the most cutting asperity, "Satan would not have the means of placing the requisite weapons in the hands of those whom he tempts to crime!" and in thus speaking, I had in mind a portion of what the unfortunate and criminal Lady Lilla Essendine had so recently been saying to me.

"What do you mean, Miss Percy? what do you mean?" asked the hag.

"I mean," was my response, "that two persons who for some years past have been more or less intimately connected with you, have this day experienced heaven's dread retribution!"

"Two persons," she cried. "Whom do you mean? whom can you mean? St. Clair?"—and her features expressed a malignant vindictiveness.

"Lady Lilla Essendine," I rejoined, "is no more. She has breathed her last."

"What! she is dead? Did she die a natural death?" exclaimed the harridan.

"Ah! well may you ask the question," I said; "well may you doubt that those who have dealt with all the frightful arts to which your skill and experience have been devoted, can have gone quietly and peaceably out of this world! Lady Lilla Essendine died of consumption. The incidents attending her death were frightful; and if I remain here to tell you all this, it is because——"

"Because you would strike terror into my soul," interjected the hag, "and fill me with horror and remorse. Well, well, it is bad enough to suffer as I have suffered! And I who ought to be rich!"

"Wretch!" I ejaculated; "can prosperity attend upon such a criminal career as your's?"

"Tell me, Miss Percy—tell me," she said; "you spoke of two? Lady Lilla is one: who is the other that has gone?"

"Who do you think ought to have been smitten by heaven's righteous judgment at the same time?" I demanded: "who but St. Clair?"

"St. Clair?" she cried; and a fiendish joy overspread her hideous features. "St. Clair! Then my Zarah may yet be avenged even from the grave! But is he really dead?"

"He perished as a suicide," I answered solemnly; "and the weapon with which self-destruction was inflicted, was the White Rose!"

"Ah!"—and Dame Betty seemed to be struck by the coincidence.

"Look!" said Beda, pointing to a bier which was that moment being borne past, covered with a large black cloth, and by the side of which two of St. Clair's footmen were walking: "look! There are the remains of him who in his lifetime was so generous a patron of your dark criminal skill!"

The hag turned to gaze upon the spectacle; and I, taking advantage of the opportunity, pulled the check-string violently; so that the coachman, comprehending the signal, lashed his horses, and the equipage rolled rapidly away. I had given no pecuniary relief to that vile woman: I did not intend to do so: for the first time in my life I had shut my heart against the picture of distress clothed in rags. And I did not repent that I had done so; for with all the strong impressions of the wretch's deep guilt on my mind, it was impossible that I could entertain any charitable feeling towards her. Indeed, I should have given her into custody then and there, only that I had the image of the dead Zarah in my mind; and moreover I had made use of Dame Betty in the case of Lady Kelvedon after I had received so many proofs of her turpitude, and after I had suspected her of that complicity in Sir George Essendine's murder which had this day been confirmed.

The equipage drove to Carshalton House, where I found my father and my cousin in the drawing-room with the Earl and Countess. They wondered why I was so late; but when I began to explain all the tragic incidents which had occurred, they listened with the deepest interest. For some time we sat conversing upon those events; and then I returned home to make a change in my toilet, for I was engaged to dine at the hospitable mansion which I had just left.

But on reaching Great Ormond Street, intelligence awaited me and Beda which afforded a suitable sequence to the retributive events which had previously rendered that day so memorable. William Lardner, who was still staying with Sir Robert Temple for the present, had been waiting a couple of hours at my house to communicate the incident to which I am alluding. It appeared that when the corpse of St. Clair was borne to his house, a woman covered with rags, pushed her way into the hall, exclaiming with a sort of frenzied excitement, " Let me look at him for a moment! Let me look at his face for a single instant!"

There was something so extraordinary in the hag's behaviour that the footmen could not comprehend it; and before they had time to recover from their surprise, or to make up their minds as to what answer they should give her, or whether they should eject her from the house, she had raised the black covering, and with a loud demoniac yell, she cried, "Ah! my Zarah is avenged!"

Then the servants recognised in that wretched ragged woman the crone who in the tribunal of the Old Bailey, on the occasion of Luigi's trial, had accused Edwin St. Clair of being the murderess of his wife or else of having connived at her self destruction. They looked at each other aghast; for they now comprehended why she exhibited such a horrible delight at thus beholding him stretched a cold corpse there. But more fearfully interesting became the scene, when sinking on her knees by the side of the bier, she raised her eyes and said in a solemn voice, " Now, my well-beloved Zarah! you may repose tranquilly in your tomb, and your spirit need not wander troubled and disturbed! Here lie the remains of the wretch who by his conduct drove you to self-destruction, even if he murdered you not outright! Detested St. Clair! even though inanimate as thou art, could I wreak my vengeance upon thee and tear thy very flesh from thy bones!"

Thus speaking, it was with a kind of spasmodic impulse—a species of passing frenzy, tigress-like and horrible—that the hag tore at the deceased's coat with her hand, as if her fingers were the claws of a ravenous wild beast. One of the footmen called out in a savage tone commanding her to be quiet; and the other rushed forward for the purpose of sezing her by the shoulders and ejecting her from the house. But the words of the former were still vibrating in the air—and the hands of the latter were only just outstretched and had not as yet touched her—when she fell suddenly backward as if stricken down by a lightning flash. An alarm was immediately raised; for the footmen actually recoiled from the bare idea of rendering any assistance to such a wretch; and it was the scullion, who rushing into the hall at hearing the cries for assistance which the lips of the footmen sent forth, pronounced that the hag was a corpse.

But how did she meet her death thus suddenly? The mystery was not immediately fathomed, though it was not very long ere it transpired. The housekeeper at Lady Lilla Essendine's villa had placed the white rose just inside the lappel of St. Clair's coat, so that it might be ready for inspection by the Coroner's Jury; and thus when the miserable old

hag fixed her talon-like fingers upon the garments of the deceased, she clawed open the coat partially—and bending so close down over the corpse as she was, she inhaled the fatal fragrance of the white rose. Yes—she perished by means of one of those beautiful and fearfully deceptive weapons which she herself had been wont to use; and in this case heaven's retribution was as righteous as in that of St. Clair himself!

There were two Coroner's Inquests next day—one upon the corpse of St. Clair, the other upon that of Dame Betty. As the reader may suppose, the incidents had created a tremendous sensation; and when it was rumoured that I should most likely be called upon to give my evidence, the effect was to gather an immense crowd about St. Clair's house long before the hour when the proceedings were to commence. I repaired thither with the Earl of Carshalton and Henry; and I unhesitatingly entered into details connected with all that I knew in reference to the white rose. My narrative was listened to with the most breathless attention; and the Coroner, in the course of some observations which he addressed to me, remarked that if I published my memoirs they would forcibly illustrate the poetic adage that " truth is stranger than fiction." I must not forget to add that the white rose which had proved so fatal in the present instance, was given to two or three celebrated analytical chemists, that a report might be made upon the nature of the poison with which it was impregnated: but it baffled all their ingenuity—and they were compelled to confess in the long run that they were unable to arrive at a satisfactory solution by means of any known tests. There was some idea at the time of sending the rose to Italy, that it might be examined by the eminent chemists of that land: but I believe that the design was ultimately abandoned — and therefore an ominous mystery still continues to enshroud that artificial flower which was as terrible as it was beautiful.

In the case of Edwin St. Clair a verdict of *Felo de se* was returned: in that of Dame Betty the verdict was to the effect that the woman had met her death by accidental poisoning. The former was buried in some dreary spot in unconsecrated ground, at the dismal midnight hour; and the corpse of the latter was sent to the workhouse, whence it was removed to a pauper's grave.

CHAPTER CXXXV.

VARIOUS MATTERS.

ONE evening—a few days after the incidents which I have just been relating—I was about to step into my carriage to proceed to Carshalton House, where I was engaged to dinner, when I was struck by beholding a species of struggle between two persons at a little distance. I should have instantaneously withdrawn my eyes and taken my seat in the carriage, were it not that one of the individuals thus engaged in conflict was too remarkable not to arrest my attention. Indeed he was none other than the hideous humpbacked dwarf whom I had first seen at Gilderoy Hemp's.

"I say you shall come!" I heard him ejaculate in his quick harsh voice; and though one arm hung motionless and useless by his side, yet with the hand of the other was he clinging most tenaciously to his opponent.

"Be off, you hideous old wretch!" cried the latter; and then to my astonishment I recognised Mr. Moss.

"There she is! there is Miss Percy!" cried the dwarf. "Come to her!"

"Miss Percy does not wish to see me," returned Moss. "I saw her the other day——"

"I don't believe a sentence of it!" interrupted the dwarf.

"Unhand me!" exclaimed Moss: "a crowd will be collecting! Come with me, if you like: Miss Percy will satisfy you that she has got no questions to ask me."

The next moment Moss and the dwarf were approaching the carriage; but the latter kept tight hold upon his companion's coat-tail, so that it was a spectacle sufficiently ludicrous to behold—that horrible-looking old man of barely three feet in height, dragging to the skirt of that young man who was double his stature. I stepped back into the house: I made a sign for them both to enter; and the moment they crossed the threshold I said to the dwarf, "You may release your grasp upon Mr. Moss: there is no account to settle between him and me."

"Well, Miss Percy," said the dwarf, "I did not know how it might be; and of course I am very sorry if I should have wrongfully suspected the young gentleman. But wonders will never cease! Here is he turning up alive, when I'm sure I thought he perished in the conflagration!—and then there was Parks who also turned up——"

"Parks?" ejaculated Moss. "What! is this possible?"—and he was seized with an air of bewildered astonishment.

"Yes — Mr. Parks lives!" I said. "I have known it for a long time past——"

"But you did not tell me so, Miss Percy," ejaculated Moss, "when I met you the other day at River House!"

"I had not time to tell you anything, Mr. Moss," I answered. "If you had waited there only a few minutes longer, I should have given you certain explanations—I should have spoken to you of Mr. Parks: but you vanished so suddenly——"

"True! true!" cried Moss; and then he again ejaculated, "But is it really possible that Parks lives? This is most providential! I have tidings for him of great importance—yes, tidings for that unhappy man of the wife and children whom he must deem lost!"

It was now my turn to give vent to an ejaculation of astonishment; and I naturally became deeply interested in the scene which was thus taking place. Moss looked at the dwarf and then at me. I comprehended what he meant; and I said to the humpback, "You need not now remain any longer. Here is something that will help you on in the world:"—and I placed a bank-note for fifty pounds in his hand.

His hideous countenance was more eloquently expressive of gratitude than even the words which he now uttered; and he took his departure.

"I thank you, Miss Percy," said Moss, "for having gotten rid of that person, in whose presence I indeed felt but little inclined to allude to those subjects which have stamped me as a villain in my own estimation and filled my soul with a remorse which never can be subdued within me!"

"You have made atonement, Mr. Moss," I said: "I have forgiven you——"

"Yes—and I have made a greater atonement still!" interjected the young man. "When I left you the other day, Miss Percy, after having restored you your fortune, I had still some hundreds of pounds left. I went upon the Continent, determined to seek some secluded place in which I might bury myself; and I accordingly proceeded to a little village called Furnes on the Belgian frontier. It was something providential—I certainly cannot call it *accidental*, which led me thither. For behold! whom should I suddenly encounter on the very day after my arrival but Mrs. Parks!"

"Is it possible?" I ejaculated. "And her children?"

"All living there likewise," responded Moss. "No—not *all*: for there is the eldest daughter Jane—I think perhaps you may have known her, Miss Percy——"

"I know her *now*," I replied: "but I did not know her at the time when I used to be a visitor at Parks's house, for she was then on the Continent with the Tremaines. But tell me—was her mother much concerned at having lost sight of her?"

"Not so," answered Moss. "There never existed much love on the part of Mrs. Parks towards Jane; and when she spoke of her the other day, she said half-coolly, half-flippantly, 'I have never seen her since I ran away from England: I have never heard of her. I suppose she is still with the Tremaines, or else getting her living by some means or another: but at all events it is very fortunate that she has not found me out to foist herself upon my humble resources.'—It was thus that the heartless woman spoke."

"Heartless indeed!" I exclaimed. "But how long had she dwelt at Furnes? It must be between thirteen and fourteen months since she and her children disappeared in so mysterious a manner; and now they are heard of for the first time after that disappearance!"

"Perhaps you are aware, Miss Percy," said Moss, "of certain particulars which followed the conflagration at Gilderoy Hemp's; for when I met your father and cousin in America I gave them the fullest explanations——"

"And they have all been repeated to me," I interjected. "Thus for instance, I know that after the conflagration you sped to Mr. Parks's house—you searched his private office—and you discovered a couple of hundred pounds in bank-notes, which you gave to Mrs. Parks."

"True," said Moss: "and in addition to that sum she had about a hundred pounds of her own —she had her jewellery, the plate, and other moveable valuables; and therewith she made the best of her way to France. Fearful of being pursued by her husband's creditors, she sought the most secluded spot which could possibly be found; and crossing the frontier, she settled at Furnes in Belgium. There she resolved to eke out her resources in the most economical manner: she was always a saving and parsimonious woman—and therefore in that little Flemish village she was enabled to practise the principle of economy accord-

ing to her own notions. To be brief, she was there living frugally and penuriously, when all of a sudden, accident—no, *providence* I should have said—led me, unhappy and conscience-stricken, to that very spot!"

"And what followed?" I asked. "You could not tell her that her husband still lived—for you then knew it not."

"No: but I told her all the truth," responded Moss, "so far as it regarded myself: I explained everything—the villanous part I had played——"

"And what said she?" I inquired.

"At first she seemed ready to spring at me with the fury of a tiger-cat," proceeded Moss: "but when I told her that I had yet a few hundred pounds left after having restored you, Miss Percy, all your fortune, and that these few hundred pounds I should then and there make over to herself, leaving me a beggar on the face of the earth ——Ah! then her humour changed, and she hesi-

tated not to accept that amount as a propitia-tion——"

"And then you came to England?" I said.

"Utterly penniless, Miss Percy, I arrived in London just now. I scarcely knew what to do; and yet I most solemnly declare to you that though in this street and so near your own dwelling, I was not coming to obtrude myself on your presence. But I once had a friend—a lawyer—who lived in this street: I thought it possible he might re-commend me to a situation—it was my only chance——"

"You have acted to me, Mr. Moss," I inter-rupted him, "in a manner which proves how deeply contrite you are for the misdeed into which temptation led you at the time of the fire. My purse is at your service——"

"A few pounds, Miss Percy—a few pounds," he said, "and no more!"

I spread a number of bank-notes before him on

the table: but I could not induce him to take more than ten pounds; and it was with tears in his eyes that he expressed his gratitude. I then proceeded to explain to him where he might find Mr. Parks and his daughter Jane; and he said, "I will suffer no delay to elapse ere I communicate to them the intelligence which must lift so heavy a weight of suspense from off their minds. It shall be alike a penitence and a pleasure for me to do this personally and not by letter,—a penitence because I shall go and encounter all the bitter reproaches which my late employer may level against me—and a pleasure because I shall have the opportunity of atoning to the utmost of my power for the evil I have done."

It was impossible not to feel for a young man who spoke in these contrite terms, and who by his actions exhibited so much real penitence. I therefore said to him, "If you fail to obtain a situation, let me endeavour to use my influence on your behalf; and if you require more money, hesitate not to apply to me for it."

With renewed expressions of gratitude Moss took his departure; and in the evening I received a note from Jane Parks, telling me that he had called—that both her own and her father's minds had sustained an immense relief—and that Mr. Parks himself was going over to Furnes with the least possible delay to join his wife and children—but that she (Jane) intended to remain in England and pursue the profession by which she was earning her bread, as she knew very well that she would be by no means likely to agree with her mother if they both lived beneath the same roof.

Nothing of any consequence occurred for the next ten days: but at the expiration of this interval Jane Parks called upon me one evening when I happened to be alone. She was evidently in a state of great mental distress; I bade her be seated and tell me what had transpired thus seriously to trouble her.

"Oh, Ellen!" she exclaimed, "however great have been the iniquities of my father towards you, he is now experiencing a terrible retribution!"

"What mean you, Jane? what mean you?" I asked quickly.

"Ah! I have often thought," she cried, "that you have not told me everything in respect to my father, and that he had in reality behaved towards you worse than I had any idea of. Whether this be so, I know not——"

"Let us avoid the topic, Jane," I said.

"Oh, you are too kind—too good, Ellen!" she ejaculated, with passionate vehemence: "you will tell me nothing to afflict me! And you are right—you are merciful and considerate!—for heaven knows I am already afflicted enough!"

"Tell me, Jane—tell me what it is?" I asked. "Something has happened to your father?"

"He has returned from Belgium," responded the afflicted young woman: "his own wife turned against him,—she vowed that he should not set foot in her house—nor share her purse—not claim any control over the children! And thus my poor father has come away heart-broken! He never could have expected such conduct on the part of his wife. But, Oh! the truth is, dear Ellen, my mother does not possess a good heart——'tis sad for me, her daughter, to say so—yet too true it is——"

"And thus your father has separated from your mother?" I exclaimed.

"Yes—and it appears that a scene of terrible violence took place," pursued Miss Parks. "My mother said that the house was her own—that she was in a land where the laws would not permit him, although her husband, to come and foist himself upon her—and that if it were otherwise, she would denounce him as a fugitive from the English Bankruptcy Court—she would surrender him up to the *gendarmes*, and have him put on board a steam-packet at Ostend to be transferred to Dover. She would not permit him to see the children—no, not his own children!" continued Jane with bitter emphasis. "And when he entreated and implored that she would alter her demeanour towards him, she overwhelmed him with a hurricane of reproaches. Alas, alas!" added Jane, weeping copiously, "too well deserved were these reproaches; for it was no doubt my father's wickedness which had destroyed the fabric of his fortunes!"

"But wickedness was also the basis," I interjected, "on which those fortunes were established. I say not this to wound your feelings, Jane—but to prove to you that whatsoever has evil at its root shall not flourish for ever."

"True—most true!" said Miss Parks. "But Oh! so long as my father was rich and prosperous, my mother cared not whence his riches came; and she willingly shared in his prosperity, without inquiring what was its source. It was not for *her* to turn round and reproach him in the hour of his adversity!"

"No, Jane," I said: "it was not for *her* thus to act. Her conduct has no doubt been heartless to a degree: for a wife should cling to her husband—and she ought to have been only too glad to allow their children to be clasped in their father's arms. But how ended this most unpleasant affair?"

"My father did not choose to create a scandal in the village," continued Jane; "and therefore, finding all his prayers and entreaties to be completely unavailing—seeing that his wife was inexorable—he yielded at length to the sad and heart-rending conviction that everything was at an end between them. For the last time he implored that he might be allowed to bestow a farewell embrace upon his children: but still the reply was in the negative. And so he departed:—he tore himself away from that cottage where he had hoped to find a home, but which had proved more coldly inhospitable than if it were the dwelling of utter strangers to which he had applied for admittance! Conceive, my dear Ellen—Oh! conceive a wife behaving thus to her own husband!—discarding him—menacing him—driving him away from her door—refusing him permission to bestow a last embrace on his children!"

"It is doubtless very terrible, Jane," I said,—"very terrible!" I repeated, shaking my head ominously. "But rest assured that heaven would not have suffered such a dread calamity to fall upon your father unless he had proved sinful against the laws of God and man. The more heavily that chastisement falls upon him, the greater will be the expiation and atonement—the more earnestly will he be led to pursue the pathway of repentance—and the better perhaps in the long run will it be for the eternal welfare of his soul!"

There was a long and solemn pause; and then I said, "You, Jane, are a good and dutiful daughter—you have not forgotten that whatsoever may have been the conduct of your father towards others, he has a right to exact obedience and to receive kindness from you. Rest assured that with you, my dear Jane, things will prosper; and if you will permit me to be of service to you——"

"No, Ellen!" she cried, with even passionate vehemence; "I will accept nothing at your hands! I can earn my own bread—and I am proud in being enabled to do so! As for my father——"

"Is he to live upon your industry?" I asked.

"No, Ellen," pursued Miss Parks: "he has declared that he will no longer do so. He has some plan in view at present—I scarcely know what—but he longs to get away from London—he has a friend in some distant county who he thinks can help him in the project which he has formed. In a word, he is about to leave me! Heart-broken and crushed down—his soul filled with the bitterest affliction—he is a man whose condition is now calculated only to excite pity, and not hatred!"

"I do not hate your father, Jane, if you mean the observation for me," I said: "but I cannot esteem him—I cannot even respect him. No—nor can I offer to do anything for him!"

I was sorry to be thus compelled to speak to the poor young woman; but I could not forget that her father was an accomplice in the murder of my grandsire. She herself did not know the fact, nor did I purpose to mention it in her hearing: but still I could not act the hypocrite by expressing sympathy for a man whom in plain terms I looked upon as a murderer. Yet, on the other hand, I felt that there was a certain duty which in common justice I had to perform, and I was now about to accomplish it.

"Some months ago, Jane," I said, "your father made a discovery of certain facts in reference to the Wakefield and Carshalton families, which were of the highest consequence to my cousin Henry—and therefore to myself. I told you then that you might give your father the assurance that he had done somewhat towards atoning for the past. I now repeat that assurance: but beyond this I can say no more. Yet with you, my dear Jane, it is very different! Never shall I forget the joy with which you came rushing into my presence at Carshalton to bring me the information which I required! Nay, interrupt me not—but listen. My cousin Henry and I had agreed together that on the day of our marriage—which is not very remote—we would beg your acceptance of five hundred pounds; and therefore you may as well permit me to give you at once this testimonial of our mutual gratitude for the part you took in procuring us that valuable information."

"My dear Ellen," answered Jane, as she hastily dashed the tears from her eyes, "I comprehend full well the delicacy of your conduct. On principle, you can do nothing for my father. He has offended you mortally: I fear that his wickedness towards you has been greater than you have suffered me to suspect. But, however that may be, certain it is that for *him* you can do nothing in a direct and positive manner. Yet you are seeking

an excuse to do everything that is generous for *me*; and you know that my father would profit by whatsoever good piece of fortune befell myself. Now, therefore, Ellen, this shall not be. I have already told you that I would receive nothing at your hands—and I regret the necessity which has compelled me to enter into this long explanation of my own conduct in so refusing. Continue to me your friendship, dear Ellen——Oh! continue it unto me——and this is all that I shall ever claim or need from you!"

With these words she pressed my hands to her lips, and then hurriedly took her departure.

Some days afterwards I received a note from Mr. Moss, informing me that he had succeeded in obtaining a good situation, and assuring me of his resolve to lead a steady, quiet, and honourable life, in order to atone for the one grand misdeed into which he had been led in a moment of temptation.

It was about the same time I received a letter from Mr. Jacobs, the house-agent at Leeds, containing intelligence to the effect that the old premises which I had inherited from my grandfather, had recently displayed such a tottering condition that it was absolutely necessary to take some immediate steps in the matter. Indeed, the house was considered dangerous: it seemed as if it were about to fall in; and if such a catastrophe were to occur, it might involve the contiguous buildings in a similar destruction, besides perilling the lives of persons passing in the street. The local authorities had threatened to interfere and to serve me with a notice either to pull down the building or else to put it into a proper condition of repair. Such was the letter which I received from Mr. Jacobs, and which I showed to my father, asking his advice upon the subject.

Having reflected for a few moments, my father said, "I myself will go to Leeds, Ellen. I will engage the services of some respectable surveyor there—and I will see what is best to be done with the property. Besides," he added, in a lower tone, "I should like to look once more into that house where you, my beloved daughter, passed so many years of your life!"

"And I will accompany you, father!" I exclaimed: "for I also should like to look once more upon the scene where my girlhood was spent. Yes—and now that heaven has showered so many precious gifts upon my head, and that by the possession of such great wealth I am enabled to do good to my fellow-creatures, it would please me well to ensure a competency to the worthy preceptress to whom I was so much indebted for whatsoever accomplishments I acquired in my younger days."

It was accordingly resolved that this little journey should be taken; and when I acquainted my cousin Henry with my intention, he smilingly and tenderly enjoined me not to remain too long away. I promised him that our absence should not extend beyond a very few days; and as he embraced me, he whispered, "At all events, dear Ellen, there is a rapturous joy in the thought that we shall speedily be united, no more to part!"

My father and I set off for Leeds, taking Beda with us. It was in the evening when we reached our destination; and although we agreed to postpone our visit to the haunted house—as the old place was called—until the following morning, yet I could not restrain my impatience to see the worthy Mrs. Kelly and to assure myself that she was well and prospering. Accordingly, after having dined at the hotel, my father and I set out for the abode of the schoolmistress; and the dusk was already closing in as we reached the little habitation where the dame dwelt. There was now a brass plate upon the door, bearing her name; and when I knocked, the summons was answered by a neatly dressed servant-girl. I was soon in Mrs. Kelly's presence, and at once clasped in her arms.

"Ah, my dear Ellen!" she said, "you have once more come back to Leeds! But I hope nothing of an unpleasant nature has brought you? —nothing connected with that man Parks?"

"Why should you think so?" I ejaculated, surprised at the observation.

"Oh, because he has been down to Leeds, I believe—he is here now——"

"Mr. Parks at Leeds?" I exclaimed: and my father likewise gave vent to an ejaculation of astonishment.

"Oh, there can be no doubt of it," rejoined Mrs. Kelly; "and it is very strange, Ellen, that I was seriously thinking of writing to you on the subject when I heard that Parks had been seen in the town; for I feared that possibly he might be endeavouring to play you some trick in reference to your house: but I went and inquired of Mr. Jacobs, who told me that he had seen nothing of Parks—and that moreover it was quite impossible for anybody to interfere with your right of possession in respect to those premises. So my mind was set at rest, and I did not trouble you with a letter."

"It is strange," I said, "that I should happen to come to Leeds at the same time as Mr. Parks: but yet I now recollect his daughter told me he was to leave London for some distant town where he possessed a friend——"

"So long as he cannot injure you, my dear Ellen," said Mrs. Kelly, "no matter!—for I remember that when you were last here, about eighteen months ago, you did not speak in very high terms of him. And Ah! dear Ellen!" continued the worthy woman, "I must again and again thank you for the noble generosity you displayed towards me on the occasion of that last visit. By purchasing for me the lease of this house, you set my mind at ease—my health improved—and I suppose that the redoubled attentions I have been enabled to bestow upon my school, gave such satisfaction to the parents of my pupils that they recommended me to all their friends; and the consequence is, dear Ellen, my schoolroom is literally crowded! And it is to you that I am indebted for all this!"

"But I have not forgotten, my dear old friend," I said, "how much I owed to your goodness in my childhood. I am now rich—yes, very, very rich—and I have come to Leeds almost on purpose to see what I can do for you. Now, listen to me!" I continued with a smile: "I have got everything settled in my mind. I shall purchase the house for you—and then you can lay by the money which you would otherwise have to pay in the shape of rent. And you must employ a teacher to assist you—you must not work too

hard—you must take care of your health—and by the arrangements I propose you will make the business of teaching a recreation henceforth instead of a labour."

Mrs. Kelly would not for a long time listen to the idea that I should purchase the house for her: but at length she yielded. I had not as yet told her that the gentleman who accompanied me was my father: but she thought he was my uncle, because the last time I was at Leeds I had spoken to her of having found an uncle. When, therefore, she learnt how closely we were connected, she was amazed; and it was also with astonishment that she listened as I went on to tell her that I possessed an income of a great many thousands a year—that I had at length recovered my grandfather's fortune, of which Mr. Parks had robbed me—that my cousin Henry was heir to the Carshalton Earldom, and that in the course of a very short time he would take the title of Viscount Ravenscliffe, so soon as the lawyers engaged in the case should have completely made out his rightful claims, of which there was indeed not the slightest doubt.

"Ah!" said Dame Kelly; "I recollect the handsome cousin with the fine brown eyes!—and I recollect his poor mother too—Mrs. Wakefield—and how affectionately she spoke of you. And I suppose, my dear Ellen," she added, with a look of good-humoured slyness, "you are to become Viscountess Ravenscliffe for the present, in anticipation of the higher title of Countess of Carshalton? There! enough, my dear girl! That blush tells the tale! God bless you—and may you be happy!"

The worthy woman embraced me cordially; and after a little more conversation, I and my father took a temporary leave of her, promising to call and see her again on the following day.

I have already said that the dusk was closing in when we had set out on this visit to Mrs. Kelly; and it was now deepening into darkness—but the street gas-lamps were lighted. Just as we were quitting the worthy woman's house, a man passed us with such an exceeding rapidity that we only obtained a momentary glimpse of him; and yet the impression made upon us both was the same—for we each gave a simultaneous start—and as I ejaculated the name of "Mr. Parks!" my father quickly replied, "Yes, I thought so!"

But scarcely were we beginning to recover from the surprise into which the sudden event had thrown us, when another individual passed us with equal rapidity, just as if he were for some purpose or another on the track of the first-mentioned.

"If that were really Parks," said my father, "depend upon it there is something wrong in that quarter! It is doubtless an officer of justice who is on his track!"

"And that it was Mr. Parks, I am convinced!" I said. "I know him as well without his spectacles as with them; and though he had the collar of his coat turned up, I nevertheless caught a glimpse of his features as the gas-light streamed upon them."

"Yes—and all this struck me likewise," interjected my father: and we continued to discuss the subject during our walk back to the hotel.

Immediately after breakfast on the following

morning, I and my father called upon Mr. Saw-bridge, the lawyer with whom I had transacted the business in reference to the lease of Mrs. Kelly's house upwards of eighteen months back; and I now inquired of him whether the said house was to be sold? He answered in the affirmative, provided that a good price was given. I requested to know this price: he named it—and I at once closed the bargain.

From the lawyer's office my father and I proceeded towards the street in which the haunted house was situated. We soon stood in front of the building, which looked darker and more dingy than ever, and displayed several threatening cracks in the brick-work between some of the windows. After having contemplated it for a few moments, we bent our way to the habitation of Mr. Jacobs, the agent. This person's office was somewhat improved since last I had seen it: there were no longer any shabbily-dressed children playing on the door-step; and whereas on the previous occasion my nostrils were assailed by blended odours of tobacco and onions, on the present there was merely the smell of the tobacco without that of the onions.

We found Mr. Jacobs sitting on a high stool at his desk: and methought that the moment he beheld me his countenance changed somewhat and an expression flitted over it as if he would rather not have seen me. But instantaneously recovering himself, he said, "Ah, Miss Percy! Come to look after the house, I suppose? Well, it's in a precious dilapidated condition!"

"I intend to do something with it," I interrupted him: "but what it is I have not quite made up my mind. We will go across and look at it. Be kind enough to give me the key."

"The key, Miss Percy?" said Mr. Jacobs. "Ah! the key to be sure!"

He opened his desk and fumbled amongst some papers: he then took down a number of keys from a nail; and having deliberately examined them all, restored them to their place. I looked at my father; and we exchanged glances expressive of the same idea—namely, that we thought there was something wrong.

"Well, Mr. Jacobs," said my father at length; "is this key forthcoming—or is it not?"

"Forthcoming, sir? of course it is forthcoming!" ejaculated Mr. Jacobs. "Only don't you see, sir? a key is a thing that one may lay one's hand on at once just as easily as one may mislay it. And to tell you the truth——"

"Well, the truth is," cried my father, "that you are a long time in producing this key, Mr. Jacobs; and I do not like the aspect of the matter. Now tell me, if you please, sir," he exclaimed, suddenly confronting the house-agent and looking at him sternly in the face, "have you seen Mr. Parks in Leeds within these last few days?"

Mr. Jacobs turned pale—then became very red—and then abruptly dashing his clenched fist down upon the counter, he cried, "Well, there is no harm done, and I'll make a clean breast of it! The fact is, I *have* seen Parks; and he has got the key of the haunted——beg your pardon——of your house, Miss Percy."

"The key of my house?" I ejaculated.

"The key of my daughter's house?" exclaimed my father. "You had better explain yourself."

"That is very easily done, sir," cried Jacobs. "Come now, don't be angry before you know the rights of the matter; for you'll soon see that there is no harm done. The fact is I did not know that Parks was in Leeds until yesterday morning, when he called to ask me if I could help him to a situation of any kind, for that he was terribly down in the world. He said that he had been disappointed by a friend, who had held out some hope which had induced him to come to Leeds, but which hope was not fulfilled. I told him I was very sorry, but that I could do nothing for him. He was in a hurry—all in a fidget like; and he went away. Last night," continued Mr. Jacobs—"I should think it must have been at about half-past nine o'clock—who the deuce should come rushing into the office but Mr. Parks, with his coat collar turned up, his hat slouched, and with quite a scared look!"

My father and I exchanged significant glances; for the time mentioned by Mr. Jacobs was the very same at which we had seen Mr. Parks rush by us at Mrs. Kelly's door in such frenzied haste.

"I couldn't think what was the matter," continued Mr. Jacobs: "but Parks soon explained it. You know perhaps that some time ago he was made a bankrupt; and he never surrendered to the court; so a warrant was granted for his apprehension. Well, it seems that the messenger of the court traced him down to Leeds and got upon his track last night."

Again did my father and I exchange meaning looks; for here was the solution of the preceding evening's incident.

"Well," continued Jacobs, "Parks was in a deuced state of agitation; and he begged me to save him. What could I do? Suppose he was traced to my house, he would soon be ferreted out—and who could tell into what trouble I might get myself? But a thought struck me. I tossed him the key of the haunted house, telling him to go and hide there; for not even Old Nick himself—saving your presence, sir, and your's too, Miss Percy—would ever think of hunting for him there. Well, to make a long story short, he cut away with the key; and to tell the truth, he hasn't brought it back again: so I suppose he must be still hiding over at the house."

The account which Mr. Jacobs just gave was stamped with truthfulness; and there was no reason to blame him for the course he had adopted in helping a fellow-creature under such circumstances. On the contrary, I was inclined to commend him; and I said a few words to that effect.

"But if this unfortunate man—guilty as well as unfortunate," I went on to observe, "has been in that house without food ever since last evening, he must be famished. Go, Mr. Jacobs, and see what can be done under the circumstances."

"I'm off at once, Miss!" cried the house-agent. "I'll take him a roll and a good slice of meat, with a drop of something to warm and cheer him; and if I can't get in the front way, it will be no difficult thing to get over into the back-yard from the neighbouring premises; and then it will be an easy matter to force open one of the ricketty old shutters."

"I think I will accompany you," said my

father. "You can remain here, Ellen, for a few minutes until our return."

I signified my assent; for I understood that my father's motive was to assure himself that there was really no collusive plot of any sinister kind between Mr. Parks and Mr. Jacobs.

I sat down in the office while those two set off, —Jacobs having previously furnished himself with the provisions to which he had alluded. The house was only a little way higher up the same street; and therefore there was no necessity for them to be very long in the accomplishment of their expedition. Accordingly, in about ten minutes they returned, with agitation and horror clearly depicted on their countenances : indeed Mr. Jacobs was perfectly aghast. I sprang up from my seat, exclaiming, "What is the matter?"

"That wretched man," said my father, in a voice that was solemn though tremulous,—"that wretched man, Ellen, has been overtaken by heaven's vengeance. He is no more!"

"What?" I ejaculated : "he is dead? Dead in the very house where he himself dealt death!"

"Eh? what?" cried Mr. Jacobs, catching at my words. "Ah! I understand! Then it is true that he and his old mother murdered your grandfather, Miss—and you know it!"

I remained silent : I did not choose to give utterance to a falsehood to shield the memory of a murderer who had evidently met his righteous doom, whatever his fate might be.

In a few minutes everything was explained. My father and Mr. Jacobs had from the neighbouring premises obtained admission into the backyard of the haunted house; and they were looking about them to ascertain which would be the most eligible means for them to enter, when they beheld a first-floor window-shutter swinging on its hinges and the window itself open. There was an immense water-butt underneath this window; and Jacobs exclaimed, "Why, Parks must have made his escape! I wonder what he has done with the key? I'll climb up, sir, and get into the house that way, and see if I can unfasten the doors from within."

There was a dust-bin close by the water-butt; and Mr. Jacobs sprang lightly upon it. But scarcely had his eyes reached the level of the top of the water-butt, when he gave vent to an ejaculation of horror and dismay, staggering back at the same time as if he were about to fall. My father was almost immediately by his side; and then the catastrophe was fully discovered. For there were the legs of a man sticking up above the water which filled two-thirds of the butt; and when the corpse was drawn forth it proved to be that of Mr. Parks.

Thus perished this man of many misdeeds!—thus died the iniquitous accomplice of his mother who had plundered me of my fortune!—and thus by a marvellous stroke of retributive justice did heaven avenge itself upon the murderer of my grandfather, upon the very premises where that black crime was perpetrated !

My father was compelled to remain in Leeds until the following day, to give his evidence at the inquest. At the same examination Mr. Jacobs, who was excessively nervous, let drop something which led to his being closely examined, and he

was compelled to repeat the words which had fallen from my lips, and which, as I have already said, he had so suddenly caught up at the moment when they were uttered. It was then proposed to summon me as a witness : but my father saved me that painful ordeal by explaining my meaning. For the sake of Jane Parks I should have assuredly kept silent relative to the deep satanic guilt of her sire in the blackest sense : but the incident to which I have just referred brought everything to light. Parks and his mother, therefore, were in their memories branded before that inquest as the murderers of my grandsire.

In reference to the awful death of Mr. Parks it can only be surmised that at some part of the night—though heaven alone can tell at what hour! whether immediately after he entered the house, or whether later—he must have heard some noise which filled him with the apprehension that the officers of justice were breaking in to seize upon him; and being well acquainted with the premises, he must have thought to escape by means of that window, the water-butt, and the dust-bin. But doubtless in the agony of his terror he made a false step ; and falling headlong, plunged into that narrow reservoir whence self-extrication was impossible.

CONCLUSION.

THE 1st of October, 1843, was a happy day for me, —a happy day likewise for my cousin Henry, whose rights by this time having been fully demonstrated by able lawyers, as they were already acknowledged by the Earl of Carshalton, had enabled him to assume the title of Viscount Ravenscliffe. This happy day beheld our hands united at the altar ; and when the ring was placed upon my finger, the handsome brown eyes shed upon me a world of love, tenderness, and devotion. It was a splendid ceremony ; and many dear friends were gathered there ; and when it was concluded, it was with the sincerest and most unfeigned fervour that they all welcomed me as the Viscountess Ravenscliffe.

On the following day another bridal took place, —a humbler one, and yet perhaps scarcely less interesting to the reader than that which I have just mentioned. It was the wedding of William Lardner and my faithful Beda.

I have little more to add,—unless it be to glance in a rapid manner at some few of the leading characters of my memoirs, so that they may be disposed of according to the facts that have come to my knowledge concerning them. And first of all I will speak of Jane Parks, who went abroad immediately after those exposures at Leeds which so terribly blackened the memory of her sire; and for several years I heard nothing of her. At length I one day received a letter, dated from Turin, and commencing with the expression of a belief that the welfare of the writer could not be a matter of indifference to me. Nor was it! On the contrary, heartily glad was I to receive those tidings from her of whom I had often thought with sorrow and with sympathy. Jane had married happily; her husband was an Italian gentleman of wealth and station; and if I do not here mention the name, it must be for reasons fully obvious to my readers. Yes—Jane is as happy as under all circumstances she can possibly be: and in that gay circle of fashion where she now moves, no one entertains the slightest suspicion that she need blush for the memory of her sire.

About two years after my own marriage, I visited Paris with my husband; and there, at a brilliant entertainment at the British Ambassador's, I beheld a distinguished-looking man, some three or four years past forty, with an elegantly dressed lady leaning upon his arm. In the latter I quickly recognised Sarah Barron—or Lady Ward, as I ought now to call her; for she had recently become the wife of the rich baronet Sir Hugh Ward, who figured in one of the episodes of my memoirs.

About a year later the newspapers announced the death of Reginald Barron, "an artist of the utmost promise, and who died of consumption." In his *studio* was found a most beautifully executed portrait of myself,—"a work of art," said the newspapers, "on which the talented deceased had evidently lavished all the powers of his great genius; for it is said by those who knew him, that he was one of the most enthusiastic admirers of the beautiful Viscountess Ravenscliffe at the time when she occupied the proud position of the first *tragedienne* of the age." Then, as I read this account, I recalled to mind the words which that singular compound of genius and of profligacy had spoken to me with so wild an enthusiasm at Tremaine Hall, when he declared "that he should devote himself to the painting of *one* grand work which should immortalise my beauty on the

painter's canvass; and that when the task should be accomplished, consumption might crown its own process of destruction!"

At the time when I am now writing, the artist's sister Sarah (Lady Ward) has likewise paid the debt of nature—as well as her husband Sir Hugh. The title is extinct; and the estates have passed into the hands of distant relatives.

My father, having seen me happily wedded to my cousin Henry, determined upon atoning for the errors of the earlier part of his life by the usefulness of his later years; and thus he resolved upon proceeding as a missionary to one of those far-off places of the earth where heathenism presents so wide a field for the zealous enterprise of the Christian instructor. There, after some years of arduous toil in the cause which he had undertaken—having made his name respected, and having experienced an almost unexampled success in his self-imposed task—he died, leaving me his blessing, with the heartfelt conviction that he had rendered himself worthy of pronouncing it.

The Earl and Countess of Carshalton are likewise numbered with the dead; and their titles are now borne by Henry and myself. But it is not because the coronet of an Earl sits upon his brow, or that the tiara of a Countess decorates mine—it is not because we are the possessors of vast wealth and broad domains,—that we are so supremely happy: but it is rather on account of that strong, faithful, and abiding love which links our hearts, and which makes home a paradise when we sit together there, smiling upon each other or meeting the fond looks of our beauteous children.

THE END.

18 JA 58